D1441454

Academic International Encyclopedia

Academic International Inc.

Published by Academic International Inc. 1990.

Also published under the title Academic American Encyclopedia.

Printed and manufactured in the United States of America.

ISBN 0-7172-2033-8

Library of Congress Catalog Card Number 89-23779

𐤂	PHOENICIAN		ETRUSCAN	
	EARLY HEBREW		EARLY LATIN	<
	EARLY ARAMAIC	**Gg**	CLASSICAL LATIN	G
	EARLY GREEK		RUSSIAN-CYRILLIC	Г
Γ	CLASSICAL GREEK	MODERN LATIN	GERMAN-GOTHIC	

G

G/g is the seventh letter of the English alphabet. Both the form of the letter and its position in the alphabet were derived from the Latin, which in turn derived it from the letter C of that alphabet by the addition of a stroke to the lower limb of C. In English speech, *G/g* is pronounced as a hard *g*, as in *get* and *go*, and is the voiced counterpart of voiceless *k*; or as soft g, with the sound of *dzh* as in *gem*, and is the voiced counterpart of *ch* (*tsh*). This second sound of *G/g* is partially shared by the letter j, as in the spellings *gaol* and *jail*, which are pronounced the same. In words recently borrowed from French, the sound *dzh* of *G/g* has become *zh* as in *gendarme*.

I. J. GELB AND R. M. WHITING

Ga [gah]

The Ga, speakers of a Kwa-Kru dialect of the Niger-Congo language family, are an African people living in the coastal region of Ghana, near the mouth of the Volta River. They are the descendants of a people that emigrated southward down the Niger and across the Volta rivers during the 17th century.

Traditionally, they were principally sea fishermen but also practiced agriculture, animal husbandry, and hunting-gathering subsistence activities. Trading, conducted mainly by women, also played an important role in their economic system. A patrilineal kinship and descent system dominated their social organization, but certain public offices and properties held by women were handed down through the female line. Husbands and wives maintained separate residences after marriage. Polygamy was practiced.

Their towns, made up of compound settlements that united for mutual defense, were politically autonomous. Magical stools symbolized the high office of town chiefs and were the center of ceremonies concerned with war and bloodshed. Traditional religious practices included ancestor worship.

Today, three-quarters of the approximately 625,000 Ga live in urban centers, with most living in Accra.

JAMES W. HERRICK

Bibliography: Kilson, Marion, *African Urban Kinsmen: The Ga of Central Africa* (1974) and *Kpele Lala: Ga Religious Songs and Symbols* (1971); Manoukian, Madeline, *Akan and Ga-Adangme Peoples of the Gold Coast* (1950).

gabbro [gab'-roh]

Gabbro is a dark-colored plutonic rock composed mainly of coarse grains of calcium-rich plagioclase FELDSPAR and PYROXENE. In addition, the rock may contain olivine, hornblende, biotite, garnet, rutile, apatite, zircon, magnetite, ilmenite, and chromite. Chemically and mineralogically, gabbro is equivalent to BASALT. Gabbros may occur as border rocks around granitic and other plutons, or as small individual plutons or dikes. Their most common occurrence is in the lower parts of large, layered complexes. Most gabbros appear to intrude the rocks surrounding them and so are thought to be of igneous origin, although some may also be produced by metamorphic processes.

WILLIAM D. ROMEY

Bibliography: Carmichael, Ian, et al., *Igneous Petrology* (1974).

Gabin, Jean [gah-ban']

The tough-tender hero of many French film melodramas, Jean Gabin, b. May 17, 1904, d. Nov. 15, 1976, surprisingly failed to find an international audience, perhaps because he was more at home suggesting action than demonstrating it. He is remembered for his roles in *Pépe le Moko* (1936), *Grand Illusion* (1937), *Port of Shadows* (1938), *The Human Beast* (1938), and *Daybreak* (1939). He gave his most remarkable postwar performance in *A Monkey in Winter* (1962).

LESLIE HALLIWELL

gable

Gable is a term used to describe the triangular upper section of a building's exterior wall where it intersects two planes of a sloped roof. The gable may be a distinct architectural element above the eaves or cornice, such as the PEDIMENT on a classical building, or it may simply describe that portion of the wall itself.

Gable, Clark

The American actor Clark Gable captivated film audiences with his straightforward and charismatic style of acting. He appears here in his role as Rhett Butler, with actress Vivien Leigh, in a scene from the Civil War epic Gone with the Wind *(1939). Gable epitomized the charm of the Hollywood leading man of the 1930s.*

Such was the brash charm of American film actor Clark Gable, b. Feb. 1, 1901, d. Nov. 16, 1960, that for 30 years he was the undisputed king of Hollywood. As a fast-talking he-man, he was noted for the force of his personality more than for acting talent. Gable appeared in such classic films as *Red Dust* (1932); *It Happened One Night*, for which he won the Academy Award (1934); *Mutiny On The Bounty* (1935); *San Francisco* (1936); and, most notably, as Rhett Butler in *Gone With The Wind* (1939). His postwar films were popular but far less memorable. He died during the filming of *The Misfits* (1961).

LESLIE HALLIWELL

Bibliography: Tornabene, Lyn, *Long Live the King* (1977).

Gabo, Naum [gah'-boh, nowm]

The Russian-American sculptor, painter, and architect Naum Gabo, b. Naom Pevsner in Bryansk, Russia, Aug. 5 (N.S.), 1890, d. Aug. 23, 1977, was one of the chief initiators of the abstract

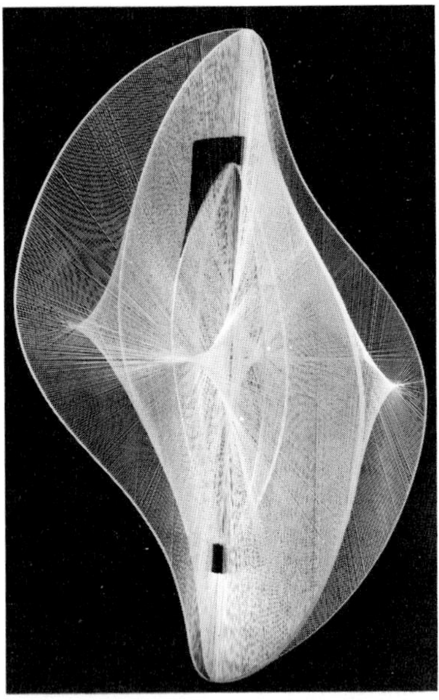

The dynamic, yet elegant, movement of Naum Gabo's Linear Construction, Number 2 *(1949), a delicate structure of plastic and nylon thread, exemplifies his mature style. Industrial materials are inherent to constructivism, a movement that Gabo helped found, and are used to define space as an abstract form integral to the design. (Municipal Museum, Amsterdam.)*

art movement CONSTRUCTIVISM. In 1910, Gabo attended the University of Munich as a medical student, but he began to study engineering in 1912 and also attended the art history lectures of Heinrich Wölfflin. In Munich, then an important art center, Gabo became friendly with Wassily KANDINSKY and began to devote his time to painting and sculpture.

Shortly after the outbreak of World War I, Gabo fled to Oslo, Norway, where he made (1915) his first "constructions." These were figurative heads and abstract forms influenced by synthetic CUBISM, and composed of intersecting planes of plywood or cardboard. Gabo's older brother Antoine Pevsner, also an artist, had joined him in Oslo in 1916 and together they returned to Russia in March 1917, following the first Russian Revolution. They were joined in Moscow by other expatriate artists such as Kasimir MALEVICH, Vladimir TATLIN, and Kandinsky. Gabo won the approval of the Communist government for his art and taught at the Moscow State Art School while engaged in a series of projects such as Serpuchov radio station (1919), which attempted to synthesize the arts of painting, sculpture, and architecture.

In 1920, Gabo began to study the aesthetic properties of movement, an interest he shared with the members of the Italian futurist movement (see FUTURISM), and constructed his *Kinetic Sculpture*. This work was followed by the *Design for Kinetic Construction* (1922) and *Monument for the Institute of Physics and Mathematics* (1925). Gabo's belief that art was an autonomous activity that could not be put to political use brought him into conflict with his colleagues and the government, and he left the USSR in 1922 for Berlin.

From 1926 to 1927 he collaborated with his brother in designing stage sets for Serge DIAGHILEV and traveled widely in Europe until 1946, when he became a permanent U.S. resident. From 1953 to 1954, Gabo taught architecture at Harvard University and executed several architectural commissions, including the U.S. Rubber Company building, New York City (1956). Gabo's major contribution to 20th-century art, however, has been in sculpture, which he succeeded in bringing into close rapport with the modern world by his use of plastics and metals. Notable examples of his work may be seen in New York's Museum of Modern Art. BARBARA CAVALIERE

Bibliography: Bann, Stephen, ed., *The Tradition of Constructivism* (1974); Gabo, Naum, *Gabo* (1957); Gabo, Naum, et al., *Circle: International Survey of Constructive Art* (1966).

Gabon [gah-bohn']

Gabon is a country on the west coast of Africa that straddles the equator. It is bounded on the south and east by the Congo, on the north by Cameroon, and on the northwest by Equatorial Guinea. Located on its 885-km (550-mi) Atlantic coastline is the capital and principal port, LIBREVILLE.

LAND AND RESOURCES

Gabon has a coastal plain that varies from 32 to 160 km (20 to 100 mi) in width. In the north and east are rugged plateaus, 300–610 m (1,000–2,000 ft) in elevation. Beyond the plateaus, to the east, mountain ranges rise to over 914 m (3,000 ft), with Mount Iboundji of the Chaillu Mountains, the highest point in the country, reaching 1,575 m (5,167 ft).

Gabon has an equatorial climate with continually high humidity and an average annual temperature of about 27° C (81° F). Rainfall occurs all year, except along the coast, where the cold Benguela Current cools and dries the air to produce two dry seasons—one from May to September, when almost no rain falls, and one from mid-December to mid-January. In the north, about 3,810 mm (150 in) of rainfalls annually; about 2,540 mm (100 in) falls at Libreville in the northwest.

The rough terrain and heavy rainfall produce many rivers that have the potential for hydroelectric development. The largest is the Ogooué, which is navigable for 354 km (220 mi) upstream and has a catchment basin of 220,000 km^2 (84,942 mi^2), draining the southern half of the country. About 75% of Gabon is covered by dense tropical rain forests with many species of trees, including mahogany, ebony, and okoume. Occasional areas of savanna interrupt the forest along the coast and in the south.

PEOPLE

Waves of migrating Negroid peoples from the northeast displaced much of the earlier Pygmy population, and today the major groups are the FANG, Adouma, Eshiras, and Okande.

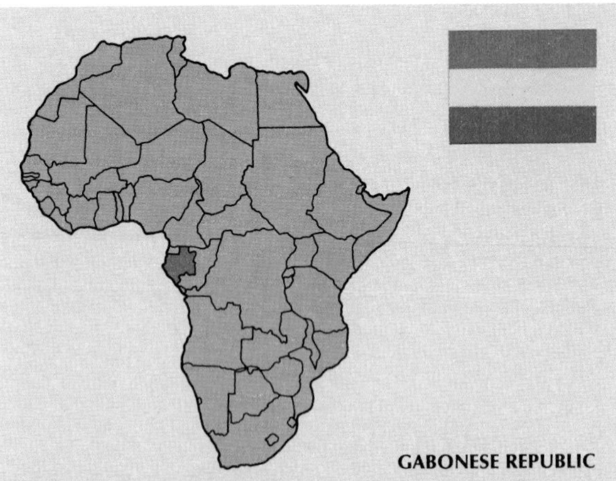

GABONESE REPUBLIC

LAND. Area: 267,667 km^2 (103,347 mi^2). Capital and largest city: Libreville (1983 est. pop., 257,000).

PEOPLE. Population (1986 est.): 1,200,000. Density (1986 est.): 4.4 persons per km^2 (11.6 per mi^2). Distribution (1986): 41% urban, 59% rural. Annual growth (1983): 1.6%. Official language: French. Major religions: Roman Catholicism, traditional religions, Protestantism.

EDUCATION AND HEALTH. Literacy (1980): 65% of adult population. Universities (1986): 1. Hospital beds (1984): 5,774. Physicians (1984): 300. Life expectancy (1983): women—51; men—47. Infant mortality (1986): 112 per 1,000 live births.

ECONOMY. GNP (1983: $3.4 billion; $3,692 per capita. Labor distribution (1983): agriculture—65%; industry and commerce—30%; government and services—5%. Foreign trade (1982): imports—$742 million; exports—$2,161 million; principal trade partners—France, Spain, United Kingdom, Italy. Currency: 1 C.F.A. franc = 100 centimes.

GOVERNMENT. Type: one-party state. Legislature: National Assembly. Political subdivisions: 9 provinces.

COMMUNICATIONS. Railroads (1986): 689 km (428 mi) total. Roads (1984): 7,500 km (4,660 mi) total. Major ports: 2. Airfields (international, 1986): 3.

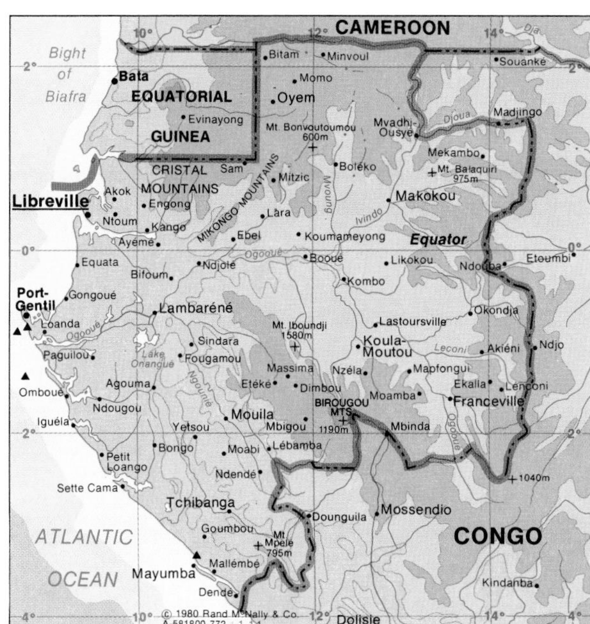

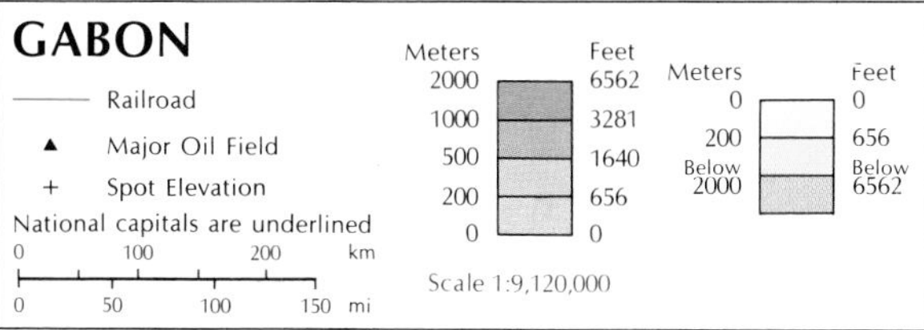

There is, however, a European minority, and French, which is the official language, is widely spoken, although the country's peoples also speak eight separate tribal languages. More than 50% of the people are Roman Catholics and Protestants, but traditional African religions prevail outside the larger towns.

Gabon is sparsely populated; most of the people live near the coast or along the river banks. Libreville is the largest city. Other urban centers include Port-Gentil, Lambaréné (the site of Albert SCHWEITZER's famous mission hospital), the mining centers of Franceville and Moamba, and the new port at Owedo, near Libreville. Education is free and compulsory between the ages of 6 and 16. Improved medical facilities have lowered the very high death rate that, until recently, caused Gabon's population to decline.

A laborer in Gabon poles logs out onto a river, where the current will carry them downstream to one of the country's many lumber mills. A major source of valuable tropical hardwoods, such as mahogany, ebony, and zingana, Gabon is also the world's largest exporter of oakum, a softwood important in the manufacture of plywood.

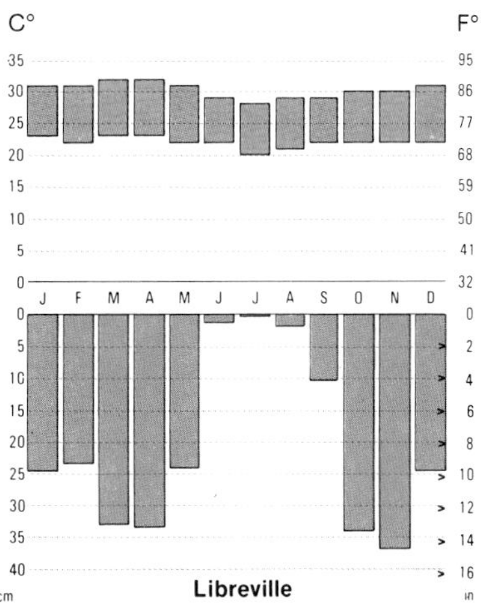

Bars indicate monthly ranges of temperature (red) and precipitation (blue) of Libreville, the capital of Gabon. Located on the west African coast, Libreville has a tropical wet-dry climate.

ECONOMIC ACTIVITY

In recent decades Gabon has experienced rapid economic growth, primarily because of its extensive mineral resources. It now has one of the highest per capita incomes in Africa. Petroleum production represents more than 80% of the country's export earnings. Gabon has about 25% of the world's known deposits of manganese, particularly in the Moamba region. Uranium and iron ore are also mined, and there are deposits of lead, zinc, and phosphate. To reduce the dependence on petroleum earnings, the government is attempting to diversify the economy and is promoting further mineral exploration.

About two-thirds of the population are subsistence farmers growing primarily manioc, bananas, yams, peanuts, and maize. Less than 1% of the land is cultivated, and more than half of all foodstuffs are imported. Forest products, which once provided more than 75% of all export earnings, now provide less than 10%. Manufacturing is limited. Tourism, fishing, and agricultural diversification are being promoted.

Rivers remain important means of internal transportation. The recently opened Trans-Gabon railroad links Libreville to Franceville and opens the interior jungle to logging, mining, and other activities. A proposed extension would facilitate exploitation of the huge high-grade iron-ore deposits at Mekambo. Pending improvement of the transit network, many of Gabon's mineral products are exported through Pointe-Noire in the Congo. Despite a continuing foreign trade surplus, Gabon experienced balance-of-payments difficulties in the late 1970s. It has since introduced reforms to reduce public spending and lower the foreign debt.

HISTORY AND GOVERNMENT

In 1839, France signed a treaty with local chiefs that gave it powers over the southern coastal regions of Gabon. The Berlin Conference of 1885 awarded all of the territory discovered by Pierre de BRAZZA to France. This area was organized (in 1910) into French Equatorial Africa, and the separate colonies of Gabon, Congo, Chad, and Ubangi-Shari were formed. Gabon achieved its independence from France in 1960, and under the 1961 constitution is a republic with a presidential form of government. Leon M'ba was the first president of the republic and presided over the unicameral National Assembly. At the death of M'ba in 1967, Omar Bongo succeeded to the presidency. Bongo introduced a one-party system in 1968 and has since been reelected unopposed. JOHN W. SNADEN

Bibliography: Ajayi, J. F., and Crowder, M., eds., *History of West Africa,* 2 vols. (1974, 1976); Barnes, J. F., *Gabon* (1986); Crowder, M., *West Africa under Colonial Rule* (1968); Gardinier, D. E., *Historical Dictionary of Gabon* (1981); Patterson, K. D., *The Northern Gabon Coast to 1875* (1975); Udo, R. K., *A Comprehensive Geography of West Africa* (1978); Weinstein, B., *Gabon* (1967).

Gabor, Dennis [gah'-bohr]

The British scientist and inventor Dennis Gabor, b. Budapest, Hungary, June 5, 1900, d. Feb. 8, 1979, won the Nobel prize for physics (1971) for his invention (1947) and later development of HOLOGRAPHY, a means of producing a three-dimensional photographic image without using a lens. Gabor began his career as an industrial research engineer in Germany but went to England with the rise of the Nazis in 1933. He began teaching in 1949 at the Imperial College of Science and Technology in London and became professor of applied electronic physics there in 1958. In 1968 he was appointed staff scientist at CBS Laboratories in Stamford, Conn.

Bibliography: Gabor, Dennis, *The Mature Society* (1972).

Gaborone [gah-buh-roh'-nee]

Gaborone (formerly Gaberones) is the capital of Botswana in south central Africa. In 1965, the year before Botswana received independence, the city replaced Mafeking, South Africa, as the country's administrative headquarters. It has a population of 79,000 (1984 est.) and is situated on the Cape-Zimbabwe railroad, close to the South African border. Primarily an administrative center with a university and national museum, it lacks a modern urban-industrial economy.

Gabriel (angel)

The angel Gabriel, an important figure in the Bible, appears first in the Book of Daniel (chapters 8 and 9) as a messenger and revealer. In the New Testament he announces the births of John the Baptist and Jesus Christ (Luke 1), and in the Book of Enoch, part of the pseudepigrapha, he is one of the seven archangels who stand close to God. Later Christian tradition made him the trumpeter of the Last Judgment. A popular figure in art, Gabriel is often pictured appearing to Mary or with trumpet raised. In Islam he is Jibril, the principal of many tales, who revealed the Koran to Muhammad.

ANTHONY J. SALDARINI

Gabriel (family)

During the 17th and 18th centuries, the Gabriel family produced a dynasty of architects that enjoyed the favor of French royalty. Two members of the family had unusually distinguished careers. **Jacques V Gabriel**, b. Apr. 6, 1667, d. June 23, 1742, was appointed first architect to the king in 1734. His most notable commissions were the royal squares at Rennes (after 1720) and Bordeaux (1735–55). In association with Jean Aubert, he created one of the outstanding private houses of the period, the Hôtel de Biron, Paris (1728–31; now the Rodin Museum).

Ange Jacques Gabriel, b. Oct. 23, 1698, d. Jan. 4, 1782, succeeded his father as first architect to the king in 1742. To fulfill Louis XV's desire for a more intimate architectural scale than the grandiose style preferred by Louis XIV, Gabriel took responsibility for the modernization and extension of the royal residences: the Palace of VERSAILLES (Grand Projet, 1742–75; Opéra, 1748–70); Château de FOUNTAINEBLEAU (Gros Pavillon, 1749–50); and Château de Compiègne (begun 1751). Public buildings commissioned from Gabriel by the crown included the École Militaire (1751–58) and the Place de la Concorde (designed 1753–55 as Place Louis XI), both in Paris.

Ange Jacques Gabriel's chief architectural triumphs were his small, blocklike structures, chastely decorated, such as the king's hunting lodges and the pleasure houses of the king's mistress, Madame de Pompadour. His masterpiece is the PETIT TRIANON (1762–68), at Versailles, a perfect cube with exterior facades derived from the architectural idiom of Andrea PALLADIO. The academic classicism of its detailing accords perfectly with the architectural theory of such contemporaries as Jacques François Blondel. The "Style Gabriel" was essentially conservative; but its sharply chiseled features and exquisite small-scale decoration represent the ultimate refinement of French classical tradition.

ROBERT NEUMAN

Bibliography: Blomfield, Reginald T., *Six Architects* (1935); Kalnein, Wend Graf, and Levey, Michael, *Art and Architecture of the Eighteenth Century in France* (1972); Tadgell, Christopher, *Ange-Jacques Gabriel*, ed. by John Harris and Alastair Laing (1986).

Gabriel (slave)

Gabriel, sometimes called Gabriel Prosser, b. *c.*1776, d. Oct. 7, 1800, was a black slave who led an abortive uprising near Richmond, Va., in 1800. Having sought in vain to develop a broad base of support, Gabriel and his followers nevertheless made plans to assault Richmond on August 30. The plot was discovered, and James Monroe, then governor of Virginia, called out the militia to round up the rebels. Gabriel fled but was brought back and hanged, along with some 35 others. The incident apparently disturbed many slaveholders, who, as Monroe said, could no longer "count with certainty" on the "tranquil submission" of the slaves.

Gabrieli (family) [gah-bree-ay'-lee]

The Gabrielis were a Venetian family, two of whose members, Andrea and Giovanni, were among the most important composers of the 16th and early 17th centuries.

Andrea Gabrieli, b. *c.*1520, d. 1586, was a pupil of Adrian Willaert at St. Mark's Basilica, Venice. Little is known of his life until 1558, when he became organist of San Geremia in Venice. He appears to have traveled extensively until he was appointed (1566) second organist of St. Mark's, later succeeding (1584) Claudio Merulo as first organist. His compositions include setting of Latin psalms, masses, and motets; several books of madrigals; and instrumental music, mostly for organ.

Giovanni Gabrieli, b. *c.*1554–57, d. Aug. 12, 1612, was a nephew and pupil of Andrea. He was organist and assistant to Roland de Lassus in Munich from 1575 to 1579. On his return to Venice, he deputized for Merulo at the first organ of St. Mark's, becoming second organist in 1584 when his uncle succeeded Merulo as first organist. With Andrea's death in 1586, Giovanni was made first organist, a post he held until he died. He had many pupils, of whom Heinrich Schütz was the most celebrated. His compositions include motets, madrigals, many pieces for ensembles of brass instruments, and organ works.

The Gabrielis' progressive, innovative style led directly to the operatic idiom of the 17th century. Andrea was a master of the art of setting texts to music. He was the first composer to assign specific instrumental parts in choral music and to pit groups of instruments against contrasting vocal groups. He was one of the first to write music for a specific combination of instruments without voices, and the first to write pieces designated as "sonatas." His organ music formed the basis of Italian organ music for a century afterward. Giovanni further developed the style of his uncle, refining the contrasts of sonorities between vocal and instrumental groups, and exploiting dynamic (loud and soft) contrasts as well. His concertos, works for opposing forces of voices and instruments, initiated the concerto concept that dominated much of baroque music. The grand Venetian style of the Gabrielis was carried by their pupils to Germany, where it vitalized German music for a century.

WILLIAM HAYS

Bibliography: Arnold, Denis, *Giovanni Gabrieli and the Music of the Italian High Renaissance* (1979); Bukofzer, Manfred, *Music in the Baroque Era* (1947); Einstein, Alfred, *The Italian Madrigal,* 3 vols. (1949; repr. 1971); Kenton, Egon, *Life and Works of Giovanni Gabrieli* (1967); Reese, Gustave, *Music in the Renaissance,* rev. ed. (1959).

Gadda, Carlo Emilio [gahd'-dah]

Carlo Emilio Gadda, b. Nov. 14, 1893, d. May 21, 1973, was one of the most influential contemporary Italian writers. His World War I diary, *Giornale di guerra e di prigionia* (Journal of War and Imprisonment, 1955), is an important example of his first attempts at a completely unique style, fusing a literary language, dialects, slang, foreign languages, and scientific vocabulary. His masterpiece, *That Awful Mess on Via Merulana* (1957; Eng. trans., 1965), is remarkable for its stylistic innovations.

LOUIS KIBLER

Gaddi (family) [gahd'-dee]

The Gaddi family, which included Gaddo, Taddeo, and Agnolo Gaddi, was prominent in Florentine painting for more than a century. **Gaddo Gaddi**, *c.*1250–1330, a contemporary of Giotto di Bondone, has been credited with several Florentine mosaics that reveal the influence of CIMABUE. Gaddo's son **Taddeo**, *c.*1300–66, was one of Giotto's most accomplished pupils and collaborators. In Taddeo's fresco cycle on the life of Mary (1332–38) in Santa Croce, Florence, he elaborated upon his master's monumental style, giving a greater sense of spatial illusion. His mature work, complex in figural detail, is well represented by his altarpiece of the Madonna and Child with saints (1353) in the Cathedral of Pistoia.

Taddeo's son **Agnolo**, fl. 1369–96, also painted in the tradition of Giotto. His major works include frescoes on the Legend of the True Cross in the choir of Santa Croce, Florence (*c.*1388–93). His highly decorated manner anticipates the style of his pupil Lorenzo Monaco. ROSA MARIA LETTS

Bibliography: Cole, Bruce, *Agnolo Gaddi* (1977).

Gaddis, William [gad'-is]

The American author William Gaddis, b. New York City, 1922, published two long novels, *The Recognitions* (1955), and *JR* (1975), whose complicated plots and loose narrative structure allowed ample opportunities for digressions into philosophy, theology, and social comment. At first received with hostility by critics, Gaddis's works have since attracted many enthusiastic readers. *Carpenter's Gothic,* another, shorter novel, was published in 1985. JEROME KLINKOWITZ

Gade, Niels [gah'-the, neels]

The founder of Denmark's national romantic school of music, Niels Vilhelm Gade, b. Feb. 22, 1817, d. Dec. 21, 1890, was that country's most celebrated 19th-century composer. Gade held various important posts, including that of assistant conductor to Felix Mendelssohn at the Leipzig Gewandhaus (1843–48). His music shows the influence of Mendelssohn and Robert Schumann as well as of Danish folk music. His compositions include eight symphonies, overtures, chamber music, a piano sonata, cantatas, and songs.

Gadolin, Johan [gah-doh-leen']

The Finnish chemist and mineralogist Johan Gadolin, b. June 5, 1760, d. Aug. 15, 1852, did early research on the rare earths (see LANTHANIDE SERIES) and was the leading Scandinavian advocate of LAVOISIER's nomenclature and theory of combustion. He investigated specific heat and the latent heat of steam, determined the composition of PRUSSIAN BLUE, and developed a method for analyzing iron ores. In the 1790s, while studying a new mineral (later named gadolinite), he discovered a material later called yttria and shown to contain several rare-earth elements. GEORGE B. KAUFFMAN

gadolinium [gad-uh-lin'-ee-uhm]

The chemical element gadolinium is a lustrous, magnetic metal of the rare earth LANTHANIDE SERIES, group IIIB of the periodic table. Its symbol is Gd, its atomic number 64, its atomic weight 157.25, and its valence +3. It is often found in association with other rare earths. Gadolinium oxide was isolated in 1880 by the French chemist J. C. G. de Marignac from the mineral gadolinite, for which the element is named. Seven gadolinium isotopes occur in nature. At least one, ^{152}Gd, is radioactive, with a half-life of 1.1×10^{14} years. With the highest neutron-absorption CROSS-SECTION of any known element, gadolinium is used in control rods in some nuclear reactors. It is also used in noise filters, in phosphors for color television, and to increase the tensile strength and electrical conductivity of some other metals.

Gadsden [gadz'-den]

Gadsden (1980 pop., 47,565), the seat of Etowah County in northeastern Alabama, is situated on the Coosa River about 95 km (59 mi) northeast of Birmingham. Iron, manganese, coal, and limestone are mined in the surrounding Appalachian foothills, and Gadsden's steel industry is the second largest in the South. Other industries manufacture rubber and electronic devices. Founded in 1846 as Double Springs, the town was renamed in 1853 for James Gadsden, who negotiated the Gadsden Purchase.

Gadsden Purchase

The Gadsden Purchase is the name given to a strip of land, now the southern part of Arizona and New Mexico, purchased by the U.S. government from Mexico in 1853. Despite the rancors of the Mexican War (1846–48), the Mexican government thereafter proved willing to arrange for more of its land to come under control of the United States—though for a price. Thus on Dec. 30, 1853, American diplomat James Gadsden (1788–1858) signed a treaty whereby Mexico ceded a rectangular strip of about 76,760 km^2 (29,640 mi^2), in the Mesilla Valley south of the Gila River, for $10 million. Negotiated by the Democratic administration of President Franklin Pierce, the treaty offered Southerners a route for a railroad to the Pacific. Before such a project could be undertaken, however, the Civil War intervened. ROBERT H. FERRELL

Gaea [jee'-uh]

In Greek mythology, Gaea (or Gaia) was the goddess of Earth and the daughter of CHAOS. She was regarded as the mother of all creation, preceding Zeus and the other Olympian gods. She gave birth to URANUS, the sky, and with Uranus she produced the TITANS. Other offspring followed, of whom some were such frightful monsters, like the CYCLOPS, that Uranus decided to imprison them in the depths of the Earth. Gaea took vengeance by instigating Uranus's castration. In Roman mythology, she was identified with Tellus and Terra.

Gaelic language: see CELTIC LANGUAGES.

Gaels [gaylz]

The term *Gael* is applied to native inhabitants of those parts of Ireland, Scotland, and the Isle of Man where languages of the Gaelic, or Goidelic, branch of Celtic (see CELTIC LANGUAGES) were traditionally spoken. Almost no monolingual Gaelic speakers survive today, and English is now the dominant language in these areas. Peasant farmers by tradition, Gaels worked at dairying, fishing, sheepherding, cattle raising, and handicrafts and cultivated cereal and vegetable crops, especially potatoes. The commercial development of peasant industries includes Scottish and Manx woolen tweeds and Irish-knit wool sweaters. ROBERT T. ANDERSON

Bibliography: O'Driscoll, R., ed., *The Celtic Consciousness* (1982).

gag rules

The gag rules were procedural rules first adopted by the U.S. House of Representatives on May 25–26, 1836, to prevent debate of the slavery question. In the 1830s ABOLITIONISTS presented thousands of petitions to Congress, calling for abolition of slavery in the District of Columbia, an end to the slave trade, and refusal of admission to the Union of more slave states. In response, a coalition of Southerners and Northern Democrats in the House secured passage of rules to stifle debate on this issue. Opposition to the rules was led by former President John Quincy Adams, who deplored the infringement of the right to petition. With the rise of antislavery sentiment in the North, he was finally able to secure repeal of the rules on Dec. 3, 1844.

Bibliography: Greenberg, K. S., *Masters and Statesmen: The Political Culture of American Slavery* (1986); Wiecek, William M., *The Sources of Antislavery Constitutionalism in America, 1760–1848* (1977).

Gagarin, Yuri [gah-gah'-rin, yoo'-ree]

The Soviet cosmonaut Yuri Gagarin, b. Mar. 9, 1934, d. Mar. 27, 1968, was the first man in space. Gagarin, an air force jet

Yuri Gagarin, a Soviet cosmonaut, became the first man in space on Apr. 12, 1961, when his Vostok 1 *spaceship orbited the Earth once and made a successful reentry. Slated to take part in the Soyuz program, Gagarin was killed in the crash of a jet trainer in 1968.*

pilot, was chosen with the first group of Soviet cosmonauts in March 1960. On Apr. 12, 1961, he was launched into orbit in the VOSTOK *1* spaceship. It reached a maximum altitude of 327 km (203 mi) and circled the Earth once before landing near the Volga River. Moscow claimed that Gagarin rode the ship all the way down, but other experts, including some Soviet sources, maintain that Gagarin bailed out of the Vostok at an altitude of 7,000 m (23,000 ft) and landed by parachute.

After a series of triumphant world tours, Gagarin was assigned as training director of the brief women-cosmonaut program (1961–63) and later returned to flight status for the SOYUZ program. When he was killed in the crash of a MIG trainer jet in 1968, he was given a state funeral and his ashes were interred in the Kremlin Wall. A prominent crater on the back of the Moon is named for him. JAMES OBERG

Bibliography: Sharpe, Mitchell, *Yuri Gagarin* (1969).

Gage, Thomas

Thomas Gage, b. 1719 or 1720, d. Apr. 2, 1787, was a British general in North America during the years preceding the outbreak of the American Revolution. He first came to America to serve in Edward BRADDOCK's expedition of 1755, and he was subsequently active in several campaigns against the French. Appointed (1760) governor at Montreal, he went to New York in 1763 as commander-in-chief of the British forces. In 1774 he became governor of Massachusetts, where he attempted to quell agitation and enforce the INTOLERABLE ACTS. It was Gage who ordered the troops to Lexington and Concord in April 1775. After the Battle of BUNKER HILL, he was recalled to England. DOUGLAS EDWARD LEACH

Bibliography: Alden, J. R., *General Gage in America* (1948).

Gaia hypothesis

The Gaia hypothesis, named for the Greek Earth goddess GAEA, holds that the Earth should be regarded as a living organism. According to this view, the BIOSPHERE, or totality of life on the planet, influences Earth processes so as to sustain and advance life. The hypothesis was first advanced by British biologist James Lovelock in 1969. It was further developed by Lovelock, along with U.S. biologist Lynn Margulis, and set forth in Lovelock's book *Gaia: A New Look at Life on Earth* (1979). The hypothesis influenced ecological and environmental studies, but it also aroused controversy over its perceived nonscientific aspects and occasionally cultish following. Lovelock subsequently modified his views to be in closer agreement with standard HOMEOSTASIS concepts of the maintenance of equilibrium in biological systems.

Bibliography: Joseph, L. E., "Britain's Whole Earth Guru," *The New York Times Magazine,* Nov. 23, 1986; Kerr, R. A., "No Longer Willful, Gaia Becomes Respectable," *Science,* Apr. 22, 1988; Lovelock, James, *The Ages of Gaia* (1988).

Gaines, Edmund Pendleton

Edmund Pendleton Gaines, b. Mar. 20, 1777, d. June 6, 1849, was a U.S. military commander of the pre–Civil War period. Born in Virginia, he was a grandnephew of Revolutionary leader Edmund Pendleton. His success against the British at Fort Erie, Ontario, during the War of 1812 won him the rank of brigadier general. Thereafter, Gaines fought in the Black Hawk and Seminole Wars. During the Mexican War, he came into conflict with his superiors and was censured for insubordination.

Gaines, Ernest J.

Ernest James Gaines, b. Oscar, La., Jan. 15, 1933, is an American writer best known for his 1971 novel *The Autobiography of Miss Jane Pittman,* a compelling account of the life of southern blacks from the time of slavery to the civil rights movement as told by its centenarian heroine, Jane Pittman. A dramatization of the novel, first televised in 1974, won nine Emmy Awards. Other works by Gaines include the novels *Catherine Carmier* (1964), *Of Love and Dust* (1967), *In My Father's House* (1978), and *A Gathering of Old Men* (1983), and a collection of short stories, *Bloodline* (1968).

Gainsborough, Thomas [gaynz'-bur-oh]

Thomas Gainsborough, b. 1727, d. Aug. 2, 1788, was one of the most accomplished English painters of the 18th century, excelling both in landscapes and portraits. A Suffolk cloth merchant's son, Gainsborough went to London in 1740 to

Thomas Gainsborough, best known for his portraits of 18th-century British aristocrats, painted The Morning Walk, *a portrait of Mr. and Mrs. William Hallett, in 1785. The fluid line and dignified elegance of the gracefully moving figures in an idyllic, wooded setting are typical of Gainsborough's late style. (National Gallery, London.)*

work as an assistant to the French engraver Hubert GRAVELOT, who had been a pupil of the rococo painter François BOUCHER. He also worked as a restorer of paintings for art dealers and thus became acquainted with work of such 17th-century Dutch landscape artists as Jacob van RUISDAEL. Gainsborough's debt to the light-hearted artificiality of the ROCOCO STYLE was tempered by his admiration for the Dutch landscape tradition and its direct observation of nature.

In 1748, Gainsborough returned to Suffolk and settled in Ipswich, where he established a reputation as a portraitist. His early, small-scale works depict their unpretentious, even homely, subjects in a setting that is often stylized but sometimes naturalistic—as in *Robert Andrews and Mary, His Wife* (*c*.1748; National Gallery, London), who sit in a verdant landscape bordering on a cornfield. Gainsborough's early portraits of prosperous English families continue a tradition that was begun by the conversation pieces of William HOGARTH, but their elegance approaches the aristocratic manner of Anthony VAN DYCK, with whose work Gainsborough later became acquainted.

Throughout his life Gainsborough painted and drew landscapes, but he was obliged to devote most of his time to portraiture, which was more esteemed and better remunerated by his contemporaries. Demand for Gainsborough's portraits steadily increased when, in 1759, he moved to the fashionable spa town of Bath. There his mature style developed in numerous portraits of the aristocracy: elegantly dressed men and women depicted full-length against idyllic imaginary landscapes. His most celebrated work, *The Blue Boy* (1770; Henry Huntington Art Gallery, San Marino, Calif.), dates from this period.

In 1768, Gainsborough became a founding member of the Royal Academy of Arts in London, where he moved in 1774, and established a large portrait practice in rivalry with his great contemporary, Sir Joshua REYNOLDS. Gainsborough now numbered members of the royal family among his patrons. Many of his finest works of these years, however, are informal portraits of his friends from the world of music and the theater. The subjects of such portraits included David Garrick, Sarah Siddons, and Johann Christian Bach.

In 1780, Gainsborough began to paint what Reynolds called his "fancy pictures." These arcadian landscapes populated with realistic bucolic figures realized his many talents in a complex synthesis. The paintings bear some resemblance to those of Jean Baptiste GREUZE, but their fanciful sensuousness and rapid brushwork recall Antoine WATTEAU.

The romantic bravura of Gainsborough's later work, which differs radically from the more sober grand manner of Reynolds, anticipates the style of J. M. W. TURNER. In Gainsborough's many landscape drawings, discovered only after his death, John CONSTABLE found encouragement for his own studies of natural scenery. Reynolds recognized Gainsborough's great contribution to English painting in *The Fourteenth Discourse*, a tribute delivered to the Royal Academy after Gainsborough's death. HOWARD BATCHELOR

Bibliography: Hayes, John, *Gainsborough as Printmaker* (1972) and *Gainsborough's Landscape Paintings*, 2 vols. (1982); Hayes, John, and Staiton, Lindsay, *Gainsborough Drawings* (1985); Leonard, Jonathan N., *The World of Gainsborough* (1969); Lindsay, Jack, *Gainsborough: His Life and Art* (1985); Reynolds, Joshua, *Discourses on Art*, ed. by Roger R. Wark (1959); Waterhouse, Ellis K., *Gainsborough* (1958).

Gaiseric, King of the Vandals [gy'-sur-ik]

Gaiseric, also known as Genseric, d. 477, was the founder of a 5th-century Vandal kingdom based in North Africa. Succeeding his brother Gunderic as king of the VANDALS and Alans in 428, Gaiseric led (429) his people from Spain to North Africa, which he gradually conquered from the Romans over the next 10 years. He then built a powerful fleet, with which he dominated the western Mediterranean, capturing and looting Rome in 455. At the time of his death he was ruler of what are now Tunisia, and parts of Algeria and Libya, along with Sicily, Corsica, Sardinia, and the Balearic Islands. The dynasty established by Gaiseric lasted until 533.

Bibliography: Goffart, Walter, *Barbarians and Romans, AD 418 to 584* (1980); Gordon, C. D., *The Age of Attila: Fifth Century Byzantium and the Barbarians* (1960).

Gaitskell, Hugh [gayts'-kul]

Hugh Todd Naylor Gaitskell, b. Apr. 9, 1906, d. Jan. 18, 1963, was leader (1955–63) of the British Labour party. Entering Parliament in 1945, he served as minister of fuel and power (1947–50), minister of economic affairs (1950), and chancellor of the exchequer (1950–51). In 1955, Gaitskell succeeded Clement Attlee as leader of the party, then in opposition. A moderate, he faced strong left-wing dissension, which contributed to Labour's defeat in the 1959 election. He finally reunited the party but died before his work bore fruit in Labour's electoral victory of 1964.

Bibliography: Hasaler, Stephen, *The Gaitskellites* (1969); McDermott, Geoffrey, *Leader Lost: A Biography of Hugh Gaitskell* (1971); Williams, P. M., *Hugh Gaitskell* (1979).

galactosemia [guh-lak'-tuh-see'-mee-uh]

Galactosemia is an inherited inability to fully metabolize the sugar galactose, a major component of milk, to glucose. The defect occurs due to the absence of one of the enzymes that act in the conversion of galactose, which can build up to toxic levels in the body. Manifestations appear early; if untreated, an infant fails to grow and usually develops brain and liver damage and cataracts. Another sugar should then be substituted for galactose in the diet. PETER L. PETRAKIS

galago [guh-lay'-goh]

The needle-clawed bush baby, or galago, Euoticus elegantulus, *is a primitive primate that nests communally in the forests of western Africa and feeds on insects and fruit. It looks more like a squirrel than a primate and has large eyes and ears, a long, bushy tail, and thick silky fur.*

Galagos, or bush babies, family Galagidae, order Primates, are small, agile African primates related to the lorises but placed in a distinct separate family. They are found throughout Africa south of the Sahara wherever trees are present. They spend much of their time in trees and can jump swiftly from branch to branch or across open grasslands. Their rapid hopping locomotion is aided by two elongated ankle bones. The larger galagos have bushy tails that aid in balancing.

ELI C. MINKOFF

Galahad, Sir [gal'-uh-had]

In the Arthurian legends, Galahad was a knight of the Round Table who succeeded in the quest for the Holy GRAIL through his unexcelled spiritual purity. Galahad was the son of LANCE-

LOT and Elaine the Fair of Astolat. He gradually replaced PARSIFAL as the hero of the Grail legends in the 13th century, when they became invested with Christian symbolism. Galahad was the king of Sarras when he died. He was taken into heaven with the Holy Grail.

See also: ARTHUR AND ARTHURIAN LEGEND.

Galápagos Islands [guh-lahp'-uh-guhs]

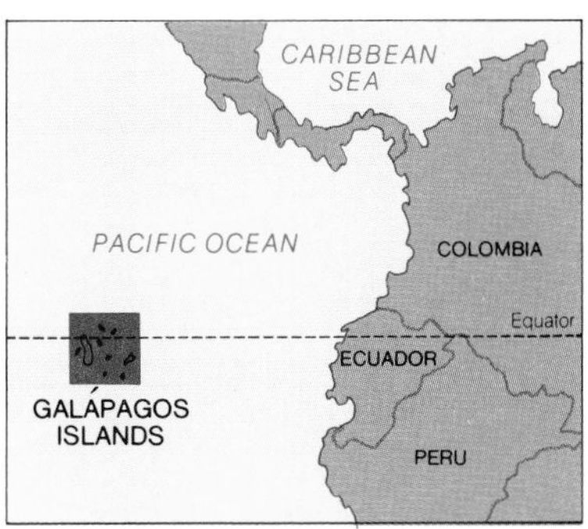

The map indicates the location of the Galápagos Islands, a volcanic archipelago in the Pacific Ocean that is administered by Ecuador. The Galápagos were made famous by naturalist Charles Darwin, who published studies of the evolutionary adaptations exhibited by many of the islands' plants and animals.

The Galápagos Islands are a group of 13 main volcanic islands and numerous islets in the Pacific Ocean about 965 km (600 mi) off the coast of South America. The islands constitute a province of Ecuador, and their official name is Archipiélago de Colón. They have a total area of 7,845 km^2 (3,029 mi^2) and a population of 9,000 (1985 est.). The capital is San Cristóbal.

Because they are located in the path of the cold Peru Current, the islands have a climate that is generally cool and dry for islands that lie on the equator. The coastal zones are desolate, but the upper slopes of the high volcanic mountains (some reaching 1,525 m/5,000 ft) receive heavy precipitation and support a dense vegetation.

The islands are noted for their animal life, with its variety of endemic species and distinctive varieties that have developed by adaptation. Best known are the giant land tortoises, the flightless cormorants, and the marine iguanas. In 1985 a fire charred Isabela Island and drew attention to the plight of the islands: increasing numbers of settlers (and of tourists) and attendant development threaten the ecological balance. Conservationists are also trying to control the species introduced by humans and to stop the poaching of protected species.

Discovered by the Spanish in 1535, the Galápagos (Spanish, meaning "tortoises") sheltered buccaneers and whalers until 1832, when Ecuador annexed and settled them. The naturalist Charles DARWIN visited the islands in 1835 and made them famous in his writings on natural selection.

Bibliography: Hickin, N. E., *Animal Life of the Galápagos* (1980); Lewin, Roger, *Darwin's Forgotten World* (1978); Perry, R., ed., *Key Environments: Galápagos* (1984).

Galatea [gal-uh-tee'-uh]

In Greek mythology, Galatea was a nymph, noted for her great beauty, who was loved by the Cyclops POLYPHEMUS. Another Galatea was a statue loved by PYGMALION, king of Cyprus. He prayed to Aphrodite that the statue might be given life. His prayer was answered, and Pygmalion and Galatea were married. The story was the model for George Bernard Shaw's *Pygmalion* (1913), which in turn was the basis for the musical *My Fair Lady* (1956).

Galaţi [gah-lahts']

Galaţi (1981 est. pop., 267,962), a city in southeastern Romania, is a major inland port on the Danube River about 130 km (80 mi) west of its mouth at the Black Sea. Iron and steel, chemicals, textiles, and furniture are manufactured in the city, which also has large shipyards and a naval base. The 17th-century cathedral is a well-known landmark. By the 15th century, Galaţi was a fishing village. Between 1837 and 1883 it was a free port, which led to the city's growth.

Galatia [guh-lay'-shuh]

Galatia was an ancient territory of central Anatolia, now part of Turkey. It was named for its early inhabitants, a branch of an Indo-European tribal confederation called CELTS or Galli (Gauls). These tribes crossed into Anatolia in 278 BC at the invitation of Nicomedes I of Bithynia, who sought their aid in war. Thereafter they began to ravage and plunder on their own. By 275 the Seleucid king Antigonus I had defeated and settled them in an area stretching from southwest to northeast through the central Anatolian plateau, the area that subsequently bore their name.

Always warlike, the Galatian tribes were employed as mercenaries and fought both against and for the Hellenic kingdoms of Anatolia. Galatia became a Roman protectorate in 85 BC. In 25 BC the Romans created a larger province of Galatia, administered from Ancyra (modern Ankara), that enclosed the Galatians between Cappadocia and the province of Asia on the west. Saint Paul's Epistle to the Galatians addressed the Christian churches founded there. LOUIS L. ORLIN

Bibliography: Magie, David, *Roman Rule in Asia Minor* (1950; repr. 1975).

Galatians, Epistle to the [guh-lay'-shuhnz]

The Epistle to the Galatians is one of the books of the New Testament. It was written by Saint Paul in answer to opponents who were trying to convince the Galatian Christians that circumcision was necessary for salvation. The letter, written about AD 54–55, is the fourth epistle in the collection of Pauline letters in the Bible.

The Galatians lived in north central Anatolia. Their faith evidently had been disturbed by the insistence of some Jewish Christians on close ties to Judaism even for gentile converts to Christianity. Paul replied by developing the theme of the efficacy of salvation in Jesus Christ. In the first two chapters, he defends his apostleship and authority. He then presents arguments from Scripture for the primacy of faith in Jesus as alone essential for salvation (chapters 3–4) and continues with an exhortation to true Christian life and freedom (chapters 5–6). This epistle and the Epistle to the Romans served as prime sources for the Reformation teaching on justification by faith.
ANTHONY J. SALSARINI

Bibliography: Bligh, John, *Galatians* (1969).

galaxies: see EXTRAGALACTIC SYSTEMS.

Galaxy, The [gal'-uhk-see]

The galaxy in which we live, usually referred to simply as the Galaxy, or the Milky Way—which is actually only the portion visible to the naked eye—is a giant spiral assemblage of several billion stars, including our Sun. Its true shape, size, and nature have only been discovered by astronomers in the 20th century. It is now known to be an immense disk-shaped object, far larger than most of the galaxies in its immediate neighborhood (the LOCAL GROUP OF GALAXIES). Its visible disk has a diameter of approximately 100,000 light-years and a height above its principal plane of about 1,000 light-years, although some kinds of objects, such as globular CLUSTERS, extend much farther above the galactic plane.

The total mass of the Galaxy can be measured by studying the motions of individual stars and clouds of hydrogen gas in different parts of the Galaxy and by applying CELESTIAL MECHANICS to calculate a total mass that will account for the observed motions. The mass can also be determined from the motions of the Galaxy's small satellite galaxies, especially the nearby dwarf elliptical galaxies, and globular clusters. Computations by both methods agree that the Galaxy's mass is possibly 1,000 to 2,000 billion times the mass of the Sun. As the Sun's mass is about average for a star in the Galaxy, the total number of stars must also be of this order. Most of these stars are invisible from the Earth, however, because the solar system lies in the dense plane of the Galaxy, where interstellar dust obscures all but its nearer parts.

The area around the Galaxy is populated by about 20 galaxies that make up a small cluster called the local group. Most of these neighbors, such as the MAGELLANIC CLOUDS, are far smaller and less luminous than the Galaxy. The only other large galaxy is the ANDROMEDA GALAXY, which is more than 2 million light-years away. It is somewhat larger and more luminous than our own galaxy and is visible to the naked eye. The Andromeda spiral differs slightly in shape from our galaxy, having a larger, smooth, amorphous central bulge and spiral arms that are less patchy.

The Sun lies a little more than 30,000 light-years from the center of the Galaxy. From our vantage point, the Galaxy appears thicker toward its center, in the direction of the constellation Sagittarius, and somewhat thinner in other directions. Because of the obscuration by dust, however, which limits our view in all directions, it is difficult to realize from observation that we are not near the center of the system.

DETERMINATION OF GALACTIC STRUCTURE

Until the 1920s it was thought that the system of stars outlined by the Milky Way was the entire universe; early attempts to understand the structure of the Galaxy were thought of as studies of the universe itself. In 1784, Sir William Herschel attempted to determine the structure of the Milky Way (he referred to his work as exploring the "construction of the heavens") by making extensive star counts through telescopes, recording the number of stars in various directions, and plotting the results in a series of maps. Assuming that all stars had ap-

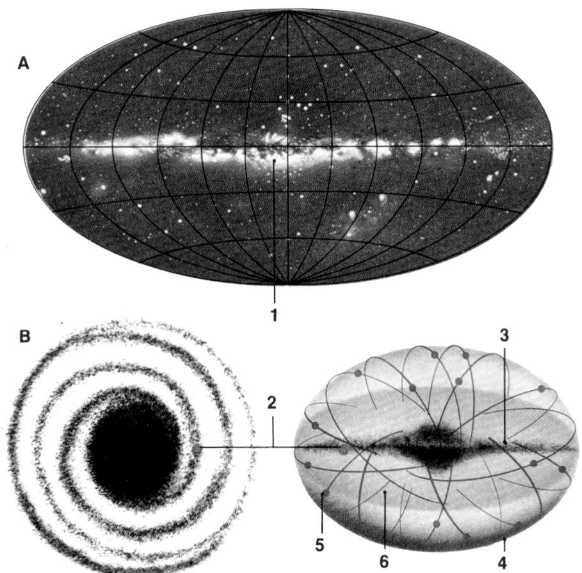

(Above) *From the Earth, the Milky Way, which lies along the plane of the Galaxy, appears as a circular band of light around the sky, which contains dust and gas, as well as stars* (A). *The dust is sufficiently dense to prevent visual observation of the Galaxy's center* (1) *in Sagittarius. A view of the Galaxy from above* (B) *reveals a spiral-shaped structure with the Sun* (2) *about 30,000 light-years from the center. An edge-on view shows a hubbed disk* (3) *surrounded by a spherical halo region* (4) *containing globular clusters* (5) *and high-velocity stars, and by an intermediate region* (6) *containing planetary nebulae.*

(Below) *This panoramic map of the celestial sphere was drawn at the Lund Observatory in Sweden on the basis of many photographs. The map illustrates 7,000 stars, the Milky Way, the Magellanic Clouds, the Andromeda galaxy, and several nebulae. The galactic center is in the Sagittarius region at the center of the map. The Great Rift, a dark cloud of interstellar dust, extends from the constellation Sagittarius to the constellation Cygnus at left center. The number of stars decreases from Sagittarius to Auriga, shown at both ends, and toward the galactic poles at top and bottom.*

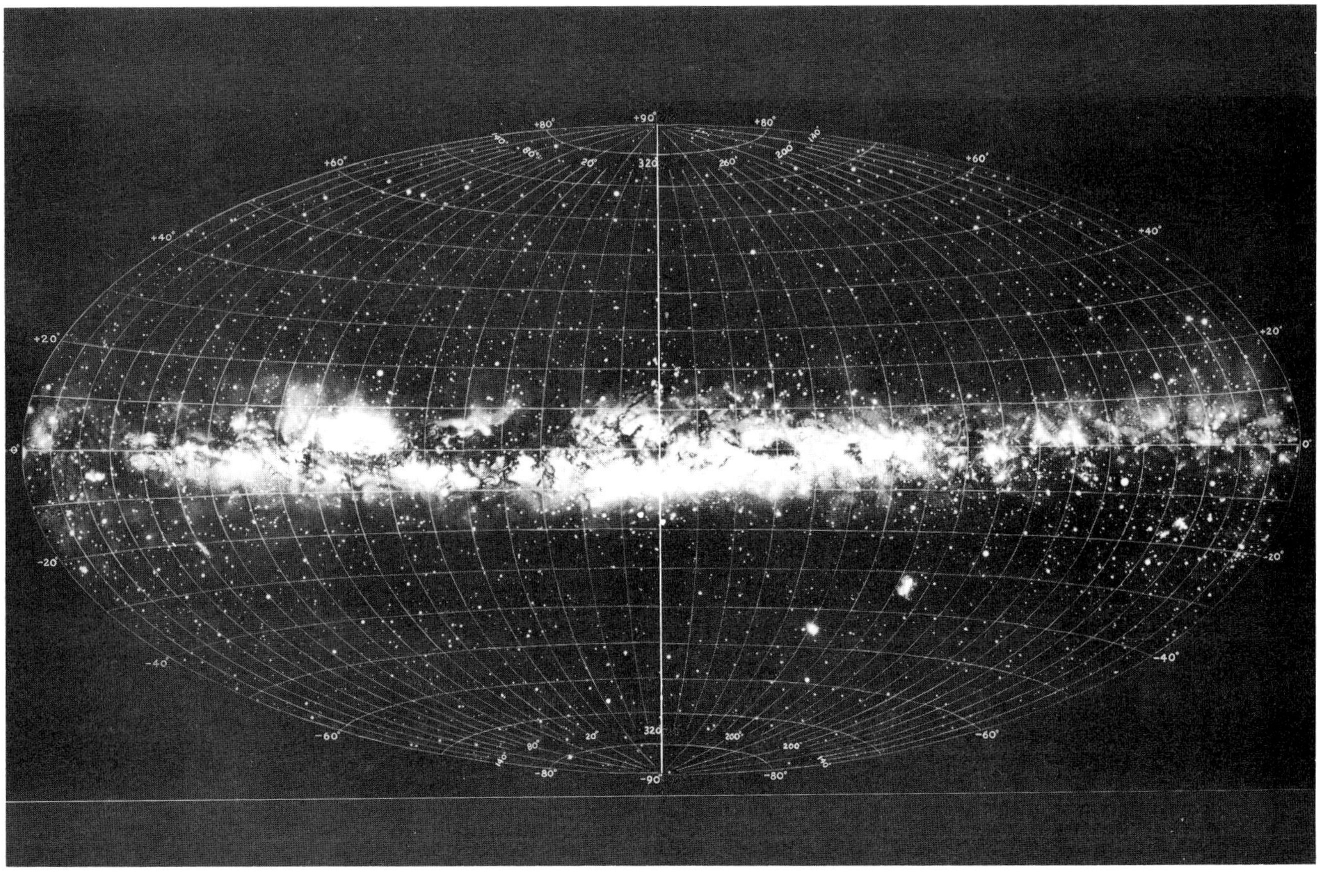

proximately the same brightness and the Galaxy was uniformly dense, Herschel calculated the extent of the system and concluded that we live in the central region of a flat, round arrangement of stars that extends far along the Milky Way.

A much more accurate view of the Galaxy resulted from Harlow Shapley's studies of globular clusters, begun in 1914. Shapley realized that dust obscured large numbers of stars along the Milky Way and discovered that making star counts was not as good a way of gauging the size of the Galaxy as determining the size of the system of globular clusters that lie above and below the obscuration of the Milky Way plane. He determined that the Galaxy is about ten times larger than previously thought, that the Sun is a considerable distance from the center, and that the clusters make up a thin, spherical halo that surrounds a bright flat disk. The detailed structure of the disk was difficult to discover because of the dust, but several astronomers, especially Jacobus C. Kapteyn in Holland and Bart J. Bok in the United States, pursued the task of trying to find a pattern, particularly a pattern of spiral arms. Only fragments of structure emerged, however, and they were found to resemble scraps of spiral arms only when stellar associations were discovered during the late 1940s.

An important breakthrough occurred in 1951, when Harvard scientists Harold Ewen and Edward Purcell made the first radio detection of the 21-cm emission line of neutral hydrogen gas in the Milky Way. By 1954, Dutch and Australian radio astronomers were ready to assemble a radio map of the Galaxy. Since radio waves pass through the dust unimpeded, this map was far more accurate than those based on visual observations. The result clearly showed a complex and beautiful spiral structure, very much like that of the giant galaxy Messier 101 or the Whirlpool Galaxy, Messier 51.

Our present view of the Galaxy is based on highly detailed radio maps of neutral atomic hydrogen gas and other sources, including hot gas clouds and gas-dust complexes that emit radiation from various molecules and parts of molecules, such as water (H_2O), carbon monoxide (CO), and hydroxyl (OH). The Galaxy consists of a slightly warped, scalloped disk of heavy-element–rich stars, gas clouds, and dust, surrounded by a tenuous spherical halo of old, heavy-element–poor stars and star clusters. The halo extends 85,000 light-years from the center and is enveloped by a corona extending to at least 200,000 light-years.

In recent years astronomers have begun to examine the core

The Very Large Array radio telescope in New Mexico produced this picture of the center of the Milky Way in 1984. Approximately 200 light-years out from the very center (lower right) *can be seen the tremendous radiowave-emitting filaments* (upper left), *approximately 150 light-years in length. The galactic plane would lie on a diagonal line drawn through the midpoints of both the core and the filaments.*

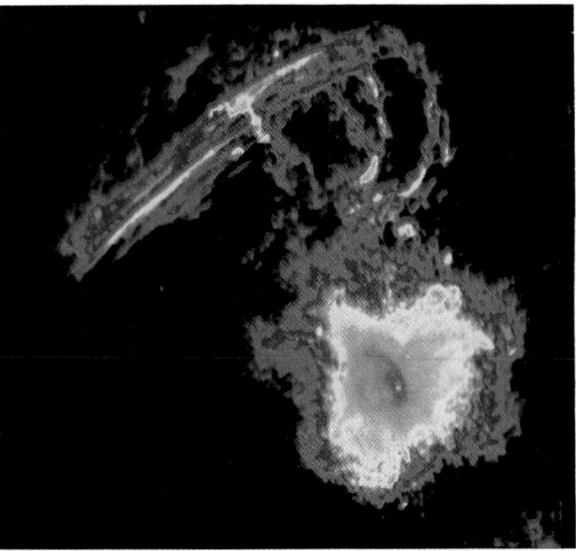

of the Milky Way in other wavelengths (see INFRARED ASTRONOMY; RADIO ASTRONOMY; X-RAY ASTRONOMY). Infrared studies have revealed a small number of fast-moving red supergiant stars within 5 light-years of the center. Strong radio and X-ray emissions from the same area suggest that a BLACK HOLE may exist in that region, and that it may be generating the extremely hot gases spiralling around the galactic center at speeds of up to 700,000 kilometers per hour. Heavy-metal synthesis, which accompanies the formation of new stars, is also thought to occur in that region. Farther out are dramatic radiowave-emitting filaments perpendicular to the galactic plane; these arcs of matter, approximately 150 light-years long, suggest that a huge magnetic field exists around the galactic core. Unrelated to these arcs are three bizarre, threadlike structures, uniformly bright and about one light-year wide and more than 100 light-years long, that cut across the central galactic regions. These threads remain unexplained but may be magnetic in structure.

COMPOSITION OF THE GALAXY

Our galaxy, like most well-studied spiral galaxies, chiefly consists of stars, gas, and dust. Studies of its visible disk indicate that most of the mass is in the stars, with only about 2% gas (mostly hydrogen) and about 0.01% dust.

The Galaxy's stars have been divided into Population I and Population II. Population I stars, prevalent in the spiral arms, include stars of all ages. They contain elements heavier than helium, in ratios comparable to those found in the Sun. Population II stars occur in the bulge around the galactic nucleus and in the spherical halo, including its globular clusters. Population II stars are about 12 to 15 billion years old and are deficient in heavy elements. These are the Galaxy's oldest inhabitants, and they are frequently offered as evidence that the Galaxy itself is 15 billion years old.

The total amount of stars, gas, and dust observed to exist in the Galaxy does not quite equal the total measured mass. It may be necessary to account for the difference by suggesting that the Galaxy contains matter in some invisible form, such as neutrinos, molecular hydrogen, black holes (collapsed large stars), or meteoroids. Recent investigations, however, suggest that the "missing mass" may be found in the corona, the composition of which is unknown; the corona may contain between 100 and 200 billion solar masses.

DYNAMICS OF THE GALAXY

In the early 20th century, as the mystery of the structure of the Galaxy was being unraveled, the motions of stars were also being determined. Astronomers recorded the slow perceived position changes of stars (proper motion) and their motions toward or away from Earth (radial velocities); the latter are easily measured by the Doppler shift of the stars' spectral lines. In 1904, Kapteyn found that stars move in two streams flowing in opposite directions along the Milky Way, one converging in the constellation of Orion and the other converging 180° away, in Scutum. The Swedish astronomer Bertil Lindblad showed that this streaming motion is simply the result of the rotation of the Galaxy. Stars traveling in nearly circular orbits around the galactic center with the Sun will have larger motions relative to the Sun either toward or away from the center—depending on whether they are approaching the nearest or farthest points in their elliptical orbits—than in the direction of motion. Therefore, we preferentially see motions toward us or away from us in these directions.

In 1927, Jan H. Oort of the Netherlands showed that the motions of stars in different parts of the Milky Way could be used to derive the properties of the rotation of the Galaxy, including the velocity of the Sun through space. When modern values are used in Oort's equations, it is found that the Sun's velocity is approximately 250 km/sec in its orbit around the galactic center. The velocities for stars at larger distances from the center are lower than in the inner part of the Galaxy. These velocity differences cause differential rotation in the disk, and they may be the primary cause of the spiral shape of the arms (and also, incidentally, of the rotation of the bodies in the solar system, including the Earth).

The dynamics of the spiral arms are still only imperfectly understood. Differential rotation will make spiral arms out of almost any structural feature in a galaxy, but the arms should only last a fraction of the age of the galaxy. It would lead to a rapid winding-up of the arms in the 50 or so rotations that have occurred since the Galaxy was formed. One possible explanation is that the arms are not constant physical entities, but are waves of high star density moving more slowly than the stars. Stars slow down and pile up temporarily in an arm because of its higher gravitational field, then pass out of the arm and proceed until they encounter the next arm.

Determinations have been made of the Galaxy's movement as a whole, relative to the rest of the universe. For example, high-altitude measurements were made of the universe's BACKGROUND RADIATION, the residual glow of the so-called "big bang" that is assumed to have occurred in the first moments of the universe (see COSMOLOGY). The measurements indicated that the Galaxy is moving, relative to the universe, in the same direction as the constellation Leo lies relative to the Earth, and with a velocity of more than 600 km/sec (373 mi/sec). The Galaxy is also moving at about 100 km/sec (62 mi/sec), relative to the center of mass of the local group of galaxies. The local group, in turn, is moving at a comparable velocity relative to the supercluster of galaxies to which it belongs. This large-scale flow of galaxies is apparently directed toward a huge, distant region of space that has been called the Great Attractor. The cause of this flow is one of the major problems occupying modern cosmology.

RADIATION FROM THE GALAXY

From a distance, the Galaxy could be detected by a wide variety of means, because it emits radiation at almost all wavelengths. It is optically bright, emitting the equivalent of approximately 200 billion Suns in visible radiation. It is a strong source of radio-line emission, especially from its large mass of neutral hydrogen. It is a source of radio continuum noise, both from the hot gas clouds in its arms and from its dense, hot nucleus. Its huge, dark, cool complexes of dust and gas emit infrared emission. It shines in the ultraviolet region, because of its very hot, recently formed stars. And it gives off X radiation from many sources. PAUL W. HODGE

Bibliography: Bok, Bart J. and Priscilla F., *The Milky Way*, 5th ed. (1981); Catchpole, R. M., "A Window on Our Galaxy's Core," *Sky & Telescope*, February 1988; Hodge, Paul W., *Galaxies* (1986); Shuter, W. L., *Kinematics, Dynamics and Structure of the Milky Way* (1983).

See also: EXTRAGALACTIC SYSTEMS; STELLAR EVOLUTION.

Galba, Roman Emperor [gal'-buh]

Galba, 3 BC–AD 69, was Roman emperor from AD 68 to 69. Respected by Augustus and Tiberius, he governed Aquitania, served (33) as consul, commanded Roman forces in Gaul, and governed (60) Hispania Tarraconensis (Hither Spain). When Nero committed suicide in 68, Galba's praetorian guards supported him as caesar, and he marched to Rome with Otho, governor of Lusitania. Galba was noted for his integrity and extreme thriftiness. When he adopted a successor, Otho was enraged and conspired with the praetorians. Galba was murdered and Otho assumed the imperial title.

Bibliography: Wellesley, Kenneth, *The Long Year, A.D. 69* (1976).

Galbraith, John Kenneth [gal'-brayth]

John Kenneth Galbraith, b. Ontario, Canada, Oct. 15, 1908, is a U.S. economist whose provocative theories have stirred national interest and debate. Galbraith taught economics at Harvard University from 1949 to 1975. He was U.S. ambassador to India from 1961 to 1963 and has also served as an economic advisor to John F. Kennedy, Adlai Stevenson, and other major political figures.

The impact of the large industrial CORPORATION on modern society has been a continuing concern in Galbraith's writing. In *American Capitalism* (1952) he suggested that the restraints on large corporations came not from competitors on the same side of the market but from "countervailing powers" on the opposite side of the market, such as large labor unions. Subsequent books, including *The Affluent Society* (1958; 4th ed., 1984) and *The New Industrial State* (1967; 4th ed., 1985), described American industrial structure as differing sharply from the traditional textbook picture. In Galbraith's view, the large corporation engages in planning to insulate itself from market forces, manages consumer demand through advertising, and emphasizes growth of output above profit maximization. As a result, the economic system favors added production even when general affluence prevails, and an imbalance develops between too many private goods, such as cars and washing machines, and too few public goods, such as education and parks.

John Kenneth Galbraith, an American economist, has advocated that the United States redirect its emphasis from the production of goods to the improvement of services. As an advisor to such political figures as Adlai Stevenson and John F. Kennedy, Galbraith has exerted considerable influence over the nation's long-range economic planning.

A versatile stylist, Galbraith has also written fiction and has served on the editorial board of *Fortune*. His other books include *The Great Crash* (1955), *The Scotch* (1964), *Ambassador's Journal* (1969), *Economics and the Public Purpose* (1973), *Money: Whence It Came, Where It Went* (1975), *A Life in Our Times: Memoirs* (1981), *The Voice of the Poor* (1983), and *Economics in Perspective* (1987).

RICHARD T. GILL

Bibliography: Gambs, John, *John Kenneth Galbraith* (1975); Munro, C. Lynn, *Galbraithian Vision: The Cultural Criticism of John Kenneth Galbraith* (1977); Okroi, Loren J., *Galbraith, Harrington, Heilbroner* (1988); Pratson, Frederick J., *Perspectives on Galbraith* (1978); Reisman, David, *Tawney, Galbraith and Adam Smith* (1982).

Gale, Zona [gayl, zohn'-uh]

A versatile American writer, Zona Gale, b. Portage, Wis., Aug. 26, 1874, d. Dec. 27, 1938, is best known for her realistic novel and play of midwestern small-town life, *Miss Lulu Bett* (1920). The dramatized version won a 1921 Pulitzer Prize. *Yellow Gentians and Blue* (1927) and *Bridal Pond* (1930) are representative of her short stories. F. M. PAULSEN

Bibliography: Simonson, Harold P., *Zona Gale* (1962).

Galen [gay'-len]

The Greek physician Galen, AD 130–200, did notable work in the field of human anatomy despite being confined to dissecting animals such as pigs, dogs, and goats. He identified numerous muscles for the first time and showed the importance of the spinal cord, noting the resulting paralysis when the cord was cut at different levels. Galen was also the first to consider the pulse a diagnostic aid. His physiological theories include concepts of blood formation, digestion, and nerve function. His written treatises survived as the medical authority until the 16th century, when Andreas VESALIUS and, later, William HARVEY amended Galen's theories.

Bibliography: Boorstin, D. J., *The Discoverers* (1985); Brain, Peter, *Galen on Bloodletting* (1986); Sarton, George, *Galen of Pergamon* (1954); Temkin, Owsei, *Galenism* (1973).

galena [guh-leen'-uh]

Galena, a lead sulfide, PbS, is the most important ore mineral of lead. Its metallic, lead-gray cubic crystals (isometric system) and cubic, perfectly cleavable masses are distinctive and characteristic. Hardness is $2^1/_2$, streak lead gray, and specific gravity 7.4–7.6. Galena is a widespread mineral deposited by hydrothermal solutions as irregular masses in dolomitized

Galena is a common, soft, dark gray or black lead sulfide mineral. The major commercial source of lead, it is usually found in metal-bearing veins as cubic crystals or as granular masses. Silver, often found as an impurity, is also extracted profitably.

limestones and in zones of contact metamorphism (see METAMORPHIC ROCK), and as veins in volcanic rocks. It often contains enough silver to be mined as an ore.

See also: ORE DEPOSITS; SULFIDE MINERALS.

Galerius, Roman Emperor [guh-lir'-ee-uhs]

Gaius Galerius Valerius Maximianus, b. AD *c.*242, d. May 311, was Roman emperor from 305 to 311. For most of his life Galerius, the son of a Thracian shepherd, was a relatively obscure soldier, but in 293 he emerged as a member of the tetrarchy established by DIOCLETIAN.

Initially a junior member (caesar) of the tetrarchy, Galerius improved his status with a decisive victory over the Persians in 297–98, and when Diocletian and Maximian retired in 305, he became the senior emperor (augustus) in the East. Although contemporary Christians held him in low esteem because he continued the persecution begun by Diocletian in 303, Galerius was an able administrator who managed to hold together an empire divided by civil war in the West. Just before his death, he issued an edict of toleration that granted freedom of worship and opened the way for the legalization of Christianity by CONSTANTINE I. JOHN W. EADIE

Bibliography: Jones, A. H. M., *The Decline of the Ancient World* (1966).

Galib, Şeyh

Galib Dede, b. 1757, d. Jan. 3, 1799, was an Ottoman Turkish poet; his pen name, Şeyh Galib, derives from his being şeyh, or sheikh ("leader"), of the *mawlawi* lodge, a mystical sect, at Galata in Istanbul. He enjoys fame for his *Divan*, a collection of lyric poems written in 1780, and for *Hüsn ü Aşk* (*Beauty and Love*), a long, allegorical romance in verse about mystical love composed in 1780. Both works were published in 1836. TALAT SAIT HALMAN

Galicia (historic region of Central Europe) [guh-lish'-ee-uh]

Galicia was the name given to the southern Polish territories annexed by Austria in the 1st and 3d Partitions of Poland (1772, 1795). The region was regained by POLAND in 1918–19. In 1939 East Galicia was annexed to the USSR; it remained part of the USSR after World War II (see UKRAINIAN SOVIET SOCIALIST REPUBLIC).

The official Austrian name for the region—Kingdom of Galicia and Lodomeria—derived from the medieval principality of Galich (Polish, Halicz), which was united with Volhynia in 1199. The region came under Mongol rule before becoming part of Poland in 1340. The Hungarians had earlier laid claim to the region, and the Austrian Habsburgs, who inherited the Hungarian crown, used this claim as a legal pretext for taking these lands in 1772.

Forming the northeastern part of the Austrian Empire, Galicia had a population of 7,316,000 in 1910; 59% spoke Polish, 31% Ukrainian, and 10% Yiddish. Ukrainians predominated in eastern Galicia and Poles in western Galicia. Poor soil, lack of significant industry, and rural overpopulation led to massive emigration around the turn of the century. In 1868, Galicia was accorded limited self-government, with Polish education and administration. Thus it was the only part of partitioned Poland in which Polish political and cultural life could develop freely. However, the late 19th century also saw the development of Ukrainian national consciousness, which provided the pretext for the later Soviet annexation of eastern Galicia. ANNA M. CIENCIALA

Bibliography: Wandycz, Piotr, *The Lands of Partitioned Poland, 1772–1918* (1976).

See also: AUSTRIA-HUNGARY; POLAND, PARTITIONS OF.

Galicia (Spain) [gah-leeth'-ee-ah]

Galicia is a historic region and former kingdom in the northwestern corner of Spain; it is bounded by the Bay of Biscay on the north, the Atlantic Ocean on the west, and Portugal on the south. LA CORUÑA is the principal industrial city, and SANTIAGO is the religious and cultural center. The population speaks a dialect closely related to Portuguese. Today the region comprises the provinces of La Coruña, Lugo, Orense, and Pontevedra. During the 6th century BC the region was settled by the Celtic Gallaeci tribe for whom the region was named. In 137 BC, Galicia was conquered by Rome. It was the independent kingdom of the Suevi tribe from AD 410 until 585, when it was conquered by the Visigoths. Occupied briefly (718–57) by the Moors, it was soon retaken and in 914 became part of the kingdom of Asturias. In the 13th century Galicia was part of Castile.

Galilee [gal'-i-lee]

Galilee was the northern province of ancient Palestine. Located east of the Sea of Galilee and the Jordan River, with the plain of Acre on the West, Galilee is roughly coextensive with the boundaries of northern Israel. The province is known as both a cultural melting pot and a major farming region because of its position on the major trade route between Egypt and Syria and its fertile land.

Jesus Christ, known as "the Galilean" (Matthew 26:69), was raised in the Galilean city of NAZARETH, and spent most of his life there. Galilee, especially the city of TIBERIAS, became the center of rabbinic learning after the fall of Jerusalem in AD 70; the Mishnah was codified and the Talmud produced there. Many 1st-century ruins of Galilean synagogues have since been excavated.

As part of modern Israel, Galilee is once again a flourishing region; Jews, Muslims, and the Druzes contribute to its heterogeneous ideologies and cultures. DOUGLAS EZELL

Bibliography: Aharoni, Yohanan, *Land of the Bible: A Historical Geography* (1967).

Galilee, Sea of

The Sea of Galilee, or Sea of Tiberias (Hebrew: Yam Kinneret; Arabic: Bahr Tabariya), is a lake in northeastern Israel. It is 21 km (13 mi) long, by 12 km (7.5 mi) at its widest point, and has an area of 166 km^2 (64 mi^2). It lies 212 m (696 ft) below sea level and has a maximum depth of 48 m (157 ft). Of the several towns and villages on its shores, TIBERIAS, on the west bank, is the largest. Agricultural settlements ring the lake, which is the source of irrigation carried by canal and tunnel as far as the Negev in southern Israel. It is also important as a fishing ground and tourist attraction.

Basalt ridges flank the basin—part of the GREAT RIFT VALLEY—that holds the Sea of Galilee, and alluvial plains are to the north and south. The lake is fed principally by the JORDAN RIVER. Drainage, from its southern end, is also provided by the Jordan. Winter rainfall averages 445 mm (17.5 in), and the mean monthly temperature ranges from 7.4° C (45.3° F) in January to 31° C (88° F) in July.

The Sea of Galilee features prominently in the New Testament, since Jesus Christ worked and preached in the towns surrounding it and is reputed to have walked on its water. MARTIN IRA GLASSNER

Galileo [gal-i-lee'-oh]

Originally known as the Jupiter Orbiter and Probe, *Galileo* is the first spacecraft designed to orbit the planet JUPITER and send a probe into its atmosphere. After repeated delays over a period of several years, *Galileo* was finally launched from a Space Shuttle on Oct. 18, 1989. Its six-year flight will take it past Venus once and Earth twice and will include fly-bys of two asteroids, Gaspra and Ida, before reaching Jupiter in December 1995. While in orbit around the planet, *Galileo* will take closer looks at the moons Io, Ganymede, Callisto, and Europa. The spacecraft contains an electric generator powered by a plutonium isotope.

Approximately 150 days before reaching Jovian orbit, the spacecraft will be separated from its atmospheric probe. The probe will then follow its own course toward Jupiter. Designed to survive to a depth at which the pressure is at least 10 times that of Earth's atmosphere at sea level, the probe will transmit data to the orbiter for relay to Earth. It will be aimed not at the famous Great Red Spot but at one of the parallel belts, or zones, considered more representative of Jupiter's dense atmosphere. In addition to transmitting information about the composition and structure of the atmosphere, the probe's instruments—in what may be an operation lasting only a half hour—will monitor lightning activity, thermal balance, the helium-hydrogen ratio, and the size of cloud particles.

JONATHAN EBERHART

Bibliography: Dornheim, M. A., "Galileo to Perform First Dedicated Study of Jupiter's Atmosphere and Satellites," *Aviation Week & Space Technology*, Oct. 9, 1989.

Galileo Galilei [gal-i-lay'-oh gal-i-lay'-ee]

Galileo Galilei, a pioneer of modern physics and telescopic astronomy, was born near Pisa, Italy, on Feb. 15, 1564. In 1581 he entered the University of Pisa as a medical student, but he soon became interested in mathematics and left without a degree in 1585.

After teaching privately at Florence, Galileo was made professor of mathematics at Pisa in 1589. There he is said to have demonstrated from the Leaning Tower that Aristotelian physics was wrong in assuming that speed of fall was proportional to weight; he also wrote a treatise on motion, emphasizing mathematical arguments. In 1592, Galileo became professor of mathematics at the University of Padua, where he remained until 1610. He devised a mechanical calculating device now called the sector, worked out a mechanical explanation of the tides based on the Copernican motions of the Earth, and wrote a treatise on mechanics showing that machines do not create power, but merely transform it.

In 1602, Galileo resumed his investigations of motion along inclined planes and began to study the motion of pendulums. By 1604 he had formulated the basic law of falling bodies, which he verified by careful measurements.

Galileo Galilei built the first astronomical telescope in 1609 and with it made observations supporting his belief in the Copernican model of the solar system, a view he was later forced to deny. One of the first to verify physical laws experimentally, Galileo overturned an accepted precept of Aristotle when he stated that falling bodies accelerate uniformly.

Late in 1604 a supernova appeared, and Galileo became involved in a dispute with philosophers who held (with Aristotle) that change could not occur in the heavens. Applying the mathematics of PARALLAX, Galileo found the star to be very distant, in the supposedly unchangeable regions of the cosmos, and he attacked Aristotelian qualitative principles in science. Returning to his studies of motion, he then established quantitatively a restricted inertial principle and determined that projectiles moved in parabolic paths. In 1609 he was writing a mathematical treatise on motion when news arrived of the newly invented Dutch telescope. He was so excited at the possible scientific applications of such an instrument that he put all other work aside and began to construct his own telescopes.

The Telescope and the Copernican Theory. By the end of 1609, Galileo had a 20-power telescope that enabled him to see the lunar mountains, the starry nature of the Milky Way, and previously unnoted "planets" revolving around Jupiter. He published these discoveries in *The Starry Messenger* (1610), which aroused great controversy until other scientists made telescopes capable of confirming his observations. The Grand Duke of Tuscany made him court mathematician at Florence, freeing him from teaching to pursue research. By the end of 1610, he had observed the phases of Venus and had become a firm believer in the Copernican HELIOCENTRIC WORLD SYSTEM. He was vigorously opposed in this belief, because the Bible was seen as supporting the opposite view of a stationary Earth. Galileo argued for freedom of inquiry in his *Letter to the Grand Duchess Christina* (1615), but despite his argument that sensory evidence and mathematical proofs should not be subjected to doubtful scriptural interpretations, the Holy Office at Rome issued an edict against Copernicanism early in 1616.

Trouble with the Church. In 1623, Maffeo Barberini, long friendly to Galileo, became pope as Urban VIII, and Galileo obtained his permission to write a book impartially discussing the Ptolemaic and Copernican systems. This became Galileo's famous *Dialogue* (1632), for which he was called to Rome for trial by the Inquisition on the grounds that in 1616 he had been personally ordered never to defend or to teach Copernicanism. In June 1633, Galileo was condemned to life imprisonment for "vehement suspicion of heresy." His *Dialogue* was banned, and printers were forbidden to publish anything further by him or even to reprint his previous works. Outside Italy, however, his *Dialogue* was translated into Latin and was read by scholars throughout Europe.

Galileo's sentence was swiftly commuted to house arrest, at first under custody of the friendly archbishop of Siena and then at his own villa in Arcetri, near Florence. There Galileo resumed and completed his Paduan studies on motion and on the strength of materials, published at Leiden as *Discourses and Mathematical Demonstrations Concerning Two New Sciences* (1638). He rightly regarded this as containing the elements of a new physics that would be carried further by his successors. Galileo died at Arcetri on Jan. 8, 1642.

Influence. Among Galileo's students was Benedetto Castelli, founder of the science of hydraulics and teacher of both Bonaventura Cavalieri and Evangelista Torricelli. Cavalieri formulated principles that were important to the development of the calculus, and Torricelli devised the barometer and explained phenomena of atmospheric pressure. Outside Italy, Galileo's influence was not great, except in making scientists conscious of the need for freedom of inquiry. As he had seen, not only religious but philosophical tradition had to yield to observation and measurement if science were to prosper.

STILLMAN DRAKE

Bibliography: Allan-Olney, Mary, *The Private Life of Galileo* (1970); Butts, R. E., and Pitt, J. C., eds., *New Perspectives on Galileo* (1978); Drake, Stillman, *Discoveries and Opinions of Galileo* (1957), *Galileo Studies: Personality, Tradition and Revolution* (1970), and *Galileo at Work—His Scientific Biography* (1978); Geymonat, Ludovico, *Galileo Galilei: A Biography* (1965); Redondi, Pietro, *Galileo: Heretic* (1987); Santillana, Giorgio de, *The Crime of Galileo* (1955); Wallace, W. A., *Galileo and His Sources* (1984).

See also: ASTRONOMY, HISTORY OF; PHYSICS, HISTORY OF.

Gall [gawl]

Gall, b. c.1840, d. Dec. 5, 1894, called Pizi in the Lakota Siouan language, was a famous SIOUX warrior who fought in the Battle of the LITTLE BIGHORN (1876) in which Gen. George Armstrong CUSTER and the 7th Cavalry were killed by Indian forces. He was a leader in the Hunkpapa section of the Sioux encampment, which was the focal point of Custer's attack, and played a vital role in the forced retreat of 1868, which confined the Indians to a reservation, and with SITTING BULL and CRAZY HORSE led Indian attempts to thwart the construction of forts and roads through the Lakota Sioux buffalo country. In late 1876, after the Little Bighorn encounter, Gall and Sitting Bull retreated into Canada. Following a dispute with Sitting Bull, Gall returned to the United States with part of the Hunkpapa band in early 1881. After a brief battle with Gen. Nelson A. MILES, he was taken as a prisoner to Fort Buford. He was released (June 1881) to the Standing Rock Indian Reservation in South Dakota, where he cultivated land and attempted to live up to treaty agreements. He converted to Christianity and is said to have attended the mission church service carrying his weapons and painted, as if for a war council. BEA MEDICINE

Bibliography: Marquis, Thomas, *Sitting Bull and Gall* (1934).

gall: see DISEASES, PLANT.

Gall, Franz Joseph [gahl]

Franz Joseph Gall, b. Mar. 9, 1758, d. Aug. 22, 1828, German physician, studied the functioning of the brain and proposed that the gray matter was the essential, active portion, whereas the white matter served as connective material. He also correctly reasoned that different parts of the brain regulate different parts of the body. His correlation of the different brain shapes with various types of emotional qualities, however, was the beginning of the pseudoscience of PHRENOLOGY.

Galla [gal'-uh]

The Galla are a Hamitic people who live in Ethiopia, where they form the largest population group, and in part of Kenya. They speak a Cushitic language of Afroasiatic stock and number about 3 million. Traditionally cattle herders and warriors, the Galla have, over the past millennium, migrated north and west from the southern border of the Ethiopian plateau, conquering peoples and being attacked in return. They tend cattle, sheep, and donkeys; some also keep horses and camels, and many have become farmers, growing mostly grain and root crops. Pastoral Galla live in nomadic bands; sedentary Galla, in villages or dispersed homesteads. Most pastoralists are pagan, but some Galla tribes adhere to Christianity or Islam. Descent, inheritance, and place of residence are determined through the male line. Marriage is polygamous, each co-wife having a separate dwelling.

The Galla were divided into a number of small chiefdoms before the 19th century, each governed by a ruler who held office for eight years and commanded the army in war. Galla males spent eight years in each of five age-grades preparing for adulthood, serving as warriors, and later performing administrative and priestly tasks. Most Galla tribes had outcast groups of smiths, leatherworkers, and hunters. The Galla owned slaves until the 1930s. PHOEBE MILLER

Bibliography: Huntingford, George W. B., *The Galla of Ethiopia* (1955; repr. 1969); Lewis, H. S., *A Galla Monarchy* (1965).

Galla Placidia, Mausoleum of [gal'-uh pluh-sid'-ee-uh]

In Ravenna, adjacent to the Church of SAN VITALE, a small, cruciform structure exists that was originally meant to be a chapel appended to the Church of San Lorenzo. Pervasive tradition has identified the building as the tomb of Galla Placidia, the remarkable Roman princess who ruled the western Roman Empire in the name of her weak son Valentinian III (425-55) until her death in 450.

The structure is important for its superb interior decoration, including its famous mosaics. In the central dome, heaven and the symbols of the four evangelists are represented. The figures of the apostles decorate the walls of the dome around the windows and the two lunettes in the cross-arms contain important figural representations. In one, the Good Shepherd is depicted in an interesting adaptation of classical models to Christian purposes; in the other, Saint Lawrence is represented with the symbol of his martyrdom and a book cabinet holding the four Gospels. The vaults, the arches, and the other two lunettes are covered with rich geometric and naturalistic decoration. These mosaics constitute an important monument in the transition from the Late Roman to the Early Christian style (see EARLY CHRISTIAN ART AND ARCHITECTURE). JOHN W. BARKER

Bibliography: Bovini, Giuseppe, *Ravenna Mosaics* (1956; repr. 1978).

Gallant, Mavis [gal'-uhnt, may'-vis]

Mavis Gallant, b. Aug. 11, 1922, is a Canadian writer whose witty short stories, some of which were first published in *The New Yorker*, are collected in *The Other Paris* (1956). Subsequent works include *My Heart Is Broken* (1964); *A Fairly Good Time* (1970), which is set in Montreal; *The Pegnitz Junction* (1973); and *The End of the World and Other Stories* (1974).

Gallatin, Albert [gal'-uh-tin]

Albert Gallatin, the U.S. secretary of the Treasury (1801-14) under Presidents Jefferson and Madison, reduced the national debt by half in the years before the War of 1812. He excelled not only as a financial expert but as a diplomat. He was largely responsible for negotiating the Treaty of Ghent (1814) and later served as minister to France and to England.

Albert Gallatin was a distinguished diplomat and U.S. financier of the early national period. Born in Geneva, Switzerland, on Jan. 29, 1761, he emigrated to America in 1780 and settled in Fayette County, Pa., where he acquired substantial landholdings. In 1790 he entered the state legislature, where he worked to secure reform of the penal code, the abolition of slavery, and the creation of a public educational system. He displayed notable financial ability and devised a plan for the liquidation of the state debt.

Distrustful of centralized government, Gallatin helped organize the Republican, or Democratic-Republican, party in Pennsylvania. As a member of the House of Representatives (1795-1801), he rendered outstanding service to the party. Jefferson named him secretary of the treasury in 1801, a post he held until 1814. By stringent governmental economy, Gallatin was able to reduce the national debt by one-half before the War of 1812. In 1814 he served as peace commissioner at Ghent and then, until 1823, as minister to France. As minister to Britain in 1826 he was successful in renewing existing agreements and arranging for the joint occupation of Oregon. Ending his public career, he thereafter moved to Long Island and served as president of the National Bank of New York from 1831 to 1839.

Keenly interested in the study of the American Indians, Gallatin published (1836) *A Synopsis of the Indian Tribes . . .*

in North America. Often called the father of American ethnology, he was instrumental in founding the American Ethnological Society in 1842, seven years before his death, on Aug. 12, 1849. HARRY AMMON

Bibliography: Adams, Henry, *The Life of Albert Gallatin* (1889; repr. 1981); Balinsky, Alexander, *Albert Gallatin: Fiscal Theories* (1958); Bender, Thomas, *New York Intellect* (1987); Walters, Raymond, *Albert Gallatin: Jeffersonian Financier and Diplomat* (1957; repr. 1969).

Gallaudet (family) [gal-uh-det']

Thomas Hopkins Gallaudet, b. Philadelphia, Dec. 10, 1787, d. Sept. 10, 1851, was an American who made important contributions to the education of the deaf. He went to England to study the oral method of teaching the deaf but preferred the sign method, which he learned at the Institut Royal des Sourds-Muets (Royal Institute for Deaf-Mutes) in Paris. He returned to the United States and established the first free school for the deaf, the American Asylum for Deaf-Mutes, in Hartford, Conn. His older son, **Thomas Gallaudet** (1822–1902), an Episcopal minister, founded a church for the deaf in New York City. His younger son, **Edward Miner Gallaudet** (1837–1917), helped establish (1864) Gallaudet College for the deaf.

Bibliography: Barnard, Henry, *Tribute to Gallaudet* (1852; repr. 1976); Boatner, Maxine T., *Voice of the Deaf: A Biography of Edward Miner Gallaudet* (1959); Degering, Etta, *Gallaudet* (1987).

Gallaudet University

Established in 1864, Gallaudet University (enrollment: 2,206; library: 174,535 volumes) in Washington, D.C., is the only liberal arts institution in the United States devoted to educating the deaf and teachers of the deaf. The library contains works dating from 1546 on the subject of deafness. On campus are an elementary and a secondary school for the deaf. In 1988, under pressure from student protests, the board of trustees appointed the institution's first deaf president.

gallbladder [gawl'-blad-ur]

The gallbladder, in humans, is a small, pear-shaped sac that stores bile, or gall, a yellowish brown or green fluid, secreted by the liver, that aids in the digestion of dietary fat. Upon stimulation by the hormone cholecystokinin, the gall bladder contracts and discharges the bile into the small intestine.

Bile contains bile salts, cholesterol, mucus, fat, lecithin, cells, cellular debris, and the breakdown products from hemoglobin. The bile salts, sodium glycocholate and sodium taurocholate, facilitate the digestion of fats and their absorption by cells lining the passage of the small intestine. The bile salts emulsify water-insoluble fats and activate lipase, a fat-digesting enzyme secreted by the pancreas. This permits transport of the fats through the watery layer of fluid that lies on the surfaces of the intestinal wall. The fatty material thereafter readily enters the intestinal-wall cells, since the cell membrane itself is a fatty substance and quite permeable to fat.

The hormone cholecystokinin is produced in the wall of the initial segment (duodenum) of the small intestine and is released into the bloodstream when the lining of the duodenum is stimulated by fatty material coming from the stomach.

Cholecystitis (inflammation), generally caused by GALLSTONES formed from calcium, cholesterol, bilirubin, and other substances, may require the removal of the gallbladder. In the absence of the organ, bile must be passed directly from the liver into the small intestine. ROY HARTENSTEIN

See also: DIGESTION, HUMAN.

Gallé, Émile [gah-yay', ay-meel']

Émile Gallé, 1846–1904, of Nancy, France, was one of the most accomplished of the artists and designers who initiated ART NOUVEAU, a late-19th-century decorative style characterized by flowing, curvilinear design and organic motifs.

Gallé first experimented with clear glass in his father's factory; he established his own factory in 1874. His glass pieces —mostly vases—were constructed of multicolored overlays, decorated with carved or etched naturalistic plant and animal forms. He also designed furniture with inlaid and carved naturalistic decoration. By 1900, Gallé's glass had become internationally famous and was widely imitated. His glass works were signed "Gallé" on the base; after his death, when his son carried on the factory (until 1910), the year was added to the mark. MARION B. WILSON

Bibliography: Duncan, Alastair, and Bartha, George, *Glass by Gallé* (1984); Garner, Philippe, *Émile Gallé* (1984).

Galle, Johann Gottfried [gahl'-e, yoh'-hahn gawt'-freet]

Johann Gottfried Galle, b. June 9, 1812, d. July 10, 1910, was a German astronomer who made the first observation of the planet Neptune, whose existence had been posited by U. J. J. LEVERRIER. The discovery was made at the Berlin Observatory in 1846, where Galle was an assistant to Johann ENCKE. In 1851, Galle began a 46-year term as university professor and director of the observatory at Breslau, where he carried out research on comets, planetoids, and meteors. He died shortly after he observed Halley's comet for the second time.

Gallegos, Rómulo [gah-yay'-gohs, roh'-moo-loh]

The Venezuelan novelist, educator, and political leader Rómulo Gallegos, b. Aug. 2, 1884, d. Apr. 4, 1969, used artistic methods acquired during his formative modernist period to portray Venezuelan rural life with a comprehensiveness and clarity that won him international acclaim. In his novels, set in the various geographical areas of Venezuela, the landscape becomes a principal force. His prolific production of novels began with *El último solar* (The Last Manor, 1920), and he secured his reputation with *Doña Bárbara* (1929; Eng. trans., 1931). Other major works include *Cantaclaro* (Chanticleer, 1934) and *Canaima* (1935), concerning an evil spirit, "Canaima," that lurks in the tropical forest. Gallegos was elected president of Venezuela on Dec. 14, 1947, but was ousted in a coup on Nov. 24, 1948. KEITH ELLIS

Bibliography: Alexander, R. J., *The Venezuelan Democratic Revolution* (1964); Dunham, Lowell, *Rómulo Gallegos: An Oklahoma Encounter and the Writing of the Last Novel* (1974); Foster, D. W., *Handbook of Latin American Literature* (1987).

galleon [gal'-ee-uhn]

The galleon was a large, 3- or 4-masted ship developed during the 15th and 16th centuries as a merchant vessel and warship. During the late 1500s it was the standard vessel of European navies (see NAVAL VESSELS). Galleons were more slender than previous sailing ships, their lines resembling those of

The galleon, a large, three-masted sailing vessel, was developed as a warship but was commonly used as an armed merchantman in trade between Europe and the New World. Its size and armament capacity made it the dominant warship of the late 16th century.

the oared GALLEY; and they were built without the earlier overhanging forecastle that had made sailing to windward almost impossible. Sir John HAWKINS streamlined the English galleons ever further, and it was his light, maneuverable fleet that defeated the heavier ships of the SPANISH ARMADA.

With the development of the galleon, naval battle tactics were revolutionized. Where earlier ships had to use oarsmen to bring them within boarding range of the enemy, the galleon could hold its position into the wind and use its broadside banks of cannon to shell enemy ships lying at a distance.

Bibliography: Anderson, Romola and Roger C., *The Sailing Ship, Six Thousand Years of History* (1927); Cipolla, Carlo, *Guns, Sails and Empires* (1966).

galley

This Venetian galley (c.1545), a merchantman, was equipped with a single lateen sail in addition to the single bank, or row, of oars on either side. Earlier galleys often employed multiple banks of oars and featured a sharply projecting bow for ramming enemy vessels.

Galleys were warships that were driven by oars in battle and equipped with sails for cruising (see NAVAL VESSELS). In use for over two millennia, the galley was the standard European battle vessel until the late 16th century, when the sail-powered, more heavily armed GALLEON began to replace it.

The earliest galleys about which much is known were Greek and Phoenician warships of early classical times. The largest of these were biremes, which had two banks of oars. By the time of the Persian Wars, the Greeks were also using triremes, galleys with three banks of oars.

Their exact design is unknown. Most likely, the oarsmen were arranged in staggered and overlapping layers, with each one pulling his own oar. This arrangement would have maximized the number of oarsmen while keeping the hull narrow for speed. The Romans and Carthaginians also used triremes; little is known about them, however, or about the later Byzantine and Arab oared warships.

A different kind of trireme became the dominant type of late medieval galley. In this type, three oarsmen, each having his own oar, shared the same bench. Instead of piercing the hull along three levels, the oars passed over the wales along the same level in clusters of three. Early modern galleys typically had about 24 banks of oars; their hulls were 36–39 m (120–130 ft) long and just over 6 m (20 ft) wide.

Beginning about 1550, the trireme was replaced by galleys in which four or more oarsmen on the same bench pulled a single large oar. This change accompanied a shift from predominantly free oarsmen to convicts and slaves. Sometimes as many as eight oarsmen were used on each bench. In the Battle of Lepanto (1571), the last great galley fight, some galleys had over 200 oarsmen.

JOHN F. GUILMARTIN, JR.

Bibliography: Anderson, Roger Charles, *Oared Fighting Ships* (1962); Guilmartin, John F., Jr., *Gunpowder and Galleys* (1975).

galley warfare

Galley warfare was an ancient form of naval warfare used in the Mediterranean from the 5th century BC. Galleys, which were long, shallow-draft vessels propelled by oars and sails, were first used as early as 3000 BC. With the introduction of the battering ram in the 10th or 9th century BC, war galleys became distinguished from commercial vessels. Around 700 BC a galley with two banks of oars was developed (the bireme), followed in 550–500 BC by the three-banked trireme. The Battle of SALAMIS (480 BC) during the Persian Wars was fought by more than 1,000 triremes. Fleets advanced in lines and attempted to cripple their opponents with the rams mounted on their prows. Grappling hooks were used to board enemy vessels.

Galley warfare was employed effectively by Rome during the Punic Wars (264–146 BC) against a seafaring adversary, the North African city of Carthage. Galleys continued to be used in naval warfare through the 16th century. The Battle of LEPANTO (1571), between Ottoman Turks and Christian forces for control of the eastern Mediterranean, was the last naval engagement in which galleys were the principal vessels used.

Galli-Curci, Amelita [gahl'-ee-koor'-chee, ah-may-lee'-tah]

Amelita Galli-Curci, b. Milan, Nov. 18, 1882, d. Nov. 26, 1963, was an Italian coloratura soprano who had great success throughout the world until a throat ailment forced her to retire. Originally a piano student in Milan, Galli-Curci was a self-taught singer. She made her debut in Rome in 1909, and a substantial career in Europe and South America followed. The soprano then arrived in the United States, where her first performance (1916), at the Chicago Opera, made her world-famous overnight. Her Metropolitan Opera debut (1921) was a triumph. Following a throat operation in 1935, Galli-Curci sang in Chicago and elsewhere, but soon after retired to California.

STEPHANIE VON BUCHAU

Bibliography: Le Massena, Clarence, *Galli-Curci's Life of Song* (1945; repr. 1978).

Galli da Bibiena (family) [gahl'-lee dah bee-bee-ay'-nah]

The Galli da Bibienas were a family of Italian theatrical designers and artists of the 17th and 18th centuries whose name, Bibiena, is derived from the birthplace of the artist **Giovanni Maria Galli**, 1625–65. Enjoying the patronage of the Habsburgs and other noble families, Giovanni Maria's sons and grandsons created theatrical settings of great beauty for weddings, funerals, balls, and operas. Their designs, in the lavishly decorated and ornate Italian baroque style, were notable for giving an illusion of immense scale by the use of perspective. The work of the Galli da Bibienas, of which little remains, is known chiefly through contemporary accounts and drawings.

Ferdinando Galli da Bibiena, 1657–1743, the eldest son of Giovanni Maria, studied architecture under Giulio Troili and painting under Carlo Cignani; on the latter's recommendation he entered the service of the duke of Parma. While employed on the duke's villa and garden at Colorno, Ferdinando began the work in scenic design that established his reputation. In 1708 he went to Barcelona to design decorations for the wedding of Charles III, pretender to the Spanish throne. In 1721, when his patron became Charles VI of Austria, Ferdinando was invited to Vienna to create scenery and decorations for the opera house and for the coronation. Elected to the Accademia Clementina in 1717, he built the Teatro del Castella (1731) in Mantua and published books on architecture.

Francesco Galli da Bibiena, 1659–1739, the second son of Giovanni Maria, studied under Carlo Cignani and Lorenzo Pasinelli. After serving as a ducal architect in Mantua, he went to Vienna, where he designed the magnificent Court Opera House (1704). His other designs include the Teatro Filarmonico (1720) in Verona, the theater in Nancy, and the Teatro Aliberti (1720) in Rome. He returned to Bologna in 1726 to direct the Accademia Clementina.

Allesandro Galli da Bibiena, 1687-1769, was Ferdinando's eldest son. An architect and painter at the court of the Palatinate elector from 1719, he is best known for his design of the Opera House (1737-42) and the Jesuit church in Mannheim (1733-56).

Giuseppe Galli da Bibiena, 1696-1757, the second son of Ferdinando, was born in Parma. The finest artist in the family, he remained in Vienna after his father returned to Italy. He created the scenery for plays and operas and designed catafalques for more than 30 court funerals. He is best known for the decorations at the Vienna Opera (completed 1742), the Dresden Opera (1747-48), and the Bayreuth Court Theater (1748). **Antonio Galli da Bibiena**, 1700-74, the third son of Ferdinando, was architect of the Teatro Communale (begun 1756) in Bologna and the Accademia del Timidi (1767) in Mantua.

Carlo Galli da Bibiena, 1728-87, the last of the Galli da Bibienas to design for the theater, was the son of Giuseppe. He worked in Germany, France, the Netherlands, England, Italy, Sweden, and Russia.

Bibliography: Mayor, A. Hyatt, *The Bibiena Family* (1940).

Gallic Wars [gal'-ik]

Julius CAESAR's campaigns in GAUL (58-51 BC) are collectively termed the Gallic Wars. In 58 BC, Gallic agitation against the Suevi, a German tribe that had recently conquered territory in Gaul, and the threat of invasion by the Helvetii, a Celtic tribe from the area that is now Switzerland, gave Caesar a pretext to advance his career through war. Lack of cavalry support almost caused Caesar's defeat by the Helvetii at Bibracte, but his legions rallied and forced the Helvetii to withdraw (58). In the same year Caesar's army defeated and killed the Suevi's leader Ariovistus in Alsace after a hard campaign.

In 57, Caesar successfully met the attacks of the Gallic tribes of the Belgae and Nervii and established Roman control over what is now Belgium and northern France. The following year he conquered the Atlantic coast, thus isolating the central Gallic tribes, and massacred the German Usipites and Tencteri, who had entered Belgium. His invasions of Germany (55) and Britain (55 and 54) accomplished little but provided much publicity for Caesar.

The winter of 54 and most of 53 were spent in suppressing sporadic revolts in northern Gaul. The biggest threat came in 52 when a coalition of tribes in central Gaul under VERCINGETORIX rose against the Romans. Caesar finally beseiged Vercingetorix at Alesia. Famine overcame the defenders while Caesar's troops defeated a Gallic rear attack. Serious Gallic resistance had now ended, but minor uprisings caused Caesar considerable frustration during 51 BC.

The Gallic Wars provided Caesar with wealth, a trained loyal army, and enormous popularity to use against his rivals at Rome. ALLEN M. WARD

Bibliography: Caesar, Julius, *The Conquest of Gaul,* trans. by S. A. Hanford (1951); Gelzer, Matthias, *Caesar, Politician and Statesman* (1968); Holmes, T R. E., *Caesar's Conquest of Gaul,* 2d ed. (1911).

Gallicanism [gal'-i-kuhn-izm]

Gallicanism is the name commonly given to a complex of theological doctrines and political positions that emphasized the relative independence from the PAPACY of the Roman Catholic church in France and the French king. The Gallican theorists argued that the decisions of ecumenical councils had supremacy over the pope (see CONCILIARISM), that all bishops were of divine institution, and that the French kings were absolutely independent of Rome in all temporal questions. A more radical form, called parliamentary Gallicanism, also argued that the church must be subordinated to the state and that the state could intervene in the church's financial and disciplinary problems. Although Gallicanism can be traced back at least to the 14th century, it reached its fullest manifestation during the 17th and 18th centuries and was best enunciated in the Four Articles, approved by LOUIS XIV in 1682. Some Gallican attitudes lingered among the French episcopacy until the middle of the 19th century. T. TACKETT

Gallico, Paul [gal'-i-koh]

The prolific and popular American writer Paul William Gallico, b. New York City, July 26, 1897, d. July 15, 1976, is best known for light, often sentimental, fiction and the professional style of his writing on a variety of subjects. Among his best known works are the novelette *The Snow Goose* (1941); the humorous series of four "Mrs. 'Arris" novels, beginning with *Mrs. 'Arris Goes to Paris* (1958), the mystery *The Hand of Mary Constable* (1964), and the disaster novel *The Poseidon Adventure* (1969; film, 1972). Gallico also wrote extensively on sports and for films.

Gallieni, Joseph Simon [gahl-lee-ay'-nee]

Joseph Simon Gallieni, b. Apr. 24, 1849, d. May 27, 1916, was a French general who worked to integrate France's colonial conquests into the FRENCH EMPIRE. He served in the Franco-Prussian War (1870-71) and later in the 1870s was sent to Africa. In the course of his colonial military and administrative career he served in the Upper Niger area, Martinique, French Sudan, Indochina, and Madagascar. In Madagascar he created a system of compulsory labor as part of his policy to have the natives raise their own standard of living.

In 1911, Gallieni declined the position of supreme commander of the French army because of ill health and age. Nonetheless, he was appointed military governor of Paris in August 1914 and raised troops to drive back the Germans in the First Battle of the Marne. He served as minister of war from 1915 to 1916 and was made a marshal of France posthumously. Gallieni wrote several works on his colonial campaigns and policies. P. M. EWY

Bibliography: Matthew, V. L., "Joseph Simon Gallieni," in *African Proconsuls,* ed. by L. H. Gann and Peter Duignan (1978).

Gallienus, Roman Emperor [gal-i-ee'-nuhs]

Publius Licinius Egnatius Gallienus, d. AD 268, was Roman emperor with his father, VALERIAN (253-60), then sole emperor (260-68). At first, Gallienus ruled in the west, capably holding off an invasion of the Alemanni (258); thereafter he was continually beset by insurrection and incursions on every front. He created a strong cavalry and replaced Senate leaders with professional soldiers as his generals, and instituted compassionate treatment of the Christians. In 268, Gallienus defeated Aureolus, who had been named emperor at Milan, but he was soon after murdered by his own staff officers, who made Claudius II emperor.

gallinule [gal'-uh-nool]

The gallinule, or moorhen, G. chloropus, *is an aquatic bird common everywhere except Australasia. Its head shield is similar to the coot's.*

Gallinule is the common name for several birds of the RAIL family, Rallidae. Like the closely related coots, gallinules are often mistaken for ducks but have cone-shaped bills. They prefer marshes with openings of shallow water congested with aquatic vegetation. Their long toes permit them to appear at times to be walking on water; actually, they are supported by lily pads and other surface growth. The common gallinule, *Gallinula chloropus,* is slate gray and drab except for a bright red forehead and red and yellow bill. It is distributed over most of the temperate regions of the world. The colorful purple gallinule, *Porphyrula martinica,* of warmer regions of the New World is deep purple with a green back, pale blue forehead plate, and red and yellow bill.

WILLIAM SANDFORD

Gallipoli campaign [guh-lip'-uh-lee]

The Gallipoli campaign of 1915 was an Allied attempt to knock Ottoman Turkey out of WORLD WAR I and reopen a supply route to Russia. The initial plan, proposed by British First Lord of the Admiralty Winston CHURCHILL, called for an Allied fleet—mostly British—to force the Dardanelles Strait and then to steam to Constantinople to dictate peace terms.

On Feb. 19, 1915, a Franco-British fleet under British Vice Admiral Sackville Carden began systematic reduction of the fortifications lining the Dardanelles. The principal fortifications were attacked on March 18. Sixteen battleships—including the powerful *Queen Elizabeth*—provided the principal firepower. Just as the bombardment had silenced the Turkish batteries, however, three battleships were sunk in an undetected minefield, and three others were disabled. The Turks had nearly expended their ammunition, many of their batteries had been destroyed, and their fire-control communications were out of action. The Allies, however, did not know this. Rear Admiral John de Robeck, who had taken command when Carden fell ill, called off the attack and withdrew his ships from the strait.

The map indicates, in chronological progression, naval and troop movements during the Gallipoli Campaign of World War I. Although an Allied force was able to land on the Gallipoli Peninsula, its advance was contained by the Turks and Germans and it withdrew.

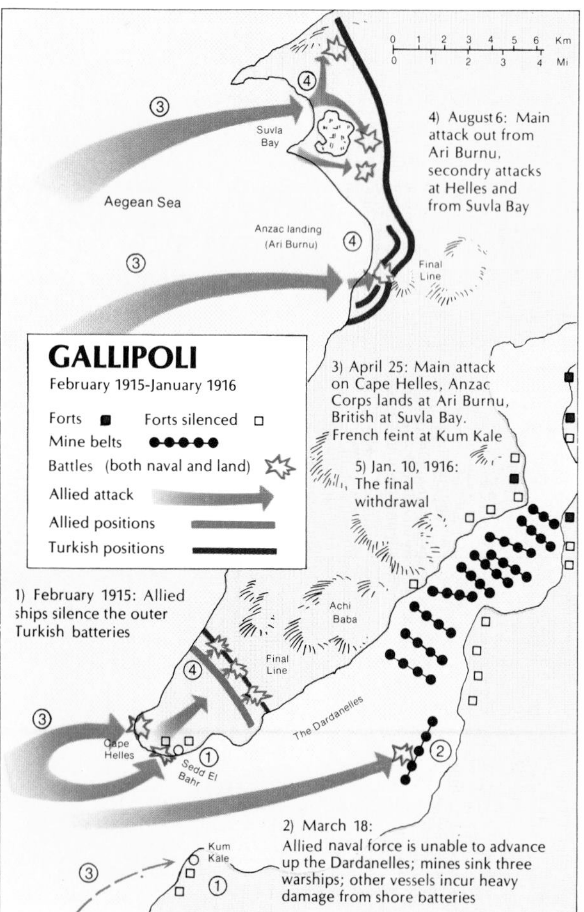

In the meantime, the Allies had hastily assembled a force of 78,000 men and dispatched it from England and Egypt to Gallipoli. As his flotilla gathered near the peninsula, however, the commanding general, Ian Hamilton, discovered that guns and ammunition had been loaded on separate ships. The transports had to steam to Egypt to be properly loaded for combat. The Turks, now alerted to the Allied plan, used the resulting month's delay to improve their defenses. Some 60,000 Turkish troops, under the German general Otto Liman von Sanders, awaited the Allies.

On April 25, British and ANZAC (Australian and New Zealand Army Corps) troops landed at several points near the tip of the peninsula. Simultaneously, on the Asiatic side of the strait, the one French division made a diversionary landing, and off Bulair, on the neck of the peninsula, a naval force attempted to distract the Turks.

The Allied troops were soon pinned down in several unconnected beachheads, stopped by a combination of Turkish defenses and British mismanagement. Losses were high. The Turks ringed the tiny beachheads with entrenchments, and the British and ANZAC troops soon found themselves involved in trench warfare.

After three months of bitter fighting, Hamilton attempted a second assault—on the western side of the peninsula. This assault lacked adequate naval gunfire support; it failed to take any of its major objectives and resulted in heavy casualties. Hamilton was relieved on October 15, and by December 10 his replacement, Gen. Charles Monro, had evacuated the bulk of the troops and supplies. The remaining 35,000 men were withdrawn without the Turks realizing it on Jan. 8-9, 1916. By contrast with the operation as a whole, the withdrawal was a masterpiece of planning and organization, with no loss of life. Estimates of Allied casualties for the entire campaign are about 252,000, with the Turks suffering almost as many casualties—an estimated 251,000.

COL. T. N. DUPUY

Bibliography: Bush, Eric W., *Gallipoli* (1975); Hamilton, Sir Ian, *Gallipoli Diary* (1920); James, R. R., *Gallipoli* (1965); Moorehouse, Alan, *Gallipoli* (1956); Liman von Sanders, Otto, *My Five Years in Turkey* (1927).

Gallipoli Peninsula

The Gallipoli Peninsula in western Turkey is a narrow, hilly projection that separates the Aegean Sea from the DARDANELLES. It was known as the Thracian Chersonese in classical times. About 80 km (50 mi) long, this remote area is separated from the rest of Turkey by the Garros Hills, which rise to a height of 915 m (3,000 ft). The port of Gallipoli, which was once an important post on the Dardanelles, is now a small fishing center and military garrison. During World War I the peninsula was the scene of the Gallipoli campaign.

Gallitzin, Demetrius Augustine [guh-lits'-in, duh-meet'-ree-uhs aw'-guhs-teen]

Demetrius Augustine Gallitzin, b. The Hague, Dec. 22, 1770, d. May 6, 1840, was an American frontier missionary and colonizer. The son of Russian aristocrats, he was raised in the Orthodox church but became a Roman Catholic in 1787 at his mother's urging. After serving in the Austrian army, Gallitzin went (1792) to the United States and entered a seminary in Baltimore, Md. In 1795 he became the first priest to obtain all his theological training and ordination in the United States. By 1799, Gallitzin had followed migrating Catholics to the Allegheny Mountains of Pennsylvania, where he built a log cabin and chapel at a colony that he named Loretto. Gallitzin, Pa., was named for him.

HENRY WARNER BOWDEN

Bibliography: Sargent, Daniel, *Mitri, or the Story of Prince Demetrius Augustine Gallitzin, 1770-1840* (1945).

gallium [gal'-ee-uhm]

The chemical element gallium is a bluish metal of group IIIA in the periodic table. Its chemical symbol is Ga, atomic number 31, and atomic weight 69.72.

Gallium is a relatively rare metal that has become important in the manufacture of SEMICONDUCTOR electronic devices. Its existence was originally detected spectroscopically; it was isolated for the first time from zinc sulfide ore in 1875 by the French chemist Lecoq de Boisbaudran, who named it after *Gallia,* the Latin name for France. Later the same year, Dmitry Mendeleyev showed that gallium was the missing group IIIA element below aluminum and above indium predicted in his theory of chemical periodicity.

Gallium is present in the earth's crust in an average abundance of 5–15 ppm. It often occurs in small amounts as Ga_2S_3 in the sulfide ores of zinc and germanium, and it is a minor component in all aluminum ores. No important mineral deposits contain a high percentage of gallium.

Most of the world's gallium is produced in the United States. The metal is recovered by controlled electrolysis of the concentrated alkaline liquors that are by-products of the extraction of aluminum and zinc from their ores. Ultrapure gallium for electronics is obtained by repeated fractional crystallization of the metal. Gallium is relatively expensive because of its low concentration in most minerals and because the metal must be extremely pure for most applications.

The pure metal has a slight bluish luster resembling that of zinc. Its melting point (29.78° C) is unusually low, and the boiling point (about 2,250° C) is not precisely known because the metal is highly active at high temperature. For this reason most of the expected applications of the low melting point and exceptional 2,200° liquid range, such as use in thermometers and related devices, are impractical. Molten gallium expands in volume by 3.2% on freezing; among all the other elements only bismuth shares this property.

Gallium normally forms compounds in the trivalent state. A +1 state also exists, but it is easily oxidized to gallium(III). A rare +2 state has been reported, but all gallium(II) compounds are unstable. At room temperature the metal is kept from corroding in air by a protective oxide film of Ga_2O_3. Corrosion occurs rapidly at high temperature, however, because the metal reduces Ga_2O_3 to Ga_2O, which evaporates to constantly expose a fresh surface. Hot molten gallium forms alloys with most other metals.

The most important gallium compounds are the semiconductors, formed with the elements phosphorus, arsenic, and antimony. The most widely used and studied compound is gallium arsenide, GaAs, which has important applications in solid-state microwave generators and photoelectric cells. It is also used in LASERS, because the light emitted from GaAs diodes (electroluminescence) is coherent and has a narrow frequency bandwidth. Gallium compounds have no known biological function, and ordinary gallium salts have very low toxicity.

PHILIP C. KELLER

Bibliography: Blakemore, John S., ed., *Gallium Arsenide* (1987); Cotton, F. A., and Wilkinson, Geoffrey, *Basic Inorganic Chemistry* (1976).

Galloway, Joseph [gal'-oh-way]

Joseph Galloway, b. West River, Md., *c.*1731, d. Aug. 29, 1803, was a prominent loyalist during the American Revolution. He was speaker of the Pennsylvania Assembly from 1766 to 1775. As a delegate to the First Continental Congress (1774), he tried to avert the imminent break with Britain. He proposed a scheme for self-government to the colonies while maintaining allegiance to the mother country, suggesting that all legislation affecting the colonies be approved both by Parliament and by a council representing the American states. The plan was rejected, and when war came Galloway sided with the British. He went to England in 1778.

Bibliography: Boyd, Julian P., *Anglo-American Union: Joseph Galloway's Plans to Preserve the British Empire* (1970); Kuntzleman, Oliver C., *Joseph Galloway: Loyalist* (1941); Newcomb, Benjamin H., *Franklin and Galloway* (1972).

gallstone [gawl'-stohn]

Gallstones, or cholelithiasis, are hard masses of stonelike material found in the GALLBLADDER or the bile duct (see LIVER). They occur in about 10 percent of the U.S. population, particularly in women. Gallstones are composed mainly of CHOLESTEROL, as well as calcium bilirubinate, calcium carbonate, or a mixture of all three. Their mechanism of formation is unknown and probably varies with their chemical nature. Predisposing factors include heredity, obesity, certain diseases, and drugs. Several kinds of metabolic defects may lead to the formation of cholesterol gallstones; abnormalities of bile composition and stasis (blocked flow) of bile may also be involved. Complications of gallstones include inflammation and, when they block the common bile, JAUNDICE.

Surgical removal of gallstones—usually by removal of the gallbladder as well—effects a cure in 95 percent of all cases. In elderly patients or those in poor health, stones may be removed nonsurgically by widening the bile duct with an ENDOSCOPE. Depending on the type of stone, the gallbladder may also be flushed with various solvents. This nonsurgical method has only limited success, however, and some solvents work slowly and can cause side effects. The nonsurgical method called lithotripsy, used in breaking up KIDNEY STONES, has been modified in several ways for the more difficult internal location of the gallbladder, including use of a computer-controlled guidance system. This modified method has been successful in clinical trials in a large percentage of cases.

CARL J. PFEIFFER

Bibliography: Dowling, R. H., and Hofmann, A. F., *The Medical Treatment of Gallstones,* rev. ed. (1982); "Test of Shock Waves for Gallstones," *Medical World News,* Nov. 9, 1987.

Gallup [gal'-uhp]

Gallup (1980 pop., 18,161), the seat of McKinley County in northwestern New Mexico, is situated on the Puerco River. Founded in 1880 as a supply base for the Atlantic and Pacific Railroad, it later flourished as a commercial center for a timber and ranching region; today coal and uranium are mined in the area. It is a major market for neighboring Indian reservations. Fort Wingate, an army ordnance depot, is nearby.

Gallup, George

George Horace Gallup, b. Jefferson, Iowa, Nov. 18, 1901, d. July 26, 1984, pioneered the development of techniques for measuring PUBLIC OPINION. He helped make the OPINION POLL one of the most characteristic institutions of 20th-century America. While director of research at New York's Young and Rubicam advertising agency, a position he held from 1932 to 1947, he founded the American Institute of Public Opinion in 1935. Gallup used market research methods to sample opinion on behalf of clients in government, business, universities, and the news media. His techniques were widely adopted, but at the time of his death the Gallup Poll was still the most respected gauge of public opinion in the United States.

Galois, Evariste [gahl-wah', ay-vah-reest']

Evariste Galois, b. Oct. 25, 1811, d. May 31, 1832, a Frenchman, made significant contributions to several branches of mathematics, including algebra, number theory, and group theory. In 1829 he published his first paper on continued fractions, followed by a paper that dealt with the impossibility of solving the general quintic (fifth-degree) EQUATION by algebraic means alone. This led to Galois theory, a branch of mathematics dealing with the general solution of equations. Tragically, Galois was killed in a duel.

ARTHUR SCHLISSEL

Galsworthy, John [gawlz'-wur-thee]

John Galsworthy, b. Aug. 14, 1867, d. Jan. 31, 1933, was an English novelist, short-story writer, essayist, and playwright. He achieved both national and international recognition in his lifetime, winning the Nobel Prize for literature in 1932. He is chiefly remembered for The FORSYTE SAGA, a series of novels that was adapted for television in the late 1960s.

The British novelist and dramatist John Galsworthy, recipient of the 1932 Nobel Prize for literature, is remembered chiefly for his three trilogies tracing the history of the fictional Forsyte family. In these and other works, Galsworthy examines the interests and mores of late Victorian and Edwardian society with both irony and compassion.

Galsworthy was educated at Harrow and New College, Oxford, and trained as a lawyer. Independently wealthy, he never had to write for his living. His works reflect his privileged background, but they also show his desire to analyze contemporary society and to document changes in it from the late Victorian age to the period following World War I. Novels such as *The Island Pharisees* (1904), *Fraternity* (1909), and *The Freelands* (1915) reveal these interests, but it is in *The Forsyte Saga,* collectively published in 1922, that he achieved his objectives most satisfactorily. This sequence of novels includes *The Man of Property* (1906), *In Chancery* (1920), and *To Let* (1921), and had two sequels, *A Modern Comedy* (1929) and *End of the Chapter* (1931–32). Galsworthy's analysis of the Forsytes and their connections illustrates the impact of the First World War on English society and explores the nature of the passion for material possessions. Other works concerning the Forsytes include *On Forsyte 'Change* and *Soames and the Flag* (both 1930).

Galsworthy's plays also reflect his interest in social documentation. They include *Strife* (1909), which led to prison reform; *The Skin Game* (1920), in which the old landed class confronts the new industrial aristocracy; and *Loyalties* (1922), which deals with racial hatred. His collections of essays include *A Sheaf* (1916), *Castles in Spain* (1927), and *Glimpses and Reflections* (1937). RICHARD FORD

Bibliography: Barker, Dudley, *The Man of Principle: A Biography of John Galsworthy* (1963; repr. 1970); Gindin, James, *John Galsworthy's Life and Art: An Alien's Fortress* (1987); Marrot, H. V., *The Life and Letters of John Galsworthy* (1935; repr. 1973).

Galt, Sir Alexander Tilloch [gawlt]

Alexander Tilloch Galt, b. Sept. 6, 1817, d. Sept. 19, 1893, was a political leader of the English-speaking community of Canada East (Quebec) before Confederation, the chief architect of the financial provisions of Canada's federal constitution, and a pioneer Canadian diplomat. A son of the Scottish novelist John Galt, he was born in London. Schooled in Canada and Britain, he became a clerk and later the commissioner of the British American Land Company, settling the Eastern Townships of Quebec.

Galt was a member of the Legislative Assembly of United Canada (1849–50, 1853–67) and then of the Canadian House of Commons (1867–72). He was active in railway promotion, especially for the Grand Trunk Railway, and he was also an early advocate of a transcontinental union for British North America. Minister of finance in Conservative administrations from 1858 to 1862 and 1864 to 1866, he was a prominent participant in the financial part of the discussions that resulted in Confederation (July–October 1867). He served as the first federal minister of finance (1867–68) in the administration of John A. MACDONALD but retired from active politics in 1872.

A member of the commission that in 1875 determined the value of the U.S. access to the Canadian inshore fisheries, Galt also undertook commercial negotiations for Canada with France and Spain in 1878–79. He was the first Canadian high commissioner in Great Britain (1880–83). D. M. L. FARR

Bibliography: Skelton, O. D., *The Life and Times of Sir Alexander Tilloch Galt* (1920; repr. 1966).

The Canadian statesman Sir Alexander Tilloch Galt was one of the architects of the Confederation of Canada. As minister of finance (1858–62, 1864–66), he took a lead in drafting the financial terms of confederation. He served briefly as finance minister (1867–68) in the first Confederation government and later was Canada's first high commissioner in Britain (1880–83).

Galt, John

The Scottish novelist John Galt, b. May 2, 1779, d. Apr. 11, 1839, chronicled the changes brought by the Industrial Revolution of the late 18th century to provincial western Scotland. Especially striking are his humor and the spellings he used in dialogues to reproduce the everyday speech of his characters. Galt's best novels are *Annals of the Parish* (1821), *The Entail* (1823), and *The Last of the Lairds* (1826). R. L. ABRAHAMSON

Bibliography: Gordon, I. A., *John Galt* (1978).

Galtieri, Leopoldo Fortunato [gal-tee-air'-ee]

Lt. Gen. Leopoldo Fortunato Galtieri, b. July 15, 1926, was president of Argentina from December 1981 to June 1982. A professional soldier, he joined the ruling military junta as army commander in chief in March 1981 and soon succeeded Gen. Roberto Eduardo Viola as president. In April 1982, Galtieri ordered the Argentine seizure of the FALKLAND ISLANDS, provoking a war with Britain. He resigned three days after Argentina's surrender. Acquitted of human rights abuses in 1985, he was convicted of wartime negligence in May 1986; in 1989 he was pardoned by President Carlos Saúl Menem.

Galton, Sir Francis [gawl-tuhn]

The British scientist Sir Francis Galton, who pioneered in the use of statistical methods for studying human heredity and intelligence, is now best remembered as the founder of modern eugenics. He also worked out the basic principles of the system of fingerprint classification still employed today.

Francis Galton, b. Feb. 16, 1822, d. Jan. 17, 1911, was an Englishman who founded the EUGENICS movement. He developed the correlation method and was an early proponent of statistical analysis as applied to mental and behavioral phenomena. He also made important contributions to the fields of meteorology, anthropometry, and physical anthropology. Galton was an indefatigable explorer and an inquirer into human intelligence.

The cousin of Charles Darwin, Galton was convinced that preeminence in various fields was principally due to hereditary factors. He was thus inclined to oppose those who stressed environmental determination of either intelligence or character; he also advocated breeding restrictions. Interest in the role of heredity led Galton to introduce the method of twin studies to examine the different contributions of nature and nurture. He also inquired into racial differences and was one of the first to employ questionnaire and survey methods, which he used to investigate mental imagery in different groups. Galton was knighted in 1909.

Bibliography: Forrest, D. W., *Francis Galton: The Life and Work of a Victorian Genius* (1974); Galton, Francis, *Inquiries into Human Faculty* (1883) and *Memories of My Life* (1908); Pearson, Karl, *Francis Galton, 1822-1911: An Appreciation* (1914-30).

Galuppi, Baldassare [gah-loop'-pee, bahl-dahs-sah'-ray]

Baldassare Galuppi, b. Oct. 18, 1706, d. Jan. 3, 1785, was an Italian composer and harpsichordist best known for his comic operas. A student of Antonio Lotti, Galuppi composed *opera buffa* with such success that he is often referred to as the father of the genre. From 1749 until the late 1760s, his works dominated the opera houses of Venice. He wrote about 112 operas—many with librettos by Carlo Goldoni and Pietro Metastasio—plus 27 oratorios and about 50 harpsichord sonatas.

ROBERT M. CAMMAROTA

Bibliography: Grout, D. J., *A Short History of Opera,* 2d ed. (1965).

Galvani, Luigi [gahl-vah'-nee]

The Italian physician Luigi Galvani, b. Sept. 9, 1737, d. Dec. 4, 1798, achieved notoriety for his experiments on "animal electricity," which led Alessandro Volta to the discovery of current ELECTRICITY. Galvani was trained at the medical school at Bologna and after graduation practiced medicine and surgery, conducted physiological research, and taught medicine at Bologna. In 1780 he undertook carefully planned and executed experiments on the effects of static electricity on nerves and muscles. Using prepared frogs, Galvani observed continual muscle contractions when the spinal cords were connected by brass hooks to an iron railing. Galvani took this as confirmation of the theory that animal nerve and muscle tissue contained an electric fluid. Volta, however, later demonstrated that the electricity did not come from the animal tissue but from the different metals—brass and iron—coming into moist contact with each other.

DAVID HOUNSHELL

Bibliography: Dibner, Bern, *Galvani-Volta: A Controversy That Led to the Discovery of Useful Electricity* (1952); Dunsheath, Percy, *Giants of Electricity* (1967).

galvanic skin response [gal-van'-ik]

The galvanic skin response (GSR) is a change in the electrical resistance of the skin. It is determined by passing a weak current through the skin and measuring changes in electricity flow or by measuring the current generated by the body itself. It has been correlated with emotion, attention, and stress and is one factor monitored by the polygraph, or LIE DETECTOR. The GSR is caused by changes in the sweat glands when they are activated by the sympathetic nervous system, not by perspiration itself.

galvanometer [gal-vuhn-ah'-muh-tur]

A galvanometer, a device named for Luigi GALVANI, is an instrument that measures the amount of electrical current by converting electrical energy into the physical displacement of a coil, which in turn moves a pointer or light beam.

In a galvanometer, a coil of fine wire is suspended between the poles of a permanent magnet, so that when the coil is magnetized as current passes through it, the like poles of magnet and coil repel each other and cause an attached pointer to deflect across a calibrated scale. When a light beam is used instead of a pointer, a mirror is mounted on the side of the moving coil and a fixed beam of light is directed at the mirror. As the coil turns, the reflected image of the light moves along a translucent, calibrated panel. The coil may be mounted on a spindle, whose ends turn on rubies or very hard steel. The direct-current ammeter is a type of calibrated galvanometer that measures larger currents; a calibrated galvanometer may also be used as a direct-current voltmeter, which measures direct voltage using Ohm's law. Galvanometers are currently being replaced by modern DIGITAL INSTRUMENTS.

LESLIE W. LEE

Bibliography: Cooper, William D., *Electronic Instrumentation and Measurement Techniques* (1978).

Galveston [gal'-ves-tuhn]

Galveston, a city in southeast Texas, lies on the northeastern end of Galveston Island at the entrance to Galveston Bay, an inlet of the Gulf of Mexico. The seat of Galveston County, it has a population of 61,902 (1980). The city is a deepwater port of entry whose economy is based on oil refining, shipbuilding, dry-cargo export, and food processing. Tourists are attracted by the mild climate and the resort facilities along its beaches. Galveston is the site of the University of Texas Medical Branch, Galveston Community College, a Coast Guard base, and Texas Maritime Academy.

Visited by Spanish and French explorers and buccaneers, Galveston was founded and laid out in 1836 by Michel B. Menard. During the Civil War it was a major Confederate supply port. Over 5,000 lives were lost and much of the city was destroyed by a hurricane that struck on Sept. 8, 1900. A massive seawall was then built to protect the city.

Galway (city) [gawl'-way]

Galway (Gaillimh), the seat of County Galway on the west central coast of Ireland, is on the River Corrib at the head of Galway Bay. The second largest city of western Ireland (after Limerick), it has a population of 37,714 (1981). Iron foundries, fisheries, and a black-marble quarry form the major industries. University College was founded in 1849. The earliest settlement dates from fortification built there in 1124; Anglo-Normans took the city in 1232. The fishing village of Claddagh is across the river, and Salthill, a popular resort, is nearby. Galway is the departure point for the ferry to the Aran Islands.

Galway (county)

Galway is a county in western Ireland on the Atlantic coast in the historic province of Connacht. The town of Galway is the county seat. The county has a population of 171,836 (1981) and covers 5,944 km^2 (2,295 mi^2). Galway is bisected from north to south by Lough Corrib. To the west the mountains of Connemara district reach 730 m (2,400 ft); silver, lead, and copper are mined there, and marble is quarried. To the east, oats, wheat, and root crops are grown, and sheep and cattle are raised. Tourism, textile manufacturing, and fishing are also important. Galway has the largest percentage of Gaelic-speakers of any county in Ireland.

Galway, James

The popular Irish flute virtuoso James Galway, b. Dec. 8, 1939, took up the flute, which his father played, after briefly studying the violin. At the age of 15 a scholarship permitted him to attend the Royal College of Music and the Guildhall School in London; later he enrolled at the Paris Conservatory. After playing in various London orchestras, he became principal flutist of the London Symphony and the Royal Philharmonic, and from 1969 to 1975 was first flutist of the Berlin Philharmonic. Galway has since pursued a highly successful soloist's career, giving concerts and making several television appearances.

Discography: collections: *Man with the Golden Flute; Magic Flute*; Mozart, Wolfgang Amadeus, *Concertos (2) for Flute.*

Gama, Vasco da [gah'-mah, vahs'-koh dah]

The Portuguese navigator Vasco da Gama led an expedition at the end of the 15th century that opened the sea route to India by way of the Cape of Good Hope. He was born about 1460 at Sines, in southwest Portugal, where his father commanded the fortress. Entering the service of the Portuguese king John II, he helped to seize French ships in Portuguese ports in 1492. He was a gentleman at court when chosen to lead the expedition to India.

Many years of Portuguese exploration down the West African coast had been rewarded when Bartolomeu DIAS rounded the Cape of Good Hope in 1488. The Portuguese then planned to send a fleet to India for spices and to outflank the Muslims in Africa. Vasco da Gama was placed in command of the expedition and carried letters to the legendary PRESTER JOHN and to the ruler of Calicut, on India's Malabar coast.

Four ships left Lisbon on July 8, 1497—the *São Gabriel,* on which da Gama sailed, the *São Rafael,* the *Bérrio,* and a storeship. They stopped in the Cape Verde Islands; from there they did not follow the coast, as earlier expeditions had, but stood well out to sea. They reached the Cape of Good Hope region on November 7.

The cape was rounded on November 22. The expedition stopped on the East African coast, broke up the storeship, and reached Mozambique on Mar. 2, 1498. There they were assumed to be Muslims, and the sultan of Mozambique supplied them with pilots, who guided them on their journey northward. They stopped in Mombasa and Malindi before sailing to the east. They crossed the Indian Ocean in 23 days, aided by the Indian pilot Ibn Majid, and reached Calicut on May 20, 1498. The local ruler, the Zamorin, welcomed the Portuguese, who at first thought that the Indians, actually Hindus, were Christians.

Unfortunately, the trade goods and presents provided by the Portuguese king were suitable for Africa, not India, and the Arabs who dominated trade in the Indian Ocean region viewed the Portuguese as rivals. As a result, da Gama was unable to conclude a treaty or commercial agreement in Calicut. After one further stop on the Indian coast, the Portuguese set out to return with a load of spices. They took three months to recross the Indian Ocean, however, and so many men died of scurvy that the *São Rafael* was burned for lack of a crew. The expedition made a few stops in East Africa before rounding the Cape of Good Hope on Mar. 20, 1499. The ships were separated off West Africa in a storm and reached Portugal at different times. Da Gama stopped in the Azores and finally reached Lisbon on Sept. 9, 1499.

Vasco da Gama, the Portuguese navigator who in 1497-98 opened a maritime trade route from Europe to India, appears in a contemporary drawing. Da Gama's voyage was less significant for the discoveries made en route than for the challenge to the Arab trade monopoly with India that it posed. (Bibliothèque Nationale, Paris.)

Da Gama's success led to the dispatch of another Portuguese fleet, commanded by Pedro Álvares CABRAL. Some of the men Cabral left in India were massacred, so Manuel ordered da Gama to India again. He was given the title of admiral and left Portugal in February 1502 with 20 ships. The Portuguese used their naval power on both the East African and Indian sides of the Indian Ocean to force alliances and establish their supremacy. Da Gama's mission was a success, and the fleet returned to Lisbon in October 1503.

Da Gama then settled in Portugal, married, and raised a family. He may have served as an advisor to the Portuguese crown and was made a count in 1519. King John III sent him to India in 1524 as viceroy, but he soon became ill and died in Cochin on Dec. 24, 1524. Vasco da Gama's first voyage to India linked that area to Portugal and opened the region to sea trade with Europe. On that foundation the Portuguese soon built a great seaborne commercial empire, with colonies in India and the Spice Islands. BRUCE B. SOLNICK

Bibliography: Correa, Gaspar, *The Three Voyages of Vasco da Gama, and His Viceroyalty,* ed. by Lord Stanley of Alderley (1869; repr. 1963); Hart, Henry, *Sea Road to the Indies* (1950); Jayne, K. G., *Vasco da Gama and His Successors, 1460-1580* (1910); Revenstein, E. G., trans. and ed., *A Journal [by an Unknown Writer] of the First Voyage of Vasco da Gama, 1497-1499* (1898; repr. 1963).

Gamaliel [guh-may'-lee-ul]

Gamaliel was a distinguished Jewish scholar and the teacher of Saint PAUL. As a member of the SANHEDRIN (supreme council of the Jews), he advised moderate treatment of the early Christians (Acts 5).

Gamaliel of Jabneh [guh-may'-lee-ul jab'-nee]

Gamaliel of Jabneh succeeded JOHANAN BEN ZAKKAI in the leadership of Jewry toward the end of the 1st century AD. A great-grandson of HILLEL the Elder, he was head of the SANHEDRIN at Jabneh, a leading center of Judaism after the siege of Jerusalem in AD 70. Gamaliel is credited with organizing the synagogue service. He also standardized the Jewish calendar, assigning fixed dates to festivals. In AD 95, Gamaliel petitioned the Roman emperor Domitian to rescind an edict expelling the Jews from the empire. NAHUM N. GLATZER

Gambetta, Léon [gahm-be-tah', lay-ohn']

Léon Gambetta, b. Apr. 2, 1838, d. Dec. 31, 1882, was a French statesman who helped to found the Third Republic. A lawyer, he gained national fame for his defense of a revolutionary agitator in 1868 and was elected to the Legislative Assembly in 1869. He served as war minister during the FRANCO-PRUSSIAN WAR (1870-71), and although he had opposed the declaration of war, he worked vigorously to avert the French defeat. After NAPOLEON III surrendered at Sedan, Gambetta helped create a government of national defense, becoming its minister of the interior. He made a dramatic escape by balloon from besieged Paris and directed a "people's war" against the Germans from southwest France.

Gambetta left office in 1871 when the National Assembly accepted Germany's humiliating peace terms. After the radical COMMUNE OF PARIS was crushed later that year, he returned to politics to help consolidate the new Third Republic. He wrote articles supporting the republic in his paper *La Republique française* and worked to unite various groups of republicans against the monarchists. In 1877, when President Patrice MACMAHON, who was a monarchist, arbitrarily dismissed the cabinet and dissolved the Chamber of Deputies, Gambetta campaigned to ensure a republican majority in the elections. After MacMahon's resignation (1879) Gambetta became president of the Chamber.

He became premier in 1881, but his cabinet did not last. His attempt to end factionalism among republicans made him appear to be an aspiring dictator. He sought to institute voting reforms, press freedoms, and laws for the separation of church and state. If successful, Gambetta might have changed the Third Republic's system to resemble Great Britain's parliamentary government, but in 1882 he was voted out of office before he could implement any of his reforms. P. M. EWY

Bibliography: Bury, J. P. T., *Gambetta and the Making of the Third Republic* (1973).

Gambia [gam'-bee-uh]

Gambia (or The Gambia) is a tiny coastal republic of West Africa. Totally surrounded by Senegal except for its Atlantic coast, the country occupies the lower and central Gambia River valley and is one of Africa's smallest nations. Its narrow strip of land is only about 24 to 48 km (15 to 30 mi) wide and stretches eastward from the Atlantic Ocean for 475 km (295 mi). Gambia gained independence from Britain in 1965.

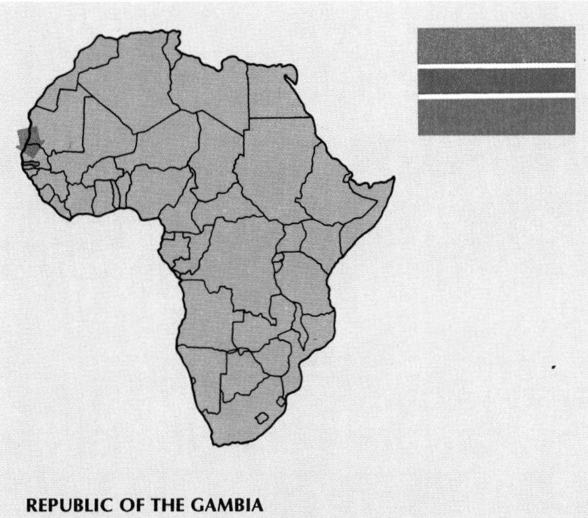

REPUBLIC OF THE GAMBIA

LAND. Area: 11,295 km² (4,361 mi²). Capital and largest city: Banjul (1983 pop., 44,536).

PEOPLE. Population (1986 est.): 774,000; density (1986 est.): 68.5 persons per km² (177.5 per mi²). Distribution (1983): 21% urban, 79% rural. Annual growth (1980–85): 2.6%. Official language: English. Major religion: Islam.

EDUCATION AND HEALTH. Literacy (1980): 20% of adult population. Universities (1987): none. Hospital beds (1980): 756. Physicians (1980): 66. Life expectancy (1980–85): women—44.1; men—40.9. Infant mortality (1984): 250 per 1,000 live births.

ECONOMY. GDP (1984): $125 million; $170 per capita. Labor distribution (1983): agriculture—75%; industry—19%; government—6%. Foreign trade (1985 est.): imports—$73 million; exports—$59 million; principal trade partners—United Kingdom, China, the Netherlands, France, West Germany. Currency: 1 dalasi = 100 butut.

GOVERNMENT. Type: republic. Legislature: House of Representatives. Political subdivisions: 6 districts, Banjul.

COMMUNICATIONS. Railroads (1987): none. Roads (1983): 3,083 km (1,916 mi) total. Major ports: 1. Major airfields: 1.

LAND, PEOPLE, AND ECONOMY

Gambia occupies a river valley and is thus a low-lying country. In the west the land adjacent to the river is very low and dominated by dense mangrove swamps. At Elephant Island, 130 km (80 mi) inland, this terrain gives way to a stretch of higher riverbanks and cliffs punctuated by marshes. About 300 km (185 mi) upstream, the cliffs are higher (6–9 m/20–30 ft) and the valley narrower.

North and south of this riverine strip are higher flats called *banto faros,* a Mandingo phrase meaning "beyond the swamp." Near the Atlantic the flats are often flooded with salt water, rendering them unsuitable for agriculture. Farther east they are free of salt, although the river periodically overflows, depositing fresh loam and supplying water necessary for rice cultivation. Beyond the *banto faros,* toward the northern and southern borders, lies higher, better-drained land that supports the cultivation of sorghum and rice, the major subsistence crops, and peanuts, Gambia's most important export. The highest point in the country, near the eastern border, rises to only 49 m (160 ft).

The climate is tropical, with a rainy season that lasts from June to October. Average annual temperatures range from 25° C (77° F) in the west to 28° C (82° F) in the east. On the coast, annual precipitation averages 1,295 mm (51 in); in the interior it averages 1,090 mm (43 in).

The peoples of Gambia may be divided into five major groups whose languages fall into two categories. The dominant Mandingo agriculturalists (316,000) and the Seranuleh traders (52,000) speak West Atlantic languages; Mande-speakers include the pastoralist Foula (105,000) as well as the WOLOF (97,000) and Jola (55,000) cultivators. Although each people has its own language, Mandingo serves as a lingua franca

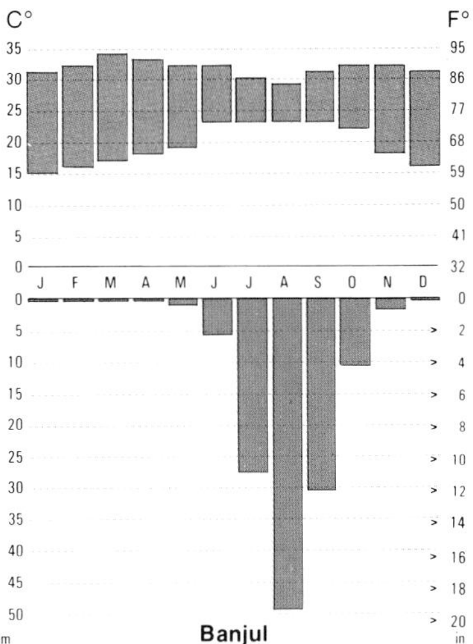

Bars indicate monthly ranges of temperatures (red) *and precipitation* (blue) *of Banjul (formerly Bathurst), the capital of Gambia. Banjul has a tropical wet-dry climate.*

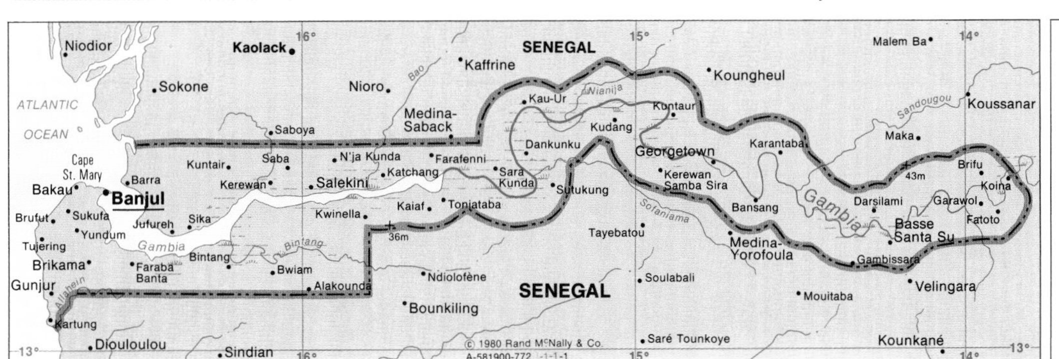

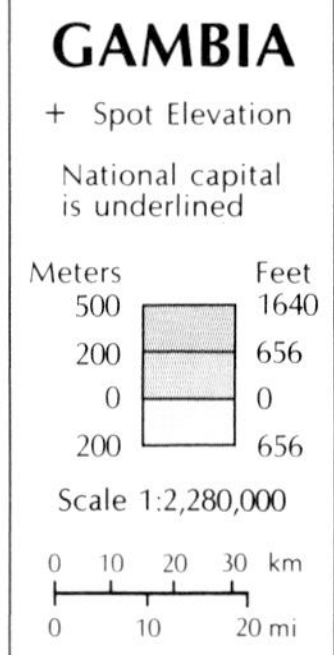

Rice has become the principal food crop cultivated in Gambia, an independent nation that occupies a narrow strip of heavily forested land along the Gambia River in West Africa. The technical aid and advisors provided by the People's Republic of China have helped Gambia increase its rice harvest to approximately 22,000 metric tons (24,250 U.S. tons) annually.

and English is the official language. About 90% of the country's inhabitants are Muslim. Most of the urban population live in BANJUL, the capital and largest city.

The Gambian economy is heavily dependent on peanuts (groundnuts) and peanut by-products, which provide nearly 90% of export earnings. Agriculture was adversely affected by drought during much of the 1980s, and the country suffers from a chronic trade deficit and relies on extensive foreign aid. Although a nascent tourist industry along with offshore oil exploration and fishing projects offer hope of internal economic diversification, the country's long-term efforts are tied to an economic union with Senegal.

HISTORY AND GOVERNMENT

Attracted by the river, most peoples of Gambia emigrated from neighboring parts of today's Senegal. By the 15th century, Mandingo settlers associated with the Mali empire had settled in the valley, founding a cluster of kingdoms that controlled trade along the river. Muslim religious wars in the 19th century resulted in the more complete Islamicization of the region and brought further immigration.

The Portuguese first reached the Gambia River in 1455 and sold trading rights to the British in 1618. In 1660 the British established a fort on Fort James Island. During the 18th century, Britain and France struggled for supremacy in the area. The British established a trading post at Bathurst at the mouth of the river in 1807 and carved out a zone of influence. In 1889, its present boundaries were settled with France, and Gambia became a crown colony. Slavery was abolished in the colony in 1906. In 1965 the colony became independent.

According to the constitution of 1970, Gambia is a republic headed by a president; Dawda K. Jawara and his People's Progressive party have ruled since independence. On Feb. 1, 1982, in the wake of a 1981 coup attempt put down with the aid of Senegalese troops, Gambia and Senegal inaugurated the Confederation of Senegambia. While each nation retains its sovereignty, the confederation provides for the integration of armed forces, coordination of foreign and domestic policies, and monetary and economic union. The president of Senegal serves as president of the confederation; the president of Gambia, as vice-president. DENNIS D. CORDELL

Bibliography: Best, Alan C. G., and Blij, Harm J., *An African Survey* (1977); Cohen, Robin, ed., *African Islands and Enclaves* (1983); Gailey, Harry A., *A History of the Gambia*, rev. ed. (1980); Gray, John M., *The History of Gambia* (1968); Quinn, Charlotte A., *The Mandingo Kingdoms of the Senegambia: Traditionalism, Islam, and European Expansion* (1972); Udo, Reuben K., *A Comprehensive Geography of West Africa* (1978).

Gambia River

The Gambia River, an important trade artery in West Africa, rises in the Fouta Djallon highlands of Guinea, West Africa. It flows north and west through Senegal and Gambia, meeting the Atlantic Ocean at Cape St. Mary, near Banjul. The middle course of the river has numerous islands, the largest being Elephant and MacCarthy islands. The river is 1,125 km (700 mi) long and navigable to large oceangoing vessels from its mouth to Kuntaur, 242 km (150 mi) upstream.

gambling

Gambling is the wagering of money or other valuables on the outcome of a game or other event. There is no historical period or culture to which gambling is unknown. Dice carved from the ankle bones of antelope have been found in prehistoric tombs and burial caves. The ancient Egyptians played atep, a game of guessing the number of upheld fingers. The classical Greeks are known to have played with astragals, the forerunner of modern dice, and Jews in biblical Israel gambled by throwing dice. The Romans were reportedly obsessed with gaming and bet heavily on gladiatorial fights and chariot races. The Roman historian Tacitus noted that the ancient Germans gambled not only wealth but liberty as well.

Although few societies have ever wholly approved of gambling, none has been able to eradicate it completely. Today the United Kingdom appears to have the most liberal gambling laws, but legal gambling can be found in many other places, among them Czechoslovakia, Ghana, France, Macao, Monaco, Puerto Rico, Scandinavia, and Yugoslavia. In the United States the forms of gambling that have been legalized vary from state to state, with Nevada, Connecticut, Rhode Island, and New Jersey among the early liberal states. By the late 1980s a majority of U.S. states ran LOTTERIES.

The games most closely associated with gambling usually involve a heavy element of chance. Whereas POKER, for instance, requires skill to play well, the outcome of the game is determined primarily by the distribution of the cards. Many casino games, such as ROULETTE and craps (see DICE GAMES), are dictated solely by chance. Betting on the outcome of sporting events—especially on HORSE RACING—or on a lottery is perhaps the most widespread legal form of gambling, and in many countries, governments have created systems to funnel through legal channels the vast amounts wagered, retaining a certain proportion for their own use.

Illegal gambling—in the United States and elsewhere—constitutes one of the largest "businesses" in existence, and its "gross" has been estimated to exceed that of its legal counterpart. Legal gambling, claim its advocates, is a means of reducing illegal-gambling profits. A great deal of the illegal gambling conducted in the United States is connected to organized crime, which is thought also to maintain a strong measure of control in legalized gambling.

Today, as throughout history, gambling is not confined to any economic stratum. Compulsive gambling is recognized as a sickness, and such organizations as Gamblers Anonymous exist for the purpose of helping individuals suffering from this problem. The methods are similar to those used by organizations that help alcoholics and overeaters. FRANK RAGLAND

Bibliography: Bergler, Edmund, *Psychology of Gambling* (1970); Findlay, John M., *People of Chance: Gambling in American Society from Jamestown to Las Vegas* (1986); Galski, Thomas, ed., *The Handbook of Pathological Gambling* (1987); King, Rufus, *Gambling and Organized Crime* (1969); Scarne, John, *Scarne's New Complete Guide to Gambling* (1986); Times Mirror Press, ed., *Gamblers Anonymous*, 3d ed. (1973).

gamboge [gam'-bohj]

Gamboge is an organic coloring substance used as a yellow pigment in watercolor paints, as a coloring agent in varnishes, and in medicine as a cathartic. It is deep brown as a solid but turns bright yellow in solution. A gum resin, gamboge is obtained by evaporating the sap from trees of the genus *Garcinia,* which are native to Southeast Asia.

game birds

Game birds are defined as any species that are hunted except for such waterfowl as ducks and geese. The most popular game birds are members of the order Galliformes, including the wild TURKEY, *Meleagris gallopavo,* family Meleagrididae; various species of GROUSE, family Tetraonidae; and QUAILS and PHEASANTS, family Phasianidae. Other important game species belong to the order Charadriiformes, including the WOODCOCK and SNIPE, family Scolopacidae; to the order Columbiformes, including DOVES, family Columbidae; and to the order Gruiformes, including RAILS, family Rallidae.

Hunting techniques are determined by the nature of the habitat and the behavior of the quarry. Upland game birds (those which live at high elevations far from the sea) are generally weak fliers and spend most of their time on the ground. They typically crouch motionless at the hunter's approach and may be easily overlooked. Specially trained dogs, such as setters and pointers, are used to detect hidden birds. When approached closely, the bird suddenly bursts into the air in a short but rapid escape flight. The speed and skill of the hunter's response will determine the success of his quest.

The wild turkey, a North American bird, and the ruffed grouse, *Bonasa umbellus,* are considered among the best upland game birds. The American woodcock, *Philohela minor,* and the ring-necked pheasant, *Phasianus colchicus,* are heavily hunted upland game birds, prized for their flesh. In contrast to upland game birds, a representative shorebird, the common snipe, *Gallinago gallinago,* provides sport because it takes off in a zigzag flight when flushed.

Game bird hunting is controlled by laws designed to limit the number of birds killed and thereby prevent excessive reduction of population. Indeed, many species of birds have become extinct as a result of excessive hunting. Attempts have been made to introduce birds into areas where they do not naturally occur in order to provide game for hunting, but most such introductions have been unsuccessful. However, the chukar, *Alectoris chukar,* the gray PARTRIDGE, *Perdix perdix,* and the ring-necked pheasant are Old World members of the family Phasianidae that have become widely established in North America since their introductions. In eastern North America the turkey has been successfully reintroduced into areas from which it had previously been wiped out because of overhunting. ROBERT J. RAIKOW

Bibliography: Rue, Leonard L., *Sportsman's Guide to Game Animals* (1968).

game laws

Game laws are statutes protecting wild birds and animals. They usually prohibit the killing of specified game except during certain periods each year. They also control hunting by limiting the number of birds or animals each hunter may kill. These controls are designed to prevent depletion of breeding stock and the consequent extinction of species. An estimated 120 kinds of mammals and 150 varieties of birds have been rendered extinct, many of them by commercial hunting.

The first game laws were established to protect the hunting prerogatives of kings and aristocrats, who employed gamekeepers to keep away poachers and severely punished those who were caught. The U.S. game conservation program is directed by the U.S. Fish and Wildlife Service in cooperation with private organizations of conservationists and sportsmen. The federal government has entered into agreements with Canada and Mexico to protect migratory birds, both by maintaining winter sanctuaries for them and by controlling hunting of them. Game-management programs have enabled some animals that were once close to extinction to flourish again, including the bison, several species of deer, and the wild turkey.

Bibliography: Sigler, William, *Wildlife Law Enforcement,* 2d ed. (1972).

game theory

The theory of games might be called the mathematics of competition and cooperation. It analyzes situations in terms of gains and losses of opposing players. It is applied widely in economics, operations research, military science, political science, organization theory, and the study of bargaining and negotiation. First formulated in the 1920s by the mathematician John von NEUMANN, it did not become well known until the publication (1944) of the monumental work *Theory of Games and Economic Behavior* by von Neumann and the economist Oskar Morgenstern. Since then many others have joined in extending and applying the theory.

Although the terminology of players, moves, rules, and payoffs might suggest a preoccupation with sports or recreation, the theory of games has seldom been of practical use in playing real games. This may be because the theory is based on idealized players who have clear motives and unlimited skill and calculating ability. Nevertheless, familiar parlor games can be used to illustrate certain aspects of game theory. Chess is a typical "game of perfect information." Because there are no hidden moves, it is possible in principle to determine whether each board position is a win for White, a win for Black, or a draw; this is the "minimax value" of the position and is discussed below. Moreover, for each player there exists an "optimal pure strategy"—a complete plan of action that guarantees him the minimax value of the starting position regardless of how his opponent plays. Poker, in contrast, is a game of "imperfect information" because decisions must be made without knowing the identity of the concealed cards. As a result, good play usually demands the use of purposely randomized behavior, or "mixed strategies." For example, certain situations call for a bluff—not based on certainty, but on a small probability. Poker also illustrates how there may be no universally best way to play, even in principle. Indeed, when there are more than two players the theory predicts only a "noncooperative equilibrium," in which each player's best strategy depends on the strategies adopted by the other players.

The mathematical cornerstone of game theory is the Minimax Theorem, discovered by von Neumann in 1928. It asserts that every finite, zero-sum, two-player game has a minimax value if mixed strategies are allowed. This means that every such game has a solution (an optimal strategy); it may, however, be difficult to find the solution. This situation is illustrated in detail in example 1 below. In this theorem, "zero-sum" means that any gain in payoff for one player represents an equal loss for the other. Many parlor games are zero-sum, but the "games" that are found in economics or in OPERATIONS RESEARCH usually are not, since wealth may be created or destroyed.

The Minimax Theorem does not apply to nonzero-sum games or games with more than two players. Nevertheless, such games do have a weaker form of solution, a noncooperative equilibrium in which no player, acting on the assumption that the other players' strategies are fixed, can gain anything by changing his own strategy. (See examples 2 and 3.) This theorem was proved in 1950 by John Nash, and these solutions are often called Nash equilibria.

The theory of cooperative games provides another approach to games with more than two players. It is concerned primarily with "coalitions"—groups of players who coordinate their actions and perhaps even pool their winnings. A cooperative game can often be put into the form of a characteristic function, $v(S)$, which expresses for each set of players S the amount they can get if they form a coalition excluding the other players. In an economic context, $v(S)$ might represent the gross product achievable by an arbitrary subset of the national economy, or, in an industry model, the prospective profit of each set of firms acting as a cartel. In a political context, $v(S)$ could be defined to be 1 for sets of legislators that have enough votes to pass a bill and 0 for sets that do not. Often, however, a single characteristic function $v(S)$ is not enough to describe the essential worth of a coalition, and more complex mathematical forms must be employed.

More than a dozen solution concepts for cooperative games have been introduced, serving different analytical purposes. One of them, introduced by Donald Gillies and Lloyd Shapley in 1953 and named the "core," is defined as the set of outcomes of the game that are "socially stable," in that no coalition has the power to force an improvement for its members. This means that if there is a characteristic function v, then the total payoff to each set of players S must be at least $v(S)$. (See Example 4, below.) Unfortunately, if coalitions are too strong the core may fail to exist, and if the coalitions are too weak, the core may include a great variety of different outcomes and not provide a satisfactory solution of the game. In many important economic applications, however, the core does give a sharp solution that is closely related to the classical equilibrium of supply and demand. For this reason, core theory is useful in mathematical economics.

Another solution for cooperative games, called the Shapley value, is defined as a weighted average of the marginal contributions $v(S) - v(S - \{p\})$ of a player p to the various coalitions S he or she might join. Unlike the core, the Shapley value is always well defined and unique, but it is not enforceable by strategic action; it merely indicates what a player should expect to get *a priori*. The Shapley value may be used in a fair appraisal of a set of conflicting claims, for example, as a basis for an adjudicated settlement (Example 4).

Example 1. Colonel Blotto is ordered to attack through the mountains. His situation resembles that of a football quarterback (see diagram).

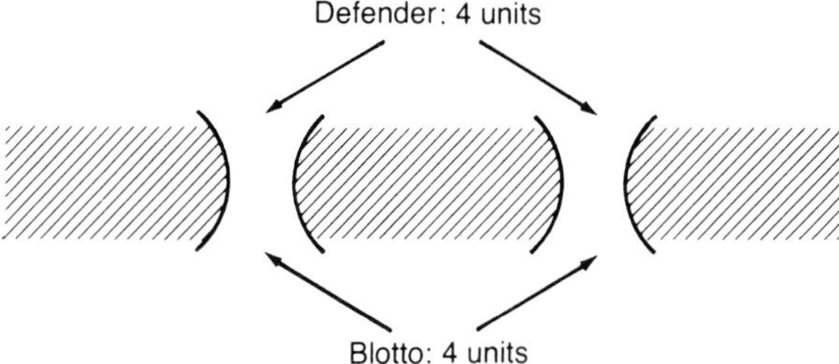

A breakthrough at either pass will bring victory, but requires a 2:1 local superiority of military strength. How should Blotto deploy his forces?

In the accompanying tabular display, "1" denotes victory for Blotto, "0" defeat, and "x:y" the strategy of sending x units to the left and y to the right. Such a table is usually called a "payoff matrix" because in many "games" there is a payment, or payoff, made from one player to another—based on the decisions that have been made.

		Defender's strategy:				
	$x:y$	4 : 0	3 : 1**	2 : 2**	1 : 3**	0 : 4
	4 : 0*	0	0	1	1	1
	3 : 1	1	0	0	1	1
Blotto's strategy	2 : 2*	1	1	0	1	1
	1 : 3	1	1	0	0	1
	0 : 4*	1	1	1	0	0

Note that no pure strategy is effective for either side. Blotto should choose equally at random one of the three strategies marked (*); he will then break through with probability 2/3 against any defense. The enemy commander should similarly mix the three strategies marked (**); his chance of stopping Blotto will then be at least 1/3. The minimax value is 2/3.

Example 2. Two prisoners are interrogated in separate cells. Each faces a 10-year sentence if incriminated by the other; otherwise the sentence will be just 3 years on a lesser charge. An additional factor is that the prosecutor has promised each prisoner a 1-year reduction in exchange for testimony against the other prisoner.

		2nd Prisoner	
		testify	be silent
1st Prisoner	testify	(9, 9)	(2, 10)
	be silent	(10, 2)	(3, 3)

In the accompanying tabular display, the ordered pair of numbers gives the sentences of the first and second prisoners. For each prisoner, "testify" is a *dominating strategy*—the best choice whatever the other does. Hence, (9, 9) is the unique Nash equilibrium and seems the only "rational" outcome for this noncooperative game. But the apparently irrational principle of "honor among thieves" leads to a distinctly better outcome (3, 3) for the thieves.

Games of this kind set up a confrontation between individual and collective rationality and are often studied experimentally for the insights they afford into social behavior.

Example 3. Three children are having a snowball fight. They throw simultaneously at 10-second intervals and are not very accurate. Abner's chance of scoring a hit on any one toss is only 4%, Becky's is 3%, and Chuck's is 2%. They can throw at either opponent but must fall down when hit. The "fighting" continues until only one (or perhaps none) remains standing.

This simple "game of survival" has not one but several Nash equilibria. The obvious one is to throw always at the more accurate opponent. The calculations are not difficult, but the result is paradoxical: Chuck wins 37.6% of the time, Becky 32.3%, and Abner 28.8%. In this case, the "fittest" individual is the least likely to survive.

A more sophisticated solution is the following: Abner's plan is to throw first at Becky, but to shift to Chuck if Chuck ever throws at him. Becky still throws at Abner, but Chuck, deterred by Abner's threat of retaliation, throws only at Becky. As in the other solution, no one can gain by changing his or her strategy, given the strategies of the other two. But now the outcome is quite different: the percentages of victory are: Abner 43.5%, Chuck 36.0%, Becky 19.2%.

There are many other solutions, both noncooperative and cooperative. Selecting the right solution concept in any multiplayer game generally requires looking beyond the physical or legal constraints and considering psychological and sociological factors, such as the credibility of threats, the firmness of commitments, and the ethics of collusion.

Example 4. Three cooperating towns, *A, B,* and *C,* wish to tie into a nearby power source. The possible transmission links and their costs are as shown in the diagram.

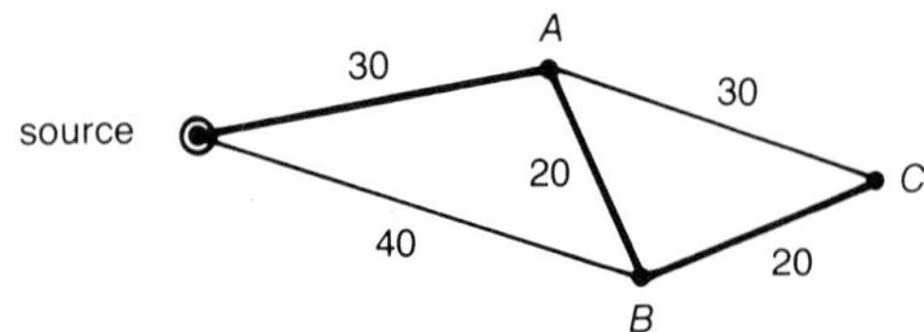

The minimum-cost connecting system (heavy lines) costs 70 units. How should this cost be allotted among the towns?

Calculating the minimum cost of each subset of towns fills out the characteristic function for this cooperative game: $v(ABC) = -70$, $v(AB) = -50$, $v(AC) = v(BC) = v(C) = -60$, $v(A) = -30$, $v(B) = -40$, and $v(\text{no links}) = 0$. Calculations of the Shapley value would indicate that towns *A, B,* and *C* should be assessed 15, 20, and 35 units, respectively. Moreover, this solution has the desirable core property that no town or set of towns is asked to pay more for this cooperative system than it would cost for it to build its own separate system. LLOYD S. SHAPLEY

Bibliography: Brams, Steven J., *Game Theory and Politics* (1975); Conway, John, *On Numbers and Games* (1976); Davis, Morton D., *Game Theory: A Nontechnical Introduction* (1983); Harsanyi, J., *Game Theory* (1982); McKinsey, John C., *Introduction to the Theory of Games* (1952); Owen, Guillermo, *Game Theory,* 2d ed. (1982); Rapoport, Anatol, *Fights, Games and Debates* (1960).

gamelan [gam'-uh-lan]

The gamelan is the Javanese and Balinese orchestra, ranging from a few players to several dozen. Except for a few string and woodwind instruments, it is a percussion group featuring xylophones, metallophones (tuned metal bars), and gongs. The various types of instruments play different rhythmic and melodic patterns. Instruments are not interchangeable between gamelans, for each orchestra has its own tuning.

The gamelan can be coupled with voices; it is used to accompany dance and the theater. The gamelan strongly influenced the musical style of Claude Debussy. The instruments for complete gamelans are housed at several American universities and European museums. ELWYN A. WIENANDT

Bibliography: Kunst, Jaap, *Music in Java: Its History, Its Theory and Its Technique,* 2 vols., 3d ed. (1973); Lentz, Donald, *The Gamelan Music of Java and Bali* (1965); McPhee, Colin, *Music in Bali* (1966).

Gamelin, Maurice Gustave [gah-muh-lan', mah-rees' gue-stahv']

Maurice Gustave Gamelin, b. Sept. 20, 1872, d. Apr. 18, 1958, was the French commander of Allied forces on the Western Front in the early stages of World War II. Commissioned in the French Army in 1893, he was a divisional commander in World War I. A believer in the MAGINOT LINE, he became (1938) chief of staff of national defense and assumed field command at the beginning of World War II. In May 1940 he was unable to resist the German invasion of France and was replaced by Maxime WEYGAND on May 19. He was later tried by France's Vichy government and interned (1943–45) in Germany.

games

Games are models of real-life situations in which—unlike real life—the issues are quite simply drawn and the participants can become engaged without all the confusions that surround everyday action and decision making. The basic function of games is to intensify human experience in ways that are relatively safe, even while they provide suspense and excitement. Typically, games simulate the more intense human experiences: physical combat, intellectual contest, and the expectancy and excitement involved in random occurrences.

This article will discuss the three basic types of games—those of physical skill, chance, and strategy—and show how these types are exemplified in board games, word games, children's games, games of fantasy, and in electronic (video) games. Details of many games may be found in separate articles on individual games (for example, MONOPOLY). Games of physical skill that have become organized sports are discussed under their separate names (BASEBALL, FOOTBALL, and so on) and in the article, SPORTS, HISTORY OF.

GAMES OF PHYSICAL SKILL

Games of physical skill are those in which the outcome is determined by the athletic abilities of the players. At the simplest level such games may not even involve competition. In some very simple cultures there are no competitive games. In these groups one is more likely to find group-effort games: a ball is kept up in the air cooperatively by all the players, or the players, holding hands, whirl around in a circle while trying not to fall over. These games are not unlike those played in early childhood in Western society. In the game of ring around the roses, all the players hold hands, form a circle, and at the end fall over on the ground together. In these group-effort games, there is an implicit contest between the

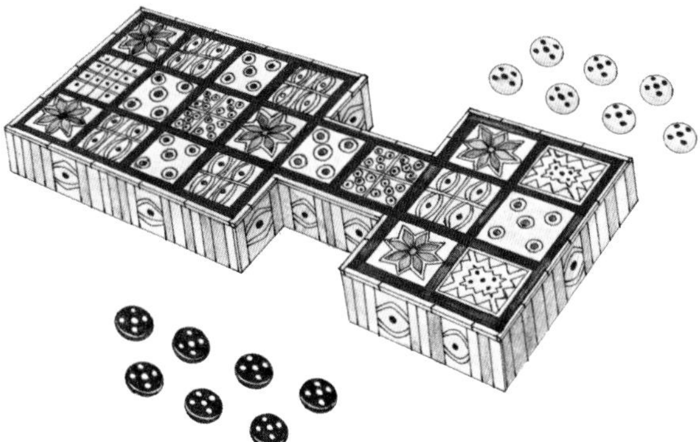

This board-and-tile game is based on a gaming board excavated from a royal tomb in the ancient city of Ur. The board, which dates from the 4th millennium BC, is believed to be the forerunner of backgammon.

players and their own natures, their lack of skill, or their clumsiness. The ability of the players to work together as a group is emphasized, and the clarity and intensity of their task and its separation from everyday life is what makes the game exciting. (In recent times an organization called the New Games Movement has been created to promote the spread of these more cooperative kinds of games. The founders argue that there is too much competition in modern life.)

Beyond the simple tribal group that must collaborate for its own survival under harsh circumstances and therefore plays only cooperative games are the many groupings in which there is some division of function that is then made a focus of competitive games. A simple example would be a game of tug o' war between men and women. There are a myriad of complex divisions that are emphasized by games involving direct physical combat and trials of skill. Perhaps the most universal game in societies that have only competitive physical-skill games are those involving spear throwing through a target rolled between two teams. The winners are those whose side gets the most spears through the target during its progress.

In modern society the simplest physical-skill games are such contests as races, archery, and darts. Most modern games, however, are combinations of physical skill and strategy. This combination is most apparent in the many varieties of ball games. American football, for example, is probably the most strategic of games involving physical skill, with its various complex plays and its control by coaches from the sidelines.

These 4th-century BC Greek terra cotta figures are playing dice. Although Sophocles ascribed the invention of dice to the Greek warrior Palamedes during the Trojan War (c.1200 BC), dice dating from the 3d millennium BC have been found in the Near East and India.

GAMES OF CHANCE

Until fairly recently, with the growth of state-sponsored lotteries, pure games of chance were not particularly welcome in the United States. Today, however, more money is spent on them and on GAMBLING than on any other types of games. They seem to have originated as a means of simulating control over the future, and they seem more likely to have appeared in societies that believed that they could discover the purposes of the gods through magical means. Today they are likely to be played by people who do not believe that they can influence the course of their lives through personal achievement, and who in consequence gain enjoyment from the magical possibilities offered by games of chance. The simplest such games usually involve some form of dice or other random number selection that determines the outcome, as in bingo or the lottery.

The games of chance known from ancient times are those which were played on a board. In most of them, players competed to complete a circuit of the board, by throwing dice to determine the number of steps that could be taken at any one turn. Although many of these games involved some strategy because some choice was available (for example, what number of pieces to move from one position to the next), they were basically games of chance. Such games as parcheesi, backgammon, and dominoes have ancient histories.

Increasingly, however, chance was combined with strategy, and real knowledge helped to determine the outcome. In Monopoly, for example, chance combined with strategy leads by cumulative steps to a winner who can buy out everyone else in the game. In games throughout history, a similar cumulative series of steps brought the player to a kingship, to the gates of heaven, to the ownership of all the cattle, or whatever ultimate end was most prized among the players. Essentially, these games were an illustration in simple form of the many steps that must be taken in personal achievement if success was to be won. The ratio of chance to strategy was a measure of the extent to which the players believed that their lives and progress were in the lap of fate or the result of their own efforts.

GAMES OF STRATEGY

Games of strategy, either by themselves (chess) or in combination with chance (poker) or with physical skill (ice hockey), are the characteristic games of the 20th century. A game of strategy is defined by the fact that its outcomes must be determined by rational decision making. This distinguishes it from games of chance where the outcomes are determined by random choices, and from games of physical skill where the outcomes are determined by athletic abilities.

In the history of civilization, games of strategy seem to have emerged when societies increased in complexity to such an extent that there was need for diplomacy and strategic warfare. In many respects the earliest games of strategy are the intelligence tests of their era. Mancala, or wari, for example, the strategic game of the African continent first played in ancient Egypt, involves each player having a number of pieces that are distributed about the playing board. At each move, each player must make estimates involving numerical skill and good judgment in order to capture the opponent's pieces. It is hard to play this game without the feeling that one is participating in one of those basic stages of civilization where the accumulation of property is what is at issue. In the Asian game of weichi, or go, on the other hand, where the players attempt to surround each other's pieces, one has the experience of a blockading kind of warfare. The Indoeuropean game of chess, by contrast, has been seen as a battle between different social orders, with the status of each member—from king to pawn—being carefully stated. Here the aim is not to surround the enemy but to capture and exterminate them.

With rules simple enough for children to learn, go is Japan's most popular board game. Players try to surround points on the board, as well as their opponent's pieces, with their own pieces. To do this well requires great strategic skill, as well as practice and patience.

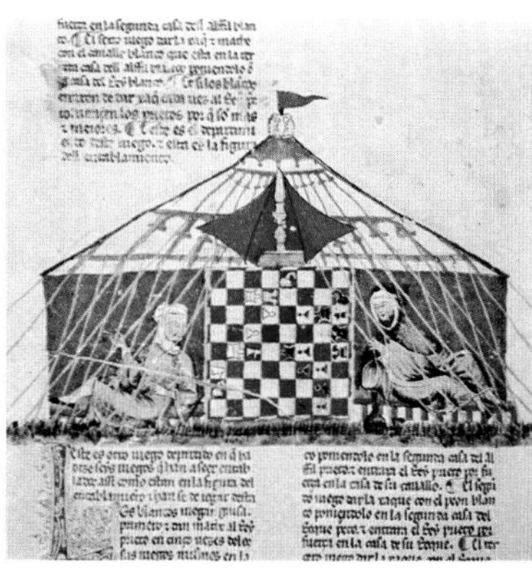

This 13th-century miniature shows King Alfonso X of Spain (r. 1252–84) playing chess. Probably originating in India during the 6th century AD, the game was introduced into Spain by the Moors during their long occupation of the Iberian peninsula. (El Escorial, Madrid.)

In modern times, many games no longer offer their winners the symbolic significance (king, owner of all the cattle) of a win. Trivial Pursuit, for example, is a game for those who believe that information is important and wish to appear superior at knowing such information, but safeguard themselves from any real contest of knowledge by characterizing their answers as "trivial." As in all other games, the player's protection from the same concern in real life is most important.

WORD GAMES AND SOLITARY GAMES

The original word game is undoubtedly the riddle, which is essentially a strategic contest over information. The player must be able to untangle the riddle's linguistic deceits in order to discover the answer. The riddle was in the first place a competition in esoteric knowledge, a game of fundamental rather than trivial pursuit. Often it was associated with magical ceremonies, and the player's life could be at stake if he or she gave the incorrect answer. (This kind of game is hardly fun, and it is important to realize that the modern definition of games as fun—that is, as posing no real danger—is a product of industrial civilization, where games are no longer a part of religious life, as many of them once were.)

The arrival of printing in the 15th century, and the spread of the ability to read, enormously increased the number of word games, even as these games lost their ancient mythological and religious connections. Today, some word games involve the guessing of enacted meanings, as in charades. Others require the guessing of correct answers based on information provided by different systems of clues. In Guggenheim or geography, players must guess the correct categories; in Botticelli, the correct person; in twenty questions, the correct word.

Many modern word games can be enjoyed solitarily. More children nowadays read riddles in books than engage in riddle contests with their peers. Just as literacy allowed people to become solitary through reading, in a way that had never before been possible, it also gave them the tools to play solitary games. These games now include mathematical puzzles, logical puzzles, and most important, word games such as the crossword puzzles that are read and worked out by thousands of persons every day.

Just as today's is a civilization in which competence with words is critical, so it is a culture in which individual and solitary achievement are also critical to success. It is not surprising, therefore, that for the first time in history many of the games of ordinary people are solitary games.

VIDEO GAMES

The most extraordinary solitary game of the age is no doubt the video game, played in games arcades and on home television screens everywhere. The video game is not simply a game of physical skill, chance, or strategy, but combines all of these to produce something completely new. There is physical skill in adjusting perceptually to the immense amount of visual information provided on the screen, information that appears with high velocity and must be adapted to quickly if the player is not to lose. Children seem to be able to learn how to manipulate these games much more quickly than do adults, suggesting that their perceptual alterness is not yet obstructed by too many preexisting ideas and strategies. Many video games are programmed to allow seemingly random events to occur, so they are also games of chance. In most games, however, decisions must be made on the basis of perceived changes or recognizable logical sequences, so strategy is also involved. Video games are in many ways a symbolic substitute for living in difficult conditions where one must learn to adapt to constantly recurring emergencies.

As yet, there has been developed no theory based on video games that might be a generalized model of how to adapt to life. One can predict that such a theory may some day be developed, because two major theories about modern life have already come out of games. The first is PROBABILITY theory, which was first developed out of games of chance in the 17th century by Blaise Pascal. The other, GAME THEORY, developed out of games of strategy in this century by John von Neumann and Oskar Morgenstern, is a system for predicting how people should behave in situations of conflict in order to win.

FANTASY GAMES

Some psychologists argue that a functioning imagination is the most important skill one can possess, but although there are games that hone one's abilities to think logically or sharpen one's athletic skills, it has taken some time for purely imaginative games to develop. The best known is Dungeons and Dragons, in which the players act out a scenario invented by the games master, leader of the game. The scenario itself is often derived from science fiction or fantasy stories with which all players are familiar. Unlike video games, where the player manipulates symbols on a screen, in Dungeons and Dragons the players become their own symbols, acting out roles as lords, monks, monsters, witches, and so forth. The game is a drama in which the outcomes are dependent on the fantasies of the master and the players, as well as on the rolls of the dice that determine how far a player may go toward the goal, whether or not his or her character has the ability to perform certain feats, and what kind of luck will accompany each move. The game may be played on a board drawn by the master, or in a location—a building, a city block—mapped to represent the world of the game.

CHILDREN'S GAMES

The first teachers of children's games are likely to be parents, and the first games are usually face games, where parents attract their infant's attention by making funny faces. Between three and six months, mother and baby learn to imitate each other's funny faces, or to rediscover each other's face hidden under a blanket. Even in these early collaborative games one sees how the excitement of the game exists in the tension between what is expected when the blanket is lifted, and what is actually there. All games require some such tension of opposites. In the second half of the first year the mother or father plays hand and body games such as "this little piggy went to market," where the child's toes personify the various piggies and the game always ends with a great tickle. After several repetitions the baby learns to anticipate the outcome, and its excitement rises until it screams with laughter at the finish. Thus are born the rising and falling emotional crescendos of games.

By the second year of life toddlers are able to mimic each other in the same way as they have mimicked their parents. By three and four years of age the child plays simple collaborative games with larger groups. These are often games of order and disorder, in which a group of children imitate each other in some unseemly fashion—all banging their blocks on the table in mounting noisiness, or all falling over in the sandpit.

By five and six years children begin to play recognizably traditional games. At the root of these games one can see the major oppositions in both animal and human culture, namely chase and escape, and attack and defense. The existence of such games among animals suggests that they must have very basic survival value for all species. Games can be distinguished from PLAY by these internal oppositions of order and disorder, chase and escape, attack and defense, win and lose. Play does not require such internal oppositions, although play shares with games the quality of being opposed to everyday life by its more schematic and caricatural nature. Both play and games mimic and mock everyday life. The little girl dressed in her mother's big shoes and oversized hat, and the soccer player spinning backwards to kick a ball into the net are both playing out-of-size roles from the perspective of everyday behavior.

From seven onward children gradually begin to play games that have less to do with symbolic survival and more to do with achievement. In general girls are less competitive than boys and play games where there is more defined turn-taking, such as jacks, hopscotch, and jump rope. Boys begin quite early to be organized into smaller-sized versions of the sports of their fathers (Little League baseball). This difference between the play of girls and boys is often repeated in the differences between men's and women's attitudes toward play, where women seem to prefer to play that is more informal, spontaneous, and collaborative, while men seek play that is organized and competitive. Whether these differences are the result of genetic patterning or learned behavior is an issue that now occupies psychologists, brain physiologists, and other scientists.

For both children and adults, games appeal because they deal with the exciting issues of the day in a way that is sufficiently simplified to be manageable within the imposed limits of space and time. In games players can invest themselves totally and passionately, without immediate concern for their everyday lives. What propels the players forward is the importance of the issues at stake in their real lives. These issues have to do with personal achievement, status, security, anxiety, and the ability to collaborate. Although game playing is treated separately from everyday life, being a good or a bad game player is a matter of fundamental importance to everyone, and in every society. BRIAN SUTTON-SMITH

Bibliography: Avedon, Elliott, M., and Sutton-Smith, Brian, *The Study of Games* (1979); Fagen, Robert, *Animal Play Behavior* (1981); Fleugelman, A., *The New Games Book* (1976); Grunfeld, Frederic V., *Games of the World* (1975); Maccoby, Michael, *The Gamesman* (1976); Sutton-Smith, Brian, *The Folkgames of Children* (1972).

games, mathematical

Mathematical games are of two types: (1) games that explicitly require mathematical reasoning in their play, and (2) games to which some mathematical theory can be applied although it is not necessary for playing the game. Mathematical puzzles are the most popular games of the first type, and mathematics itself is the most complex "game" of the first type yet devised. Games of the second type can be played without any mathematical analysis, although the players may try to mathematically analyze the game. Most gambling games are of this type, as are many "games of perfect information" (see below).

MATHEMATICAL PUZZLES

Mathematical puzzles abound in history and literature. They have been used as trials, intelligence tests, and amusements. Many fields of mathematics began with such puzzles, and many other puzzles have in turn been inspired by mathematics.

Logical puzzles require only the logical technique of DEDUCTION for their solution. The first known systematic study of such puzzles was by philosophers and mathematicians of ancient Greece. One such puzzle concerns the lawyer Protagoras, who agreed to tutor a student, contracting that the student would pay his fee when he won his first case. The student completed his studies, but accepted no clients. Protagoras later sued the student for his fee. The student argued that if he won the case, he would not have to pay, according to the court's decision; on the other hand, if he lost, he would not yet have won his first case, so he still would not have to pay, because of the original agreement. Protagoras argued that if the student won the case, he would have to pay by agreement, and if he lost, he would have to pay by court decision. How was the case resolved? One answer is: the court should decide in favor of the student. Protagoras should then sue a second time for his fee; the student would now have to pay the fee because he had already won his first case. (Note: many of the games described in this article, and many of the mathematicians mentioned, are cited in the bibliography below.)

Logical Puzzles. Logical puzzles were popular in 19th-century England, due in part to the efforts of Charles L. Dodgson (pseudonym Lewis Carroll), a mathematician and a contributor to mathematical logic. The contemporary logician Raymond M. Smullyan has published an excellent collection of logical puzzles, such as the following: an island is inhabited by two classes of people: knights, who make only true statements, and knaves, who make only false statements. Three inhabitants are conversing. Al says, "All of us are knaves." Bill says, "Exactly one of us is a knight." What are Al, Bill, and Charlie? The answer: Al cannot be a knight, for if he were a knight, his statement would be false—a contradiction of the definition of a knight. Al must therefore be a knave. Because knaves lie, Al's statement is false; thus there is at least one knight among the three. Bill and Charlie cannot both be knights, because Bill, a knight, would have lied (and knights don't lie). There must thus be exactly one knight, either Bill or Charlie. As Bill's statement is true, Bill is a knight; therefore, Charlie is a knave.

Puzzles Involving Whole Numbers. Another category of puzzles, common to many ancient cultures, involves the arithmetic of whole numbers. The earliest known systematic study of such puzzles was by the geometer Euclid, who, in the 3d century BC proposed a method for solving the following kind of puzzle.

A person buys doughnuts at $0.37 apiece and candy bars at $0.20 apiece, spending a total of $12.09. How many of each are bought? The only possible answer is 17 doughnuts and 29 candy bars. This puzzle is distinguished from the related problems of algebra in that it requires an answer in whole numbers. Otherwise, there would be many solutions containing fractions, such as 10 doughnuts and 41 and 19/20 candy bars. A more thorough study of equations having whole-number solutions was conducted 3 centuries after Euclid by Diophantus of Alexandria; hence, such equations are known as Diophantine equations.

A more popular form of number puzzle is the cryptarithm. A common example is the sum:

$$\begin{array}{r} \text{S E N D} \\ \underline{+\ \text{M O R E}} \\ =\ \text{M O N E Y} \end{array}$$

which is to be solved as a cryptogram. The symbols S, E, N, D, M, O, R, and Y represent different digits, which must be deduced. The only solution: 9567 + 1085 = 10652.

Packing Problems. Packing problems constitute another large class of puzzles. The object of such puzzles is to pack a number of pieces into a desired shape or container. The ancient Chinese game of tangrams consists of seven simple geometrical tiles that can be assembled into numerous pleasing shapes. An example of a packing problem is the following: What is the smallest rectangle that can be completely covered with an odd number of identical tiles, each shaped (as in figure 1) like a perfect square with one-quarter of it cut away?

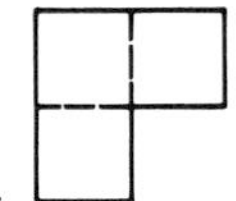
1.

The solution is shown in figure 2.

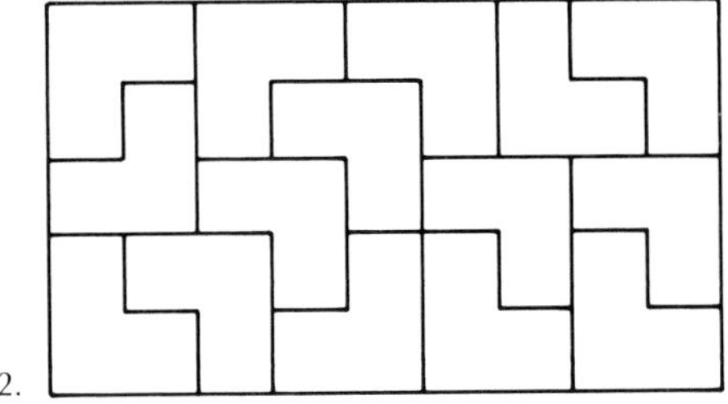
2.

The most prolific American creator of puzzles is Sam Loyd, whose popular puzzles entertained a generation of people all over the world at the turn of the century. His "15-puzzle" is still popular. It consists of a 4-by-4 tray containing 15 square tiles, numbered 1 through 15, and one empty space. The tiles can be shifted, but they cannot be lifted out of the tray. The object of the puzzle is to arrange the tiles in increasing order, as shown in figure 3.

1	2	3	4
5	6	7	8
9	10	11	12
13	14	15	

3.

The difficulty of the puzzle depends on the starting configuration—more than 20 trillion configurations are possible. Remarkably, only half of these configurations can be shifted to give the solution shown in figure 3. If the starting configuration, for example, is like figure 3, but with the "14" and "15" tiles interchanged, it is impossible to obtain the desired arrangement.

Combinatorial analysis is a branch of mathematics that investigates possible ways of arranging objects. Much of this analysis is inspired by the following puzzle first considered by the mathematician Leonhard Euler. Can the four aces (A), kings (K), queens (Q), and jacks (J) in a standard deck of playing cards be arranged in a 4-by-4 square so that each of the four rows and four columns contains exactly one card of each suit—spades (S), diamonds (D), clubs (C), and hearts (H)—and one card of each denomination? There are 144 different solutions, the following being one in which the two diagonals, as well as the rows and columns, satisfy the condition:

AS	QC	JH	KD
JD	KH	AC	QS
KC	JS	QD	AH
QH	AD	KS	JC

Generalizations of this "simple" puzzle have aided in the design of experiments and in coding theory.

WHEN MATHEMATICIANS PLAY GAMES

Mathematics can be applied to many games, even those which do not appear to be mathematical.

In the 17th century, a problem concerning a gambling game was analyzed by the mathematicians Blaise Pascal and Pierre de Fermat. Their analysis led to the development of PROBABILITY theory, one of the most useful mathematical fields. Probability theory applies to all gambling games (games of chance). It was used by Edward Thorpe to devise winning strategy for blackjack.

More recently, the development of GAME THEORY has been used in economics, military strategy, and analysis of voting

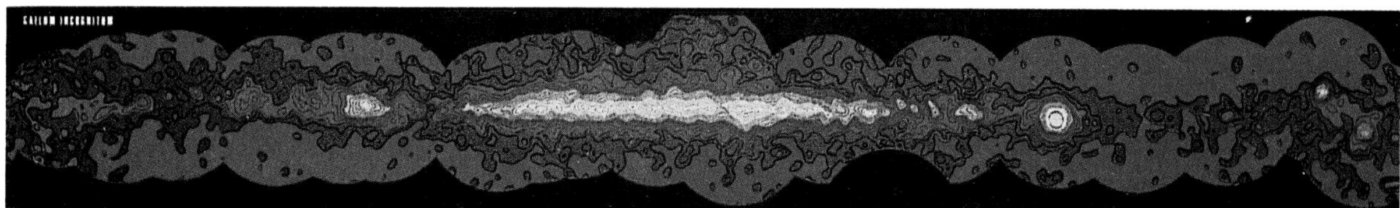

The emission of gamma rays in our Galaxy is shown in this chart by the use of colors indicating different intensities of emission. The regions of lowest intensity are in blue, ranging consecutively upward through green, red, orange, dark and pale yellow, to white regions of highest intensity. Galactic center is one such high-intensity region, as is the still more prominent Vela pulsar at the middle right.

systems. A feature of game theory is its ability to predict to what extent a person should bluff in a game.

Games of perfect information are games in which all players know the situation at all times. These games cannot contain random elements, such as dice. Chess and checkers are games of perfect information, whereas card games, where some cards are hidden from a player's view, are not. A theory of mathematics has been developed to deal with two-person perfect-information games. This theory reaches beyond games in that it probes into the heart of mathematical logic and into the mysteries of peculiar number systems.

Some games can be theoretically solved, but the strategy for obtaining the solution involves complicated calculations. Computers can easily be programmed to play such games; many programs and special-purpose computers have been made to play nim, ticktacktoe, and other solved games. Games such as chess, however, have not been solved, although a computer can be an important tool in analyzing these games. Even though no perfect strategy is known, a computer can be programmed to play skillfully, and several chess-playing computers have been commercially produced. By late 1988, computers had begun to beat chess grand masters, and the developers of these victorious computers were taking aim at the world-champion level in the future.

RECREATIONAL MATHEMATICS

Despite the connection between mathematics and games, the main reason for the popularity of both types of mathematical games is that they are recreational and fun to play. (The mathematical genius Pierre de Fermat was a lawyer by profession and pursued mathematics as a hobby.) The popularity of mathematics as a hobby today is due in part to Martin GARDNER, the author of a widely read column and publisher of numerous puzzle collections. DEAN HOFFMAN

Bibliography: Ainley, Stephen, *Mathematical Puzzles* (1983); Gardner, Martin, *Martin Gardner's Sixth Book of Mathematical Diversions from Scientific American* (1984), *Time Travel and Other Mathematical Bewilderments* (1987), and many other books; *Journal of Recreational Mathematics* (1968–); Pedoe, Dan, *The Gentle Art of Mathematics* (1958; repr. 1973); Smullyan, Raymond, *What Is the Name of This Book?* (1978).

gamma globulin: see GLOBULIN.

gamma-ray astronomy

Gamma-ray astronomy opens another window through which astronomers can observe the universe. Gamma rays (γ rays) are photons, or quanta, of extremely high-energy electromagnetic radiation, having much shorter wavelengths than X rays (see X-RAY ASTRONOMY). They are produced by nuclear processes such as fission and fusion reactions and radioactive decay. Thus γ-ray astronomy provides a means for studying the most energetic processes taking place in the universe. Conversely, however, the production of γ-rays by unshielded Soviet nuclear reactors in Earth orbit is proving a significant hindrance to such studies. The existence of these reactors has been publicly known since at least 1978 and their effects on γ-ray astronomy have been observed by scientists since 1980, but for unclear reasons the U.S. government kept the information classified until 1988.

Studies of γ rays can help explain the origin of the very high-energy particles called cosmic rays, the composition of material throughout the galaxies, and the way in which stars begin to form deep within interstellar clouds of dust and gas. By measuring the gravitational RED SHIFT in the γ-ray region of celestial spectra, astronomers can learn more about the properties of NEUTRON STAR surfaces, QUASARS, galactic cores, and the theoretically existing BLACK HOLES.

Development. The science of γ-ray astronomy did not get started until well into the 20th century. Before 1960 unsuccessful attempts were made to detect celestial γ rays with relatively simple instruments carried high into the atmosphere by balloons. Over the next ten years more sophisticated instruments were still unable to discriminate specific spectral lines of celestial γ rays from the diffuse, uniform background radiation arising from other phenomena.

In 1972 the first certain detection of celestial γ rays was made with equipment aboard the U.S. OSO-3 satellite (see OSO). In that same year another satellite, OSO-7, was used to detect γ-ray emission lines in the Sun's spectrum. Thereafter, knowledge of the γ-ray universe grew rapidly by means of such satellites as the U.S. *SAS-2* (1972–73) and the European *COS-B* (1975–82). These and other devices have found γ rays to be more intense in regions corresponding to the structures of our galaxy, probably arising from the interaction of cosmic rays with interstellar gas.

Three pulsars within our galaxy, two in or near the CRAB NEBULA and the other in the constellation Vela, are emitting γ rays in fractional-second pulses. The largest discrete source of γ rays (as well as other high-energy rays) yet discovered in our galaxy is the binary star system Cygnus X-3. Gamma rays originating from outside our galaxy have been detected emanating from Supernova 1987A. Other discrete sources thus far identified include radio and Seyfert galaxies and quasars. Unexplained bursts of low-energy γ rays have also been observed, each lasting for roughly ten seconds, at intensities that fluctuate even at the shortest resolvable time intervals. No ex-

Workers in Antarctica pipe helium into a balloon used to loft a huge gamma-ray detector in January 1988, for observations of Supernova 1987A. Fully inflated, the balloon held 0.3 million m^3 (11.6 million ft^3) of gas and was the largest ever launched there.

planation has been found for the "bursters," although one theory posits that they originate in the universe's BACKGROUND RADIATION.

Instruments. Devices for detecting γ rays include assemblies of scintillators of various types. More complicated techniques use large area detectors that, in effect, supply pictures of the tracks produced by the charged particles produced by high-energy photons. These SPARK-CHAMBER telescopes make it possible to distinguish γ-ray events and determine the arrival direction of each γ ray individually.

Higher-energy γ rays can produce detectable flashes of light in the atmosphere, through the Cherenkov effect of bombarded particles being caused to move at speeds faster than that at which light moves through the atmosphere (see CHERENKOV RADIATION). These flashes can be observed by suitably equipped ground-based telescopes. Gamma-ray detection has also been carried out from high-altitude balloons. The United States plans eventually to launch a γ-ray telescope aboard the space shuttle. MARTIN A. POMERANTZ

Bibliography: Hillier, Rodney R., *Gamma Ray Astronomy* (1984); Massey, H. S., et al., eds., *Gamma Ray Astronomy* (1981); Ramana Murthy, P. V., and Wolfendale, A., *Gamma-Ray Astronomy* (1986); Turner, K. E., ed., *Very High Energy Gamma Ray Astronomy* (1987).

gamma rays

Gamma radiation is a form of ELECTROMAGNETIC RADIATION, first detected as emissions from natural radioactive substances such as uranium, radium, and thorium. The Greek letter γ (gamma) is used to denote this phenomenon. Gamma radiation does not carry any electric charge or mass; it is a penetrating radiation. Its properties are similar to X rays; the distinction is made on the basis of origin. The sources of gamma rays are nuclear processes, whereas those of X rays are atomic. Gamma rays travel with the speed of light, 2.997925×10^{10} cm/sec.

There are several different sources of gamma radiation. After the emission of an alpha or beta particle from a parent nucleus, the daughter nucleus formed may have more energy than it would have in its normal state. The nucleus then de-excites by the emission of gamma rays carrying the excitation energy. Gamma radiation is also produced in a nuclear reaction such as the combination of a neutron with a proton to form a deuteron. When a particle such as an electron combines with its antiparticle, in this case a positron, they annihilate each other and give rise to gamma radiation.

Gamma radiation undergoes many diverse interactions with matter. Different interactions are observed at different energy ranges. Low-energy gamma radiation may be totally absorbed by an atomic electron that is then emitted. The ejected electron is known as a photoelectron, and the process is known as the PHOTOELECTRIC EFFECT. Gamma radiation can also interact with an atomic electron, sharing its energy and giving rise to the COMPTON EFFECT, in which the gamma radiation is scattered away with reduced energy and the electron is ejected. This electron is known as a Compton electron. Gamma radiation of sufficiently high energy can also interact with the electric field of the positively charged nucleus producing an electron and a positron. This phenomenon is known as pair production. When a beam of gamma radiation passes through matter, its intensity after emergence has diminished, principally as a result of the above three processes. Very high energy gamma radiation can also cause nuclear disintegration and can eject a nuclear particle such as a neutron or a proton. Mesons can also be produced by gamma radiation of extremely high energy in its interaction with atomic nuclei. R. R. ROY

Bibliography: Hurst, G. S., and Turner, J. E., *Elementary Radiation Physics* (1970; repr. 1981); Roy, R. R., and Reed, Robert D., *Interactions of Photons and Leptons with Matter* (1968).

See also: RADIOACTIVITY.

Gamow, George [gam'-ahf]

The Russian-born American physicist George Gamow, b. Mar. 4, 1904, d. Aug. 19, 1968, contributed significantly to increasing the knowledge of nuclear reactions within stars. After graduating (1928) from the University of Leningrad, he traveled in Europe. Gamow worked with Niels Bohr and Ernest Rutherford before coming to the United States in 1934. He taught at George Washington University until 1956; thereafter, he was a professor at the University of Colorado.

The Russian-American nuclear physicist and author George Gamow is known for his theoretical writing popularizing abstract physical theories. Gamow formulated theories on radioactive decay and on the organization of generic information in the living cell.

During his early years at George Washington University, Gamow collaborated with Edward Teller in the field of nuclear physics. Gamow's elaboration of the ideas of Hans BETHE led him to important conclusions about STELLAR EVOLUTION, particularly, that stars tend to become hotter as their hydrogen is depleted.

Gamow strongly supported the now generally accepted BIG BANG THEORY of the origin of the universe, first expressed by Georges Lemaître, as opposed to the steady-state theory advanced by Fred Hoyle. In the field of biochemistry, Gamow proposed (1954) that nucleic acids carry genetic code.

Gamow was noted for his popularization of science, as exemplified by his books *The Birth and Death of the Sun* (1940), *Biography of the Earth* (1941), *One Two Three . . . Infinity* (1947), and *A Star Called the Sun* (1964). STEVEN J. DICK

Bibliography: Gamow, George, *My World Line: An Informal Autobiography* (1970).

Gance, Abel [gahns, ah-bel']

The French filmmaker Abel Gance, b. Oct. 25, 1889, d. Nov. 10, 1981, began his career as a poet and dramatist. He entered the film industry in 1910, yet within five years had established himself as a screenwriter and director: *La Folie du Docteur Tube* (1915) is a fascinating example of the use of distorting lenses and mirrors for subjective effect, and *J'accuse* (1919)—Gance's first major work—is a pacifist protest against war. Films on such subjects as the end of the world and the death of Christ show the sweep of his imagination, and two immense projects of the 1920s reveal his towering ability. *La Roue* (1922) is an epic story of family life and tragedy. Even more ambitious is his epic film on Napoleon, released after three years' effort as *Napoléon vu par Abel Gance* (1927; reconstructed by Kevin Brownlow, 1980). Here he found scope for his overwhelming enthusiasm, striking technical skills, and desire to extend the limits of the film screen. After *Napoléon*, Gance was less successful, his output in the 1930s mostly undistinguished. Following a break of a dozen years, however, he did return with some zestful spectacles in the late 1950s and 1960s. ROY ARMES

Bibliography: Brownlow, Kevin, *The Parade's Gone By* (1968); Jeanne, René, and Ford, Charles, *Abel Gance* (1963).

Ganda [gan'-duh]

The Ganda are a Bantu-speaking people who constitute the largest population group in Uganda, numbering more than 1,000,000. In their traditional kingdom of Buganda, the patrilineal Ganda developed a civil administration that was more centralized and elaborately hierarchical than that of any other Bantu kingdom in the region around Lake Victoria and, perhaps, in much of precolonial Africa. When the Europeans arrived, Buganda was the largest and most powerful of the region's great states, including Ankole, Bunyoro, Busoga, Nyamwezi, Ruanda, Rundi, and others.

The heart of Buganda was the capital of the *kabaka,* or king, at KAMPALA. This center became politically and commercially the most important town in the British Protectorate (established 1894) and later in the independent nation of Uganda. Under a law known as the 1900 Agreement, the Protectorate administration gave most of the fertile land in Buganda in freehold to individuals. This led to a series of struggles between landlords and Ganda peasants who grew cotton and later coffee as cash crops. Although the Ganda practiced no complex ritual cycle of traditional seasonal celebrations, religion and politics have been closely meshed in the often violent factional struggles that have pitted groups of Christian Ganda against each other and against Muslims. RICHARD WERBNER

Bibliography: Gibbs, J. L., ed., *Peoples of Africa* (1965).

Gander [gan'-dur]

Gander (1986 pop., 10,207) is a town in Newfoundland, Canada. Its airport (opened 1939), one of the largest in North America, served as an air force base during World War II. Subsequently (until the early 1960s), it was a refueling station for commercial transatlantic flights.

Gandhara [guhn-dahr'-uh]

Gandhara was a semiindependent kingdom that flourished from the 3d century BC to the 5th century in what is now northern Pakistan. It extended from present-day Rawalpindi through the Peshawar Valley to Kabul. The region was invaded by Persian rulers in the 6th century BC. It came under Alexander the Great in 327 BC and was soon after captured by Chandragupta Maurya; subsequently it fell to the Saka dynasty (Scythians) in 95 BC, the Kushans in AD 48, and finally to the Muslims in the 7th to the 8th century. Its main city was TAXILA. Gandhara is best known for its cultural achievements, particularly its Greco-Buddhist school of sculpture.

Gandhi, Indira [gahn'-dee, in-dir'-uh]

Indira Gandhi, b. Nov. 19, 1917, d. Oct. 31, 1984, became India's first woman prime minister in 1966. The only child of Jawaharlal NEHRU, India's first prime minister, she married Feroze Gandhi (no relation to Mahatma), a lawyer who died in 1960. She was made president of the ruling INDIAN NATIONAL CONGRESS party in 1959. After her father's death in 1964, Mrs. Gandhi became minister of information and broadcasting, and she succeeded Lal Bahadur SHASTRI as prime minister in 1966.

Indira Gandhi, the daughter of India's first prime minister, Jawaharlal Nehru, dominated Indian politics for nearly two decades. Prime minister from 1966 to 1977 and again from 1980 until her assassination in 1984, she groomed her own children for public life. Her younger son, Sanjay, was regarded as her likely successor until his accidental death in 1980. Her elder son, Rajiv, elected to Parliament in 1981 and named secretary of the Congress (I) party in 1983, succeeded her as prime minister.

After India's decisive victory over Pakistan in 1971 (see INDIA-PAKISTAN WARS), she won an overwhelming electoral victory.

Mrs. Gandhi, however, was accused by her opponent of violating election laws—a charge upheld by a high court in June 1975—and her position as prime minister was threatened. These developments, and growing domestic unrest, led her to declare (June 1975) a state of emergency. She postponed elections from 1976 to 1977, suspended civil liberties, and arrested thousands of political opponents. In the March 1977 elections, her party suffered a sweeping defeat at the hands of the opposition Janata (People's) party, an uncongenial coalition of six different groups, headed by her long-time challenger Morarji DESAI. Gandhi lost her own seat along with the premiership. In 1978 she returned to Parliament as head of a Congress party faction. Although she was found guilty of contempt of Parliament in 1978, she and her Congress (I) party won an overwhelming electoral victory in 1980.

Gandhi maintained close ties with the Soviet Union but continued her father's policy of nonalignment. During her last years in office, power became increasingly concentrated in the hands of the central government, and there was growing communal strife. In June 1984 she ordered the invasion of the Golden Temple at AMRITSAR by Indian troops to quell well-armed Sikh extremists in their heavily fortified headquarters there. Later that year she was assassinated by Sikh members of her own security force. Reviewed by ROBERT I. CRANE

Bibliography: Carras, M., *Indira Gandhi* (1979); Gupta, P., *Vengeance: India and the Assassination of Indira Gandhi* (1985); Moraes, D., *Indira Gandhi* (1980); Parthasarathi, G., and Prasad, H. Y., eds., *Indira Gandhi* (1986).

Gandhi, Mahatma [muh-haht'-muh]

Mahatma Gandhi, an Indian political and spiritual leader, developed the tactics of nonviolent disobedience that forced Great Britain to grant independence to India in 1947. Until his assassination in 1948, Gandhi tried to promote unity among India's Hindus and Muslims.

Mohandas Karamchand Gandhi, leader of the Indian nationalist movement and known in his later life as Mahatma ("great soul"), was one of the greatest national leaders of the 20th century. His methods and philosophy of nonviolent confrontation, or civil disobedience, not only led his own country to independence but influenced political activists of many persuasions throughout the world.

Gandhi was born in Porbandar, India, on Oct. 2, 1869. Although his father was a chief minister for the maharaja of Porbandar, the family came from the traditional caste of grocers and moneylenders (the name *Gandhi* means "grocer"). His mother was a devout adherent of Jainism, a religion in which ideas of nonviolence and vegetarianism are paramount. Gandhi stated that he was most influenced by his mother, whose life "was an endless chain of fasts and vows." When, in the company of boyhood friends, he secretly smoked, ate meat, told lies, or wore Western clothing, he suffered intense feelings of guilt. These feelings forced him to make resolutions about his moral behavior that were to stay with him for the rest of his life.

Married by arrangement at 13, Gandhi went to London to study law when he was 18. He was admitted to the bar in 1891 and for a while practiced law in Bombay. From 1893 to 1914 he worked for an Indian firm in South Africa. During these years Gandhi's humiliating experiences of overt racial discrimination propelled him into agitation on behalf of the Indian community of South Africa. He assumed leadership of protest campaigns and gradually developed his techniques and tenets of nonviolent resistance known as *satyagraha* (literally, "steadfastness in truth").

Returning to India in January 1915, Gandhi soon became involved in labor organizing. The massacre of AMRITSAR (1919), in which troops fired on and killed hundreds of nationalist demonstrators, turned him to direct political protest. Within a year he was the dominant figure in the INDIAN NATIONAL CONGRESS, which he launched on a policy of noncooperation with the British in 1920–22. Although total noncooperation was abandoned, Gandhi continued his tactic of civil disobedience, organizing protest marches against unpopular British measures, such as the salt tax (1930), and boycotts of British goods.

Gandhi was repeatedly imprisoned by the British and resorted to hunger strikes as part of his civil disobedience. His final imprisonment came in 1942–44, after he had demanded total withdrawal of the British (the "Quit India" movement) during World War II.

Together with his struggle for political independence, Gandhi fought to improve the status of the lowest classes of society, the casteless UNTOUCHABLES, whom he called *harijans* ("children of God"). He was a believer in manual labor and simple living; he spun the thread and wove the cloth for his own garments and insisted that his followers do so, too. He disagreed with those who wanted India to become an industrial country.

Gandhi was also tireless in trying to forge closer bonds between the Hindu majority and the numerous minorities of India, particularly the Muslims. His greatest failure, in fact, was his inability to dissuade India Muslims, led by Muhammad Ali JINNAH, from creating a separate state, Pakistan. When India gained independence in 1947, after negotiations in which he was a principal participant, Gandhi opposed the partition of the subcontinent with such intensity that he launched a mass movement against it. Ironically, he was assassinated in Delhi on Jan. 30, 1948, by a Hindu fanatic who mistakenly thought his antipartition sentiment was both pro-Muslim and pro-Pakistan.

MARCUS AND VONETTA J. FRANDA

Bibliography: Borman, William, *Gandhi and Non-Violence* (1986); Erikson, Erik, *Gandhi's Truth: On the Origins of Militant Nonviolence* (1969); Fischer, Louis, *Life of Mahatma Gandhi* (1962; repr. 1983); Gandhi, M. K., *Gandhi's Autobiography*, 2d ed. (1984); Nanda, B. R., *Gandhi and His Critics* (1985); Tendulkar, D. G., *Mahatma, Life of Mohandas Karamchand Gandhi*, 8 vols., rev. ed. (1960–63; repr. 1983).

Gandhi, Rajiv

Rajiv Gandhi, b. Aug. 20, 1944, succeeded his mother, Indira Gandhi, as prime minister of India on Oct. 31, 1984. Rajiv grew up in the home of his distinguished grandfather, Jawaharlal Nehru, and earned (1965) a degree in mechanical engineering. Employed as an airline pilot from 1972, he became his mother's unofficial assistant after the 1980 death of his more politically oriented younger brother, Sanjay. In 1981 he resigned from his job to contest, and win, Sanjay's former seat in the Lok Sabha (the lower house of India's parliament); in 1983 he became a general secretary of the Congress (I) party. Appointed prime minister following his mother's assassination by Sikh extremists, he led his party to an impressive victory in the 1984 general elections. Subsequently, he faced mounting opposition that was exacerbated by rising communal tensions, economic problems, and corruption charges and called new elections in November 1989. Congress lost its majority (though it remained the largest party), and Gandhi resigned, becoming leader of the opposition.

ROBERT I. CRANE

In his first year as prime minister of India, Rajiv Gandhi was praised for signing accords to end strife in Punjab and Assam, but as communal violence in these and other areas later increased he was charged with a failure to provide India with strong leadership and a sense of direction. In 1987, he signed an accord with neighboring Sri Lanka designed to end violence between that country's Sinhalese majority and its Tamil minority. This, however, led to substantial Indian military involvement in Sri Lanka. Relations with China and Pakistan worsened.

Ganesha [guh-nesh'-uh]

Ganesha is an elephant-headed Hindu god, the son of SHIVA and Parvati. Businesspeople and others ready to embark on difficult endeavors pray to Ganesha to clear obstacles from their paths.

Gang of Four

Chinese moderate leaders, including TENG HSIAO-P'ING, used the name Gang of Four (Ssu-jen Pang) to refer to a group of leaders of the CULTURAL REVOLUTION who attempted to seize power after the death of CHOU EN-LAI in 1976. The four were arrested in September 1976, shortly after the death of MAO TSE-TUNG. They have since been blamed for the excesses of the Cultural Revolution and for China's backwardness in general and were brought to trial in 1980.

The four, all members of the politburo of the Chinese Communist party at the time of their arrest, were CHIANG CH'ING, Mao's widow; Chang Ch'un-ch'iao, a deputy premier; Wang Hung-wen, second vice-chairman of the party; and Yao Wen-yuan. They were brought to trial in November 1980 on 48 charges, including attempting to overthrow the state. Both Chiang Ch'ing and Chang Ch'un-ch'iao refused to plead guilty, claiming that their actions had been at Mao's behest, but in January 1981 they were sentenced to death (later commuted to life imprisonment). Wang Hung-wen and Yao Wen-yuan were sentenced to imprisonment for life and 20 years respectively. Chiang Ch'ing was released in 1987.

Ganges River [gan'-jeez]

The Ganges (Ganga) River, the most sacred river of Hinduism, flows across northern India and through Bangladesh. It is 2,507 km (1,557 mi) long and drains an area of 1,035,000 km^2 (409,000 mi^2). The two main headstreams of the Ganges—the Alaknanda and Bagirathi—rise in the Himalayas near Nanda Devi. Flowing south-southeast, they join northwest of Kanpur and flow southeast and east across the heavily farmed plains of Uttar Pradesh, Bihar, West Bengal, and Bangladesh, entering the densely populated delta region 320 km (200 mi) from the sea. The Ganges and Jamuna (part of the BRAHMAPUTRA RIVER) join below Dacca to form the Padma River, which then enters the Bay of Bengal through several mouths just west of Chittagong.

Major cities on the Ganges include the sacred city VARANASI; the commercial center ALLAHABAD; industrial KANPUR;

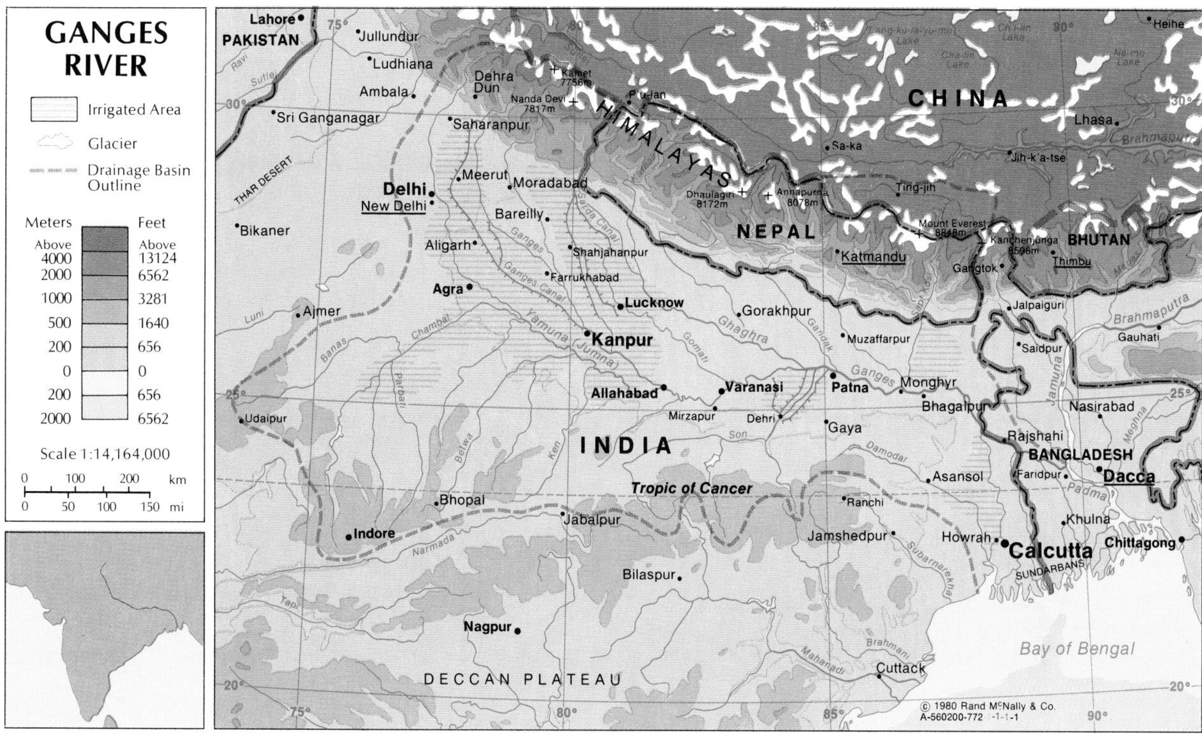

and Patna, a rice center. Crops grown in the river basin include rice and other grains, sugar, cotton, and lac trees; cattle are also raised.

Bibliography: Darian, Steven G., *The Ganges in Myth and History* (1978).

gangrene [gayn'-green]

Gangrene is the destruction of living tissue due to obstruction of its blood (and therefore oxygen) supply. Once such obstruction occurs, the gangrenous process is often caused by infection by such bacteria as *Clostridium* (gas gangrene) or a combination of streptococci and staphylococci (Meleney's synergistic gangrene).

Another common form of gangrene, diabetic gangrene, results from arteriosclerosis due to diabetes. The infection has a strong tendency to spread because the bacteria produce powerful toxins that destroy adjacent healthy tissues, making them highly susceptible to further invasion. Treatment involves heavy doses of antibiotics and the surgical removal of all affected tissue.

PETER L. PETRAKIS

gangster film: see FILM, HISTORY OF.

Gangtok [gahng'-tahk]

Gangtok (1981 district pop., 138,105) is the capital of Sikkim state, in northeast India. Its economy is based on agriculture, especially cardomom. Gangtok is the site of the noted Buddhist monastery of Runtek. Its importance as a stop on the India-Tibet trade route declined after the 1962 closing of the Tibetan border.

gannet [gan'-et]

Gannet is the common name for the birds of the genus *Morus*, family Sulidae, that migrate over the seas of the middle and upper latitudes of both the Northern and the Southern Hemisphere. Gannets are much larger (89–102 cm/35–40 in) than any of the gulls and have long, narrow, pointed wings, pointed tails, and cone-shaped bills. They are gregarious, nesting in large colonies on rocky shores and promontories. Spectacular divers, they plunge from heights of 15 m (50 ft) or more and often swim to great depths in pursuit of fish. In adult plumages, the North Atlantic species, *Morus bassanus*, is white with black wing tips and a yellow bill. Gannets are related to the boobies, genus *Sula*, of tropical seas.

WILLIAM SANDFORD

The northern gannet, or solan goose, Morus bassanus, *dives for fish from up to 30 m (100 ft) above the water. Air sacs beneath the skin protect it from the shock of impact.*

Gannett, Frank E. [gan-net']

Frank Ernest Gannett, b. Bristol, N.Y., Sept. 15, 1876, d. Dec. 3, 1957, was an American newspaper publisher. He began to build a newspaper chain during the 1920s through mergers mainly in New York State. Concentrating on gaining regional dominance, Gannett eventually owned more than 20 newspapers and 7 radio stations. In 1986 the Gannett Company—the largest U.S. newspaper group, owned 92 dailies (including *USA Today*) and 8 television and 16 radio stations.

Ganymede [gan'-ee-meed]

Ganymede, a satellite of the planet JUPITER, is the largest satellite in the solar system. It was discovered by Galileo in 1610. With a diameter of 5,276 km (3,278 mi), it is larger than the planet Mercury. Its average distance from Jupiter's center is 1,070,000 km (665,000 mi), and it takes a little more than a week to complete one orbit of the planet. Ganymede's density is not quite twice that of water, so the satellite probably has a rocky core and thick icy mantle.

Parts of Ganymede's surface are dark and heavily cratered. Interspersed are lighter regions filled with bands of parallel grooves a few hundred meters deep and several kilometers apart. Some grooves extend for thousands of kilometers, and the bands sometimes intertwine with other bands in complicated patterns. Although less heavily cratered than the dark areas, the bands are sufficiently cratered to indicate that they formed fairly early in the satellite's history. The grooves are thought to be cracks that formed as areas of the old, dark crust pulled apart. RICHARD GREENBERG

Bibliography: Morrison, David, ed., *Satellites of Jupiter* (1983).

gar

The long-nosed gar, Lepisosteus osseus, *is a predatory fish of shallow North American waters that slashes unsuspecting prey with its snout.*

Gars are long, slender, predaceous fish, characterized by a long, tooth-studded jaw and a tough, armored skin of linked, diamond-shaped scales. They belong to the family Lepisosteidae, order Lepisosteiformes. The approximately eight species of this primitive fish inhabit placid fresh waters of the New World. As adults, they feed on small fish. The largest species, the only one eaten by humans, is the giant, or tropical, gar, *Lepisosteus tristoechus,* of Mexico, Central America, and Cuba, which may reach 3.7 m (12 ft) in length. The common alligator gar, *L. spatula,* of the southeastern United States, grows to 3 m (10 ft) in length. The most common gar is the long-nosed gar, *L. osseus,* which often reaches 1 m (3.3 ft). It is abundant in the Florida Everglades but ranges northward to Canada.

Gars spawn in the spring in large groups. Their roe is poisonous. Because of the highly vascular and cellular nature of the gar's swim bladder, it functions as a lung. This accounts for the gar's ability to survive in large numbers in the often stagnant waters of the sloughs and everglades of the southern United States. A. R. EMERY

Garand, John Cantius [guh-rand']

Canadian-born John Cantius Garand, b. Jan. 1, 1888, d. Feb. 16, 1974, developed the Garand semiautomatic rifle that became the basic U.S. Army infantry weapon in World War II. Garand began work in a Connecticut cotton mill at the age of 12, and at 13 he patented his first invention, a type of jackscrew. Later, as a tool and gauge maker in Providence, R.I., he began to experiment with guns. Garand submitted a design for a machine gun to the U.S. government in 1916. He became a consulting engineer at the Springfield, Mass., armory in 1919. There he developed his gas-operated semiautomatic rifle, the M1. Patented in 1934, the M1 was adopted as the standard service shoulder weapon in 1936. After 1957 it was largely replaced by the lighter M14. FRANCES GIES

Garbo, Greta [gahr'-boh, gret'-uh]

Greta Garbo, a Swedish actress trained at the Royal Dramatic Theater of Stockholm, became one of Hollywood's first major romantic idols. In such films as Flesh and the Devil *(1927) and* Anna Christie *(1930), Garbo projected an aura of mystery and sensuality that established her as an international celebrity. The publicity-shy actress successfully made the transition from silent to sound films before retiring to a life of seclusion in 1941.*

Born Sept. 18, 1905, as Greta Lovisa Gustafsson, Garbo was brought to Hollywood from her native Sweden in 1925. MGM turned her into a beautiful, queenly actress whose ambitious films always made headlines, even if they sometimes lost money. She was known for her shyness, and her sudden retirement in 1941 enhanced the air of mystery that continues to surround her. *Flesh and the Devil* (1927) is the best of her silent melodramas. Her first talkie, *Anna Christie* (1930), was advertised with the slogan "Garbo talks!" Other notable films include *Mata Hari* (1931), *Grand Hotel* (1932), *As You Desire Me* (1932), *Queen Christina* (1933), *Anna Karenina* (1935), *Camille* (1936), *Conquest* (1937), *Ninotchka* (1939), and *Two-Faced Woman* (1941). LESLIE HALLIWELL

Bibliography: Conway, Michael, et al., *The Films of Greta Garbo* (1968); Corliss, Richard, *Greta Garbo* (1974); Walker, Alexander, *Garbo: A Portrait* (1980); Zierold, Norman, *Garbo* (1969).

Garborg, Arne [gahr'-boorg, ahr'-ne]

The Norwegian novelist, poet, playwright, and essayist Arne Garborg, b. Jan. 25, 1851, d. Jan. 14, 1924, was one of the first writers to raise Nynorsk, Norway's second language, to its present level as a richly poetic instrument for the writer. Garborg, a brilliant literary critic and a sharp observer of his contemporary cultural scene, was often criticized for his radical views. His major literary works include *Peasant Students* (1883), a study of how the values of a modern urban society destroy the moral potential of a young man, and *Haugtussa* (1895), a hauntingly powerful cycle of poems about the life of a young, weak-minded peasant girl. KJETIL A. FLATIN

Bibliography: Beyer, Harald, *A History of Norwegian Literature* (1952; repr. 1956); Støverud, Torbjørn, *Milestones of Norwegian Literature* (1967).

García Lorca, Federico [gahr-thee'-ah lohr'-kah, fay-day-ree'-koh]

Federico García Lorca, b. June 5, 1898, d. Aug. 19, 1936, was 20th-century Spain's most illustrious poet and dramatist. Since his death at age 38 in the Spanish Civil War, his influence even beyond the Spanish-speaking world has been enormous.

The eldest son of a wealthy landowner of Granada, García Lorca studied literature and law at the University of Granada before turning to writing full time. With a professor and other students he traveled through Castille in 1918, a trip that inspired a collection of prose sketches, *Impresiones y paisajes* (Impressions and Landscapes, 1918). In 1919 he went to Madrid, planning to devote himself to art, music, folklore, literature, and the theater; there he met such avant-garde figures as Salvador Dalí, Rafael Alberti, Luis Buñuel, Juan Ramón Jiménez, and Pablo Neruda. García Lorca's first play, *El Maleficio de la mariposa* (The Evildoing of the Butterfly, 1920), was neither a commercial nor an artistic success. More in tune with the times was his first volume of verse, *Libro de poemas* (Book of Poems, 1921), which helped to establish his reputation.

By 1925, García Lorca was the center of a group of poets that became known as the Generation of 1927 because in that year they honored the baroque poet Luis de Góngora on the 300th anniversary of his death. The year 1927 witnessed the production of *Mariana Pineda*, a historical play, and the publication of another book of poetry, *Canciones* (Songs). The most famous of all his poems, *Romancero gitano* (trans. as *Gypsy Ballads*, 1953), followed in 1928; using the rhythms of the traditional Spanish ballad form, this poem dealt with the closed, marginal society of Andalusian gypsies and was largely responsible, along with *Poema del Cante Jondo* (1931), for making García Lorca famous throughout the Spanish-speaking world within a few years.

During a 6-month visit to New York in 1929, García Lorca completed several works influenced by surrealism, including a book of poems, *Poet in New York* (1940; Eng. trans., 1955), which evoked the anomie and disgust he experienced there, and the play *If Five Years Pass* (1931; Eng. trans., 1941). Back in Spain García Lorca took an active role in the theater productions sponsored by the new Republican government; in 1932 he toured Spain as codirector of the La Barraca troupe. He also began to enjoy repeated success with his own plays, of which the trilogy comprising *Blood Wedding* (1933; Eng. trans., 1939), *Yerma* (1934; Eng. trans., 1941), and *The House of Bernarda Alba* (1936; Eng. trans., 1947) is his masterpiece. Brilliantly structured lyric tragedies about women, these plays strike out savagely at the paternalism and obscurantism characteristic of Spanish society. He also wrote such farces as *The Shoemaker's Prodigious Wife* (1930; Eng. trans., 1941), *The Love of Don Perlimplín with Belisa in the Garden* (1931; Eng. trans., 1941), and *Doña Rosita, the Spinster* (1935; Eng. trans., 1941).

When Gen. Francisco Franco's rebellion began on July 18, 1936, García Lorca returned to Granada. Although never affiliated with any party, he was known for his Republican sympathies, and soon after the rebels took control of the city he was arrested, imprisoned, and, 3 weeks later, shot by a firing squad and buried in a large unmarked grave.

Although García Lorca first became world famous as a martyr of the Republican cause, his fame rests on far more solid ground. In his poetry he constantly praises the human courage needed to confront the dark forces that flow beneath the surface of life, forces that are acknowledged only in dreams. He was also acutely aware of the fragility of the line separating life and death, love and hate, human and animal; and he was fascinated by metamorphoses. From beginning to end, his work exalted the ability of humans to project themselves imaginatively beyond life and beyond certain death. The moving *Lament for Ignacio Sánchez Mejías* (1935; Eng. trans., 1939) serves as a microcosm of García Lorca's mastery of the Spanish language.

PHILIP W. SILVER

The Spanish poet and dramatist Federico García Lorca established his reputation as one of Spain's finest poets with the lyrical Gypsy Ballads *(1928). Using rhythm and vivid imagery, he infused his work with a radiant and violent beauty evocative of his native Andalusia. He appears here as drawn by Gregorio Prieto.*

Bibliography: Allen, Rupert C., *The Symbolic World of Federico García Lorca* (1972); Barea, Arturo, *Lorca: The Poet and His People* (1949; repr. 1973); Campbell, Roy, *Lorca: An Appreciation of His Poetry* (1952; repr. 1970); Duran, Manuel, *Lorca: A Collection of Critical Essays* (1962); Higginbotham, Virginia, *The Comic Spirit of Federico García Lorca* (1975); Honig, Edwin, *García Lorca* (1944); Lima, Robert, *The Theatre of García Lorca* (1963); Trend, John Brande, *Lorca and the Spanish Poetic Tradition* (1956).

García Márquez, Gabriel [gahr-see'-ah mahr'-kays, gah-bree-el']

Gabriel García Márquez, b. Mar. 6, 1928, is a major Colombian novelist and short-story writer who was awarded the Nobel Prize for literature in 1982. His masterpiece, *One Hundred Years of Solitude* (1967; Eng. trans., 1970), is a family saga that mirrors the history of Columbia. Like many of his works, it is set in the fictional town of Macondo, a place much like García Márquez's native Aracataca. Mixing realism and fantasy, the novel is both the story of the decay of the town and an ironic epic of human experience.

García Márquez began his career as a reporter for *El Espectador,* for which he wrote (1955) a series of articles exposing the facts behind a Colombian naval disaster. These articles won him fame and were published in book form as *Relato de un naufrago* (The Account of a Shipwrecked Person, 1970).

García Márquez's novel *The Autumn of the Patriarch* (1975; Eng. trans., 1976) again explores the theme of decay, this time by depicting with typical exaggeration and ironic humor the barbarism, squalor, and corruption that prevail during the reign of a Latin American military dictator. Other works include three collections of short stories (*No One Writes to the Colonel,* Eng. trans., 1968; *Leaf Storm,* Eng. trans., 1972; and *Innocent Erendira,* Eng. trans., 1978), the novel *In Evil Hour* (1968; Eng. trans., 1979), and the novella *Chronicle of a Death Foretold* (1981; Eng. trans., 1983).

Bibliography: Janes, R., *Gabriel García Márquez: Revolutions in Wonderland* (1981); McMurray, G. R., *Gabriel García Márquez* (1977).

García Moreno, Gabriel [moh-ray'-noh, gah-bree-el']

Gabriel García Moreno, b. Dec. 24, 1821, d. Aug. 6, 1875, was the president of Ecuador from 1861 to 1865 and from 1869 to 1875. A journalist and lawyer, he was versed in political theory. As president, he centralized government control, reduced corruption, and signed (1862) a concordat with the Vatican that placed all education under church supervision. Construction of a road from Quito to Guayaquil permitted the first efficient transportation between the coast and the interior. He was assassinated in Quito by a group of liberals.

Garcilaso de la Vega [gahr-thee-lah'-soh day lah vay'-gah]

The Spanish Golden Age poet Garcilaso de la Vega, b. 1501, d. Oct. 14, 1536, changed the course of Spanish poetry by adapting such Italian lyrical forms as the SONNET, the ECLOGUE, the 11-syllable line, and the rhyming stanza that he called the *lira.* His important and influential works were published posthumously along with those of his friend Juan Boscán in 1543.

Garcilaso was a Renaissance humanist and courtier who served Emperor Charles V as a diplomat and soldier. His brief life ended in a battle near Fréjus, in southern France, when he was crushed by a rock hurled from a battlement. His abiding love for the married Portuguese lady Isabel Freire informs much of Garcilaso's poetry, where she appears as the shepherdess Galatea or Eliza. Although Garcilaso molded his poetry into Italinate forms, there is a strong aura of traditional Spanish courtly verse about his work. His numerous sonnets form the major part of his achievement, but his finest works are probably his three eclogues and two elegies. He infused these stylized pastoral poems with a quiet restraint and a personal note of pessimism. Their effect on later Spanish poets was considerable. ROBERTO GONZÁLEZ-ECHEVARRÍA

Bibliography: Gicovate, Bernard, *Garcilaso de la Vega* (1975); Keniston, Hayward, *Garcilaso de la Vega* (1922).

Garda, Lake [gahr'-dah]

Lake Garda, the largest lake in Italy, lies in the Piedmont region of northern Italy, 105 km (65 mi) east of Milan. Fed by the Sarca River at its narrow, mountain-guarded northern end, it is drained by the Mincio River to the south. It covers an area of 370 km^2 (143 mi^2), has a maximum width of 18 km (11 mi), and a maximum depth of 346 m (1,135 ft). Many resorts line its shores.

garden

People cultivate gardens either to produce food or for aesthetic reasons—to create pleasant surroundings harmonizing flowers, shrubs, and trees within the landscape. Gardens in the second sense comprise plants, water, natural land formations, and architectural elements. The use of these ingredients of garden design developed differently in the Islamic world, the West, and the Far East.

In the Middle East, gardens have been important as a retreat from the intense heat of the natural environment. The Persian garden is divided into two crossed axes making four quadrants, symbolizing the belief that the universe is divided by four great rivers. Irrigation provides formal pools and gentle dripping fountains to add a musical dimension. High walls and flowers create a shady oasis.

This pattern is restated in the Mogul gardens of India, most notably that surrounding the TAJ MAHAL at Agra. Rectilinear reflecting pools are lined with cypresses, a symbol of death, and brilliant floral borders make a grand approach to the white marble tomb.

The Islamic influence of the Middle East also can be seen in Spain in the magnificent Moorish gardens of the ALHAMBRA and Generalife palaces at Granada. Water dominates in the form of shimmering pools and numerous arching jets. Shrubs in pots and box hedges line the pool edges. At the Generalife, rows of clipped cypresses echo the shape of the arches bordering the garden.

In western tradition, Italian, French, and English styles, water and architectural elements fuse into dynamic forms that dramatize human control over nature. This is as different from the Far Eastern style as it is from the Middle Eastern. Italian gardens beginning in the 16th century combined balustrades, colonnades, and terraces with elaborate fountains. At the Villa Lante in Bagnaia, the water source, a woodland spring in a natural setting, culminates in a formal pool. The water at the Villa Aldobrandini in Rome emerges through spiraled columns into a niched facade complete with a statue of Atlas holding up the world. The gardens of the Villa d'Este—famous for its FOUNTAINS—those of the Villa Medici in Rome, and of the Villa Farnese at Caprarola are other notable examples of the Italian Renaissance style.

The gardens at Marly, a château built for the French king Louis XIV, were designed (1679–86) by André Le Nôtre in the mode that became the standard of palatial landscape design. They feature broad vistas of ornamental parterre gardens, fountains, pools, and statuary.

The garden at Sissinghurst Castle in England was laid out in the 1930s by diplomat Harold Nicolson and his wife, the novelist and poet Victoria Sackville-West. A compartmental garden, divided by paths, walls, and hedges into a number of separate, self-contained areas, it shows the influence of both English and continental design.

In France garden design is linked with the name André LE NÔTRE, creator of the gardens of the Palace of VERSAILLES. Two principles of the Italian garden, the axial plan and the parterre (scalloped or geometric beds with clipped shrubs forming the perimeter), were adapted in France to allow formal arrangement of the great vistas. Broad avenues were lined with symmetrical plantings of trees. The parterre developed into the *parterre de broderie*—hedges planted in elaborate "embroidered" patterns—and fountains spewed jets of water into pools shaped like the parterres. Human beings were reduced to miniature in this setting.

Many formal gardens show the influence of Versailles: those at the NYMPHENBURG PALACE, near Munich, and SCHÖNBRUNN PALACE, near Vienna, are examples, as is the summer palace (Peterhof) outside LENINGRAD, with its gilded statues, built for Peter the Great by Alexandre Le Blond (1679–1719).

The cottage-style garden with free-wheeling perennial borders is the look most associated with the English style. The graceful shaping of the English landscape is the result of centuries of garden design fluctuating between stylized continental gardens and attempts to adhere to nature. This can be seen at BLENHEIM PALACE in Oxfordshire, where a "natural" park designed by Capability BROWN contrasts with the formal east and west parterres. Another example is the 18th-century garden at Stourhead in Wiltshire, which features lakes, rolling hills, and classical temples. In the Victorian garden at Chatsworth, in Derbyshire, Joseph PAXTON constructed a large greenhouse in which he produced out-of-season fruits and vegetables and exotic, floral bedding plants.

Today numerous fine private English gardens developed in

(Above) *This painting from the Ming period (1368–1644) shows a Chinese gentleman examining antiques in a garden setting. In traditional China, a garden was a place for meditation and aesthetic pursuits, designed to suggest harmony with nature.*

(Left) *The Tofuku-ji garden in Kyoto, Japan—like the nearby Ryoan-ji—is an example of Kare-sansui, or dry landscaping. In such gardens the raked gravel often represents water, and the rocks symbolize mountains.*

the early 1900s are open to the public and are visited by thousands each year. Carefully cultivated but casual gardens at Hidcote in Gloucestershire, Sissinghurst in Kent, Exbury in Hampshire, and Crathes Castle near Aberdeen, Scotland, are influenced by William Robinson (1838–1935) and Gertrude Jekyll (1843–1932), who advocated dense plantings of familiar, indigenous species.

In the United States, Longwood Gardens in Pennsylvania and nearby Winterthur in Delaware reproduce this English style in a different setting. Examples of 18th- and 19th-century American gardens can be seen at Monticello and Williamsburg in Virginia and at the Hermitage, near Nashville, Tenn.

In the East Asian garden, no grandiose architectural implants or imposing water contrivances impinge on nature's setting. Little waterfalls, quiet streams and pools surround pavilions that shimmer in reflected light. Rocks and stones are purposefully arranged. The most significant difference between eastern and western gardens is scale. In the gardens of China and Japan the goal is the re-creation of nature in miniature.

Japan learned from China as early as the 7th century, when Japanese envoys visited the Western Park, the garden of the Sui dynasty emperor Yang Ti at Lo-Yang. As grand as Versailles later was, it had four lakes, one over 21 km (13 mi) long. From the beginning oriental gardens concentrated on harmony with nature. Lakes, islands, and rocks—elements in landscape painting as well—were aligned to stress verticality. Spiritual influences—Taoism and Buddhism in China, Shinto and Buddhism in Japan—are essential to an understanding of the Far Eastern garden.

Each turn the visitor takes in a Japanese garden is planned to open a new view. In the tea garden the path to the teahouse is made of stepping stones that direct the visitor through stopping points, a flaming maple or a pink azalea or a waterfall. Seasons are of prime importance. The garden under snow is as carefully planned as it is in spring bloom. Evergreens are a mainstay.

Zen Buddhism influenced the development of Kare-sansui, or dry landscaping. The Ryoan-ji garden near Kyoto, with its 15 rocks arranged in a bed of raked tiny stone, is a study in tension and balance; its subtleties are never completely revealed. The garden is most beautiful during a rainfall or immediately after, when the rocks glisten with moisture.

In the Japanese-style garden, serenity, austerity, balance, and asymmetry reflect the synthesis of natural elements. One part of nature represents a different element. A rock symbolizes an entire mountain; in the dry landscape the raked stones represent water. The house or pavilion, bridge, gates, islands, are all integrated into the setting.

Gardens today often reflect a synthesis of eastern and western aesthetics, as in the case of the BROOKLYN BOTANIC GARDEN AND ARBORETUM.

MARGO M. SHERMETA

Bibliography: Berrall, Julia S., *The Garden*, (1966); Coats, Peter, *Great Gardens of the Western World* (1963); Johnson, Hugh, *The Principles of Gardening* (1979); King, Ronald, *Quest for Paradise: A History of the World's Gardens* (1979); Kuck, Loraine, *The World of the Japanese Garden* (1968).

See also: LANDSCAPE ARCHITECTURE.

Garden, Mary

Mary Garden, b. Aberdeen, Scotland, Feb. 20, 1877, d. Jan. 3, 1967, was a celebrated operatic soprano. She went to the United States as a child and studied voice in Chicago. She worked with Mathilde Marchesi and was encouraged by the singer Sibyl Sanderson, who introduced her to the director of the Opéra-Comique, where she made a triumphant debut in the title role of *Louise* in Gustave Charpentier's opera. She was chosen by Claude Debussy to sing the female lead in *Pelléas and Mélisande*. After 1907, Garden often sang in the United States and scored a sensation at the Manhattan Opera House in Richard Strauss's *Salome*. She became director of the Chicago Opera for its last season in 1921–22. A glamorous and controversial artist, Garden was as well known for her acting as for her singing.

STEPHANIE VON BUCHAU

Bibliography: Garden, Mary, with Louis Biancolli, *Mary Garden's Story* (1951); Wagenknecht, Edward Charles, *Seven Daughters of the Theater* (1964).

garden city

The garden city movement of the early 20th century was inspired by the ideas and work of the English urban theorist Sir Ebenezer HOWARD. Howard's idea of a garden city was a meticulously planned self-supporting and community-owned urban center contained by a deep circle of undeveloped land called a GREENBELT. Underlying the notion of such a city was his concept of the "Town-Country Magnets." The Town Magnet's attraction for people lay in high wages, social activity, and well-lit streets; it repelled people because of the frequently great distances between home and work, the isolation people feel in crowds, slums, dirty air, and lack of sunlight. The attraction of the Country Magnet was beauty, fresh air, and health; its repulsions were lack of social activities and amusement, low wages, boredom, and cultural inertia. The garden city represents the culmination of the best of both worlds. The 19th-century utopianism of the reformers Robert OWEN and Charles FOURIER provided the intellectual impetus behind the garden city movement. Most previous utopian idealists had attempted to translate their notions of a better society into

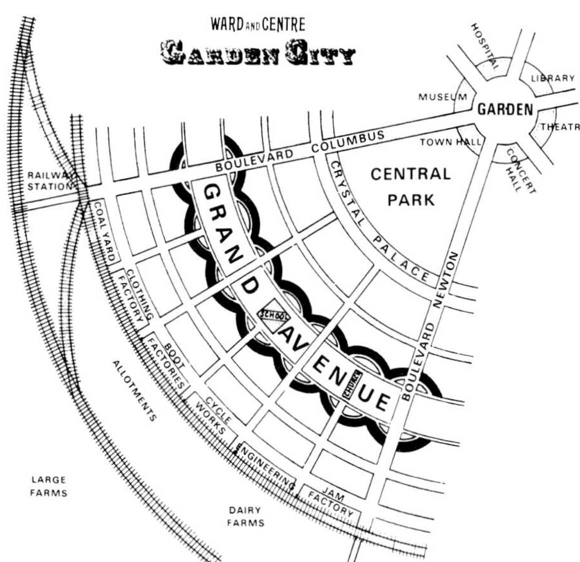

Ebenezer Howard, a British urban planner, developed the concept of a garden city, which combines the advantages of rural and urban living. His plan specifies parks, residential quarters, and industrial areas radiating outward from the cultural facilities at the city's central core.

some kind of an urban model; Howard, however, firmly believed that the proper town plan, devised as a self-contained entity incorporating specific principles in its design, would by its nature bring about social reform.

Howard's innovations included the establishment of a belt of permanently open land around the city to limit its spread; the founding of satellite cities; the return to the community of any unearned profit from the growth and prosperity of the city; community ownership and control of land; limitation of population to a predetermined size; and inclusion, within each city, of industry capable of supporting the greater part of its population.

By 1903, Howard had enough ideological and financial support to test his theories, and he started the town of Letchworth in Hertfordshire. In 1920, he helped organize a company that developed the town of Welwyn, also in Hertfordshire. In 1931 the city of Manchester founded the satellite town of Wythenshawe, designed by Barry Parker in accord with Howard's principles.

In the next 50 years, more than thirty NEW TOWNS were established in Great Britain alone. Howard's Garden-City Association became the International Garden Association, and subsequently the International Housing and Town Planning Federation. Garden cities and new towns were developed throughout Europe and the Western Hemisphere. In the United States such developments include the town of Radburn, N.J. (1929), and the greenbelt towns (organized 1936–38) of Greenhills, Ohio, and Greenbelt, Md. After World War II, the planned communities of Columbia, Md., and Reston, Va., were built, incorporating many of the physical principles of the garden city. REGINALD AND MARK ISAACS

Bibliography: Creese, Walter, *The Search for Environment: The Garden City, Before and After* (1966); Danley, Gillian, *Villages of Vision* (1975); Evans, Hazel, ed., *New Towns: The British Experience* (1973); Fishman, Robert, *Urban Utopias in the 20th Century* (1977); Howard, Ebenezer, *Garden Cities of To-Morrow* (1946); Osborn, Frederic J., *Greenbelt Cities* (1969); Smith, M. H., *The History of Garden City* (1963).

See also: URBAN PLANNING.

Garden of Eden: see EDEN, GARDEN OF.

garden heliotrope

The garden heliotrope is a course, erect, perennial plant, *Valeriana officinalis*, of the valerian family, Valerianacèae. Though native to Eurasia, it is now found in Canada and the northern United States as well. It grows to 1.5 m (5 ft) tall and has deeply divided leaves. Its tubular, fragrant flowers are white, pink, lavender, or red. The garden heliotrope should not be confused with the heliotrope, *Heliotropium*.

OLIN S. FEARING

gardenia [gahr-dee'-nee-uh]

The genus *Gardenia* comprises several species of flowering shrubs or small trees that belong to the madder family, Rubiaceae. Their flowers are sweet-scented. Gardenias are native to subtropical regions of the Eastern Hemisphere, where they grow outdoors, but they are also grown extensively indoors in greenhouses. Because of their need for warm, moist conditions, gardenias do not thrive as houseplants. Cape jasmine, *G. jasmimoides*, is a bushy shrub up to 1.8 m (6 ft) tall with glossy evergreen leaves and waxy-white, heavily scented flowers with 9 petals each. CHARLES L. WILSON

The gardenia, G. jasminoides, *an evergreen shrub from China, produces glossy white flowers.*

gardening

The ancient art of gardening—the raising of one's own flowers, shrubs, fruits, and vegetables within a limited area—is enjoying a contemporary renaissance as millions of Americans discover the satisfactions inherent in working the soil, if only on weekends. Almost everyone who has access to a bit of ground raises a few flowers, and it is estimated that perhaps half of all American families maintain vegetable gardens. In recent years seed companies have been caught short by the unanticipated rush of orders from new gardeners. The HOUSEPLANT business is booming, and plant nurseries and florists have enjoyed record sales.

Among the causes for the current enthusiasm for gardening must be counted the simple nature of gardening itself. Essentially, all that is needed to grow peas or petunias are soil, seeds, and a few basic tools. (The garden and its history as a formal art is discussed in GARDEN.)

SOIL

The successful growth of garden plants depends primarily on the quality of the soil. Soil must contain the essential nutrients to feed growing plants, and it must have a structure capable of holding air and moisture without becoming waterlogged. Soil analysis reveals nutritional deficiencies; these may be remedied through the use of FERTILIZERS, which add the phosphorous, nitrogen, potassium, and other minerals necessary for plant growth. Analysis will also determine the pH, or acidity-alkalinity index, of the soil. On a scale of 1 to 10, acid to alkaline, a pH rating of 7 is neutral—neither acid nor alkaline. Most garden plants thrive best at a pH of 6 to 7, although certain plants, such as blueberries or rhododendron, need a higher acid level. Overacidity, the more usual problem, can be decreased by adding ground limestone. In desert and semiarid regions where rainfall is low, pH ranges of 8 to 10 are common. Overalkaline soils, which may cause yellowing in plants, can be treated by adding sulfur or gypsum.

In general, soil structure is classified as sandy, clay, or loam, although most garden soils are mixtures of the three in varying proportions. A sandy soil is very loose and will not hold water. A clay soil is dense and heavy, sticky when wet, and almost brickhard when dry. Loam is a mixture of sand and clay soils, but it also contains large quantities of HUMUS, or decayed organic material, which loosens and aerates clay soil and binds sandy soil particles together. In addition, humus supplies plant nutrients. Thus, soil structure can be improved by digging in COMPOST, MANURE, PEAT MOSS, and other organic matter.

State agricultural experiment stations test soil samples, either free or for a small fee, and the report shows what fertilizer or other material is required to make the soil suitable for growing plants. A composite soil sample is obtained by mixing several cups of soil taken from an inch under the surface and from several different spots in the garden. A cup of the final mixture is then sent for analysis.

A good soil can be kept in good condition, year after year, by digging in decaying organic materials and by adding the recommended amounts of fertilizer, usually a compound commercial mixture sold at garden centers. Fertilizers should be applied only as recommended and never in excess.

Choosing a Site. Not every plant will thrive in every type of soil, nor are sunlight requirements the same for all plants. In general, however, a garden should not be situated near large trees, which not only shade the area but also draw large amounts of water and nutrients out of the soil. Areas open to the wind are to be avoided, as well as areas at the bottom of slopes because the ground there tends to retain too much water.

ANNUALS AND PERENNIALS

Most garden VEGETABLES are annuals—plants with a life span of a single growing season—or biennials—plants that are picked and eaten during their first year, although they have a two-season life span.

The FLOWER garden may contain a mixture of annuals, biennials, and perennials, plants that live more than two years. Annuals are usually easier to grow, and they produce more colorful flowers in greater abundance than do biennials and perennials. They may be planted from seed in the beds where they are to grow, or raised in seedbeds or in flats (see *seeds and seedlings*, below) and transplanted when they have grown into small plants, or seedlings. Biennials are planted either as seeds or as year-old transplants, and may not bloom during their first year in the garden. Perennials, the most difficult flowering plants to grow from seed, are usually set out as seedlings or as divisions of older plants that have become too large. Once perennials are established, they will flower for several years; their flowering period, however, is usually shorter than that of annuals.

Although they are not classed as perennials, ferns and flowers grown from bulbs will also continue to live for extended periods.

SEEDS AND SEEDLINGS

Although the seeds of many flowers and vegetables may be sown directly into well-cultivated soil, some plants are better started indoors in shallow boxes, or flats. A controlled indoor environment aids seed germination, and plants started in flats, when spring weather is still too cold to allow outdoor planting, will be well advanced by the time they are set out. Many heat-sensitive vegetables (lettuce, broccoli, and cauliflower, for example) grow far better when they are planted as seedlings and can reach maturity before the heat of midsummer.

The essential requirements for growing seeds indoors are sufficient heat to induce germination and sufficient light for seedling growth. Flats should be placed in a sunny south-facing southern exposure or under a fluorescent plant light. Damping-off, a fungus-caused disease that attacks and rots the stems of seedlings, can be controlled by sterilizing the planting soil and by being careful not to overwater flats.

Cold Frames. A cold frame is a boxlike wooden frame covered with a movable glass sash. Positioned to face south for the best exposure, the cold frame gathers and conserves sunlight and heat and acts as a miniature greenhouse in which seeds may be sown outdoors in late winter and early spring. As an additional heat source, some cold frames have an electric heating cable buried a few inches below the surface of the soil so that seedlings may be started even when outdoor temperatures are well below freezing.

PLANT CULTIVATION

If the soil furnishes sufficient nutrients and contains enough humus to hold air and water, the basic necessities for successful plant growth are present. Instructions for sowing seed or setting out transplants will be found in gardening guides, in seed catalogs, or on the seed packets themselves. Thinning instructions are also given, especially for seed-sown vegetables such as carrots.

Many gardeners use a MULCH to discourage weed growth and to help conserve soil moisture. Straw is a fine mulch for vegetable gardens; in flower beds a less noticeable mulch, such as peat moss or wood chips, is often used. Mulchless gardens require regular weeding so that weeds can be eliminated while they are small.

In dry periods the garden should be watered on a regular schedule. Morning is the best time for watering; the sun's afternoon heat may evaporate moisture too quickly, and watering at sunset may encourage the fungus growths that cause

Bright red and yellow tulips bloom beside a path in a flower garden in Williamsburg, Va. Called a mixed border, this informal arrangement of several types of spring-blooming flowers will gradually be replaced by summer varieties as the season changes.

This small backyard vegetable garden, seen in early summer, will soon provide its owners with an abundance of fresh vegetables. The tomatoes at the rear of the garden will not produce for another month or so, but beans, beets, carrots, and cauliflower are almost ready to harvest, and the green pepper plants already bear small fruits.

plant diseases, by leaving a residue of water in the soil overnight.

PLANT PESTS AND DISEASES

Many varieties of disease-resistant plants are available and are listed as such in garden catalogs. Plant diseases can be avoided by watering at the proper times; by weeding; and by removing dead plants, leaves, and other debris that often harbor injurious insects. Chemical PESTICIDES and HERBICIDES are available but should be used sparingly and with care, for many will also destroy beneficial insects and garden plants. Chemical residues left on vegetables can be harmful if they are ingested.

ORGANIC GARDENING

Organic-vegetable gardeners do not use inorganic chemical pesticides or fertilizers but depend on composts and manures for soil enrichment and for maintaining a healthy garden environment. Organic gardeners encourage beneficial insects like the ladybug, which eats plant aphids. They use natural insecticides, such as sprays made from garlic juice, whose odor and antiseptic properties are reported to repel insects. They will cluster together groups of plants that are believed to have mutually beneficial effects: marigolds planted between tomatoes, for instance, are supposed to prevent infestation of certain harmful insects, and may even repel rabbits.

Organic gardening necessitates a greater initial effort, particularly in building up the very rich soil required. Although agriculturists question many of the practices of organic gardening, its proponents claim that they can produce tastier, more nutritious vegetables and larger crops without having to rely on risky pesticides or expensive inorganic fertilizers.

DONALD WYMAN

Bibliography: Abraham, George, *Green Thumb Garden Handbook*, rev. ed. (1977); Blair, Edna, *The Food Garden* (1972); Cruso, Thalassa, *Making Things Grow Outdoors* (1971); Foley, Daniel J., *Gardening: A Basic Guide* (1973); Ogden, Samuel R., *How to Grow Food for Your Family* (1973); Rodale, J. I., and Staff, *Encyclopedia of Organic Gardening* (1959); Sunset Editors, *Basic Gardening Illustrated*, rev. 2d ed. (1975); Wyman, Donald, *Wyman's Gardening Encyclopedia*, rev. ed. (1977).

See also: FRUITS AND FRUIT CULTIVATION; GRAFTING; PLANT PROPAGATION; PRUNING; separate articles on individual flowers and vegetables.

Gardiner, Samuel Rawson

Samuel Rawson Gardiner, b. Mar. 4, 1829, d. Feb. 23, 1902, was an English historian who taught at the universities of London and Oxford. Many of his works are still considered basic sources. They include *The History of England from the Accession of James I to the Outbreak of the Civil War, 1603-1642* (10 vols., 1863-82); *History of the Great Civil War, 1642-1649* (4 vols., 1893); and *History of the Commonwealth and Protectorate, 1649-1660* (4 vols., 1903). He also wrote many textbooks and a biography of Oliver Cromwell (1901).

Gardiner, Stephen

Stephen Gardiner, b. *c.*1482, d. Nov. 12, 1555, was an English bishop at the time of the Reformation. Although he assented to King Henry VIII's declaration of royal supremacy over the English church, he nevertheless remained doctrinally conservative. At one time master of Trinity Hall at Cambridge, he later served as secretary to Cardinal Wolsey and worked for Henry's divorce from Catherine of Aragon. After his appointment as bishop of Winchester, he wrote a treatise, *On True Obedience* (1535), in which he defended the royal supremacy. He was probably the author of Henry VIII's *Six Articles*, which reasserted Catholic doctrines such as transubstantiation in the Eucharist and practices such as celibacy of the clergy. After Edward VI became king in 1547, Gardiner was removed from the royal council, was imprisoned, and lost his bishopric. When the Catholic Queen Mary I ascended the throne in 1553, Gardiner was reinstated as bishop of Winchester and was made lord chancellor. He once more accepted papal supremacy over the Church of England.

LEWIS W. SPITZ

Bibliography: Muller, James, *Stephen Gardiner and the Tudor Reaction* (1926); Muller, James, ed., *The Letters of Stephen Gardiner* (1930; repr. 1970).

Gardner, Alexander

Alexander Gardner, b. Oct. 27, 1821, d. December 1882, was a central figure in the photographic documentation of the U.S. Civil War. Emigrating from Scotland in 1856, he managed Mathew B. BRADY's Washington, D.C., studio and took many memorable war photographs for Brady before leaving his employ in 1863. In 1865 he published *Gardner's Photographic Sketch Book of the War*, which contained 100 prints carefully credited to individual photographers. Starting in 1867, Gardner photographed the West for the Union Pacific Railroad.

KEITH F. DAVIS

Gardner, Erle Stanley

The detective novelist Erle Stanley Gardner, b. Malden, Mass., July 17, 1889, d. Mar. 11, 1970, the best-selling author of his time, was the creator of Perry Mason, a Los Angeles lawyer-sleuth who appeared in Gardner's first book, *The Case of the Velvet Claws* (1933). Gardner began to practice law in 1911, specializing in the defense of indigent Mexicans and Chinese, but became a full-time writer in 1933 after the phenomenal success of his magazine stories. He also wrote, under the

The American mystery writer Erle Stanley Gardner drew on his background as a successful trial lawyer in writing his fast-paced detective stories. His best-known character, the attorney Perry Mason, first appeared in The Case of the Velvet Claws *(1933). Gardner is seen here in his law and criminology library.*

pseudonym A. A. Fair, a series of comic novels centered on the detective Bertha Cool. Although Gardner shared the low opinion of his writings held by critics, 90 of his novels have sold more than 1 million copies.

Bibliography: Hughes, Dorothy, *Erle Stanley Gardner* (1978).

See also: MYSTERY, SUSPENSE, AND DETECTIVE FICTION.

Gardner, John

The American writer John Gardner's background as a medievalist and classicist surfaced in his well-crafted novels, such as Grendel *(1971) and* The Sunlight Dialogues *(1972). Gardner was head of the creative writing program at the State University of New York at Binghamton at the time of his death in a motorcycle accident in 1982.*

Photo Jill Krementz © 1977

The American novelist, scholar, and critic John Champlin Gardner, Jr., b. Batavia, N.Y., July 21, 1933, d. Sept. 14, 1982, was best known for his voluminous and well-crafted works of fiction. His books characteristically pose metaphysical problems in fabulous and ingenious forms. The novel *Grendel* (1971) retells the Beowulf legend from the monster's point of view. His other works include the short-story collection *The King's Indian* (1974) and the novels *The Wreckage of Agathon* (1970), *The Sunlight Dialogues* (1972), *Nickel Mountain* (1973), and *October Light* (1976), which won the 1977 National Book Critics Circle Award for fiction. Gardner also produced scholarly works on the age of Chaucer; volumes of poetry; and the posthumously published *On Becoming a Novelist* (1983) and *The Art of Fiction* (1984).

Gardner, John W.

John William Gardner, b. Los Angeles, Oct. 8, 1912, founded the nonpartisan citizens' lobby COMMON CAUSE and headed it from 1970 to 1977. An educator who became an administrator, he worked (1946–65) for the Carnegie Corporation, serving as its president from 1955. President Lyndon Johnson appointed Gardner, a Republican, as secretary of Health, Education, and Welfare (1965–68), a position from which he resigned to become head (1968–70) of the National Urban Coalition. Among his books are *Excellence: Can We Be Equal and Excellent Too?* (1961; rev. ed. 1984), *Self-Renewal: The Individual and the Innovative Society* (1964; rev. ed. 1981), and *In Common Cause* (1972; rev. ed., 1973). He was educated at Stanford and the University of California (Ph.D., 1938) and was a Marine intelligence officer in World War II.

Gardner, Martin

Martin Gardner, b. Tulsa, Okla., Oct. 21, 1914, is best known for his mathematical games and puzzles, which he published in a regular column in *Scientific American* from 1956 to 1983, as well as in a continuing series of books. He graduated (1936) from the University of Chicago, where his studies included mathematics and philosophy. In books such as *In the Name of Science* (1952)—republished as *Fads and Fallacies in the Name of Science* (1957)—and *Science: Good, Bad and Bogus* (1981) he has sought to distinguish between science and pseudoscience. He has successfully explained many difficult aspects of science to the nonspecialist; for example, relativity is treated in *Relativity for the Million* (1962), and *The Ambidextrous Universe* (1964; rey. ed., 1978) discusses symmetry and aspects of astronomy.

Gardner Museum

Housing one of the major American collections of European art, the Isabella Stewart Gardner Museum in Boston reflects the avocation of its founder and patron, Isabella Stewart Gardner, b. New York City, Apr. 14, 1840, d. July 17, 1924. Her interest in art originated in 1878 at a series of lectures given by Charles Eliot Norton at Harvard University. As a result of the lectures, Gardner began collecting rare books and manuscripts. On her frequent trips to Europe, this collection was expanded to include works of fine art. Painting and sculpture became her chief interests after a trip (1886) to London, where she met the American painters John Singer Sargent and James McNeill Whistler. The latter, who painted her portrait, especially influenced Gardner, with his theories of "pure art" as a vehicle for universal values of the most humane and elevated sort.

In 1887, Gardner sent Bernard BERENSON to Europe to continue the studies of art history he began at Harvard. From 1892 until 1907, Berenson guided her in the acquisition of the works of art that form most of the current collection at Fenway Court, as the Gardner Museum building is called. Designed in the style of a 15th-century Venetian palace, the building was opened to the public after Gardner's death in 1924. Most of its furnishings and architectural details were imported from European cloisters, chapels, and palaces. The collection, which consists of Oriental and classical art and medieval, Renaissance, and post-Renaissance painting, sculpture, and decorative arts, is especially strong in paintings of the early Italian Renaissance, although the 16th and 17th centuries are also well represented. Among the important works owned by the museum are Titian's *Rape of Europa* (*c.*1559–62), Sandro Botticelli's *Death of Lucrezia* (*c.*1499), and Rembrandt's *Storm on the Sea of Galilee* (*c.*1631–36).

CARTER RATCLIFF

Bibliography: Carter, Morris, *Isabella Stewart Gardner and Fenway Court*, 3d ed. (1925; repr. 1972); Tharp, Louise Hall, *Mrs. Jack* (1965).

Garfield, James A.

James Abram Garfield became the 20th president of the United States in 1881 and was assassinated later that year. He had been an influential member of the House of Representatives for the period 1863 to 1880, but his presidency was too short to confirm the indications that he would have been the moderate, successful leader that the Republican party required in the 1880s. Garfield is now remembered mostly as the last

JAMES ABRAM GARFIELD
20th President of the United States (1881)

Born: Nov. 19, 1831, Orange Township, Cuyahoga County, Ohio
Education: Western Reserve Eclectic Institute (now Hiram College); Williams College (graduated 1856)
Profession: Teacher, Public Official
Religious Affiliation: Disciples of Christ
Marriage: Nov. 11, 1858, to Lucretia Rudolph (1832–1918)
Children: Eliza A. Garfield (1860–63); Harry A. Garfield (1863–1942); James R. Garfield (1865–1950); Mary Garfield (1867–1947); Irvin M. Garfield (1870–1951); Abram Garfield (1872–1958); Edward Garfield (1874–76)
Political Affiliation: Republican
Writings: *Diary, 1848–1874* (2 vols., 1967), ed. by H. J. Brown and F. D. Williams
Died: Sept. 19, 1881, Elberon, N.J.
Buried: Lake View Cemetery, Cleveland, Ohio

Vice-President and Cabinet Members
Vice-President: Chester A. Arthur
Secretary of State: James G. Blaine
Secretary of the Treasury: William Windom
Secretary of War: Robert Todd Lincoln
Attorney General: I. Wayne McVeagh
Postmaster General: Thomas L. James
Secretary of the Navy: William H. Hunt
Secretary of the Interior: Samuel J. Kirkwood

chief executive to be born in a log cabin and as a dark-horse candidate for the Republican presidential nomination in 1880.

Early Life. Garfield was born on Nov. 19, 1831, in Cuyahoga County, Ohio. After an impoverished childhood he attended what became Hiram College and graduated from Williams College in 1856. He returned to Hiram as principal from 1857 to 1861, but he had already concluded that "teaching is not the work in which a man can live and grow." In 1858 he married Lucretia Rudolph; two of their children, James Rudolph and Harry Augustus, gained national distinction.

Intensely religious as a youth (he was a member of the Disciples of Christ and a lay preacher), Garfield moved toward secular and political concerns in the 1850s. He studied law, became a Republican, and was elected to the Ohio Senate in 1859. When the Civil War began, he joined and helped recruit the 42d Ohio Volunteer Infantry. He fought at Shiloh and Chickamauga, rose to major general, and, as chief of staff of the Army of the Cumberland, displayed impressive talents as a planner and organizer.

Elected to Congress in 1862, Garfield began his legislative service in December 1863. For the next 17 years he concentrated on economic issues on the Appropriations and Ways and Means committees. He voted with Radical Republicans on Reconstruction but did not endorse the more stringent measures of that bloc. He was a mild protectionist in Ohio tariff politics, and he opposed greenbacks and other inflationary ideas. Scandal touched him only slightly when his modest dealings with the CRÉDIT MOBILIER company became public.

Garfield was moderately tall and wore a heavy beard. He was bookish but not intellectual and had a reputation on Capitol Hill as "one of the real jolly good fellows." Cautious and thoughtful, he appeared indecisive to some colleagues and weak to others. Yet he had ambition and resolve, and when his chance came in 1880 he was ready.

Early in 1880 the Ohio legislature elected Garfield to the Senate to succeed John SHERMAN, and he then served as Sherman's campaign manager in the race for the Republican presidential nomination. At the convention Garfield worked skillfully to block the candidacies of James G. BLAINE and Ulysses S. GRANT. In the process his appeal as a compromise candidate outshone Sherman's lackluster personality and record. By the 35th ballot a Garfield tide was running through the hall, and on the next ballot he received the nomination.

Presidency. With Chester Alan ARTHUR as his running mate, Garfield faced a difficult race against Winfield Scott HANCOCK, the Democratic nominee. The narrow victory that Garfield achieved testified to the stalemated condition of politics in the Gilded Age. His majority in the electoral college was 214 to 155, but his plurality in the popular vote was under 7,500. The Republicans won because of superior organization, a new emphasis on the tariff issue, and Democratic errors. Garfield's deft speeches at his home in Mentor, Ohio, foreshadowed the "front porch" campaigns of Benjamin Harrison and William McKinley.

Divisions within the Republican party made Garfield's cabinet and patronage choices the primary issue between his election and assassination. He named James G. Blaine secretary of state and gave greater recognition to Blaine's Half-Breed faction than to the Stalwarts led by Sen. Roscoe CONKLING of New York. Once in office, Garfield nominated an enemy of Conkling's as collector of the New York port and pushed hard to secure the appointee's Senate confirmation. Garfield's skill in this struggle indicated that responsibility had lessened his earlier irresolution. As defeat became likely, Conkling resigned his Senate seat and sought vindication and reelection from the New York legislature. When that body seemed ready to reject Conkling's bid, Garfield's ascendancy as president appeared assured.

On July 2, 1881, Garfield went to Washington's railroad station to begin a family trip. There Charles J. GUITEAU, an insane Stalwart and disappointed office seeker, shot him. Garfield lived for 11 weeks in increasing pain and failing strength and died in Elberon, N.J. on Sept. 19, 1881. Garfield quickly faded from public and historical memory. The circumstances of his assassination facilitated passage of the Pendleton Civil Service Act in 1883. His death left the Republican party confused and leaderless throughout much of the 1880s and helped delay its emergence to majority status for 15 years. LEWIS L. GOULD

Bibliography: Leech, Margaret, and Brown, Harry J., *The Garfield Orbit: The Life of President James A. Garfield* (1978); Peskin, Allan, *Garfield* (1978); Smith, Theodore Clarke, *The Life and Letters of James Abram Garfield*, 2 vols. (1925).

Garfield, John

An antiestablishment American film hero of the 1930s, John Garfield, b. Julius Garfinkle, Mar. 4, 1913, d. May 21, 1952, was a stage actor who brought a taste of New York's Lower East

Side to the Hollywood fantasy factories. He became a star in one of his first films, *Four Daughters* (1938). His rather sullen manner, however, kept him out of the top rank, despite good performances in *They Made Me A Criminal* (1939), *Pride of the Marines* (1945), *Body and Soul* (1948), and *Force of Evil* (1949).
LESLIE HALLIWELL

Bibliography: Swindell, Larry, *Body and Soul: The Story of John Garfield* (1975).

Gargallo, Pablo [gahr-gahl'-yoh, pahb'-loh]

The Spanish artist Pablo Gargallo, b. Jan. 5, 1881, d. Dec. 28, 1934, was one of the earliest sculptors to use iron in his work. He studied drawing and sculpture in Barcelona before visiting Paris in 1906. Gargallo then worked mostly in stone, but by the time of his second visit to Paris in 1911, he had switched to iron. He met Pablo PICASSO in Paris, where he was introduced to CUBISM; Picasso in turn was influenced by Gargallo's metal sculpture. Returning to Spain in 1914, Gargallo continued to work in iron and taught (1917–24) at Barcelona's Escuela Superior de Artes Oficios. He returned to Paris in 1924. An important example of his metal sculpture is his bronze *The Prophet* (1933; Musée National d'Art Moderne, Paris).
HARRY RAND

Bibliography: Read, Herbert, *A Concise History of Modern Sculpture* (1964); Selz, Jean, *Modern Sculpture: Origins and Evolution*, trans. by Annette Michelson (1963).

Gargantua and Pantagruel [gahr-gan'-choo-uh, pan-tag'-roo-el]

Gargantua and Pantagruel is the English title given to François RABELAIS's panoramic five-part satirical work. The two giants, Gargantua and his father, Pantagruel, evolve from comic and grotesque figures in the first two books (1532 and 1534) into incarnations of humanist, Christian, and Stoic ideals in the later books (1546, 1552, and 1564). In a series of tales and voyages, satire and ribaldry are mixed with serious philosophical speculation on the nature of religion, education, and politics.

gargoyle [gahr'-goyl]

Gargoyles are grotesque stone figures most commonly found on Gothic buildings at the roof or eaves. Originally the term meant the unadorned spout that extended outward from a rain gutter or parapet; the gargoyle allowed water to fall free of the building, preventing seepage and damage to masonry. Eventually the spout became a carved head or body with grotesque features. Superstition held that the gargoyle frightened away evil spirits while serving its practical function. After the introduction of the lead drain pipe in the 16th century, gargoyles primarily served a decorative function.

Garibaldi, Giuseppe [gahr-ee-bahl'-dee]

Giuseppe Garibaldi, b. Nice, July 4, 1807, was Italy's most brilliant soldier of the RISORGIMENTO and one of the greatest guerrilla fighters of all time. While serving (1833–34) in the navy of the Kingdom of Sardinia-Piedmont, he came under the influence of Giuseppe MAZZINI, the prophet of Italian nationalism. He took part in an abortive republican uprising in Piedmont in 1834.

Under a death sentence, he managed to escape to South America, where he lived from 1836 to 1848. There he took part in struggles in Brazil and helped Uruguay in its war against Argentina, commanding its small navy and, later, an Italian legion at Montevideo. The handsome warrior achieved international fame through the publicity of the elder Alexandre Dumas.

Wearing his colorful gaucho costume, Garibaldi returned to Italy in April 1848 to fight in its war of independence. His exploits against the Austrians in Milan and against the French forces supporting Rome and the Papal States made him a national hero. Overpowered at last in Rome, Garibaldi and his men had to retreat through central Italy in 1849. Anita, his wife and companion-in-arms, died during this retreat.

Disbanding his men, Garibaldi again escaped abroad,

Guiseppe Garibaldi was the leading general in the Risorgimento, the movement that unified Italy during the 19th century. With 1,000 volunteers, the "Red Shirts," Garibaldi conquered Sicily and Naples for King Victor Emmanuel II in 1860. He remains one of the most popular national heroes of Italy.

where he lived successively in North Africa, the United States, and Peru. The "hero of two worlds" could not return to Italy until 1854. In 1859 he helped Piedmont in a new war against Austria, leading a volunteer Alpine force that captured Varese and Como.

In May 1860, Garibaldi set out on the greatest venture of his life, the conquest of Sicily and Naples. This time he had no governmental support, but Premier CAVOUR and King VICTOR EMMANUEL II dared not stop the popular hero. They stood ready to help, but only if he proved successful. Sailing from near Genoa on May 6 with 1,000 Redshirts, Garibaldi reached Marsala, Sicily, on May 11 and proclaimed himself dictator in the name of Victor Emmanuel. At the Battle of Calatafimi (May 30) his guerrilla force defeated the regular army of the king of Naples. A popular uprising helped him capture Palermo—a brilliant success that convinced Cavour that Garibaldi's volunteer army should now be secretly supported by Piedmont.

Garibaldi crossed the Strait of Messina on August 18–19 and in a whirlwind campaign reached Naples on September 7. On October 3-5 he fought another battle on the Volturno River, the biggest of his career. After plebiscites, he handed Sicily and Naples over to Victor Emmanuel when the two met near the Volturno on October 26. Angered at not being named viceroy in Naples, however, Garibaldi retired to his home on Caprera, off Sardinia. Nevertheless, he continued to plot to capture the Papal States. In 1862 the Italian government, fearing international complications, had to intercept him at Aspromonte, where he was wounded in the heel. When he led another private expedition toward Rome in 1867, French troops halted him at Mentana. Subsequently, during the Franco-Prussian War (1870-71), Garibaldi led a group of volunteers in support of the new French republic.

Without Garibaldi's support, the unification of Italy could not have taken place when it did. A gifted leader and man of the people, he knew far better than Cavour or Mazzini how to stir the masses, and he repeatedly hastened the pace of events. Disillusioned in later life with politics, he declared himself a socialist. He died at Caprera on June 2, 1882.
CHARLES F. DELZELL

Bibliography: Hibbert, Christopher, *Garibaldi and His Enemies* (1965); Mack Smith, Denis, *Garibaldi: A Great Life in Brief* (1956) and, as ed., *Garibaldi* (1969); Ridley, Jasper, *Garibaldi* (1976); Trevelyan, G. M., *Garibaldi and the Making of Italy* (1911; repr. 1977), *Garibaldi and the Thousand* (1909; repr. 1976), and *Garibaldi's Defence of the Roman Republic* (1907; repr. 1971).

Garland, Augustus Hill [gahr'-luhnd]

Augustus Hill Garland, b. Tipton County, Tenn., June 11, 1832, d. Jan. 26, 1899, was an American lawyer and politician best known for his role in the 1867 Supreme Court case *Ex parte Garland.* The case arose because an 1865 law barred from law practice in the United States those, like Garland, who had served in the Confederate government during the Civil War. Garland argued successfully that the law was EX POST FACTO and thus unconstitutional.

Garland, Hamlin

A significant early American realistic writer, Hannibal Hamlin Garland, b. West Salem, Wis., Sept. 14, 1860, d. Mar. 4, 1940, is best known for his short-story collections, *Main-Travelled Roads* (1891) and *Other Main-Travelled Roads* (1910), and for the novel *Rose of Dutcher's Coolly* (1895). All are notable for their grimly realistic portrayal of Midwestern rural life. Garland's two autobiographical novels are *Son of the Middle Border* (1917) and *A Daughter of the Middle Border* (1921), which won the 1922 Pulitzer Prize for biography or autobiography.

F. M. PAULSEN

Bibliography: Ahnebrink, Lars, *The Beginnings of Naturalism in American Fiction* (1950; repr. 1961); Holloway, Jean, *Hamlin Garland: A Biography* (1960); McCullogh, Joseph B., *Hamlin Garland* (1978); Pizer, Donald, *Hamlin Garland's Early Work and Career* (1960).

Garland, Judy

Judy Garland's distinctive singing and dancing talents made her a star of Hollywood musicals during the 1940s. The onetime child actress's career became increasingly erratic, however, as she alternated between brilliant performances and extended periods of depression.

Judy Garland, originally named Frances Gumm, b. Grand Rapids, Minn., June 10, 1922, d. June 22, 1969, was one of America's most notable singers and entertainers. She began her career at age four singing with the Gumm Sisters in her father's theater and touring in vaudeville.

In 1935 Garland joined MGM, gained popularity in the Andy Hardy film series, and in 1939 won a special Academy Award for her rendition of the song *Over the Rainbow* from the film The WIZARD OF OZ. Her later films include *Babes in Arms* (1939), *Strike Up the Band* (1940), *Meet Me in St. Louis* (1944), *Easter Parade* (1948), *A Star is Born* (1954), and *Judgment at Nuremburg* (1961).

Between illnesses and breakdowns said to have originated from her early exhaustion as a young star, and her resulting dependence on alcohol, she performed in concerts throughout the world and exuded a magnetism and courage that endeared her to an international audience. Her daugher Liza MINNELLI is a singer and actress renowned for her performances in the films *The Sterile Cuckoo* (1969) and *Cabaret* (1972).

JONATHAN KAMIN

Bibliography: Edwards, Anne, *Judy Garland* (1975); Frank, Gerold, *Judy* (1975); Morella, Joe, and Epstein, Edward Z., *Judy: The Films and Career of Judy Garland* (1969).

garlic

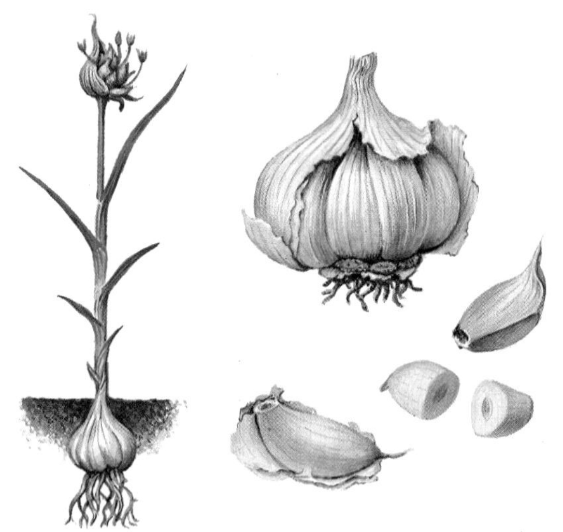

Originating in central Asia, garlic, Allium sativum, *today grows wild in southern Europe and the east central United States. It is cultivated for its bulb, containing up to 20 bulblets, or cloves, which are used to flavor many Mediterranean and Asian cuisines.*

Garlic, *Allium sativum*, a perennial herb related to the onion, is a pungent bulb composed of cloves surrounded by a thin white or purplish sheath. It is among the most ancient of cultivated plants and has long been used as a food flavoring, as a medicine, and as a germicide, since its juice contains the antibiotic oil allicin.

Because seed is rarely produced, garlic is propagated by planting individual cloves. When the green tops ripen and fall over, the bulbs are pulled. Garlic can be stored for several months if kept dry and cool. Most of the garlic in the United States is grown in California, and much of the crop is dehydrated and sold as garlic powder.

O. A. LORENZ

Garneau, F. X. [gahr-noh']

The Canadian historian François Xavier Garneau, b. Quebec, June 15, 1809, d. Feb. 3, 1866, strongly affected French-Canadian ethnic identity with his 3-volume *Histoire du Canada* (1845-48), which emphasized French contributions to Canadian culture. He lived in Europe in the early 1830s and from 1844 to 1864 held civil service posts in his native province. He was also a poet and literary journalist.

Garneau, Hector de Saint-Denys [gahr-noh', ayk-tohr' duh san-duh-nee']

Hector de Saint-Denys Garneau, b. Montreal, June 13, 1912, d. Oct. 24, 1943, was a French-Canadian poet and painter. His volume of poems, *Regards et jeux dans l'espace* (Looks and Games in Space, 1937), broke new ground in French-Canadian poetry with introspective poems using free-verse techniques and rhythms. Garneau's poems, almost all of which were written between the ages of 23 and 26, deal with the significance of death and the problems of loneliness.

Bibliography: Garneau, Saint-Denys, *Complete Poems of Saint-Denys Garneau*, trans. by John Glassco (1975).

Garner, John Nance

John Garner, b. Red River County, Tex., Nov. 22, 1868, d. Nov. 7, 1967, was a Texas politician who served (1933-41) as the 32d vice-president of the United States. A conservative Democrat, he served (1903-33) in the House of Representatives and was speaker from 1931 to 1933. In 1932, Franklin D. Roosevelt chose Garner as his running mate. Garner was not sympathetic to the NEW DEAL, however, and became estranged from Roosevelt. He challenged Roosevelt for the 1940 presidential nomination and, after losing, retired to his ranch in Texas. He was known as "Cactus Jack."

Garnerin, André J. [gahr-nair-an']

André Jacques Garnerin, b. Jan. 31, 1769, d. Aug. 18, 1823, completed the world's first parachute descent by a human. A French balloonist, he became interested in PARACHUTES in 1793 while serving as a prisoner of war in the fortress of Buda, Hungary. He toyed with the idea of using a parachute to escape, being influenced in his conceptions by the work of Jean Pierre BLANCHARD and the French physician Sébastien Lenormand. Garnerin devised a parasol-like parachute with a basket, attaching it to a hydrogen-filled balloon. On Oct. 22, 1797, he cut the parachute loose from the balloon at a height of about 915 m (3,000 ft) and descended safely to earth. He subsequently made many such descents, including the first parachute descent in England (1802). RICHARD P. HALLION

garnet

The garnets are a family of common and widespread SILICATE MINERALS found in metamorphic and some igneous rocks. The generalized chemical formula of garnets is $X_3Y_2(SiO_4)_3$, with X indicating a divalent cation, such as iron, magnesium, calcium, or manganese, and Y trivalent cation, such as aluminum, iron, or chromium. The SiO_4 indicates silica tetrahedrons—a silicon ion surrounded by four oxygen ions. The other atoms are packed between the tetrahedrons.

Natural garnets are divided into the calcium-bearing ugrandites, named after the initial letters of the calcium species *uv*arovite, *gr*ossular, and *and*radite, and the calcium-free pyralspites, named after the members *pyr*ope, *al*mandine, and *sp*essartine. Aluminum, iron, and chromium substitute freely in the ugrandites. Iron, magnesium, and manganese substitute readily for each other in the pyralspites, and all gradations between the pure species are possible. Much less substitution occurs between the two groups.

Garnets belong to the isometric crystal system and commonly occur in well-formed dodecahedral or trapezohedral crystals. Because of the tight packing of their atoms, garnets are relatively hard and dense.

Iron-rich almandine, the most common garnet, is widespread in metamorphic rocks such as schists and gneisses and in granitic igneous rocks. The magnesium garnet, favored by high pressures of formation, is found in magnesium-rich metamorphic rocks formed at great depth and may be an important mineral in the mantle of the Earth. Spessartine is found in manganese-rich gneisses and in coarse-grained, granitelike bodies called pegmatites.

The ugrandites are rarer than the pyralspites. Grossular, containing calcium and aluminum, is found in clay-rich limestones that have been metamorphosed to marble and in some contact-metamorphic deposits, or skarns, formed when an igneous rock intrudes and reacts with limestone. The calcium-iron garnet andradite and the rare calcium-chromium garnet uvarovite are also usually found in skarns.

Garnet is commonly cut as a gem (see GEMS). The dark red, Victorian garnet jewelry was made from pyrope garnets mined in Bohemia, now a part of Czechoslovakia. Grossular makes hessonite, an attractive, cinnamon brown stone, and demantoid, the green variety of andradite, is rare and highly prized. Synthetic yttrium-aluminum garnet, or YAG, is used to imitate diamond as a gem. Garnet is also used as an abrasive.
PETER B. LEAVENS

Clear garnet stones (left) *suitable for gems characteristically have 12 or 24 faces and are found in all colors except blue. A polished gem* (right) *is usually cut with a brilliant top and stepped facets below, although the cabochon, or rounded form, is sometimes used.*

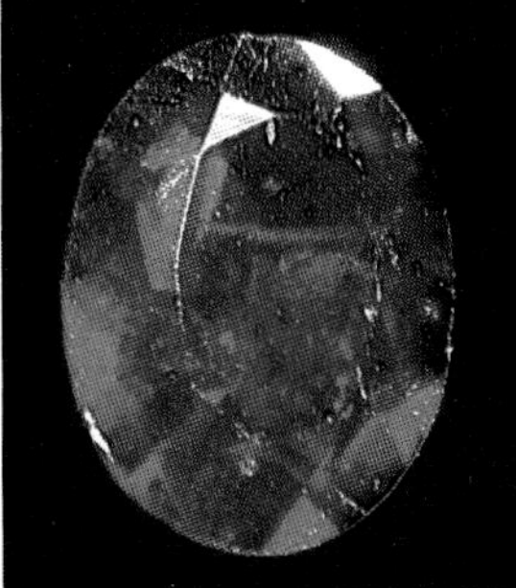

PROPERTIES OF GARNETS

Name	Formula	Common Color	Density (gm/cc)
Pyralspites			
Pyrope	$Mg_3Al_2(SiO_4)_3$	Purple red	3.58
Almandine	$Fe_3Al_2(SiO_4)_3$	Red	4.32
Spessartine	$Mn_3Al_2(SiO_4)_3$	Red to orange	4.19
Ugrandites			
Uvaroite	$Ca_3Cr_2(SiO_4)_3$	Emerald green	3.80
Grossular	$Ca_3Al_2(SiO_4)_3$	Cinnamon brown	3.59
Andradite	$Ca_3Fe_2(SiO_4)_3$	Dark brown	3.86

Bibliography: Deer, William A., et al., *Rock-forming Minerals*, vol. 1 (1962); Hurlbut, Cornelius S. Jr., and Klein, Cornelis, *Manual of Mineralogy after J. D. Dana*, 19th ed. (1977); Webster, Robert, *Gems: Their Sources, Descriptions, and Identification*, 3d ed. (1975).

Garnet, Henry Highland

Henry Highland Garnet, b. 1815, d. Feb. 13, 1882, was a black American abolitionist clergyman. Born a slave in Maryland, he escaped (1824) to New York where he obtained an education and became a Presbyterian pastor. In 1843 he called upon slaves to rise up and kill their masters, but he lost his support because of his radicalism. In 1881 he was named U.S. minister to Liberia, where he died.

Bibliography: Ofari, Earl, *Let Your Motto Be Resistance: The Life and Thought of Henry Highland Garnet* (1972).

Garnier, Jean Louis Charles

The work of the 19th-century French architect Jean Louis Charles Garnier, b. June 11, 1825, d. Aug. 3, 1898, epitomizes the exuberant ornamentation of the Second Empire style. Born of a poor family, Garnier trained in the ÉCOLE DES BEAUX-ARTS and won the Grand Prix de Rome in 1848. He returned to Paris in 1854 and worked in minor official posts until 1861 when, in competition with the most eminent architects of the time, he was chosen to design the PARIS OPÉRA (completed 1875). The opéra was intended as, and remains, the focal point of Baron Georges Eugène HAUSSMANN's replanning of Paris and the city's most conspicuous example of the ornate French neobaroque style. The Casino at Monte Carlo (1878-81) displays a similar penchant for graceful opulence, but on a smaller scale, and provided a model for resort architecture. Garnier also built the casino and baths at Vittel in 1882. The villa that he built for himself in 1872 at Bordighera, Italy, was designed in the neo-Renaissance style. Among his finest buildings is the more modest and refined Cercle de la Librairie, Paris (1878-79). ROBERT NEUMAN

Bibliography: Drexler, Arthur, ed., *The Architecture of the École des Beaux-Arts* (1976).

Garnier, Robert

The French poet and dramatist Robert Garnier, b. *c.*1544, d. Sept. 20, 1590, was the leading writer of tragedy in 16th-century France. An eloquent and imaginative poet, Garnier based many of his plays, such as *Antigone* (1580) and *Hippolyte* (1573), on classical themes and also introduced the Italian-inspired tragicomedy into France with his *Bradamante* (1582). His biblical tragedy *Les Juives* (1583) is a masterpiece of religious theater. JOSEPH A. REITER

Garnier, Tony

Tony Garnier, 1869-1948, was a French architect and city planner whose chief concern was the GARDEN CITY in the industrial age. Garnier attended the École des Beaux-Arts and won (1899) the Grand Prix de Rome. He returned to his native Lyon, where he worked as municipal architect until his death. He is known almost exclusively for his imaginative project for a *Cité Industrielle*, the plans for which were exhibited in 1901 and published in 1917. Garnier rejected the typical Beaux-Arts tendency toward rigid symmetrical organization and self-conscious monumentality in favor of a plan that conformed to the peculiarities of the site. Following the principles of the garden city, Garnier separated the residential areas from the commercial zones with GREENBELTS and recreational parks, resulting in a functional distribution of houses, factories, civic structures, and port facilities. The primary building material was concrete, and Garnier incorporated many of the latest technological innovations, including the cantilever, in his structures. Like so many of his designs, the spare, almost cubic houses daringly anticipated architecture of the future. The actual commissions that Garnier received and carried out in Lyon, such as the municipal slaughterhouse (1909-13), had relatively little influence, although his use of wide steel spans (80 m/262 ft) to roof large areas was prophetic.

ROBERT NEUMAN

Bibliography: Wiebenson, Dora, *Tony Garnier: The Cité Industrielle* (1969).

garnierite [gahr'-nee-uh-ryt]

Garnierite, a hydrated nickel and magnesium silicate—$(Ni, Mg)_6Si_4O_{11}(OH)_6 \cdot H_2O$—is an important ore mineral of nickel mined near Noumea in New Caledonia and elsewhere. It forms soft, easily crushable masses bright apple green to whitish in color with a dull luster. Hardness is 2-3 and specific gravity is 2.2-2.7. Thought by some to be a nickle-bearing SERPENTINE, garnierite is formed by the hydrothermal alteration of nickel-rich peridotites.

See also: ORE DEPOSITS.

garnishment: see ATTACHMENT (law).

Garo [gah'-roh]

The Garo are a people inhabiting a range of hills of the same name, which at present form an administrative district of ASSAM, the easternmost state of India. They number more than 300,000 and are culturally and ethnically distinct from the plains Assamese, being a tribe of the Bodo-speaking group who may have migrated there from Bhutan. Substantial numbers of Garo now live in adjacent districts of Assam and in Bangladesh. The Garo were traditionally shifting cultivators and grew rice and cotton. The latter was exchanged in the plains of Assam for commodities such as salt and dried fish. Nowadays, particularly with population pressure, they are turning increasingly to the wet cultivation of rice.

Property inheritance among the Garo is quite distinctive, in that inheritance is always through daughters. Garo parents choose one of their daughters to inherit the family homestead and to care for them in old age. When she marries, her husband moves in with her. All the other children leave the family home and set up houses of their own, either on part of the parental land or on the family land of their spouses. In earlier times the Garo were notorious for raiding and headhunting. Now many are educated, large numbers have become Christians, and the tribe is taking advantage of the rural development programs initiated by the government.

HILARY STANDING AND R. L. STIRRAT

Bibliography: Burling, Robbins, *Rengsanggri: Family and Kinship in a Garo Village* (1963).

Garonne River [gah-ruhn']

The Garonne River rises in the Maladeta massif on Spain's Pyrenees Mountains and flows northeast and then northwest 503 km (312 mi) through southwest France. It reaches the Atlantic Ocean 26 km (16 mi) north of Bordeaux through the 72-km-long (45-mi) Gironde Estuary. Its principal tributaries include the Ariège River in the Pyrenees and the Tarn, Lot, and Dordogne rivers in France. Although the river is navigable only on its lower course, the Canal du Midi links it at Toulouse with the Mediterranean. The Garonne Lateral Canal, which is 193 km (120 mi) long, runs parallel to the river from Toulouse to Castets.

Garrett, João Baptista de Almeida [guh-ret', zhwow buh-teesh'-tuh day uhl-may'-duh]

João Baptista de Almeida Garrett, b. Feb. 4, 1799, d. Dec. 9, 1854, was a Portuguese writer who became famous as a liberal politician and a leader of Portuguese romanticism. Garrett's long patriotic poems *Camões* (1825) and *Dona Branca* (1826) are the first landmarks of romantic poetry in Portugal. His prose masterpiece is *Viagens na minna terra* (Travels in My Native Land, 1846), a blend of fiction and nonfiction. He attained his greatest success in the theater. Among his dramas based on Portuguese history, *Brother Luís de Sousa* (1843; Eng. trans., 1909) is one of the finest Portuguese tragedies of the 19th century.

MARIA ISABEL ABREU

Garrett, John Work

John Work Garrett, b. Baltimore, Md., July 31, 1820, d. Sept. 26, 1889, became president of the Baltimore and Ohio Railroad Company when he led a stockholders' challenge to management in 1858. As president of the company for 26 years, he developed the railroad from a small, impoverished line to a powerful system extending from Baltimore to the Mississippi River and the Great Lakes. Garrett helped prevent abandonment of its lines to the Confederates during the Civil War. The service he provided to the North German Lloyd shipping line helped reestablish Baltimore as a major seaport.

Bibliography: Hungerford, Edward, *The Story of the Baltimore and Ohio Railroad, 1827-1927*, 2 vols. (1928; repr. 1972).

Garrett, Pat

Patrick Floyd Garrett, b. 1850, d. 1908, was the New Mexico sheriff who tracked down and shot (1881) Billy the Kid (William H. Bonney). Born in Alabama, Garrett was a buffalo hunter, cowboy, horse rancher, Texas Ranger, and twice a sheriff—once in 1880 and again in 1897. The circumstances of his death in 1908 have never been resolved.

Bibliography: Metz, Leon C., *Pat Garrett* (1974).

Garrick, David [gair'-ik]

David Garrick, b. Feb. 19, 1717, d. Jan. 20, 1779, was the greatest English actor and stage manager of the 18th century. He raised the practice of acting to a true art form and introduced a number of scenic improvements, such as hidden stage-lighting, to the English stage.

David Garrick, one of the great performers of the English stage, appears in a portrait by R. E. Pine. Once established as an outstanding thespian, Garrick became manager of the Drury Lane Theatre, where his innovative productions revived interest in the plays of Shakespeare.

Garrick was descended from a French Huguenot family that came to England in 1685. He studied with Samuel Johnson at Lichfield academy and followed the great man to London, where Garrick planned a business career in the wine trade. There he associated with Johnson's circle and, with leading stage actors such as Charles Macklin, began to play small parts in London and the provinces. Rejected by the managers of Drury Lane and Covent Garden theaters, he acted at Goodman's Fields Theatre, where as Richard III in 1741 he launched a triumphant career. He was especially noted for his expressive features and his naturalistic acting style, which determined the direction of acting technique. His great tragic roles included Hamlet, Macbeth, and Lear. His famous comedy parts included Benedick in *Much Ado About Nothing,* Able Drugger in *The Alchemist,* and Bayes in *The Rehearsal.* Garrick had a strong temper and a reputation for vanity, snobbishness, and parsimony.

As the manager of Drury Lane from 1746 to 1766, Garrick prompted significant advances in representational scene design, ended the practice of audience seating on the stage, and renewed the popularity of Shakespeare's plays, which he often emended. His own plays include *Lethe* (1740) and *Miss in Her Teens* (1747), which were published along with his others in 1768. His unsuccessful Shakespeare Jubilee at Stratford in 1769 was a program of odes, songs, and speeches by Garrick and did not include a word by Shakespeare. Reynolds, Hogarth, and Gainsborough all painted Garrick's portrait, and a great deal is known about his life from his diaries and letters and from a number of sketches by his contemporaries. He was buried in Westminster Abbey. ANDREW KELLY

Bibliography: Burnim, Kalman A., *David Garrick, Director* (1961); Davies, Thomas, *Memoirs of the Life of David Garrick, Esq.,* 2 vols. (1808); Oman, Carola, *David Garrick* (1958); Stone, George W., Jr., and Kahrl, George M., *David Garrick: A Critical Biography* (1979).

Garriott, Owen [gair'-ee-uht]

The American astronaut and geophysicist Owen Kay Garriott, b. Enid, Okla., Nov. 22, 1930, spent 59 days aboard the SKYLAB III space station in 1973. He received his doctorate in electrical engineering from Stanford University in 1960 and was selected in 1965 with the first group of scientist-astronauts. Garriott was the science pilot on Skylab III and logged almost 14 hours in three space walks. He has since served in top space posts at Johnson Space Center in Houston. In 1983 he returned to space as mission specialist aboard the SPACE SHUTTLE *Columbia,* which carried the first SPACELAB. DAVID DOOLING

Garrison, William Lloyd [gair'-i-suhn]

William Lloyd Garrison, b. Dec. 12, 1805, d. May 24, 1879, became to many of his time the personification of the American ABOLITIONIST movement. Initially a proponent of moderate abolitionism while coediting (1829–30) Benjamin Lundy's weekly *Genius of Universal Emancipation,* Garrison soon began more vehement attacks on slavery. On Jan. 1, 1831, he published the first issue of the *Liberator,* declaring slavery an abomination in God's sight, demanding immediate emancipation, and vowing never to be silenced. The *Liberator,* in continuous weekly publication through 1865, always served as a personal sounding board for Garrison's views, but it was also widely regarded as an authoritative voice of radical Yankee social reform in general.

In 1833, Garrison presided over the meeting that organized the American Anti-Slavery Society, and throughout its existence that society was closely identified with Garrison's activities and opinions. Always a believer in "moral suasion," Garrison generally insisted that slavery would be abolished only when the mass of white Americans experienced a revolution in conscience. Therefore, he called for sustained programs of agitation that aimed to convert grass-roots public opinion in favor of black emancipation and race equality.

Until the late 1830s, Garrison cooperated easily with most other major abolitionists, but by 1840 important figures like James G. Birney and Elizur Wright, Jr., had broken with him.

William Lloyd Garrison, perhaps the most outspoken champion of the abolitionist cause, published the first issue of the Liberator *in 1831 and continued to use its pages to agitate for reform for the next 35 years. Garrison alienated many by calling the Constitution "a covenant with death and an agreement with Hell," because it protected slavery.*

Garrison's espousals of anticlericalism, perfectionism, radical pacifism, and women's rights drove these individuals from the American Anti-Slavery Society. Others, however, such as Wendell Phillips and Lydia Maria Child, defended Garrison's radical doctrines and took over the society. In 1842, Garrison took the even more controversial position that Northerners should disavow all allegiance to the Union, since the Constitution protected slavery. Throughout this decade, however, he and most of his associates upheld pacifist creeds and insisted that slavery should not be ended violently.

During the 1850s, Garrison became less opposed to violence as a means for ending slavery. He condoned violent resistance to the 1850 Fugitive Slave Law, hailed John Brown's 1859 raid on Harper's Ferry, and in 1861 announced his support for war against the seceding Southern states. Throughout the Civil War, Garrison agitated for rapid and complete emancipation of the slaves; after the war he continued to insist on black equality and the creation of freedman aid programs in the old slave states. JAMES BREWER STEWART

Bibliography: Merrill, Walter M., *Against Wind and Tide: A Biography of William Lloyd Garrison* (1963); Thomas, John L., *The Liberator: William Lloyd Garrison* (1963).

garrote [guh-raht']

A garrote is an iron collar formerly used in Spain and Portugal for the execution of condemned criminals by strangulation. The victim's neck was placed in the collar, which was then tightened by a screw. The term also applies to lengths of wire or cord used by murderers to strangle their victims.

Garshin, Vsevolod Mikhailovich [gahr'-shin, fuh-see-ev'-uh-luht mee-ky'-luh-vich]

Vsevolod Mikhailovich Garshin, b. Feb. 14 (N.S.), 1855, d. Apr. 5 (N.S.), 1888, was a Russian short-story writer noted for his committed moral sensitivity. He anticipated Chekhov in his impressionism and the use of atmospheric and symbolic narrative details. Garshin's stories are also known for their unresolved conflicts and the absence of conventional plots.

At the outbreak of the Russo-Turkish War, Garshin enlisted in the army and was wounded in action. The sketches and stories that recount his military experiences, particularly "Four Days" (1877), made him famous. Among his important symbolic stories are "Attalea Princeps" (1880) and "The Red Flower" (1883). After 1880, Garshin suffered intermittent attacks of melancholy and finally committed suicide.

VICTOR TERRAS

Bibliography: Garshin, V. M., *The Signal and Other Stories,* trans. by Rowland Smith (1915).

Garstang, John [gahr'-stang]

John Garstang, b. May 5, 1876, d. Sept. 12, 1956, was an influential British archaeologist. After studying mathematics at Oxford, he became interested in archaeology and by 1899 was excavating with Sir Flinders Petrie in Egypt. During his tenure (1902-41) at Liverpool University, Garstang helped found the university's Institute of Archaeology and its publication, *Annals of Archaeology and Anthropology*. He also served (1919-26) as the director of the Department of Antiquities in Palestine and conducted (1930-36) important excavations at Jericho. In Turkey he had earlier excavated (1908, 1911) at Sakfagözü and later conducted (1936-39) work at Mersin, greatly elucidating the long cultural sequence of southeast Anatolia. Garstang's contributions to Anatolian archaeology culminated in his establishment (1947) of the British Institute of Archaeology at Ankara, which he directed and later guided in several capacities until his death. LOUISE ALPERS BORDAZ

garter snake

The 60-cm (2-ft) common garter snake, T. sirtalis, *widely distributed throughout North America, is the only snake found as far north as Alaska.*

Garter snakes, genus *Thamnophis*, family Colubridae, are the most common snakes in North America. The 12 to 19 species of aquatic and terrestrial garter snakes are found from the Atlantic to the Pacific coasts and from Costa Rica north to the Yukon, reaching farther north (67° N) than any other snake in the Western Hemisphere. Their habitats range from low-lying swamps to altitudes of 4,000 m (13,000 ft). Terrestrial forms feed largely on earthworms and insects, aquatic forms mainly on amphibians. Garter snakes are slender, the more elongate forms generally being called ribbon snakes, and they are about 0.6 m (2 ft) long. Some forms lack stripes, but the predominant pattern consists of dark brown, black, or reddish upper sides, with one to three stripes and a checkerboard pattern of blotches running the length of the body. Garter snakes generally mate in early spring, and the female delivers 12 to 70 living young in late summer.

Gärtner, Friedrich von [gairt'-nur]

The German architect Friedrich von Gärtner, b. Dec. 10, 1792, d. Apr. 21, 1847, developed the *Rundbogenstil*, or round-arch style, derived from Italian romanesque and quattrocento architecture. He studied at the Munich Academy, where he later taught, and spent his early years traveling throughout Europe. His major works were the Ludwigskirche (1829-40), the State Library (1831-40), and the university (1835-40), all on the Ludwigstrasse in Munich. The library contains medievalizing detail, colored brick, and terra-cotta in a conscious rejection of monochromatic Greek revival. The area as a whole exemplifies unified town planning within an eclectic phase of romantic classicism. ROBERT F. CHIRICO

Bibliography: Hitchcock, Henry Russell, *Architecture*, 4th ed. (1977).

Garuda [guh'-ruh-duh]

In Hindu mythology, Garuda was a creature half man and half bird, frequently depicted with a golden body, white face, and red wings. It carried Vishnu wherever he traveled; it was also the enemy of the serpents (*nagas*). In later mythology the concept of multiple garudas developed.

Garvey, Marcus [gahr'-vee]

Marcus Garvey, the leader of a black separatist movement early in the 20th century, wears a uniform signifying the presidency of his hoped-for African republic. Although Garvey anticipated the later emphasis on black culture and racial pride, in the early 1920s he alienated many by advocating separate political and economic institutions. Convicted of mail fraud in 1923, he never regained his following and died in 1940 in obscurity.

Marcus Mosiah Garvey, b. Jamaica, Aug. 17, 1887, d. June 10, 1940, organized the black nationalist movement of the 1920s in the United States. Garvey went to New York City in 1916 and recruited followers for his Universal Negro Improvement Association. Its program was to unite all black peoples through the establishment in Africa of a country and government of their own. Garvey was a magnetic speaker who dressed in a resplendent uniform and led his followers in parades through Harlem. In 1921 he claimed nearly 1 million followers.

Garvey's newspaper, *Negro World*, carried his views to all parts of the United States. He preached economic independence, pride of race, and the need for black Americans to return to Africa. Garvey organized a steamship company, the Black Star Line, to provide a commercial link among all the black peoples of the world. His methods of selling stock in the line, however, led to his conviction (1923) for using the U.S. mails to defraud. After serving nearly 3 years of a 5-year sentence, he was pardoned by President Coolidge and deported to Jamaica in 1927. Although he died in obscurity, Garvey is remembered as a national hero in his native Jamaica. RONALD L. LEWIS

Bibliography: Cronon, E. David, *Black Moses: The Story of Marcus Garvey and the Universal Negro Improvement Association*, 2d ed. (1969); Fax, Elton C., *Garvey: The Story of a Pioneer Black Nationalist* (1972); Garvey, Amy J., *Garvey and Garveyism* (1963) and *Philosophy and Opinions of Marcus Garvey* (1923-25; repr. 1976).

Gary [gar'-ee]

A port on Lake Michigan in the northwest corner of Indiana, Gary is the state's third largest city, with a population of 151,953 (1980). A principal city in the great Calumet industrial region adjacent to Chicago, it is also one of the nation's major steel centers. The United States Steel Corporation purchased land there in 1905, and soon a steel mill and a new city emerged from the coastal sloughs and sand dunes. The city was chartered in 1906 and named for Judge Elbert H. Gary, then the company's chairman of the board. The Gary plan of education, developed in the city's public schools between 1908 and 1915, was widely adopted in other parts of the United States.

Gary, Elbert Henry

Elbert Gary, b. Oct. 8, 1846, d. Aug. 15, 1927, called "Judge" because for a few years he served as a county judge in Illinois, was a corporation lawyer who became president of the Federal Steel Company in 1898. The financier J. P. Morgan put him in charge of organizing the United States Steel Corporation in 1901, and he was its chief executive officer from 1903 until his death. Gary was a strong foe of unions but introduced profit sharing and championed higher wages and better working conditions. The city of Gary, Ind., originally a steel company town, is named after him.

Gary, Romain [gah-ree', roh-man']

Romain Gary, b. Romain Kacew in Vilnius, Lithuania (now USSR), May 8, 1914, d. Dec. 2, 1980, was a French writer whose first novel, *A European Education* (1945; Eng. trans., 1960), described the Polish resistance during World War II. *The Roots of Heaven* (1956; Eng. trans., 1958), about a Frenchman imprisoned in a German concentration camp, won Gary the Prix Goncourt (1956). His later works include the autobiographical *Promise at Dawn* (1960; Eng. trans., 1961). After Gary's death by suicide it was revealed that he had written several works under the pseudonym Émile Ajar, including *La vie devant soi* (1975; trans. as *Momo,* 1978).

gas

In a strict chemical sense, a gas is any matter that is in the GASEOUS STATE, characterized by high molecular kinetic energy and the tendency to expand out of an open container. In practical use the word takes on distinct and separate meanings. NATURAL GAS refers to a natural fossil fuel that is collected in the gas phase and is easily liquefied. GASOLINE, often called, simply, gas, is a liquid mixture of hydrocarbon fuels that become gaseous in the combustion chamber of an engine. POISON GAS is used in GAS CHAMBERS and CHEMICAL AND BIOLOGICAL WARFARE.

gas chamber

A gas chamber is an airtight room in which persons are killed with poison gas. As a method of executing condemned prisoners it was first used in Nevada in 1924 (see CAPITAL PUNISHMENT). The prisoner is strapped in a chair, and sodium cyanide pellets are dropped into a bucket of acid. If the prisoner breathes deeply, death comes almost at once.

The infamous concentration camp gas chambers used in Nazi Germany's program of genocide were disguised as bathhouses. Naked prisoners were herded into them, and lethal carbon monoxide or hydrocyanic gas fumes were pumped in.

gas laws

In chemistry and physics, the behavior of gases under varying conditions of temperature, pressure, and volume may be described and predicted by a set of equations, or gas laws. These laws were determined by measurements of actual gases and are valid for all substances in the GASEOUS STATE.

The first quantitative measurements of gases were published by Robert BOYLE in 1660. He observed that if an enclosed amount of gas is compressed until it is half its original volume (V) while the temperature is kept constant, the pressure (P) will be doubled. Quantitatively, Boyle's law is $PV =$ constant, where the value of the constant depends on the temperature and the amount of gas present.

Jacques CHARLES studied (1787) the relationship between the temperature and volume of a gas while maintaining constant pressure. Charles observed that for every degree Celsius rise in temperature, the gas volume increased by 1/273 of its volume at 0° C. Charles's observations led to the concept of the absolute temperature scale, or KELVIN SCALE, because the gas would have zero volume at −273° C. The absolute temperature scale was defined so that ABSOLUTE ZERO equals −273° C. This new temperature scale allowed Charles's law to be written $V/T =$ constant, where V is the volume of the gas, T is the temperature on the absolute scale, and the constant depends on the pressure and the amount of gas present. Joseph GAY-LUSSAC studied the relationship between pressure and temperature and in 1802 formed an additional law: $P/T =$ constant. About this time John DALTON formulated his law of partial pressures: the pressure of a mixture of gases is the sum of the pressures of the constituent gases.

Boyle's, Charles's, and Gay-Lussac's laws may be combined to express a generalized gas law, $PV/T =$ constant, where the value of the constant depends on the amount of gas present and T is the absolute (or Kelvin) temperature. The generalized gas law may be written in another form: $PV/nT = R$, or $PV = nRT$; in this form it is called the IDEAL GAS law. R is the gas constant, and n is the number of moles of gas. The gas constant can be evaluated experimentally as $R = 0.082$ liter-atmospheres per Kelvin-moles. Knowing R, the fourth variable can be evaluated if any three are known.

The laws are valid for most gases at moderate temperatures and pressures. At low temperatures and high pressures, gases deviate from the above laws because the molecules move slowly at low temperatures and they are closer together on the average at higher pressures (see KINETIC THEORY OF MATTER). Both of these effects increase the attractive forces between the molecules that cause the deviations (see VAN DER WAALS EQUATION).

GERALD C. ROPER

Bibliography: Bailar, John C., Jr., *Chemistry* (1978); Jeans, James S., *An Introduction to the Kinetic Theory of Gases* (1982).

gas mask

A modern, lightweight, military gas mask protects the wearer's face, eyes, and lungs from the effects of poisonous gases. A typical mask of gas-impervious materials is tightly fitted around the face. Air (blue arrows) *is drawn in through an inlet valve in the air-purifying canister, which contains a filter for removing particles and an activated charcoal layer that absorbs and removes harmful gases. Exhaled air exits through a valve at the front of the mask.*

Invented during World War I to protect combatants' eyes and lungs from POISON GAS, gas masks are used today to filter many airborne substances—dust, asbestos fiber, vaporized paint—as well as some gases used in chemical warfare. The protective gas mask cleans the breathed air by means of a filter of chemically impregnated fibers over a bed of adsorbent material—usually activated charcoal. Another type, the closed-system rebreathing mask, uses a chemical such as sodium peroxide to react with the carbon dioxide and water from exhaled air, regenerating oxygen for breathing.

Gascoigne, George [gas-koyn']

George Gascoigne, b. *c.*1539, d. Oct. 7, 1577, was an innovative English playwright, poet, and prose writer. His drama *The Supposes* (1566), an adaptation of Ariosto's *I Suppositi,* was the first English prose comedy. *Jocasta* (1573), which Gascoigne wrote with Francis Kinwelmersh and based on Euripides' *Phoenecian Women,* was one of the earliest English blank-verse tragedies. After a scandalous youth, during which he was imprisoned for debt, he became a member of Parliament (1557–59) and fought in the Low Countries (1572–74). His *A Hundred Sundry Flowers* (1573), containing his dramas and poems, was expanded to *The Posies of George Gascoigne* (1573), which includes the earliest treatise on English prosody, "Certain Notes of Instruction." *The Steele Glass* (1576), in blank verse, is considered the first true English satire.

ROBIN BUSS

Bibliography: Johnson, Ronald, *George Gascoigne* (1971).

Gascony [gas'-kuh-nee]

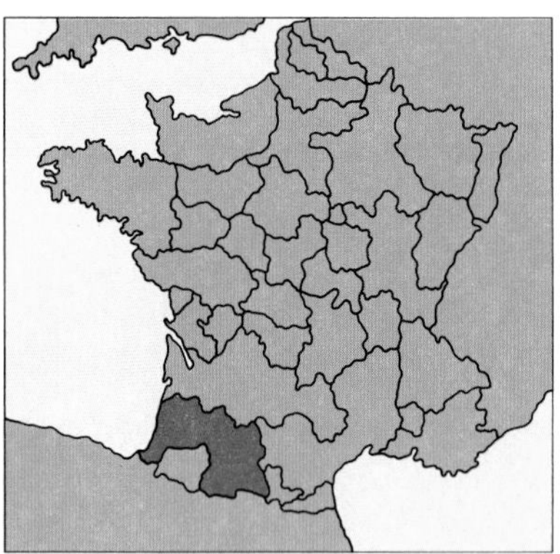

The map indicates the location of Gascony, a historic region of southwestern France. An independent duchy during part of its history, it was divided into several departments in 1790.

Gascony (French: Gascogne) is a historic region of southwestern France bordered by Béarn on the southwest, Guienne on the north, Languedoc on the east, Foix on the southeast, and Spain on the south. The name is derived from the Vascones (BASQUES), who settled here after crossing the Pyrenees from Spain in the 6th century.

The Landes, the coastal region in the west, is flat, barren, sandy country planted with pine forests. In the south the peaks of the Pyrenees exceed 3,050 m (10,000 ft). The mountain slopes are used for the summer grazing of cattle and sheep. In the fertile, populous valleys, wheat, peaches, apricots, and grapes are grown, and hydroelectric power is increasingly important. Tarbes and Bagnères-de-Bigorre, the largest market centers of the foothills, serve a growing tourist industry. Northward, the Adour, Garonne, and other rivers flowing from the Pyrenees deposited an alluvial fan of coarse pebbles, an arid moorland that supports livestock. Farther north, the rivers have deposited more fertile material in Armagnac, which produces fruit, cereals, and a brandy that rivals cognac. In the Armagnac area is the town of Auch, the traditional capital of Gascony. The Gascon people, typified by D'Artagnan, a character in the novels of Alexandre Dumas, have the reputation of being proud, eloquent, courageous, and boastful.

Known as Novempopulana in Roman times, Gascony became a semiautonomous duchy under Frankish suzerainty in the 7th century and remained a separate entity until it was joined to AQUITAINE in the mid-11th century. It came under English rule in 1154 and continued so until it was annexed by the French crown in 1453. Today Gascony corresponds to the departments of Landes, Gers, and Hautes-Pyrénées, and parts of Haute-Garonne, Tarn-et-Garonne, Lot-et-Garonne, Ariège, and Pyrénées-Atlantiques.

TIMOTHY J. RICKARD

gaseous state [gash'-uhs]

The gaseous state is one of three basic physical states of matter. In contrast to the liquid or solid states, a gas when unconfined tends to expand indefinitely, and a gas in a container always fills the container completely. This is because gas molecules contain sufficient KINETIC ENERGY to overcome basic intermolecular forces of attraction. If liquids or solids are given enough energy, as by heating, their molecules will overcome such forces and will change to the gaseous state. This is called boiling or EVAPORATION in the case of liquids and SUBLIMATION in the case of solids.

Empirical studies by chemists of the properties of gases led to a series of GAS LAWS that are of use today. These laws have been verified and modified by theoretical chemists (see KINETIC THEORY OF MATTER). Observations on the variation of the volume of a given amount of gas with pressure led to Boyle's law (1662), and variation of the volume with temperature led to Charles's law (1787) and Gay-Lussac's law (1802). These laws are summarized in the equation PV/T = constant, where P is pressure, V is volume, and T is absolute temperature. This equation, combined with AVOGADRO'S LAW (1811), led to the combined gas equation $PV=nRT$, where n is the number of moles of gas and R is a universal constant. This is also called the IDEAL GAS equation, because it is generally valid only for gases at low pressures and high temperatures. At high pressures and low temperatures the behaviors of gas molecules deviate from the ideal law because of the influence of intermolecular forces as well as the volumes of the gas molecules themselves. Chemists have attempted to modify the law so that the behaviors of all gases (so-called real gases) can be predicted (see VAN DER WAALS EQUATION).

Much of the behavior of gases, as determined by observation, is explained or predicted by STATISTICAL THERMODYNAMICS. In this treatment, the mechanical behavior of a single gas molecule is calculated, and then all molecules moving in the same manner are counted. This leads to expressions for the gas pressure and kinetic energy as a whole. It also leads to estimates of thermal conductivity, viscosity, and diffusion. All gas molecules have translational energy, and molecules with more than one atom also have rotational and vibrational energies. Not all the molecules in a given gas sample have the same energy, but methods of statistical mechanics can produce a probable energy distribution among the molecules at a given temperature. Temperature is essentially a measure of average kinetic energy of the gas. For each gaseous substance there is a certain temperature, called the critical temperature, above which the gaseous molecules cannot be liquefied by increasing pressure.

Although, theoretically, all substances can become gaseous with proper adjustment of temperature and pressure, the normal conditions of the Earth provide for only a small number of substances in the gaseous state. Some common gases are elemental nitrogen (N_2), elemental oxygen (O_2), carbon dioxide (CO_2), and water vapor (H_2O), all major ingredients of the Earth's ATMOSPHERE. Hydrogen (H_2), methane (CH_4), ammonia (NH_3), and hydrogen chloride (HCl) are examples of other important gases.

E. R. GRILLY AND A. F. SCHUCH

Bibliography: Jeans, James S., *An Introduction to the Kinetic Theory of Gases* (1982); Maron, Samuel H., and Prutton, Carl F., *Principles of Physical Chemistry* (1974).

Gaskell, Elizabeth Cleghorn [gas'-kul]

The English author Elizabeth Cleghorn Stevenson Gaskell, b. London, Sept. 29, 1810, d. Nov. 12, 1865, was an influential

Elizabeth Gaskell, an English novelist and biographer, appears in this portrait by George Richmond. A major chronicler of social conditions during the Industrial Revolution, Gaskell also wrote The Life of Charlotte Brontë *(1857), a poignant, though occasionally inaccurate, biography.*

novelist whose works focus upon social and economic themes. She was raised by her aunt in the small Cheshire village of Knutsford, an environment subsequently described in her novels. In 1832 she married the Rev. William Gaskell, a Unitarian minister, and settled in Manchester, where she assisted her husband and learned firsthand of the conditions endured by laborers in the north of England. Mrs. Gaskell's first novel, *Mary Barton* (1848), attacked the callousness of manufacturers and won the admiration of Thomas Carlyle, Benjamin Disraeli, and Charles Dickens. When Dickens began his periodical *Household Words* in 1850, he invited Mrs. Gaskell to become a regular contributor. In 1853 she published *Ruth,* a condemnation of sexual hypocrisy, and *Cranford,* a series of sketches of provincial life that were based upon her years in Knutsford. *North and South* (1855), often considered her finest novel, contrasted the socioeconomic conditions then existing in the urban north and rural south of England. A meeting with Charlotte Brontë in 1850 led to friendship, and, on Miss Brontë's death, Mrs. Gaskell wrote *The Life of Charlotte Brontë* (1857), a then controversial, but sensitive, biography.

Throughout her life Mrs. Gaskell was involved in social causes and charitable work. Her later novels, *Sylvia's Lovers* (1863), *Cousin Phillis* (1865), and the posthumously published and incomplete *Wives and Daughters* (1866), showed continuing concern with social problems and a deepening awareness of the levels of the human personality. PHILIP FLYNN

Bibliography: Brodetsky, Tessa, *Elizabeth Gaskell* (1987); Chapple, J. A., and Sharps, J. G., *Elizabeth Gaskell: A Portrait in Letters* (1982); Craik, Wendy A., *Elizabeth Gaskell and the English Provincial Novel* (1975); Duthie, E. L., *The Themes of Elizabeth Gaskell* (1980); Gerin, Winifred, *Elizabeth Gaskell* (1976); Lansbury, Coral, *Elizabeth Gaskell* (1984); Stoneman, Patsy, *Elizabeth Gaskell* (1987).

gasohol [gas'-uh-hawl]

Gasohol is a mixture of gasoline and the alcohol ethanol (or, more rarely, methanol) used as a motor fuel. Commercial quantities of ethanol can be obtained by the fermentation of agricultural wastes. During the gasoline shortages of the late 1970s, gasohol was often available to U.S. motorists for use as a gasoline extender. At that time Brazil began to produce large amounts of ethanol from sugar cane and other plant wastes; it has since come to depend on gasohol to augment its gasoline supplies. Aside from farmers, however—many of whom produce their own ethanol—few U.S. car owners now use gasohol. Although it burns more slowly, coolly, and cleanly than gasoline, and provides greater octane, in concentrated amounts it can damage the plastics and synthetic rubbers used in engines. The U.S. Environmental Protection Agency allows the addition of only 10 percent ethanol by volume (or 3 percent methanol) to unleaded gas.

gasoline [gas-uh-leen']

Gasoline, known as petrol in England, is a petroleum HYDROCARBON fuel used principally to power internal-combustion engines. Composed primarily of the ALKANES hexane, heptane, and octane, it may contain molecules with between 4 and 12 carbon atoms. The boiling range is 25° C to 180° C (77° F to 356° F), and the net calorific value is 42–44 megajoules per kilogram (MJ/kg). It is liquid at ordinary ambient temperatures but evaporates easily in air to form a flammable mixture.

Production. Gasoline is produced by distillation of crude oil and also by the cracking, or breaking up, of heavier distillation products. This cracking can be either by thermal means—that is, by maintaining heavy-oil fractions at elevated temperatures and pressures, when they break up into smaller units—or by catalytic cracking (see PETROLEUM INDUSTRY).

In catalytic cracking, the oil is fed in a stream of steam into a reaction vessel containing a catalyst—such as fine particles of FULLER'S EARTH (a hydrated aluminosilicate)—suspended in a fluidized bed. A reaction occurs in which large molecules are broken down into smaller ones. Some carbon is deposited on the catalyst, which therefore loses some of its effect and has to be regenerated in a second fluidized bed, where the carbon is burned off in a stream of air. The resultant carbon dioxide is released into the atmosphere.

Composition and Use. The burning properties of gasoline depend on the composition of the sample. One property in particular is important for automobile-engine applications. This is the tendency for hydrocarbons in the gasoline range to ignite spontaneously under the high temperature and pressure conditions inside an engine cylinder. This preignition leads to a characteristic knocking in the engine. The antiknock properties of the gasoline are measured by its OCTANE NUMBER, obtained by comparison with the behavior of isooctane. The octane number of gasolines can be increased by the use of catalytic reforming techniques. These include the use of platinum catalysts, temperatures about 550° C (1,022° F), and pressures between 1.4 and 6.9 Newtons per square millimeter (200–1,000 lb/in^2) to induce dehydrogenation and isomerization of straight-chain paraffins to more branched forms. The other method is alkylation, in which an isoparaffin is combined with an olefin to build a larger molecule with a high octane number.

The volatility of motor gasoline is important and is adjusted according to the season to insure that sufficient hydrocarbon vapor is always available for ignition even at low air-temperatures. This is done by adding extra butanes and pentanes in the winter so that the volatility is raised, and, incidentally, the flash point is lowered from the summer value of −40° C (−40° F) to a value of −45° C (−49° F).

A number of additives are incorporated in commercial gasoline blends. Some of these inhibit oxidation and gum formation during storage. Dyes are also added for identification purposes. Alcohol and surfactants may also be added to reduce carburetor icing and corrosion. In the past, tetraethyl lead was often added to increase octane ratings and improve fuel efficiency. It was found, however, that the extremely high levels of airborne lead in urban areas are directly traceable to the combustion of leaded gasoline. In 1985 the Environmental Protection Agency ruled that gasoline lead content be reduced by over 90 percent, with the goal of eventually eliminating lead altogether. The result has been a dramatic drop in airborne lead emissions, beginning with an overall 48 percent reduction in 1985.

To control the levels of other polluting emissions from automobile exhaust, engines must now be equipped with various emission control devices. The most effective is the CATALYTIC CONVERTER, which cannot operate efficiently when leaded gasoline is used. JOHN T. MCMULLAN

Bibliography: Baker, Ron, *Oil and Gas: A Production Story* (1983); Beggs, H. D., *Gas Production Operations* (1984); Goodger, E. M., *Hydrocarbon Fuels* (1975); Husselbee, William, *Automotive Emission Control* (1984).

Gasparri, Pietro [gahs-pahr'-ree]

Pietro Gasparri, b. May 5, 1852, d. Nov. 18, 1934, was an Italian cardinal who was responsible for the codification of canon law. Professor of church law at the Catholic Institute in Paris, he was called to Rome in 1901 and was put in charge of the project. Work began in 1904 and ended in 1916. Gasparri served as papal secretary of state from 1914 to 1930. His negotiations with Italian leader Benito Mussolini resulted in the LATERAN TREATY (1929) that established the Vatican as an independent state.

Gaspé Peninsula [gahs-pay']

The Gaspé Peninsula, also known as Gaspésie, is a rugged, remote area of eastern Quebec, Canada, which projects into the Gulf of St. Lawrence between Chaleur Bay and the mouth of the St. Lawrence River. It is about 240 km (150 mi) long and 115 to 135 km (70 to 85 mi) wide. Famous for its scenic views, the peninsula has a mountainous, thickly forested interior, with many lakes and rivers. Its highest peak is Mount Jacques Cartier (1,268 m/4,160 ft), in the Shickshock (Chic Choc) Mountains. Important towns include Matane, Gaspé, and Percé. The inhabitants, most of whom are French-speaking, live primarily by fishing, although some maintain marginal farms on the rocky soil. Lumbering and tourism are additional sources of income.

Gaspee [gas'-pee]

The H.M.S. *Gaspee* was a British revenue cutter that ran aground at Warwick, R.I., in June 1772. Local smugglers, resenting the cutter's interference with their activities, burned the ship and wounded its captain on June 10. The incident was one of many that caused friction between the colonists and British government on the eve of the American Revolution.

Gasperi, Alcide de: see DE GASPERI, ALCIDE.

Gass, William H. [gas]

The American author William Howard Gass, b. Fargo, N.Dak., July 30, 1924, is a leading exponent of so-called innovative fiction, in the postmodernist tradition of John Barth and Thomas Pynchon. Gass challenges the conventional conception of the relationship between artist and reality by maintaining that words themselves—not characters, themes, and ideas—make up fiction. This philosophy is articulated in *Fiction and the Figures of Life* (1970) and supported in other essay collections, such as *The World within the Word* (1978) and *The Habitations of the Word* (1984). Gass's fiction includes *Omensetter's Luck* (1966), his first novel, *In the Heart of the Heart of the Country and Other Stories* (1968), and *Willie Masters' Lonesome Wife* (1968), an illustrated and typographically variegated novella about sex and language.

Gassendi, Pierre [gahs-sen-dee', pee-yair]

Pierre Gassendi, b. Jan. 22, 1592, d. Oct. 24, 1655, was a French philosopher and scientist. He defended a form of ATOMISM drawn from Epicurus and wrote numerous commentaries on EPICUREANISM. Gassendi knew both Johannes Kepler and Galileo. He performed the experiment proving Galileo's conviction that a rock dropped from the mast of a ship would fall straight down. Gassendi thus silenced the many who claimed that if the Earth were in motion, an object dropped from a high place would not fall straight. He was also the author of a critical set of objections to René Descartes's *Meditations*. A priest, Gassendi became provost of the Cathedral of Digne in 1624. CATHERINE WILSON

Gaster, Moses [gahs'-tur]

Moses Gaster, b. Sept. 16, 1856, d. Mar. 5, 1939, was a Romanian Jewish folklorist, scholar, and early Zionist activist. Expelled (1885) from Romania for protesting official maltreatment of Jews, he was appointed (1886) to teach Slavonic literature at Oxford University. In 1887, he was named chief rabbi (*Chacham*) of the Sephardic synagogues of England and held this office until 1918. Gaster played an important part in the preliminary conferences that led to the Balfour Declaration. His many scholarly publications included studies of the Samaritans, general and Jewish folklore, history of Romanian literature, magic, and medieval romances. JOSEPH L. BLAU

gastritis [gas-try'-tis]

Gastritis is an inflammation of the stomach lining that can be caused by many factors, including irritation by agents such as drugs, alcohol, and corrosive chemicals; bacterial and viral infections; and allergies. The symptoms of acute gastritis include discomfort after eating, nausea, vomiting, and loss of appetite; they usually subside after identifying and dealing with the causative agent. Chronic gastritis, however, is more commonly the sign of some underlying disorder such as gastric or duodenal ulcers, iron deficiency ANEMIA, or other diseases that involve the stomach. Atrophic gastritis, which involves the degeneration of the stomach lining, is most often observed in older persons, including those with pernicious anemia. PETER L. PETRAKIS

Bibliography: Hamilton, Helen, *Gastrointestinal Disorders* (1985).

gastrointestinal tract disease [gas'-troh-in-tes'-tin-ul]

Diseases of the gastrointestinal system are major causes of illness and death. In developing nations malnutrition and poor sanitation predispose the populations to bacterial and parasitic infections. In industrialized nations a longer life expectancy is associated with an increase in the incidence of gastrointestinal cancer.

Congenital or Acquired Structural Lesions. Congenital pyloric stenosis is a genetically determined disorder that is more common in male infants. Thickening of the circular muscle at the pylorus, the opening from the stomach to the duodenum (first portion of small intestine), causes gastric obstruction accompanied by vomiting and dehydration. A pyloromyotomy—surgical division of the circular pyloric muscle—corrects this condition. Diverticula and strictures are the most commonly acquired structural lesions (defects). A diverticulum is a localized outpouching of the gut caused by a high pressure in the lumen (cavity) and a localized weakness of the muscle layers. Large diverticula extending from the pharynx or lower esophagus may collect food and secretions and interfere with normal swallowing. Bacterial colonization of small-intestine diverticula may cause malabsorption, and the multiple diverticula in the colon may perforate to form abscesses and cause inflammation (diverticulitis).

Abnormalities of Motor Function. The normal contraction and relaxation of the muscle layers of the gastrointestinal tract mixes food with digestive secretions, propels the intestinal content by peristaltic contraction, and prevents regurgitation by sphincter-muscle contraction. Disorders of intestinal movements may be due to neurological disease or muscle abnormalities. Hirschsprung's disease is due to a lack of nerve impulses to the anal sphincter and part of the rectum. This segment of bowel fails to relax to permit normal passage of feces; severe CONSTIPATION with distension of the colon is present from birth.

Ulcers often occur in the stomach (A) or, more commonly, the duodenum (B). They erode the mucous membrane (1) and may invade the submucous (2) and muscle (3) layers; complete perforation (4) through the wall of the gut requires treatment to prevent inflammation of the peritoneum, the membrane that lines the abdominal cavity. Gallstones (C), formed from bile pigment and cholesterol, may cause obstruction or inflammation in the gall bladder. Appendicitis, an acute inflammation of the appendix (D), requires surgical removal of that organ. Diverticulosis, or the formation of saclike diverticula (E), occurs in the colon and may lead to inflammation.

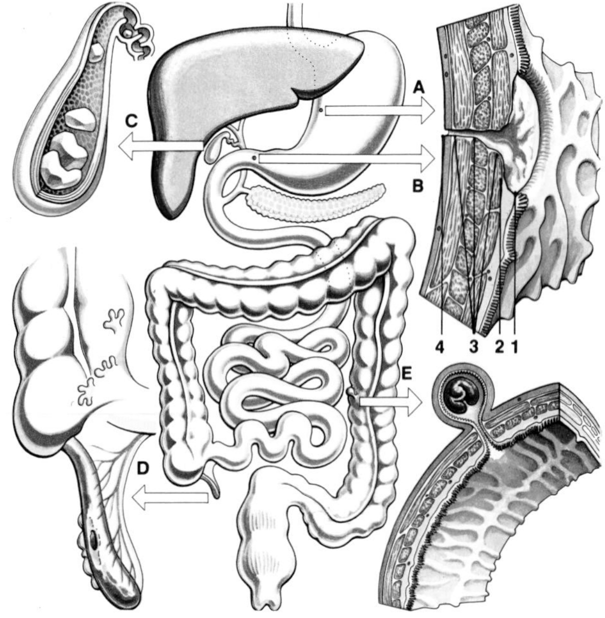

Mucosal Injury. Mucosal injury may arise due to physical or chemical agents. Two chemical agents, hydrochloric acid in the stomach and bile salts secreted into the duodenum, may cause mucosal injury. The cells that line the surface of the normal stomach protect it from acid injury. If these cells are damaged (for example, by aspirin) the acid within the stomach may leak back into the mucosa and cause erosions, or ULCERS (a partial- or full-thickness defect in the mucosa). Excessive acid secretion plays a significant role in the development of a duodenal ulcer. ANTACIDS are usually effective in relieving ulcer symptoms and in promoting ulcer healing.

The rapidly proliferating cells lining the gastrointestinal tract are sensitive to irradiation and to drugs that are used to treat cancer (chemotherapy). In the esophagus, injury may cause pain, or difficulty in swallowing; in the intestine, injury may lead to diarrhea; in the colon, radiation COLITIS may cause bleeding.

Viral, Bacterial, and Parasitic Infections. "Intestinal flu" is a common epidemic viral infection of the small bowel mucosa, causing a brief febrile (fever-present) illness with vomiting or diarrhea or both. "Traveller's diarrhea," a common and severe diarrheal illness, is usually caused by bacteria (*Escherichia coli*) that stimulates intestinal secretion of fluid. CHOLERA, caused by infection with *Vibrio cholerae* (usually due to water contamination), is a more severe diarrhea because of the production of toxins in the intestine.

Certain pathogenic bacteria, which include *Salmonella* and *Shigella*, invade the mucosa of the small bowel or colon to produce enteritis or DYSENTERY. Parasitic disease of the gastrointestinal tract, including schistosomiasis, is a major worldwide public health problem.

Diseases Causing Maldigestion and Malabsorption. The two processes that are important in the absorption of nutrients are digestion and subsequent absorption. Digestion is impaired in the case of pancreatic insufficiency when there is a lack of the major pancreatic digestive enzymes and bicarbonate. When the concentration of bile salts is depressed by hepatobiliary disease or by resection of the distal small bowel (the normal site of bile acid reabsorption and conservation), malabsorption of fat and fat-soluble vitamins causes diarrhea and deficiency of vitamins A, D, and K.

Diseases of the intestinal mucosa may cause malabsorption of many nutrients. In the tropical malabsorption syndrome (tropical sprue), mucosal damage may be due to bacterial infection, which is corrected by antibiotic therapy. In celiac sprue, cereal protein, or gluten (present in wheat, rye, barley, and oats), causes injury to the intestinal mucosa, probably by an immunological reaction.

Immunological Diseases. Deficiencies of certain immunological agents can promote intestinal infection by bacteria and parasites. Sensitivity to dietary antigens, such as cow's milk proteins, may cause local allergic reactions within the intestine, which subsequently cause diarrhea, bleeding, or leakage of plasma protein. The atrophic GASTRITIS of pernicious anemia appears to be an autoimmune disease.

Neoplastic Disease. Benign (nonmalignant) polyps are relatively common in the colon and in the stomach. In the colon these lesions may be multiple and genetically determined. Patients with a family history of multiple polyps have a high risk of developing carcinoma (malignancy) of the colon at an early age. Bleeding or a change in bowel function are important symptoms.

Vascular Lesions. Vascular malformations, with thin dilated blood vessels in the mucosa, may cause bleeding from the stomach, small intestine, or cecum. Mesenteric vascular disease may be arterial or venous. Blockage of one of the main abdominal arteries by ATHEROSCLEROSIS or by blood clot may cause tissue death (necrosis) in the small bowel.

Advances in Treatment. Patients with impaired gastrointestinal tracts can starve to death, because the method of feeding—intravenous sugar—can supply only 500 to 600 calories per day. In 1966, Stanley Dudrick was the first to apply a technique called intravenous hyperalimentation, which can supply up to 3,000 calories per day, as well as vitamins, amino acids, and minerals. "Vests" designed by Dudrick contain both the food and a pump to send the food into a large blood vessel, the superior vena cava, where it dilutes rapidly, thus preventing clots and damage. Temporarily used while patients recover from illness, surgery, or severe burns, the technique is also used to give the bowels a chance to heal in severe inflammatory disease, eliminating the need for surgery.

GRAHAM H. JEFFRIES

Bibliography: Anderson, W. A. D., ed., *Pathology*, 7th ed. (1977); Beeson, P. B., and McDermott, Walsh, eds., *Textbook of Medicine*, 14th ed. (1975); Berkow, Robert, ed., *Merck Manual of Diagnosis and Therapy*, 13th ed. (1977); Bockus, H. L., et al., *Gastroenterology*, 4 vols. (1974-76); Nugent, Nancy, *How to Get Along with Your Stomach: A Complete Guide to the Prevention and Treatment of Stomach Distress* (1978); Paulson, Moses, ed., *Gastroenterologic Medicine* (1969); Sleisenger, Marvin H., and Fordtran, John S., *Gastrointestinal Disease*, 2d ed. (1978).

gastronomy: see COOKING.

gastropod [gas'-troh-pahd]

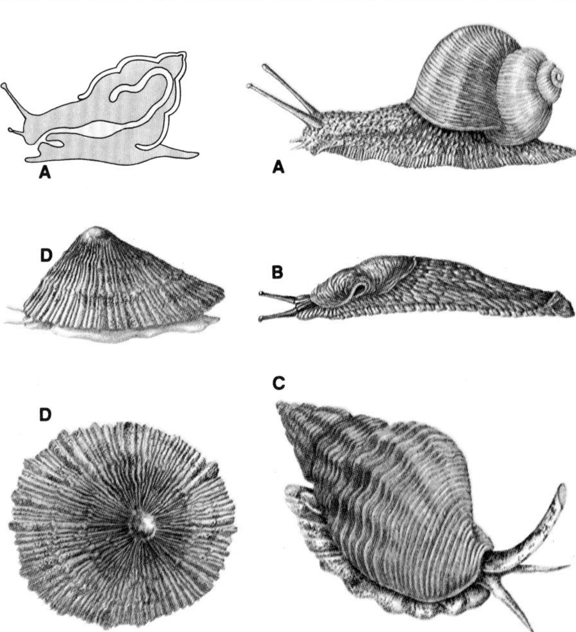

Gastropods, a class of mollusks, include the snail (A), *slug* (B), *whelk* (C), *and limpet* (D). *Virtually all gastropods have a shell, although in some, such as the slug, the shell is actually a small vestige underneath the skin. Gastropods also have a muscular foot, sensory tentacles, and a torsion, or rotation, of the internal organs.*

Gastropod is the name given to members of the largest and most diverse class in the phylum Mollusca (see MOLLUSK). The class Gastropoda contains about 35,000 living species and 15,000 fossil species of diverse form and life-styles, including SNAILS, SLUGS, ABALONES, WHELKS, PERIWINKLES, LIMPETS, and CONCHS. Although mostly marine, gastropods are also common in fresh water and are the only mollusks adapted to a terrestrial existence.

Many gastropods are characterized by a single, coiled, external shell. Some forms (abalones and limpets, for example), however, have conical or flattened shells, and sea slugs and terrestrial slugs have internalized shells or no shell at all. Gastropods have a broad, muscular, creeping foot, above which lie the internal organs and (where present) the shell. The viscera (internal organs) are asymmetrically arranged owing to the degeneration of most of the organs on one side of the body (typically the left). This imbalance lends itself to coiling (which occurs during development): the organs of the right side rotate counterclockwise through 180° to the left side, making it appear as if the organs of the right side are degenerate. The coiling, or torsion, of the organs is considered an adaptation for compactly housing the very long visceral mass of the gastropod.

Many species have a well developed head, with a concentrated central nervous system and well developed sensory structures, including eyes and olfactory and taste receptors. Aquatic forms (marine and freshwater) use gills for respiration, but terrestrial forms and those aquatic forms evolved from terrestrial ancestors have replaced gills with lunglike modifications of the mantle (tissue covering the viscera) and mantle cavity.

Gastropods are sometimes eaten by humans. Snails and slugs can be serious agricultural pests, and some serve as intermediate hosts for a variety of trematode parasites that can infect humans (see FLATWORM). STEPHEN CHARLES REINGOLD

gastroscope [gas'-troh-skohp]

The gastroscope, an instrument that permits a physician to examine the inside of the stomach, is especially valuable for detecting disorders such as ulcers or tumors that are not seen on X-ray examination. It is usually a flexible, long, slender tube containing lenses and a light so placed that a moderate amount of bending produces no distortion of the image; the fiber-optic gastroscope carries the image by means of individual glass fibers. Some gastroscopes have facilities for taking tissue samples to be examined for cancer and may have a camera. DONALD LONGMORE

See also: ENDOSCOPE.

Gates, Horatio

Horatio Gates, a military commander during the Revolutionary War, led an American army to victory over a British force under Gen. John Burgoyne at Saratoga (1777) in one of the pivotal engagements of the war. This success established Gates as a rival to George Washington for supreme command, but Gates's rout in the Battle of Camden, S.C. (1780), resulted in his removal from command.

Horatio Gates was an American general who won the Battle of Saratoga, perhaps the most significant engagement of the AMERICAN REVOLUTION. Born in England on July 26, 1727, he entered the British army and served in America during the French and Indian War (1754–63). Retiring on half pay, he immigrated to America in 1772 and bought a Virginia plantation.

Gates became adjutant general of the Continental Army in 1775. Promoted to major general in 1776, he was placed in command of the northern army. On Oct. 17, 1777, Gen. John BURGOYNE surrendered his army to Gates at Saratoga after two fierce battles. Saratoga proved to be a turning point in the war, for it convinced France to become America's ally.

Gates was appointed president of the board of war in 1777. The alleged object of the CONWAY CABAL of that year was to replace Washington with Gates as commander in chief, but there is little evidence of a real conspiracy. Taking command of the southern army in 1780, Gates was disastrously defeated at Camden, S.C., on August 16 by Gen. Charles Cornwallis. Retiring to his Virginia plantation, Gates returned to active duty in 1782 at Newburgh, N.Y. Leaving the army in 1783, he moved eventually to Manhattan Island, where he died on Apr. 10, 1806. GEORGE ATHAN BILLIAS

Bibliography: Nelson, Paul D., *Horatio Gates* (1976); Patterson, Samuel W., *Horatio Gates* (1941).

See also: SARATOGA, BATTLES OF.

Gates, Sir Thomas

Sir Thomas Gates, d. 1621, was the English governor of the Virginia colony and one of the original investors in the LONDON COMPANY that founded Virginia. Before his involvement with the company, Gates was an adventurer on the high seas, sailing (1585) with Sir Francis Drake in a raid on the Spanish and commanding his own expeditions in the 1590s. In 1609, Gates was made second in command to Lord De La Warr, first governor of Virginia. When he set sail for Virginia, his ship was wrecked at Bermuda—an incident that allegedly inspired Shakespeare's *The Tempest*; but he finally reached JAMESTOWN in May 1610. He was about to evacuate the few colonists who had survived the bitter winter when De La Warr arrived and insisted that the settlers remain. Gates later brought in new settlers and livestock and governed the colony, after De La Warr's return to England, from 1611 to 1614.

RICHARD R. BEEMAN

Bibliography: Morton, Richard L., *Colonial Virginia*, 2 vols. (1960).

Gateshead [gayts'-hed]

Gateshead (1984 est. pop., 209,600) is an industrial city in northern England. Located on the River Tyne directly across from Newcastle upon Tyne, it forms part of Newcastle's metropolitan area. Gateshead's industries include shipbuilding, coal mining, and iron and steel, glass, and chemical manufacturing. St. Mary's Church (14th century) is a well-known landmark. Originating as a small settlement outside the fortress at Newcastle, Gateshead grew rapidly during the 19th century after coal mining began.

gating circuit

A gating circuit, in electronics, selectively passes an electrical signal at a predetermined time interval or when the signal meets certain specifications. The entire realm of digital electronics is dependent on complex arrays of interconnected gating circuits called logic gates. A typical logic gate has two inputs and one output. If the gate's output is activated only when both inputs receive a signal, it is called an AND gate. If the gate's output is activated when either input receives a signal, it is called an OR gate. FORREST M. MIMS III

Gatling, Richard Jordan [gat'-ling]

The American inventor Richard Gatling, b. Maney's Neck, N.C., Sept. 12, 1818, d. Feb. 26, 1903, is best known for his crank-operated MACHINE GUN, patented in 1862. The son of a North Carolina planter, Gatling made a fortune before the Civil War from his agricultural inventions, among them a steam-powered plow. His gun was capable of firing 350 rounds a minute through its rotating multiple barrels. Although there is evidence that the Gatling was used during the war, it did not become official U.S. Army weaponry until 1866. It remained in use until 1911, when the introduction of smokeless powder made possible the gas-operated Maxim gun. *Gat,* the slang term for pistol, is derived from Gatling's name.

Bibliography: Johnson, F. R., and Stephenson, F., Jr., *The Gatling Gun and Flying Machine of Richard and Henry Gatling* (1979).

GATT: see GENERAL AGREEMENT ON TARIFFS AND TRADE.

Gatti-Casazza, Giulio [gaht'-tee-kah-zaht'-tsah]

The legendary impresario Giulio Gatti-Casazza, b. Feb. 3, 1868, d. Sept. 2, 1940, was one of the great opera administrators of the 20th century. During the 10 years (1898–1908) he was its director, he made La Scala the leading Italian opera house. In 1908 he was appointed general director of the Metropolitan Opera, a post he held for 27 years. He encouraged American composers to write operas, and produced 110 new works by internationally known composers. Among those operas were Humperdinck's *Königskinder*, Puccini's *Girl of the Golden West*, Granados's *Goyescas*, and Giordano's *Madame Sans-Gêne*. He engaged the best conductors, bringing Arturo Toscanini with him from La Scala, and improved the orchestra, chorus, and all other departments of the company. Through his administrative genius the Metropolitan reached a peak of artistic and financial success. In 1935 he retired and returned to Italy. ELLA A. MALIN

Bibliography: Gatti-Casazza, Giulio, *Memories of the Opera*, ed. by Howard Taubman (1941; repr. 1973); Kolodin, Irving, *The Metropolitan Opera, 1883-1935*, rev. ed. (1966).

Gaudí, Antonio [gow-dee']

The Catalan architect Antonio (Antoni) Gaudí i Cornet, b. June 25, 1852, d. June 7, 1926, was one of the most eccentric and original geniuses in the development of modern art. His extremely personal style evolved without any perceptible contemporary influence, and he arrived independently at an equivalent of the international ART NOUVEAU style.

The remarkable Casa Milá apartment house in Barcelona, designed by the Spanish architect Antonio Gaudí, is a fantastic construction embodying the curvilinear Art Nouveau style. Despite its fluid and organic appearance, the building is constructed of cut stone and roofed with marble slabs. Two courtyards flow into the interior with the same rhythmic pattern characteristic of the exterior. Spiraled chimneys and ironwork balconies ornament the facade.

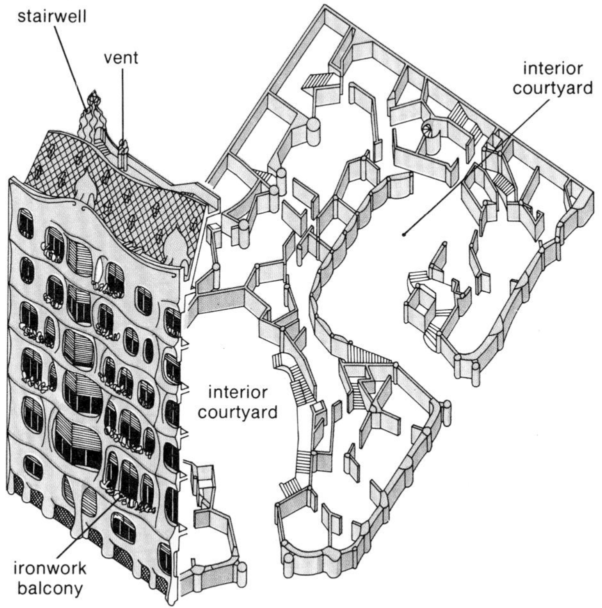

In the Palau Güell (1885-89), a town mansion for his patron Eusebio Güell, Gaudí forecast his ultimate fantastical style in this building, especially in the highly original forms of the ironwork and in the sculptural roofscape of chimneys and cornices. Güell also sponsored the spectacular Parque Güell (1900-14), a hilly site in the heart of Barcelona that Gaudí dotted with biomorphic, cavelike pavilions and galleries and linked serpentine benches completely surfaced with mosaics of broken glass tile.

In 1884, Gaudí began the monumental task that occupied him until his death and that remains unfinished, the vast Expiatory Temple of the Holy Family—the Sagrada Familia—in Barcelona. Gaudí at first continued in the Gothic Revival style set by his predecessor Francisco del Villár (1845-1922). As the building progressed, however, Gaudí revised the plans until, by 1900, the building designs were entirely without precedent, as seen in the four colossal openwork spires—outer pair, 98.4 m (323 ft), inner pair, 107 m (351 ft)—of the completed entrance facade.

Two important works are the Casa Batlló (1905-07) and the Casa Milá (1905-10) in Barcelona. In the first Gaudí transformed an existing building, creating bulging bays with bonelike frames on the lower levels, fronting the rectangular upper windows with bizarre wrought-iron balconies, and covering its undulating overall surfaces with mosaics. Even more striking is the larger Casa Milá, which resembles a rocky cliff face eroded by the weather, a naturalistic effect painstakingly created in hand-worked stone. On the roof various abstract forms enclose chimneys, ventilators, and stairwell exits, with stepped terraces covering changes in roof level. No less original are the wrought-iron balconies and window grills, which resemble masses of tangled seaweed clinging to the stratified floor levels.

Gaudí had no influence whatever beyond Barcelona until decades after his death, when his innovative forms and constructed environments were reflected in avant-garde architecture, painting, and sculpture. BETTY ELZEA

Bibliography: Cirlot, Juan E., *The Genesis of Gaudian Architecture*, trans. by J. Wittenborn (1967); Collins, George R., *Antonio Gaudí* (1960); Hitchcock, Henry-Russell, *Gaudí* (1967); Martinell, Cesar, *Gaudí*, ed. by George Collins, trans. by Judith Rohrer (1975); Sweeney, J. J., and Sert, J. L., *Antonio Gaudí, rev. ed. (1970).*

Gaudier-Brzeska, Henri [goh-dee-ay'-bur-zes-kah']

Henri Gaudier-Brzeska, b. Oct. 4, 1891, d. June 5, 1915, was a French sculptor whose considerable fame rests on a relatively small number of works produced in London between 1912 and 1914. Gaudier-Brzeska rapidly assimilated the influence of Auguste RODIN and contemporary CUBISM, and, like many other artists of his time, admired primitive African and Asian wood carving and stone carving. From 1911 he lived in London and associated with the vorticist group of artists and writers (see VORTICISM). Gaudier-Brzeska worked in wood, marble, stone, and bronze, forming heads, figures, and animals—many of which are almost miniature in size.

BARBARA CAVALIERE

Bibliography: Cole, Roger, *Burning to Speak: The Life and Art of Henri Gaudier-Brzeska* (1978); Ede, H. S., *Savage Messiah* (1972); Pound, Ezra, *Gaudier-Brzeska* (1916; repr. 1970).

Gauguin, Paul [goh-gan']

Paul Gauguin, b. Paris, June 7, 1848, d. May 8, 1903, was one of the leading figures in postimpressionist French art of the 1880s and '90s (see POSTIMPRESSIONISM). Both his personality and his principles of coloring and composition exerted a strong influence on modern painting.

Gauguin spent 4 years of his childhood with his mother in Peru—an experience of the tropics that he never forgot—and returned to France in 1855. In 1865 he joined the merchant navy and made several long sea voyages. Gauguin obtained a

The French post-Impressionist painter Paul Gauguin revitalized his art by directly experiencing primitive culture. This portrait of Tahitian Women *(1891) was painted during his first year in Tahiti. Despite the exotic dress and setting, the heavy, monumental forms of these women reveal Gauguin's classical heritage. (Louvre, Paris.)*

position with a stockbrokerage firm in 1871 and married a Dane, Mette Gad, in 1873, with whom he had five children. During this period he was essentially a "Sunday" painter, pursuing his art on weekends and in the summer, but in 1875 he met Camille PISSARRO and began to work with him to improve his drawing and painting. The financial crash of 1882-83 left him without work and prompted his decision to become a full-time artist. Successive moves—to Rouen in 1883 and to Copenhagen in 1884—brought Gauguin no commercial or critical success. Finally he abandoned his wife and family in Denmark and returned to France accompanied only by his son Clovis.

Prior to this time Gauguin's painting displayed the marks of his gradual assimilation of the principles and techniques of IMPRESSIONISM. Now he began experimenting with ceramics and sculpture, and moved rapidly toward a firmness of composition and a concern for rhythm and mass in painting. In 1887 he went to Panama and Martinique but was forced home by illness and lack of funds. In 1888, Gauguin returned to Brittany, which he had first visited in 1886. There he painted *Vision After the Sermon* (1888; National Gallery of Scotland, Edinburgh), in which Breton women returning from church see a vision of the biblical struggle between Jacob and the angel, about which the priest has just preached. The use of bold color and strongly defined forms, together with a subject that combines the visionary and the real in one composition, marked a decisive breakthrough for Gauguin. After spending a few months at Arles with Vincent VAN GOGH at the end of 1888, Gauguin passed the next few years in Brittany, where he continued to paint the local people and their way of life and simple faith, and in Paris, where he established contact with the leading writers and theorists of the symbolist movement. Although Gauguin called the style he developed in 1888 *synthetism*, he now instilled into his work qualities of mystery and suggestiveness that may be compared with symbolism in literature.

Early in 1891, Gauguin left for Tahiti, where he began a series of paintings that depict the physical beauty of the people and the myths underlying their traditional religion. The series evokes the Tahitian cycle of existence from birth through maturity to old age and death. Gauguin visited France for the last time in 1893-95, then returned to Tahiti. Plagued increasingly by ill health and poverty, he attempted suicide in 1898 after completing, by way of a last testament to his vision of Tahiti, *Where Do We Come From? What Are We? Where Are We Going?* (1897-98; Museum of Fine Arts, Boston). The paintings of his final years project an idealized vision of native life, removed from both time and actuality in its conception of the physical and spiritual dimensions of Tahitian culture. His last journey was to La Dominique in the Marquesas, where he died. MARK ROSKILL

Bibliography: Boudaille, Georges, *Gauguin: His Life and Work*, trans. by Alisa Jaffe (1964); Estienne, Charles, *Gauguin*, trans. by James Emmons (1953); Gauguin, Paul, *Noa Noa*, trans. by O. F. Theis (1957) and *Avant et Après (The Intimate Journals of Paul Gauguin)*, trans. by Van Wyck Brooks (1921); Goldwater, Robert, *Gauguin* (1957); Huyghe, René, *Gauguin*, trans. by Helen C. Slonim (1954).

Gaul [gawl]

Gaul (from the Latin *Gallia*) was the ancient name for an area roughly equivalent to modern France, Belgium, Luxembourg, and Germany west of the Rhine. In Italy, the Po Valley was called Gallia Cisalpina ("Gaul this side of the Alps") by the Romans. The CELTS, whom the Romans called Galli (Gauls), began to cross the Rhine into Gaul *c.*900 BC and by the 5th century BC had established a fairly uniform culture typified by the art of LA TÈNE. Along the Mediterranean coast Greek civilization was introduced with the founding of Massilia (now Marseille) *c.*600 BC.

To protect its ally Massilia and ensure communications with Spain, Rome annexed a strip of territory between the Cévennes and the Alps in 121 BC. Roughly equivalent to the modern Provence, this became known first as Gallia Transalpina ("Gaul across the Alps") and later as Gallia Narbonensis ("Narbonese Gaul"). Julius CAESAR conquered the rest of Gaul, called Comata ("Long-haired Gaul"), during his GALLIC WARS (58-51 BC). Three new Roman provinces eventually emerged: Belgica, Lugdunensis, and Aquitania.

Emperor CLAUDIUS I, who was born at Lugdunum (now

Lyon), admitted Gallic nobles to the Roman Senate in AD 48. He also ordered the suppression of the DRUIDS, the Celtic priests. Native deities were amalgamated with Roman counterparts, and emperor worship was encouraged. By the 4th century AD, however, Christianity predominated and weakened Celtic culture further by using Latin in worship.

In the 1st and 2d centuries AD, Gaul flourished through the export of food, wine, and pottery. In the 3d century it suffered devastating barbarian raids, however, and the Roman emperors' ineffective defense led to the creation *c.*260 of a short-lived kingdom of the Gauls. Beginning in 406 various Germanic tribes, especially VANDALS, ravaged Gaul. The Visigoths (see GOTHS), nominally Roman allies, settled in Aquitaine, where they cooperated with the Roman general Flavius AETIUS in the defeat (451) of the HUNS. By 478 the Visigoths had also acquired Narbonensis. Meanwhile, the FRANKS took over northern Gaul, and the Alamani and Burgundians settled in the east. The last Roman territory in Gaul fell to CLOVIS, king of the Franks, in 486. ALLEN M. WARD

Bibliography: Brogen, Olwen, *Roman Gaul* (1953); Ebel, Charles, *Transalpine Gaul, The Emergence of a Roman Province* (1976); Hatt, Jean-Jacques, *Celts and Gallo-Romans*, trans. by James Hogarth (1970); MacKendrick, Paul, *Roman France* (1972); Powell, T. G. E., *The Celts*, 2d ed. (1960).

See also: FRANCE, HISTORY OF; ROME, ANCIENT.

Gaulle, Charles de: see DE GAULLE, CHARLES.

Gaulli, Giovanni Battista [gah-ool'-lee]

Giovanni Battista Gaulli, called Il Baciccio, b. 1639, d. Apr. 2, 1709, was the first artist to bring Giovanni Lorenzo BERNINI's ideas of high baroque religious art (see BAROQUE ART AND ARCHITECTURE) to fruition in painting . An early study of Correggio's illusionist painted domes in Parma was crucial to Baciccio's later work in Rome, where he arrived in 1660. By means of Bernini's influence, Baciccio won the commission for the decoration of the ceiling of the church of the Il Gesù in Rome. The result was his masterpiece, a great cycle of illusionist paintings (1672-83) that includes *The Adoration of the Name of Jesus.* Baciccio's technique of combining fresco with painted stucco to create an illusion of architecture remained in use for the next 30 years. The hallmarks of Baciccio's style are use of dramatic lighting to create an upward movement within the composition and highly sculptural treatment of human figures. THOMAS W. SOKOLOWSKI

Bibliography: Enggass, Robert, *The Painting of Baciccio, 1639-1709* (1964).

gaur [gowr]

The gaur, B. gaurus, *a huge wild ox weighing more than a ton, lives in mountainous regions of southeast and central Asia.*

The gaur, *Bos gaurus,* family Bovidae, order Artiodactyla, is the largest species of wild cattle. A bull may be 3 m (10 ft) long, with a shoulder height of over 2 m (7 ft) and a weight of 1,000 kg (2,200 lb). The coat is reddish brown to black, with white stockings. Gaurs live in rocky, forested highlands, up to an elevation of 1,800 m (6,000 ft), in India and Southeast Asia. They move in herds of 5 to 20. The cow bears a single calf. EVERETT SENTMAN

Gauss, Carl Friedrich [gows]

The mathematician Carl Friedrich Gauss calculated the orbit of the asteroid Ceres after only three observations and was made director of the Göttingen observatory for his achievement. He published his work in number theory in Disquisitiones arithmeticae *and later made contributions in differential geometry and topology.*

Carl Friedrich Gauss, b. Apr. 30, 1777, d. Feb. 23, 1855, was a German mathematician who dominated the mathematical community during and after his lifetime. A child prodigy, Gauss taught himself reading and arithmetic by the age of three. Recognizing his talent, the Duke of Brunswick in 1792 provided him with a stipend to allow him to pursue his education. While still attending Caroline College (1792-95), Gauss formulated the least-squares method and a conjecture on the distribution of prime numbers among all numbers; the latter was proved by Jacques Hadamard in 1896. During this period, Gauss did not have access to a good mathematical library and therefore rediscovered many theorems that had already been accepted. The situation changed in 1795, when he went to Göttingen with its excellent library.

In 1795, Gauss discovered the fundamental theorem of quadratic residues, which deals with the concept of congruence in number theory. In 1796 he made his first mark as a serious mathematician by proving the possibility of constructing a regular 17-sided polygon using only a ruler and a compass. The next 4 years were very productive. Ideas came to him so rapidly that he could pursue only some of them. In 1799 the University of Helmstedt granted Gauss a Ph.D. degree for a dissertation that gave the first proof of the fundamental theorem of algebra.

Gauss had two major achievements in 1801. The first was the publication of his *Disquisitiones arithmeticae*, a treatise on number theory, which contained his solutions to many outstanding problems. This book set the pattern for future research and won Gauss major recognition among mathematicians. The second was caused by the discovery of the asteroid Ceres. It had been briefly observed in January 1801 but had then disappeared from view. Gauss computed the orbit using an improved theory and predicted where and when Ceres would reappear. When the prediction was proved correct, Gauss's fame spread far and wide. He subsequently accepted a financially secure position as astronomer at the Göttingen Observatory.

To fulfill his sense of civic responsibility, Gauss undertook a geodetic survey of his country and did much of the field work himself. In his theoretical work on surveying; Gauss developed results he needed from statistics and differential geometry. During the 1820s, with the collaboration of the physicist Wilhelm Weber, he explored many areas of physics, including magnetism, mechanics, acoustics, and optics. In 1833 he constructed the first telegraph. Gauss's publications were polished and finished works that opened new paths for investigation and contained the seeds of much future work. To date 12 volumes have been published. ARTHUR SCHLISSEL

Bibliography: Dunnington, G. Waldo, *Carl Friedrich Gauss: Titan of Science* (1955); Hall, Tord, *Carl Friedrich Gauss: A Biography* (1970); Schaaf, William L., *Carl Friedrich Gauss: Prince of Mathematicians* (1964); Turnball, Herbert, *The Great Mathematicians* (1929; repr. 1961).

Gaussian distribution: see NORMAL DISTRIBUTION.

Gautama, Siddhartha: see BUDDHA.

Gautier, Théophile [goh-tee-ay', tay-oh-feel']

The French poet and novelist Théophile Gautier was a pivotal figure in the transition from romanticism to naturalism in 19th-century French literature. A distinguished critic of art, dance, literature, and theater, Gautier postulated "art for art's sake" and in such works as Enamels and Cameos *(1852) exemplified his theory of austere objectivity as the sole purpose of artistic endeavor.*

Théophile Gautier, b. Aug. 30, 1811, d. Oct, 23, 1872, was one of the finest and most versatile French romantic writers (see ROMANTICISM, literature). He distinguished himself at an early age as an essayist and poet, and became a member, with Victor Hugo and Gérard de Nerval, of a flamboyant clique of writers devoted to romantic ideals. His gifts for picturesque imagery and unusual diction, apparent in *Albertus* (1832) and *Comedy of Death* (1838), reached their highest level in *Enamels and Cameos* (1852). Gautier's sensitivity to beauty and insistence on formal perfection inspired Charles Baudelaire and the PARNASSIAN movement.

After 1835, Gautier earned his living as a journalist, novelist, and travel writer. He produced numerous occasional articles and reviews for Paris newspapers, becoming an influential critic of art, literature, and the theater. His first important novel, *Mademoiselle de Maupin* (1835), was prefaced by a witty and provactive manifesto of the doctrine of "Art for Art's sake." A prolific body of prose writing followed, including *Young France* (1833), an affectionate satiric portrait of the excesses of his contemporaries; "The Dead Lover" (1836; Eng. trans., 1903), a ghost story of incomparable skill; and *The Romance of the Mummy* (1856; Eng. trans., 1863), a historical novel of ancient Egypt. Gautier traveled extensively in order to write *A Romantic in Spain* (1845; Eng. trans., 1926); *Journeys in Italy* (1852; Eng. trans., 1902); *Constantinople of Today* (1853; Eng. trans., 1854); *Voyage en Russie* (Travels in Russia, 1867); and a novel set in England, *La Belle Jenny* (1865). He also wrote two plays, but his attempts at drama were less successful than were his two ballet scripts, *Giselle* (1841) and *La Péri* (1843).

Bibliography: Grant, Richard, *Théophile Gautier* (1975); Richardson, Joanna, *Théophile Gautier: His Life and Times* (1958); Smith, Albert, *Ideal and Reality in the Fictional Narratives of Théophile Gautier* (1969) and *Théophile Gautier and the Fantastic* (1977); Tennant, P. E., *Théophile Gautier* (1975).

Gavarni, Paul [gah-vahr-nee']

Paul Gavarni was the pseudonym of Guillaume Sulpice Chevalier, b. Jan. 13, 1804, d. Nov. 24, 1866, French lithographer and caricaturist. Trained as a copperplate engraver, Gavarni became a fashion illustrator during the late 1820s. His elegant and witty portrayals of the fashionable Parisians of his day , appearing in satirical publications such as *Caricature* and *Charivari*, were popular in both France and England. The highly prolific Gavarni drew directly on the lithographic stones without using sketches or preparatory drawings; the resulting images of servant girls, courtesans, boulevardiers, and middle-class couples have an immediacy and intimacy that makes them come alive. On a visit (1847–51) to England, Gavarni observed slum dwellers and rural poor, and the harshness of the prints inspired by this experience lost him many of his earlier admirers. Gavarni's work after his return to Paris became more somber and increasingly portrayed the darker side of life, but without the mastery of his great contemporary Honoré DAUMIER. STEPHANIE M. WINKELBAUER

Gavarnie Falls [gah-vahr-nee']

Gavarnie Falls, fed by the mountain stream Gave de Pau, spills 422 m (1,385 ft) down the sheer eastern rock face of Cirque de Gavarnie, a vast, natural amphitheater in the French Pyrenees. Above the waterfall rises Pic de Marbore, a 3,256-m (10,681-ft) peak on the Spanish-French border.

gavial [gay'-vee-ul]

The gavial, *Gavialis gangeticus*, or gharial, is a crocodilian originally found in a number of river systems, including the Indus River of India and Pakistan, Ganges and Brahmaputra rivers of India and Bangladesh, and the Kaladan River of western Burma. Gavials are the sole living member of the family Gavialidae. They are one of the largest crocodilians, reaching adult lengths of 3.5 to 4.5 m (12 to 15 ft) with a recorded maximum of 6.5 m (21.5 ft). Their snout is more slender than any other crocodilian, an adaptation that allows

The Indian gavial, Gavialis gangeticus, *is a large crocodilian. Measuring 4 to 5 m (13 to 16 ft), it has a narrow, elongated snout adapted for catching fish by quick sideways movement.*

them to rapidly slash sideways in the water to catch fish, which constitute the bulk of their diet. Gavials occasionally eat birds and small mammals, but they are not known to attack humans. Since the 1950s gavials have been brought to the edge of extinction due to dam building, hide hunting, and net fishing. It is thought that no more than a hundred survive in the wild. The Indian government, however, has established several preserves with the hope of saving the species.

JONATHAN CAMPBELL

gavotte [guh-vaht']

The gavotte was a lively peasant dance in 4/4 time that was derived from the *branle*. It originated during the 14th century with the Gavots, inhabitants of the French Alpine town Gap. A line or circle of couples began the dance on the third of four beats, hopped and swayed rhythmically, and regularly exchanged kisses. In the 17th century the court of Louis XIV appropriated the gavotte, overlaid its vitality with formality, and replaced the kisses with bouquets. During the 19th century the dance's original ebullience had vanished into the virtuosic vocabulary of theatrical dance. The gavotte was often included in the dance suites of baroque composers.

BARBARA NEWMAN

Gawain, Sir [gah'-win]

In the Arthurian legends Sir Gawain was King Arthur's nephew, the son of King Lot of Orkney and Morgawse. *Sir Gawain and the Green Knight*, a 14th-century romance, is the most famous legend about him. His name and some of his attributes suggest that he was identified with or related to the Celtic sun deity.

See also: ARTHUR AND ARTHURIAN LEGEND.

Gay, John

John Gay, an English dramatist of the 18th century, is remembered chiefly for his satire of social and literary conventions. Gay's most durable work, The Beggar's Opera *(1728), lampooned genteel Italian opera by casting the dregs of English society in roles traditionally reserved for heroic characters.*

A leading poet and playwright of the English AUGUSTAN AGE, John Gay, b. June 30, 1685, d. Dec. 4, 1732, is best known for The BEGGAR'S OPERA (1728).

After grammar school Gay served a brief, unhappy apprenticeship to a merchant. A former schoolmate helped him publish his first poem, "Wine," in 1708, and thereafter he rose quickly to notice. By 1711 he had become friendly with Sir Richard Steele, Joseph Addison, and Alexander Pope. With Pope and Jonathan Swift he founded the Scriblerus Club (1714). He later held a government sinecure and in his last years enjoyed the patronage of the duke of Queensbury.

Gay's major works treat low realistic subjects and parody traditional forms and styles. *The Shepherd's Week* (1714) parodies the style of pastoral poetry, especially *The Shepheardes Calender* (1579) by Edmund Spenser; *The What D'Ye Call It* (1715) burlesques contemporary tragedy; *Trivia, or the Art of Walking the Streets of London* (1716) imitates the *Georgics* of Vergil by describing city scenes in the same manner Vergil used to describe the country. *The Beggar's Opera* ludicrously mingles elements of ballad and Italian opera in a satire on Sir Robert Walpole, who was then England's prime minister. Its vehicle is opera, but its characters are criminals and prostitutes. An unprecedented stage success in its time, it later inspired the German dramatist Bertolt Brecht to write his best-known work, The THREEPENNY OPERA (1928).

Gay's other works include *Rural Sports* (poem, 1713), *Three Hours After Marriage* (stage comedy, with Pope and John Arbuthnot, 1717), and *Fables* (2 vols., 1727 and 1738).

WILLIAM MCCARTHY

Bibliography: Gay, John, *Letters of John Gay*, ed. by C. F. Burgess (1966); Irving, William H., *John Gay: Favorite of the Wits* (1940); Melville, Lewis, *Life and Letters of John Gay* (1921).

gay activism

Gay activism is the effort to eliminate all forms of prejudice and discrimination against homosexual women and men. It may be viewed as part of a broad cultural reevaluation of the traditional male and female roles that has been fostered by the women's movement and by human potential and self-help groups, which stress individual self-realization rather than conformity to socially imposed patterns.

The impetus for gay activism came from social movements of the 1950s and '60s that demanded full individual and human rights for members of racial, religious, and ethnic minorities, and from the insistence by members of these groups on the right to cultural diversity and self-determination. It coincided with worldwide concern about overpopulation and with the so-called sexual revolution, which together challenged the procreative model of human sexuality. Gay activists, however, have emphasized human rights and dignities more than sexual freedom.

Homosexual rights organizations flourished in Germany and England from the 1860s through the 1920s, and in the 1950s several major homophile groups were established in the United States, Great Britain, and the Netherlands. The use of the term *gay activism* in the early 1970s was sparked by the so-called Stonewall Riots of June 1969, in which groups of gay men and women for the first time resisted police harassment outside a homosexual bar in New York City. Within three years the number of gay groups in the United States grew from fewer than 20 to about 1,200, and similar groups emerged in Western Europe, Latin America, Canada, Australia, and Japan.

The primary aim of U.S. organizations was the passage of civil-rights laws similar to those forbidding discrimination on the basis of race, religion, ethnic origin, and sex. They also worked for the repeal of all laws criminalizing any form of sexual behavior between consenting adults in private. Gay activists outside the United States focused principally on eliminating local discriminatory practices.

In 1973 the American Psychiatric Association removed homosexuality from its list of psychiatric disorders, an action that significantly aided gay activists lobbying for civil rights. By the late 1970s gay caucuses had formed within the major religious denominations and professional groups, and scores of gay political and legal organizations had come into being, some of them national in scope.

By 1986 more than 50 U.S. county and local governments (along with one state, Wisconsin) had enacted civil-rights protection for homosexuals. Openly gay political candidates had been elected to office, ranging from city councils to the House of Representatives. Newspapers frequently carried accounts of individual homosexuals seeking rights: to adopt children, to serve in the military, or to be ordained in the ministry.

Crucially affected by the AIDS crisis of the 1980s (see AIDS), the gay community responded in numerous ways. Such groups as the Gay Men's Health Crisis in New York City offered support and information. In Los Angeles and other cities, city councils passed ordinances protecting persons with AIDS from discrimination in jobs, housing, or health care.

THOMAS B. STODDARD

Bibliography: Adam, Barry D., *The Rise of a Gay and Lesbian Movement* (1987); Brown, Howard, *Familiar Faces, Hidden Lives* (1976); D'Emilio, John, *Sexual Politics, Sexual Communities* (1983); Katz, Jonathan, *Gay American History* (1976); National Gay Task Force, *Twenty Questions about Homosexuality* (1978); Rueda, Enrique T., *Homosexual Network: Private Lives and Public Policy* (1983); Stoddard, Thomas B., et al., *The Rights of Gay People* (1983); Vida, Ginny, ed., *Our Right to Love: A Lesbian Resource Book* (1978).

See also: CIVIL RIGHTS; HOMOSEXUALITY.

Gay-Lussac, Joseph Louis [gay-loo-sahk']

One of the leading scientists of his generation, the Frenchman Joseph Louis Gay-Lussac, b. Dec. 6, 1778, d. May 9, 1850, made his chief contributions in physical and inorganic chemistry. His earliest investigations led to the formulation of the law, sometimes credited to his countryman J. A. C. Charles, that all gases expand by equal amounts when subjected to equal increments in temperature. Subsequently he announced another fundamental generalization, that gases combine chemically in simple proportions by volume. Seized upon by the Italian physicist Amedeo Avogadro, this law helped pave the way for the modern atomic-molecular theory of matter.

Gay-Lussac was first to isolate the element boron, thus winning a rare victory over his scientific rival, Sir Humphrey Davy. Gay-Lussac enjoyed a high reputation for his exacting research in many areas of chemistry and for his novel techniques of chemical analysis, particularly volumetric analysis. In connection with the latter he introduced the terms *pipette* and *burette*.

ROBERT SILLIMAN

Bibliography: Crosland, Maurice, *The Society of Arcueil* (1967).

See also: CHEMISTRY, HISTORY OF.

Gay-Lussac's law: see GAS LAWS.

Gaza [gah'-zuh]

Gaza is the principal city in the so-called Gaza Strip. It lies in the coastal plain north of the Sinai Peninsula about 5 km (3 mi) east of the Mediterranean Sea and about 80 km (50 mi) southwest of Jerusalem. Its population, about one-fourth of which live in United Nations–supported Palestinian refugee camps, was in 1979 estimated at 120,000.

An important settlement along ancient trade routes, Gaza has been fought over since before the 15th century BC. It was one of the five cities of the Philistine League (see PHILISTINES) and is mentioned frequently in the Bible, notably as the site of the Philistine temple that Samson brought down on himself and his enemies (Judges 16). Since its capture by Arabs in the 7th century, it has been inhabited by Muslims. A part of Palestine, it was occupied by Egypt in the Arab-Israeli War of 1948 and became one of the main sites of Palestinian refugee concentration. Gaza was captured by Israel in the Six-Day War of 1967 and remains under Israeli administration.

Gaza Strip

The Gaza Strip is a narrow band of land along the western Mediterranean coast that is occupied by Israel. It is about 42 km (26 mi) long and 6.5 to 8 km (4 to 5 mi) wide and has a land area of 363 km^2 (140 mi^2). From 1917 to 1948 the Gaza Strip was part of the British mandate of Palestine. Since the Arab-Israeli War of 1948 the political status of Gaza has been unresolved, with its Palestinian residents seeking autonomy. Egypt controlled it (except for a brief period of Israeli occupation in 1956–57) until the Six Day War of 1967, when it was occupied by Israel. The Egyptian-Israeli peace treaty of 1979 provided for future negotiations concerning the strip's status, but little progress was made. In December 1987 frustrated Palestinians in the West Bank and Gaza Strip launched an *intifadah* (uprising) to end Israeli occupation.

The Gaza Strip is very densely populated, with a youthful and rapidly growing population of 559,849 (1987 est.). More than 99% of the residents are stateless Palestinian Arabs. About 75% are refugees from Israel, most of whom have lived in refugee camps since 1948. Gaza is the administrative center. The economy centers on agriculture, livestock raising, fishing, and small industry; nearly 50% of the labor force commutes to menial jobs in Israel. The climate is desertlike.

Bibliography: Roy, Sara M., *The Gaza Strip* (1986).

gazebo [guh-zee'-boh]

A gazebo is a small decorative building or garden house, usually open on all sides, offering an excellent view of the surrounding landscape. The term, a facetious combination of the word *gaze* and the Latin suffix *-ebo*, meaning "I shall," first appeared in *New Designs for Chinese Temples* (1752) by the English architect William Halfpenny and his son John Halfpenny. Gazebo also refers to an ornamental turret, or belvedere, set on the roof of a building to provide a broad view.

gazelle [guh-zel']

Gazelles *(Gazella)* are slender, graceful ANTELOPES belonging to the family Bovidae, order Artiodactyla. There are about 12

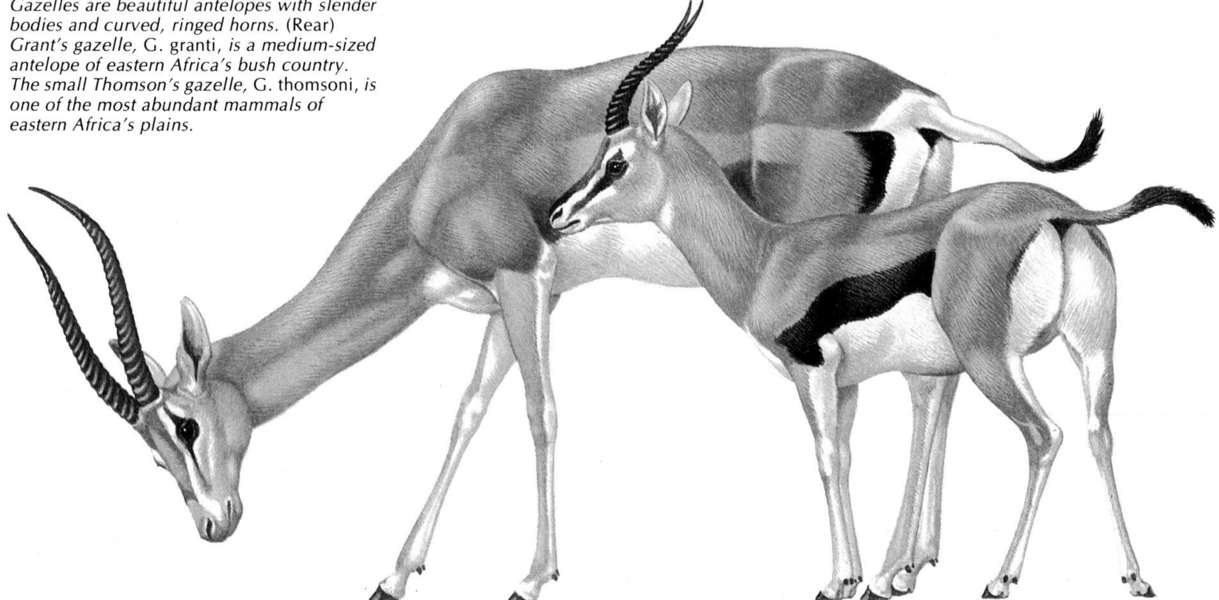

Gazelles are beautiful antelopes with slender bodies and curved, ringed horns. (Rear) *Grant's gazelle,* G. granti, *is a medium-sized antelope of eastern Africa's bush country. The small Thomson's gazelle,* G. thomsoni, *is one of the most abundant mammals of eastern Africa's plains.*

species and 50 recognized forms. The largest gazelle is the dama, or red-necked, gazelle, *Gazella damaruficollis*, of northern Africa, which stands slightly less than 1 m (3 ft) tall at the shoulder. Other species are 51 to 86 cm (20 to 34 in) tall. Gazelles have long, thin legs with two-toed hoofs. Both sexes have beautiful, black-ringed, 25- to 38-cm (10- to 15-in) horns, except for the Persian, or goitered, gazelle, only the bucks of which have horns. Grant's gazelle, *Gazella granti*, of eastern Africa has 81-cm (32-in) horns—as long as the animal is tall. Gazelles have brown or fawn-colored coats, usually with black and white markings around the face and neck, white undersides and rump, and often a horizontal band of dark color along the flanks. The ears are long and narrow. The tail is short. The large, luminous black eyes are a striking feature. Many gazelles are fast runners, and Grant's gazelle has been clocked at 80 km/h (50 mph).

Gazelles inhabit open plains from Mongolia and India to Egypt and Morocco and into tropical eastern and central Africa. Several species have become threatened because of overhunting. Gazelles graze in herds numbering from four or five to several hundred. Central and eastern African gazelles often mingle with herds of other herbivores. Like other antelopes, gazelles are ruminants, or cud-chewers. They live 10 to 12 years.

For hundreds of years the Bedouins of the Middle East have tamed gazelle fawns as pets. The name *gazelle* is derived from an Arabic word meaning "affectionate," and "gazelle-like" has become a synonym for grace and beauty.

EVERETT SENTMAN

Gdańsk [guh-dahnsk']

Gdańsk (Danzig), a port city in Poland, has a population of 467,200 (1984 est.). The city lies at the mouth of the VISTULA RIVER on the Baltic Sea; the surrounding land is low-lying, and both water defenses and dock basins were easily carved from the soft alluvium.

The ports of Gdańsk and its twin city Gdynia (to the north) are operated under a single port authority. Gdańsk's industries include shipbuilding, engineering, food processing, and chemical manufacturing. The old city consists of straight streets intersecting at right angles. In postmedieval times, Gdańsk spread outside the original walls and extended to the east, beyond the Motława, a tributary of the Vistula. The city was severely damaged during World War II but has been rebuilt and the old city restored to its former splendor.

A settlement existed there during the 10th century, but the commercial city grew up during the 12th and 13th centuries with the development of the HANSEATIC LEAGUE and Baltic trade. It became the major port of the Vistula basin and attained its greatest prosperity during the 16th and 17th centuries, when it was the principal grain market in Europe; several Renaissance graneries survive. Although Gdańsk underwent a decline during the 18th century, it remained the region's leading port until the 1920s.

In the second Partition of Poland (1793), Gdańsk, whose population was mixed German and Polish, was absorbed into Prussia. After World War I, Gdańsk was not given to the reconstituted Polish state because of its largely German population. Instead, it was constituted a free city under the sovereignty of the League of Nations. Although it was intended that Gdańsk should serve the needs of Poland, increasing difficulties with the German population led Poland to establish (1924) a new port at Gdynia in the POLISH CORRIDOR. From 1933 to 1939, Gdańsk's elected senate was dominated by the Nazis, who agitated for union with Germany. Germany's claim to annex the city was an important factor in causing World War II. At the end of the war the city was fully incorporated into Poland; most of the German majority either fled or were driven out in 1945, and the city was repopulated largely by Polish refugees from further east.

Gdańsk has long been a center of opposition to Poland's Communist government. The historic agreement allowing Polish workers to form independent unions was signed in the city on Aug. 31, 1980. On Dec. 31, 1981, a day after SOLIDARITY leaders meeting in Gdańsk called for free elections, the government abolished the labor organization and imposed martial law throughout Poland.

NORMAN J. G. POUNDS

Gdynia [guh-din'-ee-uh]

Gdynia is a major seaport in northern Poland on the Baltic Sea. Located about 19 km (12 mi) northwest of GDAŃSK (Danzig), it is part of a metropolitan conurbation that includes Sopot and Gdańsk. The population is 243,100 (1984 est.).

Port activities are the major employer, and principal exports include iron ore, lumber, coal, and food products. Gdynia is also the main base of the Polish Navy and contains several military schools.

Originally a small fishing village, Gdynia is a relatively new city. Its harbor was not developed until 1923, when the Polish government wanted an alternative to Gdańsk, which had a large German population. Much of the city was destroyed during World War II, but it has since been largely rebuilt.

gear

A gear is a toothed wheel or, less commonly, an object of some other shape with teeth cut into it, for example, a cylinder or cone. Gears are usually fastened to axles or shafts and are used to transmit rotational motion from one shaft to another. In doing this, gears change the direction of the force applied and may also change the magnitude of the force. They thus function as a machine. In fact, they are often considered a form of the wheel and axle, one of the basic SIMPLE MACHINES.

When two gears are arranged so that the teeth of one mesh, or mate, with the teeth of the other, the turning of one gear will cause the other one to turn also. If the two gears have the same number of teeth, they will turn at the same rate of rotation (angular velocity), and the applied force and turning effort (TORQUE) are changed in direction, but not in magnitude. If the gears have different numbers of teeth, however, the magnitude of the torque and the angular velocity are also changed.

A small gear (one with fewer teeth) that drives a larger one (with more teeth) will increase the torque and reduce the speed of the driven gear. The opposite arrangement (a larger gear driving a smaller gear) will decrease the torque while increasing the speed. As with other machines these effects can be described in terms of the mechanical advantage of the system, which is the ratio of the torque of the driven shaft to that of the driving shaft.

There are numerous types of gears to suit various applications. They differ in the arrangement of the teeth, the orientation of the axles, and the angle at which the teeth mesh. Spur gears are perhaps the simplest, with the teeth cut parallel to the axle. They are used to connect parallel axles. A distinction is made between external spur gears, in which the teeth are outside the wheel and point away from the axle, and internal spur gears, or planetary gears, where the teeth are cut inside one of the wheels. A rack-and-pinion arrangement may be considered to be an extreme case of external spur gears, where one of them—the rack—is infinitely large and becomes a flat strip with teeth in it. A rotational motion of the other gear—the pinion—is converted into straight-line motion of the rack and vice versa. This arrangement is used in steering systems for some automobiles, in machine tools, and on some steep railroads, where teeth on the locomotive wheels mesh with a rack imbedded in the ground, giving the locomotive improved traction. Helical gears are like spur gears except that the teeth are oblique (at an angle) to the axle rather than parallel to it. They operate more quietly, can transmit heavier loads, and can couple shafts that are not parallel. They are used in most automobile transmissions. Bevel gears have teeth cut from a conical shape. They can transmit power between axles that are not parallel; in particular, they are effective for axles at right angles, such as in the differential in the power train of automobiles, machine tools, and sewing machines. A worm-gear system consists of a worm pinion (a threaded cylinder with the threads running around the cylindrical axle, which is essentially a screw) that usually meshes at

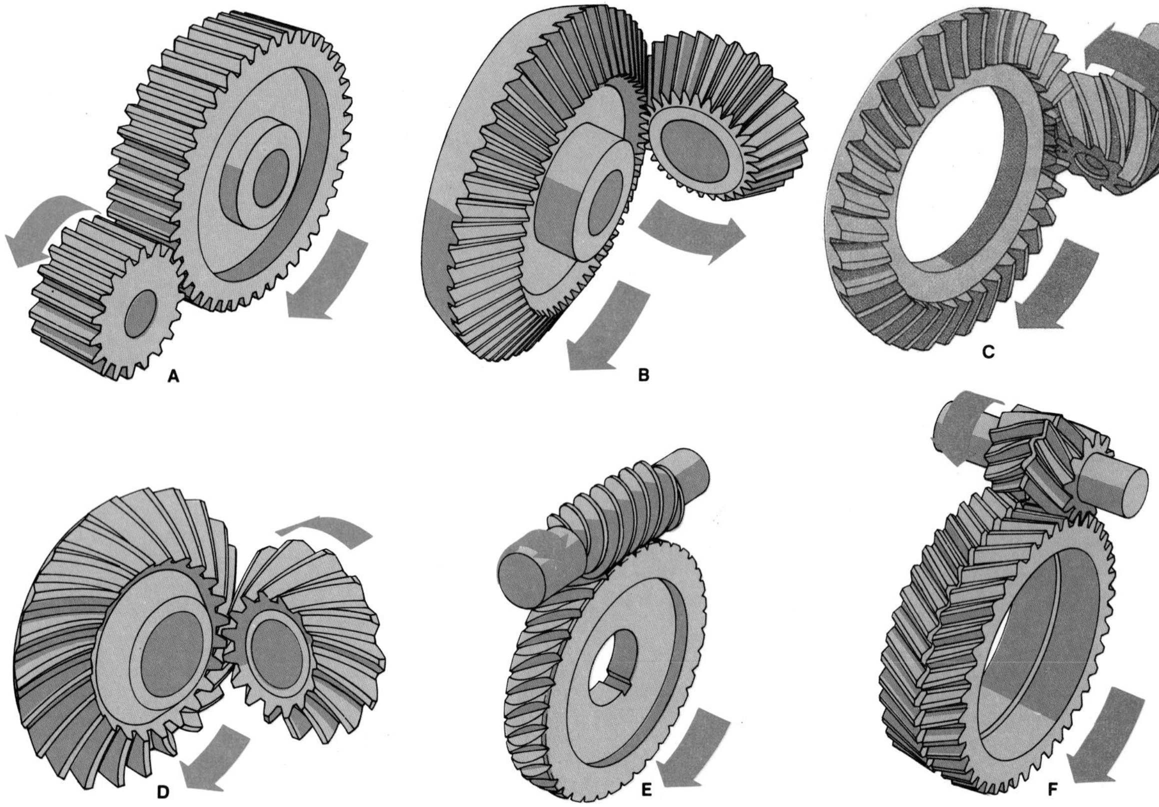

Gears are toothed wheels that are used to transmit motion from one shaft to another. Spur gears (A) have teeth cut parallel to the axis of rotation and connect shafts that are parallel to each other. Ordinary cone-shaped bevel gears (B) have straight teeth and are used to transmit power between shafts whose axes intersect. Hypoid gears (C), or bevel gears with straight teeth cut at an angle to the shaft axis, can transmit power between shafts whose axes cross each other in different planes. Spiral bevel gears (D) have teeth cut in a spiral, resulting in a larger area of contact between meshing teeth and permitting larger torques to be transmitted. In a worm gear (E) a spirally threaded worm drives a spiral-toothed gear at right angles to its own axis. Double helical gears (F) have two opposing helices cut in the same gear in order to cancel the sideways thrust generated by single spiral gears and thus reduce gear wear.

right angles with a spur gear. When the worm pinion drives the spur gear, there is a large reduction in speed and increase in torque.

Bibliography: Dudley, Darle W., ed., *Gear Handbook* (1962); Jones, Franklin D., and Ryffell, Henry, *Gear Design Simplified,* 3d ed. (1961).

Geber (Jabir ibn Hayyan) [jee'-bur]

Jabir ibn Hayyan, known in the West as Geber, is the reputed author of an extensive body of Arabic writings significant for their codification of alchemical knowledge and their transmission of Greek philosophy. The writings date from the late 8th and early 9th centuries; some may actually have been written by Jabir, but most others are the works of an Arabic school. The Latin alchemical writings under the name of Geber are of separate origin.

The works of the Jabir corpus cover all subjects—philosophy, linguistics, astrology, magic, cosmology, theology, metaphysics, the liberal arts, medicine, agriculture, and technology—but ALCHEMY predominates. This alchemy is based on the assumption that there is a natural law working in nature, according to which everything has a specific property. Alchemy deals with the relationships between these properties, how substances are used as medicines, and combinations of substances. NICHOLAS H. CLULEE

Bibliography: Federmann, Reinhard, *The Royal Art of Alchemy,* trans. by Richard Weber (1964).

gecko [gek'-oh]

Geckos are nocturnal, arboreal, generally stoutly built, insect-eating lizards found in warmer regions throughout the world. This diverse group is divided into about 75 genera and more than 400 species, constituting the family Gekhonidae. Most geckos are somber browns or grays, but some, like the brilliant green day geckos, *Phelsuma,* are brightly colored. Geckos are commonly 10 to 15 cm (4 to 6 in) in total length, with a few reaching 30 cm (12 in)—for example, the tokay gecko, *Gekko gecko,* can grow to 35.5 cm (14 in). Some of the dwarf geckos, *Sphaerodactylus,* barely exceed 2.5 cm (1 in).

Geckos have large eyes, and most species do not have movable eyelids; in these, the eyes are covered with a protective, transparent scale. Except for the primitive types, which have rounded pupils, geckos have vertical-slit pupils, which may be straight-sided or lobed. The toes of geckos vary from sim-

The banded gecko, Coleonyx variegatus, *a nocturnal desert lizard, is one of the few species with movable eyelids.*

ple claw-bearing digits to those equipped with expanded pads and concealed claws. The pads, which enable the gecko to cling even to smooth surfaces, consist of rows of plates (lamellae) covered with thousands of microscopic hooklike projections (villosities) that can catch into any minute surface irregularity. Geckos are the only lizards that can produce more than a hiss or other simple sound; vocalizations range from squeaks and clicks to croaks and barks. With rare exceptions geckos are egg-laying lizards; the eggs may be soft and parchmentlike or hard and calcareous, depending on the species.

Bibliography: Bartlett, R. D., *In Search of Reptiles and Amphibians* (1988); Halliday, T., and Adler, K., eds., *The Encyclopedia of Reptiles and Amphibians* (1986); Minelli, G., *Reptiles* (1987).

Gedda, Nicolai [ged'-ah]

Nicolai Gedda, b. July 11, 1925, is a Swedish-Russsian tenor admired for his impeccable musicianship and linguistic abilities. He made his debut (1952) at the Royal Opera, in Stockholm. That same year he recorded the role of Dimitri in Mussorgsky's *Boris Godunov* and soon achieved international recognition. Gedda made his Metropolitan Opera debut (1957) as Faust in Gounod's opera; he also sang the part of Anatol in the world premiere (1958) of Samuel Barber's *Vanessa* there. His other roles include Don Ottavio in Mozart's *Don Giovanni* and Hoffmann in Offenbach's *The Tales of Hoffmann.*

Geddes, Sir Patrick [ged'-es]

The British biologist and sociologist Sir Patrick Geddes, b. Oct. 2, 1854, d. Apr. 17, 1932, established a considerable reputation based on his contributions to theories of URBAN PLANNING. He pioneered in recognizing the need for comprehensive preliminary planning surveys of cities that would take into account historical, biological, sociological, economic, aesthetic, and geographic factors. His resultant plans for Dunfermline, Scotland, and for dozens of cities in India, remain models of rational solutions to persistent urban problems. Geddes argued that a parallel exists between human community organization and biological development and was influenced to a great extent by Charles Darwin's theories of evolution, which he studied under Thomas Henry Huxley. He taught botany at Dundee (1889–1918) and sociology at Bombay (1920–23). Geddes founded the Collège des Ecossais (Scots College) near Montpellier, France, in 1924. His major books on town planning are *City Development* (1904) and *Cities in Evolution* (1915; repr. 1949). VALENTIN TATRANSKY

Bibliography: Boardman, Philip, *Patrick Geddes, Maker of the Future* (1944); Kitchen, Paddy, *A Most Unsettling Person: The Life and Ideas of Patrick Geddes* (1975); Mairet, Philip, *Pioneer of Sociology* (1957); Stalley, Marshall, ed., *Patrick Geddes* (1972).

Geddes, Robert L.

Robert Louis Geddes, b. Philadelphia, Dec. 7, 1923, is an educator and architect whose structures reflect a concern for the social impact of architecture. Using a vocabulary derived from LE CORBUSIER and often expressed in reinforced concrete, Gedde's works stress the distinctions between public and private functions, between movement and stasis, and between multi-use and single-use areas. These traits are reflected most clearly in his master plan for Penn's Landing, Philadelphia (1959–65). His later works include the dining hall and academic building at the Institute for Advanced Study (1971), Princeton, N.J., Faner Hall at Southern Illinois University (1968–74), Carbondale, and the University of Pennsylvania hospital (1987), Philadelphia.

Geertgen tot Sint Jans [hayrt'-gen tawt sint yahns]

Geertgen tot Sint Jans, *c.*1465–*c.*1495, was a prominent Dutch painter also known as Gherrit van Haarlem. Geertgen studied with Albert van Ouwater in Haarlem, where he worked from about 1480 to 1495 while a lay brother of the Commandery (monastery) of the Knights of St. John. His art shows a strong Flemish influence as well as the influence of Dirk BOUTS and Ouwater. Moreover, Geertgen's painting has a strong individuality visible in the early *Holy Kinship* (*c.*1480; Rijksmuseum, Amsterdam). Around 1484 he painted the high altar for the Commandery; one wing survives in two panels (Kunsthistorisches Museum, Vienna), which show the *Lamentation for Christ* and the *Burning of the Bones of John the Baptist.* Later works include *John the Baptist in the Wilderness* (*c.*1490; Staatliche Museum, Berlin) and *Man of Sorrows* (Aartsbisschoppelijk Museum, Utrecht). CHARLES I. MINOTT

Bibliography: Buxton, H. J., and Poynter, E. J., *German, Flemish, and Dutch Painting* (1881; repr. 1980); Chatelet, A., *Early Dutch Painting* (1988); Panofsky, Erwin, *Early Netherlandish Painting,* 2 vols. (1953).

Geertz, Clifford [girts]

Clifford James Geertz, b. San Francisco, Aug. 23, 1926, is an anthropologist noted for studies of symbolism and culture change. He has conducted ethnographic research in Indonesia and Morocco. His writings include *The Religion of Java* (1960), *Agricultural Involution* (1963), *The Interpretation of Cultures* (1973), *Kingship in Bali* (1975), and *Works and Lives: The Anthropologist as Author* (1988). JAMES W. HERRICK

gegenschein [gay'-gen-shyn]

The gegenschein, German for "counterglow," is a faint area of diffuse light in the sky directly opposite the Sun. Keen-eyed observers report seeing this light on clear, moonless nights when its position is not in the Milky Way. Several theories have been advanced for the gegenschein. The most plausible is now thought to be that the gegenschein is caused by sunlight reflected from interplanetary particles of dust that, like the planets, orbit the Sun. FLETCHER WATSON

Gehrig, Lou [gair-ig]

Hall of Fame member Henry Louis Gehrig, b. New York City, June 19, 1903, d. June 2, 1941, nicknamed the "Iron Horse," played in a record 2,130 consecutive major league baseball games. A star athlete at Columbia University, Gehrig then played his entire career (1923–39) for the New York Yankees. Gehrig's offensive statistics are among the most impressive in baseball history. Despite playing in the shadow of Babe Ruth, the first baseman led the American League in home runs 3 times (career: 493) and in runs batted in 5 times (career: 1,991—3d all time). His lifetime batting average was .340, and slugging average, .632 (3d all time). He played in 7 World Series, of which the Yankees won 6; he was the 1936 AL Most Valuable Player; and his 23 lifetime grand slam home runs is still the major league record. Gehrig was stricken fatally with amyotrophic lateral sclerosis, often called Lou Gehrig's disease.

Bibliography: Graham, Frank, *Lou Gehrig: A Quiet Hero* (1942).

Geiger, Abraham [gy'-gur]

Abraham Geiger, b. May 24, 1810, d. Oct. 23, 1874, was a German rabbi who played an important part in the early development of Reform Judaism. He called the first conference of Reform rabbis together in 1837 and participated actively in the conferences of 1845 and 1846. Advocating a Judaism fully integrated into European culture, Geiger argued that Judaism should be considered as a religious community exclusively, without nationalistic or racial distinctiveness. Although he wrote many purely scholarly studies, his most popular work was *Das Judentum und seine Geschichte* (3 vols., 1865–71; *Judaism and Its History,* 1911), in which he presented his view of the historical course of Judaism. JOSEPH L. BLAU

Bibliography: Blau, J. L., *Modern Varieties of Judaism* (1966); Meyer, M. A., *Response to Modernity: A History of the Reform Movement in Judaism* (1988).

Geiger, Hans Wilhelm

The German physicist Hans Wilhelm Geiger, b. Sept. 30, 1882, d. Sept. 24, 1945, is best known for his pioneering research in nuclear physics and for his invention of the GEIGER COUNTER. Using this instrument, Geiger uncovered the nature of alpha and beta particles. With Ernest Rutherford, he showed (1908) that alpha particles have two units of charge, and demonstrated (1913) that the nuclear charge is about half the atomic weight. Many other results followed, including the detection of cosmic rays in 1930. ROBERT PAUL

Geiger, Rudolf Oskar Robert Williams

Rudolf Oskar Robert Williams Geiger, b. August 24, 1894, is a German meteorologist whose research on climatic conditions near ground level helped found the science of microclimatology. His observations of open fields and forest floors (*The Climate Near the Ground,* 1965) show the interdependence of heat, radiation, and air and soil moisture. Geiger has taught and done research at several German institutions, including the Meteorological Institute of the University of Munich.

Geiger counter

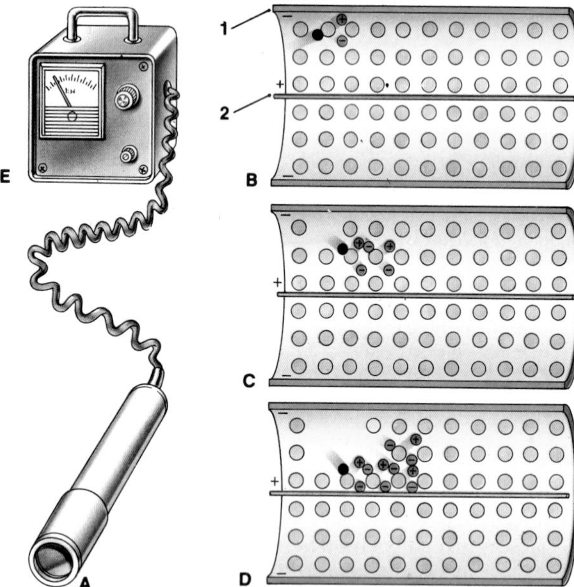

A Geiger counter detects charged particles. It consists of a metal-sheathed glass tube (A) *that encloses a negatively charged metal cylinder, or anode* (1), *and a positively charged wire, or cathode* (2). *When a high-energy particle* (black) *enters the tube* (B), *which is filled with neon gas at low pressure* (gray), *it knocks an electron* (blue) *out of a neon atom, leaving a positively charged neon ion* (red). *The electron is attracted to the anode and the ion to the cathode. Both liberate more electrons by further collisions with neon atoms* (C, D). *The resulting flow of electrons is registered on a meter* (E).

The Geiger counter, also known as the Geiger-Muller counter, is an instrument used to detect and measure the intensity of radiation, such as beta particles and cosmic rays. The device, which takes its name from the German physicists Hans GEIGER and Wilhelm Müller, may be used as a laboratory instrument, in mineral exploration, as a thickness gauge for continuous sheet materials, and as a stock level gauge in blast furnaces. It is also employed in diagnostic medical work.

The heart of the Geiger counter is the ionization tube, which may be metal, or glass with a metalized interior, and a central conductor maintained at a high positive potential with respect to the outer enclosure. The tube may contain air, argon, or other gas at or below atmospheric pressure. When the tube is exposed to nuclear radiation the gas is ionized. Negative ions or electrons are attracted to the center conductor, and positive ions are attracted to the negative enclosure. If the voltage on the tube is in the Geiger range (800–1,500 volts), each ionizing event will cause an electron avalanche (gas amplification) and will result in a large output pulse. This pulse may be received audibly in headphones or recorded electronically through counting devices.

Once begun, the discharge will continue unless something is done to stop it. Alcohol vapor can quench the pulse, but this organic material is used up with each discharge and limits the life of the tube. Quenching with a halogen gas such as chlorine or bromine is more often done. Radiation pulses change the gas from a molecular to the atomic state and back again, so there is no loss of quenching material. Tube life is indefinitely long.

The material for the tube envelope and its thickness are determined by the type of radiation to be measured. Beta rays pass through thin tube walls. Windows of mica, glass, or pliofilm are used to detect weaker ALPHA PARTICLES. GAMMA RAYS are very inefficient ionizers of gas in a counter tube. Ionization must depend upon the emission of secondary electrons from much thicker tube walls. FRANK J. OLIVER

Bibliography: Renne, Harold S., *How to Detect & Measure Radiation* (1962).

See also: DETECTOR, PARTICLE.

Geijer, Erik Gustaf [yah'-yur, ay'-rik]

Erik Gustaf Geijer, b. Jan. 12, 1783, d. Apr. 23, 1847, was a Swedish historian and poet. After studying philosophy and history at Uppsala University, he taught (1809–10) in England. Turning to conservatism after his early liberalism, he became one of the leaders and best poets of the influential Götiska Förbundet, a literary movement devoted to awakening a new Swedish national spirit. A professor at Uppsala from 1817, Geijer published works on Swedish history, including *The History of the Swedes* (3 vols., 1832–36; Eng. trans., 1845). Influenced by the socialist movement in Europe, he returned to liberalism around 1835.

Geikie, Sir Archibald [gee'-kee]

The Scottish geologist Sir Archibald Geikie, b. Dec. 28, 1835, d. Nov. 10, 1924, was a major popularizer of geology during the late 19th and early 20th centuries. He held (1871–82) the first chair of geology at Edinburgh University, and is the only geologist ever elected president of the Royal Society (1908). Geikie also worked (1855–1901) for the Geological Survey of Great Britain and was its director from 1881 to 1901. He wrote several geology textbooks, all of which appeared in multiple editions and in other languages. His book *The Ancient Volcanoes of Great Britain* (1897) contained the first chronological description of eruptions in northern Europe. He also wrote the classic *Founders of Geology* (1897; 2d., 1905; repr. 1962).

Geisel, Ernesto [gy'-sel]

Ernesto Geisel, b. Aug. 3, 1908, was president of Brazil from 1974 to 1979. A career army officer who had served in a number of military and civil administrative posts, Geisel was instrumental in planning the military coup that removed leftist president João GOULART in 1964. From 1969 to 1974 he directed the government-owned Petróleo Brasileiro (Petrobras). His expansion of the oil industry was an important factor in Brazil's spectacular economic growth. As Brazil's fourth military president since 1964, Geisel attempted to liberalize the military junta's authoritarian rule. However, he nominated his own successor, João Batista de Oliveira FIGUEIDA.

Geisel, Theodore Seuss: see SEUSS, DR.

geisha [gee'-shuh]

In Japanese society a geisha is a young woman professionally trained to entertain men, especially businessmen at restaurant parties. The conception of the geisha as a prostitute is false; the name means "artistic person," and many geisha dance, sing, or play musical instruments. Their chief function, however, is to provide light conversation. Traditionally, geisha were like indentured servants, bonded by their parents to geisha houses that boarded, clothed, and trained them. Many modern geisha are unionized, although the profession as a whole has declined in numbers since World War II. Geisha must retire when they marry; those who retire without marrying often become teachers of music or dance.

Bibliography: Dalby, Liza C., *Geisha* (1983); Scott, Adolphe C., *The Flower and the Willow World: The Story of the Geisha* (1960).

Geissler, Heinrich [gys'-lur]

The German glassblower Johann Heinrich Wilhelm Geissler, b. May 26, 1814, d. Jan. 24, 1879, earned an international reputation as a maker of glass scientific instruments. In the 1850s his standard thermometers, constructed of thin glass capillary tubes and carefully calibrated, were in demand by scientists throughout the world. Geissler also constructed glass tubes filled with rarefied gases and with electrodes sealed into the ends. These "Geissler tubes" became essential for chemists and physicists studying gases and electrical phenomena and eventually led to the discovery of cathode rays.

DAVID HOUNSHELL

gel [jel]

A gel is a solid or semisolid colloidal system, exemplified by the jelly that forms when a mixture of about 5% gelatin in hot water is allowed to cool. Although a gel is usually classed as a solid because it does not flow and is elastic, it is typically not as rigid as a conventional solid. It could, in some cases, properly be regarded as a supercooled liquid. In other colloidal systems one component forms discrete particles within a continuous, dispersing medium; in gels, however, both the solid and the liquid can be continuous, the liquid filling the interstices between the network of molecules of the solid. The liquid content in typical gels is above 90%, and it may be greater than 99% in some instances. Pectins and agar are well known for their gel-forming ability; pectins are used to make fruit jellies, and agar is used in bacteriological work. Gels formed from silica are widely used in laboratories and industry as fillers and supports for catalysts.

GEORGE GORIN

See also: COLLOIDAL STATE.

Gela [jay'-lah]

Gela is a city in Caltanissetta province in southern Sicily, Italy, on the Mediterranean Sea. A fishing port and seaside resort, it is the center of a cotton-growing region and has a petroleum-refining industry and a population of 74,789 (1981). Founded by Greek colonists from Crete and Rhodes about 688 BC, Gela itself sent out colonists to found Acragas (now AGRIGENTO) about 582 BC. Gela was sacked by Carthaginians in 405 BC and destroyed by Mamertini in 281 BC. Refounded by Holy Roman Emperor Frederick II in the 1230s, it was called Terranova di Sicilia until 1928. A landing point (July 1943) for the Allies' World War II invasion of Sicily, Gela is also known for its important Greek archaeological remains.

gelatin [jel'-uh-tin]

Gelatin is a protein obtained from the skin, tendons, and bones of animals. It is used in food products and pharmaceuticals, in many industrial processes, and for cooking. Derived from COLLAGEN, a constituent of animal skin and bone, it is extracted by treating hides and bone with lime or acid; boiling, filtering, and concentrating the material; and then drying and grinding it to produce commercial gelatin, in the form of transparent, odorless, and tasteless granules. Gelatin dissolves in hot water and congeals to form a gel as the solution cools.

Gelatin is an incomplete protein lacking the essential amino acid tryptophan, but as a food supplement it supplies several amino acids lacking in the protein of wheat, barley, and oats. Free of antigens, it does not cause allergic reactions.

In foods, gelatin is used in gelatin desserts, candy, meat products, and jellied canned soups; as an emulsifier in such foods as ice cream, marshmallows, and chiffon pie fillings; and as a stabilizer in cake fillings, icing mixers, and gum.

Gelatin's most important industrial uses are in photography, where it provides a basic ingredient in the manufacture of photographic film and paper, and in lithography and photocopying. It is used in the plastics industry to improve blending characteristics; in metallurgy to achieve greater purity in refining, as a corrosion inhibitor, and to produce bright finishes in electroplating; in drilling as a protective colloid; in agriculture as an ingredient of fertilizers, animal feeds, and sprays; and in pharmaceuticals for capsules, pill coatings, suppositories, and emulsions. Sheets of dyed gelatin are used in stage-lighting as an inexpensive substitute for glass.

Isinglass is a form of gelatin produced from the bladders of fish, and AGAR is a gelatinous seaweed extract used as a laboratory culturing medium and as a gelling agent in foods.

FRANCES GIES

Gelber, Jack [gel'-bur]

An American playwright and director, Jack Gelber, b. Chicago, Ill., April 12, 1932, scored his first success with his controversial play *The Connection* (1959), which was performed by the Living Theatre. His other plays include *The Apple* (1961), *The Cuban Thing* (1968), and *Jack Gelber's New Play: Rehearsal* (1976); all of which are concerned with the alienation of the individual from American society. BONNIE MARRANCA

Gelfond, Aleksandr Osipovich [gel'-fuhnd]

Aleksandr Osipovich Gelfond, b. Oct. 24, 1906, d. Nov. 7, 1968, was a Russian mathematician who developed basic techniques in the study of TRANSCENDENTAL NUMBERS (numbers that cannot be expressed as the solution of an algebraic equation with rational coefficients). In addition to his important work in the NUMBER THEORY of transcendental numbers, Gelfond made significant contributions to the theory of INTERPOLATION and the approximation of functions of a complex variable. Gelfond taught mathematics at the Moscow Technological College (1929–30) and then at Moscow State University.

H. HOWARD FRISINGER

Gell-Mann, Murray [gel-mahn']

Murray Gell-Mann, an American theoretical physicist, b. New York City, Sept. 15, 1929, is known for his discovery of a classification scheme for nuclear particles and their interactions, for which he was awarded the 1969 Nobel Prize for physics. The son of an Austrian immigrant, Gell-Mann worked briefly at the Institute for Advanced Study in Princeton, N.J., before joining the faculty of the University of Chicago in 1952. In 1955 he went to the California Institute of Technology, where he became a full professor in 1956.

In 1953, Gell-Mann proposed that certain subatomic particles were characterized by an invariant property that he

Murray Gell-Mann, an American theoretical physicist, won the Nobel Prize for physics in 1969 for devising an elegant and predictive classification of subatomic particles. Gell-Mann's system of particle types led him to postulate fundamental particles called "quarks" as the constituents of all nuclear particles, a theory that has spawned much productive research.

called "strangeness." He showed that strangeness was conserved in strong and electromagnetic interactions but not in weak interactions. This new conservation law was the foundation of later SYMMETRY schemes for classifying strongly interacting particles, including the so-called SU(3) symmetry introduced by Gell-Mann and, independently, by the Japanese physicist Kazuhiko Nishijima in 1961.

One of the consequences of SU(3) symmetry, also known as the "Eight-Fold Way," was the predicted existence of a new particle, the omega minus. The discovery of this particle, by N. P. Samios and R. P. Schutt in 1964, was a crucial test for Gell-Mann's theory and a turning point in particle physics. In 1963, Gell-Mann and, independently, George Zweig, a colleague at the California Institute of Technology, introduced QUARKS—particles carrying fractional electric charges—into FUNDAMENTAL PARTICLE theory to explain the organization of particle families. JOHN G. MAY

Bibliography: Berland, Theodore, *The Scientific Life* (1962); Weinberg, Steven, *The Discovery of Subatomic Particles* (1983).

Gelon, Tyrant of Gela [jee'-lahn, jay'-lah]

Gelon, *c*.540–478 BC, was a Sicilian ruler who assumed power in 491, after the death of Hippocrates, the tyrant of Gela. Gelon moved Sicily's capital from Gela to Syracuse, which became a city of great prosperity and culture. In 480 he defeated a Carthaginian invasion and extended his influence throughout Sicily. ROBIN BUSS

Gelsenkirchen [gel'-zen-kirsh-en]

Gelsenkirchen (1983 est. pop., 290,700) is an industrial city in West Germany in the state of North Rhine–Westphalia. Located along the Emscher River and the Rhine–Herne Canal less than 50 km (30 mi) northeast of Essen, it is a major inland port of the RUHR coal-mining region. Coke, iron and steel, chemicals, electronic equipment, glass, and soap are manufactured there. Historic landmarks include three castles. A village by the 12th century, Gelsenkirchen grew after 1853 as the coal mining developed. During World War II, the city suffered heavy Allied bombing.

gem cutting

Gem cutting is the art of cutting and polishing rough GEMS in order to transform them into rounded or faceted gems suitable for jewelry. The expert cutting of a gem greatly enhances its value by giving it harmonious proportions and by bringing out to the fullest its luster, brilliancy, color, and fire. A craftsman who cuts gems is called a lapidary.

The two major gem cuts are the cabochon cut and the facet cut. The cabochon cut is usually reserved for gems that are opaque (like turquoise), translucent, chatoyant (having a changing color, like opal), or asterismal (reflecting a star-shaped light, like star sapphire). A cabochon-cut gem has smooth, curved surfaces. Most gems that can produce a high degree of brilliancy, color, or fire—for example, diamonds, aquamarines, and sapphires—receive a facet cut. Facet cutting uses smooth, flat faces, which are cut into the gem at precise angles so that the greatest amount of light is refracted. Some facet-cut gems may have more than 100 facets. The two main facet cuts are the brilliant cut and the step (or trap) cut. The brilliant cut, with its kite-shaped facets, is often used on gems that are round in form, and is almost always used on diamonds. The step cut, which has trapezoidal facets, is reserved for gems that are square in form, such as emeralds and rubies.

A lapidary cuts a gem by shaping it against a grinding

Tools used to cut gemstones include an aluminum dop, or gem holder (1), *for cabochon cutting; a hardwood dop* (2), *for faceting; and a steel cleaving knife* (3), *for splitting stones. In cabochon cutting, corners and edges are first removed* (4) *by bruting, or rotating a diamond against the stone. The process is continued until the desired polished cabochon dome* (5) *is obtained. In brilliant cutting of a diamond, the edge of a pyramid cut is rounded by bruting* (6); *then facets are ground and polished, yielding a finished gem* (7–11). *Stones engraved and carved with an array of diamond-tipped tools* (12) *include a cameo* (13), *a signet ring* (14), *and a jade pendant* (15).

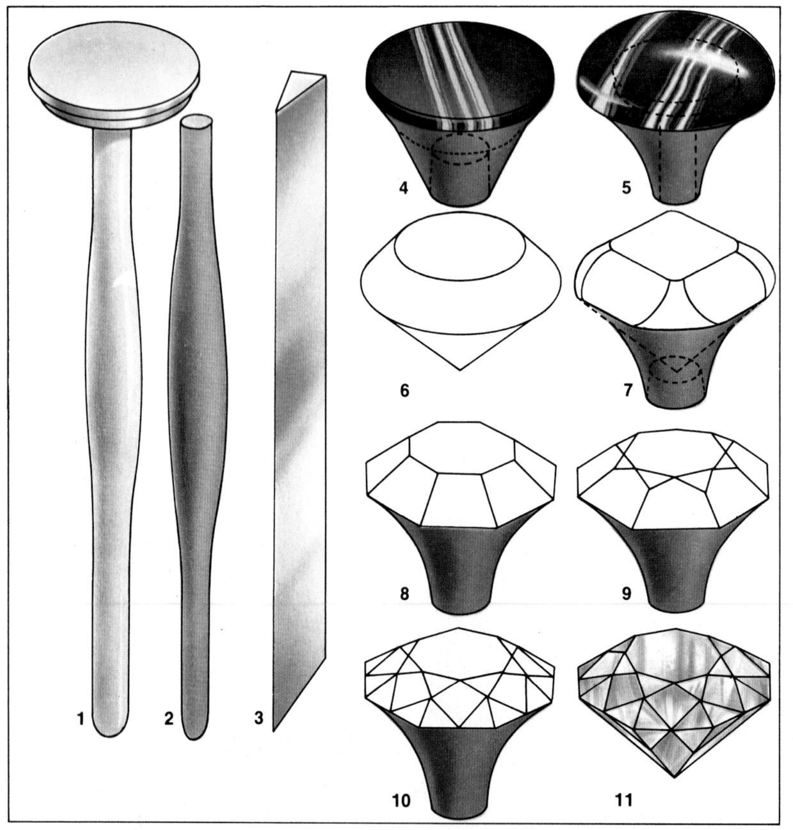

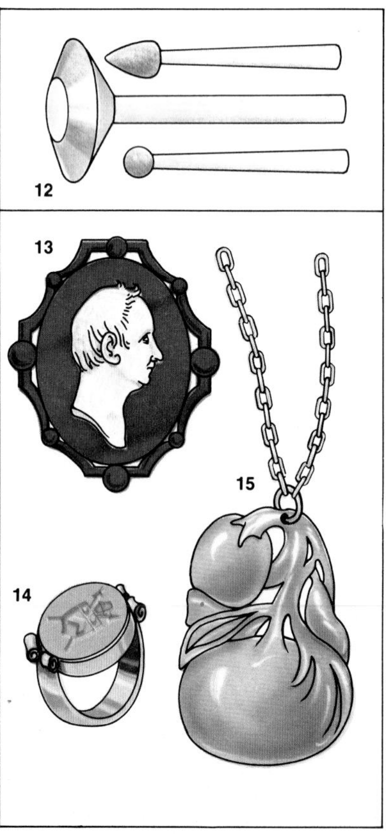

wheel, or lap, that is sprinkled with an abrasive powder. Especially hard gems are cut and polished on metal laps that use diamond powder as the abrasive. Diamond faceting was probably developed during the 15th century in the Low Countries; the full brilliant cut was perfected in Venice in the 17th century. Antwerp and Amsterdam have been leading diamond-cutting centers for over three centuries. Tel Aviv and New York City have also become important centers.

Bibliography: Perry, N. and R., *Practical Gemcutting* (1982).

Gemara: see TALMUD.

gematria: see KABBALAH.

Gemayel, Amin [juh-my'-uhl]

Amin Gemayel, b. 1942, a Lebanese Maronite Catholic and son of Pierre Gemayel, the founder of Lebanon's Phalangist party, succeeded his brother Bashir as that country's president when the latter was assassinated by political opponents in 1982. He concluded a security agreement with Israel in 1983 but was forced to repudiate it a year later under Syrian and Lebanese Muslim pressure, and his power continued to erode. When the legislature failed to agree upon a successor by the time his term expired on Sept. 23, 1988, Gemayel appointed an interim military cabinet headed by a Christian prime minister to rule the country. Muslims then appointed a rival cabinet, threatening national unity.

Gemini [jem'-in-y]

Gemini, the Twins, a constellation of the Zodiac, is seen best in the Northern Hemisphere. The two brightest stars, Castor and Pollux, are named for the twin sons of Leda in Greek mythology. Pollux is a first-magnitude star. Castor, a second-magnitude star, is a triple star, and each of its components is a double star—making six stars in all. Gemini is located by extending an imaginary line from the two bottom stars in the Big Dipper's bowl away from the handle.

Gemini program

The Gemini program was a series of piloted U.S. spaceflights in the mid-1960s. The series was authorized by Congress in 1961 as an intermediate step, between the MERCURY PROGRAM and the APOLLO PROGRAM, in the U.S. effort to land on the Moon. It was called Gemini, which means "twins" in Latin, because each piloted flight carried two astronauts into orbit.

The earlier Mercury program had demonstrated that a trained astronaut could fly in orbit for up to 34 hours. The National Aeronautics and Space Administration next had to determine whether trained crew members could endure the weightlessness of orbital freefall long enough to survive a journey to the Moon and back. This was one important objective of the Gemini program; others were to develop rendezvous and docking techniques needed for the lunar mission and to train personnel in their use.

A highly maneuverable spacecraft was required, with an elaborate life-support system that could maintain a crew for up to 14 days. A NASA team, including James A. Chamberlain and André J. Meyer, designed a two-person spacecraft, and NASA awarded the chief contract to the McDonnell Aircraft Corporation of St. Louis, Mo., on Dec. 7, 1961. Within five years, the program had achieved all of its objectives at a cost of $1,283,400,000. The flight series used the global tracking and communications network established in Project Mercury.

GEMINI HARDWARE

The Gemini capsule was a scaled-up version of the bell-shaped, blunt-ended Mercury capsule. It had 50 percent more cabin space and weighed more than twice as much, about 3,640 kg (8,000 lb). Including its reentry, retrograde, and adapter sections, the vehicle was about 5.8 m (19 ft) long and 3 m (10 ft) wide at its base. The reentry module consisted of the cabin, which contained two couches side-by-side, and a

The two-man U.S. Gemini capsule was designed for longer and more complex missions than its predecessor, the Mercury capsule. Numbers indicate attitude control thrusters (1); *equipment module* (2); *fuel, oxidant, and pressure tanks* (3); *maneuver thrusters* (4); *retro-rockets* (5); *command pilot* (6); *window* (7); *reentry attitude thrusters* (8); *landing parachute stowage* (9); *docking bar* (10); *rendezvous radar* (11); *drogue parachute storage* (12); *reentry module* (13); *instrument panels* (14); *pilot and extravehicular activity (EVA) astronaut* (15); *ejection seat* (16); *electrical equipment* (17); *and retrograde section* (18), *with four braking rockets of 930 kg (2,050 lb) thrust each.*

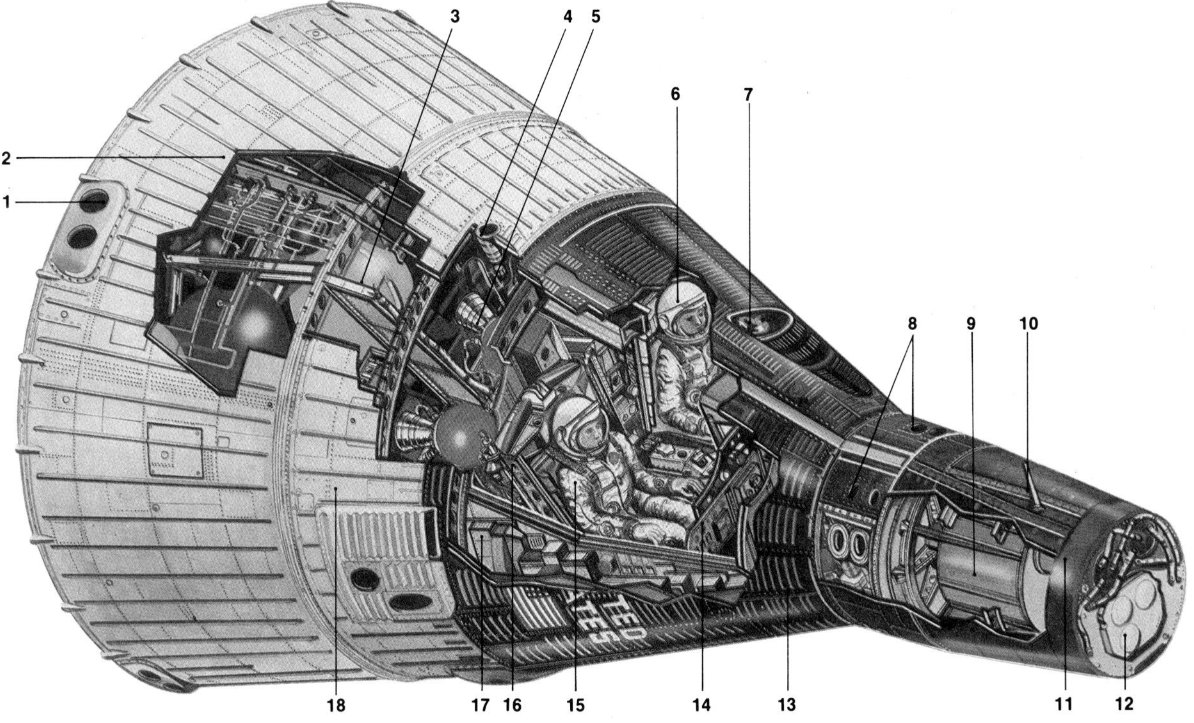

cylindrical nose containing the docking mechanism and parachutes. Behind it was the retrograde section, which contained an array of four retro-rockets to be fired in quick succession to decelerate the spacecraft for reentry. The adapter section at the rear contained the 16 engines of the Orbital Attitude and Maneuvering System (OAMS), the fuel-cell electric-power supply, and reserve oxygen. The retro-rockets and adapter were jettisoned at reentry.

The Gemini spacecraft were launched by the TITAN 2 ICBM, a two-stage rocket that was more powerful than the Atlas ICBM used in the Mercury program. To reenter, the crew separated the forward, or reentry, section from the adapter section and fired four retro-rockets of 11,100 newtons (1,100 kg/2,500 lb) of thrust each. The capsule, which was stabilized by an eight-thruster reentry control system (RCS), was designed to have lift in the high atmosphere. The pilot could control the landing point within a limited area by rolling the vehicle. The final descent was made by parachute.

GEMINI MISSIONS

The first piloted Gemini mission, *Gemini 3*, was flown by Air Force Maj. Virgil I. (Gus) GRISSOM and Navy Lt. Comdr. John W. YOUNG for three orbits on Mar. 23, 1965. Five days earlier, the Soviet cosmonaut Aleksei Leonov had spent ten minutes outside VOSKHOD *2* in the first demonstration of extravehicular activity (EVA) during orbital flight. This feat was duplicated on June 3, 1965, by Air Force Maj. Edward H. WHITE II on the four-day, 62-orbit flight of *Gemini 4* (June 3–7). He remained outside for 20 minutes in a 14-kg (31-lb) space suit designed for EVA and moved about at the end of an 8-m (25-ft) tether by firing a twin-barreled gas gun while Air Force Maj. James A. McDIVITT piloted the vessel.

The American space-endurance record was extended to eight days on the flight of *Gemini 5* (Aug. 21–29, 1965) by Air Force Lt. Col. Leroy Gordon COOPER and Navy Comdr. Charles CONRAD, Jr. They performed 17 scientific experiments and made detailed observations of the weather and ocean currents. The program next attempted to achieve rendezvous and docking with another vehicle in orbit. The original plans called for a Gemini spacecraft to dock with an AGENA rocket. The first attempt was canceled on Oct. 25, 1965, when the Agena blew up after having been launched by an Atlas missile. After an unsuccessful effort during which the launch rocket sputtered but did not lift off, *Gemini 6* was sent into orbit on Dec. 15, 1965, with Navy Capt. Walter M. SCHIRRA and Air Force Maj. Thomas P. STAFFORD aboard.

Meanwhile, the *Gemini 7* spacecraft had been launched on Dec. 4, 1965, and it was decided that *Gemini 7* would serve as the vehicle with which *Gemini 6* would rendezvous. Accordingly, Schirra piloted his craft to within one foot of *Gemini 7* on December 15;—the first successful rendezvous in space.

Gemini 6 splashed down the next day. The crew of *Gemini 7*, however—Air Force Maj. Frank BORMAN and Navy Comdr. James A. LOVELL, Jr.—went on to set a new endurance record in space: they made a controlled landing in the Atlantic Ocean on Dec. 18, 1965, after having been in orbit for 330 hours and 35 minutes. Their mission proved that trained personnel could endure a round trip to the Moon. On its 220 orbits of the Earth, *Gemini 7* had flown approximately 20 times the distance to the Moon.

Rendezvous and docking with an Agena target rocket was achieved on March 16, 1966, during the mission of *Gemini 8*, by civilian Neil A. ARMSTRONG and Air Force Maj. David R. Scott. The mission was abruptly terminated, however, when a malfunction in the Gemini OAMS thrusters forced the crew to undock and make an emergency landing in the western Pacific Ocean.

Another docking attempt was scheduled for May 17, 1966, by *Gemini 9*, but was postponed when the Agena failed to reach orbit. The crew, Stafford and Navy Lt. Comdr. Eugene A. CERNAN, finally attempted to dock on June 3 with a makeshift target adapted from Gemini parts but were prevented by a defective shroud on the target.

During the three-day flight of *Gemini 10*, Young and Air Force Maj. Michael COLLINS docked with an Agena target on July 18, 1966, and fired its engine to boost the joined vehicles to an altitude of 764 km (475 mi). On *Gemini 11* (Sept. 12–15, 1966), Conrad and Navy Lt. Comdr. Richard F. GORDON, Jr., docked with an Agena on their first orbit. They used its engine to reach an altitude of 1,368 km (850 mi).

Overheating and face-plate fogging, which had interfered with early EVA efforts, were overcome by Air Force Maj. Edwin E. (Buzz) ALDRIN, Jr., on the flight of *Gemini 12* (Nov. 11–15, 1966). After he and Lovell docked with an Agena, Aldrin succeeded in performing 2 hours and 9 minutes of continuous work outside the spacecraft. The splashdown of *Gemini 12* on Nov. 15, 1966, ended the Gemini phase of the lunar landing project. RICHARD S. LEWIS

Gemini 7 *was only 2.7 m (9 ft) away when this photograph was taken from* Gemini 6 *during the historic rendezvous of the spacecraft 258 km (160 mi) above Earth on Dec. 15, 1965. By maneuvering their craft to within 0.3 m (1 ft) of* Gemini 7, *the astronauts demonstrated that a rendezvous of moving vehicles in space would be possible. Subsequent Gemini flights also established that two orbiting vehicles could successfully dock with and separate from one another.*

Bibliography: Levine, Sol, *Appointment in the Sky* (1963); Lewis, Richard, *Appointment on the Moon*, rev. ed. (1969), and *From Vinland to Mars: A Thousand Years of Exploration* (1976); Nicolson, Isin, *Sputnik to Space Shuttle* (1983).

See also: SPACE EXPLORATION.

Geminiani, Francesco [jay-meen-ee-ahn'-ee]

Francesco Geminiani, b. Dec. 5?, 1687, d. Sept. 17, 1762, was one of the great violin virtuosos of his day and a composer of violin music. Most of his career was centered in London during George Frideric Handel's time there. A student of Arcangelo Corelli, Geminiani imitated his teacher's style in his own early works. His later violin sonatas, however, show signs of the decline of the baroque style, although they are more conservative than those of Giuseppe Tartini. Geminiani's *Rules for Playing in a True Taste on the Violin, German Flute, Violincello, and Harpsichord* (1745) and *Art of Playing on the Violin* (1751) are important sources of knowledge of performing practices of the mid-18th century. His musical compositions include trio sonatas, *concerti grossi*, and works for harpsichord. JOHN HILL

Bibliography: Boyden, David D., *The History of Violin Playing from its Origins to 1761 and its Relationship to the Violin and Violin Music* (1965); Hutchings, Arthur, *The Baroque Concert*, rev. ed. (1973); Newman, William S., *The Sonata in the Baroque Era*, 3d ed. (1972).

gems

Gemstones are unusually bright, colorful, or transparent minerals found in the rocks of the Earth. Pearl, coral, amber, ivory, shell, jet, and similar materials are also often considered gemstones, although they are the end products from processes related to living plants or animals.

Gemologists use several different tests to identify gemstones. A specially designed gem refractometer determines the refractive index—a measure of light-bending ability equal to the sine of the angle of incidence divided by the sine of the angle of refraction. Each species of gem has its own particular refractive index. The detection under a microscope of foreign inclusions and the determination of hardness by tiny test scratches made with special hardness pencils are usually sufficient additional tests. Density determination, or, more rarely, sophisticated methods of X-ray diffraction and chemical analysis, are sometimes also required.

Only about 100 mineral species (out of an estimated 3,000 known) have been found reasonably suitable for use as gems. Approximately 13 are normally found circulating widely in the gem trade, and perhaps 40 more are sometimes available to the gem collector. The remainder are mostly decorative or ornamental stones of high beauty but relatively low market value.

The cutting of gems is both a craft and an art (see GEM CUTTING). Although the techniques of carving and sculpting mineral materials date from the 3d millennium BC, optical cutting of gems began only in the late 1600s with the devising of the brilliant cut by Vincenzio Vincenti Peruzzi of Venice. Although irregularly shaped, smoothed, or tumbled gemstones have currently returned to fashion, the finest pieces of gem rough are converted primarily into patterned, faceted stones. Various combinations of flat faces or facets have been devised, all designed to bring out of the gem the greatest brilliance or color display possible. Emeralds and other attractively colored gems have different kinds of cuts, usually with large flat table facets, to display the interior color at its best.

WHAT MAKES A GEM DESIRABLE

In various cultures throughout history, certain preferences have developed for one kind of gemstone over another. These preferences, reflected in commercial price levels for gems, are based on several factors: beauty, durability, rarity, and the current fashion. Diamond or the finest jade come as close as any gemstones to meeting all these requirements. Some gemstones meet only a minimum of these requirements; for example, turquoise is beautiful and fashionable but neither particularly rare nor durable.

The beauty of a gemstone, usually revealed to its fullest only after cutting and polishing, may depend on the natural color, transparency, or some other more unusual optical effect. Most important gemstones are allochromatic; that is, the color of an individual stone depends on very slight differences in composition. Those whose color does not depend on these compositional impurities are idiochromatic. Some gemstones, because of their chemical and physical nature, are always opaque. The beauty of turquoise can be seen only by light reflected from polished surfaces. Other gems are quite transparent, transmitting light easily. The importance and beauty of transparent gemstones may be greatly diminished, however, if they contain internal flaws or bits of foreign material; blemishes are clearly visible. Totally clean, high-quality gemstones are exceedingly rare, because minerals are usually formed in nature under stress or from relatively impure materials. Inclusions of rutile, spinel, carbon, actinolite, and numerous other minerals are common.

REFRACTION, DISPERSION, DIFFRACTION, and REFLECTION are other important optical effects that produce beauty in gemstones. Different colors, or wavelengths of light, are bent, or refracted, by different amounts as they travel from the air into a cut gem. When white light, a mixture of all wavelengths, enters certain gems, its colors are dispersed or spread by differential refraction and are then reflected back out of the gem as separate color flashes. This phenomenon is quite familiar in diamond, which has excellent dispersion. Colors are also separated by diffraction, an optical process that depends on the orderly internal array of gemstone atoms or groups of atoms; among gems it is best seen in opal.

Simple reflection of light from internal flaws and inclusions in gems can also cause some remarkable and beautiful effects. Star sapphires and rubies, for example, contain thousands of needlelike foreign particles that line up uniformly in the three major directions of atomic structure for these species. Light reflecting from these three sets of needles produces asterism, a bright six-rayed, starlike reflection. If the needlelike inclusions line up in only one direction, as they somtimes do in the mineral species chrysoberyl, the reflection is in only a single ray, giving a CAT'S-EYE effect, or chatoyancy.

The durability of a gemstone depends on its toughness (its freedom from a tendency to break, cleave, or otherwise separate) and its hardness (its resistance to scratching and general abrasion). Jade is tough but only moderately hard; diamond, on the other hand, is hard but only moderately tough. Gemstones usually exceed 6 on Mohs' scale of hardness (see HARDNESS, MINERAL) and often exceed 7 or more. No comparable established standard scale for toughness exists.

The rarity of gemstones depends on two factors. Some mineral materials, such as alexandrite, just do not exist in nature in large quantities. Others, such as opal, are common, but only a small number have enough quality and beauty to be considered for gem purposes.

Fashion is one of the least predictable factors determining gemstone desirability and value. Popularity may depend on the availability and price of gems, or perhaps on a volatile fadlike preference. Diamond, ruby, sapphire, emerald, and pearl are traditionally considered as precious stones, although that term today is almost meaningless. Opal, amethyst, amber, periodot, turquoise, jet, zircon, citrine, and others seem to drift in and out of fashion.

POPULAR GEMS

The most popular and therefore the most important commercial gems include diamond, ruby, sapphire, emerald, and pearl. DIAMOND—at 10 on Mohs' scale, the hardest of all known substances—is composed of carbon and comes mostly from South Africa and the USSR. Though most highly prized when colorless, it can be yellow, blue, pink, or other colors. RUBY and SAPPHIRE are distinct varieties of the mineral species CORUNDUM, an aluminum oxide. Ruby is colored red by traces of chromium; the various colors of sapphire, however, are produced by traces of iron and titanium in the corundum. The best gem corundum is found in Sri Lanka and in the Orient at places such as Mogok in Upper Burma, near Bangkok in Thailand, and Kashmir in India. EMERALD, the rich blue green variety of the mineral species BERYL (a beryllium-aluminum silicate), gets its color from traces of chromium and a little iron. The best emeralds are from the Muzo and Chivor mines in Colombia. Fine pearls are the products of only a certain genus of oysters, *Pinctada*, which deposit layers of pearl over irritants that have gotten inside their shells (see PEARLS AND PEARLING).

A typical jewelry store may carry several other kinds of gems: blue to bluish green aquamarine, pink to peach morganite, and other varieties (including those colored yellow green to green) of beryl; the complex borosilicate TOURMALINE, which may be pink to red (rubellite), blue (indicolite), bright green or several other colors; the aluminosilicate TOPAZ, which may be sherry or muscatel wine colored, pink, green, blue, or brown; QUARTZ (silicon dioxide), whose gem varieties include AMETHYST (purple), chrysoprase (green), citrine (yellow to brown), rock crystal (colorless), and rose quartz; and OPAL, a stone often with brilliant color flashes that is usually dark and white (Australia) or transparent (anywhere from colorless to orange-to-red and found in Mexico).

Less common gems include the beryllium aluminate CHRYSOBERYL, especially its cat's-eye variety and the fascinating alexandrite variety, which appears green in daylight and red in artificial incandescent light; GARNET, such as the red Bohemian pyropes and Indian almandines; PERIDOT, a yellow green variety of the mineral species OLIVINE, a magnesium-iron silicate; the magnesium-aluminate SPINEL, in its ruby red and mauve varieties; tanzanite, a sapphire blue variety of the mineral species ZOISITE, a calcium-aluminum hydroxy silicate;

diamond (brilliant cut)
ruby
sapphire (baguette cut)
blue star sapphire
star ruby (pink)
pearl
emerald (typical emerald cut)
topaz
amethyst (quartz)
opal
chrysoberyl cat's eye
alexandrite (natural light)
alexandrite (artificial light)
garnet
peridot (olivine)
lapis lazuli
malachite
American turquoise
heliotrope
rhodonite
moss agate
carnelian
sunstone (aventurine feldspar)
aquamarine (beryl)
moonstone (adularia feldspar)
golden zircon

and spodumene, in its green to yellow green varieties or the beautiful lavender lilac kunzite variety.

Numerous other good gem species are sometimes available for collectors, including CORDIERITE, SPHENE, andalusite, benitoite, and euclase. Ornamental gemstones, beautiful but not suited for fashioning into transparent cut gems, include CORAL, nephrite and jadeite JADE, JET, LAPIS LAZULI, MALACHITE, RHODONITE, SERPENTINE, TURQUOISE, and various varieties of quartz including AGATE, JASPER, and carnelian.

COUNTERFEIT GEMS

Both now and in past centuries far more substitute and artificial gemstones have been in circulation than natural, properly identified stones. Gemstone counterfeiting is not normally intended for fraud, and fraud does not usually occur because of the materials or their manufacturers; rather it comes about from the motives of the buyer or seller. Gemstone counterfeiting caters to a market of thousands of consumers who feel they cannot afford the price of an attractive natural gem. Also, many buyers who can afford them prefer to invest in other sorts of luxury goods.

Counterfeit gemstones can be classified as substitutes, imitations, assembled gems, or synthetics. Substitute gemstones are those which can be used as plausible replacements for something more expensive. Colorless ZIRCON, colorless sapphire, and even colorless quartz are natural gemstones that, at a distance, might easily be mistaken for diamond, a common target for mimicry because of its normally high value. For close-up deception some of the newer synthetic stones are far better. Natural red garnet and red spinel are good substitutes for ruby. Two of the world's most famous "rubies," the Black Prince's Ruby and the Timur Ruby, both in the British Crown Jewels, are really red spinel. Green tourmaline can substitute for emerald. Citrine, a yellowish to brownish quartz, may replace topaz with reasonably good effect.

Imitation gems are usually made of glass or plastics. In recent years an enormous array of plastics has become available for imitations, but these materials are soft and lack brilliance, and thus are less satisfactory for the purpose than glass. Flint glasses, containing lead oxide, have higher refractive indices and tend to be more brilliant. Cheaper crown or bottle glasses are used for less expensive jewels and costume jewelry. Such gems are often poured into a preshaped mold and not even cut individually like the better flint-glass gems. Special opaque or semiopaque glasses have also been devised for imitation purposes. Jade, lapis lazuli, turquoise, and even opal have all been successfully imitated in glass.

Assembled gems are made by cementing or fusing together pieces of imitation, synthetic, or natural gem material with pieces of natural stone. For example, a colored bottom of green glass may be cemented to a top of colorless or weakly colored beryl, making a doublet. The color of the green glass dominates the stone and the top has the correct refractive index and hardness for emerald, which is a strongly colored blue green beryl. Fine opal triplets are made with a colorless quartz top, a common opal bottom, and a thin middle layer of excellent-quality, color-splashed opal. The hard quartz top not only protects the valuable opal layer from damage, but also allows its dazzling color to come through. Such triplets also help stretch out very scarce supplies of the best-quality opals. Cultured pearls are, in a sense, assembled gems, because MOTHER-OF-PEARL beads are cut and inserted into pearl oysters, which then proceed to add layers of typical lustrous nacre on top of the prepared bead. Only X-ray or sophisticated optical techniques can distinguish these assembled pearls from totally natural pearls.

Synthetic gemstones are manufactured, rather than created by nature. Emerald, ruby, sapphire, and spinel are made commercially in superb quality and in large quantities. Oddly enough, these gemstones are much superior in quality to their natural counterparts. Synthetic ruby and sapphire were first successfully made in the late 1800s by the French chemists Edmund Fremy (1814–1894) and Auguste Verneuil (1856–1913). The latter devised the flame-fusion method of ruby synthesis that is still used extensively today. In recent years the science of crystal growth has advanced greatly and permitted the synthesis of new gems that have no natural counterparts. The most successful of these at the moment are strontium titanate, a series of synthetic garnets, and cubic zirconia. Of the synthetic garnets, the yttrium aluminum garnet and gadolinium gallium garnet are among the most useful. Cubic zirconia so well matches diamond in brilliance and color dispersion that a well-cut gem of this material defies close-range visual detection. PAUL E. DESAUTELS

Bibliography: Arem, J. E., *Color Encyclopedia of Gemstones,* 2d ed. (1987); Desautels, P. E., *The Gem Collection,* rev. ed. (1980); Hurlbut, C. S., Jr., and Switzer, G. S., *Gemology* (1979); Klein, Cornelis, and Hurlbut, C. S., Jr., *Manual of Mineralogy,* 20th ed. (1985); Liddicoat, R. T., *Handbook of Gemstone Identification,* 12th ed. (1987); Van Landingham, S. L., *Geology of World Gem Deposits* (1985); Webster, Robert, and Anderson, B. W., *Gems,* 4th ed. (1983); Zucker, Benjamin, *Gems and Jewels: A Connoisseur's Guide* (1984).

gemsbok [gemz'-bahk]

The gemsbok, O. gazella, *a southern African antelope with straight or slightly curved horns that measure up to 120 cm (4 ft) in length, resembles the gazelle in both facial markings and behavior.*

The gemsbok (or gemsbuck), *Oryx gazella,* is a large ANTELOPE, belonging to the family Bovidae, order Artiodactyla. Gemsbok are 120 to 210 cm (4 to 7 ft) tall at the shoulder and may weigh over 200 kg (about 450 lb). They have horns up to 120 cm (4 ft) in length and a coat of brown and black. Gemsbok live in deserts of southern Africa. EVERETT SENTMAN

gender: see GRAMMAR.

gene

The gene is the unit of HEREDITY. Along with many other such units, it is transmitted from parents to offspring. Each gene, acting either alone or with other genes, determines one or more characteristics of the resulting organism. The totality of genes that make up the hereditary constitution of an organism is called a GENOME.

Genes occur in strands of genetic material called chromosomes (see GENETICS). In most cells each gene occupies a particular position within a specific chromosome. Chromosomes can break, however, and some of their genes may be transferred either to other places on the same chromosome or to other chromosomes. When this happens, new combinations (recombinants) of the genes are formed. Genes can also change in chemical composition. In their altered recombinant or chemically varied form, they produce different effects from the unaltered genes (see MUTATION). Depending on the characteristic transmitted by the gene, the environment may also play an important role in determining the extent to which the gene's potential effect is realized (see GENE BANK).

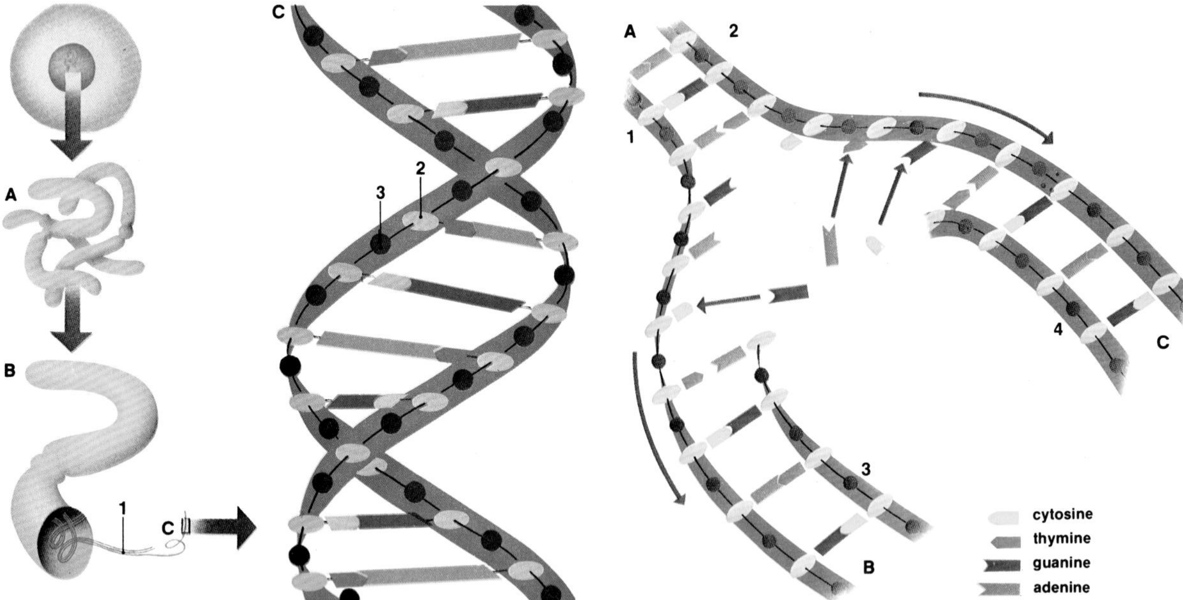

In each type of organism, the cell nucleus contains a set number of chromosomes (A), *each of which* (B) *consists of a threadlike complex of DNA and protein* (1) *coiled into a tightly packed structure. Each DNA molecule* (C) *consists of a backbone of two chains—composed of the sugar deoxyribose* (2) *and phosphate molecules* (3)*—linked by purine-pyrimidine base pairs. DNA has four bases: thymine* (magenta) *always pairs with adenine* (green), *and cytosine* (yellow) *with guanine* (purple). *The order of the bases in each chain forms the genetic code. The entire DNA molecule twists to form a double helix.*

When the DNA molecule (A) *replicates, the two strands* (1, 2) *uncoil and the base pairs separate. Free bases in the cell nucleus form bonds with corresponding bases of the DNA strands—that is, cytosine bonds with guanine and adenine with thymine. Sugar and phosphate molecules attach to the new bases and form new backbones* (3, 4) *of two new double-stranded DNA molecules* (B, C). *Each original strand thus serves as a template for the formation of a complementary new strand, a process known as semiconservative replication. DNA replication occurs in cells during the period between cell divisions.*

THE NATURE OF THE GENE

The subdivision of genetics concerned with the structure and functioning of genes at the molecular level is called molecular genetics. Since the term *gene* was first proposed by the Danish geneticist Wilhelm Johannsen in 1909, concepts of the nature of the gene have undergone great modification. Current understanding of gene structure and function at the molecular level had its origin in 1944, with the work of Canadian bacteriologist Oswald T. AVERY and American scientists Colin M. MACLEOD and Maclyn MCCARTY. They showed that the genes of bacteria are composed of the chemical compound called deoxyribonucleic acid, or DNA. This was later found to be true of the genes of most other organisms.

A further advance was made in 1953, when American biochemist James D. WATSON and English scientist Francis CRICK jointly presented their model of the structure of the DNA molecule. The molecule was shown to consist of two chains of chemical compounds called polynucleotides, the chains being twisted into the form of a coil, or double helix. Subsequently, in 1961, U.S. biochemist M. W. NIRENBERG and others figured out the relationship between the composition of DNA and the composition of the proteins produced by genes. This relationship is known as the GENETIC CODE. It later became evident that another nucleic acid, called ribonucleic acid, or RNA, also functions to carry out protein synthesis.

At first it was thought that all genes functioned in an identical manner to produce the various characteristics of an organism. Three different classes of genes, however, are now recognized. One class consists of the structural genes, whose genetic codes determine the sequences of AMINO ACIDS that go to make up proteins or the smaller molecules known as polypeptides (see PEPTIDE), including many hormones. Another class of genes has genetic codes that specify molecules that function in the physical and chemical processes involved in PROTEIN SYNTHESIS. The third gene class consists of regulatory genes, which are noncoding. They act solely as "recognition" sites for enzymes and other proteins involved in controlling protein synthesis (see OPERON).

Early studies seemed to indicate that a gene, wherever it happened to be located within a chromosome, consisted of a single continuous unit. Later it was found some genes have a region called the leader that precedes the coding segment, and a region called the trailer that follows it. In addition, the coding segment itself may actually be broken up into sections, with intervening noncoding sequences called introns between coding portions called exons.

A far-reaching advance in gene study was made in 1973, when American geneticists Stanley Cohen and Herbert Boyer demonstrated that certain enzymes, called restriction endonucleases, could be used to make cuts in a DNA molecule at certain specific sites. This produced a series of segments with identical free ends, which could join with other free ends having the appropriate complementary configuration. The result was the reestablishment of a fully functional DNA double helix. Using this procedure, called gene splicing (see GENETIC ENGINEERING), it became possible to take a gene from a human cell and transfer it to a bacterium, mouse, rat, or pig, where the human gene would function as it would in a human being. It even became possible to transfer animal genes to plants. One projected use of this procedure would be to transfer appropriate normal human genes to cells of individuals suffering from hemophilia, cystic fibrosis, or other GENETIC DISEASES. Should such transfers prove successful, they could provide a means to cure such genetic diseases through direct gene therapy.

The actual functioning of genes is complex. To understand it, the nature and structure of the nucleic acids DNA and RNA must be examined in greater detail.

DNA

DNA occurs as the genetic material in most viruses and in all cellular organisms. Some viruses, however, have no DNA. Instead, their genetic material is in the form of RNA.

Depending on the particular DNA-containing organism, most DNA is found either in a single chromosome, as in bacteria, blue-green algae, and DNA viruses, or in several chromosomes, as in all other living things. In addition to its presence in chromosomes, DNA is also found in many CELL organelles, such as plasmids in bacteria, chloroplasts in plants, and mitochondria in both plants and animals.

Structure. All DNA molecules consist of a linked series of units that are called nucleotides. Each DNA nucleotide is composed of three subunits: a 5-carbon sugar called deoxyribose, a phosphate group that is joined to one end of the sugar molecule, and one of several different nitrogen-containing bases linked to the opposite end of the sugar molecule. The four bases that predominate in DNA are called adenine and guanine (double-ringed PURINE compounds), and thymine and cytosine (single-ringed PYRIMIDINE compounds). Four different types of DNA nucleotides can be formed, depending on the base involved.

The phosphate group of each nucleotide bonds to one of the carbon atoms of the sugar molecule in the adjacent nucleotide. This forms a so-called polynucleotide chain. The DNA of most organisms consists of two polynucleotide chains that are coiled to form a double helix. The backbone, or outside margin, of each chain consists of the sugar-phosphate sequence. The bases project inward from this backbone, into the helix. The bases of one chain are attracted to bases on the other chain by means of hydrogen bonds. This holds the double helix together. Exceptions to this type of structural organization are found in some viruses with genetic material consisting of a single DNA chain.

In a DNA double helix the pairing between bases of the two chains is highly specific. That is, adenine is always linked to thymine by two hydrogen bonds, and guanine is always linked to cystosine by three hydrogen bonds. This arrangement—a purine linked to a pyrimidine—results in a molecule of uniform diameter. Because of this specific way in which DNA nucleotides are paired through certain pairs of bases, the base sequence of the two strands in the helix is said to be complementary. This means that the base sequence of either strand may be converted to that of its partner by replacing adenine by thymine or thymine by adenine, and replacing guanine by cytosine or cytosine by guanine.

Functions. The genetic material DNA has two specific functions. It provides for protein synthesis and hence for the growth and development of an organism. It also furnishes all descendants of the organism with protein-synthesizing information by replicating itself and passing a copy to each offspring. This information, known as the genetic code, lies in the sequence of bases of DNA, which specifies the sequence of amino acids in a protein. DNA does not act directly in the process of protein synthesis. Instead it acts through the formation of a particular type of RNA called messenger RNA (mRNA) during the process of transcription.

DNA replication depends on the principle of complementarity mentioned above. During the process of replication, the two strands of the DNA double helix separate from one another. As separation occurs, each base on each strand attracts its complementary base-containing nucleotide, to which it becomes attached by hydrogen bonds. For example, the base adenine attracts and bonds to the base thymine. As the complementary nucleotides are fitted into place, an enzyme called DNA polymerase performs its function. It binds the phosphate of one nucleotide to the sugar molecule of the adjacent nucleotide, forming a new polynucleotide chain. The new strand of DNA remains hydrogen-bonded to the old one, and together they form a new double-helix molecule. This type of replication is called semiconservative, because each newly formed double-stranded molecule consists of one previously existing DNA strand.

Viruses, which contain single-stranded DNA, replicate by a slightly more complicated process. When a virus enters a cell, it makes a complementary copy of itself, to which it remains attached. A virus in this condition is said to be in its replicative form (RF), temporarily becoming a double-stranded DNA virus. The two chains separate during replication, but only the recently formed strand attracts complementary nucleotides. These newly attracted nucleotides are joined together by the enzyme DNA polymerase, their base sequence being exactly the same as that of the original DNA virus. The newly formed polynucleotide chain is released from the RF of the original virus and functions alone.

Mutations. Many environmental factors can alter the structure of a DNA molecule. Some factors may be physical, and others are chemical. A mutation occurs when such alterations lead to a permanent change in the base sequence of a DNA molecule. Mutations in turn result in an inherited change in protein synthesis. Most mutations tend to be harmful in their effects, and a number of self-repair mechanisms exist to deal with the damage done to DNA by environmental factors. Processes of mutation and self-repair have been studied, for example, in the case of damage caused to DNA by exposure to ultraviolet (UV) light. The energy absorbed by DNA during UV exposure results in the formation of chemical bonds between adjacent bases of the same polynucleotide strand. This condition interferes with base pairing during replication and leads to mutations.

RNA

Ribonucleic acid, or RNA, is needed in all organisms in order for protein synthesis to occur. It is also the genetic material of some viruses, which are referred to as RNA viruses (see VIRUS).

Like DNA, all RNA molecules have a similar chemical organization consisting of nucleotides. Each RNA nucleotide, like those in DNA, consists of three subunits. One is a 5-carbon sugar called ribose, the second is a phosphate group that is attached to one end of the sugar molecule, and the third is one of several different nitrogen-containing bases linked to the opposite end of the sugar molecule. Four bases predominate in RNA: adenine and guanine (double-ringed purine compounds), and uracil and cytosine (single-ringed pyrimidine compounds).

Scientists can view nucleic acids directly by using a form of electron microscope called a scanning tunneling microscope. In the lower and main upper views, a DNA strand in its protein envelope has been coated with metal to enhance the images. In the upper insert of an uncoated DNA-protein strand, individual molecules are visible.

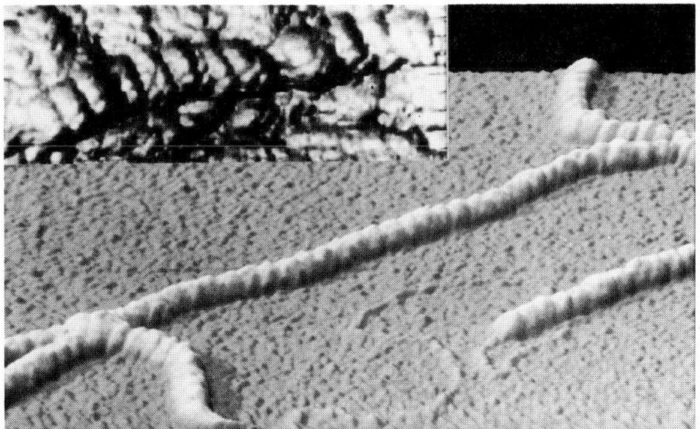

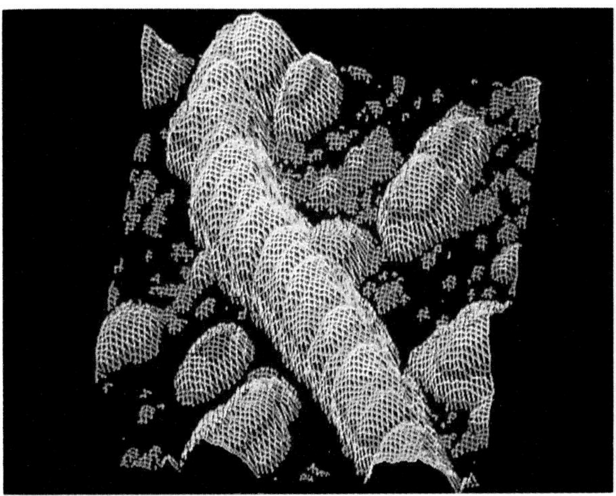

Structure. RNA differs from DNA in two aspects of its chemical organization. First, the sugar in RNA is of the ribose type, indicating that the second carbon molecule in the ring has a hydroxyl (OH) group attached to it. (In DNA the second carbon in the ring has only a hydrogen (H) atom—hence the prefix *deoxy,* meaning "lacking oxygen," in the DNA sugar deoxyribose.) Second, the base uracil is present only in RNA. (Thymine, the base comparable to uracil, is present only in DNA.) Both bases are single-ringed pyrimidines, and their nucleotides substitute for one another, depending on whether the strand is RNA or DNA.

The nucleotides of RNA are joined in a polynucleotide chain by means of bonding the phosphate of each nucleotide to a carbon atom of the adjacent nucleotide's sugar subunit. In RNA viruses the RNA is in the form of either a double or a single polynucleotide chain. In double-stranded RNA viruses, the geometric arrangement of the two polynucleotide chains is similar to that of double-stranded DNA, and the pairing between bases of the two RNA chains is highly specific. Adenine is always linked to uracil by two hydrogen bonds, and guanine is always linked to cytosine by three hydrogen bonds. Again as in DNA, the specific pairing of RNA nucleotides according to the base concerned indicates that the base sequence of the two RNA strands is complementary. Thus if the base sequence of one strand is known, then the base sequence of the other strand can be specified.

Functions. Replication of double-stranded RNA follows the pattern described for DNA. The RNA chains separate, and each base attracts an RNA nucleotide carrying the complementary base, to which it is attached by hydrogen bonds. As the complementary nucleotides are fitted into place, an enzyme called RNA replicase binds the nucleotides together, forming a new polynucleotide chain. The new strand of RNA remains hydrogen-bonded to the old strand—another example of simiconservative replication.

Single-stranded RNA viruses fall into two classes. The first group includes the polio virus that attracks the nerve cells of humans and other primates. When this type of virus enters a cell, the virus makes a complementary copy of itself, to which it remains attached. In this stage the virus is again said to be in its RF form, temporarily becoming a double-stranded RNA virus. During replication, although the two chains separate, only the recently formed strand attracts nucleotides with complementary bases. The newly attracted nucleotides are joined together by the enzyme RNA replicase. In their base sequence they are exactly the same as the original RNA virus. The newly formed chain is released from the RF of the original virus to function independently.

The second group of single-stranded RNA viruses contains some that cause tumors in animals, such as mouse leukemia virus and mouse mammary tumor virus. Upon entering a cell, this type of virus makes a complementary strand of itself. This newly formed chain, however, is composed of DNA nucleotides. The single strand of DNA in turn makes a complementary DNA strand of itself, forming a DNA double helix. The newly formed DNA double helix becomes incorporated into one of the chromosomes of the host cell, where it is replicated along with the host DNA. While in the host cell, the RNA-derived viral DNA produces single-stranded RNA viruses that leave the host cell and enter other cells. The enzyme involved in making a DNA complement of RNA is called RNA-directed DNA polymerase, or reverse transcriptase—a name based on the action of reversing the transcription process. Such viruses are also referred to as RETROVIRUSES. One of them, called HIV (for human immunodeficiency virus), invades and kills the T-helper lymphocytes of a person's immune system, resulting in the disease called acquired immune deficiency syndrome, or AIDS (see AIDS).

Types of RNA. RNA that is involved in protein synthesis is single stranded. It belongs to one of three distinct types, called ribosomal RNA (rRNA), transfer RNA (tRNA), and messenger RNA (mRNA). A cell's ribosomal RNA is associated with protein, forming bodies called RIBOSOMES. Ribosomes are the sites of protein synthesis. Ribosomal RNA varies in size and constitutes 85 to 90 percent of all the RNA in a cell.

Transfer RNA, also called soluble RNA or adapter RNA, is a group of small molecules, each of which has a specific attraction for one of the amino acids. The function of each type of tRNA is to bring its specific amino acid to a ribosome for possible inclusion in the particular protein being synthesized. The tRNA molecules consist of about 80 nucleotides structured in a cloverleaf pattern. They constitute about 5 percent of a cell's RNA.

The third type of cellular RNA, messenger RNA, constitutes 5 to 10 percent of a cell's total RNA. It acts as an intermediary between the genes located in the chromosomes, and the ribosomes located in the cytoplasm. As its name implies, mRNA carries the genetic code contained in the sequence of bases in the cell's DNA. Because the DNAs from various organisms differ only in the sequence of their bases, mRNA from different organisms must reflect this difference in base sequence. The synthesis of mRNA, called transcription, involves the formation of an RNA chain that is complementary to one of the two strands of a DNA double helix. In the transcription process, only nucleotides that contain ribose are used. In this process, uracil acts as the complement of adenine. The enzyme involved in transcription is known as RNA polymerase.

RNA as an Information Molecule. The earliest information molecule to have evolved must have been both relatively simple in structure and capable of enzymatic activity. RNA, which acts as the carrier of genetic messages in all organisms, is the simplest molecule known that has the capacity to store and transmit information.

Initially, evidence that RNA can also act as a catalyst of reactions centered on the enzyme called ribonuclease P, which consists of protein and RNA. The enzyme has been found in virtually all organisms. It is involved in the process that transforms the precursor molecules of tRNAs into their fully functional forms. Geneticists have since discovered that the RNA component of this enzyme, acting alone, can perform the catalytic activity of the enzyme, whereas the protein alone cannot. More recently, investigations have concentrated on the ribosomal-RNA specifying gene of the protozoan *Tetrahymena thermophila.* This gene consists of a noncoding sequence, or intron, between two coding portions, or exons. After transcription, the precursor RNA molecule has to have the intron-transcribed segment removed before the ribosomal-RNA molecule can become functional. It was found that the intron-specified segment snipped itself out of the precursor molecule and then spliced the two loose ends together to form the functional molecule.

These findings, that RNA is capable of catalytic activity, lend support to the concept that RNA was indeed the earliest information molecule, and that DNA must have evolved from RNA. Support for this hypothesis is found in the life cycles of RNA tumor viruses, which, upon entering cells, make DNA copies of themselves.

LOUIS LEVINE

Bibliography: Alberts, Bruce, et al., *Molecular Biology of the Cell* (1983); Carlson, E. A., *The Gene: A Critical History* (1966); Kornberg, Arthur, *DNA Replication* (1980); Suzuki, D. T., et al., *An Introduction to Genetics* (1986); Watson, J. D., *The Double Helix* (1968).

gene bank

Gene bank is a popular term used to describe repositories for GENES of living organisms. It is commonly used in the context of PLANT BREEDING, as discussed below, but it also applies to the freezing and storage of animal sperm and embryos for use in ANIMAL HUSBANDRY (see also ARTIFICIAL INSEMINATION).

Genetic variation is the raw material for the plant breeder, who must often select from primitive and wild plants, including related species, in the search for new genes. The appearance of new diseases, pests, or new virulent forms of existing disease-causing organisms makes it imperative that plant variation be preserved, because it offers a potential for the presence of disease-resistant genes not present in cultivated varieties. Also, there are demands for new characters, for example, high protein, improved nutritional factors, and fertility restoration. As a result, plant breeders require a large and diverse gene pool to meet ever-changing demands.

An understanding of crop origins and variations is necessary in assembling genetic diversity in plant crops. In certain geographical areas there has existed a rich source of variability in crop plants, but the encroachment of civilization has reduced the natural variability inherent in primitive plant forms and related species of crop plants. Agricultural progress, as a result of new breeding programs, has reduced rather than increased crop variability as improved cultivars, or varieties, are planted in wider and wider areas and old cultivars, which may contain valuable genes, are lost. Crop failures, which result in a smaller gene pool, have also led to an increased awareness of the need to preserve genetic diversity in plants.

Efforts are under way to increase collections of plant materials in various forms. Usually these are preserved as seeds, but living plants, pollen, and cell cultures may also be used. In most gene banks, seeds are usually preserved under conditions of low temperature and humidity. These collections must be periodically renewed by growing the plants and producing new seeds. Increasing emphasis is also being placed on preserving living collections of asexually propagated crops, such as fruit and nut species.

In the United States, germ plasm banks are handled in a state-federal cooperative program. Internationally, a consortium of international, government, and private organizations called the Consultative Group in International Agricultural Research established (1974) the International Board for Plant Genetic Resources (IBPGR) to promote the activities of international plant research centers that collect and preserve plant germ plasm. Initially, such centers were located predominantly in industrialized nations of the Northern Hemisphere, and developing countries supplied most of the germ-plasm material. Developing countries have complained that commercial seed companies from the developed countries have profited from the patenting and sale of the seed of new, improved plant varieties. In a 1983 meeting of the United Nation's Food and Agriculture Organization (FAO), member nations voted to bring the IBPGR under greater international control. Some industrialized nations, however, reserved their approval of the plan because of their own special agreements with seed breeders to grant patents on crop varieties; in addition, several developing countries continued their own restrictions on the shipment of germ plasm beyond their borders. The Seed Action Network, a coalition of nongovernmental organizations, met in 1988 to discuss this controversial situation. It proposed to levy a tax on the companies that sell the seeds of new plant varieties. JULES JANICK

Bibliography: Holden, J. H., and Williams, J. T., eds., *Crop Genetic Resources: Conservation and Evaluation* (1985); Plucknett, D. L., et al., *Gene Banks and the World's Food* (1987); Rubenstein, I., et al., ed., *The Genetic Improvement of Crops* (1980); Sgaravatti, E., ed., *World List of Seed Sources,* 3d ed. (1986).

See also: GENETIC ENGINEERING; GENETICS; PLANT PROPAGATION; SEED.

gene therapy: see GENETIC DISEASES.

genealogy [jen-ee-ahl'-uh-jee]

Genealogy is the study of ancestry, or family lineage. Genealogists trace lines of family ancestry and usually show their findings by means of pedigree charts, or genealogical trees. Their studies may be relevant to history, law, sociology, or eugenics. Or their appeal may be more limited and personal.

Most peoples have, at some time, venerated their ancestors, often by ancestor worship. Primitive societies, which are usually organized in tribes or clans, have often sought to trace clan ancestry to gods, legendary heroes, or animals. Clans can thus bolster their identity and strive for divine protection. Lineages were originally transmitted by oral tradition, but later literate societies began to write them down. Notable early Western examples include the genealogies of the tribes of Israel (recorded in the Bible), the Greeks, and the Romans.

Genealogies assumed particular importance in connection with the principle of inheritance—of power, rank, and property. Lists of hereditary kings were compiled by the ancient Sumerians, Babylonians, Egyptians, Indians, and Chinese. In medieval Europe feudal land-holders kept records for the transference of rank and land. Concern with descent, and thus rank, was also reflected in heraldic developments (see HERALDRY); a single coat of arms can incorporate an enormous amount of genealogical information.

In modern times, social status has depended less on pedigree, but genealogy remains of interest to many people other than scholars. The United States, for example, has numerous genealogical societies that trace people's descent. Many patriotic organizations, such as the Daughters of the American Revolution, limit membership to descendants of a particular historical group. The Mormon church has collected an enormous bank of genealogical data (official registers of births, marriages, and deaths and related documents), probably the greatest such collection in existence. Church members use these records in order to bring their ancestors posthumously into the church (see MORMONISM). Popular interest in genealogy was stimulated by the television dramatization of Alex HALEY'S ROOTS (1976); in researching this book Haley had traced his ancestry back to his African forebears. A major appeal of genealogy is that it provides people with a sense of continuity and of belonging.

Bibliography: Andereck, Paul, and Pence, Richard, *Computer Genealogy* (1985); Delson, Eric, *Ancestors* (1985); Doane, Gilbert H., *Searching for Your Ancestors,* 5th ed. (1980); Greenwood, V. D., *The Researcher's Guide to American Genealogy* (1973); Hareven, T., and Plakans, A., eds., *Family History at the Crossroads* (1987); McNaughton, Arnold, *The Book of Kings: A Royal Genealogy,* 3 vols. (1974); Pine, Leslie G., *American Origins: Sources for Genealogical Research and Records Abroad* (1960; repr. 1980) and *Heraldry and Genealogy* (1974).

General Accounting Office

As the auditing authority of the U.S. Congress, the General Accounting Office (GAO) examines the finances of almost all federal government agencies. It has statutory authority to investigate all matters relating to the receipt, disbursement, and application of public funds. It also reviews the accounting systems used by federal agencies, determines whether expenditures conform to law, and settles claims made against the United States by individuals or governments. In recent years Congress has broadened the scope of the GAO's responsibilities to include analysis of program management and policy decisions by the executive branch in diverse fields ranging from defense to health. The GAO also assists the Congress in carrying out its legislative and oversight responsibilities. The GAO, created in 1921, is headed by the comptroller general of the United States, who is appointed by the president with the consent of the Senate for a term of 15 years.

General Agreement on Tariffs and Trade

The General Agreement on Tariffs and Trade (GATT) is a treaty that has been signed by 95 nations and Hong Kong and recognized on a de facto basis by 30 others as of 1987. It took effect on Jan. 1, 1948. GATT lays down a code of conduct for international trade, based on the principles that trade should be conducted without discrimination (the MOST-FAVORED-NATION principle); that domestic industry should be protected only through customs tariffs and not through quantitative restrictions or other measures; that tariffs should be reduced through multilateral negotiations; and that member countries should consult together to overcome trade problems. GATT also established (1964) the International Trade Center, operated jointly with the United Nations Conference on Trade and Development, to assist developing nations in the promotion of their export trade. GATT is administered by a secretariat from a headquarters in Geneva.

Since the inception of GATT, a total of 8 "rounds" of trade negotiations held under its auspices have brought about far-reaching reductions in tariffs and other trade barriers. The latest round began in September 1986 with a ministerial conference at Punta Del Este, Uruguay, in which representatives agreed to hold talks over the next 3 to 4 years. One of the chief breakthroughs in the 1986 negotiations was the decision to discuss reducing barriers to service industries such as banking, insurance, and telecommunications. (Previous rounds had been limited to discussion of manufactured goods.) The delegates also agreed to consider a gradual lowering of export subsidies for agricultural products and to discuss barriers to foreign investment and "piracy" of intellectual property. During 1987 a negotiation group on textiles and clothing was established. JOHN G. STOESSINGER

General Services Administration

As the United States government's property manager and procurement agent, the General Services Administration (GSA), with 11 regional offices, operates much like a large corporation. Its activities are divided among 4 separate services—the Public Buildings Service, Federal Supply Service, Information Resources Management Service, and Federal Property Resources Service. Among its major functions are the construction and operation of federal buildings; the distribution of supplies, services, and personal property to federal agencies; the management of transportation and travel services, and the operation of federal motor pools; and the handling of telecommunications and automated data processing and the operation of Federal Information Centers. The GSA also utilizes and disposes of government-owned real property and handles the National Defense Stockpile of strategic and critical materials.

general staff

A general staff is a group of officers who assist the commanding officer of a national army in administration, planning, and coordination. The term is also used less frequently to refer to those assisting the commander of a large field unit. Staff officers have no authority to command but act as agents of the chief of staff.

The general staff concept began to develop in the 16th and 17th centuries with the growth of national armies. A prototype was created by Napoleon I, but the system was brought to its full development by the Prussian Army under Helmuth von MOLTKE, chief of the Prussian General Staff (1857–88). Moltke realized that the need to mobilize and deploy men and equipment on railroads at the onset of war required careful preparation by a trained staff during peacetime. His efforts were crowned by the crushing victories of his armies in the Seven Weeks' War (1866) and the Franco-Prussian War (1870–71).

In the United States a general staff, consisting of the chiefs of various administrative bureaus in the Department of War, was created by Congress in 1813. At the urging of Secretary of War Elihu Root, the modern general staff was introduced into the U.S. Army in 1903 with the establishment of a general staff corps and a chief of staff. (The British army general staff was created in 1906.) In 1920, under Gen. John J. Pershing, the general staff was organized into five sections: personnel (G-1), intelligence (G-2), operations and training (G-3), supply (G-4), and the War Plans Division (later renamed the Operations Division). Numerous reorganizations have occurred since then, and the navy and air force have acquired their own general staffs. The U.S. Army general-staff positions are designated as: chief of staff; vice chief; director; commander general, Army Strategic Defense Command; and deputy chiefs for operations and plans, personnel, logistics, and intelligence.

Bibliography: Dastrup, Boyd L., *The History of Army Command and General Staff* (1982); Dupuy, T. N., *A Genius for War: The German Army and the General Staff* (1977); Nelson, Otto L., Jr., *National Security and the General Staff* (1946).

general strike

A general strike is a stoppage of work by most workers in a number of different industries at the same time. It may be employed to obtain economic goals, to protest specific policies adopted by a government, or to force political concessions (see SYNDICALISM). It sometimes begins in one industry and spreads to others. General strikes in the United States have occurred only on a local basis, but in Europe some have been nationwide. The Belgian general strike of 1902 brought about universal manhood suffrage; in Russia a 1905 general strike resulted in the promise of civil liberties and other reforms; the German general strike of 1919 averted a rightist takeover. The Swedish general strike of 1909, in defiance of the practice of lockout by employers, was less successful and ended in the capitulation of the workers. In Britain in 1926 strikes in sympathy with the coal miners grew into a general strike involving 3 million workers. The strike failed and led to the Trade Disputes and Trade Union Act of 1927, which limited unions' strike powers. A general strike was called in France in 1938 to protest a government decree extending work hours and exacting penalties from strikers, but the strike failed. In the postwar period general strikes have been less frequent but have been organized on several occasions to protest government policies in Belgium, France, and Italy. A spontaneous general strike occurred in France in May 1968 when widespread protests by students sparked a walkout by workers that threatened the DE GAULLE government and led to economic concessions and some educational reforms.

Bibliography: Goodstein, Phil H., *The Theory of the General Strike from the French Revolution to Poland* (1984); Hoyles, Andrée, *Imagination in Power: The Occupation of Factories in France in 1968* (1973); Lewis, Arthur D., *Syndicalism and the General Strike* (1912; repr. 1976); Morris, Margaret, *The General Strike* (1976; repr. 1980); Shorter, Edward, and Tilly, Charles, *Strikes in France, 1830–1968* (1974).

General Theological Seminary

Established in 1817, General Theological Seminary (enrollment: 129; library: 195,000 volumes) is a coeducational institution in New York City that trains clergy for the Protestant Episcopal church. It sits on land given by Clement Clarke Moore. The seminary has a collection of Bibles that includes incunabula.

generator

A generator is a machine that converts mechanical energy into electrical energy by rotating an ARMATURE, which contains conductors, through a magnetic field. A voltage is induced in the moving conductors by an effect called ELECTROMAGNETIC INDUCTION. In order for voltage to be generated, relative motion must exist between the conductors and the magnetic field. An ENGINE, MOTOR, TURBINE, or other source of mechanical energy is used to turn the armature shaft. Generators are built in many sizes. Most electricity used today in cars, in homes, and by industry is produced by generators.

The development of the electric generator began in 1831 when Michael FARADAY in England and Joseph HENRY in the United States proved that a magnet could be made to produce

An automobile generator consists of a shaft on which is mounted an armature, composed of wires coiled around slots in a soft-iron core that is rotated between magnetic field poles and connected to a commutator for delivering direct current to external terminals.

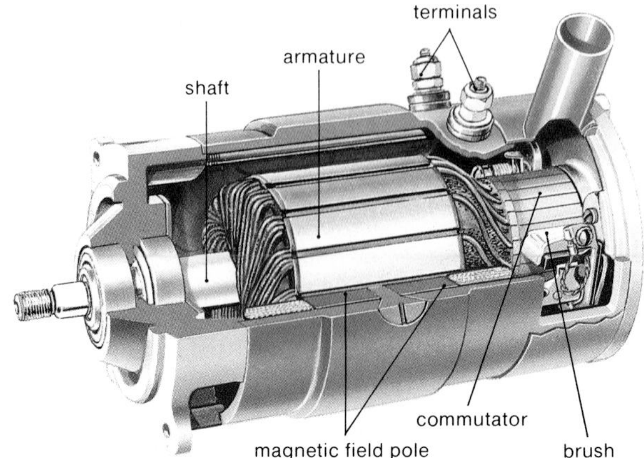

an electric current. In a classic experiment, Faraday connected a sensitive galvanometer across a coil and found that as a magnet was moved into the coil, a current flowed in the coil. As the magnet was withdrawn, a current flowed through the coil in the opposite direction. The current flow, however, occurred only while the magnet was in motion.

Faraday's experiment proved that voltage can be produced by magnetism when three conditions exist. First, a conductor must exist in which the voltage will be induced. Second, a magnetic field must be close to the conductor. Third, relative motion must occur between the magnetic field and the conductor. The conductor must be moved so as to cut across the magnetic field, or the magnetic field must be moved so that it is cut by the conductor. When the conductor or magnetic field moves, electrons within the conductor are forced in one direction or the other, creating a voltage.

Types. The two main types of generators are direct-current (DC) generators and alternating-current (AC) generators, or alternators. The DC generator rotates the conductors in a stationary magnetic field. The alternator rotates a magnetic field that is cut by the stationary conductors. Current induced in the conductors of all generators is an alternating current. The current taken from the generator, however, may be AC or DC, depending on how the generator is constructed.

The strength of the voltage induced in the conductor depends on its speed and on the strength of the magnetic field. The magnetic field may be furnished by a permanent magnet or by current flowing through field coils to form an electromagnet. When the ends of the conductor are connected to form a complete circuit, the induced voltage causes a current to flow in the external circuit.

Components. The principal components of a DC generator are the armature, commutator, field poles, brushes and brush rigging, yoke or frame, and end bells or end frames. Other components found on some DC generators are interpoles, compensating windings, and various controls and devices for regulating the generated voltage and current output.

Direct-current generators have a commutator mounted on one end of the armature shaft. The commutator rectifies or changes the alternating current in the conductors into direct current. Brushes mounted in holders ride on the rotating commutator bars and carry the direct current from the commutator to the external load circuit.

In an alternator, the armature coils, or stationary conductors, are held in place in slots in the alternator frame. The field coils are wound on poles or slots around the rotating shaft. The assembly that contains the stationary conductors is called the STATOR. The assembly that includes the rotating poles and field coils is called the rotor. Most alternators use brushes and slip rings on the rotor to pass direct current to the revolving field windings. Some alternators do not use any type of brushes or slip rings. DONALD L. ANGLIN

Bibliography: Alerich, W. N., *Electricity Four*, 4th ed. (1986); Bleaney, B. I. and B., *Electricity and Magnetism*, 3d ed. (1976); De France, J. J., *Electrical Fundamentals*, 2d ed. (1983); Ryff, P. F., *Electrical Machinery* (1988).

See also: MAGNETISM; POWER, GENERATION AND TRANSMISSION OF.

Genesis, Book of [jen'-i-sis]

Genesis, the first book of the Old Testament in the Bible, is so named because it opens with an account of the creation of the world (see CREATION ACCOUNTS). The first 11 chapters, which are heavily indebted to Mesopotamian tradition, trace the gradual expansion of humankind and the development of human culture. But they show the ambiguity of this development by incorporating stories about the sin of ADAM and EVE and about the DELUGE, both of which illustrate humankind's growing alienation from God and each other.

Following the call of ABRAHAM in chapter 12, this universal outlook appears to be lost; the focus narrows to one man and his family. Yet the traditions about Abraham, ISAAC, JACOB, and Jacob's 12 sons are linked to the earlier chapters by God's promise to bless the whole world through Abraham's descendants. Furthermore, the COVENANT established with Israel through the promise made to Abraham (22:15–18) is fundamentally the same as the covenant established with all of humankind through NOAH (9:1–17).

Although Moses has traditionally been considered the author of Genesis, modern scholars generally agree that the book is a composite of at least three different literary strands: J (10th century BC), E (9th century), and P (5th century). The interpretation of the book has led to many controversies. One of the most difficult problems has been distinguishing historical fact from symbolic narration intended to convey a religious message. J. J. M. ROBERTS

Bibliography: Rad, Gerhard von, *Genesis: A Commentary*, trans. by J. H. Marks, rev. ed. (1972); Speiser, E. A., ed., *Genesis* (1964); Youngblood, Ronald, ed., *The Genesis Debate* (1986).

Genêt, Edmond (Citizen Genêt) [zhuh-nay']

Edmond Charles Édouard Genêt, b. Jan. 8, 1763, d., July 15, 1834, was a French diplomat who served as minister to the United States in 1793. He entered the diplomatic service through the patronage of Queen Marie Antoinette and was (1789–92) chargé d'affaires in St. Petersburg. His staunch republicanism led the revolutionary government to appoint him minister to the United States. He was instructed to secure American aid, short of military intervention, for France in its war with England. Arriving in Charleston, S.C., in April 1793, Genêt was given a warm popular welcome but was coldly received by President George Washington, who disapproved of the radicalism of the French Revolution. Mistakenly believing he enjoyed popular support, Genêt defied the president's ban on outfitting privateers and threatened a direct appeal to the people. Washington requested his recall in August 1793. Fearing reprisal, Genêt never returned to France. He married a daughter of Gov. George Clinton of New York and died near Albany. HARRY AMMON

Bibliography: Ammon, Harry, *The Genet Mission* (1973).

Genet, Jean [zhuh-nay']

The French writer Jean Genet, b. Dec. 19, 1910, d. Apr. 15, 1986, was a novelist and exponent of the THEATER OF THE ABSURD. Discovered and championed by the existentialist Jean Paul Sartre, Genet was an orphan, thief, and homosexual who had spent most of his youth in prison. There he developed his personal credo: to harden himself against pain. Reversing the Christian mystic's ascent toward a state of holiness, Genet in the 1930s embarked on a satanic pilgrimage with the goal of reaching the lowest possible state of evil. *The Thief's Journal* (1949; Eng. trans., 1964) is his record of this journey, in which no aspect of suffering, sordidness, and degradation was spared him. While still in prison, Genet wrote his first novel, *Our Lady of the Flowers* (1943 and 1951; Eng. trans., 1963), a transposition and sublimation of the elements of his life. Likewise, in *Miracle of the Rose* (1943 and 1951; Eng. trans., 1966),

Jean Genet, painted by the film actor Jean Marais, was one of the most prominent figures of contemporary French literature and a vital contributor to the theater of the absurd. His own experiences as a criminal and pariah form the bases of his poems, novels, and dramas—caustic and powerful works of disturbing beauty that explore the nature of identity and evil. (Collection Viollet, Paris.)

his heroes—monsters and saints—represent aspects of the men he knew in prison, as well as extensions of himself—rootless, troubled personalities in revolt.

Genet's plays are the finest products of his art, mature reappraisals of the themes treated in his novels. In *The Maids* (1947; Eng. trans., 1954), *Deathwatch* (1949; Eng. trans., 1954), *The Balcony* (1956; Eng. trans., 1957), *The Blacks* (1958; Eng. trans., 1960), and *The Screens* (1961; Eng. trans., 1962) are seen conflicts between illusion and reality, life and death, good and evil, the strong and the weak, the old and the young, the conscious and the unconscious. Although hedonistic and ostensibly amoral, these plays nevertheless approach religious ritual and can best be understood as sacred drama, through which the audience's deepest feelings are aroused by sharing in the theatrical ceremony. As with ancient Greek theater or the Mass, the audience is offered the possibility of transformation as a result of participation. Genet is the inventor of a highly personal metaphoric imagery with a unique structure of mysterious relationships and analogies and an extraordinary violence and cruelty that produce energetically rhythmic dramatic sequences. His plays, always shocking but never vulgar, have been a powerful force in the renewal of modern drama. BETTINA KNAPP

Bibliography: Cetta, Lewis, *Profane Play, Ritual and Jean Genet* (1974); Chaudhuri, Una, *No Man's Stage: A Semiotic Study of Jean Genet's Major Plays* (1986); Coe, Richard, *The Vision of Jean Genet* (1968); Henning, S. D., *Genet's Ritual Play* (1981); Knapp, Bettina, *Jean Genet* (1968); Sartre, Jean Paul, *Saint Genet, Actor and Martyr*, trans. by Bernard Frechtman (1963); Thody, Philip, *Jean Genet* (1970).

genetic code

The genetic code is the chemical equation by which hereditary information is translated from genes into PROTEINS such as hemoglobin, insulin, and pepsin. Some proteins serve as structural material for the body, whereas others, namely ENZYMES and polypeptide HORMONES, regulate the chemical reactions of the body.

The chromosomes, located in the nucleus of the CELL, contain the nucleic acid DNA (deoxyribonucleic acid), which is the hereditary material of most organisms.The chromosome is divided into units called genes, each gene being responsible for a particular trait (see GENETICS). In biochemical terms, each gene is responsible for the manufacture of the particular protein that is involved in the development of a trait. PROTEIN SYNTHESIS takes place in the cytoplasm of the cell, so the transfer of genetic information must occur across the nuclear membrane. The constancy of the genetic code in all past and present members of the species permits the genes to have the same effects on their carriers from generation to generation.

A knowledge of how the genetic code works is important to medical research, especially in the fields of genetic diseases and genetic engineering. Improved plant- and animal-breeding methods are based on understanding the genetic code, as are studies in behavioral and developmental genetics.

THE CODON

The codon is the fundamental unit in the genetic code. An understanding of the codon, however, requires a knowledge of the structure of nucleic acid molecules. Both DNA and RNA are large chemical compounds that consist of a sequence of units called nucleotides. Each nucleotide unit consists of three smaller chemical compounds: a phosphate, a sugar, and a base (see GENE).

Nucleic Acid Bases. The essential nucleotide subunit of the genetic code is the base. Four types of bases occur in DNA: adenine (A) and guanine (G), which are double-ringed compounds called purines; and thymine (T) and cytosine (C), which are single-ringed compounds called pyrimidines. In RNA the bases used in the genetic code are adenine, guanine, cytosine, and uracil (U). Uracil is a pyrimidine that occurs in RNA wherever thymine would be present in DNA.

Combination of Bases. The key that unlocks the genetic code is the way in which the bases are arranged in sequence along the one chain of single-stranded DNA and RNA, or along one of the two chains of double-stranded DNA or RNA.

The problem of cracking the code lies in the fact that 20 different amino acids are found in proteins, but only 4 different nucleotide bases are found in nucleic acids. If each base specified an amino acid, then only 4 amino acids could be designated, causing an insufficiency of code words, or codons, for the hereditary messages to be passed on. Code words formed by 3 bases in a specific sequence, however, provide $4 \times 4 \times 4$ different combinations (64 codons), which are more than enough code words for the 20 different amino acids found in proteins. The terms *code word, codon,* and *triplet* (referring to the 3 bases) are interchangeable. The linear order of triplets in an organism's genetic material specifies the linear order of the amino acids in the protein that is produced by means of the genetic code.

Synonyms. With the exception of 3 of the 64 code words, each specifies 1 of the 20 amino acids found in proteins. Most of the amino acids have more than a single codon, whereas a few have only one triplet that codes for them. The various codons that specify a particular amino acid are referred to as the synonyms for that amino acid.

THE CODE IN OPERATION

During the manufacture of proteins the transfer of the information contained in genes takes place in two steps, transcription and translation. In transcription the hereditary material of an organism acts as a template on which an RNA polynucleotide chain, called messenger RNA (mRNA), is formed. The messenger RNA is so called because it carries the genetically coded information from nucleic acids in the cell's nucleus to ribosomes located in the cytoplasm of the cell.

During translation the mRNA becomes attached to the cell's ribosomes, which are the sites of actual protein synthesis. The sequence of the mRNA's codons determines the sequence of the amino acids in a protein. Each amino acid is carried to the ribosome by a molecule of transfer RNA (tRNA), which contains among its nucleotides a sequence of three nucleotide bases called an anticodon. The anticodon is complementary to some particular codon of the mRNA. An attraction and temporary hydrogen bonding occurs between the tRNA and mRNA. During this bonding the particular amino acid is transferred from the tRNA to the growing polypeptide chain.

Transcription from Both Strands. Geneticists originally thought that only one strand—the "sense" strand—of a double-stranded DNA molecule contained the actual genes transcribed into RNA. The other, "antisense" strand was believed to function only in replication (see NUCLEIC ACID). It has since been found that, at least in some cases, both strands of the same DNA sequence are transcribed. Whether the antisense RNA-transcript is translated into protein or remains as RNA and possibly functions as a regulator of the sense gene has not yet been established.

Starting and Stopping the Code. In order for the nucleic acid chain to be divided into genes, each carrying a specific message, signals must be present that indicate where a message begins and where it ends. The mRNA contains special nucleotides at both ends of the message—one that initiates and one that terminates the translation of the code.

The codon for methionine (AUG) is the initiator codon for protein synthesis. When first formed, all polypeptide chains have methionine as their first amino acid. During the translation process or after the protein chain is completed, however, some changes are usually made in the polypeptide chain by cellular enzymes, thereby forming the functional protein. One of these changes may be the removal of methionine.

Three nonsense codons, or terminators—UAA, UAG, and UGA—do not code for any amino acid but function only as punctuation marks in the message. No tRNAs carry anticodons for UAA, UAG, or UGA; when any of these triplets appears in an mRNA chain, the translation process stops.

CHARACTERISTICS OF THE GENETIC CODE

The genetic code has certain characteristics, described below, that determine how and under what conditions the sequence of nucleotide bases of a gene are read.

Degeneracy of the Code. Even though most of the 20 amino acids found in proteins have at least 2 codons, some have as many as 6. Any code in which 2 or more different code words have the same meaning is a degenerate code. The ability to

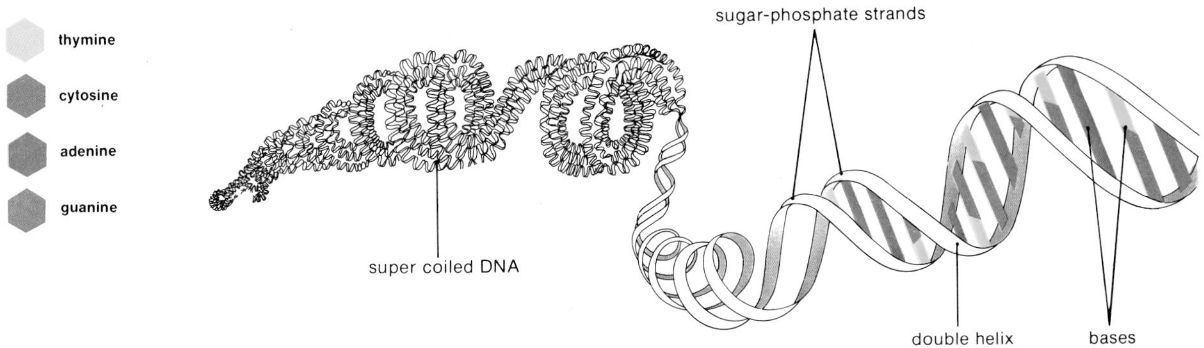

Chromosomes found in the cell nucleus of higher organisms (eucaryotes) are tightly packed structures that include various proteins and the long molecule DNA in a supercoiled form. When unraveled, the eucaryotic DNA has a ladderlike, spiral structure often called the double helix. Two strands of the double helix—each containing a sugar-phosphate sequence—are held together by bonds between two pairs of bases. One pair, the purine compound adenine and the pyrimidine thymine, bind only to each other, as do the purine guanine and pyrimidine cytosine.

use more than 1 codon to specify a particular amino acid requires as many different tRNAs for a particular amino acid as there are triplets for it in the genetic code. This correspondence between the number of codon synonyms and tRNAs results from the fact that in mRNA translation the attraction between a tRNA and a particular triplet of the mRNA depends on the correspondence of codon and anticodon.

The degeneracy of the genetic code appears to have a pattern. For all amino acids that have 2, 3, or 4 synonym codons, the first 2 bases of the relevant triplets are identical. It is only in the third base that the codons vary. For example, all triplets that specify proline start with CC (CCU, CCC, CCA, and CCG), and all codons that specify glycine start with GG, and so on. This flexibility in the third base of a triplet probably minimizes the potentially deleterious effects of a mutation or an error in translation.

Nonoverlapping Code. Although each amino acid is specified by one or more triplets, a question arises as to whether adjacent bases overlap in the formation of codons. For example, the sequence AUGUGG would, in a nonoverlapping code, specify two amino acids: methionine (AUG) and tryptophan (UGG). In an overlapping code, however, AUGUGG could specify four amino acids: methionine (AUG), cysteine (UGU), valine (GUG), and tryptophan (UGG).

A number of serious problems can arise with an overlapping genetic code. For example, asparagine is specified by codons AAU and AAC. If the genetic code were overlapping, asparagine could never follow methionine in a protein because the overlapping codon that results, UGA, is a terminator codon. In many proteins, however, asparagine does follow methionine. The same is true for all amino acids whose code letters form mutually exclusive sequences. Geneticists have therefore concluded that the genetic code is nonoverlapping.

Although the genetic code is nonoverlapping, instances are found where the same nucleotide bases form parts of more than one gene. This has been observed in viruses where the number of amino acids composing the various viral proteins exceeds the number of mRNA triplets that code for the proteins. In these situations, the same sequence of bases is read in different frames, namely, from different starting points. For example, the base sequence AUGAAUGUGUGG. . . can code for one polypeptide chain by starting with the first base at the left, but the same base sequence can simultaneously code for a second polypeptide chain if a separate round of translation begins with the fifth base from the left. Under these conditions, terminator codons for the two chains will also occur at different points of the mRNA. The resulting proteins will differ from each other in length, amino acid composition, and func-

uracil cytosine adenine guanine

first letter	second letter U	second letter C	second letter A	second letter G	third letter
U	phe	ser	tyr	cys	U
	phe	ser	tyr	cys	C
	leu	ser	term	term	A
	leu	ser	term	trp	G
C	leu	pro	his	arg	U
	leu	pro	his	arg	C
	leu	pro	gln	arg	A
	leu	pro	gln	arg	G
A	ile	thr	asn	ser	U
	ile	thr	asn	ser	C
	ile	thr	lys	arg	A
	met	thr	lys	arg	G
G	val	ala	asp	gly	U
	val	ala	asp	gly	C
	val	ala	glu	gly	A
	val	ala	glu	gly	G

gly val lys cys

When genetic information is transferred from DNA to messenger RNA (mRNA), the pyrimidine compound thymine is replaced by another pyrimidine, uracil. By means of the genetic code, the mRNA regulates the sequences of amino acids that will be bound together in a polypeptide chain to form a protein. The basic unit of the code, called a codon or triplet, consists of three bases. Each codon specifies a particular amino acid. Because there are 64 codons but only 20 amino acids, some amino acids are coded for by more than 1 codon. The table shows the amino acid (represented by its abbreviation) that is specified by each triplet. The codon AUG that specifies the amino acid methionine (met) also functions as the initiator codon for protein synthesis. The word term *in the table signifies the terminators, or nonsense codons, that end the amino acid chain. Four examples of codons and their corresponding amino acids are shown in the column to the right of the table. Thus* (from top), *GGU codes for glycine (gly); GUC codes for valine (val); AAG codes for lysine (lys); and UGC codes for cysteine (cys).*

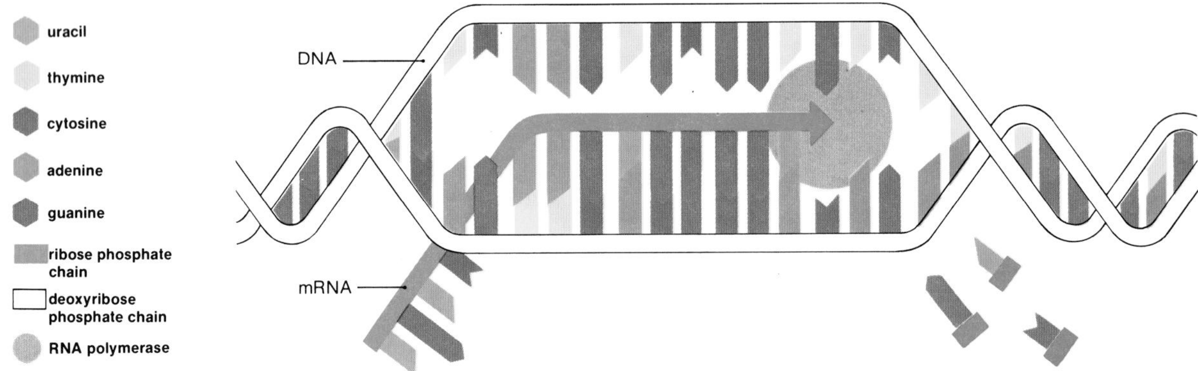

In transcription, messenger RNA (mRNA) is synthesized along a DNA template in the cell nucleus. The enzyme RNA polymerase initiates the process. Nucleotide bases of one of the two DNA strands attract a complementary sequence of bases, which form the RNA molecule. The RNA strand remains attached to the single DNA strand for a short distance; as it separates from the DNA, the double DNA strand reforms. Because the mRNA is a complementary copy of the DNA molecule, it can carry the genetic code from the DNA to the cell cytoplasm.

tion. In these situations, the base sequence of one gene may overlap that of another, or one gene may even be included within the base sequence of another gene.

Universality of the Code. Another fundamental characteristic of the genetic code is its universality—that is, a particular codon specifies the same amino acid in all organisms. For example, mammalian mRNA can be translated into mammalian protein in a test tube, using an experimental system that involves bacterial ribosomes and tRNAs. Although the origin of the genetic code is unknown, its universality suggests that its formation occurred more than 3 billion years ago.

Transfer RNA (tRNA) Identity. Each tRNA molecule has two crucial roles to play in the translation process. First, it has to become attached to a particular amino acid. Second, it has to place that amino acid in its proper place in a protein. For both tasks some recognition site must exist on the tRNA that will serve to accomplish the task.

Geneticists have known for some time that the anticodon on each tRNA is the complement of a particular messenger RNA (mRNA) codon that specifies one of the amino acids in the genetic code. Identification of the recognition site that determines which amino acid will be coupled to the tRNA has not been simple, however, because a pattern, or "code," does not seem to be involved. The most efficient arrangement would be to have one recognition site that serves both functions and hence establishes the identity of the tRNA molecule for both tasks. The most clear-cut situation would be to have the anticodon of the tRNA also act—in whatever fashion—as the recognition site for selecting the proper amino acid. Interestingly enough, this appears to be the case for more than half of the tRNAs, where any change in the anticodon of the tRNA is accompanied by a change in the amino acid selected for attachment to the tRNA.

There are other tRNAs, however, in which the amino acid recognition site is located elsewhere in the tRNA molecule. Therefore, although it has been tempting to look for a so-called "second genetic code" that would decipher the tRNA recognition sites for amino acids, such a code does not appear to exist. Disclosure of the remaining sites will have to proceed on an individual basis.

Mutation. If by any means the sequence of the DNA chain is altered, the code of one or several genes is read differently, resulting in the manufacture of different proteins. This alteration, called a mutation, sometimes results in a change in the appearance or metabolism of the organism. A mutation can be minor and relatively insignificant, or it can cause serious deformity or metabolic deficiency in the organism. On the other hand, mutations are theoretically one of the causes of changes in a species that lead to EVOLUTION.

Such an alteration may be the substitution of one base for another (base-substitution), resulting in the transformation of that particular codon. Another type of mutation entails adding or deleting one or more nucleotides from the DNA chain,

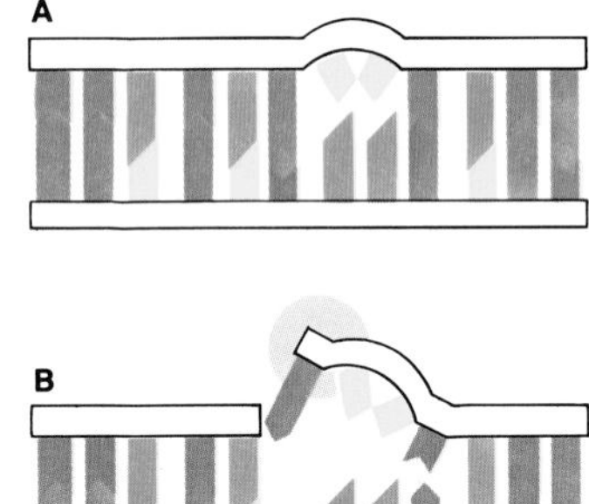

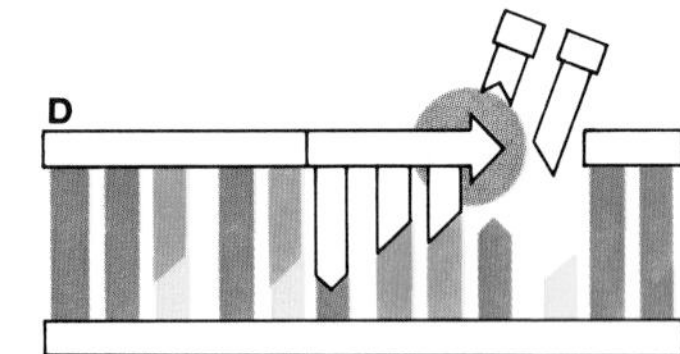

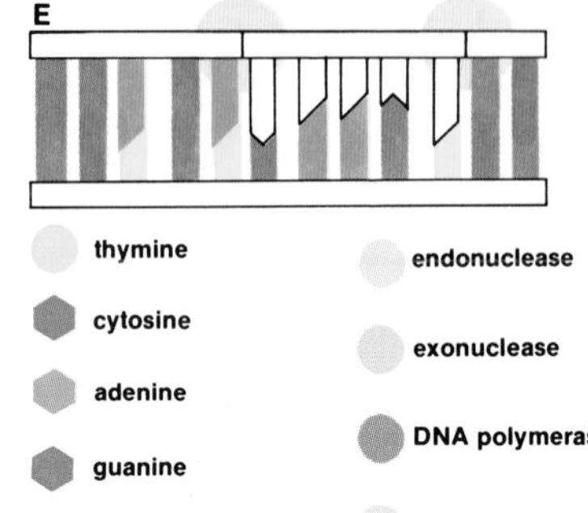

If a molecule of DNA is irradiated by ultraviolet light, damage can be caused to the molecule by the fusion (A) of adjacent thymine bases. This could potentially change the triplet sequences in the genetic code and result in the manufacture of a mutated protein. This problem can be avoided through the action of a repair mechanism, which begins when an enzyme called endonuclease severs the sugar-phosphate chain (B) near the fused thymines. An exonuclease enzyme removes a small region (C) containing the thymine dimer. DNA polymerase synthesizes the missing segment (D), using the complementary strand as a template. The final gap is closed by another enzyme, DNA ligase (E). The repair of the DNA thus maintains the integrity of the genetic information.

thereby changing the number of nucleotides in a gene. Frameshift mutation is an addition-deletion type of mutation, in which bases along the entire gene sequence are so displaced that new triplets are formed. This displacement leads to a sequence of different triplets in the mRNA transcribed from the mutated portion of the gene and is reflected in a changed amino acid sequence in the polypeptide chain produced, which may, in fact, be entirely different from the polypeptide produced by an unmutated DNA chain.

Researchers have discovered that, instead of having the entire code contained in an unbroken molecule of DNA, as in bacteria and other lower organisms, DNA in humans and other higher organisms is segmented. The segments are connected by genes called introns, which do not code for any amino acids of that protein. The entire molecule is transcribed from DNA to mRNA, and enzymes then cleave the introns from the molecule and string the genetic code segments together. Geneticists believe that the value of having the genetic code in segments is to reduce even further the possibility of extensive mutation, especially when a base is added or deleted, shifting the entire sequence of the code. It has also been found that within the section of DNA representing the intron of one gene may be located a second gene coding for an unrelated protein.

LOUIS LEVINE

Bibliography: Clark, Brian, *The Genetic Code* (1977); Dickerson, R. E., "The DNA Helix and How It Is Read," *Scientific American*, December 1983; Lewin, Benjamin, *Genes*, 3d ed. (1987); Tuite, M. F., et al., *Genetics of Translation* (1988).

genetic counseling: see GENETIC DISEASES.

genetic diseases

Genetic diseases are inherited disorders reflecting gene MUTATIONS or abnormalities in chromosome structure or number and resulting in functional or anatomical changes. Common genetic diseases include deformities, such as cleft lip and palate; metabolic disorders, such as phenylketonuria, which results in mental retardation; and albinism, which results in lack of skin pigmentation.

In the half-century between 1935 and 1985 infant mortality from infectious disease, primarily diarrhea, declined from 25% to 3%, and infant mortality from BIRTH DEFECTS increased from 5% to 15%. The frequency of chromosome abnormalities in the United States is 1 in about 150 live births. Approximately 40% of all recognized spontaneous abortions are chromosomally abnormal. Six in every 100 stillbirths have chromosome abnormalities, and 6 in every 100 neonatal deaths are associated with chromosome defects.

GENE TRANSMISSION IN FAMILIES

Gene transmission, or HEREDITY, in families is most often identified by the function of an altered GENE; its expression in a family or kindred may be charted by a family pedigree. A pedigree chart is a schematic outline of individuals in a family throughout several generations, including the sex, age, and presence or absence of a specific genetic characteristic or disease in each individual. The pedigree chart is used to determine how a particular trait or disease is transmitted.

The term *allele pair* means a pair of genes that determines a certain trait. Any number of variations in each gene of the pair can occur. In order to have blue eyes the alleles of the gene pair must be identical, both specifying blue eyes. A person having identical alleles for that characteristic is said to be homozygous. If the gene pair is not identical—for example, one allele specifies blue and the other brown—the individual is heterozygous for that trait. Alleles for blue eyes are said to be recessive, and for brown eyes, dominant. A heterozygous individual having the two different alleles in the gene pair will have brown or mixed-color eyes but never blue.

Genetic diseases can be inherited in a manner similar to that of normal traits. These diseases include single-gene disorders that are autosomal dominant, sex-linked dominant, autosomal recessive, or sex-linked recessive. They also include multifactorial disorders, resulting from more than one gene often interacting with environmental factors. Autosomal means that the gene pair is present in a chromosome pair other than the sex chromosomes.

SINGLE-GENE DISORDERS

Disorders caused by the mutation of a single gene are often called inborn errors of metabolism because they reflect alterations of a biochemical pathway. As a result of the mutation of a single gene, the final gene product normally manufactured is absent or is present in low amounts. Therefore, either an important end product is not synthesized in sufficient quantity, or an excessive accumulation of intermediate products that may be toxic occurs. Many inborn errors of metabolism are fatal in early childhood or make maintenance of proper body function difficult if not impossible.

Autosomal Dominant Genes. Autosomal dominant genes, of which more than a thousand are fully identified, are expressed in both heterozygous and homozygous individuals. Many are found to be lethal when the individual is homozygous. Dominant traits are usually expressed equally in both the male and the female. If one parent is affected, therefore, each pregnancy involves a 50% risk of recurrence. The pedigree usually reflects at least one affected member in each generation. The sex of the parent contributing the gene can also play a role in the course of the disease (see GENETIC IMPRINTING). An example is HUNTINGTON'S CHOREA, which is characterized by ceaseless, involuntary jerky movements, dementia, and finally death. Symptoms generally are manifested after 35 years of age, usually after the affected person has had offspring, 50% of whom inherit the disease.

Autosomal Recessive Genes. Autosomal recessive traits, of which 600 are fully identified, are expressed phenotypically only in homozygotic individuals. Most of these traits, if not all, result from a single-gene mutation affecting a single step in a biochemical pathway. Most autosomal recessive traits are expressed to some extent in heterozygotic individuals, although their physical appearance and general health are normal. These people are known as carriers because they can transmit the gene to their children, who manifest the disease. Usually, affected children will have unaffected carrier parents. Frequently, parents who are closely related transmit autosomal recessive disorders. The recurrence risk for heterozygous parents is 25% for each pregnancy.

TAY-SACHS DISEASE, GALACTOSEMIA, and PHENYLKETONURIA are examples of autosomal recessive disorders. Tay-Sachs disease occurs almost entirely among 4-to-6-month-old children from an Ashkenazi Jewish background. The affected gene does not produce an enzyme needed to metabolize lipids. As a result, they build up in the brain, causing neurologic deterioration and eventually death. In galactosemia the enzyme that converts the milk sugar galactose to glucose is not produced. Newborns with this disorder who are fed milk accumulate galactose in their blood. The infant develops cataracts, cirrhosis of the liver, and mental retardation. The disorder is reversible by omitting milk and milk products from the diet. Children having phenylketonuria (PKU) lack the ability to produce an enzyme that metabolizes the amino acid phenylalanine. Excess phenylalanine causes skin-pigment deficiency and mental retardation. Other such disorders include SICKLE-CELL DISEASE and thalassemia (see COOLEY'S ANEMIA).

Sex-Linked Recessive Genes. In sex-linked recessive traits, of which 125 are fully identified, the mother is heterozygous but unaffected—she is a carrier. She has a 50% chance of producing affected sons through transmission of an X chromosome carrying the gene mutation. Her daughters have a 50% chance of being heterozygous like the mother. If an affected male is able to reproduce and marries a homozygous normal female, none of his children will be affected, but all of his daughters will be heterozygous for the sex-linked gene. His sons do not inherit the disease.

MUSCULAR DYSTROPHY and HEMOPHILIA are representative sex-linked recessive disorders. In muscular dystrophy male children have weakness and degeneration of their muscles, progressing from extremities to the entire body. Hemophilia, which also affects male children with mothers who are unaffected carriers, is characterized by severe hemorrhaging and the inability of the blood to clot and heal a wound.

Sex-Linked Dominant Genes. Only a few disorders with sex-linked dominant inheritance are known, such as vitamin D–resistant rickets, which may produce severe bowing of the legs. Mutations occur on the X chromosome, so if the female carries the mutation, recurrence risks are 50% for both female and male progeny; if the male has the disorder, no sons but all of the daughters will be affected.

MULTIFACTORIAL INHERITANCE

Disorders that reflect the activity of several genes rather than one are known as multifactorial traits. In most cases the environment, especially during pregnancy, plays an important role in determining the severity of the disease in the child. Several relatively common disorders fall into this category; for example, cleft lip and palate, pyloric stenosis (obstruction of the stomach), and SPINA BIFIDA (defect of the bony spinal column). In general, the recurrence risk for parents who have an affected child is in the range of 3–5%. If one parent is affected, the risk for any pregnancy is also in the 3–5% range.

CHROMOSOME ABNORMALITIES

Chromosome abnormalities are detected with increasing frequency in birth defects. The most common type is a change in total chromosome number. In general, reduction of the total number of autosomes is incompatible with life. An infant with an extra chromosome involving virtually any autosome pair also has a limited life span, with multiple physical abnormalities and mental retardation.

The most common chromosomal abnormality is DOWN'S SYNDROME, or mongolism, which involves the chromosome designated as number 21. This defect is termed Trisomy 21 because all cells in the infant's body carry an extra number 21 chromosome. This condition occurs in 1 out of 800 liveborn infants. Maternal age is a factor in the frequency of Down's syndrome; for example, 1 out of 300 mothers in their 30s, and 1 out of 40 mothers over 40 produce such infants. Other well-described trisomies in humans are Trisomy 13 (Patau's syndrome) and Trisomy 18 (Edwards' syndrome). Both aberrations are associated with multiple birth defects, including mental retardation and limited life span. All human chromosome abnormalities can be detected in the developing fetus by the 14th to 16th week of gestation by means of amniocentesis.

Like autosomal abnormalities, aberrations of the sex chromosomes may result in impaired or absent fertility. For example, one abnormality known as 45X, or Turner's syndrome, involves anaphase lag (lag in certain stages of division of the cell nucleus). Individuals with this condition, who are classified as female, most commonly are short in stature and show impaired development of genitalia and such secondary sex characteristics as the breasts and the distribution of body hair; they are also sterile. Another abnormality, called KLINEFELTER'S SYNDROME, occurs when the individual has 47 chromosomes in the cells of the body, with an XXY sex-chromosome composition. The individual is male in appearance, tall in stature, has sparse hair distribution over the body, and is sterile.

Regardless of other sex-chromosome anomalies, when the Y chromosome is present the physical appearance is nearly always male. As the total number of sex chromosomes present increases, greater prevalence of associated birth defects and mental retardation results.

GENE THERAPY

One goal of recombinant-DNA technology (see GENETIC ENGINEERING) is the cure of human genetic diseases. A first step toward the use of gene-altered cells for this purpose has been proposed by researchers at the U.S. National Institutes of Health, in connection with an experimental cancer therapy that uses the patient's own cancer-fighting cells.

When a tumor forms, it is invaded by a special type of white blood cell called tumor-infiltrating lymphocyte (TIL). These cells can be obtained from a tumor, cultured in the laboratory to obtain large numbers of them, and then infused back into the patient. This procedure is effective in about half the patients, causing the tumor to regress by 50% or more. It is not known, however, why the treatment fails to work in other patients. Planning to use a RETROVIRUS as a vector, the researchers want to add to the TIL cells, as a marker while they are cultured, a bacterial gene that codes for resistance to the antibiotic neomycin. This will permit them to identify the marked cells and monitor their fate after they are returned to the patient, by periodically sampling the TIL cells in the tumor.

In principle, this procedure would be identical to the ones intended for use in curing human genetic diseases through gene therapy. If successful, this project will represent the first step toward achieving that goal.

GENE MAPPING AND ANALYSIS

In the late 20th century, libraries of gene probes are being developed and genes are being sequenced and characterized in detail (see GENOME). The use of gene probes permits pedigree analysis with precision; genetic risks can be assigned without the need to know the gene product. Through recombinant DNA technology and DNA-probe analysis, prenatal diagnosis is available for such disorders as Huntington's chorea, phenylketonuria, cystic fibrosis, adult-onset polycystic kidney disease, retinoblastoma, hemophilia A and B, hemoglobinopathies, and Duchenne muscular dystrophy. Such technology also promises important information on such disorders as ALZHEIMER'S DISEASE, now mapped on chromosome 21, and MANIC-DEPRESSIVE PSYCHOSIS, now mapped on chromosome 11. Various types of cancer, diabetes mellitus, and disorders associated with hypercholesterolemia may also become available to diagnosis in this way. Precision in genetic counseling and prenatal screening for disorders in families at risk will increase the odds that couples will be able to have normal, healthy children. OLIVER W. JONES, M.D.

GENETIC COUNSELING

Genetic counseling is a service available to couples who desire information or advice concerning the probability of bearing children with a genetic disease. The counselors are usually physicians; some hospitals have teams that include counselors specifically trained in genetic disease, a pediatrician, a high-risk obstetrician, a nurse, a social worker, and consultants such as a neurologist.

Couples should seek genetic counseling if they already have a defective child, if a close relative is known to have a hereditary disease, or if the mother is approximately 35 years of age or older, because women in this age group run a higher-than-average risk of bearing children with Down's syndrome and certain other chromosomal abnormalities.

Those concerned about hereditary diseases should consult their family physician or obstetrician. If the problem is not within that doctor's area of competence, the patient will be referred to a reliable counseling center.

When faced with a diagnostic problem, the genetic counselor usually begins by obtaining a family history, performing a physical examination, and ordering appropriate laboratory tests. The counselor will want to determine whether or not the problem is genetic, and if so, the mode of inheritance. A test may disclose such defects as the presence of an extra chromosome, as in Down's syndrome; the presence of abnormal hemoglobin, as in sickle-cell anemia; or the absence of a particular blood-clotting factor, as in hemophilia. Other conditions may present such striking clinical manifestations that diagnosis and counseling are possible even when the specific biochemical cause is unknown—for example, in Huntington's chorea.

Every couple faces about a 3% risk with each birth that the child will be born with a major defect of some kind. Against this background, the genetic counselor, after concluding various studies, may predict that the couple who produced a defective child face a high recurrent risk. This risk may be 25% to 50% in the case of single-gene defects, as high as 100% for certain chromosome disorders, or as low as 5% for the more common multifactorial conditions.

A defective fetus may be identified by AMNIOCENTESIS, a procedure performed in a hospital. A sample of the amniotic fluid surrounding the fetus is withdrawn through a hollow needle inserted into the mother's womb. The fluid contains fetal cells and other substances that can be studied for chromosomal or chemical abnormalities and may indicate the presence of certain birth defects. Well over 100 hereditary diseases can now be identified by amniocentesis, and the sex of the fetus can also be readily determined. Sometimes the knowledge of the sex of the fetus rules out a hereditary disorder: hemophilia, for example, occurs almost always in males, and therefore a female fetus will not be likely to have this disease.

One problem with amniocentesis is that the woman must wait until the 15th or 16th week of pregnancy before sufficient fluid has accumulated for sampling. A more recent, experimental approach is to sample placenta tissue itself, through a catheter, a process called chorionic villous sampling. This can be done as early as the 9th week of pregnancy.

Two new techniques exist for identifying fetuses carrying particular genes. One uses so-called restriction enzymes, which cut DNA only at specific "recognition sites." These sites may vary among families, yielding DNA fragments that characterize a particular lineage. If the gene causing a disease in one parent's family line happens to be located within a unique DNA fragment, the presence of such a fragment in a fetus identifies it as having the gene for the disorder. The second test involves the use of a previously obtained fragment of DNA that has been made radioactive. Such a fragment is called a probe, and it will be attracted specifically to the DNA at the site of the gene of interest. If the probe contains a normal form of the gene and the fetus contains a mutated, disease-causing form of the gene, little binding will take place between the DNA sections and very little radioactivity will be detected at the site.

GENETIC TESTING

Much of the suffering and cost of genetic diseases could be prevented if an affected child could be identified early enough to start adequate treatment. An example is the enzyme-deficiency disease phenylketonuria, one of many metabolic disorders that can be detected by the screening of blood and urine samples from newborns. Immediate dietary reduction of the amino acid phenylalanine will prevent severe mental retardation, so such screening is now mandatory in most states. An earlier approach is to identify parents at risk before they produce an affected child. For example, parents who are carriers for genes causing Tay-Sachs disease or sickle-cell anemia can be detected by blood tests and informed about the risks of producing affected offspring.

While offering much hope, however, genetic testing also raises difficult ethical questions. For example, does a patient with Huntington's chorea or muscular dystrophy or other late-developing hereditary disorders have a right to expect the traditional doctor-patient confidentiality? What is the responsibility (and liability) of physicians for warning family members at risk for inheriting the disease? At what age should persons be told that they are destined to be affected? Can industrial workers who are genetically susceptible to harm from particular substances in the workplace be excluded from certain jobs? With the rise in medical costs, should potential marriage partners or parents undergo compulsory screening and other measures to reduce the prevalence of genetic diseases? Ethical questions such as these are emerging as society begins to grapple with the field of genetic testing.

LAWRENCE J. SCHNEIDERMAN, M.D.

Bibliography: Culliton, B. J., "Gene Therapy: Research in Public," *Science*, Feb. 1, 1985; Dietz, A. A., ed., *Genetic Disease: Diagnosis and Treatment* (1983); Emery, A. E., *Elements of Medical Genetics*, 6th ed. (1983); Fletcher, J. C., *Coping with Genetic Disorders* (1982); Harper, P. S., *Practical Genetic Counseling*, 2d ed. (1984); Kolata, Gina, "Genetic Screening Raises Questions for Employers and Insurers," *Science*, Apr. 18, 1986; Merz, Beverly, "Markers for Disease Genes Open New Era in Diagnostic Screening," *JAMA*, Dec. 13, 1985; Murray, T. H., "Genetic Testing at Work: How Should It Be Used?", *Technology Review*, May/June 1985; Nichols, E. K., *Human Gene Therapy* (1988); Nora, J. J., and Fraser, F. C., *Medical Genetics*, 2d ed. (1981); Thompson, J. S. and M. W., *Genetics in Medicine* (1986); Zoler, M. L., "Genetic Tests Creating a Deluge of Dilemmas," *Medical World News*, Sept. 22, 1986.

See also: ABORTION; EUGENICS; GENETICS.

genetic engineering

Genetics is the science that studies all aspects of inherited characteristics. Genetic engineering is the application of the knowledge obtained from genetic investigations to the solution of such problems as infertility, diseases, food production, waste disposal, and improvement of a species. Included in genetic-engineering techniques are a wide range of procedures that alter the reproductive and hereditary processes of organisms. Depending on the problem, the procedures used may involve ARTIFICIAL INSEMINATION, CLONING, in vitro fertilization, species hybridization, or the direct manipulation of the genetic material itself by the recombinant-DNA technique.

NONMOLECULAR EXAMPLES

Genetic engineering has been effectively practiced in ANIMAL HUSBANDRY, HORTICULTURE, and agriculture for thousands of years. CORN has been selectively bred for food production for 7,000 years. More recently, a comparable program, involving wheat and rice, called the GREEN REVOLUTION has done much to meet the world's increasing need for food (see PLANT BREEDING). Cattle and pigs had been domesticated by 8,000 years ago and through selective breeding have become two main meat sources in the human diet.

For human diseases, successful application of a number of discoveries in the field of immunology has until recently been limited by the need for large amounts of particular types of antibodies, each specific to a given virus, protozoan, or kind of cell. In 1975 a cancer cell was fused to a spleen cell that was producing antibodies against a specific antigen. The hybrid cell (hybridoma) continued to produce the single type of antibody of its spleen-cell parent and continued to grow and divide like its cancer-cell parent. Such monoclonal antibodies are now produced in large amounts against specific microorganisms, and even against the malignant cells of some children with acute lymphocytic leukemia.

Fifteen percent of all human couples encounter various fertility problems. If the woman is fertile but the man is sterile, artificial insemination, using the sperm of another man, permits the woman to conceive. If the man is fertile but the woman has blocked fallopian tubes, eggs may be withdrawn from her ovary, fertilized by his sperm in vitro (outside the body), and later inserted into the woman's uterus (embryo

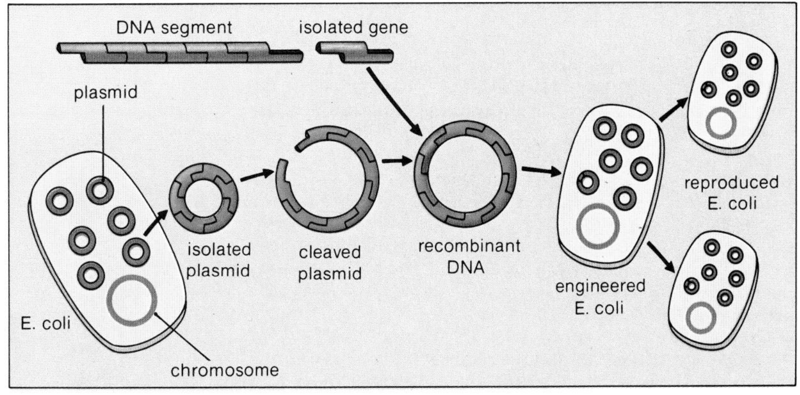

In a typical recombinant-DNA procedure, a plasmid found in E. coli, *a common intestinal bacterium, carries the foreign DNA into an* E. coli *host. The isolated plasmid and the donor DNA are cleaved by the same restriction enzyme at the same sequence of nucleotides. (Other restriction enzymes would produce different fragments for insertion in plasmids similarly formed.) The donor DNA fragment matches up with the cleaved plasmid. The recombinant-DNA molecule is then introduced into the host cell and reproduced when the cell divides. Repeated divisions produce a clone of* E. coli *containing the recombinant-DNA molecule, which may encode a useful protein, such as insulin.*

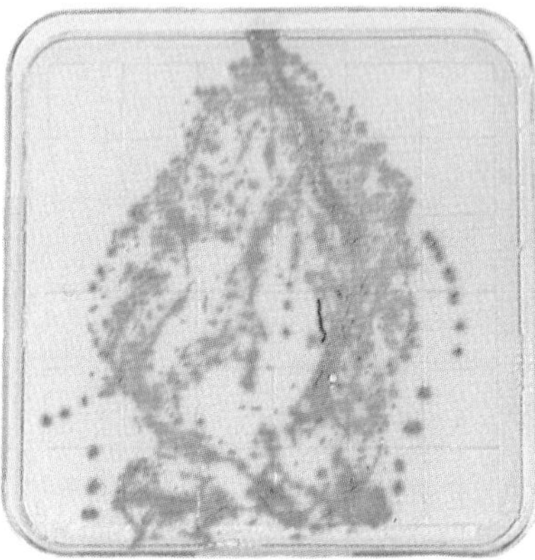

(Above) *Genetically altered bacteria are sprayed on a field of strawberries to give the plants greater protection against frost. Federal law required the wearing of special clothing, but the bacteria are considered harmless.* (Left) *Bacteria that colonize plant roots are altered to turn blue in the presence of certain chemicals. Such bacteria, when otherwise altered for testing, are easy to track and monitor.*

transplant) for completion of development and subsequent birth. This entire "test-tube baby" process was first successfully accomplished on July 25, 1978, with the birth of Louise Brown in Oldham, England.

RECOMBINANT DNA

Technique. Recombinant-DNA formation, also known as GENE splicing, is a procedure whereby segments of genetic material from one organism are transferred to another. The basis of the technique lies in the use of special enzymes (restriction enzymes) that split DNA strands wherever certain sequences of nucleotides occur. This process results in a series of donor DNA fragments that can combine with similarly formed DNA fragments from other organisms. In most experimental situations the donor DNA fragments are combined with viruses or with plasmids (small rings of self-replicating DNA found within cells). The virus or plasmid vectors carry the donor DNA fragments into cells. The combined vector and donor DNA fragment constitutes the recombinant-DNA molecule. Once inside a cell, referred to as a host, this molecule is replicated along with the host's DNA each time the host divides. These divisions produce a clone of identical cells, each having a copy of the recombinant-DNA molecule and the potential to translate the donor DNA fragment into the protein it encodes.

Applications. The use of bacteria as host cells in recombinant-DNA experiments has yielded important information on gene regulation. By using donor DNA fragments of various sizes, the location and action of the controlling units (promoter sequences) that govern the expression of particular genes have been identified (see OPERON).

Recombinant-DNA procedures involving bacteria and donor DNA fragments that translate into proteins have led to the increased availability of such medically important substances as INSULIN (for diabetes), INTERFERON (for viral infections and some forms of cancer), and growth hormone (for dwarfism). These substances were previously available only in limited quantities from their primary sources.

Another important medical application of the recombinant-DNA procedure has been the production of vaccines against a number of diseases. Heretofore, vaccination against a disease has involved the injection of killed or weakened microorganisms into a person, with the subsequent production of ANTIBODIES by the individual's immune system. This procedure has always carried the risk of there being live, virulent pathogens in the vaccine because of some error in the vaccine-producing process. Research has shown that it is the microorganism's outer surface that serves as the ANTIGEN that stimulates antibody formation. Through the recombinant-DNA procedure, it is now possible to transfer the genes that control a pathogen's surface characteristics to a harmless microorganism and use it as a vaccine against the particular disease. This has been done successfully using the harmless VACCINIA (cowpox) virus that was so effective in leading to the worldwide eradication of smallpox. For example, a strain of engineered vaccinia virus has been produced that carries the protein-coat genes for herpes simplex type I virus (cold sores), another has been engineered to act as a vaccine against the influenza virus, and a third one has been made against the hepatitis B virus. The hope is to place the protein-coat genes of various pathogenic viruses into a single strain of vaccinia virus and have it serve as a multiple-vaccination organism.

Bacteria with altered genomes, or genetic informational contents, may also be used in waste disposal. Such organisms could decompose many forms of garbage; one such strain can break down oil slicks.

Plant cells can also be used as hosts, which could have important consequences for food production. If the genes that code for the nitrogen-fixing system of certain bacteria could be transplanted into the cells of crop plants, the world's food production would dramatically increase and fertilizers would become unnecessary.

Not only can plant cells act as hosts for bacterial genes, they can also serve as recipients of animal genes. In one such gene-splicing experiment involving the firefly, which is capable of BIOLUMINESCENCE, the gene that produces the enzyme needed for light production was transferred to a tobacco plant. Subsequently, when the roots of the plant were immersed in a solution containing the necessary ingredients, the plant began to emit light. This demonstrated that animal genes, under the proper conditions, can function in plant

The world's first patented animal is a mouse whose genetic material has been altered, for research purposes, to include a gene known to cause breast cancer in humans. In the new mouse strain, half of the females develop cancer. The historic patent was issued in April 1988.

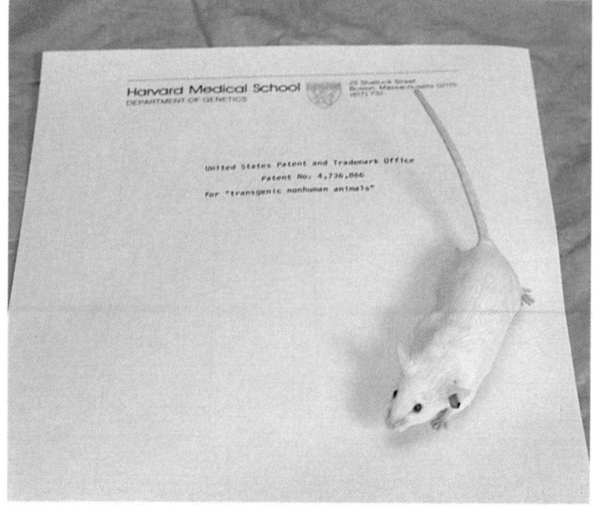

Human recombinant beta interferon is being produced in quantity in these fermentation vats. Before the advent of genetic engineering techniques, a number of biochemicals such as interferon were available for medical research and other purposes only in very small and costly amounts. The new techniques gave birth to a rapidly growing biotechnology industry.

cells. If the reverse is also found to be the case, no insurmountable barriers will exist to the transfer of genes between the animal and plant kingdoms.

Recombinant-DNA procedures have been used to study the genes of extinct animals. A zebralike animal called the quagga, for example, became extinct in the 19th century, but some quagga skins with underlying muscle tissues have been salt-preserved in museums. Enzymes were used to release DNA from these muscle cells, yielding DNA fragments representing parts of different genes. These fragments were transferred to the plasmids of bacteria, where they were replicated along with the bacterial DNA. They were then retrieved, analyzed, and compared to corresponding DNA segments of closely related living animals, revealing that the quagga DNA differs from its zebra counterpart by about 5 percent. This amount of difference indicates that the quagga and zebra shared a common ancestor about 3 million years ago. With appropriate modifications, it should be possible to use this technique to study genes from the bones and teeth of long-extinct animals.

Controversy. Questions have been raised by a number of scientists and lay people on the advisability and ethics of recombinant-DNA research. It was feared that the insertion of a disease-causing, antibiotic-resistant, or cancer-causing virus or plasmid into a bacterium like *Escherichia coli,* which lives in the human intestinal tract, could cause a deadly epidemic in the general population upon accidental release. Since 1973, however, when the recombinant-DNA technique was first demonstrated, genetic material has been transferred thousands of times without any of the feared catastrophes occurring. As a result, NIH has relaxed or eliminated most restrictions on gene-splicing work with all but pathogenic bacteria.

In 1987, after four years of legal challenges, the recombinant-DNA Advisory Committee (RAC) of the NIH gave final approval for a series of experiments involving the spraying of plants with genetically engineered bacteria to protect the plants from light frost. The bacteria commonly found on these plants secrete a protein that initiates the formation of ice crystals when the temperature drops to freezing. In the genetically modified bacteria, the gene that codes for the protein has been deleted. In the absence of the protein, ice formation does not occur until the temperature falls well below the freezing point. Normally, such a deep drop in temperature does not occur until after the harvest period has ended. The first field test of these genetically modified bacteria was conducted on Apr. 24, 1987, on a plot of strawberry plants, and similar experiments on other crops have followed. The results showed that the gene-spliced bacteria were effective.

The objection raised to the experiments, and to any method of increasing food production through the release of genetically altered microbes, is that such organisms might spread and upset the ecosystem of the area. Recent experiments, however, have shown that released bacteria remain localized and appear to present no threat to the ecosystem.

FORENSIC DNA

When DNA is subjected to restriction endonuclease enzyme activity, fragments of various sizes are formed (see GENETIC DISEASES). Except for identical twins, the pattern of sizes of the fragments from an individual is unique and can serve as a "DNA fingerprint" of that person. This fact has been crucial in identifying assailants in a number of violent crimes where the victims were unable to do so. In these cases, bloodstains or semen stains on clothing, sperm cells found in a vaginal swab taken after a rape, or root hairs of the assailant were available for analysis. Extraction of DNA from dried blood or from one of the other sources, followed by enzymatic digestion, resulted in an unambiguous match of DNA fragments with DNA obtained from cells of the accused. Where blood stains were available, clearcut DNA fingerprints were obtainable from samples that were as much as four years old.

TRENDS

In 1980 a ruling by the U.S. Supreme Court permitted the U.S. Patent and Trademark Office to grant a PATENT on a genetically engineered "oil-eating" bacterium. The bacterium was categorized as a "nonnatural manmade microorganism." Over the following eight years, some 200 patents were granted for bacteria, viruses, and plants that had been genetically modified. In 1988 a patent was granted on a mouse strain in which the cells had been engineered to contain a cancer-predisposing gene sequence (activated oncogene sequence). Technically referred to as a "transgenic nonhuman eukaryotic animal," each mouse of this type can be used both to test low doses of cancer-causing substances and to test the effectiveness of drugs considered as possibly offering protection against the development of cancer.

Successful application of the recombinant-DNA technique to medical problems has caused pharmaceutical companies to become increasingly involved in this type of research, and more than a dozen companies have been formed for the purpose of manufacturing genetically engineered microorganisms that will produce hormones, antibiotics, vaccines, interferon, and other salable substances. Universities have also been affected by the research boom. Many genetic-engineering firms have sought to subcontract some of their work to schools. These offers have raised the issue of the university's role in basic versus applied research, and the responses to these offers have been varied.

LOUIS LEVINE

Bibliography: Baines, W., *Genetic Engineering for Almost Everybody* (1988); Bolton, A., *Recombinant Products* (1984); Setlow, J., *Genetic Engineering,* vol. 11 (1989); Trevans, M., et al., *Biotechnology* (1987); Williams, J., and Patient, R., *Genetic Engineering* (1989).

genetic imprinting

The same gene can show a difference in activity depending on the sex of the parent providing the gene. This is called genetic imprinting. For example, if the gene for the disorder called HUNTINGTON'S CHOREA is inherited from the male parent, its symptoms begin in adolescence. If the female parent is the gene's source, its symptoms do not appear in the offspring until middle age. In general, genes obtained from a male parent tend to be more active than the same genes provided by a female parent. This difference appears to be linked to the relative number of methyl (CH_3) groups attached to the gene. Genes with few such groups tend to be more active.

LOUIS LEVINE

genetics

Genetics is the area of biology concerned with the study of inheritance, the process by which certain characteristics of organisms are handed down from parent to offspring. Modern genetics began in 1866, when the Austrian monk Gregor MEN-

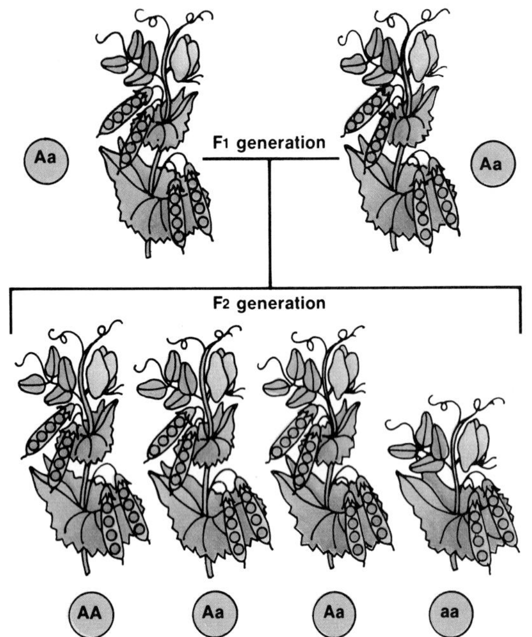

Mendel's crossing of a tall pea plant (AA) *with a short plant* (aa) *yielded all tall F_1 offspring; these, in turn, produced F_2 progeny in the ratio of 3 tall:1 short. He assumed that alleles* (A or a) *separate during gamete formation and recombine randomly in offspring. According to the law of dominance, plants with* AA *and* Aa *genotypes display the dominant trait; those with* aa *are short.*

DEL demonstrated the inheritance patterns of the garden pea, *Pisum sativum*, and provided a new way of looking at HEREDITY. Mendel's theories were based on hereditary factors, or GENES, the existence of which he deduced without seeing them or having any notion of what they were or where they were located.

Gregor Mendel's results and theories, however, went unnoticed until 1900, when Hugo De Vries in the Netherlands, Carl Correns in Germany, and Erich von Tschermak-Seysenegg in Austria—who almost simultaneously rediscovered Mendel's work and independently performed similar experiments—arrived at the same conclusions reached by Mendel. It is now known that genes dictate the characteristic structures and functions of all organisms, from viruses to redwood trees and elephants, and that these characteristics are in turn passed on from parent to offspring. It is also known that the variety of hereditary traits are caused by variations in the genes themselves.

MENDEL'S EXPERIMENTS

Mendel studied seven characteristics of the garden pea and obtained experimental results that suggested a similar hereditary mechanism for all. In one experiment, he crossed plants that differed in the characteristic of plant height. He obtained a line of pea plants that always produced tall plants and a line that always produced short plants, and he crossed the tall and short lines by transferring pollen from one plant to another. He found that the progeny (the first filial, or F_1 generation) were all tall. He then allowed these to self-pollinate and produce another generation of progeny (the F_2 generation), three-quarters of which were tall and one-quarter short.

Mendel's Laws. From these results, Mendel deduced an explanation for the mechanism of inheritance and assumed certain principles to be true: (1) hereditary factors (genes) must exist; (2) two factors exist for each characteristic; (3) at the time of sex-cell formation, the hereditary factors of a pair separate equally into the gametes (law of segregation); (4) the gametes bear only one factor for each characteristic; (5) hereditary factors for different traits sort independently of one another at gamete formation (law of independent assortment); and (6) gametes join randomly, irrespective of the factors that they carry.

The characteristic that appeared in the F_1 plants—in this case, tall plants—seemed to dominate over the one that did not appear. Mendel called tallness a dominant trait and shortness recessive; this phenomenon was referred to as the law of dominance.

A capital letter, such as *A*, is now usually used to represent the gene that determines the dominant character, and a small *a* for one that determines the recessive character. When a pair of hereditary factors, or genes, are of the same type (*AA* or *aa*), the condition is said to be homozygous for that character. On the other hand, if the two members of a pair are different (*Aa*), the condition is called heterozygous.

The F_2 plants of Mendel's experiment were composed of one-quarter *AA*, one-half *Aa*, and one-quarter *aa*. Since tallness is dominant, *AA* and *Aa* both appear tall, accounting for the three-quarter:one-quarter ratio of tall to short. The alternate forms of a gene, known as alleles, combine to produce different genetic types, or genotypes. Mendel demonstrated that the three-quarter:one quarter ratio existed for all seven characteristics of peas that he studied; he also showed that the gene pairs for the seven traits behaved independently of each other during gamete formation.

CHROMOSOMES

Mendel's knowledge of genes and their behavior was entirely theoretical. Subsequent studies of CELL structure and cell division have supplied physical evidence supporting his theories. It is now generally believed that genes behave as they do because of their location on chromosomes (see GENETIC CODE), structures found in the nucleus of each cell of an organism. Chromosomes are not all the same length, and, when stained in the appropriate way, each may show characteristic bands, thickenings, or constrictions.

The cells of each species contain a fixed and characteristic

This microphotograph shows a polytene chromosome from the salivary gland of the fruit fly Drosophila hydei. *Polytene, or many-stranded, chromosomes duplicate without cell division. The enlarged, nonbanded areas, called puffs, are associated with protein synthesis.*

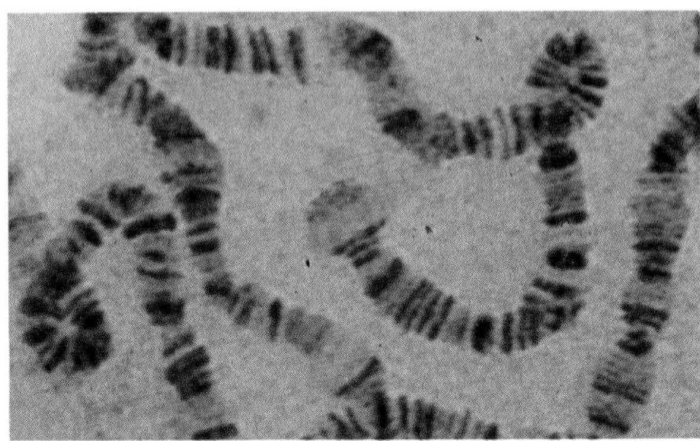

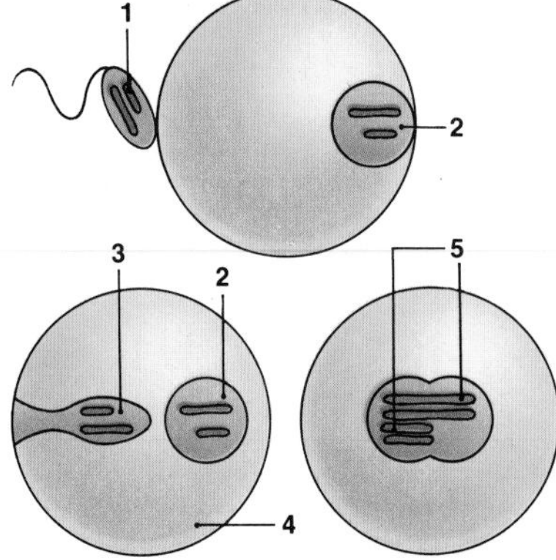

(Left) *The sperm nucleus contains a haploid set of chromosomes, two of which are shown* (1), *as does the egg nucleus* (2). *During fertilization, the sperm nucleus, in a fertilization cone* (3), *passes through the egg cytoplasm* (4) *toward the egg nucleus. The two nuclei fuse, and homologous chromosomes pair up* (5).

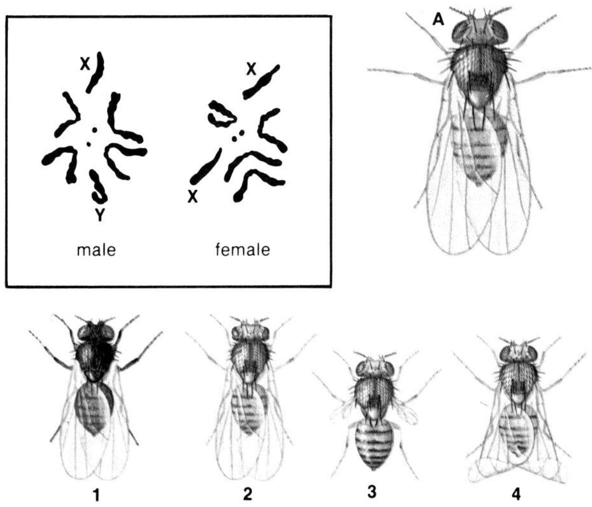

Geneticists often use the fruit fly Drosophila melanogaster (A) *in experiments: it is small (about 2 mm/0.08 in long), it reproduces every 10 to 15 days, and its cells contain 4 pairs of large chromosomes* (upper left). *The chromosome complements shown are those of male and female fruit flies. A female has 2 x-chromosomes, but no y-chromosome. Genetic damage at specific positions, or loci, on the chromosomes produces certain mutations, including black bodies* (1), *bar-shaped eyes* (2), *vestigial wings* (3), *and curled wings* (4).

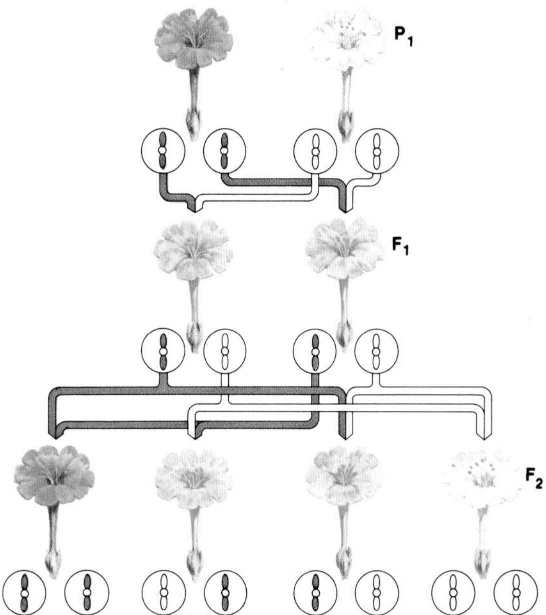

Flowers of four-o'clock plants, Mirabilis jalapa, *illustrate the principle of incomplete dominance: heterozygous offspring express an intermediate character rather than the dominant trait. The crossing of a four-o'clock containing red alleles with a plant containing white alleles yields plants with pink flowers (F_1 generation). If the pink four-o'clocks are crossed, the alleles combine to produce offspring (f_2) that are red, pink, and white in the ratio of 1:2:1. In the case of complete dominance, the comparable ratio would be 3 red:1 white in the F_2, while the F_1 would have been all red.*

number of chromosomes. Some organisms, such as fungi and single-celled algae, have only a single set, or haploid number (n), of chromosomes in their cell nuclei. The somatic cells of most higher organisms, including humans, contain two sets, or a diploid number ($2n$), of chromosomes. Still other organisms, such as mosses, ferns, and horsetails, alternate between diploid and haploid during different stages of their life cycles. Human cells contain two sets of 23 different chromosomes ($2n = 46$); pea cells contain two sets of seven ($2n = 14$); the cells of the haploid mold *Neurospora* contain a single set of seven ($n = 7$).

Meiosis. In diploid cells, gene pairs are located at specific sites (loci) on each chromosome. These gene pairs can be composed of either two identical genes or two alleles. A diploid cell therefore contains two genes for each hereditary characteristic. The gametes (sex cells) of diploid organisms, however, contain only a haploid (n) number of chromosomes; the union of two gametes, one from each parent, produces a diploid ($2n$) zygote, from which the offspring develops.

The process of cell division by which such gametes are produced is called meiosis. It takes place in the testes and ovaries of animals, in the anthers and ovaries of higher plants, and in the sporophyte ($2n$) stage of organisms that alternate between haploid and diploid. In meiosis a single diploid cell divides into two haploid cells, each of which divides into two more haploid cells. During this process, the two sets of chromosomes separate, thereby separating the members of the gene pairs. Each of the four resulting gametes therefore contains only one gene for each characteristic, and different gametes from the same parent may carry different alleles.

Mendel's postulates may therefore be restated in physical terms as follows: (1) genes are located on chromosomes; (2) genes occur in pairs, occupying specific loci on a chromosome pair; (3) the first meiotic division separates the chromosome pairs, producing an equal separation of the members of a gene pair in the product cells; (4) since there are two cell divisions and only one replication of chromosomes, the chromosome number is halved; (5) different gene pairs on separate chromosome pairs behave independently of each other; and (6) collision of egg and sperm is a chance process.

Linkage and Crossing-Over. In the early 1900s, Thomas Hunt MORGAN used the fruitfly *Drosophila melanogaster* to test a situation that Mendel did not encounter, namely, that in which two gene pairs are located on the same chromosome pair. In this case they do not behave independently, since genes that are on the same chromosome tend to stay together during meiosis, a phenomenon known as linkage. The linked combinations, however, can be separated by breaking and rejoining the chromosome, a process known as crossing-over. This process occurs regularly during meiosis and randomly between any pair of chromosomes in a bundle of four. A crossover can only be detected genetically if it involves two heterozygous gene pairs (the alleles producing distinct gene products). The positions of crossovers can be detected, however, under a microscope, where they appear as cross-shaped structures called chiasmata.

Mapping. Crossing-over can be used to produce a chromosome map showing the relative positions of the loci of the known gene pairs. Two organisms having homozygous gene pairs are bred, and the offspring (F_1) has heterozygous gene pairs (AaBb):

$$\frac{\mathrm{A\ \ B}}{\mathrm{A\ \ B}} \times \frac{\mathrm{a\ \ b}}{\mathrm{a\ \ b}} = \frac{\mathrm{A\ \ B}}{\mathrm{a\ \ b}}(\mathrm{F_1})$$

This heterozygote is then crossed with a tester strain of the genotype *aabb*, a standard tool known as a testcross. The progeny of a testcross are screened for the appearance of the genotype *A*a*bb* and *aa*B*b*, which can only arise from crossovers. The frequency of these types is a standard measure and is assumed to be proportional to the distance between the two loci on their chromosome. Using different combinations of gene pairs, an internally self-consistent map can be constructed in which the number of map units is defined as the percentage of progeny in a testcross derived from a crossover.

The Role of Chromosomes. It is now known that genes are lengths of a threadlike chemical called deoxyribonucleic acid (DNA) and form a continuous string that constitutes the chromosomes. Several researchers have attempted to explain the significance of the long assemblages of genes in chains, or chromosomes. First, some combinations of genes have adaptive value and need to be inherited as a package. Having

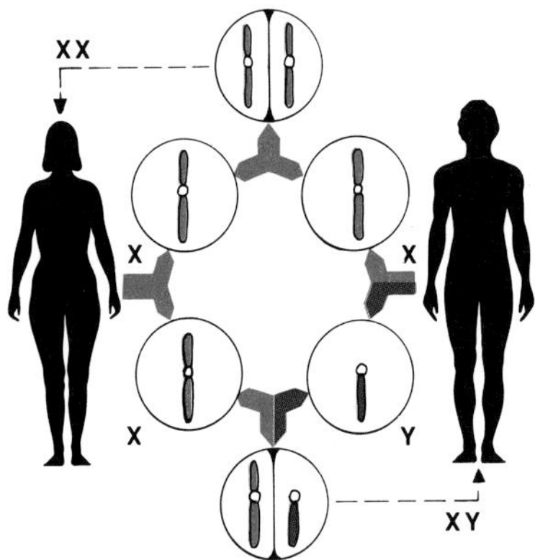

Human cells contain one pair of sex chromosomes, XX in females and XY in males. Ova contain only the X chromosome; spermatozoa possess either X or Y. At fertilization, the chance of an XX or XY pair being formed is about equal. Sex-linked characteristics arise from genes on the X chromosome, which have no counterpart on the Y chromosome.

them linked closely on one chromosome is one way of ensuring this. Second, genes with related functions often need to be activated simultaneously; their proximity allows them to be activated by one common switch mechanism. Third, the packaging of genes into units facilitates the orderly production of daughter cells in cell division.

Crossing-over and independent assortment of genes result in combinations of genes in progeny that are different from the parental arrangements. This process, called recombination, is believed to be an important mechanism for generating new genotypes. Recombination most frequently occurs among genes widely separated from each other; closely linked genes, however, have a reduced chance of rearrangement.

POLYGENES AND CONTINUOUS VARIATION

Mendel explained the phenomenon of discontinuous hereditary variation, which is expressed in separate and distinct phenotypes that are associated with a particular kind of allele, such as tall versus short or wrinkled versus smooth. Continuous variations occur in many phenotypes, however, such as length or weight, and form an apparently unbroken range

The X chromosome (but not the Y) carries genes for coat color in cats, which accounts for the observation that nearly all tortoiseshell cats are female. If a female carrying a black gene on each X chromosome is crossed with a male carrying a ginger gene on its X chromosome, only the female (XX) offspring can possess both types of genes; their coats have a black-and-ginger "tortoiseshell" pattern. Male offspring are black because their X chromosome carries a black gene; the Y chromosome lacks a corresponding gene for coat color.

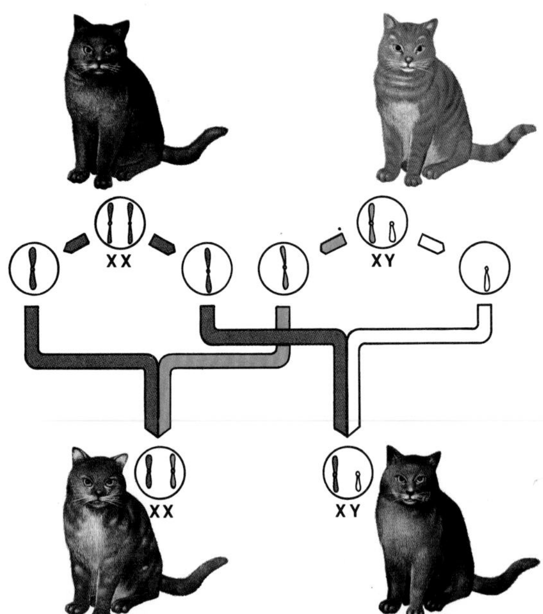

from one extreme to another. This phenomenon, known as polygenic inheritance, results from the complex interaction among a set of genes. Human skin color, in shades ranging from dark brown to pinkish white, is a good example of a trait determined by polygenes. Only an infinite number of polygenes, however, could give a perfectly continuous variation.

GENE-ENVIRONMENT INTERACTION

The phenotype of an organism is shaped not only by its genotype but also by the interaction of that genotype with the environment. Wilhelm Johannsen first demonstrated this phenomenon in his work (1903) on the inheritance of seed weight in dwarf beans.

It is often difficult—as in the case of human intelligence—to determine the relative contribution of genetic and environmental factors to a particular phenotype. In the case of rabbits, a dominant gene for yellow fat in rabbits will produce yellow fat only if the rabbit is fed plant leaves.

SEX DETERMINATION

The sex of an organism is usually an inherited phenotype. In haploid forms, alleles of one gene pair can determine sex, but in higher organisms sex is often associated with a special pair of chromosomes called sex chromosomes. For example, human cells contain 22 pairs of autosomes, or nonsex chromosomes, and one pair of sex chromosomes. Women possess two identical sex chromosomes (X and X) and men possess two different sex chromosomes (X and Y). The presence or absence of the Y chromosome determines sex in humans; therefore, the Y contains the genes for sex determination. In many higher plants, anthers and ovaries are located on separate plants (dioecism), and some of these have an X/Y-like chromosomal determination of sex.

In humans, the X chromosome bears genes that affect traits having nothing to do with the sex. Because they are located on the X, however, they show a special inheritance pattern different from autosomal gene inheritance; the Y chromosome apparently has no counterpart. Red-green color blindness and hemophilia are two genetic traits determined by X-linked genes. The X and the Y chromosomes are able to separate into equal numbers of sperm in the male and produce a 1:1 ratio of males to females in the eggs that they fertilize.

THE NATURE OF THE GENE

The genetic material of most organisms, DNA, is a double-stranded helix comprising a long chain of nucleotide bases with a sugar-phosphate backbone, as proposed by James D. Watson and Francis H. C. Crick in 1953. Eucaryotic cells contain two kinds of DNA sequences: unique DNA, one copy present in a haploid gene set; and repetitive DNA, identical copies (one million or more) found dispersed throughout the chromosome. The unique segments probably contain regular genes. The function of repetitive DNA segments is not known, although they may be involved either in chromosome pairing or in regulating the activity of the unique sequences.

DNA of eucaryotic organisms is formed into nucleosomes—small, beadlike units, each consisting of about 200 base pairs of DNA and a complex structure of proteins known as histones. Nucleosomes help package the DNA into the chromosome—an average human chromosome is about 0.005 mm in length yet contains about 50 mm of DNA.

During mitotic cell division chromosomal replication produces two daughter cells, each of which contains identical DNA, assuring the stability of the hereditary material. The DNA replication is semiconservative, which means that free nucleotides hydrogen-bond to each half of the separate DNA strands, resulting in two new DNA double helices. Each of the new double helices consists of one-half old and one-half newly formed strands.

Genes of the DNA in eucaryotic organisms (RNA in some viruses) control phenotype by coding for the structure of PROTEINS, which are the main structural and catalytic molecules in an organism; hair, muscle, skin, tendons, and enzymes are all proteinaceous. During PROTEIN SYNTHESIS, the order of the nucleotide pairs in DNA dictates the corresponding order of amino acids that give proteins their specific shape and function. The protein-building information in DNA is copied into a single-stranded molecule, called messenger RNA (mRNA).

The mRNA then moves to the cytoplasm, where protein synthesis occurs. The nucleotides in mRNA can be thought of as letters that are read in groups of three, called codons, each codon standing for an amino acid. The amino acids are transported to the mRNA by transfer RNA molecules, and the protein is assembled on the surface of ribosomes.

In humans the DNA in each cell contains about 3 billion base pairs, distributed among 22 sets of autosomal chromosomes and one set of sex chromosomes in the nucleus as well as one set of chromosomes in each mitochondrion. If all of this DNA were stretched out, it would have a length of about 1 m (3 ft), but the DNA is tightly compressed into the chromosomes, which, if stretched out, would have a total length of only about 0.0001 m (0.004 in). Only about 2 percent of a person's DNA forms the actual genes, as well; the rest constitutes either noncoding "spacer" regions between genes or noncoding "intron" regions within genes. The amount of DNA per cell varies tremendously within both animal and plant kingdoms and is unrelated to the taxonomic group concerned (see GENETIC CODE; GENOME).

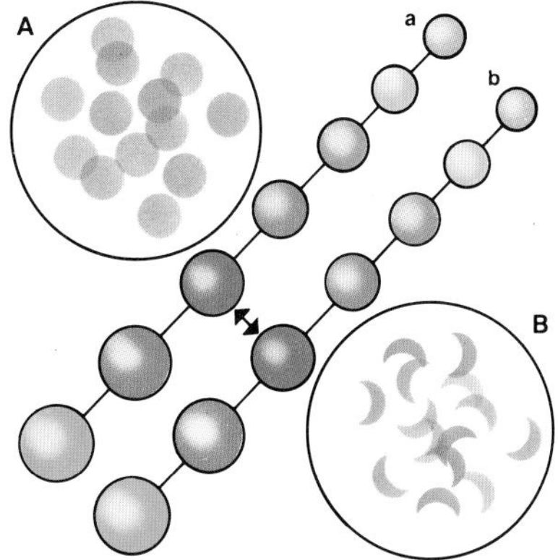

Normal red blood cells (A) *depend on a gene that controls the production of normal hemoglobin* (a), *a protein containing chains of amino acids* (colored disks). *A mutant form of the gene causes a change of one amino acid in the protein chain* (b), *leading, in homozygotes, to the sickle-shaped red blood cells* (B), *resulting in sickle-cell disease.*

MUTATION

MUTATION is the process by which genes change from one form to another. Mutations may be caused by such mutagens as X rays, ultraviolet rays, nitrous acid, ethyl methane sulfonate, and nitrosoguanidine; less frequently, mutations may occur spontaneously as a result of accidental changes in the chemistry of the cell. Because mutation is random, haphazard change, most mutants contain damaged genes that are nonfunctional. Mutants usually do not live long in nature; geneticists and breeders, however, may keep mutants alive for study or for use in producing new plant and animal forms that have characteristics desirable for agriculture.

A mutation in DNA usually results in an altered nucleotide sequence, either by substitution, addition, deletion, or insertion, which is translated into an altered amino-acid sequence that usually produces a change in the organism's normal body function. The alteration of amino acids can have a drastic effect on function, as in the case of sickle-cell hemoglobin. A mutation of the chromosome can cause similar effects. Mutations of cells other than sex cells are considered to be a primary cause of cancer in those tissues.

All humans carry quite a large number of deleterious and lethal mutant genes that are recessive. Each mating is a kind of a lottery, in which the offspring reveal whether or not the parents' mutations are at identical loci. For example, if both parents are heterozygous (*Aa*) for a gene pair in which the recessive allele is deleterious, then 1/4 of their children will show GENETIC DISEASE of the kind controlled by that locus. Genetic counseling can often help prospective mates in determining whether such diseases can occur in their offspring (see also GENETIC IMPRINTING).

GENES IN DEVELOPMENT

Most organisms start life as single cells (zygotes) and grow into massive multicellular bodies with cells of considerable differences in form and function. This process, which involves growth and differentiation, is called DEVELOPMENT. Although skin cells, liver cells, brain cells, and so on are highly differentiated, they are all derived from the original zygote as a result of the high-fidelity copying of DNA during mitotic division. Cell specialization is achieved by a complex process whereby different genes are active in different tissues.

The best examples of gene regulation are found in bacteria, where genes of related function are grouped on the chromosome together with a special class of regulatory genes to form an operon, which is a kind of control unit. The operon theory was proposed by François Jacob and Jacques Monod in 1961. Regulatory genes, usually responding to environmental cues, either assist or prevent the passage of the mRNA synthesis enzyme, RNA polymerase, along the operon, thereby controlling gene activity. No satisfactory examples of operons have been found at present in higher organisms, but some of them do have special sequences of nucleotides that control developmental processes. These sections of DNA have been called "homeoboxes." There are at least 6 homeoboxes in human DNA and at least 20 in *Drosophila* DNA. Each homeobox consists of 180 nucleotide pairs and codes for the production of a protein that can bind to DNA, thus placing it in a position to control transcription. Evidence exists that the protein encoded by a homeobox functions to regulate batteries of genes involved in development. In addition to humans and *Drosophila,* homeoboxes have been found in such organisms as yeasts, sea urchins, earthworms, and toads.

GENES IN CYTOPLASMIC ORGANELLES

Although most genes are found in the chromosomes of the nucleus, two kinds of cytoplasmic organelles, mitochondria and chloroplasts, also contain certain genes. Phenotypes determined by these genes are inherited through the female parent. Maternal or uniparental inheritance has been studied in microorganisms, notably the unicellular algae, Chlamydomonas, and several fungi. In Chlamydomonas, a variety of drug-resistant and morphological phenotypes are involved. In fungi, sensitivity to certain drugs can be cytoplasmically inherited, as can some kinds of poor growth phenotypes.

The mitochondria and chloroplasts carry their own DNA, which is circular and unlike nuclear DNA in nucleotide composition. They also contain their own autonomous protein-synthesizing system, many parts of which are coded by organellar DNA genes. Many other components of the mitochondria and chloroplasts, such as cytochromes, are coded by genes of nuclear DNA. These organelles are therefore composed of a mixture of components with DNA blueprints located in both the nucleus and the organelle.

Mitochondrial genes also code for proteins involved in the production of adenosine triphosphate (ATP), the key energy molecule of cells. Recently it has been discovered that people suffering from Leber's hereditary optic neuropathy (LHON) have a defect in a mitochondrial gene that codes for a protein involved in the first step of ATP production. LHON is a rare disease that causes the optic nerve to degenerate in young adults, leading to blindness. It has been hypothesized that other maternally inherited genetic diseases exist that are caused by mutations in mitochondrial DNA.

The specific synthesizing machinery of the mitochondrion, together with its shape and size, have suggested to some that the mitochondrion is a vestige of a primitive symbiotic association with bacteria. Similarly, the structure and functions of a chloroplast are reminiscent of the primitive blue-green algae. This kind of evolution, in which complexity results from the adoption of an internal collection of simpler cells, is called hereditary symbiosis and may have been important in the development of modern cells.

GENES IN POPULATIONS

Mendelian genetics can predict the inheritance patterns within families, but one should not expect to see similar patterns and ratios in populations, which are complex mixtures of different families. A different approach, called POPULATION GENETICS, is used to analyze genetic distribution in populations.

In order to understand the analytical procedures involved in population genetics, assume that a chromosome locus contains two alleles (*A* and *a*) of one gene. The gene pool of a population is derived by considering each diploid individual to be one cell bearing two genes at that locus. The total number of *A* and *a* genes in a population is calculated and an allele frequency for each is obtained. Usually, the frequency of *A* is called *p*, and the frequency of *a* is called *q*, where $p + q = 1$ (or 100%). The allele frequencies are the main determinants of the genetic structure of populations. If mating is random, for example, there will be p^2 of *AA*, 2 *pq* of *Aa*, and q^2 of *aa*. This distribution, which is stable if all other factors are constant, is named Hardy-Weinberg equilibrium for its discoverers. At its most fundamental level, evolution is little more than a change in relative allele frequencies.

The actual values of *p* and *q* at each locus are determined by the complex interaction of many forces, including mutation from *A* to *a*, mutation from *a* to *A* (reversion, which is usually less frequent than forward mutation), chance fluctuation due to small populations (producing genetic drift of allele frequencies), and natural selection for or against certain genotypes. In turn, selection can be directional, ultimately eliminating one allele from the population, or stabilizing, favoring intermediate genotypes and tending to maintain several alleles and phenotypes in an interbreeding population, a phenomenon called genetic polymorphism.

Preliminary results of a different form of genetic study of human evolution aroused controversy at the 1987 meeting of the American Anthropological Association. The research involved analyses of mitochondrial DNA in placental samples from women with a worldwide distribution of ancestry. Such DNA is inherited only from the mother, and through mutation studies the researchers hoped to trace human ancestry back to a "single" source—some generation of first humans. The results of a team of geneticists working at the University of California, Berkeley, suggested a human family tree with roots in sub-Saharan Africa some 140,000 to 200,000 years ago. Another team, at Emory University, proposed a common ancestor of similar age but in southeastern Asia. Anthropologists expressed considerable skepticism, however, about these results of what came to be known as the "Eve" hypothesis. Most anthropologists consider that the first true humans appeared much longer ago (see PREHISTORIC HUMANS).

MODERN GENETICS

Genetics is an important aspect of many areas of pure and applied biology. Viral genetics, microbial genetics, plant genetics, animal genetics, and human genetics focus research on specific types of organisms. Research in molecular genetics involves studies on chemical structure and function; cytogenetics on location of the genetic material in cells and on cell division; developmental genetics on the genetic function in embryological phenomena; behavior genetics on the role of the gene in regulating behavior; and population genetics on the evolutionary process.

At the applied level, genetics is of direct use in understanding genetic diseases and environmental mutation. It is used in plant and animal breeding to improve the quality and quantity of food. It also is a tool in basic research by which complex biological processes can be analyzed, often at the molecular level.

A. J. W. GRIFFITHS

Bibliography: Ayala, F. J., *Population and Evolutionary Genetics* (1982); Briggs, David, and Walters, Max, *Plant Variation and Evolution* (1969); Burnet, F. M., *Endurance of Life: The Implications of Genetics for Human Life* (1978); Dobzhansky, Theodosius, *Genetics of the Evolutionary Process* (1970); Goodenough, U., *Genetics*, 3d ed. (1983); Lerner, I. Michael, and Libby, William J., *Heredity, Evolution, and Society*, 2d ed. (1976); Levine, Louis, *Biology of the Gene*, 3d ed. (1980); Lewontin, R. C., Rose, Steven, and Kamin, L. J., *Not in Our Genes: Biology, Ideology and Human Nature* (1984); McKusick, V. S., *Mendelian Inheritance in Man*, 7th ed. (1986); Malacinski, G. M., *Developmental Genetics of Higher Organisms* (1988); Merrell, D. J., *Ecological Genetics* (1981); Mertens, Thomas R., ed., *Human Genetics: Readings on the Implications of Genetic Engineering* (1975); Rothwell, N. V.,

This map shows the distribution of the human blood group gene B throughout the world. The highest frequency (25% to 30%) of gene B occurs in Central Asian populations. The incidence of the gene generally decreases as distance from this center increases; it is lowest among the original populations of Australia and the Americas. Such maps can be used to study past migrations of populations.

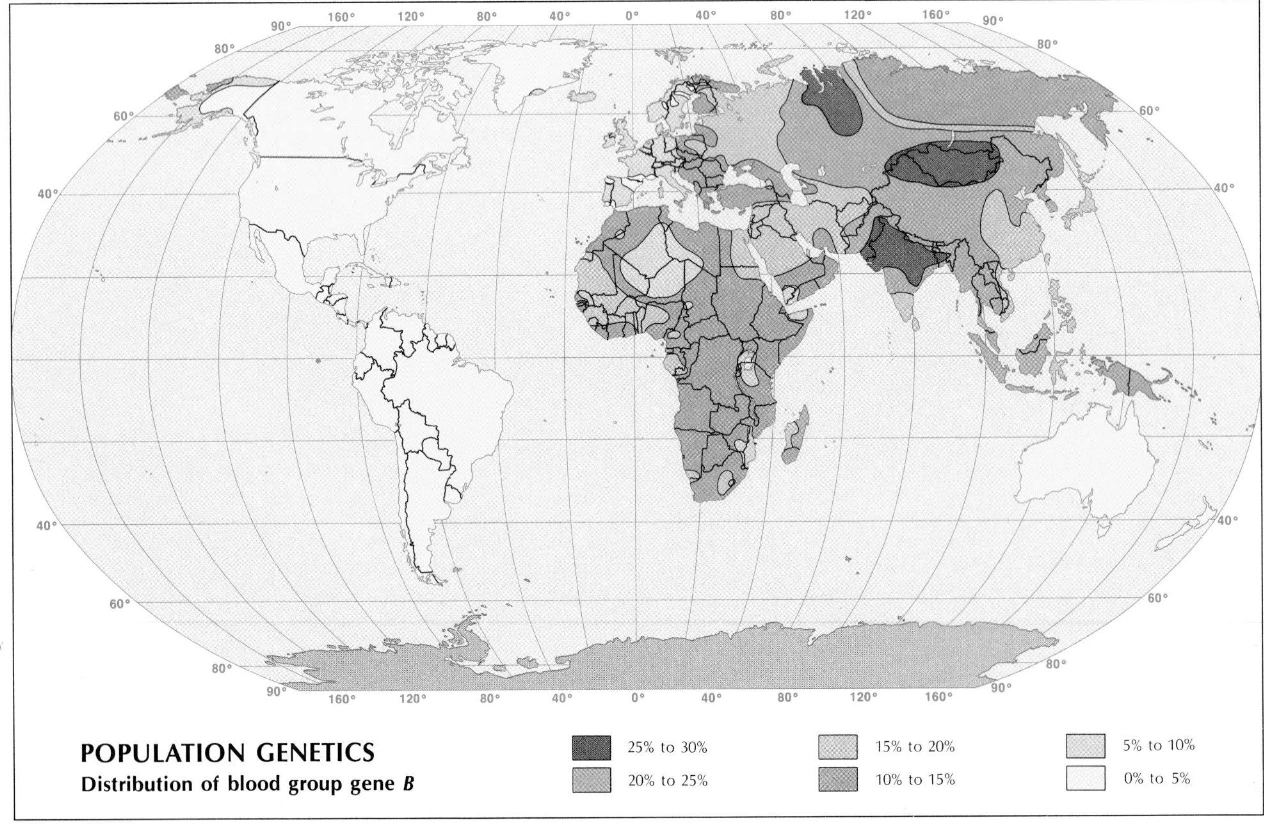

Understanding Genetics, 4th ed. (1988); Scandalios, J. G., *Molecular Genetics of Development* (1987); Spiess, E. B., *Genes in Populations* (1977); Stent, G. S., and Calendar, R., *Molecular Genetics* (1978); Suzuki, D. T., Griffiths, A. J., and Lewontin, R. C., *An Introduction to Genetic Analysis,* 3d ed. (1986); Watson, J. D., et al., *The Molecular Biology of the Gene,* 2 vols. (1987).

Geneva [juh-neev'-uh]

Geneva (French: Genève; German: Genf) is the third largest city in Switzerland and capital of the canton of Geneva, in the western part of the country. The population of the city is 159,900 (1986 est.). Located at the southwest tip of Lake Geneva, it is known for its parks and boulevards and for its view of the Mont Blanc massif.

The city of Geneva is the intellectual and economic center of the French-speaking area of Switzerland and has many contacts with nearby France. It still retains its early importance as a transportation center, but its economy is based primarily on service industries, especially international organizations, finance, watchmaking, printing, and the manufacture of electrical machinery, jewelry, and handicrafts.

Contemporary City. Geneva is famous for having been the seat of John CALVIN in the 16th century. The school of theology at the University of Geneva remains a center of Calvinist studies; the university is also renowned for its programs in botanical and international studies. In the 19th and 20th centuries, Geneva blossomed into an international city; international and ecumenical organizations ranging from the International Red Cross to the World Health Organization and the World Council of Churches have their headquarters there. Between the two world wars it was the seat of the League of Nations. The League's chief facility, the Palace of Nations, is now the European office of the United Nations.

The international flavor of the city has attracted multinational organizations and facilitated Geneva's rise as an international banking center; it has also given the city a unique character. A popular place to live, the city has grown rapidly since 1945 and has recently experienced ecological and crowding problems. A rich cultural life is provided by the university, several museums, theaters, a conservatory, and the Orchestre de la Suisse Romande.

History. Geneva was founded by a Celtic tribe, the Allobroges, who settled in the 1st century BC at the tip of Lake Geneva, at one of the few convenient crossings of the Rhône River. Geneva was Christianized under the Romans, and trade developed along routes across the mountains to France and Italy. During the Middle Ages the bourgeoisie resisted the power of resident bishops supported by Burgundy and turned to the counts of Savoy, who began appointing the bishops in the 15th century.

The city adopted Protestantism in 1535; this led to war with Savoy. In 1536, Calvin established theocratic rule that lasted well past his death in 1564. He made Geneva a political and religious center and involved the city in several religious wars. The dukes of Savoy were ultimately repulsed in 1602. The atmosphere in Geneva gradually became more tolerant, and in the 18th century many radical thinkers were drawn there. Following French occupation (1798) and forced membership in Napoleon I's Helvetic Republic, Geneva joined the Swiss Confederation in 1815.

JONATHAN E. HELMREICH

Geneva, Lake

Lake Geneva (French: Lac Léman; German: Genfersee) is a crescent-shaped lake that lies in the Alps of southwestern Switzerland and southeastern France. The largest of the Alpine lakes, it has an area of 580 km^2 (224 mi^2). The lake is 72 km (45 mi) long, 14 km (8.5 mi) wide, and 310 m (1,017 ft) deep; its mean depth is 152 m (500 ft).

Lake Geneva is essentially a widening of the RHÔNE RIVER, which enters the lake at its eastern end and exits at the city of Geneva in the extreme west. Fluctuations, called seiches, probably caused by changes in atmospheric pressure, cause the entire lake to rock rhythmically from shore to shore. Its deep, clear waters support some 20 species of indigenous fish. The Alps, to the east and south, and the Jura Mountains, to the west and north, provide dramatic mountain backgrounds. Lakeside resorts include Montreux and Vevey in Switzerland and Évian-les-Bains in France. Modern highways and railroads ring the lake, and frequent steamship service is offered.

Geneva, University of

The University of Geneva (enrollment: 11,500; library: 1,600,000 volumes) is a francophone institution in Geneva, Switzerland. It was founded (1559) as an academy by John Calvin. During the 18th century the university was a center of French Protestant theology.

Geneva conferences

Geneva, Switzerland, the home of the League of Nations and of some branches of the United Nations, as well as numerous other international organizations, has been the site of many international conferences. Among the most significant meetings held there have been the World Disarmament Conference of 1932–37 and the conference of 1954 to effect a settlement of the war in Indochina.

Disarmament Conference. The World Disarmament Conference was the last effort to achieve armaments limitation in the period before World War II. Disarmament had been a major

Geneva, a canton capital in western Switzerland near the French border, has developed into a center of international banking and finance. Attracted by the city's location in central Europe and by Switzerland's traditional neutrality, many international organizations, including the European offices of the United Nations and the International Red Cross, have established their headquarters in Geneva.

objective of the LEAGUE OF NATIONS since its establishment after World War I, but the reluctance of certain powers, most notably France, to disarm without adequate security guarantees had blocked agreement. From 1926 on the league had sponsored meetings of a preparatory commission to lay the groundwork for a disarmament conference. The United States and the USSR, although not then league members, took part in these talks.

The Disarmament Conference opened in Geneva in February 1932 with 60 nations represented. Because delegates could not agree on either the budgetary limitations proposed for air, land, and naval forces, or the categories of weapons to be restricted, the conference made no headway. Various plans were suggested, including one by U.S. president Herbert HOOVER that proposed a one-third reduction in the defense components of armed forces, but to no avail. France remained insistent on security and Germany on its right to equality with the other powers. After adjourning in March 1933, the representatives met again the following October. Germany, now the Nazi government of Adolf Hitler, withdrew, however, from both the conference and the league. This move destroyed any chances for success, and although the conference continued to meet sporadically until April 1937, it reached no agreement.

Indochina Conference. The Geneva Conference of 1954 was called to settle the war between France and the Communist-backed VIET MINH in Indochina. Since 1946, when French forces returned to Vietnam after World War II, the French had been unable to overcome the opposition to their rule. French losses in the Battle of DIEN BIEN PHU (March–May 1954) led the United States, Britain, the USSR, and France to call the Geneva Conference. Representatives of those powers, as well as of the Indochinese nations, Communist China, and North and South Korea, met from April until July 1954.

The French, Vietnamese, Cambodian, and Laotian representatives quickly agreed to draw a cease-fire line along the 17th parallel, effectively dividing Vietnam into two countries: Communist in the north and French-backed in the south. An international control commission was established to supervise the settlement, but its provisions were violated by both sides. The agreement to reunify Vietnam by holding elections within two years was not honored by South Vietnam, and the Geneva Accords became the subject of later controversy (see VIETNAM WAR). DONALD S. BIRN

Bibliography: Cable, James, *The Geneva Convention of Nineteen Fifty Four on Indochina* (1986); Northedge, F. S., *The League of Nations* (1986); Randle, Robert, *Geneva Nineteen Fifty Four* (1969); Scott, George, *The Rise and Fall of the League of Nations* (1973).

Geneva conventions

The Geneva conventions are a series of international agreements to provide for the humane treatment of the wounded, prisoners of war, and civilians in time of war. The first Geneva convention "for the amelioration of the condition of the wounded and sick of armed forces in the field" was signed in Geneva, Switzerland, in August 1864. Representatives of 16 countries pledged to respect the neutrality of civilians and of medical personnel and hospital ships bearing the emblem of the RED CROSS and to treat the war wounded humanely.

Other conventions were added in 1899, 1907, and 1929, covering such things as maritime warfare and treatment of prisoners of war. Four more conventions in 1949 extended and codified the laws of war. They recognized the fact that warfare had become total, thus erasing the distinctions between the civilian home front and the war front.

The fourth convention of 1949 sought to broaden the protection of civilians menaced by saturation bombings and other manifestations of total war. It forbade such abuses as deportation, the taking of hostages, torture, collective punishment and reprisals, and racial, religious, national, or political discrimination.

Bibliography: Roberts, Adam, and Guelff, Richard, eds., *Documents on the Laws of War* (1982).

See also: DUNANT, JEAN HENRI; HAGUE CONFERENCES; WAR CRIMES.

Genevieve, Saint [jen'-uh-veev]

Saint Genevieve, 422–500, is the patron saint of Paris. According to tradition, she inspired the city to resist an attack by the Huns in 451. Feast day: Jan. 3.

Genghis Khan, Mongol Emperor [jeng'-gis kahn]

The MONGOL leader Genghis Khan was one of the great conquerors in the history of the world. Born *c.*1167, he was the son of Yesügei, leader of a small tribe in northeastern Mongolia, in an area adjacent to the modern border with the Soviet Union. Yesügei was poisoned when Temüjin (Genghis Khan's name as a youth) was about 10 years old, and the orphaned boy later entered the service of Toghril Khan, the most powerful Mongol ruler of the time. Struggle and bloodshed characterized the succeeding years until 1206, when Temüjin united the warring Mongol tribes and was proclaimed Genghis Khan ("universal ruler") of the Mongol chieftains. (The name also appears as Jenghiz Khan.)

In 1207, Genghis Khan led the Mongols on the first of the series of destructive, bloody invasions that would result in the conquest of much of the Asian mainland. After defeating the CHIN empire in northern China, the Mongols occupied Peking in 1215. Extending their expeditions to the shores of the Caspian Sea, the Mongol warriors penetrated the steppes of Russia and totally defeated the Russian army by 1223. They did not, however, follow up their victory with a conquest of the cities to the west; instead they returned eastward. The empire established by Genghis Khan eventually extended from the Pacific Ocean to the Black Sea, and from Siberia to the northern borders of mainland Southeast Asia.

Genghis Khan, the Mongol leader who conquered a vast Asian territory that stretched from the Pacific in the east to the Black Sea in the west, appears in this illustration from a 13th-century Chinese album. After uniting the traditionally hostile nomadic tribes of Mongolia, Genghis Khan created one of the largest land empires in history. (National Palace Museum, Taipei.)

Genghis Khan's success as soldier, conqueror, and ruler resulted largely from his military organization, strategy, and mobility, all of which gave him a consistent advantage over opponents who were often weaker and less well organized. Although he never learned to read, he left behind a system of law that probably represented more than a mere codification of existing practices. He died on Aug. 18, 1227, and was buried in a secret location in Mongolia. RICHARD BUTWELL

Bibliography: Brent, Peter, *Genghis Khan* (1976); Chambers, James, *The Devil's Horsemen* (1985); Grousset, René, *Conqueror of the World* (1967); Lamb, Harold, *Genghis Khan* (1927; repr. 1981); Lister, Richard, *Genghis Khan* (1969).

genius: see INTELLIGENCE.

genius (mythology)

In Roman mythology a genius was a guardian spirit that protected an individual throughout his or her life. Every living person was endowed with a specific genius to whom yearly offerings were made, generally on the person's birthday. In addition to the individual's genius there were genii who protected tribes, towns, places, and the Roman state. A particularly important genius was the *Genius populi Romani*, guardian of Rome. The accomplishments of an individual were often attributed to his or her genius.

Genji: see TALE OF GENJI, THE.

Gennep, Arnold van [je-nep']

Arnold van Gennep, b. Apr. 23, 1873, d. May 7, 1957, was a French ethnographer and folklorist noted for the influential work *The Rites of Passage* (1909; Eng. trans., 1961). In it he theorized about the significance of ceremonies marking the transition of individuals or groups from one status in society to another (see PASSAGE, RITES OF). JAMES W. HERRICK

Genoa [jen'-oh-uh]

Genoa (Italian: Genova) is the capital of Genoa province and the Liguria region in northwestern Italy. It has a population of 735,600 (1985 est.) and is located about 120 km (75 mi) south of Milan on the Gulf of Genoa, the northern portion of the Mediterranean's Ligurian Sea. Genoa is Italy's most important seaport and one of the largest in Europe. The city is built up from the port area into the surrounding hills, which reach an elevation of 115 m (378 ft).

Contemporary City. Genoa's economy is dominated by its port activities and by the rail, air, and highway transportation systems that service the shipping industry. Genoa is the major embarkation point for the agricultural and industrial products of northern Italy and much of central Europe. It is also a leading passenger port on the Mediterranean. After the reconstruction and enlargement of Genoa's port facilities in the 1950s—they had been damaged by Allied bombing during World War II—Genoa's annual trade grew dramatically. In addition to shipping, important industries include shipbuilding, iron and steel production, and the manufacture of such diverse products as textiles, munitions, paper products, chemicals, locomotives, cement, and aircraft supplies. Genoa is also an important banking, commercial, and insurance center.

Genoa is noted for its medieval, Renaissance, and baroque palaces, including the Ducal Palace (begun 1291). The Doria Tursi Palace (16th century) is now used as the city hall. The Cathedral of San Lorenzo dates from the 10th century, and the churches of Sant' Ambrogio and the Annunciation are important examples of baroque architecture. Genoa has several museums, such as those in the Bianco Palace and the Rosso Palace. The University of Genoa (founded 1243) is an important learning center. The city also has commercial colleges and a school of navigation. Famous Genoans have included Andrea DORIA, Christopher Columbus, and Nicolò Paganini.

History. By the 5th century BC, Genoa was already an important trade center of the Ligurians, a pre-Roman people of northern Italy. The city flourished under Roman rule, which began in the 3d century BC; although it was destroyed by Carthage, it was quickly rebuilt. After the fall of Rome the city suffered numerous Germanic and Arab invasions. It became a free commune, or republic, in the 12th century, and its maritime power increased. In the 13th century it gained control of Sardinia and Corsica and also held possessions in the Greek Islands and in the Black Sea, defeating its rival, Pisa, in 1284. The Crusades brought Genoa great wealth, and for a time it was Venice's chief rival in trade with the East until its defeat in the War of Chioggia (1378–80).

Beginning in the 14th century, Genoa went through a long period of foreign domination, although its nominal independence was preserved. France, Milan, Spain, and Austria all controlled the city at various times. In 1796 the French ousted the Austrians, and Genoa's formal independence came to an end. It became part of the Ligurian Republic, and in 1805, Napoleon I annexed it to France. At the end of the Napoleonic era, the Congress of Vienna (1815) gave the city to the Kingdom of Sardinia. In 1861 the city was absorbed into the newly unified Kingdom of Italy.

The city prospered as part of the new kingdom, although its republican traditions remained strong. During World War II, Genoa was a center of underground resistance to the Axis, and the Genoans staged a successful insurrection against the Germans in April 1945. DANIEL R. LESNICK

genocide [jen'-uh-syd]

Genocide (Greek *genos*, "race," and Latin *cide*, "killing") is the persecution or destruction of a national, racial, or religious group. Years before the word *genocide* was coined by the Polish-American scholar Raphael Lemkin in 1944, genocide was practiced by the Russians in their pogroms against the Jews and by the German Nazis, who systematically killed ethnic groups including Jews, Poles, and gypsies. A more recent example is the slaughtering (1972–79) of various tribal groups by the former president of Uganda Idi AMIN DADA. The tribunal at the NUREMBERG TRIALS (1945–46) of Nazi war criminals declared that persecution of racial and religious groups was a crime under international law. In 1948 the General Assembly of the United Nations approved the Convention on the Prevention and Punishment of the Crime of Genocide, which took effect in 1951. The nations that ratified the convention agreed that genocide was a matter of international concern, even if committed by a government within its own territory. Any nation can ask the United Nations to take action to prevent or suppress acts of genocide. The United States is a signatory of the Genocide Convention, but the U.S. Senate, which is reluctant to subject American citizens to the jurisdic-

Genoa, a provincial capital in the Ligurian region of northwestern Italy, is the nation's busiest seaport. The city's highly developed harbor facilities have been a major source of revenue since the Middle Ages.

tion of any international tribunal, for many years refused to ratify it; it finally did so in 1986.

Bibliography: Horowitz, Irving, *Taking Lives: Genocide and State Power,* 3d ed. (1981); Walliman, Isidor, and Dobkowski, Michael, *Genocide and the Modern Age* (1987).

genome

The genome of an organism is the totality of genes making up its hereditary constitution. In the late 1980s, two research projects were proposed concerning the human genome. The goal of one would be to determine the exact location of all the genes—50,000 to 100,000, plus regulatory elements—on their respective chromosomes (see GENETICS). The goal of the other would be to establish the sequence of nucleotides—estimated to be about 6 billion pairs—of all the genes (see GENETIC CODE). Both goals are possible and would be of great medical benefit, but they would take at least a decade to complete at an estimated cost of $3 billion. The U.S. National Institutes of Health (NIH) and Department of Energy are mainly involved in the projects, with the assistance of the National Science Foundation and the Howard Hughes Medical Institute. Nobel Prize winner James WATSON has been chosen to head the new Office for Human Genome Research at the NIH.

LOUIS LEVINE

Bibliography: Office of Technology Assessment, *Mapping Our Genes: Genome Projects—How Big, How Fast* (1988).

genre [zhawn'-ruh]

Genre, a French word rendered in English as "type," "kind," or "form," is a term that describes works of literature according to their shared thematic or structural characteristics. The attempt to classify literature in this way was begun by ARISTOTLE in the POETICS, where he distinguishes TRAGEDY, EPIC, and COMEDY and recognizes even more fundamental distinctions between DRAMA, epic, and LYRIC poetry. Classical genre theory, established by Aristotle and reinforced by HORACE, is regulative and prescriptive, attempting to maintain rigid boundaries that correspond to social differences. Thus, tragedy and epic are concerned exclusively with the affairs of the nobility, comedy with the middle or lower classes.

Modern literary criticism, on the other hand, does not regard genres as dogmatic categories, but rather as aesthetic conventions that guide, but are also led by, writers. The unstable nature of genres does not reduce their effectiveness as tools of critical inquiry, which attempts to discover universal attributes among individual works, and has, since classical times, evolved theories of the NOVEL, ODE, ELEGY, PASTORAL, SATIRE, and many other kinds of writing. A dominant contemporary genre theory is that of Northrop FRYE, whose *Anatomy of Criticism* (1957) presents a comprehensive typology of literature.

HOWARD BATCHELOR

genre painting

Genre painting (from the French word *genre,* meaning "type" or "kind") is a term applied to works that depict secular scenes of everyday domestic work or recreation. The term is commonly used to distinguish such paintings from works of a religious, historical, or ceremonial character, which tend to elevate their subjects above the mundane level of ordinary existence. Genre painting, which is characterized by realism (see REALISM, art), first appears as an element in early Renaissance art and northern European 15th-century religious painting. The frescoes *Good Government* (1339) in the Palazzo Publico, Siena, by Ambrogio Lorenzetti (see LORENZETTI family) and the illuminated manuscript the *Très Riches Heures du Duc de Berry* (*c.*1416; Musée Condé, Chantilly, France) by the LIMBOURG BROTHERS, combine glimpses of the daily life of the time with political and devotional themes. Genre scenes play a far larger part in the work of Albrecht DÜRER and Pieter Bruegel (see BRUEGEL family), which led to the full flowering of genre painting in 17th-century Holland. Among the Dutch masters of the form were Gabriel METSU, Adriaen van OSTADE, Jan STEEN, and Jan VERMEER. Their work, as distinct from the closely related forms of conversation piece and portraiture, was informal and anecdotal, depicting anonymous figures engaged in familiar activities. Since the 17th century numerous styles of painting have evolved that may be assigned to this category, and genre painting may now be graded as a fundamental, if not predominant, form of artistic expression.

CHARLES MINOTT

Bibliography: Chepp, Mark, et al., *Low-Life in the Lowlands: 17th Century Dutch and Flemish Genre Painting* (1974); Sitwell, Sacheverell, *Narrative Pictures: A Survey of English Genre and Its Painters* (1938); Spike, John, *Giuseppe Maria Crespi and the Emergence of Genre Painting in Italy* (1986).

gentian [jen'-shuhn]

The gentian, native to southern Europe, is a herbaceous plant that bears showy, trumpet-shaped flowers. When dried, its roots yield the drug gentian, which is used as a tonic and as a stimulant to digestion.

Gentian is the common name for any of some 350 species of mostly perennial herbs of the genus *Gentiana* in the gentian family, Gentianaceae. Gentians are found throughout the world except in Africa and occur chiefly in cool temperate or mountainous regions. In the Alps they grow in large masses, with conspicuous flowers. Species range in height from about 10 cm (4 in) to more than 3.5 m (12 ft). The tubular white, yellow, blue, or purple flowers occur singly or in small clusters. They show an increasingly specialized adaptation to different types of insects. The simpler forms are rather open, with their nectar readily accessible to short-tongued insects. Intermediate forms are longer, and their nectar is taken by certain kinds of bees. The most advanced forms have deeply tubular flowers whose nectar is obtainable only by long-tongued butterflies. Gentian roots contain bitter glucosides that have been used medicinally.

OLIN S. FEARING

gentian violet

Gentian violet, also known as crystal violet, Basic Violet 3, and hexamethylrosaniline chloride, is a shiny, dark green powder that can be used as a dye or as an anti-infective agent. In aqueous solution it is applied externally against certain bacteria, molds, and fungi; taken internally in enteric-coated tablets, it is effective against pinworms.

Gentile, Giovanni [jayn'-tee-lay]

Giovanni Gentile, b. May 30, 1875, d. Apr. 15, 1944, was the self-proclaimed philosopher of Italian FASCISM and a major figure in the rise of Hegelian thought in Italy in the early decades of the 20th century. A professor of philosophy at the universities of Palermo and Pisa, he lectured at the University of Rome from 1917 until his death. As minister of education in Benito MUSSOLINI's first cabinet, he presided over a purge of liberals and democrats from Italian education.

Gentile's best-known works, *The Theory of Mind as Pure Act* (1916; Eng. trans., 1922) and his 1917 study, *Logic as a*

Theory of Knowing, develop a philosophy that he called "actual idealism." While denying that any philosophy can transcend actual human experience through an appeal either to matter or a realm of timeless forms, he defended the view that human experience is fundamentally mental or spiritual. Human spirituality finds its fulfillment in the creation and defense of the state. PETE A. Y. GUNTER

Bibliography: Holmes, Roger Wellington, *The Idealism of Giovanni Gentile* (1937; repr. 1960).

Gentile da Fabriano [jayn'-tee-lay dah fahb-ree-ah'-noh]

Gentile da Fabriano, *c.*1370–1427, born Gentile di Nicolò di Giovanni di Massio, was one of the major Italian painters of the early 15th century who worked in the International Gothic style (see INTERNATIONAL STYLE, art). He began working in northern Italy, where his reputation was well established when he received a commission in 1409 to execute the frescoes (now destroyed) in the Doge's Palace in Venice. Other commissions took him to Brescia, Siena, Florence, Orvieto, and Rome. Among his many works now lost were important frescoes in the basilica of Saint John Lateran in Rome, which were completed by Antonio PISANELLO after Gentile's death.

His most famous works are two large altarpieces: *Adoration of the Magi* (1423; Uffizi, Florence), commissioned by the wealthy Florentine Palla Strozzi for his family chapel in the sacristy of Santa Trinità in Florence; and a large polyptych, *Quaratesi Polyptych* (1425), made for the Quaratesi family in Florence, whose panels are now dispersed in museums in London, Florence, Rome, and Washington, D.C.

The *Adoration of the Magi* is generally considered the quintessential International Gothic style painting. The main panel depicts the Virgin and Child with the three Magi and a throng of attendants dressed in elaborate and richly colored costumes. Birds, monkeys, dogs, horses, camels, and leopards participate in an exotic procession set in a fairy-tale landscape. The work is characterized by sinuous lines and elegant decorative effects, with little concentration on volume or depth.

Gentile's style is often contrasted with the monumental style of his Florentine contemporary MASACCIO. Gentile's influence, which was extensive, can be seen in the works of his followers Jacopo Bellini (see BELLINI family) and Pisanello, among others. TANIA M. BAYARD

The Adoration of the Magi *(1423), by Gentile da Fabriano, an Italian master of the International Gothic style, was painted for the church of Santa Trinità in Florence. The painting is considered the finest of the artist's extant works. (Uffizi, Florence.)*

Bibliography: Castelfranchi Vegas, Liana, *International Gothic Art in Italy*, trans. by B. D. Phillips (1966); Christiansen, Keith, *Gentile da Fabriano* (1981); Marle, Raimond van, *The Development of the Italian Schools of Painting*, vol. 8 (1927).

Gentileschi (family) [jen-tee-les'-kee]

The Lute Player *(1626), a late work by the Italian baroque painter Orazio Gentileschi, modifies Caravaggio's realistic, chairoscuro style by infusing it with a Florentine delicacy and attention to detail. The grand gesture and the monumental composition reflect Orazio's Roman Renaissance heritage. (National Gallery, Washington.)*

Orazio Gentileschi and his daughter Artemisia were Italian painters inspired by Michelangelo CARAVAGGIO's naturalism, which they transformed into their own personal styles.

Orazio Gentileschi, *c.*1563–*c.*1639, was trained by his half brother Antonio Lomi in Florence and went to Rome in the late 1570s. Little is known of his early work there. He knew Caravaggio, whose influence can be seen in Orazio's paintings done between about 1605 and 1615, such as the *Judith* (*c.*1610; Wadsworth Atheneum, Hartford, Conn.). At this time he also painted in fresco, collaborating with Agostino Tassi. Active in Rome and the Marches until 1621, Orazio traveled in northern Italy (Genoa and Turin) until about 1623, when he visited France. The brighter, more elegant compositions of this period, such as his *Rest on the Flight into Egypt* (*c.*1626; Louvre, Paris), appealed to such painters as Philippe de CHAMPAIGNE. In 1626, Orazio went to London and became court painter to Charles I, for whom he executed numerous works.

Artemisia Gentileschi, *c.*1593–1651, first studied painting with her father and then with his colleague Agostino Tassi. In

1612, Tassi was accused of raping Artemisia, but the case was dismissed. Artemisia left Rome (1621) for Florence, where she established a reputation for her paintings of biblical and mythological heroines. In *Judith with the Head of Holofernes* (*c*.1625; Detroit Institute of Arts), a composition that she repeated several times, the impact of Caravaggesque CHIAROSCURO is pronounced. During the 1620s she visited Genoa and Venice and by 1630 had settled in Naples, where she remained—except for a visit (*c*.1638) with her father in London—until her death. Her role in the dissemination of Caravaggesque realism was significant: she influenced the French painter Simon VOUET in Rome and inspired such artists as Bernardo Cavallino and Massimo Stanzione in Naples.

EDWARD J. SULLIVAN

Bibliography: Bissell, R. Ward, "Artemisia Gentileschi: A New Documented Chronology," *The Art Bulletin*, June 1968, and *Orazio Gentileschi and the Poetic Tradition in Caravaggesque Painting* (1982); Moir, Alfred, *The Italian Followers of Caravaggio* (1967); Sterling, Charles, "Gentileschi in France," *Burlington Magazine*, April 1958.

Gentz, Friedrich von [gents]

Friedrich von Gentz, b. May 2, 1764, d. June 9, 1832, was a German political theorist, publicist, and statesman. He is remembered for his relentless polemic campaign against Napoleon I and, more generally, for his opposition to revolutionary movements in early 19th-century Europe. As a young man at the University of Königsberg, he became a disciple of the philosopher Immanuel KANT; like Kant, he was a supporter of the popular movement that culminated in the French Revolution. Gentz's *Missive* (1797) to King Frederick William III of Prussia urged freedom of the press and of commerce. In his masterpiece, *On the Sources and Character of the Wars against the French Revolution* (1801), however, he sounded the conservative themes that were increasingly to characterize his career. In 1812 he became secretary to the Austrian leader Klemens von Metternich, agreeing with his new benefactor that in an age of decay the sole function of a statesman is "to prop up mouldering institutions." A powerful figure in Austrian and European politics, he was secretary at the congresses of Vienna (1814–15), Aix-la-Chapelle (1818), Troppau (1820), Laibach (1821), and Verona (1822). His clear, objective writings are regarded as significant sources for the understanding of his times.

PETE A. Y. GUNTER

Bibliography: Mann, Golo, *Secretary of Europe* (1946; repr. 1970); Sweet, Paul R., *Friedrich von Gentz, Defender of the Old Order* (1941; repr. 1970).

geocentric world system [jee-oh-sen'-trik]

The geocentric world system was the Earth-centered view of the universe systematized by ARISTOTLE in the 4th century BC, elaborated by PTOLEMY in the 2d century AD, and universally accepted until the HELIOCENTRIC WORLD SYSTEM was expounded by COPERNICUS in the 16th century. The geocentric system of hierarchical spheres is prominent in Dante's *Divine Comedy*.

STEVEN J. DICK

Bibliography: Dreyer, John L., *A History of Astronomy from Thales to Kepler*, 2d ed. (1953).

See also: ASTRONOMY, HISTORY OF.

geochemistry [jee-oh-kem'-is-tree]

Geochemistry is the application of chemistry to geologic problems. Its primary focus is the distribution and migration of the elements (particularly the rarer ones) in Earth materials. It most often refers to a method of prospecting for buried ore deposits by analyzing soil, water, and vegetation. Geochemistry also touches upon mineralogy, petrology, oceanography, and economic geology.

Geochemistry began as a science in the early 19th century in Germany and Sweden with the accumulation of analytical data on rocks and minerals. Later, the chemistry of ore deposits, particularly as related to hot springs and volcanic emanations, attracted much attention in France. Only toward the end of the 19th century was geochemistry recognized as a discipline in its own right, and extended to the study of chemical changes that are part of geologic processes. Especially notable in the early 20th century were the work of chemical analysts, particularly F. W. Clarke and H. S. Washington of the United States Geological Survey, the synthesis of planetary chemistry by V. I. Vernadsky in Russia, and the beginning of systematic efforts to duplicate natural chemical changes under laboratory conditions at the Geophysical Laboratory of the Carnegie Institution of Washington. After World War I, the Norwegian geochemist V. M. Goldschmidt used the newly developed techniques of X-RAY DIFFRACTION and rapid spectrographic analysis (see SPECTROSCOPY) to determine the rules that govern the occurrence of rare elements in rocks and minerals. Only since World War II, however, has the field attracted many scientists and has the term *geochemistry* been widely used.

DIFFERENTIATION OF EARTH MATERIALS

On a planetary scale the most striking chemical feature of the Earth is that its material is separated into three distinct layers: a core extending out from the center about halfway to the surface, primarily composed of metallic iron; a MANTLE making up most of the rest of the Earth, composed in large part of compounds containing the four elements iron, magnesium, silicon, and oxygen; and a thin outer crust, variegated in composition but far richer in compounds of sodium, potassium, aluminum, silicon, and oxygen than the materials beneath it. Outside the solid crust are the oceanic liquid water and the atmospheric gases. How the planet's original material came to be segregated or differentiated in this way is unknown, but the process probably involved melting of at least part of the Earth, followed by heavy materials settling toward the center and light materials rising toward the surface. Recent studies indicate that the Moon and Mars underwent a similar geological history. Although much of the Earth may have been molten at some time in the distant past, at present the mantle and crust are largely solid, and only the outer part of the core is liquid.

Chemical changes have occurred in the crust and upper mantle all through the Earth's 4½-billion-year history and continue today. New rock is formed and added to the crust by molten LAVA that comes to the surface along the mid-oceanic ridges and solidifies there. The lava originates as MAGMA in a part of the upper mantle where temperatures are close to the melting point. Locally, large bodies of this liquid rock ascend through fissures and pour out on the sea bottom, forming BASALT. This dark-gray rock, richer in iron and magnesium than most surface rocks, composes most of the ocean floor. Carried by currents (CONVECTION CELLS) in the hot, plastic mantle beneath, it is being slowly rafted away from the mid-ocean rises by seafloor spreading. At some continental margins (SUBDUCTION ZONES) the basaltic layer, together with the thin veneer of sediments on its surface, is carried down into the mantle, its temperature rising as it descends. The temperature ultimately becomes high enough for basalt and sediment to begin melting. The first melt, rich in silicon, sodium, and potassium, is lighter than the rocks around it and rises through fissures, some to emerge at the surface and build VOLCANOES, and some to solidify under the surface and form BATHOLITHS of GRANITE.

This process, which constantly adds new material to the existing continents, is probably the one that has operated gradually throughout geologic time to build the continents. In its chemical aspects, the process involves removing elements typical of granite (sodium, potassium, aluminum, silicon) from basalt and returning the basalt's iron and magnesium back to the mantle. The reactions occurring today represent a late stage in the long history of differentiation of the Earth's original materials. The continents are islands of silicon-rich scum, or slag, accumulated on top of a huge circulating system of heavier materials rich in iron and magnesium. The process's chemistry is similar to the operation of a blast furnace, in which silicon-rich slag forms on top of molten iron, although more complex.

THE ROCK CYCLE

Granite is formed by the solidification of molten rock at great depths, but slow movements in the solid crust eventually bring much of it to the surface, where, exposed to air and water, it undergoes slow chemical changes called WEATHERING. Aluminum minerals are very slowly changed to CLAYS, making the rock soft and vulnerable to disintegration. Iron in the granite's minor, dark-colored minerals is oxidized, giving the yellow and brown iron-oxide stains common on rock surfaces. Much of the sodium, potassium, and calcium is dissolved in rainwater and carried into streams and ultimately into the ocean. Only the very resistant minerals, especially QUARTZ (silicon dioxide), are left as the weathered rock disintegrates; these, moved by wind and water, are worn down to form grains of sand. Part of the clay and sand accumulates on the granite surface to form SOIL, part is carried by streams and deposited as layers of SEDIMENT on plains or in the ocean. Such layers eventually harden into SEDIMENTARY ROCKS.

Through EROSION AND SEDIMENTATION granite's original chemical constituents become separated and then redeposited to form new kinds of rock. As sedimentary layers (strata) pile up on one another in a GEOSYNCLINE, the lowest part of the pile may sink to great depths and become chemically altered to METAMORPHIC ROCK by high pressure and temperature. Ultimately, some of this material may begin to melt. Metamorphism and partial melting take place on a large scale in sedimentary piles (eugeosynclines) near certain continental margins, where subduction, the movement of the seabed under a continent, crumples the sedimentary layers and drags them down, with basalt, into the mantle. The sediment and basalt form new granite melt, completing what is known as the rock cycle: granite is originally formed from partly melted basalt and sediment; the granite is raised to the surface and weathered; sedimentary rock is formed from the weathered material; then metamorphism of the sedimentary rocks occurs and new granite is generated by partial melting. The cycle is not quite closed because light minerals (compounds of silicon, sodium, potassium, and aluminum) are added to the continents, and heavy minerals rich in iron and magnesium are added to the mantle.

SEAS, AIR, AND LIFE

Geochemistry is concerned not only with these transformations in the Earth's solid materials but also with the envelopes of water and atmospheric gases that surround the planet. The water and gases have come primarily from the Earth's interior, probably mostly in the early part of geologic history, and have undergone continual chemical changes. Dissolved material from the land has poured into the ocean, forming seawater salt, and much of this material has precipitated out of the water as marine sediment. Long ago a balance was reached, the addition of each element to the ocean being compensated by its deposition in sediment, so that for much of geologic time the composition of SEAWATER has remained nearly constant. The composition of air has changed profoundly: initially large amounts of carbon dioxide were present, but only traces of oxygen; now oxygen is a major gas and carbon dioxide is a minor constituent. This change was largely caused by the development of living organisms.

The origin of LIFE on the Earth's surface is one of the most fascinating questions for geochemists. If the original ATMOSPHERE consisted mainly of carbon dioxide, nitrogen, and water vapor, complex organic molecules could have been formed from these gases by lightning discharges, ultraviolet light from the Sun, or simply the heat of molten rock from volcanoes. If such molecules dissolved in the warm water of shallow seas, a type of molecule probably would form that was capable of duplicating itself. Many steps in this progression from simple gases to living organisms remain to be traced, but the general progression is evident.

Once life had established itself, the geochemistry of the Earth's surface changed slowly but profoundly. Of particular importance was PHOTOSYNTHESIS in green plants, by which carbon dioxide was converted into organic compounds and free oxygen released to the air. Operating over two billion years, this activity could have changed the atmosphere from one dominated by carbon dioxide to one with oxygen as a major constituent. The Earth's present oxygen-rich atmosphere is unique in the solar system. It has permitted development of the higher forms of animal life and makes oxidation a major part of the weathering of rocks and minerals.

Living creatures also have a strong influence on the chemistry of sedimentary rocks. Many marine organisms use the dissolved calcium carbonate of seawater to build CALCITE and ARAGONITE shells, and others use SILICA. Remains of these organisms have accumulated in enormous quantities to form beds of LIMESTONE, which is mostly calcium carbonate, and CHERT, mostly silica. When the soft parts of dead organisms are deposited in restricted environments out of contact with air, the organic matter slowly changes to simpler compounds. Coal, petroleum, and natural gas accumulate from such changes. Organisms influence other geochemical processes less directly, for example, in the formation of some iron and manganese ores.

APPLICATIONS OF GEOCHEMISTRY

During all chemical changes involving the major elements of the Earth's crust and upper mantle, the minor elements partly follow the major elements and partly separate from them. Geochemists study the processes of separation in order to understand how some of the rare elements are concentrated into ORE DEPOSITS. During the cooling of a granite PLUTON, for example, the last liquid remaining as magma crystallizes is a water-rich solution, part of the water coming from the molten granite and part from surrounding rocks. In this hot water are dissolved elements such as copper and gold, the atoms of which do not fit easily into the crystal structures of the major granite minerals. Movement of the water into surrounding cooler rocks can form veins or disseminated ores of these valuable metals. Again, dilute solutions of rare metals are sometimes added to seawater, either by streams or by submarine volcanic activity, and if chemical conditions and ocean currents permit, the metals may precipitate to form high concentrations in sediments (see OCEANIC MINERAL RESOURCES).

Not only the distribution of elements, but the distribution of ISOTOPES as well, has become a major subject of geochemical research. Isotopes of a few light elements are slightly separated in ordinary geochemical processes, and the subtle variations in their distribution often shed light on the origin and history of rocks and minerals. The isotopes of elements produced by radioactive decay have a special interest because analyses for these isotopes make possible the RADIOMETRIC AGE-DATING of geologic materials.

One branch of geochemistry has proved useful to the mining industry. This is a technique of exploration for ore deposits that are hidden by soil, vegetation, or thick sediments laid down by streams. For example, if a copper deposit exists beneath a layer of soil, the soil may look no different from soil elsewhere, and the deposit would be missed by ordinary prospecting methods. The soil above the deposit may, however, contain copper from weathering of the ore, and sensitive analysis can detect it. The hidden deposit may also become evident through abnormal copper concentrations in nearby vegetation, or in the water and sediments of streams that drain the area. Geochemical prospecting, the technique of finding such clues, is a major tool in mineral exploration, along with geologic mapping and geophysical surveys.

Geochemistry has become a part of environmental health as more is learned about how human and animal well-being depends on trace elements in plants, soil, and water. Some of the rarer elements—mercury is an example—are toxic in even minute quantities. Others, like selenium and fluorine, are essential for life in trace amounts but toxic in larger amounts. Deficiencies or excesses of a number of elements must be remedied, and geochemical knowledge of their distribution and mobility is necessary.

KONRAD B. KRAUSKOPF

Bibliography: Berner, Elizabeth and Robert, *The Global Water Cycle* (1986); Bowie, S., and Thornton, I., eds., *Environmental Geochemistry and Health* (1985); Brown, G. C., and Mussett, A. E., *The Inaccessible Earth* (1981); Krauskopf, K. B., *Introduction to Geochemistry*, 2d ed. (1979); Levinson, A., *Introduction to Exploration Geochemistry* (1974); Saxena, S. K., ed., *Chemistry and Physics of Terrestrial Planets* (1986); Thornton, I., ed., *Applied Environmental Geochemistry* (1984).

See also: EARTH, HEAT FLOW IN; EARTH, STRUCTURE AND COMPOSITION OF; PETROLOGY; PLATE TECTONICS.

geode [jee'-ohd]

Geodes are rock cavities partially lined with layers of tiny crystals along their inner walls. Geodes of quartz, dolomite, and calcite are common. Many are banded, as in agate, and resemble rough, rocky balls until they are opened to reveal their crystalline interiors.

Geodes are slightly flattened spherical mineral bodies that contain layers of inwardly radiating crystals surrounded by a layer of cryptocrystalline quartz. New crystal layers frequently grow on the terminations of old layers, often nearly or completely filling the geode. Geodes typically range in size from less than 5 cm (2 in) to more than 30 cm (12 in) in diameter, but can be much larger. The crystals usually are composed of quartz. They also may be composed of the carbonate minerals calcite, dolomite, aragonite, and ankerite; of the oxide minerals hematite and magnetite; or of the sulfide minerals pyrite, chalcopyrite, and sphalerite. The sulfide minerals, when present, are most often innermost; the carbonate minerals usually are next to the outermost chalcedonic layer.

Geodes occur in limestones and some shales, where they have formed by the expansion of a cavity filled with a salt solution. Silica-bearing waters coagulate into a gel, which surrounds the salt solution. As the water surrounding this silica gel becomes less saline, internal pressures are created by the osmotic action seeking to equalize the salinity imbalance. These pressures cause the geode to expand until equilibrium is reached. Dehydration of the gel and subsequent crystallization occur, along with shrinkage and cracking of the geode wall. Mineral-bearing waters percolate into the geode and deposit crystals on the cavity wall. Subsequent periods of crystallization may follow, leaving the characteristic layers of crystals.

Bibliography: Berry, L. G., and Mason, Brian, *Mineralogy,* 2d ed. (1983).

geodesic dome [jee-oh-des'-ik dohm]

The U.S. pavilion at Montreal's Expo '67, designed by R. Buckminster Fuller, is a geodesic dome constructed of interlocking steel struts and plexiglass panels. The 60-m-high (200-ft) structure housed a series of platforms exhibiting U.S. achievements in the arts and sciences.

The geodesic dome was developed by the American designer R. Buckminster FULLER after World War II as a low-cost and efficient method of space-frame, modular construction. Fuller employed standardized parts, usually spherical forms with triangular or polygonal facets made of bamboo, wood, plastic, aluminum, or any other material from cardboard to prestressed concrete. The architectural significance of these domelike structures made of interconnected, self-supporting members lies in their high structural efficiency, in which a large area may be enclosed without internal supports, a minimum of material is required, and construction time is brief. The principle has been widely adopted in the United States by industry and the military sector. During the 1960s, geodesic domes, which can be insulated and are suitable for all climates, became popular as an alternative, or "people's," technology. They have been used as exhibitions halls, as in the U.S. pavilions at the Seattle World's Fair (1962) and at Expo '67 in Montreal. The dome's design principles also have been utilized for sports arenas and greenhouses.

Bibliography: Fuller, R. Buckminster, *Inventions* (1983); Howell, Ruth Rea, *The Dome People* (1974); Marks, Robert W., *The Dymaxion World of Buckminster Fuller* (1960); Popko, Edward, *Geodesics* (1968).

geodesy: see EARTH, SIZE AND SHAPE OF; EARTH, GRAVITATIONAL FIELD OF; GEOPHYSICS SURVEYING.

geoduck [goo'-ee-duhk]

The geoduck is a very large burrowing CLAM, *Panope generosa,* in the family Hiatellidae. Its shell measures up to 18 cm (7 in) long, and the clam itself may weigh 3 kg (6.5 lb) or more. Geoducks are found in the intertidal zone from Alaska to Baja California, Mexico. They burrow deeply into mud or sand, extending long siphons to the surface of the burrow to allow for circulation of water within their bodies.

STEPHEN C. REINGOLD

Geoffrey of Monmouth

Geoffrey of Monmouth, d. 1155, bishop of Saint Asaph in Wales, wrote the *Historia Regum Britanniae* (1135–39), which introduced the Arthurian legend (see ARTHUR AND ARTHURIAN LEGEND) into Western literature. Shakespeare's *King Lear* is based on Geoffrey's work, which was essentially folklore.

geographical linguistics

Geographical linguistics, the study of variations in language within a geographical area, is concerned primarily with dialectal variations, that is, variations of dialect within an area whose inhabitants speak the same language. The study of geographical linguistics is therefore also called dialect geography or dialectology. In a broader sense the field also includes the study of how different languages spoken in the same area interact, and what characteristics they have in common.

Geographical linguistics overlaps SOCIOLINGUISTICS and HISTORICAL LINGUISTICS. In the former case differences in dialect or language within an area often correlate with social differences. In the latter case the variations encountered at a particular time are the product of historical developments, and investigation of these developments can shed light on the current situation.

Idiolects and Dialects. No two individuals speak in exactly the same way; everyone has a unique form of speech, or idiolect. Nevertheless, for communication to be possible, each speaker's idiolect must generally correspond to the idiolects of others. To the extent that people are in close communication, their idiolects will tend to be similar. When communication is more limited because of geographical separation or other reasons, however, differences between forms of speech may become more numerous. In such cases one group of people may have common speech characteristics that another group does not share, even though the groups speak the same language. Any variety of a language that distinguishes one group from another is called a dialect.

WORD GEOGRAPHY OF THE EASTERN UNITED STATES

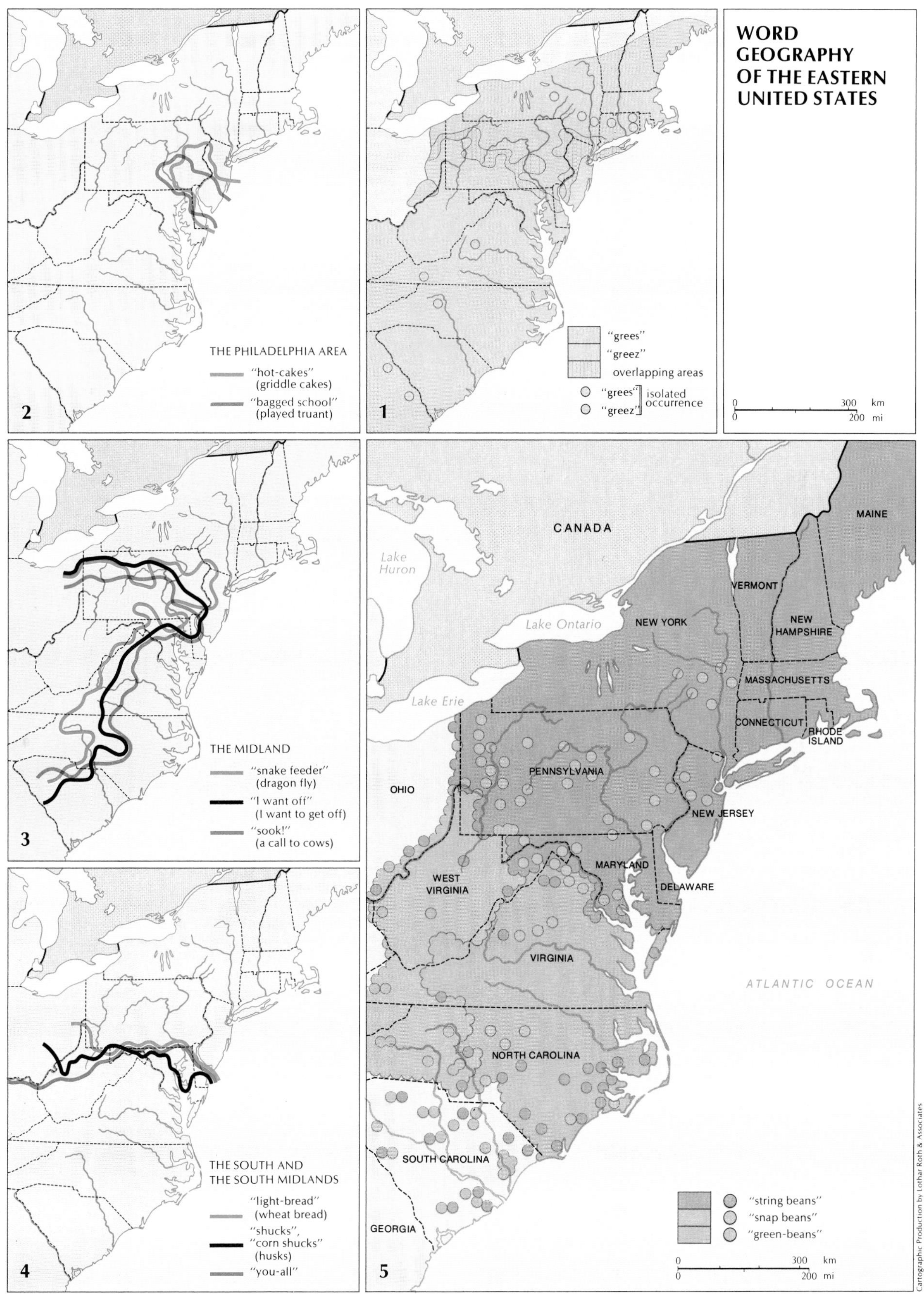

Cartographic Production by Lothar Roth & Associates

In areas that have been settled for centuries and where most of the inhabitants rarely travel far from home, each village can have its own dialectal peculiarities. Even where there is a much higher degree of population mobility, regions may differ in dialectal features. For example, it is possible to draw a line on a map of the United States cutting across New Jersey, Pennsylvania, Ohio, Indiana, and Illinois. North of the line the predominant pronunciation of the word *grease* when used as a verb rhymes with *fleece* (shown as *grees* on Map 1); south of the line it rhymes with *freeze* (shown as *greez* on Map 1). A line on a map that separates an area where a specific linguistic feature is typically found from other areas where it is absent or occurs only infrequently is called an isogloss. A set of maps of this sort—each dealing with a different linguistic feature of a language area—is a linguistic atlas.

Linguistic Atlases. Compiling a linguistic atlas is time-consuming and expensive. Many years may separate inception from completion. This was the case with the earliest such enterprise, founded by Georg Wenker in 1876. He mailed a questionnaire to schooteachers in more than 40,000 localities throughout Germany and asked them to translate a set of sentences into their local dialects. The *Deutscher Sprachatlas,* based on Wenker's data, first began publication a half century later, in 1926.

Another pioneering work was the *Atlas linguistique de la France* of Jules Gilliéron, which appeared between 1902 and 1910. He relied on the fieldwork of one carefully trained investigator, Edmond Edmont, who traveled to 639 selected locations scattered throughout France, presenting a questionnaire to informants and taking down their answers.

Interviewing informants directly has been the preferred technique in the many linguistic surveys undertaken since then. The goal of one particularly ambitious survey, initiated in 1930, was to produce a linguistic atlas of the United States and Canada. Some parts of the atlas have been published; much of it remains to be done.

Isoglosses: Analysis of Speech Patterns. Certain patterns are noticeable when the maps of a linguistic atlas are compared. Often a set of isoglosses radiate from a single center, or focal area. This is generally a center of prestige, whether for political, economic, or cultural reasons, from which characteristic features of speech have been adopted by the surrounding population. Philadelphia, for example, is such a focal area. (As shown in Map 2, the expressions *hot cakes* and *bagged school* originated there and spread into surrounding areas.)

The tendency to imitate the speech of those with more prestige is a most powerful force in promoting change in dialects. Those who are considered members of an elite are frequently imitated in other ways as well, so that isoglosses often coincide with the diffusion of other features of culture, such as the design of houses and types of food.

Features of speech in a focal area may spread throughout a region, until only the marginal areas on the outskirts preserve the older forms, called relic forms. In the pronunciation of Boston and the neighboring port cities, the sound of *r* in such words as *far* and *farm* was lost. This type of pronunciation came to characterize all of New England east of the Connecticut River, except for a few outlying points.

Sometimes a bundle of isoglosses follows approximately the same course. Such a bundle, for example, delimits the Midland area of the eastern United States, including most of Pennsylvania and dividing the western mountain region of Virginia and the Carolinas from the rest of the South (see Map 3). This bundle reflects earlier patterns of population migration because more settlers in the Southern highlands came from Pennsylvania than from the coastal South.

Isoglosses may also coincide with political boundaries, as, for example, the Southern use of *you-all* as the plural of *you,* which extends only up to the Mason-Dixon Line (see Map 4). Isoglosses run along such lines because, like natural barriers such as mountain ranges, political boundaries can constitute long-term obstacles to communication or to the extension of influence from centers of prestige.

Because isoglosses often crisscross one another, reflecting competing influences on the speech of the inhabitants of a region, assigning a particular locality unambiguously to a single major dialect area is sometimes difficult. Most of West Virginia, for example, would go with the South on the basis of the use of *you-all* or the pronunciation of the vowel in words like *time.* It would, however, belong with Pennsylvania as part of the Midland region if the greatest weight were given to the retention of the sound of *r* in *far* and *farm,* or to such vocabulary items as *green beans* instead of the Southern *snap beans* or the Northern *string beans* (see Map 5).

Isoglosses are much less clear-cut in the western United States than in the East, bearing out the general principle that dialect differences are more striking in older, established areas than they are in recently settled areas. Nevertheless, differences are also observable in the West; one such instance is the more Northern pronunciation of *egg* with a short *e* in San Francisco and Los Angeles, whereas in the surrounding nonurban areas *egg* rhymes with *vague.*

Sociological Factors. As the last example indicates, language variation has a social as well as a geographical dimension, and often reflects the contrast between urban and rural populations as well as differences in age, sex, class, or ethnic identity. Regional features found in the speech of some members of a community may be adopted more generally by all members of a particular socioeconomic or ethnic subgroup as a way of reinforcing their sense of belonging. This fact was demonstrated in classic studies by William Labov on Martha's Vineyard and in New York City. Population shifts may also transform features that originally characterized the dialects of a geographical area into marks of membership in a social class or ethnic group, as with the Southern features of black English in Northern cities. (For further discussion, see SOCIOLINGUISTICS.)

Furthermore, the same speaker may command several different registers or styles of language. People will not necessarily use the same vocabulary, grammar, or pronunciation at a job interview that they will in talking to close friends. In many parts of the world, the difference between the informal and formal varieties is so great that learning the latter is comparable to learning another language. One grows up with the local dialect at home but studies the standard language in school.

This situation, known as diglossia, prevails, for example, in much of the area that includes the Netherlands, the northern half of Belgium, Germany, Austria, and the German-speaking part of Switzerland. In these areas a network of local dialects of great diversity exists. Those dialects which are neighboring, including those on opposite sides of a national boundary, are mutually intelligible; those which are at geographical extremes, even within the same country—for instance, in the vicinity of Hamburg in the north and in Bavaria in the south—differ to such an extent that communication between speakers of one and the other, without recourse to the standard language, is almost out of the question. In these circumstances, the standard languages, which are relatively uniform everywhere, serve the essential function of permitting communication beyond the confines of the local community.

Local dialects are forms of a language that are just as authentic as the standard form. Standard languages always originated as local dialects, or amalgams of several dialects; they became more widely used, not for any inherent qualities that they possessed, but because of the socially or politically dominant position of the people who spoke them. Thus Standard English developed out of the speech of London, Standard French out of that of Paris, and Standard German out of the fusion of dialects employed by the official bureaucracies in the central and southern German seats of power in the Holy Roman Empire of the 14th to 16th centuries.

Once a standard language has been adopted as a medium of expression in literature, government, and education, it becomes better adapted to such uses than dialects that have never been called upon to perform the same functions.

Bilingualism. In diglossia, two closely related forms of speech serve distinct functions within a community; the same can be true of two or more different languages as well. In India, for example, an educated person may use English with professional colleagues, Hindi with merchants, and a regional lan-

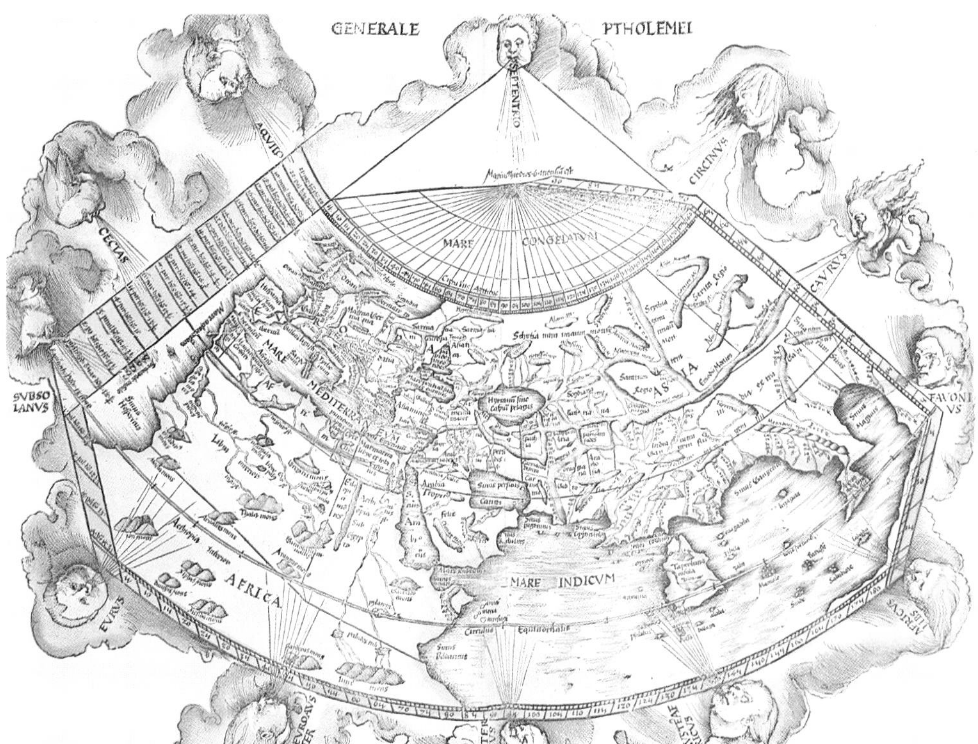

This 15th-century map of the known world was, like many others of its period, based on an atlas compiled by the Greco-Egyptian cartographer Claudius Ptolemy during the 2d century. Ptolemy's Geography, *derived from earlier Phoenician sources, listed the latitudes and longitudes of thousands of places in Europe, Asia, and Africa and gave instructions on the preparation of accurate maps based on mathematical computation. Despite numerous substantial errors, including a considerable underestimation of the Earth's circumference, Ptolemy's work remained the standard cartographic text until the 16th century.*

guage that is radically different from both, such as Bengali or Marathi (which themselves have formal and informal varieties), with friends and family.

Such bilingualism or multilingualism can lead to changes in one or more of the languages in use. In extreme cases of change resulting from language contact, the outcome may be a PIDGIN, a form of speech with simplified grammar and reduced vocabulary that evolves as a means of intercommunication among speakers of mutually incomprehensible languages.

Even without such explosive transformations, multilingualism can eventually lead to the spread of linguistic features over a group of otherwise dissimilar languages spoken in the same geographical area. Western Europe, the Balkans, the Caucasus, southern Africa, India, and Southeast Asia are all linguistic areas of this kind, where languages of diverse origin share a set of similar features. FRANKLIN E. HOROWITZ

Bibliography: Bailey, Richard, and Robinson, Jay L., eds., *Varieties of Present-Day English* (1973); Carver, Craig, *American Regional Dialects: A Word Geography* (1987); Cassidy, Frederic, ed., *Dictionary of American Regional English,* vol. 1 (1985); Davis, Lawrence, *English Dialectology* (1983); Kurath, Hans, *Studies in Area Linguistics* (1972); Montgomery, Michael, and Bailey, Guy, *Language Variety in the South* (1986); Weinreich, Uriel, *Languages in Contact* (1953; repr. 1974).

geographical societies

Numerous privately and governmentally sponsored geographical societies function in countries around the world. Basically, their goals are to encourage, sponsor, and, in some cases, financially support worthwhile geographic research. The results are printed and disseminated in the various journals published by the societies. The International Geographical Union (1923) is a worldwide organization of geographers. In the United States, the American Geographical Society of New York (founded 1852) and the Association of American Geographers (1904) are of particular note to the geographer. The NATIONAL GEOGRAPHIC SOCIETY (1888) in Washington, D.C., however, is better known by the public because of its monthly magazine, its maps, and the programs it produces for television. In Britain the Royal Geographical Society (1830) has made invaluable contributions, sponsoring many expeditions of exploration. ROBERT S. WEINER

geography

Geography is the study of spatial variation on the Earth's surface and of humankind's relation to its environment. Of essential concern to the geographer are spatial patterns and the interrelations of climate, landforms, vegetation, soils, population, economic activities, and political units, either on a global scale or in a more limited area. Geography is thus an exceedingly complex discipline that can be subdivided into numerous specialized areas. The geographer seeks to explain the location of various elements in the environment and to describe and establish the spatial patterns of these elements. The processes that form and change these patterns are also analyzed. One principal means to this end is the map, which for the geographer is an indispensable research tool as well as a visual representation (see MAPS AND MAPMAKING).

HISTORY AND EVOLUTION OF GEOGRAPHY

Early Geographers. Many consider geography one of the oldest academic disciplines. Its antecedents may be traced to ancient Greece, where they were called by such names as natural history or natural philosophy. In fact, most of the ancient Greek geographers, such as THALES OF MILETUS (6th century BC) and HERODOTUS (5th century BC), were actually philosophers or historians. Much of their geographic writings described their physical environment. Indeed, the word *geography* is derived from the Greek, meaning "Earth description." The physical environment and the location of natural phenomena were of utmost importance to the Greeks.

The Greeks dominated most of the known Western world, especially the eastern part of the Mediterranean Sea. They traveled this area in search of trade and new lands to colonize. The clear skies of the Mediterranean were essential in the first attempts of Greek sailors to navigate the seas; wind patterns merited equal consideration in terms of speed and safety. Perhaps most important to the evolution of the discipline, the Greeks wrote down their observations and thoughts for succeeding generations. Notable are the Greek studies of the Nile River in Egypt, which described its annual flooding and the development of its delta. In the 5th century BC, Herodotus ascended the river to the first cataract and wrote a description of it, stating his hypothesis about the Nile's source.

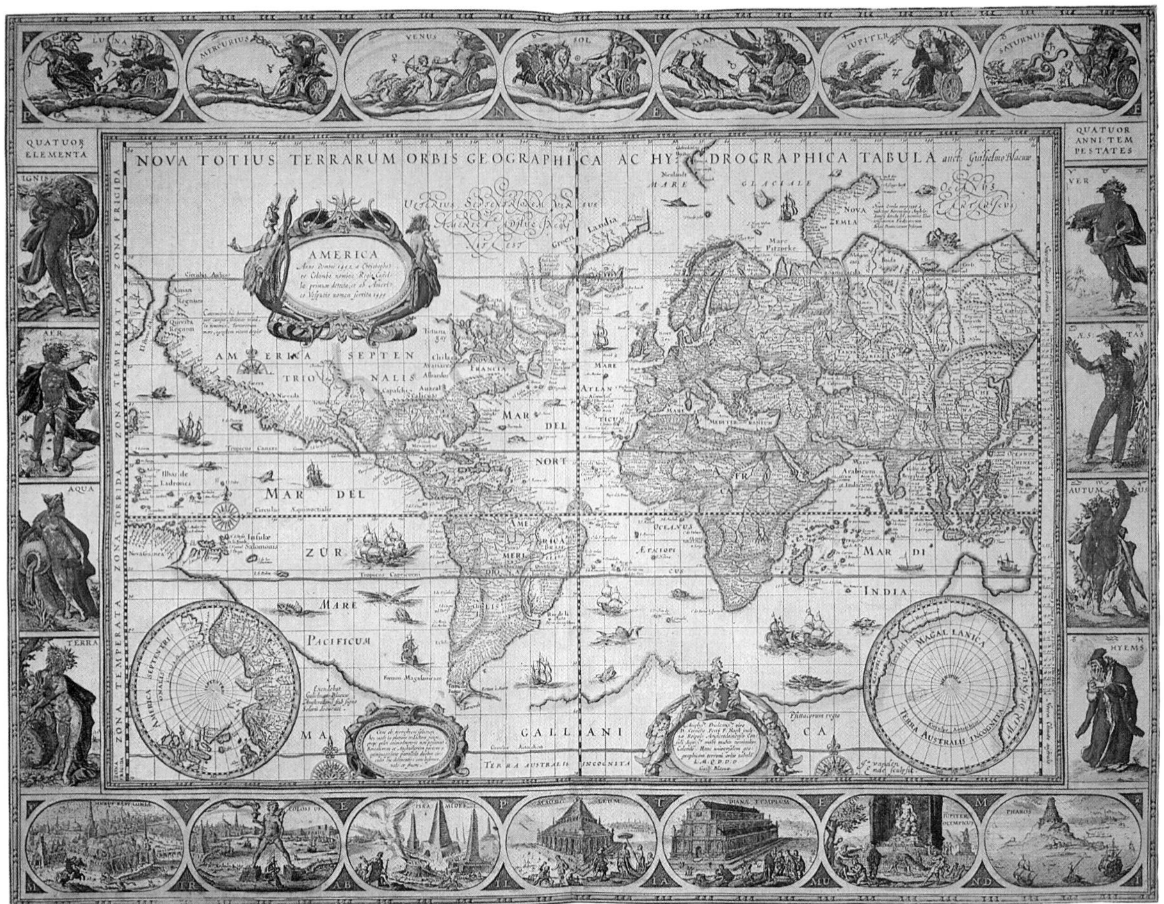

A world map by the Dutch cartographer Willem Blaeu employs the technique devised by Gerardus Mercator in 1569 for transferring the curved meridians of a globe to a two-dimensional chart with straight meridians. The borders of Blaeu's map portray (left) *the four elements—fire, air, water, and earth;* (top) *celestial bodies of the solar system;* (right) *the four seasons; and* (bottom) *the Seven Wonders of the World.*

The Greeks also observed the planet as a whole. ARISTOTLE (4th century BC) is most often credited with conceiving the Earth as a sphere, a conclusion he arrived at by using philosophical reasoning and astronomical observations. His speculation about the Earth's shape was seconded by ERATOSTHENES, librarian of Alexandria. The latter's *On the Measurement of the Earth* gives his calculation of the circumference of the Earth; he based his computation on a limited, measured arc of longitude. The astronomer HIPPARCHUS of Rhodes (2d century BC) developed a location system of lines on the surface of the Earth, the forerunners of latitude and longitude.

STRABO (*c.*63 BC–AD 21) wrote *Geography,* a 17-volume work that describes through firsthand observation the world known to him from Gaul and Britain to India and from the Black Sea to Ethiopia. Although his descriptions of lands and peoples are often marred by omissions and errors, he advanced the study of geography by substituting divisions based on natural boundaries (such as mountain ranges and drainage systems) for the less permanent and artificially drawn political units and thus became the father of regional geography.

PTOLEMY of Alexandria (fl. AD 121–51), perhaps the most famous ancient geographer, further systematized the geographical study of areas by classing regions in terms of size and detail from the general study of large tracts (chorography) to the detailed physical description of small areas (topography). He drew a map of the then-known world that, considering the knowledge available in his day, is remarkably accurate. His eight-volume *Guide to Geography* consisted of a list of all known places tabulated according to longitude and latitude, a system he devised himself.

After the collapse of the Roman Empire, the heritage of Greek geography was preserved in the Arab world. All the geographic works of Ptolemy were translated into Arabic. There were, however, regressions. After about AD 900 indications of longitude and latitude were no longer given on maps. Nevertheless, the Arabs made important contributions to a more profound knowledge of the world. In the 12th century al-IDRISI devised a refined system of climate classification. The great 14th-century explorer IBN BATTUTA found, on his travels through Africa and Asia, concrete evidence that refuted Aristotle's thesis that hot regions of the world would be too warm for human habitation. In the same century IBN KHALDUN wrote an important historical-geographic treatise.

Age of Discovery. Although the Crusades had stimulated European interest in the outside world, it was not until the Renaissance, when the voyages of Bartolomeu DIAS, Vasco da GAMA, and Christopher COLUMBUS in the late 15th century ushered in the so-called age of discovery, that there was a concomitant renewal of interest in world exploration, geographic description, and mapping.

As early as 1507 the German cartographer Martin Waldseemüller (*c.*1470–*c.*1521) produced a map of the world that clearly indicated both North and South America. It was on this map that the term *America* was first applied to any part of the New World. Fifteen years later Ferdinand MAGELLAN's party circumnavigated the Earth, thereby confirming its global shape. This information allowed for greatly increased accuracy of measurements and observations, which again aided the new breed of mapmakers, such as Gerardus MERCATOR, a Dutchman. Mercator published a series of maps that in terms of accuracy surpassed anything previously produced. This included his famous navigation chart (1569), which introduced the map projection bearing his name, with its parallels and meridians at right angles.

Geography as an academic discipline was rejuvenated by Bernhardus Varenius (1622–50), who, in his *Geographia Generalis* (1650), established the concepts of topical geography and regional geography. He considered the distribution of topics (especially physical topics such as winds and seas) over the surface of the Earth and tried to interrelate their causes and effects. This work may be said to have dominated the field for the following 150 years. Although some 18th-century philosophers and writer-scholars, such as Kant, Goethe, and Montesquieu, took an interest in the human topics of geography (the interaction of humanity and the environment), the general development of the discipline had, by the 19th century, reached a stage of stagnation and was closely identified with GEOLOGY.

Founders of Modern Geography. During the 19th century there was a renewed effort to develop geography as a descriptive science. Contributions toward that end were made by the German geographers Alexander von HUMBOLDT, Carl Ritter, and FRIEDRICH RATZEL. The first two have sometimes been called the founders of modern scientific geography, although neither was trained as a geographer. Humboldt laid the foundations of plant geography, performing field work in Europe, South America, Central America, and Asiatic Russia before he wrote his five-volume masterwork, *Kosmos* (1845–62). This work is a summary and exposition of the laws and conditions of the physical universe, yet it is imbued with the humanism that was Humboldt's hallmark.

Ritter, whose interest in geography was stimulated by Humboldt, is credited with introducing humankind into geographical studies, particularly humanity in relationship to its environment. Ratzel took Ritter's human geography still further, subdividing it into anthropogeography and political geography, both of which he dealt with in separate works. He also made investigations into cultural geography, especially in North America, but he is best known for his organic theory of the state, in which he compares the evolution of the state to that of a living organism.

In the United States, geography was not pursued by university scholars until the end of the 19th century and the first part of the 20th century—about the same time that the United States emerged as a world power. Many of the early American geographers, such as Ellen Churchill Semple, were former students of Ratzel in Germany.

German and French Schools. This period in the history of geography was marked by the development in the 19th century of the geographic philosophy referred to as either determinism, environmentalism, or the German school of thought. Determinism held that the environment was the deciding factor in a person's way of living and his or her economic development. One American geographer, Ellsworth HUNTINGTON, whose work reflects Ritter's influence, expressed the idea that the climate determined the extent and character of a people's capacity for physical work and intellectual development. Thus, he concluded, a stimulating climate, such as that of the temperate zones, spurs the development of higher civilization, but people who inhabit the constantly hot and humid lands of the tropics face a major barrier to their development.

Determinism began to decline during the 1930s and was eventually discredited. Earlier in the century, however, another geographical philosophy had emerged. This French school of thought, called possibilism, held that people had a choice in determining their development within the physical environment. In other words, the choices that people made determined the extent of their cultural advancement. Thus, although neither humans nor their environment existed in isolation, neither was able to control the other, and humans, therefore, were the ultimate master of their destiny. Paul Vidal de la Blache was a notable proponent of this theory.

Quantitative Revolution. During the 1960s a major change took place in the methodology of geographic research. The desire to make geography more scientific, or at least more intellectually acceptable as a discipline, led to the adoption of statistical methods as a major research technique. Location (or spatial) analysis, as this new aspect of geography is called, seeks to analyze and explain the factors that control humankind's spatial organization, specifically by statistical methods and models. Mathematically constructed models became tools useful to the geographer in coping with rapidly accumulating knowledge, and they could also be used to predict future trends or spatial patterns.

This was not the first time statistics had been used for geographical research. As early as the 1920s and '30s, Torsten Hägerstrand in Sweden and Walter CHRISTALLER in Germany had used statistical techniques. Only in the 1960s, however, did significant growth in statistical methodology occur.

Since the late 1960s, other new techniques have aided the analysis of geographic information. Two developments have been most significant: the electronic computer and remotely sensed imagery of the Earth from satellites.

APPROACHES TO GEOGRAPHY

Two principal approaches to the study of geography have developed: topical, or systematic, and regional. Regional and topical geography are often pursued in combination. Topical geography is the study of the spatial organization or locational distribution of a specific phenomenon and its relation to human presence. Medical geography, an example of topical geography, studies the distribution of disease-causing organisms and their relation to local populations.

Regional geography concerns all aspects of a relatively small area and compares that area with other areas. A region can be defined by physical criteria or by sociopolitical criteria. For example, a region may be an area receiving 100 mm (4 in), or less, of rainfall annually, or an area where more than 50% of the population are under the age of 15.

BRANCHES OF GEOGRAPHY

Physical Geography. Physical geography studies the natural conditions and processes on the Earth's surface and the resulting spatial structures; it includes several subdisciplines.

1. Geomorphology studies landforms, or the Earth's relief features, and examines their origins and evolution. The field is a bridge between geography and geology.

This infrared photograph taken over southwestern Arizona includes the Colorado River (center, lengthwise) *and farmland, which appears as patches of red. The photograph was taken from an Earth Resources Technology Satellite (ERTS).*

2. Biogeography, or ecogeography, is the study of plant and animal distribution. Plant geography, or phytogeography, and zoogeography are allied with ECOLOGY, which studies the relationships of plants and animals to their habitat.
3. Climatology examines the distribution of weather patterns, their seasonal changes, and what shapes the patterns.

Human (or Social) Geography. Human geography studies the changing spatial distributions of people and their activities and their interaction with the natural environment. It draws on the knowledge of the related social sciences but is particularly concerned with spatial analysis and description.

1. Cultural geography examines the distribution of cultural groups or of specific cultural traits such as religions, languages, architecture, place names, or burial rites.
2. Population geography studies the numbers and distribution of people and the changing patterns of distribution.
3. Economic geography deals with the location of economic activities and analyzes the reasons for location. Included are such subdivisions as agricultural geography, manufacturing geography, and transportation geography.
4. Historical geography is concerned with the local or regional environments of humankind as they existed in the past. This involves assessing both historical events and the role of the natural environment.
5. Political geography is the study of governmental units as observed on the landscape. This can involve the regional study of a specific political unit or the effect of political phenomena on an area.
6. Urban geography analyzes the origin and growth of cities as well as the spatial arrangement within cities. Many of the new statistical methods used in modern geography were introduced by urban geographers.

ROBERT S. WEINER

Bibliography: Carter, George F., *Man and the Land: A Cultural Geography*, 3d ed. (1975); De Blij, Harm J., *Essentials of Geography: Regions and Concepts*, 2d ed. (1978); Douglas, Ian, *The Urban Environment* (1984); Forbes, Dean K., *The Geography of Underdevelopment* (1985); Hartshorne, Richard, *Perspectives on the Nature of Geography* (1959); Matthews, John A., *Quantitative and Statistical Approaches to Geography: A Practical Manual* (1981); Pounds, Norman J. G., *Political Geography*, 2d ed. (1972); Strahler, A. N. and A. H., *Modern Physical Geography*, 2d ed. (1983); Thoman, Richard S., and Corbin, Peter, *The Geography of Economic Activity*, rev. 3d ed. (1974); Whyte, Robert O., *Spatial Geography* (1982).

See also: AERIAL PHOTOGRAPHY; CENTRAL PLACE THEORY; EXPLORATION; GEOPOLITICS; REMOTE SENSING.

geologic time

One of the most important discoveries of modern science has been the age of the Earth and the vast length of time encompassed by its history. The scale of this history, in the millions and billions of years, is recognized as geologic time.

Most cultures incorporate some form of creation mythology, for example, the biblical Book of Genesis. In the mid-17th century an Irish churchman Bishop James USSHER added the years in the biblical genealogies and concluded that the Earth was created in 4004 BC. This idea persisted for a long while, although the 18th-century French scientist Georges Louis Leclerc, comte de BUFFON, reasoned that the Earth cooled from an originally molten body and that this would have required at least 75,000 years.

Buffon had to recant, but development of the principle of UNIFORMITARIANISM in the late 1700s and early 1800s provided geologists with new grounds for arguing that the Earth is far older than anyone had imagined.

Similarly, in 1859, Charles DARWIN recognized that millions of years were necessary for small evolutionary changes to accumulate and produce the variety of life we see today. Because they lacked definitive, precise data, however, 19th-century geologists could only guess at the age of the Earth. In the meantime, an accurate, relative geologic time scale had been developed, which placed the main events of geologic history in their proper sequence.

THE RELATIVE TIME SCALE

The relative time scale comprises four major intervals, called eras. The oldest, or PRECAMBRIAN, includes ancient rocks whose only fossils are microorganisms and the layered mounds (stromatolites) built by blue-green algae. The next era, the PALEOZOIC, was dominated by marine invertebrate life, although arthropods, mollusks, vertebrates, and plants that invaded land later in the era began rapidly to expand.

After many forms of marine life had become extinct, the MESOZOIC ERA began with a new radiation of marine life and the dominance of reptiles on land. This era also closed with a number of extinctions, particularly among the reptiles, such as the dinosaurs, and some marine groups.

Finally, the CENOZOIC, or Present, Era, is characterized by the dominance of mammals, insects, and flowering plants on land, and still another radiation of marine life.

During the late 19th and early 20th centuries, scientists, in an attempt to determine the Earth's age, measured the present rates of physical processes and tried to extrapolate these rates to the past. Estimates based on the yearly addition of salt to the oceans yielded ages of about 90 million years, whereas others, based on the rate of accumulation of sedimentary rock, ranged from 3 to 500 million years. These methods were fraught with uncertainties and unproved assumptions. Thus the English physicist Lord KELVIN resurrected Buffon's methods and, using better data, calculated that the Earth had existed for 25 to 100 million years.

Kelvin also reasoned that the Earth and Sun had been formed at the same time, and that, given conventional energy sources, the Sun could have emitted energy at its present rate for only about 40 million years. Geologists and biologists familiar with the geologic and FOSSIL RECORDS regarded these figures as being far too low, but they lacked the quantitative data necessary to refute Kelvin.

ABSOLUTE AGE DATING

In 1896 the French physicist Henri Becquerel discovered radioactivity—the spontaneous decay of certain elements and forms of elements. In 1906, R. J. Strutt (later 4th Baron Rayleigh) demonstrated that the heat generated by this process refuted Kelvin's arguments.

Then an American chemist, B. B. Boltwood, found (1905-07) that in the decay of uranium (U) to lead (Pb), the ratio Pb/U was consistently greater, the older the rock containing these elements. Thus if the rate of radioactive decay could be determined, it could be used to calculate absolute ages for the geologic time scale.

The radioactive decay rate is unaffected by normal chemical and physical processes and is exponential. The decay rate for each radioactive isotope is characterized by a particular half-life—the time required for half of the remaining radioactive "parent" to decay to its stable "daughter." For example, suppose a certain radioactive substance has a half-life of 1 million years. After a million years half of it will remain, after another million years a quarter will remain, after still another million years an eighth will remain, and so on, virtually to infinity. The geologic age of a rock can be calculated by estimating the amounts of parent and daughter elements that were originally present in the rock, measuring the amounts that are now present, and calculating the number of half-lives that must have passed to bring parent and daughter to current levels.

The classic techniques of dating rocks by utilizing radioactivity, called RADIOMETRIC AGE-DATING, involve the decay of isotopes of uranium to lead, rubidium to strontium, potassium to argon, or carbon to nitrogen. With the exception of the carbon isotope, C^{14}, all of these have half-lives long enough so that they can be used to determine the Earth's great age. Carbon^{14}, which has a short half-life, is useful only for dating substances in the late QUATERNARY PERIOD. Several techniques devised in recent years substantiate the earlier dates, as well as increase the variety of datable materials.

CALIBRATING THE RELATIVE SCALE

Radiometric dating techniques have shown that the oldest rocks are approximately 3.8 billion years old, that the Paleozoic Era began about 570 million years ago and the Mesozoic

GEOLOGIC TIME SCALE

Era	Period	Epoch	Approximate Duration (millions of years)	Approximate Beginning (millions of years ago)
Cenozoic	Quaternary	Holocene	10,000 years ago to the present	
		Pleistocene	1.7	1.7
	Tertiary	Pliocene	9	12
		Miocene	14	26
		Oligocene	12	38
		Eocene	16	54
		Paleocene	11	65
Mesozoic	Cretaceous		70	135
	Jurassic		55	190
	Triassic		35	225
Paleozoic	Permian		55	280
	Carboniferous: Pennsylvanian		40	320
	Carboniferous: Mississippian		25	345
	Devonian		55	400
	Silurian		25	425
	Ordovician		75	500
	Cambrian		100	600
Precambrian (Proterozoic, Archeozoic)			3,200	3,800

Era about 230 million years ago, and that the Cenozoic Era has occupied the last 65 million years. In addition, meteorites (which are probably material left over from the formation of the solar system) and rocks from the Moon (the surface of which has not been altered by atmospheric weathering and erosion or by tectonic processes) indicate that the Earth and the remainder of the solar system originated 4.65 billion years ago. (See also: EARTH, GEOLOGICAL HISTORY OF.)

Most radioactive elements occur in igneous and metamorphic rocks, whereas nearly all fossils, on which the relative time scale is based, occur in sedimentary rocks. If igneous rock such as a lava flow or an ash bed is intercalated in a sequence of sedimentary strata, the assignment of a radiometric date to the sediments is relatively easy. In other instances, geologists must analyze regional relationships in an attempt to relate radiometrically dated crystalline rocks and sedimentary strata. For example, if a sedimentary formation is cut by an igneous intrusion that is 250 million years old, the geologist knows that the strata are older than this, but not how much older. If the intrusion is truncated by an overlying sedimentary formation, the geologist knows that these strata are less than 250 million years old but not how much less. But if this second sedimentary formation is intruded by a second igneous body dated at 200 million years, the second set of strata must be between 200 and 250 million years old. Thus, geologists can continue to refine the calibration of radiometric and relative time scales. LEIGH W. MINTZ

Bibliography: Eicher, Don, *Geologic Time,* 2d ed. (1976); Gould, Stephen Jay, *Time's Arrow, Time's Cycle: Myth and Metaphor in the Discovery of Geologic Time* (1987); Mintz, Leigh W., *Historical Geology,* 2d ed. (1977); Zeuner, Frederic E., *Dating the Past: An Introduction to Geochronology,* 4th ed. (1946; repr. 1970).

geology

Geology, derived from the Greek *geo,* "earth," plus *logos,* "study," deals with the study of the planet Earth—the materials of which it is made, the processes that affect Earth materials, the products formed in the Earth, and the history of the planet and its inhabitants since its origin.

Geologists study the composition of Earth materials and the various geological processes in order to locate and exploit the Earth's mineral resources. They also investigate earthquakes, volcanoes, and other geologic hazards in order to predict and minimize the damaging effects of these natural phenomena. Geologists study geologic history to determine the former positions of the continents and oceans, to ascertain the nature of ancient climates, and to trace the evolution of life as revealed in the FOSSIL RECORD.

Geology draws heavily from other sciences; Earth science and the basic sciences overlap in many areas of investigation. For example, chemistry is used to analyze the rocks and minerals of the Earth's crust. Biology aids in understanding the nature of prehistoric organisms. Thus, botany provides information about ancient plants, and a knowledge of zoology is

A geologist observes at close hand the active Kilauea crater of Hawaii's Mauna Loa volcano. The scientific study of volcanic activity, which extends back to the days of ancient Rome, has been essential to the growth of geologic knowledge. The Scottish scientist James Hutton correctly theorized in the 19th century that granite and basalt are rocks that solidified from a molten state produced by volcanic or deeper-lying Earth processes. His work helped to dispel older notions that all rocks were the sedimentary products of Noah's flood.

essential to the understanding of prehistoric animals. Physics helps to explain the various physical forces that affect the Earth and how Earth materials respond to these forces. Findings from astronomy reveal where the Earth fits into the universe, and astronomers have also attempted to explain the origin of the Earth.

SUBFIELDS

Because of its broad scope, geology has been divided into two major divisions: physical geology and historical geology. Physical geology deals with the composition of the Earth, its structural arrangement, the movements within and on the Earth's crust, and the myriad geologic processes by which the Earth is, or has been, changed. The principal subfields of physical geology include mineralogy, the study and classification of MINERALS; PETROLOGY, dealing with the origin, structure, occurrence, and history of rocks; and structural geology, which has to do with the deformation of rocks and their structural attitude or arrangements. PLATE TECTONICS is closely related to structural geology but generally treats the deformation and historical evolution of the Earth's larger structural features. GEOMORPHOLOGY is concerned with the general configuration of the Earth's surface and the origin, development, and classification of landforms. Economic geology has to do with geologic processes and materials that can be utilized by humans, and GEOPHYSICS and GEOCHEMISTRY rely on data derived from the study of the physics and chemistry of the Earth. More specialized subfields of physical geology include seismology (the study of EARTHQUAKES and the Earth's interior), volcanology (the study of VOLCANOES and volcanic phenomena), glaciology (the study of GLACIERS and glacial phenomena), environmental geology (geological studies related to human environmental concerns), engineering geology (the application of the geological sciences to engineering practice), and marine geology, or geological oceanography (that aspect of the study of the ocean which deals specifically with the ocean floor and the ocean-continent margins; see OCEAN AND SEA).

Historical geology is concerned with the evolution of the Earth and its inhabitants from their origin to the present day. Subfields include STRATIGRAPHY, dealing with the study, interpretation, and correlation of rock strata, and paleontology, the study of prehistoric plants and animals as revealed by their fossils and related to the chronology of the Earth's history. Geochronology is the study of time in relationship to the history of the Earth, and PALEOGEOGRAPHY deals with the physical geography of all or part of the Earth's surface at some time in the geologic past. More specialized are PALEOCLIMATOLOGY (the study of climates of the geologic past), PALEOECOLOGY (the study of the relationship between ancient organisms and their environment), PALEOMAGNETISM (the study of the Earth's magnetic field over geologic time), and MICROPALEONTOLOGY (the study of microscopically small fossils).

The major branches of historical geology—like those of physical geology—overlap in a number of areas and are interdependent. Thus the unification of physical and historical geology leads ultimately to a better understanding of the Earth.

HISTORY OF GEOLOGY

Although geology is a relatively young science, humans have long been interested in the Earth. Prehistoric people utilized stones as tools and weapons, formed clay into pottery, and sought shelter in rocky caves. But their knowledge of the Earth was restricted to the ground beneath their feet or the limited areas that they could explore on foot.

Ancient Myths. Curiosity probably prompted early humans to pick up stones that later became tools. Fear undoubtedly spurred speculation about such cataclysmic events as earthquakes and volcanic eruptions. In early interpretations such geologic phenomena were explained by means of unworldly or supernatural forces. According to an early Hindu legend, the Earth was supported by eight elephants that stood on the back of a giant turtle. The turtle, believed to be an incarnation of the god Vishnu, rested on the back of a coiled cobra, the symbol of water. When any of these creatures moved, the Earth would vibrate, producing an earthquake. In Japanese folklore, earthquakes are caused by a giant catfish that lives in mud beneath the Earth. The fish can only be controlled while pinned beneath a huge "keystone" possessing magical powers. When the catfish frees itself and thrashes about, earthquakes are produced.

Ancient Greek and Roman Beliefs. As early as the 4th century BC, ARISTOTLE taught that the Earth was a sphere. He also believed that streams originated from springs and that minerals were formed from "exhalations" of the Earth. He said that earthquakes were caused when "pent-up" winds burst to the surface after being trapped in subterranean channels.

Titus Lucretius Carus, an early Roman, wrote that quakes were caused by the collapse of the roofs of great caverns. Other ancient Romans speculated about volcanic eruptions. Indeed, the term *volcano* probably derives from the island of Vulcano, one of the Lipari or Aeolian Islands in the Tyrrhenian Sea off the coast of Sicily. This island's active volcano was assumed to be the home of Vulcan, Roman god of fire. Vulcan was the blacksmith of the gods, and when his forge was heated, smoke issued from Vulcano's crater. The volcanic explosions were thought to be caused by Vulcan pounding on his anvil.

Other ancients pondered the origin of fossils. In the 5th century BC, ANAXIMANDER of Miletus noted fossil fish well above sea level and concluded that fish had been the ancestors of all living things, including humans. XENOPHANES of Colophon (5th century BC) found fossils of marine organisms far inland and correctly inferred that they represented the remains of sea-dwelling animals. Approximately 100 years later HERODOTUS of Halicarnassus found nummulites (large foraminifera) in Egyptian limestones. He said that these small, disk-shaped fossils were lentils left over from the slaves who built the pyramids. Herodotus also stated that lower Egypt had been formed from sediment deposited by the Nile. Because its roughly triangular shape resembles the Greek letter Δ, he named that region the delta. Today this term is used to describe similar river-laid deposits in all parts of the world.

In the 4th century BC, EMPEDOCLES of Agrigentum recognized fossils in Sicily. He proposed that plants, animals, and humans had appeared in this order because each depends on its predecessor for survival—an "evolutionary" approach far ahead of its time. Aristotle and THEOPHRASTUS of Lesbos also collected fossil fish, and the latter made one of the earliest attempts to classify minerals.

Medieval Thought. There were few attempts to solve the Earth's mysteries during the Middle Ages. No distinction was made between rocks, minerals, and fossils as the terms are now understood. Early in the 11th century, however, AVICENNA, a Persian physician and Islamic scholar, perceived basic geologic processes that were not to be understood for centuries. He recognized water and wind as erosional agents, flooding of the land by prehistoric seas, the development of solid rock from soft, water-deposited sediment, the formation of soils, and fossils as the remains of ancient animals. Avicenna also grasped the importance of time in geological processes. A less important contribution was made by ALBERTUS MAGNUS, a 13th-century German scholar who wrote about rocks, minerals, and mountains.

The Renaissance: An Awakening. Interest in the Earth was rekindled early in the Renaissance by LEONARDO DA VINCI. He recognized the true nature of fossils and refuted the then-popular notions that fossils were freaks of nature or devices that Satan had put in the rocks to lead people astray. His approach to the study of the Earth was modern in that he explained features in the rocks in the light of natural processes that could still be observed.

In the mid-16th century Georg Bauer, a German writing under the name of Georgius AGRICOLA, wrote on the origin of mountains, minerals, and underground water. Two of his books, *De natura fossilium* (1546) and *De re matallica* (1556), laid the foundations for mineralogy and mining geology.

The 17th Century. In 1667, Nicolaus STENO, a Danish physician and theologian, published the first true treatise on geology. He wrote on processes of sedimentation, the origin of rocks, the formation of crystals and fossils, and the interpretation of rock strata. His *Prodromus* (1669) established criteria for differentiating between freshwater and marine sediments. He was the first to recognize the principle of superposition—that the lower layers in a sequence of rock strata must be older than those deposited above them. He also stated that rock layers were formed from beds of sediment that were originally laid down in a nearly horizontal position—the principle of original horizontality. Steno was also the first to note that the crystal faces of a given mineral always have the same angle with respect to each other. This is now known as the law of constancy of interfacial angles.

Despite advances in the 17th century, however, the concept of geologic time was not understood. The creation of the Earth and the geologic record were still explained in terms of biblical chronology. Accordingly, the creation was believed to have taken place in 4004 BC, a date based on the calculations of James USSHER, a mid-17th-century Irish bishop.

18th- and 19th-Century Advances. Modern geologic thought began to develop in the 18th century and expanded steadily in the 19th. Benoit de Maillet, a French consul to Egypt, was probably the first to note that older rocks contain fewer fossil species than do younger rocks. He also concluded that layered rocks were deposited over long spans of time. In his *Telliamed* (de Maillet spelled backward) he wrote of the formation of the Earth and of the origin of animals.

Giovanni ARDUINO, an Italian mineralogist, wrote on metamorphism and attempted to arrange rocks chronologically from youngest to oldest. He classified them as "primitive" or "primary," "secondary," and "tertiary." The last term is still used today.

Two major geological controversies emerged during the late 18th century, both of which were largely resolved by Scottish geologist James HUTTON. The first centered around the neptunism/plutonism debate. Proponents of neptunism, led by German minerologist Abraham Gottlob WERNER, held that all bedrock had been precipitated in an ancient universal sea. Accordingly, fossils were seen as victims of Noah's flood, and granite and basalt were believed to be the oldest deposits of an ancient sea. Proponents of plutonism, led by Hutton, acknowledged that sedimentary build-up occurred, but held that most rock had solidified from an original molten mass. Neptunism was eventually discounted when granite and basalt were proven to be igneous rocks.

The second controversy involved CATASTROPHISM, a then widely held doctrine that the Earth's major physical features were caused by periodic, worldwide catastrophes. Hutton shared the belief that the Earth had undergone great changes, but he saw no concrete evidence for catastrophism. He proposed that all past geologic events were somehow connected, that the most important events occurred over immense time

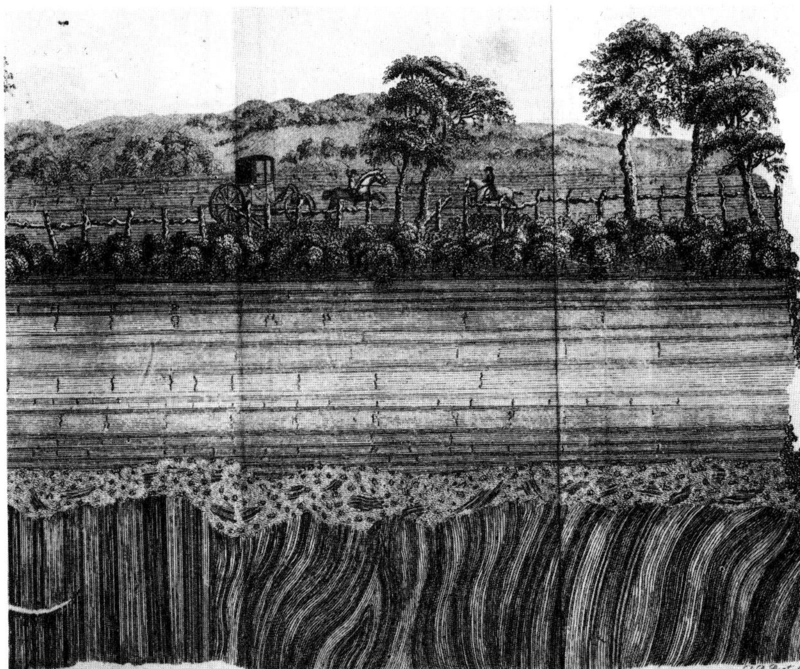

An engraving (left) *from James Hutton's* Theory of the Earth *(1795) shows horizontal rock strata resting on inclined layers. Hutton, often called the founder of modern geology, attributed such unconformities to gradual folding and erosion together with deposition of surface strata rather than to sudden catastrophic events. A modern field geologist* (below) *uses methods similar to those used by Hutton.*

periods, and that they continue to occur in the present. Hutton's concepts, which became known as UNIFORMITARIANISM, established the significance of geologic time and provided the cornerstone of future geologic thought.

Field studies and mapmaking burgeoned in the 19th century. William SMITH, an English civil engineer, observed that each layer of rock contained fossils characteristic of that particular stratum, and that such strata might be identified by their fossils and thus correlated over wide areas. He laid the foundation for stratigraphical paleontology and published the first geologic map of England. William Maclure, a Scottish geologist who settled in Virginia, published the first maps of what was then the United States in 1809.

Near the end of the 19th century, geologists began to abandon a 6,000-year age for the Earth, and many thought that the Earth was at least tens of millions of years old. In 1896 radioactivity was discovered by Henri Becquerel, a French physicist. This paved the way for the 20th-century development of RADIOMETRIC AGE-DATING, which has found some rocks to be 3.8 billion years old.

Geology in the 20th Century. With an understanding of geologic time and with Hutton's concept of uniformitarianism to guide them, 20th-century geologists began to forge geology as it is known today. Increasing knowledge of radioactive minerals, rates of decay, and decay products led to the development of the long-awaited "geologic clock," which suggests that the Earth is at least 4.6 billion years old. New sophisticated instruments and research techniques have been developed; the Earth is now studied from ships, aircraft, and orbiting satellites.

In 1912, Alfred WEGENER, a German meteorologist, put forth his theory of CONTINENTAL DRIFT. He proposed that a single protocontinent—Pangaea—had broken apart and the fragments had drifted away to form the continents as they are known today. Wegener's revolutionary proposal was rejected for decades, but in the early 1960s, geologist Harry H. HESS and Robert S. Dietz, a geological oceanographer, developed the theory of SEAFLOOR SPREADING. This theory, along with a better understanding of paleomagnetism, led to the theory of plate tectonics, or global tectonics. This important and now widely accepted theory assumes that the several moving plates of the Earth's crust are formed by volcanic activity at the oceanic ridges and destroyed in great seafloor trenches at the margins of the continents. One of the great geologic theories of all time, plate tectonics has revolutionized geologic thought and stimulated global research.

The concept of plate tectonics has advanced research in marine geology, and special attention is being directed to the ocean basins. Deep-sea cores recovered by research vessels have confirmed seafloor spreading and yielded much information about the composition and geologic history of the ocean floor. Studies of the continental shelves have provided clues to valuable deposits of oil and natural gas. Radar and infrared imagery from high-altitude aircraft and satellites are being used to study volcanoes and potential earthquake faults and to locate accumulations of valuable mineral deposits.

In the laboratory, computer models are being developed to assist in solving geological problems. The mass spectrometer, scanning electron microscope, and computerized axial tomography are probing rocks, minerals, and fossils as geologists use evidence from the past to understand the present and predict the future. WILLIAM H. MATTHEWS III

Bibliography: Adams, Frank D., *The Birth and Development of the Geological Sciences* (1938; repr. 1954); Dott, Robert H., and Batten, Roger L., *Evolution of the Earth*, 4th ed. (1988); Judson, Sheldon, Kauffman, Marvin E., and Leet, L. Don, *Physical Geology*, 7th ed. (1987); Levin, Harold L., *Contemporary Physical Geology*, 2d ed. (1986), and *The Earth through Time*, 3d ed. (1988); Mather, Kirtley L., and Mason, Shirley L., *A Source Book in Geology* (1939); Moore, Ruth E., *The Earth We Live On: The Story of Geological Discovery*, 2d ed. (1971).

geomagnetism: see EARTH, GEOMAGNETIC FIELD OF.

geometric isomer: see CONFIGURATION; ISOMER.

geometry

Geometry is a mathematical system that is usually concerned with points, lines, surfaces, and solids. All mathematical systems are based on undefined elements, assumed relations, unproved statements (postulates and assumptions), and proved statements (theorems); different sets of assumptions give rise to different geometries.

HISTORICAL DEVELOPMENT

Geometric figures first appeared over 15,000 years ago in both practical and decorative forms such as shapes of buildings and pottery, cave paintings, and decorations on pottery. The word *geometry* is derived from the Greek words for "Earth" and "measure." In this context geometry was originally used at least 5,000 years ago by Egyptian surveyors who tried to reestablish the boundaries of fields that were obliterated by the annual flooding of the Nile River. Prior to the work (*c*.600 BC) of the early Greek philosophers, geometry consisted of rules that produced useful, approximate results—but not always accurate by modern standards.

Ancient reports that THALES OF MILETUS (fl. *c*.600 BC) developed the first general theorems for geometry are now in dispute. PYTHAGORAS OF SAMOS (fl. *c*.540 BC) tried to explain all aspects of the universe in terms of counting numbers, which he frequently represented by sets of objects arranged in geometric shapes. For example, there were the triangular numbers 1, 3, 6, 10, 15, . . . , $(1/2)n(n + 1)$; square numbers 1, 4, 9, . . . , n^2; and so forth. Magnitudes—measures of quantities that could not be represented by counting numbers—were represented by lengths of line segments. Line segments were used to develop a geometric algebra of magnitudes. Geometric procedures corresponding to most of the usual laws of algebra were developed to solve for the positive roots of linear and quadratic equations with positive coefficients.

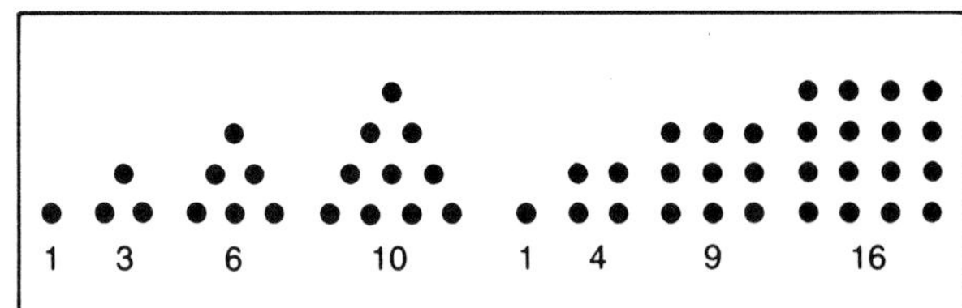

TRIANGULAR NUMBERS AND SQUARE NUMBERS

Plato (fl. *c*.400 BC) emphasized geometry in his Academy and used the five regular POLYHEDRONS to explain the scientific phenomena of the universe. ARISTOTLE, a pupil of Plato, developed the laws of logical reasoning. The mathematics taught in Plato's Academy was structured by EUCLID (fl. *c*.300 BC) into a logical system. For 2,000 years the geometry of Euclid's *Elements* was assumed to be the one true geometry. Despite doubts about Euclid's parallel postulate, all attempts to derive it from his other four postulates or to develop other geometries without it were futile until the 19th century. The tremendous productivity of mathematicians in the 19th and 20th centuries has led to the development of several types of geometries, some of which are identified below.

TYPES OF GEOMETRIES

Euclidean Geometry. The most common geometry is EUCLIDEAN GEOMETRY, which appears to explain the universe in which

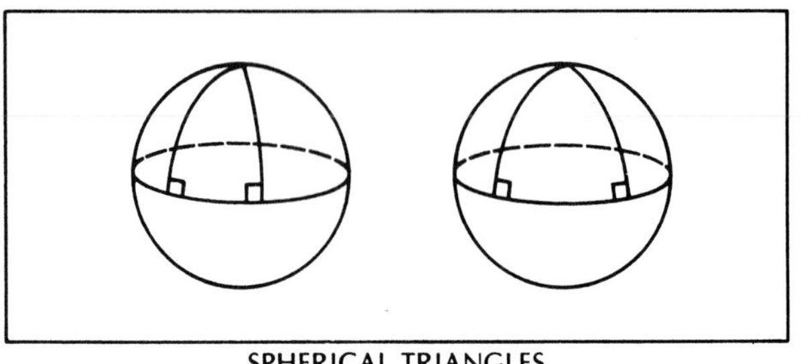
SPHERICAL TRIANGLES

humans live. Applications of it are found in nearly all aspects of daily activity as well as in the development of all industrial and scientific products. One of its postulates assumes the existence of one and only one line that is both parallel to a given line *m* and contains a given point that is not a point of the line *m*. The two non-Euclidean geometries were developed from efforts to prove Euclid's parallel postulate and are based on alternatives to it.

Other Approaches. Spherical geometry, the geometry of points on a sphere, can be easily visualized. Because the Earth is approximately spherical in shape, this geometry has practical applications in navigation and surveying. The surface of a given sphere is a two-dimensional space because each point may be located (identified) by two coordinates. For example, points (positions) on the Earth may be identified by latitude and longitude. On this two-dimensional surface the shortest distance between two points is measured along a spherical line called a GREAT CIRCLE, that is, a circle obtained as the intersection of the sphere and a plane that contains the center of the sphere. Spherical geometry is a study of points and spherical lines under the assumptions imposed by considering the two-dimensional spherical surface as a part of three-dimensional Euclidean space.

Angles formed by spherical lines have the same measures as the angles formed by the planes that determine the spherical lines in the model. SPHERICAL TRIGONOMETRY is the study of triangles on a sphere, or spherical triangles.

Transformations of a Euclidean plane onto itself are often considered in terms of translations (sliding motions) and rotations (about a point). Only four two-dimensional geometries exist that have two distinct types of transformations and have lines such that line segments have the properties of intervals of real numbers. If a geometry requires that two distinct lines have at most one common point, then spherical geometry is excluded, and the only geometries possible are Euclidean geometry and the two NON-EUCLIDEAN GEOMETRIES (elliptic geometry and hyperbolic geometry). As in the case of spherical geometry, each of the non-Euclidean geometries may be studied by using a model in Euclidean space. These models and theorems of Euclidean geometry may be used to derive theorems of each of the non-Euclidean geometries. Each of the three geometries (Euclidean, elliptic, and hyperbolic) is consistent if the set of real numbers is consistent. Also, any one of the three geometries may be the actual geometry of the entire universe.

Coordinates, which were first used by APOLLONIUS OF PERGA (fl. *c.*225 BC) to identify points on a conic and developed further by Oresme (fl. *c.*1360), René DESCARTES (1596–1650), and Pierre de FERMAT (1601–65), are used extensively today in the study of geometries. They are usually called Cartesian coordinates, in recognition of Descartes's work on coordinate systems (see COORDINATE SYSTEMS, mathematics). Because ordered sets of coordinates can be handled algebraically for any number of coordinates, geometries of any number of dimensions may be considered algebraically. ALGEBRAIC GEOMETRY is the study of geometry in terms of coordinates and algebraic representations of figures.

After Renaissance artists began to use PERSPECTIVE in their work, artists and mathematicians used sequences of perspectivities to obtain projectivities and develop PROJECTIVE GEOMETRY. Efforts to represent three-dimensional figures by plane figures led to the development of DESCRIPTIVE GEOMETRY.

ARCHIMEDES (287–212 BC) used small elements of volume to derive a formula for the volume of a sphere. The use of such small elements (infinitesimals) led to the development of analysis (calculus) and DIFFERENTIAL GEOMETRY.

Many geometries may be considered studies of properties that are invariant (unchanged) under a group of transformations. A hierarchy of geometries may be obtained by considering the effect of removing various assumptions from Euclidean geometry. From this point of view, Euclidean geometry is a study of CONGRUENT FIGURES. Any two congruent figures have the same area and the same shape. If only the requirement that area be preserved is removed (while retaining the requirement that the shape remain the same), the geometry of similar figures (corresponding figures having the same shape) is obtained. If only the requirement that shape be preserved is removed (while requiring that the area remain the same), equiareal geometry (the study of corresponding figures having the same area) is obtained. If both requirements (area and shape) are removed, affine geometry is obtained.

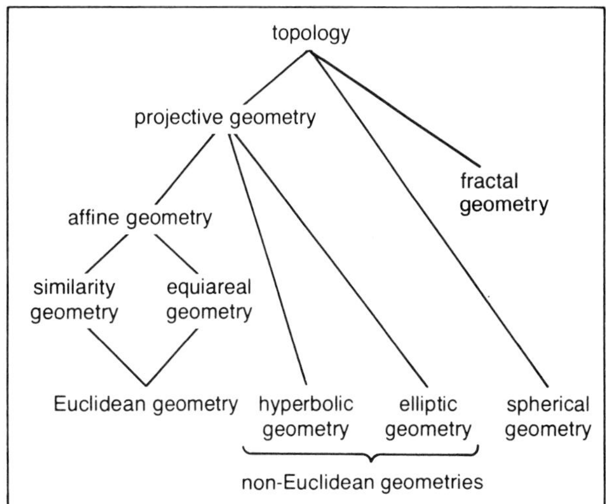

BRANCHES OF GEOMETRY

Affine geometry is the geometry used by artists when a horizon (ideal) line is added to the Euclidean plane. In Euclidean geometry, lines correspond to lines, and parallel lines correspond to parallel lines. In affine geometry, any two lines that have a point of the horizon line in common are regarded as parallel lines. If this special property of the horizon line is removed and the horizon line is treated as indistinguishable from any other line, no parallel lines exist, and the subject is called projective geometry. The study of lines that are allowed to correspond to linear continua (curves) is called TOPOLOGY. Two-dimensional topology is sometimes loosely referred to as "rubber sheet geometry" because it does not allow cutting apart or sealing together, but deformations are permitted. This representation is correct only for a special case of topology but may help to clarify the subject matter of topology. Formally, topology is the study of properties that are invariant under bicontinuous and biunique transformations; that is, the transformations are continuous and unique, and the inverse of each transformation is continuous and unique. Topology is the most general geometry in the hierarchy of the branches of geometries shown in the accompanying figure.

LOGICAL STRUCTURE

Each of the 13 books of Euclid's *Elements* opens with a statement of the definitions required in that book. In the first book the definitions are followed by the assumptions (postulates and common notions) that are to be used. There follows a set of propositions (theorems) with proofs. The logical structure of the exposition of the proofs has influenced all scientific thinking since Euclid's time. This logical structure is essentially as follows:

1. A statement of the proposition.
2. A statement of the given data (usually with a diagram).
3. An indication of the use that is to be made of the data.
4. A construction of any additional lines or figures.
5. A synthetic proof.
6. A conclusion stating what has been done.

Modern refinements of logical procedure have long since shown that Euclid's work needs modification. The recently developed fractal geometry, for example, requires a more abstract, general definition of dimension than Euclid's. Furthermore, mathematicians today think of such Euclidean statements as "a point is that which has no part" and "a line is breadthless length" as descriptions rather than definitions, and they recognize that any logical system must contain some undefined terms (see GÖDEL, KURT). The need for modern refinements, however, does not detract from the significance of Euclid's work and its profound influence on the development of mathematics. BRUCE E. MESERVE

Bibliography: Hilbert, David, and Cohn-Vossen, Stephen, *Geometry and the Imagination* (1952); Jacobs, Harold R., *Geometry,* 2d ed. (1987); Melzak, Alex Z., *Invitation to Geometry* (1983).

geometry, fractal

A modern mathematical theory that radically departs from traditional EUCLIDEAN GEOMETRY, fractal geometry describes objects that are self-similar, or scale symmetric. This means that when such objects are magnified, their parts are seen to bear an exact resemblance to the whole, the likeness continuing with the parts of the parts and so on to infinity. Fractals, as these shapes are called, also must be devoid of translational symmetry—that is, the smoothness associated with Euclidean lines, planes, and spheres. Scaling symmetry without translational symmetry yields nonstandard scaling—a rough, jagged quality maintained at every scale at which an object can be examined. The quintessential nature of fractals is reflected in their etymology. The word was coined by mathematician Benoit B. Mandelbrot from the Latin verb *frangere,* "to break," and the related adjective *fractus,* "irregular and fragmented."

The simplest fractal is the Cantor bar (named for the 19th-century German mathematician Georg CANTOR). One may be constructed by dividing a line in 3 parts and removing the middle part. The procedure is repeated indefinitely, first on the 2 remaining parts, then on the 4 parts produced by that operation, and so on, until the object has an infinitely large number of parts each of which is infinitely small.

Fractals are not relegated exclusively to the realm of mathematics. If the definition is broadened a bit, such objects can be found virtually everywhere in the natural world. The difference is that "natural" fractals are randomly, statistically, or stochastically rather than exactly scale symmetric. The rough shape revealed at one length scale bears only an approximate resemblance to that at another, but the length scale being used is not apparent just by looking at the shape. Moreover, there are both upper and lower limits to the size range over which fractals in nature are indeed fractal. Above and below that range, the shapes are either rough (but not self-similar) or smooth—in other words, conventionally Euclidean.

A computer can use the concept of fractals to generate a wide range of complex shapes. Here, for example, a basic plane is repeatedly subdivided into smaller and smaller self-similar triangles. This same process can be continued to the limits of the capacity of the computer. The resulting network can be manipulated by adding random factors to produce a desired simulation of a complex terrain.

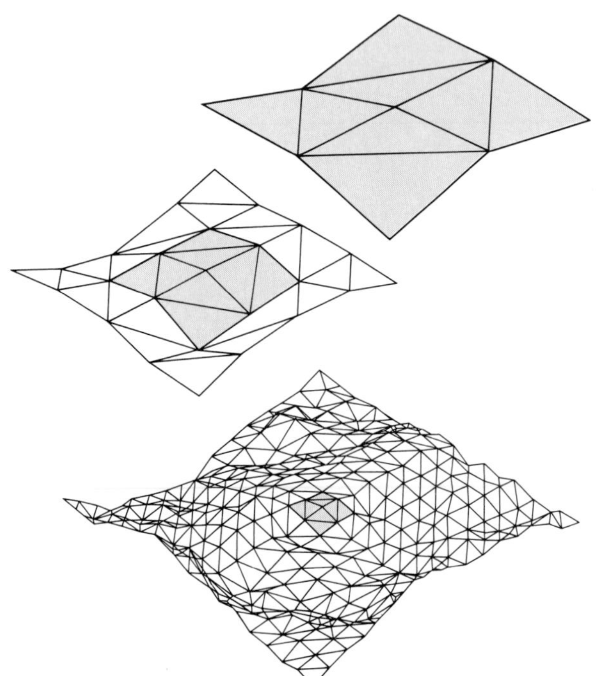

Whether natural or mathematical, all fractals have particular fractal dimensions. These are not the same as the familiar Euclidean dimensions measured in discrete whole integers—1, 2, or 3—but a different kind of quantity. Usually noninteger, a fractal dimension indicates the extent to which the fractal object fills the Euclidean dimension in which it is embedded. A natural fractal of fractal dimension 2.8, for example, would be a spongelike shape nearly 3-dimensional in appearance. A natural fractal of fractal dimension 2.2 would be a much smoother object that just narrowly misses being flat.

Background. The roots of fractal geometry can be traced to the late 19th century, when mathematicians started to challenge Euclid's principles (see GEOMETRY). Fractional dimensions were not discussed until 1919, however, when the German mathematician Felix Hausdorff put forward the idea in connection with the small-scale structure of mathematical shapes. His work, as completed by the Russian mathematician A. S. Besicovitch, was a forerunner of fractal dimensionality. Other mathematicans of the time considered such strange shapes as "pathologies" that had no significance.

This attitude persisted until the mid-20th century and the work of Mandelbrot, a Polish-born French mathematician who moved to the United States in 1958. His 1961 study of similarities in large- and small-scale fluctuations of the stock market was followed by work on phenomena involving nonstandard scaling, including the turbulent motion of fluids and the distribution of galaxies in the universe. A 1967 paper on the length of the English coast showed that irregular shorelines are fractals whose lengths increase with increasing degree of measurable detail. By 1975, Mandelbrot had developed a theory of fractals, and publications by him and others made fractal geometry accessible to a wider audience. The subject began to gain importance in the sciences.

Mandelbrot later also investigated another fractal terrain, that of shapes distorted in some way from one length to another. These fractals are now called nonlinear, since the relationship between their parts is subject to change. They retain some degree of self-similarity, but it is a local rather than global characteristic in them. The general definition of the word *fractal* may need further refinement, to indicate more precisely which shapes should be included by the term.

The most intriguing of the nonlinear fractals thus far has been the mathematical set named after Mandelbrot by the American mathematicians John Hubbard and Adrien Douady. The more the set is magnified, the more its unpredictability increases, until unpredictability comes to dominate the bud-like shape that is the set's major element of stability. The set has become the source of stunning color COMPUTER GRAPHICS images. It is also important in mathematics because of its centrality to dynamical system theory. An entire Mandelbrot set is actually a catalog of dynamical mathematical objects—that is, objects generated through an iterative process called Julia sets. These derive from a work done by a French mathematician, Gaston Julia, on the iteration of nonlinear transformations in a complex plane.

Impact on the Sciences. Scientists have begun to investigate the fractal character of a wide range of phenomena. Researchers are interested in doing so for the practical reason that behavior on a fractal shape may differ markedly from that on a Euclidean shape. Physics is by far the discipline most affected by fractal geometry. In condensed-matter, or sold-state, physics, for example, the so-called "percolation cluster" model used to describe critical phenomena involved in phase transitions and in mixture of atoms with opposing properties is clearly fractal. This has implications, as well, for a host of attributes, including electrical conductivity. The percolation cluster model may also apply to the atomic structure of

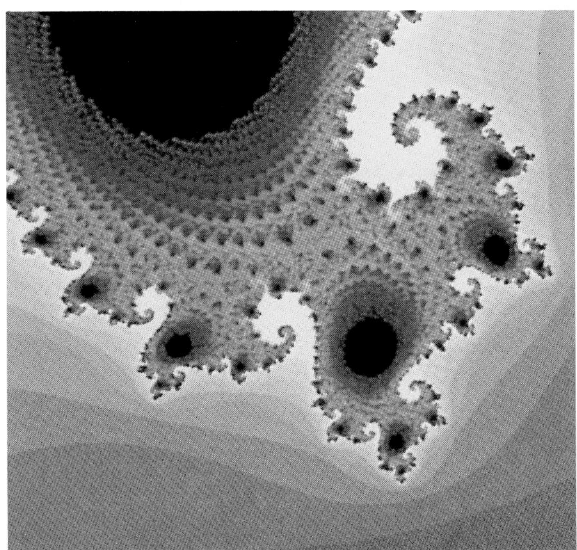

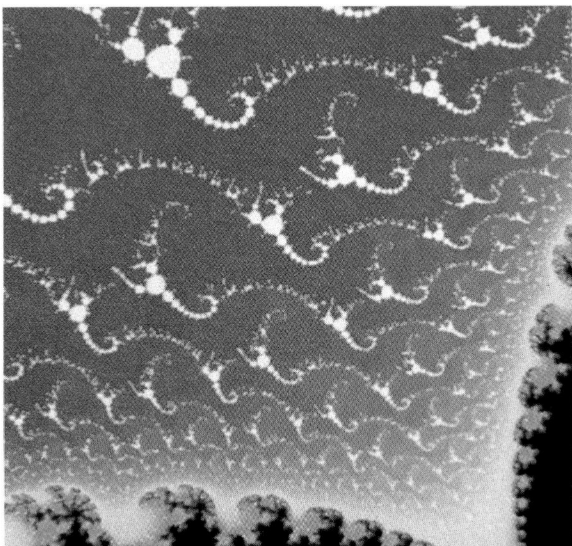

Computer graphics produced these striking fractal images derived from a mathematical set known as the Mandelbrot set, named after Benoit Mandelbrot, the founder of modern fractal geometry. The set's major element of stability is a somewhat budlike shape. As the set is magnified, however, through a repeating process known as a Julia set, its unpredictability increases. The result is a potentially infinite variety of geometrical patterns that can be colored by the computer to produce such images as those seen here. The Mandelbrot set has become popular for its intriguing beauty, but it represents an important contribution to dynamical system theory, as well.

glasses, gels, and other amorphous materials, and their fractal nature may give them unique heat-transport properties that could be exploited technologically.

Another major area of condensed-matter physics to invoke the concept of self-similarity is that of kinetic growth, in which particles are gradually added to a structure in such a way that once they stick, they neither come off nor rearrange themselves. In the case of the simplest model of kinetic growth, the most important physical phenomenon to which it applies appears to be the fingering of a less-viscous fluid (water) through a more viscous fluid (oil) lodged in a porous substance (limestone and other kinds of rock). A more complex model explains the growth of colloidal agglomerates.

Mathematical physics, for its part, has a particular interest in nonlinear fractals. When dynamical systems—those which change their behavior over time—become chaotic, or totally unpredictable, physicists describe the route they take with such fractals (see CHAOS THEORY). Called strange attractors, these objects are not real physical entities but abstractions that exist in "phase space," an expanse with as many dimensions as physicists need to describe dynamical physical behavior. One point in phase space represents a single measurement of the state of a dynamical system as it evolves over time. When all such points are connected , they form a trajectory that lies on the surface of a strange attractor. Most physicists who study chaos do so with carefully controlled laboratory setups of turbulent fluid flow. Individual strange attractors have been identified for different kinds of turbulent fluid flow, suggesting the existence of numerous routes to chaos.

Although not concerned with fractals to the same extent as physics, other sciences have discovered them. In biology the anomalous thermal relaxation rate of iron-containing proteins has been explained as resulting from the fractal shape of the linear polymer chain that makes up all proteins. The distribution pattern of atoms on the protein surface, a different aspect of protein structure, also appears to be fractal. Many more fractals have been detected in geology, including both random exterior surfaces—ragged mountains and valleys—and interior fracture surfaces in the brittle crust. Earthquake processes for small tremors appear to be fractal in time as well as space, since these quakes occur in self-similar clusters rather than at regular intervals. Meteorology provides a different kind of space-time fractal: the contour of the area over which tropical rain falls is self-similar, and the amount of rain that falls varies in a self-similar fashion over time.

Finally, on the interface of science and art, computer-graphics specialists, using a recursive splitting technique, have produced striking new fractal images of great statistical complexity. Landscapes made this way have been used as backgrounds in many motion pictures; trees and other branching structures have been used in still lifes and animations.

MORT LA BRECQUE

Bibliography: Gleick, James, *Chaos: Making a New Science* (1987); Mandelbrot, Benoit, *The Fractal Geometry of Nature* (1982); Peitgen, H. O., and Richter, Peter, *The Beauty of Fractals* (1986).

geomorphology [jee-oh-mohr-fahl'-uh-jee]

Geomorphology, from Greek words for *earth* and *form,* is the study of landforms and landscapes, particularly from the standpoint of origin. Unlike PHYSIOGRAPHY, a branch discipline restricted to classifying landscapes, geomorphology seeks to relate specific landforms to the formative processes that operate in different environments.

H. F. GARNER

Bibliography: Selby, M., *Earth's Changing Surface* (1985).

geophysics [jee'-oh-fiz-iks]

Geophysics, one of several EARTH SCIENCES, is the application of the principles and techniques of physics to the study of the Earth and its environment. It encompasses not only studies of the solid Earth but also of the oceans and atmosphere, the outer atmosphere, fields, particles, and planets within the solar system, and the relationship of the Sun and the planets.

SOLID-EARTH GEOPHYSICS

Studies of the solid Earth's shape, composition, physical properties, and fields are the subjects of several disciplines.

Geodesy is concerned with the shape of the Earth, its gravity field, and its orbital parameters, and with changes in the shape of the Earth brought about by tidal and tectonic forces. Studies of this shape and the gravity field lead to an understanding of the distribution of mass within the Earth. Variations of orbital parameters, such as changes in the pole of rotation and the length of the day, are measured at International Latitude Observatories established in a number of countries. The Earth's shape is measured both by conventional geodetic instruments and by satellites that measure the geopotential surface (geoid). The gravity field is studied by direct surface measurements and by analyses of the effect of the field on satellite trajectories.

Seismology is the study of EARTHQUAKES and related phenomena. Central to the field is the study of seismic waves generated by earthquakes and other disturbances, such as underground nuclear explosions. Seismic waves, sound waves that travel through the solid earth, are of two principal types: body waves, which travel directly through the Earth; and surface waves, which travel along an interface of contrasting sound velocities, most prominently the surface of the Earth. Body waves propagate in two phases. In P, or compressional, waves, particle motion is parallel to the direction of wave propagation; in S, or shear, waves, particle motion is perpendicular to the direction of wave travel. By carefully timing the arrival of the waves, seismologists are able to study the physical properties of the deep interior of the Earth. Similarly, by locally monitoring seismic waves generated artificially by explosions, exploration geophysicists can determine underground structures that may indicate mineral deposits.

Seismology also involves the study of earthquakes themselves: the mechanisms, modes, and locations of occurrence, as well as their prediction. This part of seismology overlaps with the field of tectonophysics, which is concerned with deformations in the Earth. These range from the small deformations produced by tides to PLATE TECTONICS and mountain building (OROGENY). Central to this field is the science of rock mechanics, the study of the physical processes responsible for the deformation of rock under the temperature and pressure conditions of the Earth's interior.

Geomagnetism and PALEOMAGNETISM have to do with the nature of the Earth's magnetic field and the history of this field over GEOLOGIC TIME. The Earth's main field, a dipole with poles offset approximately 11° from the rotational poles, is thought to result from the convective motion of conductive fluids, principally iron, in the Earth's outer core. This motion produces the field by induction. When a rock containing magnetic minerals (for example, magnetite) is formed, these minerals retain a magnetism that is oriented in the direction of the Earth's magnetic field at that time. Scientists have shown that the magnetic poles have wandered with respect to the location of the present continents (POLAR WANDERING) and that the polarity of the main magnetic field reverses periodically. These discoveries have made it possible to measure CONTINENTAL DRIFT and to devise a geologic time scale for such events.

The study of VOLCANOES—their origin, behavior, and mode of occurrence—is the subject of volcanology. This science, especially with regard to the origin of the MAGMAS that generate volcanoes, overlaps with the fields of GEOCHEMISTRY, PETROLOGY, and mineralogy.

OCEANS AND ATMOSPHERE

Investigation of the fluid envelopes of the Earth, both liquid and gaseous, have more in common with each other than with solid-earth geophysics.

METEOROLOGY is concerned with the behavior of the lower ATMOSPHERE. In that region the atmosphere is sufficiently dense to behave according to the laws of fluid mechanics. Thus the general circulation of the atmosphere and the origin of weather and CLIMATE come under the heading of meteorology. Surface observations are now made in conjunction with global monitoring by satellite.

The study of the oceans is usually broken into chemical, biological, and physical branches; only the latter, physical OCEANOGRAPHY, is considered a branch of geophysics. Oceanography, concerned with the fluid part of the oceans, is distinct from marine geophysics, the study of the ocean floors. Major fields of study are the structure of the oceans—as expressed by variations of salinity, pressure, and temperature—and ocean circulation, currents, tides, and waves.

The study of the HYDROSPHERE of the Earth—water that is not only in the oceans and atmosphere but on land, in lakes, rivers, and underground—is the domain of the HYDROLOGIC SCIENCES. In studies of the HYDROLOGIC CYCLE, hydrology merges with both oceanography and meteorology; other areas are GROUNDWATER hydrology and LIMNOLOGY (the study of lakes).

OUTER ATMOSPHERE AND SOLAR SYSTEM

Beyond 50 km (30 mi) above the Earth and extending into interplanetary space, matter is sufficiently diffuse to be strongly ionized by solar radiation; its behavior is determined largely by electromagnetic fields. The Sun gives off a continuous stream of charged particles (plasma) called the SOLAR WIND. The Earth's magnetic field forms a repulsive sheath about 100,000 km (62,000 mi) in diameter, called the MAGNETOSPHERE, that changes continuously in response to changes in the solar wind arising from solar flares and other variations in the solar cycle. Magnetospheric physics is concerned with the nature of these fluctuations. Within the magnetosphere, the upper atmosphere (50 to 2,000 km/30 to 1,250 mi) is diffuse and highly ionized. The study of the upper atmosphere, called aeronomy, includes many electrical phenomena, such as AURORAS and the VAN ALLEN RADIATION BELTS, as its subjects.

The fields of solar and interplanetary physics involve studies of processes within the Sun and their effects on solar radiation, the solar wind, and planets and other members of the solar system. Planetology is the study of the major and minor planets, with a view toward reconstructing the evolution of the Earth and of the solar system in general. Earth satellites and planetary probes have greatly expanded this field through the return of samples of lunar materials, the landing of scientific instruments on Venus and Mars, and flights past Mercury, Jupiter, Saturn, and Uranus and several satellites of the last three planets, as well as some comets. Evidences of volcanism on Mars and Venus, for example, and even the very different volcanic processes currently at work on Jupiter's satellite Io, all aid in understanding the forces that shaped the Earth's own, unique volcanic history.

INTERNATIONAL COOPERATION

Geophysics requires extensive data-gathering systems, such as global seismograph networks, weather satellites, oceanographic research vessels, and space probes. The first fully international cooperative venture began with the INTERNATIONAL GEOPHYSICAL YEAR (IGY) of 1957–58. This highly successful project has led to numerous international programs, most of which are sponsored by the International Union of Geodesy and Geophysics. Like most member nations, the United States participates through its national organization, the AMERICAN GEOPHYSICAL UNION.

CHRISTOPHER H. SCHOLZ

Bibliography: Allegre, Charles, *The Behavior of the Earth* (1988); Bates, C. C., and Gaskell, T. F., *Geophysics in the Affairs of Man* (1982); Mareš, Stanislav, *Introduction to Applied Geophysics* (1984); Wesson, P. S., *Cosmology and Geophysics* (1979).

See also: EARTH, GEOLOGICAL HISTORY OF; OCEAN-ATMOSPHERE INTERACTION.

geopolitics [jee-oh-pahl'-i-tiks]

Geopolitics is the study of the influence of geography, along with economics and demography, on the politics of a nation. Geopolitics helps in understanding forces that affect the politics of national states, especially their foreign relations.

Geopolitics had its beginnings in the early 20th century in the work of the Swedish political scientist Rudolf Kjellén, a follower of the German geographer Friedrich RATZEL. The British geographer Sir Halford J. MACKINDER maintained that the Euro-Asian "heartland" (comprising most of the USSR) was of strategic importance; he warned that a resurgence of German power after World War I might lead to world dominance if Germany were to control Europe and Russia. Karl Haushofer's German school of geopolitics in the 1920s promoted similar ideas that were used by the Nazis to justify their *Lebensraum* program of territorial expansion. MANIFEST DESTINY was a geopolitical theory promoted in the United States during the 19th century. ROBERT S. WEINER

Bibliography: Sprout, Harold and Margaret, *Toward a Politics of the Planet Earth* (1971).

George, David Lloyd: see LLOYD GEORGE, DAVID.

George, Henry

The 19th-century American social reformer Henry George advocated a single-tax solution for the inconsistencies of existing tax laws. In his treatise, Progress and Poverty *(1880), he outlined a plan aimed at abolishing all forms of taxation except land taxes.*

Henry George, b. Philadelphia, Sept. 2, 1839, d. Oct. 29, 1897, was an American social reformer whose *Progress and Poverty* (1880) won him international fame. In it he asserted that working the land was a natural right and that landlords were not entitled to reap the profits from it. He advocated a tax on land equal to its total economic rent—that is, the amount by which its value exceeded the value of land in other, less productive uses. Such a tax, he said, would eliminate the need for other taxes. His exposition of the SINGLE TAX theory made George a much-sought-after lecturer. In 1886 he ran for mayor of New York City; he was defeated, although he ran ahead of Theodore Roosevelt.

Bibliography: Barker, Charles A., *Henry George* (1955; repr. 1974); Oser, Jacob, *Henry George* (1974); Rose, Edward J., *Henry George* (1968).

George, Jean Craighead

Jean Craighead George, b. July 2, 1919, is an American writer and illustrator. She is best known for such children's books as *My Side of the Mountain* (1959), a contemporary classic, and *Julie of the Wolves* (1972), which won the 1973 Newbery Medal. George writes her books, which introduce the reader to the world of nature, with the accuracy of a naturalist and an artist's eye for beauty in unlikely places. She has written dozens of books and has illustrated many of them.

George, Lake

Lake George, a long (51 km/32 mi), narrow (up to 6 km/4 mi wide) glacial lake, lies in the foothills of the Adirondack Mountains in northeastern New York. It has a depth of 120 m (400 ft) and drains into Lake CHAMPLAIN to the north through a series of falls and cascades. Located in a region of great natural beauty, Lake George mainly serves recreational purposes. Named for George II in 1755, it was the site of several important battles in the French and Indian War and the American Revolution.

George, Saint

Saint George, the patron saint of England, may have been a martyr in Palestine before AD 300, but no actual details of his life are known. The legend that he saved a Libyan princess by killing a dragon arose in the 12th century, possibly from the myth of PERSEUS, who slew a sea monster near the site of George's supposed martyrdom. His status as patron of England probably originated with the foundation of the Order of the Garter under his patronage about 1347. George is also patron of Portugal, Aragon, Catalonia, and Lithuania. Feast day: Apr. 23.

Bibliography: Barclay, Alexander, *The Life of Saint George*, ed. by William Nelson (1955); Budge, E. A., trans., *George of Lydda, The Patron Saint of England* (1930; repr. 1977).

George, Stefan [gay'-ohr-ge, shtef'-ahn]

Stefan George, b. July 12, 1868, d. Dec. 4, 1933, was one of Germany's great lyric poets in the romantic-symbolist tradition. He was also profoundly controversial in his private life and politics.

After leaving school, George spent several years (1888–92) traveling in Europe and mixing in literary circles. In Paris, which particularly attracted him, he met the French symbolist poets Stéphane Mallarmé and Paul Verlaine. He soon began writing verse in the new style—finely wrought visions of poetic moods and landscapes. In his early twenties, George had already produced such collections of lyrical, but often esoteric, poems as *Hymns* (1890), *Pilgrimages* (1891), and *Algabal* (1892).

George was influenced by Friedrich NIETZSCHE, whom he considered one of the elite whose duty was to purify German language and culture. By the age of 24, George had attained sufficient stature to found his own elitist literary society, "The George Circle." The group included some of the most influential writers and critics at the turn of the century and, in 1892, founded a journal, *Blätter für die Kunst* (Pages for Art). Following a book of historical costume-poems, *Die Bücher der Hirten* (Books of the Shepherds, 1895), George composed some of his finest verse in *Das Jahr der Seele* (The Year of the Soul, 1897).

In 1903, during a difficult time in his life, George became infatuated with a 15-year-old boy, "Maximin," and sublimated the experience into a poetic, even mystical, encounter, *Der siebente Ring* (The Seventh Ring, 1907), celebrating Maximin as a new god. *Der Stern des Bundes* (The Star of the Covenant, 1913) continued the notion of a select league or circle. George's last book, *Das neue Reich* (The New Kingdom, 1928), prophesied an era in which Germany would become a new Greece.

Although George's personal stance was elitist, he was by no means proto-Nazi; when the Nazis came to power, George emigrated to Switzerland, where he died the same year.

George's poems, translated into English as *Poems* (1943) and *The Works of Stefan George* (1949), helped to shape modern German poetry, including the works of Hugo von Hofmannsthal and Rainer Maria Rilke. DAVID H. MILES

Bibliography: Goldsmith, Ulrich K., *Stefan George* (1970); Metzger, Michael and Erika, *Stefan George* (1972).

George Eastman House

The International Museum of Photography at George Eastman House in Rochester, N.Y., maintains a collection of more than 500,000 photographs, probably the best in the world, and a collection of nearly 5,000 motion pictures. Opened in 1947 at the home of George EASTMAN, founder of Eastman Kodak Company, the museum is especially rich in 19th-century photographs. At the core of these holdings are two collections: that of the Viennese historian of photography, Dr. J. M. Eder; and that of the visionary French collector, Gabriel Cromer.

The museum also houses an extensive historical collection of photographic equipment and a large library. PETER GALASSI

See also: NEWHALL, BEAUMONT.

George of Poděbrady, King of Bohemia

[pawd'-yuh-brahd]

George of Poděbrady, b. Apr. 23, 1420, d. Mar. 22, 1471, was the last national monarch of Bohemia (1458–71). After becoming the leader of the moderate HUSSITES (Utraquists) in 1444, George represented the main source of stability in Bohemia during the minority of LADISLAS V. In 1448 he seized Prague and became the administrator, and later regent, of Bohemia. After Ladislas's death (1457), George was elected king. His continued allegiance to Hussitism, however, brought him papal excommunication, as well as the military intervention of MATTHIAS CORVINUS of Hungary, who conquered Moravia (1468) and was elected king (1469) by the Catholic nobility. George died in the midst of this struggle, after naming Vladislav II (1471–1516), the son of CASIMIR IV of Poland, as his successor. Although his rule was seldom peaceful, George appears to have embodied the religious and national aspirations of his people. Moreover, his proposal for a league of princes to deal with general European problems made him an early champion of European unity. S. B. VARDY

Bibliography: Heymann, Frederick G., *George of Bohemia: King of Heretics* (1965); Odložilík, Otakar, *The Hussite King: Bohemia in European Affairs, 1440-1471* (1965).

George Town: see PENANG.

George Washington Bridge

The George Washington Bridge links the island of Manhattan, New York City, with Fort Lee, N.J., across the Hudson River. It has a clear span of 1,067 m (3,500 ft), which made it the longest suspension BRIDGE in the world when it was completed (1931). Designed by the famous bridge engineer O. H. AMMANN, and with a second deck and stiffening trusses added in 1959–62, the bridge now carries 14 lanes of traffic on the two decks, which are suspended from four main cables, each 0.9 m (3 ft) in diameter and built up of 26,474 parallel wires. Because of notable innovations in its erection, the bridge may be regarded as the first bridge to use modern methods of cable spinning.

The latticed steel towers at each end of the bridge, over which the suspension cables pass, are 179 m (595 ft) high, and each is built of 18,450 metric tons (20,500 U.S. tons) of steel. The bridge, together with its approaches, cost $248 million. SIR HUBERT SHIRLEY-SMITH

Bibliography: Shirley-Smith, Hubert, *The World's Great Bridges* (1965).

George Washington University, The

The George Washington University (enrollment: 21,000; library: 750,000 volumes), in Washington, D.C., was established as Columbian College in 1821 by a group including President James Monroe. George Washington had planned for the university, but the shares he left to endow it were worthless. It is a private university with graduate schools of law, medicine, and international affairs.

George I, King of England, Scotland, and Ireland

George I, elector of Hanover, succeeded to the British throne on the death of Queen ANNE in 1714. The succession was determined by the Act of SETTLEMENT of 1701, which passed over the legitimate but Roman Catholic representatives of the STUART line in favor of the Protestant house of HANOVER, descended from the daughter of James I.

Born on Mar. 28, 1660, in Hanover, George received a thorough education in the military and diplomatic arts. He became elector in 1698. After succeeding to the British throne, he remained staunchly German in his attachments and objectives. His constant aim was the aggrandizement of Hanover,

George I, the founder of the Hanoverian dynasty of British monarchs, succeeded Queen Anne in 1714. A German prince (he was elector of Hanover), he spoke no English and took little interest in Britain's domestic affairs. As a result, the power of his ministers, most notably Robert Walpole, grew enormously.

and it was due largely to his use of the British fleet that he successfully completed the acquisition of Bremen and Verden for Hanover in the Great NORTHERN WAR. In England George caused much controversy by his uncompromising support for the WHIG PARTY against the Tories and by his tendency to take advice on matters of state from his Hanoverian counselors. The uprising of the JACOBITES in 1715, several Jacobite conspiracies, and the SOUTH SEA BUBBLE in 1720 all presented threats to the security of his dynasty.

George quarreled both with his wife, Sophia Dorothea (1666–1726), whom he divorced and incarcerated (from 1694 until her death) in punishment for her alleged infidelity, and with his son, Prince George, who consorted with his political opponents. The prince succeeded to the throne as George II when George I died on June 12, 1727. PAUL LANGFORD

Bibliography: Hatton, Ragnild, *George I* (1979).

George II, King of England, Scotland, and Ireland

George II succeeded to the British throne and the electorate of Hanover on the death of his father, George I, in 1727. Born on Nov. 10, 1683, in Hanover, he remained largely Hanoverian in his interests, although, unlike his father, he learned fluent English. He visited the electorate regularly during most of his reign and sometimes utilized his position as king of England to the advantage of his German territory.

Although George has been represented as a king manipulated by his own ministers—notably Sir Robert WALPOLE and the duke of NEWCASTLE—and by his highly intelligent wife, Queen Caroline (1683–1737), he was by no means a weak monarch. He played a larger part in the direction of foreign and military policy than most contemporaries suspected, and at Dettingen (1743), in the War of the AUSTRIAN SUCCESSION, was the last British monarch to appear in person on the battlefield. His reign witnessed the final collapse of the JACOBITES after their uprising of 1745 and closed with Britain's brilliant successes in the SEVEN YEARS' WAR (1756–63) under the leadership of William PITT the Elder. George had long detested Pitt, but he eventually came to recognize his merits.

George's son, Frederick, predeceased him, so when George II died on Oct. 25, 1760, he was succeeded by Frederick's son, George III. Although he was vulnerable to management by others, he was undoubtedly a knowledgeable and skillful politician, within the narrow framework of Hanoverian interests in which he worked. PAUL LANGFORD

Bibliography: Plumb, J. H., *The First Four Georges, 1714-1830* (1975); Williams, Basil, *The Whig Supremacy* (1962).

George III, King of England, Scotland, and Ireland

George III was the longest reigning of male British monarchs. Born on June 4, 1738, he was the son of Frederick, prince of

George III saw a great expansion of Britain's commercial empire during his lengthy reign (1760-1820) despite the loss of the American colonies. The latter years of his rule were marred by his sufferings from a rare metabolic disorder known as porphyria, which ultimately cost him his sanity and his sight and led to the appointment of the prince of Wales as regent in 1811.

Wales, and the grandson of George II. He succeeded his grandfather in 1760, his father having died in 1751.

George had high but impractical ideas of kingship. On his accession he sought to rule without regard to party, to banish corruption from political practice, and to abandon the Hanoverian preoccupations of his predecessors. The chief minister chosen to implement his new system of politics, the 3d earl of Bute (1713–92), however, was an unpracticed politician who merely succeeded in disrupting the established politics of the day without creating a viable alternative. The result was 10 years of ministerial instability and public controversy, which ended only in 1770 with the appointment of Frederick, Lord NORTH, an able and congenial minister.

Although never an autocratic monarch in the sense that his opponents contended, George III was always a powerful force in politics. He was a strong supporter of the war against America, and he viewed the concession of independence in 1783 with such detestation that he considered abdicating his throne. At the same time he fought a bitter personal feud with the Whig leader Charles James FOX, and his personal intervention brought the fall of the Fox-North ministry in 1783. He then found another minister, William PITT, the Younger, who suited him. Even as late as 1801 he preferred, however, to force Pitt to resign as prime minister rather than permit CATHOLIC EMANCIPATION, a measure that he interpreted as contrary to his coronation oath to uphold the Church of England.

George III's later years were made wretched by severe attacks of porphyria, an illness that had already afflicted him seriously in 1788. Although physiological in origin, the disease destroyed his reason for prolonged periods and ultimately compelled him to submit to the establishment of a formal REGENCY in 1811. The regent was his oldest son, the future George IV, one of 15 children borne him by his wife, Queen Charlotte.

George III was bitterly criticized by Whig historians of his own and later days. But 20th-century scholarship has somewhat redressed the balance, and he is now seen as a strong-minded but public-spirited monarch who perhaps ascended the throne at an overly young and impressionable age. He learned quickly, however, and developed into a shrewd and sensible statesman, although one of conservative views. To the court he brought a sense of public duty and private morality that proved popular in a society already being transformed by the evangelical revival. He showed considerable interest in agricultural improvement and was an avid collector of paintings and books. The best loved of the Hanoverian rulers, he enjoyed a personal reputation that stood his house in good stead during the disastrous reign of his son George. George III died on Jan. 29, 1820.

PAUL LANGFORD

Bibliography: Brooke, John, *King George III* (1972); Butterfield, Herbert, *George III and the Historians,* rev. ed. (1959); Pares, Richard, *King George III and the Politicians* (1953; repr. 1967); Watson, J. Steven, *Reign of George III, 1760–1815* (1960).

Appointed (1811) prince regent because of the mental instability of his father, George III, George IV finally succeeded to the throne in 1820. The British public disliked his extravagant lifestyle and rallied to the support of his estranged wife, Caroline of Brunswick, when he attempted to divorce her. During George IV's 10-year reign, the prestige and political influence of the monarchy suffered a steady decline.

George IV, King of England, Scotland, and Ireland

George IV, who served as prince regent from 1811 to 1820 (see REGENCY) before succeeding his father, George III, to the throne, brought the standing of the British monarchy lower than at any other time in its modern history. Born on Aug. 12, 1762, he consorted as a young man with his father's parliamentary opponents, including Charles James FOX. In 1785 he illegally married Mrs. Maria Fitzherbert. He subsequently denied the marriage in order to secure Parliament's payment of his debts, and in 1795 he married Princess Caroline of Brunswick, whom he later attempted to divorce on his accession as king. Although long an ally of the Whigs, he declined to bring them into power when he became regent, and he was thereafter associated with deeply conservative causes, especially the maintenance of official discrimination against Roman Catholics and Protestant dissenters. His personal profligacy and his treatment of Queen Caroline brought him great unpopularity. He spent extravagant sums on the arts. Some of the richest portions of the royal collection and, above all, the ROYAL PAVILION AT BRIGHTON remain as monuments to his cultural interests. He died on June 26, 1830, and was succeeded by his brother, WILLIAM IV.

PAUL LANGFORD

Bibliography: Fulford, Roger, *George IV,* 2d ed. (1949); Hibbert, Christopher, *George IV, Prince of Wales, 1762–1811* (1974) and *George IV, Regent and King, 1811–1830* (1975).

George V, King of England, Scotland, and Ireland

George V, king of Great Britain from 1910 until 1936, was held in deep affection by the British people. Active in constitutional and political affairs, he relinquished his German titles in 1917 and changed the name of the royal house from Saxe-Coburg-Gotha to Windsor.

George V succeeded his father, EDWARD VII, to the British throne in 1910. Born on June 3, 1865, he pursued a naval career until the death (1892) of his older brother made him second in line to the throne of his grandmother, Victoria. In 1894 he married Princess Mary of Teck.

At the beginning of his reign George was involved in two crises—one over reform of the House of Lords (1910–11) and the other over Irish HOME RULE (1912–14). His conduct in these and, later, his choices of Stanley BALDWIN as prime minister in 1923 and Ramsay MACDONALD as head of the national government in 1931 generated some controversy. Nonetheless, he won popular affection, despite his gruff personality, by his visits to the troops during World War I and later by his Christmas radio broadcasts. During the war he changed the name of the royal family to WINDSOR. George's silver jubilee in 1935 was celebrated with elaborate festivities. He died on Jan. 20, 1936, and was succeeded by his oldest son, EDWARD VIII.

DON M. CREGIER

Bibliography: Judd, Denis, *The Life and Times of George V* (1973); Rose, Kenneth, *King George V* (1984).

George VI, King of England, Scotland, and Ireland

George VI assumed the British throne in 1936, when his elder brother, Edward VIII, abdicated. During World War II, George VI concentrated on bolstering public and military morale by visiting battle fronts and severely bombed areas. He died in 1952, following surgery for cancer.

George VI succeeded to the British throne on the abdication of his brother, EDWARD VIII, in 1936. Born on Dec. 14, 1895, he was the second son of the future George V. In 1923 he married Lady Elizabeth Bowes-Lyon.

A shy man, George VI struggled successfully to overcome a speech defect and won wide respect for his dedication and courage. During World War II, to encourage morale, he risked his life visiting war zones and recently bombed cities. He also created the George Cross for civilian gallantry, awarding it to the people of Malta for heroism under air attack. He and his consort, Queen Elizabeth, made notable state visits to France (1938), Canada and the United States (1939), and South Africa (1947). The king's frail health was weakened, and his life probably shortened, by his determination to carry on with his public duties despite serious illness. He died on Feb. 6, 1952, and was succeeded by his elder daughter, ELIZABETH II.

DON M. CREGIER

Bibliography: Donaldson, Frances, *King George VI and Queen Elizabeth* (1977); Wheeler-Bennett, Sir John, *King George VI: His Life and Reign* (1958).

George I, King of Greece

George I, b. Dec. 24, 1845, d. Mar. 18, 1913, succeeded OTTO I on the Greek throne in 1863. The second son of King Christian IX of Denmark, he was nominated as king of the Hellenes by Britain, France, and Russia and then elected by the Greek National Assembly. During his reign the territory of Greece was considerably extended by the cession of the Ionian Islands by Britain (1864) and the acquisition from Turkey of Thessaly and Arta (1881) and, later, of Epirus, Macedonia, and Crete (1913). The last territories were won as a result of the First BALKAN WAR, at the end of which George was assassinated.

K. M. SMOGORZEWSKI

George II, King of Greece

The eldest son of King CONSTANTINE I, George II, b. July 20, 1890, d. Apr. 1, 1947, was king of the Hellenes from 1922 to 1924 and again from 1935 to 1947. He went into exile after the British and French forced his father to abandon the throne in June 1917. Constantine returned in late 1920, and when he was compelled to abdicate after Greece's defeat by Turkey in Asia Minor, George became king on Sept. 27, 1922. In the aftermath of an abortive military revolt (October 1923) involving proroyalist officers, republicans in military and civilian circles pressed George into leaving Greece. In the early spring of 1924, a republic was declared.

The republic fell when ardent royalists engineered the restoration of the monarchy in the autumn of 1935. George II returned in November 1935, hoping to reconcile opposing factions. When moderate methods failed to improve conditions, he approved the establishment of a dictatorship under Ioánnis METAXÁS in August 1936. The German invasion of Greece in the spring of 1941 drove George into exile. A plebiscite on Sept. 27, 1946, approved his return, but he died soon after.

S. VICTOR PAPACOSMA

Georgetown (Cayman Islands)

Georgetown (1985 est. pop., 8,900) is the capital of the CAYMAN ISLANDS in the West Indies. The city is located on the excellent natural harbor of Grand Cayman. It is a center of tourism, banking, fishing, and boatbuilding.

Georgetown (Guyana)

Georgetown is the capital of Guyana. Situated at the mouth of the Demerara River on the northeastern coast of South America, its port handles Guyanan sugar and rice products, gold, and bauxite. The population (1985 est., 200,000) is mixed East Indian, African, and European. At first an English settlement called Georgetown, it was occupied (1784) by the Dutch, who changed the name to Stabroek; it was renamed Georgetown in 1812. With wide avenues and canals, this tropical city contains some of the best-preserved British colonial architecture in the Caribbean. The University of Guyana is there.

Georgetown University

Established in 1789 and operated by the Jesuits, Georgetown University (enrollment: 11,986; library: 1,500,000 volumes), in Washington, D.C., is the oldest Roman Catholic institution of higher learning in the United States. Among its professional schools are the School of Foreign Service (1919), the first school in the country for the training of diplomats, and the School of Languages and Linguistics (1949).

Georgia

Georgia is the largest state east of the Mississippi River. Its territorial domain extends from the Sea Islands on the Atlantic shore to the forested mountains of the southern Appalachians. Georgia is bounded on the east by South Carolina and the Atlantic Ocean, on the west by Alabama, on the north by Tennessee and North Carolina, and on the south by Florida.

A distinctive feature of Georgia is the paradox of old and new—often side by side. The forces generating change throughout the American South can readily be seen in Georgia. The state has experienced major economic growth in recent years, and Atlanta has emerged as the major urban center of the southeastern United States. In 1976 a native Georgian, Jimmy Carter, was elected president of the United States, the first southerner to occupy the nation's highest office since Reconstruction.

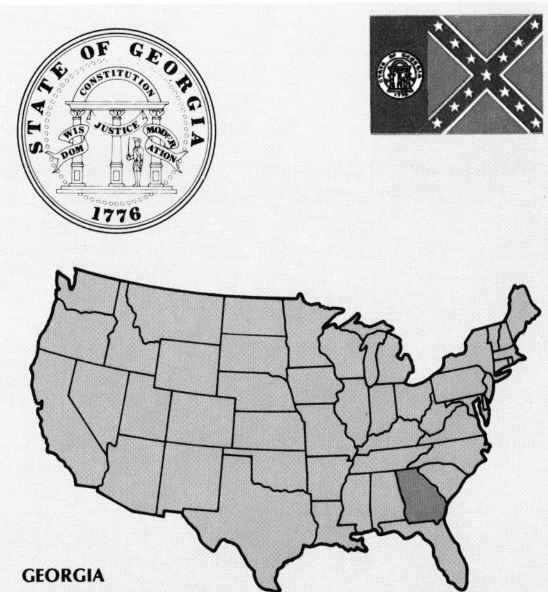

GEORGIA

LAND. Area: 152,576 km^2 (58,910 mi^2); rank: 21st. Capital and largest city: Atlanta (1986 est. pop., 421,910). Counties: 159. Elevations: highest—1,458 m (4,784 ft), at Brasstown Bald; lowest—sea level, at Atlantic coast.

PEOPLE. Pop. (1987 est.): 6,222,000; rank: 11th; density: 41.4 persons per km^2 (107 per mi^2). Distrib. (1986): 64.3% metro., 35.7% nonmetro. Av. ann. change (1980–87): +2.0%.

EDUCATION. Public enrollment (1986): elem.—777,991; sec.—318,434; higher—147,269. Nonpublic enrollment (1980): elem.—20,800; sec.—6,000; combined—54,100; higher (1986)—47,854. Institutions of higher education (1985): 80.

ECONOMY. State personal income (1986): $82.1 billion; rank: 12th. Median family income (1979): $17,414; rank: 37th. Nonagricultural labor distribution (1986): manufacturing—565,000 persons; wholesale and retail trade—670,000; government—459,000; services—506,000; transportation and public utilities—167,000; finance, insurance, and real estate—145,000; construction—156,000. Agriculture: income (1986)—$3.2 billion. Fishing: value (1986)—$25 million. Forestry: sawtimber volume (1987 prelim.)—92.3 billion board feet. Mining: value (1985)—$946 million. Manufacturing: value added (1985)—$27 billion. Services: value (1982)—$9.6 billion.

GOVERNMENT (1989). Governor: Joe Frank Harris, Democrat. U.S. Congress: Senate—2 Democrats; House—9 Democrats, 1 Republican. Electoral college votes: 12. State legislature: 56 senators, 180 representatives.

STATE SYMBOLS. Statehood: Jan. 2, 1788; the 4th state. Nicknames: The Empire State of the South, Peach State; bird: brown thrasher; flower: cherokee rose; tree: live oak; motto: Wisdom, Justice, and Moderation; song: "Georgia on My Mind."

LAND AND RESOURCES

Five physiographic regions are identifiable within Georgia: the CUMBERLAND PLATEAU, BLUE RIDGE MOUNTAINS, Ridge and Valley Region, PIEDMONT PLATEAU, and Coastal Plain. Lookout Mountain and Sand Mountain in the northwest corner of Georgia are remnants of the modest synclinal structure associated with the Cumberland Plateau. The surface elevations of these plateau remnants are 450 to 550 m (1,500 to 1,800 ft). The Blue Ridge Mountains extend into northern Georgia from adjacent Tennessee and North Carolina; the highest elevations in the state are found there. The narrow valleys and forested mountains are a major recreational resource. Springer Mountain (1,164 m/3,820 ft) is the southwestern terminus of the APPALACHIAN TRAIL. The Ridge and Valley region extends across northeast Georgia from Alabama to Tennessee. A group of low and open valleys 150 to 250 m (500 to 825 ft) above sea level are separated by ridges that extend 200 to 250 m (675 to 825 ft) above the valley floors. These three mountain provinces—the Cumberland Plateau, Blue Ridge Mountains, and Ridge and Valley area—as a group account for about 15% of Georgia's land area.

The Piedmont is the rolling upland plain south of the mountains. The northern margin of the Piedmont has an average elevation of 360 m (1,200 ft). The Piedmont's southern margin, which follows a line from Columbus to Augusta, is at an elevation of 150 m (500 ft). Local relief on the Piedmont is normally not more than 30 to 60 m (100 to 200 ft), but several MONADNOCKS exist with elevations that make them distinctive on the rolling Piedmont surface, such as Mount Yonah at 967 m (3,173 ft).

The fall line is associated with the point at which the unconsolidated materials of marine origin forming the Coastal Plain overlap with the geologically older rocks of the Piedmont. In Georgia the fall line extends through the cities of Macon, Columbus, Milledgeville, and Augusta. The border area is marked by low hills—the Sand Hills—that contrast with the low relief of the Coastal Plain. The outer, or Atlantic, edge of the Coastal Plain is composed of offshore islands—including St. Simons, Jekyll, St. Catherines, Sapelo, and Cumberland—and tidal marshes and low marine terraces. One such poorly drained terrace is occupied by the OKEFENOKEE SWAMP, a national wildlife refuge.

Soils. The soils of Georgia are varied, depending upon topographic character, drainage, and the underlying parent material. The slopes of the three mountain regions prohibit their soils from being used for cropland agriculture. The valley soils of the Ridge and Valley region, which are formed from limestone, are highly productive, however. Piedmont soils range from sandy loams to clay, but the rolling character of the Piedmont, in combination with the practice of intensive row cropping, has contributed to extensive and severe erosion damage. During the past five decades much of the Piedmont has been converted to grassland or forest, and the potential for continued resource destruction has been greatly reduced. The soils of the Coastal Plain are light, deep, and sandy.

Climate. A humid subtropical climate with mild winters and hot moist summers is characteristic of most of Georgia. The average annual precipitation varies from about 1,015 mm (40 in) in central Georgia to more than 1,900 mm (75 in) in northeast Georgia. One of two annual precipitation maxima occurs in February or March, when between 100 and 150 mm (4 and 6 in) of rain may be expected because of the high seasonal incidence of cyclonic activity over the southeastern United States. The second maximum occurs in June and July, when precipitation from thunderstorm activity may bring 100 to 180 mm (4 to 7 in) monthly.

The number of summer days when the temperature exceeds 32° C (90° F) are numerous, but in the mountain areas and the hilly Piedmont cool evenings bring welcome relief. Winters are mild, but significant variation occurs from south to north in Georgia. Snow cover lasting more than one or two days or exceeding 50 mm (2 in) occurs only in the mountainous fringe of north Georgia. The great day-to-day variability in winter weather is caused by the interaction of polar and subtropical air masses. Atlanta's extreme low temperatures are rarely below −10° C (14° F).

Vegetation and Animal Life. Forest, Georgia's most common landscape component, covers nearly 70% of the state; forest area has increased by more than 10,000 km^2 (3,860 mi^2) since the 1930s. Complexes of longleaf and slash pines cover most of the Coastal Plain, and loblolly and shortleaf pines forest the Piedmont. A forest of oak and pine is dominant on the upper Piedmont, changing to oak and hickory forest in the mountains. The declining acreage for cropland has allowed extensive forest regrowth of pine.

Georgia has a thriving wildlife population. Bears are limited mainly to the mountain regions and Okefenokee Swamp, but deer, squirrel, raccoon, and bobcat are numerous throughout the state in a habitat enhanced by the extensive forest and grassland. Many of the rivers, reservoirs, and coastal bays and thousands of farm ponds are available for recreational purposes. Lake Sidney Lanier, northeast of Atlanta, is the largest water body in the state. Bass, crappie, bream, and catfish are sought by freshwater-fishing enthusiasts.

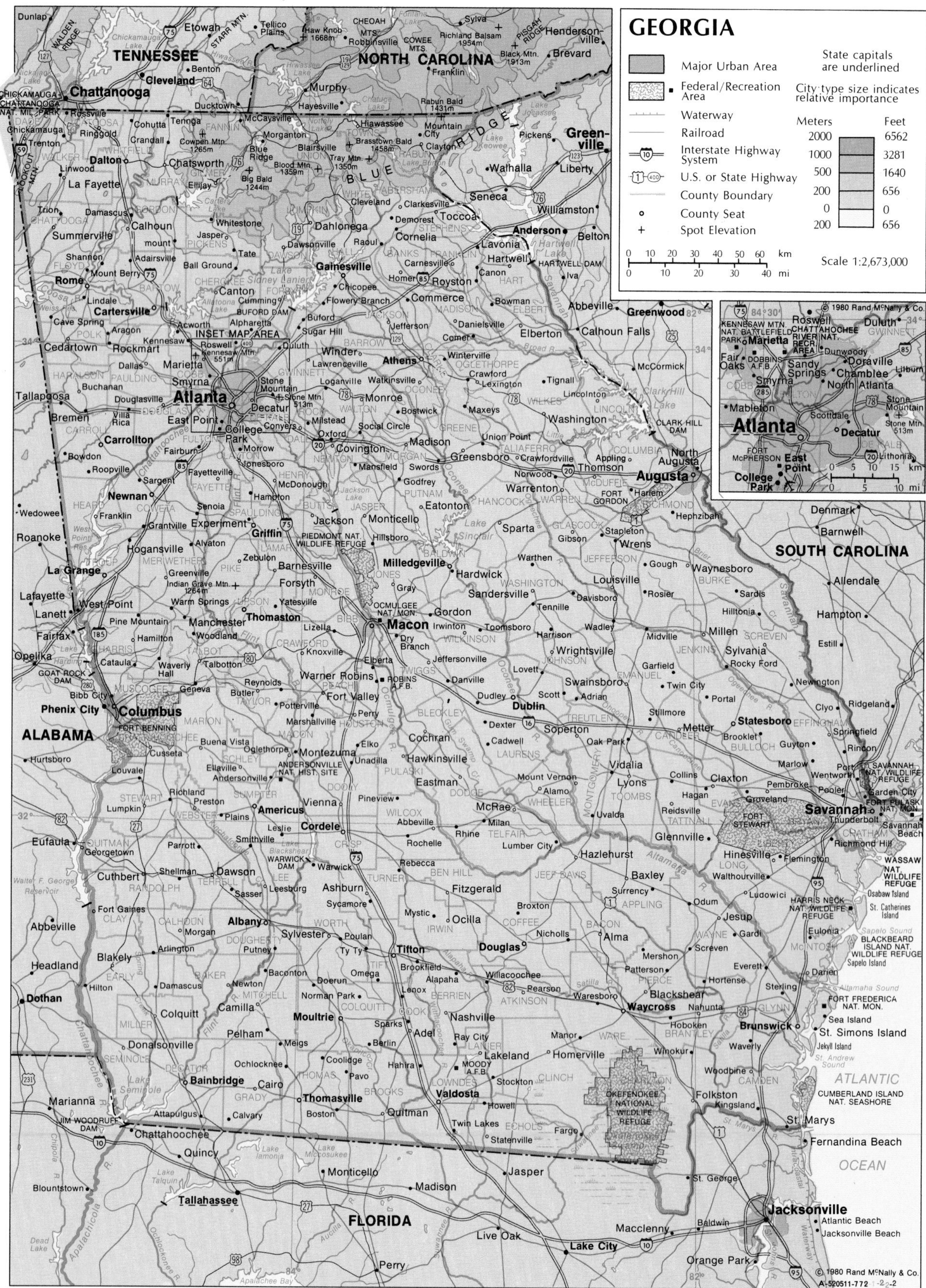
GEORGIA
Major Urban Area
Federal/Recreation Area
Waterway
Railroad
Interstate Highway System
U.S. or State Highway
County Boundary
County Seat
Spot Elevation
State capitals are underlined
City type size indicates relative importance
Meters
Feet
2000
6562
1000
3281
500
1640
200
656
0
0
200
656
Scale 1:2,673,000
km
mi
TENNESSEE
NORTH CAROLINA
SOUTH CAROLINA
ALABAMA
FLORIDA
ATLANTIC
OCEAN
BLUE RIDGE
Chattanooga
Cleveland
Dalton
Rome
Cartersville
Gainesville
Atlanta
Decatur
East Point
College Park
Marietta
Smyrna
Athens
Augusta
Macon
Milledgeville
Columbus
Phenix City
La Grange
Griffin
Newnan
Carrollton
Albany
Americus
Cordele
Tifton
Valdosta
Thomasville
Bainbridge
Moultrie
Waycross
Brunswick
Savannah
Statesboro
Dublin
Douglas
Jacksonville
Tallahassee
Anderson
Greenville
Greenwood
INSET MAP AREA
OKEFENOKEE NATIONAL WILDLIFE REFUGE
FORT BENNING
FORT STEWART
FORT GORDON
ROBINS A.F.B.
MOODY A.F.B.
PIEDMONT NAT. WILDLIFE REFUGE
CUMBERLAND ISLAND NAT. SEASHORE
FORT FREDERICA NAT. MON.
St. Simons Island
Sea Island
Jekyll Island
Fernandina Beach
St. Marys
© 1980 Rand McNally & Co.
A-520511-772

Okefenokee Swamp, extending from the southeastern part of Georgia into northern Florida, is the largest preserved freshwater swamp in the United States. A sizable portion of the swamp—1,189 km² (459 mi²)—designated the Okefenokee National Wildlife Refuge, is a sanctuary for threatened species, such as the American alligator, and for numerous varieties of migratory waterfowl.

Drainage. Most of Georgia's major river systems have headwaters in the uplands of north Georgia. The SAVANNAH RIVER follows much of Georgia's eastern boundary, and the Altamaha system drains eastern Georgia to the Atlantic. The CHATTAHOOCHEE and Flint rivers join the Appalachicola after draining much of western Georgia. Numerous dams have been constructed for power, flood control, and recreational purposes. Large areas of the Coastal Plain experience poor drainage, and rivers crossing this area are generally sluggish. The humid climate and limited use of water resources in south Georgia, however, furnish a basis for substantial future agricultural and industrial growth. In southwestern Georgia AQUIFERS underlay the soil and make irrigation possible.

PEOPLE

Georgia's population was 5,463,105 in 1980. Between 1970 and 1980 the population increased by 19.1%. Although the state's overall population density is 36 persons per km² (94 per mi²), it is considerably lower in most areas of the south Georgia plains and the northern mountains.

In 1980, 62.4% of Georgia's population lived in urban areas. ATLANTA, with a standard metropolitan statistical area population of 2,029,710 (1980), is the largest city and functions as the state capital, as a wholesale and retail center, and as the southeastern regional commercial center. Growth in the Atlanta area has been rapid for several decades. More than one-third of the total population of the state lives within Atlanta's metropolitan area. AUGUSTA, COLUMBUS, and MACON—the fall line cities—each has a metropolitan population of more than 200,000. SAVANNAH (1980 pop., 141,390) is Georgia's oldest city and has managed to retain its historic charm even while functioning as a major Atlantic port. The following smaller cities serve as regional centers: ALBANY, ATHENS, Gainesville, Rome, Valdosta, and Waycross. Forty percent of the rural population of Georgia is not economically involved in farming but instead works in factories.

Many of Georgia's early settlers came from Virginia and the Carolinas, bringing with them the plantation concept and slaves and thereby establishing early a demographic pattern that included large numbers of blacks and whites. In 1980 there were 1,465,457 blacks in Georgia, which comprised 27%

Atlanta, the capital and largest city of Georgia, is located in the north central portion of the state, bordering foothills of the Appalachian Mountains. Virtually devastated during the Civil War, Atlanta was rebuilt and is today a leading center of commerce and transportation in the southeastern states.

(Above) *A high-relief carving in the granite face of Stone Mountain is a memorial to Confederate leaders—Jefferson Davis* (left), *Robert E. Lee, and Stonewall Jackson* (not shown). *Gutzon Borglum designed and began carving the memorial in 1916, but the work was not completed until 1970.*

(Left) *Stone Mountain, which rises to a height of 513 m (1,683 ft) above the surrounding plain, is one of the largest granite monadnocks in the world.*

of the total population. The Baptists constitute the largest religious denomination in Georgia; Methodists, Presbyterians, and Roman Catholics are other religious groups with significant memberships.

Education. A system of statewide elementary and high schools is supported with state and local tax funds. Beginning in 1985 the state required that high school students pass a standardized test of minimum skills in order to graduate. Public higher education is organized as the University System of Georgia and includes junior colleges, 4-year colleges, and universities. (See GEORGIA, STATE UNIVERSITIES AND COLLEGES OF.)

Tourism and Recreation. Tourism is becoming a major economic activity. Georgia has numerous historic sites: Savannah, an early settlement center, which was built along exacting specifications; Atlanta and environs, the site of major Civil War battles; and the coastal zone with its relics of former plantation systems. Automobile traffic that crosses the state en route to Florida adds to the tourism income. The mountains and the Sea Islands are contrasting environments for the many summer vacationers from Georgia and surrounding states. Georgia has many state-supervised recreation areas.

Georgia's growth and progress in the past two decades is nowhere seen more sharply than in Atlanta and its environs. The city now has a symphony orchestra; boasts major league baseball, football, and basketball teams; and has become a major convention and culture center. Atlanta's location at the junction of several interstate highways at the southern end of the Appalachians makes it a crossroads city, benefiting from exchange and interaction with other regions. The folk art and culture of the mountain people have fostered crafts fairs and handwork exhibits, often in conjunction with music festivals.

ETOWAH MOUNDS, near Cartersville in northwestern Georgia, are remnants of prehistoric Indian constructions. To the west President Franklin D. Roosevelt's Little White House in WARM SPRINGS is now a national shrine. Tybee Lighthouse, still standing at the mouth of the Savannah River, was originally built in 1736 by James Oglethorpe; its replacement was reconstructed after the Civil War in 1867. STONE MOUNTAIN, with its Confederate memorial, is east of Atlanta.

Georgia's communications needs are served by daily and weekly newspapers. Numerous television and radio stations broadcast from within the state.

ECONOMY

Manufacturing and wholesale and retail trade account for about 60% of all nonfarm employment in Georgia. Although agriculture no longer dominates employment in Georgia, many workers still are engaged in industries related to farming and farm products. Poultry production is a major industry, with most processing plants centered in Gainesville in north Georgia. The mean per capita income in Georgia is somewhat below the national average.

Agriculture. Although greatly reduced as a source of employment, agriculture has undergone a major transformation. Georgia agriculture is modern and mechanized, and the former strong economic dependence upon cotton has been replaced with a diversified agricultural economy based upon the production of soybeans, corn, peanuts, tobacco, poultry, cattle, and horticultural and orchard crops. Much of Georgia's crop production is concentrated on the Inner Coastal Plain. The Piedmont, once an established farming region, is now characterized by farmers who operate small part-time cattle farms but who earn most of their income from employment in towns and cities.

Forestry. The extensive pine forests of the state are the basis for an important sector of the economy. Sawtimber and pulpwood for paper manufacturing are produced in large quantity. Georgia's forests are also noted as sources of tars and resins.

Mining. Although Georgia does not have a major mineral base, it ranks among the leading U.S. states in the value of its nonfuel mineral production. Granite and marble are quarried throughout the state. Kaolin, a fine-grained clay found in central Georgia, is a major export.

Manufacturing. Manufacturing in the South was a minor economic activity until well after the Civil War. In the late 19th century, however, new attitudes toward economic development, a surplus of agricultural labor, and cotton and power resources lured textile manufacturers from New England to the Piedmont. Poor and landless white tenants have taken advantage of this employment opportunity, but the surplus black agricultural laborers have joined the steady migrant stream to the North.

In the post–World War II years Georgia has undergone an economic revolution. The growth of textile manufacturing continues, particularly the carpet industry of northwest Georgia. Apparel manufacturing has become a leading Georgia industry and is primarily located in the many small towns and cities of rural areas. Other industries include transportation equipment, pulp and paper, food processing, and electrical machinery.

Transportation. The first settlements in the state developed along the waterways leading from the coast; after a decline, water transport is again gaining importance. Railroad and truck transportation serve the bulk of the state's transit needs.

(Above) *Tobacco, Georgia's second most valuable cash crop, dries outside a barn near Waycross. The city of Waycross was named for its location at a point where nine railroads and five highways converge.* (Left) *Georgia leads all states in the production of peanuts, a crop that contributes more than $500 million annually to the state economy. Peanut farming on a large scale began after a boll weevil infestation during the 1920s destroyed much of Georgia's cotton crop.*

Airlines, primarily in the Atlanta area, provide access to all major national cities.

Energy. The Tennessee Valley Authority power system does not serve the state, so Georgia must import fuel. Its proximity to the Appalachian coal field is advantageous. Hydroelectric plants along rivers contribute 20% to the power needs of Georgia; coal and natural gas fuel the remaining steam generators.

GOVERNMENT AND POLITICS

Georgia's ninth state constitution became effective in 1977 and provides for a government composed of legislative, executive, and judicial branches. The executive branch is headed by a governor who holds office for a 4-year term. Other officers include a lieutenant governor, attorney general, comptroller general, commissioner of agriculture, commissioner of labor, secretary of state, state superintendent of schools, and treasurer.

Legislative power is granted to a General Assembly that is composed of the Senate and House of Representatives. The judicial system includes a supreme court, a court of appeals, and superior courts. Local government is vested in cities and counties. Georgia is divided into 159 counties, most of which are governed by boards of commissioners.

From 1917 to 1962, Georgia's General Assembly members were elected through a county-unit primary system that allocated legislative seats on the basis of county population size. The least populous counties were represented by one legislator, while the eight most urban counties were allotted three representatives. This system gave the rural areas of the state an inordinately great opportunity to control legislation. In 1962 the U.S. Supreme Court declared the county-unit system to be unconstitutional. Since that decision, seats have been apportioned solely on the basis of population, independent of the number per county.

Georgia has been a Democratic state since the period following Reconstruction. Local and state politics remain overwhelmingly Democratic, but on the national level extremely liberal Democrats have been rejected by the basically conservative Georgia voters.

HISTORY

The earliest known inhabitants of present-day Georgia are thought to have been MOUND BUILDERS, predecessors of the CHEROKEE and CREEK Indians inhabiting the area at the time of European arrival. Hernando DE SOTO crossed Georgia in 1539-40, vainly searching for precious metals and gems, but he established no settlements on the mainland.

Savannah, the first European settlement in Georgia, was established in 1733 by James OGLETHORPE—a British general and member of parliament—for economic and philanthropic reasons. King George II of England granted a charter to Oglethorpe in order to provide a new home for the poor of England. In 1752 the trustees turned over control of the colony to the royal government. Georgia became actively involved in the AMERICAN REVOLUTION in 1778 when the British captured Savannah. This seizure was followed by the eventual British seizure of all Georgia except for Wilkes County, northwest of Augusta.

Settlement had first expanded along the coastal zone and Sea Islands. Interior settlement occurred later, between 1770 and 1840, when settlers moved southwestward from Virginia and the Carolinas. That it took nearly seven decades after 1770 to complete the settling process of the state was in no small part due to the resistance of the Creek and Cherokee Indians. In a series of land cessions, the Creeks were pushed westward from river to river, until by 1826 all Creek Indian lands had been seized. During the following 12 years the Cherokee Indians of north Georgia—an Indian nation remarkably advanced and rapidly acculturating—were also deprived of their territory. In 1838 the federal government forcibly removed the Cherokee people to lands in western territory, an exodus that would come to be known as the "trail of tears."

A restored home in Savannah reflects an Italian Renaissance revival style which had become popular in the antebellum South. An important port city on the Atlantic coast, Savannah was the site of the first English settlement in Georgia during the colonial period.

Portions of Georgia, such as the Pine Barrens of southeast Georgia and the southwest, remained sparsely populated until well after the Civil War. Along the coast and on the Sea Islands a black culture known locally as "Gullah" developed among the slaves tending the cotton and rice fields.

The advance of settlement between 1780 and 1840 was encouraged by improved cotton-ginning technology and the increased markets for cotton in Europe. The corollary of this was an intense demand for land, for slaves, and for the removal of Indians. The expansion of the planter system not only set distinctive demographic patterns but established a social, economic, and political structure that prevailed in the state well into the 20th century.

The CIVIL WAR was a period of disruption and destruction in Georgia. The Union army of General William Tecumseh SHERMAN crossed the state in 1864. After burning Atlanta in November of that year, he and his 60,000 men moved eastward, reaching Savannah in 29 days and leaving devastation in their wake. During RECONSTRUCTION the Georgia legislature's refusal to ratify the 14th AMENDMENT placed the state under military rule. Georgia was readmitted to the Union in 1870.

Although slavery was declared illegal, planters and ex-slaves adopted a tenancy system that kept many blacks and whites in poverty until the system's demise after World War II. In addition, few late 19th-century European immigrants coming to the United States settled in Georgia, leaving the prevailing social system undisturbed.

The decade of the 1920s was significant in Georgia's history because of the rapidity with which agriculture declined in the state. Boll weevil infestations during the period virtually destroyed the cotton crops, forcing workers off the land. The out-migration from the farms and from the state as a whole exceeded any movement into Georgia, but the population continued to increase because of a high birthrate. The great northward migration during this century, however, reduced the black population from the 47% of 1900 to 27% in 1980.

The post-World War II era has been one of economic development and new social attitudes—amounting to an economic and social revolution. Business has greatly expanded and many new jobs have been attracted to Georgia, especially to Atlanta and its environs. The state continued to prosper through the 1980s, a decade that saw setbacks in some other U.S. regions.

The CIVIL RIGHTS movement and its achievements in the 1960s have particularly altered urban life in Georgia. Blacks have united to become a political force in Georgia's cities and, in turn, a vocal element in the state and in the nation.

JAMES S. FISHER

Bibliography: Bartley, Numan V., *The Creation of Modern Georgia* (1983); Coleman, Kenneth, *A History of Georgia* (1977); Garrison, Webb B., *Oglethorpe's Folly: The Birth of Georgia* (1982); Hepburn, Mary A., *Local Government in Georgia* (1986); Hodler, Thomas W., and Schretter, Howard A., *The Atlas of Georgia,* ed. by Rebecca McCarthy (1986); Saye, Albert B., *Constitutional History of Georgia, 1732–1968,* rev. ed. (1970).

Georgia, state universities and colleges of

All of the colleges and universities in the University System of Georgia are coeducational and all offer the bachelor's degree; all but one grant graduate degrees. The **University of Georgia** (1785; enrollment: 25,230; library: 2,300,000 volumes) at Athens, the oldest state-chartered university in the United States, is a land-grant school. It has programs in the liberal arts and sciences and schools of law, pharmacy, journalism, veterinary medicine, and forest resources. **Georgia Institute of Technology** (1885; enrollment: 10,958; library: 1,600,000 volumes) at Atlanta has undergraduate and graduate curricula emphasizing chemistry, architecture, engineering, and business. Its library contains U.S. Atomic Energy Commission reports and U.S. Army Map Service maps. **Southern Technical Institute** (1948; enrollment: 3,610; library: 75,000 volumes), formerly a division of the Georgia Institute of Technology, is at Marietta. **Georgia State University** (1913; enrollment: 21,366; library: 912,875 volumes) at Atlanta and the **Medical College of Georgia** (1828; enrollment: 2,320; library: 112,000 volumes) at Augusta have undergraduate and graduate programs.

State colleges with liberal arts and teacher education programs leading to bachelor's and master's degrees are: **Albany State** (1903; enrollment: 1,893; library: 127,847 volumes); **Armstrong State** (1935; enrollment: 2,680; library: 132,000 volumes) at Savannah; **Augusta** (1925; enrollment: 4,091; library: 364,000 volumes); **Columbus** (1958; enrollment: 3,985; library: 195,080 volumes); **Fort Valley State** (1895; enrollment: 1,837; library: 166,910 volumes), founded as a land-grant college for blacks; **Georgia** (1889; enrollment: 3,795; library: 140,409 volumes) at Milledgeville; **Georgia Southern** (1906; enrollment: 6,526; library: 337,511 volumes) at Statesboro; **Georgia Southwestern** (1906; enrollment: 2,259; library: 136,705 volumes) at Americus; **Kennesaw** (1963; enrollment: 5,821; library: 110,000 volumes) at Marietta; **North Georgia** (1872; enrollment: 1,979; library: 111,257 volumes), a liberal arts military college at Dahlonega; **Savannah** (1890; enrollment: 2,011; library: 153,400 volumes); **Valdosta** (1906; enrollment: 6,095; library: 230,000 volumes); and **West Georgia** (1933; enrollment: 6,250; library: 248,657 volumes) at Carrollton.

Georgian Bay

Georgian Bay, in south central Ontario, Canada, is an inlet of Lake HURON, from which it is separated by the Bruce (or Saugeen) Peninsula and Manitoulin Island. It is 190 km (120 mi) long and 80 km (50 mi) wide and is the site of Georgian Bay Islands National Park. First explored (1615) by Samuel de Champlain, it was named for King George IV by an English naval officer.

Georgian poetry

Named after the reigning English monarch, George V, Georgian poetry emphasized the pastoral aspects of nature in traditional verse forms employing simple, direct language. It is represented in five anthologies edited by Edward Marsh between 1912 and 1922. Wordsworth was an important influence, but the Georgians lacked his philosophical vision and verbal intensity. Representative poets include Rupert BROOKE, Walter DE LA MARE, John DRINKWATER, Robert GRAVES, John MASEFIELD, and Wilfred OWEN.

KARL BECKSON

Bibliography: Ross, Robert H., *The Georgian Revolt: Rise and Fall of a Poetic Ideal, 1910–1922* (1965).

Georgian Soviet Socialist Republic

The Georgian Soviet Socialist Republic is one of the 15 constituent republics of the USSR. It is located in Transcaucasia, on the Black Sea, and borders on Turkey and the Armenian, Azerbaijan, and Russian republics. Its area is 69,700 km^2 (26,900 mi^2), and the population is 5,171,000 (1984 est.). The republic's capital is TBILISI.

The topography of Georgia consists of the Greater CAUCASUS MOUNTAINS in the north, a central valley, and the uplands of the Lesser Caucasus to the south. The climate varies from semiarid in the interior, where vineyards dominate, to humid-subtropical along the coast, where tea and lemons are grown.

The Georgians, who constitute 67% of the population, are a Caucasian language group with a distinct alphabet; and they adhere to the Eastern Orthodox religion. The major cities in addition to Tbilisi include Kutaisi (210,000) and Rustavi (142,000; 1984 est.).

Georgia is one of the few parts of the USSR climatically suitable for the cultivation of warm-weather crops. It supplies tea, citrus, wines, and fruits to the Soviet market. Tbilisi and Kutaisi are centers for the nation's silk textile and automobile industries. Important manganese deposits are mined at Chiatura. The mountainous terrain offers many sites for hydroelectric plants; the largest, on the Inguri River, began generating power in 1978.

Politically, the Georgian SSR encompasses 3 autonomous areas, each based on an ethnic group. The Abkhaz Autonomous Republic in the northwest, with an area of 8,600 km^2 (3,320 mi^2) and a population (1982 est.) of 513,000, is based on a Caucasian ethnic group. The Adzhar Autonomous Republic, on the Turkish border, has an area of 3,000 km^2 (1,160 mi^2) and 385,000 people, and is based on the Adzhars, Turkicized Georgians. The South Ossetian Autonomous Oblast, in the Greater Caucasus, covers 3,900 km^2 (1,500 mi^2) and has a population of 99,000, primarily Ossetians of Iranian-language stock.

Known to the Greeks and Romans as COLCHIS (western Georgia) and Iberia (eastern Georgia), the region adopted Christianity while under Byzantine influence in the 4th century. Between inroads by the Arabs, Mongols, Turks, and Persians, Georgian states flourished briefly in the Middle Ages and in the second half of the 18th century before union with Russia in 1801. The overthrow of the tsar in 1917 brought independence before the Bolsheviks assumed control in 1921. Nationalist feeling, which sparked several revolts in the early days of Soviet rule, was again expressed by mass demonstrations in 1989. THEODORE SHABAD

Bibliography: Allen, W. E., *A History of the Georgian People,* new ed. (1978); Lang, D. M., *The Georgians* (1966), *The Last Years of the Georgian Monarchy, 1658–1832* (1957), and *A Modern History of Soviet Georgia* (1962).

Georgian style

Georgian is the term applied to the architectural and decorative art styles that flourished in England during the reigns of the first four Georges (1714–1830). The period began with the revived Palladianism (see PALLADIO, ANDREA) of Richard Boyle, earl of BURLINGTON (Chiswick House, London; begun 1725), and the baroque style of William KENT. Toward 1750 the style lightened under the influence of the ROCOCO STYLE (Chesterfield House, London; now demolished), although the rococo was never completely accepted in England; it is seen in perhaps its purest form in the silver work of Paul de Lamerie (1688–1751). The rococo spirit encouraged outré styles such as Gothic and Chinese; all three can be seen in the furniture designs (published 1754–62) of Thomas CHIPPENDALE. German rococo porcelains strongly influenced those made in the factories of Chelsea (see CHELSEA WARE), Bow, and Derby. The rococo had virtually disappeared from the furniture designs (published 1788) of George HEPPLEWHITE, but from 1760 onward Robert ADAM's influential and increasingly refined neoclassical style appeared (see NEOCLASSICISM, art). Adam often designed every detail of his interiors, including furniture and carpets. The neoclassical equivalent in ceramics is seen in Wedgwood wares (see WEDGWOOD, JOSIAH). The architect Henry HOLLAND, much influenced by the French, carried refinement even further (Southill; 1795–99); refinement is also seen in Thomas SHERATON's delicate and rectilinear furniture designs (1791–94). The ages of walnut and mahogany were succeeded by that of satinwood. From 1800 the influences of Louis XVI and EMPIRE STYLE furniture, together with the archaeological Greek, Roman, and Egyptian designs of Thomas Hope (1769–1831), produced the REGENCY STYLE (until about 1840); it was accompanied in architecture by the GREEK REVIVAL. The rich and grand silverwork of Paul Storr (1771–1844) is Regency par excellence. The style coarsened until, by 1835, the decline of the classical tradition made Victorian eclecticism possible. JOHN MORLEY

Bibliography: Fry, Roger, *Georgian Art, 1760–1820* (1929; repr. 1977); Hussey, Christopher, *Georgian Houses,* 3 vols. (1988); Summerson, John, *Georgian London,* 3d ed. (1978; repr. 1989).

GEOS

GEOS (Geodetic Earth Orbiting Satellite) is a series of satellites developed for the National Aeronautics and Space Administration (NASA) as part of its overall program to study the Earth's surface, shape, and gravitational field. *GEOS 1* (also known as EXPLORER *29*) was launched on Nov. 6, 1965, from (then) Cape Kennedy by a DELTA vehicle into an orbit with an apogee of 2,280 km (1,414 mi), a perigee of 1,116 km (693 mi), and a period of 120 min. The initial satellite weighed 175 kg (385 lb) and carried an optical and radio Doppler beacon, range and range-rate transponder, and 322 small prisms to reflect laser beams from Earth. *GEOS 2* (also known as *Explorer 36*) was launched on Jan. 11, 1968; *GEOS 3,* launched on Apr. 9, 1975, weighed 336 kg (750 lb) and featured a 597-cm (235-in) boom, which acted to stabilize the satellite. The GEOS series added greatly to the knowledge of the Earth's true shape. A balloon satellite similar to ECHO and known as PAGEOS (Passive Geodetic Satellite) was not officially a part of the GEOS series but accomplished similar objectives.

GEOS (from Geostationary Scientific Spacecraft) is also the name given to a satellite developed for the European Space Agency to study the energetic particle flux and electrical and magnetic fields at a constant distance from the Earth. *GEOS 1* was launched by a Delta from Cape Canaveral on Apr. 20, 1977, but a rocket malfunction caused the satellite to enter into the wrong orbit. MITCHELL SHARPE

geosynchronous satellite: see SATELLITE, ARTIFICIAL.

geosyncline [jee-oh-sin'-klyn]

A geosyncline is a large, usually elongate depression in the crust of the Earth, which during subsidence has accumulated very great thicknesses (thousands of meters) of sedimentary, and usually also volcanic, rocks. Although some geologists have extended the concept of geosyncline to include any subsiding region that has accumulated a significant thickness of sediments, most now restrict the term to the large troughs from which the construction materials for strongly folded mountains originate.

EARLY THEORIES

The geosyncline concept originated in 1857 with the American stratigrapher and paleontologist James Hall (1811–98). On the basis of his extensive surveys in New York State and the Midwest, Hall observed that the areas that had the thickest accumulation of sediments subsequently became sites of extensive deformation and mountain building. Observing that fossils of shallow-water organisms were found throughout the extensive thickness of sediments, Hall concluded that water depths in the subsiding trough were generally shallow, and that the basin must have subsided slowly as it was filled with sediments. He further speculated that the weight of accumulating sediments was the cause of the subsidence.

The initiation and continuance of crustal subsidence by sediment weight alone, however, are contrary to the requirements of ISOSTASY; a volume of relatively light sediment cannot displace the same volume of the much denser mantle material on which the crust floats. This problem was recognized (1873) by James Dwight DANA, who coined the term *geosynclinal,* since modified to geosyncline. Dana realized that some additional force must cause the downwarping of the geosyncline, and that the release or reversal of this force allows the accumulated deposits to rise up as mountains. By the end of the 19th century it was commonly supposed that contraction of the Earth due to progressive cooling caused the folding. This idea faded with the advent of modern geophysics and the discovery of radioactivity, an internal heat source for the Earth. Geologists also began to find tensional, as well as compressional, features in geosynclines.

European geologists, meanwhile, were developing divergent views. Concentrating their studies on the Alps, they found evidence of deep-water deposition in that former geosyncline. This evidence conflicted with the predominant American view, based on studies of the Appalachians, that geosynclinal sediments originated primarily from shallow water. It soon became evident that both shallow- and deep-water sediments and fossils are to be found in the same geosyncline. The German geologist Wilhelm Hans Stille (1876–1966) distinguished in 1940 between the deep, rapidly subsiding eugeosyncline and the more slowly subsiding, shallow-water miogeosyncline. The eugeosyncline contains extensive volcanic deposits, and even though it accumulates the thickest deposits, not enough sediment reaches its depths to keep pace with subsidence. The miogeosyncline, which usually stands between the eugeosyncline and the craton (the central, relatively stable portion of the continent), contains virtually no volcanic deposits, and sedimentation rates here are almost always sufficient to keep up with subsidence. Geosynclines are typically formed along the margins of the craton and are evidently a result of the instability and geological mobility of the zone linking thick continental crust with low-lying, relatively thin oceanic crust.

THE GEOSYNCLINAL CYCLE

The development cycle of geosynclines has been a subject of intense interest during the mid-20th century. Geosyncline development often fits a general pattern. First, sediments accumulate in the subsiding geosynclinal trough along a cratonic margin, with volcanic materials and deep-water sediments accumulating in the peripheral eugeosyncline. Next, folding, deformation, and overthrusting centered in the eugeosyncline occur, often displacing eugeosynclinal deposits over the miogeosyncline. Third, metamorphism and placement of large intrusive igneous rock masses occurs, particularly in the eugeosyncline. This is followed by uplift of the eugeosyncline, formation of marginal troughs, and renewed sedimentation (see MOLASSE). The compressive stresses then relax, and trough basins form within the mountain range, often accompanied by outpourings of basaltic lava. Erosion then completes the cycle.

The task of modern geosyncline study has been the identification of modern geosynclines and the reconciliation of the geosynclinal cycle with PLATE TECTONICS. Here again American and European investigators have initially diverged. The U.S. model for the modern geosyncline is most often the marginal deposits of the Gulf of Mexico and the Atlantic coast. These reach geosynclinal thicknesses and show most of the characteristics of the miogeosyncline, but without the eugeosynclinal elements (deep-water sediments and volcanic rocks). European geologists have looked more to the deep-ocean trenches and the associated island-arc systems for a modern analogue of the ancient geosyncline.

Recognizing the profound differences among continental margins (previously cited by Stille), the British geologists A. H. Mitchell and H. G. Reading have attempted a synthesis of continental margins, geosynclines, and plate tectonics. They have identified five situations where contemporary geosynclines are forming. Among these, the most important distinction is the presence or absence of a deep-ocean trench, or SUBDUCTION ZONE. The Atlantic-type continental margin has no subduction zone; it is the trailing edge of a continent adjacent to a spreading ocean. The edge of the continent receives miogeosynclinal deposits, while deep-water sediments accumulate off the edge of the continent on the continental rise. The Atlantic-type margin corresponds to the earliest stages in the geosynclinal cycle. The Pacific-type continental margin has an active subduction zone in which ocean crust is consumed either immediately adjacent to the continent (west coast of Central and South America) or at some distance from shore (northwest Pacific). Fully developed eugeosynclinal activity, including active volcanism and intense deformation, comes with the development of the Pacific-type margin, which develops around a shrinking sea. The Pacific-type margin is apparently necessary to initiate mountain building. If the adjacent ocean is eventually completely consumed by subduction, the continents on either side collide, resulting in Himalayan-type mountain building.

PAUL S. BOYER

Geosynclines are long, narrow, seafloor depressions where thick layers of sediment from the adjoining crustal blocks accumulate (A) *as the sea bottom subsides* (B). *As the crustal blocks move together, large masses of sedimentary layers are squeezed together, folded, and uplifted to form geanticlines, or ridges* (C), *which, if above the water, divide the geosyncline into separate basins. The crustal blocks eventually move so close together that compressive forces fold and raise the sediment between them into mountain ranges* (D).

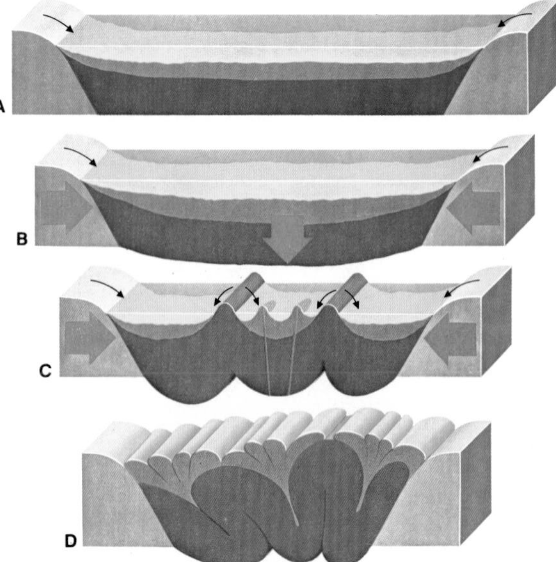

Bibliography: Burk, Creighton A., and Drake, Charles L., eds., *The Geology of Continental Margins* (1974); Jacobs, J. A., et al., *Physics and Geology*, 2d ed. (1974); Seyfert, C. K., and Sirkin, L. A., *Earth History and Plate Tectonics* (1973); Windley, Brian F., *The Evolving Continents* (1977); Wyllie, Peter J., *The Dynamic Earth* (1971).

geothermal energy

Geothermal energy is the heat energy that occurs naturally within the Earth. The molten interior contains vast quantities of thermal energy; although some diffuses upward to the surface and is dissipated, temperatures within the Earth remain fairly constant, apparently maintained by the decay of radioactive material. Geothermal energy therefore represents a potentially inexhaustible source of energy, which has been tapped by humans for centuries but, until recent years, only on a small scale (see ENERGY SOURCES).

In some regions of the world, particularly in the zone of tectonic activity surrounding the Pacific Ocean, MAGMA may occur at depths of only a few kilometers. GROUNDWATER trickling down to the hot rocks overlying the magma chambers can be heated to temperatures as high as 205°–260° C (400°–500° F). Where topography permits, the heated water may rise to the surface as HOT SPRINGS. In a few areas where the water is prevented from reaching the surface, some of it may turn to steam. Energy also can be derived from heated rocks in the absence of groundwater.

Heating Use. Geothermal fluids may be used directly for heating homes and greenhouses and for industrial purposes, if they occur near populated areas. Iceland is the most notable example. About 65% of its homes and much of its greenhouse produce depend on groundwater heat. Parts of Budapest, some Paris suburbs, and several communities in the Soviet Union are also heated in this way. In the United States, most of Klamath Falls, Oreg., and parts of Boise, Idaho, depend on geothermal heating. Examples of the industrial use of geothermal fluids are found in Iceland and New Zealand. In addition, such countries as Denmark and Sweden are experimenting with the use of geothermal fluids in heat-pump installations that also burn sewage.

Power Generation. The greatest potential for large-scale use of geothermal energy is in the generation of electric power. Geothermal steam has been used in Larderello, Italy, since 1904 to produce power. Other nations with geothermal power plants include China, Indonesia, Japan, Kenya, Mexico, New Zealand, the Philippines, and the Soviet Union. The largest plant in the world is in the United States, near Geyserville, Calif. (north of San Francisco), where steam has been used to produce power since 1960. The present generating capacity there is about 1,140 megawatts (MW), and the potential capacity is estimated to range up to 4,000 MW. Drilling into the steam pockets is a difficult process, however, and the steam itself is corrosive and contains dissolved gases, particularly hydrogen sulfide, that are difficult to remove.

No other region in the United States is known to possess geothermal steam in sufficient quantities, although the Pacific Northwest is under study. Sources of geothermal hot water are much more numerous, particularly in such western states as California, Nevada, New Mexico, and Utah. Much of this water has a temperature of only 95°–150° C (200°–300° F), too low for economic power generation by conventional methods. When the temperature is above 200° C (400° F), however, the water may be partially "flashed" into steam by reducing the pressure on it, and the steam can be used to drive turbines. Cooler water may be used to boil a secondary fluid, such as isobutane, whose vapor may then be used in special turbines. The efficiency of this so-called binary process may be increased by placing the heat exchangers at depth.

The use of geothermal water for power production is still in the development stage. Water at such sites as Salton Sea, Calif., is several times more saline than ocean water and thus poses serious design and operating problems. Also, because the temperature of geothermal water is relatively low, plants require vast quantities and are not very efficient. Furthermore, withdrawing geothermal water from geologically unstable regions may cause SUBSIDENCE and possibly earthquakes. One possibility being explored is the use of portable turbines that make use of both water and steam.

Also being studied is the use of hot rocks themselves to heat water for power production. Experimental projects are underway in Cornwall, England, and at Los Alamos, N. Mex. In the Los Alamos experiment, two deep wells have been drilled into solid rock. Cold water, forced into one of the wells at a pressure of 492 kg/cm^2 (7,000 lb/in^2), fractures the hot, crystalline rock, creating a network of cracks that increases the hot surface area. The water, heated to 190° C (374° F), is forced up the second well to the surface, where its heat is used to run a small electric power plant. It is then returned to the rock to be heated once more. Hot dry rock is found almost everywhere, but hotter rocks closer to the surface are more common in geologically active areas, such as the U.S. western mountain regions.

Outlook. Estimates of what proportion of U.S. electric power supply will be produced from geothermal energy by the year 2000 range from approximately 1% by the U.S. Bureau of Mines to at least 15% by some proponents of geothermal energy. The rapid growth anticipated in the 1980s, however, has been hampered both by lack of funding and by technological problems. J. S. DOOLITTLE

Bibliography: Bowen, R., *Geothermal Resources* (1980); Edwards, L., et al., eds., *Handbook of Geothermal Energy* (1982); Nemat-Nasser, S., ed., *Hydraulic Fracturing and Geothermal Energy* (1983).

See also: EARTH, HEAT FLOW IN.

Gera [gay'-rah]

Gera (1983 est. pop., 128,247) is a city in East Germany, located along the White Elster River about 55 km (35 mi) southwest of Leipzig. It is a rail and industrial center, producing machinery, tools, furniture, leather products, textiles, and musical instruments. Gera was first mentioned in written sources in 995. From 1564 to 1918, it served as the capital of the Reuss princes, whose castle (built 1686–1735) still stands. Gera was almost completely destroyed by fires in 1639, 1686, and 1780.

geranium [juh-rayn'-ee-uhm]

Geranium is the generic name of the cranesbills, or true geraniums, and is also commonly applied to the showy garden and greenhouse plants of the genus *Pelargonium.* Both genera are members of the geranium family, Geraniaceae.

The cranesbills include more than 300 species distributed throughout the cooler regions of the north temperate zone and the mountains of the Southern Hemisphere. Most are annual or perennial herbs with erect to spreading stems, deeply lobed, opposite leaves, and flowers with five sepals, five overlapping petals alternating with small glands, and ten stamens. Some are commonly cultivated. Among the best known are the blood-red geranium, *Geranium sanguineum,*

Florists' geraniums, genus Pelargonium, *are hardy house plants. The Martha Washington geranium* (left), P. domesticum, *and the common geranium* (right), P. hortorum, *are two popular varieties.*

and the meadow geranium, *G. pratense,* both natives of Europe and Asia with large, purple flowers, and the wild cranesbill, *G. maculatum,* a common woodland species of eastern North America with large, rose purple flowers.

The storksbills, or florists' geranium, genus *Pelargonium,* include about 280 species of mostly succulent perennial herbs, subshrubs, and vines native to southern Africa. Although similar to *Geranium,* the flowers of *Pelargonium* are irregular; two petals differ from the others in size, structure, or markings and lack glands between them. JOHN EBINGER

Bibliography: Yeo, Peter, *Hardy Geraniums* (1985).

Gérard, François Pascal Simon, Baron [zhay-rahr', frahn-swah' pahs-kahl' see-mohn', bah-rohn']

Baron François Pascal Simon Gérard, b. May 4, 1770, d. Jan. 11, 1837, was a French painter of historical subjects and portraits. He was a student of Jacques Louis DAVID, the foremost neoclassical artist (see NEOCLASSICISM, art) of the time, whose influence is visible in Gérard's noted work *Cupid and Psyche* (1798; Louvre, Paris). Gérard's success was assured in 1800 by the commission from Napoléon Bonaparte for his official portraits. Gérard painted almost 300 portraits of the most important people in France—for example, his elegant portrait of the *Comtesse Regnault de Saint-Jean d'Angély* (1798; Louvre). PHILIP GOULD

Bibliography: Friedlaender, Walter, *David to Delacroix,* trans. by Robert Goldwater (1952); Wilson, Michael, *French Paintings after 1800* (1984).

Gerasa [jair'-uh-suh]

The town of Jerash, located 48 km (30 mi) north of Amman, Jordan, is the site of the well-preserved remains of the Greco-Roman city of Gerasa. Probably founded by Semites, the settlement became important after annexation to the Roman province of Syria in 63 BC. This initiated a period of prosperity based on caravan trade, agriculture, and mining that reached its zenith in about AD 150. The city was organized along a grid of wide, colonnaded streets. These expanded at the two major intersections to form small, circular piazzas containing scenic four-pillar monuments and, at the south gate, a large oval forum. Other monuments include a triumphal arch, a stadium, two theaters, several baths, a fountain, and temples. The richly decorated sanctuary of Artemis dominates the town center, which also contains the well-preserved remains of 13 Early Christian churches. JOHN P. OLESON

Bibliography: Harding, G. Lankester, *The Antiquities of Jordan,* 2d ed. (1967).

gerbil [jur'-bul]

The large, naked-soled gerbil, Tater indica, *like other gerbils, is adapted to life in arid regions and rarely drinks water, obtaining almost all of the water it requires from the foods that make up its diet.*

Gerbils, family Cricetidae, are soft-furred, burrowing rodents inhabiting arid regions in Africa and Asia. They have elongated hind legs, with which they can make kangaroolike leaps, and, usually, long tails. The 100 or more species are grouped into 10 or 12 genera. The fur is usually of sand or earth colors, and the larger species, *Rhombomys,* may reach 200 mm (nearly 8 in) in body length. The popular American pet is the Mongolian gerbil, *Meriones unguiculatus.* Some species are called jirds, and one species, *Pachyuromys duprasi,* with a short, thick tail, is also called the fat-tailed mouse.

Gerhardt, Charles Frédéric [zhay-rahr', shahrl fray-day-reek']

The French chemist Charles Frédéric Gerhardt, b. Aug. 21, 1816, d. Aug. 19, 1856, was one of the first to treat organic compounds as a single structure in contrast to the earlier dualistic view, which held that they consisted of electropositive and electronegative parts. In close collaboration with Auguste LAURENT, Gerhardt classified organic acids and alcohols as members of homologous series and partially reformed atomic weight values and molecular sizes. In his theory of types, he classified organic compounds into water, ammonia, hydrogen, and hydrogen chloride types, in which an organic radical replaced a hydrogen atom or atoms (see ORGANIC CHEMISTRY).

AARON J. IHDE

geriatrics [jair-ee-at'-riks]

Geriatrics is the branch of medicine that treats the problems of AGING. It is more restricted in scope than gerontology, the scientific study of the clinical, biological, historical, and sociological aspects of OLD AGE.

Medical treatment of elderly persons presents a challenge, because many of them have numerous physical problems that complicate and interfere with diagnosis and treatment of any single illness. Diseases of one organ system place stress on other systems; furthermore, some diseases do not produce the symptoms in the elderly that are usually seen in younger persons. Many older people also have nutritional deficiencies because of limited incomes, poor dental status, and other problems (see NUTRITIONAL-DEFICIENCY DISEASES). In addition, the elderly run increased risks of complications from surgery, and convalescence takes longer because damaged tissues recover more slowly; the longer periods of bedrest can also lead to pneumonia, bedsores, and circulatory disorders. Drugs are metabolized more slowly, as well, and their effects are prolonged in the body.

Some diseases that occur in younger people become increasingly common among persons over the age of 65. Among them are CARDIOVASCULAR DISEASES: ATHEROSCLEROSIS, angina, other HEART DISEASES, and STROKE are common causes of disability and death. The elderly also have a higher incidence of CANCER, especially prostate cancer, multiple myeloma, chronic lymphatic leukemia, lymphoma, and basal cell carcinoma. Chronic diseases that develop earlier in life also often present severe health problems in the elderly because the metabolism becomes slower with age. For example, gangrene of the foot occurs in elderly persons with DIABETES mellitus because of poorer circulation in the extremities.

Some diseases are of special concern in the elderly, such as bone disorders (see BONE DISEASES). Thus OSTEOPOROSIS, or decrease in bone mass, mainly affects women after menopause; the bones become brittle, and even minor injuries can produce major fractures. Also limited to the elderly is PAGET'S DISEASE, the slowly progressive deformation of bone. Osteoarthritis (see ARTHRITIS), which affects all elderly persons to some degree, can also cause joint deformities, swelling, and pain. When the weight-bearing joints are affected, instability can result; this is a common cause of falling and FRACTURES. Some degenerative neurological diseases such as PARKINSON'S DISEASE occur almost exclusively among the elderly, as does accidental HYPOTHERMIA, the sudden drop in body temperature in response to cooler air temperatures; the latter effect is caused by age-related changes in the nervous system.

Mental disorders of physical or other origin are also a problem of old age. Thus senile dementia (see SENILITY) is a progressive deterioration of personality and intellect that can occur in the seventh and eighth decades of life. Several causes exist, including small vessel hemorrhages in the brain, viral infections of the brain, severe head injuries, tumors, alcoholism, vitamin deficiencies, pellagra, multiple sclerosis, and even lead or carbon monoxide poisoning. ALZHEIMER'S DISEASE, which is caused by deterioration of brain cells, has similar symptoms but begins in the fifth or sixth decades of life. In addition, DEPRESSION in the elderly can have symptoms almost identical to senile dementia; loss of interest in life, memory lapses, and living in the past are common in both conditions. Problems such as the loss of a spouse and friends, or the stress of living on a fixed income, account for the high frequency of depression in elderly persons; the suicide rate among persons over 65 is the highest of any age group.

Few medical schools in the United States offer training programs in geriatrics. In spite of the increasing over-65 population, fewer than 400 physicians in the United States were specializing in geriatrics by the late 1970s. The National Institute on Aging, which is part of the Public Health Service, funds most of the research on aging, and the American Geriatrics Society and the Gerontological Society promote education in geriatrics. MEDICARE and the Veterans Administration fund most of the health care for the elderly in the nation.

WILLIAM A. CHECK

Bibliography: Crandall, Richard C., *Gerontology* (1980); Ebersole, Priscilla, and Hess, Patricia, *Toward Healthy Aging* (1981); Exton-Smith, A. N., *Geriatrics* (1979); Hodkinson, H. M., *An Outline of Geriatrics* (1981); Reichel, William, ed., *Clinical Aspects of Aging* (1983).

Géricault, Théodore [zhay-ree-koh', tay-oh-dohr']

Best known for his painting *The Raft of the Medusa,* Jean Louis André Théodore Géricault, b. Sept. 26, 1791, d. Jan. 26, 1824, was one of the most gifted French artists of the 19th century. After studying for a time with Carle Vernet—about whom Géricault said, "One of my horses would have devoured six of his"—he became a pupil of Pierre Guérin. Géricault was deeply impressed by the impassioned military paintings of Antoine Jean GROS, and in 1812 he exhibited *The Charging Chasseur* (Louvre, Paris), a flamboyant Gros-like vision of valor. As a complement, he exhibited *The Wounded Cuirassier* (Louvre) at the Salon of 1814.

Géricault continued his studies in Rome in 1816–17, in part to escape from a scandalous love affair with his aunt. He drew many classical subjects (for example, *Centaur Abducting a Nymph;* Louvre) in a crude and rugged style with which he had experimented earlier, but he also sketched contemporary subjects. After witnessing the annual race of the riderless horses during the Roman carnival, Géricault began developing this theme in numerous studies for a monumental master-

The Raft of the Medusa *(1819), Théodore Géricault's interpretation of a disaster, was initially acclaimed more for its political implications than for its artistic merit. This painting embodies the emotionality of romanticism and the immediacy of realism. (Louvre, Paris.)*

piece, but he never carried this project through.

Géricault returned to Paris in 1818. The following year he caused a sensation with his *Raft of the Medusa* (Louvre), an enormous canvas depicting survivors of a shipwreck that the government had been blamed for mishandling. He turned this event into a monumental history painting, a heroic scene of ghastly suffering and Michelangelesque nude figures.

Géricault traveled to England in 1820, where he was impressed by the English painters of animals and by John CONSTABLE. In England he sketched English street life and painted *Racing at Epsom* (1821; Louvre). In 1822, Géricault returned to Paris in poor health and subsequently suffered a riding accident. He continued to paint genre scenes in the restrained manner that he had developed in England, and sometimes portrayed everyday scenes with a bleak grandeur (*The Lime Kiln,* 1822; Louvre). At the instigation of the psychiatrist Dr. Georget, Géricault painted a haunting yet objective series of portraits of the insane in 1822-23 (for example, *The Kleptomaniac,* Museum of Ghent).

KENNETH BENDINER

Bibliography: Berger, Klaus, *Géricault and His Work,* trans. by Winslow Ames (1955; repr. 1978); Eitner, Lorenz, *Géricault* (1982).

Gerlache de Gomery, Adrien de, Baron
[zhair-lahsh' duh gohm-ree', ah-dree-an' duh]

A Belgian naval officer, Adrien Victor Joseph de Gerlache, b. Aug. 2, 1866, d. Dec. 4, 1934, led a scientific expedition to Antarctica in 1897-99. When its ship, *Belgica,* got trapped in pack ice for 13 months, the party—which included Roald AMUNDSEN—became the first to spend a winter in Antarctica. Gerlache subsequently conducted oceanographic research in the Arctic and helped plan Ernest SHACKLETON's British Imperial TransAntarctic Expedition (1914-17).

germ warfare: see CHEMICAL AND BIOLOGICAL WARFARE.

Germain, Lord George [jur'-muhn]

George Sackville Germain, 1st Viscount Sackville, b. Jan. 26, 1716, d. Aug. 26, 1785, was British secretary of state for the American colonies during the American Revolution. He was known as Lord George Sackville until 1770 and then as Lord George Germain until he became Viscount Sackville in 1782.

Entering the British army, he was wounded and captured at Fontenoy (1745) in the War of the Austrian Succession. During the Seven Years' War he served as second-in-command of the Saint-Malo expedition in 1758. When he failed to lead a cavalry charge needed to complete the victory at Minden (1758), he was disgraced and dismissed from the service.

Germain virtually directed the Revolutionary War in America as secretary of state for the colonies—a position he held from 1775 to 1782. Many critics charged him with the British errors of strategy, but recent scholarship suggests that he was blamed too much. Germain had personality conflicts with Generals William Howe, Guy Carleton, and Henry Clinton, favored John Burgoyne and Charles Cornwallis in their independent-minded operations, and tried to control the conduct of the war too strictly from London. These measures contributed significantly to Britain's ultimate defeat. When his resignation was announced, two motions were introduced claiming the Minden incident made him unfit for a peerage, but he was nonetheless created Viscount Sackville.

GEORGE ATHAN BILLIAS

Bibliography: Marlow, Louis, *Sackville of Drayton* (1948; repr. 1973).

German Academy of Sciences at Berlin: see AKADEMIE DER WISSENSCHAFTEN DER DDR.

German art and architecture

German art and architecture, as defined in this article, refers to the artistic production of the many principalities and kingdoms that were united into a single German state in 1871. The art and architecture of Austria, although they share the same German cultural heritage, are treated in a separate article (see AUSTRIAN ART AND ARCHITECTURE).

THE CAROLINGIAN AND OTTONIAN PERIODS

Although the beginnings of German art can be traced back to pre-Christian times, it was not until the Carolingian age (8th and 9th centuries AD) that a significant artistic and architectural style began to emerge in the German lands. The Frankish king Charlemagne, whose realm included much of present Germany, and whose northern capital was the German city of Aachen, sought to revive the glories of the Roman Empire in both the political and the cultural spheres. He gathered scholars and artists at his court and imported entire libraries from Italy and Byzantium, providing local artists with classical (Roman) and Byzantine models. Byzantine influence can be seen in Charlemagne's Palatine Chapel (790-805) in Aachen, which is probably based on the church of San Vitale in Ravenna; classical influence is visible in the Carolingian Gatehouse at Lorsch, inspired by the Arch of Constantine in Rome (see CAROLINGIAN ART AND ARCHITECTURE). In the art of manuscript illumination, the *Godescalc Gospels* (781-83; Bibliothèque Nationale, Paris) shows how German artists of the period strove to integrate classical forms with their native tradition. The miniature *Christ Enthroned* from that manuscript blends the illusionism of classical imagery with the abstract Irish ornamentation characteristic of the north. The figure of Saint Matthew in Charlemagne's *Coronation Gospels* (800-10; Nationalbibliothek, Vienna) is derived from ancient depictions of philosophers and poets at work (see ILLUMINATED MANUSCRIPTS).

After the breakup of Charlemagne's empire in the 9th century, a period of political, economic, and cultural decline ensued, in which little artistic activity took place. These years of strife ended in the 10th century when Emperor Otto I and his successors (the Saxons, or Ottonians) reestablished stability in Germany. In the intervening period, ties between northern Europe and the Mediterranean cultural centers had loosened, and Ottonian architects and artists, though not entirely independent of Carolingian and Roman-Byzantine models, developed a vernacular style of their own (see OTTONIAN ART AND ARCHITECTURE).

This style is apparent in perhaps the most important ecclesiastical structure of the period, Saint Michael's church at Hildesheim (1001-31). Like the churches of the Carolingian period, it has a Roman basilican nave with symmetrical towers at the east and west ends, but it also has an additional transept and is entered from the north and south. An important innovation was the adoption both of the crossing square as a module for the dimensions of the nave and of the alternate support system that subsequently became a standard feature of many later medieval churches. The figures on the bronze doors (1015)

The Cathedral at Worms (1110–81) is typical of German Romanesque architecture, which was centered in the Rhineland during the 11th and 12th centuries. Seen in this view of the exterior are the eastern and western apses, with twin circular towers containing staircases, an octagonal tower with pointed roof crossing the nave, double bays and rib vaulting supporting the nave, and a small polygonal choir that was added in1234. The scale of the cathedral, which dwarfed other churches, was meant to symbolize the church's power. The height of the towers serves as an expression of the relationship between the Church and the spirit.

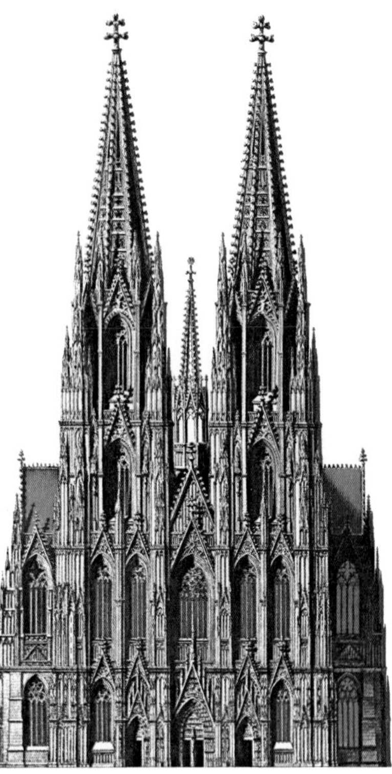

The soaring verticality and multiplicity of form displayed in the facade of Cologne Cathedral are typical of Gothic architecture. This, the largest Gothic church in northern Europe, was begun in 1248, but the nave and the two spires shown here, each 157 m (515 ft) high, were built between 1842 and 1890, from the original specifications.

of this church, which were cast in a single piece for the first time since ancient Rome, not only anticipate the reinstatement of large-scale sculpture in the period that followed, but also testify to the developing vernacular Ottonian style. In contrast to the classical calm of the *Coronation Gospels,* an expressive force characterizes the pantomimic poses and gestures of the bronze figures. Similarly, the wooden *Gero Cross* (969–76) expresses the suffering of the crucified Christ far more viscerally than any Carolingian or Early Christian work of art.

Such dramatic expression is often found as well in the manuscripts of the period. As the *Gospel Book of Otto III* (983–1002; Bayerische Staatsbibliothek, Munich) illustrates, many Ottonian illuminators also renounced the clarity, calm, and illusionism of classicism in favor of a heightened expressionism, manifested in the jerky gestures and hinged movement of the figures in the manuscript.

THE ROMANESQUE PERIOD

Following the death of the last Ottonian ruler in 1024, the Salian dynasty came to power, marking the beginning of the Romanesque period in Germany. Perhaps the most important achievement of the era was the development of the groin vault, which allowed architects to construct masonry ceilings that could both admit light and resist the fires that destroyed many pre-Romanesque structures with their flat, timber roofs.

Speyer Cathedral (1082–1106) is one of the earliest fully vaulted Romanesque churches, and its innovations made possible the later expansion of the Mainz and Worms cathedrals. Like most other Romanesque structures, it is blocky in appearance, and its exterior surface, in contrast to that of its Ottonian predecessors, is richly articulated, reflecting the cathedral's interior organization.

Other architectural developments of the period show the influence of the Cluniac and Cistercian orders spreading from France into Germany in the 12th and 13th centuries. Not only churches, but also chapter houses, dormitories, and other types of monastic buildings began to receive advanced architectural treatment.

Although elsewhere in Europe outdoor stone sculpture underwent a revival in the Romanesque period after its almost complete disappearance in the 8th and 9th centuries, this did not happen in German territories. Carved reliefs with figures, so ubiquitous on the exteriors of French, Spanish, and Italian Romanesque cathedrals, were exceptional in Germany, where the highest quality sculpture could be found instead on church furnishings such as choir screens, tombs, baptismal fonts, and reliquaries and in the form of small ivory carvings. Additionally, with the enlargement of windows in Romanesque cathedrals, stained glass became a more important art form. Among the most impressive remaining examples—and the only one still in its original location—is the cycle of five prophets in Augsburg Cathedral (*c.*1120–30).

THE GOTHIC PERIOD

The Gothic style was slow to take hold in German-speaking territories, and it was not until the second half of the 13th century, after the major French Gothic monuments had been built, that German cathedrals began to lose their Romanesque character. Two of the major examples of German Gothic architecture, Strasbourg Cathedral (nave begun 1235) and Cologne Cathedral (begun 1248), reflect the influence of French structures, the former of Saint Denis and the latter of Amiens.

Yet the Germans did make two unique contributions to European Gothic. The first originated in the north, where the lack of sandstone necessitated the use of brick in the con-

The Four Horsemen of the Apocalypse *(1498) is one of a series of 15 woodcuts by the German Renaissance painter and graphic artist Albrecht Dürer. In Dürer's imagination, God's final judgment falls on terrified humanity in the form of three soldiers who ride with Death.*

struction of Gothic architecture. This building material precluded the intricate detailing of Gothic sandstone cathedrals, thereby imposing an austerity and clarity of overall design quite unlike the complexity of southern Gothic structures. The second, the *Hallenkirche* (hall church), was probably of French origin, but it was developed most fully in the large urban centers of Germany. As is illustrated by an early example of this type, Saint Elizabeth at Marburg (1233–83), the aisles of these hall churches rise to the same height as the nave.

Early Gothic German sculpture also reflected French influence, as is evident in the *Bamberg Rider* (late 13th century), which, mounted on a pier in Bamberg Cathedral, bears stylistic similarity to the royal figures at Reims. Both this work and the sober *Ekkehart and Uta* (c.1250–60) from the choir of Naumburg Cathedral illustrate the growth of realism during the 13th century, which continued throughout the 14th and 15th centuries. Indeed, while Renaissance idealism flourished in Italy in the latter 15th century, contemporaneous Gothic German sculpture, particularly in the accomplished, yet very different hands of Tilman RIEMENSCHNEIDER and Veit STOSS, remained tied to the realistic and expressive late Gothic mode.

In the field of painting, the most important development was the evolution of painting on wood panels in the 14th century, and later on canvas. Though the influence of the Sienese dominated in the 14th and early 15th centuries, by 1450, Netherlandish sources were equally if not more important. In the north, Stephen Lochner (1400–51) joined the influence of Jan van Eyck with the tradition of the International Style to produce what is sometimes referred to as a "soft" or flowing style, quite unlike the blocky, "hard" forms of Konrad WITZ in the south. Martin SCHONGAUER, who was strongly influenced by Rogier van der Weyden, not only headed a large painting workshop, but was probably the century's most skilled northern master of the new technique of copper engraving, which was developed in the 1430s and widely replaced the woodcut by the second half of the century.

RENAISSANCE AND BAROQUE

Early-16th-century German art reflects a sudden awareness of the Italian Renaissance and its preoccupation with theory, humanistic subject matter, mythology, and history. Many German artists traveled to Italy to study the art and ideas firsthand, while others learned about it indirectly, through Italian engravings and printed treatises that made their way to northern Europe.

The greatest of the German Renaissance artists was unquestionably Albrecht DÜRER, who synthesized the realistic and expressive German with the more idealized, humanistic Italian tradition. An exceptionally talented painter of religious and secular themes, Dürer was also among history's greatest masters of the woodcut and engraving. Hans HOLBEIN the Younger was a particularly accomplished portraitist who, like Dürer, combined the monumentality and sculpturesque forms of Italian painting with the northern realistic tradition. Other

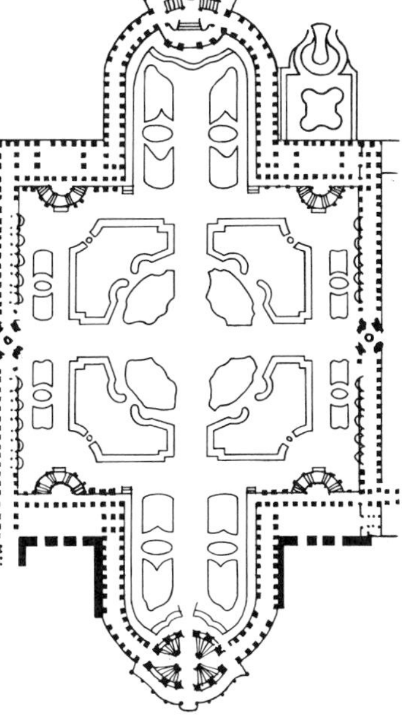

The Zwinger (1711–22) of the Dresden Palace is an open-air arena for ceremonies such as tournaments and festivals. This rare example of secular high baroque architecture in northern Germany was built by Matthäus Popplemann. The view on the left is of the West Pavilion, with sculptural decorations by Balthasar Permoser. On the right is the ground plan of the Zwinger, showing single-story galleries and stone pavilions arranged around a court with fountains and pools.

The interior of the church of the Benedictine Abbey at Ottobeuren, near Memmingen, Bavaria, typifies the south German rococo style of architecture. Designed by Johann Michael Fischer, it achieves a dynamic effect by decoration rather than structure.

German Renaissance artists of great accomplishment were Albrecht ALTDORFER, Lucas CRANACH the Elder, Hans BALDUNG-GRIEN, and Matthias GRÜNEWALD. The last was unique in his almost complete rejection of Renaissance classicism. A brilliant colorist, he was not interested in the construction of monumental, idealized figures in the Italian manner, and his celebrated *Isenheim Altarpiece* (*c.*1510–15) elevated the realism of the German tradition to new expressive heights.

The German Renaissance was remarkably short lived, for by 1530 the Reformation had effected an almost complete halt in the production of religious imagery, and painters in Protestant regions thereby lost the patronage of the church, formerly their best source of income. Many artists could support themselves only through book illustration and portrait painting, and for a number of them this was insufficient.

This dismal artistic climate continued throughout the mid-17th century in Germany, and it was not until well after the Thirty Years' War (1618–48) that a new generation of German artists could contribute to international artistic developments. This occurred above all in the field of architecture, which received considerable impetus from the numerous Italian and Austrian architects who, because of the dearth of capable Germans, had been called to Germany to execute architectural commissions. The leading German architects Johann Balthasar NEUMANN, the DIENTZENHOFER family, and the ASAM BROTHERS learned a great deal from such Austrians as J. B. Fischer von Erlach and Johann Lukas von Hildebrandt. Among the most remarkable examples of the late baroque-rococo style that flourished above all in Catholic Bavaria are Neumann's Vierzehnheiligen church near Bamberg (begun 1743), the Asams' Saint John Nepomuk (1733–46) in Munich, and the Ottobeuren Abbey church (1748–62) by Johann Michael FISCHER.

Characteristic to all is a decorative exuberance, established through the use of light, luminous color, undulating ground plans and structural forms, and the integration of architecture with painting and sculpture. Indeed, in many cases architects called on foreign artists to contribute painted and sculptured additions to their structures, and perhaps the greatest frescoes of the period were executed by the Italian painter Tiepolo in the Würzburg Residenz (1751–53). (See BAROQUE ART AND ARCHITECTURE.)

NEOCLASSICISM AND ROMANTICISM

The neoclassicists of the late 18th and early 19th centuries turned again for inspiration to the art of ancient Greece and Rome. Their ideas were articulated by the German painter Anton Raphael MENGS in his treatise *Considerations on Beauty and Taste in Painting* (1762). Neoclassicism taught that the arts should serve an educational function, and the foundation of many German museums in the 19th century, as well as academies of art in Berlin, Munich, Düsseldorf, and Dresden, owed much to the impact of neoclassical theory. The leading architect of the period was Karl Friedrich SCHINKEL, whose many buildings in Berlin include the New Guard House (1818), the Schauspielhaus (1821), and the Altes Museum (1824–28). Leo von KLENZE had a similar impact on Munich through his city planning, as did Gottfried SEMPER in Dresden.

Paralleling the growth of neoclassicism was an interest in romantic themes and styles, particularly among painters. Artists such as Caspar David FRIEDRICH, Philipp Otto RUNGE, and the Nazarene artists Johann Friedrich OVERBECK, Peter von Cornelius (1783–1867), and Karl Philipp Föhr (1795–1818) all rejected the academic and classical direction and pursued an art based on either landscape or literary and biblical themes. Painters of the middle and late 19th century, including Adolf von MENZEL, Wilhelm LEIBL, and Max LIEBERMANN, became increasingly interested in a realist aesthetic, though some, such as Anselm FEUERBACH and Hans von Marées (1837–87), continued to paint in a classicizing vein.

THE TWENTIETH CENTURY

A number of regional expressionist groups developed early in the 20th century. Composed of Wassily KANDINSKY, Alexey von JAWLENSKY, Franz MARC, and Paul KLEE, among others, Der

The German Romantic painter Caspar David Friedrich painted the awesome Landscape on the Island of Rügen *in 1818. The human figures in the foreground are dwarfed by the grandeur of the white cliffs and the sea beyond. (Sammlung Oskar Reinhart, Winterthur.)*

(Right) *A pioneering example of modern architecture, the Fagus shoe last factory (1911) at Alfeld-an-der-Leine, near Hildesheim, West Germany, was the first structure to be built with the metal and glass curtain walls that became standard in the later International Style. It was designed by Walter Gropius and Adolf Meyer; Gropius went on to become (1919) the founder of the Bauhaus, a school that had a decisive influence on 20th-century architecture and design.*

(Below) *Max Beckmann's* The Night *(1918–19) is a chaotic group of figures engulfed in despair. The work expresses the fear and confusion of the German people during World War I. (Kunstsammlung Nordrhein-Westfalen, Düsseldorf.)*

BLAUE REITER (The Blue Rider) society was established in Munich, its idealistic purpose being to rejuvenate society through a spiritual art based on the intimate relationship of man and animal to nature. The leading spirit of the group was Kandinsky, whose paintings reached the verge of abstraction about 1910. In contrast, Die BRÜCKE (The Bridge) painters—Ernst Ludwig KIRCHNER, Emil NOLDE, Erich HECKEL, and Karl SCHMIDT-ROTTLUFF, among them—pursued a more intense, directly expressive art similar in sensibility to the primitive objects from which it drew inspiration. Centered in Dresden and later in Berlin, the art of Die Brücke was one of fierce expressionism, as opposed to the more lyrical style of Der Blaue Reiter.

Also predominant in the early decades of the 20th century was an interest in the applied arts. This movement has its roots in the Jugendstil (style of youth) of the 1890s, when artists such as August Endell (1871–1915), Peter BEHRENS, Bernhard Pankok (1872–1943), and Hermann Obrist (1863–1927) applied their taste for organic, curvilinear forms of both the fine and decorative arts, including paintings, typography, furniture design, and crafts of every sort. The rapid industrialization of Germany soon found expression in the Werkbund movement, which involved the creation of an expressly modern and functional design vocabulary that might be applied to the products of machine technology. Although this positivist approach to art and industry was interrupted by World War I, the widespread devastation of Germany during the years 1914–18 only encouraged the social concerns of artists, designers, and architects in the 1920s.

The applied art movement reached its fullest expression in the BAUHAUS (house of building), founded in Weimar in 1919 and subsequently located in Dessau and Berlin. Led by architects Walter GROPIUS, Ludwig MIES VAN DER ROHE, and Marcel BREUER, and by painters and sculptors such as Oskar SCHLEMMER, László MOHOLY-NAGY, Lyonel FEININGER, and Josef ALBERS, the Bauhaus sought to apply the most advanced, and generally geometric, formal concepts to the arts. It became the 20th century's most influential school of architecture and design.

A more cynical response to World War I and modern culture was expressed by the Berlin Dada group. Politically motivated, and responding to the militarism associated with the war, artists such as Georg GROSZ, Otto DIX, Raoul Hausmann (1886–1971), and Richard Huelsenbeck (1892–1974) assaulted the Weimar government through their polemical art. Often manipulating photography and collage, while issuing rhetorical campaigns against the state, the German form of Dada, though short-lived, was nevertheless an aggressive application of art for political purposes. The post–World War I period also produced a number of great yet essentially independent artists, among them Max ERNST and Kurt SCHWITTERS and the expressionist Max BECKMANN.

All these progressive movements were brought to a standstill by the rise of Nazism in the early 1930s. In 1937 the work of Germany's most accomplished vanguard artists was exhibited in the notorious Entartete Kunst (degenerate art) exhibition in Munich. Abused and mistreated by the Nazis, most of the work in the exhibition was sent to Switzerland, where it was sold at auction. Faced with the loss of their livelihood at the hands of censors, and unable to purchase art supplies legally, most of Germany's most advanced artists and architects emigrated to France or the United States. Under Hitler's direction, the avant-garde was replaced by a highly political form of neoclassical painting, sculpture, and architecture, much of which was destroyed at the conclusion of World War II.

Although Germany produced little important art in the decade following World War II, since 1960 influential work has again been produced on German soil, particularly in the form of expressionist painting. The predominant figure in this development has been Joseph Beuys (1921–). As a teacher at the Art Academy in Düsseldorf in the 1960s, and through his own work, Beuys has influenced such painters as Anselm Kiefer (1945–), Jörg Immendorf (1945–), Georg Baselitz (1938–), and Markus Lüpertz (1941–). While working in a variety of expressive painting modes, these artists have all dealt in their work with the problems of being an artist in the late 20th century and with themes relating to German literature and culture. Notable among contemporary West German architects is Gottfried BÖHM.

MARIA MAKELA

Bibliography: Lindemann, Gottfried, *History of German Art: Painting, Sculpture, Architecture* (1971); Metropolitan Museum of Art, *German Masters of the Nineteenth Century: Paintings and Drawings from the Federal Republic of Germany* (exhibition catalogue, 1981); Metropolitan Museum of Art, *Gothic and Renaissance Art in Nuremberg, 1300–1550* (exhibition catalogue, 1986); Picton, Harold, *Early German Art and Its Origins from the Beginnings to about 1050* (1939); Roh, Franz, *German Art in the Twentieth Century* (1968); Royal Academy of Arts, London, *German Art in the Twentieth Century: Painting and Sculpture, 1905–1985* (exhibition catalogue, 1985).

German and Austrian music

From medieval times until the mid-20th century composers working in the German-speaking countries of central Europe created a rich and varied literature that has come to be regarded as the backbone of the Western art music tradition. Obviously, composers working elsewhere also made important and unique contributions, many of which left traces on the German style. Italy, for instance—an important center of musical activity from the end of the medieval era through the late 18th century—originated not only opera, but early forms of the instrumental sonata and concerto and the vocal cantata. The French turned some of these Italian forms to their own uses, revamping them to reflect a local concern for courtly elegance, and thereby giving them a recognizably Gallic form. Together with composers from Italy and the Netherlands, French musicians forged the basis of the polyphonic style, in which several melodic parts proceed simultaneously.

The Germans at first resisted many of these foreign developments; when they adopted them, however, they brought them to extraordinary heights of sophistication. By the beginning of the 19th century, German and Austrian composers were creating new forms and genres of their own. The classical style—a proportioned approach to organizing thematic and harmonic materials that informs the sonatas and symphonies at the core of the modern concert repertoire—was largely developed in the German musical centers (especially Vienna) in the late 18th and early 19th centuries. As this classicism unfolded into romanticism, with its grander structures, the Germans and Austrians retained the historical initiative, and they held it firmly into the 20th century.

THE MIDDLE AGES

Although today West Germany, East Germany, and Austria are three separate countries, historically they form a single cultural region, the musical history of which is tied to both its geography and its political and religious development. Its location in the center of Europe made it a crossroads for cultural ideas.

In its origins, the German musical tradition was influenced by those of the ancient Romans, the Magyars, the Slavs, and the early Germanic peoples themselves. It can be precisely traced from the early Christian era, when the Gregorian chant, or PLAINSONG, served as a uniform code by which religious observance could be celebrated in music. In Austria the use of plainsong dates back to the 5th century, and it flourished at monastic centers in Salzburg and elsewhere in the 8th century. At that time, the lands that were to become Germany were part of the Frankish empire, which reached its height under the rule of Charlemagne. In 843 the German lands were partitioned from those corresponding to present-day France and Italy; in 962 the German-dominated Holy Roman Empire was founded when Otto I (the third in the line of German kings) was crowned emperor by the pope.

Because the early German monarchs regularly moved their courts, centers of court life (and its attendant musical traditions) did not immediately take root. As in Austria, however, the monasteries remained centers of musical activity. By the 10th and 11th centuries, German monks were compiling musical treatises by the dozens, some of these addressing the subject from a purely philosophical point of view, others dealing with practical concerns. In practical terms, in fact, the German monks were introducing variants into the traditional plainsong formulas, in the hope of highlighting the chants' expressive qualities. This led to freer, inspired compositions, such as the extraordinary sequences, hymns, and songs of the Abbess Hildegard von Bingen (1098–1179), probably the first great woman composer and certainly one of the era's great intellects. Besides her numerous compositions, she wrote a morality play, plus texts on medicine, nature, and sacred topics. She also corresponded with popes, emperors, and kings, who regularly sought her advice.

Outside the abbeys and monasteries, religious music was taking another form. A folk-music tradition had slowly emerged in Germany, and as it developed, German missionaries turned it to sacred use, creating a parallel literature of sacred folk songs, sung in the vernacular rather than in Latin.

The vernacular tradition in court music, from the 11th through the 14th century, was reflected in the art of the minnesinger. Influenced by the French troubadours and trouvères, but writing in a style that also reflected the gestures of native folk melodies and even plainchant, the minnesingers composed chivalric epics of courtly love, usually in a monodic style (one melody line, accompanied instrumentally). Among the greatest of the minnesingers were WALTHER VON DER VOGELWEIDE, NEIDHARDT VON REUENTHAL, and Heinrich von Meissen (known as Frauenlob, c.1255–1318). The minnesingers were often of noble birth, but by the 14th century they were supplanted by the MEISTERSINGERS—primarily middle- and lower-class artisans—who established guilds and schools for the cultivation of their compositional craft. The meistersingers cultivated a conservative style, devoid of the polyphony that composers of other countries were exploring.

THE RENAISSANCE AND EARLY BAROQUE PERIODS

Polyphony began making headway in Germany in the 15th century when the Netherlands-born composers Heinrich ISSAC and Roland de LASSUS (Orlando di Lasso), along with such native composers as Ludwig Senfl (1490–1543), expanded the languages of court and church composition, both in Vienna and in the larger German cities. Instrumental music also came of age at this time; dance music was played in the home, and in the church, performance on the organ was more highly developed in Germany than anywhere else in Europe. Music was, by this time, the province not only of the court and church, but of town governments, which often employed musicians for civic purposes.

In the 16th century the Protestant Reformation had a strong effect on the music of the German cities that came under Martin Luther's influence. The primary musical expression of Luther's reformed church was the CHORALE—a polyphonic setting of a simple sacred hymn, sung in the vernacular. These hymns were extremely popular when they were introduced, and they held the central place in Lutheran church music for more than a century. Their popularity was abetted by the newly invented printing press, which had been turning out music books in Germany as early as 1511 and which was quickly put to the task of producing Luther's hymnals. In Austria, Lutheranism and its church music reigned only briefly: by 1600 the chorale tradition there was in decline.

One of the few Germans whose sacred music did not rely heavily on the chorale was the 17th-century composer Heinrich SCHÜTZ, the first German composer to compose works that fully reflected the developments of the Netherlands and Italian composers of the time. Consequently, his distinctive and vital choral settings (usually on biblical texts) came to be renowned throughout Europe. Schütz also composed a now-lost opera, *Dafne,* in 1627, long before the genre became fashionable in Germany.

Quite a few German composers of the 17th century left works that have survived not only as fine historical examples, but as lively music that has remained in the active repertoire. Michael PRAETORIUS, in his *Syntagma musicum,* offers vivid examples of dance and instrumental work popular in his day, and composers such as Johann Jacob FROBERGER, Johann PACHELBEL, Jan Reincken (1623–1722), and Dietrich BUXTEHUDE brought refinements to the art of solo keyboard writing.

THE LATER BAROQUE

These composers were the immediate predecessors of Johann Sebastian BACH, who as a young man studied their works and probably heard some of them play. For posterity, the figure of Bach dominates the first half of the 18th century; in his own time, he was more highly regarded as a keyboard virtuoso than as a composer, primarily because he devoted himself to perfecting the ornate contrapuntal style of his predecessors, at a time when younger composers—including his own sons, Johann Christian BACH and Carl Philipp Emanuel BACH—were developing the more streamlined *stil galant* (elegant style), which pointed the way to the classic era.

From today's perspective, Bach's music stands as the culmination of the polyphonic style that began in the Renaissance. Among his legacy are four brilliant orchestral suites, concertos for the violin, keyboard, and various wind instruments, the Brandenburg Concertos, hundreds of choral works (ranging from small- and moderately scaled motets and cantatas to the grander Passion settings), and a large body of works for solo violin, cello, organ, lute, and harpsichord. His most astonishing compositions, however, are a group of pieces probably intended as exemplary treatises and not performed during Bach's life. Among these are the Mass in B Minor, the two books of *The Well-Tempered Clavier,* and the work Bach died before completing, *The Art of Fugue.*

George Frideric HANDEL and Georg Philipp TELEMANN were Bach's contemporaries, but they were far more cosmopolitan than he—and far more famous. Handel left Germany fairly early, traveling through Italy (where he became enamored of opera) and finally settling in England, where he composed his best known orchestral works and oratorios. Telemann, who held a variety of posts in Germany and Poland (where he absorbed some of that country's colorful folk influences) before settling in Hamburg, was the most prolific of them all: among his works are 40 operas, 600 orchestral suites, 44 Passion settings, 700 cantatas, and countless concertos and sonatas.

Telemann wrote in a simpler, more direct style than Bach or Handel—a style that reflected the public's weariness of dense, cerebral counterpoint and its preference for well-crafted but light-spirited dance music and unadorned but emotionally direct sacred works. The new style was also, however, a more overtly dramatic one: individual movements were composed of contrasting themes, which despite the music's veneer of simplicity, had to be carefully balanced. This change in taste reflected a change in the social structure of music making in the wake of the Thirty Years' War. As the resources of the German towns were depleted by the war, the municipally supported guilds gave way to amateur, but highly polished, ensembles of university students and other part-time players.

THE CLASSIC ERA

In the 1740s, however, Berlin, Dresden, and Mannheim emerged as centers where orchestras (and orchestral music) grew and flourished. In Berlin, Frederick the Great (Frederick II of Prussia)—a composer himself—brought together an orchestra that included C. P. E. Bach, the flute virtuoso and theorist Johann Joachim QUANTZ, and other brilliant players. He also established an opera house there. Mannheim, too, was known for its large and brilliantly polished orchestra, which its composers—among them Johann Stamitz (see STAMITZ family) and Franz Xaver Richter (1709–87)—exploited in a unique symphonic style that used dramatic dynamic contrasts.

By the end of the 18th century the front line of musical development shifted to Austria, where Franz Joseph HAYDN, beginning under the patronage of the Hungarian Esterhazy family in the 1760s, established himself in the following decades as the most esteemed composer of his time. The Esterhazy princes proved to be generous patrons who let Haydn experiment freely with forms and ensemble deployments; as a result, he was able to shape the string quartet, symphony, and sonata into their modern forms. Expanding on the *stil galant* notion of contrasting themes, for instance, he wrote works that were the embodiment of the sonata form—essentially a two-theme, three-part symmetrical structure containing an exposition, a development section, and a recapitulation (thus quite distinct from the early two-part Italian sonata form). In his late years Haydn worked as a composer-at-large, fulfilling commissions from Paris and London, and considering Vienna his home. All told, he composed 104 symphonies, plus chamber works, operas, and oratorios.

Haydn is said to have predicted the preeminence of Wolfgang Amadeus MOZART when Mozart was just a child, and indeed, the young Mozart was one of music's most brilliant prodigies. Under the tutelage of his father, Leopold, he learned the basics of composition as well as keyboard and violin performance, and before he was ten years old he had astounded Europe's royalty with his abilities and composed his first symphonies. Eventually he would compose 41 of these (although some musicologists argue that certain overtures should be counted into the total, bringing Mozart's complete symphonic output to more than 60), steadily improving on the structural integrity of the form while couching it in a brilliantly expressive language.

Mozart excelled at every genre he essayed, from chamber music to solo piano sonatas, orchestral works, and opera. Yet while the music flowed from his pen with astounding speed, it nevertheless bears a consistent stamp of genius. In opera, Mozart began by working within the newly sprouted tradition of the singspiel, a German-language genre that combines the spoken dialogue of the comic theatre with musical interludes and arias. His contributions—including *The Abduction from the Seraglio* (1782) and *The Magic Flute* (1791)—are not only the genre's greatest examples, but paved the way for the more ambitious forms of German opera that would evolve during the following century.

Haydn and Mozart began a revolution in music that was brought to fruition in the works of Ludwig van BEETHOVEN. Born in the Rhineland, Beethoven moved to Vienna to study with Haydn and spent the rest of his life there. These were heady times: in literature and art, the age of romanticism was dawning; in the political world, revolution was in the air. On the heels of the American and French revolutions, antimonarchist sentiments sprang up in Germany, along with declarations of liberty and equality for the nonaristocratic masses.

Johann Sebastian Bach (left) *was the greatest German composer of the baroque period, but his genius was recognized only after his death. Wolfgang Amadeus Mozart* (center) *and Ludwig van Beethoven* (right), *who followed him, were European celebrities in their own lifetimes.*

Beethoven was caught up in this revolutionary and romantic fervor, and although his patrons were members of Vienna's aristocracy, he made it clear that he considered himself their equal (or perhaps their better) by virtue of his talents.

His aristocratic friends did not challenge him. Beethoven's early works show an affinity for the style of Haydn—but also an impatience with the constraints of the classic style. In 1804 (by which time he was almost entirely deaf), he embarked on what he called "a new way," unveiling his Third Symphony (the *Eroica*)—a work of enormous proportions, for the time, and an implied internal program that showed Beethoven grappling with the romantic notion of a heroic ideal. Thereafter, many of his works seemed to deal with idealized, lofty concepts, and in the spirit of the romantic literature he was reading (particularly the works of Goethe, for whose play *Egmont* he composed incidental music), he heightened the dramatic contrasts of his musical language in order to capture the passions and the conflicts implicit in his subjects. His output was much smaller than Bach's, Haydn's, or Mozart's. There were only 9 symphonies, 5 piano concertos, 1 violin concerto, a single opera (*Fidelio,* recast several times between 1803 and 1814, and never entirely successful), 32 piano sonatas, and chamber music (including 16 progressively brilliant string quartets). The expanse of ground, however, that this body of work covers is phenomenal.

THE ROMANTIC AGE

The generations that followed Beethoven looked up to him as a towering musical giant whose footsteps could never be adequately filled. Yet several of the German and Austrian composers who ventured forth in Beethoven's shadow found that while he had pointed the way toward the expressive romantic style, he had by no means explored all the available routes. Thus the rest of the 19th century was populated by a stream of individual stylists. Working in Vienna, Franz SCHUBERT composed music that, while less stormy than Beethoven's, was equally passionate. Schubert expressed these passions through his sweetly harmonized chamber works, symphonies, and piano sonatas. The medium he excelled in, however, was the song, or lied, of which he composed some 600. Using the sparest of performing forces—a solo voice, with piano accompaniment—Schubert set lengthy cycles of poems in a way that made the cycle's organic development clear while delving into the fine shades of emotion that each phrase in each song was meant to convey.

In Germany, meanwhile, Felix MENDELSSOHN composed an array of orchestral, choral, and chamber works that were as exquisitely melodic as Schubert's, while Robert SCHUMANN expressed himself most successfully through the piano. Schumann was a more eccentric composer than Schubert, and his music is less consistently well wrought. Many of his pieces, however—for instance, his *Papillons,* the *Symphonic Etudes,* and *Carnaval*—contain an ingenious spark. Schumann's wife, Clara Wieck (1819–96), was also a talented composer, although she made her reputation primarily as a pianist.

This drawing by Erald Kaiser, done in 1847, portrays Robert and Clara Schumann. Inspired by the German romantic school of poetry, both Schumann and his wife composed piano music and vocal songs renowned for their elegance and melodic clarity. During this period song (lied) *composition flourished in German music.*

Besides composing, Schumann published a journal of musical criticism and philosophy, wherein he appraised the work of his predecessors and contemporaries. One young composer he was particularly impressed with was Johannes BRAHMS, a native of Hamburg whose conservative inclinations led him to compose works that looked back at classical structural models while taking full advantage of the large-scale romantic orchestra, with all its thunder and coloration. His four symphonies are extensions of what he considered a Beethovenian ideal, as (on a smaller scale) are his finely crafted chamber works. Like many of his contemporaries, Brahms also addressed himself to lieder, and although these have been generally overlooked, many of them are as beautifully expressive as Schubert's.

GERMAN MUSIC DRAMA

If Brahms represents the conservative side of 19th-century music, Richard WAGNER was the radical force intent on driving the art forward. Wagner's métier was opera, a form that had come of age, in Germany, with the works of Carl Maria von WEBER. In *Der Freischutz* (1821) and *Euryanthe* (1823), Weber took a crucial step beyond the limits of the singspiel tradition by giving the orchestra an unprecedented importance in expressing the works' drama and emotionality. Beyond that, he pioneered the use of leitmotiv, a brief musical theme that represents a specific character, object, emotion, or trait, and that regularly returns to evoke the characteristic it represents. In a sense, the leitmotiv brought to opera the kind of thematic organization that the symphony and sonata had enjoyed (the difference being that the sonata's themes were organized according to a proportional logic, whereas the deployment of the leitmotiv was dictated by the dramatic context).

Wagner expanded the use of the leitmotiv considerably, making his orchestra as crucial to the furtherance of the drama as any of his leading characters. Wagner's harmonic language was marked by an unbridled use of chromaticism, which gave the music an almost mystical aura. Because he scored operas for an unusually large orchestra, Wagner required singers with powerful, dramatic voices—the only kind capable of rising over his rich orchestration to put forth his larger-than-life characterizations. Many of his operas are grandly nationalistic works that revolve around episodes, characters, and legends of the distant Teutonic past. His crowning achievement is the four-part *Ring* cycle (1848–74), a truly epic drama based on the myths of the ancient gods.

The complexity and scale of Wagner's works have never been surpassed, but his successors found other ways to bring the art of opera composition forward. Richard STRAUSS chose an array of subjects for his stage works, and in some of his early operas—*Salome* (1905) and *Elektra* (1908)—he shocked audiences with both his plot choices and the evocative, chromatic music he used. On the other hand, in works such as *Der Rosenkavalier* (1911), *Intermezzo* (1923), and *Capriccio* (1941), he struck an interesting balance between his modern tonal language and orchestral texturing, and an almost neoclassical sense of elegance and proportion.

Strauss's most lasting orchestral works are his symphonic tone poems. Like his operas, these are a varied lot, ranging from sprightly character pieces, such as *Till Eulenspiegel's Merry Pranks* (1895), to the more serious *Also Sprach Zarathustra* (1896) and *Ein Heldenleben* (1898).

Concurrently, other composers created works that exploited the timbres of the orchestra and the resources of the opera house in a lighter, more popular way. Among the most illustrious of them were Johann STRAUSS, Jr., an Austrian orchestra leader celebrated for his lavish, colorfully orchestrated waltzes and his operetta *Die Fledermaus* (1874); the German composer Albert Lortzing (1801–51), whose energies were directed almost entirely to operetta; and Franz LEHAR, a Hungarian-born Viennese composer who, with works like *The Merry Widow* (1905), brought the art of operetta into the 20th century.

This caricature silhouette by Otto Böhler depicts the 19th-century composer Richard Wagner as a giant surrounded by his tiny critics. Criticism, especially in the press, persisted from 1843 in reaction to Wagner's operatic reforms and musical innovations. The genius of his vision was fully recognized only during the 20th century.

THE TWENTIETH CENTURY

In Austria, Anton BRUCKNER and Gustav MAHLER continued to push the multimovement symphony further along the path that Haydn, Mozart, Beethoven, and Brahms had traveled. But just as Wagner brought new dimensions to opera, Bruckner and Mahler expanded the scope of the symphony (and, in Mahler's case, the orchestrally accompanied song cycle) to epic lengths, at the same time demanding a broader coloristic palette and a great degree of orchestral virtuosity. Their sprawling canvases embody a searing emotional intensity and a sense of self-revelation. They mark the zenith of the expressive romantic style.

Mahler's successors in the early 20th century felt that the language of romanticism had been taken to its limit. Arnold SCHOENBERG composed his early works, including the massive *Gurrelieder* (1901–13) and the dark, mysterious string sextet *Transfigured Night* (1899), in a style that seemed the outgrowth of Brahms's and Mahler's romantic aesthetic. By 1920, however, he had developed a method of composition in which he arranged the 12 tones of the scale in a series, and then used the permutations of the series as the thematic material on which he based his works. Actually, this form of composition (called the TWELVE-TONE SYSTEM or SERIAL MUSIC) is less confining than might be supposed, for a work could use several series, each of which could be broken into shorter components and subjected to all the traditional forms of thematic metamorphosis (including inversions, retrogrades, transposition, augmentation, and diminution). Serialism, as Schoenberg saw it, was simply a tool whereby composers could find fresh material, free from the constraints of major and minor tonalities. Later composers brought serialism to greater extremes, serializing not only pitches but rhythms, tone colors, and dynamics.

Schoenberg, along with his two greatest disciples—Alban BERG and Anton von WEBERN—worked in Vienna, were the central figures in what was known as the Second Viennese school. Each pursued a different route, and taken together, their works show the variety of styles the twelve-tone school allowed: Schoenberg adapted his method to the traditional chamber and orchestral forms, while Webern left a body of compact, concise miniatures and Berg—in many ways the most enduring of the three—composed two full-scale operas, *Wozzeck* (1921) and *Lulu* (1935), plus a gorgeously romantic violin concerto (1935) and a handful of songs and chamber works.

The advent of the Nazis brought an end to Germany's dominance of the musical world. The music of Schoenberg and his followers was declared "decadent"—as was the much more popularly based theatrical music of Kurt WEILL, and the neo-baroque and neo-classical music of Paul HINDEMITH, a prolific and practical composer who rejected the serial approach. Schoenberg, Weill, and Hindemith fled to the United States, as did hundreds of other composers, performers, authors, and artists from Germany, Austria, and other European countries that came under German domination in the 1930s.

The German composing tradition was slow to recover from this devastation, and although postwar Germany has been particularly receptive to new music by foreign composers, few native composers have achieved global renown. Among those who have are Karlheinz STOCKHAUSEN, an influential composer of electronic music and of works combining electronic tape and conventional instruments, and Hans Werner HENZE whose operas, symphonic scores, and chamber works run the stylistic gamut from avant-garde to almost neo-romantic.

ALLAN KOZINN

Bibliography: Grout, Donald, *A History of Western Music* (1960); Harewood, Earl of, ed., *The New Kobbe's Complete Opera Book* (1969); Lang, Paul Henry, *Music in Western Civilization* (1941); Robertson, Alec, and Stevens, Denis, eds., *The Pelican History of Music* (1960–86); Rosen, Charles, *The Classical Style: Haydn, Mozart, Beethoven* (1971); Sadie, Stanley, ed., *The New Grove Dictionary of Music and Musicians* (1980); Schonzeler, Hans-Hubert, ed., *Of German Music: A Symposium* (1976); Simpson, Robert, ed., *The Symphony* (1966–67); Strunk, Oliver, *Source Readings in Music History* (1950); Tovey, Donald Francis, *Essays in Musical Analysis* (1935–44): Ulrich, Homer, *Chamber Music* (1966).

(Left) *This portrait of Gustav Mahler, a composer and conductor, dates from the 1890s, when he was conducting in Hamburg and writing his early symphonies. His music's grandiose quality is leavened by folk elements and the German romantic spirit. Mahler's later symphonies brought to a close the romantic era.*

(Below) *The Austrian composer Arnold Schoenberg began to work on atonal music during the early 1900s. This work led him to formulate his 12-tone technique, a form of serial music. Schoenberg was active as a teacher of musical theory in both Europe and the United States.*

German Confederation

The German Confederation was a loose grouping of German states created (1815) by the Congress of Vienna (see VIENNA, CONGRESS OF) to replace the Holy Roman Empire. The confederation was rendered largely ineffective by the rivalry between Austria and Prussia, and it was dissolved after the Prussian defeat of Austria in the Seven Weeks' War (1866).

German Democratic Republic: see GERMANY, EAST AND WEST.

German East Africa

German East Africa was a former German colony comprising the areas of most of Rwanda, Burundi, present-day Tanzania, and part of Mozambique. The Germans controlled the region from 1884 until World War I, after which most of the area was mandated to Great Britain.

German language: see GERMANIC LANGUAGES.

German literature

German literature, which comprises the literatures of Germany, Austria, and the German-speaking part of Switzerland, has always tried to integrate foreign influences, especially those of classical antiquity and France. Thus it is not surprising that the concept of a German literary tradition did not emerge before the 17th century; in fact, not before the end of the 18th century was Germany able to express its national identity in literary terms.

Germany, for centuries a region divided by religious strife, was late in achieving political unity (see GERMANY, HISTORY OF). The loose federation of small German principalities had no capital city as a dominant cultural center. This lack of national unity proved beneficial, however, because German literature developed in regional centers, and the resulting diversification of cultural trends prevented sterile uniformity.

EARLY AND MEDIEVAL GERMAN LITERATURE

Writings in the Old High German language, in use from *c.*800 to *c.*1050, mirror the conflict between the heroic tradition of the Germanic tribes with their concepts of honor, valor, and fate and the Christian gospel of humility, renunciation, and love. Among the earliest extant poems, the *Song of Hildebrand* (*c.*800; Eng. trans., 1906), an alliterative verse fragment, is genuinely pagan in its emphasis on fate, whereas the *Heliand* (*c.*830), an epic poem about the life of Christ, is an attempt to synthesize the old and the new: the savior becomes a Germanic duke, and the Christian message is presented in traditional heroic imagery. Otfried von Weissenburg's *Evangelienbuch* (Book of Gospels, completed *c.*870) set the precedent for a new Christian literature consisting of biblical paraphrases. This work, the first by an identifiable German author, introduced end-rhyme into German poetry. During the 10th century the monasteries were centers of culture, and Old High German was replaced by Latin. Three secular works merit attention: the *Waltharius Manufortis* (*c.*930; trans. as *Walter of Aquitaine,* 1950), which introduced classical hexameter; *Ecbasis Captivi* (*c.*940), the earliest extant beast fable in German literature; and *Ruodlieb* (*c.*1050; Eng. trans., 1959), a tale of the adventures of a young hero. HROSWITHA VON GANDERSHEIM (fl. after 950), the first known German woman writer, was a nun who used the Roman playwright Terence as a model for her morality plays.

During the Middle High German period (*c.*1050–*c.*1300), German literature reached impressive heights of achievement in its first Golden Age (*c.*1180–*c.*1220). Secular culture, perpetuated by minstrels (see MINSTRELS, MINNESINGERS, AND TROUBADOURS), now became the concern of the knights who celebrated COURTLY LOVE in complex lyrics. Among the minnesingers who, influenced by Provençal troubadours, produced an abundance of songs, WALTHER VON DER VOGELWEIDE attained a unique position. He overcame literary convention by turning away from empty gallantry to express powerful emotions of love, and by transforming the short poem of proverbial wisdom into a political weapon of satire and patriotism.

The Arthurian legends (see ARTHUR AND ARTHURIAN LEGEND) popular in contemporary French literature also formed the basis of German heroic poetry. The idealized world of chivalry was counterbalanced by religious restraint in the work of HARTMANN VON AUE, especially in *Der arme Heinrich* (*c.*1195; trans. as *Henry the Leper,* 1905). GOTTFRIED VON STRASSBURG, unchallenged master of elegant poetic style, glorified sensual passion in his unfinished TRISTAN AND ISOLDE. WOLFRAM VON ESCHENBACH created one of the most profound works of German literature in his *Parzival* (*c.*1210; Eng. trans., 1956), which symbolizes, in the quest for the Holy Grail, the search for eternal salvation. In the NIBELUNGENLIED (*c.*1200; Eng. trans., 1904) an anonymous author tried to combine the archaic legends of popular tradition with the refinement of the age by describing the exploits of the warrior Siegfried in the setting of courtly love and chivalry. Despite its humane sympathy, the poem retains a tragic, somber fatality.

LATE MIDDLE AGES AND 16TH CENTURY

Late medieval literature reflects the decline of knighthood and the rise of the city burghers. The high style of chivalry was frequently parodied, and human folly was satirized by such writers as Sebastian BRANT and Johann Baptist FISCHART. The numerous plays, legends, and merry tales of Hans SACHS exemplify the coarse humor of this period. Popular literature flourished, and CHAPBOOKS, simple prose versions of verse romances, were widely read. These were important collections of folklore, as were the adventures of the prankster Till EULENSPIEGEL. The FAUST legend appeared in several versions at this time.

In the hands of the MEISTERSINGERS, who cared only for observing literary conventions, poetry degenerated into a mechanical practice of matching rhymed lines. Prose writing, however, improved and acquired stylistic refinement and expressive quality. The mystics Meister ECKHART and Johannes TAULER contributed to this development as did JOHANNES VON TEPL in *The Bohemian Plowman* (*c.*1400; Eng. trans., 1958).

Martin LUTHER's translation of the Bible into German, and his beautiful religious songs, had a considerable effect on German culture. Some of the greatest literary works of the period, however, written in Latin by the humanists Ulrich von HUTTEN and Johannes Reuchlin (1455–1522), contributed to the European Renaissance. The REFORMATION forced these poets and scholars to take sides in the religious conflict. As a result the application of neoclassical principles to German poetry was delayed until the 17th century.

THE 17TH CENTURY

Writers of this period were obsessed with the idea that German was equal if not superior to the languages of neighboring countries. Academies (*Sprachgesellschaften*) were therefore founded in order to establish a pure language and correct grammar. The rules of literary neoclassicism were first formulated (1624) by Martin Opitz. In drama the separation of tragedy and comedy was rigorously observed. Seneca was the model for the tragedies of Andreas GRYPHIUS and Daniel Caspar von Lohenstein, whereas the Jesuits developed their own religious theater in Latin. In poetry the sonnet and the alexandrine verse were the preferred forms. The creation of bold images, musical effects, and new word combinations served to enrich the German language. Among the numerous skillful poets, Paul Fleming (1609–40), Gryphius, and Christian Hofmann von Hofmanns-Waldau (1617–79) are outstanding. The voluminous novels of the period are forgotten; only the ribald humor and colorful realism of Hans GRIMMELSHAUSEN survives. The visionary Jakob BÖHME profoundly influenced the mystics of this century.

THE 18TH AND 19TH CENTURIES

During the first half of the 18th century a controversy concerning poetic theory took place between proponents of rigid French classicism in drama and those who championed the merits of religious epic poetry. The creative production of both factions remained insignificant. The uselessness of the controversy was demonstrated by Gotthold LESSING, who introduced a new concept of tragic experience. He replaced courtly tragedy with bourgeois drama and repeatedly praised William Shakespeare for his craftsmanship. Lessing's *Minna von Barnhelm* (1767; Eng. trans., 1930) remains the unsurpassed masterpiece of German comedy; his *Nathan the Wise* (1779; Eng. trans., 1955) is a stirring call for religious tolerance. In his critical writings Lessing created a German prose style of clarity and wit.

Christoph Martin WIELAND added grace and playfulness to the language and flavored his verse and prose with subtle irony. *Oberon* (1780; Eng. trans., 1798) is his best-known epic poem; *The History of Agathon* (1766; Eng. trans., 1773) emphasizes the psychological growth of character. Friedrich Gottlieb KLOPSTOCK created in his *Odes* (1771; Eng. trans., 1848) a new poetic language of dynamic expression. He influenced the young STURM UND DRANG generation with his religious fervor and patriotic zeal.

Sturm und Drang (1770–85). This movement praised original genius, demanded a poetry of strong passions, and found new models in Shakespeare's plays and in simple folksongs. Johann Gottfried von HERDER disseminated these ideas among youthful writers who included Johann Wolfgang von GOETHE and Friedrich Wilhelm Joseph von SCHILLER. The first novel of this movement, Goethe's THE SORROWS OF YOUNG WERTHER, brought its author international acclaim and disseminated the tenets of ROMANTICISM throughout Europe. The literary aim of German romanticism during this period was the presentation of passion, regardless of considerations of traditional form. In later works, however, Goethe strove to endow his creations with the advantages of self-discipline. *Wilhelm Meister's Apprenticeship* (1795; Eng. trans., 1824), the classic BILDUNGSROMAN, was the outcome of this aim.

The Second Golden Age. In Weimar during the early 19th century Goethe and Schiller collaborated in creating works of enduring merit. Their goal was to integrate the ancient classical tradition into German romanticism. In Jena, August Wilhelm and Friedrich von SCHLEGEL, the mystic NOVALIS, and the poet Ludwig TIECK formed the first romantic circle. This was followed by other groups in Berlin and Heidelberg, whose members included Achim and Bettina von ARNIM; Clemens BRENTANO; Joseph, Freiherr von EICHENDORFF; and Ernst Theodor Amadeus HOFFMANN—famous as lyric poets and storytellers. Jacob and Wilhelm GRIMM stimulated interest in early Germanic literary traditions. Two other writers of this period stand apart: Friedrich HÖLDERLIN, whose poems achieved a synthesis of ancient Greek forms and modern sensibility, and Heinrich von KLEIST, who expressed his chaotic view of the world in passionate dramas and powerful short stories.

Postromanticism. After 1830 the grandiose period of German literature came to an end. The so-called Biedermeier poets (see GERMAN ART AND ARCHITECTURE) reacted by withdrawing into the realm of the family and idyllic nature. This resignation was replaced in the poems of Heinrich HEINE by new political directions and a realistic outlook. Many progressive writers had to go into exile after the revolution of 1848 (see GERMANY, HISTORY OF), among them Karl MARX and Carl SCHURZ. Throughout the 19th century the forms introduced by Goethe and Schiller prevailed: in poetry, the *Lied* derived from folksongs; in drama, the historical tragedy in blank verse; in prose, the novella, an artistically structured story centered on an extraordinary event. Annette Elisabeth von DROSTE-HÜLSHOFF and Eduard MÖRIKE were the leading poets; Franz GRILLPARZER and Christian Friedrich HEBBEL, the dramatists; Jeremias GOTTHELF, Gottfried KELLER, Conrad Ferdinand MEYER, Wilhelm RAABE, Adalbert STIFTER, and Theodor STORM, the storytellers. Far ahead of his time was Georg BÜCHNER, who rejected bourgeois values and wrote such plays as *Woyzeck* (1850; Eng. trans., 1957), in which he anticipated modern styles. The ideas of Friedrich Wilhelm NIETZSCHE, who rejected the idealistic philosophy of Georg Wilhelm Friedrich HEGEL and Arthur SCHOPENHAUER, dominated German thought throughout the earlier part of the 20th century.

THE 20TH CENTURY

Because German realism had been tempered by a strong romantic tradition, NATURALISM came as a shock when it was introduced after 1885 by Gerhart HAUPTMANN and Arno HOLZ. Hauptmann was able to overcome the narrow restrictions of naturalistic theory and, with sympathetic understanding, created convincing dramatic characters. Arthur SCHNITZLER, a contemporary of Sigmund Freud's, added a Viennese flavor to his erotic, melancholy plays.

SYMBOLISM was introduced as a reaction to naturalism about 1900 by the poets Stefan GEORGE, Rainer Maria RILKE, and Hugo von HOFMANNSTHAL. They wrote some of the most beautiful poems of modern world literature.

Expressionism is a collective term for the style of certain poets and dramatists who were active between 1910 and 1925 (see EXPRESSIONISM, literature). Before the war such poets as Gottfried BENN, Georg TRAKL, and Georg Heym created apoca-

(Below) *Johann Wolfgang von Goethe, one of the principal figures in German literature, influenced the development of the late-18th-century Sturm und Drang period and the classicism of the early 19th century. Goethe, whose work encompassed such fields as science, music, art, and philosophy, as well as literature, has been called the last "universal man."*

(Above) *Friedrich Schiller, a dramatist, poet, and philosopher, profoundly influenced, along with Goethe, the direction of German literature. Schiller's early historical dramas, such as* The Robbers *(1781), focus on the issue of political freedom; his later historical dramas, such as* Wilhelm Tell *(1804), explore the question of moral freedom.*

Rainer Maria Rilke is considered one of the foremost lyric poets of 20th-century German literature. In such works as New Poems *(1907–08), he used symbolism and skillfully manipulated language and rhythm to evoke the essence of his subject. According to Rilke, "Verses are not . . . simply feelings; they are experiences."*

lyptic visions or experimented with style. Toward the end of World War I and during the early years of the German republic, dramatists, notably Georg KAISER and Ernst TOLLER, tried to revolutionize the theater. In the meantime the novel gradually developed from the refined realism of Theodor FONTANE, the chronicler of Prussian aristocracy and Berlin's lower middle class, to the epic canvases of Hermann BROCH, Alfred DÖBLIN, Thomas MANN, and Robert MUSIL. They portrayed the social, intellectual, and emotional problems of their time and refined narrative techniques in the manner of Marcel Proust or James Joyce.

Literature under the Nazis. Modern German literature was brutally suppressed by the Nazis. Most writers had to go into exile after 1933, and many were unable to return home after the war. In 1945, Germany was a cultural vacuum. There was an acute need to reestablish contacts with the outside world, and work that had been ignored or suppressed had to be rediscovered. A writer who had been known only as author of a few minor prose sketches—Franz KAFKA—appeared as a great novelist. Bertolt BRECHT, who had written his best plays in exile, also became recognized as a classic modern writer. His theory of EPIC THEATER and the alienation effect was applied by the Swiss dramatists Friedrich DÜRRENMATT and Max FRISCH, who represented German drama in the 1950s.

German Literature since World War II. The literature of the postwar period has presented a wide variety of styles and trends of thought. The West German postwar literary resurgence was organized around GRUPPE 47, to which belonged the novelists Heinrich BÖLL, Günter GRASS, and Uwe JOHNSON, who became the leading literary voices of the postwar era.

In recent decades, new writers—especially those willing to experiment with new forms and styles—have created an international readership for German literature in translation. Authors now widely read—in addition to the Gruppe 47 writers—include the poets Ingeborg BACHMANN and Paul CELAN; the playwrights and novelists Peter WEISS and Peter HANDKE; and the East German novelist Christa WOLF. CHRISTOPH HERING

Bibliography: Demetz, Peter, *Postwar German Literature* (1970); Garland, Henry, and Garland, Mary, eds., *The Oxford Companion to German Literature* (1976); Hamburger, Michael, *A Proliferation of Prophets: Essays on German Writers from Nietzsche to Brecht* (1984); Heller, Erich, *In the Age of Prose* (1984); Ritchie, James M., ed., *Periods in German Literature* (2 vols., 1967, 1970); Taylor, Ronald, *Literature and Society in Germany, 1918–45* (1980).

German longhaired pointer

The German longhaired pointer is a setterlike breed believed to have been derived from crosses of the old German hawking dog, which was a breed similar to spaniels, the French spaniel, and probably the Gordon setter. The German longhaired pointer was popular in Germany in the early 1900s and is now recognized by the Canadian Kennel Club.

The dog averages between 63.5 and 68.5 cm (25 to 27 in) in height at the shoulders and 25 and 29.5 kg (55 to 65 lb) in weight. It has a long head, hanging ears, and a long tail. Its coat is smooth, slightly wavy, and preferably either a solid liver brown or white with liver brown patches.

German measles

German measles, or rubella, is a contagious but mild viral disease common in children and young adults. The early symptoms, similar to those of the common cold, are often followed by a skin rash that first appears on the face and neck and then rapidly spreads to the trunk and extremities. Lymph nodes on the back of the neck become swollen and tender. Symptoms usually disappear without complication in about a week. Many people may have had German measles without knowing it, because a skin rash is not always present. Natural infection apparently produces lifelong immunity. Pregnant women who become infected by rubella have a high risk of giving birth to a baby with serious defects, including blindness, cardiovascular disorders, or mental retardation. Vaccination is therefore recommended before the childbearing age, although the immunity provided is weaker than that from natural infection. PETER L. PETRAKIS

German music: see GERMAN AND AUSTRIAN MUSIC.

The literature of modern Germany reflects the influence of Nietzsche, Freud, and politics in its concern with philosophy, psychology, and the dialectics and complexities of 20th-century society. Bertolt Brecht (left) *developed his drama into terse and moving studies of the politics of the human condition. Thomas Mann* (center) *and Hermann Hesse* (right), *both of whom received Nobel Prizes for literature, Mann in 1929 and Hesse in 1946, used character studies to explore intellectual and philosophical arguments.*

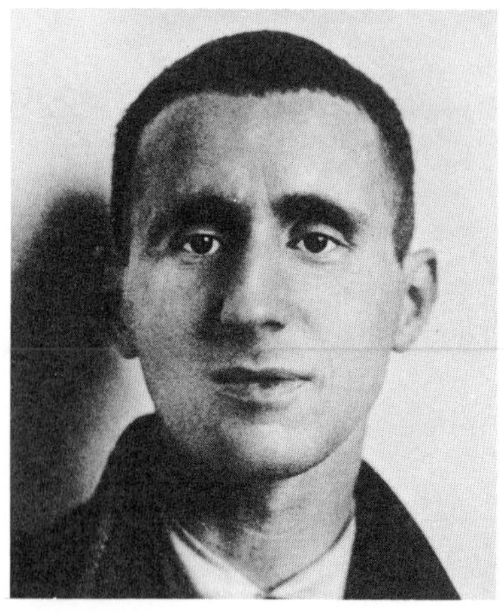

German shepherd

The German shepherd, or Alsatian, is a powerful, intelligent dog with a long body and short fur. Although shepherds are often pale or white, breeders prefer the characteristic, rich tan-and-black coloring.

The German shepherd dog, known as the Alsatian in Britain, is one of the most widely known and popular breeds of purebred dogs in the world. For 14 years, until displaced by the doberman pinscher in 1977, the breed was the second most popular—after the poodle—in the United States. The breed is a descendant of earlier German herding and farm dogs. Today's German shepherd was developed in the latter part of the 19th century by methodical breeding. German shepherds are commonly selected to be army dogs, police dogs, or guide dogs for the blind. They are medium-sized, powerful animals; the males can be up to 65 cm (26 in) in height and weigh 38.5 kg (85 lb); the females are slightly shorter and weigh a little less. The dense coat may be black and tan, gray, or solid black.

JOHN MANDEVILLE

Bibliography: Bennett, Jane G., et al., *The Complete German Shepherd Dog*, 4th ed. (1970); Strickland, Winifred G., and Moses, James A., *The German Shepherd Today* (1974).

German shorthaired pointer

The German shorthaired pointer, or kurzhaar, was developed in the late 19th century by German hunters interested in an all-purpose sporting breed. The older, heavier German pointers, descendants of Spanish pointers and various hounds, were mated with English pointers and possibly other gundogs to produce the desired animal. The German shorthaired pointer can scent and point game and retrieve on both land and water. The breed was recognized by the American Kennel Club in 1930.

The German shorthaired pointer was bred from the pointer, bloodhound, foxhound, and other breeds. Considered one of the finest all-purpose sporting dogs, it is an excellent pointer, can retrieve on land and in water, and has a highly developed sense of smell.

German shorthairs resemble pointers. Males stand to 62.5 cm (25 in) high at the shoulders and weigh about 32 kg (70 lb). The tail is docked at about two-fifths of its length. The smooth coat is light or dark brown, with or without grayish white or dark-brown to liver-colored patches.

JOHN MANDEVILLE

Bibliography: Maxwell, C. Bede, *The New German Shorthaired Pointer*, 3d ed. (1975).

German wirehaired pointer

The German wirehaired pointer is an all-around hunting dog similar to the German shorthaired pointer in its general shape and abilities. The wirehair, however, has a double-layered coat that provides additional protection against jagged underbrush.

The German wirehaired pointer, or drahthaar, resembles the German shorthaired pointer in all ways except for the coat. The wirehaired pointer has a two-layered coat: the undercoat is a soft, dense insulating covering, and the outercoat is straight, harsh, and wiry. The wirehaired pointer was developed in Germany, during the last half of the 19th century, from the German shorthaired pointer and several other pointing breeds, including the pudelpointer. The breed very quickly became popular in its native land. Introduced to the United States in the 1920s, it was officially recognized by the American Kennel Club in 1959.

JOHN MANDEVILLE

Bibliography: Compere, Newton, *How to Raise and Train a German Wirehaired Pointer* (1966).

germander [jur-man'-dur]

Germander is the common name for plants of the genus *Teucrium*, in the mint family, Labiatae. The approximately 300 species of germander are perennial herbs or shrubs. They are widely distributed but occur chiefly in the Mediterranean area, with about 12 species in North America. They commonly bear showy clusters of tubular or bell-shaped flowers.

OLIN S. FEARING

Germanic languages

Germanic languages, which form a subfamily of INDO-EUROPEAN LANGUAGES, are spoken today by 540 million people in many parts of the world but chiefly in Europe and North America. Traditionally, Germanic languages comprise three major branches: West Germanic, North Germanic, and East

Germanic. (Individual languages and the number and distribution of speakers are shown in Table 1.)

TABLE 1: DISTRIBUTION OF GERMANIC LANGUAGES

West Germanic		
English	369 million speakers	England, Ireland, United States, Canada, New Zealand, Australia, South Africa, India
German	120 million speakers	Germany, Austria, Switzerland, parts of Alsace-Lorraine
Netherlandic (Dutch and Flemish)	20 million speakers	Netherlands and Belgium
Afrikaans	6 million speakers	South Africa
Yiddish	5 million speakers	East and South Europe, United States
Frisian	½ million speakers	North Sea Coast—Holland to Schleswig-Holstein
North Germanic		
Swedish	10 million speakers	Sweden, Finland
Danish	5 million speakers	Denmark
Norwegian	5 million speakers	Norway
Icelandic	220,000 speakers	Iceland
Faeroese	37,000 speakers	Faeroes Islands
East Germanic		
Gothic, Vandalic, Burgundian, Rugian, and Heruler (all dead languages)		

SEPARATION FROM INDO-EUROPEAN

The Germanic languages broke away from other Indo-European languages before 500 BC, forming a clearly distinguishable and independent group of closely related dialects, usually referred to as Proto-Germanic. A more-or-less regular series of sound changes, described by GRIMM'S LAW and called the First Sound Change, was one of the distinguishing features of this separation. The changes can be illustrated by using Latin words to represent the Indo-European sounds, and English words to represent the Proto-Germanic, or primitive Germanic:

TABLE 2: FIRST SOUND CHANGE

Indo-European	p	t	k	(not st sp sk)	b	d	g
Proto-Germanic 1.	f	ϕ	χ	(later h)	p	t	k
2.	v	ð	γ	not initially			
usually	ƀ	d	g				

For the sounds in row 2, the Dane Karl Adolf VERNER discovered the rule (Verner's Law) that if the main stress was not immediately before the sound, the sound became voiced; that is, f *θ* χ became v ð g. Latin/English: *pater/father*, *piscis/fish*, *tres/three*, *frater/brother*, *centum/hundred*, *cornu/horn*, *septem/seven*, *labium/lip*, *duo/two*, *ager/acre*.

EAST, NORTH, AND WEST GERMANIC

Today no general agreement exists as to the correctness of the traditional division into East, West, and North Germanic subgroups, which took place after the Proto-Germanic period and was completed by the time of Christ (5th to 1st century BC). The West Germanic grouping in particular is questioned because it is apparent that language elements of German, English, Netherlandic, and Frisian go back to three groups of which the Ingvaeones are most frequently named.

East Germanic. The oldest surviving Germanic literary text—fragments of a Bible translation made by Ulfilas, bishop of the West Goths (d. *c.*385)—was written in Gothic. The preserved fragments of an East Gothic manuscript of the translation from the 6th century are referred to as the *Codex argenteus* (silver book). Since the Goths had no written language, Ulfilas took the Greek uncial alphabet, added to it a few Latin and runic letters, and thus created an alphabet for his translation.

North Germanic. The North Germanic languages all descend from Old Norse and have several distinctive features in common. The definite article is added as a suffix to the noun; for example, "the book" is boken, with *-en* signifying "the." The passive is formed by adding *-s* to the end of the verb, or *-r* is changed to *-s* in the present tense (*-st* in Icelandic): jag kallar, "I call"/ jag kalla*s*, "I am called"/ jag kallade, "I called"/ jag kallade*s*, "I was called."

Old Norse separated into West Nordic and East Nordic. West Nordic comprises Old Icelandic (12th–15th century), which became Icelandic; Old Norwegian, which became Landsmål, now called Nynorsk (modern Norwegian); and Faeroese, also called Faeroic. East Nordic comprises Old Swedish, which evolved into Swedish, and Old Danish, which became modern Danish.

West Germanic. All West Germanic languages have one thing in common; they all doubled consonants except *r* before *i* or *j* after short vowels, and sometimes before *l*, *r*, and *w*—a process called gemination. This may be demonstrated as follows: Gothic sa*t*jan / West Germanic sa*tt*(i)an / German se*tz*en; Gothic a*k*r / West Germanic a*kk*r / German A*ck*er. West Germanic shared with North Germanic the change of *z* to *r*, and *ē* to *ā*: Gothic mai*z*a ("more") / Old Saxon mē*r*o / Old Norse mei*r*o; Gothic g*ē*bum ("we gave") / Old Saxon g*ā*bum / Old Norse g*ā*fum. English and Netherlandic also share several sound characteristics: 1) *n* drops before fricative sounds: German u*n*s, fü*n*f / English us, five / Netherlandic vijf, but o*n*s; 2) consonants in both are palatalized: German *K*inn, *T*ag, la*g* / English *ch*in, da*y*, la*y*.

Anglo-Frisian (Ingvaeonic in the broadest sense) includes English and Frisian. The bases for English are the dialects of the Angles, Saxons, and Jutes, who emigrated to England from Schleswig-Holstein about AD 450. Anglo-Saxon or Old English existed until the 12th century, Middle English until 1450, and New English since then. (See ENGLISH LANGUAGE.)

The German-Netherlandic group includes Low German and High German. Low German splits into Low Franconian, which becomes Netherlandic (Dutch and Flemish); and Low Saxon, which has a three-stage evolution: Old Saxon or Old Low German (AD 800–1200) becomes Middle Low German (1200–1600), which in turn becomes modern Low German or Plattdeutsch (1600–). High German subdivides into Middle German and Upper German.

Geographically, the dividing line between Low German and High German (the Benrath line) is located near the Düsseldorf-Magdeburg parallel. The set of sound changes that took place in the High German area, but not in the Low German, English, or Dutch areas, is called the Second Sound Change, or the High German Sound Shift.

TABLE 3: SECOND SOUND CHANGE

Other Germanic languages:	p	t	k	b	d	g
High German:	pf	ts	(kχ)	(p)	t	(k)
	f	s	χ			

The sounds *pf, ts,* kχ appear initially, in gemination, and after consonants; but after *r* and *l*, *pf* becomes *f*. The sounds *f, s,* and χ appear in the middle of a word and at the end of a word after vowels. (Examples are shown in Table 4.)

TABLE 4: SECOND SOUND CHANGE

	Netherlandic	English	Swedish	Danish	German
p > pf	*p*ond	*p*ound	*p*und	*p*und	*Pf*und
	a*pp*el	a*pp*le	ä*pp*le	æ*b*le	A*pf*el
	hel*p*en	hel*p*	hjäl*p*a	hjæl*p*e	hel*f*en
t > ts	*t*ien	*t*en	*t*io	*t*i	*z*ehn
	*t*ellen	*t*ell	*t*ala	*t*ale	*z*ählen
	har*t*	hear*t*	hjär*t*a	hjer*t*e	Her*z*
p > f	ho*p*en	ho*p*e	ho*pp*as	ha*b*e	ho*ff*en
t > s	ui*t*	ou*t*	u*t*	u*d*	au*s*
k > χ, ç	boe*k*	boo*k*	bo*k*	bo*g*	Bu*ch*
d > t	*d*ag	*d*ay	*d*ag	*d*ag	*T*ag

WRITING AND SPELLING
Aside from Gothic, for which Ulfilas invented an alphabet, before the year 600, no written Germanic existed except for a few single words and short sentences in runic characters, for example, ᛒᛟᛊᛟ ᚠᚱᚨᛗᛏ ᚱᚢᚾᚨ = "Boso cut or wrote (the) runes." More of these have been found in Scandinavia and Britain than in Germany. After 600, when Christian monks tried to write the Germanic languages in Latin characters, they experienced many difficulties because Latin and Germanic sounds do not resemble each other very closely.

Written Dutch is fairly uniform in spelling, grammar, and vocabulary, but spoken Dutch has a number of dialects as well as an official spoken form. Written Dutch evolved from the Flemish spoken in Flanders and Brabant in the 15th century; modern spoken Dutch, however, grew out of the vernacular of the province of Holland.

Afrikaans arose from the Dutch spoken by the Boers, who emigrated from the Netherlands to South Africa in the 17th century. Its written form dates only from the mid-19th century. Its basic Dutch vocabulary has been greatly expanded with native African and English borrowings.

Yiddish, although it is not a national language, is spoken by Jews all over the world. It arose (*c.*1100) out of a blend of a number of German dialects in the ghettos of Central Europe, and from there it spread to other parts of the world. Phonetically, Yiddish is closer to Middle High German than is modern German. Its vocabulary is basically German, but it has been enlarged by borrowings from Hebrew, Slavic, Romance languages, and English.

VOCABULARY
Only about 25 percent of the vocabulary of modern Germanic languages can be traced directly back through West and North Germanic to Indo-European. Ninety percent of Gothic vocabulary is Indo-European. The pronouns (I, my, you), nouns of kinship (father, mother, brother), parts of the body (eye, ear, arm), domestic animals (hound, ox, steer), and common activities (build, bite, go, stand, sit, know) are such words. Some of the most common Germanic words, however, have baffled etymologists; these include such terms as *broad, bring, dumb, hold, rain, drive, drink,* and sea-terms such as *sea, cliff, leak,* among others.

Latin vocabulary and grammar have influenced the Germanic languages extensively. The most important Latin influences occurred during the Reformation and the rise of humanism (15th and 16th centuries). Many Greek words were also borrowed at that time. The great influence of French on English after the Norman invasion (1066) produced a hybrid language that is West Germanic in grammar and basic vocabulary, but is French in most words of five letters or more (Germanic: is, am, it, of, for, the, this; French: senior, editor, ultimately). French culture and language have given hundreds of loanwords and related ideas to most other Germanic languages, although their effect is not as great as on English.

Within the Germanic languages extensive borrowing of vocabulary is evident. English words, for example, abound in present-day German, Dutch, Afrikaans, and most Scandinavian languages. Italian, Spanish, the Slavic languages, Arabic, and others have also enriched the Germanic vocabulary.

MORPHOLOGY
The Germanic languages have two adjective declensions, a strong and a weak. The weak forms are used generally after articles, demonstrative pronouns, and possessive adjectives; the strong are used independently. The number of these forms is reduced greatly in Danish, Swedish, and Netherlandic. The comparison of adjectives and adverbs in Germanic differs from that in the Romance languages. Generally, *-r* and *-st* endings are added: long, longer, longest; Swedish, lång, längre, längst.

The eight cases of Indo-European nouns, adjectives, and pronouns were reduced to four, and sometimes even fewer, in Germanic. Free stress (accent) became recessive, and precise accent rules became dominant, with the first root syllable in Germanic carrying the stress. Umlauting, a process of modifying vowel sounds, took place extensively (w*o*man, w*o*men; f*oo*t, f*ee*t). A system of strong verbs developed as the result of vowel alternation (ablaut), as in sing, sang, sung, and a unique way of forming the past tense using weak verbs (jump, jump*ed*) was created, probably by adding a form of *did* to the verb (I jump-*did* = I jump*ed*). The number of strong verbs in Germanic is steadily being reduced, and the system does not seem to permit the creation of new strong verbs. Conversely, the number of weak verbs is increasing.

ARVAL L. STREADBECK

Bibliography: Baugh, Albert C., *A History of the English Language* (1957); Cook, A. B., *Introduction to the English Language, Structure and History* (1969); Haugen, Einar, *The Scandinavian Languages* (1976); Jesperson, Otto, *Language, Its Nature, Development and Origin* (1954); Lehmann, Winifred P., *A Reader in Nineteenth Century Historical Indo-European Linguistics* (1967) and *Historical Linguistics* (1962); Lockwood, W. B., *An Informal History of the German Language, with Chapters on Dutch and Afrikaans, Frisian and Yiddish* (1965); Meillet, Antoine, *General Characteristics of the Germanic Languages,* trans. by William Dismukes (1970); Moulton, William G., *The Sounds of English and German* (1962); Muller, Siegfried, *The World's Living Languages* (1964); Pei, Mario, *The Story of English* (1967) and *The World's Chief Languages* (1967); Seymour, R. K., *A Bibliography of Word Formation in the Germanic Languages* (1968); Streadbeck, A. L., *A Short Introduction to Germanic Linguistics* (1966); Waterman, John T., *A History of the German Language* (1966); Weinrich, Uriel and Beatrice, *Yiddish Language and Folklore: A Selective Bibliography* (1959); Williams, J. M., *Origins of the English Language* (1975).

Germanic law

Germanic law was the unwritten, customary law of the GERMANIC PEOPLES from their entry into recorded history until the end of the early Middle Ages. It was not the law of a unified people or state. Early Germanic law had three characteristics.

It was customary law, not statute law or the work of a legislator. The law seemed to live in the consciousness and conviction of each individual. It was attached to people, not to territory, and it was regarded as unalterable.

It was unwritten law, transmitted orally. Legal rules were expressed simply, formally, and directly. Legal acts, moreover, had to be visible or audible; requirements were established for specific formalities, for witnesses or even for an assembly, and for the use of legal symbols.

Germanic Society. The Germanic peoples were divided into groups, and all their law was originally group law. The oldest and most important group was the *Sippe,* or kindred, composed of males linked by blood ties from their forefathers and of others who were included as a result of marriage. The *Sippe* fulfilled several public obligations. It was a federation for peace among the members, and thus entitled them to law and freedom. It provided protection, especially of the honor of the members; it established guidelines for military service and for land settlement.

The *Sippe* was divided into houses, each under the control of the male head of the family. His power (*Munt*) extended over his wife, children born to his wife and recognized by him, and his free domestic servants. The *Munt* was primarily a power over persons, but it also carried with it a duty of protection. In the earliest times, land was not owned, and movables belonged not to individuals but to the house.

The Written Record. Under the influence of the Roman and Christian cultures of the lands they conquered, the Germanic peoples began to reduce their customs to writing. By the time this occurred, the kings had begun to make law; indeed, the Visigoths (see GOTHS) and LOMBARDS made no outward distinction between old customary and new kingly law.

The first written collections of Germanic law date from about the 5th century. For the Visigoths the comprehensive *Codex Euricianus* (*c.*475) is the earliest collection and shows the considerable influence of ROMAN LAW. Shortly thereafter, however, in 506, Alaric II promulgated the *Lex Romana Visigothorum* ("Breviary of Alaric"), a compilation based on Roman sources for the Romans living in his territories. Then, for the Goths alone, Leovigild (d. 586) issued a revised *Codex.* The very important *Lex Visigothorum* (*c.*654) of King Reccesvinth once again applied to both Visigoths and Romans and contained Germanic customary law.

The Burgundians had the *Lex Burgundionum* (501), promulgated by King Gundobad. It applied to Germans and in disputes between Romans and Germans. The same king issued (506) a separate code for Romans, the *Lex Romana Burgundionum,* but this seems to have had no practical importance.

Collections of Lombard laws began with King Rothair's Edict of 643, which was distinguished by clear systematization and exactness of expression. Later kings added new laws. Lombard law was closely related to that of the Saxons, Anglo-Saxons, and North Germans. Of all the Germanic laws, it alone was subjected to scholarly treatment, especially in the law school at Pavia. W. A. J. WATSON

Bibliography: King, P. D., *Law and Society in the Visigothic Kingdom* (1972); Wallace-Hadrill, J. M., *The Barbarian West 400–1000,* 3d ed. (1966).

See also: LAW, HISTORY OF.

Germanic peoples

Classical writers were aware of localized tribes of Germans (speakers of a Germanic language) perhaps as early as 600 BC. Substantial political contact, however, did not occur until the late 2d century BC when the Cimbri and Teutons attacked Italy. Julius CAESAR and TACITUS in his *Germania* (AD 98) provide most of the available information about the early Germans. Groups such as the Treveri, Nervii, and Tencteri were important during the mid-1st century BC. Later, the Frisians, Marcomanni, Quadi, GOTHS, VANDALS, and LOMBARDS are mentioned. The FRANKS, SAXONS, Alamans (also called Suevi), and Burgundians became more important in the West, and small groups such as the Heruli, Rugii, and Turcilingi are mentioned only briefly in the sources.

For most of the period through the late 5th century what is known about the Germanic peoples comes from classical writings of this era. Much has also been learned about the developing Iron Age culture of these peoples from archaeological evidence. Additional written sources became available with the appearance of GERMANIC LAW codes in the late 5th and early 6th centuries and the histories of writers like Jordanes and Gregory of Tours in the 6th century and BEDE in the early 8th century.

The Germanic peoples are generally credited with or blamed for destroying the Roman Empire and bringing an end to classical civilization. From the 2d to the 11th century various Germanic peoples, including VIKINGS, invaded, ravaged, and devastated great parts of Western Europe. Much wealth was consumed in defending the "civilized world" from these "barbarians," and countless lives were lost in these conflicts. Although they certainly played a role in destroying the Roman Empire, they also played an important role in building a new society within the framework of the Roman fortified *civitates,* the Christian religion, and Latin culture. Only in fringe areas far distant from Rome such as Britain did the Germanic language dominate within what had been the empire.

The Germanic contribution to the new medieval culture was largely that of human resources and military vitality. After having been absorbed in what is today France by the dominant Romance-Christian culture, these peoples proceeded to convert the less Romanized peoples east of the Rhine and educate them to the values of ancient civilization.

BERNARD S. BACHRACH

Bibliography: Bury, J. B., *The Invasion of Europe by the Barbarians* (1928; repr. 1967); Wallace-Hadrill, J. M., *The Barbarian West, 400–1000,* 3d ed. (1967).

Germanicus Caesar [jur-man'-i-kus see'-zur]

The Roman general Germanicus Caesar, b. May 24, 15 BC, achieved success on the battlefield as well as great personal popularity. His father was Nero Claudius Germanicus Drusus (see DRUSUS family), the brother of TIBERIUS; the latter adopted young Germanicus in AD 4. Germanicus married Agrippina, a granddaughter of Emperor AUGUSTUS.

He fought under Tiberius in Pannonia and Dalmatia (AD 7–9) and on the Rhine (AD 11). Consul in 12, Germanicus was appointed commander in Germany and Gaul (France). After Augustus's death (14) he suppressed a mutiny in the legions of Lower Germany. During 14–16 Germanicus launched a series of campaigns against the German leader ARMINIUS. These struggles proved inconclusive, and Tiberius (now emperor) recalled Germanicus, who celebrated a triumph in 17 and served a second consulship in 18. Sent to the east, Germanicus subdued Cappadocia and Commagene, organizing them into provinces.

After a visit to Egypt, Germanicus suddenly fell ill at Antioch. He voiced suspicion that he had been poisoned by the Roman governor of Syria before he died on Oct. 10, 19. Germanicus's children included CALIGULA, who became emperor (r. 37–41), and AGRIPPINA II, mother of the emperor NERO (r. 54–68). Germanicus's brother was also emperor as CLAUDIUS I (r. 41–54).

germanium [jur-mayn'-ee-uhm]

The chemical element germanium, semimetal of group IVA in the periodic table, is of central importance in the manufacture of SEMICONDUCTOR materials and devices. Its symbol is Ge, atomic number 32, and atomic weight 72.59. The German chemist Clemens A. Winkler first isolated the element in 1886 from the mineral argyrodite, a mixed sulfide of silver and germanium, and named it after his homeland. Germanium is widely distributed in the Earth's crust, with an average abundance of about 7 grams per metric ton. The element is usually found as a minor component in sulfide ores of copper, zinc, tin, lead, and antimony.

Germanium has a brittle metallic appearance, a melting point of 937.4° C, and a boiling point of 2,830° C. It crystallizes in a cubic structure similar to diamond but has a hardness of only 6 on Moh's scale (diamond is 10). The ultrapure element is an intrinsic semiconductor, which accounts for its major use in solid-state electronics. It forms compounds in the +2 and +4 oxidation states. The +2 state is both easily reduced to the element and easily oxidized to Ge(IV), so that tetravalent germanium compounds are the most common. The chloride and oxide, $GeCl_4$ and GeO_2, are the most important compounds because of the role they play in the production of the pure element.

Ultrapure germanium can be produced in near-crystalline perfection more easily than other semiconductors. For this reason alone, the electronic properties of germanium have been studied more than those of any other solid. The earliest semiconductor research was done with this element, and William Shockley used germanium to make the first transistor in 1948.

Germanium is recovered by treating enriched wastes and residues from zinc sulfide ores, pyrometallic ores, and coal with hydrochloric acid to form the volatile liquid $GeCl_4$, which is extracted with carbon tetrachloride and purified by distillation. The tetrachloride is treated with demineralized water to precipitate the dioxide GeO_2, which is then reduced to germanium with hydrogen. The ultrapure element is obtained by zone refining, a selective fusion-recrystallization process that concentrates impurities in the melt.

Germanium dioxide is finding increasing use in special optical materials. Fused GeO_2 glasses have transmission characteristics greatly superior to quartz (SiO_2) glasses in the infrared portion of the spectrum. PHILIP C. KELLER

Bibliography: Cotton, F. A., and Wilkinson, Geoffrey, *Basic Inorganic Chemistry* (1976); Hampel, C. A., ed., *The Encyclopedia of the Chemical Elements* (1968); Rochow, E. G., *The Metalloids* (1966).

Germanus of Auxerre, Saint [jur-mayn'-uhs, oh-sair']

Saint Germanus, c.378-448, was a Roman advocate who ruled part of Gaul before becoming bishop of Auxerre in 418. He was probably the teacher of Saint PATRICK. He spent his personal fortune on charitable works and made two journeys to Britain. The first journey (429) was made at the request of Pope Celestine I, who commissioned Germanus to eliminate

PELAGIANISM in Britain. On the second journey (447), he led British troops to victory over the Picts and Saxons. Feast day: July 31.

Germany, East and West

Germany, a unified country from 1871 to 1945, is now divided into two states, the Federal Republic of Germany (West Germany) and the German Democratic Republic (East Germany). Located in central Europe, the states are bordered on the north by the North Sea, Denmark, and the Baltic Sea; on the east by Poland, Czechoslovakia, and Austria; on the south by Liechtenstein and Switzerland; and on the west by France, Luxembourg, Belgium, and the Netherlands.

Following Germany's defeat at the end of World War II, the country was divided into four zones of occupation by the Allies—France, Great Britain, the United States, and the USSR. In 1949, West Germany was created from the combined British, French, and U.S. zones, and East Germany was soon created from the Soviet-occupied zone. Throughout the postwar period West Germany has been allied with the West, whereas East Germany is a Communist state, closely tied to the USSR and the other Soviet-bloc nations.

BERLIN, the capital of Germany, was also divided into occupation sectors after the war and subsequently partitioned. East Berlin is now the capital of East Germany. West Berlin is now a West German enclave surrounded by East German territory.

The two Germanies have each undergone spectacular economic recovery and growth during the postwar period. For both, regional economic cooperation has been a key element: West Germany is a member of the EUROPEAN ECONOMIC COMMUNITY (EEC), and East Germany belongs to the COUNCIL OF MUTUAL ECONOMIC ASSISTANCE (Comecon or CMEA).

LAND AND RESOURCES

Five major physiographic regions may be differentiated in the two Germanies: the North German Lowlands, the Southern Transitional Borderlands, the Central Uplands (Mittelgebirge), the Alpine Foreland, and the Alps.

North German Lowlands. This hilly region, extending south from the Baltic Sea coast, is part of the Great Plain of Europe. The plain was covered by Quaternary deposits, which are partially of glacial origin. The Baltic and the North Sea coasts have numerous indentations, but because coastal waters are shallow the area is deficient in natural harbors. The infertile soils require intensive tillage and fertilization.

Southern Transitional Borderlands. To the south of the lowlands is a transitional belt of thinly layered morainic material with highly fertile loess soil. The borderlands include a number of lowland embayments, most notably the Cologne Bay in the southwest. Most of West Germany's coal and lignite deposits are located in the borderlands. The Mittelland Canal is a vital artery in the region.

Central Uplands. A faulted area composed of worn-down fragments of the late Paleozoic system, the Central Uplands are heavily forested and consist of dissected hills, inactive volcanoes, plateaus, and granite massifs. The highland areas include the scarplands of Swabia and Franconia in the southwest; the HARZ Mountains, Thuringian Forest, and Saxon Uplands in the north and east; and the Bohemian Forest in the southeast. Of the many ridges and valleys of the region, the most picturesque is the valley of the Middle Rhine River, which flows in an 80-km-long (50-mi), often-narrow, steep gorge from Bingen to Bonn. The Rhine is Europe's busiest waterway and the gorge is a famous tourist attraction.

Alpine Foreland and the Alps. The Alpine Foreland, located to the northeast of the Alps, has the appearance of a broad plain. Rivers rise in the Alps and cross the foreland in broad, marshy valleys. Only the Danube is navigable. A small part of the ALPS lies within Germany, in the extreme south. Germany's highest mountain peak, the Zugspitze (2,963 m/9,721 ft) is located south of Munich.

Drainage. Germany has an extensive network of rivers, most of which drain into the Baltic and North seas. The major exception is the DANUBE, which flows into the Black Sea. The RHINE RIVER is navigable throughout West Germany. The Mo-

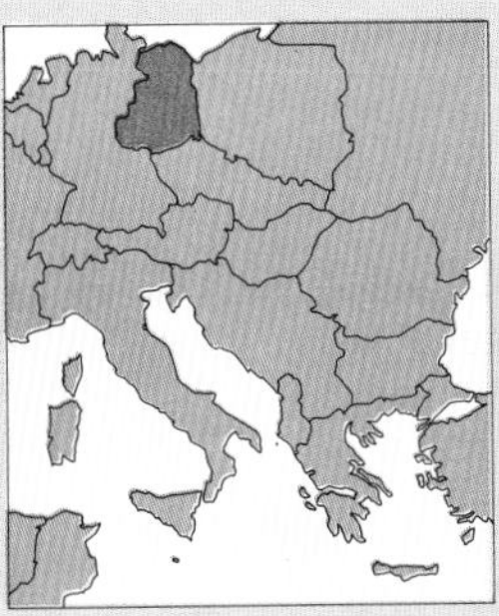

GERMAN DEMOCRATIC REPUBLIC (EAST GERMANY)

LAND. Area: 108,568 km^2 (41,918 mi^2). Capital and largest city: East Berlin (1985 est. pop., 1,196,900).

PEOPLE. Population (1987 est.): 16,700,000; density (1987 est.): 154 persons per km^2 (399 per mi^2). Distribution (1987): 77% urban, 23% rural. Annual growth (1987): 0.0% Official language: German. Major religions: Protestantism, Roman Catholicism.

EDUCATION AND HEALTH. Literacy (1985): 100% of adult population. Universities (1987): 7. Hospital beds (1985): 170,000. Physicians (1985): 37,000. Life expectancy (1983): women—75.1; men—69.1. Infant mortality (1986): 9.6 per 1,000 live births.

ECONOMY. GNP (1984): $93.6 billion; $5,600 per capita. Labor distribution (1984): agriculture—10.7%; mining and manufacturing—41%; construction—6.9%; transportation and communication—7.4%; trade—10.1%; services—23.9%. Foreign trade (1984): imports—$22.9 billion; exports—$25.1 billion; principal trade partners—USSR, Czechoslovakia, West Germany, Poland. Currency: 1 DDR mark = 100 pfennige.

GOVERNMENT. Type: Communist state. Legislature: Volkskammer. Political subdivisions: 15 districts.

COMMUNICATIONS. Railroads (1984): 14,226 km (8,840 mi). Roads (1984): 47,380 km (29,440 mi) total. Major ports: 4. Major airfields: 4.

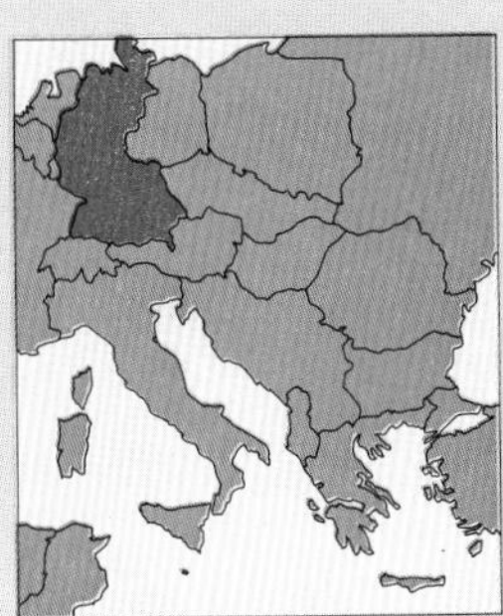

FEDERAL REPUBLIC OF GERMANY (WEST GERMANY)

LAND. Area: 248,577 km^2 (95,976 mi^2). Capital: Bonn (1985 est. pop., 292,600). Largest city: West Berlin (1985 est. pop., 1,852,700).

PEOPLE. Pop. (1987 est.): 61,000,000; density (1987 est.): 245 persons per km^2 (636 per mi^2). Distr. (1987 est.): 85% urban, 15% rural. Ann. growth (1987): −0.2%. Off. language: German. Major religions: Protestantism, Roman Catholicism.

EDUCATION AND HEALTH. Literacy (1985): 100% of adult population. Universities (1985): 42. Hospital beds (1984): 678,708. Physicians (1985): 153,895. Life expectancy (1982–84): women—77.5; men—70.8. Infant mortality (1986): 9.5 per 1,000 live births.

ECONOMY. GNP (1986): $667.3 billion; $10,940 per capita. Labor distribution (1985): agriculture—5.4%; industry—41.6%; services and other—34.7%; trade and transport—18.2%. Foreign trade (1985): imports—$157.5 billion; exports—$182.4 billion; principal trade partners—France, the Netherlands, Italy, United Kingdom, United States, Belgium-Luxembourg. Currency: 1 Deutsche mark = 100 pfennige.

GOVERNMENT. Type: Federal republic. Legislature: Federal Parliament. Political subdivisions: 10 states.

COMMUNICATIONS. Railroads (1984): 68,512 km (42,571 mi) total. Roads (1984): 490,045 km (304,500 mi) total. Major ports: 11. Major airfields: 8.

GERMANY
Major Urban Area
Railroad
Canal or Waterway
Spot Elevation or Depth
National capitals are underlined
City type size indicates relative importance
0 20 40 60 80 100 km
0 20 40 60 mi
Scale 1:4,413,000
Meters
4000
2000
1000
500
200
0
0
200
Feet
13124
6562
3281
1640
656
Sea Level
0
656
NORTH SEA
BALTIC SEA
DENMARK
NETHERLANDS
BELGIUM
LUXEMBOURG
FRANCE
SWITZERLAND
AUSTRIA
CZECHOSLOVAKIA
POLAND
WEST GERMANY
EAST GERMANY
NORTH FRISIAN ISLANDS
EAST FRISIAN ISLANDS
Deutsche Bay
Kieler Bay
Mecklenburger Bay
Pomeranian Bay
BLACK FOREST
SCHWÄBISCHE ALB
THURINGIAN FOREST
ORE MTS.
BOHEMIAN FOREST
ALPS
Hamburg
Bremen
Hannover
Kiel
Lübeck
Rostock
Schwerin
West Berlin
East Berlin
Magdeburg
Leipzig
Dresden
Halle
Karl-Marx-Stadt (Chemnitz)
Erfurt
Szczecin
Prague
Dortmund
Essen
Düsseldorf
Cologne
Bonn
Frankfurt am Main
Mannheim
Karlsruhe
Stuttgart
Nuremberg
Munich
Augsburg
Regensburg
Würzburg
Kassel
Braunschweig
Osnabrück
Bielefeld
Münster
Wiesbaden
Mainz
Saarbrücken
Strasbourg
Basel
Zurich
Salzburg
Innsbruck
Linz
Luxembourg
Liège
Arnhem
Groningen
© 1980 Rand McNally & Co.
A-561000-772

SELLE (German: Mosel) and the MAIN rivers are its chief tributaries. Chief tributaries of the Danube are the INN, Isar, and Naab rivers. Other important rivers are the ELBE, ODER, SPREE, WESER, Ems, and Saale. Lake CONSTANCE, Germany's largest lake, is located in the Alps.

Climate. Germany's climate is generally temperate. Because of moist, warm winds from the Atlantic Ocean, the west experiences fairly mild winters and summers. The average annual temperature in northwestern Germany is about 10° C (50° F); in the southwest it averages 12° C (53° F) yearly. The east experiences a more continental climate with cold winters and short, hot summers. Annual temperatures average about 2° to 4° C (3.6° to 7.2° F) lower than in the west. Baltic Sea harbors are frequently closed by ice during the winter.

Precipitation is evenly distributed throughout Germany, with the heaviest rainfall—from 864 to 1,016 mm (34 to 40 in)—occurring in the highlands. The coast has an annual average precipitation of 762 mm (30 in), and the east receives from 406 to 508 mm (16 to 20 in).

Flora and Fauna. More than one-quarter of the land is still under forest cover, mostly in highland regions. Coniferous trees, especially pine and fir, constitute two-thirds of the timber stands. Deciduous species, which include birch, beech, chestnut, oak, and walnut, grow mainly in the warmer area of west central and southwest Germany. Vines flourish in the Rhine, Moselle, and Danube River valleys.

Wild fauna are limited in number and variety to such species as the red and roe deer, although wild boars inhabit some forested areas. Less common species found in remote areas include the bear, wolf, fox, wildcat, otter, and badger.

The harmful effect of pollutants on Germany's forests has become a major concern with the proliferation of exhaust fumes and industrial waste.

PEOPLE OF WEST GERMANY

Language and Religion. Although the German language is spoken by both West and East Germans, it always has been distinguished by its many regional dialects. The standard language, *Hochdeutsch* (High German), is taught in school, but despite the influence of radio and television, most people still speak their own dialects (see GERMANIC LANGUAGES). Schleswig-Holstein has a small Danish minority.

West Germany's constitution guarantees "undisturbed practice of religion." About 90% of the population belong to Christian churches, roughly divided between Roman Catholic and Evangelical (a union of Lutheran and Reformed) with a small number in other Christian denominations. Evangelical Protestants are the majority in the north, and Catholics are concentrated in the south. Jews, once a large minority, today constitute only about 0.1% of the population.

Demography. The postwar influx of refugees and expellees from Eastern Europe and East Germany resulted in a rapid growth of West Germany's population, which increased by about 13 to 14 million between 1950 and 1980. Thereafter the combination of a decline in immigration and a lowered birth rate caused the population to level off and decrease slightly. The country now has one of the lowest birthrates in the world.

Of the major European nations, only the Netherlands and Belgium are more densely inhabited than West Germany. Distribution is uneven, however, with the major concentration in the heavily industrialized west. The Ruhr conurbation constitutes only about 2% of the land area, but it is the home of nearly 10% of West Germans.

Between 80% and 90% of West Germany's inhabitants are classified as urban dwellers, but the percentage of the population so classified has been decreasing in recent years. The

(Left) *Neuschwanstein Castle, located in the Bavarian Alps and begun in 1869, was inspired by three operas—*Lohengrin, Parsifal, *and* Tannhäuser*—all written by the German composer Richard Wagner.*

The Schwarzwald, or Black Forest, is a mountain range in southwestern West Germany. The range, a resort area with many rivers and lakes, extends approximately 145 km (90 mi) roughly parallel with the Rhine. Its once-dense coniferous forests have been severely affected by acid rain.

The tower of the Kaiser Wilhelm Gedächniskirche, damaged during World War II, looms above the recently constructed memorial church along the Kurfürstendamm, West Berlin's major commercial boulevard. The older church has been preserved in its ruined state as a reminder of the city's sufferings during World War II.

principal cities, in order of size, are West Berlin, HAMBURG, MUNICH, COLOGNE, ESSEN, FRANKFURT AM MAIN, DORTMUND, DÜSSELDORF, STUTTGART, BREMEN, DUISBURG, HANNOVER, NUREMBERG, BOCHUM, WUPPERTAL, BIELEFELD, MANNHEIM, BONN, GELSENKIRCHEN, MÜNSTER, KARLSRUHE, WIESBADEN, Mönchengladbach, BRUNSWICK, KIEL, AUGSBURG, AACHEN, Oberhausen, KREFELD, LÜBECK, Hagen, MAINZ, SAARBRÜCKEN, KASSEL, and FREIBURG IM BREISGAU.

Education and Health. West Germany's adult population is virtually 100% literate. Educational and cultural matters in West Germany are the responsibility of the individual states, and thus school curricula vary widely among them. School attendance is compulsory for 9 years—from the ages of 6 to 15—in most states and for 10 years in some. All public education is free. Kindergarten, which originated in Germany, is for children ages 3 to 6. All children attend 4 years of primary school and then choose between 3 types of secondary schools. The 9-year high school, or GYMNASIUM, is required for university admission. About half of West Germany's students attend the 5-year secondary school (the *Hauptschule*), which specializes in vocational education. The intermediate school (*Realschule*) provides technical education. This system has been criticized on the grounds that children must decide on their curriculum too early in their education and find it difficult to switch schools. A new type of school, the comprehensive school (*Gesamtschule*) combines the curricula of all three types of traditional school.

The oldest university, at Heidelberg, was founded in 1386. Other venerable universities include Freiburg (1457), Munich (1472), Tübingen (1477), Marburg (1527), and Göttingen (1737). More than 20 new universities have been founded since 1965. The linguist and philosopher Wilhelm von Humboldt (1767–1835) is considered the father of the university system as it developed in the 19th century, when German universities were pioneers in changing and expanding their curricula to keep abreast of advances in science. They set a new world standard by a skillful and successful combination of teaching and research. Modern-day curricula—partly in response to student unrest during the 1960s and '70s—have greatly broadened, aim at equal education for all, and provide more professional education. The number of students attending universities increased from 6% of those leaving high school in 1950 to 25% in 1980.

West Germany's national wealth has resulted in a high standard of health care. About half of all deaths result from heart and circulatory-system ailments, a rate comparable with the other highly developed countries. Compulsory health insurance programs cover health, accident, and disability costs.

Communications. Newspapers are the most important source of news, but news magazines such as *der Spiegel* and *Stern*

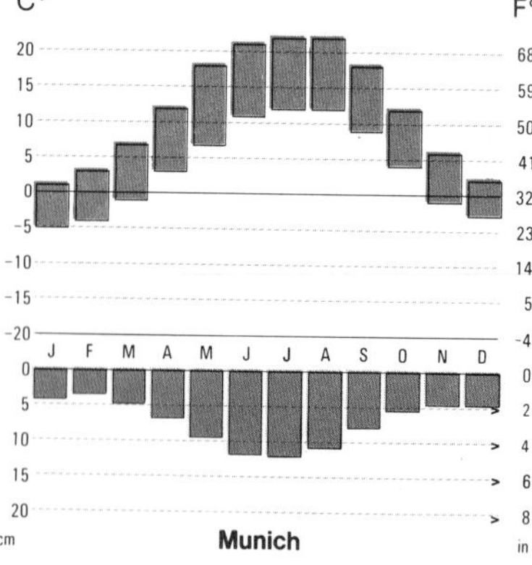

Bars indicate monthly ranges of temperature (red) and precipitation (blue). Munich, located in the southern highlands of Bavaria, has the high precipitation and moderate temperatures characteristic of a marine west-coast climate. Berlin, on the northern plain, has the fairly constant precipitation and moderate temperatures of the continental humid zone. The climate changes gradually from north to south, as the moderating maritime influences of the North and Baltic seas are increasingly countered by extremes of continental weather systems in the south.

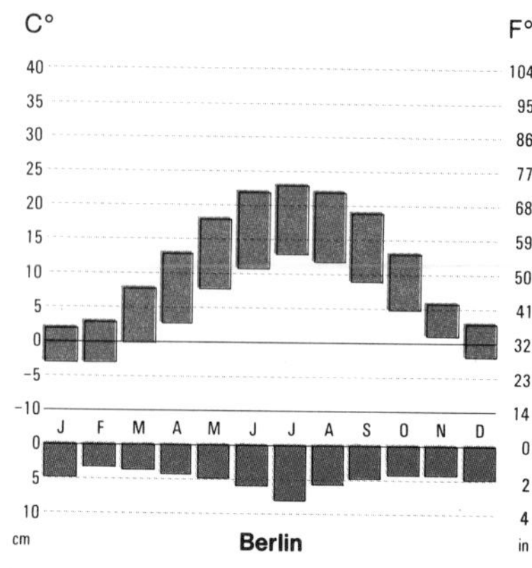

East Berlin's Alexander Platz, one of the city's largest public squares, contains department stores, hotels, and the World Clock, which indicates the time in national capitals around the world. The square was constructed as part of an urban redevelopment project.

are also very popular. The broadcasting media are organized as public corporations. They are self-governing but are charged with the responsibility of presenting a comprehensive picture of German society. Most West German households own a radio and a television.

Sociocultural Patterns. West German societal structure has undergone fundamental changes in the 20th century. The nobility have lost their predominant role, and a middle class has become dominant, especially since the early 1950s. The upper-middle class comprises mostly private-enterprise managers, professionals, and owners of large farms. In general, a high standard of living can be achieved only if both partners in a marriage are employed. Foreign workers (*Gastarbeiter*), most of them from Mediterranean countries, began to play a role in West German industry during the mid-1950s and have since become a permanent feature of West German life. Their presence has caused a certain amount of friction with the German population, and they have often been subject to discrimination. The stresses of postwar changes have been evident in the radical, violent politics of some left-wing fringe groups and neo-Nazi organizations, in student unrest, and in demonstrations against nuclear arms. Environmentalism, represented by the Green party, won support from a substantial minority of voters in the 1980s.

PEOPLE OF EAST GERMANY

As in West Germany, the population in East Germany is basically homogeneous, except for a small (0.2%) Slavic minority, the Sorbs, or Wends. Religious practice is permitted, and most people belong to the Evangelical church, although there is a small Catholic minority. Church membership, however, has declined since the Communist regime was instituted.

The population is about one-fourth that of West Germany. Its per capita income, however, is much lower, although it is the highest among the Comecon nations. Even though the population increased after World War II, a sizable outflow of new immigrants and local residents subsequently occurred until 1961, when construction of the BERLIN WALL virtually halted emigration. Partly because the percentage of those in the child-bearing age group is lower than average, the country has a zero growth rate.

Much of the northern part of the country is sparsely settled. Its only population center is ROSTOCK, one of East Germany's main seaports. The population in and around East Berlin has greatly increased since the establishment of East Germany. The southern part of the country traditionally has been densely settled, especially in the fertile loess lowlands. The leading cities of the south are LEIPZIG, DRESDEN, KARL-MARX-STADT, and MAGDEBURG. Other important industrial towns are HALLE, ERFURT, ZWICKAU, JENA, and Cottbus. East Berlin and its neighboring city of POTSDAM together have a population of more than 1.3 million. New industrial dormitory towns include Halle-Neustadt, Eisenhüttenstadt, Neu-Hoyerswerda, and Schwedt.

Education and Health. Education in East Germany is free and compulsory, and the population is virtually 100% literate. The system, under complete state control, is based on a 10-year polytechnical school for basic education, stressing science and technology. Higher education is available to those who have completed the basic program and 2 to 4 years of apprentice training in a professional school, vocational school, or specialized adult institute. East Germany has more than 50 institutions of higher education, including 7 universities. All education is strongly influenced by the Soviet model, and this is clearly reflected in the broadening of admission policies for higher education with priority given to party and workers' groups.

As in West Germany, health standards are high. Also as in West Germany, heart and circulatory-system diseases are the principal causes of death. Compulsory insurance covers health, disability, unemployment, and other costs.

Communications. The Communist party publishes East Germany's principal newspapers and controls radio and television broadcasting. Many television and radio programs from West Germany are popular in East Germany and are accessible to most of the population.

Sociocultural Patterns. Society in a Communist state is dominated by the party (the bureaucracy and high government officials) and a group of technicians. Members of the party and especially those in leading positions have many privileges, and a clear class distinction exists between party members, less than 10% of the total population, and others.

ECONOMIC ACTIVITY IN WEST GERMANY

Germany experienced an industrial revolution following its political unification in 1871. Soon it exceeded other European countries in production and trade. Despite its defeat and territorial losses during World War I, Germany continued its economic progress until World War II. By a superhuman effort and with the help of MARSHALL PLAN aid from the United States, West Germany's economy quickly revived after the war. By early 1950 the standard of living exceeded the prewar level, and today it is one of the highest in Europe.

Agriculture, Forestry, and Fishing. Only a small minority of the West German population is engaged in agriculture, forestry, and fishing. When Germany was partitioned after World War II, most of the arable land went to East Germany. Nevertheless, today West Germany is largely self-sufficient in food production in most years. About one-third of the total land area is arable.

Oats, barley, rye, wheat, and potatoes are the chief food crops. Barley is of special importance for the brewing of beer, and oats predominate in the moist regions along the Baltic coast and the North Sea. Sugar beets and fodder are grown on the loess soils at the foot of the Central Uplands. Vegetable production is widespread. Industrial crops, such as hemp, flax, tobacco, and sunflowers, are of increasing importance. Animal husbandry is significant.

The North Sea is the main fishing ground. Almost half of the fish landed are cod and redfish. The small forestry industry produces timber, pulp, and their products.

Mining and Energy. Only about 2% of the labor force works in mining and power production. Coal, potash, and lignite are West Germany's basic mineral resources. Small deposits of iron ore, lead, zinc, and copper are also mined. The RUHR VALLEY is the center of rich coking coal and other types of coal (about 80% of West Germany's production), with the

Wearing traditional knickers and vest, members of a brass band give an open-air concert in their town square. West Germans from all regions of the country have perpetuated local traditions, reflecting the strength of regional loyalties within the modern nation.

Diners enjoy a meal at a sidewalk cafe in the Marienplatz, the center of the old city of Munich. Munich, which historically has been the most important city of Bavaria, is the third largest urban center of West Germany after West Berlin and Hamburg.

Saar and the region near Aachen contributing the remainder. Lignite deposits, concentrated in the Cologne vicinity, occur in thick deposits close to the surface. Hard-coal production has declined significantly since 1970, while lignite production has undergone a moderate increase.

Among the energy sources, petroleum, nuclear power, and natural gas all play a role in the German economy. West Germany is independent in coal requirements. Although some petroleum is extracted from the North Sea, most of this important energy source must be imported. Domestic natural gas is produced in areas bordering the Netherlands and the North Sea. About one-third of the nation's electric power is nuclear generated.

Manufacturing. West Germany is one of the world's great industrial powers, but its economy tended to be sluggish during the 1980s. Its industries are generally located in a belt across the central part of the country extending from Aachen on the German-Belgian border to the border of Czechoslovakia. About 40% of the labor force are engaged in industry. Steel and chemicals are the leading products. Other major goods are automobiles, other transportation equipment, heavy machinery, aluminum, diverse small consumer goods, and precision instruments.

Services and Tourism. The service sector—including finance, trade, and public employees—engages a large portion of the labor force. West Germany's tourist industry is important to the economy. Popular tourist areas include the Alps, the Rhine valley, coastal resorts, resorts and spas in the Central Uplands, and the BLACK FOREST.

Trade. Free trade within the EEC has played a major role in increasing West Germany's foreign commerce. Food constitutes about one-tenth of its total imports; raw materials account for about a quarter and include sizable quantities of natural rubber, petroleum, and ores. Additional imports include such manufactured goods as machinery and automobiles. Exports include a wide range of industrial goods, raw materials and fuels, and food items.

The countries of the EEC account for the majority of West Germany's total exports and imports. Major export markets besides the EEC are the United States, the non-EEC European nations, and Japan. Intrazonal trade (between the two Germanies) is increasing, but this trade is more important to East Germany than it is to West Germany; West Germany is one of the GDR's main trade partners.

Transportation. The most important means of transportation is the federal railways; the rail network of nearly 70,000 km

Karl Marx Platz, Neubrandenburg's central square, blends traditional and modern architectural styles. The city, which is located in East Germany's northern lowlands, served as capital of the duchy of Mecklenburg-Stargard during the 14th and 15th centuries.

(20,000 mi) is 35% electrified. Road traffic has been growing rapidly and competing with the railroads; four-fifths of passenger transportation is by private car. West Germany has 7,400 km (4,600 mi) of express highways, which are called Autobahns.

The canals and navigable rivers within Germany are important for bulk transport. The Rhine-Main-Danube Canal, scheduled for completion by the mid-1980s, will enable vessels to travel from the North Sea to the Black Sea. The merchant fleet consists of 9 million gross tons registered. Lufthansa is the official and only West German airline.

ECONOMIC ACTIVITY IN EAST GERMANY

Economic recovery after World War II took longer in East Germany, which was occupied by the USSR and was forced to pay considerable reparations in the form of shipments of entire factories and industrial goods. East Germany is now, however, one of the world's leading industrial nations, with a gross national product of $135.4 billion (1980).

Agriculture and Forestry. This sector employs only about 11% of the total labor force. Under the Communist regime 95% of the farmland has been gradually collectivized. The impact of this collectivization and the resistance offered by the traditional farmers, indicated by the poor performance of farming, was felt in the food rationing that had to be continued throughout the 1950s. With industrial employment becoming more attractive and the aging of the farm labor force, a shortage of people willing to work on farms has been a serious problem for East Germany. Collectives average 5,000 ha (12,355 acres). Land use for agriculture varies from 20% in sandy soils to as much as 75% in the fertile loess soils of the Southern Transitional region. Of the cereal crops, more rye is produced than wheat, and industrial crops are increasing. Increased area sown for fodder crops is an indication of the growing importance of livestock.

About 27% of East Germany is covered by forests, and 75% of this is regarded as primarily wood producing. In 1979, 8.8 million m^3 (310.8 million ft^3) of wood was cut. An active afforestation program is underway, in part to offset overcutting during the war and early postwar years.

Mining, Manufacturing, and Power. More than 40% of the labor force works in these sectors. East Germany is mineral poor and depends almost exclusively on Soviet raw materials. Potash, lignite, and a small but growing natural gas industry constitute most of the mining sector. Additionally, small amounts of iron, copper, tin, silver, and salt are also mined.

Despite its dependence on imports, East Germany has built a highly technically oriented industrial sector, producing iron and steel, machine tools and engineering equipment, optics, and precision equipment. Other important industries include textiles and food.

In 1978, East Germany's energy consumption by fuel types was: coal 68.9%, oil 21.3%, natural gas 6.6%, and hydro and nuclear electricity 3.2%. East Germany hopes to rely on nuclear production for 20% of its electricity by 1990.

Services. The tertiary sector employs only about 20% of East German workers. Tourism is a relatively small industry, with less than 1 million foreign tourists in 1978. Spas and health resorts are popular attractions, as are Leipzig, with its well-known trade fair, and Berlin.

Trade. Two-thirds of East Germany's volume of foreign trade is with Comecon members, and half of it is with the USSR. West Germany is now also an important trading partner, and East Germany benefits from a large interest-free credit (about $312 million in 1983) from West Germany. East Germany's principal exports are machinery, precision and optical instruments, chemicals, and textiles and clothing.

Transportation. East Germany's transportation network was greatly disrupted by the new borders and the changes in direction of goods and passenger traffic after World War II. Of more than 40 prewar routes that crossed into West Germany, only 5 remain open. Motor transport has become increasingly important since the 1960s and today plays an important role in short-distance haulage. Railroads carry freight over longer distances and dominate passenger service.

Natural waterways provide north-south routes, and canals provide mostly east-west connections. Interflug, the national airline, offers regular links with many countries.

GOVERNMENT AND POLITICS OF WEST GERMANY

The federal constitution of West Germany, the Basic Law, was put into effect at a constitutional convention in 1949. The constitution provides for a president, a largely ceremonial post. The legislative branch consists of two houses: the Bundestag, or House of Representatives, and the Bundesrat, or Federal Council. Half the members of the Bundestag are elected by winning a majority of the votes in given constituencies. The other half of the seats are distributed among the parties on the

Factories in the Ruhr River valley have been producing large quantities of iron and steel since the 19th century. Heavily bombed during World War II, the Ruhr was rebuilt and is now the center of West Germany's steel, chemical, and petroleum-products industries.

The valleys and plateaus of West Germany's Central Uplands are dotted with small farms, which produce a variety of grains and other crops. The heavily forested hills of the region are a major source of timber, which is used primarily for manufacturing paper.

The Rhine-Main-Danube Canal, under construction in the 1980s, flows through the fertile river valleys of south central Germany. The purpose of the canal is to link the tributaries of the Rhine with those of the Danube, providing a waterway from Rotterdam to the Black Sea.

basis of votes cast for party lists in each state. Only parties gaining at least 5% of the votes cast nationally receive seats under this system of proportional representation. The Bundesrat is composed of delegations appointed by the government of each state according to the size of its population; delegation members vote as a bloc. The Bundesrat can also veto legislation passed by the Bundestag. West Berlin sends 4 representatives to the Bundesrat and 22 representatives to the Bundestag, but because of its special legal status, its members have only limited voting rights.

The federal chancellor is the head of the government and is nominated by the federal president and elected by the Bundestag. Cabinet ministers are nominated by the chancellor and approved by the president.

Individual state governments have considerable power—the right to levy taxes, to establish educational and cultural policies, and to maintain police forces. Each state's chief official is a president elected by popular vote. Each state has its own parliament. The ten states (*Länder*) are Baden-Württemberg (see BADEN; WÜRTTEMBERG), BAVARIA, BREMEN, HAMBURG, Hessen (HESSE), Lower Saxony, North Rhine-Westphalia (see WESTPHALIA), Rhineland-Palatinate (see RHINELAND; PALATINATE), SAARLAND, and SCHLESWIG-HOLSTEIN.

The Federal Constitutional Court is the supreme judicial authority in West Germany. This court guarantees the Basic Law and rules in disputes between the federal government and the states. The Supreme Federal Court is the highest court in civil and criminal cases. Each state has local courts, district courts, and a court of appeals.

West Germany has three main political parties—the Christian Democrats, with whom the Christian Social Union in Bavaria is closely associated (CDU/CSU); the Social Democratic party (SPD); and a smaller party associated with the CDU/CSU in the present government, the Free Democratic party (FDP). The Greens, an antinuclear group that opposes West Germany's membership in the NATO alliance, gained 42 parliamentary seats in the 1987 elections. Helmut KOHL of the CDU/CSU has been chancellor since 1982.

GOVERNMENT AND POLITICS OF EAST GERMANY

The German Democratic Republic (GDR) was officially founded in October 1949, and in 1954 the USSR granted autonomy. The present constitution dates from 1968, although it was amended (1974) to link the GDR officially with the USSR. For most of its history the GDR has been a highly centralized single-party state with political institutions modeled on those of the USSR.

The government of East Germany consists of the 24 members of the Council of State (Staatsrat), although their influence has been much reduced in the last few years. The chairman of the council is the head of state. The Council of Ministers leads the government, and its chairman functions as the prime minister. The legislative body is a 500-member unicameral parliament (Volkskammer), with most of its members belonging to the dominant Socialist Unity party (SED), the Communist party. The most important official is the general secretary of the central committee of the SED, who now also chairs the Council of State. Four other small parties work closely with the SED. East Germany has a Supreme Court and numerous local courts constitutionally responsible to parliament.

Local government consists of 15 districts (*Bezirke*) including Berlin. The districts replaced (1952) the former prewar states of BRANDENBURG, MECKLENBURG, SAXONY, THURINGIA, and Saxony-Anhalt.

HISTORY SINCE 1945

After the German capitulation in World War II the Allies—the United States, France, Great Britain, and the USSR—divided Germany into four occupation zones. Berlin, located within the Soviet zone, was at first jointly administered by the four powers, each occupying a sector of the city. According to the terms of the Potsdam Conference (August 1945) Germany lost its territory east of the Oder and western Neisse rivers (see ODER-NEISSE LINE) to Poland and a major part of East Prussia to the USSR. Together the lands totaled about 25% of the former German Reich. Following the Potsdam Conference 5.5 million ethnic Germans were expelled from Poland, and 3.5 million Sudeten Germans were expelled from Czechoslovakia. Perhaps another 4 million Germans left their ancestral homes in Romania, Yugoslavia, and Hungary, most of whom settled in areas that became West Germany. Cooperation between the

These women are assembling electronic instruments, one of East Germany's chief products, in a Berlin factory. The East German economy has expanded rapidly since the 1960s, making the nation the most highly industrialized country of the Eastern European bloc.

USSR and the Western Allies ceased in March 1948, when the USSR left the Allied Control Council.

When all hope of Soviet cooperation in solving Germany's problems was abandoned in mid-1948, the Western powers agreed to establish a West German state, which was founded on Sept. 21, 1949. Konrad ADENAUER was elected chancellor. On May 5, 1955, full sovereignty was restored when the occupation regime was eliminated. West Germany had been transformed from a defeated enemy to a valuable partner. Under the CDU/CSU government of Chancellor Adenauer (1950–63) the "economic miracle" occurred.

The Soviet zone was structured on the Soviet model, but only after the creation of West Germany was East Germany officially founded (October 1949). An anti-Soviet uprising in June 1953 was easily crushed by Soviet troops. Many citizens fled to West Berlin and West Germany, resulting in construction of a barbed-wire fence along its entire border and, finally, in the Berlin Wall in August 1961. By then about 3.5 million people had left East Germany.

In 1955, West Germany became a member of the North Atlantic Treaty Organization (NATO). It was more firmly linked with Western Europe when it became one of the founding members of the EEC. In 1958 rearmament began. In 1957–59 the East and West German governments resumed discussions for reunification, but no agreement could be reached.

The enclave of West Berlin had come under pressure when the USSR cut off the city from all transport links to the West for 10 months (1948–49). The BERLIN AIRLIFT, the huge effort by U.S. and British airfleets to supply West Berlin, forced the USSR to reopen the transport routes. In 1958 the USSR again issued an ultimatum, but the Western powers were united in refusing to capitulate. In June 1962 a partial agreement was reached whereby the USSR would no longer dispute the right of the Western powers' presence in West Berlin and would accept the existing links between West Berlin and the rest of West Germany.

Political tranquillity, which had been the mark of West German politics since its founding, was interrupted when Chancellor Adenauer was forced to resign in 1963, and his economics minister, Ludwig ERHARD, became the new West German chancellor. Erhard won the 1965 election, but differences within his party forced his resignation (1966). With Erhard's resignation, a grand coalition was formed by the CDU/CSU and the SPD with Kurt Georg Kiesinger as federal chancellor and Willy BRANDT as foreign minister.

In 1969 a new party coalition was formed between the SPD and FDP, with Brandt as chancellor and the FDP leader Walter SCHEEL as foreign minister. For the first time the CDU/CSU had become an opposition party. The new government established an entirely new policy for relations with East Germany and the Soviets, known as *Ostpolitik*. A series of treaties was signed between West Germany and the USSR, Poland, and East Germany. This new policy aroused much opposition in West Germany, led by the Christian Democrats. The new *Ostpolitik* has greatly eased West Germany's position vis-à-vis the Eastern European countries and has strengthened the position of West Berlin.

In May 1974, Chancellor Willy Brandt resigned following the exposure of a spy on his staff. He was succeeded by Helmut SCHMIDT (SPD). The SPD/FDP coalition was victorious in the 1976 election, but in 1982 the FDP switched its support to the CDU/CSU, enabling that party to return to power under Helmut Kohl. The Kohl government gained a secure majority in the election of March 1983, and won a second but closer victory in January 1987.

Political conditions in East Germany were tightly controlled by the SED, which was formed in 1946 by a forced merger between the Communist and Social Democratic parties. Under the leadership of Walter ULBRICHT from 1950 to 1971, East Germany became a member of the Warsaw Treaty Organization and Comecon in the 1950s. As part of the *Ostpolitik,* East and West Germany concluded a treaty recognizing one another's borders and sovereignty in 1972. In the same year the four Western powers and the USSR signed a treaty regarding the status of Berlin.

In 1989, influenced by the new openness of the Gorbachev regime in Moscow and by democratic reforms in neighboring Poland and Hungary, a popular demand for change once again rose in East Germany. Beginning in the summer, nearly a quarter of a million East Germans fled to the West through Hungary and Czechoslovakia, provoking a crisis that forced the resignation of party chief Erich HONECKER, the dismantling of the hated Berlin Wall by his brief successor, Egon Krenz, and extensive liberalization.

Bibliography:

GENERAL: Ardagh, John, *Germany and the Germans* (1987); Fritsch-Bournazel, Renata, *Confronting the German Question,* trans. by Caroline Bray (1988); McClelland, Charles, and Scher, Steven, eds., *Postwar German Culture* (1974); Mellor, Roy, *The Two Germanies: A Modern Geography* (1978); Turner, Henry, *The Two Germanies since 1945* (1987); Whetten, Lawrence, *Germany East and West* (1981).

EAST GERMANY: Keefe, E. K., et al., *Area Handbook for East Germany* (1972); Sandford, Gregory, *From Hitler to Ulbricht: The Communist Reconstruction of East Germany* (1982); Schneider, Eberhard, *The G.D.R.: The History, Politics, Economy and Society of East Germany* (1978); Sontheimer, Kurt, and Bleek, Wilhelm, *The Government and Politics of East Germany* (1976).

WEST GERMANY: Balfour, Michael, *West Germany,* rev. ed. (1982); Childs, David, and Johnson, Jeffery, *West Germany: Politics and Society* (1981); Hartrich, Edwin, *The Fourth and Richest Reich* (1980); Kloss, Gunther, *West Germany: An Introduction* (1976); Laqueur, Walter, *Germany Today* (1985).

See also: GERMAN ART AND ARCHITECTURE; GERMAN AND AUSTRIAN MUSIC; GERMAN LITERATURE.

Germany, history of

For nearly 2,000 years, German history has been marked by two major features. First, important political, social, and religious differences have divided Germany. Even after the country's belated political unification in 1871, these divisions raised questions about whether Germany can be thought of as a single entity. The second major feature is Germany's exposed geographical position in the heart of central Europe. Without natural boundaries and overshadowed during much of its history by more powerful neighbors, Germany has been a frequent battleground. This geographical situation has made Germans highly conscious of the need for security.

ANCIENT GERMANY

When the Romans first attempted to conquer the German lands late in the 1st century BC, they found them inhabited by a variety of GERMANIC PEOPLES, comprising perhaps 4 million individuals. Exact knowledge of their origins is lacking, but it seems likely that these tribes migrated from Scandinavia and the territory between the Elbe and Oder rivers between 1000 and 100 BC, displacing the CELTS as they did so. These ancient Germans came as conquerors, but they quickly settled down to pastoral and agricultural pursuits. Their simple log houses were grouped into villages, and the nearby fields were owned and tilled communally. Tribal government was primitively democratic. Assemblies of freemen made all important decisions, except in times of war, when elected kings temporarily held unlimited power. The ancient Germans worshiped a variety of gods and goddesses, whom they viewed as powerful but not as omnipotent or eternal. Because these deities were thought to be capricious and vengeful, human and other sacrifices were made to propitiate them.

Both before and after the arrival of the Romans, various Germanic tribes emigrated from Germany, impelled mainly by the very forces that had brought them there in the first place—overpopulation and scarcity of land. Some whole tribes, or large segments of them, found new homes; they included the Visigoths in Spain, the Vandals in North Africa, and the Angles and Saxons in England. Others, such as the Teutons and Cimbri, were defeated and destroyed. Hence, modern Germans are the descendants of only a few of the original tribes.

The Romans, for all their efforts to conquer Germany between 12 BC and AD 16, met with only limited success. The Germans held their ground tenaciously, and Roman leadership varied in quality. In AD 9, German forces under ARMINIUS annihilated three Roman legions in the Battle of Teutoburg For-

Charlemagne, the subject of this 9th-century bronze equestrian statue, extended Frankish rule as far east as the Elbe. The division of his empire by his grandsons eventually created (870) two Frankish realms: the East Frankish kingdom (Germany) and the West Frankish kingdom (France).

est. The Romans were able to avenge that defeat but not to consolidate their rule in most of Germany nor to establish the Elbe as their outermost European frontier. Instead, they fell back to a 4,800-km (3,000-mi) fortified border, called the *limes,* which extended from the Rhine to the Danube.

The fact that only a small part of southwestern Germany came under Roman hegemony had far-reaching effects. Most of Germany experienced little or no contact with the civilizing influences of Greco-Roman culture. Political allegiances remained with local leaders and traditional customs and were not transferred to a common state with unified laws and administration. Moreover, a pattern of division between a Romanized west and a barbarian east was established; over the centuries this cleavage would reappear in a variety of political and religious forms.

THE FRANKISH KINGDOM AND EMPIRE (481-919)

As the German tribes overran the Roman Empire in the 5th century, one tribe, the FRANKS, expanded from its base in northwest Germany until it controlled territories stretching from the Atlantic Ocean in the west to Bavaria and Thuringia in the east. The first great leader of the Franks, CLOVIS (r. 481-511), established the MEROVINGIAN dynasty, which lasted until 751. Clovis forged his empire by combining conquest, murder, and intrigue with conversion to Christianity. The last was by no means least in importance, since the substantial power of the Christian clergy in Gaul (essentially modern France and Belgium) greatly facilitated the consolidation of Clovis's rule. Once Clovis himself had adopted Christianity and allied with the church, it was only natural for him and his successors to sponsor the activities of missionaries in the eastern reaches of his realm. Thus the Frankish kingdom began the merger of Roman, German, and Christian elements that was the foundation of medieval German culture.

Charlemagne. The decline of the Merovingian dynasty in the 8th century placed power in the hands of royal officials, one of whom, CHARLES MARTEL (r. 714-41), established a new line of Frankish kings. This CAROLINGIAN dynasty was named after its greatest figure, Charles I (r. 768-814), better known as CHARLEMAGNE. Charlemagne conquered still more lands in Germany, including Bavaria in the east and Saxony in the north. To the SAXONS, particularly warlike and unruly, he gave the choice of death or conversion to Christianity.

Charlemagne made additional conquests in Italy and Spain. When the pope crowned him emperor on Christmas day of the year 800, Charlemagne was recognized as master of a revived Roman Empire in the West. But this restoration was more nominal than real because the economic disintegration that had undermined the original Roman Empire made it difficult to create a centralized state in so vast a realm. Hence, Charlemagne's traveling inspectors, called *missi dominici* ("the king's emissaries"), were able to provide only minimal administrative control over local officials.

This partial restoration and extension of political order was accompanied by a rebirth of interest in learning, which has been called the Carolingian Renaissance. To his palace at AACHEN in northwest Germany, Charlemagne brought scholars from all over Europe for the purpose of setting educational standards for the empire's monastery schools. The most important of these scholars, ALCUIN, had left his native England to supervise Charlemagne's own palace school. One of Alcuin's Frankish pupils, Einhard (*c.*770-840), wrote a biography of his emperor that is a major source of our knowledge of the period. Other Carolingian scholars copied classical manuscripts in a more modern form of writing, the Carolingian miniscule, thus preserving these works for future generations (see CAROLINGIAN ART AND ARCHITECTURE).

Civil War and Disruption. These promising developments were slowed or even, in some cases, reversed after Charlemagne's death. Not only did his empire rest almost entirely on the force of his own personal genius, but he himself had stipulated that his lands should be divided among his heirs after his death, according to the long-standing German tradition. The result was almost a century of civil war among the heirs and the eventual emergence (870) of two Frankish kingdoms, that of the West Franks (France) and that of the East Franks (Germany). The general political chaos of these decades was complicated by invasions of barbarian VIKINGS and MAGYARS. Central government became all but impossible, and the great landed nobles of the realm asserted their local powers. FEUDALISM took hold in most of Germany as a means of preserving a modicum of law and order.

MEDIEVAL GERMANY (911-1517)

The last Carolingian king of the East Franks was Louis the Child (r. 899-911). On his death (911), LOTHARINGIA (Lorraine) was the only East Frankish duchy to transfer its allegiance to the Carolingian king of the West Franks. The dukes of BAVARIA, FRANCONIA, SAXONY, and SWABIA—the other so-called

Otto I (left), founder of the Holy Roman Empire, presents Jesus with a model of Magdeburg Cathedral in this 10th-century plaque. As German king (936-73; emperor from 962), Otto extended German power into eastern Europe. (Metropolitan Museum of Art, New York.)

Frederick I kneels in submission to Pope Alexander III after Frederick's army was routed by the Italians in 1176. Under the terms of this reconciliation, Frederick acknowledged Alexander as the true pope and abandoned his attempts to assert authority in Italy.

stem duchies—initially elected the duke of Franconia king of Germany as CONRAD I. In 919, however, they turned to the house of Saxony as their best defense against the Magyars.

Saxon, Salian, and Hohenstaufen Dynasties. The first two Saxon kings, HENRY I and his son, OTTO I, were able to reassert the strength of a centralized monarchy. They stopped the Magyar onslaught and expanded German holdings into Eastern Europe—the so-called DRANG NACH OSTEN. Working closely with the church, they also established effective administrative machinery that succeeded in keeping the ambitious rival German dukes in line. Equally important in controlling the other dukes was the Saxon kings' claim to the title of Holy Roman emperor. When Otto I founded the HOLY ROMAN EMPIRE in 962, he gained both a powerful ally in the papacy and new sources of taxes in northern Italy. To maintain these advantages, however, his successors were frequently obliged to preoccupy themselves with Italian affairs instead of attending to matters at home.

Early in the 11th century, the Saxon line of monarchs died out, and the German princes began to elect a series of Salian (Franconian) kings. Of these, HENRY III (r. 1039-56) brought imperial control over the church to its pinnacle, deposing three rival popes in 1046 and nominating four popes in succession. His successor, HENRY IV, however, faced a resurgent papacy, which not only resisted lay control of the church but also did so in alliance with the German princes, who sought to win back the powers taken from them by the kings. This struggle, usually called the INVESTITURE CONTROVERSY, lasted until 1122 and ended essentially in victory for the papacy and the German nobility. The German king's powers over the church and the great German princes were gravely weakened, and the process of feudalization in Germany was accelerated.

The HOHENSTAUFEN dynasty increased the power of the monarchy briefly. First elected to the throne in 1138, the Hohenstaufens held it, despite vigorous challenge from the rival WELF family, until 1254. The dynasty's greatest figure, FREDERICK I (r. 1152-90), known as Barbarossa, chose to work within the feudal structure as a partner of the great princes. Although he acquired the valuable province of Burgundy by marriage and subdued most of Italy by force, his successors were overwhelmed by a resurgent papal-aristocratic alliance and by French and English intervention. Only the brilliant FREDERICK II (r. 1212-50) was able to restore a measure of order, but he was so absorbed in Italian affairs that he neglected Germany. Hence, at a time when England and France were being welded into modern nation-states, Germany fell once more into the hands of regional princes.

There were sufficient intervals in this turbulent age to permit some economic progress and cultural achievement. Cities and commerce made a solid comeback, and by the end of the period there were no fewer than 1,600 cities and towns of varying size in Germany, many of them crowned by impressive Romanesque cathedrals. The early 13th century was also the peak of the medieval German court epic, represented most notably by WOLFRAM VON ESCHENBACH, and of *Minnesang*, or lyric love poetry, whose great genius was WALTHER VON DER VOGELWEIDE.

Consolidation of Princely Rule. None of Frederick II's successors was able to regain the imperial powers that had been usurped by the German princes. The period immediately following Frederick's death—the so-called Interregnum—was one of particular chaos. During this period the Hohenstaufen were finally extinguished, and foreign princes contested for the imperial title. In 1273, RUDOLF I of the house of HABSBURG was elected king. The German princes were suspicious of Habsburg territorial ambitions, however, and elected a series of kings from other dynasties in succession to Rudolf. One of these kings, LOUIS IV (r. 1314-46) of the Bavarian house of WITTELSBACH, had to fight off a challenge from a Habsburg

The map indicates the political divisions and dynastic holdings within the Holy Roman Empire about 1176, the year in which the Hohenstaufen emperor Frederick I (Barbarossa) was defeated by the Lombard League in the Battle of Legnano. The Lombard League, an alliance of north Italian cities, supported Pope Alexander I against Frederick's ambitions to dominate the Italian peninsula.

(Left) *Merchants ply their trade along the busy waterfront of Hamburg, one of the cities of northern Germany that were linked in a loose confederation known as the Hanseatic League. During the 13th and 14th centuries, the league held a virtual monopoly on commerce throughout the Baltic.*

antiking, Frederick the Fair (*c.*1286–1330; r. 1314–26). Consistently opposed by the papacy, Louis rallied the support of the German princes for his 1338 declaration asserting the authority of these princes to elect the emperor without confirmation by the pope.

CHARLES IV (r. 1347–78) of the house of Luxemburg, formally acknowledged the principle of elective monarchy with the GOLDEN BULL, of 1356, which regularized elections by naming seven electors: the archbishops of Mainz, Trier, and Cologne, the duke of Saxony, the margrave of Brandenburg, the count palatine of the Rhine, and the king of Bohemia. Far from endorsing or deliberately encouraging disorder, the Golden Bull accepted the political realities of an age in which unified monarchy had become impossible in Germany. Real power rested with the princely and ecclesiastical states, the imperial free cities, and the imperial knights.

Rise of the Habsburgs. If the imperial title had lost much of its significance, it remained valuable to the ambitious Habsburgs as a symbol of sovereignty. From 1438, members of the ruling dynasty of AUSTRIA were elected Holy Roman emperors, with only one short break (1740–45), until the empire's dissolution in 1806. Acquiring Burgundy, the Low Countries, Spain, and much of Italy by marriage, they came closest to restoring full dignity to the imperial crown. The ablest of the early Habsburgs, MAXIMILIAN I (r. 1493–1519), decreed "Eternal Peace" in 1495 in order to control the unruly imperial knights and restore order in his divided realm. He also created an imperial court of justice (Kammergericht) to help enforce his decrees.

(Right) *Holy Roman Emperor Maximilian I extended the power of the Habsburg dynasty by his own marriage to the Burgundian heiress Mary and his son's marriage into the Spanish royal house. Throughout his reign (1493–1519), Maximilian strove to curtail the power of the Valois dynasty, which ruled France.*

The German princes, jealous of their powers and still fearful of Habsburg ambitions, responded by demanding an imperial governing council (Reichsrat) to control imperial policies. As constituted in 1500, it included several of the great princes and representatives of the imperial free cities. It did not, however, evolve into an effective organ of representative government. The princes were more interested in hamstringing the emperors than they were in assuming the burden of statesmanship, and the additional divisions generated by the Reformation overwhelmed the council and left Germany as fragmented as ever.

But political fragmentation did not retard growth in other areas. Germany's economic advances since the Middle Ages and its recovery from the calamity of the Black Death (1347–50; see BUBONIC PLAGUE) were best mirrored in the prosperity of the great cities. Not least among them were the great northern trading cities that banded together into the HANSEATIC LEAGUE, centered in LÜBECK. The expansion of trade, commerce, and industry in the 15th century was paralleled by ma-

Holy Roman Emperor Charles V (center), *whose dynastic holdings included Spain, the Netherlands, and portions of Italy, as well as the traditional Habsburg territories of Austria, personally presided over the Diet of Augsburg (1530), convened in an attempt to reconcile differences between Catholics and Protestants in Germany. Despite his enormous power, Charles was unable to curb the spread of the Reformation, which further eroded imperial authority in Germany. (Bibliothèque Nationale, Paris.)*

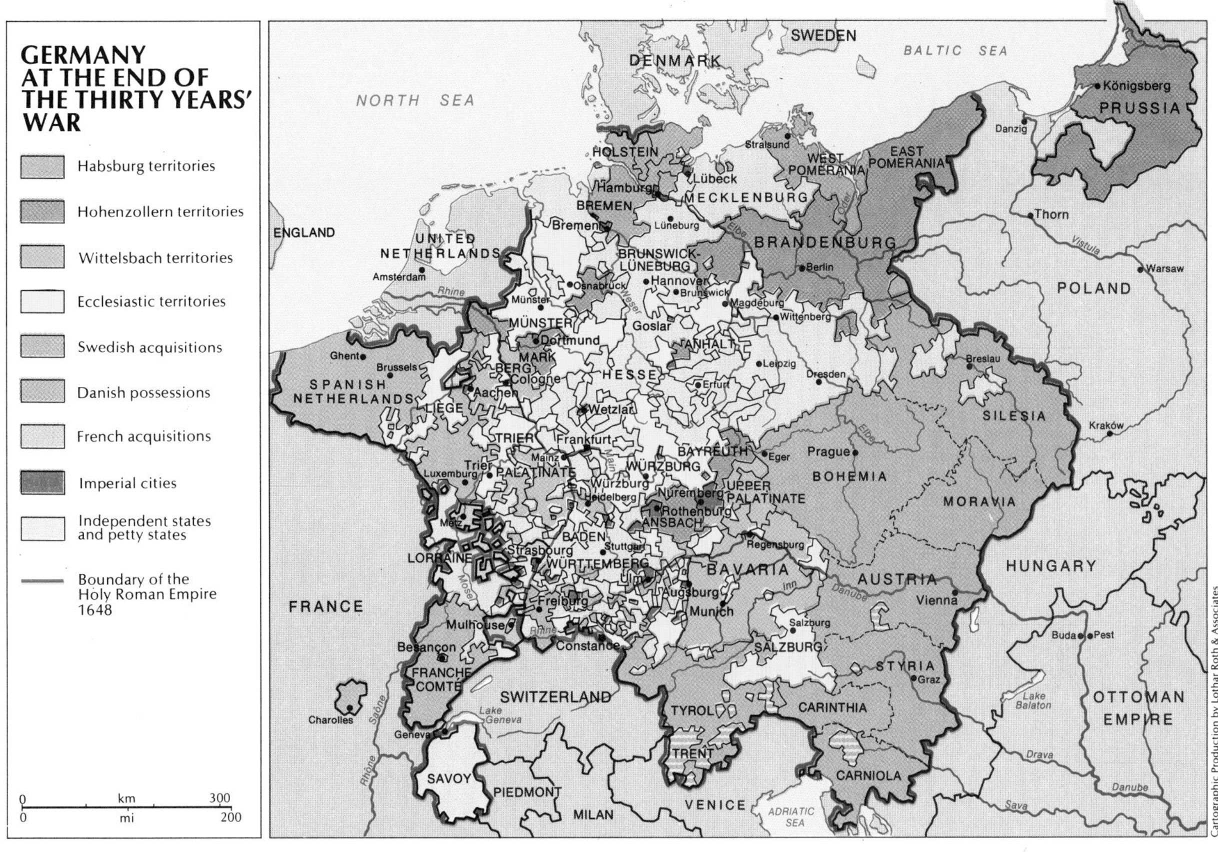

The map of central Europe indicates the major territorial acquisitions formalized by the Treaty of Westphalia (1648), which concluded the Thirty Years' War. This conflict (1618-48), in which the German Protestant principalities in alliance with Denmark, Sweden, and France fought imperial, Spanish, and Bavarian forces to a standstill, physically devastated Germany, and left it politically fragmented.

jor technological development, most notably the invention of movable type, attributed to Johann GUTENBERG of Mainz. The printing press had a major cultural impact on the succeeding era, which was also distinguished by the achievements of artists such as Albrecht DÜRER, Hans HOLBEIN the Younger, Lucas CRANACH, and Matthias GRÜNEWALD.

RELIGION AND ABSOLUTISM (1517-1789)

On Oct. 31, 1517, Martin LUTHER nailed to a church door in Wittenberg his 95 theses condemning the sale of INDULGENCES by the Roman Catholic church. This event is usually taken to mark the beginning of the Protestant REFORMATION.

The Reformation. Luther's revolt against what he regarded as abuses by the Roman Catholic church swiftly became entangled in larger political and social issues. The peasants of much of Germany, chafing under the oppressive rule of aristocratic landowners, drew some unwarranted political conclusions from Luther's religious independence and rose in the revolt known as the PEASANTS' WAR in 1524. The revolt was suppressed, with Luther's help, but religious and social radicalism lived on in the ANABAPTIST sects.

Still more important were the political uses to which the higher orders of the empire put LUTHERANISM. Always on the lookout for ways to strengthen their hand against the staunchly Catholic emperor and covetous of the church's property, tax powers, and legal jurisdiction, many of the German princes enthusiastically embraced the Protestant religion. Emperor CHARLES V (r. 1519-56) found himself confronted simultaneously with a revolt by the Lutheran princes and free cities, organized into the League of Schmalkald, and a massive Turkish invasion of southeastern Europe. After a long and desperate struggle, the religious wars ended in a stalemate with the Peace of Augsburg (1555; see AUGSBURG, PEACE OF), which in effect recognized Lutheranism as the religion of most of northern and central Germany. Although the settlement was a great victory for Protestantism, it helped to perpetuate and intensify Germany's political disintegration.

Thirty Years' War. The Peace of Augsburg did not solve Germany's basic political and religious problems and hence could be nothing more than a truce. It had called for the maintenance of the religious and political status quo of 1555, but Lutheranism and CALVINISM, a rival Protestant sect, continued to make progress in Germany—to the horror of Catholic princes and church leaders. Nor had the Habsburg emperors given up their goal of making the Holy Roman Empire into a modern, unified state.

These conflicting developments produced the THIRTY YEARS' WAR (1618-48), a series of four related wars. In it the Protestant states barely held their own, although they were aided by the acquisitive Swedes and by the French, who wanted to undermine their great rivals, the Habsburgs, by keeping Germany divided and weak. When hostilities were ended by the Treaty of Westphalia (1648; see WESTPHALIA, PEACE OF), devastated Germany was still torn hopelessly apart, a collection of more than 300 virtually sovereign states without effective central government.

Rise of Brandenburg-Prussia. Although a few of these states, such as Bavaria and Saxony, achieved a measure of wealth and power, the state that was ultimately to unify Germany arose from unpromising beginnings. BRANDENBURG, in origin a small march (military frontier) state created on lands conquered from the Slavs on the north German plain in the 13th century, began to expand under its vigorous HOHENZOLLERN rulers in the 17th century. Its most important early acquisition was the duchy of PRUSSIA, which had been conquered by the TEUTONIC KNIGHTS in the 13th century and secularized in 1525; Prussia passed by inheritance to the margrave of Brandenburg in 1618. The territories of Brandenburg were further augmented by the Treaty of Westphalia.

Frederick II (the Great) of Prussia used the efficient army created by his predecessors to challenge the dominance in Germany of Habsburg Austria. He seized Silesia from Austria in the War of Austrian Succession (1740-48) and retained it through the Seven Years' War (1756-63), in which Prussia faced a coalition formed by Austria, Russia, and France.

The most prominent of the early Hohenzollern rulers were FREDERICK WILLIAM, elector of Brandenburg (r. 1640-88), and his grandson FREDERICK WILLIAM I (r. 1713-40), king of Prussia (the rulers of Brandenburg-Prussia had assumed the title "king in Prussia" in 1701). They built an army that was far larger than those of other states of comparable population. Their purpose was defensive because Prussia had suffered hideously during the Thirty Years' War. However, King FREDERICK II (r. 1740-86), later called the Great, used the army to expand Prussia's borders. As a result of the war of the AUSTRIAN SUCCESSION (1740-48) and the SEVEN YEARS' WAR (1756-63), Frederick won the valuable province of SILESIA from Austria. He also participated (1772), with Russia and Austria, in the first of three successive partitions of Poland (see POLAND, PARTITIONS OF). Like the other so-called enlightened despots of the 18th century, Frederick used authoritarian methods to modernize his government and society; he did not, however, go so far as to antagonize the powerful Prussian nobles, known as JUNKERS.

When Frederick died, Prussia was the largest and most significant northern state in divided Germany. Austria, with its imperial Habsburg dynasty, was still considered the dominant German state. However, its wars with Prussia had revealed serious weaknesses, and the centralizing reforms of MARIA THERESA and her son, emperor JOSEPH II, another enlightened despot, antagonized some of the Habsburgs' disparate subjects.

These often chaotic years of religious and dynastic struggles caused German economic and cultural life to decline, although the astronomy of Johannes KEPLER and the novel *Simplicissimus* (1669; Eng. trans., 1924) by Hans Jakob von GRIMMELSHAUSEN were significant exceptions. Partial recovery during the 18th century helped to produce magnificant BAROQUE ART AND ARCHITECTURE and the equally monumental baroque and classical music of Johann Sebastian BACH, Wolfgang Amadeus MOZART, and Franz Josef HAYDN.

NATIONALISM AND UNIFICATION (1789-1871)

During the wars of the French Revolution and the Napoleonic period, Germany was conquered by the French. The chief impact of this conquest was to instill a sense of unity and nationalism in the German people. Even before the French intrusions, Johann Gottfried von HERDER had popularized German nationalism, urging Germans to cast off their servile imitation of the French. The humiliation of outright domination by French overlords, however, crystallized into the determination to free and unite Germany. Prussia, although defeated by NAPOLEON I, carried out drastic military and social reforms and ultimately led the other German states in the victorious War of Liberation against the French in 1813. (See FRENCH REVOLUTIONARY WARS; NAPOLEONIC WARS.)

German Confederation. The dreams of German patriots were smashed by the peacemakers at the Congress of Vienna (1814-15; see VIENNA, CONGRESS OF). They restored most of the major princes while retaining Napoleon's simplified structure of only about three dozen, instead of three hundred, states. These states were bound loosely together in the GERMAN CONFEDERATION. Like the Holy Roman Empire, which Napoleon had dissolved in 1806, the Confederation was dominated by the Habsburgs, who now called themselves emperors of Austria. For the time being, Prussia took a back seat, contenting itself with instituting (1834) the ZOLLVEREIN, a tariff union that included most of the German states.

In the following decades the forces of entrenched conservatism, seemingly personified by the Austrian foreign minister Klemens von METTERNICH, were increasingly challenged by liberal ideas drawn from the French revolutionary example and by nationalism.

Demands for change and an economic depression combined to produce the REVOLUTIONS OF 1848. Liberal concessions were granted in virtually all the German states, and representatives were elected to a national convention, the FRANKFURT PARLIAMENT, to unite Germany and provide it with a liberal constitution. However, divisions among the revolutionaries and the dogged opposition of conservative Prussia, whose king, FREDERICK WILLIAM IV, contemptuously refused to rule over a united German constitutional monarchy, caused the revolution to collapse in 1849.

Bismarck's Unification of Germany. The cause of German nationalism was taken up again in 1862 by Prussia's new minister-president, Otto von BISMARCK. A conservative Prussian patriot, he was determined to steal the nationalist issue from the liberals and assure Prussian leadership in a united Germany. In a series of three wars, in each of which he managed to make his adversary appear the aggressor, he eliminated first Danish, then Austrian, and finally French influence from Germany. The war against Denmark (1864), fought in alliance with Austria, resulted in the Danish cession of SCHLESWIG-HOLSTEIN. A quarrel over the administration of the ceded territory gave Bismarck his pretext for attacking and defeating Austria in the SEVEN WEEKS' WAR (1866). With Austria carefully excluded from German affairs, Bismarck formed (1867) the North German Confederation, uniting the northern German states under a federal government dominated by Prussia. Three years later, during the FRANCO-PRUSSIAN WAR (1870-71), the southern German states agreed to join the federation, and on Jan. 18, 1871, the Prussian king WILLIAM I was crowned emperor of a new German Reich at Versailles.

The Revolutions of 1848 were aimed at securing constitutional government in the various German states and a united Germany. More radical, republican groups, such as the one shown meeting here in Berlin, played a peripheral role.

The rise of German industrialism was delayed somewhat by the lack of a strong, central government. During the 1850s, however, the German states more than doubled their industrial output, creating the favorable economic conditions that led to the formation of a powerful, unified Germany.

In the name of Prussian authoritarianism and militarism, and with "blood and iron" tactics, Bismarck had succeeded where the German liberals had failed. Overwhelmingly eclipsed by the turn of events, most liberals hastened to make their peace with Bismarck. Germany was united, but its political maturation had been drastically retarded.

The years of growing German national consciousness were also great ones for German culture. Classical idealism reached its highest expression in the poetry and drama of Johann Wolfgang von GOETHE and the music of Ludwig van BEETHOVEN. Lasting influence on the development of philosophy was exerted by G. W. F. HEGEL, while romantic music found two of its geniuses in Robert SCHUMANN and Richard WAGNER.

IMPERIAL GERMANY (1871-1918)

Bismarck fastened an appropriately authoritarian political structure on the newly formed nation. The German Empire retained the constitution he had created for the North German Confederation. It provided for a democratically elected parliament, the REICHSTAG, but granted it only the limited powers of fiscal appropriation and debate. Germany was organized on a federal basis, with certain powers reserved to the states. But in the national government, real power lay with the Prussian

The map indicates the stages of the unification of Germany during the 19th century. The German Confederation, created in 1815, collapsed when Prussia defeated Austria in 1866. The North German Confederation united the northern German states under a government dominated by Prussia. During the Franco-Prussian War (1870-71) the southern German states joined the federation to form the German Empire.

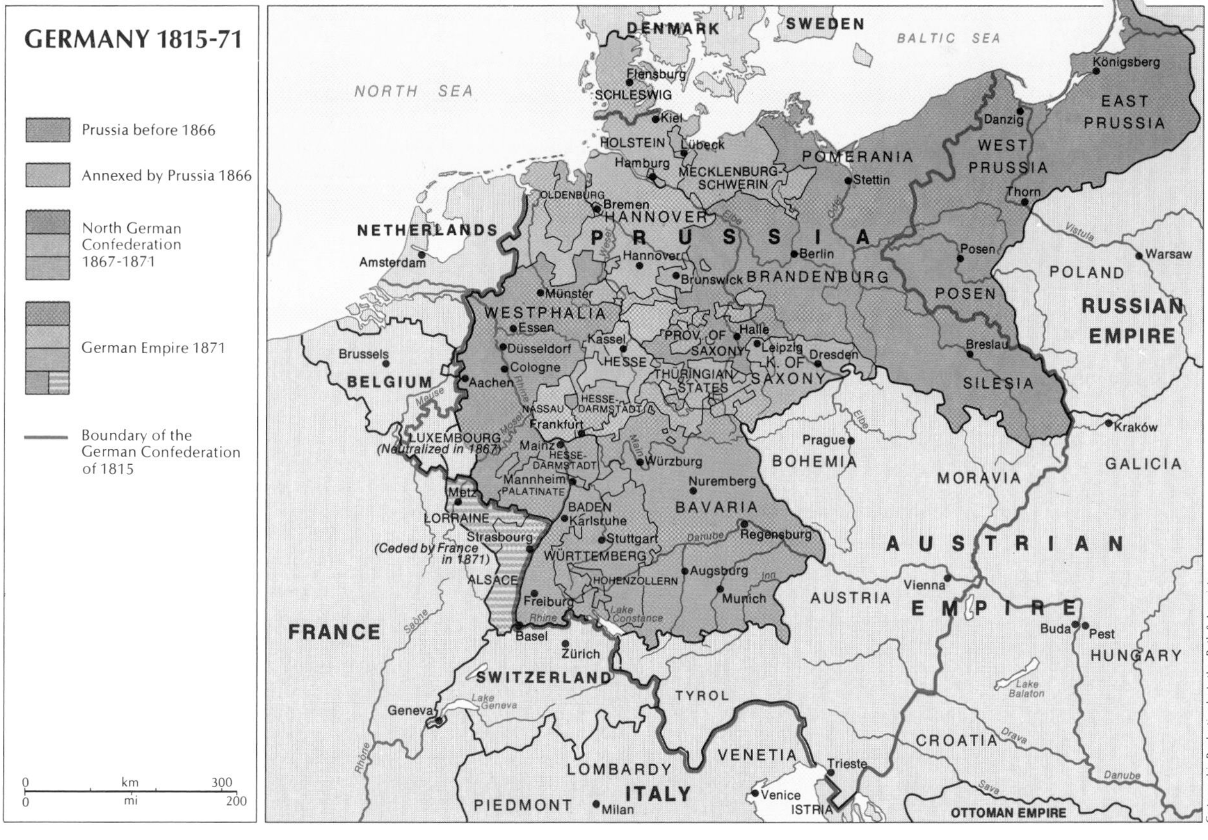

GERMANY 1815-71

Prussia before 1866

Annexed by Prussia 1866

North German Confederation 1867-1871

German Empire 1871

Boundary of the German Confederation of 1815

0 km 300
0 mi 200

Cartographic Production by Lothar Roth & Associates

King William I of Prussia is proclaimed German emperor at Versailles in 1871. The architect of this triumph and of the whole political process of German unification was Otto von Bismarck, who stands at the foot of the dais in a white uniform.

A famous British cartoon, "Dropping the Pilot," satirizes the dismissal in 1890 of Bismarck by Germany's ruler, Emperor William II. The emperor's reckless militarism and ambitions for personal glory contributed to Germany's disastrous participation in World War I.

king, who was also the German emperor (*Kaiser*), and his advisors. As long as William I ruled (until 1888), his chancellor, Bismarck, was given his way on virtually every issue.

Bismarck's Rule. In order to manipulate the Reichstag, Bismarck formed coalitions of parties that were based at least as much on opposition to real or imagined internal enemies as on concrete political issues. At first he allied with his former foes, the liberals, to encourage the growth of industrial and commercial capitalism in Germany. Simultaneously, he fought the large Roman Catholic minority and its political arm, the Center party, as enemies of the new state. This campaign, known as the KULTURKAMPF, produced only short-term benefits since the Catholics, assisted by some non-Catholics, resisted doggedly.

Bismarck ended the Kulturkampf in 1878 only because he wanted to run Germany with the help of new partners, the conservatives. He had concluded that the best way to deal with a severe economic depression was to protect German industry and agriculture with tariffs, a policy more acceptable to conservative than to liberal minds. The enemy, too, changed. This time it was Germany's mildly Marxist party, the Social Democratic party (SPD), that represented the growing industrial working class. In the 1880s, Bismarck had the SPD outlawed as subversive and tried to win over the German workers with the world's first comprehensive social security system. However, he was no more successful in suppressing the socialists than he had been with the Catholics. By 1890 he had lost control of the Reichstag and was contemplating the use of force to overturn the constitution when the new emperor compelled him to resign.

Bismarck's foreign policy was far sounder than his domestic politics. Convinced that Germany had all the territory it needed, he promoted European stability by isolating France and diverting its attention to colonial expansion overseas. He won important allies for Germany by the TRIPLE ALLIANCE with Austria and Italy (1882) and the Reinsurance Treaty with Russia (1887). He endorsed a policy of German colonial expansion only belatedly and half-heartedly, and then mainly to secure support for his domestic policies from nationalists and from industrial and commercial interests.

William II's Policies. William I was succeeded briefly by his son FREDERICK III and then by his grandson WILLIAM II (r. 1888–1918). The young William appreciated neither Bismarck's assumption that only Bismarck could govern Germany nor his heavy-handed attempts to bludgeon minorities into submission. After forcing the Iron Chancellor to retire (1890), the new emperor attempted to dominate German politics himself even though he did not possess the intelligence and emotional stability necessary to do so. William seriously attempted to conciliate the German working class, dropping the anti-socialist laws and extending the social security system. But he would not make concessions to the idea of political democracy, stubbornly resisting demands by the SPD and middle-class liberals for reform of Prussia's old, undemocratic constitution and for the granting of real powers to the Reichstag. The growth of reform sentiment and outrage over William's frequent blunders produced all the ingredients for a constitutional confrontation on the eve of World War I.

Not the least of the reformers' complaints concerned William II's inept foreign policy, in which he was guided by the foreign office official Friedrich von HOLSTEIN and by Bernhard von BÜLOW, who became foreign secretary in 1897 and chancellor in 1900. Unsure of his ability to maintain alliances with both Russia and Austria in view of their rivalry in the Balkans, the emperor opted for Austria and let the Reinsurance Treaty with Russia lapse in 1890. Four years later, France concluded an alliance with Russia. Then, instead of behaving with appropriate caution, William followed the advice of Admiral Alfred von TIRPITZ in launching a naval arms race with Britain. He also plunged into colonial adventures and thus further antagonized both Britain and France. By 1909, when Bülow was succeeded as chancellor by the more sober Theobald von BETHMAN-HOLLWEG, Germany had only one reliable ally, Austria-Hungary.

These serious flaws were less apparent at the time than they might otherwise have been because of imperial Germany's dazzling economic, scientific, and cultural achievements. Encouraged by government subventions and the close collaboration of bankers and industrialists, Germany experienced most of its economic growth between 1870 and 1910. Although German industrialization had gotten underway long after Britain's, by 1910 German steel production was more than twice that of Britain. German science and technology, supported by a sophisticated university system, came to be regarded as the world's best. At the same time, the early novels of Thomas MANN, the late romantic music of Johannes BRAHMS and Richard STRAUSS, and the apocalyptic philosophy of Friedrich NIETZSCHE helped maintain Germany's reputation as a major cultural center.

World War I. These signs of vitality suggested that Germany might peacefully have solved its political and social problems over a period of time. However, its defeat in WORLD WAR I denied it that possibility. Excessively eager to support its ally Austria in a dispute with Russia over Serbia, Germany helped precipitate war in 1914 by sending an ultimatum to Russia and, when it was rejected, declaring war on both Russia and France, in accordance with the rigid war plan devised by Alfred von SCHLIEFFEN. Most Germans, even the SPD, supported the war effort at first, but their mood began to change when no swift victory could be won and terrible food shortages developed. Increasing numbers of them wondered whether the government was more interested in conquests than in a fair peace treaty. When, in November 1918, it was obvious that Germany had to sue for peace, the German people rose in revolt against their leaders. Even the German generals pressed for the emperor's abdication. William went into exile in the Netherlands, and the Social Democrats took over the government, proclaimed a republic, and brought the war to an end.

WEIMAR AND NAZI GERMANY (1918–45)

It is one of the great tragedies of modern history that Germany's first encounter with democratic government was associated with defeat and misery. The Social Democrats, accepting the support of the army in order to maintain order, suppressed several Communist revolts, including those in Berlin and Bavaria. Early in 1919 a freely elected constituent assembly met in Weimar to write a constitution giving direct governing power to the Reichstag. SPD leader Friedrich EBERT was named president of the new Weimar Republic, and Philipp SCHEIDEMANN formed a coalition government of the SPD, the Center party, and a liberal group. This government soon resigned rather than sign the Treaty of Versailles, the vindictive settlement imposed by the PARIS PEACE CONFERENCE. However, Germany really had no choice. In June 1919 the Weimar Assembly voted to comply with the treaty, which deprived Germany of large amounts of land, people, and natural resources and forced it to pay enormous REPARATIONS.

Crisis and Recovery. The attempt to root parliamentary democracy in Germany was beset from the beginning by grave problems. There were so many political parties—at least six major and many more minor ones—that it was hard to form stable coalitions for effective government. Militant minorities—the Communists on the far left and monarchists and racists on the opposite extreme—sometimes resorted to force in efforts to overturn the republic. Notable among these efforts was the MUNICH PUTSCH of 1923, in which the tiny National Socialist party led by Adolf HITLER made a somewhat farcical attempt to seize power in Bavaria. The continuing unrest made the national government even more dependent on the basically conservative army.

The year 1923 was one of major crisis. The payment of reparations, in both cash and kind, had placed an enormous strain on a country already bankrupted by more than four years of war. As inflation had mounted, Germany had suspended payment in 1922, provoking the French to occupy the Ruhr area in January 1923. Workers in Ruhr mines and factories resisted by striking, but such resistance contributed to inflation, which brought on economic collapse. The situation was saved in November 1923 when the ablest of Germany's republican politicians, Gustav STRESEMANN, introduced a new currency and improved Germany's relations with the Western nations, paving the way for foreign loans and a more reasonable schedule of reparations payments.

Members of the Spartacus League, a revolutionary socialist group, march through the streets of Berlin during the "Spartacist Revolt" of January 1919. This Communist uprising was ruthlessly suppressed, and its leaders, Rosa Luxemburg and Karl Liebknecht, were killed.

During the later 1920s, therefore, the German economy revived, and politics settled down. Also, during those years, a remarkable avant-garde culture blossomed in Germany, extending from the epic theater of Bertolt BRECHT, to the BAUHAUS school of functional art and architecture, to the relativity physics of Albert EINSTEIN, and to the existential philosophy of Martin HEIDEGGER.

This new Germany was cut down in its infancy by the onset of the Depression of the 1930s and the Nazi seizure of power. Depression conditions once more radicalized politics and so divided the parties in the Reichstag that parliamentary government became all but impossible. From 1930 on, government functioned by emergency decree. The Communists profited briefly from this radicalization, but the main beneficiary was Hitler's National Socialist, or Nazi, party, which had the twin attractions of appearing to offer radical solutions to economic problems while upholding patriotic values. By 1932 it was the largest party in the Reichstag. The following year President Paul von HINDENBURG appointed Hitler chancellor after allowing himself to be convinced by generals and right-wing politicians that only the Nazi leader could restore order in Germany and that he could be controlled.

Nazi Dictatorship. Most Germans who supported Hitler during his rise to power did so out of desperation, scarcely knowing what he planned to do. They received much more than they had bargained for. After half-persuading, half-coercing the Reichstag to grant him absolute power, Hitler lost no time in founding a totalitarian state, known unofficially as the THIRD REICH—supposedly in the tradition of the Holy Roman Empire and the unified German Empire set up by Bismarck. When confronted by demands from Storm Trooper (SA) leader Ernst ROEHM and others for a second revolution that would make good on Nazi claims to socialist ideals, Hitler purged Roehm and his associates on the weekend of June 30, 1934. Four years later, he forced out two of the top generals on trumped-up charges in order to assure himself of full control of the expanding German armed forces. Thanks to a ruthless secret police (the GESTAPO) and a CONCENTRATION CAMP system under the direction of SS (Schutzstaffel) leader Heinrich HIMMLER, known enemies of NAZISM were put away and potential ones terrorized.

Hitler's virulent racism gave rise to a cruel system of ANTI-SEMITISM. The Nuremberg Laws of September 1935, which deprived Jews of most civil rights, were supplemented by other measures designed to rid Germany of Jews. These measures were to culminate in a policy of deliberate extermination during World War II, taking the lives of approximately 6 million European Jews. More immediately, however, a concerted state program of ending unemployment with public works projects and a restoration of business confidence produced remarkable economic recovery in Germany. Joseph GOEBBELS's efficient propaganda ministry controlled the media to assure that Hitler would be viewed as a genius and Nazi Germany as the best of all possible worlds. Given this combination of coercion, achievement, and thought control, it is perhaps not surprising that there was little resistance, aside from limited opposition from the churches and the army.

World War II. Hitler's foreign-policy goals were determined by his belief that Germany was overpopulated and needed to conquer Europe in order to secure *Lebensraum* (living space) in Poland and Russia. Concealing his real goals before 1939, he hoodwinked Europe's diplomats into appeasing him with concessions—as at the MUNICH CONFERENCE of 1938. The 1936 remilitarization of the Rhineland, from which troops had been banned by the Versailles treaty; the annexation of Austria (the so-called Anschluss) in 1938; and the dismemberment of Czechoslovakia in 1938–39 were all accomplished without effective interference by the other European powers.

When Britain and France finally declared war (Sept. 3, 1939) after the German invasion of Poland, Hitler found himself involved in war on a much larger scale than he had expected and for which Germany was not adequately prepared. A series of initially successful *Blitzkriege* (lightning campaigns)

(Above) *Adolf Hitler, an Austrian-born soldier, assumed leadership of the National Socialist German Workers' (NAZI) party after Germany's defeat in World War I. Using his position as chancellor, and later as führer, Hitler transformed the nation into a militarist Fascist state.* (Left) *Hitler delivers one of his charismatic orations before troops at a rally in Nuremberg.*

against Poland (1939), western Europe (1940), and the USSR (1941) made him temporary master of most of Europe. But, unable to destroy Britain and Russia, Hitler found himself confronted by an overwhelmingly powerful enemy coalition, including (after December 1941) the United States. Germany's main European ally, Fascist Italy, soon collapsed, and its Asian ally, Japan, fought an essentially independent war. The German collapse began in mid-1944 when the Allies invaded France and strategic bombing began to reduce German armament production. When Hitler committed suicide in Berlin in April 1945, Germany was largely in ruins and at the mercy of the countries it had ravaged. (See WORLD WAR II.)

The map of Germany (1933–42) shows, in chronological progression, how Hitler conducted his campaign to expand the Lebensraum *("living space") of the Third Reich. Not appearing on the map are the extensive areas in North Africa and the Soviet Union controlled by the military forces of the Reich and its Axis allies.*

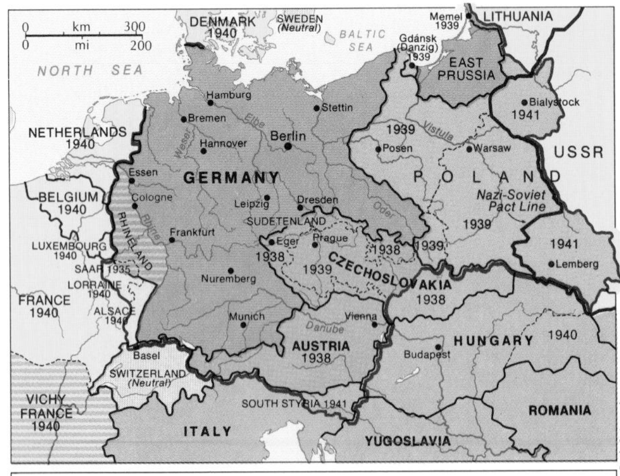

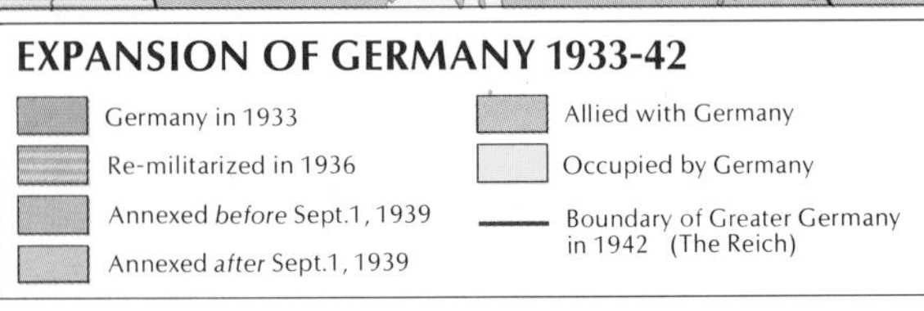

GERMANY SINCE 1945

The victorious Allies managed to agree to give most of eastern Germany to Poland and the USSR, to divide what was left into four zones of occupation, and to try the major Nazi war criminals before an International Military Tribunal at Nuremberg (see NUREMBERG TRIALS). However, they could not agree on whether or how to reunite the four occupied zones. As COLD WAR tensions grew, stimulated in part by the German situation itself, the temporary dividing line between the Soviet zone in the east and the British, French, and U.S. zones in the west hardened into a permanent boundary. In 1949, shortly after the Western powers permitted their zones to unite and restore parliamentary democracy in the Federal Republic of Germany, the Russians installed a puppet regime of German Communists in the east, creating the German Democratic Republic.

For more than 20 years the leaders of the West German government refused to recognize the legitimacy of the East German regime, claiming that only they truly represented the whole German nation. They even refused to establish diplomatic ties with countries that did recognize the German Democratic Republic. However, following the advent of a more flexible and realistic SPD government in West Germany, visits across the border by both heads of state in 1970 resulted two years later in a basic treaty amounting to reciprocal recognition. The disunity that has always been a feature of German history seems to be firmly institutionalized for the foreseeable future.

For information on contemporary Germany, see GERMANY, EAST AND WEST.

DONALD L. NIEWYK

Bibliography: Barraclough, Geoffrey, *The Origins of Modern Germany*, 2d ed. (1947; repr. 1984); Berghahn, Volker, *Modern Germany* (1982); Calleo, David, *The German Problem Reconsidered: Germany and the World Order, 1870 to the Present* (1978); Craig, Gordon A., *Germany, 1866–1945* (1978); DuBoulay, F. R. H., *Germany in the Late Middle Ages* (1983); Holborn, Hajo, *The History of Modern Germany*, 3 vols. (1959–69; repr. 1982); Mann, Golo, *The History of Germany since 1789*, trans. by Marion Jackson (1968); Pinson, Koppel S., *Modern Germany: Its History and Civilization*, 2d ed. (1966); Reinhardt, Kurt F., *Germany: 2000 Years*, 2 vols., rev. ed. (1961); Stern, Fritz, *Dreams and Delusions: The Drama of German History* (1987); Thompson, James W., *Feudal Germany*, 2 vols. (1928; repr. 1962).

See also: EUROPE, HISTORY OF; GERMAN ART AND ARCHITECTURE; GERMAN AND AUSTRIAN MUSIC; GERMAN LITERATURE.

Germinal [zhair-mee-nahl']

Germinal (1885; Eng. trans., 1901) is a novel by Émile ZOLA written in the tradition of French NATURALISM, which portrays people as the victims of heredity and environment. A story of the hardships of impoverished coal miners at the time of the great strike of 1884, *Germinal* is a great socialist labor novel as well as a study in social Darwinism. The novel concentrates on the socialist Étienne Lantier and the Meheu family, all of whose members must work in the mines. It is among the most famous of the 20 novels that constitute Zola's Rougon-Macquart cycle. JANE COLVILLE BETTS

Bibliography: Grant, Elliott M., *Zola's "Germinal": A Critical and Historical Study* (1970); Smethurst, Colin, *Emile Zola: Germinal* (1974).

germination [jur-min-ay'-shuhn]

Germination is the resumption of growth of a plant seed, spore, or bud after a period of DORMANCY. The main feature of germination is the increased rate of respiration, that is, the biologic "burning," or oxidation, of carbohydrate to provide energy for metabolism and growth. The viability, or the ability to germinate after prolonged periods of time, varies greatly among different species. The spores of mosses and other lower plants reputedly remain viable for thousands or even millions of years, but this belief has not been substantiated. Among the best documented spore survivals are those of slime molds, which may remain viable for more than 50 years. Some seed plants, however, have shown remarkable viability. The seeds of toadflax, *Spergula arvensis*, found in Denmark, sprouted after 1,700 years. The record for dormancy is held by the Arctic lupine, *Lupinus arcticus*, whose seeds were found in the frozen permafrost layer of earth in the Yukon, Canada, in 1954 and were determined by the radiocarbon method to be at least 10,000 and possibly as much as 15,000 years old. These seeds germinated in a laboratory in 1966.

Bibliography: Mayer, A. M., et al., *The Germination of Seeds*, 2d ed. (1976; repr. 1982).

Germiston [jur'-mis-tuhn]

Germiston, a city in Transvaal province, South Africa, is located 14 km (9 mi) east of Johannesburg. It is South Africa's largest railroad junction, with a population of 116,559 (1980). The city has the world's largest gold refinery. Its other industries produce explosives, machine tools, munitions, and furniture. ALAN C. G. BEST

Gernsback, Hugo [gurnz'-bak]

Editor, publisher, and inventor in the new field of radio, Hugo Gernsback, b. Aug. 16, 1884, d. Aug. 19, 1967, is best known for his founding of *Amazing Stories* (1926), the first magazine devoted to "scientifiction" (as Gernsback called it)—a new genre of fiction based loosely on science laced with a good deal of fantasy. Other, rival magazines quickly followed, and eventually SCIENCE FICTION became an established field of imaginative writing. The annual HUGO AWARD, given to the best new science fiction of the year, is named in his honor.

Born in Luxembourg, Gernsback emigrated to the United States in 1904 and in 1908 founded *Modern Electrics*, the first radio magazine (later incorporated with *Popular Science*). He founded several other magazines in the field of radio and established his own technical publishing company as well.

Gérôme, Jean Léon [zhay-rohm']

The French painter and sculptor Jean Léon Gérôme, b. May 11, 1824, d. Jan. 10, 1904, was one of the most notable academic artists of the second half of the 19th century. After studying first (1839) in the studio of Paul Delaroche and subsequently (1845) with Charles Gleyre, Gérôme achieved immediate acclaim for his *Cockfight* (1847; Louvre, Paris), which has remained his most famous painting.

Following his appointment (1863) as professor at the École des Beaux-Arts and his election (1865) to the Institut de France, he became even more conservative and classically oriented, concentrating on meticulously drawn and highly finished depictions of historical episodes from ancient times, such as *Pollice verso*, or *Thumbs down* (1874; Phoenix Art Gallery, Ariz.) and *The Death of Caesar* (1867; Walters Art Gallery, Baltimore, Md.). Because Gérôme was devoted to the French academic tradition, which stressed detailed realism and lofty subject matter, he became a staunch opponent of impressionism and other modern movements, calling them the shame of French art. From about 1878 he turned his attention to sculpture, often innovatively combining marble with bronze, precious stones, and ivory. BARBARA CAVALIERE

Bibliography: Boime, Albert, *The Academy and French Painting in the 19th Century* (1971); Reff, Theodore, ed., *Exhibitions of Classicizing Art* (1981).

Geronimo [jur-ahn'-i-moh]

Geronimo, a leader of the Chiricahua Apaches, conducted a series of raids against both Mexican and American settlements in the Southwest. In 1876 the tribe was confined to Arizona's San Carlos Reservation, but Geronimo and his followers repeatedly escaped. After eluding a pursuing federal army for nearly a year, Geronimo finally surrendered to Gen. Nelson Miles in 1886.

Geronimo, b. 1829 in southern Arizona, d. Feb. 17, 1909, was an APACHE war leader noted for his guerrilla raids against Mexican and later U.S. troops in the American Southwest. A member of the Deindai band of the Chiricahua Apache, he was called *Goyathlay* (meaning "one who yawns") in Apache. In 1850 the ambush killing of his first wife and children kindled in Geronimo an undying hatred of Mexicans. As leader of the avenging Apache at Arispe in Sonora, he performed such daring feats that the Mexicans singled him out with the sobriquet *Geronimo* (Spanish for "Jerome"). Some attributed his numerous raiding successes to powers conferred by supernatural beings, including a reputed invulnerability to bullets.

Geronimo's war career was linked with that of his brother-in-law, Juh, a Chiricahua chief. Although he was not a hereditary leader, Geronimo appeared so to outsiders because he often acted as spokesman for Juh, who had a speech impediment. In 1875, U.S. authorities branded Geronimo the chief opponent of the policy to consolidate all Apache and called for his hanging to end the disruption. When the Chiricahua were forcibly removed (1876) to arid land at San Carlos, in eastern Arizona, Geronimo fled with a band of followers into Mexico. He was soon arrested and returned to the new reservation. For the remainder of the 1870s, he and Juh alternated between raiding attacks and a quiet life on the reservation, but with the slaying of an Apache prophet in 1881, they returned to full-time hit-and-run raiding activities from a secret camp in the Sierra Madre Mountains.

In May 1882, Apache scouts working for the U.S. army surprised Geronimo in his mountain sanctuary, and he agreed to return with his people to the reservation. After a year of farming, the sudden arrest and imprisonment of the Apache warrior Ka-ya-ten-nae, together with rumors of impending trials and hangings, prompted Geronimo to flee on May 17, 1885, with 35 warriors and 109 women, children and youths. In January 1886, Apache scouts penetrated Juh's seemingly impregnable hideout. This action induced Geronimo to surrender (Mar. 25, 1886) to Gen. George CROOK. Geronimo later fled but finally surrendered to Gen. Nelson MILES on Sept. 4, 1886. The government breached its agreement and transported Geronimo and nearly 450 Apache men, women, and children to Florida for confinement in Forts Marion and Pickens. In 1894 they were removed to Fort Sill in Oklahoma. Geronimo became a rancher, appeared (1904) at the Louisiana Purchase Exposition in St. Louis, sold Geronimo souvenirs, and rode in President Theodore Roosevelt's 1905 inaugural parade.

FRED W. VOGET

Bibliography: Adams, A. B., *Geronimo: A Biography* (1971); Barrett, S. M., ed., *Geronimo's Story of His Life* (1906; repr. 1970); Debo, Angie, *Geronimo: The Man, His Time, His Place* (1976); Faulk, O. B., *The Geronimo Campaign* (1969).

gerontology: see GERIATRICS; MEDICINE.

gerrhosaurid [jair-oh-sohr'-id]

Gerrhosaurids are African and Madagascan lizards resembling the skinks, to which they are closely related. They were formerly often placed in a separate family, Gerrhosauridae, but today most herpetologists include them in the subfamily Zonurinae of the family Cordylidae. Gerrhosaurids are found in rugged and hilly grass or scrub country, preferring dry, open terrain. They are ground dwellers, and most have strong limbs, including the Sudan plated lizard, *Gerrhosaurus major.* Several genera, however, including the whip lizards, *Tetradactylus,* have degenerate or absent legs. The largest members of this group are the Madagascan girdled lizard, *Zonosaurus maximus,* and the rock plated lizard, *G. validus,* of southeastern Africa, both of which reach slightly over 61 cm (2 ft) in length. Gerrhosaurids typically have head shields fused to the skull, bony cores in the body scales, a deep fold of skin along each side of the belly, and a long tail. All species lay eggs and feed mainly on insects. (See GIRDLE-TAILED LIZARD.)

JONATHAN CAMPBELL

Gerry, Elbridge [gair'-ee, el'-brij]

Elbridge Gerry was a signer of the U.S. Declaration of Independence, a congressman, governor of Massachusetts, and vice-president of the United States (1813–14).

Born in Marblehead, Mass., on July 17, 1744, he graduated from Harvard College in 1762 and entered his father's shipping business. An early advocate of American independence, Gerry served in the Massachusetts Provincial Congress (1774–75) and the Continental Congress (1776–80, 1783–85). He was a delegate to the Constitutional Convention of 1787, but refused to sign the Constitution because it did not agree with his ideas on republicanism.

Gerry was elected to the House of Representatives in 1789, after declaring that he would support the Constitution. Retiring in 1793, he returned to government service in 1797 when President John Adams appointed him a member of the mission to France that became involved in the XYZ AFFAIR. At odds with his fellow negotiators, John MARSHALL and Charles C. Pinckney (see PINCKNEY family), Gerry tried to negotiate separate terms after they left France. He was elected governor of Massachusetts in 1810 and reelected in 1811. In 1812 he signed into law a redistricting bill designed to ensure continued majorities for his party, the Democratic-Republicans; this political maneuver was named the gerrymander after him. In 1812 he was elected vice-president under James MADISON. He died in that office on Nov. 23, 1814.

GEORGE ATHAN BILLIAS

Bibliography: Billias, George Athan, *Elbridge Gerry: Founding Father and Republican Statesman* (1976).

gerrymander [jair'-ee-man-dur]

A gerrymander is an election district whose boundaries have been redrawn by the party in power for its own political ad-

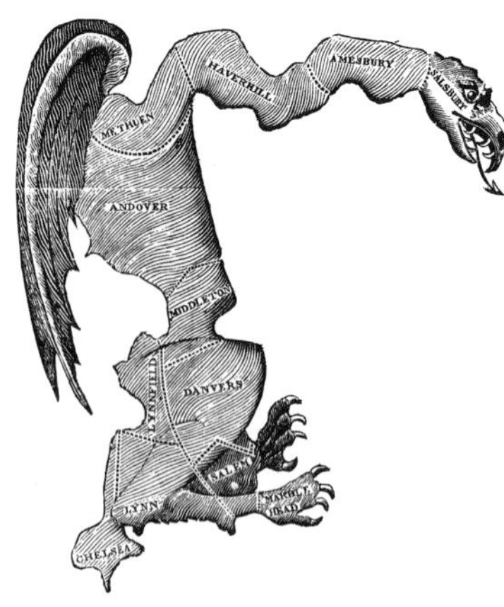

In 1812 the Massachusetts legislature rearranged the senatorial districts to favor the dominant Democratic-Republican party. One strangely shaped district in Essex County was caricatured as a salamander and was soon dubbed a "gerrymander," after Gov. Elbridge Gerry.

vantage, usually by excluding areas in which the opposing party is strong or including areas in which it is weak. The word originated in 1812, during Elbridge Gerry's second term as governor of Massachusetts, when the legislature redistricted the state so as to give the Democratic-Republicans an advantage in state senatorial elections. One of the new senatorial districts was particularly sprawling. An artist jokingly added wings, claws, and teeth to its outline, prompting the suggestion that it resembled a salamander. Benjamin Russell, a staunchly Federalist newspaper editor, gave it the name *Gerrymander,* referring to the Democratic-Republican governor.

The U.S. Supreme Court has ruled that legislative districts must contain roughly equal numbers of people, but legislatures are still permitted to draw district lines so as to give a particular party or faction an electoral advantage.

Bibliography: Griffith, Elmer C., *The Rise and Development of the Gerrymander* (1907; repr. 1974); Musgrove, Philip, *The General Theory of Gerrymandering* (1976).

See also: APPORTIONMENT; BAKER V. CARR; REYNOLDS V. SIMS.

Gershwin, George and Ira [gur'-shwin]

The composer of *Rhapsody in Blue* and PORGY AND BESS, George Gershwin, b. Brooklyn, N.Y., Sept. 26, 1898, d. July 11, 1937, was one of America's most versatile and popular song writers. With his brother Ira, b. Dec. 6, 1896, d. Aug. 17, 1983, he was also the creator of the first musical comedy to win the Pulitzer Prize for drama, *Of Thee I Sing.* A talented pianist, George left school at age 15 to become a "song plugger" in New York's Tin Pan Alley. His brother Ira fared poorly at the piano but compensated for this deficiency years later by writing the words to most of George's songs.

"Swanee" (1919), popularized by Al Jolson, was Gershwin's

The American composer George Gershwin gained renown for his popular Broadway musicals of the 1920s. He began his career as a jazz pianist and created a landmark in American musical development with Rhapsody in Blue *(1924), in which the style of the piano concerto is blended with a symphonic jazz idiom.*

first hit song. From 1920 to 1924 he wrote songs for the *George White's Scandals* revues and met Paul Whiteman, who commissioned him to write a jazz piece for a concert at Aeolian Hall in New York City. The result, *Rhapsody in Blue* (1924), was orchestrated by Ferde Grofé and first performed, with Gershwin as piano soloist, with great success. The conductor of the New York symphony, Walter Damrosch, asked Gershwin for a symphonic work, and the composer complied with his *Concerto in F* (1925). After further studies in composition, Gershwin wrote other classical-oriented works such as *An American in Paris* (1928) and *Second Rhapsody* (1931). Meanwhile, with his brother Ira as lyricist, he had also composed the musical shows *Lady Be Good* (1924), *Strike up the Band* (1927), *Girl Crazy* (1930), and *Of Thee I Sing* (1931).

One of Gershwin's deepest ambitions was the creation of an American opera, and this ambition he achieved with *Porgy and Bess* (1935), based on the book by DuBose Heyward and with lyrics by Heyward and Ira Gershwin. The opera was Gershwin's last major work. He died of a brain tumor two years later in Hollywood, where he and Ira had been writing songs for films.

Bibliography: Jablonski, Edward, *Gershwin* (1987); Jablonski, Edward, and Stewart, L. D., *The Gershwin Years,* rev. ed. (1973); Kendall, Alan, *Gershwin* (1987); Rosenberg, Deena, *The Brothers Gershwin* (1989); Schwartz, Charles, *Gershwin: His Life and Music* (1973).

Gerson, Jean le Charlier de [zhair-sohn']

Jean le Charlier de Gerson, b. Dec. 13, 1363, d. July 12, 1429, was a French theologian and chancellor of the University of Paris who was instrumental in ending the Great SCHISM (1378–1417) of the Western church. He studied at the College of Navarre in Paris and succeeded Pierre d'AILLY as chancellor in 1395, a position he held until his death. Although he is best known for his works on theological, pastoral, and mystical themes, Gerson also wrote on philosophy and education.

Gerson's most active years coincided with the Great Schism, a period during which the Christian church was divided by rival claimants to the PAPACY. He played a leading role at the Council of CONSTANCE (1414–18), which finally settled the schism. At the council he advocated CONCILIARISM, the theory that an ecumenical council of the church can overrule a pope; he saw this as the only solution to the critical situation of his day.

Gerson devoted his last ten years to a life of asceticism. During this time he wrote a number of treatises on the church, defending his position on councils while adhering to the idea of papal primacy. His most important work is *Montagne de contemplation* (The Mountain of Contemplation, 1397), in which he proposed his mystical teachings.

THOMAS E. MORRISSEY

Bibliography: Brown, D. C., *Pastor and Laity in the Theology of Jean Gerson* (1987); Pascoe, L., *Jean Gerson: Principles of Church Reform* (1973).

Gersonides: see LEVI BEN GERSHON.

Gesell, Arnold [guh-zel']

Arnold Lucius Gesell, b. Alma, Wis., June 21, 1880, d. May 29, 1961, was an American psychologist who conducted child development studies. He received a doctorate in psychology in 1906 as a student of G. Stanley Hall. In 1911, while studying for an M.D. at Yale, he founded the Yale Clinic of Child Development to study retarded children. He introduced the use of motion pictures to psychological research in 1924 and one-way observation techniques in 1930. With Louise Ames and Frances L. Ilg he wrote a popular syndicated column about children. In books such as *The First Five Years of Life* (1940) and (with Ilg) *The Child from Five to Ten* (1946), he emphasized the cyclical nature of development.

Gesner, Konrad von [ges'-nur]

Konrad von Gesner, b. Mar. 26, 1516, d. Dec. 13, 1565, was a Swiss physician and naturalist best known for his manuscript *Bibliotheca Universalis* (1545), which contained summaries of all the then-known books in Latin, Greek, and Hebrew. He described all the known animals of his era and is believed to be the first scientist to publish illustrations of fossils.

Bibliography: Ley, Willy, *Dawn of Zoology* (1960); Sarton, George, *Six Wings: Men of Science in the Renaissance* (1957).

Gestalt psychology [ge-shtahlt']

Originally, Gestalt psychology was a system of psychology concerned with the nature of PERCEPTION. Just prior to World War I, German researchers such as Kurt KOFFKA, Wolfgang KÖHLER, and Max WERTHEIMER began studying the way in which perception was influenced by the context or configuration of elements perceived. (*Gestalt* translates from German roughly as "configuration" or "pattern.") They argued that the relationship among components, rather than their fixed characteristics, determines what is perceived. Thus a person perceives a whole or pattern that may be much more than the collection of individual elements: for example, an oval shape is perceived as the round top of a table in the context of a dining room. Research studies in Gestalt psychology have attempted to determine the necessary and sufficient conditions for this perceptual transformation.

Since the 1950s the term has been adopted to describe psychotherapies that share assumptions loosely related to the Gestalt psychology of perception. Gestalt psychotherapies, pioneered by Fritz PERLS, assume that the human organism responds holistically to life events—that separation of mind and body is artificial. The theory emphasizes awareness and the accurate perception of oneself, of one's needs, and of the world. The aware person is able to regulate and balance his or her experience. Experience can become unbalanced when the person avoids awareness of unpleasant events—the holistic response or Gestalt is then broken and incomplete. Incomplete or unfinished Gestalten may be carried with an individual and may interfere with later experiences of a similar nature. The aware person lives in the present and is not unduly influenced by past or future events.

LYNN REHM

Bibliography: Koffka, Kurt, *Principles of Gestalt Psychology* (1967) and *Growth of the Mind* (1980); Köhler, Wolfgang, *Gestalt Psychology,* new ed. (1970; repr. 1980), and *The Task of Gestalt Psychology* (1969); Perls, Frederick, et al., *Gestalt Therapy Verbatim* (1959; repr. 1988).

Gestapo [ge-stah'-poh]

The Geheime Staatspolizei (Secret State Police), known as the Gestapo, was, together with the SS (Schutzstaffel, or Black Shirts), the mainstay of power of the German National Socialists under Adolf HITLER. Originally formed (1933) by Hermann GOERING as a political police unit in the state of Prussia, it gradually came under the control of Heinrich HIMMLER. In February 1936, Hitler decreed the Gestapo to be a national secret police and forbade judicial appeals against its decisions.

The day-to-day operations of the Gestapo were handled by Heinrich Müller, supervised by Reinhard Heydrich, and after January 1943 by Ernst Kaltenbrunner, under the overall authority of Himmler as leader of the SS. At its height, in 1943–45, the Gestapo had 40,000 to 50,000 employees.

The Gestapo's task was to suppress opposition to the regime inside Germany and, after World War II began, in the occupied territories. Its six sections dealt with all forms of possible opposition, from political to religious. Subsection Four of the second section, handling religion, dealt with the Jews and was headed by the notorious Adolf EICHMANN. Its methods included savage interrogation techniques, torture, outright murder, and imprisonment in CONCENTRATION CAMPS. The Gestapo instituted the concentration-camp system and, with the help of the SS, put about 4 million Jews in these camps for extermination. The Gestapo and SS also formed the so-called Einsatz groups, which followed the advancing German armies and murdered an additional 2 million Jews as well as many others termed *undesirables.*

Bibliography: Delarue, Jacques, *The Gestapo: A History of Horror,* trans. by Mervyn Savill (1964; repr. 1986).

gestation [jes-tay'-shuhn]

Gestation is the process by which the females of viviparous animals—those which give birth to live young—carry the young internally from conception to birth. In mammals it is synonymous with pregnancy (see PREGNANCY AND BIRTH). The gestation period, or interval between fertilization and birth, varies considerably among the different mammalian species. Examples, given as mean length in days, are Syrian hamster 16, mouse 20, rabbit 31, dog 61, cat 63, pig 113, sheep 148, human 267, cattle 284, horse 337, Indian elephant 645. The period is obviously related to the size of the adult, but there may also be a complementary adaptive adjustment to the time of the mating season, so that the young are born when food is abundant. The young of marsupials are born in a very immature state, and the period of gestation is generally shorter. It is said to be only 12 days in the Virginia opossum.

VIVIPARITY occurs in some species of many classes of animals, including coelenterates, insects, fish, and reptiles, as well as mammals. It is an adaptation that safeguards the young during the early and highly vulnerable stages of development, but at the cost of reduced numbers of progeny and greatly increased physiological demands on the females.

In ovoviviparous animals the female does little beyond furnishing shelter within her body for the eggs to develop so that hatching and birth are effectively simultaneous events. In true viviparity, on the other hand, the shell and food reserves within the egg are minimal or absent, and the developing embryo becomes parasitic on the mother. True viviparity is characteristic of the higher mammals, including the marsupials, which nourish the fetus internally through a placenta, which connects fetus and mother. In addition to supplying nutrition, the placenta performs the fetal respiratory and excretory functions by exchanging substances between the blood of the mother and that of the fetus.

The initiation and termination of gestation are signaled, and its maintenance regulated, by hormones produced principally in the pituitary gland, the ovaries, the chorion, and the placenta. The details vary greatly, even between species as closely related as sheep and goats, so that general statements are difficult to formulate; however, the maintenance of pregnancy appears to be dependent upon a continuous supply of a progestogen, which in most species investigated is specifically the SEX HORMONE progesterone. C. E. FORD

Bibliography: McKenzie, John, *An Introduction to Developmental Biology* (1976); Moore, Keith, *The Developing Human,* 2d ed. (1977).

See also: DEVELOPMENT.

Gesualdo, Carlo [jay-zoo-ahl'-doh]

Carlo Gesualdo, prince of Venosa, b. *c.*1560, d. Sept. 8, 1613, was one of the leading Italian MADRIGAL composers of the Renaissance. The audacious musical style of his late works and the tragic events of his personal life have earned him a notoriety unequaled in musical history. He was born into one of the oldest and most noble families of Naples and was the nephew of Saint Charles Borromeo. He had already become a composer of some distinction when in 1590 he ordered the murder of his wife and her lover, which caused a scandal that spread throughout Italy. His second marriage in 1594 to a princess of the d'Este family brought him into contact with the court of Ferrara, where he resided for a few years and where his first four books of madrigals were published (1594–96). He published two other books of madrigals and three volumes of sacred music. Gesualdo's late works, in which contrapuntal and homophonic elements mingle freely, are remarkable for the intensity of their musical expression and for their highly personal style. They are characterized, above all, by daring harmonic progressions and striking chromaticism of a kind that suggests the music of Richard Wagner. FRANK D'ACCONE

Bibliography: Watkins, Glenn, *Gesualdo, the Man and His Music* (1973).

Gethsemane [geth-sem'-uh-nee]

Gethsemane is the place on the Mount of Olives near Jerusalem where Jesus Christ was betrayed by Judas Iscariot and arrested while praying with his disciples after the Last Supper. The name (Matt. 26:36; Mark 14:32) may have meant "oil vat," suggesting a stand of olive trees. John's Gospel (18:1) refers to the site as a garden; hence, the composite designation, the Garden of Gethsemane. Despite several conjectures, the site is not precisely identifiable today.

Getty, J. Paul [get'-ee]

Jean Paul Getty, b. Minneapolis, Minn., Dec. 15, 1892, d. June 6, 1976, amassed an enormous fortune estimated at more than $1 billion. With backing from his father, a successful oil man, Getty entered the oil business in Oklahoma. By the time he was 23 he had made his first $1 million. During the depression years of the 1930s he put together a network of companies through stock purchases. The Tidewater, Skelly, and Getty companies were the primary links in his vast domain. He lived most of his life in hotel rooms, and his chief indulgence was collecting art. He owned a 16th-century estate in England, Sutton Place, and established the Getty Museum in Malibu, Calif. Among his books were *My Life and Fortunes* (1963), *How to Be Rich* (1966), and *As I See It* (1976).

Bibliography: Lund, Robina, *The Stately Gnome: An Intimate Biography of J. Paul Getty* (1978).

Getty Museum

The J. Paul Getty Museum was founded in 1954 by the oil magnate and art collector on his estate overlooking the Pacific Ocean in Malibu, Calif. The collections, originally displayed in a Spanish-style villa, are now housed in a sumptuous and meticulously researched re-creation of the Villa of the Papyri (begun 2d century BC) in Herculaneum, buried by the eruption of Mount Vesuvius in AD 79. Opened in 1974, the museum and its gardens were designed to enhance Getty's Greek and Roman art collection, which includes the *Lansdowne Hercules* (AD *c.*130) from Hadrian's Villa near Rome, the *Mazarin Venus* (AD *c.*117–38), and the *Getty Bronze* (late 4th century BC), a life-size statue of Greek youth.

Among the museum's Renaissance and baroque paintings are outstanding works by Thomas Gainsborough, Georges de La Tour, Peter Paul Rubens, and Sir Anthony van Dyck. Characteristic paintings by Sir Lawrence Alma-Tadema and Adolphe William Bouguereau round out the collection. The superlative collection of French decorative arts from about 1670 to 1790 is displayed in galleries and period rooms and includes signed pieces by André Charles Boulle and Jean Henri Riesener. Getty bequeathed (1976) the museum an endowment in excess of $700 million, which had appreciated to $1.1 billion by the time the funds were actually transferred in 1982. The museum is thus by far the richest in the world.

EDWARD T. MCCLELLAN

Bibliography: Garrett, S., *Guidebook: The J. Paul Getty Museum,* 4th ed. (1978); Neuerberg, N., *Herculaneum to Malibu* (1975).

Gettysburg [get'-eez-burg]

Gettysburg, site of the great Civil War battle (July 1–3, 1863), is situated in rolling fruit-orchard country in southern Pennsylvania. The borough has a population of 7,194 (1980) and is the seat of Adams County. It has been a college community since before the Civil War, the seat of a theological seminary and of Gettysburg College. The town has iron mines and granite quarries, but most important to its economy is the 1,380-ha (3,409-acre) National Military Park, which draws thousands of visitors every year. Adjoining the battlefield is the farm of Dwight D. Eisenhower. The borough was founded in the 1780s and named for James Gettys, to whom William Penn originally granted the land.

Gettysburg, Battle of

The Battle of Gettysburg, one of the most important battles of the U.S. Civil War, was fought at Gettysburg, Pa., on July 1–3,

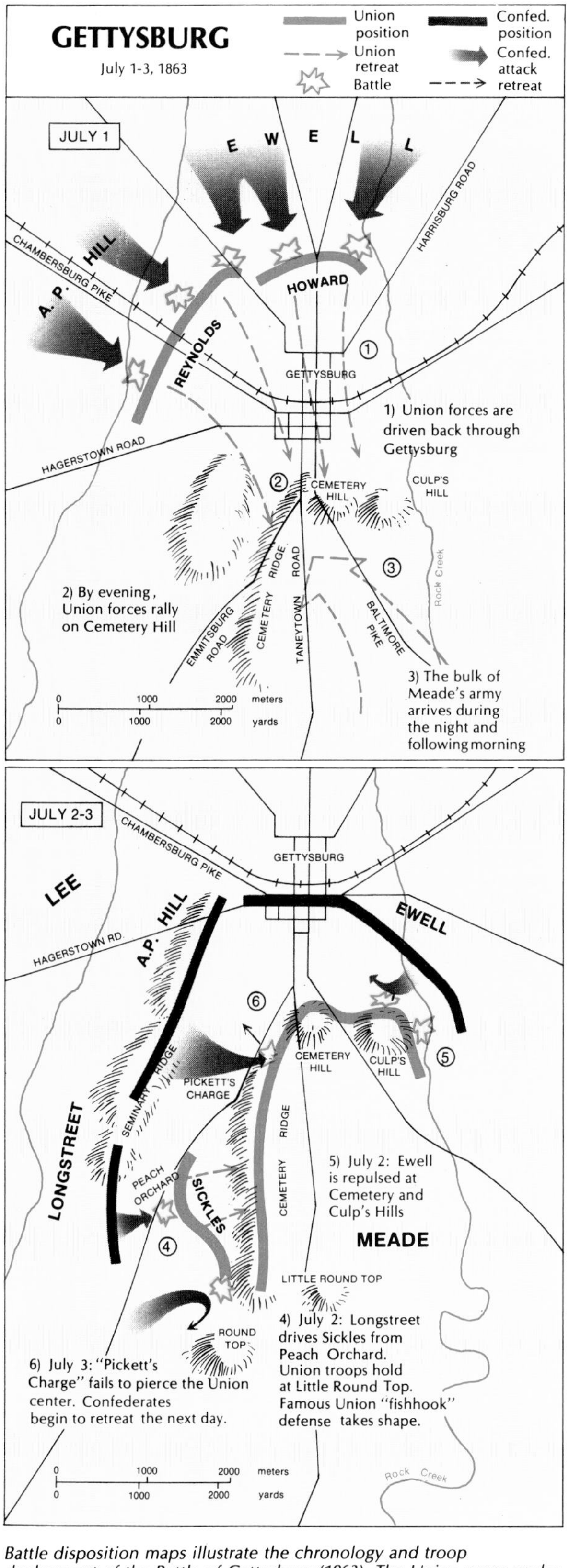

GETTYSBURG
July 1-3, 1863

Union position
Union retreat
Battle
Confed. position
Confed. attack
retreat

JULY 1

EWELL
A. P. HILL
HOWARD
REYNOLDS
CHAMBERSBURG PIKE
HARRISBURG ROAD
HAGERSTOWN ROAD
GETTYSBURG
CEMETERY HILL
CULP'S HILL
RIDGE ROAD
CEMETERY
EMMITSBURG ROAD
TANEYTOWN ROAD
BALTIMORE PIKE
Rock Creek

1) Union forces are driven back through Gettysburg

2) By evening, Union forces rally on Cemetery Hill

3) The bulk of Meade's army arrives during the night and following morning

0 1000 2000 meters
0 1000 2000 yards

JULY 2-3

LEE
A.P. HILL
EWELL
LONGSTREET
SICKLES
MEADE
CHAMBERSBURG PIKE
HAGERSTOWN RD.
GETTYSBURG
SEMINARY RIDGE
PICKETT'S CHARGE
CEMETERY HILL
CULP'S HILL
CEMETERY RIDGE
PEACH ORCHARD
LITTLE ROUND TOP
ROUND TOP
Rock Creek

5) July 2: Ewell is repulsed at Cemetery and Culp's Hills

4) July 2: Longstreet drives Sickles from Peach Orchard. Union troops hold at Little Round Top. Famous Union "fishhook" defense takes shape.

6) July 3: "Pickett's Charge" fails to pierce the Union center. Confederates begin to retreat the next day.

0 1000 2000 meters
0 1000 2000 yards

Battle disposition maps illustrate the chronology and troop deployment of the Battle of Gettysburg (1863). The Union army, under George G. Meade, halted the Confederate invasion and forced Robert E. Lee's army to retreat, a turning point of the Civil War.

1863. Gen. Robert E. LEE invaded Pennsylvania for strategical and logistical reasons. His army of about 75,000 encountered the Union Army of the Potomac, about 90,000 strong, under Gen. George G. MEADE on the outskirts of Gettysburg on July 1. In a battle of considerable movement, Lee tested first the Union right (July 1) and then, in an assault led by Gen. James LONGSTREET, the left (July 2). On July 3, Gen. George PICKETT led perhaps the most famous charge in American military history against the Union center. Only 5,000 of his original force of 15,000 survived the repulse.

Lee watched the survivors return and confessed, "It is all my fault." Gettysburg, a military and logistical disaster for the South, cost Lee 20,000 men (killed and wounded) and 30,000 arms. Meade lost almost as many men. The battle had considerable psychological effect on both North and South, calling forth President Lincoln's Gettysburg Address. Occurring in the same week that Vicksburg fell to Gen. Ulysses S. Grant, Gettysburg put the Confederates on the defensive in the east.

FRANK E. VANDIVER

Bibliography: Catton, Bruce, *The Final Fury* (1974); Coddington, Edwin B., *The Gettysburg Campaign* (1968); Dowdey, Clifford, *Death of a Nation* (1958); Perisco, Joseph E., *My Enemy, My Brother: Men and Days of Gettysburg* (1977).

Gettysburg Address

On Nov. 19, 1863, President Abraham Lincoln dedicated a national cemetery on the battlefield at Gettysburg, where a few months earlier over 7,000 men had died. Although Lincoln's address received little attention at the time, it has since come to be esteemed as one of the finest speeches in the English language.

> Fourscore and seven years ago our fathers brought forth on this continent a new nation, conceived in liberty and dedicated to the proposition that all men are created equal. Now we are engaged in a great civil war, testing whether that nation or any nation so conceived and so dedicated can long endure. We are met on a great battlefield of that war. We have come to dedicate a portion of that field as a final resting-place for those who here gave their lives that that nation might live. It is altogether fitting and proper that we should do this. But in a larger sense, we cannot dedicate, we cannot consecrate, we cannot hallow this ground. The brave men, living and dead who struggled here have consecrated it far above our poor power to add or detract. The world will little note nor long remember what we say here, but it can never forget what they did here. It is for us the living rather to be dedicated here to the unfinished work which they who fought here have thus far so nobly advanced. It is rather for us to be here dedicated to the great task remaining before us—that from these honored dead we take increased devotion to that cause for which they gave the last full measure of devotion—that we here highly resolve that these dead shall not have died in vain,

Abraham Lincoln was asked to deliver a speech at the ceremony dedicating a national cemetery at the site of the Civil War battle at Gettysburg, Pa. His brief remarks on Nov. 19, 1863, known as the Gettysburg Address, contain one of the most concise and eloquent definitions of democracy, a "government of the people, by the people, for the people."

that this nation under God shall have a new birth of freedom, and that government of the people, by the people, for the people shall not perish from the earth.

Bibliography: Barton, William E., *Lincoln at Gettysburg* (1930; repr. 1971); Berns, Laurence, et al., *Abraham Lincoln: The Gettysburg Address and American Constitutionalism* (1976); Nevins, Allan, ed., *Lincoln and the Gettysburg Address* (1964).

Geulincx, Arnold [gur'-links]

Arnold Geulincx, b. Jan. 31, 1624, d. November 1669, was a Flemish Cartesian philosopher who was one of the proponents of OCCASIONALISM. Originally a Roman Catholic, Geulincx adopted Calvinism in 1658. He taught at Louvain and, later, at Leiden. His major works, *Ethica* and *metaphysica vera,* were published posthumously.

According to Geulincx, body and mind cannot affect each other. A person's intention to move his body is merely the occasion on which God, the only real cause, produces the movement. Since minds cannot affect bodies, people cannot control their actions; they can only control their wills. Accordingly, Geulincx's ethics stresses a humbling of the will.

Geyl, Pieter [hayl, pee'-tur]

Pieter Catharinus Arie Geyl, b. Dec. 15, 1887, d. Dec. 31, 1966, was a Dutch historian, whose work is valued for his critical scholarship and broad view of the history of the Netherlands. Geyl was professor of Dutch history at London University (1919-35) and later at Utrecht. During World War II he was interned by the Germans. His 3-volume *Geschiedenis van de Nederlandse stam* (History of the Dutch People, 1930-37) is his most important work.

geyser [gy'-zur]

A geyser is a HOT SPRING that periodically throws hot water and steam into the air, sometimes to a great height and for a considerable length of time. The word *geyser,* which means to "gush forth," comes from Iceland, where there are about 30 active geysers. The most notable, the now dormant Great Geysir, threw a tremendous jet of hot water and steam to a height of 70 m (230 ft) about every 6 hours. Twenty large geysers and perhaps 100 smaller ones occur in Kamchatka, USSR. Most of those in New Zealand have been destroyed by GEOTHERMAL ENERGY development in recent years. New Zealand, however, is famous for the world's record geyser, Waimangu, which, between 1902 and 1905, played to 450-m (1500-ft) heights every 5 to 30 hours. By far the largest number—about 200—and the most spectacular ones are in Yellowstone National Park.

A geyser results from the superheating of pressurized water in contact with hot volcanic rocks in deep, interconnecting chambers (A). *As the superheated water expands, it drives out some of the water above it, which reduces the pressure. The superheated water immediately flashes into steam, which violently drives out a column of water and steam through the surface opening* (B). *Groundwater then flows back into the chambers* (C), *and the process is repeated.*

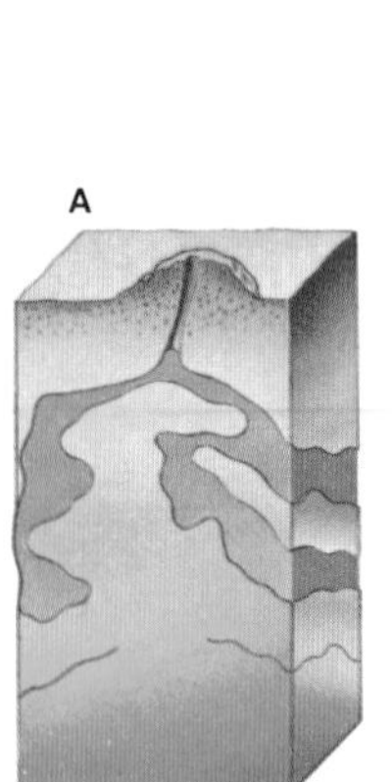

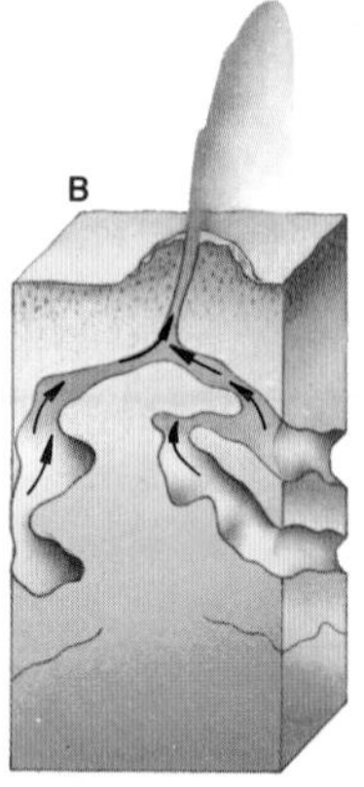

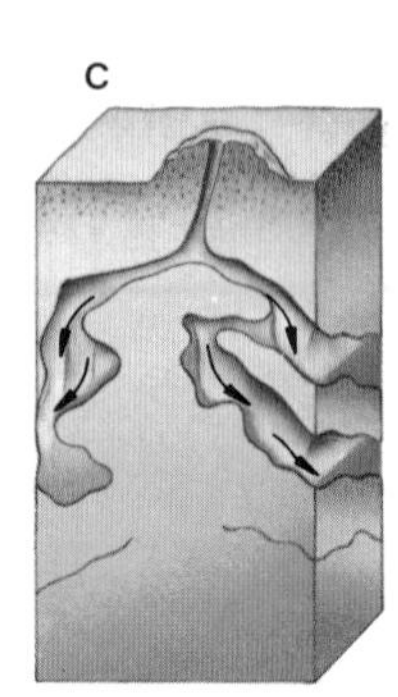

"Old Faithful," the most famous geyser in the Yellowstone Park area of the United States, is so named because it has sent, for more than 100 years, a column of hot water and steam to a height of about 50 m (165 ft) for periods of 2 to 5 minutes at intervals of 30 to 90 minutes.

Geysers are located near geologically recent (within the last 1 million years) volcanic activity, especially in regions where precipitation is heavy. Yellowstone National Park is a huge collapsed volcano that erupted about 600,000 years ago, and the geysers of New Zealand, Iceland, and Kamchatka, USSR, are all located near active volcanoes.

In order to function, a geyser must have a source of heat, a reservoir where water can be stored until it reaches an unstable temperature, an opening through which to eject hot water and steam, and underground channels for replenishing the supply of fresh water after an eruption. A geyser erupts when some of its hot water expands explosively into steam, growing a thousandfold in volume. Water under pressure can remain liquid at temperatures above its normal boiling point. In a geyser, the weight of the upper water exerts pressure on the lower water, permitting the latter to reach much higher temperatures than the upper water before turning to steam. As the deep water becomes hotter and lighter, a blob of superheated water forms, suddenly rises to the surface, and explodes into steam. The explosion churns up all the water in the geyser reservoir, triggering renewed upward movement of hot water, and further explosions. The geyser is then in full eruption. Some geysers empty nearly all of their reservoirs during an eruption by emitting a powerful and continuous column of hot water and steam. The emptied reservoir is hot, and the eruption is usually topped off with a persistent roaring jet of steam. Other geysers produce little water and steam, ridding themselves of excess heat by a series of powerful explosions, the typical action of a fountain or pool geyser. Immediately after an eruption water again flows into the underground reservoir, heating begins, and the process repeats itself.

A complete cycle may take minutes, hours, days, or years. Some geysers erupt regularly, others sporadically; some are active briefly, then become inactive, only to rejuvenate at a later time; new geysers come into being while others become dormant. Many of the changes in eruption patterns are associated with changes in barometric pressure, earthquake activity, and variations in the gravitational pull of the Sun and the Moon on the Earth. OLD FAITHFUL, the most famous geyser in Yellowstone Park, plays a column of hot water and steam into the air for 2 to 5 minutes, reaching a height of about 50 m (165 ft), at intervals of 30 to 90 minutes. Steamboat Geyser (also in Yellowstone), now the largest active geyser in the world, unexpectedly erupted in March 1978 after 9 years of dormancy. Water was thrown to heights of 150 m (500 ft) for nearly 15 minutes, and steam gushed forth for about 40 hours. Grand Geyser, perhaps the most magnificent in Yellowstone, now erupts about three times a day, although it too has had dormant periods. It erupts with a series of 6 or 8 explosive bursts at intervals of several minutes, throwing fans of water and jetting steam to heights of about 70 m (230 ft).

Geyser water is usually heavily laden with dissolved SILICA MINERALS, which precipitate out when the discharged water cools. This produces huge (up to 5 m/15 ft high) cones and terraces of SINTER, the nozzles and pools so common in geyser basins. JOHN S. RINEHART

Bibliography: Barth, T. F. W., *Volcanic Geology, Hot Springs, and Geysers of Iceland* (1950); Kaysing, Bill, *Great Hot Springs of the West*, rev. ed. (1984); Keefer, W. R., *The Geologic Story of Yellowstone National Park* (1972); Loam, Jayson, *Hot Springs and Hot Pools of the Northwest*, 2d ed. (1985); Rinehart, John S., *A Guide to Geyser Gazing* (1976); Schreier, Carl, *Yellowstone's Geysers, Hot Springs and Fumaroles* (1987).

geyserite: see SILICA MINERALS.

Gezelle, Guido [he-zel'-e]

Guido Gezelle, b. May 1, 1830, d. Nov. 27, 1899, was a Roman Catholic priest and teacher, and one of the greatest 19th-century Flemish poets. Independent of all literary movements, he ushered in a rebirth of Flemish poetry with his volume *Kerkhofblommen* (Graveyard Flowers, 1858); his poetry was a unique mixture of traditional literary Dutch with the dialect of his own West Flanders. His passionate literary and nationalistic beliefs led to conflicts with ecclesiastical and educational authorities, which caused him to stop writing poetry (1870–75); during this time he wrote essays and translations. But Gezelle returned to the brilliance of his earlier poetry in *Tijdkrans* (Time's Garland, 1893) and *Rijmsnoer* (String of Rhymes, 1897). Typically, the poems in these volumes deal with nature, religion, and Flemish nationalism and display an original use of rhyme, metaphor, and sound. THEO D'HAEN

Bibliography: Gezelle, Guido, *Poems/Gedichten*, bilingual edition, trans. by Christine d'Haen (1972).

Gezer

Gezer (modern Tell Jezer) is a large mound located 11 km (7 mi) southeast of Ramla in present-day Israel. Guarding a major strategic crossroads, it was one of the most important Canaanite cities. Occupied since the 4th millennium BC, Gezer was first fortified during the Middle Bronze Age (*c*.1900–1550 BC) with a massive stone wall 16 m (52 ft) wide. Just inside were placed, slightly later, ten enormous standing stones set on a north-south line; they were intended as a religious installation, as the "High Place." Under Solomon, the city, like MEGIDDO and HAZOR, became a major stronghold and was provided with a casemate wall and gateway of two square towers and three pairs of buttresses. About two centuries later a subterranean water system was constructed. Numerous inscriptions have been found, including an early Hebrew calendar dating from the 10th century BC and six Roman boundary stelae recording the name *Gezer.* Excavations took place from 1902 to 1909 and from 1964 to 1973. JONATHAN N. TUBB

Ghana [gah'-nuh]

Ghana is an independent country of West Africa located on the Gulf of Guinea of the Atlantic Ocean. It is bounded on the west by the Ivory Coast, on the north by Burkina Faso, and on the east by Togo. Its capital city is ACCRA, on the southern coast. Ghana was formerly the British colony of the Gold Coast and was the first black African colony to receive independence (Mar. 6, 1957). The country takes its name from the medieval empire that was located to the northwest of the present state.

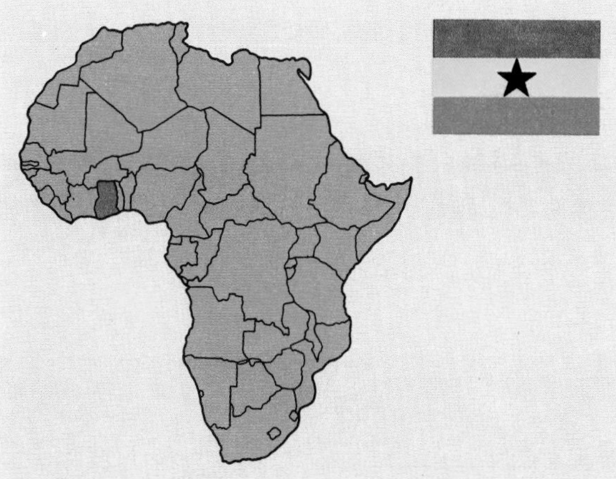

REPUBLIC OF GHANA

LAND. Area: 238,539 km² (92,100 mi²). Capital and largest city: Accra (1984 pop., 964,879).

PEOPLE. Population (1988 est.): 14,400,000; density (1988 est.): 60.4 persons per km² (156.4 per mi²). Distribution (1987): 31% urban, 69% rural. Annual growth (1987): 2.8%. Official language: English. Major religions: traditional religions, Christianity, Islam.

EDUCATION AND HEALTH. Literacy (1985): 53% of adult population. Universities (1986): 3. Hospital beds (1981): 20,582. Physicians (1982): 1,435. Life expectancy (1980–85): women—51.7; men—50.3. Infant mortality (1987): 94 per 1,000 live births.

ECONOMY. GNP (1986): $5.13 billion; $390 per capita. Labor distribution (1986): agriculture—55%; trade, government, and services—27%; manufacturing—18%. Foreign trade (1985): imports—$731 million; exports—$617 million; principal trade partners—United States, United Kingdom, West Germany, Nigeria. Currency: 1 cedi = 100 pesawas.

GOVERNMENT. Type: military rule. Legislature: Parliament (suspended). Political subdivisions: 8 regions, Greater Accra.

COMMUNICATIONS. Railroads (1985): 953 km (592 mi) total. Roads (1985): 28,300 km (17,585 mi) total. Major ports: 2. Major airfields: 1.

LAND AND RESOURCES

Most of Ghana is composed of lowlands; more than half the country has an elevation less than 150 m (500 ft). Along the eastern border of the country are the Akwapim Hills, which have an average elevation of 460 m (1,500 ft) and include Mount Afadjato (885 m/2,905 ft), the highest point in the country. The 550-km (340-mi) coastline is mostly sandy beaches backed by plains and saltwater lagoons. Stretching inland from the coast, and covering about one-third of the country, is the forest belt that produces most of Ghana's cacao and timber. North of the forest belt are the savanna and plains at elevations from 120 to 400 m (400 to 1,300 ft).

Climate. Ghana has a tropical climate influenced by two air masses: the hot, dry, dust-laden continental air mass from the Sahara in the north, and the warm, humid marine air mass from the Atlantic in the south. Consequently, rainfall varies from more than 2,025 mm (80 in) in the southwest to less than 1,000 mm (40 in) in the north, where the Saharan influence is strongest. Temperatures are equable, the annual average being about 25° C (78° F).

Drainage. The VOLTA RIVER, which dominates the drainage system, has a basin that covers all but the southwestern third of the country. The artificially created Lake VOLTA, behind the Akosombo Dam, extends 400 km (250 mi) northwest along the river and covers about 3% of the country's land area. The Tano and Pra rivers drain directly into the sea.

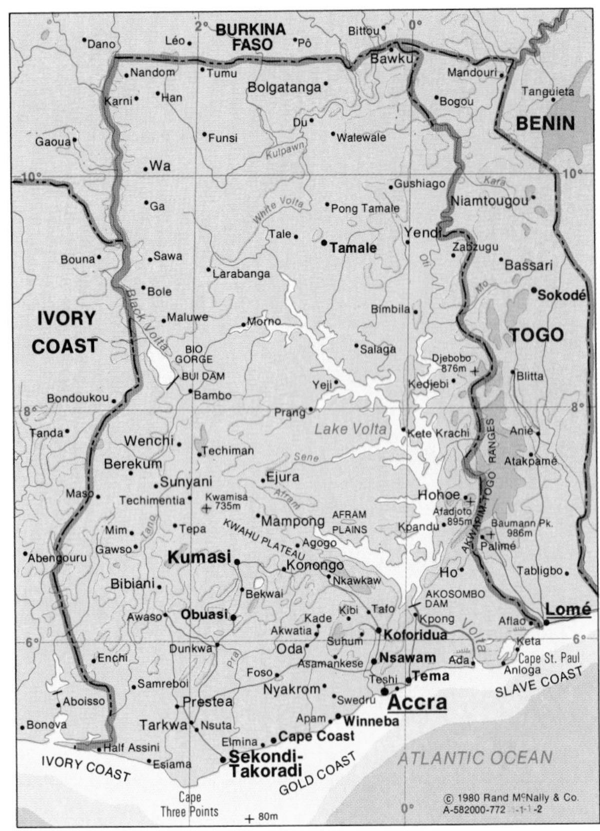

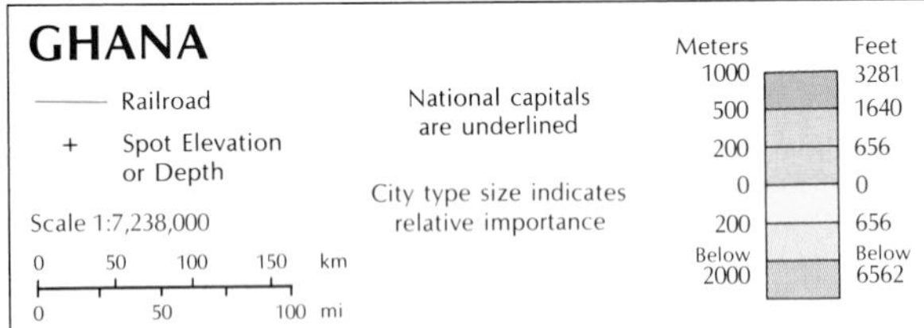

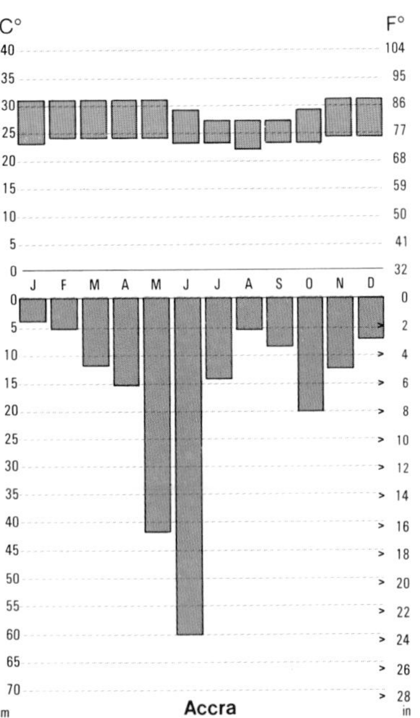

Vegetation and Animal Life. Natural vegetation in Ghana is tropical rain forest in the southwest and savanna—mostly grasslands with scattered trees—in the drier north. The savanna zone extends south to the coast around Accra, the only place in West Africa where this occurs, because of the low rainfall in that area. Much of the tropical forest has been cleared for agriculture, and the formerly rich African fauna has been depleted because of human population pressure, although large mammals such as lions, antelope, elephants, and buffalo still occur.

PEOPLE

Of the more than 75 ethnic groups in Ghana, the AKAN, EWE, GA, and Mole-Dagbani are the largest. Although broad cultural similarities exist, ethnic groups are separated by varying rules of descent systems and residence patterns. Languages fall into the Gur or Kwa groups of the Niger-Congo family, but each ethnic group is associated with a separate dialect, and the larger groups sometimes speak several dialects. English is the official language and is taught in the schools.

About 21% of the population maintain traditional animistic beliefs. Christianity is the religion of some 63% of the population; Roman Catholics are the largest single group, although the combined Protestant sects number twice as many. About 16% of the population are Muslim.

Demography. Urban centers are experiencing rapid growth, and nearly one-third of the population now live in cities. The largest cities, in descending order, are Accra, Kumasi, Tamale, Tema, and SEKONDI-TAKORADI. Many Ghanaians work in neighboring countries. High population densities are found in two areas: in the south—a triangular area, with its base along the coast and its apex at Kumasi—which contains about one third of the population; and in the northeast, a strip along the border with Burkina Faso. Elsewhere population densities are low, reflecting the extensive (rather than intensive) agricultural methods.

Education and Health. In 1974 free, mandatory, primary and middle-school education was introduced in state schools and in government-supported missionary schools. The resulting education system is considered one of the best in Black Africa. The University of Ghana (1948) at Legon, near Accra, is the country's leading university.

Life expectancy and infant mortality rates are close to the average for Africa. Hospitals and clinics are provided by the government and by Christian missions.

Cultural Life. The arts are closely allied to traditional religions. The visual arts are dominated by wood carving, especially masks, and the most important performing arts are dancing and music. Important institutions are the National Cultural Centre in Kumasi and the Arts Council of Ghana, located in Accra.

ECONOMIC ACTIVITY

At independence, in 1957, Ghana was the world's largest producer of cacao and had substantial cash reserves. In an effort to create a socialist state as rapidly as possible, large sums of money were spent on industrialization, state farms, and pub-

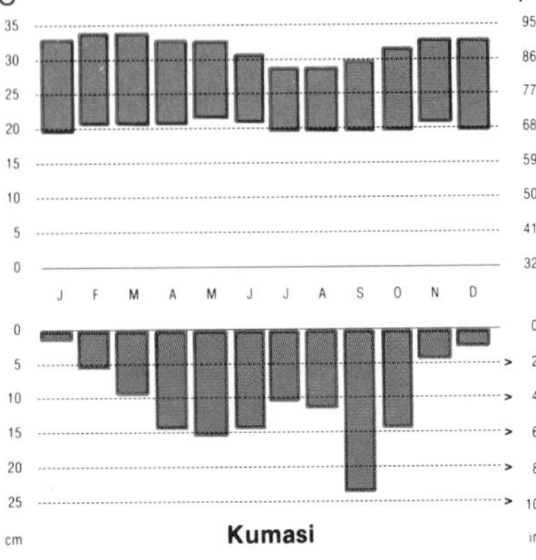

Annual climate charts for two cities in Ghana illustrate the major climate zones in that West African nation. Bars indicate monthly ranges of temperatures (red) and precipitation (blue). Accra, the nation's capital and leading seaport, has a steppe climate moderated by a tropical rainy season. Kumasi, a regional capital located 185 km (115 mi) northwest of Accra, has a tropical wet-dry climate.

(Left) *The hydroelectric station at the Akosombo Dam supplies virtually all of Ghana's electricity, for both industrial and domestic use. Some power is also exported to Benin and Togo. Finished in 1964, the Akosombo Dam created huge Lake Volta, an important source of water for irrigation and of fish, Ghana's principal source of protein.*

(Right) *Accra is the capital, most populous city, and principal port and transportation center of Ghana. The site was long occupied by villages of the Ga ethnic group, and by the late 17th century European traders had constructed fortified trading posts there. In 1877 the city became the capital of the British Gold Coast colony.*

lic works projects, and by 1966 the country was badly in debt. Governmental programs have since been considerably curtailed. Aging trees, low prices paid to growers, and adverse weather conditions contributed to a decline in vital cacao production during the 1970s and 1980s. Government attempts to revitalize the cacao industry have met with little success, and the overall lack of economic growth has led many Ghanaians to seek employment outside the country.

Manufacturing and Energy. The small-scale production of consumer goods such as processed foods, textiles, beverages, cigarettes, plywood, and furniture are important to the economy. Large manufacturing enterprises, however, are often underutilized and unprofitable due to chronic shortages of imported raw materials and spare parts. The hydroelectric plant at the Akosombo Dam (operational 1966), with an ultimate capacity of 976,000 kW, accounts for 99% of Ghana's electricity production. The Volta Aluminum Company at Tema generally uses more than 60% of the electricity generated there to smelt imported alumina, although smelting was halted (1983) after a prolonged drought drastically cut power output.

Agriculture, Forestry, Mining, and Fishing. Cacao dominates the cash-crop production and accounts for about 45% of the country's exports. The principal food crops are cassava and other root crops, corn, and sorghum; few cattle are kept due to the presence of the disease-carrying tsetse fly. Logs and sawn timber account for 2% of exports by value, and gold, diamonds, manganese, and bauxite for another 17%. Offshore oil deposits are being exploited for domestic use. There is some fishing in Lake Volta and along the coast.

Transportation and Trade. Ghana's railroads are concentrated in a triangle connecting Kumasi with Sekondi-Takoradi and Accra. Roads, about 25% of which are paved, are located mostly in the southern third of the country. Ghana is heavily dependent on imported food, petroleum, consumer goods, and capital equipment. Despite severe import restrictions, the balance of trade remains generally unfavorable.

GOVERNMENT

Ghana's third constitution, promulgated in 1979, was suspended following the 1981 military coup. The country is governed by a provisional national defense council which rules by decree; the chairman of the council is head of state.

HISTORY

Medieval Ghana, the empire that flourished from the 9th to the 13th century, was centered slightly north of the headwaters of the Senegal and Niger rivers in present-day Mali and should not be confused with the modern state of Ghana. The name "Ghana" was chosen for the Gold Coast with the assumption that migrants from the ancient kingdom settled the coastal region.

Initial contact with Europeans occurred when the Portuguese reached West Africa in the early 1400s. They soon established trade relations with the people of the Gold Coast. The West African slave trade began in the mid-1400s, when the Portuguese transported some Africans to meet their own labor shortage. The Portuguese built Elmina Castle on the coast in 1482. The Dutch, seeing the profits of slave trading, conquered the Portuguese bases in West Africa, and by 1642 they controlled the Gold Coast forts. Between 1500 and 1870, an estimated 10 million slaves left Africa, about 19% of them from the Gold Coast.

The British, who from about 1660 were the chief competitors of the Dutch, greatly increased their involvement in the Gold Coast between 1850 and 1874, by which time they had practically broken the authority of traditional African rulers. By 1898 the boundaries of the British Gold Coast were established. The British developed the infrastructure of the colony in an effort to lure British private investments to the area.

The very developments that improved the economic status of the colony eventually led to the rise of nationalism and the end of colonialism. The expanded economy required skilled African labor for subordinate positions. The emergence of an educated African elite, combined with a changed world opinion, ultimately led to independence. In 1947 the British- and American-educated Kwame NKRUMAH organized a nationalist party, and ten years later the colony attained full independence, with Nkrumah as president. His one-party state, however, suffered from inefficiency and corruption and was overthrown by the army in 1966. The military ruled the nation until 1979, when elections were held to return the country to civilian rule. Hilla Limann, who became president, was deposed in December 1981. The coup leader, former flight lieutenant Jerry RAWLINGS, worked to reverse the nation's economic decline.

RONALD D. GARST

Bibliography: Agbodeka, Francis, *Ghana in the Twentieth Century* (1972); Apter, David, *Ghana in Transition,* 2d ed. (1972); Austin, Dennis, *Ghana Observed* (1976); Boateng, E. A., *A Geography of Ghana,* 2d ed. (1966); Howard, Rhoda, *Colonialism and Underdevelopment in Ghana* (1978); Pellow, Deborah, and Chazan, Naomi, *Ghana* (1986); Ray, Donald, *Ghana* (1986).

Ghats [gahts]

The Ghats (Hindi, "steps") are two mountain ranges bordering the Deccan Plateau in southern India. The Western Ghats, with an average height of 915 to 1,525 m (3,000 to 5,000 ft), extend about 1,600 km (1,000 mi) along the coast of the Arabian Sea. They are the watershed for the Godavari, Kistna, and Cauvery rivers; the Palghat Gap is their only break. The Eastern Ghats, a discontinuous series of hills, average height 610 m (2,000 ft), extend about 1,450 m (900 mi) from the Mahanadi Valley to the Nilgiri Hills along the Bay of Bengal.

Ghazali, al- [gaz-ah'-lee, ahl]

Abu Hamid Muhammad al-Ghazali, b. 1058, d. Dec. 18, 1111, a theologian, mystic, and apologist, is one of the most revered personalities in the Muslim world. In his spiritual autobiography, *al-Munqidh min al-Dalal* (The Deliverer from Error), he describes the great crisis that forced him in 1095 to abandon his brilliant professional career in Baghdad and to search for an inner, direct knowledge of the reality of God. He adopted the life of a wandering ascetic and mystic, visited Damascus, Jerusalem, and Mecca, and lived with some disciples in his birthplace, Tus (in present-day Iran), before he was persuaded to return (1106) to his teaching career. He retired to Tus in 1110. Of his more than 50 books, the *Tahafut* (The Incoherence of the Philosophers) and the *Ihya 'Ulum al-Din* (The Revival of the Religious Sciences) are particularly important.

WILLEM A. BIJLEFELD

Bibliography: Ormsby, E., *Theodicy in Islamic Thought* (1984); Watt, W. Montgomery, *Muslim Intellectual* (1963) and *The Faith and Practice of al-Ghazali* (1963; a trans. of *al-Munqidh).*

Ghaznavids [guhz'-nuh-vids]

The Ghaznavids were a Muslim Turkish dynasty that ruled an empire in what is now Afghanistan and eastern Iran from 977 to 1087, at times expanding into the Punjab and the Indus valley and laying the foundation for the spread of Islam into the Indian subcontinent. They were champions of Sunnite Islam against the Shiite Buyid dynasty in Iran. The greatest Ghaznavid ruler was MAHMUD OF GHAZNI (r. 998–1030), patron of the Persian poet Firdawsi. Conflicts among Mahmud's sons led to the breakup of the Ghaznavid empire in the century after his death. Impressive examples of Ghaznavid architecture survive in the imperial capital, Ghazni, and other parts of Afghanistan.

STANFORD J. SHAW

Bibliography: Bosworth, C. E., *The Ghaznavids* (1973) and *The Later Ghaznavids* (1977).

Ghelderode, Michel de [gel'-duh-rohd]

The prolific Belgian dramatist Michel de Ghelderode, b. Apr. 3, 1898, d. Apr. 1, 1962, gained an international reputation following Jean Louis Barrault's controversial Paris production (1949) of Ghelderode's *Fastes d'enfer* (1929; trans. as *Chronicles of Hell,* 1960). His French-language plays, however, written to be performed by either puppets or actors, had been known in Belgium in Flemish translation since the 1920s. Highly stylized mixtures of the satiric and mystical, full of lustiness and lyricism, Ghelderode's plays evoke the color and grotesqueries of medieval Flanders as depicted by Bruegel or Bosch and are written in a language influenced especially by the literature of 17th-century Spain. Of 50 plays written by Ghelderode, *Escurial* (1927; Eng. trans., 1958), *La Mort du Docteur Faust* (The Death of Dr. Faust, 1928), *Pantagleize* (1929; Eng. trans., 1958), *Sire Halewyn* (1934; Eng. trans., 1958), *Hop! Signor* (1935), and *L'École des bouffons* (School for Jesters, 1937) are most representative.

Ghent [gent]

Ghent (Flemish: Gent; French: Gand) is the capital of the province of East Flanders in northwestern Belgium and the second largest city in the country. The population is 234,251 (1986 est.). Its location at the junction of the Scheldt and Lys rivers early made it a trading center. It remains Belgium's second largest port after Antwerp.

Called the "city of flowers" because of its nurseries, Ghent is also known for its textiles. Other industries include oil refining and the manufacture of steel, chemical dyes, and paper. Ghent is a major tourist center; attractions include the castle of the counts of Flanders (reconstructed 1180), the medieval belfry and town hall, the cathedral of Saint Bavon (12th–16th centuries), and scenic quays. Among the city's many art masterpieces is the *Adoration of the Holy Lamb,* a polyptych altarpiece by Hubert and Jan Van EYCK.

Ghent's weaving industry was prominent by the 13th century and influenced its politics for years. The strong middle class retained a degree of independence despite the nominal rule of the counts of Flanders and dukes of Burgundy. The city pursued an independent policy under the leadership of the ARTEVELDE family during the Hundred Years' War and resisted Habsburg rule during the 16th century. Its economy later declined but was revived when the region was occupied by French Revolutionary armies. Europe's first cotton spinning mill was built there in 1800, and cotton textile manufacture soon replaced the making of wool cloth as the dominant industry.

JONATHAN E. HELMREICH

Bibliography: Nicholas, David, *The Metamorphosis of a Medieval City: Ghent in the Age of the Arteveldes* (1987).

Ghent, Treaty of

The Treaty of Ghent, signed on Dec. 24, 1814, officially ended the WAR OF 1812 between Great Britain and the United States, although the slowness of communications allowed a major battle to be fought at New Orleans early in 1815. The American negotiators at Ghent included John Quincy Adams, James

Bayard, Henry Clay, and Albert Gallatin; the British were represented by William Adams, Admiral Lord Gambier, and Henry Goulburn. The treaty was an agreement to stop fighting, to restore any occupied territory, and to establish boundary commissions to settle problems along the Canadian-United States border. REGINALD HORSMAN

Bibliography: Engelman, Fred L., *The Peace of Christmas Eve* (1962).

Ghent altarpiece: see EYCK, JAN VAN.

Gheorghiu-Dej, Gheorghe [gay-ohr'-gue-dayzh, gay-ohr'-gay]

Gheorghe Gheorghiu-Dej, b. Nov. 8, 1901, d. Mar. 19, 1965, became first secretary of the Romanian Communist party in 1945. He was premier of Romania from 1952 to 1955 and president of the state council from 1961 until his death. He became a member of the outlawed Communist party in 1930 and in 1933 was sentenced to 12 years in prison as a strike organizer. Escaping in 1944, he became (1945) the party's general secretary and served in the Communist-led coalition government that established the People's Republic in 1947. After an intraparty struggle, Gheorghiu-Dej made himself premier in June 1952. He resigned that office in 1955 but in 1961 assumed the equivalent post of president of the state council. He initiated Romania's industrialization program.
K. M. SMOGORZEWSKI

ghetto [get'-oh]

The ghetto was originally a Jewish quarter or a separate area of a city for Jews. Although the word was first used in English in the 17th century, segregation of Jews, or ghettoization, began much earlier.

Institution of the Ghettos. Some of the earliest ghettos were voluntarily established by Jewish communities in the cities of Europe and the Middle East in which they settled during the DIASPORA. From the 12th century on, Jews were often required by law to live apart from Christians in their own sections, sometimes surrounded by walls and accessible only through controlled portals. In medieval Spain, for example, they lived in the *Juderías* ("Jewish area"); in Germany, in the *Judengasse* ("Jew's street or row"); in Prague, in the *Judenstadt* ("Jew's city"); in Venice, in the *ghetto* (on the site of a foundry). Jews dwelt freely in most parts of the Muslim world until the 18th century, after which they were often required to live in special areas away from mosques and other holy places. This was especially characteristic of Persia, Yemen, and Morocco, where remnants of the old ghettos still exist. In Western Europe, the last ghetto (Rome) was officially abolished in 1870. In the 1930s, however, the Nazis in Germany revived the enforced ghettoizing of Jews, but only as a temporary step in their plan for the Final Solution, the total extermination of European Jewry.

Ghetto Culture. Ghetto culture, often oversimplified by depictions of 19th-century Jews living in the *shtetls* (Jewish towns) of Eastern Europe, was in fact highly varied and stratified. Professionals, artisans, merchants, and laborers, as well as Talmudic scholars, were usually found within the gates. What almost all ghettos had in common, however, was a certain amount of imposed autonomy. They ran their own political, social, and economic affairs through religious and secular councils, often with the consent, and sometimes at the insistence of, the external authorities. The ghetto dwellers had various relations with the world outside. At times their members performed special functions for others, such as lending money to government officials or members of the aristocracy in lands where such activity was forbidden to Christians, or collecting taxes, or peddling soft goods and hardware in other parts of the city and to peasants in the hinterlands. Their limited contacts, specialized occupations, and unusual garb set them apart and often reinforced the prejudices of those who used the ghetto-dwelling Jews as easy scapegoats for the ills of society. As scapegoats, ghetto Jews in Tsarist Russia were the target of government-organized riots called POGROMS.

The most famous instance of Jewish resistance to the HOLOCAUST took place in the Warsaw ghetto, an area into which almost 500,000 Jews, many from outside the city, had been herded in the early 1940s. In the spring of 1943, after a revolt lasting nearly 30 days against impossible odds, the Warsaw ghetto was completely destroyed, and all but a handful of Jews perished. The following year the Nazis liquidated most of the other ghettos in Poland and the surrounding areas.

Non-Jewish Ghettos. In recent years the word *ghetto* has been used to label any area of confinement or voluntary residence of minority populations. One hears of Gypsy ghettos in Spain, Algerian ghettos in France, and, especially, black, Puerto Rican, and Chicano ghettos in the United States. (Hispanic ghettos are often called *barrios*.) In these areas one finds many of the characteristics so often associated with Jewish quarters: the evidence of discrimination, often manifest in segregation; dual allegiances created by the fact that the ghetto dwellers are subject to but not of the dominant society; communal bonds created out of a need for defensive insulation against the outer world; and, sometimes, local institutions to help care for group members.

The most famous black ghetto is Harlem, a section of New York City. Every large American city has its own "Harlem." Among the better known are Watts in Los Angeles, the South Side of Chicago, Hough in Cleveland, Roxbury in Boston, and Bedford-Stuyvesant in Brooklyn.

Like many Jewish ghettos, those of other ethnic groups have been painful reminders to the inhabitants of their "second-class citizenship." They are also places of refuge and cultural strength and are incubators of great talent in the arts and humanities. "From the ghetto" is a common theme of many young writers whose works often combine the bitterness of confinement with a sense of comradeship to give outsiders a glimpse into what, for many, is an unfamiliar world.
PETER I. ROSE

Bibliography: Clark, Kenneth B., *Dark Ghetto* (1965); Connolly, Harold X., *A Ghetto Grows in Brooklyn* (1977); Hapgood, Hutchins, *The Spirit of the Ghetto* (1967; repr. 1983); Kusmer, Kenneth L., *A Ghetto Takes Shape: Black Cleveland, 1870–1930* (1976); Marcus, Jacob, *The Jew in the Medieval World* (1938; repr. 1975); Osofsky, Gilbert, *Harlem: The Making of a Ghetto* (1966); Shulman, Nisson, *Authority and Community: Polish Jewry in the Sixteenth Century* (1986); Wilson, William Julius, *The Truly Disadvantaged: The Inner City, the Underclass, and Public Policy* (1987); Wirth, Louis, *The Ghetto*, rev. ed. (1956; repr. 1982).

See also: ANTI-SEMITISM; HOLOCAUST; INNER CITY; JEWS.

Ghibellines: see GUELPHS AND GHIBELLINES.

Ghiberti, Lorenzo [gee-bair'-tee]

"The Story of Jacob and Esau" is one of the ten reliefs constituting Lorenzo Ghiberti's Gates of Paradise. *The elegantly draped figures were first modeled in wax, then cast in bronze. Despite their swirling Gothic drapery, these bronzes mark the Renaissance's true beginning because of Ghiberti's feeling for the body's structure.*

Lorenzo Ghiberti's Gates of Paradise *(1425–52) were greatly admired by Michelangelo and are among the masterpieces of Early Renaissance art. The ten reliefs show scenes from the Old Testament, and the figures' modelling and the composition demonstrates Ghiberti's command of the classical style. (Baptistry, Florence.)*

The creator of some of the most admired sculpture of the Renaissance, Lorenzo Ghiberti, b. Florence, *c.*1381, d. Dec. 1, 1455, is best known for his bronze doors for the Baptistery in Florence. Sharing the Renaissance ideals of humanism with his contemporary artists, Ghiberti based his art on close study of nature and the classical tradition. From his goldsmith stepfather and from studying the works of northern artists, he learned the techniques of working with metals in the Late Gothic style. After early work as a painter he was mainly occupied with sculptural commissions from Florentine guilds for two buildings: the Florence Baptistery and the church of Or San Michele. For the Baptistery door commission (1403), Ghiberti's *Abraham and Isaac* bronze relief (Bargello, Florence) won the competition over Filippo BRUNELLESCHI, Jacopo della QUERCIA, and others. Between 1403 and 1424, Ghiberti worked on the 28 bronze high reliefs for his first set of doors. The earlier reliefs show some characteristics of the Late Gothic (see GOTHIC ART AND ARCHITECTURE) or International Style (see INTERNATIONAL STYLE, art), blended with innovative Renaissance features. During this period he also cast the larger-than-life bronze figures for Or San Michele: *St. John* (1414–46), *St. Matthew* (1419–22), and *St. Stephen* (1425–28).

In 1425, Ghiberti was commissioned to do the second pair of doors for the Baptistery. This consisted of ten pictorial reliefs, numerous figures and busts, and a festooned frame. The reliefs were cast by 1437 and finished, gilded, and installed by 1452. The work so closely complements Leon Battista ALBERTI'S theories in his pioneering *Treatise on Painting* (1435) that he has been proposed as Ghiberti's inspiration.

According to Giogio VASARI, Ghiberti was the first to imitate antique art. He also revived the technique of casting large-scale figures. His illusionistic reliefs *Jacob and Esau* and *Solomon and Sheba*, for the "gates of paradise," exemplify the Renaissance style in their perfection of design, their variety within harmonious balance, and the decorum of the individual figures.

Ghiberti's style in general is an illustration of the Renaissance preoccupation with visual and intellectual harmony. In his concern for classical nobility and grace, his work presents a contrast to the violent expressiveness of DONATELLO, the human warmth of Luca della Robbia (see DELLA ROBBIA family), and the forcefulness of Jacopo della Quercia. Yet he shares with them the shaping of the Renaissance style in the categories of freestanding and relief sculpture. Ghiberti was also a writer on art and is the author of the earliest surviving autobiography by an artist. MILES CHAPPELL

Bibliography: Goldscheider, Ludwig, *Ghiberti* (1949); Krautheimer, Richard, *Ghiberti's Bronze Doors* (1971); Krautheimer, Richard, with Krautheimer-Hess, Trude, *Lorenzo Ghiberti* (1956; repr. 1970).

See also: BRONZES, ITALIAN ART AND ARCHITECTURE; RENAISSANCE ART AND ARCHITECTURE; SCULPTURE.

Ghirlandaio, Domenico [geer-lahn-dah'-ee-oh]

Domenico Ghirlandaio, the last important Florentine painter of the Early Renaissance, painted the famous portrait Old Man with His Grandson *(1480), which shows scrupulous attention to painterly detail. The exchange of tender expression, combined with an emphasis on physical rectitude, bears the strong imprint of Italian humanism, which permeated the arts in the Renaissance. (Louvre, Paris.)*

The naturalistic style of the Florentine painter Domenico Ghirlandaio, 1449–94, is the culminating expression of the careful observation and representation of visual reality that characterized early Renaissance painting. Ghirlandaio worked almost exclusively in Florence except for a trip to Rome (1481–82) to paint frescoes in the SISTINE CHAPEL. In Ghirlandaio's paintings, figures, architecture, landscape, and still-life elements are all represented with precise and prosaic reality. His works generally avoid effects that might be termed dramatic, imaginative, or poetic; his beautiful color, technical excellence, clear expression of narrative content, and compositional balance make his paintings masterpieces.

Ghirlandaio was a prolific artist; he once stated that he wished he could cover the entire circuit of the Florentine city walls with frescoes. His successful completion of many large projects while maintaining a high level of quality attests to his skill as an entrepreneur. His large work shop included his brother Davide, his brother-in-law Sebastiano Mainardi, and many other assistants and apprentices including, for a brief period, the young Michelangelo.

Ghirlandaio's greatest accomplishments are the decorative narrative schemes that he devised for Florentine family chapels. Those in the Sassetti Chapel at Santa Trinità (1483–86) and the Tornabuoni Chapel at Santa Maria Novella (1485–90) survive virtually intact. These decorative ensembles exalt Ghirlandaio's patrons and their friends, as well as life in 15th-century Florence in general. Ghirlandaio's panel paintings demonstrate his absorption of the Flemish oil technique, which allowed him to achieve ever more impressive naturalistic effects. His realistic style lent itself especially well to portraiture.

Bibliography: Borsook, Eve, *The Mural Painters of Tuscany*, 2d ed. (1981); DeWald, Ernest T., *Italian Painting, 1200–1600* (1961; repr. 1978): Freedberg, Sydney J., *Painting of the High Renaissance in Rome and Florence*, 2 vols., 3d ed. (1985).

Ghose, Aurobindo: see AUROBINDO, SRI.

ghost

A ghost is the spirit of a dead person capable of making itself seen or heard by the living. Belief in, and worship of, ghosts was common in ancient societies and is still found today (see ANCESTOR WORSHIP). In Europe belief in ghosts dates back to ancient times and was widespread during the Middle Ages. The belief declined somewhat in the ensuing centuries, but was revived in the 19th century when SPIRITUALISM came into vogue.

The forms ghosts are believed to take differ from culture to culture. They can include the solid or transparent likeness of the deceased, strange lights, or a disembodied voice. Poltergeists are disruptive ghosts who move or break objects. There is no scientifically accepted evidence of the existence of ghosts.

Bibliography: Cohen, David, *The Encyclopedia of Ghosts* (1984; repr. 1987); Finucane, F. C., *Appearances of the Dead* (1984).

ghost dance

The ghost dance refers to a type of messianic movement that arose (1870-78) among Indians of the western Great Basin and later (1887–95) spread to Plains Indians. It expressed a desperate longing for the restoration of the past—a return to a life free of hunger, epidemic disease, and the bitter warring and divisiveness that accompanied the Indians' subjugation by whites. Prophets "died," visited God, and returned with the message that the dead would soon join the living in a world where game was plentiful and all lived happily together in the old way. Followers were admonished to purify themselves, speak the truth, love one another, and to dance a special dance to hasten the event. Prophets held that a tidal wave of new earth would cover the alien whites and Indian nonbelievers and renew the land. The ghost dance precipitated armed conflicts with the U.S. government, which brought a rapid end to the movement.

An earlier prophetic tradition centered in eastern British Columbia and Washington emphasized an imminent destruction of the world, return of the dead, and change to more righteous ways and may have been the ultimate source of the later movement.

The ghost-dance belief began among the PAIUTE of Nevada with the revelations of the shaman Tävibo in 1870. Between 1887 and 1889 the prophet WOVOKA "died" and returned with a ritual dance to hasten the renewal of the world and return of the ancestors. News of Wovoka's prophecies quickly reached the plains and prompted followers among the ARAPAHO, Northern CHEYENNE, and Oglala SIOUX. Ghost-dance teachings especially excited the Sioux at Pine Ridge, N.Dak., who were embittered from reduced rations and in despair from diseases and from natural disasters that cut down crops and cattle. During the battle at WOUNDED KNEE (1890), in which hundreds of Sioux warriors, women, and children were massacred, many wore "ghost shirts" emblazoned with eagle, buffalo, and morning-star decorations.They believed that these symbols of powerful spirits would protect them from the soldiers' bullets. The tragedy at Wounded Knee effectively put an end to the ghost dance, although some Plains tribes performed it until 1895 or incorporated aspects of the ritual into their culture, as in the ghost-dance handgame of the PAWNEE.

FRED W. VOGET

Bibliography: Bailey, Paul, *Wovoka, the Indian Messiah* (1957); LaBarre, Weston, *The Ghost Dance: Origins of Religion* (1970); Mooney, James, *The Ghost-Dance Religion and the Sioux Outbreak of 1890* (1965); Spier, Leslie, *The Prophet Dance of the Northwest and Its Derivatives: The Source of the Ghost Dance* (1935; repr. 1977); Utley, Robert M., *The Last Days of the Sioux Nation* (1963).

ghost story

A ghost story, in literature, is a SHORT STORY that focuses on the interactions between live characters and the spirits of dead characters. The ghost may appear to exact revenge upon a wrongdoer or to comfort a loved one left behind. The usual purpose of a ghost story is to frighten the reader. A ghost story differs from a supernatural FOLKTALE in that it is a written fiction, whereas a folktale is an oral narrative often said by the teller to be true.

Although ghosts have appeared in the written literatures of all cultures, they were, up until the 19th century, only peripheral elements to the main stories. The modern ghost story's main antecedent was the GOTHIC ROMANCE, exemplified by Horace WALPOLE's *Castle of Otranto* (1764). Sir Walter SCOTT wrote the first stories that could truly be called ghost stories in the 1820s. The genre soon became very popular in Great Britain, fueled by the proliferation of anthologies and by the practice, developed by literary magazines, of devoting Christmas issues to the genre. The rising interest in SPIRITUALISM also contributed to the popularity of ghost stories. Famous practitioners of the genre include Charles DICKENS, Nathaniel HAWTHORNE, Henry JAMES, Edgar Allen POE, SAKI, and Algernon Blackwood.

Bibliography: Cox, M., and Gilbert, R. A., eds., *The Oxford Book of English Ghost Stories* (1986).

ghost towns

Ghost towns are settlements that have been abandoned by their inhabitants. Because of their rapidly changing economic fortunes, many frontier towns of the American West underwent spectacular fluctuations in population. A few thousand persons might be attracted to a mining camp in the course of a few months and just as quickly leave again. Many communities, mining towns in particular, were established far from major transportation routes in places where an inhospitable climate made living difficult and uncomfortable. If the glittering economic promise of such places proved an illusion, the rootless population usually moved on.

Some of these towns made the transition to a more stable economy by becoming market centers for the region around them or by establishing mills for processing ores. Many others, however, declined into small villages or disappeared. Because of the value of building materials, departing settlers usually stripped an abandoned town of everything they could carry, and only rarely can a true ghost town of empty, decaying buildings be found. St. Elmo, Colo., is one of a few exceptions. In most cases only a few artifacts and the foundations of buildings can be seen.

Many communities called ghost towns actually kept a small population, and after a later restoration of saloons, corrals, hotels, and stores, they have enjoyed a growing trade of tourists in search of the "true West." Examples are Virginia City, Nev.; Central City, Colo.; Tombstone, Ariz.; and Nevada City, Calif. Religious and political utopian settlements, like Kaweah in California, also have virtually vanished. ELLIOTT WEST

Bibliography: Eberhart, Philip, *Guide to the Colorado Ghost Towns and Mining Camps,* 4th ed. (1968); Moore, T. W., *Vanishing Western Ghost Towns with Lamentations* (1986); Weis, Norman D., *Ghost Towns of the Northwest* (1971) and *Helldorados: Ghosts and Camps of the Old Southwest* (1977); Wolle, Muriel S., *The Bonanza Trail: Ghost Towns and Mining Camps of the West* (1953; repr. 1975).

Ghosts

Ghosts (1881), Henrik IBSEN's revolutionary drama, is one of the most important examples of modern theatrical realism. The play's frank discussion of marital infidelity, its hint at incest, and mention of syphilis shocked Victorian audiences in both Europe and America. The play centers on Helene Alving, a respected widow who suppresses the truth about her debauched husband, Captain Alving. Only when she learns to reject the conventionality and social hypocrisy represented by Pastor Manders is she liberated from the "ghosts" of the past. This demands recognizing that her son Oswald is going mad from hereditary syphilis, the disease that killed her husband, as well as taking personal responsibility for contributing to her husband's dissoluteness through her rejection of spontaneity. The flawless economy of Ibsen's play is based on a number of interwoven psychological discoveries that propel the plot to its final crisis.

Bibliography: Lyons, Charles R., *Critical Essays on Henrik Ibsen* (1987).

G.I. Bill of Rights

The G.I. Bill of Rights is the popular name for a series of U.S. programs that provide educational and economic assistance to veterans of World War II, the Korean War, and the Vietnam War. Congress passed the first G.I. Bill, called the Servicemen's Readjustment Act, in 1944. Previous legislation had provided special assistance for disabled veterans, but this bill was designed to assist healthy soldiers in reentering the civilian world by helping them with the problems they would face when a war ended. For example, those who had been drafted from jobs might find that the industry they had been working in had been converted to wartime production and that, for the time being, their jobs no longer existed. Those whose educations had been interrupted might find they no longer had scholarships or that their parents could not help them finish their schooling.

The educational benefits proved to be the most popular part of the program. All veterans who had served 90 days or longer and who had been honorably discharged were eligible for educational benefits. The duration of the benefits depended on the length of service, from one year of full-time education or vocational training for veterans who had served 90 days, up to a maximum of 48 months. The government paid the tuition costs and standard educational fees and provided a tool allowance for veterans training for skilled occupations. It also provided a living allowance. With some variations, the program was reinstated for veterans of the Korean and Vietnam wars. The existing education benefits program was terminated in 1976, although eligible Vietnam veterans could use benefits until 1989. In 1987, after a three-year trial period, Congress voted to make a voluntary educational-benefits program available to all following military service, with the beneficiaries paying a small share toward the benefits.

More than 7.8 million veterans of World War II took advantage of the educational provisions of the G.I. Bill. By the late 1980s, well over 20 million veterans of the three wars had received training or educational assistance under the various G.I. Bills. After World War II, educational institutions had not been prepared for the sudden arrival of millions of veterans. In meeting the needs of these students, often different from the needs of prewar students, the universities furthered the democratization of U.S. higher education. DALE KOCH

Bibliography: Addlestone, D. F., et al., *The Rights of Veterans* (1981); Levitan, Sar A., and Zickler, Joyce K., *Swords into Ploughshares: Our GI Bill* (1973); Mosch, Theodore R., *The GI Bill* (1975); Olson, Keith W., *The G.I. Bill, the Veterans, and the Colleges* (1974).

Giacometti, Alberto [jah-koh-met'-tee]

The Swiss sculptor Alberto Giacometti, b. Oct. 10, 1901, d. Jan. 11, 1966, was primarily concerned with reporting the precise visual perception of objects and their relationship to the enveloping space.

The son of the impressionist painter Giovanni Giacometti (1868–1933), Alberto had extensive early artistic exposure. In 1919 he studied sculpture at the École des Arts-et-Métiers in Geneva, and in 1920 he accompanied his father to the Venice Biennale. During his 2 years in Italy, Giacometti familiarized himself with medieval, Renaissance, baroque, and Egyptian art. Thus, upon his arrival in Paris in January 1922 to spend 3 years at the Académie de la Grande-Chaumière under the auspices of the sculptor Émile Antoine BOURDELLE, he was already well acquainted with the history of art.

The attenuated, ghostly effect of Giacometti's Walking Man II *(1960) is surrealistic. The sculpture's proportions and monumental scale result, however, from his study of Egyptian, archaic Greek, and primitive art. (Rijksmuseum Kroller Muller, Otterlo, Netherlands.)*

In 1925, Giacometti opened his own studio and began to sculpt in a cubist manner (see CUBISM). Under the influence of Henri LAURENS, Jacques LIPCHITZ, and the primitive art of Africa and Oceania, he developed compact pieces, such as *The Couple* (1926; Museum of Fine Arts, Zurich). He also created open cagelike forms, which are exemplified by the *Palace at 4 A.M.* (1932; Museum of Modern Art, New York City), which he executed during his affiliation (1929–35) with the surrealist movement (see SURREALISM, art).

After working for a decade (1925–35) almost exclusively from his imagination, Giacometti became discontented and turned to figuration.

His mature sculpture is typified by attenuated bronze figures with scarred or eroded surfaces. In *Composition with Seven Figures and a Head or The Forest* (1950; Reader's Digest Association, Pleasantville, N.Y.) Giacometti confronted the relationship of the figure to the space around it. The result is a group of isolated figures placed in a void, a space that becomes an obstacle to communication between individuals. The psychological implications of compressed space and the indistinctness caused by the frenetic surface handling is apparent in the painting *Head of a Man* (1961) and in the sculpture *Monumental Head* (1960), both in the Hirshhorn Museum and Sculpture Garden, Washington, D.C. These works assert humanity's universality and are the culmination of Giacometti's relentless examination of spatial phenomena.

HARRY RAND

Bibliography: Fletcher, V. J., et al., *Alberto Giacometti* (1988); Hohl, Reinhold, *Alberto Giacometti* (1972); Juliet, Charles, *Giacometti* (1986); Lord, James, *A Giacometti Portrait* (1965; repr. 1980) and *Giacometti: A Biography* (1985); Sartre, Jean Paul, "The Paintings of Giacometti," in *Essays in Aesthetics*, trans. by W. Baskin (1963).

Giaever, Ivar [jay'-vur, ee'-vahr]

The Norwegian-born American experimental physicist Ivar Giaever, b. Apr. 5, 1929, shared the 1973 Nobel Prize for physics for the demonstration of a fundamental effect of superconductivity in transistors. Giaever emigrated to Canada in 1954 and the United States in 1957 and made his discovery at the General Electric research laboratory in Schenectady, N.Y., where he has worked since 1958.

MICHAEL MEO

Giamatti, A. Bartlett [jee-uh-mah'-tee]

Angelo Bartlett Giamatti, b. Boston, Apr. 4, 1938, d. Sept. 1, 1989, succeeded Peter Ueberroth as commissioner of baseball in April 1989. Although he had served (1986–89) as president of the National League and was a lifelong baseball fan, Giamatti's choice had been considered somewhat unlikely. A medieval and Renaissance scholar (*The Earthly Paradise and the Renaissance Epic*, 1966; *The Play of Double Senses: Spenser's "Faerie Queene,"* 1975), he taught (1966–78) English and comparative literature at Yale and served (1978–86) as its president.

Giambologna: see BOLOGNA, GIOVANNI DA.

Giannini, Amadeo Peter [jah-neen'-nee, ah-muh-day'-oh]

Amadeo Peter Giannini, b. San Jose, Calif., May 6, 1870, d. June 3, 1949, founded the Bank of America and controlled the world's largest private banking system at the time of his death. The son of an Italian immigrant, at 13 he went to work in the produce business in San Francisco. Giannini became a partner in the firm but sold his interest in 1901 to go into banking. His Bank of Italy, founded in 1904, survived the earthquake and fire of 1906 and then grew rapidly through his innovative system of branch banking. Renamed (1930) the Bank of America and later subsumed (1968) by BankAmerica Corp., the bank prospered, although in 1986–87 BankAmerica, then the nation's second-largest bank holding company and in difficulties, acted to fend off takeover efforts.

Bibliography: Bonadio, Felice A., and Cavaioli, Frank J., *A. P. Giannini: Banker, Philanthropist, Entrepreneur* (1985).

giant schnauzer: see SCHNAUZER.

giant toad

The giant toad, B. marinus, *lives in a wide range of habitats throughout Central and South America. Secreted by parotid glands in the skin, its poison is highly toxic to small animals.*

The giant toad, *Bufo marinus,* in the family Bufonidae, grows to 23 cm (9 in) in length. Adult males are brown in color; adult females and young are light yellowish, with brown spots. It is found from south Texas to the Amazon Basin of South America, and it ranges from sea level to elevations of about 1,500 m (5,000 ft).

Giant toads were introduced into many tropical islands to help control insects, but the plan backfired because they also devour beneficial native fauna. Remarkably prolific, a single female can produce 35,000 eggs in a single year.

JONATHAN CAMPBELL

giantism: see ENDOCRINE SYSTEM, DISEASES OF THE.

giants

In folklore and mythology, giants are primeval creatures of immense size, usually humanlike but evil and cruel. In Greek mythology the Gigantes were a race born from the blood of URANUS after the latter had been castrated by his son CRONUS. They rebelled against Zeus and the Olympian gods but were defeated—symbolizing the triumph of civilization over barbarism—and were buried in the Earth. Thus they were thought to cause earthquakes and volcanic eruptions. In Norse mythology, the Mountain Giants were also represented as powers of the Earth, and the Frost Giants were associated with winter storms. Like their Greek counterparts, the Norse giants were the enemies of the gods; the giants and most of the gods were to destroy each other at the great final battle of RAGNAROK.

In European folklore giants usually appear as cannibalistic ogres whose stupidity makes it possible to defeat them by trickery. Examples in English folklore include Cormoran and Blunderbore, who were mastered by Jack the Giant Killer. In the mythologies of peoples of the Western Hemisphere, giants often have the form of birds or other animals. The Indians of the North American Great Plains believed that giants were the first race of people on Earth.

Belief in giants was often related to the myth that men had degenerated to their present condition from a golden age in which they had been taller and stronger. This myth was inspired, in part, by fossil bones of huge extinct animals and by massive prehistoric mounds and stone circles and alignments such as Stonehenge.

Giant's Causeway

The Giant's Causeway is a promontory on the northern coast of Northern Ireland. It is composed of thousands of basalt columns, mostly irregular hexagons, and is divided into three sections—the Little, Middle, and Grand causeways—the last extending more than 200 m (about 700 ft).

The causeway was formed when a lava flow cooled quickly and contracted to form the hexagonal pattern. The columns

The Giant's Causeway is a prismatic basalt formation of volcanic origin located on the northeastern coast of Ireland. Legend states that the formation was created by giants as part of a road to the island of Staffa, where a similar formation occurs.

reach a maximum diameter of 50 cm (20 in) and a maximum height of 6 m (20 ft). Seen from above, the causeway resembles a giant checkered pavement.

Giap, Vo Nguyen: see VO NGUYEN GIAP.

Giardia [jee-ahr'-dee-uh]

Giardia, *Giardia,* are any of several flagellated PROTOZOA of the small intestine in humans and other vertebrates. Found worldwide, *Giardia* are not fatal, but *G. intestinalis* may cause diarrhea, cramps, and nausea. This condition is highly contagious. The organism has two nuclei and four pairs of flagella. See PARASITIC DISEASES.

J. F. MCCLELLAN

Giauque, William Francis [jee-ohk']

The American physical chemist William Giauque, b. Niagara Falls, Ontario, Canada, May 12, 1895, d. Mar. 28, 1982, did significant work in chemical thermodynamics, particularly on the behavior of substances at very low temperatures, for which he was awarded the 1949 Nobel Prize for chemistry.

Giauque determined accurately the entropy of a large number of substances near absolute zero, and he proved that the third law of thermodynamics, which states that at absolute zero a perfect crystal has zero entropy, was a fundamental law of nature. He also discovered how a strong magnet could be used to produce temperatures very close to absolute zero.

ROBERT J. PARADOWSKI

gibberellins [jib-uh-rel'-inz]

Gibberellins, such as gibberellic acid, are growth-regulating substances in plants noted for their marked stimulation of stem growth (see HORMONE, PLANT). They were first studied in Japan in the 1920s, when it was found that the rice-disease fungus *Gibberella fujikuroi* produced substances that caused the stems of seedlings to elongate extensively before they died. Gibberellins are used commercially to promote flowering and fruit development.

gibbon [gib'-uhn]

Gibbons are long-armed APES of the order PRIMATES, family Hylobatidae, which also includes the SIAMANG. They live in rain forests from northeastern India to Borneo. There is one genus, *Hylobates,* and four to six species are recognized. Gibbons stand 40 to 64 cm (16 to 25 in) high and weigh up to 8 kg (about 17 lb). The coat is dense and shaggy and ranges from black to brown or gray, varying greatly even within species. They have relatively the longest legs of any apes and can run with agility, holding their even longer arms in the air. They are best known for their speed and grace in swinging from limb to limb through the trees, using the movement called brachiation in which the hands serve only as hooks. Gibbons live in small groups and feed mainly on fruit.

ELI C. MINKOFF

A lar gibbon, H. lar, swings easily from tree to tree as it makes a loud whooping sound. A screaming troop of lar gibbons can be heard for several kilometers. Such troops consist of up to about 15 family members. Each troop maintains its own territory within a forest, but during the day several troops may gather and feed peacefully in regions between territories.

Gibbon, Edward

Edward Gibbon, considered one of the greatest English historians, was the author of *The History of the Decline and Fall of the Roman Empire.* This work, published in six volumes from 1776 to 1788, is a masterpiece of both history and literature. Its breadth of treatment, accuracy of detail, and elegant style are among its strong points. However, Gibbon's negative treatment of Christianity and his bitter irony also made the work a subject of controversy.

Gibbon was born at Putney, near London, on Apr. 27, 1737. Although a sickly youth, he went to Magdalen College, Oxford, in 1752. Fourteen months later, however, he became a Roman Catholic and was expelled from the university. His father then sent him to Lausanne, Switzerland, where he studied French literature and the Latin classics, thus laying the

Edward Gibbon, the great 18th-century English historian, produced in his work The History of the Decline and Fall of the Roman Empire *(1776–88) both a broad historical interpretation and a literary masterpiece. A stout, pompous man, Gibbon was often ridiculed. Nonetheless, he was recognized as a man of genius, and his circle of friends included Sir Joshua Reynolds and the actor David Garrick.*

foundation of his vast erudition. He was also reconverted (1754) to Protestantism. Although he left Lausanne in 1758, he was to return many times.

Between 1763 and 1765 Gibbon toured Europe. While he was in Rome, "musing amidst the ruins" as he later described it, the idea of writing the history of the later Roman Empire came to him. He spent the next 20 years at the task. From 1774 to 1783 he was also a member of Parliament. Gibbon died in London on Jan. 16, 1794. His *Miscellaneous Works,* which included his memoirs, was published posthumously (1796).

Bibliography: Bond, Harold L., *The Literary Art of Edward Gibbon* (1960); De Beer, Sir Gavin, *Gibbon and His World* (1967); Gibbon, Edward, *Memoirs of My Life and Writing,* ed. by George A. Bonnard (1969); Jordan, David P., *Gibbon and His Roman Empire* (1971); Low, D. M., *Edward Gibbon, 1737-1794* (1937); Swain, Joseph W., *Edward Gibbon the Historian* (1966).

See also: DECLINE AND FALL OF THE ROMAN EMPIRE, HISTORY OF THE.

Gibbons, Grinling

Grinling Gibbons, b. Apr. 4, 1648, d. Aug. 3, 1721, the leading English wood-carver of the late 17th and early 18th centuries, was celebrated for astonishingly naturalistic carvings of birds, flowers, fruit, and foliage, which rivaled the finest European decorative sculpture of the period. In 1671, Gibbons's work came to the attention of Charles II, who later commissioned him to execute a considerable amount of ornamental woodwork. He subsequently worked for William and Mary in the royal palaces of Kensington and Hampton Court. By the 1690s, Gibbons was the most famous craftsman among the many builders and decorators employed by Sir Christopher Wren at SAINT PAUL'S CATHEDRAL, London. Gibbons's work at Saint Paul's included some exterior stonecarving and the intricately carved ornaments of the choir stalls, organ-case, and bishop's throne. In 1714 he was appointed master carver in wood to George I. Gibbons also provided interior ornaments for the town and country houses of the nobility, and examples of his work exist at Petworth Place, Sussex (1692).

REVIEWED BY KATHRYN B. HIESINGER

Bibliography: Bullock, Albert E., ed., *Grinling Gibbons and His Compeers* (1914); Green, David, *Grinling Gibbons: His Work as Carver and Statuary, 1648-1721* (1964); Tipping, Henry A., *Grinling Gibbons and the Woodwork of His Age* (1914).

Gibbons, James

James Gibbons, b. Baltimore, July 23, 1834, d. Mar. 24, 1921, was an American Roman Catholic archbishop and the second American to be named a cardinal. He grew up in Ireland, but returned to the United States in 1853 to study for the priesthood. Ordained in 1861, he spent four years as a parish pastor and chaplain in military hospitals in Baltimore. In 1868 he was consecrated a bishop and was appointed to organize the vicariate apostolic of North Carolina. He was subsequently made bishop of Richmond, Va. (1872) and archbishop of Baltimore (1877). In 1886, Pope Leo XIII named him a cardinal.

James Gibbons, Roman Catholic archbishop of Baltimore and a cardinal, was a key leader of the American Catholic church during its years of enormous growth in the late 1800s. At a time when Rome was skeptical of the ultraliberalism of its U.S. congregation, Cardinal Gibbons mediated between secular and church authorities, stressing unity and modifying new ideas.

As the principal leader of American Catholicism during the period of its greatest growth, Gibbons was instrumental in achieving Roman Catholic integration into American society. His vocal patriotism and his endorsement of the separation of church and state helped to overcome traditional Protestant hostility: his concise exposition of Catholic doctrine, entitled *The Faith of Our Fathers* (1876) was widely read by non-Catholics. Conversely, he defended the American church-state relationship at the Vatican and prevented a papal condemnation of the unionizing efforts of the KNIGHTS OF LABOR movement. In 1889, Gibbons became the first chancellor of the Catholic University of America. The extent of his prestige was shown when President Taft personally led the celebration of the 50th anniversary of his ordination in 1911.

Bibliography: Cross, Robert D., *The Emergence of Liberal Catholicism in America* (1958); Ellis, John Tracy, *Life of James Cardinal Gibbons,* 2 vols. (1952).

Gibbons, Orlando

The celebrated English composer Orlando Gibbons, baptized Dec. 25, 1583, d. June 5, 1625, is best known for his madrigals and music for the Anglican church. He was a chorister (1596-98) at King's College, Cambridge, and matriculated there in 1598. In 1605 he was appointed organist of the Chapel Royal, a post he held until his death. He was named (1619) virginalist to the king, and in 1623 he became organist of Westminster Abbey. His father, William, three of his brothers, and his son Christopher were also musicians.

In 1612, Gibbons published *The First Set of Madrigals and Motets of 5 Parts,* which includes the well-known "The Silver Swan." As a group his madrigals are more austere than those of his contemporaries. Examples of his excellent chamber music are found in *Fantasies of Three Parts* (c.1610) for viols. His keyboard works include six pieces printed in *Parthenia* (1611), a collection (including pieces by William Byrd and John Bull) of music for the virginal. Gibbons composed about 40 anthems, some of which are choral throughout (full anthems), and some (verse anthems) that include sections for one or more solo voice parts with accompaniment, as in *This is the Record of John.* He also composed a poignant fantasia for voices and viols based on the traditional cries of London street peddlers. His music generally tends to be somewhat reserved but is not without emotional qualities.

Bibliography: Fellowes, Edmund H., *Orlando Gibbons and His Family,* 2d ed. (1951; repr. 1970) and *The English Madrigal Composers,* 2d ed. (1948); Meyer, E. H., *English Chamber Music* (1946).

Gibbons v. Ogden

The case of *Gibbons* v. *Ogden* (1824) resulted in the United States Supreme Court interpretation of the so-called commerce clause of the U.S. Constitution and was one of Chief Justice John MARSHALL's most important decisions. The New York legislature had granted exclusive rights to navigate New York's waterways by steam vessels to the inventors and entrepreneurs Robert Fulton and Robert Livingston. In turn Aaron Ogden obtained permission from the holders of the franchise to navigate between New York and New Jersey but was confronted by competition from Thomas Gibbons, a citizen of New Jersey who ran steamboats between Elizabethtown and New York City.

Chief Justice Marshall invalidated the New York monopoly on the grounds that the state law was in conflict with the act of Congress under which Gibbons had been granted a license. He maintained that commerce includes navigation, that the government's power to regulate it included the power to "prescribe the rule by which commerce may be governed," and that Congress might deal with commerce wherever it existed, including within a state, when it was connected with interstate or foreign commerce. Eventually, Marshall's doctrine that commerce includes any transactions across state lines, combined with the doctrine of implied powers he enunciated in McCulloch v. Maryland (1819), permitted a broad range of congressional regulation of activities ranging from business enterprises to race relations.

Robert J. Steamer

Gibbs, James

James Gibbs's Radcliffe Camera (1739–49), a library at Oxford University, is a monumental tribute to the dome, reflecting the diverse influences of Mannerist and baroque styles. The exterior is an eclectic synthesis typical of Italian Mannerism. The interior, which articulates the building's two concentric cylinders by means of a strongly linear ornamentation, suggests the restraint of Christopher Wren's baroque style.

The Scotsman James Gibbs, b. Dec. 23, 1682, d. Aug. 5, 1754, was the most important London church architect of the early 18th century. In 1703, Gibbs went to Rome to study for the priesthood, but after one year at the Pontifical Scots College he took up painting and then architecture, which he studied under the Italian architect Carlo Fontana. He returned (1709) to London, where he executed (1714) his first important commission, St. Mary-le-Strand Church, an example of his early, individual, neobaroque manner. His most distinguished achievements are St. Martin-in-the-Fields, London (1721–26), whose design became the prototype for many parish churches in England and the United States, and the Radcliffe Camera of Oxford University (1739–49).

Gibbs's eclectic architectural style reflects the influence of Sir Christopher Wren, but he later took up the popular Palladian manner (see Palladio, Andrea), especially in St. Martin-in-the-Fields, an original combination of a steeple with a portico facade. The originality of the Radcliffe Library lies in Gibbs's use and understanding of the Mannerist style.

Gibbs's designs were influential because they were published in books. *A Book of Architecture* (1728) and *Rules for Drawing The Several Parts of Architecture* (1732) were widely used in both England and the American colonies. Other notable creations by Gibbs are the Palladian mansion of Ditchley in Oxfordshire (1720–22) and King's College Fellows' Building at Cambridge (1724–30); the latter best demonstrates Gibbs's ability to combine Mannerist and Palladian elements in a successful, controlled design.

Valentin Tatransky

Bibliography: Downes, K., *English Baroque Architecture* (1966); Little, B., *The Life and Work of James Gibbs* (1955); Summerson, J., *Architecture in Britain, 1530–1830* (1970).

Gibbs, Josiah Willard

The theoretical physicist and chemist Josiah Willard Gibbs, b. New Haven, Conn., Feb. 11, 1839, d. Apr. 28, 1903, was one of the founders, along with Ludwig Boltzmann, of statistical mechanics. The son of a professor of sacred literature at Yale, Gibbs received one of the first Ph.D. degrees granted in the United States from Yale's new graduate school in 1863, in engineering. He taught at Yale until his death. In the early 1870s, Gibbs began his studies in thermodynamics. His first scientific paper, "Graphical Methods in the Thermodynamics of Fluids," discussed the relationships among entropy, energy, temperature, pressure, and volume in thermodynamic systems. He used a geometric (graphical) approach in diagraming the system in two dimensions. Another paper published later the same year extended his geometry to three dimensions. The Cambridge physicist James Clerk Maxwell became an enthusiastic supporter of Gibbs. Boltzmann referred to Gibbs in 1883, and, most important, Wilhelm Ostwald translated the papers of Gibbs into German in 1892. Gibbs's longest and most important paper, "On the Equilibrium of Heterogeneous Substances," appeared in 1876–78. This study incorporated into a single thermodynamic system chemical, elastic, surface, electromagnetic, and electrochemical phenomena. The application of these ideas to chemistry led to a better understanding of chemical equilibrium in systems composed of several phases.

Sheldon J. Kopperl

Bibliography: Rukeyser, Muriel, *Willard Gibbs* (1942; repr. 1964); Wheeler, Lynde, *Josiah Willard Gibbs: The History of a Great Mind*, rev. ed. (1952).

gibbsite: see BAUXITE.

Gibraltar [juh-brawl'-tur]

Gibraltar is a British territory located on a peninsula 6 km² (2.25 mi²) in area that extends 5 km (3 mi) into the Mediterranean Sea from southeastern Spain and dominates the Strait of Gibraltar, which connects the Mediterranean to the Atlantic Ocean. The peninsula consists of the Rock of Gibraltar, a high ridge of limestone and shale rising 426 m (1,396 ft) above sea level, and a low-lying isthmus, 1.6 km (1 mi) long, connecting it to the mainland. The northern and eastern sides of the rock are steep cliffs, but its southern and western sides slope more gradually in a series of terraces. The city of Gibraltar, which contains two-thirds of the territory's 29,000 people (1983 est.), is situated on the lowest of these terraces. Summer temperatures average about 22° C (71° F), and annual rainfall averages 865 mm (34 in). Tourism and services to shipping are the main industries.

Gibraltar and Mount Abyla, which is located across the strait on the Moroccan coast, have long been known as the Pillars of Hercules. According to classical myth, Hercules created the Strait of Gibraltar by forcing apart Gibraltar and Mount Abyla in order to let water into the Mediterranean.

Government. Gibraltar is administered by a governor appointed by the British crown. The governor commands the

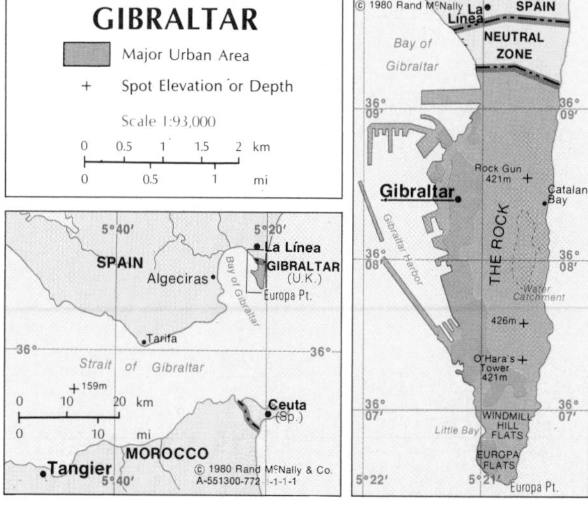

The Rock of Gibraltar is an imposing promontory dominating the surrounding peninsula. Strategically located at the gateway between the Mediterranean Sea and the Atlantic Ocean, Gibraltar is a valuable military base and the subject of a long dispute between Spain and Great Britain.

British garrison that runs the large naval base, air field, and artillery emplacements in the territory and is responsible for all defense and internal security matters. Since 1969 control of municipal affairs has been vested in a board of ministers that is responsible to a 15-member elected House of Assembly. All Gibraltarians (those who can trace residency on Gibraltar through the male line back to before 1925) may vote, as may those with special British residency permits.

History. Because of the strategic value of its location and topography, Gibraltar has always been a prized military possession. It was conquered by the successive Mediterranean empires of the Phoenicians, Carthaginians, Romans, Vandals, and Visigoths. In 711 it was taken by Muslim Moorish forces, who built (725) a massive castle that partly remains today. It was retaken by the Spanish in 1462. In 1704 it was captured by the British, to whom Spain formally ceded it in the Treaty of Utrecht (1713). When the Suez Canal opened in 1869, Gibraltar became even more important as a military and supply link on the Mediterranean route from Great Britain to India. It was the site of a strategic naval base during the two world wars.

In 1967 the residents of Gibraltar voted by referendum to remain a British crown colony, and a new constitution was adopted in 1969. In the latter year, the Spanish government closed the border between Spain and Gibraltar. The border was partially (1982), then totally (1985) reopened, but Spain still pressed its claim to the peninsula. PAUL C. HELMREICH

Bibliography: Dennis, Philip, *Gibraltar* (1977); Howes, Henry W., *The Story of Gibraltar* (1946); Stewart, John D., *Gibraltar: The Keystone* (1967).

Gibraltar, Strait of

The Strait of Gibraltar is the 60-m-long (36-mi) channel that separates Europe (Spain) from Africa (Morocco) at the western end of the Mediterranean Sea. The strait is 13 km (8 mi) across at its narrowest point. Its current is two-layered; the upper layer moves east into the Mediterranean, carrying oxygen and nutrients, and the lower, saline layer moves west, or outward. The strait is deepest in the east; the relative shallowness of the western end (320 m/1,050 ft) causes it to retain the warmth of the Mediterranean's water. The strait is named for the Spanish promontory that was once named Jebel Tariq or Mount Tariq in honor of the Berber leader who began the Muslim conquest of Spain in 711.

Gibran, Kahlil [juh-brahn', kah-leel']

A Lebanese poet who emigrated to the United States, Kahlil Gibran, b. Jan. 6, 1883, d. Apr. 10, 1931, is best known for his poetic parables and aphorisms, contained in such works as *The Prophet* (1923) and *Sand and Foam* (1926). Gibran was influenced by Nietzsche but was also highly religious and dealt with such abstractions as God, love, and woman. The very scope of his subjects and the sentimentality with which he presents them are serious problems in his work, but these characteristics may well be the source of his popularity. He also wrote Arabic poetry and was a skillful artist, producing drawings similar in style and feeling to those by the English poet-illustrator William Blake. CHARLOTTE SOLOMON

Bibliography: Gibran, Kahlil and Jean, *Kahlil Gibran: His Life and World* (1974); Hawi, Kahlil S., *Kahlil Gibran: His Background, Character, and Works* (1972).

Gibson, Althea

Althea Gibson, b. Silver, S.C., Aug. 25, 1927, was the first black person to win major titles in tennis. She won the Italian championship in 1956 and again in 1957, a year in which she also won Wimbledon and the U.S. championship. She repeated her singles victories at Wimbledon and Forest Hills in 1958 and ranked number one in the world among women players in both 1957 and 1958. Gibson's strength as a tennis player was her powerful serve and volley. She later became a moderately successful professional golfer.

Bibliography: Gibson, Althea, *I Always Wanted to Be Somebody* (1958).

Gibson, Bob

Robert Gibson, b. Omaha, Nebr., Nov. 9, 1935, was an American baseball pitcher who won 251 games in the 1960s and '70s and was outstanding for his strikeout records. He also had a brief basketball career with the Harlem Globetrotters. Gibson joined the St. Louis Cardinals, the only team he played for in the major leagues, in 1959. He pitched the Cardinals to World Series triumphs in 1964 and 1967, and in the 1968 series, which the Cardinals lost, he struck out 35 men, including 17 in one game. He had 3,117 strikeouts in his career. Gibson won the Cy Young Award as the National League's best pitcher in 1968 and 1970, retired in 1975, and was inducted into the Hall of Fame in 1981.

Bibliography: Gibson, Bob, and Pepe, Phil, *From Ghetto to Glory: The Story of Bob Gibson* (1968).

Gibson, Charles Dana

A popular American illustrator, Charles Dana Gibson, b. Sept. 14, 1867, d. Dec. 23, 1944, was widely known for his pen-and-ink drawings of the "Gibson Girl," which influenced fashions and publications for 20 years. This Victorian "glamour girl," born on his drawing board in the early 1890s, and his sentimental, humorous, and sometimes gently satirical pictures of social life appeared in many publications, including the old humor magazine *Life*. His books include *The Education of Mr. Pipp* (1899), another popular Gibson character. Although Gibson was also critically acclaimed as a painter in oils, he is mainly remembered as a social satirist and the delineator of the spirit of an era. ROBERT V. HUDSON

Bibliography: Gibson, Charles D., *The Gibson Girl and Her America*, ed. by Edmund Gillon (1969).

Gibson, Edward

The American astronaut Edward George Gibson, b. Nov. 8, 1936, is a physicist who helped set the 84-day U.S. space-endurance record. He earned his doctorate in engineering from the California Institute of Technology in 1964 and was selected with the first group of scientist-astronauts in 1965. Gibson is the author of *The Quiet Sun*, a solar physics textbook.

Gibson was science pilot on SKYLAB III. In addition to operating the Apollo telescope mount, Gibson performed stellar and cometary observations. He resigned from NASA in 1974 to conduct research on Skylab solar data, then worked in West Germany as a space science consultant. He rejoined NASA and returned to flight status in 1977.

DAVID DOOLING

Gibson, Josh

Joshua Gibson, b. Buena Vista, Ga., Dec. 21, 1911, d. Jan. 20, 1947, was considered the greatest hitter of the black baseball leagues in the United States before blacks were allowed to play in the major leagues. Called the "Black Babe Ruth," Gibson hit about 800 home runs in the 17 years he played, including 75 in the 1931 season.

Although statistics were often undocumented in the Negro National League, Gibson was the league's leading hitter four times and had a lifetime batting average of .347. A catcher, he played mostly for teams in and around Pittsburgh. He died suddenly in early 1947, the year Jackie Robinson became the first black player in the major leagues. In recognition of his accomplishments, Gibson was inducted into the Baseball Hall of Fame in 1972.

Gibson Desert

The Gibson Desert, in east-central Western Australia and the Northern Territory, is an uninhabited region of sandhills, extending about 840 km (520 mi) east to west and 400 km (250 mi) north to south. Ernest Giles explored and crossed it in the 1870s and named it for a companion, Alfred Gibson, who died while searching for water.

Giddings, J. Louis [gid'-ingz]

James Louis Giddings, Jr., b. Apr. 10, 1909, d. Dec. 9, 1964, was an American archaeologist and professor at Brown University. He is noted for his excavations at CAPE DENBIGH, Alaska, where he found a remarkably complete record of the Arctic Small Tool tradition, a prehistoric tool culture that spread from western Alaska across the Arctic between 4000 and 1000 BC. Among his books are *The Archaeology of Cape Denbigh* (1964) and the posthumously published *Ancient Men of the Arctic* (1967).

Gide, André [zheed]

André Gide was one of the major French literary figures of the first half of the 20th century. In awarding him the Nobel Prize for literature in 1947, the Nobel jury spoke of his works—a lifelong study of man's mind and soul, beginning with the confessional *Cahiers d'André Walter* of 1891—as a major contribution to humanism.

Gide, b. Nov. 22, 1869, d. Feb. 19, 1951, was the son of a Sorbonne professor who died when André was 11. He was brought up in a strict Protestant atmosphere by his solicitous and protective mother. His world was bounded by women: his mother, her English companion, his grandmother in Provence, and his cousins in Normandy. He married his cousin Madeleine in 1895, but the union proved tragic.

The French author André Gide, writing during the first half of the 20th century, influenced the development of modern literature with his introspective writing and experimental narrative techniques. As a novelist, critic, and dramatist, Gide addressed the problems of personal freedom within the confines of conventional moral and ethical codes.

As a young man, Gide sought an escape from the stuffy confines of home and relatives by going to literary gatherings. His early works, written in the 1890s, were influenced by symbolism. A trip to North Africa and his discovery of a homosexuality free of shame set him in open rebellion against his family and polite society. Gide went on to become a champion of sincerity in all its forms, defending the right of each person to choose and to change his mind.

He waged his war against conformity in prose pieces, in plays, in the press, and on the lecture platform. *Fruits of the Earth* (1897; Eng. trans., 1949) preached Nietzschean paganism in musical and visually evocative language. *Strait Is The Gate* (1909; Eng. trans., 1924) depicted the folly of denying the flesh, although in *The Immoralist* (1902; Eng. trans., 1930), perhaps his best-known work, he had already demonstrated the evils of sensual indulgence. Gide believed that values are relative, that truth may always be found on both sides of an issue, so that any new book might contradict its predecessor.

Although the tone of Gide's books is usually quite serious, *Lafcadio's Adventures* (1914; Eng. trans., 1927) proved that he could also use humor effectively. Its whimsical young hero, Lafcadio, is a firm believer in acting on impulse, equally capable of risking his life to rescue someone from a burning building and of pushing a stranger off a fast-moving train. The heroine of *The Pastoral Symphony* (1919; Eng trans., 1931) is another sort of innocent, a blind girl victimized by a Swiss pastor whose love for her exceeds Christian charity.

Lafcadio and the pastor were still on Gide's mind when he composed what could be considered his greatest novel, *The Counterfeiters* (1925; Eng. trans., 1927). This comprehensive summary of Gide's views on life and art examines the literal and figurative significances of counterfeiting in a complicated design that continues to fascinate literary critics.

In the journals, plays, and miscellaneous pieces that occupied Gide for the rest of his life, we encounter the rebel who believed in courage, fervor, and individual freedom. Gide was a man of action as well as a thinker. He denounced political and social evil wherever he found it, in colonialism or in capitalism, and was always prepared to change his position (as he did on Soviet Communism) when he felt he had been mistaken.

As head of the eminent *Nouvelle Revue Française*, Gide fostered the best in French writing, publishing works by Proust, Claudel, Valéry, Giraudoux, and others who now rank with him as the great literary figures of the period.

LAURENT LESAGE

Bibliography: Cordle, Thomas, *André Gide* (1969); Fowlie, Wallace, *André Gide: His Life and Art* (1969); Gide, André, *Journals*, 4 vols., trans. by Justin O'Brien (1889-1949); Guerard, Albert, *André Gide*, 2d ed. (1969); Ireland, G. W., *André Gide: A Study of His Creative Writings* (1970); Littlejohn, David, ed., *Gide: A Collection of Critical Essays* (1970); Painter, George, *André Gide: A Critical Biography* (1968).

Gideon [gid'-ee-uhn]

Gideon was the biblical judge and warrior who saved the Israelites from the annual raids of the nomadic Midianites. Because of his opposition to the worship of Baal and his dramatic victories, he was offered the kingship of Israel. But he refused it because he believed that God was Israel's only king. The Gideon tradition is related in Judges 6-8.

Gideon v. Wainwright

In the case of *Gideon* v. *Wainwright* (1963) the U.S. Supreme Court, speaking through Justice Hugo BLACK, overruled *Betts* v. *Brady* (1942), in which an earlier majority had held that the 6th AMENDMENT's guarantee of the right to counsel applied only to trials in federal courts, that it was not essential to a fair trial, and that it was not incorporated into the DUE PROCESS clause of the 14TH AMENDMENT. Clarence Gideon had been charged with breaking and entering a poolroom in Florida, was found guilty by a jury, and had been sentenced to five years in prison. Gideon had not been represented by counsel even though he had requested that the state appoint a lawyer for his defense.

Justice Black argued that the 14th Amendment's guarantee of due process embraced the 6th Amendment's right to counsel. The case was significant in that it made one Provision of the BILL OF RIGHTS that had previously applied only to the federal government apply also to state criminal proceedings. Prior to the decision in *Gideon,* the Supreme Court had used the 14th Amendment to apply to the states only the rights guaranteed in the 1ST AMENDMENT (freedom of speech, press, religion, assembly, and petition) and in the 4TH AMENDMENT (freedom from unreasonable search and seizure).

ROBERT J. STEAMER

Bibliography: Lewis, Anthony, *Clarence Earl Gideon and the Supreme Court* (1972) and *Gideon's Trumpet* (1964).

Giedion, Sigfried [gee'-dee-ohn, zeek'-freet]

The Swiss architectural historian Sigfried Giedion, b. Apr. 14, 1893, d. Apr. 10, 1968, was trained in engineering and later influenced by such teachers as Heinrich WÖLFFLIN. Giedion, who is best known for his work *Space, Time, and Architecture* (1941), applied his historical approach to contemporary architectural events. In the words of Walter GROPIUS, he was "the first to place in a historical perspective the conversion of the American economy to mechanical production methods with its profound psychological and cultural consequences."

Giedion was secretary general of CIAM, or the Congrès Internationaux d'Architecture Moderne (International Congresses of Modern Architecture), from the organization's inception in 1928 until 1954. He taught at the Federal Institute of Technology in Zurich, at the Massachusetts Institute of Technology, and at Harvard University, where he was the first Charles Eliot Norton Lecturer in 1938-39. Giedion died one day after completing his last book, *Architecture and the Phenomena of Transition* (1969; Eng. trans., 1971).

REGINALD AND MARK ISAACS

Gielgud, Sir John [geel'-gud]

The English actor Arthur John Gielgud, b. Apr. 14, 1904, is the grand-nephew of actress Ellen Terry and is one of the foremost actors of the English-speaking stage. He made his debut in 1921 with the Old Vic theater and achieved his first popular success in the play *Richard of Bordeaux* in 1932. His speaking voice is remarkable for its diction and tone, which enable him to sustain the melody of a poetic line without losing its drama.

Gielgud's most notable roles include Hamlet (1934), Jack Worthing in Oscar Wilde's *The Importance of Being Earnest* (1939), Benedick in *Much Ado About Nothing* (1952), and Spooner in Harold Pinter's *No Man's Land* (1975). He is also a producer and director and has appeared in a number of films. He was knighted in 1953.

ANDREW KELLY

Bibliography: Gielgud, John, *Distinguished Company* (1973) and *Early Stages*, rev. ed. (1976); Hayman, Ronald, *John Gielgud* (1971).

Sir John Gielgud, British director, producer, and one of the finest Shakespearean actors of his time, was knighted in 1953 for his contributions to the British theater.

Gierek, Edward [gyair'-ek]

Edward Gierek, b. Jan. 6, 1913, was the political leader of Poland from Dec. 20, 1970, when he succeeded Władysław Gomułka as first secretary of the Polish United Workers' party, to Sept. 6, 1980. Previously a coal miner and first secretary of the party organization in Silesia, Gierek took office at a time of serious unrest over food prices. Under his leadership Poland expanded its trade with the West and undertook a costly effort to industrialize and to make consumer goods more available. Gierek acquiesced in the visit (1979) of Pope John Paul II to Poland, the first visit by a pope to a Communist country. New food price increases sparked worker demonstrations in 1976 and a wave of strikes beginning in July 1980. Gierek's dismissal came after the strikes forced him to concede the rights of workers to strike and to form independent unions.

K. M. SMOGORZEWSKI

Gierke, Otto Friedrich von [geer'-ke]

The German legal theorist Otto Friedrich von Gierke, b. Jan. 11, 1841, d. Oct. 10, 1921, greatly influenced European legal thinking by studying and advocating the use of early Germanic law to create a legal foundation of a unified Germany. Von Gierke insisted that German law was distinct from individualistic Roman law in its unique emphasis on creative , freely organized social groups. Although von Gierke's early thoughts on decentralized government influenced the drafting of the Constitution of the WEIMAR REPUBLIC (1919) and pluralist theory in Great Britain, von Gierke himself firmly espoused the authoritarian *Reich* headed by an emperor.

Bibliography: Lewis, John D., *The Genossenschaft-Theory of Otto von Gierke: A Study in Political Thought* (1935).

Gieseking, Walter [gee'-zuh-king]

Walter Gieseking, b. Nov. 5, 1895, d. Oct. 26, 1956, was a distinguished German pianist, best known for his sensitive performances of the music of the French impressionist composers. Trained at the conservatory in Hanover, he made his debut in London in 1923 and concertized widely thereafter in Europe and in the United States. His playing was characterized by great precision and complete control of coloristic nuances. He recorded extensively, including the complete solo piano music of Wolfgang Amadeus Mozart, Claude Debussy, and Maurice Ravel.

F. E. KIRBY

Bibliography: Schonberg, Harold C., *The Great Pianists* (1963).

Gifford, William [gif'-urd]

The English author William Gifford, b. April 1756, d. Dec. 31, 1826, was editor (1809-24) of the influential *Quarterly Review* from its foundation. He made his name as a satirist, and his conservative tastes established the *Quarterly* as forum for hostile criticism of young writers, especially the romantic poets.

ROBIN BUSS

gifted, education of the: see SPECIAL EDUCATION.

gigaku [gi-gah'-koo]

Gigaku is the Chinese form of Buddhist processional drama introduced to Japan in 612 by the Korean performer Mimashi. Actors wearing masks impersonated Buddhas, demons, and men in comic sketches that ridiculed lust, violence, and other human sins. Masks for the characters Brahman and Garuda are of Indian origin. The more sophisticated BUGAKU gradually supplanted Gigaku in court functions, and, although several hundred masks remain, Gigaku ceased being performed at least 500 years ago. JAMES R. BRANDON

Gigantopithecus [ji-gan-toh-pith'-uh-kuhs]

Gigantopithecus is a genus of giant fossil apes of the Pliocene to Pleistocene epochs. In 1935, G. H. R. von Koenigswald purchased from a Chinese druggist in Hong Kong huge molar teeth belonging to this then unknown fossil ape, which he named *Gigantopithecus blacki*. Since that time, several lower jaws and many teeth belonging to this genus have been found in sites in India and China. The evolutionary position of this massive ape is uncertain. Because it possessed rather small canine teeth relative to the huge size of the jaw, this hominid-like trait may closely ally *Gigantopithecus* to prehistoric humans. ALAN MANN AND NANCY MINUGH

Gigli, Beniamino [jeel'-yee, ben-yah-meen'-oh]

One of the great singers of his generation, the Italian tenor Beniamino Gigli, b. Mar. 20, 1890, d. Nov. 30, 1957, was known for his powerful and expressive voice. He made his opera debut as Enzo in Ponchielli's *La Giaconda* in 1914. He made his American debut (1920) at the Metropolitan Opera as Faust in Boito's *Mefistofele* and remained with the company for 12 years. Although Gigli was admired especially for his Verdi and Puccini, he sang French and German roles with equal success. He returned (1939) to Italy and remained there during World War II; returning to the United States in 1955, he gave a series of highly successful concerts.

ELLA A. MALIN

Bibliography: Gigli, Beniamino, *Memoirs* (1957).

Gijón [hee-hohn']

Gijón (1981 pop., 255,969) is a city in northwestern Spain, situated on the Bay of Biscay. The city is an important seaport and transportation hub, industrial center, and tourist resort. Its leading manufactures include chemicals, steel, and ships.

Settled by the Romans on a previously inhabited site, Gijón was taken by the Moors early in the 8th century. One of the first cities to be recaptured (722) by the Spanish Christians, it was capital of the kingdom of Asturias until 791.

Gijsen, Marnix [hay'-suh, mahr'-niks]

Marnix Gijsen is the pseudonym of Jan Albert Goris, b. Antwerp, Oct. 20, 1899, a Flemish poet, novelist, journalist, and critic. His poetry, such as *The House by the Leaning Tree* (1925; Eng. trans., 1963), earned him an important place in the expressionist movement. Gijsen is also noted for *The Book of Joachim of Babylon* (1948; Eng. trans., 1951), a novel written in the form of a biblical allegory and for works that are the result of his 20 years in the United States: *Good and Evil* (1950) and *Armageddon* (1965). His *Candid Opinions on Sundry Subjects* (1964) is a collection of essays in English.

Gila monster [hee'-luh]

The Gila monster, *Heloderma suspectum* and its close relative, the beaded lizard, *H. horridum*, the only poisonous lizards in the world, make up the family Helodermatidae. The venom is produced by glands in the lower jaw and is conducted by grooves in the upper and lower teeth. The bite is rarely fatal to humans but is extremely painful. The Gila monster acquired its name from the Gila Basin of Arizona; the

The venomous Gila monster, H. suspectum, *is not dangerous unless carelessly handled. It hunts at night and if necessary can go without food for months, living on the fat stored in its tail.*

beaded lizard, from its scales, which in this family do not overlap but merely adjoin one another, like rows of beads. The Gila monster, found from southern Utah and Nevada to Mexico, grows to about 50 cm (20 in) in overall length and is blackish brown with irregular, pinkish or orangish areas. The beaded lizard, found in western Mexico, grows to about 81 cm (32 in) overall, and is black and yellow. The thick, blunt tail of both species serves for fat storage. This enables the lizards to go for long periods without food. Their diet consists mainly of eggs, young birds, small mammals, and lizards.

JONATHAN CAMPBELL

Bibliography: Schmidt, K. P., and Inger, R. F., *Living Reptiles of the World* (1957).

Gila River

The Gila River rises in southwestern New Mexico and flows about 1,015 km (630 mi) west and southwest to join the COLORADO RIVER at Yuma, Ariz. Its main tributaries include the San Francisco, San Pedro, Santa Cruz, Salt, Agua Fria, and Hassayampa rivers. Many dams along its course, including Coolidge and Painted Rock, impound its waters for flood control, hydroelectricity, and irrigation projects in the otherwise arid region. The remains of prehistoric Indian dwellings can be seen in the river's valley at Gila Cliff Dwellings (New Mexico) and Casa Grande (Arizona) national monuments.

Gilbert, Cass

Cass Gilbert, b. Zanesville, Ohio, Jan. 28, 1858, d. May 17, 1934, designed some of the most important commercial and civic landmarks in New York City. After studying at the Massachusetts Institute of Technology and in Europe, he gained professional experience in the prestigious firm of MCKIM, MEAD AND WHITE. He established his reputation by winning two important architectural competitions, the first for the Minnesota State Capitol in St. Paul (1896) with a design modeled on Saint Peter's Basilica in Rome, and the second for the U.S. Customs House in New York City (1905). Gilbert was particularly successful in designing tall buildings. The Gothic verticality of his most famous skyscraper, the WOOLWORTH BUILDING (1913), was judged by his contemporaries a satisfying means of expression for a 60-story building. Gilbert was also chief architect of the GEORGE WASHINGTON BRIDGE (1927), whose magnificent steel towers he originally planned to cover with stonework in medieval style. LEON SATKOWSKI

Bibliography: Kidney, Walter C., *The Architecture of Choice: Eclecticism in America, 1880–1930* (1974); Thompson, Neil B., *Minnesota's State Capitol: The Art and Politics of a Public Building* (1974).

Gilbert, Grove Karl

Grove Karl Gilbert, b. Rochester, N.Y., May 6, 1843, d. May 1, 1918, was an outstanding U.S. geologist of the late 1800s and early 1900s. Gilbert joined the westward movement as a member of the Ohio, Wheeler, and Powell geological surveys. He skillfully combined the techniques of physics, engineering, and geology in an approach that contrasted strongly with those of such notable contemporaries as W. M. DAVIS, C. E. DUTTON, and J. W. POWELL, all of whom he knew well. He is especially noted for his classic *Report on the Geology of the Henry Mountains* (1877) and for his studies of glacial Lake Bonneville (see LAKE, GLACIAL). After 1900 he turned his attention to new fields, including hydraulic mining techniques and hydrology. His hydrologic research included one of the earliest experimental flume studies, which led him to formulate what has been called Gilbert's law of stream capacity, which states the relationship between river runoff volume and sediment-carrying capacity. H. F. GARNER

Bibliography: Pyne, Stephen, "The Mind of Grove Karl Gilbert," in *Theories of Landform Development*, ed. by W. N. Melhorn and R. C. Flemal (1975; repr. 1980).

Gilbert, Sir Humphrey

Sir Humphrey Gilbert, b. *c.*1539, d. Sept. 9, 1583, was an English soldier and colonizer who failed in his attempt to establish the first permanent English colony in North America. After studying military science at Oxford, Gilbert joined the army and was wounded in France (1563). In 1566 he wrote *Discourse*, published ten years later, in which he expressed his belief in the existence of a NORTHWEST PASSAGE. He fought in Ireland from 1566, eventually attaining the rank of colonel. He crushed the Munster rebellion there in 1569 and was knighted the next year.

In 1571 he served in Parliament for Plymouth. The next year he commanded an expedition to aid the Dutch Revolt against the Spanish. His plans for colonization, originally applied to Ireland, were transferred to the New World. In 1578, Elizabeth I granted Gilbert a charter that permitted him to settle any lands not already held or claimed by Christians. He set sail the next year, but his fleet broke up, and he was forced to return to England.

A second colonizing expedition was planned, and the voyage began in June 1583. It reached St. John's Bay, Newfoundland, in August and claimed the territory in the name of the queen. After one ship was lost, the remainder of the expedition headed for England. Gilbert's ship, the overloaded *Squirrel*, sank en route. BRUCE B. SOLNICK

Bibliography: Quinn, D. B., ed., *The Voyages and Colonising Enterprises of Sir Humphrey Gilbert*, 2 vols. (1940); Slafter, C., ed., *Sir Humfrey Gylberte and His Enterprise of Colonization in America* (1966).

Gilbert, William

The English physician William Gilbert (also known as William of Colchester), b. May 24, 1544, d. Dec. 10, 1603, is known for his early studies on electricity and magnetism. His *De magnete* (1600) propounded the theory that the Earth was a giant lodestone with north and south magnetic poles. His theory that the Earth exerted a magnetic influence throughout the solar system was a precursor to the modern conception of gravity as an attracting force between masses. Gilbert was among the first to divide substances into electrics (spar, glass, amber) and nonelectrics. CATHERINE WILSON

Bibliography: Harré, Romano, *Early Seventeenth Century Scientists* (1965).

Gilbert, Sir William S.: see GILBERT AND SULLIVAN.

Gilbert Islands: see KIRIBATI.

Gilbert and Sullivan

Gilbert and Sullivan were among the most successful collaborators in all music. Their OPERETTAS are enjoyed for their satirical wit, comic plots and characters, and tuneful music.

William Schwenk Gilbert, b. Nov. 18, 1836, d. May 29, 1911, wrote drama criticism, verse, and stage pieces before working with Sullivan. Arthur Seymour Sullivan, b. May 13, 1842, d. Nov. 22, 1900, a bandmaster's son, began his musical training

The musical collaboration of the composer Sir Arthur Sullivan (left) *and the librettist Sir William Gilbert* (right) *resulted in 14 comic operas that satirized and burlesqued Victorian manners. Works such as* H.M.S. Pinafore *(1878),* Patience *(1881), and* The Mikado *(1885) have delighted audiences throughout the world.*

as a choirboy. He later studied at the London Royal Academy and in Leipzig. Even before collaborating with Gilbert, he had composed prolifically: hymns, cantatas, oratorios, piano pieces, songs, and orchestral works.

Sullivan's early ventures into comic opera, with writer F. C. Burnand, resulted in *Cox and Box* and *The Contrabandista*, in 1867. But his work with Gilbert brought out the best in each man: from Gilbert a waggish wit and pungent satire, from Sullivan an almost inexhaustible lyricism and a perfectly matched musical wit.

Their first collaboration, *Thespis, or the Gods Grown Old* (1871), was unsuccessful. *Trial by Jury* (1875), though not a success at first, was unusual in being a one-act operetta without spoken dialogue. *The Sorcerer* (1877) began their public acclaim, as well as their association with Richard D'OYLY CARTE's company, which was organized for their productions. *H.M.S. Pinafore* (1878) and *The Pirates of Penzance* (1879) brought them to the peak of their fame, which extended to the United States. *Patience* (1881), *Iolanthe* (1882), *Princess Ida* (1884), and especially *The Mikado* (1885) consolidated their success and were followed by *Ruddigore* (1887), *The Yeomen of the Guard* (1888), and *The Gondoliers* (1889). A quarrel between them temporarily halted (1890–93) their production, to the public's dismay. Reconciled, they attempted two more operettas, *Utopia Limited* (1893) and *The Grand Duke* (1896), but without their earlier deftness.

Knighted in 1883, Sullivan was under pressure to compose more serious works; he responded with his grand opera *Ivanhoe* (1891) and five more operas, and died exhausted. Gilbert was knighted in 1907, and at age 74 he died trying to save a drowning woman. JOHN W. BARKER

Bibliography: Ayre, L., *The Gilbert and Sullivan Companion* (1972); Eden, D., *Gilbert and Sullivan* (1986); Goodman, A., *Gilbert and Sullivan's London* (1986); Hayter, C., *Gilbert and Sullivan* (1987); Hibbert, C., *Gilbert and Sullivan and Their Victorian World* (1976); Hughes, G., *The Music of Arthur Sullivan* (1960); Jefferson, A., *The Complete Gilbert and Sullivan Opera Guide* (1984); Pearson, H., *Gilbert, His Life and Strife* (1957); Wilson, R., and Lloyd, F., *Gilbert and Sullivan: The Official D'Oyly Carte Picture History* (1984).

Gilbreth, Frank and Lillian [gil'-breth]

A husband and wife engineering team, Frank Bunker Gilbreth, b. Maine, July 7, 1868, d. June 14, 1924, and Lillian Moller Gilbreth, b. California, May 24, 1878, d. Jan. 2, 1972, developed the TIME AND MOTION STUDY to increase the efficiency and output of industry. Married in 1904, the Gilbreths launched an industrial consulting firm in Providence, R.I., which they later moved to Montclair, N.J. In 1911, Frank Gilbreth published *Motion Study,* which was followed by a series of books on industrial efficiency, written in collaboration with his wife. The Gilbreths' application of efficiency methods to their home and their 12 children was described by 2 of the children, Frank B. Gilbreth, Jr., and Ernestine Gilbreth Carey, in *Cheaper by the Dozen* (1949; film, 1950) and *Belles on Their Toes* (1950; film, 1952).

See also: INDUSTRIAL MANAGEMENT.

Gilded Age

The Gilded Age is a term used to describe the post-Civil War period in U.S. history. A satirical novel, *The Gilded Age* (1873), by Mark Twain and Charles Dudley Warner gave the period its name. The era, one of rapid industrialization, was characterized by the ruthless pursuit of profit, government corruption, conspicuous consumption, and vulgarity in taste.

gilding [gil'-ding]

The art and technique of decorating metal, wood, plaster, or other objects with a covering of gold is called gilding. In gilding, gold in leaf or powder form is applied by a special process. This process can also be used for "gilding" with other metals, such as silver and aluminum. The purpose of the metal covering may be either ornamental or protective.

The technique of gilding dates from the oldest civilizations. Wood and metal were gilded by the ancient Egyptians and later by the Romans. Gilding is mentioned in many places in the Old Testament. Oriental civilizations also gave importance to the technique, and it continues to be practiced in Asia. Modern uses for gilding include the decoration of picture frames, furniture, pottery, and leatherwork, as in ornamental bookbinding.

Two principal processes are used to coat surfaces with gold or another metal: the mechanical processes and the chemical processes. The first of these methods refers to the direct application of the prepared metal to the surface to be gilded by the artisan. To gild copper, for example, the artisan cleans and prepares the metal surface, lays the gold leaf on the surface, and applies heat. The surface is then burnished to bring up the color of the gold. Similar techniques are used for gilding other metals. To gild wood, the surface is carefully smoothed by sanding and then primed with glue size (glue mixed with water) followed by the application of several coats of whiting, a substance that glazes the surface and enables the metal gilding to adhere to it. Finally gold size (an adhesive) is applied. Then the surface is burnished and lacquered.

There are several chemical processes whereby gilding can be achieved. These include techniques known as cold gilding, wet gilding, and fire or wash gilding. In all of these the gold is chemically combined with some other substance at some stage. Preparation and finishing stages are similar to mechanical gilding processes. Pottery and porcelain are gilded by chemical means.

The techniques of gilding are complex, and a high degree of technical skill is required by the artisan. Thus gilded objects have always been items of luxury and value.

Bibliography: Shearman, William M., *Metal Alloys and Patinas for Casting* (1976).

See also: ELECTROPLATING.

Gilead [gil'-ee-ad]

In the Bible, Gilead is the name of the fertile region east of the Jordan and northeast of the Dead Sea. An area of rugged highlands, it was known for its pastures, vineyards, olive groves, and especially for the proverbial "balm of Gilead," a medicinal resin. It was at Gilead that David took refuge during the rebellion of Absalom.

Gilels, Emil

Known for his interpretations of Beethoven, Russian pianist Emil Grigoryevich Gilels, b. Oct. 19 (N.S.), 1916, d. Oct. 14, 1985, made his debut at the age of 13. He studied with Yakov Tkatch and Berthe Ringold at the Odessa Conservatory. Upon graduation in 1935 he studied with Heinrich Neuhaus at the Moscow Conservatory. Gilels won three major international piano competitions: 1st prize at Moscow in 1933, 2d prize in Vienna in 1936, and 1st prize in Brussels in 1938. He performed in recital and as orchestra soloist throughout Europe and in the Far East and appeared frequently in the United States. When he made his U.S. debut in 1955, he was the first Soviet artist to perform in the United States since Sergei Prokofiev in 1921. ELLA A. MALIN

Gilgamesh, Epic of [gil'-guh-mesh]

The Epic of Gilgamesh is a long Akkadian poem on the theme of human beings' futile quest for immortality. A number of earlier Sumerian stories about Gilgamesh, the quasi-historical hero of the epic, were used as sources, but the Akkadian work was composed about 2000 BC. It exists in several different recensions, none of them complete.

In the story, Gilgamesh and his friend Enkidu seek immortality through fame, but when Enkidu dies, Gilgamesh finds fame hollow. Unable to accept the finality of death, he goes to Utnapishtim, the Babylonian counterpart of the biblical NOAH, to learn the secret of his immortality. Utnapishtim explains that he received it due to the unique circumstances of the flood, but he consoles the dejected Gilgamesh with news about a plant of life. A snake swallows the plant before Gilgamesh can use it, however, and he finally returns home, reluctantly accepting death as inevitable. The Bible has a similar deluge story (see DELUGE) and shares the epic's general cultural views. The similarities probably derive from a common source in the body of ancient legend. J. J. M. ROBERTS

Bibliography: Heidel, Alexander, *The Gilgamesh Epic and Old Testament Parallels* (1949); Pritchard, J. B., ed., *Ancient Near Eastern Texts Relating to the Old Testament* (1955).

See also: DILMUN.

gill

The gill is an organ found in a wide variety of multicellular, usually aquatic animals. It functions in respiration, the exchange of gases between the body and the environment. Basically, the gases involved are oxygen and carbon dioxide, and usually the environment is water, but it may be moist air, as in the case of crustacean beach fleas. Obtaining oxygen is a greater physiological problem for aquatic animals than for air breathers, because oxygen's diffusion, or migration, is much slower in water than in air. The problem is handled in several ways. Although diverse in appearance and location on the body, gills typically have three important characteristics to facilitate gaseous exchange: (1) a large surface area, usually achieved by repeated branchings or intricate foldings; (2) a rich supply of blood vessels, to increase the volume of blood used to carry the gases; and (3) thin walls—frequently only two cells wide—separating the blood supply from the surrounding water.

Gills are found in aquatic invertebrates, in the larvae of aquatic amphibians, and in fishes. Gills may be extensions of body appendages such as legs, as in certain crustaceans; extensions of the body wall, as in the larvae of certain aquatic insects; or modifications of other parts of the body. Two types of gills, external and internal, are found in vertebrates. External gills, which look like feathery projections arising behind the head, are formed as derivatives of the skin covering the pharyngeal arches (the skeletal supports in the throat region). External gills are found in the tadpoles of certain am-

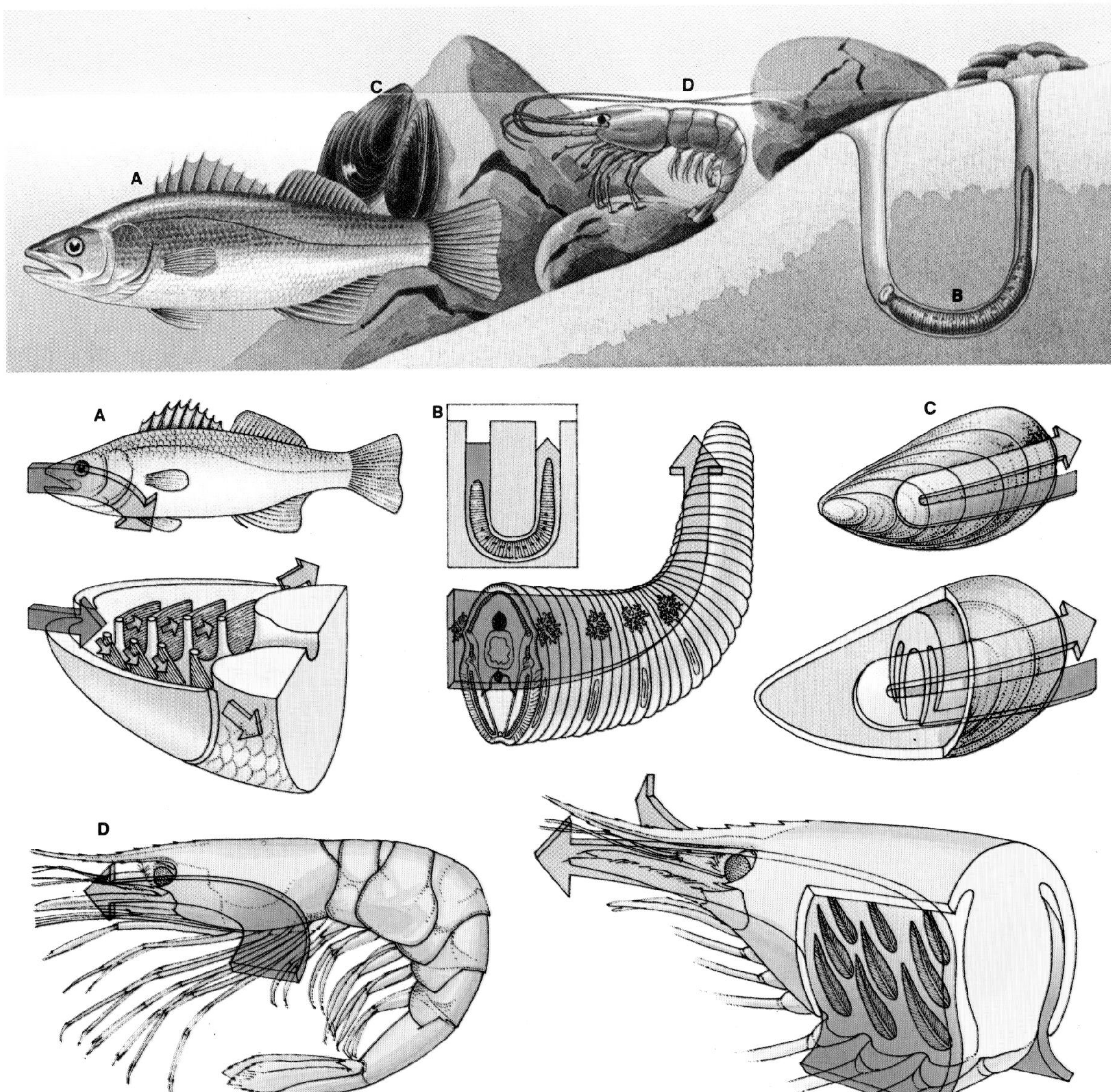

Gills, which are respiratory organs, allow many aquatic animals to breathe oxygen from water. In a teleost fish (A), water flows into the mouth and through four pairs of arched gills. The gills have an abundance of capillaries, which pick up oxygen from the water and release carbon dioxide. A lugworm (B) uses paired gills located on each side of its body, used in a similar manner to gills of fish. A mussel (C), like many bivalve mollusks, has a siphon that sucks water into internal gills and another for expelling water from its shells. A prawn (D) has five sets of featherlike gills located near its thoracic legs; water moves into the body through the gills and is forced out through the prawn's mouth.

phibians and in the larvae of a few bony fishes, such as the African lungfish. Internal gills, characteristic of fishes, consist of a series of filaments arranged on the paired pharyngeal arches in jawed fishes or within pharyngeal pouches in jawless fishes.

MICHAEL H. HORN

Gill, Sir David

Sir David Gill, b. June 12, 1848, d. Jan. 24, 1914, was a Scottish observational astronomer. During his tenure (1879–1907) as royal astronomer at the Royal Observatory, Cape of Good Hope, he determined the solar parallax with an accuracy unsurpassed until the 1960s and compiled the first photographic star catalog (the *Cape Photographic Durchmusterung*). Under Gill, the observatory became one of the best equipped and most respected in the world.

Gill, Irving

The architect Irving Gill, b. Syracuse, N.Y., 1870, d. 1936, transformed the southern California Mission tradition of building into a striking expression of modern architectural style. He worked in Chicago for Louis Sullivan and later settled in San Diego. His early projects, such as the Burnham House in San Diego (1906), are derived from Frank Lloyd WRIGHT's prairie style houses, but his later designs were simple cubes with white stucco outer walls often combined with California redwood interiors. Rejecting applied ornament, he declared: "We should build our houses simple, plain and substantial as a boulder, then leave the ornamentation of it to Nature, who will tone it with lichens, chisel it with storms, make it gracious and friendly." His masterpiece is the Dodge House in Hollywood (1916; destroyed), which was built of reinforced concrete. Gill's achievements were technical and social as well. The Lewis Courts houses in Sierra Madre (1910) indicate his concern for worker's housing, and the La Jolla Women's Club (1913–14) pioneered in the use of tilt-slab construction. The Panama Pacific Exhibition in San Francisco (1915) turned public taste toward an elaborate Spanish Revival style, however, and Gill received considerably fewer commissions from then on. LEON SATKOWSKI

Bibliography: McCoy, Esther, *Five California Architects* (1960).

Gillespie, Dizzy [guh-les'-pee, diz'-ee]

John Birks "Dizzy" Gillespie, b. Cheraw, S.C., Oct. 21, 1917, is a jazz trumpeter-composer-bandleader most noted for creating BEBOP along with Charlie Parker and Thelonious Monk. Early musical training from his father led Gillespie to formal study and a long career in jazz. He was one of Cab Calloway's featured soloists in the early 1940s and played in several other prominent big bands, including that of Earl Hines. A fine musician and a superb technician, by 1945 he had helped evolve the complex and difficult bop mode. One of the most popular of present-day jazz artists, Gillespie has led his own groups—from big bop bands to small combos—in tours throughout the United States and much of the rest of the world. JONATHAN KAMIN

Bibliography: James, Michael, *Dizzy Gillespie* (1961).

Gillette, William H. [juh-let']

William Hooker Gillette, b. July 24, 1853, d. Apr. 29, 1937, was an American playwright and actor who was noted for his portrayal of cool, unruffled men of action. He rose to stardom in his plays *Held by the Enemy* (1886) and *Secret Service* (1895). Gillette's most famous play, *Sherlock Holmes,* was first produced in New York in 1899, with Gillette in the title role. He revived the play many times in the United States and England. He also played the lead in one silent film, *Sherlock Holmes* (1916).

Gilliatt, Penelope [gil'-ee-uht]

An English writer and award-winning film critic, Penelope Gilliatt, b. March 25, 1932, wrote film reviews regularly for *The New Yorker* magazine from 1968 to 1979. Her novels, including *One by One* (1965) and *A State of Change* (1967), and numerous short stories are noted for their precise characterizations. She has also written stage plays, screenplays for television, and the screenplay for the film *Sunday Bloody Sunday* (1971). Her early criticism is collected in *Unholy Fools* (1973).

Gillot, Claude [zhee-loh']

Claude Gillot, b. Apr. 27, 1673, d. May 4, 1722, was the first significant French artist to depict the Italian Comedy. Although limited in training he was inventive and versatile, designing fashions, drawing caricatures, and producing about 300 engravings. He was in demand as a decorator after creating scenery for the opera. Antoine WATTEAU, who worked five years for Gillot, transformed his COMMEDIA DELL'ARTE theme into poetic evocations unlike Gillot's amusing moments from actual performances. In Gillot's *Scene from the Two Coaches* (c.1707; Louvre, Paris), stock characters making the emphatic gestures necessitated by the Italian dialogue appear before buildings that disappear in the rapidly receding perspective of the stage. JOAN C. SIEGFRIED

Bibliography: Fosca, François, *The Eighteenth Century, Watteau to Tiepolo,* trans. by Stuart Gilbert (1952).

Gillray, James [gil'-ray]

James Gillray, b. Aug. 13, 1756, d. June 1, 1815, was the outstanding English caricaturist of the golden age of British political satire. He began as a letter engraver, but after a brief career as a strolling player, he entered the Royal Academy in 1778. He also studied under Francesco Bartolozzi, an engraver, and this dual tuition improved the drawing of his prints and gave him a sound printmaking technique. At first he produced a variety of engravings, but by the mid-1780s he had become a specialist in political cartoons, inventing his own subjects and producing his own plates. Everyone and everything became a target for his devastating burlesques: George III, William Pitt the Younger, Napoleon, Whigs, and Tories were all victims of his savage wit. During his industrious career he produced nearly a thousand prints, but his activity ended in insanity in 1810. MALCOLM CORMACK

Bibliography: Gillray, James, *The Satirical Etchings of James Gillray,* ed. by Draper Hill (1976); Katanka, Michael, and Rickword, Edgell, *Gillray and Cruikshank* (1973).

Gilly, Friedrich [zhil'-ee]

Friedrich Gilly, b. Feb. 16, 1772, d. Aug. 3, 1800, was a German architect who, like his French contemporaries Étienne Louis Boullée and Claude Nicolas Ledoux, worked in the neoclassical style (see NEOCLASSICISM, art). He is better known for his grandiose and unrealized neoclassical projects than for his executed designs. A staunch proponent of the ideals of neoclassicism, Gilly expressed his ideas most fully in his 1797 design for a monument to Frederick II (the Great) of Prussia. This unexecuted complex was to consist of a Doric temple—one of the earliest revivals of this Greek architectural type—raised on a large, starkly geometric substructure. Also notable is his 1798 design for a national theater in Berlin, which he based on a strikingly severe conception closely akin to 20th-century architecture. ROBERT NEUMAN

gillyflower [jil'-ee-flow-ur]

Gillyflower is a species of stock, *Matthiola incana,* in the mustard family, Cruciferae. Gillyflower, or imperial stock, is a biennial or perennial or is sometimes raised as an annual, and ranges from compact, dwarf races to plants about 75 cm (2.5 ft) tall. The fragrant flowers occur in a variety of colors. OLIN S. FEARING

Gilman, Charlotte Perkins

Charlotte Perkins Gilman, b. July 3, 1860, d. Aug. 17, 1935, was known to her contemporaries as one of America's most prominent feminist intellectuals. Today, she is best remembered for "The Yellow Wallpaper" (1892), a short story depicting the mental breakdown of a young wife. *Women and Economics* (1898), her major theoretical work, explores the American woman's economic dependency. After a divorce (1894), then an uncommon practice, Gilman supported herself by writing and editing and produced a feminist journal, *The Forerunner* (1909–16). Afflicted with cancer, she committed suicide. Her autobiography, *The Living of Charlotte Perkins Gilman,* was published the same year.

Bibliography: Nies, Judith, *Seven Women* (1977).

Gilman, Daniel Coit

Daniel Gilman, b. July 6, 1831, d. Oct. 13, 1908, was the first president of The Johns Hopkins University. After 16 years as librarian and professor at Yale, he left in 1872 to serve as president of the University of California. Three years later he accepted the presidency of the new Johns Hopkins University, which was to be modeled on European universities. Johns Hopkins, free of both church and political control, emphasized academic freedom, graduate study, and research. Under Gilman's leadership, Johns Hopkins helped set the pattern for American postgraduate education. In 1901, Gilman resigned to become the first president (1902–04) of the Carnegie Institution of Washington, D.C.

Bibliography: Flexner, Abraham, *Daniel Coit Gilman* (1946); Franklin, Fabian, *The Life of Daniel Coit Gilman* (1910; repr. 1973).

Gilman, Lawrence

The American music critic and writer Lawrence Gilman, b. July 5, 1878, d. Sept. 8, 1939, was best known for his astute program notes for the concerts of the New York Philharmonic and Philadelphia orchestras. In 1901 he became music critic of *Harper's Weekly,* a post he held for 12 years. From 1915 to 1923 he was music, drama, and literary critic of the *North American Review,* and from 1923 until his death he was music critic of the *New York Herald-Tribune.* Gilman's books include *Edward MacDowell* (1905), *The Music of Tomorrow* (1906), *Music and the Cultivated Man* (1929), *Wagner's Operas* (1937), *Toscanini and Great Music* (1938). He also set to music three poems by W. B. Yeats. ELLA A. MALIN

Bibliography: Engel, Carl, "Lawrence Gilman," *Musical Quarterly,* January 1940.

Gilmer, Elizabeth Meriwether: see DIX, DOROTHY.

Gilmore, Dame Mary

Mary Jean Gilmore, b. Aug. 16, 1865, d. Dec. 3, 1962, is generally acknowledged as the grande dame of Australian literature. Her first collection of warm and patriotic poems, *Marri'd,* appeared in 1910. Other works include *The Tilted Cart* (1925), *The Wild Swan* (1930), *The Rue Tree* (1931), *Old Days: Old Ways* (1934), and *Battlefields* (1939). She was made a dame commander of the British Empire in 1937.

Gilroy, Norman Thomas [gil'-roy]

Norman Thomas Gilroy, b. Sydney, Jan. 22, 1896, d. Oct. 21, 1977, was the first Australian-born cardinal. After working in the postal department and as a telegraph operator, he served on a troopship in the Gallipoli Campaign of World War I. Gilroy studied in Rome and was ordained a Roman Catholic priest in 1923. From 1924 to 1931 he was secretary to the Apostolic Delegation in Australia, in 1931 he became secretary to the bishop of Lismore, and in 1935 he was named bishop of Port Augusta. From 1940 until his retirement in 1971, Gilroy was archbishop of Sydney. He was created a cardinal in 1946 and was knighted by Queen Elizabeth II in 1969.

Gilson, Étienne [zheel-sohn', ay-tee-en']

Étienne Gilson, b. June 13, 1884, d. Sept. 19, 1978, was a French historian and proponent of Thomism, the philosophy of Thomas Aquinas. A graduate of the Sorbonne, he taught at the universities of Lille and Strasbourg prior to holding chairs of medieval philosophy at the Sorbonne and, later, at the Collège de France. He was instrumental in founding (1929) the Institute of Medieval Studies at the University of Toronto and became its director. In 1946, Gilson was elected to the French Academy.

Gilson's publications include both pure history and works of critical interpretation. Among his many works are *Descartes' Concept of Liberty and Theology* (1913), *Moral Values and the Moral Life* (1925), *The Spirit of Medieval Philosophy* (1936), and *The Philosopher and Theology* (1960). According to Gilson, there have been only three great metaphysicians: Plato, Aristotle, and Aquinas; by balancing faith and reason, religion and science, the philosophy of Aquinas can fill the dangerous void left by the failures of modern philosophy.
PETE A. Y. GUNTER

Bibliography: O'Neil, Charles J., *Étienne Gilson Tribute* (1959); Pegis, Anton, ed., *A Gilson Reader* (1957).

gin [jin]

Gin is an alcoholic beverage made by distilling fermented mixtures of grains and flavoring the resulting alcohol with juniper berries. The name is derived from the French word *genièvre* (juniper). First made in 17th-century Holland, the manufacture and popularity of gin spread quickly throughout Europe, and variations of the Dutch formula began to appear. Today Holland gin is a comparatively heavy-bodied, lower-proof beverage; London gin is dryer and more potent; Plymouth, or Old Tom, gin is a sweeter variety. Sloe gin, a popular English drink, is flavored and tinted with sloe berries, the fruits of the blackthorn tree, and is sweetened by the addition of sugar. Other fruits, herbs, or spices may also be used to flavor gin.

Along with vodka, another colorless, almost tasteless liquor, gin has grown in popularity in recent years. It is rarely drunk by itself, but is used as the alcoholic base for such mixtures as the martini (gin and vermouth) and the gin-and-tonic.

In 1689 the English, who had previously imported distilled liquors, began to encourage the domestic manufacture of spirits from English grain. Gin, which could be cheaply made and sold, rapidly became the solace and the scourge of the nation's poor. In the early 1700s about 1 million gallons of gin were distilled annually, and in addition, much of the grain alcohol produced in Ireland and Scotland found its way into the English gin trade. By the 1740s gin consumption had reached 20 million gallons annually. Since there were few restrictions on its sale, anyone with a spare room and access to a distillery could open a gin shop, and contemporary estimates counted one such establishment for every six houses in London.

Appalled by the steeply rising mortality rate—attributable, in part, to urban alcoholism—and by the disastrous effects of widespread public drunkenness, Parliament passed the Gin Act in 1736. Although the act imposed heavy duties on both distillers and retailers of gin, its effect was minimal because the production of bootleg gin was impossible to control. It was only with the imposition of stiff excise taxes on gin production and the rigid control of its retail sale through a series of laws regulating public houses that the kind of mass inebriation depicted by Hogarth (*Gin Lane,* 1751) disappeared from the English scene.

See also: WHISKEY.

gin rummy: see RUMMY.

Ginastera, Alberto [hee-nah-stay'-rah]

Alberto Evaristo Ginastera, b. April 11, 1916, d. June 25, 1983, was the foremost Argentine composer of his generation. At first he was closely identified with Argentine musical nationalism, embodied in such works as *Argentine Dances* (1937), for piano; *Estancia* (1941), a ballet; *Overture to The Creole Faust* (1943); and *Pampeana* no. 3, "Symphonic Pastorale" (1954), for orchestra. In the 1950s, however, Ginastera gradually withdrew from musical nationalism, trying instead to create a personal synthesis of various contemporary musical techniques. In the 1960s he won acclaim for his operas *Don Rodrigo* (1964) and *Bomarzo* (1967). *Bomarzo* seemed to have everything to attract a modern audience: sex, violence, perversion, death, serialism (see SERIAL MUSIC), and aleatoric devices (see ALEATORY MUSIC). The opera was a sensation, as was its successor, *Beatrix Cenci* (1971). In 1962, Ginastera organized and became director of the Latin American Center for Advanced Musical Studies in Buenos Aires, an institute for the study of contemporary techniques of composition.
DIKA NEWLIN

Bibliography: Austin, William A., *Music in the Twentieth Century* (1966); Salzman, Eric, *Twentieth-Century Music: An Introduction,* 2d ed. (1974).

ginger [jin'-jur]

Ginger is the spice made from the rhizome, or enlarged underground stem, of the herbaceous perennial plant *Zingiber officinale.* Native to southern Asia, ginger has been an important commodity since ancient times and is widely cultivated in Africa, India, the Orient, and the West Indies, particularly in Jamaica.

The plants grow 60 to 90 cm (2 to 3 ft) high, with long, narrow leaves and pale green flowers. The plant is vegetatively reproduced by planting its rhizome segments. The fleshy, aromatic rhizomes are commonly referred to as roots; they are harvested when the plant is about 1 year old and are washed,

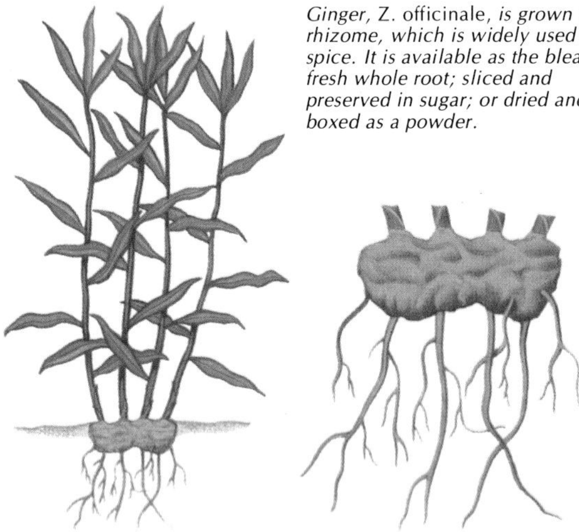

Ginger, Z. officinale, is grown for its rhizome, which is widely used as a spice. It is available as the bleached, fresh whole root; sliced and preserved in sugar; or dried and boxed as a powder.

dried, bleached by liming or by the sun, and then shipped, peeled or unpeeled.

The rhizomes are processed in several different ways. Preserved ginger, produced almost exclusively in China, is made by boiling tender rhizomes in a sugar solution and packing them in syrup or in a sugar coating. Unpeeled rhizomes may be scalded in boiling water before drying to make black ginger; without scalding, the product is green ginger. When parboiled, peeled, and bleached, the rhizomes are marketed as white ginger. Fresh gingerroot and dried, ground ginger are the most common commercial forms.

Ground ginger is widely used as a food seasoning. Ginger oil is used in perfumes and fruit flavorings. The oleoresin, which contains the essential oil, is used in making ginger-flavored beverages, sauces, and chutneys.

Several lesser varieties of ginger are also cultivated. Japanese ginger, *Z. mioga,* is grown in Japan and Hawaii, where its pungent young leaves are used in salads, fish, and soybean dishes. Wild, or bitter, ginger, *Z. zerumbet,* grows in southeastern Asia and Malaysia; its young shoots are cooked as a vegetable. *Asarum canadense,* the native North American wild ginger, has rhizomes that may be used as the true ginger.

ARTHUR O. TUCKER

Bibliography: Rosengarten, Frederic, Jr., *Book of Spices,* rev. ed. (1981).

ginger lily

The ginger lily, *Hedychium coronarium,* also known as the butterfly lily, is a tall herb with large, fragrant, whitish flowers borne in a cluster at the end of the stem. Although it resembles a lily, it is a member of the ginger family, Zingiberaceae. It is a native of tropical and subtropical areas of the Old World but has been introduced and cultivated in many other countries. The ginger lily is often used in Hawaiian leis.

gingham [ging'-uhm]

A yarn-dyed fabric identified by woven-in plaids, checks, or stripes of two or more colors, gingham was originally of cotton, but it now may contain synthetic fibers as well. (In yarn-dying, threads are dyed before the cloth is woven, in contrast to a print, in which the color is printed on the fabric after weaving. Gingham has been a common fabric for generations. Its name may be derived from a Malay word, *genggang,* meaning "striped." Combed gingham has fine, even yarns, and is used for better grades of women's and children's dresses, aprons, men's shirts, pajamas, and curtains; carded gingham is a medium-grade fabric used for apparel and household textile goods.

gingivitis [jin-juh-vy'-tis]

Gingivitis is an inflammation or degeneration of the gums, specifically the gingival tissue, that results most often from bacterial plaque (microbial colonies on teeth). It may also result from impacted food or from systemic disorders such as vitamin C deficiency (SCURVY) and endocrine disturbances (DIABETES mellitus). Gingivitis may progress to periodontitis (PYORRHEA), where supporting bone is lost. Prevention and treatment include good oral hygiene and control or correction of local and systemic factors.

PETER L. PETRAKIS

ginkgo [ging'-koh]

The ginkgo, or maidenhair tree, *Ginkgo biloba,* is the only living species of the family Ginkgoaceae, which were GYMNOSPERMS that thrived about 175 to 200 million years ago. It is a medium-sized, deciduous tree, growing up to 36 m (120 ft) in height. Its fan-shaped leaves have two lobes and parallel veins. Male ginkgo trees bear cones and female trees bear pairs of ovules, or seeds, at the end of each flower stalk; when ripe, the fleshy seeds fall to the ground and emit a strong, unpleasant odor.

Native to southeastern China, ginkgoes are now distributed worldwide. They are hardy in moderate climates and are commonly planted in Europe and North America as ornamentals or to line streets. For centuries the ginkgo was used to landscape monastery and temple grounds in China and Japan. The Chinese also used ginkgo extracts for medicinal purposes, and U.S. scientists have synthesized a compound found in ginkgoes that may be used to treat asthma and other ailments.

The exact ancestry of the ginkgo is uncertain, but it is thought to have originated from seed ferns, which are extinct groups of gymnosperms. Abundant fossil remains of *Ginkgo* date from the Permian age, over 200 million years ago. Many species of this tree apparently developed rapidly after that time, reaching peak distribution and abundance in the Jurassic Period, about 130 million years ago, when several different genera of ginkgoes and about 50 species of the genus *Ginkgo* were evolving. At present, the group is represented by only a single species, which includes several cultivated varieties.

SIDNEY F. GLASSMAN

The ginkgo, G. biloba, native to southeastern China, is the remaining species of a tree family that existed 175 to 200 million years ago. The tree bears fan-shaped leaves and clusters of tiny flowers. Its fruit yields a sweet, nutlike seed prized as a delicacy in China.

Ginsberg, Allen [ginz'-burg]

Allen Ginsberg, b. Newark, N.J., June 3, 1926, is an American poet and leading apostle of the BEAT GENERATION. His first published work, *Howl and Other Poems* (1956), sparked the SAN FRANCISCO RENAISSANCE and defined the generation of the 1950s with an authority and vision that had not occurred in the United States since T. S. Eliot captured the anxiety of the 1920s in *The Waste Land.* Ginsberg's bardic rage against mate-

Allen Ginsberg became a prophet of the Beat Generation with Howl *(1956), an assault in verse on American materialism. A cultural rebel, Ginsberg has proclaimed his outrage in books of poetry and in public readings and performances. He won the National Book Award for* The Fall of America *in 1974.*

rial values, however, was in a voice very different from Eliot's scholarly mourning for the loss of the spirit. In his second major work, *Kaddish* (1961), a poem on the anniversary of his mother's death, Ginsberg described their anguished relationship. In the 1960s, while vigorously participating in the anti–Vietnam War movement, he published several poetic works, including *Reality Sandwiches* (1963) and *Planet News* (1969). *The Fall of America* received the National Book Award for 1974. *Collected Poems, 1947–80* contains all of his important work. Ginsberg sees himself as a part of the prophetic tradition in poetry begun by William Blake in the 18th century and continued by Walt Whitman in the 19th century. He names his contemporary influences as William Carlos Williams and his friend Jack Kerouac. JOHN TYTELL

Bibliography: Gifford, Barry, ed., *As Ever: The Collected Correspondence of Allen Ginsberg and Neal Cassady* (1977); Ginsberg, Allen, *Journals: Early Fifties, Early Sixties,* ed. by Gordon Ball (1977); Hyde, Lewis, ed., *On the Poetry of Allen Ginsberg* (1984); Portuges, Paul, *The Visionary Poetics of Allen Ginsberg* (1978).

ginseng [jin'-seng]

Ginseng is a perennial herb of the genus *Panax*. The root of the ginseng has for centuries been reputed to be a panacea for cancer, rheumatism, diabetes, sexual debility, and aging. The claims date back to ancient China, and the root was long of great value there; Europe did not hear of it, however, until 1642, when the explorer Alvaro Samedo returned with a report of the restorative properties of Oriental ginseng (later named *P. pseudoginseng*), which he reported was being sold for twice its weight in silver.

The American ginseng, P. quinquefolius, *grows wild in North American woodlands. It stands up to 60 cm (2 ft) tall, has leaves up to 15 cm (6 in) long, and bears greenish white flowers.*

In 1713, Émile Jartoux, a Jesuit cartographer working in northern China, reported ginseng's effectiveness and power among the Chinese. His fellow Jesuit, Joseph François Lafiteau, read the report in Quebec, and after a diligent search found (1718) in the woods near his mission an almost identical species, *P. quinquefolius,* wild American ginseng. (A smaller American species, *P. trifolus,* is known as dwarf ginseng.) Demand for the American root grew in China, and many colonists and settlers, including Daniel Boone, hunted it avidly. Millions of pounds were uprooted, dried, and exported in the China trade. Eventually the slow-maturing plant, native to cool woods from Quebec to Oklahoma, was almost extinct. Cultivation began in the late 19th century, but the Chinese market balked at the cultivated American product, and many investments were lost.

Today China and Korea export ginseng to the West, where its popularity has grown in recent years. Soviet scientists claim to have found substances in ginseng that stimulate endocrine secretions and act as a tonic to the cardiovascular system. Medical research in the West, however, has failed to substantiate these claims.

Bibliography: Harding, A. R., *Ginseng and Other Medicinal Plants,* rev. ed. (1972); Fulder, S., *About Ginseng, the Magical Herb of the East* (1984); Kimmens, Andrew C., *Tales of the Ginseng* (1975).

Ginzberg, Asher: see ACHAD HA-AM.

Ginzberg, Louis [ginz'-burg]

The Jewish scholar Louis Ginzberg, b. Lithuania, Nov. 28, 1873, d. Nov. 11, 1953, was one of this century's foremost authorities in rabbinic literature. He emigrated to the United States in 1899 and was a professor at New York's Jewish Theological Seminary from 1902. His best-known work is the monumental 7-volume *Legends of the Jews* (1909–38), in which he compiled the folklore scattered throughout the Midrash and Talmud, tracing the stories to their sources. He also wrote an important commentary on the Palestinian Talmud, studying in detail the development of rabbinic theology.

Bibliography: Ginzberg, Eli, *Keeper of the Law: Louis Ginzberg* (1966).

Ginzburg, Natalia [gints'-boorg]

Natalia Levi Ginzburg, b. July 14, 1916, is an Italian writer noted for her poetic and deceptively simple literary style. Most of her novels treat with sensitivity the solitude of a female protagonist within a family group. These include *The Dry Heart* (1947; Eng. trans., 1949), *All Our Yesterdays* (1952; Eng. trans., 1956), and the autobiographical *Family Sayings* (1963; Eng. trans., 1967). *The Little Virtues* (Eng. trans., 1985) is a collection of essays written between 1944 and 1962.

LOUIS KIBLER

Ginzburg, Vitaly Lazarevich [ginz'-boork, vee-tahl'-ee lah-zahr'-uh-vich]

The Russian physicist Vitaly Lazarevich Ginzburg, b. Oct. 4, 1916, is known for his research on high-energy physics, the behavior of matter under extreme conditions, and radio astronomy. He heads the theoretical physics department of the Physics Institute of the Academy of Sciences of the USSR.

STEVEN J. DICK

Gioberti, Vincenzo [joh-bair'-tee, vin-chen'-tsoh]

Vincenzo Gioberti, b. Apr. 5, 1801, d. Nov. 26, 1852, was an Italian philosopher and statesman. Ordained (1825) a Roman Catholic priest, he was exiled (1833–46) on charges of involvement in a republican plot. It was during this period that he wrote his most significant philosophical works. His system, called ontologism, is summarized in the formula, "Being creates existence, and existence returns to being." God is identified with being; all else is merely existence. Gioberti composed many popular political works, advocating a federal union for Italy. He held several political positions in the kingdom of Sardinia before retiring to private life in 1849.

Giocondo, Fra Giovanni [joh-kohn'-doh, frah joh-vahn'-nee]

Fra Giovanni Giocondo, b. *c.*1433, d. July 1, 1515, was an Italian scholar and engineer whose writings, especially a 1511 edition of Vitruvius, were frequently consulted by contemporary architects. As an engineer he worked all over Italy and in France for Charles VIII and Louis XII, mostly as an advisor. He is known to have been engaged (1476–88) in Verona on the Loggia del Consiglio, at Poggioreale in Naples (*c.*1490), on the defenses of Venice (*c.*1506), and in Paris (1500–08) on the Pont-de-Notre-Dame. In 1514 he was appointed by Pope Leo X to assist Raphael at SAINT PETER'S BASILICA in Rome.

DAVID CAST

Bibliography: Heydenreich, Ludwig H., and Lotz, Wolfgang, *Architecture in Italy: 1400–1600* (1974).

Giolitti, Giovanni [joh-lit'-tee, joh-vahn'-nee]

Giovanni Giolitti, b. Oct. 27, 1842, d. July 17, 1928, was one of the ablest Italian political leaders of the modern era. A member of Parliament from 1882 until his death, he was premier five times between 1892 and 1921. Under his leadership, Italy prospered, the suffrage was democratized, and social security was introduced. He also kept the government neutral in labor disputes. Giolitti guided Italy into the ITALO-TURKISH WAR over Libya in 1911 but opposed entry into World War I. His reputation, however, remains controversial; some of his electoral victories were linked with corruption. He was ready to accept the support of new political forces such as the Catholics after 1904 and the Fascists after World War I. At first, he supported the government of Benito Mussolini, thinking he could tame it, but after November 1924 he withdrew his support.

CHARLES F. DELZELL

Bibliography: Giolitti, Giovanni, *Memoirs of My Life*, trans. by Edward Storer (1923); Salomone, A. William, *Italian Democracy in the Making, 1900–1914* (1945).

Giono, Jean [joh-noh']

The French writer Jean Giono, b. Mar. 30, 1895, d. Oct. 8, 1970, is noted for novels that are rustic, poetic, and pagan in their praise of benevolent nature. His early works, reflecting his Mediterranean origins and tastes, include *Colline* (1920; trans. as *Hill of Destiny*, 1929), *Un de Baumugnes* (1929; trans. as *Lovers are Never Losers*, 1931), and *Harvest* (1930; Eng. trans., 1939). Representative of Giono's later works, which he called "chroniques," is *The Hussar on the Roof* (1951; Eng. trans., 1953).

JOSEPH A. REITER

Bibliography: Goodrich, Norma L., *Giono: Master of Fictional Modes* (1973); Redfern, Walter D., *Private World of Jean Guiono* (1967).

Giordano, Luca [johr-dahn'-oh]

Luca Giordano, b. Oct. 18, 1632, d. Jan. 3, 1705, was a Neapolitan baroque painter whose prolific output—at least 5,000 oil paintings—earned him the nickname "Luca fa presto" (Luke the speedy). He probably studied first in Naples with his father, Antonio Giodano, a copyist, and with Jusepe de RIBERA. At the age of 13 he went to Rome where he became an assistant to Pietro da CORTONA. The influence of many painters, including Paolo VERONESE and Cortona, is evident in his work. Among Giordano's many fresco commissions were the ceiling in the ballroom of the Medici-Riccardi Palace in Florence (1682–83), the ceilings in the ESCORIAL in Spain (after 1692), and the ceiling of the Certosa de San Martino in Naples (1704). Other Neapolitan painters of the late 17th and 18th centuries, including Giovanni Battista Tiepolo (see TIEPOLO family), were influenced by Giodano's light colors and animated style.

TANIA M. BAYARD

Bibliography: Waterhouse, Ellis K., *Italian Baroque Painting*, 2d ed. (1969); Wittkower, Rudolf, *Art and Architecture in Italy: 1600–1750*, 3d ed. (1973).

Giordano, Umberto

Umberto Giordano, b. Aug. 27, 1867, d. Nov. 12, 1948, was an Italian composer of VERISMO operas. Son of a poor artisan, he studied at Naples Conservatory, where he wrote instrumental works and his first opera. Encouraged by the publisher Sonzogno, Giordano achieved his first success, *Mala vita* (1892), which identified him with the new school of blood-and-thunder melodrama. His fourth opera, *Andrea Chenier* (1896), was a triumph, and on it his fame largely rests. Giordano's subsequent *Fedora* (1898) is his only other opera that is performed with any frequency, but among the total of 12, *Siberia* (1903) and *La Cena della Beffe* (1924) bear mentioning.

JOHN W. BARKER

Giorgione [johr-john'-ay]

The Italian painter Giorgione, b. Castelfranco, Veneto, *c.*1477, played a pivotal role in the development of the High Renaissance in early-16th-century Venetian painting. Little is known of his career, however, and few of his paintings have been authenticated. He probably received some training in Venice in the 1490s with Gentile and Giovanni Bellini (see BELLINI family). According to Giorgio Vasari, Giorgione soon surpassed those masters and began to imitate the coloring and hazy modeling (*sfumato*) of LEONARDO DA VINCI. In 1508 he worked on frescoes on the facade of the Fondaco dei Tedeschi and on a group portrait of the Council of Ten in Venice (now lost). It can be inferred from 16th-century descriptions of Venetian collections that Giorgione also executed commissions for numerous private patrons. He died of the plague in September or October 1510.

Our knowledge of Giorgione's works and reputation comes from the 16th-century writers Marcantonio Michiel, Vasari, Ludovico Dolce, and Paolo Pino and from the 17th-century writers Carlo Ridolfi and Marco Boschini. Based on Michiel and early sources, modern scholars are restrictive and generally unanimous in accepting as Giorgione's the following works: the *Castelfranco Madonna* (*c.*1500; cathedral, Castelfranco, Veneto); *Judith* (*c.*1504; Hermitage, Leningrad); *Portrait of a Youth* (Staatliche Museum, Berlin); *The Tempest* (*c.*1503; Accademia, Venice); *Venus*, finished by TITIAN (*c.*1507;

Giorgione's The Tempest *(c.1503) has been celebrated for the mysterious, sensual associations of its unidentified subject. The painting, one of the few unquestioned works of Giorgione, was commissioned by Gabriele Vendramin, the young scion of one of the wealthiest aristocratic families in 16th-century Venice.*

Gemäldegalerie, Dresden, East Germany); *Portrait of a Young Woman* (1506; Kunsthistorisches Museum, Vienna); and *The Three Philosophers,* finished by SEBASTIANO DEL PIOMBO (Kunsthistorisches Museum, Vienna). This group of paintings has established a sense of Giorgione's style against which numerous other paintings attributed to him have been measured. Strongly argued attributions include *Self Portrait of David* (Herzog Anton-Ulrich Museum, Brunswick, West Germany); *Christ Carrying the Cross* (Isabella Stewart Gardner Museum, Boston); *The Knight of Malta* (Uffizi Gallery, Florence); *Portrait of a Man* (Fine Arts Gallery, San Diego, Calif.); *Portrait of an Old Woman* (Accademia, Venice); and *Adoration of the Shepherds* (National Gallery, Washington, D.C.). A further group of paintings that comprises *Pastoral Concert* (Louvre, Paris); *The Concert* (Pitti Palace, Florence); *St. George* (Cini Collection, Venice); and *Christ Carrying the Cross* (Scuola di San Rocco, Venice) are regarded by some as the work of Giorgione but are sometimes attributed to the young Titian.

In Vassari's view, Giorgione introduced the "modern manner," or High Renaissance, in Venetian painting. This view is based not only on his style, subject matter, and type of work but also on his personality as an artist.

Giorgione was a musician and poet as well as a painter, and he moved in the most cultivated circles of Venice. Venetian poetry was then dominated by the revival of the Arcadian poets, and his painting deals with subjects also treated by contemporary writers such as Jacopo Sannazaro, Ludovico Ariosto, and Pietro Bembo. Although he painted large-scale public commissions, his paintings primarily were small-scale easel pictures done for cultivated private patrons. While history or narrative painting was the Renaissance artist's major concern, Giorgione produced nonnarrative "mood scenes" such as *The Tempest* or *The Pastoral Concert*, the subjects of which elude easy and precise identification. Breaking with the linear contours and closed compositions of the Bellinis, he developed open forms with soft contours defined by warm light, creating a subtle balance between the highlights and transparent shadows. Giorgione's influence on his contemporaries was profound, particularly on Titian, who collaborated with him in the early years and finished one or more of his paintings. Titian mastered Giorgione's innovations and developed them throughout his long career. Because Giorgione diminished the importance of subject matter and emphasized the purely expressive content of his paintings, recent critics have claimed that he anticipated much of modern art.

MILES CHAPPEL

Bibliography: Baldass, Ludwig von, *Giorgione,* trans. by J. Maxwell Brownjohn (1965); Coletti, Luigi, *All the Paintings of Giorgione* (1962); Pignatti, Terisio, *Giorgione,* trans. by Clovis Whitfield (1971); Vasari, Giorgio, *The Lives of the Painters, Sculptors and Architects,* trans. by William Gaunt (1908; repr. 1963); Zampetti, Pietro, *The Complete Paintings of Giorgione* (1968).

Giotto di Bondone [joht'-toh dee bohn-doh'-nay]

The leading Florentine painter of his generation, Giotto di Bondone, b. *c.*1267, d. Jan. 8, 1337, created a revolution in painting that set Italian Renaissance art on the course it would follow for centuries. Giotto broke free of the flat, ethereal Byzantine manner of his Italian predecessors by painting convincing human figures with the semblance of weighty pieces of sculpture placed within a convincing illusion of space. Giotto dramatized religious narratives with a keen comprehension of human behavior in a way that later artists seldom equaled or surpassed.

Little of Giotto's career has been documented. A late tradition claims that he was trained by his most famous Florentine predecessor, CIMABUE. As noted in Dante's *Purgatorio* in the early 14th century, Giotto's reputation soon surpassed Cimabue's. It is possible that more fundamental influences on Giotto's style were the works of Pietro CAVALLINI in Rome and the sculptures of Nicola and Giovanni PISANO.

Giotto's relationship with the Master of the St. Francis cycle and the Isaac Master, who painted frescoes in the church of San Francesco in Assisi, has aroused considerable debate among specialists. Despite some similarities in style, most critics no longer believe that Giotto and either of these Masters are the same person. In Giotto's lifetime his most famous work was the mosaic *Navicella* (*c.*1300; Saint Peter's, Rome), which is now all but destroyed.

The iconography of Giotto's Betrayal *(c.1305), from his fresco cycle in the Arena Chapel, Padua, follows a typical medieval pattern. The artist, however, has introduced a kind of psychology of relationships in his representation of human facial and bodily movement.*

Giotto's major extant work and the touchstone of his artistic personality is found in Padua, where he frescoed (*c.*1305) almost the entire inner surface of the Arena Chapel for the wealthy Enrico Scrovegni. At the bottom of a depiction of the Last Judgment covering the entrance wall, Scrovegni is shown presenting the chapel, in the form of a model, to the Virgin. On the other walls, three ranges of paintings narrate the life of the Virgin and of Christ. In each incident Giotto, like a skilled stage director, arranges his "actors" across the surface of each scene and within a shallow stagelike space so that the drama attains a climactic visual focus. In the well-known scene of the Lamentation, somber, blocklike figures surround the body of Christ within the space while all glances and gestures and even the diagonal line of the hill draw our eyes to Mary's embrace of her dead son.

Giotto's works in Florence include the *Ognissanti Madonna* (*c.*1310; Uffizi), a large wooden panel painting. In the 1320s he also painted frescoes in the chapels of the Bardi and Peruzzi families in the church of Santa Croce. These later frescoes have a broader format than his earlier Paduan paintings.

Giotto's fame also led to work for the king of Naples between 1328 and 1334; nothing remains of his work there. In 1334 he was made director of public works for Florence and designed the cathedral's bell tower *(campanile).* Giotto influenced almost all Florentine painters in the first half of the 14th century. MASACCIO in the early 15th and MICHELANGELO in the early 16th century are the true heirs to his style of weighty figures and dramatic narration.

THOMAS BUSER

Bibliography: Cole, Bruce, *Giotto and Florentine Painting: 1280-1375* (1976); Eimerl, Sarel, *The World of Giotto* (1967); Schneider, Laurie, ed., *Giotto in Perspective* (1974); Smart, Alastair, *The Assisi Problem and the Art of Giotto* (1971); Stubblebine, James, ed., *Giotto: The Arena Chapel Frescoes* (1969); White, John, *Art and Architecture in Italy: 1250-1400* (1966).

See also: FRESCO PAINTING; ITALIAN ART AND ARCHITECTURE; RENAISSANCE ART AND ARCHITECTURE.

Giovanni, Nikki [joh-vah'-nee]

Nikki Giovanni, b. July 6, 1943, is an American poet known for her exploration of the new attitudes toward black consciousness that became current in the 1960s. Some of her poems are portraits of individuals, such as "Aretha Franklin" and "Angela Davis" (from *Black Feeling/Black Talk/Black Judgment,* 1970) or those in her later volume, *The Women and the Men* (1975). Among her other works are an autobiography, *Gemini* (1971), and *A Poetic Equation: Conversations between Nikki Giovanni and Margaret Walker* (1974).

Bibliography: Baldwin, James, and Giovanni, Nikki, *A Dialogue* (1973).

Giovanni da Montecorvino

Giovanni da Montecorvino, 1247–1328, was an Italian Franciscan friar who founded the earliest Roman Catholic missions in India and China. After missionary work in Armenia and Persia, he was commissioned (1289) by Pope Nicholas IV to travel east carrying papal letters to the rulers of the East. Setting out from Persia in 1291, he went to India, where he stayed a year, and reached the Mongol court in Peking, China, in 1294. Working mainly alone, he made numerous converts and translated the New Testament into Uighur. In 1307, Pope Clement V named him archbishop of Peking and patriarch of the Orient. Although he never returned to the West, Montecorvino's letters record his experiences in the East.

Bibliography: Dawson, Christopher, ed., *The Mongol Mission* (1955).

Giovanni di Paolo

Giovanni di Paolo, baptized Nov. 19, 1403, d. between January and Mar. 27, 1482, was an eclectic yet distinctive Sienese painter whose special gift for depicting narratives is evident both in his panel paintings and in illuminated manuscripts. Many fragments of the altarpieces he painted from 1426 on for churches in Siena are now dispersed in various European and American collections. Giovanni borrowed artistic ideas from his Sienese contemporary, SASSETTA, as well as from such 15th-century Florentine masters as LORENZO MONACO, Fra ANGELICO, and DONATELLO. He was indifferent, however, to his Florentine contemporaries' preoccupation with perspective. Instead, the Sienese painter created fantastic, seemingly endless vistas that were uniquely his own, such as that in *St. John Entering the Wilderness* (n.d.; Art Institute of Chicago).

Among the other influences pervasive in Giovanni's work are the richly decorated but naturalistically detailed style of GENTILE DA FABRIANO, who was active in Florence in the 1420s, and the art of Giovanni's 14th-century Sienese predecessors, DUCCIO DI BUONINSEGUA, Simone MARTINI, and the LORENZETTI family. Giovanni's *Purification of the Virgin* (1447–49; Pinacoteca, Siena) resembles a painting of the same subject by Ambrogio Lorenzetti more than a hundred years earlier (1342; Uffizi Gallery, Florence). Here, as throughout his work, however, the style is unmistakably Giovanni's: decorative, sometimes even dainty, but also agitated and expressionistic to a degree unparalleled in his sources. EDITH W. KIRSCH

Bibliography: Brieger, Peter, et al., *Illuminated Manuscripts of the Divine Comedy,* 2 vols. (1969); Os, H. W. van, "Giovanni di Paolo's *Pizzicaiuolo Altarpiece,*" *Art Bulletin,* Summer 1971; Pope-Hennessy, John, *Giovanni di Paolo* (1937).

Gippius, Zinaida Nikolayevna: see HIPPIUS, ZINAIDA NIKOLAYEVNA.

giraffe [juh-raf']

The giraffe, *Giraffa camelopardalis,* family Giraffidae, order Artiodactyla, is the tallest of all animals, as much as 5.5 m (18 ft) high. A series of valves in the vessels of the vascular system ensures a blood supply to the head. The shoulder height may be up to 3.7 m (12 ft), and the weight 1,400 kg (3,000 lb). There are usually three skin-covered horns, two on top of the head and one between the eyes. Sometimes an additional pair of hornlike knobs is also present on the back of the head. Patterns and shades of dark patches on the tawny coat,

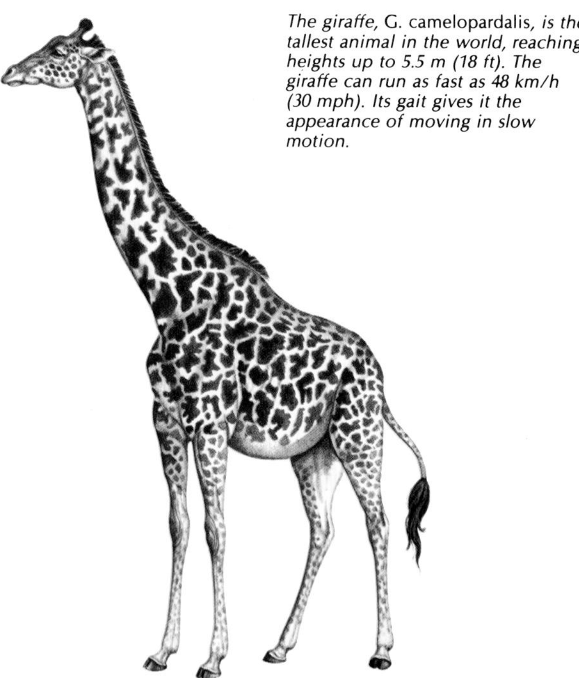

The giraffe, G. camelopardalis, *is the tallest animal in the world, reaching heights up to 5.5 m (18 ft). The giraffe can run as fast as 48 km/h (30 mph). Its gait gives it the appearance of moving in slow motion.*

which help conceal the animals when they stand in the shade of trees, vary among the subspecies. The long tongue is used for plucking leaves from trees. Giraffes live on tree-dotted grasslands south of the Sahara in Africa. Their chief foods are acacia and mimosa leaves. When startled, a giraffe can gallop up to 48 km/h (30 mph) for a moderate distance. The female gives birth to a single young, rarely twins. The life-span is from 15 to 20 years. EVERETT SENTMAN

Bibliography: Dagg, Anne I., and Foster, J. Bristol, *The Giraffe: Its Biology, Behavior and Ecology* (1976).

Giralda [hee-rahl'-dah]

The Giralda, the bell tower of the Cathedral of Seville, Spain, is one of the finest examples of Moorish tower architecture. Erected (1184–96) as the minaret of the mosque (destroyed) of Seville, the simple square tower (60 m/197 ft high) was surmounted in 1568 by an ornate Renaissance cupola, designed by Hernan Ruize, which houses the cathedral bell. The name is derived from the weathervane, or *giraldillo,* that graces the top of the structure in the form of a female figure representing Faith. The total height of the tower, including cupola and weathervane, is 97 m (320 ft).

Girard, Stephen [jur-ahrd']

Stephen Girard, b. May 20, 1750, d. Dec. 26, 1831, an American businessman and banker, began his career as a merchant seaman and eventually owned a fleet of ships. In 1812 he established the Bank of Stephen Girard and in 1813 underwrote the sale of government war bonds. He played a key role in setting up the Second Bank of the United States in 1816, underwriting most of its capital stock. When he died, he was worth about $7 million. Most of his fortune went to establish Girard College in Philadelphia, Pa., a preparatory school for boys that opened in 1848.

Bibliography: Minnegarde, Meade, *Certain Rich Men* (1970).

Girardon, François [zhee-rahr-dohn']

The French sculptor François Girardon, b. Mar. 17, 1628, d. Sept. 1, 1715, was a key figure in the classical movement that dominated 17th-century French art. The powerful patronage of the chancellor of France, Pierra Séguier, enabled him to study in Rome, and then in Paris under François Anguier (see ANGUIER BROTHERS). In 1657 he was admitted to the French Academy of Painting and Sculpture, which under the autocratic leadership of Charles LE BRUN had become the supreme arbiter of artistic taste in France. As he rose through the ranks of the Academy, holding successively the posts of professor (1659), rector (1674), and chancellor (1695), Girardon made significant contributions to Le Brun's aesthetic program, which stressed the primacy of reason and the faithful emulation of classical models. After collaborating with Le Brun in decorating the Louvre (1663-71) and the Versailles gardens (1666-75), he executed on his own the tomb of Cardinal Richelieu (1675-94; Chapel of the Sorbonne, Paris), a three-figure composition of classical formalism. Thereafter he received many royal commissions, including his bronze equestrian statue of *Louis XIV* (1683-99; destroyed 1792) and his famous *Rape of Proserpina* (1677-99), which was a baroque criticism of Giovanni da BOLOGNA's Mannerist sculpture, the *Rape of the Sabine Women*. Girardon died on the same day as Louis XIV, in whose service he had created much of his oeuvre.

NANETTE SALOMON

Bibliography: Blunt, Anthony, *Art and Architecture in France, 1500-1700*, 2d ed. (1970).

Giraud, Henri Honoré [zhee-roh', ahn-ree' ohn-ohr-ay']

The French general Henri Honoré Giraud, b. Jan. 18, 1879, d. March 11, 1949, was cofounder with Gen. Charles DE GAULLE of the French Committee of National Liberation during World War II. After service in World War I, he was a commander in Morocco (1922-25, 1930-36). When Germany invaded France in 1940, Giraud—in command of the sector—was captured. Escaping in 1942, he took part in the Allied invasion of North Africa and became commander in chief of French forces. After the assassination (December 1942) of Admiral Jean François DARLAN, he also became French high commissioner in Africa. Although he linked his administration with de Gaulle's Free French movement in the French Committee, formed in June 1943, differences with de Gaulle forced his retirement in April 1944. Giraud served in the postwar Constituent Assembly in Paris.

Giraudoux, Jean [zhee-roh-doo']

Hippolyte Jean Giraudoux, b. Oct. 29, 1882, d. Jan. 31, 1944, was a French dramatist who wrote 15 plays, most initially staged by the actor-director Louis JOUVET and later internationally acclaimed. Giraudoux was also a prose writer and served France as a diplomat and government official.

Giraudoux was born in the village of Bellac and studied at the École Normale Supérieure. In his youth he traveled extensively—to Germany, Italy, the Balkans, Canada, and the United States, where he spent a year (1906-07) as an instructor at Harvard. Returning to France, he served in World War I, was twice wounded, and became the first writer ever to be awarded the wartime Legion of Honor.

The French writer Jean Giraudoux satirized society in novels, tragedies, and deceptively whimsical dramas. Many of his works use ancient or supernatural backgrounds to introduce the element of fantasy while voicing concern over the absence of morality in human nature.

His worldwide importance rests on such plays as *Amphitryon 38* (1929; Eng. trans., 1938), *Judith* (1931), *Tiger at the Gates* (1935; Eng. adaptation of *La Guerre de Troie n'aura pas lieu*, 1955, by Christopher FRY), *Ondine* (1939; Eng. trans., 1961), and *The Madwoman of Chaillot* (1945; Eng. trans., 1949), which was published and produced posthumously. Giraudoux also wrote five novels, the best known being *My Friend from Limousin* (1922; Eng. trans., 1923) and *Bella* (1926; Eng. trans., 1927), and numerous short stories. He was one of France's outstanding essayists during the interwar years, best known for such literary studies as *Racine* (1930) and such political studies as *Pleins Pouvoirs* (Full Powers, 1939). At the start of World War II he served as minister of information under Premier Édouard Daladier.

Giraudoux's dramatic and narrative style is a rich and inimitable blend of allusive prose, allegory, fantasy, and political and psychological perceptions. He tempered tragic themes with rueful comedy, as though he wished to unite the contrasting qualities of Racine, Molière, Maeterlinck, and Baudelaire.

ALBERT C. BERMEL

Bibliography: Cohen, Robert, *Giraudoux: Three Faces of Destiny* (1968); Lemaître, Georges, *Jean Giraudoux: The Writer and His Work* (1971); LeSage, Laurent, *Jean Giraudoux, His Life and Works* (1959); Mankin, Paul, *Precious Irony: The Theatre of Jean Giraudoux* (1971).

See also: MADWOMAN OF CHAILLOT, THE.

girdle-tailed lizard

The armadillo lizard, Cordylus cataphractus, *is a slow-moving girdle-tailed lizard. Scales on its head, back, and legs protect it from attack.*

Girdle-tailed lizards are any of 23 species constituting the family Cordylidae and are characterized by a spiny tail. The spines consist of the raised, projected keels of large body scales that encircle the tail in successive whorls. In some species the whorls of spiny scales may extend along the body. The spines provide protection: the armadillo lizard, *Cordylus cataphractus,* for example, when attacked in the open, rolls onto its back, curls its tail over its belly, and then clutches it in its mouth, presenting a prickly ball to its enemies.

Girdle-tailed lizards inhabit grasslands, particularly in rocky areas, in southern Africa, but one species, *C. cordylus,* is found as far north as Ethiopia. Four species, the snake lizards, *Chamaesaurus,* have degenerate or missing legs. All members of the family bear living young, usually two to four, and are carnivorous, feeding on insects, worms, and other small invertebrates.

JONATHAN CAMPBELL

See also: GERRHOSAURID.

Girl Scouts of the U.S.A.: see SCOUTING.

Girodet-Trioson, Anne Louis [zhee-roh-day' tree-oh-zohn']

The French painter Anne Louis Girodet-Trioson, b. Jan. 5, 1767, d. Dec. 9, 1824, bridges the neoclassical and romantic traditions (see NEOCLASSICISM, art; ROMANTICISM, art). At the age of 18 he joined the studio of Jacques Louis DAVID and quickly gained the favor of his master. After he won the Prix de Rome in 1789, Girodet-Trioson's career was launched as a painter of classical subjects and of themes drawn from history and from contemporary literature. During the French Revolution, he was forced to flee from Rome to Naples, and then to Venice and Genoa before returning to Paris in 1798. At the Salon of 1798 he exhibited several portraits, including one of *J. B. Belly* (1796–97; Versailles). Girodet, also a skilled illustrator, created drawings for editions of Vergil, Racine, and Chateaubriand. Among his most important paintings are *The Sleep of Endymion* (1793; Louvre, Paris), *Deluge* (1806; Louvre), *Napoleon Receiving the Keys of Vienna* (1808; Versailles), and *The Burial of Atala* (1808; Louvre).

Toward the end of his life Girodet gave more attention to literary pursuits and the writing of poetry than to painting. He was elected to the French Academy of Fine Arts in 1815 and became a chevalier of the Legion of Honor in 1816.

PHILIP GOULD

Bibliography: Friedlaender, Walter, *David to Delacroix* (1963); Levitine, George, *Girodet-Trioson: an Iconographical Survey* (1978); Rosenblum, Robert, *Transformations to Late Eighteenth Century Art* (1967).

Girondists [jir-ahn'-dists]

During the FRENCH REVOLUTION, the Girondists (properly, Girondins) were the deputies who went to the Legislative Assembly and the National Convention from the department of Gironde. Notable orators, these men were prominent as "patriots" in 1791–92 when they advocated war against Austria and expressed the general suspicion of the intentions of King LOUIS XVI. When the Republic was established, however, they sought to moderate the Revolution and to curb the power of Paris—policies that led to their downfall and execution in 1793. By extension, the name *Girondists* is often applied by historians to many others supposedly associated with them. Leaders of the group included Jacques Pierre BRISSOT DE WARVILLE and Jean Marie and Jeanne Manon Philipon ROLAND DE LA PLATIÈRE.

M. J. SYDENHAM

Bibliography: Sydenham, M. J., *The Girondins* (1960).

Giroux, André [zhee-roo']

André Giroux, b. Dec. 10, 1916, a French-Canadian writer who won the Prix Montyon and the Quebec Province Prize for his novel *Au délà des visages* (Beyond Faces, 1948), also won the Governor General's Award for *Malgré tout, la joie* (In Spite of Everything, Joy, 1959). He has written radio scripts and a film script and has contributed articles to *Revue de l'Université Laval.*

Girtin, Thomas [gurt'-in]

Thomas Girtin, b. Feb. 18, 1775, d. Nov. 9, 1802, together with J. M. W. Turner, revolutionized the art of WATERCOLOR and introduced the romantic style in English LANDSCAPE PAINTING. He was apprenticed to Edward Dayes in 1788, and from 1792 he produced topographical scenes for the antiquarian publisher James Moore. In about 1795 he began copying and studying the works of CANALETTO, John Robert Cozens (see COZENS family), Giovanni Battista PIRANESI, and Richard WILSON, which broadened the scope of his art and introduced a greater sense of atmosphere to his landscapes. From 1796 he traveled extensively in England, Scotland, and Wales in search of picturesque scenery, and in 1801–02 he visited Paris. On his return he exhibited an enormous panorama of London, *The Eidometropolis.* Girtin's final works, such as *The White House at Chelsea* (1800; Tate Gallery, London), introduced a personal note of tranquility into landscape painting, and his technique of broad washes and open compositions led the way to the poetic visions of the romantic era.

MALCOLM CORMACK

Bibliography: Girtin, Thomas, and Loshak, David, *The Art of Thomas Girtin* (1954); Hardie, Martin, *Water-colour Painting in Britain*, ed. by Dudley Snelgrove, with Jonathan Mayne and Basil Taylor, vol. 2 (1967).

Girty, Simon [gurt'-ee]

The American frontiersman Simon Girty, b. 1741, d. Feb. 18, 1818, became known as the Great Renegade after transferring allegiance from the patriots to the British during the American Revolution. Girty, who had served (1759–74) as an Indian interpreter at Fort Pitt (Pittsburgh), joined the British at Fort Detroit in 1778. Thereafter he led Indian war parties against the Americans, reputedly encouraging the torture of prisoners. Following the Revolution he promoted Indian attacks on American pioneers in the Ohio country. He settled in Canada when the British abandoned Detroit in 1796.

Bibliography: Boyd, Thomas A., *The White Savage* (1928); Butterfield, C. W., *History of the Girtys* (1890).

Giscard d'Estaing, Valéry [zhees-kahr' des-tan', vah-lay-ree']

Valéry Giscard d'Estaing, president of France from 1974, was defeated in his bid to gain reelection in 1981. He had been criticized for the rates of unemployment and inflation, as well as for his aloof and aristocratic style. Another issue was his acceptance of a gift of diamonds made by Emperor Bokassa of the Central African Empire. It appeared, however, that the main reason for his defeat was the French people's wish for a change of government.

Valéry Giscard d'Estaing, b. Feb. 2, 1926, was president of France from 1974 to 1981. The son of a prominent financier and economist, he attended the École Polytechnique and the École Nationale d'Administration before entering government service in 1952 in the Ministry of Finance. In 1956 he was elected to the National Assembly and in 1959 became secretary of state for finance.

Giscard founded (1962) the pro-Gaullist Independent Republican party (now the Republican party). From 1962 to 1966 he was minister of finance in Charles de Gaulle's coalition cabinet, but he was dropped from the cabinet in 1967. After that year's March election, which returned him to the Assembly, he became more critical of some of de Gaulle's policies. He became minister of finance again in 1969 under de Gaulle's successor, Georges Pompidou.

As president, Giscard moved France away from its policy of self-reliance toward fuller cooperation with other countries and reduced state controls on the economy. He also implemented an intensive nuclear-power program and built up France's independent nuclear deterrent. In the 1981 presidential election he was defeated by his Socialist rival, François MITTERRAND.

K. M. SMOGORZEWSKI

Bibliography: Giscard d'Estaing, Valéry, *French Democracy: The French President Evaluates the France of Today, His Own Administration, and His Hopes and Plans for the Future* (1977).

Giselle: see BALLET.

Gish, Dorothy and Lillian [gish]

The Gish sisters (real name De Guiche) were among the earliest American film stars, especially known for their work in such D. W. GRIFFITH films as *Orphans of the Storm* (1922). Dorothy Gish, b. March 11, 1898, d. June 4, 1968, made occasional talking films, such as *The Cardinal* (1963), but had a

Lillian (left) *and Dorothy* (right) *Gish appear in a scene from one of their most important films,* Orphans of the Storm *(1922). The Gish sisters rose to stardom in silent films directed by D. W. Griffith. Their popularity declined somewhat with the advent of talking films.*

rather desultory career. Lillian Gish, b. Oct. 14, 1896, remained more in the public eye, from her early appearances in *Birth of a Nation* (1914), *Broken Blossoms* (1918), and *Way Down East* (1920) to such sound films as *Duel in the Sun* (1946), *Night of the Hunter* (1955), and *The Comedians* (1967). In her eighties she was still starring in television movies and lecturing in universities. LESLIE HALLIWELL

Bibliography: Gish, Lillian, *Dorothy and Lillian Gish*, ed. by James E. Frasher (1973); Gish, Lillian, and Pinchot, Ann, *Lillian Gish: The Movies, Mr. Griffith and Me* (1969).

Gislebertus [jis-ul-bair'-tuhs]

The 12th-century French sculptor Gislebertus was the leader of an unusually homogenous group of sculptors that carved the figural capitals and the doorway sculpture of the cathedral of Saint Lazarus, at Autun in Burgundy, between about 1125 and 1135. Gislebertus's work represents a high point of Burgundian Romanesque sculpture (see ROMANESQUE ART AND ARCHITECTURE). His signature, *Gislebertus hoc fecit*, is found in the tympanum over the west entrance of the cathedral. The tympanum portrays in high relief the Last Judgment, with heaven and the saved to the left of the central figure of Christ, and hell and the damned to the right. The lintel illustrates the raising of the dead. The figural capitals inside the church display a myriad of subjects, mostly drawn from the Bible and the lives of saints. The sculptural style of Gislebertus and his assistants is marked by a use of extraordinarily delicate linear patterns, an elongation of human body proportions, and the frequent use of fluttering drapery edges. RONALD E. MALMSTROM

Bibliography: Grivot, Denis, and Zarnecki, George, *Gislebertus, Sculptor of Autun* (1961).

Gissing, George Robert [gis'-ing]

George Robert Gissing, b. Nov. 22, 1857, d. Dec. 28, 1903, was an English novelist whose work marks the transition from Victorian melodrama to modern realism. His promising scholarly career was cut short when he was expelled from college and jailed for having stolen to support a prostitute whom he wished to marry and reform. A life of unremitting literary toil followed, often bordering on poverty, recorded in his popular novels *New Grub Street* (1891) and *The Nether World* (1889). From his first book, *Demos* (1886), the subjects of his 22 novels were the poor and the shabby genteel, the world earlier described by Dickens but treated here without Dickens's humor or optimism.

Gissing was influenced by French and Russian novelists, but English Victorian propriety denied him the freedom and honesty of European literary naturalists. He wrote about and lived among the lower classes without being one of them; his own ideal remained the life of classical scholarship and scholarly seclusion evoked in *By the Ionian Sea* (1901) and *The Private Papers of Henry Ryecroft* (1903). PHILIP FLYNN

Bibliography: Collie, Michael, *George Gissing: A Biography* (1977); Korg, Jacob, *George Gissing: A Critical Biography* (1963); Tindall, Gillian, *The Born Exile: George Gissing* (1974).

Gist, Christopher [gist]

Christopher Gist, *c.*1706–1759, an American frontiersman, in 1750–51 became the first white man to carefully explore the Ohio River lands in southern Ohio and northeastern Kentucky. The following winter he explored the area between the Monongahela and Great Kanawha rivers. Gist accompanied George WASHINGTON as a guide on the latter's mission to the Forks of the Ohio in 1753–54 and twice saved his life. He was also the guide on Edward BRADDOCK's ill-fated expedition (1755) against Fort Duquesne.

Gitlow v. New York [git'-loh]

In the case of *Gitlow* v. *New York* (1925) the U.S. Supreme Court announced two major doctrines. First, it held that the guarantee of FREEDOM OF SPEECH of the 1ST AMENDMENT is applicable to the states through the DUE PROCESS clause of the 14TH AMENDMENT. Second, it ruled that a state might validly restrict freedom of speech through statutes prohibiting seditious utterances. Benjamin Gitlow, a leader of the Left Wing Section of the Socialist party, had been convicted of violating New York's criminal anarchy statute by advocating and teaching "the doctrine that organized government should be overthrown by force, violence and unlawful means."

Following a cryptic statement that the Court assumed that "freedom of speech and of the press . . . are among the personal rights and 'liberties' protected by the due process clause of the Fourteenth Amendment from impairment by the states," the opinion by Justice Sanford nevertheless went on to uphold Gitlow's conviction. The state might, asserted Sanford, "suppress the threatened danger in its incipiency" and need not wait until the spark had "burst into a swelling and destructive conflagration." This has been called the "bad tendency test," as opposed to Justice Holmes's "clear and present danger doctrine" enunciated in SCHENCK V. UNITED STATES (1919). ROBERT J. STEAMER

See also: DENNIS V. UNITED STATES.

Giulini, Carlo Maria [joo-lee'-nee]

The Italian conductor Carlo Maria Giulini, b. May 9, 1914, began his career on radio and conducting opera. After graduating (1939) from the Conservatory of Music of Santa Cecilia in Rome, he studied conducting with Bernardino Molinari at the Accademia Musicale. Between 1946 and 1953, he was conductor of the orchestras of Radio Roma and Radio Milano. In 1951 he made his opera debut with *La Traviata* at La Scala, where he became principal conductor (1953–56). Invited by Fritz Reiner in 1955 to conduct the Chicago Symphony, he was principal guest conductor of that orchestra for nine seasons (1969–78). In 1978 he became conductor and music director of the Los Angeles Philharmonic. ELLA A. MALIN

Discography: Beethoven, L. v., *Symphonies Nos. 3, 6–9;* Brahms, J., *Symphonies Nos. 3, 4;* Bruckner, A., *Symphony Nos. 7, 9;* Mahler, G., *Symphonies Nos. 1, 9; Mozart, W. A., Symphonies Nos. 40, 41;* Schubert, F., *Symphony No. 9; Verdi, G., Requiem.*

Giulio Romano [jool'-yoh roh-mah'-noh]

The Italian architect and painter Giulio Romano, b. *c.*1499, d. Nov. 1, 1546, was a follower of RAPHAEL and one of the founders of MANNERISM. He began working in Raphael's workshop as a boy, and by the time of Raphael's death in 1520, he had become one of the leading artists working in Rome. He helped complete several projects begun by Raphael, among them the *Transfiguration* (1517–22) and the *Stanza dell'Incen-*

Giulio Romano, one of Raphael's foremost students, painted The Bath of Cupid and Psyche *(1527–31) for Federigo II Gonzaga of Mantua. Giulio's innovative Mannerist style exhibits a tension that contrasts with the classicism of his teacher. (Palazzo del Te, Mantua, Italy.)*

dio di Borgo (1514–17) in the Vatican. Giulio's work cultivated Raphael's elegance and sophistication and demonstrated the Mannerist tendency to strain and contradict classical principles of style.

In 1524, Federigo II Gonzaga invited Giulio to Mantua, where he dominated the artistic life of the area as an architect and decorator until his death. His masterpiece is the Palazzo del Te (1527–34), designed for Federigo. The building's exterior exhibits the Mannerist characteristics of capriciousness and variety. The interior is equally ingenious: the beehive-shaped *Sala dei Giganti* is completely painted with a scene of Jupiter repulsing an attack of giants and is so designed that visitors to the room feel that they are about to be crushed by the fall of the giants. After Federigo's death in 1540, Giulio continued working in Mantua for Cardinal Ercole Gonzaga. During this final period he began work on the rebuilding of the cathedral in Mantua; he also built (*c.*1544) a Mannerist-style house for himself and his family. THOMAS BUSER

Bibliography: Hartt, Frederick, *Giulio Romano* (1958).

Giunta Pisano [joon'-tah pee-zah'-noh]

Giunta Capitini, called Pisano, a Pisan painter who died between 1255 and 1267, is well known for his painted crucifixes portraying the pathetic, dead Byzantine Christ. In his signed crucifixes, such as the one at San Francesco at Assisi (*c.*1236, now lost) or the later ones (*c.*1250, Museo Civico, Pisa, and San Domenico, Bologna) the gentle posture of Christ is marked by a pronounced sway. This characteristic of Byzantine style also influenced CIMABUE and Coppo di Marcovaldo. ALAN P. DARN

Bibliography: Dewald, Ernest, *Italian Painting 1200–1600* (1961); White, John, *Art and Architecture in Italy, 1250–1400* (1966).

Giurgola, Romaldo [joor'-goh-lah, roh-mahl'-doh]

Romaldo Giurgola, b. Rome, Sept. 2, 1920, is one of the leading American architects. After studying architecture at the University of Rome and at Columbia University (M.S., 1951), he moved to Philadelphia, where he taught (1954–66) at the University of Pennsylvania. There he became a colleague and disciple of Louis Kahn. From 1966 to 1971 he was chairman of the architecture department at Columbia University. The work of his firm, Mitchell/Giurgola Architects, has included revealingly analyzed and effectively articulated educational buildings, such as the University Museum Wing at the University of Pennsylvania (1971), Columbus East High School, Columbus, Ind. (1973), The Student Union in Plattsburgh, N.Y., and the Graduate Studies Center, The American College, Bryn Mawr, Pa. (1980). His work has also included government and commercial buildings, forming an elegant, urban symmetry—for example, The Insurance Company of North America, Philadelphia (1974), Penn Mutual Tower, Philadelphia (1975), the Volvo corporate headquarters, Göteborg, Sweden (1984), and Parliament House, Canberra, Australia (1988), by Mitchell/Giurgola/Thorp architects. C. RAY SMITH

Givenchy, Hubert de: see FASHION DESIGN.

Giza [gee'-zuh]

Giza is the administrative capital of Giza governorate, Egypt. It is located on the west bank of the Nile River opposite CAIRO, to which it is linked by bridges over the islands of Roda and Gezira. The population of Giza is 1,509,600 (1983 est.). A prosperous suburb of Cairo, Giza is noted for its shopping districts, zoological and botanical gardens, and museum of agriculture. Its industrial establishments include cotton textile plants, breweries, and film studios. The University of Cairo (1924), the largest in Egypt, is also located there.

Some 8 km (5 mi) southwest of Giza are the Great SPHINX and the three large PYRAMIDS of Khufu (Cheops), Khafre, and Menkaure, built between 2613 and 2494 BC. One of the Seven Wonders of the Ancient World, these great monuments are a major tourist attraction in Egypt.

gizzard [giz'-urd]

The gizzard is the thick-walled section of the stomach of crocodilians, birds, and some other animals, including earthworms. The walls of the gizzard have heavy layers of muscle, the action of which, with the help of swallowed grit, grinds the food of seed-eating birds. ROBERT J. RAIKOW

Gjellerup, Karl Adolph [yel'-ur-up]

Karl Adolph Gjellerup, b. June 2, 1857, d. Oct. 11, 1919, was a Danish novelist and poet and, with Henrik Pontoppidan, was corecipient of the Nobel Prize for literature in 1917. Although he had a degree in theology, he was an atheist and antitheological writer. Influenced by Wagner and Schiller, Gjellerup used classical and Germanic themes. His works include the novels *En Idealist* (An Idealist, 1878) and *The Pilgrim Kamanita* (1906; Eng. trans., 1911), which reflects his interest in Buddhism and the Orient, and the plays *Brynhild* (1884) and *Wuthorn* (1893).

Gla [glah]

Gla, located 40 km (25 mi) from Thívai (Thebes), Greece, is the site of a Late Bronze Age Mycenaean fortress. Situated between the ancient cities of Thebes and Orchomenos in Boeotia, it is identified by some with Arne, mentioned in Homer's Iliad. Gla occupies a hill that may have been an island on the north edge of an extensive lake that once filled the Copas basin. The walls surround an area about 3 km (2 mi) in circumference—larger than the area inside any other known Mycenaean fortress. The simple palace plan differs from those of other fortresses that have been excavated. Work on the palace may not have been completed, and it appears that no private houses were built. The palace was destroyed by fire and the fortress abandoned at about the same time that other Mycenaean citadels were overwhelmed, toward the end of the Bronze Age (*c.*1200 BC). SINCLAIR HOOD

Bibliography: Vermeule, Emily T., *Greece in the Bronze Age* (1964).

glaciers and glaciation

A glacier is a large mass of mobile, permanent ice formed on land by the consolidation and recrystallization of snowflakes. It may move down a slope by gravity, or spread outward in all directions because of its own thickness. Glaciers may terminate on land, in the ocean, or in a lake. They vary in size

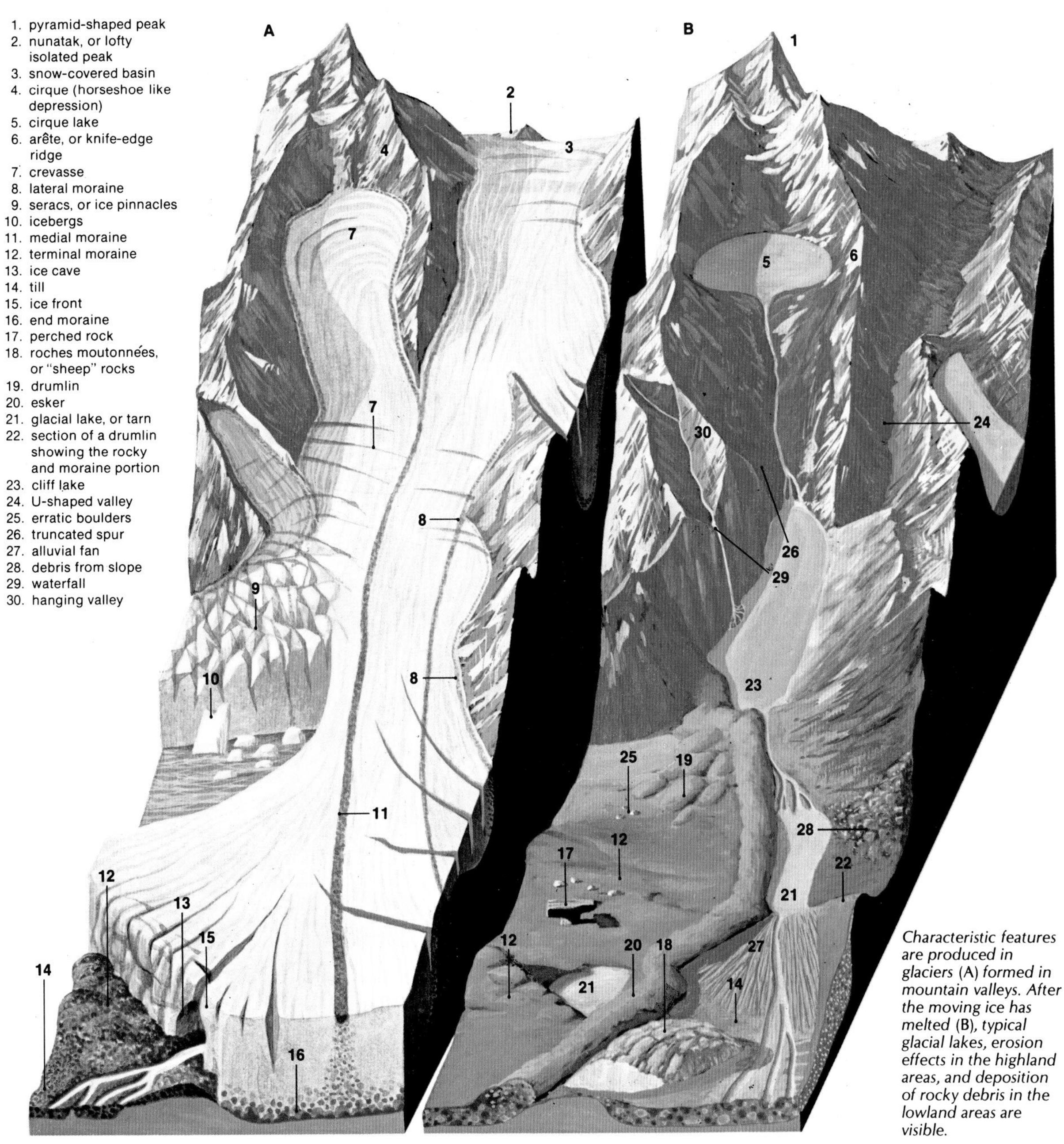

*Characteristic features are produced in glaciers (**A**) formed in mountain valleys. After the moving ice has melted (**B**), typical glacial lakes, erosion effects in the highland areas, and deposition of rocky debris in the lowland areas are visible.*

from small features about 1 km (0.6 mi) long to the great Antarctica ice sheet, which covers 12,500,000 km² (4,826,000 m²). They are found today in all of the great mountain ranges of the world, where they number in the tens of thousands, and on all of the continents except Australia. Glaciers store about 75 percent of the Earth's fresh water.

ICE SHEETS

An ice sheet is a dome-shaped glacier covering an area of more than 50,000 km² (19,300 mi²). It moves outward in all directions and is not greatly impeded by topography. The Antarctic and Greenland ice sheets are the only ones now in existence, but during the Pleistocene Epoch ice sheets covered the northern parts of both North America and Europe. If the area covered is less than 50,000 km², the glacier is called an ice cap.

Today. About 91 percent of the world's glacial ice is locked up in the ANTARCTIC ice sheet, which covers an area about 1½ times as large as the contiguous United States. The greatest thickness of ice measured in the Antarctic ice sheet is 4,300 m (14,000 ft); its average thickness is thought to be about 2,000 m (6,500 ft). Calculation shows that if the Antarctic ice sheet were to melt completely, SEA LEVEL around the world would rise more than 60 m (200 ft), destroying much of the world's wealth.

The lowest air temperature ever recorded anywhere was −88.3° C (−126.9° F) at the Soviet Vostok Station on the Antarctic ice sheet. The mean annual precipitation of snow in the central parts of the ice sheet is less than 5 cm (2 in) (water equivalent), although in some coastal areas it is considerably greater. This central part of the ice sheet is therefore about as arid as most of the great deserts. Estimates of the accumulation and ablation rates for the whole of the ice sheet suggest that it is currently growing. The Earth's crust has been depressed by the great weight of the Antarctic ice sheet; the great depth of the Antarctic continental shelf resulted from this depression.

The GREENLAND ice sheet is smaller and the climate is less rigorous.

Pleistocene. During the PLEISTOCENE EPOCH, large ice sheets, much like the one covering Antarctica today, blanketed the northern parts of North America and Europe (see ICE AGES). These ice sheets advanced and retreated several times during the past few million years, and the climate between some advances was similar to that of the present. The successive ice sheets in North America had areas generally greater than the present day Antarctic ice sheet, and were centered in Canada, from which they moved outward in all directions. The Earth's crust was successively depressed by the weight of the ice, but the crust rebounded to approximately its original position each time the ice retreated. The ice sheets in Europe, although smaller, behaved in the same way as the North American ice sheets. The geology of the glaciated regions differs greatly from that of the non-glaciated areas farther south. During some of the successive glacial advances, sea level was about 100 m (330 ft) lower than now, because a large amount of ocean water was locked up as glacial ice. The last ice sheet, as it moved down from Canada, pushed the climatic zones southward. This is why the bones of musk oxen have been found in Arkansas, caribou bones in Connecticut, and reindeer bones in the Côte d'Azur region of France.

TYPE OF GLACIERS

An ice shelf is an extensive, thick, flat, floating sheet of ice that is attached to the land on one or more sides and terminates in the ocean in a vertical ice cliff, generally 30 m (100 ft) high, from which many of the huge tabular ICEBERGS break off. Ice shelves are found mainly in Antarctica, although some occur in the Arctic. The Ross Ice Shelf in Antarctica is the best known. Nourished by snowfall, land ice, and perhaps by bottom freezing, it moves outward from the coast an average of 30 m/yr (100 ft/yr) and covers an area almost as large as Texas. Although appearing to be flat, it rises gently from the ocean inland, varying in total ice thickness from 100 m (330 ft) near the ocean to more than 700 m (2,300 ft) inland.

An alpine, mountain, or valley glacier flows down a valley. Tens of thousands of them exist at the present time. Fed by snow from one or more CIRQUES and confined by the walls of preexisting stream-cut valleys, they are much longer than they are wide. Some are less than a kilometer long, but the Hubbard Glacier in Yukon Territory and Alaska, one of the longest, is over 100 km (68 mi) in length. Most move less than a meter (3 ft) a day. The longer ones generally have tributaries.

A piedmont glacier is a thick, extensive sheet of ice formed on the lowlands at the foot of mountains when a valley glacier becomes unconfined and expands on leaving its valley. Some of the larger piedmont glaciers are formed by the spreading out and coalescing of two or more valley glaciers. The best known is Alaska's MALASPINA GLACIER, which covers 4,200 km^2 (1,600 mi^2) and is about 600 m (2,000 ft) thick.

Outlet glaciers, found in Greenland, Iceland, and Antarctica, are fed from the margin of an ice sheet or ice cap and move through a pass in a coastal mountain range down into a preexisting valley. Tidewater glaciers, found only in rugged coastal regions of high latitudes, are sources of icebergs.

GLACIER MOVEMENT

It has long been known that glaciers move. Movement has been demonstrated by the invasion of ice onto ground earlier uncovered, by G. J. Hugi's observation that his hut on the Unteraar Glacier in Switzerland moved about a mile downstream between 1827 and 1840, and by the displacement of surface markers on glaciers. The sliding of a glacier over the bedrock beneath it and the internal deformation of the ice are responsible for the movement.

The majority of valley glaciers move only a meter (3 ft) each day. Some valley glaciers in Alaska and elsewhere, called surging glaciers, however, can attain daily speeds of more than 60 m (200 ft). Ice sheets as a whole move much more slowly than valley glaciers.

SURFACE FEATURES

The surface features of a glacier may be large (medial moraines and crevasses) or small (glacier tables and cryoconite holes). A medial MORAINE is a surface ridge of material near the middle of a glacier. It is aligned parallel to the flow lines of the glacier and moves down a valley with it. Medial moraines are formed immediately downstream from the point where the lateral moraines along the sides of two coalescing glaciers unite. A trunk glacier formed from a number of tributary flows will usually have as many medial moraines on it as it has tributary glaciers.

Crevasses, wedge-shaped cracks or fissures in the surface of an ice sheet or glacier, are formed by tensile stresses set up by ice movement. Though sometimes over 20 m (70 ft) wide and hundreds of meters long, they are usually less than 35 m (120 ft) deep. In winter they are often hidden by snow bridges, making travel dangerous.

A glacier table is a large block of stone resting on an ice pedestal, which may rise 3 m (10 ft) or more above the surface of a glacier. A glacier table is formed when the stone is large enough to insulate the ice immediately beneath it from the sun's radiation. The pedestal gets higher as the surface of the glacier is lowered by ABLATION.

If, however, a fragment or a small quantity of dust on the ice does not insulate, but instead conducts heat to the ice beneath it, the material will melt its way down into the glacier and form a cryoconite hole. Such holes are commonly nearly vertical, less than 1 m (3 ft) deep, and a few centimeters or so wide.

GLACIATION

The covering of the land by glacial ice is called glaciation, and the uncovering that results as glaciers retreat is called deglaciation. During either stage the processes of EROSION AND SEDIMENTATION operate to drastically modify the landscape. Glaciers and ice sheets erode by abrasion and quarrying. Abrasion occurs when the fine particles and fragments held at or near the base of a glacier are scraped across the bedrock immediately beneath. Quarrying, or plucking, is the removal by a glacier of blocks of rock from the bedrock over which it moves.

STRIATIONS, glacial polish, and grooves are small features resulting from abrasion. ROCHES MOUTONNÉES are larger features formed by both abrasion and quarrying. The largest topographic features resulting from glacial erosion are the U-shaped valleys formed by the deepening and widening of preexisting river valleys. These valleys, when deglaciated, are characterized by steep, high cliffs, tributary hanging valleys, truncated spurs, waterfalls, and other glacial features. They afford some of the most magnificent and spectacular scenery on earth; Yosemite Valley in California is a classic example. FJORDS are glaciated valleys invaded and drowned by the sea.

Till (see TILL AND TILLITE), loose, unstratified glacial DRIFT, covers millions of square kilometers in North America and Europe and is being deposited now by modern glaciers. Till contains everything from clay-sized particles to large boulders, and varies in general from less than 1 m (3 ft) to more than 150 m (492 ft) in thickness. In New England, till contains so many boulders that it makes farming difficult, but in other regions good soil has developed on it.

When the terminus of a glacier neither advances nor retreats but remains more or less stationary for some time, a ridge of till called an end moraine is deposited along the ice margin. The moraine formed by any kind of glacier at its farthest advance is called a terminal moraine. Some valley glaciers have formed terminal moraines hundreds of meters high. Some of the world's most beautiful lakes are dammed by moraines and occur in glaciated valleys.

In the Alps, Scandinavia, and the Pacific Northwest, glaciers supply great quantities of MELTWATER to the rivers during the dry, warm summer months when there is little rainfall. This water is important for agricultural, industrial, and domestic use. The meltwater streams transport and deposit large quantities of sand and gravel, as well as very fine-grained sediment called rock flour. When the sand and gravel form a long, narrow deposit confined in a valley, a valley train is formed. An outwash plain is formed by the coalescence of sand and gravel deposits from the many streams that issue from the margin of an ice sheet. These deposits frequently bury blocks of ice, which long after burial are melted out, forming a hollow surrounded by sand and gravel. These hollows, called KETTLES, are common on Cape Cod, Mass., and some contain lakes. Glacial sand and gravel deposits are used to build roads and make concrete and are important sources of GROUNDWATER. ROBERT L. NICHOLS

Bibliography: Embleton, Clifford, and King, Cuchlaine A. M., *Glacial and Periglacial Geomorphology,* 2 vols., 2d ed. (1975); Flint, Richard F., *Glacial and Pleistocene Geology* (1957) and *Glacial and Quaternary Geology* (1971); Holmes, Arthur, *Principles of Physical Geology,* 2d ed. (1965); Leet, L. Don, et al., *Physical Geology,* 5th ed. (1978); Strahler, Arthur N., *The Earth Sciences,* 2d ed. (1971); Sugden, D. E., and John, B. S., *Glaciers and Landscape* (1976).

See also: DRUMLIN; ESKER; KAME; VARVED DEPOSIT.

Glacier National Park

Glacier National Park occupies 4,102 km² (1,584 mi²) in northwestern Montana on the southern borders of Alberta and British Columbia, Canada. In 1932 the U.S. park was linked with the adjoining 1,349-km² (521-mi²) Waterton Lakes National Park in Alberta to form the Waterton-Glacier International Peace Park.

Located on the Continental Divide, the park conserves a rugged and beautiful section of the Rocky Mountains. Fifty small glaciers feed hundreds of lakes, rivers, and waterfalls among the region's mountains. Forests of cedar, hemlock, fir, spruce, and pine alternate with stands of larch, aspen, alder, and birch, and a colorful variety of wild flowers grow in the alpine meadows. Among the park's 100 species of animals are grizzly and black bear, elk, mountain goat, cougar, bighorn sheep, and wolverine. Some 1,600 km (1,000 mi) of trails and the 84-km (52-mi) Going-to-the-Sun Highway afford access to the park's interior.

Bibliography: Radlauer, Ruth S., *Glacier National Park* (1977).

Glackens, William [glak'-enz]

Chez Mouquin, painted by William Glackens in 1905, evokes the gaiety and sophistication of Parisian café life. After visiting France, Glackens abandoned his realistic style for a bright and colorful impressionism. (The Art Institute of Chicago.)

A member of the ASHCAN SCHOOL, or The Eight, the American painter William James Glackens, b. Philadelphia, Mar. 13, 1870, d. May 22, 1938, was one of a group of artists whose search for realism challenged the genteel academicism of an earlier generation. Glackens studied at the Pennsylvania Academy of the Fine Arts where Robert HENRI had earned prominence as a teacher. With his friends John SLOAN, George LUKS, and Everett SHINN, Glackens worked as a newspaper artist, reporting the events of the day through illustrations. After traveling to Europe in the mid-1890s, Glackens returned to the United States and settled in New York City, where Robert Henri had gathered other Philadelphia artists. In 1908, in defiance of their rejection by the National Academy, Glackens, Henri, and six other artists participated in a counter-exhibition entitled "Eight Independent Painters," or The Eight, at the Macbeth Gallery in New York.

As a realist, Glackens could not be considered innovative in his methods. His early works, influenced by Henri and Edouard MANET, were painted in dark colors and with robust brushwork. After his travels in France introduced him to impressionism (see IMPRESSIONISM, art), his later paintings used the light, bright palette of Pierre Auguste RENOIR and a fragmented impressionist touch. Although he desired to address his art to contemporary life, he was only briefly involved with Ashcan-school subjects. Glackens was naturally drawn to society, and his most celebrated paintings are of fashionable life. His depictions of festive café scenes, such as *Chez Mouquin* (1905; Art Institute of Chicago) or of the cosmopolitan world of New York's Washington Square, are characteristic of his art. DAVID TATHAM

Bibliography: Brown, Milton W., *American Painting from the Armory Show to the Depression* (1955); City Museum of Saint Louis, *William Glackens in Retrospect* (1966); Glackens, Ira, *William Glackens and the Ashcan Group* (1957).

Gladden, Washington

Solomon Washington Gladden, b. Feb. 11, 1836, d. July 2, 1918, was an American Congregational clergyman and a pioneer in the SOCIAL GOSPEL movement. Educated at Williams College, he served several churches before becoming pastor of the First Congregational Church of Columbus, Ohio, in 1882. From that platform he interpreted the biblical criticism and liberal theology of his day through sermons, lecture tours, and many books. He advocated applying Christian principles to social problems, with particular attention to the rights of labor. His writings include *Social Salvation* (1902) and the hymn "O Master, Let Me Walk with Thee." JOHN F. PIPER, JR.

Bibliography: Handy, Robert T., ed., *The Social Gospel in America, 1870-1920* (1966).

gladiators

In ancient Rome, gladiators—professional combatants drawn from the ranks of prisoners of war, criminals, slaves, and volunteer freedmen—competed as public entertainment at festival games. Such combats were held in Rome as early as 264 BC as part of memorial ceremonies. Although some gladiators fought wild animals, the combats generally featured a pair of human contenders. The gladiators fought in various styles, depending on their background and training. Unless the audience or emperor indicated that he should be spared, a defeated gladiator usually lost his life. Increasingly elaborate, the imperial games sometimes exhibited thousands of pairs of gladiators in a series lasting several months; some private individuals sponsored fights with as many as 100 pairs. Despite their condemnation by many observers, the gladiatorial contests persisted until the early 5th century AD.

Bibliography: Grant, Michael, *Gladiators* (1967).

gladiolus

Gladiolus, *Gladiolus,* is any of several corm-producing flowering plants that belong to the iris family, Iridaceae. They produce swordlike leaves and spikes of funnel-shaped flowers.

Gladiolus species G. byzantinus (left) *and* G. hybrida (right) *can be cross-pollinated to produce a surprisingly colorful crop of hybrids. The flowers are favorites of horticulturists and home gardeners.*

Most species are native to South Africa, but many new varieties and hybrids have been developed. Few other flowers thrive over such a wide geographic area. They are propagated primarily from corms. CHARLES L. WILSON

Gladstone, William Ewart [glad'-stuhn]

William Ewart Gladstone, four times Liberal prime minister of Britain, was an Olympian figure in 19th-century British politics. The son of a Liverpool merchant, he was born on Dec. 29, 1809, and educated at Eton and Oxford. He entered Parliament in 1832 as a Canningite Tory.

An erudite classicist and High Church Anglican given to soul-searching, Gladstone always sought to apply morality to politics. He became (1843) president of the Board of Trade under Sir Robert PEEL and with Peel began to support more liberal positions, including repeal of the CORN LAWS in 1846. After the ensuing split in the Tory party, Gladstone gradually moved into Liberal circles, finding much in common with Richard COBDEN and John BRIGHT. He served as chancellor of the exchequer in Lord ABERDEEN's coalition (1852-55) and by 1859 was ready to assume the same office as a Liberal under Viscount PALMERSTON, continuing tax reforms and securing a commercial treaty with France. By 1865 he had developed liberal views on the rights of nonconformists, disestablishment of the Church of Ireland, and electoral reform. He was well on the way to becoming "the people's William" when the death of Palmerston and resignation of Lord John RUSSELL gave him leadership of the Liberals in 1866.

Gladstone's first and most successful government (1868–74) was marked by disestablishment of the Irish church, the Irish Land Act (to protect the peasants against abuses by their landlords), abolition of religious tests in universities, open competition in the civil service, the Secret Ballot Act, and other reforms. However, a pro-Anglican bias in the Education Act of 1870 contributed to his electoral defeat in 1874.

William Ewart Gladstone, one of the outstanding statesmen of the Victorian age, served as prime minister of Great Britain four times between 1868 and 1894. As leader of the Liberal party, Gladstone campaigned vigorously for tax reforms, an end to Britain's colonial expansion, and the establishment of home rule in Ireland, an issue that split the Liberal party.

Gladstone resigned the Liberal leadership in 1875, but he reentered the political arena to chastise (1876) his Conservative rival Benjamin DISRAELI for indifference to Turkish atrocities in the Balkans. After vigorous electioneering in the Midlothian campaign (1879-80)—the first such political campaign in British history—Gladstone returned to power in 1880. His second government carried (1884) the third REFORM ACT but was discredited by colonial setbacks, especially the failure to relieve Charles George GORDON at Khartoum, and fell in 1885.

In his third, short-lived ministry (1886) Gladstone attempted unsuccessfully to give Ireland home rule (see HOME RULE BILLS). Not always adept in handling colleagues and followers, he now split them on this issue; Joseph CHAMBERLAIN led the defection of the Liberal Unionists, who favored the continuing union of Britain and Ireland. The home rule issue also dominated Gladstone's fourth ministry (1892-94)—a second Home Rule Bill was defeated in 1893—and diverted the Liberals from constructive domestic policies. Gladstone finally resigned in 1894, however, in a dispute over the naval budget, peace and retrenchment remaining his strongest passions.

Gladstone died on May 19, 1898. Though he had failed in two ambitions—abolition of the income tax and settlement of the Irish question—and showed an uncertain touch in foreign and colonial affairs, the "Grand Old Man" had shaped the LIBERAL PARTY of the Victorian era. DONALD SOUTHGATE

Bibliography: Feuchtwanger, E. J., *Gladstone* (1975); Magnus, Sir Philip, *Gladstone* (1954; repr. 1963); Morley, John, *The Life of William Ewart Gladstone*, 3 vols. (1903; repr. 1972).

Glamorgan [gluh-mohr'-guhn]

Glamorgan (also called Glamorganshire) was the most industrialized county in Wales, containing over half the population, until 1974, when the local government of Wales was reorganized. The region is located in the southeastern portion of Wales, bordered on the south by the Bristol Channel. CARDIFF is the former county seat and leading port.

The south of the region is a low, fertile plain where vegetables are grown and stock and dairy cattle are raised. The land gradually rises inland to mountains in the north. Coal resources located there attracted steel and iron manufacturing and tin-plating industries to urban centers including SWANSEA, Caerphilly, and Port Talbot.

After the Normans conquered the region during the late 11th century, they organized it as a lordship. Beginning in the late 18th century Glamorgan became heavily industrialized. The region suffered during the depression of the 1930s because of severe unemployment, but following World War II an industrial revival took place through government planning and aid. In 1974, Glamorgan was divided into the four counties of GWENT, and Mid, South, and West Glamorgan.

gland

A gland is an organ that secretes substances into or out of the body. Glands vary in complexity from the unicellular mucus-secreting goblet cells of the intestine to the multicellular glands of the endocrine system, some of which secrete several HORMONES. There are three general categories of glands: exocrine, endocrine, and mixed.

Exocrine glands discharge their products onto an epithelial surface, either directly or through ducts. Examples of exocrine glands are the sweat, tear, mammary, and salivary glands and glands that provide lubrication for the genitals during sexual intercourse.

Glands of the ENDOCRINE SYSTEM secrete hormones directly into the blood or lymph circulatory systems, which transport these hormones to body tissue. These glands include the pituitary, thyroid, parathyroid, and adrenal glands and the testes and ovaries. The duodenum is also considered an endocrine organ. It secretes several hormones that affect other parts of the digestive system.

An example of a mixed-function gland is the pancreas. Its exocrine secretion, pancreatic juice, contains digestive enzymes and is discharged into the small intestine. Its endocrine secretions, the hormones insulin and glucagon, are secreted directly into the circulatory system for the regulation of carbohydrate and lipid METABOLISM. PETER L. PETRAKIS

glanders [glan'-durz]

An infectious disease, mainly of horses, mules, and donkeys, glanders is caused by the bacterium *Pseudomonas mallei*. The disease is decreasing in incidence and is now absent from North America. Human cases are rare and usually follow the handling of infected horses. The illness may be sudden and feverish, or chronic and recurrent. Ulcers develop in the mucous membranes of the nostrils, and lymph glands enlarge. The skin form of glanders, called farcy, is typified by abscesses beneath the skin, which break down and form ulcers. Untreated human disease is usually fatal; treatment is with streptomycin and sulfonamides. J. MICHAEL S. DIXON, M.D.

Glaser, Donald [glay'-zur]

The American physicist Donald Arthur Glaser, b. Cleveland, Ohio, Sept. 21, 1926, is known for his invention of the BUBBLE CHAMBER (1952), for which he received the 1960 Nobel Prize for physics. This device detects elementary atomic particles by photographing the vapor bubbles they leave when passing through a tank of heavy liquid maintained close to its boiling point. RAYMOND J. SEEGER

Glasgow [glaz'-goh]

Glasgow, the largest city and major port of Scotland, is situated on the River Clyde, in western Scotland, about 32 km (20 mi) inland, in a coal- and iron-mining area. The city has a population of 733,800 (1985 est.). Printing is an important industry, and the city produces ships, heavy machinery, chemicals, textiles, paper products, liquor, and foodstuffs. Glasgow's landmarks include the cathedral (12th–15th century), the Trades House (1794), the Kelvingrove Art Galleries and Museum, the Hunterian Museum, and the Burrell Collection (opened 1983). The University of Glasgow was established in 1451 and the University of Strathclyde in 1964.

About 550, Saint Kentigern (also known as Saint Mungo) reputedly founded a religious settlement on the site. A bridge across the Clyde was completed in 1350, and thereafter the city steadily grew as a market center. As trade with the New World developed, Glasgow rapidly became an important Atlantic port. Later, supplies of U.S. cotton led to the development of a textile industry. When the U.S. Civil War cut off the cotton supply the city developed varied industries. As new factories appeared, nearby residential sections turned into slums. Glasgow became notorious for its dreadful housing conditions in areas such as the Gorbals, but these conditions are being eliminated.

Bibliography: Keating, M., *The City That Refused to Die* (1988).

Glasgow, Ellen

Ellen Glasgow, b. Richmond, Va., Apr. 22, 1874, d. Nov. 21, 1945, was a highly respected novelist whose best work concerns the reshaping of the South after the Civil War. *Barren Ground* (1925), generally considered her finest novel, deals with the survival strategies, both economic and emotional, of a young woman working a depleted farm. Her *Vein of Iron* (1935) was a fictional treatment of life during the Depression. She was an acute observer of manners and could be bitingly satiric, as in *They Stooped to Folly* (1929). Glasgow won a Pulitzer Prize for *In This Our Life* (1941). *The Woman Within* (1954), her posthumously published autobiography, describes her literary ascent and lifelong struggle with deafness.

Bibliography: Raper, J. R., *Without Shelter: The Career of Ellen Glasgow* (1971; repr. 1982); Saunders, C., *Writing the Margins* (1987); Wagner, Linda W., *Ellen Glasgow: Beyond Convention* (1982).

Glasgow, University of

Founded in 1451 on the model of the University of Bologna and reconstituted in 1577, the University of Glasgow (enrollment: 11,800; library: 1,400,000 volumes) is a Scottish coeducational institution. It has faculties of arts, divinity, engineering, law, medicine, veterinary medicine, social science, and science. The library, dating from the 15th century, has about 500 incunabula, and the university's Hunterian Museum (1807) contains collections of coins, fine arts, and minerals.

Glashow, Sheldon

American physicist Sheldon Lee Glashow, b. New York City, Dec. 5, 1932, shared the 1979 Nobel Prize for physics with Abdus Salam and Steven WEINBERG for their work leading to the development of the ELECTROWEAK THEORY. This theory unites electromagnetism and the weak nuclear force, two of the FUNDAMENTAL INTERACTIONS of nature, into a single gauge theory (see UNIFIED FIELD THEORY). Glashow earned a Ph.D. from Harvard University in 1958 and later joined (1966) the faculty of Harvard, where he was named Higgins professor of physics in 1979. In 1983 he moved to the theoretical physics department of Texas A&M University.

glasnost [glahz'-nohst]

Glasnost (Russian for "publicity" or "openness") is a word used by Soviet leader Mikhail GORBACHEV to describe his policy of disclosure. Until Gorbachev came to power in March 1985, the Soviet media had not reported candidly about activities of the government, foreign affairs, disasters, and shortcomings in the Soviet system. Gorbachev introduced a new tolerance for criticism, a broader range of opinions in the press and in the arts, and a more accurate rendering of Soviet history. The new freedom given to the media and to the intelligentsia has led to the rehabilitation and publication of formerly forbidden writers, such as Nikolai Gumilev and Vladimir Nabokov, and suppressed works, such as Boris Pasternak's *Doctor Zhivago* (1958).

Glasnost was an essential first step in the carrying out of Gorbachev's economic and political reforms (PERESTROIKA), encouraging people to contribute to the debate on what kind of reform was needed. This allowed the expression, not only of liberal ideas, but also of conservative and extreme nationalist views. By late 1989 this had resulted in the emergence of nationalist movements in many of the Soviet republics and helped to bring about dramatic changes in the Soviet-dominated countries of Eastern Europe. RONALD GRIGOR SUNY

Glaspell, Susan [glas'-pel]

An American dramatist and novelist, Susan Glaspell, b. Davenport, Iowa, July 1, 1882, d. July 27, 1948, and her husband, George Cram COOK, founded (1915) the PROVINCETOWN PLAYERS in Provincetown, Mass. There they produced their joint one-act satire on psychoanalysis, *Suppressed Desires* (1915), and Glaspell's *Trifles* (1916). Her play *Alison's House* (1930) won the 1931 Pulitzer Prize. Other plays include *Inheritors* and *The Verge* (both 1921).

Bibliography: Waterman, Arthur E., *Susan Glaspell* (1966).

glass

Glass is an amorphous substance made by heating a mixture of such materials as sand, sodium carbonate, and limestone to a temperature of about 1,300° C (2,400° F). It is made continuously in large tanks; powdered raw materials are fed in at one end, and a molten strip or plate of glass emerges at the other end. The glass is heated by oil or gas flames over the melt, or by metal electrodes in the melt.

HISTORY OF GLASSMAKING

Glass was used in Egypt for decorative objects, mainly as a colored glaze on stone or pottery beads, before 3000 BC. The art of making glass was perfected about 1500 BC in Egypt and

In this drawing of a 16th-century glassworks, glass is made in large, clay pots fired in a cone-shaped, wood-fueled furnace. Workers gather molten glass from "glory holes" on the sides of the furnace. A glass vessel is swung in the air to cool it (foreground). *A worker shapes a glass mass on a marver* (center). *A glass vessel is being blown* (rear).

the Near East. GLASSBLOWING, which was probably discovered about 50 BC in Phoenicia, greatly extended the types of objects that could be made of glass. It also made them easier to fabricate and more transparent. The art of glassblowing spread rapidly throughout the Roman Empire, and GLASSWARE became common and relatively inexpensive.

Beginning in the 11th century, several new centers of glassmaking arose in western Europe. In Bohemia, ash from plants (potash, which is high in potassium) was used as a raw material to make a glass with a lower melting point. The most important European center of glassmaking developed near Venice, where new compositions, colors, forming techniques, and artistic skills developed. The Venetians added manganese, in the form of the mineral pyrolucite, to oxidize iron impurities in glass, clarifying the glass and removing the green or brown tint caused by the reduced state of iron. By adding lead, borate, and more soda to glass they increased its working temperature range and were able to make more intricate shapes, thinner blown glass, and finer enamels. They also learned to color the glass with special additives. Venetian glass was preeminent in Europe until the 18th century.

So-called crystal was developed in England in the late 17th century to compete with Venetian *cristallo* glass. Purer raw materials, oxidation of iron, and addition of lead gave a more transparent glass; this transparency, together with the higher index of refraction resulting from the addition of lead, gave sparkle to faceted cut glass. London became an important center of glassmaking at this time.

In the 19th century techniques of glassmaking advanced rapidly. The scientific community's growing need for improved optical glass stimulated the development of manufacturing processes that would strictly control bubbles, stria, refractive index, and color. Michael FARADAY advanced scientific understanding of glass and characterized it as "a solution of different substances, rather than a strong chemical compound," a view that is still valid.

Clay pots heated by a wood fire were used to melt glass until about 1800, when coal and then oil and gas became the preferred fuels. Pot or batch melting of glass is used now only for specialty, laboratory, and some optical glasses.

Production of Flat Glass for Windows. Traditionally, window glass was made by hand by either the crown or cylinder process. In the crown process a gob of glass was blown out and one side of the resulting globe was flattened. A solid iron rod was attached to the flat part and the blowing pipe detached. The globe was then reheated and rotated until it formed a flat disk about 1 m (3 ft) in diameter. Panes of glass were cut from the disk after it was slowly cooled. The part attached to the rod was the "bull's eye," which can still be seen in some older windows. In the cylinder process the blower made a large cylinder that was then split open and flattened. Cylinder glass was also made by machine.

In the early part of the 20th century the Fourcault and Colburn processes for drawing sheet glass directly from the glass melt were developed. When used in conjunction with a continuous glass-melting furnace these processes are capable of producing large quantities of flat glass of reasonable quality. Until recently, plate glass of the highest quality was made by flowing the glass from the furnace through rollers. The rough-surfaced glass is then ground and polished by large automatic machines. This process requires a large capital investment but is economical since it produces large quantities of glass continuously. The ground and polished plate glass is very flat but is more costly than sheet glass that is drawn directly from the melt. The sheet glass surface has a fine fire-polished finish, but shows some surface distortion because of variations in processing conditions as the glass is drawn from the melt.

In the 1950s a new method of making relatively inexpensive flat glass of high quality was developed in England by Alistair Pilkington, of the Pilkington Glass Co. In this float process a continuous strip of glass from the melting furnace floats onto the surface of a molten metal, usually tin, at a carefully controlled temperature. The flat surface of the molten metal gives the glass a smooth surface as it cools. After cooling the glass becomes rigid and can be handled on rollers without damag-

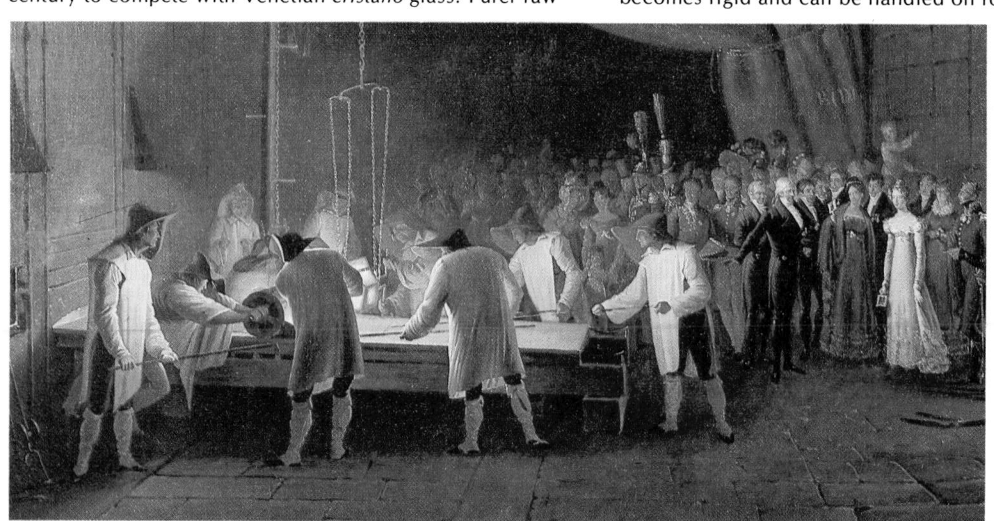

The first factory for producing cast plate glass was established in the late 17th century. In this painting (c.1820), the duchesse de Berry watches as molten glass is poured onto an iron casting table. As the glass cooled, an iron roller pressed it to the desired thickness. Plate glass was used primarily for mirrors.

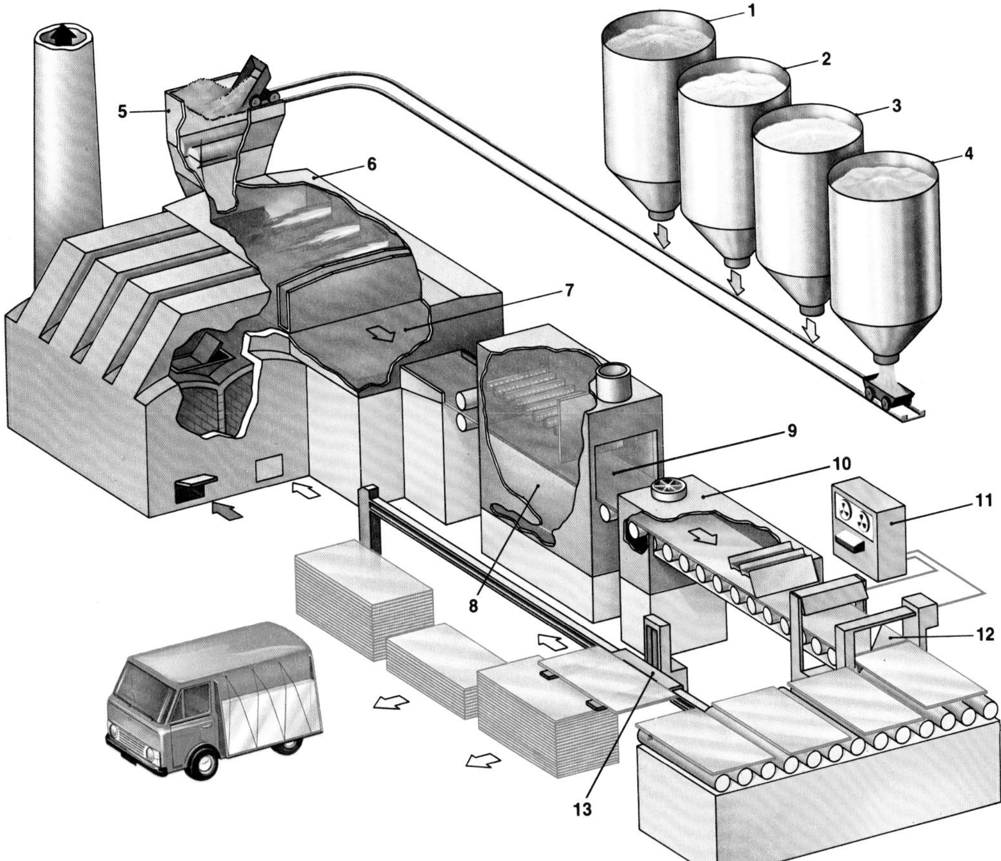

The float glass process is widely used to make flat, distortion-free plate glass. Weighed amounts of glass scrap (1), lime (2), sodium carbonate (3), and silica (4) are blended in a mixing hopper (5) and melted in an oil-fired regeneration furnace (6); high temperatures are attained when contact is made between incoming air (blue arrow) and the hot furnace brick. Molten glass (7) flows between rollers, then floats along the surface of a bath of molten tin (8) under a controlled temperature in the absence of oxygen. As the glass moves along the bath, it is gradually cooled and emerges as a uniformly thick, rigid, flat sheet (9), which is passed through a cooling unit, or annealing lehr (10), to relieve internal stresses. After annealing, a computer (11) controls the subsequent cutting (12) and stacking (13) of specified lengths of glass plate.

ing the surface finish. The glass can be formed at high speeds and is much less expensive to produce than similar quality glass made by grinding and polishing. As a result, many glass manufacturers have converted to the float process, and today most flat glass is made by this process.

Production of Glass for Other Uses. Glass containers such as BOTTLES and jars are made by blowing hot glass into a mold on a continuous machine. Light bulbs are also made by blowing hot glass into a mold, but in this case the glass is fed from the melting furnace as a ribbon, rather than an individual gob of glass, and a special nozzle blows glass from the ribbon into a mold. This high-speed ribbon machine produces more than one light bulb every two seconds.

Glass objects such as plates, tumblers, and vases can be made inexpensively by pressing hot glass in a mold. This pressed glass was popular in the United States in the 19th century because it was cheaper than imported crystal. In this method a gob of hot glass is placed in a metallic mold, and a metallic plunger is forced into the mold to form the glass into the desired shape. Patterns in the mold surface are thus pressed onto the glass. Pressed glass can also be made continuously using automatic feeders for molds on a rotating bed.

TYPES OF GLASS

The most important commercial glasses are the silicates, in which silica (SiO_2) sand is a major constituent. A variety of types of silicate glasses are produced for different uses.

Soda Lime. Because soda-lime glass can be melted at a relatively low temperature, is easy to form, has good chemical durability, and is inexpensive, it accounts for about 90% of all glass produced. A typical commercial soda-lime glass is composed of 72% silica (SiO_2), 15% soda (Na_2O), 5% lime (CaO), 4% magnesia (MgO), 2% alumina (Al_2O_3), and 1% boric oxide (B_2O_3). Also present are impurities in the raw materials and small amounts of special additives, such as antimony oxide to help remove bubbles from the glass melt. Soda-lime glass has a relatively high thermal expansion coefficient of $9.2 \times (10)^{-6}$ per degree Celsius and is thus easily subject to thermal shock. It has a softening temperature of about 700° C (1,292° F). The softening temperature is technically defined as the temperature at which a rod 0.3 m (1 ft) long and 0.76 mm (0.03 in) in diameter elongates 0.04 in (1 cm) per minute. More simply, it is technically defined as the temperature above which the glass can be readily formed and worked. Soda-lime glass is often called soft glass because of this relatively low softening temperature.

Soda-lime glass is used for windows, mirrors, and flat glass of all kinds; for containers such as bottles, jars, and tumblers; for light bulbs; and for many other purposes.

Pyrex. Pyrex (the most common brand of borosilicate glass) was developed at Corning Glass Works to provide thermal and chemical properties superior to those of soda-lime glass while retaining reasonably low melting temperatures (1,300–1,400° C/2,370–2,550° F). This kind of glass contains about 81% SiO_2, 13% B_2O_3, 4% Na_2O, and 2% Al_2O_3. It has a low thermal expansion coefficient of 3.3×10^{-6} per degree Celsius, giving it good resistance to thermal shock. It is more resistant to chemical attack than soda-lime glass because it contains less alkali (sodium). Pyrex glass has a softening point of about 820° C (1,500° F) and is sometimes termed hard glass because its softening point is considerably higher than that of soda-lime glass. Pyrex is more expensive than soda-lime glass because it must be melted at a higher temperature and the borate raw material is relatively expensive.

Pyrex borosilicate is used in cooking and laboratory ware, in automobile headlights, and in other applications requiring superior resistance to thermal shock and greater chemical durability. Pyrex was used for the 200-in (5-m) mirror in the Mount Palomar telescope because of its low thermal expansion coefficient.

Lead Silica. A variety of lead glasses are important as low-melting sealing and solder glasses and for use in lead crystal glassware. A typical sealing glass is composed of 77% SiO_2, 9%

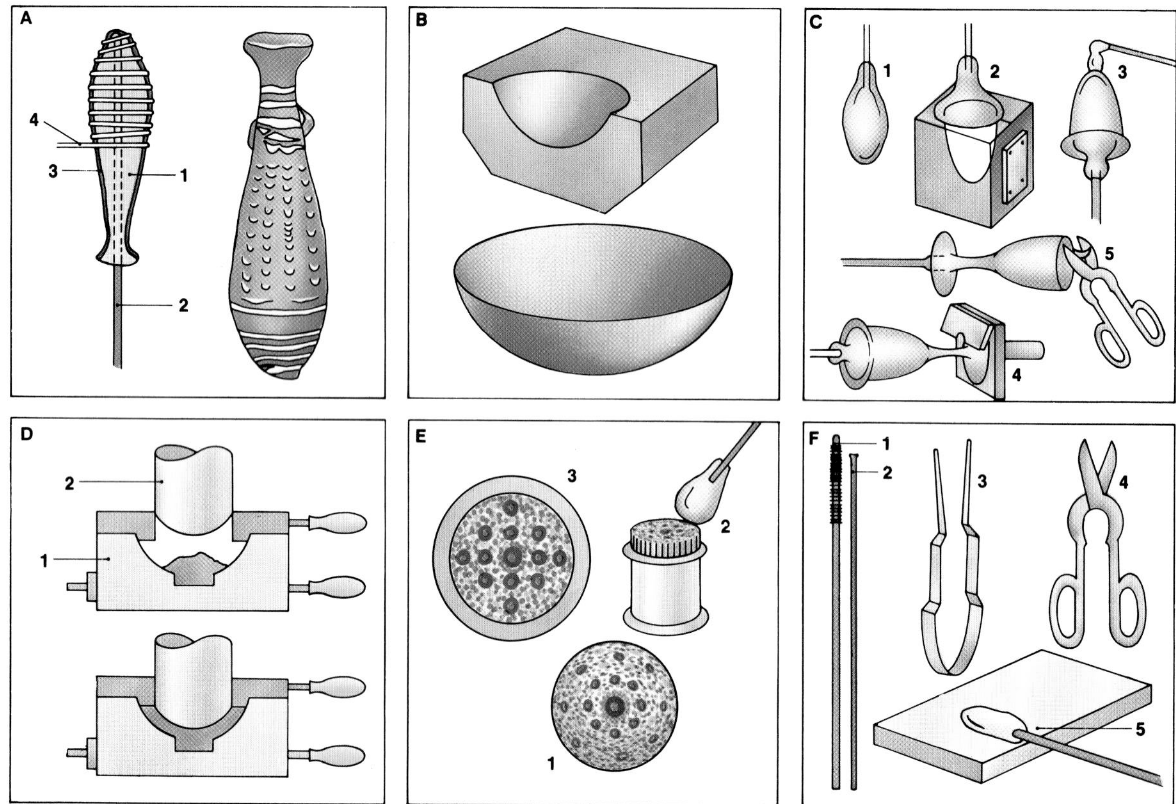

The glass-shaping techniques illustrated here have been in use for centuries, and many are still used in making fine glassware. (A) *The ancient Egyptians used the sand-core method to make glass bottles. The sand core* (1), *supported on a copper or bronze rod* (2), *was dipped in molten glass* (3) *and then wrapped with threads of hot, softened glass* (4). (B) *Pressing molten glass into open molds produces cups, bowls, and dishes.* (C) *A wineglass is made by gathering a mass of molten glass at the end of a long, hollow blowpipe* (1), *shaping the mass by blowing it in a mold* (2), *adding a stem* (3), *shaping the foot* (4), *and trimming the rim* (5). (D) *In the relatively modern technique of press molding, a mass of molten glass is poured into a metal mold* (1), *and a metal plunger* (2) *presses the glass mass into the desired shape.* (E) *A decorative Millefiori paperweight* (1) *is made by filling a cylindrical mold with rods of colored glass* (2) *and incorporating them in a molten glass mass* (3), *which causes the rods to fuse, as well as surrounding them with a clear covering.* (F) *Glassworking tools include a blowpipe* (1) *and a pontil, or punt* (2), *a solid rod that is used to hold the molten glass mass; tongs* (3); *shears* (4); *and a marble slab* (5), *on which softened glass is smoothed.*

Na_2O, 5% K_2O, 8% PbO, and 1% CaO, giving a thermal expansion coefficient of 9.3×10^{-6} per degree Celsius and a softening point of 630° C (1,166° F). Lead glass for fine crystal contains much more lead.

Fused Silica. A glass of special interest is fused silica, which is pure SiO_2. Because the highest melting point of crystalline silica, cristobalite, is 1,710° C (3,110° F), fused silica must be melted at a higher temperature. Few materials are suitable as containers at such high temperatures; graphite and refractory metals such as tungsten, which are used commercially for this purpose, are expensive. Although fused silica is quite costly to produce, it is widely used because of its great purity, optical transparency, high temperature and chemical durability, and resistance to thermal shock—it has a thermal expansion coefficient of 0.5×10^{-6} per degree Celsius.

These properties make fused silica especially appropriate for use as arc tubes in lamps, as crucibles for melting high-purity semiconductors, as optical parts, as containers for high-temperature processing, and, recently, as telescope mirrors. Mirrors of fused silica in the 5-m (200-in) range have been made; they were fabricated in one solid piece at temperatures above 1,800° C (3,272° F).

PROPERTIES OF GLASS

Structure. Glass technology has traditionally defined glass as an inorganic product of fusion that has been cooled to a rigid condition without crystallization (see CRYSTAL). But it is also possible to make glass without cooling it from the molten state; for example, it may be deposited from vapor or from a liquid solution such as sodium silicate in water (water glass). Moreover, organic materials such as polymers and even alcohol can be cooled to a glassy state. Thus it seems better to define glass as an amorphous solid, where solid is defined as a rigid material that does not flow when subjected to moderate forces. A material is amorphous when its molecules have no regularity in their arrangement on a scale larger than a few times the size of the molecular constituents.

To form glass a liquid must be cooled rapidly enough to prevent its crystallization. Thus viscous liquids, which crystallize slowly, are more likely to form glasses than fluid liquids. If cooled fast enough, materials not normally thought of as glassy, such as some metals and ALLOYS, can be made into glasses. Such amorphous metals were first made by "splat cooling," in which a globule of liquid metal is thrown against a rotating metal plate. The liquid is spread into a thin film that cools very rapidly. Amorphous metals have unusual properties and are being studied intensively.

The basic structural element of silicate glasses on the atomic level is a three-dimensional network of silicon-oxygen bonds. The bonds are arranged regularly on a short-range scale (a few atomic distances), but at a longer distance there is no regular pattern to the arrangement of atoms. This random network structure contrasts with the regular long-range arrangement of atoms in crystals (see SILICA AND SILICATE MINERALS).

As modifying oxides, such as those of sodium and calcium (soda and lime), are added to pure silica, the silicon-oxygen network is progressively broken up, leading to the lower viscosities and lower melting and softening temperatures of glasses containing these oxides. Even in these glasses the silicon-oxygen network is still the basic structural element, providing coherence and strength.

Strength. Although the network structure of silicate glass is extremely strong, glass itself is very brittle. Brittle materials fracture more readily than their structure leads one to expect because of tiny flaws or cracks in their surfaces. When glass is loaded with a tensile (pulling) force, the force at the tips of these flaws is multiplied many times, and the flaw or crack grows until it breaks. Glass is also subject to fatigue; that is, it becomes weaker when it is loaded for a period of time, as a result of the reaction of water vapor with the glass.

Glass can be strengthened by a process called tempering. This is done by cooling the surface of the glass more rapidly than the interior. The surface becomes rigid first, and when the interior cools and contracts it pulls on the surface, causing a residual compressive stress. This can be done relatively easily and inexpensively during processing, but it is hard to control and often results in nonuniform surface stress. It is commonly used for strengthening glass windows and doors.

Chemical tempering is another way to strengthen glass by developing a compressive stress in its surface. In this process smaller sodium ions in the glass are replaced by larger potassium ions. This "stuffing" of a larger ion into the glass causes a compressive stress in the glass surface, and is accomplished by treating the glass in a fused potassium salt, such as potassium nitrate, at about 400° C (752° F). This process is more expensive than ordinary tempering by rapid surface cooling, but is more easily controlled and leads to a more uniform stress. It is now used for strengthening eyeglass lenses.

Electrical Conductivity. The electrical conductivity of glass results from the motion of alkali ions, usually sodium, in the glass. These ions are the most mobile because they are the most loosely bonded in the glass structure. Even pure fused silica, which has a concentration of alkali ions of less than one part per million, conducts electricity through the transport of sodium and lithium ions. At room temperature, however, these ions are not very mobile, so glass is a good insulator. At this temperature any electrical conductivity of bulk glass results from surface conductivity. How this surface conductivity is produced remains uncertain, but it probably results from the motions of ions such as sodium in a layer on the glass surface. The surface conductivity is strongly influenced by ambient humidity; in dry air it is low, but in moist air it can be high, especially in glasses containing sodium, such as soda-lime glass (see CONDUCTION, ELECTRIC).

The electrical (or dielectric) breakdown of glass is related to two factors: surface conductivity and strength. Thus a strong glass with low surface conductivity has the highest breakdown strength and makes the best electrical insulator.

Color. Glass can be colored by adding particular compounds: chromates for green, copper and cobalt for blue, copper or selenium for red, and manganese for purple. The common green of bottles results from the addition of oxidized iron, and brown is made by adding a combination of iron and sulfur. Very small metal particles in glass can color it deeply; for instance, the addition of gold produces ruby-colored glass.

Fluorescent glasses have recently been used in lasers and as optical elements for amplifying laser light; one type of fusion reactor being tested involves many fluorescent glass lenses.

The potential optical clarity of fused silica has led to its application as a transmission medium for optical signals in FIBER OPTICS. Glass thus used must have low optical absorption for lengths up to a mile, and fused silica fibers meeting these requirements are now being mass-produced. Impurity and defect levels in such fibers must be very low to prevent optical absorption. These fibers are produced by combining glasses of different refractive indexes (see REFRACTION), carefully controlled by special additions; one glass is used as a core, another as a surface cladding. Optical fibers have begun to replace metallic cables for long-distance signal transmission.

Although glass has found wide technological applications, it is still a valuable artistic and decorative medium. The technical developments in glassblowing and glass forming, in coloring, in clarity, and in flexibility of working temperature have provided the artist with continuing fresh possibilities for expression.

ROBERT H. DOREMUS

Bibliography: Babcock, C. L., *Silicate Glass Technology Methods* (1977); Corning Museum of Glass, *A Survey of Glass Making from Ancient Egypt to the Present,* new ed. (1977); Doremus, Robert H., *Glass Science* (1973); Scholes, S., *Modern Glass Practice,* 7th rev. ed. (1975).

Glass, Carter

Carter Glass, b. Lynchburg, Va., Jan. 4, 1858, d. May 28, 1946, was a U.S. legislator who sponsored some of the most important banking laws of the 20th century. A Virginia Democrat, Glass served in the House of Representatives from 1902 to 1918. In 1913 he wrote and sponsored the law setting up the Federal Reserve System. Glass was Woodrow Wilson's secretary of the treasury (1918–20). As U.S. senator (1920–46) he sponsored several banking acts, among them the GLASS-STEAGALL ACT (1933), which curbed bank speculation and established the FEDERAL DEPOSIT INSURANCE CORPORATION.

Bibliography: Kennedy, Susan, E., *The Banking Crisis of 1933* (1973); Smith R., and Beasley, N., *Carter Glass* (1939; repr. 1972).

Glass, Philip

Philip Glass, b. Baltimore, Md., Jan. 31, 1937, is one of the leading avant-garde composers of his generation. After receiving traditional training at the University of Chicago and the Juilliard School, Glass became interested in synthesizing the musical traditions of East and West. Rhythm—rather than melody, harmony, and thematic development—forms the core of Glass's work, which is often characterized by the repetition of a small number of notes and note cycles. His many compositions include the instrumentals *Music in 5ths* (1969) and *Glassworks* (1982); the operas *Satyagraha* (1980) and *Akhnaten* (1984); and, in collaboration with Robert WILSON, the 4½-hour one-act opera *Einstein on the Beach* (1976) and the fifth act of the massive, multimedia *Civil Wars* (1984).

glass ceramics

A glass ceramic is a GLASS in which fine, uniform crystals are grown by treating with controlled heat, producing higher strength, chemical durability, and electrical resistivity than ordinary glass. Also, glass ceramics can be made with low thermal expansions, giving good resistance to thermal shock. They are important materials for use as cookware, radar domes, electrical insulators, and telescope mirrors.

Glass ceramics are usually made from lithium-aluminum-silicate or magnesium-aluminum-silicate. Titania (TiO_2) or phosphate (P_2O_5) is added to the basic material as a nucleating agent, to initiate the formation of the crystals. To produce a glass ceramic, a glass article is formed by conventional methods. It is then heated so that crystals form and grow throughout the glass. The resultant product is a composite structure of fine crystals held together in a glassy matrix.

Because the crystals scatter light, glass ceramics that contain a high density of crystals are white and opaque, resembling porcelain. Glass ceramics, however, can be produced that are translucent or even transparent, for use as heat-resistant optical materials.

ROBERT H. DOREMUS

Bibliography: McMillan, Peter W., *Glass Ceramics* (1964).

glass harmonica

The story of the glass harmonica, originally called "armonica," begins in the 17th century with tuned musical glasses, the results of centuries of experimenting with vessels of various materials. The actual instrument, however, originated in 1761 with Benjamin Franklin who, intrigued by the fashionable European craze, applied his ingenuity to inventing a more efficient mechanism. Threading a concentric series of glass bowls on a spindle and mounting them in a trough partially filled with water, he rotated them by means of a treadle. Sound was made by touching the moist rims of the rotating glasses with the fingertips; dynamics were controlled both by speed and pressure. The instrument had its virtuosos, notably

Marianne Davies and Marianne Kirchgessner, and composers among whom were Johann Adolf Hasse, Jan Ladislav Dussek, and Wolfgang Amadeus Mozart. After the early decades of the 19th century, the instrument fell into disuse.

ROBERT A. WARNER

Bibliography: King, A. Hyatt, "Musical Glasses," in *The New Grove Dictionary of Music and Musicians,* 6th ed. (1980).

Glass Menagerie, The

The Glass Menagerie (1944) was Tennessee WILLIAMS's first success, and it may be his best play. Characterized by a strong autobiographical element, the play is narrated by Tom Wingfield, who participates in the vignettes that portray his family's failures in a St. Louis tenement. Amanda, his mother, is a former Southern belle who lives in the past while struggling with the poverty that has overtaken her. Laura, his crippled sister, lives in a world of make-believe, symbolized by her collection of glass animals. Tom himself tries to escape reality, through movies. His abortive attempt, at Amanda's insistence, to provide a "gentleman caller" for his sister climaxes the family's frustrations.

MYRON MATLAW

Bibliography: Falk, Signi L., *Tennessee Williams,* 2d ed. (1978).

glass snake

Glass snakes are legless lizards of the genus *Ophisaurus,* family Ahguidae. They are identifiable as lizards by the presence of ear openings and movable eyelids, which snakes lack. The glass snake has the ability to break off its tail near the base; since the tail is about 2/3 of the lizard's total length, the lizard itself appears to break in half. There are 10 species of glass snakes, with 3 native to the United States. The eastern glass snake, *O. ventralis,* is the longest lizard in the United States, reaching about 1 m (3 ft) in length. Glass snakes eat worms, snails, insects, small lizards, and similar prey.

Glass-Steagall Acts

The Glass-Steagall Acts (1932, 1933) were among several pieces of legislation aimed at reforming the U.S. BANKING SYSTEM after its near collapse in the early years of the Great Depression. Both acts were sponsored by Sen. Carter GLASS—who in 1913 had been instrumental in establishing the FEDERAL RESERVE SYSTEM—and Rep. Henry B. Steagall. The 1932 act liberalized the terms under which member banks could borrow from the Federal Reserve. The 1933 act (also known as the Banking Act of 1933) established the FEDERAL DEPOSIT INSURANCE CORPORATION, which guaranteed the savings of bank depositors, separated commercial from investment banking, regulated the interest that banks could pay on time deposits, and increased the power of the Federal Reserve Board. The regulations of the 1933 act, although still in effect in the early 1980s, came increasingly under question by legislators who favored bank deregulation.

glassblowing

Glassblowing is a process in which glass objects are formed by forcing air into a gob of molten GLASS. Discovered in the 1st century BC in the Near East, perhaps in Phoenicia, the process led to a great increase in the manufacture of useful glass articles. Before the invention of glassblowing, glass articles were made by covering a shaped core with a layer or coils of molten glass. Glassblowing was considerably quicker and simpler than this cumbersome process; it also facilitated the manufacture of thin and transparent glass.

In blowing glass a gob of molten glass is gathered on the end of a blowpipe, through which air is blown to form the glass into a hollow sphere. The size, shape, and wall thickness of the glass are controlled by the pressure of the air, the angle at which the pipe is held, and the speed at which the glass cools. The glass is formed into different shapes by the glassblower with simple tools as he or she twirls the pipe on a special bench. During this shaping process the glass is reheated as needed to allow easy forming. Air blown periodically into the object also helps to shape it.

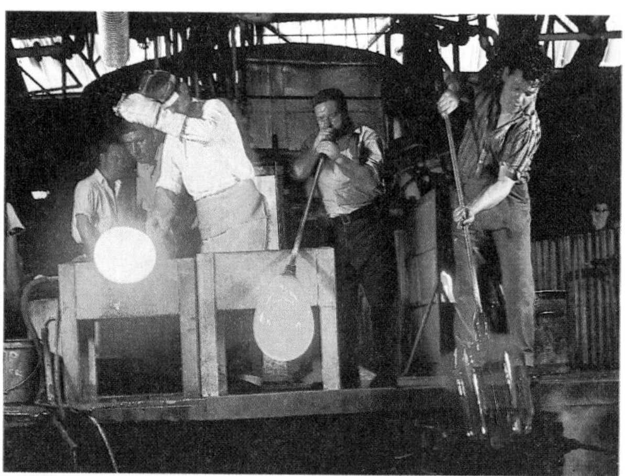

A two-piece iron mold is used for blowing large jars and bottles. A blown-glass blank (left) *is inserted and reblown inside the mold* (center). *Steam prevents contact between the glass and the sides of the mold, and the finished bottle* (right) *has a smooth surface.*

Many glass articles are manufactured continuously by blowing glass. Continuous BOTTLE-making machines and machines for jars and tumblers operate by blowing gobs of glass into a mold. The ribbon machine for making light bulbs is another example, in which glass from the ribbon is blown into molds at rates up to 2,000 bulbs per hour.

ROBERT H. DOREMUS

Bibliography: Douglas, R. W., and Frank, S., *A History of Glassmaking* (1972); Kulasiewicz, Frank, *Glassblowing* (1974); Littleton, Harvey, *Glassblowing: A Search for Form* (1971).

glassfish

Glassfish is the common name for several kinds of fishes characterized by transparent bodies. Most commonly it refers to the popular aquarium fishes of the genus *Chanda,* in the snook family, Centropomidae. Some classifications place them in a family of their own, Chandidae, or with related forms in the family Ambassidae. These glassfishes are found in fresh and brackish waters in southern Asia and grow from 5 to 10 cm (2 to 4 in) long. Their bodies are so transparent that part of the skeleton and some internal organs can be clearly seen. The transparent-bodied icefishes of the family Salangidae are also known as glassfish.

glassware, decorative

Objects made of GLASS have been prized as ornaments and decorative ware from the time of the most ancient civilizations in Mesopotamia to the present. The inherent qualities of glass—lustrousness, beauty, color, and fragility—and its adaptability to numerous forms account for much of this popularity. STAINED GLASS, its most important application in the fine arts, is discussed under that heading elsewhere in the encyclopedia.

Ancient Glass. Because glass objects are fragile, few have survived from ancient times. Among the earliest pieces of decorative glass from Egypt, dated back to 2500 BC, are beads and unguent jars of dark blue glass with colored overlay designs in a zigzag pattern. These jars were not made from blown glass, but were built up around a core of sand. The technique of glass blowing is presumed to have been invented about the 1st century BC by the Phoenicians.

Although some glass was made during the Mycenaean period, most of the examples of glass found in Greece date from about 600 BC on. Much of this glassware resembles the Egyptian prototypes in technique and may have been imported. Hand-blown glass bottles were made in Rome by the late 1st century BC. These bottles and the popular MOSAICS of the period were probably the work of glass blowers from Alexandria, Egypt, and Syria. (Syrian glass workers are known to

By the 18th dynasty, (c.1500 BC), distinctive glassmaking techniques were developed by the Egyptians. The decorations on these Egyptian blue jars (left) *were produced by combing threads of glass into the jars. (Metropolitan Museum of Art, New York City.) A notable example of Roman reticulated glass is the 4th-century Lycurgus Cup. When viewed in reflected light, it is green* (bottom left), *and when viewed in transmitted light, it is red* (bottom right). *(British Museum, London.)*

have traveled as far north as Reims, in France.) A unique type of Roman glass known as *millefiori* ("thousand flowers") consisted of long canes of variously colored glass that were cut into small segments and implanted into glass bowls to form a pattern. Roman CAMEO glass was made by applying a white overlay to blue glass and carving away part of the overlay. Glass that has been buried in the earth for a long time acquires an opalescent quality that is caused by the flaking of the surface. This appearance is considered a "disease," but in very old examples, such as Roman bottles, this rainbowlike surface adds to both its value and appeal.

Islamic Glass. Glass produced in Damascus and Aleppo beginning in the 9th century is generally classified as Islamic glassware. In the Middle East the art of enameling glass (see ENAMEL) was brought to its highest peak, with the glass itself serving merely as a base for the heavily enameled and gilded vases and mosque lamps.

Medieval European Glass. By the late 12th century, glassmaking was a thriving industry in Venice. A type of clear and colorless Venetian glass made with soda was called *cristallo* (crystal). It was sparsely enameled, in contrast to the heavily enameled Islamic products. One of the distinctive types of glass made by the Venetians is *lattimo*, also called *latticino* or *vetro di trina* (lace glass), in which alternate bands of opaque glass are drawn in wave patterns across the clear glass. The Venetians were the first to develop the stems of wine glasses as we know them today, but the stems eventually evolved into overly intricate shapes, known as "wings," that were far from being utilitarian.

During the Middle Ages in northern Europe, glass made with soda was largely superseded by Waldglas, a type of glass made with potash. This glass tended to be yellow, green, or brown, depending on the impurities present in its molten state. Despite Venice's attempt to retain a monopoly on the production of glass, many Venetian glassblowers traveled northward, particularly to the Netherlands and England, thus spreading the Venetian styles and technique. An exception was Germany, where robust shapes were developed that have no resemblance to Venetian glass. Cylindrical shapes of clear glass were enameled with scenes and figures drawn in a primitive manner that were sometimes derided as "peasant-like." Another shape that was developed by the 15th century was a style of goblet called a *rümer* (or *roemer*), which was used for white wines. These goblets had heavily knobbed bases, and after the invention of wheel engraving, the bowls were profusely engraved.

Northern Renaissance Glass. By the 16th century glass was being produced in Silesia and Bohemia. Bohemian bottles, decanters, and goblets achieved an international popularity in the 19th century. They consisted of a clear base, on which designs in deep tones of red, green, and blue were overlaid, with gilding sometimes added as well.

The glass products of the Low Countries reflect both Venetian and German influences, being less flamboyant than the Venetian style and characterized by a refinement of such German shapes as the rümer. The Low Countries also originated the diamond-pointed instruments that were used to engrave glass. (Wheel engraving was later introduced from Germany.)

English and Irish Glass. Most of the early glass factories in England employed Venetian workers, and one house is

Techniques in glassmaking and decorating developed throughout Europe, with Venice as the glassmaking center from the 15th century onward. (Above) *Examples of 16th-century Venetian glass are shown* (left to right): *blue vase with* vetro di trina *decoration; enameled plate; standing cup; and dragon-stem goblet. (Corning Museum of Glass, New York.)* (Center) *This German or Dutch 18th-century drinking glass with enameled decoration is typical of the peasant glassware of the period. (Museum of Fine Arts, Boston.)* (Right) *An enameled blown-glass decanter by William Beilby exemplifies the style of English rococo glass produced during the mid-18th century. (Philadelphia Museum of Art.)*

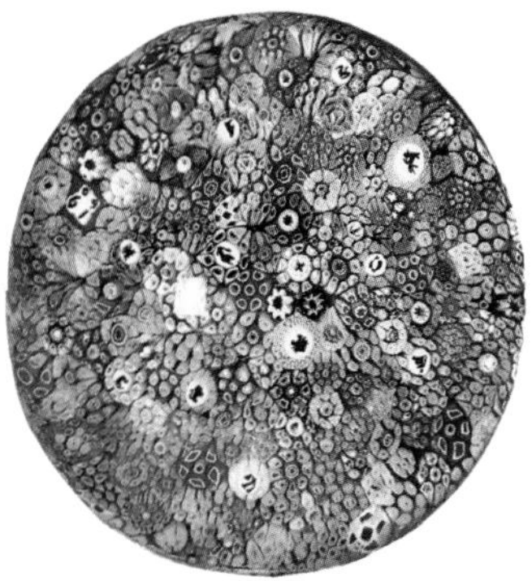

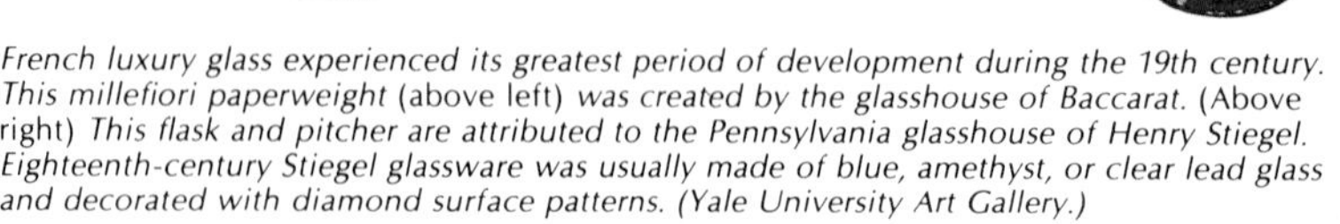

French luxury glass experienced its greatest period of development during the 19th century. This millefiori paperweight (above left) *was created by the glasshouse of Baccarat.* (Above right) *This flask and pitcher are attributed to the Pennsylvania glasshouse of Henry Stiegel. Eighteenth-century Stiegel glassware was usually made of blue, amethyst, or clear lead glass and decorated with diamond surface patterns. (Yale University Art Gallery.)*

known to have sent designs to Venice to be produced there. Until the 18th century, English glass was sent to Holland to be diamond-engraved and diamond-stippled. Some glass may also have been enameled in Holland. A variety of styles were developed for the stems of English wine glasses, including baluster shapes, faceting, opaque and colored twists, and molded pedestals. By the 18th century both English and Irish glass became renowned for their brilliance, which was achieved by the addition of lead to the raw metal. To avoid the government excise tax (first imposed in 1745) that was placed upon prospering glass companies, several Englishmen started glass houses in Dublin, Cork, and Waterford (see WATERFORD GLASS). When this tax was extended to Ireland in the early 1800s, most of the companies closed down. A recent revival of the Irish glass industry has occurred in both Galway and Waterford.

French Glass. Very little is known about the early glass factories in France. By the 19th century, French glass was noted for the quality of its cutting and engraving. Three centers that became famous for their paperweights were Clichy, St. Louis, and Baccarat, which is also renowned for the excellent shapes of its other glass products. In 1875, Emile GALLÉ, the famous French ART NOUVEAU designer, opened a glass house to produce his own creations; he applied a tinted overlay in relief designs in naturalistic shapes on an opaque glass base. The foremost 20th-century designer of the ART DECO style was René LALIQUE who used a heavy, molded glass for many items, including perfume bottles. His lighting fixtures were especially designed for the modernistic interiors of the 1920s.

Swedish Glass. The earliest glassworks in Sweden were established at Kungsholm in 1676 (and closed in 1815). As Venetian workmen were employed at the factory, the Venetian influence is apparent in the modeling of the goblets, wine glasses, and chalices made there. The English influence became dominant at Kosta, Gotëborg, and other glassworks in the 18th century. Beginning in 1917, with assistance from the Swedish Society of Arts and Crafts, the companies at ORREFORS and Kosta began to employ artists in order to raise the quality of their products. Simon Gate and Edward Hald were successful creators of glassware at Orrefors, and Edvin Ollers was the leading designer at Kosta. At the Paris Exposition in 1925 the Grand Prix was awarded to the Orrefors glass works.

American Glass. Although several attempts were made to establish small glassworks in the colonies during the 17th century, the first successful glass factory in America was founded in 1739 by Caspar Wistar in Salem County, N.J. It produced a kind of glassware known as South Jersey-type glass. The factory primarily produced bottles and other utilitarian objects in green, brown, and an odd shade of terra-cotta. Two factories were established by Henry William STIEGEL in Pennsylvania, one at Elizabeth Furnace (1763) and the other at Manheim (1768). Among his creations were amethyst-colored bottles

During the late 19th and early 20th century the Tiffany Glass Company originated the art nouveau style in American glassware. (Above) *The Tiffany lamp combines a leaded glass shade and bronze base.*

(Left) *This engraved Gazelle Bowl (1935) was designed by Sidney Waugh for the Steuben Glass Company.*

that were dip molded and patterned, and cordial bottles in both clear and deep-blue glass that were decorated with colored enamel designs. By the early 19th century, glassworks had been established in Keene, N.H.; East Manchester, Conn. (Pitkin Glass Works); and Frederick, Md. (the New Bremen Glass Manufactory, which was founded by John Frederick Amelung in 1784). A glasshouse was started at Sandwich, Mass. (the Boston and Sandwich Glass Company), in 1825 by Deming Jarves, the inventor of press-molded glass. Sandwich pressed glass was produced in many colors as well as in clear glass. In addition to cup plates, the most widely reproduced items are dolphin candlesticks in yellow. Among the decorative types of glass produced, beginning in the 1880s, were Satin glass, Amberina, Peach Blow, Burmese, and Favrile. Favrile, a glass with a metallic sheen, was the creation of Louis Comfort TIFFANY, who studied under Emile Gallé. The prestigious glass objects of the 20th century from the Steuben Glassworks (see STEUBEN GLASS), which is now operated by the Corning Glass Company, Corning, N.Y., are made of wheel-engraved glass with a deep luster, each individually designed by well-known artists. The Corning Museum of Glass, founded in 1951, has the most comprehensive historical collection in the world.

MARION B. WILSON

Bibliography: Daniel, Dorothy, *Cut and Engraved Glass, 1771-1905* (1950; repr. 1973); Gros-Galliner, Gabriella, *Glass: A Guide for Collectors* (1970); Haynes, Edward B., *Glass Through the Ages*, rev. ed. (1964); Kämpfer, Fritz, and Beyer, Klaus G., *Glass: A World History, The Story of 4000 Years of Fine Glass-Making*, trans. by Edmund Launert (1966); McKearin, Helen and George, *American Glass* (1941); Mariacher, Giovanni, *Glass from Antiquity to the Renaissance* (1970); Neuburg, Frederic, *Ancient Glass* (1962); Polak, Ada B., *Modern Glass* (1962); Schwartz, Marvin D., *Collector's Guide to Antique American Glass* (1969); Weiss, Gustav, *The Book of Glass* (1971).

See also: ANTIQUE COLLECTING; ARCHAEOLOGY; CHANDELIER; EGYPTIAN ART AND ARCHITECTURE; ISLAMIC ART AND ARCHITECTURE; JEWELRY; MESOPOTAMIAN ART AND ARCHITECTURE; PERSIAN ART AND ARCHITECTURE; ROMAN ART.

glassy state

The glassy, or vitreous, state of matter is exhibited by certain inorganic and organic substances. A GLASS appears solid, but its molecules are not arranged in crystalline form and it does not show the well-defined phase changes characteristic of solids. Instead it grows plastic and soft when heated and, on cooling, grows increasingly viscous until the limit of viscosity is reached and it appears solid again. Its molecules are randomly distributed, as in a LIQUID, and a glass may in fact be considered a supercooled liquid. If a glass is kept molten for a long time, crystals may form on its surface—a process called devitrification. The most useful glasses are the inorganic, which generally are transparent, hard, and brittle and have a high shear strength, low thermal expansion, and low electrical and thermal conductivity. Nonflammable and inert to most chemicals, they are useful as containers, windows, lenses, mirrors, insulators, and dielectrics. Their main ingredient is silica, SiO_2; other oxides are added to modify the glass for a particular use. A. F. SCHUCH AND E. R. GRILLY

Bibliography: Doremus, R. H., *Glass Science* (1973).

Glauber, Johann Rudolf [glow'-bur]

The German chemist Johann Rudolf Glauber, b. *c.*1604, d. March 1670, was an inventor of laboratory techniques and equipment, such as bead and flame tests and the distillatory furnace, that were important in the development of modern chemistry. He prepared many new chemicals, such as the salt still known as Glauber's salt; urged the application of chemistry in industry; and wrote widely. NICHOLAS H. CLULEE

glauberite [glow'-bur-yt]

The EVAPORITE mineral glauberite, a sodium and calcium sulfate ($Na_2Ca(SO_4)_2$), occurs sparingly in the deposits left by evaporation of saline lakes. It forms brittle, tabular, and prismatic crystals (monoclinic system) with vitreous luster, pale-yellow or gray color, good basal cleavage, and slightly salty taste. Hardness is 2½–3, streak white, and specific gravity 2.7–2.9. Glauberite also occurs as isolated crystals.

Glauber's salt [glow'-burz]

Glauber's salt is the hydrated form of sodium sulfate. Its chemical formula is $Na_2SO_4{\cdot}10H_2O$. Glauber's salt is used commercially as an inexpensive substitute for SULFURIC ACID, H_2SO_4, as a flux in metallurgy, and as an ingredient in pharmaceuticals, in paper and glass production and textile dyeing and printing, and in standardizing dyes.

glaucoma [glaw-koh'-muh]

Glaucoma is an EYE disease in which the optic nerve is damaged as a result of an imbalance between the production and draining of the watery fluid produced by cells behind the lens of the eye. The relative increase of fluid pressure in the eyeball that can cause such damage varies among individuals. Glaucoma is a major cause of BLINDNESS.

The normal eye continually produces a fluid that flows into the anterior chamber of the eyeball and eventually drains through tiny channels between the cornea and iris. A number of different disease processes can cause these channels to become blocked. The fluid pressure then builds within the eyeball and, over a period of months or years, can damage the optic nerve. This condition, called chronic open-angle glaucoma, is the most common form of the disease; the risk of its onset increases from middle age onwards. No pain is involved, and the loss of peripheral vision is so gradual that it may go unnoticed for a long time.

A less common condition, called acute narrow-angle glaucoma, results from a sudden and complete blockage of the drainage channels due to abnormal eye structure, injury to the eye, certain drugs, or systemic disorders such as diabetes. The risk of its onset also increases after middle age. The onset, sometimes preceded by preliminary attacks, is marked by

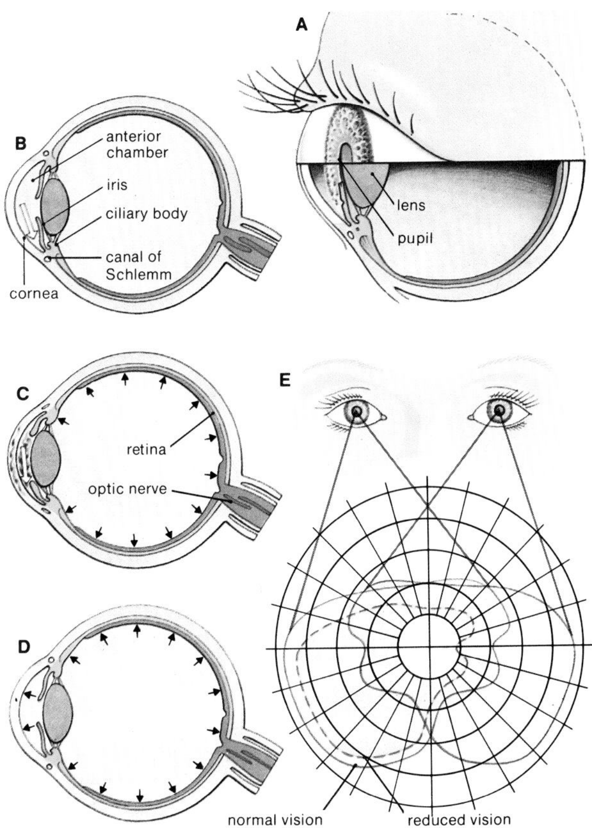

Glaucoma occurs when fluid pressure within the eye (A) *increases. Under normal conditions* (B), *aqueous fluid, which is produced by the ciliary body, flows into the anterior chamber and drains into blood vessels through the canal of Schlemm, located near the angle formed by the cornea and the iris* (arrow). *If the angle is narrow* (C), *the opening of the canal may become obstructed, resulting in acute-angle glaucoma. Pressure builds and is transmitted* (black arrows) *to the retina and the optic nerve. If the angle is wide* (D), *blockage may still occur in part of the drainage system; chronic open-angle glaucoma results, and peripheral vision* (E) *is gradually reduced.*

pain, eye redness, blurred vision, and haziness of the cornea. Only one eye is usually affected at a time, but the other is likely to be affected later. Predisposition to both forms of glaucoma tends to run in families.

The peripheral vision lost in undetected chronic glaucoma cannot be restored. For this reason, regular examinations by an ophthalmologist are recommended for its early detection, especially after the age of 40. Chronic glaucoma is treated by drugs that increase fluid outflow or decrease fluid production; tetrahydrocannabinol, the active agent in marijuana, has also proved useful in reducing pressure within the eye. If drugs do not check the condition, however, surgery may be recommended to open drainage channels. Such surgery is essential following an attack of acute glaucoma, in order to prevent visual impairment. Drug therapies and modern surgical techniques, including the use of laser beams, have shown a high rate of success in treating the disease; the use of ultrasound is also being tested. THOMAS P. MATTINGLY AND MELVIN L. RUBIN

Bibliography: Leychecker, W., and Crick, R. P., *All about Glaucoma* (1981); Portney, G. L., *Glaucoma Guidebook* (1977).

Glaucus [glaw'-kuhs]

In Greek mythology, Glaucus was the name of the following characters: (1) a sea-god who loved SCYLLA before her transformation into a monster; (2) a son of MINOS who as a child fell into a honeypot and was smothered; (3) the father of BELLEROPHON; (4) a brother of the seer LAOCOÖN; and (5) a Trojan ally who exchanged armor with DIOMEDES.

glaze

A glaze is a smooth, glassy coating applied to CERAMIC objects in order to add color and decoration to the surface or to vary its texture. The glaze forms a hard, nonporous surface that is easily cleaned.

Glazes are usually made from powdered glass combined with colored oxides of such elements as cobalt, chrome, manganese, or nickel. The mixture of powders is suspended in water and applied to the ceramic surface by spraying, brushing, or dipping. The glaze is then dried and fixed onto the ceramic surface by firing. During firing, the glass softens and flows over the ceramic surface to a greater or lesser extent, and reacts with the ceramic substrate to form a strong, adherent bond to it. Various components such as alkali oxide, borates, and lead oxide can be added to the glaze to make it soften at a lower temperature, so that it flows more easily during firing and smooths out roughness and defects in the ceramic surface.

If a glaze is applied to a fired ceramic substrate, a second firing is necessary to melt and bond the glaze to the substrate. It is also possible to apply a glaze to an unfired ceramic, and fire both the glaze and substrate together. Two firings make possible a greater range of colors and textures.

The suspension, or slip, in which the glaze is applied to the ceramic surface must have particular properties to ensure that the glaze is easy to apply, does not run as it is drying, and adheres well both when wet and after drying. These slip properties are often obtained by adding a small amount of clay to the suspension, and by controlling the amount of water in the slip and the size of the powder's particles. Organic-surface-active agents (detergents) also can be added to a slip to improve its properties.

Often fine crystals grow in the glaze, making it more translucent or opaque. Crystals also give a dull, or mat, surface finish. The crystals nucleate and grow in the glassy glaze in much the same way as they do in GLASS CERAMICS. Crystal growth can be encouraged by heating the fired glaze for a time at a temperature somewhat below the firing temperature.

Glazes craze, or develop fine cracks, if the thermal expansion of the glaze varies significantly from that of the substrate. Thus the glaze composition must be designed with an expansion coefficient close to that of the substrate. On the other hand, an artist may wish to induce crazing for its different appearance and texture (crackle glaze); the larger the difference in expansion the finer the craze.

Colors in glazes are controlled by adding coloring agents to the glassy components of the glaze. A wide variety of colors is possible, depending upon the agent added, the base composition of the glaze, the color of the substrate, and the state of oxidation in the kiln.

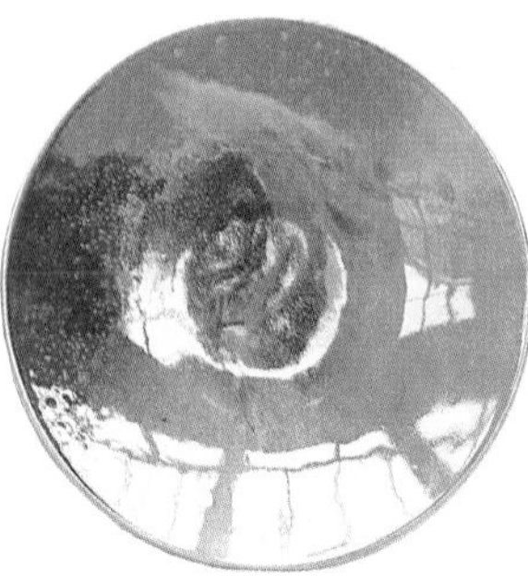

Colors obtained in glazing depend in part on the atmosphere within the kiln. A copper oxide glaze turns blue when fired in an oxidizing atmosphere (as on the base of the vase and at the left side of the plate); in a reducing atmosphere the same glaze becomes a brilliant red.

Special effects in glazes can also be produced. If salt is added to the kiln during firing, the glaze develops a fine orange-peel texture, which can be uniform or spotty depending upon conditions. A glaze that froths during firing gives a rough surface of broken bubbles known as a blister glaze.

ROBERT H. DOREMUS

Bibliography: Chappell, James, *Potter's Complete Book of Clay and Glazes* (1977); Green, David, *Pottery Glazes,* rev. ed. (1973); Hopper, Robin, *The Ceramic Spectrum* (1983); Ruscoe, William, *Glazes for the Potter* (1974); Wood, Nigel, *Oriental Glazes* (1978).

Glazer, Nathan [glayz'-ur]

Nathan Glazer, b. New York City, Feb. 25, 1923, is an American sociologist who specializes in ethnic studies and urban affairs. Glazer graduated from the City College of New York, worked as an editor for *Commentary* magazine, received his Ph.D. from Columbia University, and has been a professor at the University of California and at Harvard University. Much of his writing has been for magazines and deals with contemporary political and social issues.

With David Riesman and Reuel Denney, Glazer wrote *The Lonely Crowd: A Study of the Changing American Character* (1950), dealing with the effects of modern culture on personality. He collaborated with Daniel Patrick Moynihan on *Beyond the Melting Pot* (1963; 2d ed., 1970) and wrote *Affirmative Discrimination* (1976) and *Ethnic Dilemmas, 1964–1982* (1983).

Glazkov, Yury Nikolayevich [glaz'-kawf, yoo'-ree nee-koh-ly'-e-vich]

The Soviet cosmonaut Yury Nikolayevich Glazkov, b. Oct. 2, 1939, served as flight engineer on the brief SOYUZ *24* flight in early 1977. Glazkov, an air force engineering officer, joined the cosmonaut team in 1965. Along with crew commander Viktor GORBATKO, he served on the backup crew for the aborted *Soyuz 23* space flight in October 1976, which failed to link up with the SALYUT *5* space station. Subsequently, Gorbatko and Glazkov were launched on Feb. 7, 1977, on *Soyuz 24,* and spent 16 days aboard the Salyut before closing it down and returning to Earth.

JAMES OBERG

Glazunov, Aleksandr Konstantinovich [glah-zoo'-nawf]

Aleksandr Konstantinovich Glazunov, b. Aug. 10, 1865, d. Mar. 21, 1936, was a distinguished Russian composer of orchestral, chamber, and piano music. He was a child prodigy whose first teacher was his mother, a pianist. At age 15 he became a pupil of Rimsky-Korsakov, and at age 17 his first symphony was performed, conducted by Mily Balakirev. He became a masterly writer for the orchestra, composing a variety of works in the medium. Glazunov taught at the St. Petersburg Conservatory from 1899, and was its director from 1905 until 1928; he then left Russia and settled in Paris, where he died. His works include several symphonic poems; nine symphonies, the last unfinished; string quartets; two piano concertos; and solo piano, organ, and vocal works. With Rimsky-Korsakov he completed Borodin's unfinished opera *Prince Igor.* His violin concerto in A minor and the ballets *Raymonda* (1898) and *The Seasons* (1899) have enjoyed considerable popularity.

MILOS VELIMIROVIC

Bibliography: Malko, Nicolai, *A Certain Art* (1966).

Gleason, Jackie [glee'-suhn]

Herbert John "Jackie" Gleason, b. Brooklyn, N.Y., Feb. 26, 1916, d. June 24, 1987, was an entertainer and television producer. He began his career as an emcee in Brooklyn's Folly Theatre, and in 1949 he gained popularity in the television series "The Life of Riley." He headlined "The Jackie Gleason Show," which ran intermittently on television from 1952 to 1970, and achieved star status as Ralph Kramden, a bus driver in the weekly television show "The Honeymooners." In 1959, Gleason won a Tony Award for the musical comedy *Take Me Along*. He is also remembered for his performance as Minnesota Fats in the film *The Hustler* (1961) and for his later comedic roles in such films as *Smokey and the Bandit* (1977) and *Nothing in Common* (1986). FRANK MANCHEL

Bibliography: Allen, Steve, *The Funny Men* (1956); Bishop, Jim, *The Golden Ham* (1956).

glee

A glee is a composition for unaccompanied male voices that flourished in England in the 18th and early 19th centuries. Normally a glee is comparatively short and contains several contrasting sections, mostly in a homophonic (chordal) style using short phrases and frequent changes of rhythm. The term *glee* comes from the Anglo-Saxon *gligge*, which means "music," and does not indicate that glees are necessarily gleeful. Several societies were formed in England for the performance of glees and other vocal part music. One of these was the Glee Club, founded in London in 1783. The term *glee club* is now used to describe choral groups that perform short works of various types.

Gleizes, Albert [glez]

The French painter Albert Gleizes, b. Paris, Dec. 8, 1881, d. June 23, 1953, was an influential proponent of CUBISM. Originally an industrial designer, Gleizes began painting impressionist-style works about 1900, but under the influence of Paul Cézanne he gradually began to simplify forms and colors. This simplification process led inevitably to the radical austerity of cubism, which Gleizes joined Georges Braque and Pablo Picasso in exploring. In 1912, Gleizes and Jean Metzinger published the important book *Du cubisme* (Eng. trans., 1913), which helped provide the movement with its theoretical foundations. Gleizes's own cubist paintings, of which *On Brooklyn Bridge* (1917; Guggenheim Museum, New York City) is representative, are marked by precise patterns of abstraction. In later years Gleizes became deeply religious and sought to breathe new life into religious art through cubism.

Bibliography: Robbins, Daniel, *Albert Gleizes, 1881–1953* (1964).

Glencoe, Massacre of [glen-koh']

Glencoe, a valley in western Scotland, was the site of a massacre of members of the MacDonald clan in 1692. The MacDonald chief had failed, probably as a result of deliberate hindrance, to meet the deadline for the Highland clans to swear allegiance to the new king of England, WILLIAM III. As a result Sir John Dalrymple, a secretary of state for Scotland, sent a regiment of Campbells, a rival clan, to punish the MacDonalds in Glencoe for a week before attacking and killing 38 of them on Feb. 13, 1692. The massacre left deep anti-English and anti-Campbell feelings among the Scots.

Bibliography: Linklater, Magnus, *The Story of Glencoe* (1983); Prebble, John, *The Massacre at Glencoe* (1975).

Glendale

Glendale is a city in southwestern California, 13 km (8 mi) north of Los Angeles. It lies at the southeastern end of the San Fernando Valley in the Verdugo Hills. Primarily a residential community, it has a population of 139,060 (1980). The city's industries produce aircraft, pharmaceuticals, optical instruments, and films. Founded in 1886 on the former Rancho San Rafael, the first Spanish land grant in California (1784), the city was incorporated in 1906. Forest Lawn Memorial Park, a well-known cemetery, is located there.

Glendower, Owen [glen-dow'-ur]

Owen Glendower, *c.*1354–*c.*1416, was a Welsh prince who led the last major Welsh revolt against English rule. A dispute with an English neighbor touched off (1400) his revolt against HENRY IV, whom he had earlier supported. He first allied himself with Henry's enemies, the PERCY family, but after their defeat (1403) sought French aid. By 1404 he controlled most of Wales, but English forces under Prince Henry (later HENRY V) gradually captured his strongholds. By 1412, Glendower had disappeared into the Welsh mountains.

Glenn, John H., Jr.

John H. Glenn, Jr., a former military pilot, was chosen in 1959 as one of the original group of astronauts. On Feb. 20, 1962, he became the first American to orbit the Earth. Glenn has served as a Democratic senator from Ohio since 1975.

The American astronaut and senator John Herschel Glenn, Jr., b. Cambridge, Ohio, July 18, 1921, was the first American to orbit the Earth. Glenn became a Marine Corps pilot in 1943 and flew in combat in World War II and the Korean War. In 1957 he became the first man to fly faster than sound from New York to Los Angeles, covering the distance in 3 hours, 23 minutes in a F8U Crusader. He was a test pilot when selected as one of the original seven astronauts in 1959.

On Feb. 20, 1962, Glenn's 4-hour, 56-minute flight aboard *Friendship 7* (*Mercury-Atlas 6*), the third flight of the MERCURY PROGRAM, took him around the globe three times to a splashdown in the Atlantic Ocean. Although a signal during the flight indicated that *Friendship 7*'s heat shield was loose, the craft's retrorockets were fired and the reentry went without incident.

Deciding to enter politics, Glenn resigned from the space program (1964) and the Marine Corps (1965). In 1974 he was elected to the U.S. Senate as a Democrat from Ohio. He won easy reelection in 1980 and 1986. A prominent moderate, he was considered a serious potential presidential candidate when, in 1983, he announced his bid for the 1984 nomination. He suffered early losses in the primaries, however, and withdrew from the race in March 1984. DAVID DOOLING

Bibliography: Van Riper, Frank, *Glenn: The Astronaut Who Would Be President* (1983); Wolfe, Tom, *The Right Stuff* (1979).

Glidden, Joseph Farwell

An Illinois farmer, Joseph Farwell Glidden, b. Charlestown, N.H., Jan. 18, 1813, d. Oct. 9, 1906, invented the first commercially successful BARBED WIRE, making possible the development of the North American Great Plains by providing cheap fencing to protect crops and confine herds. In 1873, Glidden and a friend, Jacob Haish, applied for barbed wire patents two months apart. After litigation, Glidden was awarded a patent on Nov. 24, 1874. In 1875, Glidden helped found the Barb Fence Company of De Kalb, Ill. He sold his half interest a year later, but patent royalties won him a large fortune.

glider

A glider is a type of heavier-than-air AIRCRAFT that has no engine or has only a small auxiliary engine. Early gliders were not capable of sustained flight, but they did form a vital step-

The long, thin wings of a glider, or sailplane, enable the craft to remain aloft by soaring on rising air currents. Gliders, the first heavier-than-air vehicles to achieve sustained flight, are flown today both for recreation and as a competitive sport.

ping-stone in the development of the airplane. Such pioneers as Otto LILIENTHAL, Octave CHANUTE, and Percy Pilcher had some early success with gliders, but their experiments (1893-99) pointed out fundamental problems involving stability and control. In 1900-02, Orville and Wilbur WRIGHT accomplished the vital process of learning how to fly a stable glider; they then fitted (1903) an engine onto their aircraft. With the development of the powered airplane, interest in gliders waned until the 1920s, when German glider designers created more efficient machines characterized by their extremely long-span slender wings (wings of high aspect-ratio), which could produce greater lift at lower speeds, allowing the glider to travel further horizontally for a given drop in altitude. By finding and taking advantage of updrafts, a glider pilot could also extend a flight and in some cases stay aloft almost indefinitely. Gliders have also been used by military forces landing invasion troops and supplies.

Today's competition glider, or sailplane, is built to fit the rules of particular classes, which specify such things as the wing dimensions and equipment of the glider. A glide ratio exceeding 40—in other words, the glider can fly more than 40 units horizontally for each unit of altitude it falls—is possible with today's gliders. On all except the calmest days this capability allows at least some attempt at soaring; on particularly favorable days a skilled pilot may cover several hundred kilometers. The record for distance covered in a straight line is 1,461 km (907.8 mi), and the altitude record, set over California, is 14,102 m (46,266 ft), which is a respectable height even for powered aircraft.

Modern sailplanes are constructed chiefly from glass-fiber, often with carbon fiber to stiffen the wing spars. The pilot sits in a reclining position under a large transparent canopy. Wing flaps, airbrakes, water ballast, and a braking parachute are common features.

BILL GUNSTON

Bibliography: Allen, R. C., *The Theory of Flight for Glider Pilots,* 2d ed. (1969); Carter, William T., *Soaring,* ed. by Carroll V. Glines (1973); Coates, Andrew, *Jane's World Sailplanes and Motorgliders* (1978); Piggott, Derek, *Gliding; A Handbook on Soaring Flight,* 3d ed. (1972).

See also: AERIAL SPORTS FLIGHT, HUMAN-POWERED.

gliding: see AERIAL SPORTS.

gliding lemur: see COLUGO.

Glière, Reinhold Moritzovich [glee-air']

Reinhold Moritzovich Glière, b. Jan. 11, 1875, d. June 23, 1956, was an eminent Russian composer and conductor. He studied (1891) violin and composition at the Kiev Music School and attended (1894-1900) the Moscow Conservatory. In 1914, Glière became director of the Conservatory in Kiev. From 1920 until his death he was professor of composition at the Moscow Conservatory. Glière traveled extensively in the Soviet Union, collecting folk melodies of the various European and Asiatic republics, and many of his works are based on the music of these cultures. He composed an opera, six ballets, orchestral and band music, chamber music, and songs. His pupils included Serge Prokofiev, Aram Khachaturian, and Nicolai Miaskovsky.

ROBERT M. CAMMAROTA

Bibliography: Krebs, Stanley D., *Soviet Composers and the Development of Soviet Music* (1970); Schwarz, Boris, *Music and Musical Life in Soviet Russia 1917-1970* (1972).

Glinka, Mikhail Ivanovich [gleen'-kah]

Mikhail Ivanovich Glinka, b. June 1 (N.S.), 1804, d. Feb. 15 (N.S.), 1857, is universally considered the father of RUSSIAN MUSIC. He received desultory musical instruction, including piano lessons from John Field during his education in St. Petersburg, and wrote several unimportant youthful pieces. Glinka spent some time in Berlin, where he received elementary instruction in composition from Siegfried Dehn. The two major musical influences in his life were the folk music that he grew up with in the country and the operas of Vincenzo Bellini and Gaetano Donizetti.

Inspired with the idea of creating a true Russian opera, Glinka turned to a court official, Baron G. F. Rosen, who gave him the libretto of *Ivan Susanin; or, A Life for the Tsar,* a celebration of the Romanov dynasty and Russian patriotism in which the characteristics of Russian and Polish national music are vividly contrasted. First performed in 1836, the opera was an immediate success. For the first time, genuine Russian music was heard on the operatic stage with stunning effect, particularly in the choral scenes. This highly original music is interlarded, however, with set pieces in the ubiquitous Italian operatic style of the time. Glinka's second opera, *Ruslan and Lyudmila* (1842), based on a tale by Aleksandr Pushkin, was less successful, although it contains some striking and original scenes. Glinka again used Russian sources, but he also employed Oriental music, Viennese dance music, and Italian operatic conventions.

Glinka's orchestral works include the symphonic poem *Kamarinskaya* and two overtures, *Jota Aragonesa* and *Summer Night in Madrid,* inspired by a visit to Spain. In his many songs are combined a Russian character, a cosmopolitan polish, and a thorough knowledge of the voice.

MARTIN COOPER

Bibliography: Brown, David, *Mikhail Glinka* (1974); Calvocoressi, M. D., and Abraham, Gerald, *Glinka* (1936); Seaman, Gerald, *History of Russian Music* (1967).

globe

A globe is a three-dimensional cartographic representation of a sphere. Terrestrial globes, usually of the surface of the Earth or the Moon, give the user an image with equal distances, equal areas, and equal angles—characteristics impossible on a two-dimensional map. Celestial globes show the relative positions of heavenly bodies in the sky as seen by an observer from the surface of the sphere. Globes are constructed of gores, elongated strips with pointed ends. Each is printed so that, when all gores are applied to a spherical base, a continuous image results.

The earliest globes were celestial, made of stone or copper by astronomers of ancient Mesopotamia, Egypt, and Greece. Crates of Mallus, a Greek astronomer, is thought to have made the first terrestrial globe in the 2d century BC. Martin Benhaim, a German, is credited with making the first modern globe in 1492.

Globe Theatre

The Globe was the most renowned theater of Elizabethan and Jacobean London. It was corporately owned and managed by the Burbage family and the player company called the CHAMBERLAIN'S MEN (later, the KING'S MEN), with which William SHAKESPEARE was associated. It was built on Bankside, south of the Thames, in 1599, using timbers from the dismantled Theatre, London's first playhouse. Destroyed in 1613 by a fire that started in its thatched roof, it was immediately rebuilt and survived until demolished in 1644. C. WALTER HODGES

See also: BURBAGE, RICHARD; ELIZABETHAN PLAYHOUSE.

globular cluster: see CLUSTER, GLOBULAR.

globule [glahb'-uel]

A globule is the astronomical term for a relatively small, dense interstellar cloud that obscures optical light. It is thus a small galactic NEBULA. Many of these objects were discovered in the early days of astronomical photography by E. E. Barnard, who referred to them as dark nebulae or dark clouds. The extinction they produce is caused by the interstellar dust particles they contain. The density of atoms and molecules in these globules, estimated from the observed amounts of extinction, together with a reasonable assumption of the ratio of gas to dust, is often as high as 10^8 particles per cm^3.
DONALD E. OSTERBROCK

globulin [glahb'-yuh-lin]

A globulin is a protein that is insoluble in pure water, in contrast to an albumin, which is soluble. Globulins are widely distributed in plants and animals. Human blood serum contains several globulins that differ in molecular size, amino acid composition, solubility, and the rate at which they migrate during an analytical procedure called electrophoresis. Serum globulins are classified on the basis of electrophoretic mobility. Antibodies of the immune system are γ-globulins. Total serum globulin increases during recovery from infection. Such β-globulins as transferrin transport iron, heme, and, less often, copper and zinc throughout the human body.
PETER L. PETRAKIS

glockenspiel [glahk'-en-speel]

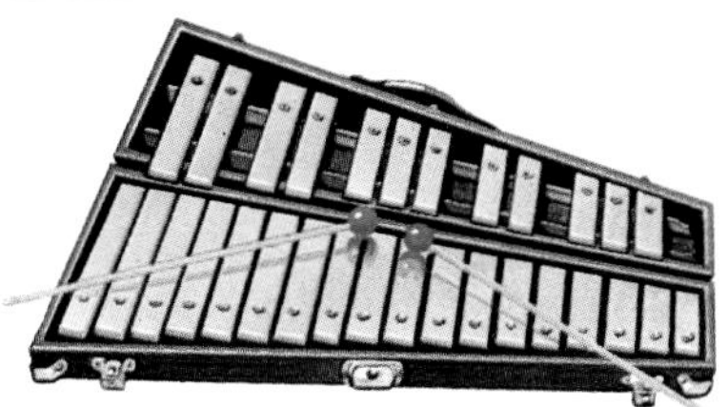

The glockenspiel is a percussion instrument in modern orchestras. It consists of a set of thin steel bars arranged in two rows in the manner of a keyboard and played with wooden mallets. It produces delicate bell sounds.

The German word *Glockenspiel* translates as "bell chime" and has been used to mean both carillon and a set of small BELLS. The term now is generally restricted to tuned graduated metals bars that produce bright, silvery tones. The bars may be struck indirectly from below by means of a carillon keyboard—providing a quiet practice instrument—or a common keyboard—allowing facility in playing simultaneous pitches. It may also be struck directly from above by mallets, allowing a variety of tone quality regulated by the choice of beaters and the use of tuned resonators suspended on the underside of the instrument. A noteworthy early orchestral use occurs in Mozart's *The Magic Flute* (1791). Since then the glockenspiel has been used effectively in music where its distinctive tone color is appropriate. The bell lyre is a portable and visually colorful form ubiquitous in marching bands.
ROBERT A. WARNER

Bibliography: Blades, James, *Percussion Instruments and Their History*, 2d ed. (1975); Blades, James, and Montague, Jeremy, *Early Percussion Instruments* (1976); Marcuse, Sybil, *Survey of Musical Instruments* (1975).

Gloeocapsa [glee-oh-kap'-suh]

Gloeocapsa is a genus of the BLUE-GREEN ALGAE. *Gloeocapsa* occur on wet rocks or soil, and some are aquatic. They are unicellular organisms that reproduce by simple fission and occur singly or in colonies of 2, 4, or 8 cells with several concentric sheaths.

Glomar Challenger: see DEEP SEA DRILLING PROJECT.

Glorious Revolution

The Glorious Revolution is the name given to the overthrow in 1688 of the Roman Catholic JAMES II of England and the accession to the throne of his daughter MARY II and her Dutch Protestant husband, WILLIAM III. Invited to invade England by seven English noblemen, William hoped to bring England into the imminent War of the GRAND ALLIANCE against France. He feared that James would ally himself with the French king LOUIS XIV or that James's favoritism toward his Catholic subjects would so provoke the Protestant majority as to cause another civil war, thus making England impotent in Europe.

The invitation was sent to William on June 30, 1688; when he arrived in November, his partisans rose in rebellion in Yorkshire and elsewhere. William's triumph was bloodless; James's forces, under John Churchill, later duke of MARLBOROUGH, deserted, and James himself fled. When William and Mary were made joint sovereigns (1689), they acquiesced in a Declaration and BILL OF RIGHTS, which opened the road to constitutional monarchy. MAURICE ASHLEY

Bibliography: Ashley, Maurice, *The Glorious Revolution of 1688* (1968); Pocock, J. G., ed., *Three British Revolutions, 1641, 1688, 1776* (1980); Trevelyan, C. M., *The English Revolution, 1688-89* (1938).

glory-bower

Glory-bower is the common name for a large genus, *Clerodendrum,* of plants with showy clusters of white, violet, purple, or red flowers. Many are grown as garden ornamentals. The approximately 400 species include woody herbs, vines, shrubs, and small trees. Members of the vervain family, Verbenaceae, they are native to the tropics and subtropics of the Old World.

glossolalia: see TONGUES, SPEAKING IN.

Gloucester (England) [glahs'-tur]

Gloucester, in west central England on the River Severn, is the county seat of Gloucestershire. About 56 km (35 mi) northwest of Bristol, it is a major inland port linked to the Bristol Channel by the River Severn and a ship canal. Gloucester has a population of 92,133 (1981) and is a market center for a cattle- and grain-growing region. The city's industries manufacture airplanes, railroad cars, farm equipment, lumber, cutlery, and rope. Gloucester's magnificent cathedral, built mostly in the 11th century (the 68.6-m/225-ft tower was completed c.1450), contains the tomb of Edward II. Other landmarks include the churches of Saint Mary-de-Lode and Saint Mary-de-Cript (both 11th century). There are church schools and inns dating from the 15th to the 17th century and a notable folk museum.

The Britons established a settlement on the site, but the founding date is generally considered to be AD 97, when the Romans built Glevum where they bridged the Severn. As England became united, the city became a royal residence, and it was incorporated in 1483.

Gloucester (Massachusetts)

Gloucester is a major fishing port and summer resort located on Cape Ann in northeastern Massachusetts. It has a population of 27,768 (1980). Since its settlement in 1623, its economy has been based on fishing. Henry Wadsworth Longfellow's *The Wreck of the Hesperus* concerns the nearby Reef of Norman's Woe. Rudyard Kipling's *Captains Courageous* tells of Gloucester fishermen, who are commemorated by Leonard Craske's statue, *The Man at the Wheel* (1923). With the declining numbers of haddock, halibut, and mackerel, the fishing catch now consists mainly of cod, whiting, lobster, and shrimp, much of which is frozen in Gloucester plants.

Gloucester, Humphrey, Duke of

Humphrey, duke of Gloucester, b. 1390, d. Feb. 23, 1447, was the younger brother of King HENRY V of England. During the minority of his nephew, HENRY VI, Humphrey was forced to share power with his brother John, duke of Bedford, and Cardinal Henry BEAUFORT. He was a disturbing political influence, defending the lands of his wife JACQUELINE OF HAINAUT against England's ally, PHILIP THE GOOD of Burgundy, and later championing a war policy in France against the peace efforts of Beaufort. Humphrey's enemies humiliated him by convicting (1441) his second wife, Eleanor Cobham, of sorcery. Humphrey died mysteriously after being arrested.

GEORGE HOLMES

Bibliography: Vickers, K., *Humphrey, Duke of Gloucester* (1907).

Gloucestershire [glahs'-tur-shir]

Gloucestershire, a county in west central England, is located immediately east of the border with Wales. The county covers an area of 2,643 km² (1,020 mi²), and its population is 509,200 (1984 est.). The city and port of GLOUCESTER is the county seat and principal commercial center. Cheltenham is famous for its spa and private schools, most notably Cheltenham College (1841) and Cheltenham Ladies' College (1853).

Gloucestershire is bisected by the River SEVERN; in the fertile river valley wheat, barley, and fruits are grown, and dairy cattle are raised for milk and cheese production. In the east the beautiful Cotswold Hills support sheep and stock raising as well as tourism. The Forest of Dean is located in the west, where limestone is mined. The county has remains from the Iron Age, Roman (especially at Cirencester), Saxon, and Norman periods.

gloves

Gloves are hand coverings with a separate sheath for each finger, unlike the simpler mitten. They can be made of fine leather or heavier hide, fur, knitted or woven cotton, silk, wool, or linen. Until the 19th century, when technology made possible machines that could mass-produce apparel, gloves were among the costliest items of clothing, and from early times they were associated with royalty and priests and were seen as symbolic of high rank or of religious purity.

Linen gloves were found in the tomb of the ancient Egyptian King Tutankhamen (14th century BC). Gloves are mentioned in the works of Homer and Herodotus and were worn by upper-class Romans. In the early Middle Ages, linen or silk gloves, embroidered and decorated with gems, were part of a bishop's liturgical costume; similar highly decorated gloves were worn by kings at their coronations. Both ladies and gentlemen wore leather gauntlets while hawking, and knights used armored gauntlets—heavy leather gloves covered with small iron scales.

The peak of ornateness in glove styles was reached in 16th- and 17th-century Europe, when glove cuffs became wide and heavily embroidered and were embellished with ribbon and lace. Queen Elizabeth I was renowned for her collection of jeweled and ornamented gauntlets, many of them scented with rare perfumes. During the Renaissance the most elegant gloves were made in Spain, although France and Italy were also major glove-making centers.

In 1834 a French glover, Xavier Jouvin, invented a punch press that could cut out six gloves simultaneously. This press and a new machine for sewing glove seams were the foundation of an industry that was producing inexpensive cotton and leather gloves by the millions by the end of the 19th century.

The New York town of Gloversville, in Fulton County, was an early glove-making center in the United States. Today, Gloversville and its surrounding towns produce half the leather gloves made in America.

Bibliography: Beck, S. William, *Gloves: Their Annals and Associations* (1883; repr. 1969).

See also: COSTUME.

glowworm [gloh'-wurm]

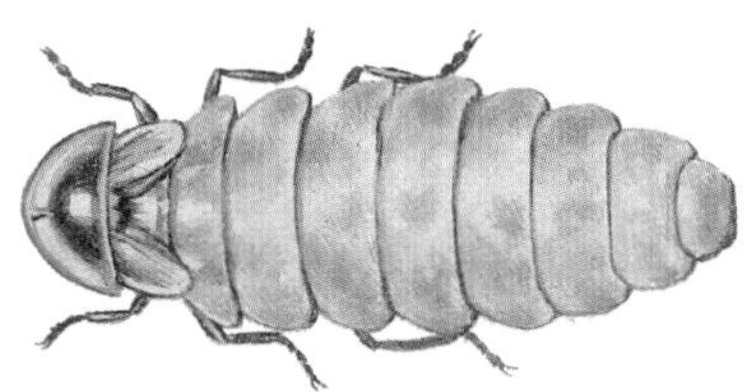

Some female adult glowworms, family Phengodidae, resemble glowworm larvae; both produce iridescent green light. Similar, wingless, luminescent females and larvae in the firefly family, Lampyridae, are also called glowworms.

Glowworm is the common name for the larvae and some adults of beetles of the family Phengodidae, a group of insects closely related to the fireflies, or lightning bugs. Glowworms live on the ground or under logs and bark, where they prey upon other insects. They have a row of light-producing organs along each side of the body, and these produce a luminous glow with almost no heat (see BIOLUMINESCENCE). It is not yet known whether the light serves any function.

Larvae and wingless adult females of some species of fireflies, and a few other light-producing insect larvae, are also popularly called glowworms.

DAVID J. HORN

gloxinia [glahk-sin'-ee-uh]

Gloxinia, S. speciosa, requires a warm, humid room in which to grow properly. The effort needed to nurture this plant is rewarded by a profusion of velvety flowers.

Gloxinia, *Sinningia speciosa,* is a flowering plant belonging to the gesneriad family, Gesneriaceae. It is Brazilian in origin and produces richly colored, showy, bell-shaped flowers that are violet, purple, white, or reddish, often marbled or spotted with darker shades.

Glubb, Sir John Bagot [gluhb]

Sir John Bagot Glubb, b. Apr. 16, 1897, d. Mar. 17, 1986, was a British army officer who commanded the Arab Legion from 1939 to 1956. In 1930, Glubb was sent to the British mandate of Transjordan (now Jordan) as assistant commander of the Arab Legion. He became commander in 1939 and turned it into the best army in the area. Known as Glubb Pasha, he continued to head the army after Jordan became independent in 1946. In 1956, however, King Hussein I, bowing to Arab nationalist pressure, removed him from command. His writings include *The Story of the Arab Legion* (1948) and a 3-volume history of the Arab world (1963–65).

glucagon [gloo'-kuh-gahn]

Glucagon is a hormone produced by the pancreatic islets of Langerhans. Its secretion is stimulated by the lowering of glucose concentration in the blood. Glucagon stimulates the breakdown of glycogen, a starchlike substance, to its glucose subunits, and the biochemical conversion of certain amino acids into glucose. Glucagon thus overcomes the glucose deficiency and helps ensure an adequate supply of glucose for oxidation into energy for body activities.

In general, the effects of glucagon are antagonistic (opposite) to those of another pancreatic hormone, INSULIN, secretion of which tends to increase when blood glucose is high. The effect of these antagonistic actions is to maintain blood glucose concentration within normal limits.

Bibliography: Foa, P. P., and Bajaj, J. S., eds., *Glucagon* (1978).

Gluck, Alma [gluk]

The American soprano Alma Gluck, b. Bucharest, Romania, May 11, 1884, d. Oct. 27, 1938, was brought to the United States as a child and attended public schools and college in New York State. She made her Metropolitan Opera debut (1909) as Sophie in Jules Massenet's *Werther*, and during her 3 years with the company she sang more than 20 roles. Gluck retired from opera in 1912 and embarked on a successful concert career. She gave her final concert at the Manhattan Opera House in 1925. Her second husband was the violinist Efrem Zimbalist. ELLA A. MALIN

Gluck, Christoph Willibald [gluk, kris'-tohf vil'-i-bahlt]

Christoph Willibald Gluck, b. July 2, 1714, in Erasbach, near Nuremberg, Germany, was one of opera's profoundest reformers. Following preliminary education by Jesuit priests, Gluck was sent to Prague, where he learned to sing and play the violin, the cello, and the organ. While in Milan as a court musician he had his first instruction in music theory from Giovanni Battista Sammartini. In 1741, Gluck composed *Artaserse* to a text by Pietro METASTASIO, continuing in the accepted Italian convention of *da capo* arias for single voices sung by characterless castrati.

Gluck later went to Paris, where he met Jean Philippe Rameau and heard some of his operas. He then went to London, where he was commissioned (1746) to compose an opera in celebration of the victory at Culloden. London's opera public had been educated by George Frideric Handel and Gluck's opera sounded thin and pallid by comparison. Deciding that his style was at fault, Gluck toured Europe for three years as conductor of an Italian opera company. In 1750 he married a wealthy Viennese heiress, Marianna Pergin.

He continued to compose, and by 1757 he was famous in Vienna and was knighted by the pope. Gluck observed the new French plays and comic operas in vogue in Vienna, which he exploited for their deeper musical experience in flesh-and-blood characters. His ballet *Don Juan* saw great success in 1761. Gluck renounced Metastasio and his conventions with *Orpheus and Eurydice* (1762). His librettist, Ranieri Calzabigi, provided a text dealing with personal human conflicts and emotions, while Gluck's score contained unadorned melodies. The recitatives were orchestrally accompanied, and the chorus functioned as a corporate character.

The German-born composer Christoph Willibald Gluck reformed baroque opera when he broke with the traditional Italian operatic form and rejected superfluous musical ornamentation. Gluck instead concentrated on creating a close integration of the dramatic and musical elements of opera.

All this caused a sweeping change in the art of opera. With Gluck's *Alceste* (1767) opera finally became true music drama. His *Iphigenia in Aulis* was produced (1774) by the Paris Opera upon a promise from the composer to supply five more operas. One of these was the revised *Orpheus,* with added numbers and a tenor as Orpheus instead of a contralto (which was unacceptable in Paris). Gluck met with personal opposition from Paris's reigning Italian composer, Niccolò PICCINNI, although the two men respected each other.

Armide (1777) and *Iphigenia in Tauris* (1779) were his last two successes in an output that included 29 Italian and 12 French operas. In 1779, Gluck stopped composing; he died of a stroke in Vienna on Nov. 15, 1787. ALAN JEFFERSON

Bibliography: Berlioz, Hector, *Gluck and His Operas,* trans. by Edwin Evans (1915; repr. 1973); Einstein, Alfred, *Gluck,* trans. by Eric Blom (1936; repr. 1972); Howard, Patricia, *Gluck and the Birth of Modern Opera* (1963); Newman, Ernest, *Gluck and the Opera* (1967; repr. 1976).

glucocorticoid

A glucocorticoid is any of a group of steroid hormones that includes corticosterone, cortisol, and cortisone. Produced in the outer layer, or cortex, of the adrenal gland, these hormones regulate protein and carbohydrate metabolism, as well as body reactions to stress. Examples of stress are infections, injuries, extreme hot and cold, and physical exertion. Glucocorticoids cause adaptive physiological changes to occur that allow a person to cope with such stresses. Symptoms of glucocorticoid deficiency, as in ADDISON'S DISEASE, are loss of appetite, weakness, low blood sugar, water retention, tendency to go into shock on exposure to stress, and oversecretion of the melanocyte-stimulating hormone by the pituitary gland; this results in a brownish skin pigmentation.

Glucocorticoids, particularly cortisone, are useful in the treatment of rheumatoid arthritis and other inflammatory diseases by limiting their spread, although serious side effects such as peptic ulcers, weakening of the bones (osteoporosis), and aggravation of diabetes mellitus usually limit their use. Other medical uses include the treatment of allergic reactions and of various skin diseases. PETER L. PETRAKIS

glucose

Glucose, $C_6H_{12}O_6$, is the most common MONOSACCHARIDE, or simple SUGAR. It is usually obtained from sugarcane or sugar beets, where, combined chemically with another monosaccharide, fructose, it forms the disaccharide sucrose. Synthesized in plants by the process of PHOTOSYNTHESIS, glucose (also called dextrose) is an energy-rich CARBOHYDRATE, important in human nutrition.

glucose tolerance test

The glucose tolerance test (GTT) is used to identify abnormal glucose metabolism in DIABETES MELLITUS and certain other diseases. In the usual procedure, a patient who has fasted 18 to 24 hours drinks a concentrated solution of glucose, and glucose concentration is measured in blood and urine samples taken at ½, 1, 2, and 3 hours after ingestion. In healthy individuals, glucose concentration rises to about twice the normal level within the first hour and returns to normal within two hours; little or no glucose is excreted in the URINE. In diabetics, blood glucose rises to a much higher level, the return to normal levels is delayed three hours or more, and a large amount of glucose is excreted in the urine. The diabetic's response is due to lack of INSULIN, a hormone required for the removal of glucose from the blood. There is also a GTT for HYPOGLYCEMIA. In a hypoglycemic, the blood sugar level is abnormally low, and sugar is absent in urine.

glue: see ADHESIVE.

gluon

Gluon is the whimsical name given to the subatomic particle held responsible for "gluing," or binding together the QUARK constituents of protons and neutrons. Believed to be carriers of the strong nuclear force (much as photons are carriers of the electromagnetic force), gluons are theorized to exist in eight kinds, corresponding to the eight transformations that can change the "color" of quarks; the three noncolor transformations are accounted for by two gluons. Gluons also bind with each other to form particles called glueballs.

Bibliography: Ishikawa, Kenzo, "Glueballs," *Scientific American,* November 1982.

glycerol [glis'-ur-awl]

Glycerol, or glycerin, a nontoxic liquid with a slightly sweet taste, is a commercially important alcohol. Its ability to absorb water makes it a valuable humectant (moisturizing agent) for tobacco and foods, which it also sweetens, and an emollient (softening agent) for skin conditioners. It is also used in the production of pharmaceuticals, plasticizers, alkyd resins, and the explosive nitroglycerin. Glycerin is derived from fats and vegetable oils as a by-product in soap manufacture and from propylene through chlorination and HYDROLYSIS. It is soluble in water and other polar solvents but insoluble in nonpolar organic solvents. Its chemical name is 1,2,3-propanetriol, and the structural formula is $CH_2OHCHOHCH_2OH$.

glycogen

Glycogen, $(C_6H_{10}O_5)_n$, is a natural polymer made of many GLUCOSE molecules strung together. Also called animal starch, glycogen is an example of a POLYSACCHARIDE. Some glucose molecules, which provide the body with energy upon oxidation, are stored in the liver in the form of glycogen.

glycol [gly'-kawl]

A glycol, also called a dihydric alcohol or diol, is a type of ALCOHOL that has two hydroxyl groups (OH), each bonded to different carbon atoms of an aliphatic carbon chain. The most common glycol is ethylene glycol, $(CH_2OH)_2$, used as an automotive antifreeze and in the production of polyester fibers, pharmaceuticals, and explosives.

Low-molecular-weight glycols are colorless, water-soluble liquids. As the molecular weight increases, the solubility in water decreases and the melting point, boiling point, and viscosity increase. Glycols undergo all of the reactions of alcohols. Simple glycols are usually synthesized from the corresponding unsaturated hydrocarbon. ELBERT H. HADLEY

glycolysis: see METABOLISM.

glycoside [gly'-kuh-syd]

Glycoside compounds are a large family of plant chemicals composed of a sugar bonded to a nonsugar component called a glycon. The sugar generally is GLUCOSE. Long before anything was known about their chemistry, glycosides were used as natural dyes, drugs, and condiments. An ancient vegetable dye called MADDER, for example, was the first glycoside whose chemical structure was determined. Willow bark, which contains a glycon related to aspirin, was used to treat fever and acute rheumatism. Mustard seeds, long used as a pickling flavoring, contain a glycoside called sinigrin, and so on.

The properties of glycosides—crystalline solids, bitter taste, and limited solubility in water—and their chemical make-up have led botanists to postulate that plants may use glycosides to store harmful substances. This hypothesis has been supported by the observation of a chemical, called 2-chloroethanol, that breaks the dormancy of tubers. Plant tissue converts the chemical to a glycoside:

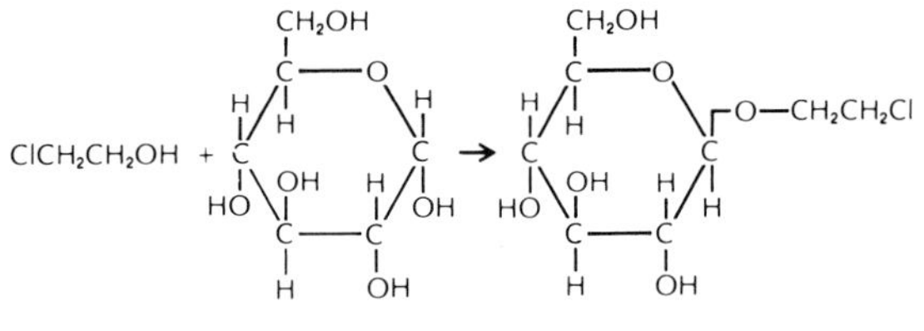

$ClCH_2CH_2OH$ + *D*-glucose → 2-chloroethyl-β-*D*-glucopyranoside

2-chloroethanol *D*-glucose 2-chloroethyl-β-*D*-glucopyranoside

Other possible functions of the glycoside in plants are movement of harmful material to tissues where it can eventually be shed, and movement of decorative materials (such as pigment) from the leaves to the flowers or fruits. Still, the detoxification thesis is important and is also supported by animal research. Thus, the urine of a dog fed hydroquinone will subsequently contain the following compound:

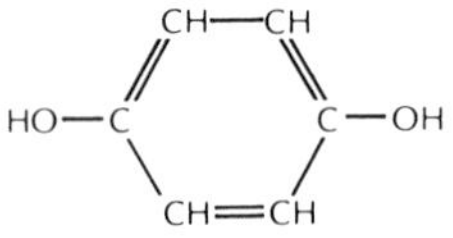

hydroquinone

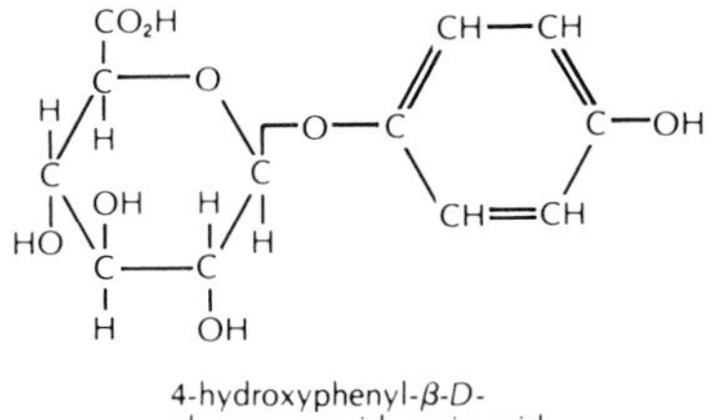

4-hydroxyphenyl-β-*D*-glucopyranosiduronic acid

This compound is also related to the glycosides.

K. THOMAS FINLEY

Glyndebourne Opera Festival [glynd'-burn]

Famous for its opera productions, the Glyndebourne Festival in England was inaugurated in 1934 by John Christie and his wife, the singer Audrey Mildmay. This renowned summer festival began on a high artistic level with a production of Mozart's *The Marriage of Figaro*; Fritz Busch was made permanent conductor and Carl Ebert stage director. Rudolf Bing became general manager in 1935, a post he held until 1948 (minus the years of World War II, when the festival was suspended). Moran Caplat succeeded (1948) Bing as general manager, and Vittorio Gui succeeded Busch as permanent conductor in 1951. An international roster of singers, conductors, and designers have participated each summer in a repertoire that includes traditional, rarely heard classical, and contemporary operas. These have included Gottfried von Einem's *The Visit,* Leon Janáček's *The Cunning Little Vixen,* Benjamin Britten's *The Rape of Lucretia,* Igor Stravinsky's *The Rake's Progress,* Hans Werner Henze's *Elegy for Young Lovers,* and Nicholas Maw's *The Rising of the Moon.* Among the guest artists have been Joan Sutherland, Régine Crespin, Geraint Evans, Birgit Nilsson, Montserrat Caballé, and Teresa Berganza. Guest conductors have included Sir Thomas Beecham, Ernest Ansermet, Sir Georg Solti, Bernard Haitink, and Carlo Maria Giulini. Glyndebourne makes its own recordings, telecasts its productions, and has a touring company. ELLA A. MALIN

Bibliography: Blunt, Wilfred, *John Christie of Glyndebourne* (1968); Brody, Elaine, and Brook, Claire, *The Music Guide to Great Britain* (1975); Hughes, Spike, *Glyndebourne,* rev. ed. (1981).

Glyptothek [glip-toh-tayk']

The sculpture museum Glyptothek (from the Greek *glyptos,* "carved," and *theka,* "gallery") in Munich was built (1816–30)

by the Bavarian king Maximilian I. It was one of the several buildings lining the Königsplatz undertaken by Maximilian and Louis I, of which two, the Propylaeon and the Glyptothek, were designed by the architect Leo von KLENZE. The building consists of an unfenestrated block that runs through an octastyle (eight-column) Greek Ionic portico in the center. It is a free interpretation of Greek motifs; the gallery was designed to house the bold archaic pedimental sculpture from the temple of Aphaia at Aegina, Greece (*c*.490 BC), installed and restored by Bertel THORVALDSEN. Inside, the galleries are divided into subunits, each capped with low saucer masonry domes. Although the exterior was not greatly damaged, bombardment during World War II completely destroyed the interiors, which have been rebuilt without the original detailed stucco relief carving. LELAND M. ROTH

Gmelin, Leopold [guh-mel'-een]

The German chemist Leopold Gmelin, b. Aug. 2, 1788, d. Apr. 13, 1853, a professor of chemistry and medicine at Heidelberg, discovered potassium ferricyanide, wrote on mineralogy, and made a chemical study of digestion, gall, and blood. With Friedrich Tiedemann he discovered pancreatine and taurine, and identified cholesterol in blood and choline in bile. Expanded revisions of Gmelin's 3-volume *Handbuch der inorganischen Chemie* (1817–19) continue to be published. VIRGINIA F. MCCONNELL

gnat: see MIDGE.

gnatcatcher [nat'-kech-ur]

The blue-gray gnatcatcher, P. caerulea, *a tiny bird of the warbler family, has a long, mobile tail. Gnatcatchers are insectivorous birds.*

Gnatcatcher is the common name for the birds of the genus *Polioptila,* which is a New World group of the so-called Old World warbler family, Sylviidae; this family also includes the KINGLETS of North America. Gnatcatchers are tiny (9–13 cm/ 3.5–5 in), graceful, constantly active woodland dwellers that are given to aerial acrobatics in pursuit of flying insects. Most species are resident in small areas of tropical America, but the migratory blue-gray gnatcatcher, *P. caerulea,* nests in the eastern and southwestern United States. WILLIAM F. SANDFORD

Gnathostomata [nay-thoh-stoh'-muht-uh]

Gnathostomata, in some classifications, is a superclass of the subphylum Vertebrata (phylum Chordata), containing seven classes of backboned animals with jaws. This is in contrast to the superclass Agnatha, which contains the backboned animals without jaws: lampreys, hagfish, and the extinct ostracoderms. The seven classes of jawed vertebrates are as follows: the extinct Placodermi fishes, the cartilaginous Chondrichthyes fishes (sharks), the bony Osteichthyes fishes (herring, trout), the Amphibia (salamanders, frogs), the Reptilia (turtles, snakes), the Aves (birds), and the Mammalia (humans, horses).

Gnathostomata is also the name of a superorder of invertebrates in the class Echinoidea, containing SEA URCHINS, SAND DOLLARS, and related forms. STEPHEN C. REINGOLD

gnatwren [nat'-ren]

Gnatwrens are three species of small, insect-eating birds in the family Sylviidae or, in some classifications, Polioptilidae. Found from Mexico to Brazil and Peru, they inhabit the dense understory of tropical forest. Somewhat resembling American gnatcatchers, they are 9 to 13 cm (3.5 to 5 in) in length, with long, narrow tails cocked sharply upwards.

Gneisenau, August Wilhelm Anton, Graf Neithardt von [guh-ny'-zen-ow, grahf nyt'-hahrt fuhn]

August Wilhelm Anton Gneisenau, b. Oct. 27, 1760, d. Aug. 23, 1831, was a Prussian field marshal who was one of the chief organizers of Napoleon I's final defeat. He joined the Prussian army in 1786 and achieved prominence as a result of his defense of Kolberg against the French (1807). After Prussia had accepted the harsh peace of Tilsit (1807), Gneisenau worked with General von SCHARNHORST to modernize the army. Succeeding Scharnhorst as chief of the general staff in June 1813, he was the principal strategist in the War of Liberation; the plan of the Battle of Leipzig (Oct. 16–19, 1813) was mostly his work. Gneisenau resigned from the army in 1816, but returned to service to help crush a Polish insurrection in 1831. K. M. SMOGORZEWSKI

gneiss [nys]

Gneiss is a coarse- to medium-grained banded METAMORPHIC ROCK formed from igneous or sedimentary rocks during regional metamorphism. Rich in FELDSPARS and QUARTZ, gneisses also contain mica minerals and aluminous or ferromagnesian silicates. In some gneisses thin bands of quartz-feldspar minerals are separated by bands of micas; in others the mica is evenly distributed throughout. Common orthogneisses (gneisses formed from igneous rocks; those formed from sedimentary rocks are called paragneisses) are similar in composition to GRANITE or GRANODIORITE, and some may have originally been LAVA flows.

Augen gneiss is a variety containing large eye-shaped grains (augen) of feldspar. Injection gneisses are formed by injection of veinlets of granitic material into a SCHIST or some other foliated rock. Banded gneisses called migmatites are composed of alternating light-colored layers of granite or quartz-feldspar and dark layers rich in biotite. Some migmatites were formed by injection, others by segregation of quartz and feldspars. The origin of a gneiss can usually be determined by its chemical composition and mineral content. ANNA HIETANEN

Gnetum [neet'-uhm]

Gnetum is the only genus in the family Gnetaceae, a group of broad-leaved gymnosperms. Most members of the genus are small tropical trees and climbing vines found in the Eastern and Western Hemispheres. The leathery evergreen leaves are simple, ovate to oblong. The plants are usually dioecious.

gnome: see FAIRY.

gnosticism [nahs'-ti-sizm]

Gnosticism is a term derived from a Greek word for knowledge (*gnosis*) and applied to a philosophical and religious movement that influenced the Mediterranean world from the 1st century BC to the 3d century AD. It expressed itself in a variety of pagan, Jewish, and Christian forms. Its name is derived from the fact that it promised salvation through a secret knowledge or understanding of reality possessed by its devotees.

Gnosticism was considered a heresy by orthodox Christians, and the Manichaeans, whose beliefs were influenced by it, were persecuted during the Middle Ages. Here Dominican inquisitors are shown burning books of the Albigenses, a Manichaean sect that attracted followers in France during the 12th and 13th centuries. A nonheretical work rises miraculously from the fire.

Previously known mostly from the writings of its Christian opponents, gnosticism can now be studied in a collection of original documents found near the Egyptian town of NAG HAMMADI in 1945. Despite the complex diversity of gnostic groups and their teachings, the basic doctrines of gnosticism formed an identifiable pattern of belief and practice. A pervasive dualism underlay much of gnostic thought. Good and evil, light and darkness, truth and falsehood, spirit and matter were opposed to each other in human experience as being and nonbeing. The created universe and human experience were characterized by a radical disjunction between the spiritual, which was real, and the physical, which was illusory. This disjunction resulted from a cosmic tragedy, described in a variety of ways by gnostic mythology, as a consequence of which sparks of deity became entrapped in the physical world. These could be freed only by saving knowledge that was revealed to a spiritual elite by a transcendent messenger from the spirit world, variously identified as Seth (one of the sons of Adam), Jesus, or some other figure. Renunciation of physical desires and strict asceticism, combined with mystical rites of initiation and purification were thought to liberate the immortal souls of believers from the prison of physical existence. Reunion with divine reality was accomplished after a journey of the soul through intricate systems of hostile powers.

Associated in legend with SIMON MAGUS, a Samaritan sorcerer mentioned in Acts 8:9–24, gnosticism probably originated in the Near East as a synthesis of Oriental and Greek ideas before the advent of Christianity. It reached the height of its influence as a Christian sect in the middle of the 2d century AD, when it was represented by the Egyptian teachers BASILIDES and VALENTINUS. As Christian orthodoxy was defined in the period that followed, gnosticism began to decline and gradually was pushed to the periphery of the Christian world or driven underground by the persecution of church leaders. Some gnostic tendencies found their way into later Christian monasticism, while others survived among the MANDAEANS and adherents of MANICHAEISM.

Modern scholars continue to study the Nag Hammadi documents for an understanding of gnosticism. Some emphasize its charismatic spirituality and transcendental radicalism, and others see it as a chaotic amalgam of escapist myth and unhistorical speculation. Few would deny its direct formative influence in the life of early Christianity or its general impact on Judaism and Christianity as a part of the cultural milieu in which those religions worked out their institutional identities.

JAMES BRASHLER

Bibliography: Jonas, Hans, *The Gnostic Religion* (1963); Pagels, Elaine, *The Gnostic Gospels* (1981); Robinson, James M., *The Nag Hammadi Library* (1977).

gnotobiotics [naht-oh-by-aht'-iks]

Gnotobiotics (Greek for "known life") is the study of biological systems that are either free of contaminating microorganisms or contain microorganisms that have been identified. The purpose of developing a gnotobiotic system is to eliminate confusion in the interpretation of scientific data that could result if an experimental system were contaminated with unknown microorganisms.

PETER L. PETRAKIS

GNP: see GROSS NATIONAL PRODUCT.

gnu: see WILDEBEEST.

go

Go is an oriental game played on a board marked with 361 points that are formed by the intersections of 19 horizontal and 19 vertical lines. The game also uses 361 pieces, called stones—181 black and 180 white—which are round and slightly convex on each side. The rules of go are very simple although the strategy is immensely complicated. Each player alternately places a stone on an empty intersection, trying either to control territory or to capture an opponent's stones. Stones are captured when they are completely surrounded by an opponent's stones and there are no unoccupied adjacent intersections. The player with more occupied intersections wins the game.

Go is known as I-go in Japan and wi-ch'i in China, where an early version of the game, Yi, is mentioned in the entry for the year 546 BC in the Tso Chuan chronology. The game was introduced to Japan in AD 735, where it was played by professionals in the royal court. Philosophical importance was attached to go, and a go academy was established by Japan's first national champion. Go appeared in the United States as go-bang in the 19th century and enjoys a growing following in the West.

Bibliography: Iwamoto, Kaoru, *Go for Beginners* (1972); Korschelt, O., *Theory and Practice of Go,* trans. by George Leckie and S. P. King (1965).

Goa, Daman, and Diu [goh'-uh, duh-mahn', dee'-oo]

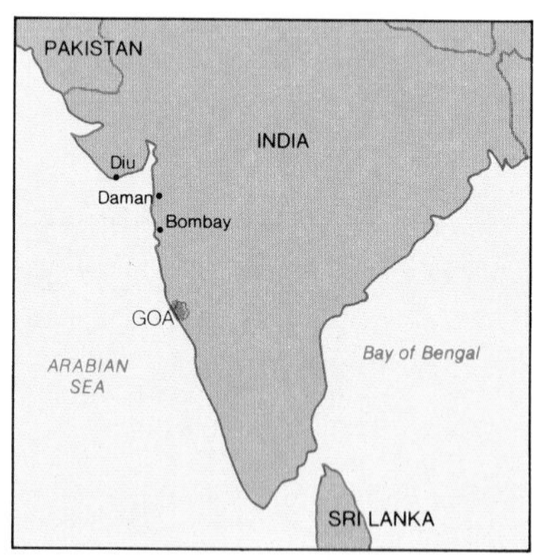

Goa, Daman, and Diu, three former Portuguese colonial possessions in western India, now form a union territory with representation in the Indian parliament. Portugal acquired all three during the 16th century. The Portuguese colonial presence was not brought to an end until 1961, when Indian troops occupied the three territories.

Goa is a union territory of India and a former Portuguese colony (1510–1961). It is located in west India between the Western GHATS and the Arabian Sea, about 400 km (250 mi) south of Bombay. Its official name is the Union Territory of Goa, Daman, and Diu, and it has a population of 1,082,117 (1981). The territory has an area of about 3,800 km^2 (1,480 mi^2). The capital, Panjim, retains a Portuguese colonial ambience. Its churches include the Basilica Bom Jesus, which contains the tomb and shrine of St. FRANCIS XAVIER. Goa has a warm, tropical climate with an average annual temperature of 26° C (78° F). Its climate and the picturesque beaches along its 100-km (62-mi) coast make it a tourist center during the winter. Heavy rains occur from June to September.

Nearly 40% of the people of Goa are Christians, mainly Roman Catholics. Most others are Hindus. Marathi and Konkani are the principal local languages.

Goa's port, Marmagao, the second largest in India in terms of tonnage, exports a sizable amount of iron ore mined in Goa. India annexed Goa in 1961, ending 451 years of Portuguese rule.

ASHOK K. DUTT

goat

The goat, *Capra,* is a mammal, related to the SHEEP, with backwardly arching horns and a short tail. Goats have played an important role in supplying human needs since prehistoric times, and still do so in certain areas.

Approximately 400 million goats exist throughout the world, most of them in India, China, Turkey, Ethiopia, Iran, and Brazil. More than 200 breeds are recognized. The most important products that goats yield are milk, cheese, butter, mohair, and leather. Certain goat cheeses are highly prized, as is the leather made from the skin of young goats. Because they can feed by browsing, goats are valuable in some areas for brush control.

Both milk goats, *Capra hircus,* and mohair-producing goats, *C. angorensis,* were probably domesticated from a wild species known as the pasang, or Grecian ibex, found in Anatolia and Persia.

Mohair Goats. The most important mohair-producing breed, the Angora, originated in Turkey; in the United States, Angoras are concentrated in Texas. The average yield of mohair is 3 kg (7 lb) annually, obtained in two clippings.

Milk Goats. The principal breeds of milk goat in the United States are the Saanen, Nubian, Toggenburg, French Alpine, and La Mancha. California and the New England states are the principal areas of milk goat production.

The Saanen breed, the largest Swiss breed, is white or light cream with a flesh-colored muzzle. White is preferred. A Saanen produces about 900 kg (2,000 lb) of 3.5 percent butterfat milk in a year. Does weigh 61 kg (135 lb) and bucks 84 kg (185 lb) or more.

The Toggenburg is also a breed of Swiss origin. The color is typically fawn to brown, with white stripes down the face and white on the legs and rump. The hair may be long, short, or curly, and wattles may or may not be present. They typically give about 725 kg (1,600 lb) per year of 3 percent milk. Does weigh 57 kg (125 lb), and bucks 73 kg (168 lb) or more.

The Nubian breed originated in England from native goats and importations from Egypt, India, and North Africa. They have short, glossy hair ranging from black through shades of red to white, with spotted or dappled patterns. They may be horned or hornless and have long, drooping ears. The milk has a high fat content, and production of 680 kg (1,500 lb) of milk a year may be expected. Does weigh 59 kg (130 lb), and bucks 79 kg (175 lb) or more.

French Alpine goats are noted for their colors, which vary from pure white to shades of fawn, gray, red, brown, and black, and combinations of these colors in the same animal. Does weigh about 57 kg (125 lb) and bucks about 77 kg (170 lb). They produce about 725 kg (1,600 lb) of milk of medium butterfat content.

The America La Mancha was developed by crossing the La Mancha, a short-eared Spanish breed, with the dairy breeds. They may be any color, vary in size, and have very short ears or no external ears at all. The breed was recognized by the American Dairy Goat Association as a separate breed in 1958.

CONNELL JEAN BROWN

Bibliography: Gregory, Diana, *Dairy Goats* (1976); Salmon, Jill, *Goatkeepers Guide* (1976); Sims, John A., and Johnson, Leslie E., *Animals in the American Economy* (1972).

goatfish

The goatfishes, or surmullets (family Mullidae, order Perciformes), are common fishes of warm seas. They have elongate and slightly compressed bodies with two widely separated dorsal fins. A small, ventrally placed mouth is well suited for obtaining food from sand or mud. A pair of barbels on the chin, having chemosensitive organs, serves to find crustaceans, worms, and small fish as the goatfish sweeps rapidly

The domestic goat, Capra hircus, *a member of the cattle family Bovidae and related to the sheep, serves as a source of milk, hair and wool, leather, and meat. Major U.S. dairy breeds include the Saanen* (1), *which yields high milk production over a long period, and the smaller Toggenburg* (2). *Both are sturdy, hornless varieties of Swiss origin. The British Alpine* (3), *a cross between the Saanen and the Toggenburg, is black with the Toggenburg's white markings; it is noted for its high milk output. A cross of Asian and British varieties, the Anglo-Nubian* (4) *gives milk with a high butterfat content. The Granada* (5) *is a black, hornless dairy breed raised in Spain. Mohair is made from the long, fine hair of the Angora goat* (6), *which was originally bred in Turkey and is now the single largest breed in the United States.*

The spotted goatfish, Pseudupeneus maculatus, *living inshore in the American Atlantic, drags its barbels along the bottom to find food.*

over the bottom or probes deeply into the sediments. The highly esteemed red mullet of Europe is a goatfish; it is the essential ingredient of the famous fish soups of many parts of the Mediterranean. Occasionally its flesh is poisonous.

C. P. IDYLL

goatsucker

Goatsucker is the common name for birds of the family Caprimulgidae; the name is derived from an ancient belief that they sucked milk from goats at night. Goatsuckers are medium-sized (19–32 cm/7.5–13 in), drab, mottled birds with short, wide bills and, in many species, long rictal bristles. Most are nocturnally active. The names of several New World species—for example, WHIP-POOR-WILL, chuck-will's-widow, and poorwill—are imitative of the birds' repetitious calls. All are chiefly insectivorous, sweeping through the air to capture flying insects in their wide mouths. More than 500 mosquitoes have been found in the stomach of a common NIGHTHAWK, *Chordeiles minor,* of the Americas. Goatsuckers have small, weak feet and usually rest on the ground. On narrow, elevated perches such as limbs and wires, they lie lengthwise.

WILLIAM F. SANDFORD

Gobbi, Tito [gohb'-bee, tee'-toh]

The Italian operatic baritone, Tito Gobbi, b. Oct. 24, 1915, d. Mar. 5, 1984, mastered a repertoire of nearly 100 roles. He made his debut in Rome in 1938, and at La Scala in 1942. His American debut (1948) took place at the San Francisco Opera. In 1956 he began his long association with the Metropolitan Opera as Scarpia in Puccini's *Tosca,* to great acclaim. Known for his fine acting, he sang at most of the major opera houses in Europe and North and South America and had a parallel directing career.

ELLA A. MALIN

Discography: *The Art of Tito Gobbi*; Puccini, Giacomo, *Gianni Schicchi* and *Tosca*; Verdi, Giuseppe, *Falstaff, Nabucco,* and *Otello.*

Gobelins [gawb-lan']

The National Manufactory of Gobelins, the most important French tapestry factory, was founded on the outskirts of Paris as a dye works in the 15th century by Jean Gobelin. A tapestry-weaving workshop was added in 1601 by two Flemish artisans, and in 1662, Louis XIV purchased the manufactory, which then became a center for the production of tapestries and furniture for the royal palaces. Charles LE BRUN was director of the manufactory from 1663 until 1690, supervising a staff of weavers in low-warp and high-warp workshops. In 1664, Le Brun provided designs for three sets of tapestries—*The Elements, The Seasons,* and *The Story of Alexander*—followed in 1665 by *The Story of the King,* which glorified in 14 tapestries important events of the reign of Louis XIV.

The painter Pierre MIGNARD succeeded Le Brun as director (1690), but the factory was closed in 1694 because of the king's financial difficulties, and the weavers were dispersed. The factory was reopened in 1699 solely for the production of tapestries, and the first series woven there was the popular *Portières of the Gods,* designed by Claude III Audran (1658–1734). Other important sets woven during the 18th century included *The Story of Don Quixote,* designed by Charles Antoine Coypel (1714), *The Story of Esther* by Jean François de Troy (from 1739), and *The Gods* by François Boucher (from 1758).

Although the factory survived the French Revolution, it did so in a radically reorganized form, and it was not until the First Empire (1804–14) that Napoleon revived production on a large scale to furnish his imperial palaces. Gobelin tapestries of this period include a set of *Napoleonic Subjects* (from 1806). During the Second Empire (1852–70) Gobelins again served as an imperial factory and produced tapestries for Napoleon III. The fall of the Second Empire and the insurrection (1871) of the Commune of Paris nearly ruined the factory, but it has survived to this day and since 1937 had functioned under the patronage of the state as a branch of the Mobilier National.

Reviewed by KATHRYN B. HIESINGER

Bibliography: Cole, Charles W., *Colbert and a Century of French Mercantilism,* 2 vols. (1939); Weigert, R. A., *French Tapestry* (1962).

Gobi [goh'-bee]

The Gobi, Asia's largest desert, covers an area of about 1,295,000 km^2 (500,000 mi^2) in Mongolia and the Inner Mongolia region of China. The name is Mongolian for "place without water." The desert extends 1,600 km (1,000 mi) east to west, with a maximum north to south measurement of 966 km (600 mi). It is a region of plateaus averaging 900 m (3,500 ft) above sea level, broken by hills and by the ALTAI MOUNTAINS, whose peaks exceed 3,700 m (12,000 ft).

The desert consists mostly of a shallow layer of gravel over

The Gobi Desert, extending across southern Mongolia into northern China, is one of the most sparsely populated areas on Earth. The prevailing winds have lifted the soil cover from the Gobi and deposited it in China, resulting in the sand dunes and sparse grass cover of the desert.

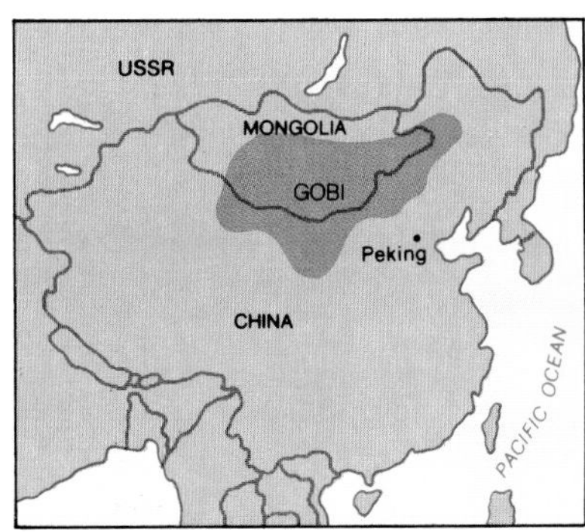

The Gobi Desert, which occupies portions of China and Mongolia, is a vast plateau bordered by mountain ranges. Due to its elevation and northerly location, and because it is subject to continental climatic influences, the Gobi experiences the most extreme range of temperatures of any of the world's deserts.

granite, slate, and other rocks. Annual rainfall averages about 200 mm (8 in) in the east and less than 76 mm (3 in) in the west. The climate is continental, and temperatures range from highs of 50° C (113° F) in July to lows of −40° C (−40° F) in January. Small, brackish lakes exist, but wells and springs supply potable ground water. An ocean covered part of the area in the Permian Period (280 to 230 million years ago), but for the last 100 million years the Gobi has become increasingly dry. Vegetation is scarce and consists primarily of tough grasses, sage, and niter bush. The diverse wildlife includes gazelles, wild asses, jerboas, pit vipers, sandgrouse, and owls. The desert is home to scattered groups of Mongol nomads, who herd camels, goats, and sheep. The population density is less than 1 person per km^2 (3 per mi^2).

The Gobi became widely known through the writings of Marco POLO, who reached it in the 13th century. For centuries it has been the site of numerous caravan routes, and today it is crossed by several railroads and highways. Sven HEDIN and Roy Chapman ANDREWS explored the Gobi in the 20th century, discovering artifacts of Bronze Age and earlier peoples, as well as fossilized dinosaur eggs of the Mesozoic Period (230 to 65 million years ago).

Bibliography: Hedin, Sven A., *Across the Gobi Desert*, trans. by H. J. Cant (1931; repr. 1968).

See also: DESERT; TAKLA MAKAN DESERT.

Gobineau, Joseph Arthur, Comte de [goh-bee-noh']

Joseph Arthur, comte de Gobineau, b. July 14, 1816, d. Oct. 13, 1882, was a French novelist, historian, and anthropologist best known for his racial theories, which are said to have influenced such major figures as Richard Wagner, Friedrich Nietzsche, and Adolf Hitler. Prominent in French social circles, Gobineau first attracted attention among his contemporaries with his novels, of which the best known is *Les Pléiades* (1874). While serving as a diplomat in Europe, Iran, and South America he wrote his *Essai sur l'inégalité des races humaines* (Essay on the Inequality of Human Races, 1853-55), setting forth his theory of the supremacy of the white race and describing what he considered to be the characteristics inherent in other races. Gobineau wrote several scholarly works, including a 2-volume history of Persia and a study of cuneiform.

Bibliography: Biddiss, Michael D., *Father of Racist Ideology: The Social and Political Thought of Count Gobineau* (1970); Rowbotham, Arnold H., *The Literary World of Count Gobineau* (1929; repr. 1973).

goblin: see FAIRY.

goby [goh'-bee]

The striped goby, Tridentiger trigonocephalus, *is a spiny-finned fish found in the waters off the coast of Southeast Asia.*

The gobies, family Gobiidae, order Perciformes, are abundant fishes that inhabit bottom, near-shore areas in tropical and temperate seas. Their pelvic fins are modified to form a suctorial disc. Gobies are small; one Philippine species is the smallest vertebrate known, reaching a length of 3 mm (0.12 in). The mudskippers, *Periophthalmus* and *Boleophthalmus*, are tropical gobies that spend most of their lives on land. The frilled goby, *Bathygobius sorporator*, exhibits remarkable learning ability. If trapped when the tide recedes, a fish that has been swimming over the area can jump unerringly from one pool to another.

C. P. IDYLL

God

In Western culture, which for the last 2,000 years has been dominated by the Judeo-Christian tradition, the word *God* generally refers to one supreme holy being, the divine unity of ultimate reality and of ultimate goodness. God, so conceived, is believed to have created the entire universe, to rule over it, and to bring it to its fulfillment.

In the Old Testament, God was called YHWH, pronounced Yahweh by most scholars; the exact pronunciation of the name was lost because it was rarely enunciated. In its place was read Adonai ("Lord"). The written combination of the tetragrammation YHWH with the vowels of Adonai was traditionally rendered as Jehovah in English Bibles. Although the meaning of YHWH is disputed, it is frequently translated as "He who is" and probably designates YHWH as creator. In ISLAM, ALLAH stands for a similar notion.

Thus, as a functioning word, God in the first instance refers to the central and sole object of religious commitment—and so to the center of WORSHIP, PRAYER, and religious MEDITATION. Secondarily, God has been the object of religious and philosophical reflection, the supreme object of THEOLOGY and of most forms of speculative metaphysics.

God is a puzzling and elusive notion, by no means easy to define. As the supreme being, the creator and ruler of all, God transcends all creaturely limits, distinctions, and characteristics. If something is definable only by its distinctions from other things, its limits, and its special characteristics, how is it possible to define the source of all things, which is not limited, distinguished, or peculiar? God is in neither time nor space; he/she/it transcends all substances and causes; he is neither dependent on nor an effect of other things. Thus, he cannot be spoken of simply as a being among other beings lest he be conceived as a mere creature and thus not God. For these reasons, the concept of God inevitably tends toward that of the transcendent absolute of much speculative philosophy: impersonal, unrelated, independent, changeless, eternal. In some theologies, the concept moves into even more distant realms of abstraction. God can only be described negatively, as the negation of all that is experienced here and now, for example, as nontemporal, nonphysical, and unchanging.

In Jewish and Christian belief, however, God is also in some way personal, righteous, or moral, concerned with people and their lives and therefore closely related to and active within the world and the course of history. The reflective problems in this concept of God, the subject of debates throughout Western history, therefore, have a dual source: God, whatever he may be, is unlike ordinary things that can be described, and the notion of God includes certain dialectical tensions or paradoxes (absolute-relative, impersonal-personal, eternal-temporal, changeless-changing) that defy ordinary powers of speech and of definition. In approaching the divine, religiously or philosophically, one first of all encounters mystery and, with that, special forms or rules of speech—a characteristic as old as religion itself.

VARIATIONS IN THE CONCEPT OF GOD

Ideas of god vary widely from religion to religion and from culture to culture.

Many Gods. In primitive cultures that conceive of human life as totally upheld and threatened by (and thus subordinate to) strange and uncontrollable natural and social powers, all such powers and forces—in animals, totems, rivers, trees, moun-

This 13th-century illustration portrays God as the architect of the universe. In the Judeo-Christian tradition, God is both a transcendant creator and a personal, moral force in history. In other cultures God is purely impersonal, an ultimate principle that defies definition.

tains, kings and queens, tribes, ancestors, holy men and women—participate in and manifest holy power. Here the divine is undifferentiated; it is universally present in important objects and persons. In other ancient cultures that conceive of the person as unique and differentiated from natural and social forces and recognize the role of personal power in politics, these varied natural and cultural forces are personified or symbolized by gods and goddesses who control, work through, and manifest themselves in these powers. For example, ARES was the Greek god of thunder and of war; APHRODITE, the goddess of love and beauty; and APOLLO, the god of light and order. The worship of many gods, known as POLYTHEISM, characterized the religions of most of the ancient world. In every case, a deepening sense of unifying order in reality was accompanied by a drive toward a unity of these plural forces, toward MONOTHEISM.

Impersonal World Order. In many advanced civilizations, the divine appears, not as a person, but as order or harmony; it is thus impersonal, universal, and omnipresent. Clear examples of this view are the *Tao* of TAOISM and the notion of the *Logos* in STOICISM. Both are ultimately an impersonal and unifying principle of the world. Other forms of this view appear in the hymns to Indra in HINDUISM and in the worship of Ahura Mazda, the god of light, in ZOROASTRIANISM. In each of these religions, there is a dualistic principle: an impersonal order, harmony, or light represents the divine; but disorder, chaos, or matter represents the rest of reality. In modern philosophy and theology, the process thought of Alfred North WHITEHEAD also emphasizes the divine as order, against an opposing principle of reality, creativity.

Undifferentiated Unity. Some religions conceive of the divine as the undifferentiated unity of all, a unity in and beyond all manifestations, powers, and persons. The ultimate becomes not only the whole of reality as its unity and ground, but it is so far beyond finite reality that it becomes relatively unintelligible and relatively unreal. In these cases, of course, the divine is thoroughly beyond ordinary speech and even beyond positive analogies, for language deals with the determinate and the finite. The clearest expression of this transcendence of all being and all thought is found in Mahayana BUDDHISM, which describes the ultimate principle in negative assertions and names it a Nothingness, or Voidness. In this notion of the divine the originating religious categories of power, person, and order are infinitely transcended as characteristics essentially related to finitude and therefore antithetical to the divine. Correspondingly, the religious practices of meditation and the religious hope of ultimate release also transcend relations to nature, tribe, society, the course of history, and even all religious praxis and symbols. Such religions regard the Western notion of God, with its implication of personal being and its emphasis on the life of the self in this world, as an extremely inappropriate and even insulting way of regarding their own ultimate principle.

PARADOXES OF THE BIBLICAL CONCEPT

The paradoxes or dialectical tensions characteristic of the Western understanding of God are derived from the Bible. In the Old Testament, God transcends all the limited and special forces and powers of the human experience. On the other hand, his central characteristic, or mode of self-manifestation, is his concern for and relation to history. Although he manifests his power in nature, the main arena for divine activity is the sequence of historical events related to the calling, the establishment, and the protection of his chosen people. In this activity, moreover, God reveals himself as moral or righteous, the source of the moral law, and is quick to punish those, even his chosen ones, who defy this law. He is, however, also a God of mercy, patience, faithfulness, and GRACE. This God of history, COVENANT, judgment, and promised redemption is assumed to be, and often clearly affirmed to be, the ruler of all events.

These aspects of the notion of God reappear, with some modification, in the New Testament. There the one God is also concerned with history, judgment, and redemption, but his central manifestation is JESUS CHRIST, through whom God's will for mankind is revealed, his judgments are made known, and his power to save is effected. The New Testament writers generally use the word *God* to designate the God of the Old Testament. Christ is understood as the fulfillment of the Messianic promise and as the Son, or LOGOS. His relation to God the Father and the HOLY SPIRIT led to the development of the Christian doctrine of the TRINITY. Both Jewish and Christian theology therefore display a dialectical tension between God's transcendence over nature and history as creator and ruler, and his personal, moral participation in history for the sake of humankind.

PHILOSOPHIC APPROACHES

As the symbolic center of Western Christendom down to the ENLIGHTENMENT, and as the fundamental concept in its understanding of nature, society, and human existence, God was the object of endless philosophical and theological speculation. During the long period in which Western culture understood itself and the world largely through the framework of Greco-Roman philosophy (*c.*200–1400), the notion of God was shaped with the help first of Platonic and then of Aristotelian categories. Because of Greek philosophy's bias toward transcendent, changeless, eternal realms of being, this religious tradition greatly emphasized the absolute nature of God: God was understood as pure act, utterly independent, changeless, nontemporal, and unrelated. The active, related, personal aspects of God manifested themselves chiefly in piety and through numerous angelic and saintly representatives.

During the REFORMATION, which emphasized the primacy of Scripture, the personal, purposive, active side of the biblical God again achieved prominence, and the philosophical side receded: God's judgments and his mercy toward humans were considered his central attributes. The transcendent and eternal aspect of this personal God was expressed in the eternal mystery and changelessness of his all-determining will, especially the electing and providential will, rather than in the mystery and changelessness of the divine being.

The subsequent divergence of modern thought from Greco-Roman traditions led to the introduction of new philosophical options emphasizing change, process, and relatedness. They give expression to a new dynamic and immanent interpretation of God and can be found in systems such as PROCESS PHILOSOPHY. While recognizing and affirming in some sense God's absoluteness, eternity, and invulnerability, many modern theologians emphasize his participation in the passing of time, active relatedness to events, and consequent changeableness; they argue that such a view is closer to the biblical notion than is the older Greek view.

Knowability of God. Throughout history certain returning questions have been answered in different theological and philosophical terms. Perhaps the most debated question has been whether God is to be known by reason, by faith, or by experience. Each solution has had powerful and persuasive adherents. Those who argue that God can be known by reason offer one version or another of the classical proofs of God's existence: the cosmological proof from the existence of the world; the teleological proof from the order of the finite world; the ontological proof from the implications of the very concept of God as a perfect and necessary being; and the moral proof from the implications of moral experience. They argue that any theology intellectually respectable enough to speak to modern, intelligent men and women must be grounded in rational philosophy. Those who believe God can be known only by faith tend to be skeptical of such philosophical proofs and possess a perhaps more transcendent image of God. For them, the God of rational theology, proven and tailored by thinking processes, is merely the creature of humanity's own wayward wisdom. God himself must speak to humankind if he is to be known rightly, or even at all, and therefore faith, as a response to divine REVELATION, is the only path to a true knowledge of God. Finally, there are those who assert that God can be known neither by reason nor by faith but only by direct experience.

Reality of God. The secular climate of today's world has led to a reconsideration of the old issue of the reality of God, which has been denied by many humanistic liberals and by most modern Marxists. The appearance of the so-called death-of-God theologies in the 1960s introduced the issue into the Jewish and the Christian religious traditions themselves where it has been the subject of considerable debate. Although most theologians have not followed the lead of the "God is dead" school, there is little question that today no theology can proceed, either by reason, faith, or experience, without raising and in some measure answering this primary query about the reality of God. Is the notion of God, which correlates so closely with the self-understanding of humankind, merely a projection of humanity's self-consciousness onto an unresponding cosmos? Many solutions have been proposed to this question, but the answer ultimately rests on faith. LANGDON GILKEY

Bibliography: Angeles, Peter A., *Problem of God: A Short Introduction* (1974); Bowker, John, *The Sense of God* (1977); Collins, James Daniel, *God in Modern Philosophy* (1959); Cooke, Bernard J., *The God of Space and Time* (1972); Dewart, Leslie, *The Future of Belief* (1968); Dumery, Henry, *The Problem of God in Philosophy of Religion*, trans. by Charles Courtney (1964); Gilkey, Langdon, *Maker of Heaven and Earth* (1959); Hick, John H., *Existence of God* (1964); Kaufman, Gordon D., *God the Problem* (1972); Murray, John C., *The Problem of God: Yesterday and Today* (1964); Ráez, István, *The Unknown God* (1970); Ward, Keith, *The Concept of God* (1975).

See also: CHRISTIANITY; JUDAISM; PRIMITIVE RELIGION; RELIGION.

Godard, Jean Luc [goh-dahr', zhawn luek]

One of the most influential film directors of the 1960s, Jean Luc Godard, b. Paris, Dec. 3, 1930, of Swiss parents, is best known for his innovative NEW WAVE films and for his increasingly radical approaches to politics and art. His experimental use of the hand-held camera, jump cuts, and flash-shots; his disregard for cinematic continuity; and his recourse to question-and-answer sessions within films to illustrate philosophical dialectics have done much to revolutionize cinema in the past 25 years.

The French film director Jean Luc Godard became prominent during the late 1950s as a leading member of the New Wave cinema group. A master of improvisatory filmmaking, Godard is shown here directing actress Brigitte Bardot in Masculin-Féminin *(1966).*

A lively and controversial contributor to the important journal *Cahiers du Cinéma* from 1952 on, Godard made several shorts before directing his first feature, *Breathless* (1959). In *Le Petit Soldat* (The Little Soldier, 1960), on the Algerian War, and other films, Godard combined documentary with fictional footage in an attempt to arrive at a truth beyond art or reality.

Godard's early films dealt with the nature and contradictions of modern society. Of particular interest to him was the place of women in society. *Une Femme est une femme* (A Woman is a Woman, 1961), a film on male-female relationships with a happy ending, was followed by the more biting and ironic *My Life to Live* (1962), on prostitution, *Une Femme mariée* (A Married Woman, 1964), *Masculin-Féminin* (1966), and *Two or Three Things I Know About Her* (1966). Their themes rested on the notion of woman as object, but his approach brought into question the entire commodity-advertising nexus of today's consumer society—as did his more blatant attacks on materialism, *Alphaville* (1965) and *Weekend* (1968). In such films as *Made in USA* (1966), *La chinoise* (1967), and *Sympathy for the Devil* (1968), starring the Rolling Stones, Godard subordinated considerations of plot and pared down his visual imagery to a few static tableaux, becoming more overtly Marxist and didactic.

After a car accident in 1971, Godard produced the autobiographical *Tout va bien* (Everything's Fine, 1972). Other later films include *Numéro deux* (1975), *Every Man for Himself* (1980), *First Name: Carmen* (1983), *Detective* (1984), and *Hail Mary* (1985). GAUTAM DASGUPTA

Bibliography: Barr, Charles, et al., *The Films of Jean-Luc Godard* (1970); Kawin, Bruce F., *Mindscreen: Bergman, Godard, and the Language of First-Person Film* (1978); MacCabe, Colin, *Godard: Images, Sounds, Politics* (1981); Roud, Richard, *Jean-Luc Godard* (1970).

Goddard, John [gahd'-urd]

John Goddard, b. Dartmouth, Mass., 1723, d. 1785, was a leading Newport, R.I., cabinetmaker. He is notable for his contribution to the development of blockfront furniture decorated with stylized scallop shells, which remained a hallmark of Newport cabinetmaking. Apprenticed at an early age to Job Townsend, Goddard married (1746) his employer's daughter and established his own business. Goddard's sons continued their father's business until 1804.

Reviewed by KATHRYN B. HIESINGER

Goddard, Robert

The American physicist Robert Hutchings Goddard, b. Oct. 5, 1882, d. Aug. 10, 1945, laid the foundations of modern rocket and astronautics technology. He earned his master's and doctoral degrees in physics at Clark University, in Worcester, Mass., where he later taught. On his own time and money, Goddard conducted research on improving solid-propellant rockets. Further experiments were conducted under a grant from the Smithsonian Institution, and in 1919 the Smithsonian

Robert Goddard, an American physicist, pioneered research in rocketry that culminated in 1926 with the launching of the first successful liquid-fuel rocket. Goddard's experiments and his treatise, A Method of Reaching Extreme Altitudes *(1919), met an unenthusiastic reception in the American scientific community before World War II. The wartime development of Germany's V-2 rocket, however, demonstrated the practical applications of his research.*

published a 69-page summary of his results, entitled *A Method of Reaching Extreme Altitudes.*

The most noted milestone in Goddard's work came on Mar. 16, 1926, when he fired the world's first successful liquid-propellant rocket. A simple pressure-fed rocket that burned gasoline and liquid oxygen, it traveled only 56 m (184 ft) but proved that the principle was valid. Goddard's future work was dedicated to developing more powerful rockets and more complex systems. He later received grants from Harry F. Guggenheim and the Guggenheim Foundation that proved invaluable when he moved his work to Roswell, N.Mex. During World War II the U.S. government was unconvinced of the rocket's worth as a weapon and put Goddard to work on rocket-assisted-takeoff units for aircraft.

In 1951, Goddard's widow and the Guggenheim Foundation filed a joint patent infringement claim against the U.S. government. In 1960 a $1 million settlement granted the government the rights to more than 200 patents covering "basic inventions in the field of rockets, guided missiles and space exploration." Goddard's records were later published as *The Papers of Robert H. Goddard* (1970). The National Aeronautics and Space Administration named its Goddard Space Flight Center in his honor. DAVID DOOLING

Bibliography: Dewey, A. P., *Robert Goddard, Space Pioneer* (1962); Goddard, R., *The Papers of Robert H. Goddard,* 3 vols. (1970); Lehman, M., *This High Man: The Life of Robert H. Goddard* (1963).

See also: ROCKETS AND MISSILES.

Goddard College

Established in 1938, Goddard College (enrollment: 1,114; library: 66,800 volumes) is a private liberal arts college in Plainfield, Vt. It is a well-known experimental college, with a work-study program, no prescribed courses, and evaluations of student performance that are not reduced to numerical or alphabetical scales.

Goddard Space Flight Center

Goddard Space Flight Center, located in Greenbelt, Md., is the main U.S. facility for tracking and controlling unmanned spacecraft and for relaying data from manned spacecraft. It is also in charge of unmanned Earth-oriented missions and some astronomy missions. Goddard was established in 1958 shortly before the National Aeronautics and Space Administration (NASA) was formed, with the intention that it would become part of the new agency. The center is named in honor of Robert H. Goddard. DAVID DOOLING

Godden, Rumer [gahd'-en, roo'-mur]

Rumer Godden, b. Sussex, England, Dec. 10, 1907, is an author known principally for her novels and children's stories. Several of her works draw on experiences in India, where she spent her childhood and some of her adult life. *Black Narcissus* (1939; film, 1947) concerns Anglican nuns in India and anticipated one of her best-known novels, *In This House of Brede* (1969), which details life in a Benedictine convent.

The Indian setting and Godden's recurrent theme of the mystery of childhood and the transition to adolescence are combined in *The River* (1946; film, 1951). Other works focusing on children are *An Episode of Sparrows* (1955; film, 1957), about London street urchins, and *The Greengage Summer* (1958; film, *Loss of Innocence,* 1961), a mystery. Godden also wrote *Two under the Indian Sun* (1966), an autobiography coauthored by her sister Jon; many children's books; a biography of Hans Christian Andersen (1955); and a book of poems, *In Noah's Ark* (1949). Recent books include *Five for Sorrow, Ten for Joy* (1979) and *The Dark Horse* (1981).

Bibliography: Simpson, Hassell A., *Rumer Godden* (1973).

Gödel, Kurt [gur'-dul]

Kurt Gödel, b. Apr. 28, 1906, d. Jan. 14, 1978, was a Czech-born American mathematician and logician. He is best known for his proof of Gödel's undecidability theorems, which state that any rigidly logical mathematical system contains questions that cannot be proved or disproved on the basis of the AXIOMS within the system. These results were an epochal landmark in 20th-century mathematics, indicating that mathematics is not a finished object, as was previously believed. Gödel's proof first appeared in a German technical journal in 1931. This paper ended nearly a century of attempts to establish axioms that would provide a rigorous basis for all mathematics. Gödel also helped develop geometric models for Einstein's theory of relativity. He became a member of the faculty of the University of Vienna in 1930, where he belonged to the school of logical positivism. In 1940 he immigrated to the United States; he was a professor at the Institute for Advanced Study, in Princeton, N.J., from 1953 to his death.

H. HOWARD FRISINGER

Godey, Louis Antoine [goh'-dee]

Louis Antoine Godey, b. June 6, 1804, d. Nov. 29, 1878, was an American publisher who cofounded (1830) the *Lady's Book,* changing its name to *Godey's Lady's Book* on the withdrawal of his partner. The leading American women's magazine of the 19th century, it dominated its field for more than 50 years under the guidance of Godey and Sarah Josepha HALE, his longtime coeditor. The magazine is best remembered for its richly illustrated fashion plates, but *Godey's Lady's Book* also published the works of the period's leading writers and was an influential supporter of women's causes, including education. It reached a record circulation of 150,000 in 1858. Godey was the first American magazine publisher to leave an estate in excess of $1 million. His magazine outlived him by 20 years, until 1898. CHARLES T. DUNCAN

Bibliography: Entrikin, Isabella, *Sarah Josepha Hale and Godey's Lady's Book* (1946).

Godfrey, Arthur [gahd'-free]

An American entertainer, Arthur Godfrey, b. New York City, Aug. 31, 1903, d. Mar. 16, 1983, became a popular radio and television personality with his blend of informality and sophistication. Godfrey began his radio career in the early 1930s and soon became known for his relaxed style and his success in promoting products that he endorsed. On Dec. 8, 1948, he launched his first television program, "Arthur Godfrey's Talent Scouts."

Bibliography: Godfrey, Jean and Kathy, *Genius in the Family* (1962).

Godfrey of Bouillon

Godfrey of Bouillon, b. *c.*1060, d. July 18, 1100, was a leader of the First CRUSADE and the first ruler of the Latin Kingdom of Jerusalem. Son of Count Eustace II of Boulogne and heir to the duchy of Lower Lorraine, Godfrey was excluded from his inheritance by Holy Roman Emperor Henry IV until 1082. In

1096, with his brothers, Godfrey joined the First Crusade. After the conquest of Jerusalem in 1099, he was elected ruler of the kingdom but took only the title of "Defender of the Holy Sepulcher." He repulsed an Egyptian incursion before his death at Jerusalem. His brother Baldwin I succeeded him.
C. M. BRAND

Bibliography: Anderssohn, John C., *The Ancestry and Life of Godfrey of Bouillon* (1947); Riley-Smith, Jonathan, *The Crusades: A Short History* (1987).

See also: JERUSALEM, LATIN KINGDOM OF.

Godiva, Lady [guh-dy'-vuh]

Lady Godiva, fl. 1040–80, was an English noblewoman who, according to legend, rode naked through Coventry in order to persuade her husband, Earl Leofric of Mercia, to lighten the taxes on the townspeople. In one version, she was observed by only a tailor, the original Peeping Tom, who was struck blind.

Godkin, Edwin Lawrence [gahd'-kin]

An influential American journalist, Edwin Lawrence Godkin, b. Moyne, Ireland, Oct. 2, 1831, d. May 21, 1902, was the founder and long-time editor of The NATION. After reporting on the Crimean War for the *London Daily News*, Godkin emigrated to the United States in 1856, studied law in New York, and covered the Civil War for the *Daily News*.

In 1865 he launched *The Nation*, which quickly became the country's foremost weekly magazine of commentary. He sold it in 1881 to Henry Villard, owner of the *New York Evening Post*, but remained as its editor. Two years later he became editor in chief of the *Post*.

In his trenchant, moralistic commentaries, which made him one of the most influential social critics in post–Civil War America, Godkin opposed expansionism, was a moderate on Reconstruction, and advocated free trade and reforms of currency and the civil-service system. He is also known for several books critical of U.S. society, including *Unforeseen Tendencies of Democracy* (1898).
DONALD H. JOHNSTON

Bibliography: Armstrong, William M., *E. L. Godkin: A Biography* (1978) and *E. L. Godkin and American Foreign Policy, 1865–1900* (1957; repr. 1977).

Godoy, Manuel de [goh-doy']

Manuel de Godoy y Álvarez de Faria, b. May 12, 1767, d. Oct. 4, 1851, chief minister of Spain from 1792 to 1798 and from 1801 to 1808, led his country into disastrous wars. He joined the royal bodyguard in 1784 and soon after became the lover of Maria Luisa, whose husband succeeded to the throne as CHARLES IV in 1788. Charles made Godoy chief minister in 1792.

Godoy's domestic policies were enlightened, for he weakened the Inquisition and supported education. Unfortunately he lacked talent for diplomacy. Spain entered the war against revolutionary France in 1793, but after a series of defeats Godoy concluded the Treaty of Basel (1795), for which he was awarded the title Prince of Peace. In 1796, Godoy allied Spain with France and thus subjected his country to several defeats by the British. This pattern was repeated after Godoy, out of office from 1798 to 1801, resumed power; the Spanish fleet was destroyed at the Battle of TRAFALGAR (1805). In 1808 a popular uprising overthrew Charles in favor of his son FERDINAND VII. Godoy was arrested but released later in the year after French intervention in Spain. He spent the rest of his life in Paris.
DANIEL R. HEADRICK

Bibliography: Chastenet, Jacques, *Godoy: Master of Spain*, trans. by J. F. Huntington (1953; repr. 1971); Hilt, Douglas, *The Troubled Trinity: Godoy and the Spanish Monarchs* (1988).

Godthåb [gawt'-hawp]

Godthåb (1986 pop., 10,972) is the capital and largest town of Greenland. Since Greenland achieved home rule in 1979, the Greenlandic name Nuuk has been used increasingly for the town. It lies on an ice-free fjord and has large fishing and fish-processing industries. Greenland's legislature and a teachers college are there. The town was founded in 1721 by Hans Egede, a Norwegian missionary.

Godunov, Aleksandr [goh'-duh-nof]

The Soviet dancer Aleksandr Godunov, b. Sakhalin Island, USSR, 1950, began his ballet training at the age of nine in the State Ballet School of Riga, Latvia. Godunov became a member of the Moiseyev Young Ballet in 1967 and made his debut (1971) with Moscow's Bolshoi Ballet as Prince Siegfried in *Swan Lake*. Continuing his training under Alexei Emilyanov, Godunov became the favorite partner of prima ballerina Maya PLISETSKAYA and was awarded the gold medal at the 1973 Moscow International Ballet Competition. On the Bolshoi Ballet's 1973–74 U.S. tour he received glowing reviews, especially for his spectacular performances of the title role in *Spartacus*. During the company's 1979 U.S. tour Godunov defected. His superb dancing made him an instant star when he joined American Ballet Theatre in the same year. Since 1982 he has danced as a guest artist; he also acted in the movie *Witness* (1985).
EDWARD T. MCCLELLAN

Godunov, Boris: see BORIS GODUNOV, TSAR OF RUSSIA.

Godwin, Mary Wollstonecraft: see WOLLSTONECRAFT, MARY.

Godwin, William [gahd'-win]

William Godwin, b. Mar. 3, 1756, d. Apr. 7, 1836, was an English writer and the author of *An Enquiry Concerning Political Justice* (2 vols., 1793), an influential work of political and philosophical anarchism. Godwin stressed that humans, shaped by environment and governed by reason, are innately good and free to act without restriction. His ideas influenced the later romantic poets. His novel *The Adventures of Caleb Williams* (1794) was both a psychological thriller and an indictment of society. In 1797 he married Mary WOLLSTONECRAFT, who died giving birth to their daughter Mary Wollstonecraft SHELLEY.
ROBIN BUSS

Bibliography: Marshall, Peter, *William Godwin: Philosopher, Novelist, Revolutionary* (1984); Philp, Mark, *Godwin's Political Justice* (1986).

Godwin Austen

Godwin Austen, officially named K2, is the world's second highest peak and is located in northern Kashmir, Pakistan, in the KARAKORAM RANGE of the Himalayas. It has an elevation of 8,611 m (28,250 ft). It was the second peak to be measured in the 1856 survey of the Karakoram Range (hence, K2) and was originally named for its first surveyor, Henry Haversham Godwin-Austen (1834–1923). Numerous attempts to reach its snow- and glacier-covered summit failed until an Italian team, led by the geologist Ardito Desio, succeeded in 1954.

Goebbels, Joseph [geb'-els]

Paul Joseph Goebbels, b. Oct. 29, 1897, d. May 1, 1945, was propaganda minister of the National Socialist regime in Germany. Reared a Roman Catholic, he received his doctorate in literature and history at Heidelberg in 1922, joined the National Socialist party the same year, and was elected to the Reichstag in 1928. Five years later, when Adolf HITLER came to power, Goebbels became minister of popular enlightenment and propaganda, with control over the press, radio, film, the theater, literature, and art. Goebbels did not simply block off undesirable information or commentary through totalitarian censorship; he shrewdly exploited the captive media in a carefully orchestrated campaign supporting the National Socialist party line.

A small man with a deformed foot, Goebbels did not measure up to the physical standards of the ideology he propa-

Joseph Goebbels, Adolf Hitler's minister of propaganda, addresses a German National Socialist party rally in 1937. A dynamic orator and highly efficient master of propaganda techniques, Goebbels orchestrated public opinion in order to favor and support Hitler's regime.

Hermann Goering, a German aviation hero during World War I, became one of the leaders of the National Socialist party. As air minister (from 1933) he organized the Luftwaffe (German air force), and as plenipotentiary of the 4-year economic plan (from 1936) he directed the nation's economy. Goering was designated as Hitler's successor in 1939 and named Reichsmarschall *in 1940. Reverses in the war discredited him, however, and he lost influence after 1943.*

gated. His virulent anti-Semitism and antiintellectualism notwithstanding, he was a brilliant intellectual who had studied under the prominent Jewish scholar Friedrich Gundolf, and his wife, Magda, had been reared in a Jewish household. Moreover, contrary to his image as one of Hitler's earliest and most loyal stalwarts, Goebbels had actually demanded his expulsion from the party in 1926. But after Hitler had won him over and entrusted him with the party leadership in Berlin, Goebbels came to idolize his leader. He kept the faith until the end. When Hitler committed suicide at the end of World War II, Goebbels and his wife poisoned their six children and then took their own lives. DONALD S. DETWILER

Bibliography: Bramstedt, Ernest K., *Goebbels and National Socialist Propaganda, 1925–1945* (1965); Goebbels, Joseph, *The Goebbels Diaries, 1939–1941,* ed. and trans. by Fred Taylor (1982), *The Goebbels Diaries, 1942–1943,* trans. by Louis F. Lochner (1948), and *Final Entries 1945: The Diaries of Joseph Goebbels,* ed. by Hugh Trevor-Roper, trans. by Richard Barry (1978); Heiber, Helmut, *Goebbels,* trans. by John K. Dickinson (1972); Herzstein, Robert, *The War That Hitler Won: Goebbels and the Nazi Media Campaign* (1986).

Goehr, Alexander

Peter Alexander Goehr, b. Aug. 10, 1932, is a German-born English composer. The son of conductor Walter Goehr, he studied at Royal Manchester College and, in Paris, attended classes by Olivier Messiaen. Goehr produced musical programs for the BBC from 1960 to 1968 and has held teaching and conducting posts in England and the United States. His basically serial techniques are modified by modal and other composing styles. Major works include a violin concerto (1961–62); an opera, *Arden Must Die* (1966); a work for musical theater, *Shadowplay* (1970); a piano trio (1966); String Quartet no. 2 (1971–72); and *Sinfonia* (1980).

Goerdeler, Karl Friedrich [gur'-de-lur]

Karl Friedrich Goerdeler, b. July 31, 1884, d. Feb. 2, 1945, was a leader of the German resistance to Adolf Hitler. He was mayor of Leipzig (1930–37) before resigning to organize opposition to the Nazi regime. After the unsuccessful attempt to assassinate Hitler on July 20, 1944, Goerdeler, who was to have been chancellor in the new government, was executed.

Bibliography: Ritter, Gerhard, *German Resistance: Carl Goerdeler's Struggle against Tyranny,* trans. by R. T. Clark (1958; repr. 1970).

Goering, Hermann [gur'-ing]

Hermann Wilhelm Goering (or Göring), b. Jan. 12, 1893, d. Oct. 19, 1946, was second only to Adolf HITLER in the German National Socialist regime and the one man in Hitler's inner circle with a distinguished social and military background. The son of the first German imperial commissioner of South West Africa, Goering was a highly decorated World War I flyer, having succeeded Manfred von RICHTHOFEN in command of the latter's famous air squadron.

Goering became a National Socialist in 1922 and took part in the abortive MUNICH PUTSCH of 1923. Elected to the Reichstag in 1928, he became its presiding officer in 1932, the year before Hitler came to power. During the 1930s he accrued enormous power as Prussian minister-president and minister of the interior; chief of the GESTAPO (secret police—with his ally Heinrich HIMMLER in operational control); minister of aviation and, with the rank of field marshal, commander in chief of the air force; and economic dictator of the Third Reich, directing the four-year plan (for economic mobilization).

Goering was ferociously efficient in his earlier years, but his personal vitality was later sapped by morphine addiction. During World War II his influence with Hitler was undermined by the failure of the air force (Luftwaffe), first against the British and then against the Soviets. Captured by the Allies in 1945, he was tried as a major war criminal by the International Military Tribunal at Nuremberg (see NUREMBERG TRIALS). He was condemned to execution but cheated the hangman by taking poison. DONALD S. DETWILER

Bibliography: Göring, Hermann, *The Political Testament of Hermann Göring,* trans. by H. Blood-Ryan (1939; repr. 1972); Mosley, Leonard, *The Reich Marshal* (1974); Overy, R. J., *Goering* (1984); Swearingen, Ben, *The Mystery of Hermann Goering's Suicide* (1985).

Goeritz, Mathias [gur'-its]

Mathias Goeritz, b. April 1915, is a sculptor and architect who left his native Germany before World War II and settled in Mexico in 1949. He is best known for abstract, monumental sculptures that complement large architectural projects. His Mexican works include the knife-edged Towers of Satellite City (with Luis BARRÁGAN, 1957) and the conical Automex Towers (1964).

GOES

GOES (Geostationary Operational Environmental Satellites) is a series of meteorological satellites placed in geosynchronous orbits. It is a program of the U.S. National Oceanic and Atmospheric Administration (NOAA). The satellites provide pictures day and night at a rate of one every 30 minutes. *GOES 1* was launched on Oct. 16, 1975, *GOES 2* on June 16, 1977, and *GOES 3* on June 16, 1978. *GOES 4,* orbited on Sept. 9, 1980, also provides vertical water-vapor and temperature profiles of the atmosphere, as do subsequent entries in the series. *GOES 5, GOES 6,* and *GOES 7* were orbited on May 22, 1981, Apr. 28, 1983, and Feb. 26, 1987, respectively. *GOES 7,* which remains functional, is also the first geosynchronous weather satellite in SARSAT, the international satellite search and rescue service (see SARSAT). MITCHELL R. SHARPE

The Portinari Altarpiece *(c.1476) is the masterpiece of the Flemish painter Hugo van der Goes. Admired for its realism, the painting also contains curious disjunctions in scale between the various figures. While the purpose of this triptych was religious, it also indicated the limitations of Flemish naturalism. Tommaso Portinari, the donor, and his family are portrayed on the wings of the triptych. (Uffizi Gallery, Florence.)*

Goes, Hugo van der [hoos]

The work of the Flemish painter Hugo van der Goes, b. *c.*1435-40, d. 1482, occupies an important position in the century-long transition between medievalism and humanism, which occurred in Northern European art between 1425 and 1525. Van der Goes explored the possibilities of portraying religious intensity through expressions of individual feeling—gestures and facial expressions—and far surpassed his predecessors in his ability to portray psychological complexities. Van der Goes's early life is obscure, but in 1467 he was accepted as a master in the painters guild of Ghent. The paintings attributed to him from this time until 1474-76, when he painted his best-known work, the *Portinari Altarpiece* (Uffizi, Florence), were in the decorative, narrative Gothic style. In the *Portinari Altarpiece,* however, he introduced a distinction between the intellectual abstraction of the angels, which he painted in the Gothic style, and the human emotions exhibited by Saint Joseph, Mary, and the shepherds—the apprehensive Joseph; the sorrowing Mary; and the awestruck and wondering shepherds. The altarpiece was commissioned by Tommaso Portinari, an Italian banker living in Bruges, for the Florentine church of San Egidio; its Italian destination was acknowledged by the inclusion of pieces of Italian majolica and Venetian glass in the foreground of the painting. It was enthusiastically received by contemporary Florentine painters, particularly Domenico GHIRLANDAIO, who borrowed van der Goes's shepherds for his *Adoration of the Shepherds* (1485; Santa Trinita, Florence).

About 1475, van der Goes entered the monastery of the Red Cloister near Brussels and became a lay brother. In his later years he became subject to increasingly severe attacks of depression, and his work took on a compulsive intensity, which can be seen in the *Death of the Virgin* (*c.*1480; Musée Communal, Bruges). This painting, in which the introverted and personalized mourning of each Apostle precludes unified composition, is nonetheless a masterful study of individual emotions. Van der Goes attempted suicide in 1481, and died insane the following year. ROWLAND ELZEA

Bibliography: Friedlander, Max J., *Early Netherlandish Painting* (1969) and *From Van Eyck to Bruegel* (1956); Wittkower, Rudolf and Margot, *Born Under Saturn* (1963).

Goethals, George Washington [goh'-thulz]

George Washington Goethals, b. Brooklyn, N.Y., June 29, 1858, d. Jan. 21, 1928, an officer in the U.S. Army Corps of Engineers, directed the building of the PANAMA CANAL. Graduating from West Point in 1880, Goethals gained experience in canal and harbor construction over two decades. In 1907, President Theodore Roosevelt appointed Goethals chief engineer of the Isthmian Canal Commission. The following year, Goethals became the administrator of the Canal Zone, dealing also with the logistics of housing and feeding 30,000 workers. When the canal opened in 1914, Goethals remained as governor of the Canal Zone until 1916. During World War I he served as a director of supply for U.S. troops.

Bibliography: Fast, Howard M., *Goethals and the Panama Canal* (1942).

Goethe, Johann Wolfgang von [gur'-te]

Generally recognized as one of the greatest and most versatile European writers and thinkers of modern times, Johann Wolfgang von Goethe, b. Aug. 28, 1749, d. Mar. 22, 1832, profoundly influenced the growth of literary ROMANTICISM. Best known for his lyrical poetry, for the far-reaching influence of his novels, and particularly for his dramatic poem FAUST (Part 1, 1808; Part 2, 1832; Eng. trans., 1838), Goethe also made substantial contributions to biology and to the history and philosophy of science.

For ten years a leading political figure, Goethe was an acute observer of the great social and intellectual revolutions of the late 18th century and one of the earliest thinkers to explore the implications of the Industrial Revolution.

Goethe's major significance, however, is as an extremely sensitive and vulnerable individual who struggled through a wide range of human crises and left a critical record of this experience.

Johann Wolfgang von Goethe, one of the greatest figures of German culture, encompassed literature, science, music, and philosophy within his work. His early poems and novels display the sensibilities characteristic of the Sturm und Drang *movement; his later works, culminating in* Faust *(1808-32), superbly synthesize knowledge, philosophy, and art.*

LIFE

Goethe was born in Frankfurt am Main into a well-to-do middle-class family. His father, Johann, withdrew from public life and educated his children himself. Goethe's six-volume autobiography, *Aus meinem Leben: Dichtung und Wahrheit* (1811-22; trans. as *Memoirs of Goethe*, 1824), recalls his upbringing as a chaotic experience, but it may have been the most stimulating possible nourishment for his synthesizing mind.

At the age of 16, Goethe began his studies at the university in Leipzig, then a leading cultural center. There he wrote his earliest poems and plays. In 1770 at the university in Strasbourg he came under the influence of Johann Gottfried von HERDER, who introduced him to the works of Shakespeare. In 1771, Goethe received a licentiate in law at Strasbourg and during the next 4 years practiced law with his father and wrote two works that brought him literary celebrity. (See Works and Influences section below.) In 1775 he was invited to the ducal court of Karl Augustus in Saxe-Weimar, where he held (1775-86) numerous high offices and spent most of the remainder of his life. During his early years there he also wrote the beautiful and mysterious lyrics to Charlotte von Stein, a married woman 7 years his senior.

During a 2-year sojourn in Italy (1786-88), Goethe recognized that he was an artist and resolved to devote the rest of his life to writing. The decision did not promise to be a happy one at first; his return to Weimar was followed by years of alienation from court society. Many of his friends were offended by his living with young Christiane Vulpius, who bore him a son in 1789. To legitimize the child, Goethe married Christiane in 1806.

Goethe spent much of his time in nearby Jena and from 1794 to 1805 developed an intense collaboration with Friedrich SCHILLER, a union that many regard as a high point in German letters. However problematic Goethe's decision to withdraw from public life may have been, it did lead to his most important literary and scientific achievements. Goethe's creative powers persisted through his sixties and seventies, and he died in Weimar at the age of 82.

WORKS AND INFLUENCES

In his early twenties Goethe achieved fame in Germany with the play *Goetz of Berlichingen* (written, 1771; publ., 1773; Eng. trans., 1799), which scorned fashionable literary correctness, formalism, and cosmopolitanism. It drew its inspiration from Shakespeare and from Goethe's native genius and embodied the thinking of his early friend and mentor, Herder. Soon after, Goethe became famous throughout Europe with a sentimental and individualistic novel in the style of Jean Jacques Rousseau, The SORROWS OF YOUNG WERTHER (1774; Eng. trans., 1779). During his first ten years in Weimar, Goethe published nothing of further note, although he did collect many of his previously published works in the eight-volume *Goethes Schriften* (Goethe's Writing, 1787-90).

The highly lyrical BILDUNGSROMAN (developmental novel) that Goethe worked on for much of his life, *Wilhelm Meister's Apprenticeship* (1795; Eng. trans., 1824), was a disappointment to admirers of *Werther*, but it was praised and emulated by the later generation of German romantic writers as the exemplary form, and it continued to influence the novel well into the 20th century.

Most celebrated during his lifetime as the author of *Faust*, Goethe was also known for the satirical *Reynard the Fox* (1794; Eng. trans., 1855) and the rather saccharine epic *Hermann and Dorothea* (1798; Eng. trans., 1801), both written in remarkably fine hexameters. His so-called classical dramas, *Iphigenie auf Taurus* (final version, 1787; Eng. trans., 1793) and *Torquato Tasso* (1790; Eng. trans., 1827), were much admired during the 19th century, as were the ballads he wrote in collaboration with Schiller.

Some of his mature works began to be appreciated only in the 20th century, including the second part of *Faust*, the subtly ironical *Elective Affinities* (1809; Eng. trans., 1872), and the deeply passionate lyrical cycle, *West-Eastern Divan* (1819; Eng. trans., 1877). Other works, such as the sensual hexameters of *Roman Elegies* (1795; Eng. trans., 1876) and *Wilhelm Meister's Travels* (1821; Eng. trans., 1824), a highly discursive continuation of the earlier novel, are only now receiving recognition.

Goethe himself expected to be remembered as a scientist. Biology has long recognized its debt to him, especially for the concept of morphology, which is fundamental to the theory of evolution. He thought his most important work was *Zur Farbenlehre* (3 vols., 1810; trans. as *Goethe's Theory of Colors*, 1840), in which he undertook to discredit Newtonian science. This effort brought Goethe into disrepute with 19th-century positivists, but the current emphasis on perception appears to be sympathetic to Goethe's point of view, and the first volume of *Zur Farbenlehre* contains the first comprehensive history of science.

Goethe's careful attention to sociological factors makes him an important forerunner of many modern thinkers. Similarly, current literary scholarship finds in Goethe an early advocate of such concepts as *Weltliteratur*, or comparative literature, and of the decisive role played by the reader in giving meaning to a literary work.

EVALUATION

In our time Goethe is especially noted for recognizing the dehumanizing demands of the industrial epoch, particularly the demand for specialization, and for successfully meeting them without forfeiting his humanity. He was able to do so largely through the synthesizing power of his intellect and his great personal candor.

Goethe was probably greatest as a lyric poet, and his other works often take their strength from lyricism. In the history of GERMAN LITERATURE he is credited with setting the tone for entire movements, for introducing new forms, such as the novella, and for profoundly influencing other forms, such as the novel. The history of Goethe criticism suggests that no generation of scholars can comprehend his entire output. Currently he is particularly admired for the humor and irony of such works as *Faust* and *Wilhelm Meister*, which were long taken quite seriously.

The full implications of his science may also elude today's thinkers. As determinism ceases to characterize science, however, it is finding greater tolerance for a Goethean world in which all phenomena tend to merge. To him, poetry and science were one. Wide-eyed, astonished, but intensely participative, he surveyed the larger context of every human experience.

H. G. HAILE

Bibliography: Blackall, Eric, *Goethe and the Novel* (1976); Fairley, Barker, *A Study of Goethe* (1947; repr. 1977); Goethe, Johann W. von, *Autobiography*, 2 vols., trans. by John Oxenford (1975); Gray, Ronald, *Goethe: A Critical Introduction* (1967); Haile, H. G., *Artist in Chrysalis: A Biographical Study of Goethe in Italy* (1974); Lange, Victor, ed., *Goethe: A Collection of Critical Essays* (1967); Robertson, J. G., *The Life and Work of Goethe* (1932; repr. 1973); Staiger, Emil, *Goethe*, 3 vols. (1952-59).

goethite [guh'-tyt]

The widespread iron ore mineral goethite, an iron hydroxide, FeO(OH), is a common weathering product. It usually forms stalactitic masses with concentric or radiating internal structure. Color is yellowish to dark brown, hardness 5-5½, streak yellow, cleavage perfect, and specific gravity 3.3-4.3. Goethite is often associated with and indistinguishable from limonite in the gossan of sulfide mineral deposits, in tropical laterite, and in bog deposits.

Goff, Bruce Alonzo [gawf]

The American architect Bruce Alonzo Goff, b. Alton, Kans., 1904, d. Oct. 6, 1982, designed buildings that are unusual because of the way in which he combined expressionistic and functional forms. A prodigy who began his apprenticeship with a Tulsa firm at age 12, Goff admired Frank Lloyd WRIGHT's organic forms and carried them much further, as in the Bavinger house (1950-55) near Norman, Okla.—a spiral-shaped structure with circular rooms hung from a central mast. While appearing to be fantastic, each Goff design is shaped to fulfill his client's needs.

J. MEREDITH NEIL

Bibliography: Cook, Jeffrey, *The Architecture of Bruce Goff* (1978).

Goffman, Erving [gawf'-muhn]

Erving Goffman, b. Mannville, Alberta, June 11, 1922, d. Nov. 19, 1982, who taught (1968–82) sociology and anthropology at the University of Pennsylvania, was known for his analysis of implicit social rules governing nonverbal interactions. He demonstrated in numerous books, including *The Presentation of Self in Everyday Life* (1965), that an individual's most casual actions, such as eye movements and body posture, are calculated toward communicating a positive impression.

Gog and Magog [gahg, may'-gahg]

In the prophecy recorded in Ezekiel 38–39, Gog, ruler from the land of Magog, is to be destroyed when he attacks Israel. Symbolic of the conflict between good and evil, the theme reappears in Revelation 20:8, where both are agents of Satan.

Gogarten, Friedrich [goh'-gahr-ten]

Friedrich Gogarten, b. Jan. 13, 1887, d. Oct. 16, 1967, was a German Lutheran theologian known for his interpretation of culture and history. According to Gogarten, a major biblical theme is that humans are responsible for their own history. Secularization is therefore to be considered a normal process in religion and is the result of biblical teaching. One of his most celebrated works was *Demythologizing and History* (1953; Eng. trans., 1955).

Gogh, Vincent van: see VAN GOGH, VINCENT.

Gogol, Nikolai [goh'-gul]

Nikolai Gogol, Russian author of the novel Dead Souls *(1842) and the play* The Inspector General *(1836), first gained success with* Evenings on a Farm near Dikanka *(1831–32), a collection of stories set in the Ukraine.*

The novelist and short-story writer Nikolai Gogol, b. Mar. 31 (N.S.), 1809, d. Mar. 4 (N.S.), 1852, one of the most gifted Russian writers of his time, was a seminal force in 19th-century Russian literature. His extraordinary originality left its mark not only upon the novel, to which he imparted a strain of realism and social protest, but upon literary style in general, which he developed in directions different from Pushkin's innovations. His genius is not easy to characterize, for he was by turns a comic buffoon and a humorless religious fanatic. Celebrated above all for his bizarre comic vision, his work anticipates qualities in modern literature that are grouped under the label of ABSURDISM.

The son of a petty Ukrainian aristocrat, Gogol at age 19 moved to the capital, Saint Petersburg, where he sought success by publishing his narrative poem *Hans Küchelgarten* (1829). Disastrous reviews caused him to buy up and burn the unsold copies and to flee Russia briefly. After his return he attempted an acting career, worked in a government office while studying painting, and taught in a girls' boarding school. His first literary success came with the story collection *Evenings on a Farm near Dikanka* (2 vols., 1831–32), for which the rich folklore of the Ukraine, its Cossack traditions, and the parochial life-style of its people provided most of the raw material. He then taught (1834) medieval history at St. Petersburg University before publishing more Ukrainian stories under the title *Mirgorod* (1835).

Although Gogol was convinced that his labors would bring great benefits to his countrymen, his self-confidence was undermined by a recurrent fear that spiritual weakness would keep him from his high destiny. For Gogol, spiritual weakness, or evil, consists in the eternal human tendency to worship what is worthless. The conflict between Gogol's idealistic strivings and his sad, cynical view of human propensities became vividly apparent in the stories "The Portrait" and "Nevsky Prospect" in *Arabesques* (1835). This dark vision shaped the trivia-ridden, sometimes phantasmagoric, comic world of his greatest masterpieces—the drama The INSPECTOR GENERAL (1836), the novel DEAD SOULS (1842), and the stories "The Nose" (1836) and "The Overcoat" (1842).

Gogol spent many of his productive years abroad, living in Rome, with interruptions, from 1836 to 1848. There he became progressively more preoccupied with religion, coming to believe that he had been called by God to reveal through his art the path of righteousness in an evil world. He resolved to make *Dead Souls* the first part of a kind of contemporary *Divine Comedy*, but despite a decade of labor he believed he had failed, in part two, to give satisfactory expression to his positive religious ideas. This he did in *Selected Passages from Correspondence with Friends* (1847), which was, however, politically and socially reactionary. This work was strongly condemned by liberals, especially the influential critic Vissarion G. BELINSKY, who had previously understood Gogol narrowly as a satirist of social abuses and injustice in autocratic Russia. After this, Gogol gradually sank into the religious obsessions that darkened his last years. In a fit of despair, just ten days before his death, he burned the manuscript of the second part of *Dead Souls*.

KENNETH N. BROSTROM

Bibliography: Erlich, Victor, *Gogol* (1969); Lavrin, Janko, *Gogol* (1926; repr. 1972); Lindstrom, Thais S., *Nikolay Gogol* (1974); Maguire, Robert A., ed., *Gogol from the Twentieth Century* (1974); Nabokov, Vladimir, *Nikolai Gogol* (1961); Setchkarev, Vsevolod, *Gogol: His Life and Works*, trans. by Robert Kramer (1965); Troyat, Henri, *Divided Soul: The Life of Gogol*, trans. by Nancy Amphoux (1973); Zeldin, Jesse, *Nikolai Gogol's Quest for Beauty* (1978).

goiter [goy'-tur]

Goiter is an enlargement of the thyroid gland, an endocrine gland located in the lower part of the front of the neck. The hormones of the thyroid gland are thyroxine and triiodothyronine, which regulate the rate of metabolic activity throughout the body. Iodine is an essential part of their molecular structure. Simple goiter is an enlargement of the thyroid that occurs in reaction to insufficient iodine in the diet and is characterized by underproduction of the thyroid hormones. It is believed that the proliferation of thyroid tissue allows more effective capture of whatever iodine is available for the synthesis of thyroxine. Simple goiter can be reversed or prevented by dietary iodine supplements such as iodized salt. Exophthalmic goiter is an enlargement of the thyroid due to unknown causes that is accompanied by excessive production of thyroxine. This causes a marked increase in the metabolic rate, nervousness, muscle weakness, rapid and irregular heartbeat, and, occasionally, protrusion of the eyeballs, or exophthalmos, from which the name of the disease is derived. Tumors of the thyroid can produce similar effects if they involve the hormone-producing cells. Exophthalmic goiter is often treated with antithyroid drugs, radioiodine, or surgery.

PETER L. PETRAKIS

Bibliography: DeGroot, Leslie, and Stanbury, John, *The Thyroid and Its Diseases*, 4th ed. (1975).

See also: ENDOCRINE SYSTEM, DISEASES OF THE.

Gokstad ship burial [gawk'-stahd]

The Gokstad ship, one of the finest surviving vessels of the VIKINGS, was found (1880) beneath a burial mound in southern Norway, some 80 km (50 mi) south of Oslo. Dating from about AD 900, it measures more than 23 m (75 ft) long and 5.25 m (17 ft) wide. It evidently served as a seagoing longship.

The Gokstad vessel was built of oak and pine, with a heavy wooden keel and high prow and stern; it is less ornate in construction than the Oseburg ship (see OSEBURG SHIP BURIAL). Its overlapping planks were nailed together and lashed to 19 ribs and cross members. There were 16 oar holes on each side of the hull and 32 shields mounted one over the next along the gunwales. A huge square sail was carried upon a single mast, whose yard measured 11 m (36 ft) across. Steering was effected by means of a steering oar fixed at the aft end on the starboard side. Associated grave goods found at Gokstad include a wealth of domestic utensils and funerary offerings.

DENNIS W. HARDING

gold

The chemical element gold, atomic number 79, symbol Au (from the Latin *aurum*), is a soft, lustrous yellow, malleable metal. Its atomic weight is 196.967; it belongs to group 1B along with copper and silver.

OCCURRENCE

Although the Earth's crust averages a mere 0.004 grams of gold per ton, commercial concentrations of gold are found in areas distributed widely over the globe. Gold occurs in association with ores of copper and lead, in quartz veins, in the gravel of stream beds, and with pyrites (iron sulfide, FeS_2). Seawater contains astonishing quantities of gold, but so much energy is required for its recovery that the process is not economical. The ancients found quantities of gold in Ophir, Sheba, Uphaz, Parvaim, Arabia, India, and Spain. By the time of Christ, written reports were made of deposits in Thrace, Italy, and Anatolia.

The greatest early surge in gold recovery followed the first voyage of Columbus. From 1492 to 1600, Central and South America, Mexico, and the islands of the Caribbean Sea contributed significant quantities of gold to world commerce. Particularly important were Colombia, Peru, Ecuador, Panama, and Española (Haiti). During the 17th century these regions contributed 61% of the world's newfound gold. In the 18th century they supplied 80%, over 48 million troy oz (0.5 billion grams).

Following the discovery (1848) of gold in California, North America became the world's major supplier of the metal (see GOLD RUSH). Smaller amounts were discovered in Australia beginning in 1851. From 1850 to 1875 more gold was discovered than in the previous 350 years. By 1890 the gold fields of Alaska and the Yukon edged out those in the western United States, and soon the African Transvaal exceeded even these. Today the world's unmined reserves are estimated at 1 billion troy oz (31 billion g), about half in the Witwatersrand area of the Republic of South Africa. Gold deposits are also found in Wales, Hungary, and the Ural Mountains of the USSR.

The distribution of gold seems to validate the theory that gold was carried toward the Earth's surface from great depths by geologic activity, perhaps with other metals as a solid solution within molten rock. After this solid solution cooled, its gold content was spread through such a great volume of rock that large fragments were unusual; this theory explains why much of the world's gold is in small, often microscopic particles. The theory also explains why small amounts of gold are widespread in all igneous rocks; they are rarely chemically combined and seldom in quantities rich enough to be called an ore.

Because of its poor chemical reactivity, gold was one of the first two or three metals (along with copper and silver) used by humans in its elemental state. Because it is relatively unreactive, it was found uncombined and required no previously developed knowledge of refining. Its first uses are unknown, but it was probably used in decorative arts before 9000 BC. Even civilizations that developed little or no use of other metals prized gold for its beauty (see GOLD AND SILVER WORK).

PHYSICAL AND CHEMICAL PROPERTIES

Elemental gold has a melting point of 1,063°C and a boiling point of 2,966°C. In addition to its softness, it is both the most malleable and most ductile of all elements. This means, respectively, that gold can be hammered into extremely thin sheets (approaching a small number of atoms), and it can be drawn into extremely fine wires. Gold in the form of very thin sheets is called gold leaf, and it has many decorative uses. Elemental gold is an excellent conductor of electricity and heat, surpassed only by the other members of group 1B, copper and silver

Gold usually forms compounds (and complexes) by giving up either one or three of its valence electrons. It is commonly alloyed with other metals, as in jewelry, in proportions that yield desired hardnesses and colors. An alloy of gold, silver, and copper, in which the amount of silver predominates, is called "green gold." An alloy of the same three elements in which copper predominates, is called "red gold." An alloy of gold and nickel is called "white gold." The purity of alloyed gold is expressed by the karat system, where the percent of gold by weight is given as a fraction of 24. Therefore pure gold is 24 karat, whereas 18-karat gold is 18/24, or 75%, gold by weight. Gold dissolves in very few solvents, among them AQUA REGIA and cyanide solutions (used in extraction). When it does dissolve, it is generally by forming complexes. Gold also forms amalgams with mercury and as such is used in dentistry.

MINING

Gold is obtained by two principal mining methods—placer and vein mining—and also as a by-product of the mining of other metals. Placer mining is used when the metal is found in unconsolidated deposits of sand and gravel from which gold can be easily separated due to its high density. The sand

(Left) *Gold is usually found in a native (uncombined) state but is often alloyed with another metal, frequently silver, copper, palladium, or platinum, in amounts from 1% to 50% that must be separated by various refining methods.* (Right) *Johannesburg, the most important mining center in South Africa, is seen beyond mounds of slag, a waste product created by metallurgical refining processes. South Africa produces more than two-thirds of the world's gold supply, as well as large amounts of copper, diamonds, and iron.*

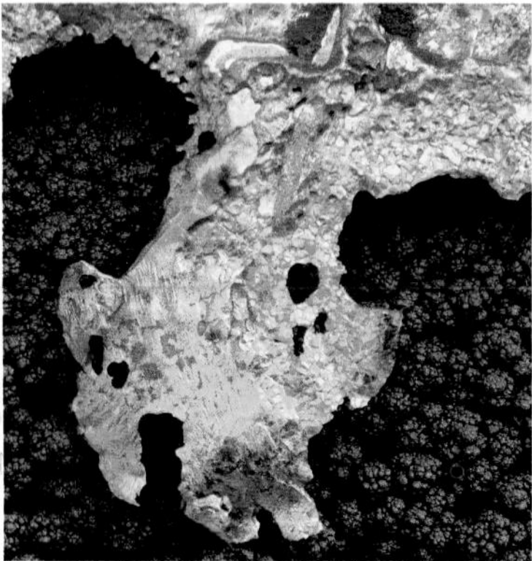

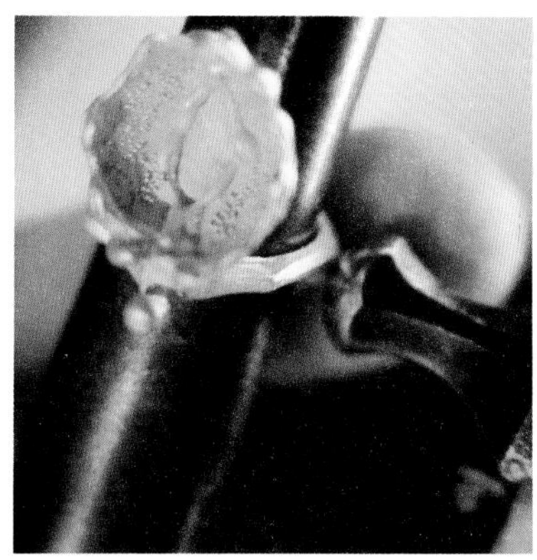

(Left) *Gold bricks weighing 13 kg (35 troy lb) are used as currency reserves. Gold was first used for coins by the Lydians of Anatolia during the 7th century* BC. (Center) *Electrolytic refining purifies gold alloy. When electrolyzed in a chlorine solution by direct and alternating currents, the anode, silver-containing gold, dissolves and deposits 99.95% pure gold on the gold cathode; the silver remains on the anode.* (Right) *A jeweler creates a gold ring. Gold's extreme malleability makes possible simpler metalworking techniques.*

and gravel are suspended in moving water; the much heavier metal sinks to the bottom and is separated by hand. The simplest method, called panning, is to swirl the mixture in a pan rapidly enough to carry the water and most of the gravel and sand over the edge while the gold remains on the bottom. Panning is the classic method used by the forty-niners and is immortalized in story, art, and song (see GOLD RUSH).

Much more efficient is a sluice box, a U-shaped trough with a gentle slope and transverse bars firmly attached to the trough bottom. The bars, which extend from side to side, catch the heaviest particles and prevent their being washed downslope. Sand and gravel are placed in the high end, the gate to a water supply is opened, and the lighter material is washed through the sluice box and out the lower end. The materials caught behind the bars are gleaned to recover the gold. A similar arrangement catches the metal on wool, and may have been the origin of the legend of Jason's search for the GOLDEN FLEECE.

Another variation of the placer method is called hydraulic mining. A very strong stream of water is directed at natural sand and gravel banks, causing them to be washed away.The suspended materials are treated much as if they were in a giant sluice box. Today's most important placer technique is dredging. In this method a shovel of several cubic meters capacity lifts the unconsolidated sand and gravel from its resting place and starts the placer process. Sometimes the shovel rests on a floating barge and cuts its own channel as it moves forward sifting the materials; as it moves it discharges the tailings behind it. The barge floats in a tiny pond that moves as the barge does. This method is called paddock dredging and is probably the least destructive to the environment. Vein, or lode mining, is the most important of all gold recovery methods. Although each ounce of gold recovered requires the processing of about 100,000 ounces of ore, there is so much gold deposited in rock veins that this method accounts for more than half of the world's total gold production today. The gold in the veins may be of microscopic particle size, in nuggets or sheets, or in gold compounds. Regardless of how it is found, the ore requires extensive extraction and refining.

More gold than that recovered by placer mining, but less than by vein mining, is produced as a by-product of copper, lead, and zinc production. The gold found in the sludge left over from the refining of such metals is present in quantities sufficient to make recovery profitable. One-third of all gold is obtained from such by-products.

EXTRACTION AND REFINING

In obtaining gold from vein ore, the ore is first crushed in rod or ball mills. This process reduces the ore to a powdery substance from which the gold can be extracted by amalgamation with mercury or by placer procedures. About 70% is recovered at this point. The remainder is dissolved in dilute solutions of sodium cyanide, NaCN, or calcium cyanide, $Ca(CN)_2$. The addition of metallic zinc to these solutions causes metallic gold to precipitate. This precipitate is refined by smelting. The purification is completed by electrolysis similar to that previously described for copper, and the sludge produced will contain commercial quantities of silver, platinum, osmium, and other rare-earth metals.

USES

One of the principal uses of gold today is as a currency reserve. Gold was for centuries used directly as currency along with silver. During the 19th century it assumed a role as the sole basis of the currencies of most nations; paper MONEY was directly convertible into gold. World War I disrupted this system. The original GOLD STANDARD was gradually abandoned (the United States stopped minting gold coinage in 1934), and the dollar eventually emerged as the principal unit of international monetary transactions (see EXCHANGE RATE). Since the 1970s gold has been bought and sold on the market, with widely fluctuating prices, and gold reserves maintain only a very indirect relationship with the values of currencies and economic systems.

There is a large and rapidly growing demand for gold in industrial processes. Its relatively high electrical conductivity and extremely high resistance to corrosion make the metal critically important in microelectrical circuits. Minute quantities dissolved in glass or plastic sheets prevent the passage of infrared radiation and make an efficient heat shield. Because of its chemical stability, gold is in demand for bearings used in corrosive atmospheres. It is also plated on surfaces exposed to corrosive fluids or vapors. Many other industrial uses demand the properties unique to gold. Its lack of toxicity and its compatability with living systems make it indispensable in dentistry and medicine, and its beauty has made it outstanding in the arts and crafts since the beginning of written history.

CHARLES HOWARD

Bibliography: Cohen, Daniel, *Gold: The Fascinating Story of the Noble Metal through the Ages* (1976); Einzig, Paul, *The Destiny of Gold* (1972); Faulk, Terry R., *Simple Methods of Mining Gold* (1969); Gajda, George, *Gold Refining,* 2d ed. (1977); Green, Timothy, *The New World of Gold* (1982); Jastram, Roy W., *The Golden Constant: The English and American Experience, 1560–1976* (1977); Marx, Jenifer, *The Magic of Gold* (1978); Massey, A. G., et al., *The Chemistry of Copper, Silver and Gold* (1975); Puddephatt, R. J., *The Chemistry of Gold* (1978); Wigley, Thomas, *The Art of the Goldsmith and Jeweler* (1977).

Gold, H. L.

The Canadian-American science fiction writer Horace Leonard Gold, b. Montreal, Apr. 26, 1914, was the editor of *Galaxy* magazine from its inception in 1950 until 1961. His stories, many published under pseudonyms, often concern the psychological and social effects of technological progress. They include *Five Galaxy Short Novels* (1958), *Mind Partner* (1961), and the story "What Will They Think of Last?" (1976).

Gold, Herbert

The American novelist Herbert Gold, b. Cleveland, Ohio, Mar. 9, 1924, has been recognized for his vivid and highly finished style and for his bold portrayal of character. A prominent theme in his works is the individual's struggle for a sense of heroism or glamor while adjusting to the circumstances of contemporary American life. Among his most-admired novels are *The Man Who Was Not With It* (1956), a story of carnival life, and *The Fathers* (1967), a semifictional tribute to the life and career of his father, who had immigrated to the United States from Russia.

Bibliography: Gold, Herbert, *My Last Two Thousand Years* (1972); Hassan, Ihab, *Radical Innocence* (1961).

Gold, Michael

Michael Gold was the pen name of the American novelist, playwright, essayist, and social critic Irwin Granich, b. New York City, Apr. 12, 1894, d. May 14, 1967. As an editor (1921-22) of *Liberator,* a socialist journal, he wrote extensively about proletarian literature. Gold's proletarian novel *Jews Without Money* (1930) is an important document of urban social protest.

Gold, Thomas

The Austrian-born American astronomer Thomas Gold, b. May 22, 1920, is one of the founders of the now generally discounted STEADY-STATE THEORY in COSMOLOGY. He is also known for his explanation of PULSARS as spinning NEUTRON STARS. Gold graduated from Cambridge University (1942, 1946) and in 1959 became professor of astronomy and director of the Center for Radiophysics and Space Research at Cornell University.

STEVEN J. DICK

Gold Coast: see GHANA.

gold rush

Although gold had been mined in western Georgia in the late 1830s, the greatest gold rush in the history of the United States began with the discovery of gold at Sutter's Mill on the American River in northern California on Jan. 24, 1848. When word reached San Francisco, thousands from that city and other parts of California flocked to the region. The great rush, however, began in 1849. California's population grew from about 14,000 in 1848 to 100,000 in 1850. That number increased to 250,000 by late 1852 and to 380,000 by 1860. While the majority of immigrants were from the United States, forty-niners also came from China, Australia, many Latin American nations, and all parts of Europe to prospectors' camps like Yreka, Spanish Bar, and Grass Valley.

George Northrup of Minnesota displays some of the equipment wielded by California gold prospectors in this daguerreotype (c.1860). The discovery of gold in California in 1848 touched off a massive rush, the first of its kind, into the western territories that the United States had recently acquired through its war against Mexico.

Over the next decade, three mining regions developed in California. The first was in the mother-lode region of the Sierra Nevada from Sutter's Mill south to Mariposa. The second was to the north in Nevada County. The third area, in the northern coastal ranges west of Shasta, was never exploited fully because of its isolation and rough terrain.

The earliest placer miners sought the eroded gold in the form of dust, flakes, and nuggets. Found in stream beds and in gravels laid down by ancient rivers, this supply of gold was exhausted quickly, and miners were forced to turn to other techniques requiring greater cooperation, sophistication, and expenditure. Eventually deep mines were dug to tap the original deposits of gold. Rock was hauled to the surface, crushed, and treated to extract the precious dust. Such work, however, required huge amounts of capital, and the individual placer miner either went to work as a wage laborer, returned home, or wandered on to gold strikes in Colorado, Nevada, Idaho, Montana, and Arizona between 1859 and 1890. Subsequent gold strikes in Australia (1851), the TRANSVAAL (1886) in South Africa, the KLONDIKE (1896), and ALASKA (1898) produced similar sequences of events.

The gold rush drew not only fortune hunters but also merchants, artisans, and farmers to the American West. This boom in turn encouraged construction of wagon roads and railroads and attracted essential outside capital. Gold production provided wealth for an expanding American economy and stimulated technological advances later used elsewhere in the United States and the world.

ELLIOTT WEST

Bibliography: Chidsey, D. B., *The California Gold Rush* (1968); Lewis, Oscar, *Sea Routes to the Gold Rush* (1949); Paul, Rodman W., *California Gold* (1947) and *Mining Frontiers of the Far West* (1963); Trimble, William J., *The Mining Advance into the Inland Empire* (1914; repr. 1972).

gold and silver work

Gold and silver were among the first metals to be worked and were prized by the earliest civilizations as tokens of wealth and symbols of power. Gold, which naturally occurs in a pure state, was made into ornaments as early as 3000 BC, but silver, which is usually found compounded with other substances, was not used until techniques of SMELTING were discovered during the BRONZE AGE.

The arts of the goldsmith and silversmith are closely allied to those of the jeweler (see JEWELRY), enameler (see ENAMEL), sculptor, and engraver. Gold and silver were first worked by hammering, and methods of decoration, such as embossing and engraving, followed quickly. Techniques of manipulating metal, which include CASTING, enameling, and WELDING AND SOLDERING, have changed little to this day.

The earliest surviving goldwork, made about 3000 BC, is simple Egyptian jewelry (see EGYPTIAN ART AND ARCHITECTURE), but excavations at Ur (Iraq) have yielded sophisticated work made only 500 years later, which suggests that the Sumerians were the first goldsmiths. The influence of the Sumerian civilization (see MESOPOTAMIAN ART AND ARCHITECTURE) spread through western Asia and toward the Mediterranean, where, on the site of TROY, the archaeologist Heinrich Schliemann (1822-90) discovered a large hoard of gold jewelry dating from about 2500-2300 BC. During the Egyptian Middle Kingdom (*c.*2133-1786 BC) metalworkers attained a very high degree of skill, working in every decorative technique, including repoussé, ajouré, chasing and engraving, granulation, wirework, enameling, and lapidary work. The tomb of TUTANKHAMEN, who reigned during the Egyptian New Kingdom (1570-1085 BC), contained a wealth of fine gold ornaments.

By 2000 BC advanced techniques of filigree work and granulation were known to Minoan goldsmiths in Crete, whose work was ultimately derived from Asian styles (see MINOAN ART). Excavation of the royal burials of MYCENAE has revealed fine gold- and silverwork in the form of vases, drinking cups, jewelry, and weapons. At about the same time, copper and gold were worked in primitive techniques in the British Isles. The splendid *lunulae* (crescent-shaped neck ornaments) of the Irish Early Bronze Age were made during the period of about 1800 to 1500 BC, and the unique sheet gold cape with

The high level of artistry attained in the metalwork of ancient cultures is seen in the brilliant decoration of this Egyptian throne (c.1350 BC) (above) *from the tomb of Tutankhamen (Egyptian Museum, Cairo), and in the delicate filigree of this Colombian pendant* (left) *dating from the 13th-14th centuries AD.*

repoussé decoration found in Wales (British Museum, London) has been dated to about 1400 BC. The famous Celtic gold torcs, or neck rings, date from the 4th to the 1st century BC (see CELTIC ART).

From 850 to 700 BC, after a period of great poverty that followed the Mycenaean civilization, superb goldwork was produced in Greece, Anatolia, and Phoenicia (see PHOENICIAN ART). During the Hellenistic Age exceedingly fine and innovative jewelry was produced, and later Etruscan and Roman work was largely a continuation of these styles (see ETRUSCANS; ROMAN ART AND ARCHITECTURE).

Outstanding goldwork and silverwork in other parts of the world include Persian artifacts of the 5th and 4th centuries BC, such as the Oxus treasure (British Museum) and the treasure from SUSA (Louvre, Paris). There are numerous references to goldwork and jewelry in the literature of the Indo-Aryan civilization of northern India (*c.*1400–*c.*1000 BC). The earliest surviving Indian piece of importance is the Bimaran gold reliquary (*c.*100 BC–AD *c.*100; British Museum), a superb example of repoussé work set with rubies. Very little early goldwork and silverwork from China has been discovered, but the HAN dynasty (202 BC–AD 220) produced some refined gold jewelry.

South and Central America, where the Spanish sought the legendary El Dorado, are very rich in gold and silver. The earliest gold artifacts in America, made by the primitive techniques of cold hammering and repoussé, were probably created in the Andean region of Peru about 2000 BC. It was not until a comparatively late date (AD *c.*300–800), however, that the INCAS acquired the important skill of casting. According to contemporary European descriptions, the 16th-century treasure of Montezuma, last ruler of the AZTECS, was filled with the finest goldwork. Unfortunately, none remains, for all of it was plundered by the Spanish and melted down.

Wealthy citizens of the Roman Empire owned luxurious jewelry and silver plate that was often decorated in relief with naturalistic forms. Roman styles were adopted by Byzantine metalworkers (see BYZANTINE ART AND ARCHITECTURE) and even influenced the work of the SASSANIAN period in Persia (6th and 7th centuries). The *Antioch Chalice* (AD *c.*500; Cloisters, New York City), a silver-gilt cup discovered near the important metalworking center of Antioch and thought at one time to incorporate the Holy Grail, marks a transition between late Roman and early Byzantine style.

The *Reliquary of the True Cross* (AD *c.*930; Limburg Cathedral, Germany), made in the palace workshops at Constantinople (now Istanbul), is representative of Byzantine workmanship. Its configuration of rich enamels and precious stones is typical of a style that influenced much ecclesiastical goldsmiths' work in the centuries following.

During the Middle Ages most goldwork and silverwork was made for the church, and many goldsmiths were monks. The German Benedictine monk Theophilus wrote *De Diversis Artibus* (Of Many Arts, *c.*1110–40; Eng. trans., 1961), an important treatise on the craft. The churches of Western Europe abound in gold and silver reliquaries, crucifixes, chalices, and other sacred vessels. One of the few surviving pieces of secular work is the gold and enamel *Royal Cup of the Kings of France and England* (1380; British Museum).

During the Middle Ages and before, the goldsmith was the most highly honored of all artists, mainly because he worked with precious materials. This attitude gradually changed during the Renaissance (see RENAISSANCE ART AND ARCHITECTURE), when the artist's skill was valued more highly than his materials. Thus arose a distinction between the artist and the artisan that has persisted to this day. This distinction was strengthened when, after the Spanish discovery of America, large quantities of silver and gold became available for domestic use. Great artist-goldsmiths continued to flourish, however, in the courts of Europe. Outstanding among these

Two representative pieces of the metalwork of the early and late Middle Ages, are the 8th-century Ardagh Chalice (left) *(National Museum of Ireland, Dublin) and a French reliquary shrine (c.1340)* (below). *(Metropolitan Museum of Art, New York City.)*

(Above) *The 16th-century saltcellar of Francis I of France exemplifies the work of Benvenuto Cellini (Kunsthistorisches Museum, Vienna). Its ornate style contrasts with the functional designs of early-18th-century metalwork, typified by the silver teapot and stand* (right). *(Metropolitan Museum of Art.)*

(Above) *This silver and silver-gilt covered bowl (1930–40), created by the French silversmith Jean Puiforcat, reflects the elegant line and pure form that distinguish much of his work. Puiforcat was one of the foremost Art Deco designers. (Metropolitan Museum of Art, New York City.)*

men was Benvenuto CELLINI, whose best-known work is the gold and enamel saltcellar (1540–44; Kunsthistorisches Museum, Vienna) made for Francis I of France. Cellini's considerable fame once overshadowed that of the Nuremberg goldsmith Wenzel Jamnitzer (see JAMNITZER family), whose work was sometimes mistakenly attributed to Cellini. Jamnitzer, who was goldsmith to the Habsburg emperors, excelled in a fashionable Renaissance style that incorporated natural objects—shells, plants, and reptiles, often cast directly from nature—in the form and decoration of a work. The Flemish Van Vianen brothers (Adam, 1565–1627, and Paul, 1568–1613) devised the curious auricular style of silversmithing, precursor of the ROCOCO STYLE. The last of the great court goldsmiths was Johann Melchior Dinglinger (1664–1731), whose patron was the extravagant Frederick Augustus I, elector of Saxony (Augustus II, King of Poland). Dinglinger was the master of every conceivable technique, and his ingenious decorative fantasies are still preserved in the "Green Vaults" of the palace treasury at Dresden.

Eighteenth-century goldsmithing and silversmithing became increasingly utilitarian and consisted largely of decorative articles for domestic use in palaces or middle-class households. The work of Paul de Lamerie (1688–1751), a French Huguenot who settled in England, typifies this trend. Juste Aurèle MEISSONNIER, an innovative designer and master of the rococo style in gold and silver, spent his life working in Paris as a royal goldsmith. Although none of his work has survived, it is known through his engravings, which influenced other metalworkers of his time.

A heavy neoclassical style with lavish classical motifs pervaded Europe in the early 19th century, when Napoleon I assumed Roman imperial grandeur.

The Industrial Revolution then began to affect metalworking techniques, and the goldsmith became an entrepreneur with a staff of designers and craftsmen. These developments can be studied in the work of George Richards Elkington (1801–65) and Charles Christofle (1805–63), innovative and scientifically minded craftsmen who evolved methods of mass production in order to meet the growing needs of the middle class and employed the finest contemporary designers for more prestigious work.

In the later 19th century the British ARTS AND CRAFTS MOVEMENT led a reaction against the uniformity caused by industrial methods of production. In the field of metalwork the most important theoretician and practitioner was the architect Charles Robert Ashbee (1863–1942), who sought to revive the skills of ancient craftsmanship. The artist-goldsmiths of today have continued this practice. BETTY ELZEA

Bibliography: Aldred, Cyril, *Jewels of the Pharaohs* (1971); Belli Barsali, Isa, *Medieval Goldsmith's Work*, trans. by Margaret Crosland (1969); Blakemore, Kenneth, *The Book of Gold* (1971); British Museum, London, *Jewelry through 7,000 Years* (1976) and *Wealth of the Roman World A.D. 300–700* (1977); Goetz, Hermann, *India, Five Thousand Years of Indian Art* (1959); Honour, Hugh, *Goldsmiths and Silversmiths* (1971); Kuntzsch, Ingrid, *A History of Jewels and Jewelry* (1981); Link, Eva M., *The Book of Silver* (1973); Mason, John A., *The Ancient Civilizations of Peru* (1957); Strong, Donald E., *Greek and Roman Gold and Silver Plate* (1966); Talbot-Rice, David, *Art of Byzantine Era* (1963); Taylor, Gerald, *Art in Silver and Gold* (1964) and *Silver* (1956); Von Solodkoff, A. *Russian Gold and Silver Work* (1981).

gold standard

The gold standard was an international monetary system in which the value of a currency was defined in terms of a fixed quantity of gold. Paper currency was freely convertible into gold, and both might circulate as money. The heyday of the gold standard was between 1870 and the outbreak of World War I in 1914, when the English pound dominated international trade and prices remained fairly stable. At the end of the war, however, the United States was the only Western country where paper money was still convertible into gold coins. European countries returned slowly to a modified gold standard, but by the mid-1930s, few central banks were required to hold stocks of gold in order to meet liabilities.

Because increases in the money supply were tied to the amount of gold held in national coffers, the gold standard enforced an inflexibility in EXCHANGE RATES, which had little reference to economic conditions. By the late 1950s, U.S. DOLLARS had almost entirely replaced gold in international transactions. While most countries continued to use it as a reserve asset, the importance of gold lessened until, by the 1970s, it was only one of several means of payment, which, in addition to dollars, also included such monetary mechanisms as the Special Drawing Rights, or "paper gold," issued by the INTERNATIONAL MONETARY FUND. LYNN TURGEON

Bibliography: Jastram, Roy W., *The Golden Constant: The English and American Experience, 1560–1976* (1977); Wright, Quincy, ed., *Gold and Monetary Stabilization* (1982).

Goldbach conjecture [gohld'-bahk]

The Goldbach conjecture is an unproved conjecture in NUMBER THEORY. It states that every even integer (except 2) is a sum of two PRIME NUMBERS. For example, $4 = 2 + 2$, $10 = 3 + 7$, and $100 = 47 + 53$. It has been verified, using a computer, that every even integer up to 10^8 (100 million) is a sum of two primes, but the general conjecture has never been proved or disproved. In 1974, however, the Chinese mathematician Jing-run Chen proved that every sufficiently large even integer is a sum of a prime and an integer with at most two prime factors. WILLIAM W. ADAMS

Bibliography: Apostal, Tom, *Introduction to Analytic Number Theory* (1976).

Goldberg, Arthur J.

Arthur Joseph Goldberg, b. Aug. 8, 1908, was a labor lawyer in Chicago and special counsel to the AFL-CIO when he was appointed secretary of labor by President John F. Kennedy in 1961. In 1962, Kennedy appointed him to the United States Supreme Court. He reluctantly resigned in 1965 when President Lyndon B. Johnson asked him to become U.S. ambassador to the United Nations. He resigned from that post in 1968 to return to the practice of law in New York City. He was the unsuccessful Democratic candidate for governor of New York in 1970.

Bibliography: Goldberg, Dorothy, *Private View of a Public Life* (1975); Lasky, Victor, *Arthur J. Goldberg: The Old and the New* (1970).

Goldberg, Bertrand

The Chicago architect Bertrand Goldberg, b. July 17, 1913, has designed high-rise buildings that depart from conventional, rectangular form. Marina City in Chicago (1966), a complex with two circular towers containing apartments, parking, and commercial services, is his most striking project. The petal-shaped plan of the towers provides a flexible framework for apartments of different sizes, and its innovative concrete structure uses flat arches to support the balconies, thus giving the exterior an undulating effect. American critics view Goldberg's work as eccentric, but his designs have been favorably received in Europe. LEON SATKOWSKI

Bibliography: Cook, John W., and Klotz, Heinrich, *Conversations with Architects* (1973).

Goldberg, Rube

The American cartoonist Reuben Lucius Goldberg, b. San Francisco, July 4, 1883, d. Dec. 7, 1970, created drawings of absurdly complex devices for performing simple tasks, designs that he attributed to the fictitious Professor Lucifer Gorgonzola Butts. The term *Rube Goldberg* is now part of the American idiom, denoting a complex or roundabout means of doing something that actually or seemingly could be done more simply.

After receiving (1904) a degree in engineering from the University of California, Goldberg began his career as a sportswriter and cartoonist for the San Francisco newspapers. In 1907 he moved to New York and, while working for the *New York Evening Mail* (1907-21), created and began syndicating (1915) several series of cartoons including "Boob McNutt" and "Mike and Ike." He won (1948) the Pulitzer Prize for editorial cartooning while employed as an editorial cartoonist by the *New York Sun*. Goldberg's drawings are collected in such works as *Foolish Questions* (1909), based on a cartoon series of the same name, and *Rube Goldberg vs. the Machine* (1968).

Bibliography: Marzio, Peter C., *Rube Goldberg: His Life and Work* (1973).

Golden Ass, The

The Golden Ass, entitled *Metamorphoses* by its author, the Roman philosopher and rhetorician Lucius APULEIUS, is a picaresque Latin romance that tells of the magical transformation of a young man into an ass. The story is related by the ass, who becomes the reluctant property of a gang of robbers and undergoes many ludicrous and shameful adventures before being restored to human form by the favor of the goddess Isis. The realistic details of the work give an engaging colloquial account of everyday life in Apuleius's time, and the narrative is embroidered with numerous tales, including the beautiful myth of CUPID and PSYCHE, which has frequently been imitated by later writers.

Bibliography: Walsh, P. G., *The Roman Novel* (1970).

Golden Bough, The

The Golden Bough: A Study in Magic and Religion (1890), by Sir James FRAZER, presents a large amount of information about parallel primitive beliefs and customs. Its basic theses are that human thought and behavior evolved from the magical to the religious to the scientific and that the archetypal ritual is the sacrifice of the tribal priest-king (exemplified by the deaths of Adonis, Osiris, the priest of Nemi, and the Norse god Baldur) in order to ensure the well-being of the society. Frazer's theories are no longer accepted in toto, but they exerted great influence on 20th-century literature and anthropology.

Bibliography: Downie, R. Angus, *Frazer and the Golden Bough* (1970); Vickery, John B., *The Literary Impact of the Golden Bough* (1973).

Golden Bowl, The

The Golden Bowl (1904), the last novel by American author Henry JAMES, is the story of two marriages and a fable of redemption through human love and understanding. The symbolically complex plot centers on an affair between Prince Amerigo, husband of the heroine Maggie Verver, and her friend Charlotte Stant, who is married to Maggie's wealthy father, Adam. Maggie and Adam become aware of the liaison, but conceal this knowledge with tact and self-sacrifice. The prince gains new depth of character when he becomes aware that Maggie has known the truth. The golden bowl, which has a hidden flaw, symbolizes the flawed relationships of the characters and the prince's moral weakness.

Golden Bull

A Golden Bull, from the Latin *bulla,* meaning "seal," was an important document with a gold seal attached, issued by a medieval ruler. The Golden Bull (1222) of King ANDREW II of Hungary enumerated the rights and privileges of the nobility. The Golden Bull (1356) of Emperor CHARLES IV served as a constitution for the HOLY ROMAN EMPIRE. So many controversies had arisen about princely rights in the election of emperors that Charles decided to promulgate basic regulations. His Golden Bull named seven electors: the archbishops of Mainz, Cologne, and Trier; the king of Bohemia; the count palatine of the Rhine; the margrave of Brandenburg; and the duke of Saxony. It defined their ceremonial functions, prescribed their judicial powers, and regulated succession in their principalities. No role was assigned to the popes, who were thus *de facto* excluded from a voice in imperial elections.

RAYMOND H. SCHMANDT

Golden Calf

In the Bible, the Golden Calf was an idol made by AARON for the Israelites while MOSES was on Mount Sinai receiving the TEN COMMANDMENTS. When Moses saw the idol, he was enraged and destroyed it (Exodus 32). Similar representations had a prominent place in other religions.

golden chain

Golden chain is a small tree, *Laburnum anagyroides,* of the pea family, Leguminosae, native to Europe and often cultivated for its yellow flowers, which hang in chainlike clusters up to 30 cm (12 in) long. Golden chain grows to 9 m (30 ft) high, with fruit pods containing up to eight seeds. The plant, particularly the seed, is poisonous. OLIN S. FEARING

golden cup

Golden cup is a hardy perennial herb, *Hunnemannia fumariae-folia,* of the poppy family, Papaveraceae, native to Mexico. It grows to a height of 60 cm (2 ft) and has divided leaves covered with a powdery bloom, and bright yellow flowers about 6.5 cm (2.5 in) in diameter. When cultivated, it is grown from seeds as an annual. OLIN S. FEARING

Golden Fleece

In Greek mythology the Golden Fleece was the treasure wrested from a dragon in Colchis by JASON and the Argonauts, after MEDEA had drugged the dragon. Jason and Medea then fled, carrying the fleece on Jason's ship, the Argo. Some ancient writers, for example, STRABO, believed that this fleece was covered with alluvial gold. Others held that what Jason sought was not gold, but amber. APOLLONIUS OF RHODES thought it was a ram's fleece used as a priest's costume, or the sign of Aries the Ram, or some other sacred cult object. After the Argo's return this prize was spread on the bridal couch of Jason and Medea, thus sanctifying their royal union.

NORMA L. GOODRICH

Golden Gate

The Golden Gate is the strait linking San Francisco Bay with the Pacific Ocean. It is 5 km (3 mi) long, 1.6-3.2 km (1-2 mi) wide, and deep enough (90 m/300 ft) to accommodate large oceangoing vessels. Sir Francis Drake may have landed in the area, but actual discovery of the strait is attributed to Francisco de Ortega in 1769.

Golden Gate Bridge

The Golden Gate Bridge (1933-37), with its span of 1,280 m (4,200 ft) at the entrance to San Francisco Bay, in the heart of the earthquake belt, is one of the world's most famous BRIDGES. The two main cables, each of 0.93 m (3 ft) diameter, pass over the top of cellular steel towers 227 m (746 ft) high and support a six-lane roadway and two footpaths. Great difficulties were encountered in building the bridge foundations; one foundation had to be built inside a huge concrete cofferdam made on the ocean bed. The overall cost of the bridge was less than $35 million. Like many bridges, the Golden Gate attracts suicides. As of June 1977, 604 people had jumped from it.

SIR HUBERT SHIRLEY-SMITH

Bibliography: Cassady, Stephen, *Spanning the Gate: Building the Golden Gate Bridge* (1977).

Golden Horde, Khanate of the

The Khanate of the Golden Horde was the name given to the MONGOL state established in south Russia as a result of GENGHIS KHAN's bestowal of that area on his son Juchi in 1223. Actual conquest of the area was undertaken by Juchi's son BATU KHAN, who by 1240 had destroyed Kiev, the most important Russian state of that time. His conquest of Kievan Russia was the major factor in the decline of Russia from one of the most advanced to one of the most backward European nations in the succeeding centuries. The name *Golden Horde* is derived from the colorful tents of the Mongol encampments.

This group of Mongols merged with the TATARS and other Turkic peoples such as the CUMANS (or Kipchaks), adopting their language and their religion—Islam. As a result their state is also known as the Kipchak Khanate. Headquartered in the Lower Volga region in a series of capitals called Sarai, they imposed a system of strict vassalage on the Russian princes, who were required to pay heavy tribute. Internal divisions—principally between the Blue (eastern) and White (western) hordes—weakened the khanate, enabling DIMITRY DONSKOI of Moscow to defeat the Mongols at Kulikovo in 1380 and TIMUR to conquer the state from 1389 to 1395. Subsequently, the Golden Horde broke up into separate khanates of Astrakhan, Crimea, and Kazan.

RICHARD BUTWELL

Bibliography: Grousset, René, *The Empire of the Steppes: A History of Central Asia,* trans. by Naomi Walford (1970).

Golden Notebook, The

The first major novel by Doris LESSING, *The Golden Notebook* (1962) explores the experiences of Anna Wulf, a South African writer who lives in London. The work is divided into five sections: one is the novel, *Free Women,* that Anna is writing; the other four consist of Anna's notebooks, each devoted to a separate aspect of her life. Although some critics have interpreted the novel as dealing with the problems of liberated women, *The Golden Notebook* actually details the struggle to become free. Anna, who possesses an acute political consciousness, tries to order her world but fails. In the end, she is unsure whether she has won anything at all, and the term *free woman* has become charged with irony.

CHARLOTTE D. SOLOMON

golden retriever

The golden retriever, so named because of its burnished gold color, is a powerful swimmer. The dog has a thick, water-resistant coat.

The golden retriever is a powerful dog with a dense, water-repellent coat that may range in color from light blond to a deep, lustrous, golden red. Males are about 61 cm (24 in) high at the shoulders and weigh up to 34 kg (75 lbs); females are slightly smaller.

Sir Dudley Marjoribanks played a significant role in the breed's development in the mid-19th century, when he bred a dog on his estate near Inverness, Scotland, to suit the local hunting conditions. The breed apparently derived from the yellow puppy that occasionally appeared in litters of the normally black, wavy-coated (or flat-coated) retriever. Initially the breed was called yellow retriever, but in 1913 the dogs were separated as yellow, or golden, retrievers, and in 1920 the name *yellow* was dropped.

JOHN MANDEVILLE

Bibliography: Fischer, Gertrude, *The Complete Golden Retriever* (1974); Sawtell, Lucille, *All About The Golden Retriever* (1973).

golden section

A golden section is a line segment that has been divided into two parts in such a way that the ratio of the longer part (a) to the shorter part (b) is equal to the ratio of the entire segment ($a + b$) to the longer part (a). This can be indicated symbolically as $a/b = (a + b)/a = \phi$, and this ratio, ϕ, is called the *golden ratio.* The concept of a golden section is of historical importance in aesthetics, art, and architecture. It has often been thought that a form, including the human form, is most pleasing when its parts divide it in golden sections. A related concept is the *golden rectangle,* which is a rectangle that has adjacent sides with lengths in the golden ratio. The ancient Greeks felt that the golden rectangle had proportions that were the most aesthetically pleasing of all rectangles; the shape appears in many works from antiquity to the present. It is especially prevalent in RENAISSANCE ART AND ARCHITECTURE. A golden rectangle has the property such that if a square with side equal to the rectangle's short side is marked off, the remaining figure will be another golden rectangle; this process can be repeated indefinitely.

Golden sections also have interesting mathematical properties. Since $a/b = (a + b)/a$, it follows that $a^2 - ab - b^2 = 0$. If this quadratic equation is solved for a in terms of b, the solution is $a = b\,(1 \pm \sqrt{5})/2$. Using only the positive value, $\phi = a/b = (1 + \sqrt{5})/2$, which is approximately equal to

Golden ratios are illustrated in this sequence of golden rectangles and corresponding golden sections. The three largest golden rectangles shown have sides a *and* b, a′ *and* b′, *and* a″ *and* b″, *respectively.*

1.618. It is also true that $\phi^2 = \phi + 1$ and $1/\phi = \phi - 1$. Using approximate numerical values, $1/\phi = 0.618$, $\phi = 1.618$, and $\phi^2 = 2.618$. The golden ratio arises in FIBONACCI SEQUENCES and in the construction of some regular polygons; it is also useful in numerical analysis. JOE K. SMITH

Bibliography: Cook, Theodore A., *The Curves of Life* (1978); Budden, F. J., and Wormell, C. P., *Mathematics Through Geometry* (1964).

goldenrain tree

The goldenrain tree, K. paniculata, *native to China, is an ornamental tree whose abundant flowers the Chinese have long used as a medicine and whose seeds they make into necklaces.*

The goldenrain tree, *Koelreutria paniculata,* is a small deciduous tree of the family Sapindaceae. Native to China, Korea, Taiwan, and Fiji, it has been introduced into the United States and is widely planted in the Midwest. It is coarsely open-branched and flat-topped and has masses of upright, yellow, pyramidal blooms in midsummer. CHARLES L. WILSON

goldenrod

Goldenrod is a genus, *Solidago,* in the sunflower family, Compositae, of about 130 species of mostly North American hardy, perennial herbs that bloom in late summer or autumn. It is related to the aster and typically has a slender, unbranched stem with short-stalked or stalkless leaves and small, yellowish flower heads borne in complex clusters. Widespread throughout the United States, goldenrod has been erroneously blamed for the hayfever caused by ragweed *(Ambrosia).* Some species, however, are toxic because they contain high concentrations of nitrates or diterpenes or because of contamination with fungi. A yellow dye can be prepared from the flowers of some species. OLIN S. FEARING

Canada goldenrod, Solidago canadensis, *a perennial herb, is easily identified by its showy yellow flower clusters. Goldenrod is wrongly thought to be a cause of hay fever.*

Goldfaden, Abraham [gohld-fah′-den]

The Ukrainian-born playwright and composer Abraham Goldfaden, b. July 24, 1840, d. Jan. 9, 1908, was a dominant force in the rise of YIDDISH THEATER. After his theater was banned in Russia, he toured Western Europe and immigrated to the United States in 1903. His early comedies, *Shmendrik* (1877) and *The Kuni Lemels* (1880), are good-natured satires that combine song, poetry, and spectacle, but his later plays are more popular. *Shulamit* (1880) deals with the colorful world of biblical Jerusalem, and *Bar Kochba* (1882) deals with the last revolt of the Jews against the Romans. Goldfaden's songs are known by Jews throughout the world. SOL LIPTZIN

goldfinch

The American goldfinch, Carduelis tristis, *named for the male's distinctive yellow plumage, breeds from mid- to late summer, depending on the supply of thistle and other seeds.*

Goldfinches are birds that include several species of the genus *Carduelis,* order Passeriformes, family Fringillidae, to which also belong SISKINS and greenfinches. They are sometimes placed in the genus *Spinus.* These birds are distributed throughout Europe and North America. They measure about 10–14 cm (4–5 in) and have short, notched tails. The American goldfinch, *Carduelis tristis,* frequents bushes, trees, and fields and is fond of thistle and sunflower seeds. The male has breeding plumage that is bright yellow with a black cap, wings, and tail. The female, young, and male in winter have dull, olive brown plumage. In the lesser goldfinch, *Carduelis psaltria,* of the southwestern states and Pacific coast, the male has a black or dark green back. ROBERT J. RAIKOW

Bibliography: Newton, Ian, *Finches* (1973).

goldfish

The goldfish is a domesticated form of a carplike fish, *Carassius auratus,* native to East Asia and known as *funa* in Japan. In the wild state, *C. auratus* is olive or dark brown, grows to a length of 30 cm (1 ft)—some have reportedly reached 60 cm (2 ft) in length—and weighs up to 4.5 kg (10 lb). When the reddish gold domesticated form escapes to the wild, it reverts in only a few generations to the original dull colors. In North America such reverted fish are called johnny carp or simply wild goldfish.

In North America, where they have been distributed widely, wild goldfish are found as far north as southern Canada. The domesticated variety appears to have originated about 1,000 years ago in China, where they were court pets of the Sung dynasty. They reached Japan about 1500 and Europe (Portugal) in the early 17th century. The most common color in goldfish is a brassy red or orange, but many others are known. Pink fish are often incorrectly called scaleless because the scales lack the amino acid guanine and are difficult to see. One officially recognized form, the shubunkin, does in fact lack scales; its skin color is a mixture of blue, red, white, black, and gold. Goldfish are hardy, peaceful aquarium fish that eat a variety of foods, but the fancier forms generally require warmer water, above 15° C (59° F), than the plainer forms. Hatching occurs in about 8 days in cool water, about 17° C (62° F). The newly hatched fish are nourished by their attached yolk sacs for the first 48 hours, after which they begin to feed on microscopic organisms. Goldfish have been known to live 30 or 40 years. A. R. EMERY

Bibliography: Evans, Anthony, *The Care and Breeding of Goldfish* (1957).

Goldie, Sir George [gohl'-dee]

Sir George Dashwood Taubman Goldie, b. May 20, 1846, d. Aug. 20, 1925, was a British empire-builder in Africa. Commissioned (1865) in the Royal Engineers, he traveled widely in Africa. In 1879 he formed the United African Company, a commercial concern designed to promote British influence in the Niger River region. In 1886 the British government granted a charter to his enterprise, renamed the Royal Niger Company, whereby the company obtained administrative powers in the area later called Nigeria. Goldie became the company's governor in 1895. In 1900 the company's territories passed under direct British colonial control. Goldie was later an alderman of the London County Council (1908–19). L. H. GANN

Bibliography: Flint, John F., *Sir George Goldie and the Making of Nigeria* (1960).

Golding, William

William Golding, one of the most original post-World War II British writers, is best known for his allegorical novel Lord of the Flies *(1954), a bleak examination of human nature. Moral degeneration is seen as inevitable in the absence of social controls against greed and competition.*

William Gerald Golding, b. Cornwall, Sept. 19, 1911, is a prominent English novelist, an essayist and poet, and winner of the 1983 Nobel Prize for literature. Golding's often allegorical fiction makes broad use of allusions to classical literature, mythology, and Christian symbolism. Although no distinct

The goldfish has been bred in a variety of shapes and colors, all of which are considered variants of the original species, Carassius auratus. *The celestial goldfish is so named because its bulging, globular eyes are turned upward. The veiltail has a short, heavy body and a long, sheer, double tail. The lionhead has rounded, blisterlike growths on its head that form a "mane." The telescope black moor, a black goldfish, has large globular eyes that point forward.*

thread unites his novels and his technique varies, Golding deals principally with evil and emerges with what has been characterized as a kind of dark optimism.

Golding's first novel, LORD OF THE FLIES (1954; film, 1963), introduced one of the recurrent themes of his fiction—the conflict between humanity's innate barbarism and the civilizing influence of reason. *The Inheritors* (1955) reaches into prehistory, advancing the thesis that humankind's evolutionary ancestors, "the fire-builders," triumphed over a gentler race as much by violence and deceit as by natural superiority. In *Pincher Martin* (1956) and *Free Fall* (1959), Golding explores fundamental problems of existence, such as survival and human freedom, using dreamlike narratives and flashbacks. *The Spire* (1964) is an allegory concerning the hero's obsessive determination to build a great cathedral spire regardless of the consequences. His later works include *The Scorpion God* (1971), a collection of three short novels; and two major novels, *Darkness Visible* (1979) and *A Moving Target* (1982).

Golding studied English literature and philosophy at Oxford, served in the Royal Navy during World War II, and has been a schoolmaster and lecturer. He is a fellow of the Royal Society of Literature. In addition to his novels, Golding has published a play, *The Brass Butterfly* (1958); a book of early verse, *Poems* (1934); and a collection of essays, *The Hot Gates and Other Occasional Pieces* (1966).

Bibliography: Babb, Howard S., *The Novels of William Golding* (1970); Biles, Jack I., and Evans, Robert O., eds., *William Golding* (1978); Johnston, Arnold, *Of Earth and Darkness: The Novels of William Golding* (1980); Tiger, Virginia, *William Golding* (1974).

Goldman, Edwin Franko

Founder of the well-known Goldman Band, Edwin Franko Goldman, b. Jan. 1, 1878, d. Feb. 21, 1956, was a distinguished American bandmaster. He studied composition with Antonin Dvořák at the National Conservatory in New York City, and for 10 years he was a cornetist in the orchestra of the Metropolitan Opera. He organized his first band in 1911, and in 1918 he began the Goldman Band outdoor concerts, performing on university campuses and in public parks and later touring the United States. In 1945 the band performed for servicemen in Japan and the Philippines. Goldman composed numerous marches and other band music and became a founder and honorary life president of the American Bandmaster's Association.

Goldman, Emma

The American anarchist Emma Goldman infused her spirited lectures, publications, and demonstrations with a passionate belief in the freedom of the individual. Deported to the USSR in 1919, she continued her radical advocacy in Europe. Goldman described her political and personal growth in her autobiography, Living My Life *(1931).*

The American anarchist Emma Goldman, b. Russia, June 27 (N.S.), 1869, d. May 14, 1940, combined the anarchist traditions of the European immigrants with native American radicalism. After a brief marriage in Rochester, N.Y., she entered into a lifelong relationship with the anarchist Alexander Berkman (d. 1936) in New York City. During the HOMESTEAD STRIKE (1892), their plan to precipitate an anarchist uprising by assassinating the industrialist Henry Clay FRICK failed and backfired. Consequently, Goldman repudiated such acts. She rejected all institutions of force and exploitation: private property, wage slavery, religion, marriage, the state, and militarism. She envisioned a communist society of free individuals linked through federated association, contributing according to ability, and taking according to need.

Goldman was imprisoned for hindering conscription in 1917 and deported (1919) to the USSR, a decade after her ex-husband's naturalization was nullified in order to cancel hers. Disillusioned by Bolshevik repression, she left the Soviet Union in 1921 and became (1925) a British subject through a sham marriage. Her last crusade was to aid the Spanish anarchists during the Spanish Civil War (1936–39).

FRED GREENBAUM

Bibliography: Drinnon, Richard, *Rebel in Paradise: A Biography of Emma Goldman* (1961); Goldman, Emma, *Living My Life* (1931); Goldman, Emma, and Bergman, Alexander, *Nowhere at Home: Letters from Exile*, ed. by Richard and Anna Maria Drinnon (1975); Shulman, Alex, *To the Barricades: The Anarchist Life of Emma Goldman* (1971).

Goldmark, Karl

Karl Goldmark, b. May 18, 1830, d. Jan. 2, 1915, was an Austro-Hungarian composer, instrumentalist, and music critic. The son of a cantor, Goldmark studied at the Vienna Conservatory in 1847–48. His overture, *Sakuntala,* first performed in 1865, established his reputation. The most successful of his six operas was *The Queen of Sheba* (1875), but perhaps his best-known work today is *The Rustic Wedding Symphony,* first performed in 1878. Goldmark also wrote concertos, chamber music, piano music, songs, and choral works.

ROBERT M. CAMMAROTA

Bibliography: Goldmark, Karl, *Notes from the Life of a Viennese Composer,* trans. by Alice Goldmark Brandeis (1927).

Goldmark, Peter Carl

The Hungarian-born American inventor Peter Carl Goldmark, b. Dec. 2, 1906, d. Dec. 7, 1977, invented the long-playing phonograph record (LP) and developed systems for broadcasting color television and for viewing recorded film cassettes on television screens by using electronic video technology. After studying in Berlin and Vienna, Goldmark moved to England in 1931 and to the United States in 1933. He worked for the Columbia Broadcasting System from 1936 to 1971; after 1944 he was in charge of engineering research and development at CBS Laboratories. In 1940, Goldmark began work on color television broadcasting. He developed a rotating-disk method that was almost approved by the federal government in 1950. In 1948 he introduced the long-playing phonograph record, which revolutionized the recording industry. The LP had more and narrower grooves than a conventional record and revolved more slowly (33⅓ revolutions per minute). Goldmark's last major technological achievement was the development of an electronic video recording system that played video cartridges through a standard television receiver.

Bibliography: Goldmark, Peter C., *Maverick Inventor* (1973).

Goldoni, Carlo [gohl-doh'-nee]

Carlo Goldoni, b. Venice, Feb. 25, 1707, d. Feb. 6, 1793, was an Italian dramatist whose plays completely reformed Italian comedy. The son of a doctor, Goldoni took a law degree at Padua University in 1731 and practiced law in Venice and Pisa while pursuing his primary interest in the theater. After an unsuccessful first play, *Amalasunta* (1732), a tragedy, he turned to comedy. In 1734 he joined the Imer company of players at the San Samuele theater in Venice, for which he wrote the tragicomedy *Belisario* that year, as well as scenarios for the COMMEDIA DELL'ARTE.

Goldoni sought to reform traditional Italian comedy, in which masked figures presented stock characters in improvised farces. He believed that comedy should reflect nature, and, following the example of Molière, he depicted the foibles of the middle and lower-middle classes, offering a realistic portrayal of character absent from the commedia dell'arte.

He introduced this new style in his first successful play, *La Putta honorata* (The Respectable Girl, 1749). Other famous plays include *La Bottega del Caffè* (*The Coffee Shop*, 1750) and *The Mistress of the Inn* (1753; Eng. trans., 1958). In all, between 1748 and 1762, Goldoni wrote about 133 comedies in Italian and Venetian dialect for two Venetian companies. After 1762 he wrote in French for the Italian theater in Paris, where he enjoyed great success at the courts of Louis XV and Louis XVI. After the Revolution he died in poverty.

Bibliography: Riedt, H., *Carlo Goldoni*, trans. by U. Molinaro (1974).

Goldschmidt, Meyer Aron [gawl'-shmit]

Meyer Aron Goldschmidt, b. Oct. 26, 1819, d. Aug. 15, 1887, was a Danish writer of novels, essays, and stories that reflect the Jewish culture of his homeland. He began a career as a journalist in 1837 and achieved a reputation as a satirist in his own political journal, *Corsaren* (1840-46). In 1845, Goldschmidt produced the novel *The Jew of Denmark* (Eng. trans., 1852). From 1847 to 1859 he published the cultural periodical *Nord og Syd* (North and South), in which he serialized his novel *Hjemløs* (1853–57), translated by Goldschmidt as *Homeless, or A Poet's Inner Life* in 1861. Goldschmidt developed an ethical system that he called "nemesis," by which good and evil are balanced in each individual's life.

Bibliography: Ober, Kenneth H., *Meyer Goldschmidt* (1976).

Goldsmith, Myron

The architect Myron Goldsmith, b. Chicago, Sept. 15, 1918, chief structural engineer of the Chicago branch of SKIDMORE, OWINGS, AND MERRILL, is an heir of those 19th-century Chicago architects who pioneered the development of the structural building. Goldsmith's early designs include a hangar for San Francisco International Airport that uses concrete columns and steel beams, shaped according to the theoretical curvature of their stresses. His most elegant project is the KITT PEAK NATIONAL OBSERVATORY in Arizona (1962). LEON SATKOWSKI

Goldsmith, Oliver

Oliver Goldsmith, b. Kilkenny West, Ireland, Nov. 10, 1730?, d. Apr. 4, 1774, was an Anglo-Irish author of prose, drama, and poetry who achieved literary success with "The Traveller" (1764), a poem praising English freedom but attacking the social evils that concentrated wealth in the hands of a few and drove the poor to emigrate to America. His greatest poetic triumph, "The Deserted Village" (1770), laments the passing of a simple rural life in the face of agricultural consolidation by the great landowners. The fame brought by these poems enabled Goldsmith to associate comfortably with such prominent writers and artists as Edmund Burke, David Garrick, Sir Joshua Reynolds, and Samuel Johnson.

Oliver Goldsmith, an Anglo-Irish novelist and playwright, avoided debtor's prison by publishing The Vicar of Wakefield *(1766), a classic of English literature. Through his essays and farcical plays, such as* She Stoops to Conquer *(1773), Goldsmith led English theater away from the sentimental comedies in vogue during the 18th century.*

When Goldsmith arrived (1756) in London, he became a remarkably versatile but hopelessly improvident professional writer, constantly on the edge of poverty. His most substantial work at that time was *The Citizen of the World* (1762), a collection of mildly satiric essays on English life as viewed by an imaginary Chinese visitor. He also wrote two successful plays, *The Good-Natured Man* (1768) and SHE STOOPS TO CONQUER (1773), a witty attack on the sentimental drama of the day. The VICAR OF WAKEFIELD (1766), Goldsmith's only novel, is a mixture of humor, satire, and the melodrama and sentimentality that he deplored on the stage. An idyllic and moral tale, it was much admired in the 19th century. JOHN RICHETTI

Bibliography: Ginger, John, *The Notable Man* (1977); Swarbrick, A. P., ed., *The Art of Oliver Goldsmith* (1984); Wardle, Ralph, *Oliver Goldsmith* (1957; repr. 1969).

Goldstein, Joseph L.

American molecular geneticist Joseph Leonard Goldstein, b. Sumter, S.C., Apr. 18, 1940, is noted for his work on CHOLESTEROL metabolism. Goldstein obtained his M.D. from the Southwestern Medical School of the University of Texas in 1966, and for the next four years he studied the genetic aspects of heart disease at the National Heart Institute and the University of Washington. In 1972, at the University of Texas Health Science Center, he and Michael S. Brown began studying inherited high blood cholesterol, an important factor in HEART DISEASES. For discovering that persons with this condition are deficient in cell receptors for cholesterol, and for elucidating the mechanisms of cholesterol extraction from the blood, Goldstein and Brown were awarded the 1985 Nobel Prize for physiology or medicine.

Goldstone Tracking Station

Goldstone Tracking Station is the main data-acquisition station for deep-space probes. It is operated by the nearby JET PROPULSION LABORATORY (JPL) at Pasadena, Calif. Goldstone's main instruments, two parabolic dish antennae 26 m (85 ft) and 64 m (210 ft) in diameter, are capable of tracking probes past the orbit of Jupiter. DAVID DOOLING

Goldwater, Barry M.

Barry Goldwater, a prominent U.S. senator from Arizona (1953–65, 1969–87), became a leader of the Republican party through his articulation of a conservative political philosophy. Running against Lyndon Johnson in the 1964 presidential election, Goldwater suffered one of the most decisive defeats in American history, largely because of the electorate's apprehension over his allegedly extremist position on the issue of nuclear weapons.

U.S. Senator Barry Morris Goldwater, b. Phoenix, Ariz., Jan. 1, 1909, was the unsuccessful Republican presidential candidate in 1964. Goldwater was elected to the Senate from Arizona in 1952. A staunch conservative, he became a spokesman for right-wing Republicans in their campaign against big government, advocating instead greater state and local powers. He vigorously opposed federal welfare appropriations as socialistic and sought to curb public ownership of utilities. A strong anticommunist, Goldwater supported American military intervention in Vietnam and criticized efforts to achieve détente with the USSR. He was decisively defeated by Lyndon Johnson in the 1964 presidential election. Goldwater was reelected to the Senate in 1968, 1974, and 1980.

Bibliography: Goldwater, Barry, *The Conscience of a Conservative* (1960) and *Where I Stand* (1964); Hess, Karl, *In a Cause that Will Triumph: The Goldwater Campaign and the Future of Conservatism* (1967); Kessel, John H., *Goldwater Coalition* (1968).

Goldwyn, Samuel [gohld'-win]

The American film producer Samuel Goldwyn, a founder of Goldwyn Pictures Corporation, later Metro-Goldwyn-Mayer, dominated the Hollywood film industry for more than 30 years. Using screenplays by some of the best writers of the time, Goldwyn produced films of outstanding technical quality and great popular appeal.

Samuel Goldwyn, b. Warsaw, Aug. 27, 1882, d. Jan. 31, 1974, considered Hollywood's greatest independent producer, was involved in two of the most important mergers in the history of the U.S. FILM INDUSTRY. A colorful figure known for his malapropisms and mangled but expressive syntax, Goldwyn nevertheless translated his high technical and moral standards into the production of films that were admired both for their craftsmanship and fine pictorial qualities.

An immigrant whose original name was Goldfisch, Goldwyn worked in the glove trade before joining his brother-in-law, Jesse Lasky, and Cecil B. De Mille in founding (1913) the Lasky Feature Play Company. Their initial venture, *The Squaw Man* (1914), was one of the first feature-length films made in the United States.

Following the Famous Players-Lasky merger (1916), Goldwyn left the company to join with Edgar and Arch Selwyn in establishing (1916) Goldwyn Pictures Corporation, in Culver City, Calif.; the corporate name, an amalgamation of Goldfisch and Selwyn, 2 years later became his own. Goldwyn's break with the Selwyns in 1922 in turn paved the way for the merging of the Goldwyn company into the Metro-Goldwyn-Mayer Corporation, in which Samuel Goldwyn sold his entire interest in 1924.

Thereafter, as an independent producer until 1959, Goldwyn personally financed and supervised his films (made in his own studios with stars and other players contracted to him), releasing them through United Artists and RKO. His most creative association, that with director William Wyler, resulted in such films as *Wuthering Heights* (1939), *The Little Foxes* (1941), and the highly acclaimed *The Best Years of Our Lives* (1946). Goldwyn retired in 1960 after his last film production, *Porgy and Bess* (1959).

Bibliography: Easton, Carol, *Search for Sam Goldwyn: A Biography* (1976); Goldwyn, Samuel, *Behind the Screen* (1923); Griffith, Richard, *Samuel Goldwyn: The Producer and His Films* (1956); Marx, Arthur, *Goldwyn: A Biography of the Man behind the Myths* (1976).

golem [goh'-luhm]

The Hebrew word *golem* means "unformed mass." It appears once in the Bible (Psalm 139:16) to refer to a human as an incomplete substance. The golem of medieval legend was a clay robot activated by magical words. In the famous tale of Rabbi Loew of Prague, the golem was a servant made of clay and brought to life by placing a piece of paper inscribed with the name of God under its tongue. Fearing that the creature, which had run amok, would desecrate the Sabbath, the rabbi destroyed it. ROSALIND DARROW SHOR

golf

Golf, a game of Scottish origin, is one of the most popular recreational and competitive sports in the world. Each participant uses a variety of clubs to drive a small ball into a succession of either 9 or 18 designated holes, over a course designed to present obstacles, in as few strokes as possible. In the United States alone more than 18 million people play golf, including 8,200 professional players. Golf tournaments in the United States and elsewhere are popular with spectators as well as with players and since the 1960s have received wide television coverage.

History. Roman emperors apparently played a relaxing game called *paganica*, using a bent stick to drive a soft, feather-stuffed ball. Over the next 5 centuries the game developed on several continents and eventually evolved into the popular

(Left) *A golfer's equipment includes spiked shoes, a glove, and a golf bag* (1), *which may contain up to 14 clubs; woods* (2); *wedges and irons* (3); *a putter* (4); *tees* (5); *and golf balls* (6). *Woods are used to hit the ball great distances, and irons are used for accuracy and height. A putter is used to tap the ball into the hole.* (Center) *The golfer prepares to hit the ball.*

(Below) *To play a par-4 hole, the golfer assumes the correct grip* (1) *and drives from the tee* (2). *At 131 yd (120 m) from the hole, the golfer makes an approach shot* (3) *and lands in a sand trap, where he or she "explodes" the ball onto the green* (4) *then putts it into the hole* (5).

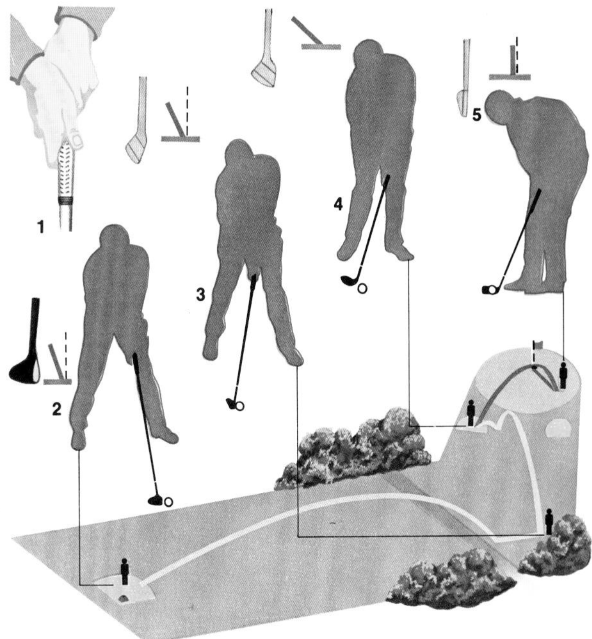

MASTERS CHAMPIONS

1934 Horton Smith
1935 Gene Sarazen
1936 Horton Smith
1937 Byron Nelson
1938 Henry Picard
1939 Ralph Guldahl
1940 Jimmy Demaret
1941 Craig Wood
1942 Byron Nelson
1943–45 No tournaments
1946 Herman Keiser
1947 Jimmy Demaret
1948 Claude Harmon
1949 Sam Snead
1950 Jimmy Demaret
1951 Ben Hogan
1952 Sam Snead
1953 Ben Hogan
1954 Sam Snead
1955 Cary Middlecoff
1956 Jack Burke
1957 Doug Ford
1958 Arnold Palmer
1959 Art Wall, Jr.
1960 Arnold Palmer
1961 Gary Player (S.Afr.)
1962 Arnold Palmer
1963 Jack Nicklaus
1964 Arnold Palmer
1965–66 Jack Nicklaus
1967 Gay Brewer
1968 Bob Goalby
1969 George Archer
1970 Billy Casper
1971 Charles Coody
1972 Jack Nicklaus
1973 Tommy Aaron
1974 Gary Player (S.Afr.)
1975 Jack Nicklaus
1976 Ray Floyd
1977 Tom Watson
1978 Gary Player (S.Afr.)
1979 Fuzzy Zoeller
1980 Seve Ballesteros (Sp.)
1981 Tom Watson
1982 Craig Stadler
1983 Seve Ballesteros (Sp.)
1984 Ben Crenshaw
1985 Bernhard Langer (Ger.)
1986 Jack Nicklaus
1987 Larry Mize
1988 Sandy Lyle (U.K.)
1989 Nick Faldo (U.K.)

U.S. OPEN CHAMPIONS

1895 Horace Rawlins
1896 James Foulis
1897 Joseph Lloyd
1898 Fred Herd
1899 Willie Smith
1900 Harry Vardon (U.K.)
1901 Willie Anderson
1902 L. Auchterlonie
1903–05 Willie Anderson
1906 Alex Smith
1907 Alex Ross
1908 Fred McLeod
1909 George Sargent
1910 Alex Smith
1911–12 John McDermott
1913 Francis Ouimet
1914 Walter Hagen
1915 Jerome D. Travers
1916 Charles Evans, Jr.
1917–18 No tournaments
1919 Walter Hagen
1920 Edward Ray (U.K.)
1921 James M. Barnes
1922 Gene Sarazen
1923 Bobby Jones
1924 Cyril Walker
1925 William MacFarlane
1926 Bobby Jones
1927 Tommy Armour
1928 Johnny Farrell
1929–30 Bobby Jones
1931 Billy Burke
1932 Gene Sarazen
1933 Johnny Goodman
1934 Olin Dutra
1935 Sam Parks, Jr.
1936 Tony Manero
1937–38 Ralph Guldahl
1939 Byron Nelson
1940 W. Lawson Little
1941 Craig Wood
1942–45 No tournaments
1946 Lloyd Mangrum
1947 Lew Worsham
1948 Ben Hogan
1949 Cary Middlecoff
1950–51 Ben Hogan
1952 Julius Boros
1953 Ben Hogan
1954 Ed Furgol
1955 Jack Fleck
1956 Cary Middlecoff
1957 Dick Mayer
1958 Tommy Bolt
1959 Billy Casper
1960 Arnold Palmer
1961 Gene Littler
1962 Jack Nicklaus
1963 Julius Boros
1964 Ken Venturi
1965 Gary Player (S.Afr.)
1966 Billy Casper
1967 Jack Nicklaus
1968 Lee Trevino
1969 Orville Moody
1970 Tony Jacklin (U.K.)
1971 Lee Trevino
1972 Jack Nicklaus
1973 Johnny Miller
1974 Hale Irwin
1975 Lou Graham
1976 Jerry Pate
1977 Hubert Green
1978 Andy North
1979 Hale Irwin
1980 Jack Nicklaus
1981 David Graham (Aus.)
1982 Tom Watson
1983 Larry Nelson
1984 Fuzzy Zoeller
1985 Andy North
1986 Ray Floyd
1987 Scott Simpson
1988–89 Curtis Strange

BRITISH OPEN CHAMPIONS

1860 Willie Park
1861–62 Tom Morris
1863 Willie Park
1864 Tom Morris
1865 A. L. Strath
1866 Willie Park
1867 Tom Morris
1868–70 Tom Morris, Jr.
1871 No tournament
1872 Tom Morris, Jr.
1873 Tom Kidd
1874 Mungo Park
1875 Willie Park
1876 Bob Martin
1877–79 J. Anderson
1880–82 Bob Ferguson
1883 Willie L. Fernie
1884 Jack Simpson
1885 Bob Martin
1886 D. L. Brown
1887 Willie Park, Jr.
1888 Jack Burns
1889 Willie Park, Jr.
1890 John Ball
1891 Hugh Kirkaldy
1892 Harold H. Hilton
1893 Willie Auchterlonie
1894–95 J. H. Taylor
1896 Harry Vardon
1897 Harold H. Hilton
1898–99 Harry Vardon
1900 J. H. Taylor
1901 James Braid
1902 Alex Herd
1903 Harry Vardon
1904 Jack White
1905–06 James Braid
1907 Arnaud Massy (Fr.)
1908 James Braid
1909 J. H. Taylor
1910 James Braid
1911 Harry Vardon
1912 Edward Ray
1913 J. H. Taylor
1914 Harry Vardon
1915–19 No tournaments
1920 George Duncan
1921 Jack Hutchison (U.S.)
1922 Walter Hagen (U.S.)
1923 Arthur G. Havers
1924 Walter Hagen (U.S.)
1925 James Barnes (U.S.)
1926–27 Bobby Jones (U.S.)
1928–29 Walter Hagen (U.S.)
1930 Bobby Jones (U.S.)
1931 Tommy Armour (U.S.)
1932 Gene Sarazen (U.S.)
1933 Denny Shute (U.S.)
1934 T. Henry Cotton
1935 Alfred Perry
1936 Alfred H. Padgham
1937 T. Henry Cotton
1938 R. A. Whitcombe
1939 Richard Burton
1940–45 No tournaments
1946 Sam Snead (U.S.)
1947 Fred Daly (Irel.)
1948 T. Henry Cotton
1949–50 Bobby Locke (S.Afr.)
1951 Max Faulkner
1952 Bobby Locke (S.Afr.)
1953 Ben Hogan (U.S.)
1954–56 Peter Thomson (Aus.)
1957 Bobby Locke (S.Afr.)
1958 Peter Thomson (Aus.)
1959 Gary Player (S.Afr.)
1960 Kel Nagle (Aus.)
1961–62 Arnold Palmer (U.S.)
1963 Bob Charles (N.Z.)
1964 Tony Lema (U.S.)
1965 Peter Thomson (Aus.)
1966 Jack Nicklaus (U.S.)
1967 Roberto de Vicenzo (Arg.)
1968 Gary Player (S.Afr.)
1969 Tony Jacklin
1970 Jack Nicklaus (U.S.)
1971–72 Lee Trevino (U.S.)
1973 Tom Weiskopf (U.S.)
1974 Gary Player (S.Afr.)
1975 Tom Watson (U.S.)
1976 Johnny Miller (U.S.)
1977 Tom Watson (U.S.)
1978 Jack Nicklaus (U.S.)
1979 Seve Ballesteros (Sp.)
1980 Tom Watson (U.S.)
1981 Bill Rogers (U.S.)
1982–83 Tom Watson (U.S.)
1984 Seve Ballesteros (Sp.)
1985 Sandy Lyle
1986 Greg Norman (Aus.)
1987 Nick Faldo
1988 Seve Ballesteros (Sp.)
1989 Mark Calcavecchia (U.S.)

PROFESSIONAL GOLFERS ASSOCIATION CHAMPIONS

1916 James M. Barnes
1917–18 No tournaments
1919 James M. Barnes
1920 Jack Hutchison
1921 Walter Hagen
1922–23 Gene Sarazen
1924–27 Walter Hagen
1928–29 Leo Diegel
1930 Tommy Armour
1931 Tom Creavy
1932 Olin Dutra
1933 Gene Sarazen
1934 Paul Runyan
1935 Johnny Revolta
1936–37 Denny Shute
1938 Paul Runyan
1939 Henry Picard
1940 Byron Nelson
1941 Vic Ghezzi
1942 Sam Snead
1943 No tournament
1944 Bob Hamilton
1945 Byron Nelson
1946 Ben Hogan
1947 Jim Ferrier
1948 Ben Hogan
1949 Sam Snead
1950 Chandler Harper
1951 Sam Snead
1952 Jim Turnesa
1953 Walter Burkemo
1954 Chick Harbert
1955 Doug Ford
1956 Jack Burke
1957 Lionel Hebert
1958 Dow Finsterwald
1959 Bob Rosburg
1960 Jay Hebert
1961 Jerry Barber
1962 Gary Player (S.Afr.)
1963 Jack Nicklaus
1964 Bobby Nichols
1965 Dave Marr
1966 Al Geiberger
1967 Don January
1968 Julius Boros
1969 Ray Floyd
1970 Dave Stockton
1971 Jack Nicklaus
1972 Gary Player (S.Afr.)
1973 Jack Nicklaus
1974 Lee Trevino
1975 Jack Nicklaus
1976 Dave Stockton
1977 Lanny Wadkins
1978 John Mahaffey
1979 David Graham
1980 Jack Nicklaus
1981 Larry Nelson
1982 Ray Floyd
1983 Hal Sutton
1984 Lee Trevino
1985 Hubert Green
1986 Bob Tway
1987 Larry Nelson
1988 Jeff Sluman
1989 Payne Stewart

Scottish game known as *golfe*. Various European countries had games resembling *paganica—cambuca* in England, *jeu de mail* in France, and in the Netherlands *het kolven,* which was played in the American colonies as early as 1657. The Scottish game, however, is the direct ancestor of the modern game. The first formal golf club, the Company of Gentlemen Golfers, now the Honourable Company of Edinburgh Golfers, was established in Edinburgh in 1744. It codified the first set of rules, which helped eliminate local variations in play. The Royal and Ancient Golf Club, established 10 years later at Saint Andrews, Scotland, became the official ruling organization of the sport. Its rules committee, along with the United States Golf Association, still governs golf.

Golf in the United States. The first golf club and course in the United States was the Saint Andrews Golf Club of Yonkers, established in Yonkers, N.Y., in 1888. The first national tournament in the United States was held in 1895. Through a succession of outstanding players, including Walter HAGEN, Bobby JONES, Ben HOGAN, Sam SNEAD, Arnold PALMER, and Jack NICKLAUS, Americans assumed a dominant role in the sport. Before this long list of American champions began, however, an Englishman, Harry VARDON, helped popularize the sport in the United States. Vardon was a six-time British champion between 1896 and 1914. He made two extended tours of the United States, in 1900 and 1913, winning the U.S. Open on his first tour and losing to a young American, Francis Ouimet, on his second. Americans marveled at his style and ability and began to copy him. Jones was one of those he influenced. Jones and Hagen became standouts whom Americans could emulate in the era following Vardon's visit. For many years, however, golf was a sport played almost exclusively by the rich, even though many of the tournament golfers came from humble backgrounds. Not until the 1960s, when Arnold Palmer captured the imagination of the public, did golf become universally popular. Palmer's ascendancy coincided with the increased coverage of sports on television. At the same time, the number of municipal golf courses was rising. By the start of the 1980s there were about 13,000 golf courses, public and private, in the United States, which had become the largest training ground in the world for outstanding golfers. This fact was reflected in the professional standings, where young Americans, attracted by the popularity and large purses of major tournaments, each year dominated lists of the top 20 players, measured by the amount of money won in Professional Golfers Association tournaments. Among the major men's tournaments are the Masters, the U.S. Open, the British Open, and the PGA. Women golfers have their own tour, sponsored by the Ladies Professional Golf Association, the governing body for about 450 women professionals. Their two major tournaments are the LPGA and the U.S. Women's Open. One or both of these championships have been won by such outstanding golfers as Babe Didrikson ZAHARIAS, Mickey WRIGHT, Kathy WHITWORTH, and Nancy LOPEZ-MELTON. Although professional golf has thoroughly overshadowed amateur competition since the retirement (1930) of Jones, the annual U.S. Amateur championships continue to be played, and intercollegiate play is widespread and governed by the National Collegiate Athletic Association (NCAA), which sponsors yearly national championship tournaments with both team and individual competition for both men and women.

International Play. Golf is played, to some extent, in most countries of the world. In Japan, for instance, golf is sometimes regarded as the national pastime. The World Cup (professional) and the World Amateur Team Championship are the most significant international tournaments. The former, held annually since 1953, awards both a team and an individual prize. The latter, held biennially since 1958, is strictly a team competition and has been dominated by the United States. The Ryder Cup is a biennial men's professional competition between a U.S. team and one representing England, Scotland, and Ireland. The Ryder Cup, begun in 1927, has been won only three times by the Europeans. The Walker Cup and Curtis Cup are amateur competitions for men and women respectively, between teams from the United States and the British Isles (England, Scotland, and Ireland). The for-

This golf course is in Palm Springs, a wealthy southern California resort community that regularly hosts such prestigious professional tournaments as the Bob Hope Desert Classic. During the first 4-5 months of the year, all professional events are played in warm climates, and the PGA and LPGA tours do not move into the northern United States until summer. Of the three Grand Slam events played annually in the United States, the sites of two—the U.S. Open and the PGA—vary from year to year, whereas the site of the third—the Masters—remains constant at Augusta National golf course in Georgia.

Jack Nicklaus watches as his putt rolls toward the cup during a professional tournament. Nicklaus, who has won 20 major titles and about $5 million in prize money, was the dominant figure on the men's tour from the mid-1960s into the 1980s.

mer began in 1922 and since 1947 has taken place in odd-numbered years. Curtis Cup competition began in 1932 and is held in even-numbered years. The U.S. teams have won the majority of both these matches.

Rules. The basic golf rules are internationally uniform for both men and women. A player is permitted to carry a selection of up to 14 clubs of varying shapes, sizes, and lengths. The U.S. golf ball is a minimum of 1.68 in. (4.26 cm) in diameter; the British ball is slightly smaller. The game changed considerably in the early 20th century when the B. F. Goodrich Company of Akron, Ohio, invented a lighter, tightly wound, rubber-threaded ball, which replaced the gutta-percha ball used in the 19th century.

A golf course generally has 18 holes spread over a landscaped area that customarily includes a number of hazards—water, rough, sand traps (also known as bunkers), trees—that are designed to make the game more difficult. Difficulty is also increased by the varying distances among holes. Play on each hole is begun at the tee area, from which players "tee off," or "drive" the ball into the fairway. At the end of the hole—which can vary in length from about 150 to 600 yd (135 to 550 m)—is the putting green, which surrounds the actual hole, or "cup," into which the ball must be putted in order to complete the hole. Saint Andrews in Scotland, Augusta National in Georgia (site of the annual Masters tournament), and Pebble Beach in California have some of the most famous and difficult courses.

Golf is usually played by groups of two to four people who move throughout the course together, each participant taking a turn to play his or her ball. The ball must be played as it lies, except in unusual circumstances when the rules allow for the ball to be moved to a slightly better position. In stroke competition the total number of strokes used to move the ball from the tee to the hole is recorded as the player's score for that individual hole. The player who uses the fewest strokes to complete the course is the winner. In match play scores are compared after every hole, and a player wins, loses, or halves (ties) each hole.

As the game has developed, the courses have become more difficult to play, and the most successful players are those who are able to drive the ball more than 200 yd from the tee, approaching most holes with less than three shots. Each course has established an average number of shots (par) necessary to reach a hole (usually depending on length), and thus an average number of shots needed to complete the course. Most championship-caliber professionals score in the mid-60s to low 70s, depending on the tournament and course. Golfers use a peculiar and distinct language to describe their scoring—a birdie is a score on any one hole that is one stroke less than par; an eagle, two less than par; and a bogey, one more than par. A hole in one, the rarest of golfing events, is scored when a player drives the ball into the hole with only one stroke.

ERIC LINCOLN

Bibliography: Browning, Robert, *A History of Golf,* rev. ed. (1985); Gallwey, W. Timothy, *The Inner Game of Golf* (1981); Golf Digest Editors, *The One Hundred Greatest Golf Courses and Then Some* (1986); Golf Magazine Editors, *Golf Magazine's Encyclopedia of Golf,* rev. ed. (1978); Hogan, Ben, *Five Lessons: The Modern Fundamentals of Golf* (1957; repr. 1986); Ward-Thomas, Pat, et al., *The World Atlas of Golf* (1976); Wind, Herbert W., *The Story of American Golf,* 4th ed. (1986).

Golgi, Camillo [gohl'-jee, kah-mil'-loh]

Camillo Golgi, b. July 7, 1843, d. Jan. 21, 1926, an Italian physician, shared the 1906 Nobel Prize for physiology or medicine with Santiago RAMÓN Y CAJAL for their work in neuroanatomy. Golgi developed a method for staining nerve tissue by using silver salts, and in 1898 he described a cytoplasmic organelle of cells known as the Golgi apparatus. He was a professor of histology at the University of Pavia for many years until his death.

Golgi apparatus

The Golgi apparatus is an organelle common in the CYTOPLASM of all eukaryotic CELLS and is believed to act as a storage site for newly synthesized materials within the cell and as a "packaging" system for such secretions as hormones. Named for the Italian anatomist Camillo Golgi, the Golgi apparatus consists of a series of flattened sacs and round vesicles of membranous material. The apparatus takes up the products of the ENDOPLASMIC RETICULUM by accepting them into small vesicles. It then moves the products to larger vesicles where they are transferred to other parts of the cell. Hormones and some enzymes are transferred to the surface for release from the cell.

Bibliography: Whaley, W. G., *The Golgi Apparatus* (1975).

Goliath [guh-ly'-uhth]

In the Bible, Goliath was a Philistine warrior of great stature. When he challenged the Israelites to single combat, the youthful DAVID (later king) responded and vanquished him with a single stone from his sling (1 Sam. 17).

goliath frog

The goliath frog, C. goliath, *is a giant frog measuring about 30.5 cm (12 in) in length. It is found only in the mountains of a small area in west central Africa.*

The shy and elusive goliath frog, *Conraua goliath,* family Ranidae, is the largest known frog. It reaches a body length of 30.5 cm (12 in) and overall length from nose to toe of about 91 cm (3 ft); specimens in excess of 3.2 kg (7 lb) have been collected. Goliath frogs inhabit cascading mountain streams in a restricted range in west central Africa (Mbini and Cameroon). They are prized as food by the Bayele, a

tribe of pygmies, who also value their thigh bones for their presumed power to bring good luck. Formerly much sought after by zoological parks, the goliath frog is now protected by law.
JONATHAN CAMPBELL

Goltzius, Hendrik [gohlt'-see-us, hen'-drik]

Hendrik Goltzius, 1558–1617, was a Dutch Mannerist artist best known for his engravings and chiaroscuro woodcuts. He learned engraving in Haarlem where he copied drawings by Bartholomäus Spranger. A brief Italian journey (1590) resulted in a tempering of his style with classical elements and the influence of Raphael. Goltzius was also famous for his large pen drawings and small, naturalistic landscape studies.
EDWARD J. SULLIVAN

Bibliography: University of Connecticut Museum of Art, *Hendrik Goltzius and The Printmakers of Haarlem* (1972).

Gombrich, Sir Ernst H. [gohm'-brik, airnst]

Sir Ernst Hans Josef Gombrich, b. Mar. 30, 1909, is an art historian best known for his book *Art and Illusion* (1959) and his studies of Renaissance art. Educated in Vienna, he went to England in 1938. After serving with British Intelligence during World War II, he joined (1947) the staff of the Warburg Institute, London University, where he was director from 1959 to 1976. Many of his writings, including *Art and Illusion* and *The Image and the Eye* (1982), deal with the visual arts in their relationship to the history and psychology of perception. He treats his other main interest, Renaissance art, in relation to iconography, the history of patronage, and the intellectual concerns of the period.
JACQUELINE V. FALKENHEIM

Bibliography: Gombrich, E. H., *Meditations on a Hobbyhorse, and Other Essays on the Theory of Art* (1963), *Norm and Form,* 2d ed. (1971), and *The Story of Art,* 13th rev. ed. (1980).

Gombrowicz, Witold [gahm-broh'-vich, vee'-tohld]

The most distinguished Polish writer of the 20th century, Witold Gombrowicz, b. Aug. 4, 1904, d. July 25, 1969, clearly revealed his iconoclasm in his first volume of short stories, *Pamiętnik z okresu dojrzewania* (Memoirs of Immaturity, 1933), when he wrote: "Wherever I see some mystique, be it virtue or family, faith or fatherland, there I must commit some indecent act." In novels and plays notable for their highly individualistic prose style, Gombrowicz continued to use the weapons of absurd exaggeration and the insights of a philosopher to debunk the values and institutions of his age—masculinity, honor, liberalism, and civilization, among others. For Gombrowicz, true humanity was achieved by breaking with the categories and definitions imposed by society, a feat that he accomplished most dramatically in the brilliant comic novel *Ferdydurke* (1938; Eng. trans., 1961). This novel helped gain him an international following and a new popularity in post-Stalinist Poland, where his previously banned works were allowed to be published and then were promptly suppressed. A resident of Argentina from 1939 to 1963, Gombrowicz moved to France in 1964. His plays, especially *Yvonne, Princess of Burgundy* (1938; Eng. trans., 1969); his novels *Transatlantyk* (1953), *Pornography* (1960; Eng. trans., 1966), and *Cosmos* (1965; Eng. trans., 1967); and his essay-diaries for the years 1953–61 gradually won him increased recognition for his originality, reflected in the International Publishers Prize, which he received in 1967.
MICHAEL KANDEL

Bibliography: Thompson, Ewa M., *Witold Gombrowicz* (1979).

Gómez, Juan Vicente [goh'-mes, hwahn vee-sayn'-tay]

Juan Vicente Gómez, b. *c.*1857, d. Dec. 17, 1935, was dictator of Venezuela from 1908 to 1935. He joined Cipriano CASTRO's army of revolution in 1899 and, after Castro won control of Venezuela, was appointed vice-president in 1902. In 1908, while Castro was in Europe, Gómez seized control.

An uneducated but cunning man, Gómez controlled Venezuela's military forces. When he himself was out of office, he ruled through puppet presidents. Gómez served as the elected president in 1910–14, 1922–29, and 1931–35. His administration was known for its tight controls and suppression of all dissent. The stability that resulted, however, helped Venezuela pay off its enormous debts and encouraged foreign companies to develop a flourishing petroleum industry in the country. Although unmarried, Gómez had a large family, many of whose members he placed in government positions. He instituted public works projects and at the same time amassed land and businesses for himself and his family.

Bibliography: Clinton, Daniel J., *Gómez, Tyrant of the Andes* (1936; repr. 1969).

Gompers, Samuel [gahm'-purz]

The American labor leader Samuel Gompers organized (1886) the American Federation of Labor and served almost continuously as its president and chief spokesman until his death in 1924. Gompers advocated business unionism, stressing the economic objectives of organized labor and discouraging political affiliations.

Samuel Gompers, b. London, Jan. 27, 1850, d. Dec. 13, 1924, was a U.S. labor leader who founded the American Federation of Labor. At the age of 14 he became a cigarmaker in New York City and joined the Cigarmakers' Union. He rose to become the first president of the American Federation of Labor in 1886—remaining in that position, except for the year 1895, until his death—and served as an advisor to the Council of National Defense during World War I. Gompers championed "business unionism," advising union leaders to build their unions and bargain with employers for economic gains. For Gompers the aims of labor were better wages, hours, and working conditions, not political reform. He was viewed as essentially conservative: opposed to industrial unions, government regulation, and the widening of the labor movement to include blacks, women, and unskilled workers. Although the powers of his position were limited, Gompers built the AFL into the largest labor organization in the country.

Bibliography: Livesay, Harold, *Samuel Gompers and Organized Labor in America* (1978).

See also: AMERICAN FEDERATION OF LABOR AND CONGRESS OF INDUSTRIAL ORGANIZATIONS.

Gomułka, Władysław [guh-mul'-kuh, vlah-dis'-lahf]

Władysław Gomułka, b. Feb. 6, 1905, d. Sept. 1, 1982, was a Polish Communist leader. He was born into a working-class family near Krosno and trained as a mechanic. He became a Communist activist in 1926 and was imprisoned in 1932–34. After a year at the International Lenin School in Moscow, he returned to Poland and was again imprisoned (1936–39).

Gomułka's rise in Polish Communist ranks began during World War II. In November 1943 he became secretary general of the Polish Workers' party in German-occupied Poland. In

December 1945 he became first secretary of the party, vice-premier, and minister of regained territories—the Oder-Neisse lands acquired from Germany. He lost these positions in 1948 during Stalin's purge of suspected deviationists among the Communists of Eastern Europe. After a period of imprisonment, Gomułka returned to power in October 1956, a time of political unrest. He was able to win popular support and Soviet approval of a somewhat more liberal "Polish road to socialism." Later, Gomułka's regime became increasingly repressive, anti-Semitic, and mired in economic problems. A drastic increase in food prices in December 1970 precipitated rioting by workers that led to Gomułka's resignation.

ANNA M. CIENCIALA

Bibliography: Bethell, Nicholas, *Gomułka: His Poland and His Communism* (1969); Dziewanowski, M. K., *The Communist Party of Poland: An Outline of History*, rev. ed. (1977); Morrison, J. E., *The Polish People's Republic* (1968).

gonadotrophin [goh-nad-uh-troh'-fin]

Gonadotrophins are HORMONES that influence the development and functioning of the ovaries and testes. The main source of follicle-stimulating hormone (FSH) and luteinizing hormone in both men and women is the anterior portion of the pituitary, an endocrine gland located within the skull. The placenta is the source of chorionic gonadotrophin in pregnant women.

The anterior pituitary gonadotrophins have different effects in each sex. FSH in women promotes the development of ovarian follicles, which contain the maturing ova; in men the hormone stimulates testicular development and initiates sperm production. Luteinizing hormone in women stimulates final development of the follicle, triggers ovulation, and promotes the development of the corpus luteum, and endocrine tissue that forms in the ruptured follicle; in men the hormone stimulates the testes to produce the male hormone testosterone, which in turn promotes sperm cell production and the development of other male characteristics. The placental chorionic gonadotrophin helps maintain a proper uterine environment for the developing fetus until the end of pregnancy.

PETER L. PETRAKIS

Bibliography: Moudgal, N. R., *Gonadotrophins and Gonadal Function* (1974); Saxena, B. B., et al., *Gonadotrophins* (1972).

Gonçalves, Nuno [gun-sahl'-vuhs, nun'-yoh]

Nuno Gonçalves, the greatest Portuguese painter of the 15th century, was active in Lisbon from about 1450 until his death, sometime before 1492. He was court painter to Alfonso V and is best known for his large altarpiece painted on six wood panels for São Vicente de Fora, Lisbon (National Museum, Lisbon). Represented on the panels are Saint Vincent, contemporary political and religious leaders, and other unidentified figures. Gonçalves's style is rooted in Flemish art and derives inspiration from Jan van EYCK and Dirk BOUTS, especially in the stark realism of facial detail in the panels. Gonçalves showed little interest in creating a precise space for his figures, who are projected against undefined backgrounds. He influenced many Portuguese painters of the 16th century.

EDWARD J. SULLIVAN

Bibliography: Dos Santos, Reynaldo, *Nuno Gonçalves* (1955); Smith, Robert C., *The Art of Portugal 1500-1800* (1968).

Gonçalves Dias, Antônio

Antônio Gonçalves Dias, b. Aug. 10, 1823, d. Nov. 3, 1864, is regarded as Brazil's national poet, and his *Song of Exile* (1843), with its evocative first line, "My land has palm trees," is that country's best-known poem. Educated in Portugal at the University of Coimbra, he wrote of love and of his country in *Primeiros Cantos* (First Songs, 1846), *Segundos Cantos* (Second Songs, 1848), and *Ultimos Cantos* (Last Songs, 1851). The unfinished Indian epic, *Os Tambiras* (1857), and a dictionary of the Tupi language (1858) reflect his interest in ethnology. Acting on behalf of the government, he surveyed the school system in North Brazil and participated in a scientific expedition to the Upper Amazon Valley. He was returning to Brazil from Europe when he died in a shipwreck.

Bibliography: Kennedy, J. H., "Goncalves Dias, National Bard of Brazil," *Negro History Bulletin*, January 1974.

Goncharov, Ivan Aleksandrovich [guhn-chuh-rawf']

Ivan Aleksandrovich Goncharov, b. June 18 (N.S.), 1812, d. Sept. 27 (N.S.), 1891, was a Russian novelist best known for his novel *Oblomov*. After graduating (1834) from Moscow University, he joined the civil service. His modest career was highlighted by a voyage to Japan as secretary to the admiral in charge of a Russian expedition to the Far East (1852-54); he subsequently published a travelogue of this voyage, *The Frigate Pallas* (1856; Eng. trans., 1858). Goncharov's first successful work of fiction was a short novel, *A Common Story* (1847; Eng. trans., 1917), but his fame rests on *Oblomov* (1859; Eng. trans., 1915). The novel's central character, Oblomov, has a keen mind and a worthy soul, but his incurable inertia causes him to while away his life. Oblomov was initially interpreted as symbolizing the decaying Russian gentry, but he may also be viewed as a universal human type. The term *Oblomovism* has since been used to describe mental apathy. Goncharov's third novel, *The Precipice* (1869; Eng. trans., 1915), is far inferior to *Oblomov*. He also wrote poetry, short stories, critical essays, and memoirs.

VICTOR TERRAS

Bibliography: Ehre, Hilton, *Oblomov and His Creator* (1973); Lyngstad, Alexandra and Sverre, *Ivan Goncharov* (1971); Setschkareff, Vsevolod, *Ivan Goncharov: His Life and Works* (1974).

Goncharova, Natalia Sergeyevna [guhn-chuh-rawv'-uh]

Natalia Goncharova, b. Russia, June 16 (N.S.), 1881, d. Oct. 17, 1962, was a painter prominent in rayonism, the Russian abstract art movement invented by her husband Mikhail Larionov about 1911-12. After studying (1891-96) for a degree in history in Moscow, she took up (1898) sculpture, then became a painter in 1904. In her early paintings she adapted the Russo-Byzantine icon tradition to a sophisticated modern manner. The rayonist manifesto (1913) described the movement as a synthesis of CUBISM, FUTURISM, and ORPHISM, concerned with spatial forms derived from the patterns of rays reflected from various objects. From 1910 to 1914, Goncharova painted a series of nonfigurative compositions in brilliant colors, disintegrating landscape forms into rays of light. She also designed sets and costumes for the Diaghilev Ballet.

BARBARA CAVALIERE

Bibliography: Chamot, Mary, *Goncharova* (1972); Gray, Camilla, *The Russian Experiment in Art: 1863-1922* (1971).

Goncourt, Edmond de and Jules de [gohn-koor']

Edmond de Goncourt, b. May 26, 1822, d. July 16, 1896, and Jules de Goncourt, b. Dec. 17, 1830, d. June 20, 1870, were brothers who collaborated in one of the world's most famous literary partnerships. The cultured but neurotic products of a wealthy, aristocratic French family, they wrote pioneering social history and art criticism, a number of documentary novels, and, from 1851, the *Journal des Goncourts* (9 vols., 1887-95; Eng. trans., 1937), which is still a valuable source for French 19th-century social and literary history.

The Goncourts' joint historical studies include *Histoire de la société française pendant la Révolution* (History of French Society During the Revolution, 1854), *Histoire de la société française pendant le Directoire* (History of French Society During the Directory, 1855), and *The Woman of the Eighteenth Century* (1862; Eng. trans., 1927). They also educated public taste on the subject of 18th-century art. Studies of Watteau, Boucher, Fragonard, Greuze, Chardin, and others were collected in *French Eighteenth-Century Painters* (1859-75; Eng. trans., 1948). Later, Edmond contributed to

Western understanding of Japanese art with *Outamaro* (1891) and *Hokousaï* (1896).

The Goncourts' novels had an impact on Zola and other naturalist writers (see NATURALISM, literature), but most are now regarded as having greater historical than artistic significance. *Germinie Lacerteux* (1864; Eng. trans., 1955), a study of moral collapse, and *Madame Gervaisais* (1869), on religious mania, still have their admirers. So too do Edmond's *La Fille Elisa* (1877; Eng. trans., 1959), on prostitution, and *Les Freres Zemganno* (1879), on circus life. JOHN CRUICKSHANK

Bibliography: Baldick, R., *The Goncourts* (1960); Grant, R. B., *The Goncourt Brothers* (1972); Jarman, L. M., *The Goncourt Brothers* (1982).

Gond [gahnd]

The Gond are a people of central India divided among the states of Madhya Pradesh, Maharashtra, Andra Pradesh, and Orissa. They number more than 3,300,000 and are generally classified as a tribal group because of their Dravidian language, Gondi, and their distinctive customs. Today, however, many Gond speak the dominant language of their region and, similarly, the kinship patterns and the Hindu religious observances of the area are practiced along with Gondi ones, resulting in great cultural variation.

The Gond people are highly differentiated in terms of economy and social organization. Many were traditionally shifting cultivators living in small, impermanent forest settlements. The Raj Gond, on the other hand, are a feudal society with an elaborate hierarchy of local rajas linked by blood and marriage. Powerful Gond kingdoms controlled large areas of central India for several centuries until they were finally overcome by the stronger MARATHA rajas in the 18th century. Culturally, all Gond are linked by cults of clan and ancestors, by the custom of erecting carved stone or wooden memorials to the dead, and by participation, to a greater or lesser extent, in a common tribal tradition safeguarded by a hereditary caste of bards. HILARY STANDING AND R. L. STIRRAT

Bibliography: Elwin, Verrier, *Leaves from the Jungle: Life in a Gond Village* (1958); Furer-Haimendorf, Christoph von, *The Raj Gonds of Adilabad* (1948).

Gonder [gahn'-dur]

Gonder (also Gondar) is the capital of Begemdir and Simen province in northwestern Ethiopia, of which it was once (*c.*1636–*c.*1860) the capital. The population is 68,848 (1984 est.). About 2,286 m (7,500 ft) above sea level, it is reached by roads and by air. It is the site of notable ruins of castles, palaces, and churches.

gondola [gahn'-duh-luh]

A gondola is a small, highly maneuverable boat used on the canals of Venice. Originally a much larger boat holding 12 oarsmen, by the 16th century the gondola had assumed the shape it still retains: long, narrow, keelless, with a tapered prow and stern that rise above the water. The single oarsman, or gondolier, propels the boat from a standing position near the stern. Gondolas average about 9 m (30 ft) in length and are slightly more than 1 m (3 ft) in width. The seven-pronged metal *ferro* that decorates the prow weighs over 18 kg (40 lb) and acts as a counterbalance to the oarsman's weight.

Once sumptuously decorated, most Venetian gondolas have been painted a somber black since 1562, when a city ordinance banned public ostentation. In the mid-19th century, before the era of steam power, Venice had a fleet of over 10,000 gondolas. Today, there are around 500, and their functions have largely been taken over by *vaporetti* (little steamers) and other powered boats.

Gondwanaland [gahnd-wah'-nuh-land]

Gondwanaland is the "supercontinent" from which Africa, South America, Australia, Antarctica, and India split off during the JURASSIC PERIOD (between 190 and 135 million years ago). The conclusion that the southern continents were once connected is based on widespread evidence of CARBONIFEROUS and PERMIAN continental glaciation and by the discovery of widespread fossiliferous deposits with an assemblage of distinctive fossil plants, of which the fern genus *Glossopteris* is most conspicuous. Usually spoken of as an arrangement of landmasses during the Permian Period, Gondwanaland is likely to have persisted from more ancient times and lasted until the middle of the MESOZOIC ERA, when rifted parts resembling the present continents first appeared. The name originated in a region of India where the flora *Glossopteris* is extensive. JAMES M. SCHOPF

Bibliography: Campbell, K. S. W., ed., *Gondwana Geology* (1975); Hallam, A., *A Revolution in the Earth Sciences* (1973); UNESCO, *Gondwana Stratigraphy* (1969).

Gone With the Wind

Gone With the Wind (1936), a best-selling novel by Margaret MITCHELL, received the Pulitzer Prize in 1937 and inspired an enormously popular motion picture (1939). Set in Georgia during and after the Civil War, the novel follows the career of a self-centered belle, Scarlett O'Hara. Determined to regain the possessions her family has lost during the war, Scarlett uses and discards men to gain these ends. Although she loves Ashley Wilkes, a genteel aristocrat, her real match is Rhett Butler, whose toughness equals her own. Such people, devoid of scruples, flourish in the postwar era, while the gentler ones, like Ashley, belong to a society that is "gone with the wind." CHARLOTTE D. SOLOMON

Bibliography: Edwards, A., *Road to Tara* (1986); Harwell, Richard B., ed., *"Gone With the Wind" as Book and Film* (1983).

gong

The gong is thought to have originated in China, where it was known by the 6th century AD. Unlike the bell, which vibrates most strongly at its rim, the gong resonates at its center, with vibrations diminishing toward the edge of the rim.

A circular PERCUSSION INSTRUMENT, the gong may be tuned or of indefinite PITCH; it is common in Oriental and Asian musical life but relatively specialized in Western music. Gongs are suspended or cradled on cords, and they must be struck in the center because they lack resonance at the edges. They were known in China before the 6th century, and spread through Asia and Africa before being introduced into Europe. Gongs are important components of the Javanese GAMELAN and the gagaku, the Japanese court orchestra. By the end of the 18th century, Western composers had begun to introduce gongs into concert music. ELWYN A. WIENANDT

Bibliography: Blades, James, *Percussion Instruments and their History* (1970).

Góngora y Argote, Luis de [gohn'-goh-rah ee ahr-goh'-tay]

Luis de Góngora y Argote, b. July 11, 1561, d. May 23, 1627, was one of the most important representatives of the baroque movement in Spanish literature. His poetry, characterized by an erudite vocabulary, Latinate syntax, constant classical allusions, and abundant imagery, is an outstanding example of the 17th-century poetic movement known as *culteranismo* (see GONGORISM).

The Spanish poet Luis de Góngora y Argote's baroque and deliberately obscure style gave rise to the term Gongorism. *His work is known for its originality of language and for an allusive, contrived formality. This portrait of Góngora is by Velázquez. (Museum of Fine Arts, Boston.)*

Góngora's poetry was not directed toward the masses, and he did not seek publication of his work; as a result, all of his major works were published posthumously. These include the *Fable of Poliphemus and Galatea* (1613; Eng. trans., 1961), a retelling of the story, from OVID'S METAMORPHOSES, about the love of Galatea by the cyclops Polyphemus, who kills Galatea's lover, Acis, out of jealousy. Góngora also wrote a burlesque version of the classical story of *Píramo y Tisbe* (Pyramus and Thisbe, 1618).

Góngora's most important work is the unfinished *Solitudes* (1613; Eng. trans., 1931), a lengthy lyric poem, of which only one of the projected four sections had been completed at his death. Although he claimed a hidden meaning for the work, it has little plot in the ordinary sense. It consists of descriptions of the persons and natural phenomena seen by a lovelorn youth, shipwrecked on the shore of a strange land—the rustic life of the shepherds who give him shelter; a country wedding party, ceremony, and banquet; the life of fishermen who receive him in their humble dwelling.

The poetry of Góngora was not received with unanimous approval; it was the subject of a lively debate. Particularly prominent among his critics were QUEVEDO Y VILLEGAS and Lope de VEGA. Although Góngora had important 17th-century followers and was praised by Cervantes, his poetry was subsequently held in little esteem until it was rediscovered in the 20th century. His works, collected in a modern edition in 1921, a few years before the tercentenary of his death, had a profound influence on Spanish poetry in the early 20th century. DANIEL EISENBERG

Bibliography: Foster, David and Virginia, *Luis de Góngora* (1973).

Gongorism [gawng'-guh-rizm]

Gongorism is an affected poetic style of 16th- and 17th-century Spain, full of neologisms, Latinate and Greek diction, and dislocated word order. The style is named for Don Luis de Góngora y Argote, who established this school of baroque Spanish poetry at the same time that similarly affected styles appeared as euphuism in England and Marinism in Italy. JANE COLVILLE BETTS

Bibliography: Kane, Elisha K., *Gongorism and the Golden Age* (1928).

goniometer [goh-nee-ahm'-uh-tur]

The goniometer is a mechanical instrument used to establish and inspect angles, precise to within 0.1 second of arc. It is of massive construction to minimize vibration, consisting of a table that rotates about a vertical axis and carries a divided circle, a collimator telescope, and microscope readers. Another telescope is permanently fixed to the base. The goniometer is used in crystallography and in the manufacture of prisms and optical components. DOUGLAS M. CONSIDINE

Gonium [goh'-nee-uhm]

Gonium is a genus of unicellular organisms, in the phylum Chlorophyta (green ALGAE), that occur as simple colonies and are found in fresh water. Each colony, shaped like a flat plate, consists of 4, 8, 16, or 32 cells embedded in a gelatinous matrix. The colony swims as a unit by means of the coordinated beating of FLAGELLA and reproduces sexually and asexually.

gonorrhea [gahn-uh-ree'-uh]

Gonorrhea is a specific infection caused by the bacterium *Neisseria gonorrhoeae,* commonly called gonococcus. It is one of the most common VENEREAL DISEASES. The bacterium can primarily infect only certain parts of the body: the urethra, uterine cervix, rectum, throat, and eyes. The vast majority of cases are acquired by sexual contact.

Initial symptoms of gonococcal urethritis appear an average of 2 to 10 days after a person becomes infected. The urethra is the site most often infected in men. Most men develop a combination of burning on urination and a thick, pus-laden discharge from the tip of the penis. Three percent of men show no symptoms at all. Women are usually infected in the uterine cervix, but only a minority experience burning on urination or a vaginal discharge. Infection in the throat or rectum almost never produces symptoms, and infection of the eyes results in pain, redness, and discharge.

If the infection is untreated in women, it can lead to pelvic inflammatory disease (see UROGENITAL DISEASES), and subsequently some of these women have difficulty becoming pregnant. The disease may result in infection of the joints (arthritis). During birth, babies may contract gonococcal eye disease from an infected mother. Silver nitrate drops placed into the eyes of newborns kill the gonococcus if present. Treatment with antibiotics is usually highly effective. Both sexual partners must be treated. The gonococcus has become increasingly resistant to commonly used antibiotics, however, and in 1977 a new strain was discovered that inactivated penicillin but is curable with other drugs. In 1985 a potential gonorrhea vaccine was developed that showed promise in early clinical testing. MICHAEL F. REIN, M.D.

Bibliography: Hart, Gavin, *Sexually Transmitted Diseases,* 3d rev. ed. (1984); Noble, R. C., *Sexually Transmitted Diseases,* 3d ed. (1984); Skinner, F. A., et al., eds., *Gonorrhea* (1978).

Gonzaga (family) [gohn-tsah'-guh]

The Gonzaga family ruled Mantua, Italy, from the early 14th century to 1707 and Montferrato from 1536 to 1707. **Luigi Gonzaga**, *c.*1268–1360, inaugurated the family's rule in Mantua by wresting control from the Bonacolsi family in 1328. **Gian Francesco Gonzaga,** 1394–1444, an astute diplomat and soldier, was also the patron of Vittorino da Feltre, the creator of humanistic educational ideals. **Francesco II**, 1466–1519, a leader against the French at the beginning of the ITALIAN WARS, made Mantua a cultural center. The Gonzagas were dukes of Mantua from 1530 and of Montferrato from 1575. The extinction (1627) of the direct line led to the War of the Mantuan Succession (1628–31), in which France and Spain backed rival claimants. The French branch of Gonzaga-Nevers won and ruled both duchies until it died out in 1707.

BENJAMIN G. KOHL

Bibliography: Brinton, Selwyn, *The Gonzaga Lords of Mantua* (1927).

Gonzales, Pancho [gahn-zahl'-es, pahn'-choh]

Richard Alonzo Gonzales, b. Los Angeles, May 9, 1928, is an American tennis champion. A fierce, volatile player, Gonzales often played his most breathtaking tennis after losing his temper. Respected for his powerful first serves, he captured the U.S. singles championship in 1948 and 1949, two U.S. Clay Court championships, and the U.S. Indoor title in 1949. Gonzales dominated professional tennis in the 1950s. In 1958, at his peak, he played a series of challenge matches in the United States with Lew Hoad of Australia and defeated Hoad by a wide margin. Gonzales was 40, old for a champion, when tennis became "open" in 1968, allowing amateurs to compete against professionals. In 1969 he won the longest match in the history of Wimbledon, 22–24, 1–6, 16–14, 6–3,

Pancho Gonzales, playing at the age of 43, makes a backhand return during a match against Manuel Orantes in 1971 at Wimbledon, which Gonzales won. A self-taught athlete who won the U.S. professional men's singles championship eight times between 1953 and 1961, Gonzales remained active on the pro tour well into the 1970s.

11–9, opposing Charlie Pasarell. In 1970, Gonzales twice defeated Rod Laver, then ranked number one in the world.

Bibliography: Frayne, Trent, *Famous Tennis Players* (1977).

González, Julio [gohn-thah'-leth, hool'-ee-oh]

The Spanish sculptor Julio González, b. Sept. 21, 1876, d. Mar. 27, 1942, learned metalwork techniques from his father, a goldsmith. He studied painting at the Barcelona Academy and in 1900 moved to Paris, where he met Pablo Picasso. He worked primarily as a painter until 1926, drawing inspiration from the cubist aesthetic (see CUBISM) of Picasso and his associates. In the early 1930s, however, he began to devote himself entirely to sculpture, and he produced the innovative abstract works in welded iron for which he is chiefly known. González's idea of sculpture as a drawing in space evolved from his interest in the theories of the constructivist group (see CONSTRUCTIVISM), whose influence is apparent in *Head* (1934; Museum of Modern Art, New York City). His work inspired the sculptors Anthony Caro and David Smith.

Bibliography: Rowell, Margit, *Julio González* (1983); Withers, Josephine, *Julio Gonzáles: Sculpture in Iron* (1978).

González Márquez, Felipe

Felipe González Márquez, b. Mar. 5, 1942, became prime minister of Spain in December 1982. After studying at the University of Louvain in Belgium, he joined the clandestine Socialist party, outlawed under the dictatorship of Francisco Franco. He became the party's leader in 1974 and emerged as a popular political figure when democratic rule was reestablished after Franco's death. As premier, González pursued a moderate leftist policy, leading Spain into the European Community and conducting a successful campaign to maintain its ties with NATO. He remained in office despite Socialist losses in the elections of October 1989.

Gonzalo de Córdoba: see FERNÁNDEZ DE CÓRDOBA, GONZALO.

Good Friday

Good Friday is the Christian commemoration of the death of JESUS CHRIST, observed on the Friday before EASTER. Originally, it was a day of fasting in preparation for the unitive celebration of the death-resurrection-exaltation of Jesus; no liturgy was held on that day. In the 4th century, at Jerusalem, a procession was staged from Gethsemane to the sanctuary of the cross, followed by readings about the passion. This was the beginning of the Good Friday observance as it is now known.

In the Catholic tradition, the liturgy of the day consists of reading the passion, the ceremony of the veneration of the cross, and communion from the sacrament consecrated the day before. The service of preaching on the seven last words, of Jesuit origin, has become popular in Protestantism.

REGINALD H. FULLER

Good Hope, Cape of

The Cape of Good Hope is a small, rocky peninsula jutting into the Atlantic Ocean near the southern tip of Africa in Cape Province of South Africa. The tip of the cape rises in a sheer cliff to a peak 260 m (850 ft) above the ocean. Thought by early sailors to be the extreme southern point of the continent, the cape is noted for winds and currents that are more dangerous than those off Cape Agulhas (the true southern tip), slightly to the southwest. Called the Cape of Storms by Bartolomeu DIAS, who first sighted it in 1488, it was renamed by King John II of Portugal when the riches of Oriental trade flowed around it. The Cape of Good Hope Nature Reserve was established on the cape in 1939.

Good Neighbor Policy

The efforts made by the administration of U.S. president Franklin D. ROOSEVELT to improve relations with Latin America were known as the Good Neighbor Policy. Roosevelt pledged to be a "good neighbor" in his inaugural address in 1933, and the phrase was soon linked to American policy in the Western Hemisphere. At the Pan American Conference in Montevideo, Uruguay, in December 1933, the United States signed a convention forbidding intervention by one state in another's affairs. The following year Roosevelt ended the 19-year occupation of Haiti by U.S. Marines and abrogated the PLATT AMENDMENT, which had made Cuba a virtual U.S. dependent. The United States continued to adhere to the policy of nonintervention when Bolivia and Mexico expropriated American property in 1937–38. The Good Neighbor approach and cultural exchange programs improved hemispheric relations and paved the way for cooperation on security during World War II. However, relations deteriorated again, despite the creation of the ORGANIZATION OF AMERICAN STATES (1948) and the ALLIANCE FOR PROGRESS (1961).

DONALD S. BIRN

Bibliography: Guerrant, Edward O., *Roosevelt's Good Neighbor Policy* (1950); Wood, Bryce, *The Making of the Good Neighbor Policy* (1961).

Good Soldier Schweik, The [shvayk]

A humorous and satirical Czech antiwar novel by Jaroslav HAŠEK, *The Good Soldier Schweik* (1920–23; Eng. trans., 1930) was extolled by the Germans until the rise of nazism. The protagonist, Schweik, makes a mockery of the army by appearing to be such a bungler and an innocent that he inadvertently undoes everyone and everything around him. Nonetheless, he emerges unscathed from military prison, an insane asylum, the mishandling of his superior's love life, accusations of being a spy, and being sent to the Russian front. One of the great comic creations of all time, Schweik is, like many antiestablishment heroes, considered crazy by the crazy society in which he finds himself.

JANE COLVILLE BETTS

Goodall, Jane

Jane Goodall, b. Apr. 3, 1934, is a British animal behaviorist best known for her long-term observations of chimpanzees in the wild. She is associated with both the Gombé Stream Research Center in Tanzania and Stanford University. Her work has led to an appreciation of individual differences among nonhuman primates and the discovery of tool use and man eating among chimpanzees. Goodall's writings include *My Friends the Wild Chimpanzees* (1967), *In the Shadow of Man* (1971), and *The Chimpanzees of Gombé: Patterns of Behavior* (1986), a summary of her research.

JAMES W. HERRICK

Goodbye, Mr. Chips

Goodbye, Mr. Chips (1933; film, 1939; musical film, 1969), a short sentimental novel about an English schoolmaster written by the English author James HILTON, was an immediate best-seller when it first became available in the United States in 1934. For Americans in particular, Mr. Chipping symbolized the best in British tradition. The book consists of flashbacks over a long life of quiet dignity, humor, and richness of experience loyally spent in the service of the boys, despite personal loss, World War I, and a new educational outlook that threatens to displace him. JANE COLVILLE BETTS

Goodenough, Ward

Ward Hunt Goodenough, b. Cambridge, Mass., May 30, 1919, is an anthropologist noted for his role in developing componential analysis, a semantic approach to the investigation of cultural systems. A professor at the University of Pennsylvania, he has conducted fieldwork among the Trukese of Micronesia. His writings include *Description and Comparison in Cultural Anthropology* (1981). JAMES W. HERRICK

Goodhue, Bertram Grosvenor [gud'-hue, bur'-truhm grohv'-nur]

The American architect Bertram Grosvenor Goodhue, b. Pomfret, Conn., Apr. 28, 1869, d. Apr. 24, 1924, joined the firm of Cram and Wentworth in Boston, advocates of the English GOTHIC REVIVAL style of church building, in 1891.

Outstanding examples of Goodhue's early work include Saint Thomas' Church, Fifth Avenue, New York City (1913), and the chapel of the U.S. Military Academy, West Point, N.Y. (1908). In 1914, Goodhue established his own office in New York City and continued to design churches. He became influenced by Spanish colonial architecture and designed many buildings and houses in southern California in that style. Other works of this later period include Saint Bartholomew's Church, New York City (1917–19), and the State Capitol at Lincoln, Nebr. (1934). RON WIEDENHOEFT

Bibliography: Kidney, Walter C., *The Architecture of Choice: Eclecticism in America, 1880–1930* (1974).

Goodman, Benny

The "King of Swing" during the SWING era of the 1930s and '40s, the clarinetist Benjamin David Goodman, b. Chicago, May 30, 1909, d. June 13, 1986, led one of the greatest of the big bands. Although Fletcher Henderson's band had been playing swing for several years (and Goodman used many Henderson arrangements), from the mid-1930s, Americans danced to Goodman's music. In addition to his band, the Benny Goodman Trio, with drummer Gene KRUPA and pianist Teddy Wilson—the first black musician to be featured with a popular white group—was formed in 1935. It soon expanded to include vibraphonist Lionel HAMPTON, guitarist Charlie CHRISTIAN, and many other jazz greats. After 1945, Goodman played almost exclusively with small groups. He also played as a soloist with classical orchestras. DONALD IVEY

Bibliography: Connor, D. Russel, and Hicks, Warren W., *B. G. on the Record* (1969); Goodman, Benny, *The Kingdom of Swing* (1939).

Goodman, Nelson

Nelson Goodman, b. Somerville, Mass., Aug. 7, 1906, is an American philosopher known for his work in philosophy of science and theory of knowledge. He was educated at Harvard and has taught at Tufts, the University of Pennsylvania, and Brandeis. Goodman has produced important studies in inductive logic, causal theory, structure of theories, and linguistic systems. He is a proponent of NOMINALISM, holding that only individuals exist. Among his principal works are *The Structure of Appearance* (1951), *Fact, Fiction, and Forecast*, 4th ed. (1983), *Problems and Projects* (1972), and *Of Mind and Other Matters* (1984). E. DARNELL RUCKER

Goodnight, Charles

Charles Goodnight, b. Macoupin County, Ill., Mar. 5, 1836, d. Dec. 12, 1929, was a Texas Ranger, cattle rancher, and powerful figure in the Texas Panhandle. He lived an active life from his early years, when he fought Indians on the frontier. Goodnight established ranches and cattle trails in New Mexico, Wyoming, and Colorado, and in 1876 started a ranch in Texas that eventually covered nearly 400,000 ha (1,000,000 acres) of range. He organized a stockmen's association to pacify the Panhandle, and was also a breeder of Angus cattle, crossing them with buffalo to produce the cattalo.

Bibliography: Haley, J. Evetts, *Charles Goodnight: Cowman and Plainsman* (1949; repr. 1977).

Goodrich, Benjamin F.

Benjamin Franklin Goodrich, b. Ripley, N.Y., Nov. 4, 1841, d. Aug. 3, 1888, founded the B.F. Goodrich Company. Having been a medical student, he served as an army surgeon during the Civil War. Then he went into the real estate business, which led Goodrich and a partner into buying a rubber goods factory. After an initial failure, they moved to Akron, Ohio, and established (1870) Goodrich, Tew & Company, which manufactured various rubber products and was the predecessor of the present firm.

Goodyear, Charles

Charles Goodyear, b. New Haven, Conn., Dec. 29, 1800, d. July 1, 1860, was an American inventor who developed the vulcanization of rubber. Working in his father's failing hardware business, he learned the impracticality of Brazilian gum rubber, which turned sticky when hot and brittle when cold. In 1830 he began a determined search for an improved product. After several false starts, he accidentally found that a heated mixture of rubber and sulfur gave the desired properties: improved strength, stability, and elasticity. This discovery came early in 1839, but Goodyear did not obtain a U.S. patent until 1844; by then, Thomas Hancock had studied Goodyear's samples and received a British patent.

Goodyear promoted his process in products ranging from rubber utensils, furniture, and wall coverings to a rubber suit that he wore. Even after Goodyear was granted his patent, however, several competitors infringed on his rights and made handsome profits. He had no affiliation with the company named after him, and even the term *vulcanization* was coined by an English rival. Goodyear spent much of the rest of his life in debtors' prisons, his health and personal life suffered considerably, and he died a poor man. DENNIS SIMANAITIS

Bibliography: Hooper, Meredith, *Everyday Inventions* (1976); Regli, Adolph, *Rubber's Goodyear: The Story of a Man's Perseverance* (1959).

Goolagong, Evonne [goo'-luh-gawng', ee-vahn']

Evonne Fay Goolagong Cawley, b. July 31, 1951, is an outstanding Australian tennis player. After winning many amateur titles as a teenager, she turned professional in 1970. In 1971 she won her first major singles title, the French and Wimbledon championships, and the Associated Press Female Athlete of the Year award. With her aggressive style of play, Goolagong has won three Australian Open titles, as well as the 1974 and 1976 Virginia Slims titles. She won again at Wimbledon in 1980.

goose

The goose is a web-footed water bird of the family Anatidae, which also includes the duck and swan. Geese find much of their food on land, since they are largely vegetarian and enjoy browsing on grasses. They also eat various grains. Male geese are referred to as ganders, the female is the goose, and young are called goslings. The plumage of the sexes is alike. Geese are monogamous and pair for life; usually both sexes care for the young.

Geese have played an important role in the lives of humans. They were hunted as an important source of food, both for meat and eggs. They also serve as food today, more commonly in Europe than in North America. Goose feathers have been used as ornaments of dress as well as for insulation.

The Canada goose, Branta canadensis (left), *a favorite North American game bird, is easily recognized by its black head and white cheeks. The snow goose,* Anser caerulescens (center), *and the white-fronted goose,* A. albifrons (right), *inhabit subarctic and Arctic regions.*

Goose down is used widely in quilts, jackets, and other items for comfort and warmth. Goose down can be carefully plucked from live birds. Several pluckings a year are possible. The quills of the larger contour feathers were once commonly used as pens. Domestic geese are also sometimes used as "watchdogs" because they hiss and honk at strangers.

Among wild geese the Canada goose, *Branta canadensis,* is probably the best known. As the human population has grown and destroyed former breeding grounds, the Canada goose has been breeding in larger numbers along streams, lakes, and ponds closer to urban centers. Such adaptations may assure the continuation of the species. Other well-known wild species are brant, snow geese, and blue geese. The more common domesticated varieties are the Toulouse, Emden, African, and Chinese—names that indicate the many years of association between geese and humankind in all the major regions of the world. SAMUEL C. GUNDY

Bibliography: Owen, Myrfyn, *Wild Geese of the World* (1980); Romashko, Sandra, *Wild Ducks and Geese of North America* (1977); Soames, Barbra, *Keeping Domestic Geese* (1980).

Goose Bay

Goose Bay is a village and the site of a large air force base at the western end of Lake Melville in Labrador, Canada. The base was built in 1941 by the Canadian government, and during World War II, it was used by the U.S. and Canadian air forces. It is now a U.S.-Canada early warning detection site.

gooseberry

Gooseberry is the common name for several low, spiny shrubs that, together with CURRANTS, constitute the genus *Ribes* of the family Saxifragaceae, and for the edible red or green fruit that they bear. Gooseberries are native to the temperate Northern Hemisphere, extending into the South American Andes; because they are hosts to white pine blister rust, they are prohibited in some areas of the United States. They are widely grown as garden fruit but are not commercially important. The name is also applied to a number of mainly tropical, edible fruits, such as the Cape, or Barbados, gooseberry (*Physalis* species), the hill gooseberry *(Rhodomyrtus tomentosa),* the country gooseberry *(Averrhoa carambola),* and the Chinese gooseberry, or KIWI fruit. One species of PHYLLANTHUS, *P. acidus,* is known as the gooseberry tree.

goosefish

The goosefish, *Lophius americanus,* family Lophiidae, is a large-mouthed marine predator found from Newfoundland to Brazil. A similar species, *L. piscatorius,* inhabits coastal waters of Europe and West Africa. The goosefish measures about 100 cm (39 in) in length and weighs about 16 kg (35 lb). It has a flattened body, a large head, and one dorsal spine that has a long, flexible "fishing rod" with a lure at the end.

goosefoot

Goosefoot is the common name for the genus *Chenopodium* in the goosefoot family, Chenopodiaceae. It contains about 250 species of hardy, weedy, annual or perennial herbs of wide distribution. Goosefoots, extending to a height of 3 m (10 ft), typically are strongly scented and are often hairy, glandular, or covered with a mealy powder. The flowers are small, greenish, and borne in clusters. Lamb's-quarters, or pigweed, *C. album,* is sometimes used as a potherb in the United States; it is high in nitrates, however, and in large quantities may be toxic to both humans and cattle. In the Andes Mountains of South America the seeds of *C. quinoa* are eaten as a boiled or toasted cereal or they are ground into flour. OLIN S. FEARING

Goossens, Sir Eugene [gaw'-senz]

Eugene Goossens, b. May 26, 1893, d. June 13, 1962, was a distinguished English conductor and composer. He studied in Bruges (1903–06), Liverpool (1906–07), and London (1907–11); his principal teacher of composition was Sir Charles Stanford. He played violin in the Queen's Hall Orchestra from 1911 to 1915 and was assistant to Thomas Beecham from 1916 to 1920. In 1921 he formed his own orchestra and also conducted opera and the Russian Ballet at Covent Garden. From 1923 to 1931 he conducted the Rochester (N.Y.) Philharmonic Orchestra and then succeeded Fritz Reiner as conductor of the Cincinnati Symphony (1931–46). He was conductor of the Sydney Symphony and director of the New South Wales Conservatorium in Australia from 1947 to 1956. A prolific composer, Goossens was knighted in 1955. LEONARD A. PEARLMAN

Bibliography: Goossens, Eugene, *Overture and Beginners* (1951).

GOP: see REPUBLICAN PARTY.

gopher [goh'-fur]

Gophers are burrowing rodents of North and Central America that belong to the family Geomyidae. They are sometimes called pocket gophers because they have cheek pouches for carrying food. There are 5 genera and about 25 species. The animals have stout, heavyset bodies with short necks, legs, and tails. Gophers are 13 to 45 cm (5 to 18 in) long. The coat

The plains pocket gopher, Geomys bursarius, *is found in prairies of the midwestern United States. The five strong claws on each powerful forelimb enable it to dig rapidly through the soil.*

varies from whitish or brown through black. The eyes and ears are small. The lips can be closed behind the incisors, enabling the gopher to gnaw dirt without getting it into the mouth. Gophers destroy crops by tunneling under growing plants and eating the roots. EVERETT SENTMAN

Gorbachev, Mikhail [gahr-bah-chawf']

Mikhail Sergeyevich Gorbachev, b. Mar. 2, 1931, is general secretary of the Soviet Communist party and president of the USSR. Born and raised on a collective farm in the Stavropol region, Gorbachev worked as a young man at a machine tractor station. He studied law at Moscow University and joined the Communist party in 1952. Rising in the ranks, he became party leader of the Stavropol region in 1970. A protégé of KBG chief Yuri ANDROPOV, Gorbachev was elected to the party's Central Committee in 1971. In 1978 he was brought to Moscow as an agricultural expert, and he became a full member of the Politburo in 1980. When Andropov was chosen head of the party in 1982, Gorbachev aided the ailing leader in his reform efforts. After the deaths of Andropov and his short-lived successor Konstantin CHERNENKO, Gorbachev, who had emerged as the dominant figure in the Soviet hierarchy, was elevated to the top party position in March 1985.

Gorbachev immediately embarked on a sweeping program of economic and political reforms (PERESTROIKA). He curbed the use of alcohol, called for greater labor discipline and productivity, and announced a new policy of openness in the media (GLASNOST). He encouraged intellectuals to speak out and allowed more freedom in the writing of Soviet history. Gorbachev advocated greater initiative from below, less direction by the bureaucracy, and more reliance on market forces. In 1988–89 he carried out a thorough reorganization of the party and government, and modified the electoral system to allow for greater democracy. He showed great skill in handling the crises caused by the Chernobyl nuclear accident (1986), the nationalist unrest that emerged in the Baltic states, Armenia, Moldavia, and other Soviet republics in the late 1980s, and the disruption resulting from his economic reforms. In foreign affairs Gorbachev restored friendly relations with the West, disengaged the Soviet Union from its war in Afghanistan, and sought to end the long-standing quarrel between the USSR and China. In Eastern Europe he renounced the "Brezhnev doctrine" by which the Soviets had claimed the right to intervene militarily in the Warsaw Pact countries.

RONALD GRIGOR SUNY

Mikhail Gorbachev, who assumed leadership of the USSR in 1985, initiated revolutionary changes in the Soviet system, virtually dismantling a tightly controlled police state that had been in existence since the 1920s. While ushering in a new era of freedom in the USSR and Eastern Europe, Gorbachev's reforms also caused further strain to an already troubled Soviet economy.

Bibliography: Aslund, Anders, *Gorbachev's Struggle for Reform* (1989); Lewin, Moshe, *The Gorbachev Phenomenon* (1988).

Gordian knot [gohr'-dee-uhn]

In Greek legend, the Gordian knot was an intricate knot tied by Gordius, king of Phrygia. An oracle foretold that he who untied the knot would rule all of Asia. According to the story, Alexander the Great cut the knot with his sword. Thus "cutting the Gordian knot" came to mean solving a difficult problem by forceful action.

gordian worm

The gordian worm, or hairworm, is any of about 250 species of unsegmented worms making up the phylum Nematomorpha. It is slender and hairlike, dark brown or black, and ranges in length from about 6 mm (0.25 in) to more than 1 m (3 ft). The larval stages are parasitic in arthropods, such as aquatic insect larvae or beetles or crickets. The adults are free-living in sea and fresh water and are believed not to feed, merely serving as a reproductive stage. STEPHEN C. REINGOLD

Gordimer, Nadine [gohr'-di-mur, nay-deen']

Nadine Gordimer, b. Nov. 20, 1923, is a highly praised South African writer who has written novels and short stories about the tensions of life under apartheid. Among her best novels are *The Lying Days* (1953), *The Late Bourgeois World* (1966), *A Guest of Honour* (1970), and *Burger's Daughter* (1979). *A Sport of Nature* (1987) envisions a future in which black majority rule in South Africa has become a reality. Gordimer's short-story collections include *Six Feet of the Country* (1956), *Livingstone's Companions* (1971), and *Something Out There* (1984).

Bibliography: Clingman, S., *The Novels of Nadine Gordimer* (1986).

Gordin, Jacob [gohr'-din, yah'-kuhb]

Jacob Gordin, b. May 1, 1853, d. 1909, was a Russian-born playwright whose serious plays ushered in the golden age of Yiddish theater after his immigration to the United States in 1891. Among the more than 70 plays that Gordin wrote, adapted, or translated are *The Jewish King Lear* (1892), which applies the Shakespearean theme of children's ingratitude to the problems of a generational conflict between a patriarchal parent and his modernized children; *God, Man, and the Devil* (1900), a philosophical tragedy that explores the individual's internal struggle with good and evil forces; and *The Kreutzer Sonata* (1902), an English translation of which was produced in 1906. SOL LIPTZIN

Bibliography: Lifson, D. S., *The Yiddish Theatre in America* (1965).

Gordion [gohr'-dee-uhn]

Remains of Gordion (or Gordium), a city of ancient PHRYGIA, are located near Yassihöyük village, 100 km (60 mi) southwest of Ankara in central Turkey. Preserved in legend as the site where Alexander the Great cut the GORDIAN KNOT, the Phrygian capital was first investigated by German archaeologists. Systematic excavations conducted by an American team from 1950 onward have concentrated on the Phrygian periods (8th–4th century BC) of the city mound and its associated cemeteries. Notable is the largest burial tumulus (53 m/174 ft high), popularly called the Midas Tomb for the renowned Phrygian king, with its remarkable wooden chamber and funerary gifts. Earlier phases documented within the city mound include 3d-millennium BC remains and the so-called Hittite Cemetery of the 2d millennium BC. In the early 2d century BC, Gordion, then only a small town, was abandoned under Galatian attacks. Artifacts from Gordion are preserved in a local site museum and in the Ankara Archaeological Museum.

LOUISE ALPERS BORDAZ

Bibliography: Macqueen, J. G., *The Hittites and their Contemporaries in Asia Minor* (1975); Metzger, Henri, *Anatolia II* (1969).

Gordon, Adam Lindsay

Adam Lindsay Gordon, b. Oct. 19, 1833, d. June 24, 1870, was an Australian poet who also achieved fame as a jockey. Raised in England, he emigrated (1853) to Australia, where he popularized the ballad form of poetry. He was the first Australian poet to have a wide readership, although much of his fame came after his suicide. Representative works are *Sea Spray and Smoke Drift* (1867) and *Bush Ballads and Galloping Rhymes* (1870). LEON CANTRELL

Bibliography: Hutton, Geoffrey, *Adam Lindsay Gordon* (1978).

Gordon, Caroline

The American Southern novelist Caroline Gordon, b. Oct. 6, 1895, d. Apr. 11, 1981, celebrated the virtues of agrarian life. Her first success was *Aleck Maury, Sportsman* (1934), the story of a teacher who sustains his inner life by hunting and fishing. Her later novels include *The Strange Children* (1952), a satire on intellectuals. Among her critical works are *The House of Fiction* (1950), written with her husband, Allen Tate, and *How to Read a Novel* (1957).

Bibliography: Fraistat, R. A., *Caroline Gordon as Novelist and Woman of Letters* (1984).

Gordon, Charles George

The British general Charles George Gordon, famous for his military exploits in China and his administrative reforms in Egypt, oversaw the defense of Khartoum against a 10-month (1884–85) siege by the Mahdists. The fall of Khartoum—and death of Gordon, a popular hero—2 days before relief forces reached the garrison excited much public indignation against William Gladstone's government in Great Britain.

Charles George Gordon was a British general who won renown for his dramatic but unsuccessful defense of Khartoum (1884–85) against the Sudanese rebels led by the MAHDI.

Born near London on Jan. 28, 1833, Gordon was commissioned in the British Army in 1852 and fought in the Crimean War (1853–56). In 1860, during the Second OPIUM WAR, he joined the British forces in China, taking part in the capture of Peking. The Chinese government later (1863) made him commander of the peasant force known as the Ever-Victorious Army, which helped to suppress the TAIPING REBELLION. He returned (1865) to London a famous figure, popularly known as "Chinese Gordon."

In 1873, Gordon joined the service of the Egyptian khedive as governor of the province of Equatoria, on the upper Nile. From 1877 to 1880 he was also governor-general of the Sudan and was extremely active in suppressing the slave trade and putting down revolts. Four years later he was sent back to the Sudan to evacuate Egyptian forces from Khartoum, then threatened by the Mahdi's army. Disobeying the orders to evacuate, Gordon defended the city against siege from March 1884 until Jan. 26, 1885, when the rebels broke through and massacred the entire garrison. Two days later a British relief force reached the city.

Bibliography: Nutting, A., *Gordon of Khartoum* (1966); Tames, R., *General Gordon* (1983); Trench, C. C., *The Road to Khartoum* (1979).

Gordon, Cyrus H.

Cyrus Herzl Gordon, b. Philadelphia, Pa., June 29, 1908, is a professor of Hebrew and a linguist who was one of the first to write (1940) a grammar of Ugaritic, an extinct language of Northern Syria. His other works include *Evidence for the Minoan Language* (1966), *Forgotten Scripts* (1968; rev. and enl. ed., 1982), and numerous books and articles on Near Eastern language, literature, and culture.

Gordon, John Brown

The American military and political leader John Brown Gordon, b. Upson County, Ga., Feb. 6, 1832, d. Jan. 9, 1904, was a distinguished Confederate general and later an important and revered political figure in Georgia. After practicing law and working as a mine developer, he joined Robert E. Lee's Confederate army in Virginia at the outbreak of the Civil War in 1861. He fought well in every campaign, rising to head a brigade in 1862, a division in May 1864 under Jubal A. Early, and finally, in the winter of 1864 as a lieutenant general, he commanded Stonewall Jackson's old II Corps.

Gordon was a brilliant orator, and after the war he served as U.S. senator from Georgia (1873–80, 1891–97) and governor of Georgia (1886–90). He headed the United Confederate Veterans from 1890 until his death.

Bibliography: Tankersley, Allen P., *John B. Gordon: A Study in Gallantry* (1955).

Gordon, Judah Leib

Judah Leib Leon Gordon, b. Judah Loeb Ben Asher in Vilna, Lithuania, Dec. 7, 1830, d. Sept. 16, 1892, was a writer and journalist who became a key spokesman for the Jewish enlightenment. Writing in both Hebrew and Russian, he championed social, religious, and cultural reform. After serving as a teacher in Jewish government schools, he became secretary of the Jewish community of St. Petersburg and director of the Society for the Diffusion of Enlightenment among the Jews in Russia and, later, editor of a Hebrew daily. After the pogroms of 1881–82, he recommended Jewish migration to Western countries and Palestine. LAWRENCE H. SCHIFFMAN

Bibliography: Rhine, A. B., *Leon Gordon: An Appreciation* (1910); Waxman, Meyer, *A History of Jewish Literature*, vol. 3 (1960).

Gordon, Richard F., Jr.

The American astronaut Richard Francis Gordon, Jr., b. Seattle, Wash., Oct. 5, 1929, flew on the second manned mission to the Moon. He became a navy pilot in 1953 and was selected as an astronaut in 1963. On his first space mission (1966) he piloted *Gemini 11* (see GEMINI PROGRAM) with commander Pete CONRAD. The 3-day flight included two space walks for Gordon. On *Apollo 12* (1969; see APOLLO PROGRAM) he was command module pilot and stayed in lunar orbit while Conrad and Alan BEAN explored the Moon's surface. He retired from the navy and NASA in 1972. DAVID DOOLING

Gordon, Ruth

The American actress Ruth Gordon, b. Wallaston, Mass., Oct. 30, 1896, d. Aug. 28, 1985, also achieved success as a writer of drama and television plays. She won an Academy Award (1969) as best supporting actress for her role in *Rosemary's Baby* (1968). Gordon, who made her stage debut in 1915, is the author of such plays as *Leading Lady* (1948) and *A Very Rich Woman* (1965), as well as the autobiographical *Myself among Others* (1971), *My Side* (1976), *An Open Book* (1980), and *Shady Lady* (1981). RITA M. PLOTNICKI

Gordon Riots

The Gordon Riots were violent anti-Catholic demonstrations that occurred in London in June 1780. In 1778, Parliament had passed a Catholic Relief Act, which lifted some of the restrictions on British Roman Catholics (see CATHOLIC EMANCIPATION).

This legislation was protested by Protestant fanatics such as Lord George Gordon (1751-93), who in 1779 formed the Protestant Association to secure repeal of the act. On June 2, 1780, Gordon led a crowd of some 50,000 people to present a petition to Parliament. The march turned into a week-long riot, in which Catholic chapels were destroyed, public buildings attacked, jails set afire, and prisoners freed. It took some 10,000 troops to quell the disorder, in which several hundred people were killed and injured. Gordon was charged with high treason but acquitted.

Bibliography: Hibbert, Christopher, *King Mob* (1958); Kazantzis, Judith, *The Gordon Riots* (1967).

Gordon setter

The Gordon setter displays the smooth, flowing gait and stamina of other setters but works closer to the hunter. Its dark color makes it unfavorable for hunting in the woods. It is named for the duke of Gordon, a Scottish nobleman responsible for developing the breed.

The Gordon setter is a breed of dog similar to the English setter and the Irish setter. It is black with distinctive tan markings about 2.5 cm (1 in) in diameter over the eyes, on the sides of the muzzle, on the throat, chest, the inside of the hind legs, the forelegs from the carpus to the toes, and around the anus.

Popular with hunters in Scotland for years, the Gordon setter is somewhat more thickset than the Irish setter and, consequently, a slower worker. This is largely a result of the effort of Alexander, Fourth Duke of Gordon in the late 1700s. The Gordon setter is the least popular of the three setter breeds.

JOHN MANDEVILLE

Bibliography: King, Bart, *How to Raise and Train a Gordon Setter* (1965).

Gore, Charles

Charles Gore, b. Jan. 22, 1853, d. Jan. 17, 1932, was a theologian and bishop of the Church of England. An acknowledged leader of the High Church movement, Gore was editor of *Lux Mundi* (1889), a work designed to establish a proper relationship between the Catholic faith and modern intellectual and moral problems.

Gore was also a founder of the Christian Social Union and in 1892 was one of the original members of the monastic Community of the Resurrection. He was successively bishop of Worcester (1902), Birmingham (1905), and Oxford (1911). Of his many works, *The Ministry of the Christian Church* (1888), revised and reprinted many times as *The Church and the Ministry,* has become a theological classic.

JOHN E. BOOTY

Bibliography: G. L. Prestige, *The Life of Charles Gore* (1935).

Gore, Thomas P.

Thomas Pryor Gore, b. Dec. 10, 1870, d. Mar. 16, 1949, was a U.S. senator from Oklahoma for many years (1907-21, 1931-37). Totally blind by 1890, he was known as "the Blind Orator." A leading Democrat in Oklahoma Territory from 1901, he entered the Senate when Oklahoma became a state in 1907 and was a major spokesman for farmers' interests. He was the grandfather of the writer Gore Vidal.

Bibliography: Billington, Maurice Lee, *Thomas P. Gore: The Blind Senator from Oklahoma* (1967).

Goren, Charles H.

Charles Henry Goren, b. Mar. 4, 1901, is an American expert on the card game BRIDGE. In 1949 he introduced a point-count system of bridge bidding that became nearly universal in the United States. Goren practiced law in Philadelphia, but his interest in bridge steadily increased. He wrote over 50 books on the game, the first of which was *Winning Bridge Made Easy* (1936). Another, *Contract Bridge Complete* (1951), was a best seller. In these works he presented his system of allocating points for honor cards and suit distribution in a bridge hand and for determining the correct bids from the sum of points. Goren also wrote daily and weekly bridge columns and presented bridge shows on radio and television.

Bibliography: Goren, Charles, *Goren's Bridge Complete,* rev. ed. (1973).

Gorey, Edward

Edward Gorey, b. Chicago, Feb. 22, 1925, a well-known author and illustrator, is largely a self-taught artist. His literary interests led him, in the early 1950s, to found the Poet's Theater in Boston, with Frank O'Hara and V. R. Lang. Although Gorey has worked extensively as an illustrator for other authors, he is best known for books composed entirely of his own work. Combining a gloomy severity with a sly, sinister wit, his drawings portray eccentric individuals in genteel, often Victorian, settings. His stories and poems give a macabre flavor to the most innocent literary traditions. Since the publication of his first book in 1953, Gorey has found an appreciative audience among both children and adults. His recent work includes set designs for the Broadway production of *Dracula* (1977).

Bibliography: Gorey, Edward, *Amphigorey* (1972), *Amphigorey Too* (1975), and *The Loathsome Couple* (1977).

Gorges, Sir Ferdinando [gohr'-jez]

Sir Ferdinando Gorges, b. 1568, d. May 24, 1647, played an important role in the early English development of New England, although he himself never visited America. His long military career included service in France and the governorship of Plymouth, England (1595-1602, 1603-29). In 1620, Gorges obtained a royal charter for the Council for New England, a company that received land rights to all of North America between 40° and 48° north latitude (from Philadelphia to the Gaspé Peninsula). During its 15-year history it issued large and overlapping land grants that became the basis of five New England colonies: Plymouth, Massachusetts Bay, New Hampshire, Maine, and part of Connecticut. One of the grants (1622), a huge tract between the Merrimack and Kennebec rivers, went to Gorges and his chief associate, John MASON. In 1629 they divided the area, Gorges receiving the region between the Piscataqua and Kennebec rivers; a royal charter later confirmed (1639) Gorges' title and made him lord proprietor of Maine.

Although sympathetic to PLYMOUTH COLONY, Gorges was hostile to the MASSACHUSETTS BAY COMPANY, whose initial land grant (1628) had preempted much of the council's domain. He succeeded in having the crown reclaim the Massachusetts charter for a time. Massachusetts survived this challenge, however, and in 1677 bought out the Gorges family's claims to Maine.

OSCAR ZEICHNER

Bibliography: Burrage, H. S., *Gorges and Grant of Province of Maine* (1923); Preston, R. A., *Gorges of Plymouth Fort: A Life of Sir Ferdinando Gorges* (1953).

Gorgias [gohr'-jee-uhs]

Gorgias of Leontini (Sicily), *c.*480–380 BC, was a Greek SOPHIST philosopher famous in his time as a teacher of rhetoric. He led a diplomatic delegation from Leontini to Athens in 427 BC, and figures prominently in Plato's dialogue *Gorgias,* where he is a foil for Socrates. Gorgias is best known for his treatise *On Nature or the Nonexistent,* in which he argued that (1) nothing exists; (2) if anything exists, it cannot be known; and (3) if it can be known, it cannot be communicated to others. It is not certain whether he meant this extreme skeptical position to be taken literally, or whether his arguments were intended as a demonstration of rhetorical skill. This and most of his other works are known only from the writings of other philosophers, the originals having been lost. Two surviving rhetorical exercises, *Helen* and *Palamedes,* are attributed to him.

Bibliography: Kerferd, G. B., *The Sophistic Movement* (1981); Plato, *Gorgias,* trans. by Terence Irwin (1979).

Gorgon [gohr'-guhn]

In early Greek mythology, the Gorgon was a monster of the underworld. In later tradition, the Gorgons were the three daughters of sea-god Phorcys and Ceto: Stheno, Euryale, and MEDUSA. They had writhing snakes for hair and were so ugly that the sight of them turned beholders into stone. Medusa, who was mortal, was killed by PERSEUS.

Gorgosaurus [gohr-guh-sohr'-uhs]

Gorgosaurus (Greek: *gorgos,* "terrible"; *saurus,* "lizard") was one of the last of the large carnivorous dinosaurs. Its remains have been found in the Late Cretaceous (100 to 65 million years ago) rocks of North America and possibly of eastern Asia. The animal is probably the same as *Albertosaurus,* an older name that was given to less complete remains. Like all theropods, *Gorgosaurus* was bipedal, with long, powerful hind legs; greatly shortened arms and hands; a long, heavy tail; and a large head armed with sharp, bladelike teeth. It was a smaller version (2 to 3 tons) of its closely related near contemporary TYRANNOSAURUS. JOHN H. OSTROM

Bibliography: Colbert, E. H., *Dinosaurs: An Illustrated History* (1983); Glut, D. F., *The New Dinosaur Dictionary* (1982).

gorilla [guh-ril'-uh]

The gorilla, *Gorilla,* is a member of the family Pongidae, or great APES, which also includes the chimpanzee and orangutan. Together with the lesser apes—a group that includes the gibbon and the siamang—the great apes are close relatives of the monkeys and of humans, and all belong to the order PRIMATES.

The gorilla is the largest living primate: males sometimes reach 180 cm (6 ft) in height and in nature weigh between 135 and 180 kg (300 and 400 lb). Females are shorter and weigh about half as much as the males. In years past, some captive males attained weights greater than 270 kg (600 lb), but for health reasons captive gorillas are no longer allowed to become so overweight.

Gorillas become sexually mature at 6–9 years of age and live about half as long as a human. Single infants are born following a pregnancy of 8½ months, are partially weaned by 1 year, but remain with the mother for at least 3 years. The hair on the male's back turns silver-gray with maturity, giving rise to the term "silverback" for adult males.

There are three geographic variants, or races, of gorilla, all of which are found in the African rain forest: the western lowland gorilla (*Gorilla gorilla gorilla*), the mountain gorilla (*G. gorilla beringei*), and the eastern lowland gorilla (*G. gorilla graueri*). The mountain gorilla, in comparison to the western lowland gorilla, has longer, thicker, more intensely black hair, suited to its colder, montane forest habitat, less flaring of the nostrils, a broader chest, and shorter arms and legs. The eastern lowland gorilla is intermediate between the other two races with respect to these physical characteristics.

A silverback gorilla, G. gorilla, *is an adult male whose hair on its back has turned from black to silver gray. A silverback is the dominant male of its troop and defends females and infants from intruders.*

Gorillas are the most terrestrial of the great apes, their bulky size making them ill-suited to tree dwelling. Locomotion on the ground is quadrupedal, and the knuckles of the hands are used to support the upper body, in contrast to the monkeys, who use the palms. Youngsters and females with infants demonstrate their arboreal heritage, however, by building sleeping nests in trees each night.

Gorillas live in family groups that consist of a single male leader, or silverback; some younger, black-backed males, possibly sons of the silverback; several adult females; and varied numbers of juvenile and infant offspring. The size of the group varies with geographic location and the availability of food.

Contrary to popular misconceptions, gorillas are not aggressive, bloodthirsty monsters, but rather amiable vegetarians. They spend most of their day, apart from a midday rest period, foraging for food. When gorilla groups meet, fighting is rare. Females and youngsters of different groups frequently intermingle for periods of time. When tension does develop between silverbacks of two groups, it is generally relieved in nonaggressive ways such as impressive displays of chest beating, which serve to reduce actual conflict.

The gorilla is threatened with extinction in its natural habitat by various human activities, and its last chances for survival may be a few gorilla sanctuaries in Africa and the zoos and other captive environments that maintain gorillas in other parts of the world. RONALD D. NADLER

Bibliography: Fossey, D., *Gorillas in the Mist* (1983); Schaller, George B., *The Mountain Gorilla: Ecology and Behavior* (1963).

Göring, Hermann: see GOERING, HERMANN.

Gorky [gohr'-kee]

Gorky is the capital of Gorky oblast in the Russian Soviet Federated Socialist Republic of the USSR. It is situated on the Volga River, at the mouth of the Oka, a tributary. The city has a population of 1,392,000 (1984 est.). Originally named Nizhni Novgorod, it was the site of Russia's largest annual trade fair in the 19th century.

Gorky is one of the USSR's largest industrial cities, known mainly for its automotive and shipbuilding industries. It also has a wide range of machine-manufacturing, apparel, and food-processing factories. An oil refinery operates in the southeast suburb of Kstovo. Electric power is supplied in part by the Gorky hydroelectric station, on the Volga, upstream from the city. Gorky has a university and a polytechnic institute.

The city is divided into an old town, which is located on high ground on the right bank of the Oka, and newer sections on the lower left bank of the Oka. Noteworthy in the old town is a kremlin, or fortress, dating from the 16th century, which overlooks the Oka-Volga confluence. The kremlin contains the Cathedral of the Archangel Michael, which was completed in 1631 and is now a museum. Most residential and industrial areas are on the low bank, where the old fairground was located. The Gorky auto plant is southwest of the old town, and the shipyards are at Sormovo, northwest of the old town. Because of its defense industries, Gorky is closed to foreign tourists.

One of the oldest Russian cities, Nizhni Novgorod was founded in 1221. It was annexed to Moscow in 1392 but plundered by the Tatars in 1520 and 1536. Because of its favorable location on important waterways, it developed into a major commercial center. In 1932 the city was renamed for the writer Maksim Gorky, who was born there in 1868.

THEODORE SHABAD

Gorky, Arshile

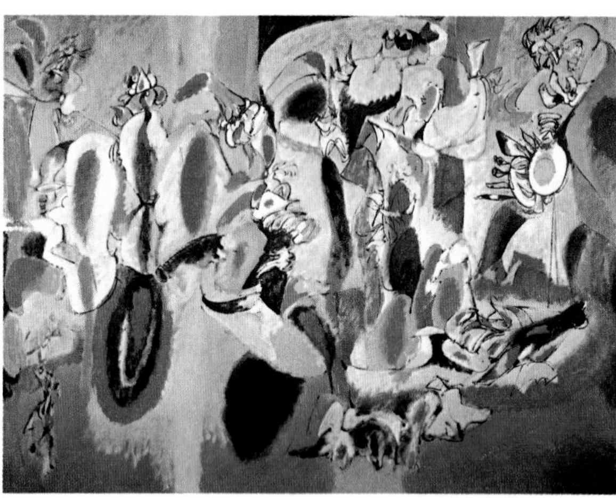

The sexual imagery of Arshile Gorky's The Liver Is the Cock's Comb *(1944) points to the inspiration of surrealism in early abstract expressionism. Biomorphic forms set the pattern for Gorky's late style (1944–46). Vibrant colors and black lines indicate the influence of Kandinsky and Miro. (The Albright-Knox Art Gallery, Buffalo.)*

Arshile Gorky, b. Armenia, Oct. 25, 1904, d. July 21, 1948, is best known for his postsurrealist abstract paintings of the 1940s, which were an important contribution to the first generation of American ABSTRACT EXPRESSIONISM. Gorky came to the United States in 1920. He painted *The Artist and His Mother* in 1926, a work in which he began his process of abstraction and individuation that led him from the styles of Paul Cézanne, Pablo Picasso, Wassily Kandinsky, and Joan Miró to his original brand of biomorphism, a sensuously symbolic multiple imagery derived from his intimate study of nature. His biomorphic abstraction began with his series *Image in Xhorkam* (from 1936). Important for Gorky were his friendships with Willem de Kooning and John Graham. Chief among his works of the 1940s are *The Liver Is the Cock's Comb* (1944; Albright-Knox Gallery, Buffalo, N.Y.) and *The Bethrothal II* (1947; Whitney Museum, New York City). Gorky committed suicide following several tragedies in his personal life.

Bibliography: Levy, Julien, *Arshile Gorky* (1966); Rosenberg, Harold, *Arshile Gorky: The Man, The Time, The Idea* (1962); Schwabacher, Ethel K., *Arshile Gorky* (1957); Seitz, William C., *Arshile Gorky: Paintings, Drawings, Studies* (1962).

Gorky, Maksim

The Russian writer Maksim Gorky, pseudonym of Aleksei Maksimovich Peshkov, b. Mar. 28 (N.S.), 1868, d. June 18, 1936, gained worldwide renown as a spokesman for the downtrodden and despised through his novels, stories, dramas, and memoirs. This role, together with his active involvement in the revolutionary movement, his friendship with Lenin, and his leadership in establishing SOCIALIST REALISM as a dominant trend in postrevolutionary Russia, assured his canonization in the USSR as "the great proletarian writer."

Gorky (meaning "the bitter") was born into an impoverished middle-class family of Nizhni-Novgorod (renamed Gorky). At the age of five, after the death of his father, he went to live with his maternal grandparents; the harshness of that household, along with its moments of beauty, were later captured in the memorable vignettes of *My Childhood* (1913–14; Eng. trans., 1915), the brilliant first part of Gorky's autobiographical trilogy, which also includes *In the World* (1915; Eng. trans., 1917) and *My Universities* (1923; Eng. trans., 1952).

Sent to work at the age of 8, Gorky for many years led a difficult, penurious, increasingly aimless life, finally becoming a hobo. His many odd jobs and adventures, however, brought him into contact with thousands of ordinary Russians and provided him with voluminous material for his later work. Rebellious, freedom-loving tramps, in fact, became the heroes of Gorky's early stories, which reflect the author's permanent belief in the possibility of a more fulfilling and beautiful existence for all. It was, in turn, the success of these stories, including "Makar Chudra" (1892) and "Chelkash" (1895), that ended his own vagabondage.

Although Gorky later rejected the hoboes' antisocial nihilism, he remained attracted to the personalities of willful men who had the strength to shape life. This is evident in his novels about Russian merchants, *Foma Gordeyev* (1899; Eng. trans., 1955) and *The Artamonov Business* (1925; Eng. trans., 1948), as well as in his memoir *V. I. Lenin* (1924).

Social protest led inevitably to political commitment. Gorky's youthful contacts with radicals in Kazan and elsewhere brought him to the attention of the police, and because of his association with Russian Marxists after 1900 his election to the Russian Academy of Sciences was annulled (1902) by the government. He was later imprisoned for participation in the revolutionary events of 1905 and released only after foreign luminaries, in response to the international success of his powerful drama *The Lower Depths* (1902; Eng. trans., 1906), made formal protests to the tsar. Gorky then left Russia. A trip to the United States in 1906 to raise funds for the revolutionary movement failed in part because his insistence on traveling with his mistress alienated influential people. After completing *Mother* (1906; Eng. trans., 1911), a crude but still widely read revolutionary novel, and *City of the Yel-*

The Soviet writer Maksim Gorky exercised considerable influence in post-revolutionary Russia because of the proletarian themes of his works. He became a confidant of Lenin and served Stalin as a propagandist. Since his death, Gorky has been recognized as the founder of socialist realism, an artistic movement encouraged in many Marxist nations.

low Devil (1906), a polemical attack on the United States, he settled in Capri, where he remained until 1913. Here he wrote some of his best works, including *The Small Town Okurov* (1909), *The Life of Matthew Kozhemyakin* (1910; Eng. trans., *c.*1960), and *My Childhood.*

Gorky's assertive nonconformity again surfaced following the Bolshevik coup in 1917, when his outspoken criticism of the party leadership led to the suppression of his newspaper *New Life.* Gorky at this time performed a great service to Russian culture by his largely successful efforts to save pre-revolutionary works of art from destruction and hundreds of writers, artists, and scholars from starvation and, on occasion, the firing squad.

Suffering anew from recurrent pulmonary tuberculosis and dissatisfied with political developments, Gorky again left (1921) the USSR to settle in Sorrento. The Bolsheviks, however, desired Gorky's return for reasons of prestige, and in 1928 he responded to their urgings. Thereafter, he increasingly became the chief literary propagandist for Stalin's hardening dictatorship and the socialist realism subsequently imposed on creative artists, although he continued to protect individual writers. Some mystery surrounds his sudden death in 1936 while under medical treatment; the logic of events during the era of the great purges, however, suggests that Stalin may have hastened his demise.

In addition to his fiction and autobiography, Gorky will be remembered for his magnificent *Reminiscences of Tolstoy, Chekhov, and Andreyev* (1905, 1919, 1922; Eng. trans., 1949; new ed. 1968). He was at work on a multivolume novel of Russian life over four decades, *The Life of Klim Samgin,* at the time of his death. KENNETH N. BROSTROM

Bibliography: Gourfinkel, Nina, *Gorky,* trans. by Ann Fesbach (1960; repr. 1975); Hare, Richard, *Maxim Gorky: Romantic Realist and Conservative Revolutionary* (1962); Kaun, Alexander S., *Maxim Gorky and His Russia* (1931; repr. 1968); Levin, Dan, *Stormy Petrel: The Life and Work of Maxim Gorky* (1965); Weil, Irwin, *Gorky* (1966).

Gorton, John Grey

John Gorton, the 24th prime minister of Australia (1968–71), was elected as a liberal party candidate, but eventually resigned over policy disputes within the party. During his stay in office, he focused on both domestic and foreign issues, especially aboriginal rights and the development of military defense systems in Asia.

John Grey Gorton, b. Sept. 9, 1911, was prime minister of Australia from 1968 to 1971. He belonged to the left wing of the basically conservative Liberal party, and his outspoken views, together with his pursuit of liberal reforms, led to his removal from office by his colleagues.

After service as a pilot in World War II, Gorton was elected to the Senate for Victoria in 1949. He served as minister of the navy (1958–63), minister of works (1963–66), and minister for education and science (1966–68). Described by his critics as a "one-man band," Gorton was seldom out of the public eye, and the press relished accounts of his activities.

Gorton became prime minister in 1968 on the death of Harold HOLT. In that position he tried to strengthen the Australian alliance with the United States. Although he denounced Australians who demonstrated against the Vietnam War, he tolerated their heckling with patrician self-assurance. One of Gorton's major problems as prime minister was the independence movement in Papua New Guinea, a territory administered under United Nations charter, and his handling of it led to his downfall. He was successful, however, in winning better opportunities and education for the Aborigines of Australia. After losing a Liberal party vote of confidence, he resigned in March 1971 in favor of William MCMAHON. He served for a time as minister of defense in 1971 and retired from politics in 1975. A. R. G. GRIFFITHS

Bibliography: Reid, Alan D., *The Power Struggle* (1969); Trengrove, Alan, *John Grey Gorton: An Informal Biography* (1969).

Gorton, Samuel

Samuel Gorton, *c.*1592–1677, was the Anglo-American founder of a religious sect known as the Gortonites. Born in England, he seems to have received no formal education, but he influenced a small group of followers with forceful sermons. Gorton denied belief in a Trinity, claiming that only Jesus Christ was divine and that union with him would make an individual perfect. He emigrated to America in 1637 and immediately offended both the clergy and civil officials of Massachusetts by criticizing their control over religious affairs. Within a year he moved to Rhode Island, where he established (1632) the settlement later called WARWICK. The Boston courts arrested him on charges of heresy, blasphemy, and political subversion, but by 1648 his legal disputes had come to a peaceful end, and he continued preaching until his death. The Gortonites remained an active sect for about a century.

HENRY WARNER BOWDEN

Bibliography: Janes, L. G., *Samuel Gorton* (1896).

Gosford, Archibald Acheson, 2d Earl of [gahz'-fohrd]

Lord Gosford, b. Aug. 1, 1776, d. Mar. 27, 1849, was governor in chief (1835–37) of British North America. He sat in the British House of Commons before inheriting his title (1807) and from 1811 was a representative Irish peer in the House of Lords. As governor in chief of Canada, Gosford was ordered to report on conditions in Lower Canada (Quebec). He recommended "conciliation without concession" toward the French Canadians, a policy that pleased neither the French nor the English. He resigned only days before the REBELLIONS OF 1837.

Gosnold, Bartholomew [gahz'-nohld]

Bartholomew Gosnold, d. Aug. 22, 1607, was an English navigator who explored the coast of New England in 1602 and gave Cape Cod its name. An active promoter of American colonization, he was involved in the formation of the London Company and was one of the founders of Jamestown, Va., in 1607.

gospel music

The term *gospel music* embraces several types of song, all of which share an emotional, personal identification with the biblical text and a rich musical vocabulary. Of the various types, the gospel music sung in black Baptist churches is perhaps the most important, because it has influenced not only white gospel forms but also certain styles of popular music. Unlike the SPIRITUAL, which is rooted in the formal Protestant hymn, black gospel music is extemporaneous, highly emotional, and joyful. Based on a sung dialogue between congregation and preacher, with the preacher setting the text and the congregation supplying musical affirmation, gospel music inspires a "fire and excitement that sometimes, without warning, fill a church, causing [it] to 'rock' " (James Baldwin, *The Fire Next Time*). In the 1940s, Mahalia JACKSON, Clara Ward, and Sister Rosetta Tharpe began recording gospel-style music. In the 1950s and '60s, church-trained musicians took the style into popular music. Singers like Aretha FRANKLIN and James BROWN recorded what came to be known as SOUL, a style that reproduces the vocal devices of gospel: use of falsetto, bent and sliding tones, shouts, and the stretching-out of a single sung syllable over many notes.

White gospel music, sung at Protestant revival meetings, was similar to black gospel music in its spontaneity and emotional fervor. A popular offshoot of white revivals was the gospel hymn, which can be traced to evangelists Dwight L. MOODY and Ira D. Sankey, who exposed large audiences to such hymns and composed many others. White quartet and family gospel groups now dominate this genre; in addition, a youth-music movement, largely in the South, has developed a repertoire of pop-gospel music.

Bibliography: Blackwell, Lois S., *Wings of the Dove: The Story of Gospel Music in America* (1978); Heilbut, Tony, *The Gospel Sound,* rev. ed. (1985); Sankey, Ira D., et al., *Gospel Hymns* (repr. of 1895 ed.); Shaw, Arnold, *The World of Soul* (1970); Warrick, Mancel, and Hillsman, Joan R., *The Progress of Gospel Music* (1977).

Gospels: see BIBLE.

Gossaert, Jan [gohs'-airt]

Jan Gossaert, called Mabuse, *c.*1478–*c.*1533, was one of the earliest Northern Renaissance painters to popularize the Italianate style in the Low Countries. By 1503 he was classified as a free master in the Antwerp painters' guild, and about 1507 he entered the service of Philip, duke of Burgundy. His earliest Mannerist paintings (see MANNERISM), such as the *Holy Family* altarpiece (*c.*1505; Museum National de Arte Antiga, Lisbon), are richly detailed, ornate, and somewhat crowded. Gossaert's early influences were Gerard DAVID, Albrecht DÜRER, Jan van EYCK, and Hugo van der GOES. In 1508-09 he traveled to Italy and was much impressed by what he saw there, which was complemented by his later study of prints by Jacopo de' BARBARI and Marcantonio RAIMONDI. His many nudes, including *Venus and Cupid* (*c.*1521; Musées Royaux des Beaux-Arts, Brussels), were greatly influenced by his Italian experience. He was also known for his sober, realistic portraits, such as the *Merchant* (Philadelphia Museum of Art).

EDWARD J. SULLIVAN

Bibliography: Friedländer, Max J., *Early Netherlandish Painting,* vol. 8 (1930), trans. by Heinz Norden (1972).

Gossage, William [gahs'-uhj]

A pioneer of the British chemical industry, William Gossage, b. 1799, d. Apr. 9, 1877, was an English manufacturer of alkali, a chemical that was necessary for the production of glass, cloth, and other products and one of the first substances to be industrially synthesized. Alkali production generated quantities of hydrochloric acid gas, which would have caused immense pollution problems had it not been for Gossage's invention, a clay-lined masonry tower containing running water that absorbed the gas. The process also made possible the recovery of hydrochloric acid.

FRANCES GIES

Gossec, François Joseph [goh-sek']

François Joseph Gossec, b. Jan. 17, 1734, d. Feb. 16, 1829, became one of France's most influential musicians in the 18th century. Born in the Netherlands, he settled in Paris (1751), holding various posts until 1770 when he founded the Concert des Amateurs. In 1773 he became director of the Concert Spirituel, and in 1784 he organized the École Royale de Chant, which later became the Paris Conservatory (1795). Gossec was also a composer of symphonies (influenced by those of Johann Stamitz) and string quartets. Although he composed much, little of Gossec's music is performed today.

Göteborg [yuh-te-bawr']

Göteborg, the seat of Göteborg och Bohus county in southwestern Sweden, is that country's second largest city and chief seaport. The population is 424,085 (1984 est.). Located on the Göta River near where it empties into the Kattegat, the port has direct access to the Atlantic. The Göta Canal runs between Stockholm and Göteborg, and the city is connected to most parts of Sweden by rail lines and domestic air service. Nearby shipbuilding facilities are the largest in the country, and the industries in Göteborg produce automobiles, office machines, textiles, foodstuffs, paper, leather, and wood products.

The old parts of the city contain the cathedral (1633), Kristine Church (1648), the law courts (1672), the town hall (1750), and the opera house (1859). There are art, natural history, and folk museums, botanical and amusement parks, and a university (1891), as well as technical and other schools.

In 1619, King Gustav II Adolf founded Göteborg on the site of a previous settlement, giving Sweden a port on its southwest coast. The city prospered, especially during the Napoleonic Wars, when Göteborg remained open while many European ports were blockaded by France.

Gotha (aircraft) [gaw'-thuh]

Germany's Gotha G.III, the third in a series of twin-engine biplane bombers, replaced the slow, cumbersome Zeppelins that had been used for bombing during the early stages of World War I. With a range of 840 km (522 mi) at a speed of 140 km/h (87 mph), the Gotha was known for its daylight bombing raids over London in 1917.

The Gotha was a large, twin-engine, long-range bomber developed by the Germans soon after the advent of World War I. The Gotha had a double wing connected by three sets of braces, or struts, on each side of the body. Commencing with the G.II design of 1916, the series continued with a few G.IIIs fitted with a pair of 260-horsepower Mercedes D.IVA units and the addition of a fuselage tunnel to enable the dorsal gunner to aim his weapon to fire rearward below the tail surfaces. The major production Gotha G models were the pusher Mercedes D.IVA-powered G.IV and G.V designed with 23.7 m (77'9¼ in) unequal-span wings. By mid-1917 these two variants had replaced the Zeppelins formerly used for bombing raids against England. Improved defenses, however, forced the Gothas to operate at night until, by the spring of 1918, the high attrition rate of the aircraft compelled the Germans to cease their use.

PETER M. H. LEWIS

See also: AIRCRAFT, MILITARY.

Gotha (city) [goh'-tah]

Gotha (1980 est. pop., 57,892) is a city in southwestern East Germany, situated on the Leine Canal, 35 km (22 mi) east of the West German border. Gotha is a rail junction and its industries produce transportation equipment, precision instruments, chemicals, and textiles. Publishing has been an important industry since the 18th century, when the famous publishing house of Justus Perthes (now Hermann Haack) was established. Many historic landmarks are there, including Saint Margaret's Church (first built in the 12th century, rebuilt in 1652), the town hall (begun 1567), and 16th-, 17th-, and 18th-century palaces.

By 775 a Frankish settlement was established there. Much of the city was destroyed (1567) during the religious wars of the Reformation. The city became the residence of the dukes of Saxe-Gotha in 1639; from 1826 to 1918 it served as the residence of the dukes of Saxe-Coburg-Gotha.

Gothic art and architecture

The term *Gothic* was first used during the Italian Renaissance to characterize all the monuments of the Middle Ages because they were contemptuously regarded as the products of barbarian Goths and therefore utterly lacking in artistic merit. Subsequently, however, the term was restricted to the art and architecture of those centuries immediately following the Romanesque period and preceding the Renaissance. As the last medieval period, the Gothic age has now also come to be regarded as one of Europe's outstanding artistic eras.

EARLY AND HIGH GOTHIC ARCHITECTURE

Gothic architecture, arising out of the 12th-century heyday of the Romanesque (see ROMANESQUE ART AND ARCHITECTURE), remained the dominant expression of the Gothic period and outlasted all of the other Gothic arts well into the 16th century. Whereas a vast number of noteworthy secular buildings were produced in the Gothic style, it was in the service of the church, the most prolific builder of the Middle Ages, that the new architectural ideas were formulated and brought to their fullest fruition. Although by 1400 Gothic architecture had become international in scope, its creative heartland was in northern France in an area stretching from the royal domain around Paris, including Saint-Denis and Chartres, to the region of the Champagne in the east and southward to Bourges. Within this restricted area, in the series of cathedrals erected in the course of the 12th and 13th centuries, the major innovations of Gothic architecture took place.

Gothic architecture is not easily defined. Although rib vaulting and the pointed arch (see ARCH AND VAULT) are its most characteristic features, both were widely used in Romanesque churches. Only when diagonal ribs are used in direct conjunction with pointed transverse arches in the vaulting of an interior can a structure be identified as Gothic. This type of rib vaulting was the decisive factor in the evolution of the French cathedrals. Because they were concentrated in those few small areas from which the ribs spring, the outward thrusts of the vaults—deflected downward by the pointed transverse arches—could be more easily counteracted by narrow buttresses and by external arches, or flying buttresses, invented at NOTRE DAME DE PARIS sometime after 1163. With these structural advantages, the thick Romanesque walls could be replaced with translucent walls of STAINED GLASS, and the builders were also able to erect vaulted interiors of unprecedented heights.

Early Gothic Architecture. In France, Gothic architecture appeared sporadically in a number of different locales in the early decades of the 12th century. But the creative phase of Gothic architecture that was to lead to the building of the great northern cathedrals began in 1144 with the completion, under the patronage of Abbot SUGER, of the ambulatory (aisle circling the apse) and radiating CHAPELS of the royal ABBEY of SAINT-DENIS just outside Paris. Instead of being separated in Romanesque fashion, the chapels now opened out into each other, forming a single flowing space called a chevet, while the slender supports of the vaults and the expansive windows further de-emphasize the solids.

The innovations at Saint-Denis led in the 1160s to a series of bold experiments. Still adhering to the general features of the French Romanesque churches—a three-aisled NAVE, a TRANSEPT, and a semicircular chevet, with a three-story elevation consisting of a groundfloor ARCADE, a gallery over the side aisles and a CLERESTORY—the architects of the Early Gothic cathedrals sought, often in complicated ways, to open

(Left) *The Cathedral of Notre Dame (1163–c.1250), located on Paris's Île de la Cité, is a magnificent amalgam of the Gothic stylistic elements that developed during the more than 150 years of its construction and renovation. Such features as the lofty, rib-vaulted nave, flying buttresses, large clerestory windows, and delicate stone tracery, which extends from the rose windows to the adjoining facade, create the quality of weightless verticality that contrasts sharply with the massive architecture of the preceding Romanesque period.*

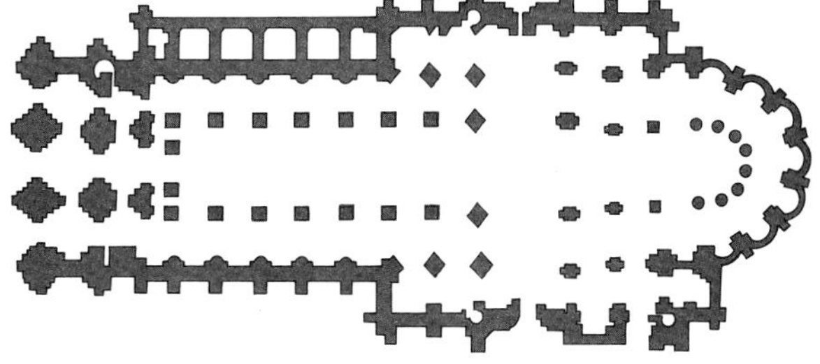

(Below) *The plan of the Abbey Church of Saint Denis, Paris, indicates the chevet, or ambulatory, around the high altar at the east* (right) *end of the church. (1137–44; nave, c.1231.)*

up the solid walls and to attain added height by inserting still another story between the galleries and the clerestory. Known as a TRIFORIUM, this additional story is nothing more than a narrow passageway contrived in the thickness of the wall immediately below the clerestory windows and faced on the open inner side with a small arcade. Although minor in size, the triforium was to become a standard feature in later Gothic churches.

Notre Dame de Paris, in its original unremodeled form (with circular openings instead of a triforium), and the five-towered Cathedral of Laon, both begun in the 1160s, are two of the most successful of these experiments in four-story elevation; the interior of Notre Dame de Paris attained a height of 35 m (115 ft), unprecedented for its time. These results, however, involved complexities that demanded a solution, and it was in the rebuilding of CHARTRES CATHEDRAL, begun immediately following a catastrophic fire in 1194, that they were resolved. By dispensing with the gallery over the side aisles of the nave, but retaining the narrow band of the triforium, Chartres returned to a simpler three-story design. Height was achieved by the creation of a huge clerestory as tall as the groundfloor arcade and, in each bay, embracing two large lancet windows surmounted by a ROSE WINDOW. In one stroke the architect of Chartres had created a clarified and integrated formula for the elevation of a Gothic interior that, in spite of all subsequent changes in style, was to be endlessly repeated in the later churches.

High Gothic Architecture. Chartres inaugurated the High Gothic period; it culminated in the great Coronation Cathedral of REIMS, begun in 1210. Somewhat cold and intellectual in design, overwhelming in scale, and, like Chartres, ponderous in its masonry structure, the internal proportions of Reims are as classical in their way as those of the Parthenon. A notable contribution of Reims to the development of later Gothic architecture was bar tracery, or stone framework of a Gothic window, invented by its first architect for the windows of the apsidal chapels. The earlier plate tracery, such as that in the clerestory of Chartres, consists essentially of a series of openings in a masonry wall constructed in horizontal courses. In bar tracery these separate openings are absorbed into a single large window, which is then subdivided into tall lancets by thin upright monoliths, the so-called mullions. The openwork

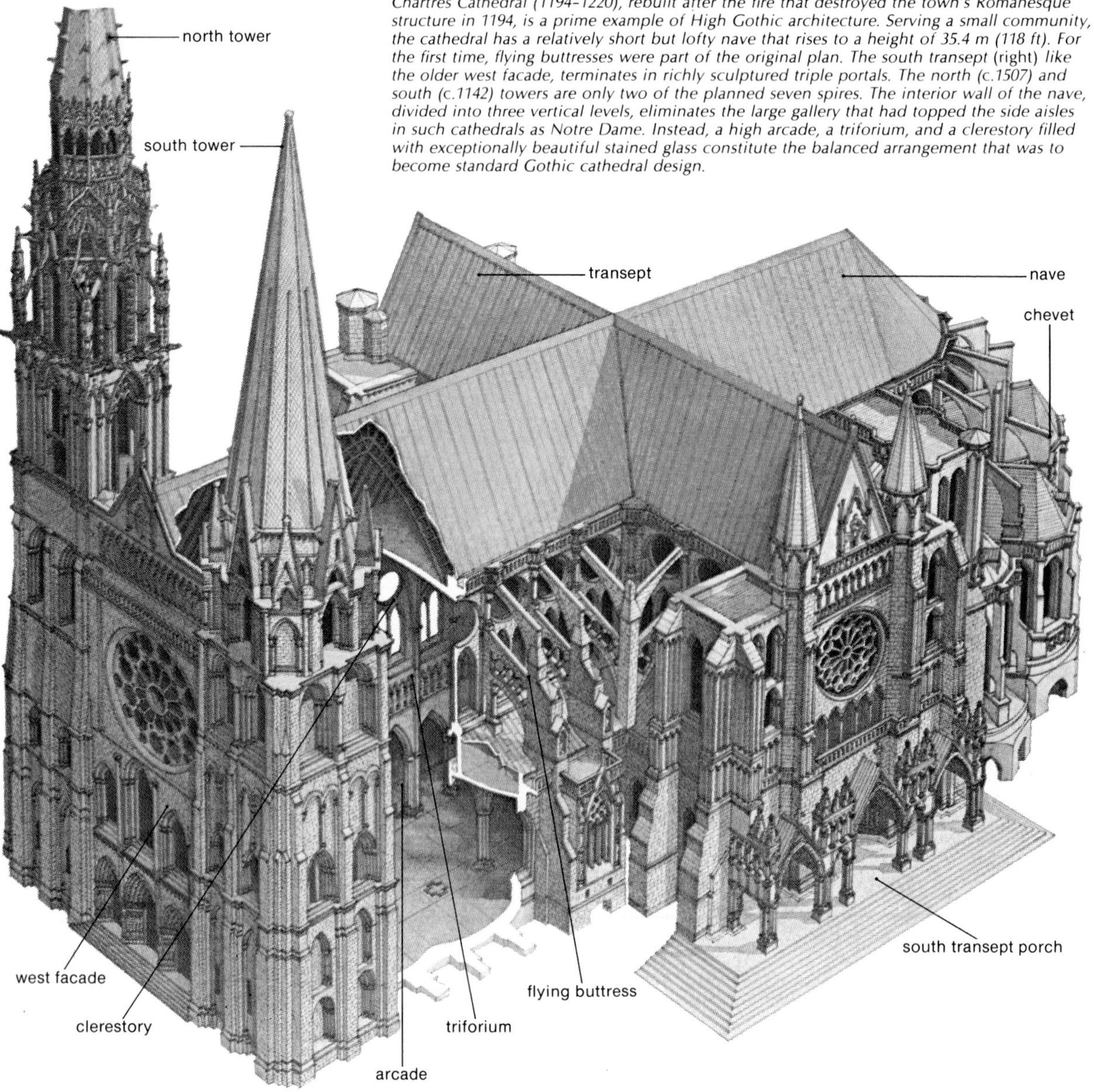

Chartres Cathedral (1194-1220), rebuilt after the fire that destroyed the town's Romanesque structure in 1194, is a prime example of High Gothic architecture. Serving a small community, the cathedral has a relatively short but lofty nave that rises to a height of 35.4 m (118 ft). For the first time, flying buttresses were part of the original plan. The south transept (right) like the older west facade, terminates in richly sculptured triple portals. The north (c.1507) and south (c.1142) towers are only two of the planned seven spires. The interior wall of the nave, divided into three vertical levels, eliminates the large gallery that had topped the side aisles in such cathedrals as Notre Dame. Instead, a high arcade, a triforium, and a clerestory filled with exceptionally beautiful stained glass constitute the balanced arrangement that was to become standard Gothic cathedral design.

The vast interior of Laon Cathedral (1160-1225), an example of early Gothic style, extends the length of 21 architectural divisions, or bays, and terminates in a nonprojecting eastern facade. Like its contemporary, Notre Dame de Paris, Laon has a majestic 4-story design, with a full gallery and a third level (here a triforium) between the aisle galleries and the clerestory.

tracery in the head of the window is fashioned somewhat in the manner of a cutout.

The Cathedral of Bourges, begun in 1195, rivals Chartres and Reims in providing a High Gothic solution to the problems of church design. Here height is achieved from below by means of an extraordinarily lofty groundfloor arcade, thus reducing the dimensions of the clerestory to approximately those of the triforium. The soaring 42-m (138-ft) nave of AMIENS CATHEDRAL (begun 1220), chronologically following Reims, represents a transitional stage in which attenuation and aspiring verticality are again stressed, while the tracery of the large clerestory windows is a further elaboration of the simpler design of Reims. In 1225 a Reims architect undertook the rebuilding of Beauvais Cathedral. Basing his groundfloor design on the gigantic, lofty arcades of Bourges, a height of 48 m (157 ft) was reached by superimposing on the arcades an almost equally tall clerestory, thus creating one of the loftiest continuous interiors ever attempted.

Of the early 13th-century west facades destined for the cathedrals, only those of Laon and Notre Dame de Paris were brought to completion as originally planned, each a contrast to the other—the upward-thrusting facade of Laon is sculpturesque and dynamic where Notre Dame de Paris is planar and recessive. The cavernous triple portals of Laon were amplified in those of Amiens, which, in part, provided the models for the five gabled portals of Bourges.

Rayonnant or Late Gothic Architecture. The last of the great cathedrals, Beauvais, was begun the year before Louis IX came to the throne in 1226. Early in his long reign there emerged a new phase of Gothic architecture known as Rayonnant (see RAYONNANT STYLE), a term derived from the radiating spokes of the immense rose windows that form an important, but by no means essential, feature of this new style. Height was no longer the dominant goal. Rather, the aim of Rayonnant architecture was the further elimination of solid masonry by piercing the triforium wall with traceried windows. A more unified internal effect was also achieved by continuing the vaulting shafts uninterruptedly from pavement to vault and by linking the clerestory windows and the triforium arcade into one interrelated design.

The rebuilding of Saint-Denis was the first major undertaking in the Rayonnant. Beginning in 1232 the whole of the church, with the exception of the ambulatory and west facade, was reconstructed in the new style to supply additional space for the series of royal tombs. The structure that best epitomizes the spirit of the Rayonnant, however, is the SAINTE-CHAPELLE, the shrinelike chapel erected (1242-48) on the Parisian Île-de-la-Cité. It was commissioned by Louis IX as a fitting receptacle for the Crown of Thorns he had acquired from the Latin emperor Baldwin II of Constantinople. Piers, arches, and tracery formed a delicate armature for the jeweled medallions of the stained-glass windows that completely fill the spaces between the slender vaulting shafts.

Stained-Glass Windows. The windows of Gothic churches were progressively enlarged—not to allow more light to penetrate into the interior, but to increase the areas reserved for the stained glass. With their full complement of stained-glass

(Left) *The south transept of Reims Cathedral (1211-90) contains one of the magnificent rose windows for which this coronation cathedral is noted. The sharply pointed arches and the compound piers, which form unbroken lines from floor to vault, give Reims a sense of exalted grandeur.* (Right) *The intricate facade of Amiens Cathedral (1220-88), completed during the 15th century, combines the structure of the earlier facade with the ornamentation and abundant sculpture typical of late Gothic cathedral design.*

windows, the interiors of Gothic structures were actually darker than those of many a Romanesque church. It was a luminous darkness, however, alive with the refracted glow of the glass, an effect that can still be appreciated at Chartres, Bourges, and the Sainte-Chapelle.

The subject matter of stained-glass windows can be divided into two categories. The lancets of the clerestory are generally occupied by large figures of saints and prophets, sometimes of immense size, and thus easily distinguishable from below. The more detailed episodes from the Bible and the legends of the saints, rendered with an effective economy in design, are illustrated in small medallions in the windows of the aisles and of the ambulatory chapels that are nearer to the observer. Throughout the first half of the 13th century the color scheme was dominated by a brilliant ruby red and a dark saturated blue. With the lighter tonality of the later glass and with the introduction of grisaille glass—white glass infused with gray patterns—the earlier mystic darkness was dispelled.

Influence of French Gothic Architecture. The impact of French Gothic architecture on much of continental Europe was profound. The scheme of Bourges, with its gigantic arcade and short clerestory, was repeated only once in France, at Le Mans, but it served as the direct model for the Spanish cathedrals of Toledo (begun 1227) and Burgos (begun 1221). By 1509, when the new cathedral of Salamanca was begun, it had long been part of indigenous Spanish architecture. The giant arcade and the French semicircular chevet were used in the cathedrals of Palma de Mallorca (begun 1306), Barcelona (begun 1298), and Gerona (begun 1312). The nave of Amiens served as the inspiration for the Cathedral of León (begun *c.*1255). In Germany the towers of Laon were copied at Bamberg (*c.*1237) and Naumburg (*c.*1237) and its four-story elevation emulated in the Cathedral of Limburg-an-der-Lahn (begun 1211). French High Gothic forms appear throughout Saint Elizabeth's Church (begun 1235) at Marburg, and at Cologne the cathedral (begun 1248), rivaling Beauvais in height, transports to the banks of the Rhine the Rayonnant choir of Amiens.

England and Italy were the exceptions to this pervasive influence across the continent. The Gothic churches of Florence, in a uniquely Italianate style, and the style reminiscent of a French cathedral facade at Siena (begun 1284) and Orvieto (begun 1290) were but stages of the progression toward the Renaissance of Filippo BRUNELLESCHI. In England, French Gothic intrudes decisively only twice: once in the 1170s at CANTERBURY CATHEDRAL and again in Henry III's rebuilding of WESTMINSTER ABBEY (begun 1245), designed along the lines of Reims but modified by Parisian Rayonnant. With these exceptions, England continued to be highly original and independent. Eschewing the emphasis on height and the logical constructionalism of French Gothic, the English churches stressed horizontality in the elevation and an extreme elongation in plan. Double transepts were sometimes included, and a square east end was usually substituted for the French polygonal chevet. Typically English as well was the multiplication in the number of vaulting ribs, some purely decorative.

EARLY AND HIGH GOTHIC SCULPTURE

Like its Romanesque antecedents, Gothic sculpture was at first predominantly an architectural adornment on church portals. Like the new forms of the Early Gothic cathedrals, it can also

(Above) *The upper chapel of La Sainte Chapelle, Paris (1243–48), a reliquary shrine built by King Louis IX, is the culmination of Gothic attempts to replace heavy walls with radiant stained glass. Only the supporting piers interrupt the chapel's beautifully preserved lancet and rose windows.*

(Right) Notre Dame de la Belle Verrière, *one of the most magnificent examples of mid-12th-century stained glass, is in the cathedral of Chartres, itself an exemplar of High Gothic style. This window, together with the lancet windows of the west facade, was preserved during the fire of 1194 and restored to the cathedral during its reconstruction.*

The Cathedral of Siena (c.1226–1380), like other structures of central and southern Italy, incorporates Gothic elements in a strongly Mediterranean design. The heavy walls and flat roof, requiring no buttresses, are given horizontal emphasis by the alternating white and black marble. The campanile, domed crossing, and relatively few windows further accentuate the Romanesque traditions. The freely sculptured facade, geometric in emphasis, contrasts with the delicate unity achieved in the facade of Amiens.

be said to have originated at Saint-Denis in the triple portals of the west facade, consecrated in 1140. But at Saint-Denis this Proto-Gothic sculpture was still overwhelmingly Romanesque in character. It was only at Chartres, in the somewhat later west portals of about 1155 that survive from the older cathedral, that Gothic overtones began to manifest themselves, particularly in the work of the outstanding sculptor, the so-called headmaster, who was responsible for the central portal. Here in the TYMPANUM the Romanesque theme of the Apocalyptic Christ surrounded by symbols of the four Evangelists had been reinterpreted in boldly conceived plastic forms, while a new human quality, unknown in Romanesque sculpture, pervaded the benign figure of the blessing Savior. The major innovation of this Proto-Gothic style, however, was the so-called statue-columns in the lateral embrasures of the portal: the tall over-life-size figures reiterate in their columnar form the colonnettes to which they are attached. Eventually the statue-column led to the freestanding monumental statue, a form of sculpture hitherto unknown in the Middle Ages.

In France during the next few decades, the west portals of Chartres inspired a host of similar portals with statue-columns and also gave rise to one of the outstanding creations of medieval Spain—the sculptural ensemble of the cathedral at Santiago da Compostela, appropriately known as the Pórtico de la Gloria (1168–88). Nevertheless, all these monuments retained to some degree the imprint of their Romanesque heritage. In the 1180s, however, in northern Europe as well as in England, a more relaxed period in all the arts began, in which the more rigidly controlled Romanesque figure style was replaced by a feeling of grace, sinuosity, and freedom of movement. This so-called classicizing style culminates around 1210 in such notable works as the great series of sculptures on the north and south transept portals of the new Cathedral of Chartres. The classical quality of this phase of Gothic sculpture is clearly seen in the group of the *Visitation*, of about 1230, on the west-central portal of Reims cathedral, created at a time when the statue-column had at last completely emancipated itself from its rigid columnar form.

Veiled like a Roman matron, the Virgin of the *Visitation* turns toward her older cousin Elizabeth in a contrappostal (twisted) pose reminiscent of a classical Greek statue. Unclassical, however, is the curving sway of her body that was to become the typical stance of so many later Gothic statues. At the left, the neighboring group of the *Annunciation* demonstrates the reaction against this classicizing phase. Although by an inferior sculptor, the more restrained Virgin of the *An-*

Jamb statues (c.1225–45) from the west portal of Reims Cathedral, the Annunciation (left) *and the earlier* Visitation (right), *illustrate the rapid change in Gothic sculpture from the hieratic, somewhat stiff* Visitation *figures to the graceful smiling angel in the* Annunciation.

The German statue Bamberg Rider *(c.1230-40), the earliest surviving equestrian statue since those of classical Rome, transforms the knightly ideal seen in French sculpture into an intensely expressive and realistic style. Reluctant to mimic French architectural sculpture, German Gothic artists developed a highly individual and striking style of freestanding statuary.*

The Virgin of Paris, *early-13th-century sculpture from the coronation portal of Notre Dame, embodies the mannered elegance characteristic of the late High Gothic. Artfully pretty and unrealistic in pose, the Virgin nevertheless retains the playful appeal initiated by the smiling angel of Reims cathedral.*

nunciation, in a severe style derived from Amiens, possesses the clear volumetric definition lacking in the *Visitation* group. In the announcing angel (*c.*1250), Gothic sculpture had finally come into its own. Instead of the confused impressionistic surface treatment of the drapery in the *Visitation*, that of the angel is given a structural solidity by the large angular V-folds of his mantle and the long tubular forms of his undergarment that break sharply around his feet. His smiling features, clustered curls, and mannered pose all belong to a later stage of the Reims sculpture that synthesizes naturalistic forms with courtly affectations and a delicate spirituality.

It was in Germany, however, that Gothic statuary, influenced by that of Reims, achieved its fullest plastic expression. At Bamberg, the sculptor of a group of the *Visitation* in the interior of the cathedral, inspired by the figures at Reims, was also responsible (*c.*1240) for the Bamberg *Rider*, the first truly monumental equestrian statue of the later Middle Ages. Although the identity of the regal horseman remains unknown, no other work so impressively embodies the chivalrous ideal of the medieval ruler.

The stylistic evolution of Gothic sculpture, briefly traced thus far, was accompanied by the introduction of new themes in the subject matter of the sculptured portals, reflecting the growing intensification of the cult of the Virgin Mary. In the 1170s, for the first time on a cathedral portal, her death, her assumption, and her crowning by Christ in Heaven are represented on the tympanum of the main doorway of the Cathedral of Senlis near Paris. From then on a coronation portal was included among the doorways of the major Gothic cathedrals. On the west facades of Laon and Reims the crowning of Mary had even supplanted the traditional subject of the Last Judgment as the major theme of the central portal.

Along with this development a new type of cult statue of the Virgin, standing and holding the Christ Child, was introduced between 1215 and 1220 on the central pier of the coronation portal on the west facade of Notre Dame de Paris. By the middle of the 13th century this new type, now in the manneristic idiom of the angel of Reims, assumes a more intimate and maternal character as the swaying figure of the Virgin playfully balances the Christ Child on the outward thrust of her hip—an image that in the ensuing centuries was to be disseminated in an infinite variety of versions throughout Western Europe.

DECORATIVE ARTS

In Paris during the reign of Louis IX the decorative arts tended to emulate the arts of the churches. In the series of Moralized Bibles of the second quarter of the 13th century, as in the *Bible Moralisée* (*c.*1230-40; Bibliothèque Nationale, MS 11560) in Paris, the columns of medallions that frame the illustrations in these vast picture books frankly imitate stained-glass windows. In the 1260s the large metal shrines, or reliquaries (see RELIQUARY), of the saints assumed the aspect of diminutive Rayonnant churches, and the decorative gables surmounting the traceried roses of the windows on the exterior of the Sainte-Chapelle were copied in the miniatures of the *Psalter of Louis IX* (1253-70; Bibliothèque Nationale, Paris). The forms and mannerisms of the monumental sculpture are in turn reflected in the willowy figures of the *Psalter* illustrations. From this same period the delicate ivory of the *Virgin with the Christ Child* (*c.*1260; Louvre, Paris) from the Sainte-Chapelle was directly inspired by the large statue formerly on one of the portals of the chapel and preserved in a modern Parisian church.

The decorative arts assumed a more independent role in the first half of the 14th century. The expressionistic tendencies in Germany resulted in the creation of devotional works of extraordinary pathos. About 1300 the misnamed Plague Crosses of polychromed wood appeared, in which the emaciated, broken body of the Savior hangs from a forked cross, as in the *Forked Cross* (*c.*1304; Santa Maria im Kapitol) in Cologne. Later a new type of the mourning Virgin, seated and holding the dead body of Christ across her lap—the so-called *Pietà*—is given its most harrowing evocation in the statuette in Bonn (polychromed wood, 14th century; Rheinisches Landesmuseum).

In Parisian ILLUMINATED MANUSCRIPTS, as illustrated in a page from the *Belleville Breviary* (1323-26; Bibliothèque Nationale, Paris; MS Lat. 10488), decorated by Jean PUCELLE in the 1320s, the lettering, the vignette at the beginning of the text, the vine borders with their butterflies and other creatures, and the little scenes at the bottom of the page all contribute to a totally integrated effect that established an enduring precedent for later illuminators. More significant for the future, however, was the rendering of the little barrel-vaulted room in the vignette. Here Pucelle used the new art of linear PERSPECTIVE borrowed from the contemporaneous illusionistic painting (see ILLUSIONISM) of the Italian Proto-Renaissance.

LATE GOTHIC PERIOD

Although Paris had been the leading artistic center of northern Europe since the 1230s, the ravages of the Black Death and the outbreak of the Hundred Years' War in the middle of the 14th century drastically changed the situation. Paris became only one among several other independent artistic centers, while the most talented artists were those imported from French and Belgian Flanders.

The International Style. As a result of this dissemination of artistic currents a new pictorial style emerged in which, as foreshadowed by Pucelle, Gothic elements were combined with the developing illusionistic art of the Italian painters. This INTERNATIONAL STYLE in art has sometimes been described as Gothic. In this context, however, the term can only be understood as a qualitative adjective, because by definition illusionistic painting lies outside the medieval artistic conceptions of the Gothic period. Gothic sculpture, however, remained unaffected by the Italian Renaissance. Its naturalistic tendencies led to new developments. In Paris around 1387 the lifelike figures of Charles V and his queen (Louvre, Paris) from the Hospice Chapel of the Quinze-Vingts herald the revival of the standing-portrait statue, a form of sculpture unknown in the West after late Roman times.

Late Gothic Sculpture. The most momentous works were those produced for Philip the Bold, duke of Burgundy, by the Flemish sculptor Claus SLUTER, whose art culminates in the series of prophets surrounding the so-called *Well of Moses*, created between 1395 and 1404 at the Chartreuse de Champmol in Dijon. Breaking away entirely from the soft, pliant aristocratic types current in the 14th century, Sluter conceived his prophets in terms of rugged Flemish patriarchs. In the Moses he emphasized enormous breadth in the voluminous folds of the cape, and in the bald-headed Isaiah he created a highly individualized figure worthy of Donatello. Although after his death, in 1406, the influence of Sluter expanded over much of Europe, by 1500 the era of Gothic sculpture was drawing to its close.

Late Gothic Churches. The last phase of French Gothic architecture was the Flamboyant (see FLAMBOYANT STYLE), so named for the flamelike quality of its intricate curvilinear decoration. Among its new decorative motifs was the acutely pointed ogee arch, formed of two double curves. The major ornamentation of this ebullient style was reserved for the exterior. The interior of the churches underwent a drastic simplification by eliminating the capitals of all the PIERS, which were reduced to plain masonry supports, from which the moldings of the vaulting ribs gradually emerge. But the ribs themselves formed an intricate network of ever more complicated patterns. These features are also observable in the German churches, as in the interior of the Lorenzkirche (1439–77) in Nuremberg.

Although it was already underway by the 1380s, the great flowering of Flamboyant architecture did not occur in France until the first half of the 16th century, when several of the older cathedrals, such as Beauvais, received magnificent transept facades in the new style, while smaller Flamboyant churches proliferated everywhere. In Germany the most ubiquitous manifestation of Late Gothic architecture is in the form of the hall church wherein three aisles are all of the same height, as in the choir of the Nuremberg Lorenzkirche. Never prone to imitation, the English builders devised their own Late Gothic style—the PERPENDICULAR GOTHIC STYLE—using a traceried rectangular panel as a module for both window tracery and wall decoration and even, in modified shapes, for the new type of fan vaulting that reached its apogee in the

This full-page illumination from the Psalter of Paris *(c.1223), produced during a period of flourishing stained-glass design, reflects the influence of this art in its heavy lines and dominant hues of brilliant red, blue, and green. Later illuminators increasingly sought to portray three-dimensional figures in their paintings. (Bibliothèque de l'Arsenal, Paris.)*

(Above) *Claus Sluter's awesome figure of Moses, part of the* Well of Moses *(1395–1404) in the Carthusian monastery of Champmol, Dijon, represents the late-Gothic return to robust, realistic sculpture.* (Left) *The intricate fan vaults of King Henry VII's chapel (1502–12), Westminster Abbey, are some of the most elaborate extensions of Gothic stone tracery produced in the English Perpendicular style. The increased use of decorative rather than structural ribs, beginning in the 14th century, culminated in this delicate stone lacework.*

Chapel (1502-12) of Henry VII at Westminster Abbey, where it is combined with gravity-defying pendentives.

Late Gothic Secular Buildings. Late Gothic architecture, however, is not confined to churches. The roster of important secular buildings is almost endless. In Belgium the series of civic halls began very early with the huge belfried Cloth Hall (1304-80; destroyed 1915) of Ypres and continued to the apogee of Late Gothic, the Hôtel de Ville (1448-63) of Louvain. In France the civic buildings culminated in the vast Flamboyant Gothic Palais de Justice (1499; damaged 1944) at Rouen. In the earlier periods the austere castles had been little affected by developments in ecclesiastical architecture, but in the 1380s the grim fortresses began to be transformed into pleasure palaces. From this period stems France's earliest important monument in the Flamboyant style, the large traceried screen surmounting the triple fireplace (1384-86) added to the ancient castle hall of the Palais des Comtes at Poitiers.

The 15th-century castellated House of Jacques Coeur (1443-51) at Bourges is the grandest of the many Late Gothic town mansions including the elegant Hôtel de Cluny (1485) in Paris, now appropriately transformed into a museum for the arts of the Middle Ages. All over France, from Josselin (early 16th century) in Brittany to Amboise (1483-1501) and BLOIS (1498-1515) on the Loire, new *châteaux* were being erected in the Flamboyant style. Late Gothic secular architecture also developed its own architectural vernacular, from the Venetian Gothic of the Ca d'Oro (Golden House; c.1430) and the DOGE'S PALACE (1424-1529) to the Tudor Gothic of HAMPTON COURT (1515-36) on the Thames and the Collegiate Gothic of Oxford and Cambridge (15th and 16th centuries). In the 17th and 18th centuries, however, few attempts were made to build in a Gothic style. The great resurgence came with the GOTHIC REVIVAL of the 19th century, responsible for London's famous Houses of Parliament, or WESTMINSTER PALACE (begun 1840). In such original creations as Liverpool's Anglican Cathedral (completed 1979) and the nave of SAINT JOHN THE DIVINE in New York (still in progress), the Gothic Revival has lasted to the present day. WILLIAM M. HINKLE

Bibliography: Aubert, M., *The Art of the High Gothic Era,* trans. by P. Gorge (1965); Avril, F., *Manuscript Painting at the Court of France, the Fourteenth Century, 1310-1380* (1978); Branner, R., *Gothic Architecture* (1961); Deuchler, F., *Gothic Art,* trans. by V. Menkes (1973); Evans, Joan, *Art in Medieval France, 987-1498* (1969); Frankl, Paul, *Gothic Architecture,* trans. by D. Pevsner (1963); Grodecki, Louis, *Gothic Architecture,* trans. by I. Mark (1977); Harvey, John, *Cathedrals of England and Wales* (1974); Kidson, P., *Sculpture at Chartres* (1958; repr. 1975); Mâle, Emile, *The Gothic Image,* trans. by Dora Nussey (1958); Martindale, A., *Gothic Art from the Twelfth to the Fifteenth Century* (1967); Porcher, Jean, *Medieval French Miniatures,* trans. by J. Brown (1960); Sauerländer, W., *Gothic Sculpture in France, 1140-1270,* trans. by J. Sonderheimer (1972); Stoddard, W. S., *Monastery and Cathedral in France* (1966); Swaan, Wim, *The Gothic Cathedral* (1969).

See also: ARCHITECTURE; ART; CATHEDRALS AND CHURCHES; ENGLISH ART AND ARCHITECTURE; FLEMISH ART AND ARCHITECTURE; FRENCH ART AND ARCHITECTURE; GERMAN ART AND ARCHITECTURE; ITALIAN ART AND ARCHITECTURE; MONASTIC ART AND ARCHITECTURE; PAINTING; SCANDINAVIAN ART AND ARCHITECTURE; SCULPTURE; SPANISH ART AND ARCHITECTURE.

Gothic Revival

The Gothic Revival style of architecture, which dominated much of the building activity of mid-19th-century Europe and the United States, originated in the mid-18th-century vogue for "gothick" architectural fantasies. Essentially a part of the romantic movement, this dilettante preference for Gothic picturesqueness, epitomized by Horace WALPOLE's villa at Strawberry Hill (1770), outside London, was transformed in the 1830s into a serious moral crusade for the supposedly superior Christian virtues represented by medieval Gothic art and architecture. As an indisputably Christian style, Gothic was championed by many as being superior to the classical revival style popular in the early 19th century.

The standard-bearers of the ideological phase of the Gothic Revival were John RUSKIN and Augustus PUGIN, whose book *Contrasts* (1836) became the manifesto of the movement. Significantly, the building in which the revivalists' aspirations were first embodied was also England's foremost national monument—the new Houses of Parliament, or WESTMINSTER PALACE, designed in 1836 by Sir Charles BARRY with Pugin's indispensable assistance. This immense project included, beside the architectural elements, all the interior furnishings and decoration.

The enthusiasm engendered by the Houses of Parliament elicited a tremendous spate of neo-Gothic building activity, particularly by Sir George Gilbert SCOTT, who designed no less than 39 cathedrals and minsters, in addition to numerous smaller buildings in the Gothic mold. Although many of his projects seem not as well designed as those executed by such lesser-known architects as George Edmund Street, Scott did create one of the true masterpieces of the Gothic Revival—the Albert Memorial (1864-72) in London.

The Gothic Revival had strongly nationalistic overtones in northern Europe, where each country prided itself on its own Gothic heritage. In Germany, the centerpiece of the revival was the completion of Cologne Cathedral (1842-80), a formidable undertaking jointly sponsored by Catholics and Protestants as a symbol of the imminent reunification of the German nation. This nationalistic component was absent, however, in the United States, where the new architectural vogue was enthusiastically received. New York City alone possesses three important early landmarks of the revival: Richard UPJOHN's famous Trinity Church (1840-46), James REN-

The intricate decoration and soaring design of the Albert Memorial (1864-72; London) exemplifies Gothic Revival architecture. The Albert Memorial, which emulated medieval Gothic style, was created by Sir George Gilbert Scott, a leading figure of the movement.

WICK's ensemble of Grace Church and its parish buildings (1843–46), and Renwick's ambitious design for SAINT PATRICK'S CATHEDRAL (1858–79).

Although several early-20th-century skyscrapers, such as Cass GILBERT's 60-story French Gothic WOOLWORTH BUILDING (1913; New York City), were executed in the Gothic style, the revival as a coherent movement had largely spent itself by the late 19th century, its momentum slowed by the fantastic cost of medieval-type craftsmanship and its aesthetic program undermined by more forward-looking artistic movements.

WILLIAM M. HINKLE

Bibliography: Bright, Michael, *Cities Built to Music: Aesthetic Theories of the Victorian Gothic Revival* (1984); Clark, Kenneth, *The Gothic Revival* (1950); Germann, Georg, *The Gothic Revival in Europe and Britain*, trans. by Garald Onn (1972); Howe, Katherine, and Warren, David, *The Gothic Revival Style in America* (1976); Macaulay, James, *The Gothic Revival* (1975).

Gothic romance

The earliest Gothic romance, a class of novel dealing in the mysterious and supernatural, which emerged shortly after the establishment of the novel form itself, was Horace WALPOLE's *Castle of Otranto* (1764). Reacting against the literalism and confined domesticity of Samuel RICHARDSON, Walpole indulged a contemporary taste for the "Gothic," which for the 18th-century reader conjured up a medieval world of barbarous passions enacted in picturesque melodramatic settings of ruined castles, ancient monasteries, and wild landscapes. Within a plot designed for suspense, a delicate feminine sensibility is subjected to the onslaught of elemental forces of good and evil. Sanity and chastity are constantly threatened, and over all looms the suggestion that evil and irrationality will destroy civilization. Walpole's invention, inspired by a general awakening of interest in the past, brought the subconscious within the range of the novel, and implicitly challenged the rational confidence of his time. His Gothic romance, which immediately encouraged numerous imitators, is the earliest expression in English literature of the nascent romantic movement (see ROMANTICISM).

The Gothic romance flourished in its original form until 1820 and produced, in addition to a great many minor novelists, three writers of considerable stature. Ann RADCLIFFE's *Mysteries of Udolpho* (1794) typifies one style of gothic narrative, in which a persecuted heroine survives numerous assaults to arrive at last at a happy ending in the arms of a handsome young man. (Radcliffe's rather tame horrors were justly mocked by Jane AUSTEN in *Northanger Abbey,* 1818.) Matthew Gregory LEWIS added a stronger content of terror and sheer nastiness in *The Monk* (1796), but the finest work in this genre was *Melmoth the Wanderer* (1820), a Faustian novel by the Irish clergyman Charles Robert Maturin. Other notable Gothic works include William BECKFORD's *Vathek* (1786), William GODWIN's *Caleb Williams* (1794), Mary SHELLEY's FRANKENSTEIN (1818), and the Waverley novels of Sir Walter SCOTT, which fully exploit the romantic appeal of history.

The Gothic strain also played a large part in the development of the American novel and appears in the work of Nathaniel HAWTHORNE, Edgar Allan POE, and Henry JAMES, as well as that of contemporary writers such as John HAWKES. The modern "thriller" and detective novel may also be regarded as remote descendants of the Gothic romance. The "Gothic" paperback novels popular in the 1970s and 1980s owe much to the plots devised by the English novelist Daphne DU MAURIER.

HOWARD BATCHELOR

Bibliography: Berenbaum, L. B., *The Gothic Imagination* (1981); MacAndrew, E., *The Gothic Tradition* (1980); Summers, Montague, *The Gothic Quest* (1938); Varma, D. P., *The Gothic Flame* (1957).

Goths

The Goths were a GERMANIC PEOPLE who probably migrated from southern Scandinavia sometime before the time of Christ. By the 3d century the Goths had settled in the areas around the Black Sea and were staging periodic raids on Roman territory. Those who settled in the area of the modern Ukraine came to be known as Ostrogoths. Those who settled in the region of the Danube were called Visigoths.

During the 4th century the Visigoths coexisted peacefully with the Romans, farming and trading agricultural products and slaves for luxury goods. The Visigoths adopted many elements of Roman culture. Some of them became literate in Latin. In the middle of the century substantial numbers of the Visigoths accepted ARIANISM.

The Huns' drive westward pushed the Visigoths into territory controlled by the Roman Empire. The resulting conflict culminated in a great Visigothic victory at Adrianople in 378 and led to an alliance with the empire. But the Visigoths were fickle allies; under ALARIC I they sacked Rome in 410 and in 418 settled in Aquitaine in southwestern France. During the last half of the 5th century the Visigoths expanded their control to Spain, but in 507–08 the Franks under CLOVIS drove them from most of Aquitaine.

The Visigoths in Spain conquered (585) the Suevi and drove out (629) the Byzantines. In 589, King Reccared converted the Visigoths to orthodox Christianity, and King Reccesvinth tried (*c.*654) to unite the various inhabitants of Spain under a single law (see GERMANIC LAW). Social, political, religious, and regional differences in Visigothic Spain, however, led to frequent regicide and to civil war. Spain came under the domination of the Muslims in 711.

The Ostrogoths were conquered (*c.*370) by the Huns. Under THEODORIC THE GREAT the Ostrogoths moved west, and Theodoric became king of Italy (493–526). He was succeeded by his daughter Amalasuntha, who was murdered in 535 by her husband and co-ruler, Theodahad. Her allies, the Byzantines, soon attacked Italy, but the Ostrogoth forces held out until 553. The Byzantines, and later the Lombards, took control of Italy.

BERNARD S. BACHRACH

Bibliography: Burns, T. S., *A History of the Ostrogoths* (1984); Thompson, E. A., *The Goths in Spain* (1969); Wallace-Hadrill, John M., *The Barbarian West, 400–1000,* 3d ed. (1967).

Gotland [gaht'-luhnd]

Gotland, the largest island (3,023 km²/1,167 mi²) in the Baltic Sea, lies 80 km (50 mi) off the Swedish coast. Together with the smaller islands of Fårön, Gotska Sandön, and Karlsö it constitutes a county of Sweden. The island has a population of 55,346 (1980), and Visby is the administrative center. Gotland is a low, undulating limestone plateau. A temperate, sunny climate and ample fertile soil support the raising of sugar beets, cereals, and sheep. Tourism, fishing, and stone quarrying are important industries.

Settled during the Stone Age, Gotland early developed extensive trade with the people of northern Europe. By the 12th century Visby was an important town of the Hanseatic League. Beginning in 1361, when Denmark captured it, control of Gotland was disputed by several nations. Trade routes shifted, however, and by the time Sweden gained lasting control in 1645, it was impoverished.

Götterdämmerung: see RING OF THE NIBELUNG, THE.

Gottfried von Strassburg [gawt'-freet fuhn shtrahs'-boork]

Gottfried von Strassburg, *c.*1170–*c.*1215, was a medieval German poet whose incomplete version of the TRISTAN AND ISOLDE legend, *Tristan* (*c.*1210), was one of the most influential poems of the period. It is particularly significant for the mystically tinged conception of love it advances, which marks a departure from the troubadours' conception of courtly love. That the work is unfinished is perhaps no accident; after Tristan's pure and undying love for Isolde has been exalted above the claims of wedlock, it becomes difficult to follow the fable, which has him marry another woman when his illicit love is thwarted. Gottfried's idealization of Tristan's love is conveyed sometimes by explicit statement, sometimes by subtle modification of his immediate source, Thomas of Britain. Thus, the lovers' retreat in the forest becomes an idyllic temple of love from which the rightful husband is allegorically and practically excluded. This scene is the culmination of Gottfried's decorative yet lucid style, which became a model for authors of the next generation. Other, inferior poets continued the work. PAUL SALMON

Bibliography: Batts, Michael S., *Gottfried von Strassburg* (1971).

Gottheil, Gustav [gaht'-hyl, gus'-tahv]

Gustav Gottheil, b. Prussia, May 28, 1827, d. Apr. 15, 1903, was a leader of American Reform Judaism. Educated in Berlin and Halle, he served as rabbi in Manchester, England, and lectured at the university there from 1860 to 1873. Upon invitation from Temple Emanu-El in New York City, Gottheil immigrated to the United States in 1873 and served as senior rabbi of that synagogue until 1899. He prepared (1886) the first Jewish hymnbook in the United States, founded the Association of Eastern Rabbis, helped establish the Jewish Publication Society of America, and was one of the founders of the Federation of American Zionists, later known as the Zionist Organization of America. SAUL S. FRIEDMAN

Gotthelf, Jeremias [gawt'-helf, yay-ray-mee'-ahs]

The Swiss writer Jeremias Gotthelf, b. Oct. 4, 1797, d. Oct. 22, 1854, was one of the creators of the German village tale. His life as a pastor in the Swiss village of Lützelflüh, in the Emmental, inspired most of his stories. His works are characterized by a masterful depiction of human motivations, didactic moral and religious purpose, robust humor, and—parallel to developments in European literature at the time—a studied realism. Gotthelf's best-known novels are *Ulric the Farm Servant* (1841; Eng. trans., 1888) and its sequel, *Uli, der Pächter* (Ulric the Tenant Farmer, 1847). Gotthelf's most popular novella is *The Black Spider* (1842; Eng. trans., 1975).
JAMES M. MCGLATHERY

Bibliography: Waidson, H. M., *Jeremias Gotthelf: An Introduction to the Swiss Novelist* (1953).

Göttingen [gurt'-ing-en]

Göttingen is a city in eastern West Germany in Lower Saxony state. Situated along the Leine River, it is 145 km (90 mi) from the East German border. Its population is 132,537 (1982 est.). Manufactures include precision instruments, pharmaceuticals, electrical equipment, and processed foods. The University of Göttingen (1737) and many of the research institutes of the Max Planck Scientific Society are there. Among Göttingen's many historic landmarks are the Rathaus, or town hall, and the Church of Saint John, both dating from the 14th century, as well as medieval fortifications.

By 953 a village called Gutingi existed on the site. In the 14th century Göttingen joined the Hanseatic League and prospered as a trade center. During the Reformation Göttingen accepted Protestantism and suffered heavy damage during the ensuing religious wars of the 16th century. The establishment of the university during the 18th century ushered in a new growth period.

Gottlieb, Adolph [gaht'-leeb]

Adolph Gottlieb, b. New York City, Mar. 4, 1903, d. Mar. 4, 1974, was a prominent member of the abstract expressionist group of artists (see ABSTRACT EXPRESSIONISM). After studying painting in New York City with John Sloan and Robert Henri, and in Europe, Gottlieb exhibited regularly in the 1930s with the avant-garde artists Ilya Bolotowsky and Mark Rothko. From 1941 to 1951, Gottlieb painted several "pictographs"—monochromatic paintings composed of abstract symbols arranged on a grid understructure. In the early 1950s he explored the relationship between floating forms and dense masses in a series of imaginary landscapes. Gottlieb's interest in object placement and his growing emphasis on expressive color led to his "Burst" paintings. In *Burst* (1957; Collection of Ben Heller), he reduced the imagery to two shapes on a white

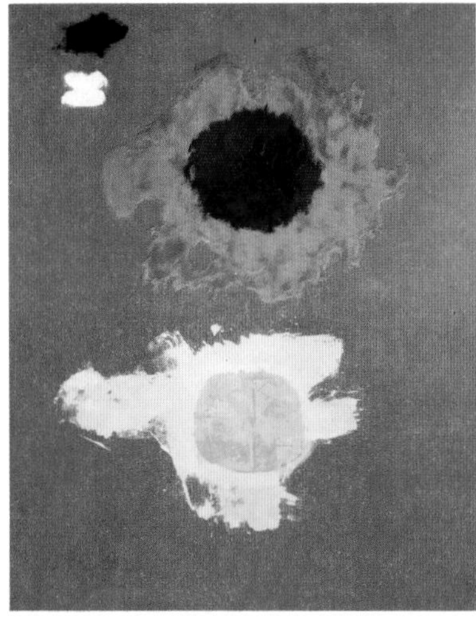

Adolph Gottlieb was a leading figure of American abstract expressionism when he painted Etendue Rouge *(1960). Gottlieb juxtaposes contrasting forms while using vivid, vibrant colors. (Sydney Janis Gallery, New York City.)*

ground, without reference to the canvas edge. Although extremely large, Gottlieb's "Burst" paintings are poetic and intimate works that present a subtle interplay of colors, shapes, and density. LISA M. MESSINGER

Bibliography: Doty, Robert, and Waldman, Diane, *Adolphe Gottlieb* (1968); Sandler, Irving, *The Triumph of American Painting: A History of Abstract Expressionism* (1970); Siegel, J., "Adolph Gottlieb at 70: Interview," *Art News*, December 1973.

Gottschalk, Louis Moreau [gaht'-shawk]

Louis Moreau Gottschalk, b. New Orleans, May 8, 1829, d. Dec. 18, 1869, was a celebrated American composer, pianist, and conductor. His German-English father and French mother were well educated and socially prominent. Gottschalk's musical abilities were evident early and at the age of 12 he was sent to Paris to study, remaining for 6 years. In 1849 he made his professional debut as a pianist in Paris. He embarked on concert tours of France and Switzerland (1850) and Spain (1851–52), winning great acclaim with both for performance and composition. He made his American debut in New York in 1853, then conducted his orchestral works at mammoth music festivals, again to wild acclaim. He spent the years 1856–62 wandering about the Caribbean islands. In 1865 he performed in California, after which he lived and performed for a few years in South America, continuing to enjoy phenomenal popularity. An attack of yellow fever caused his death in Rio de Janeiro at the height of his fame.

Gottschalk's salon pieces for piano contain a blend of Creole and American Negro musical characteristics. Programmatic ideas dominate his orchestral works, many of them inspired by Spanish subject matter. Long neglected, much of Gottschalk's music has been revived in recent years.
HOMER ULRICH

Bibliography: Doyle, J. G., *Louis Moreau Gottschalk* (1983); Loggins, Vernon, *Where the Words End: The Life of Louis Moreau Gottschalk* (1958).

Gottwald, Klement [gawt'-vahlt, klay'-ment]

Klement Gottwald, b. Nov. 23, 1896, d. Mar. 14, 1953, was the Czech Communist leader who established Czechoslovakia's Communist regime in 1948. A Communist party member from 1921 and party secretary from 1929, he spent the years of World War II in the USSR. He returned to Prague to become deputy premier (1945) and then premier (July 1946) in the postwar coalition government of Eduard BENEŠ. On June 14, 1948, after the forced resignation of Beneš, Gottwald became president of the now de facto single-party state. He was responsible for a major purge of Communist party members, including Rudolf Slansky, the party's secretary general, who was executed with ten others in November 1952.
K. M. SMOGORZEWSKI

gouache [goo-ahsh']

Gouache is paint made from opaque water color but with the addition of white pigment and a higher proportion of binder, such as gum arabic. The presence of a larger quantity of vehicle (the liquid in which pigments are mixed) creates the opaque effect, while the white pigment produces the characteristic brilliant, light-reflecting quality, as opposed to the luminosity of watercolors. Gouache paintings are commonly executed on paper in a spontaneous, *alla prima* manner. The technique has frequently been used for making preliminary studies for large oil paintings. VALENTIN TATRANSKY

Bibliography: Doerner, Max, *The Materials of the Artist and Their Use in Painting*, rev. ed. (1962; repr. 1984); Mayer, Ralph, *The Artist's Handbook of Materials and Techniques*, 4th ed. (1981).

Goujon, Jean [goo-zhohn']

Jean Goujon, *c*.1510–*c*.1568, was the most accomplished sculptor of the French Renaissance. His first documented work, the Corinthian columns of the organ loft in the Church of Saint Maclou, Rouen (1541), demonstrates that Goujon had already acquired a profound knowledge of classical architecture and may have been trained as an architect. In 1544, Goujon collaborated with Pierre LESCOT on the rood screen of Saint Germain l'Auxerrois, Paris. The central panel, a Pietà (Louvre, Paris), is an example of Goujon's mature style, an entirely personal synthesis of classical Renaissance motifs. In mid-century he executed his finest work, including the sculptures for the *Fountain of the Innocents* (1547–49; Louvre, Paris), which are figures carved in shallow relief within an architectural framework. Goujon's depictions of human figures in motion recall classical Greek sculpture. He commented on sculptural ornament in an appendix to an edition of the work of the Roman architect Vitruvius (1547), for which he also did woodcut illustrations. NANETTE SALOMON

Bibliography: Blunt, Anthony, *Art and Architecture in France, 1500-1700* (1953; repr. 1977).

Goulart, João [goo-lahr', zhwow]

João Belchior Marques Goulart, b. Mar. 1, 1918, d. Dec. 6, 1976, was president of Brazil from 1961 to 1964. A protégé of Getúlio Dornelles VARGAS, Goulart served (1953–54) as Vargas's minister of labor, industry, and commerce and was vice-president (1956–61), first under Juscelino KUBITSCHEK and then under Jânio Quadros. After Quadros's resignation in August 1961, Goulart became president. His reputed Communist leanings led the military to insist on restricting his presidential powers, but a plebiscite in 1963 restored them. Goulart's administration was marked by inflation and labor unrest. He was ousted by a military coup in April 1964.

Bibliography: Dulles, John F., *Unrest in Brazil: Political-Military Crises, 1955–1964* (1970).

Gould, Benjamin Apthorp [goold]

The American astronomer Benjamin Apthorp Gould, b. Boston, Sept. 27, 1824, d. Nov. 26, 1896, was the founder of the *Astronomical Journal* (1849) and of the Argentine National Observatory. He was educated at Harvard College and at the University of Göttingen, Germany, where he worked under C. F. Gauss. After serving a brief and tempestuous term as director of the Dudley Observatory in Albany, N.Y., he moved (1870) to Argentina. He remained there for 15 years, producing catalogs that contained positions for more than 100,000 southern stars. The *Astronomical Journal* did much to enhance the reputation of American astronomy.

Gould, Chester

The American cartoonist Chester Gould, b. Pawnee, Okla., Nov. 20, 1900, d. May 11, 1985, helped introduce the adventure comic strip by creating *Dick Tracy* in 1931. The strip, which first appeared in the *Chicago Tribune* and was later widely syndicated, portrays explicit violence but always stresses that crime does not pay. Gould's characters, such as Pruneface, B. O. Plenty, and Gravel Gertie, are highly imaginative. The strip's hero, Dick Tracy, is thought to have been inspired by J. Edgar Hoover. ROY PAUL NELSON

Gould, Glenn

The brilliant Canadian pianist Glenn Gould, b. Toronto, Sept. 25, 1932, d. Oct. 4, 1982, retired from concertizing at the peak of his success in 1964. He made his professional debut (1946) as soloist with the Toronto Symphony. In 1955 he gave his first U.S. recitals in Washington, D.C., and New York City, and in 1957 he made his European debut in Berlin. Gould was the first North American pianist invited (1957) by the Soviet government to perform in the USSR. After leaving the concert stage, he concentrated on making recordings, which he considered a distinct art form. Often cited for his creative, if not always popular, interpretations, Gould was best known for his playing of J. S. Bach. ELLA A. MALIN

Bibliography: Page, Tim, ed., *Glenn Gould Reader* (1984); Sachs, Harvey, *Virtuoso* (1982).

Gould, Gordon

Gordon Gould, b. New York City, July 17, 1920, is credited with conceptualizing the LASER in 1957. Independent of Gould, Charles Hard TOWNES realized the same idea in 1958. Because Gould had not immediately applied for patents (as Townes had), Townes was long given credit for the idea. Gould finally won laser patents in 1977, 1979, and 1987.

Gould, Jay

The railroad builder and speculator Jay Gould, b. Roxbury, N.Y., May 27, 1836, d. Dec. 2, 1892, was one of the most successful and notorious "robber barons" of the 19th century. He was the son of a poor farmer and went to work early in his life. At age 21, with savings of $5,000, he invested in the leather business and began speculating in railroad stocks. By the age of 31 he was a director of the Erie Railroad. With Daniel DREW and James FISK he waged the "Erie war" to prevent Cornelius Vanderbilt (see VANDERBILT family) from gaining control of the railroad. They issued illegal stock and bribed state legislators, making fortunes in the process. Gould became president of the Erie and continued to speculate in its stock. In 1869, Gould and Fisk almost cornered the gold market until the U.S. Treasury released some of its own gold stocks, leading to the BLACK FRIDAY panic of Sept. 24, 1869. The resulting public indignation forced Gould to resign (1872) as director of the Erie.

Gould proceeded to move into and out of a number of railroad companies—the Wabash, the Texas and Pacific, the Missouri Pacific, and the Union Pacific. He won control by shrewd stock purchases and ruthless competition with other lines. At the time of his death he owned the Missouri Pacific system, the Western Union Telegraph Company, and the Manhattan Elevated Railroad.

Bibliography: Grodinsky, Julius, *Jay Gould: His Business Career, 1867–1892* (1957; repr. 1981); Klein, Muary, *The Life and Legend of Jay Gould* (1986).

Gould, Morton

The American pianist, composer, and conductor Morton Gould, b. Richmond Hill, N.Y., Dec. 10, 1913, blends popular and serious music in compositions that emphasize American themes. Much of Gould's professional experience has been in radio: he conducted (1934–43) a program for contemporary American music on station WOR, and he was a staff musician and conductor at NBC and CBS. In 1965 he was engaged by Radio City Music Hall as composer and conductor. Among his compositions are scores for Broadway musicals, films, ballets (including *Fall River Legend*), and symphonic works with American themes such as *Symphony of Spirituals* and *Cowboy Rhapsody*. ELLA A. MALIN

Gould, Stephen Jay

American paleontologist Stephen Jay Gould, b. New York City, Sept. 10, 1941, is an evolutionary theorist and a writer of popular works on natural history and the role of science in society. Obtaining his Ph.D. from Columbia University in 1967, Gould joined and has remained on the staff of Harvard University. With others, he has advanced the debated concept that major evolutionary changes take place in sudden bursts (see EVOLUTION). Among his award-winning books are *The Panda's Thumb* (1980) and *The Mismeasure of Man* (1981); the latter traces the historical development and social misuse of supposed intelligence-measuring techniques.

Gounod, Charles [goo-noh']

Charles François Gounod, b. Paris, June 17, 1818, d. Oct. 18, 1893, was the composer of *Faust*, one of the most popular operas in the repertoire. Gounod's father was a painter, his mother a pianist. Gounod entered (1836) the Paris Conservatory, won (1839) the Prix de Rome, and spent two and a half years in Italy, where he studied church music and composed a mass. From 1852 to 1860 he was director of the choral society Orphéon, for which he wrote choral music. In 1866 he was elected a member of the Institut de France; he was made an officer of the Legion of Honor in 1888. His autobiographical *Memoirs of an Artist* was published in 1896.

The premiere of *Faust* at the Théâtre-Lyrique in Paris in 1859 was only moderately successful. Ten years later, however, after Gounod had made revisions in the score and added a ballet, the work was produced at the Paris Opéra to acclaim. Since then *Faust* has been performed in virtually every opera house in the world. Gounod's operas *Roméo et Juliette* (1867) and *Mireille* (1864) are also frequently performed; his 10 other operas (one incomplete) were unsuccessful. His most popular short piece is his "Ave Maria"; for its accompaniment he used a keyboard prelude by Johann Sebastian Bach—thus it is also known as the Bach-Gounod "Ave Maria." (Gounod referred to it as a prank and was said to have deplored its popularity.) Also popular is the whimsical *Funeral March of a Marionette*. Gounod had a deep understanding of the voice and was a skillful orchestrator. His works include 23 masses, 6 oratorios (including *The Redemption*), 2 symphonies, 3 string quartets, piano pieces, and incidental music for plays.

FARLEY HUTCHINS

Charles Gounod, a 19th-century French composer, achieved fame with his lyrical opera Faust, *first performed in 1859. Intending to enter the priesthood, he had studied theology for two years before dedicating himself to a career in music. Although Gounod was best known for his popular operas, he also wrote numerous sacred compositions.*

Bibliography: Cooper, Martin, *French Music from the Death of Berlioz to the Death of Fauré* (1951); Demuth, Norman, *Introduction to the Music of Gounod* (1950); Harding, James, *Gounod* (1973).

gourd [gohrd]

Gourds are a large and diverse group of plants belonging to the family Cucurbitaceae and related to pumpkin and squash. They are grown for their fruits, which occur in a great variety of sizes, shapes, and colors. Many gourds are raised as ornamentals, and the hard shells of some are used for making utensils such as dippers. The yellow-flowered gourd, *Cucurbita pepo,* the most common American type, produces small, smooth or knobby fruits in several shapes and colors. Bottle gourds, genus *Lagenaria,* may reach a length of 1.5 m (5 ft) and are used in India as sounding boxes for certain musical instruments. Gourds of genus *Luffa* have a spongelike interior that, when dried, can be used as a dishcloth. Some gourds are edible, and the buffalo gourd, *C. foetidissima,* with roots and seeds rich in starch and oil, is being studied as a potential commercial crop on arid lands.

Gourds are used primarily for decoration, although some hard-shelled varieties are turned into drinking cups. Their long vines bear broad palmate leaves and yellow flowers. They are harvested in autumn and waxed or varnished for preservation.

Gourds are cultivated as are pumpkin or squash. The seeds are planted directly in the soil, and the plants are harvested when the fruits are mature and hard.

O. A. LORENZ

Gourmont, Remy de [goor-mohn', ruh-mee' duh]

A French writer and critic, Remy de Gourmont, b. Apr. 4, 1858, d. Sept. 27, 1915, was an influential advocate of literary experimentation. Beginning in 1889 he contributed extensively to *La Mercure de France,* a periodical that helped promote the symbolist movement in literature. Gourmont's novels and plays, depicting intellectual, unheroic characters, are overshadowed by his critical writings and linguistic studies.

Bibliography: Aldington, Richard, *Remy de Gourmont, a Modern Man of Letters* (1928); Burne, Glenn S., *Remy de Gourmont: His Ideas and Influence in England and America* (1963).

gout [gowt]

Gout is a disease marked by recurrent acute attacks of ARTHRITIS, the result of deposits of monosodium-urate crystals around the joints and tendons. These crystals occur when abnormally high amounts of uric acid are present in the body (hyperuricemia). The presence of hyperuricemia distinguishes gout from other forms of arthritis because more than 95 percent of persons with gout are hyperuricemic; it is not, however, the sole cause.

Almost all gouty patients are men, usually over 30 years old. Primary gout appears to involve a heredity factor. A genetically sex-linked defect in purine metabolism leads to increased purine production, called the Lesch-Nyhan syndrome, resulting in a high uric acid concentration. Secondary gout develops as a result of other causes, such as another disease. Excessive cell breakdown, as in hemolytic anemia, results in overproduction of urate. Diuretic drugs used to treat high blood pressure can induce hyperuricemia and result in clinical gout.

Gout usually begins with pain and inflammation of a joint, often the big toe. Acute attacks are treated with the drug COLCHICINE. One treatment is aimed at preventing crystal deposits of urate. Excretion of urate by the kidney is aided by uricosuric drugs along with high fluid intake, which increases the urine output.

Bibliography: Copeman, W. S. C., *A Short History of the Gout and the Rheumatic Diseases* (1964).

Gouthière, Pierre Joseph Désiré [goo-tee-air']

Pierre Gouthière, 1732–*c.*1813, was one of the finest fondeurs-doreurs, or finishers of cast bronzes, in France during the reign of Louis XVI. In 1758, Gouthière became a maître-doreur, and after marrying the widow of his employer, the gilder François Cériset, he opened a shop on the quai Pelletier, Paris. From 1769 to 1777 he was employed mainly by the court and developed a technique of mercury gilding whereby highly burnished and matte finishes were combined within the same piece. Gouthière's clients were slow to pay, and he was declared bankrupt in 1788. His firm did not survive the French Revolution, and Gouthière died in poverty.

REVIEWED BY KATHRYN B. HIESINGER

government

Government comprises the set of legal and political institutions that regulate the relationships among members of a society and between the society and outsiders. These institutions have the authority to make decisions for the society on policies affecting the maintenance of order and the achievement of certain societal goals. This article provides an overview of the types of government, the ways authority can be distributed, the divisions of government, and the functions of government. Separate articles deal with the origins and development of the concept of the STATE, the theoretical and practical development of REPRESENTATION, LAW, and the study of government (see POLITICAL SCIENCE).

The power of a government over its own citizens varies, depending on the degree to which it is free of limitations and restraints. The power of a government abroad also varies, depending on the human and material resources with which it can support its FOREIGN POLICY. Governments range in size and scope from clans, tribes, and the shires of early times to the superpowers and international governments of today. Until recent times some governments were strong enough to establish EMPIRES that ruled not only their own people but other peoples and states across national, ethnic, and language boundaries. The present-day counterpart of the empire is the superpower that is able to lead or dominate other countries through its superior military and economic strength. Within the modern nation-state, government operates at many different levels, ranging from villages to cities, counties, provinces, and states.

TYPES OF GOVERNMENT

ARISTOTLE, a Greek political philosopher of the 3d century BC, distinguished three principal kinds of government: MONARCHY, ARISTOCRACY, and polity (a kind of enlightened DEMOCRACY). The differences among them chiefly concerned whether power was held by one, by a few, or by many. Aristotle thought that the selfish abuse of power caused each type to become perverted, respectively, into tyranny, OLIGARCHY, and a lower form of democracy characterized by mob rule. Monarchy tended to become tyrannical because it vested authority in a single ruler. Aristocracy, a government based on birth and privilege, in which the rulers governed for the good of the whole society, tended to become oligarchy as a consequence of restricting political power to a special social and economic class; only a few members of the class would have enough drive and ability to acquire the power to govern. The polity, likewise, would deteriorate into ochlocracy or mob rule if the citizens pursued only their selfish interests.

Aristotle's classifications suited the societies of ancient times, but they do not correspond to the power structure of later societies. Modern writers have developed a variety of schemes for classifying governments, based on the nature of the ruling class, the economic system, the government's political institutions, the principles of authority, the acquisition and exercise of power, and other factors. Some influential writers on government include Thomas HOBBES, Baron de MONTESQUIEU, Jean Jacques ROUSSEAU, Karl MARX, Gaetano MOSCA, Vilfredo PARETO, and the sociologist Max WEBER.

Monarchy. The most common form of government from medieval times to the early part of the 20th century was monarchy, or rule by a hereditary king or queen. Monarchy passed through three basic stages, varying according to the nation and the political and economic climate. The first stage was that of the absolute monarch. In the Christian part of the world during the Middle Ages, a conflict developed between the pope and the kings who recognized his spiritual authority. The pope wanted to expand the power of the church beyond spiritual matters to include the temporal realm. But some kings proclaimed that God had given them the right to rule, and by proclaiming this DIVINE RIGHT they were able to give legitimacy to their reigns and limit the pope's power. (See CHURCH AND STATE; INVESTITURE CONTROVERSY.)

Limited monarchy was the second stage. Kings depended on the support of the most powerful members of the nobility to retain their thrones. In England and some other Western European countries, the nobility placed limits on the power of the ruler to govern. This was done in England, for example, through the MAGNA CARTA. Threatened with the loss of political and financial support, even the strongest kings and emperors had to accept a system of laws that protected the rights and privileges of powerful social and economic classes.

The third stage in the evolution of monarchy was the constitutional monarchy. Present-day monarchs are nearly all symbolic rather than actual rulers of their countries. (A few exceptions can be found in Africa and Asia.) In such monarchies as Great Britain, the Netherlands, and Sweden, governing power is now in the hands of the national parliaments.

Constitutional Government. Today most governments derive their legitimacy from national CONSTITUTIONS that provide a legal framework for their rule and specify how power is to be exercised and controlled. Even one-party states, such as the USSR, the Communist-bloc countries of Eastern Europe, and other nations in Africa, Asia, and South America, have found it necessary to establish formal constitutions. In democratic countries the constitution can be amended or replaced by popular vote, either directly or through a system of elected representatives. In authoritarian one-party systems, however, all political power, including that of revising the constitution, resides with the leaders of the party. The constitution may thus be only a paper facade, and in order to understand how the country is governed one must examine the actual political process.

Democracy. Representative government in the modern world is based not only on a constitution that provides for it but on the actual rule of law—the assurance that provisions of the constitution will be enforced. It requires that citizens be free to organize competing POLITICAL PARTIES, engage in political CAMPAIGNS, and hold ELECTIONS according to agreed-upon rules. Democratic governments vary in structure. Two common forms are the parliamentary and the presidential. In the parliamentary form of government, as in Australia, Britain, Canada, or India, all political power is concentrated in the parliament or LEGISLATURE. The prime minister or premier and the officers of the cabinet are members of the parliament. They continue in office only as long as parliament supports—or has "confidence" in—their policies. In the presidential form of government, as in France and the United States, the voters elect a powerful chief executive who is independent of the legislature but whose actions are delimited by constitutional and other legal restraints.

Dictatorship. As a form of government, DICTATORSHIP is principally a 20th-century phenomenon. The dictator, often a military leader, concentrates political power in himself and his clique. There is no effective rule of law. The regime may or may not have a distinctive political IDEOLOGY and may or may not allow token opposition. The main function of a dictatorship is to maintain control of all governmental operations. There have been only a few cases—Indira GANDHI in India and several military dictatorships in Latin America—in which authoritarian dictators have relaxed their control and have even allowed open general elections.

The totalitarian dictatorship, as in the USSR, Nazi Germany, or Communist China, is much more thoroughgoing. It seeks to control all aspects of national life, including the beliefs and attitudes of its people. It has a set of ideas that everyone is expected to embrace, such as revolutionary MARXISM or counterrevolutionary FASCISM. The ruling group uses all the means of organization and propaganda that are available in a modern society. At its most extreme, as during the leadership of Joseph STALIN in the USSR, the power of the dictator may become more absolute than in any of the earlier forms of tyranny. Such gross power in the hands of one person results inevitably in the development of what has been called a cult of personality. The leader is credited with almost infallible wisdom, because to admit that he or she may be wrong would deprive the regime of its authority. In Communist countries the cult of personality appears to be giving way to the dominance of a group of party leaders—a ruling oligarchy. The administrative complexities of managing a modern industrial state are too great to be monopolized by an individual such as Stalin or MAO TSE-TUNG. The regimes continue to claim infallibility for their parties and doctrines, but not for the leaders. Examples of 20th-century dictators in addition to those already mentioned include Idi AMIN DADA (Uganda), Kemal ATATÜRK (Turkey), Fulgencio BATISTA and Fidel CASTRO (Cuba), Francisco FRANCO (Spain), Ferdinand MARCOS (Philippines), Benito MUSSOLINI (Italy), Juan PERÓN (Argentina), and Antonio SALAZAR (Portugal).

DISTRIBUTIONS OF AUTHORITY

Effective government in any form requires a workable method for distributing authority within the country. The larger and more diverse the jurisdiction of the government, the stronger the tendency toward a federal system in which authority is "layered" or distributed among different levels, as in the United States or Canada. In countries with a relatively homogeneous population and with a common tradition, language, and sense of national history, the central governments may not be federal but unitary—that is, they may retain most of the administrative power at the center, as in France. Loosely allied autonomous states sometimes join together to create a type of central government known as a confederation, in which the central government exists only at the pleasure of the sovereign members—as in the United States under the ARTICLES OF CONFEDERATION of 1781.

Federal Systems. The United States and India with their state governments, Canada and China with their provincial governments, and the USSR with its republics are examples of workable federal systems in large nations with very diverse populations. Other federal states include Argentina, Australia, Brazil, Czechoslovakia, Mexico, Nigeria, and West Germany. The national governments of these countries are clearly more powerful than those of their subdivisions, even though the constitutions delegate many powers and responsibilities to the subnational units. In certain prescribed policy areas a state government may have a high degree of autonomy. In the United States, for example, state legislatures pass laws having to do with state affairs, state administrators carry them out, and state judiciaries interpret them.

Federal systems also include autonomous local governments such as county governments and MUNICIPAL GOVERNMENTS—in cities, boroughs, townships, and villages. Local governments may stand in a relationship to their state governments that corresponds to that of state governments with the national government. The citizens in each jurisdiction elect many of the public officials. In addition, certain special districts exist with a single function, such as education or sanitation, and have their own elected officials.

The layers of government in a federal system may not be clearly defined in practice. Often the different levels compete for control of functions and programs. In the United States and other countries the tendency over the years has been for the national government to become much more involved in areas that once were the exclusive domain of state or regional governments. Cooperative interaction between state and federal governments has become common, leading to a complex, interlocking relationship. In the United States, for example, national and state governments both appropriate funds for cities, with the consequence that the affairs of a large city such as New York or Chicago are partly determined by political decisions made in the national capital at Washington, D.C., and in the state capital at Albany or Springfield. In addition, the distribution of authority has become even more complex and varied with the rise of large metropolitan areas—the MEGALOPOLIS—and the corresponding new local governmental organizations such as the Port of New York Authority. Political scientists are fond of saying that the federal system in the United States, with its involuted layers, is more akin to a marble cake than a layer cake. In the USSR, on the other hand, the federal organization—reflecting ethnic subdivisions—exists principally for administrative purposes, while all real power is concentrated in the central government and in a dominant subnational unit—the Russian Soviet Federated Socialist Republic.

Unitary States. In unitary states the national government performs all the governmental functions. Subnational national units administer matters within their jurisdiction, but their powers are set and delegated by the national authority. The national government retains the police power—the inherent power of a government to provide for the health, safety, and welfare of its citizens. The power to tax also rests almost entirely with the national government. Likewise, all significant laws are national in scope.

Most nations are unitary states, but their institutions and processes may differ markedly. Great Britain, for example, is considered a unitary system, yet a certain degree of regional autonomy exists in Northern Ireland, Scotland, and Wales, and local county governments perform certain fairly autonomous functions. In France, however, strict control over the administrative territorial subdivisions called *départements* and *arrondissements* is exercised by the national government. In other unitary states, in eastern Europe, for example, there exists only token territorial decentralization.

Confederations. Confederation produces the weakest central government. Member states in a confederation retain their sovereignty, delegating to the central government only those powers that are essential for its maintenance. The individual states jealously guard their power to tax and to make their own laws. The central government serves as a coordinating instrument to protect the interests of all its members. It also represents the confederation in dealings with outside governments, but its actions are subject to the review and approval of the confederated states. The weakness of the confederate form of government led the United States to abandon that system in 1789 after only 8 years, although the South attempted to adopt such a system during the U.S. Civil War (see CONFEDERATE STATES OF AMERICA). Confederations, however, have also served other nations—Germany and Switzerland, for example—as a preliminary step towards a more unified government. No modern nation-state is organized along confederate lines, yet certain international organizations, such as the British COMMONWEALTH OF NATIONS, the EUROPEAN COMMUNITY, the FRENCH COMMUNITY, and the NORTH ATLANTIC TREATY ORGANIZATION, have some aspects of a confederation.

DIVISIONS OF GOVERNMENT

Various political thinkers have distinguished types of government activity. Montesquieu was the first, however, to urge the creations of three separate institutions or divisions of government—the executive, legislative, and judicial—a distinction that became common in almost all modern constitutions. Some governmental structures, notably the United States, are based on the principle of SEPARATION OF POWERS at nearly every level. Executive, legislative, and judicial powers are divided into three branches of government, creating a system of checks and balances among them. The balance does not remain constant, since the dynamics of politics produces competition between the branches. Nevertheless, the separation of powers has helped to protect citizens from arbitrary and capricious actions on the part of any of the three branches. Such protection is crucial in the areas in CIVIL RIGHTS—those constitutionally guaranteed rights that shield the citizen from tyrannical actions by government. The historical record shows that in times of grave national emergency, when the central government needs more power, the public is willing to grant it. The executive branch usually predominates at such times (see PRESIDENT OF THE UNITED STATES).

Proponents of the separation of powers bring an additional argument in its favor: they point out that the system diminishes the influence of SPECIAL-INTEREST GROUPS, or factions, over any one branch of government or over the government as a whole. The struggle for influence among organized pressure groups is common to every governmental system. It is difficult for even the strongest special-interest group to dominate a government in which the executive is elected by the entire population, members of the legislature represent different geographical constituencies, and the judges are appointed by the executive with the approval of the legislature.

Not all states, of course, have such clear divisions of government, nor do divisions necessarily guarantee personal liberties. Parliamentary democratic systems, for example, tend to merge legislative and executive functions yet control the exercise of power by constitutional methods of sharing it. Authoritarian states may, however, be constitutionally bound to have separate organs of government yet actually concentrate power in the executive.

FUNCTIONS OF GOVERNMENT

Maintenance of Authority. One of the principal functions of government is to remain in power. Governments do not relinquish their authority unless compelled to do so. Many of the actions of politicians and civil servants can be explained by the need to maintain and enhance their power.

Every government strives to increase its legitimacy in the eyes of the people. It may identify itself with ancient traditions, with hope for the future, or with fear of a common enemy. Some governments employ repression, never relaxing their vigils against real or imagined opponents. Even democracies, when threatened, are likely to engage in a search for subversives and "enemies of the people."

When a regime draws its main support from a privileged class or group that decreases in numbers and strength, when a government becomes ineffective domestically or against external threats, or when a society's consensus on the principles and goals of government evaporates, a government tends to lose authority. The French monarchy in the 18th century and the Russian monarchy in the 20th were based on aristocracies that had lost much of their legitimacy in the eyes of the people. Eventually they were unable to enforce their laws, and REVOLUTIONS swept them from power. The Weimar Republic of Germany and the French Third and Fourth Republics lost authority largely because of their ineffectiveness. The lack of consensus in the United States was an important factor in the onset of the Civil War. Governments tend, therefore, to foster widespread ideological commitment to the nation through patriotic ceremonies, propaganda, and civic education; they employ armed forces and intelligence-gathering organizations for national defense; they maintain police and prison systems to ensure domestic order; and they undertake the administration of supervisory, regulatory, and enterprisory functions to carry out national goals by establishing various bureaucracies to handle the complexities of each function.

Administration. All governments recognize the principle that the public must be protected and served. The citizen, in effect, surrenders a degree of individual sovereignty to the government in return for protection of life and property and the delivery of essential services. Governments supervise the resolution of conflicting interests, the workings of the political process, the enforcement of laws and rights, and the monitoring of national income (see INCOME, NATIONAL) and INTERNATIONAL TRADE; they regulate economic and social relationships among individuals and private organizations; and they carry out enterprises such as in production of military goods, provision of postal services, and ownership of power utilities and public works. Among the most basic services provided by government are the printing and coining of MONEY, the provision of roads, sewers, water, education, and SOCIAL AND WELFARE SERVICES.

Governments have also taken on wide-ranging regulatory functions. The proper scope of government intervention in economic life has always been controversial. In the 16th and 17th centuries some governments adopted policies called MERCANTILISM, designed to increase national industrial power at the expense of other nations. They imposed strict regulations on foreign trade. In the 19th century the LAISSEZ-FAIRE and FREE TRADE ideas of Adam SMITH and John Stuart MILL influenced governments to leave economic affairs as much as possible to private business. In the mid-20th century the belief spread that governments should provide directly for the welfare of their citizens.

With the growth of the WELFARE STATE, governments began to provide services such as SOCIAL SECURITY and HEALTH INSURANCE. But the scope of GOVERNMENT REGULATION is now much broader than that. In the United States the government sets minimum wages, limits the rates charged by railroads and public utilities, buys farm commodities to keep prices up, runs airport control towers, forbids the sale of harmful foods and drugs, sets standards for gasoline consumption by automobiles, requires manufacturers to install antipollution devices, and monitors the safety of factories. Federal, state, and local governments in the United States also engage directly in economic activity. They are involved in TAXATION, formulate budgets, produce and consume goods, sell electric power, lend money to farmers and exporters, and insure bank deposits.

In other countries governments intrude even farther into the workings of the economy. In Western Europe governments own and operate telephone, radio, and television services, railroads, coal mines, and aircraft companies. In some countries, such as Sweden and Great Britain, the entire health system is also run by the state. In the USSR and other countries with Communist governments, the state controls the entire economic life of the nation. Private ownership is restricted to items of personal property and, in some countries of Eastern Europe, small farms. All economic planning is centralized in the government and its bureaucracies.

INTERNATIONAL GOVERNMENT

In modern times national governments have become increasingly involved with one another in supranational systems. The LEAGUE OF NATIONS, established in 1919, grew to include 94 members. It collapsed in World War II but was succeeded by the UNITED NATIONS (UN), which had 151 members in 1979. The UN, like the League, is a voluntary association generally without power to act unless the five permanent members of the Security Council agree. It has, however, served as a forum for international debate and a convenient meeting ground for negotiations.

Associated with the UN are a number of specialized organizations that perform important governmental functions. They include the FOOD AND AGRICULTURE ORGANIZATION, the INTERNATIONAL ATOMIC ENERGY AGENCY, the INTERNATIONAL CIVIL AVIATION ORGANIZATION, the INTERNATIONAL LABOR ORGANIZATION, the INTERNATIONAL MONETARY FUND, the Universal POSTAL UNION, the UNITED NATIONS EDUCATIONAL, SCIENTIFIC, AND CULTURAL ORGANIZATION, the WORLD HEALTH ORGANIZATION, the International Bank for Reconstruction and Development (WORLD BANK), and the International Telecommunication Union.

The specialized agencies have enabled national governments to cooperate in many practical matters such as setting standards, extending technical and financial assistance to developing countries, eliminating or controlling epidemic diseases, and establishing an international monetary system.

THOMAS B. HARTMANN

Bibliography: Finer, S. E., *Comparative Government* (1974); McLennan, Barbara N., *Comparative Political Systems* (1975); Ridley, F., *The Study of Government* (1975); Stevenson, Thomas H., *Politics and Government* (1973).

Government Printing Office, United States

The Government Printing Office (GPO) was established by the U.S. Congress in 1860 to print and distribute federal government publications. These now include the CONGRESSIONAL RECORD, covering the business of Congress, and over 25,000 publications of government agencies. The GPO prints pamphlets explaining social security and other governmental benefits, as well as publications on subjects of interest to homemakers and farmers. Lists of its publications may be obtained from the Superintendent of Documents, Government Printing Office, Washington, D.C., 20242.

government regulation

Regulation is the practice in which governments seek to influence the behavior of individuals or organizations, especially private business firms, by imposing and enforcing legal obligations. As a method of economic intervention, regulation is intended to serve governmental goals, such as protecting the public from various harms, while leaving most business decisions to the discretion of management and the test of the market. It is a kind of halfway house between unfettered private enterprise, on the one hand, and public ownership or detailed ECONOMIC PLANNING on the other.

In the United States regulation extends to numerous industries and aspects of economic activity; it is carried on by state and local governments as well as the federal government. Several industries have been heavily regulated by the federal government—including agriculture, banking, securities, telecommunications, radio and television broadcasting, energy, and transportation. In some cases this regulation has been reduced or was eliminated in the 1970s and 1980s. Besides regulating particular industries, the federal government also regulates many or all industries with respect to certain aspects of business performance; these include wages and hours, labor relations, employment discrimination, environmental pollution, workplace safety, product safety, trade practices, and industry structure. In all, about 55 federal agencies with approximately 80,000 employees are engaged in some form of regulation.

State governments play a role in implementing some federal regulatory programs, and states act on their own authority to regulate certain industries (such as insurance) and occupations (from electricians to bartenders to medical doctors). These regulatory policies vary widely from state to state. Finally, there is considerable regulation in the form of local ordinances, much of it concerned with building practices, health and sanitation, and land-use planning.

Although Americans often believe that the hand of government is peculiarly burdensome in the United States, government control is even more extensive in many other developed economies. Typically, outside the United States, the gas, electric-power, telephone, and railroad industries and at least one of the major television networks are publicly owned. Some countries, such as Sweden and West Germany, have regulations requiring that labor representatives participate formally in corporate policy-making. In Japan, the ministry of trade and industry plays a large role in planning industrial development. In the so-called command economies of communist countries, of course, the state owns and directly operates all of the significant enterprises.

THE CONTROVERSIAL ROLE OF REGULATION

The proper role for government regulation has long been controversial. Under the policies of MERCANTILISM dominant in Europe in the 16th, 17th, and 18th centuries, governments attempted to control manufacturing, trade, and shipping to achieve a favorable balance of trade and increase national wealth. Mercantilist doctrines were discredited by 18th-century economists such as Adam SMITH, who proposed that governments should refrain from interfering with the market—which, he said, leads selfish individuals to benefit others as if by a "hidden hand." The resulting ideology of LAISSEZ-FAIRE liberalism was dominant in Great Britain and the United States during the 19th century. Some regulation was introduced, however, and in the 20th century it was expanded greatly.

Today's liberals (unlike the bearers of that label in the 19th century) often advocate regulation to mitigate social and economic problems they associate with unregulated private enterprise. Conservatives usually oppose such plans—arguing that regulation merely diminishes freedom and makes the economy less efficient. Taking a kind of middle position, many economists argue that markets are "imperfect" and government intervention may be appropriate in several well-defined circumstances: (1) if there is a monopoly (see MONOPOLY AND COMPETITION); (2) if the cost of obtaining and using information (say, about food additives) prevents consumers or others from choosing intelligently; (3) if economic activities affect third parties (for example, by pollution); or (4) if certain goods (such as police service or local parks) are by their nature consumed collectively and hence cannot be sold successfully to individuals.

EARLY REGULATION

Throughout American history, as the scholars Merle Fainsod and Lincoln Gordon have observed, regulation has been "initiated by particular groups to deal with specific evils as they arose, rather than inspired by any general philosophy of governmental control." The first significant regulatory programs were adopted, at the state level, to control businesses in a position to exercise arbitrary power. In Massachusetts, for example, a bank commission was created in 1838, direct supervision by the legislature having been tried and judged inadequate. The state also regulated railroads to prevent excessive rates, and in 1869 a railroad commission was created as an advisory body to strengthen implementation of existing laws. As in much of the U.S. regulatory experience, these Massachusetts programs generally lacked the resources and legal powers needed for effective enforcement.

The federal government first assumed a major regulatory function to deal with railroads. In the 1870s protest by the National GRANGE, focusing on charges of unreasonable and discriminatory rates, led to new or increased regulation of railroads in a number of states. But state regulation proved ineffective, and in the Interstate Commerce Act of 1887, Congress created the INTERSTATE COMMERCE COMMISSION (ICC) and gave it modest authority to oversee the industry. Similarly, Congress superseded state regulation of trusts and monopolies in the SHERMAN ANTI-TRUST ACT of 1890.

The ICC is an independent regulatory commission, a type of administrative agency used earlier by the states and subsequently in much federal regulation. Designed to be independent of the executive branch, such agencies are headed by a commission whose members (usually 5 or 7) are appointed by the president to fixed and staggered terms of office, with no more than a bare majority to be chosen from the same political party. Congress has often preferred this arrangement partly because, along with ordinary executive authority, the commissions have been given "quasi-legislative" powers to determine policy and "quasi-judicial" ones to decide cases. Besides the ICC, the principal independent regulatory commissions now in existence are the CONSUMER PRODUCT SAFETY COMMISSION (1972), the FEDERAL COMMUNICATIONS COMMISSION (1934), the FEDERAL RESERVE BOARD (1913), the FEDERAL TRADE COMMISSION (1914), the NATIONAL LABOR RELATIONS BOARD (1935), the NUCLEAR REGULATORY COMMISSION (1975), and the SECURITIES AND EXCHANGE COMMISSION (1934). Other regulatory programs are administered by agencies located in the executive branch, such as the Antitrust Division of the Justice Department; the FOOD AND DRUG ADMINISTRATION (1931), in the Department of Health and Human Services; the OCCUPATIONAL SAFETY AND HEALTH ADMINISTRATION (1970), in the Department of Labor; the National Highway Traffic Safety Administration, in the Department of Transportation; and the ENVIRONMENTAL PROTECTION AGENCY (1970), which is independent of any cabinet department.

REGULATION AND THE COURT

The growth of regulation occasioned a half-century of eventful debate over the interpretation of the U.S. Constitution. In MUNN V. ILLINOIS (1877), a case involving the Granger laws, the Supreme Court upheld the states' authority to regulate industries, such as railroads and grain elevators, that are "affected with a public interest." For much of the period from the 1880s to the 1930s, however, a bold Court vetoed numerous regulatory laws, both state and federal, as unconstitutional. In UNITED STATES v. E. C. KNIGHT COMPANY (1895), which narrowed the Sherman Act, and HAMMER v. DAGENHART (1918), which invalidated a federal ban on goods produced by child labor, it held that federal authority to "regulate interstate commerce" did not extend to production. In other cases, such as LOCHNER v. NEW YORK (1905), it used the due-process clauses of the 5th and 14th Amendments to invalidate regulatory measures as "unreasonable" or "arbitrary and capricious." The Court's construction of the commerce clause was defensible legally, though surely impractical; its use of the guarantees of due process to enforce substantive policies, such as a strict notion of freedom of contract, was more strained. In all, as Justice Oliver Wendell Holmes pointed out, dissenting in *Lochner,* the Court was reading the Constitution as embodying "a particular economic doctrine."

The Court's assertiveness ended abruptly in 1937, as a result of confrontation with President Franklin D. Roosevelt's program to end the Depression. After the Court had struck down major parts of Roosevelt's NEW DEAL and this had led to an escalating conflict with the president, one of the conservative justices switched his position and the Court removed itself as an obstacle to regulation. Since then, the Court has prohibited state regulation only if it conflicted with federal responsibility, and has enforced no limits to federal control. The federal courts still review the actions of regulatory agencies on statutory grounds, exhibiting a new activism in recent years. In many of these cases they have ended up demanding more regulation. In *Sierra Club* v. *Ruckelshaus* (1973), for example, the Supreme Court ordered the Environmental Protection Agency (EPA) to establish a major program to prevent deterioration of air quality in unpolluted areas. In making these demands, some have argued, the courts are prone to overlook the technical and administrative complexities of regulatory issues.

THE EXPANSION OF FEDERAL REGULATION

Most of the expansion of the federal regulatory role took place in three waves, each occurring during a period of general political ferment and governmental activism. The Democratic party, which has been more liberal and less responsive to business than the Republican party, has controlled Congress in each of these periods; much of the time a Democrat also occupied the White House. Several major regulatory acts, the first wave of expansion, owed their impetus largely to the Progressive movement from 1900 to World War I. These include the Pure Food and Drug Act of 1906 (see PURE FOOD AND DRUG LAWS), the Hepburn Act of 1906 (which strengthened railroad regulation), and several major laws adopted in President Woodrow Wilson's highly productive first term: the Federal Reserve Act (1913), the CLAYTON ANTI-TRUST ACT (1914), and the Federal Trade Commission Act (1914).

A second wave emerged from the economic chaos of the Depression of the 1930s, which led to widespread distrust of the unregulated workings of capitalism. Regulation was created or expanded for industries that were held responsible for the Depression (banking and the stock exchanges); that seemed to be victims of it (agriculture, coal, airlines, trucking); or for which regulation had previously been sought on other grounds (radio, telephone, food, drugs). In the NATIONAL LABOR RELATIONS ACT, or Wagner Act (1935), labor unions won a long-sought federal guarantee of a right to collective bargaining.

Much of the New Deal regulation, like the earlier regulation of railroads, was PUBLIC UTILITY-type regulation of prices and service. In the standard form of such regulation, the agency decides an appropriate rate of return on investment for firms in the industry, establishes a rate base (the current value of this investment), and determines allowable costs of service. Finally, it sets prices intended to produce sufficient revenue to cover those costs and provide the appropriate rate of return. Since the firm is allowed to make money on its entire investment, officials must scrutinize a multitude of management decisions—for example, whether American Telephone and Telegraph really needs a new microwave link between Chicago and Denver. Favored by economists only where monopoly is unavoidable, versions of such regulation were also extended during the 1930s to transportation industries—described as "sick" or "infant" industries—whose structure was highly competitive.

A common complaint about the Progressive Era and New Deal regulatory programs has been that they are often "captured" by the industries they are supposed to regulate: that is, the industry becomes the dominant force in the agency's political environment and largely controls its decisions. Though this sometimes occurs, the phenomenon has been overrated. For example, the CIVIL AERONAUTICS BOARD (CAB)—often cited as the classic case of a captured agency—was created in the first place partly to assist the airlines, and its policies, though in some ways protective of the industry, did not bestow abnormal profits.

The third, and most consequential, expansion was largely a product of the liberal activism and skepticism toward business of the 1960s and 1970s. Promoted by a network of citizens' organizations, whose most prominent spokesman was Ralph NADER, the measures of this period often sought "social" objectives (such as health or racial equality) instead of the "economic" objectives (reasonable rates or stable service) more characteristic of earlier regulation. In numerous laws, Congress established or expanded regulatory programs in four areas of social concern: (1) CONSUMER PROTECTION (with laws on trade practices, truth-in-lending, automobile safety, consumer products safety, prescription drug safety and efficacy, and other subjects); (2) environmental protection (including air pollution, water pollution, pesticide safety, strip mining, noise control, and toxic substances); (3) workplace safety (the Occupational Safety and Health Act of 1970 and a separate measure protecting miners); and (4) civil rights (certain provisions of the CIVIL RIGHTS ACT of 1964 and other laws, dealing with discrimination in employment and access for the handicapped). In addition, the inflation and energy crises of the mid-1970s produced a brief experiment with general wage and price controls and longer-lasting controls for petroleum products and natural gas.

In contrast to previous regulation, which usually covered a single industry, some of the recent social regulation has broad scope—affecting a large part of the economy. It has been correspondingly difficult to administer and expensive to comply with. Established by presidential order in 1970, and strengthened by a dozen significant laws of the succeeding decade, the Environmental Protection Agency (EPA) quickly became the largest federal regulatory agency, with about 11,000 employees and a budget of $5.6 billion in 1980. Compliance with its requirements was estimated to cost, by 1978, over $7 billion in capital expenditures alone. Partly because the environmental and the workplace-safety regulatory programs involve huge administrative tasks, such as inspecting tens of thousands of places of business, the states were given a large role in their implementation.

DEREGULATION AND REGULATORY REFORM

Since the mid-1970s the dominant trend in regulatory policy has been to prune away some of the excesses of existing programs. Besides a generally conservative trend in politics, this reflects a broader concern that existing regulatory programs may be hindering the overall performance of the economy. They probably do so—but not to a great extent. Some scholars have concluded that regulation may have contributed in small measure to slowing economic growth, depressing the growth of productivity, and increasing inflation.

The most successful reform effort has been to cut back price and entry regulation in industries where regulation has merely suppressed competition. Procompetitive reform began administratively as early as the late 1960s, with relaxation of controls on stock brokerage commissions and telecommunications services. It became a force to be reckoned with as of 1978—when the Air Transportation Deregulation Act completely removed price and entry controls in the airline industry and ordered the abolition, by 1985, of the CAB. (The airlines are still regulated with respect to safety by the FEDERAL AVIATION ADMINISTRATION.) Subsequent legislation substantially reduced anticompetitive regulation in the trucking, bus, railroad, and banking industries. In the same period the quite different form of regulation that held energy prices below market levels in the middle and late 1970s was also largely eliminated.

The effects of deregulation have been much debated. Clearly, it has caused at least temporary instability in some industries: airlines have scrambled to restructure their route systems and a few have gone bankrupt in the process; consumers have had to choose their own long-distance telephone carriers; and a group of aggressive firms has broken down barriers that once separated several sorts of banking and kept the whole industry apart from other kinds of financial service. But, on the whole, deregulation has had precisely the effects its advocates had promised. In several industries it has demonstrably pushed down average prices, forced improvement in efficiency, and promoted innovation.

A less successful effort has been made to control the costs of health, safety, and environmental regulation. Presidents Gerald Ford and Jimmy Carter both established special advisory units to oversee regulatory agencies and create pressure to limit costs. President Ronald Reagan, even more determined to reduce costs, empowered the U.S. Office of MANAGEMENT AND BUDGET to review new regulations and require changes as a condition for their issuance. The main strategy in the effort to control costs has been to subject regulations to cost-benefit analysis—a set of methods for assessing whether their potential benefits in health, safety, or other values are worth the costs to be imposed on industry and passed on, for the most part, to consumers. Cost-benefit analysis is controversial, however, because its results are highly sensitive to debatable choices of methods and assumptions and because, critics say, its stress on measurable effects creates a bias against the intangible values often served by regulation.

In addition, cost-conscious reformers have proposed to amend statutes, especially the Clean Air Act and the Occupational Safety and Health Act, that instruct agencies to pursue a primary goal, such as protection of health, and give them no mandate to weigh the costs. Partly because the Reagan administration's aggressive rhetoric and militant early appointees in some agencies polarized debate, there has been no significant progress on such amendments—nor on other legislation to make regulation more efficient. The Reagan administration's main impact on regulatory policy has been to loosen some regulations administratively (an approach stymied in several instances by the courts) and to weaken enforcement by sharply cutting agency budgets.

The post-Reagan period seems to promise a return to more balanced regulatory politics. To be sure, there will be continued efforts to limit costs. But there will also be intensified regulatory effort to deal with serious problems—such as acid rain and toxic chemicals—that have not yet been adequately addressed.

PAUL J. QUIRK

Bibliography: Bardach, Eugene, and Kagan, R. A., *Social Regulation: Strategies for Reform* (1982); Derthick, Martha, and Quirk, P. J., *The Politics of Deregulation* (1985); Eads, G. C., and Fix, Michael, *Relief or Reform: Reagan's Regulatory Dilemma* (1984); Fainsod, Merle, and Gordon, Lincoln, *Government and the American Economy*, 3d ed. (1959); Kahn, A. E., *The Economics of Regulation*, 2 vols. (1970–71); Melnick, R. S., *Regulation and the Courts: The Case of the Clean Air Act* (1983); Reagan, M. D., *Regulation: The Politics of Policy* (1987); Shepherd, W. G., *Public Policies toward Business*, 7th ed. (1985); Wilson, G. K., *Business and Politics: A Comparative Introduction* (1985); Wilson, J. Q., ed., *The Politics of Regulation* (1980).

governor

In the United States a governor is the elected chief executive of a state. The office evolved from the post held in prerevolutionary times by the royal governor appointed by the British crown to administer a colony. The chief task of a modern governor is to formulate and execute state policy. As leader of his or her party the governor can influence legislation, and through the preparation of the budget, one of the main gubernatorial functions, he or she establishes state priorities. A governor also has the power to summon special sessions of the legislature, to veto legislation (except in the state of North Carolina), and to issue pardons and commute sentences in cases that do not involve treason or impeachment. In addition, the governor acts as commander in chief of the state militia. Most governors serve 4-year terms, although about a fifth of the states have 2-year terms. Many states set no limit on the number of terms a governor may serve; some stipulate a limit of one term or two successive terms. Governors may be removed from office through IMPEACHMENT by the state legislature and, in 12 states, by RECALL. Because of the political power wielded by the governor, the position has been one of the traditional stepping-stones to the presidency.

Bibliography: Bentley, Judith, *State Government* (1978); Halacy, D. S., *Government by the States* (1973); Ogg, Frederic A., and Ray, P. Orman, *Ogg and Ray's Essentials of American State and Local Government*, 10th ed. (1969); Ransone, Coleman B., *The Office of Governor in the United States* (1956).

governor-general

Governor-general is the name sometimes given to the chief executive of a country's present or former territorial possessions, colonies, or dependent areas. Other titles for the same post are governor-in-chief and captain general. Governors-general under a monarchy personally represent the crown; in other systems they represent the government. They are often citizens of the country or colony that they govern and may be either selected by the people of the area in which they serve or appointed by the government of the mother country.

Governors-general have been responsible for administering the possessions of Great Britain, the Netherlands, Portugal, and Spain, and the overseas territories and departments of France. The post has frequently been retained even after an area has achieved independence and the governor-general no longer represents a controlling government. In the British COMMONWEALTH OF NATIONS, for example, Australia, Canada, and New Zealand are among the countries that have governors-general.

The powers of the office of governor-general vary in accordance with the specific systems adopted in different countries throughout the world. In Canada, for instance, the governor-general has little real authority and mainly functions for symbolic and ceremonial purposes. In dependent territories, the governor-general has more extensive executive authority, and in some possessions or colonies, such as those of Portugal, governors-general have ruled autocratically. The French system also accorded governors-general fairly broad powers, although these were abridged in 1958, following the creation of the FRENCH COMMUNITY.

When contemporary governors-general occasionally do assert their limited authority, their actions are regarded as highly controversial, as in the case of the dissolution of the Australian Parliament and the dismissal of Prime Minister Gough WHITLAM by Governor-General Sir John KERR in 1975.

Bibliography: Henige, David P., *Colonial Governors from the Fifteenth Century to the Present* (1970).

Governors Island

Governors Island is situated about 450 m (1,500 ft) off the southern tip of Manhattan Island in upper New York Bay. It covers about 70 ha (173 acres). Owned by the U.S. government, it serves as the area headquarters of the U.S. Coast Guard. Originally acquired by the Dutch in 1637 and named Nutten Island, it was taken by the English in 1664 and renamed (1698) Governors Island. Historic buildings on the island include the Governor's House (18th century), Fort Jay (1794–98; rebuilt 1806), and Castle Williams (1811).

Gower, John [gow'-ur]

John Gower, *c.*1330–1408, was an English poet whose work, although largely neglected today, was once favorably compared with that of his friend Geoffrey Chaucer. Gower wrote in Latin and French, but his masterpiece is the long poem in English, *Confessio Amantis* (*c.*1390). Mixing medieval learning with classical stories often taken from the Latin poet Ovid, it discusses the Seven Deadly Sins and also develops the theme of courtly love with considerable rhetorical skill and delicacy.

ROBIN BUSS

Bibliography: Fisher, John H., *John Gower* (1964).

Gowon, Yakubu [goh'-wahn, yah-koȯ'-boo]

Yakubu Danjuma Gowon, b. Oct. 19, 1934, led Nigeria's government during the Nigerian civil war of 1967-70. Gowon was educated at the Government College at Zaria, Nigeria, and in England. A career officer, he became the Nigerian army's chief of staff after the coup of January 1966; following the countercoup of July 1966, Gowon became head of the military government. The next year, the IBOS of the eastern region formed the secessionist state of BIAFRA under Chukemeka OJUKWU, and Gowon led the war against them. Following the Nigerian government's victory in 1970, Gowon initiated a policy of reconciliation. In 1975 he was deposed by a bloodless coup.

L. H. GANN

Bibliography: Červenka, Zdenek, *The Nigerian War, 1967-1970* (1971); Crowder, Michael, *The Story of Nigeria,* 3d ed., rev., (1973); Gowon, Yakubu, *Faith in Unity* (1970).

Goya, Francisco de [goy'-ah, frahn-thees'-koh]

Francisco José de Goya y Lucientes, b. Mar. 31, 1746, was a brilliantly imaginative Spanish painter and engraver. After studying in Saragossa he established himself about 1774 in Madrid, where his brother-in-law, the painter Francisco Bayeu (1734-95), helped him obtain commissions from the royal tapestry manufactory. For his tapestry cartoons (see CARTOON, art), executed between 1775 and 1792, Goya rejected the customary mythological scenes, adopting instead the genre subjects (see GENRE PAINTING) that Jean Honré FRAGONARD was establishing in France. Goya depicted the open-air amusements attended by Madrid's upper classes, who often appeared dressed as majos and majas, Madrid's popular types. In *The Picnic* (1776; Prado, Madrid) he used the luminous colors, subtle gradations, and undulating rhythms characteristic of the ROCOCO STYLE, to make natural objects more graceful and harmonious. His juxtaposition of light and shade demonstrates that the baroque painters Diego VELÁZQUEZ and REMBRANDT van Rijn were the masters Goya acknowledged after nature itself.

Goya's keen observation of nature is revealed in his portraits, which were in great demand following his appointment in 1786 as court painter to Charles III. Unlike Veláquez, whose luminous paint spiritualized Philip IV, king by divine right to the 17th-century mind, Goya did not idealize his royal and upper-class subjects, especially after a near-fatal illness in 1792-93 left him totally deaf and less impressed with the world. His later portraits, such as *The Duchess of Alba* in

Francisco de Goya's painting The Third of May, 1808 *(1814-15) memorializes the execution of Madrid citizens by Napoleon's troops of occupation. The intense drama and brutality of the act is depicted in glowing color and nocturnal light, apotheosizing the plight of these and all victims of political tyranny. Another painting,* The Second of May, 1808, *depicts its antecedent atrocity with equal strength. (Prado, Madrid.)*

Francisco de Goya's nightmarish etching and aquatint There Is a Lot to Suck *is no. 45 of 80 prints comprising his first great series,* Los Caprichos *(1796–98). Goya, combining the two graphic techniques to their fullest advantage, creates a terrifying scene dominated by three grotesque creatures cackling together over their victims. (Copperplate; Calcografia Nacional, Madrid.)*

the costume of a maja (1797; Hispanic Society Museum, New York City), are remarkable for their acute observation of personality, their social implications, and their new, striking color. Goya's sympathy with liberal reform movements may have prompted his unflattering depictions of the corrupt and reactionary Spanish royal family. In *The Family of Charles IV* (1800; Prado), the awkward poses and fatuous features of the royal persons contrast oddly with their brilliantly painted, splendid costumes, a disparity that makes the painting satirical.

After Napoleon's invasion of Spain in 1808, and the savage guerrilla warfare that followed, Goya executed two large canvases representing tragic events of the war. In his passionate and monumental *The Third of May, 1808* (1814; Prado), the horror and cruelty of war are evoked by the stark image of a group of Spaniards about to be shot by a French firing squad. The victims are each differentiated by writhing gestures and grimaces of despair; but the faceless soldiers, who are seen from behind, are lined up like automatons, denoting the inhuman nature of their task.

Goya's reaction to war led him to invent macabre caricatures of the irrational bestiality of human behavior, something he had already begun in a series of etchings, *Los caprichos* (1796–98), that are ironic treatments of familiar social events. The French occupation of his country brought this side of Goya's artistic vision to full realization in *The Disasters of War,* a series of etchings made between 1810 and 1814. These were followed by *Bullfighting* (1815–16) and finally by *Los proverbios* (c.1813–18), in which Goya offered a vision of the world populated by monstrous personifications of evil. These last etchings have counterparts in the paintings that Goya executed on the walls of a house near Madrid that he bought in 1819. These black paintings, now in the Prado, are nightmarish images prompted by the aging painter's reflections on human nature.

To avoid the repressions of the restored monarchy, Goya lived in voluntary exile in Bordeaux, France, from 1824 until his death on Apr. 16, 1828. He executed such portraits as that of his liberal friend, Don Tiburcio Pérez (1820; Metropolitan Museum, New York City), in which the subject is portrayed with simple human dignity against a background of neutral color. Goya had many outspoken admirers among early-19th-century French romantic painters and writers, and his art contributed to the formation of the French impressionist style.

Bibliography: Chabrun, Jean, *Goya,* trans. by Maxwell Brownjohn (1965); Chastenet, Jacques, *Goya* (1964); Gassier, Pierre, *The Drawings of Goya* (1975); Gassier, Pierre, and Wilson, Juliet, *The Life and Complete Works of Francisco Goya* (1971); Guidol, José, *Goya,* trans. by Ricilla Muller (1965); Klingender, F. D., *Goya in the Democratic Tradition* (1948); Licht, Fred, *Goya: The Origins of the Modern Temper in Art* (1979); Lopez-Rey, José, *Goya's Caprichas, Beauty, Reason and Caricature* (1953); Poore, Charles, *Goya* (1938); Schickel, Richard, *The World of Goya* (1968).

Goyen, Jan van [goy'-en]

Jan van Goyen, b. Jan. 13, 1596, d. Apr. 27, 1656, was a prolific Dutch landscape painter and etcher. A student of Esaias van de Velde in Haarlem, van Goyen worked for most of his life in The Hague. His early paintings show the influence of van de Velde and other early 17th-century artists such as Hendrik van AVERCAMP and Hercules SEGHERS.

About 1630 van Goyen's style changed; the horizon in his paintings became lower and the subject simpler. Atmospheric tonality began to dominate over color, leading to nearly monochromatic landscapes in tones of gray or brown. During this period his work had an affinity with that of contemporaries Salomon van Ruysdael and Pieter de Molyn. His paintings of dunes (for example, *Village and Dunes,* 1647; Allen Memorial Museum, Oberlin College, Ohio), river landscapes, and views of Leiden and The Hague place van Goyen as a leader in bringing atmosphere to Dutch LANDSCAPE PAINTING. In the 1640s van Goyen became more concerned with color, and a full chromatic range is present in his later pictures. About 1,200 of his paintings survive and van Goyen is represented in most of the world's major museums and collections.

Van Goyen is believed to have speculated with his earnings as a painter; he was a picture dealer and an appraiser and made investments in tulips and real estate. These ventures were not successful, and despite recognition and influence, van Goyen had financial difficulties all his life.

CHARLES I. MINOTT

Bibliography: Rosenberg, Jakob, et al., *Dutch Art and Architecture: 1600–1800* (1966); Stechow, Wolfgang, *Dutch Landscape Painting of the Seventeenth Century* (1966).

Goyen, William

An American author, critic, and editor, Charles William Goyen, b. Trinity, Tex., Apr. 24, 1915, d. Aug. 30, 1983, was noted principally for fiction that explores the tenuous relationship of fantasy, memory, and reality. Set mostly in the Southwest, his novels include *The House of Breath* (1950; rev. 1975), *In a Farther Country* (1955), and *Come, the Restorer* (1974).

Bibliography: Goyen, William, *The Collected Short Stories of William Goyen* (1975).

Goytisolo, Juan [goy-tee-soh'-loh]

The contemporary Spanish novelist Juan Goytisolo, b. 1931, has lived in exile in France, the United States, and Mexico since 1957. His early novels deal with post–Spanish Civil War society in an almost documentary fashion. His more recent works abandon realism and traditional novelistic form. *Mark of Identity* (1966; Eng. trans., 1969), *Count Julian* (1970; Eng. trans., 1974)—ranked as his masterpiece—and *Juan the Landless* (1975; Eng. trans., 1977) are stylistically experimental diatribes against the traditions of his estranged homeland.

ROBERTO GONZÁLEZ-ECHEVARRÍA

Bibliography: Schwartz, Kessel, *Juan Goytisolo* (1970); Ugarte, Michael, *Trilogy of Treason* (1982).

Gozzi, Carlo, Conte [goht'-tsee]

The Italian dramatist Carlo Gozzi, b. Dec. 13, 1720, d. Apr. 4, 1806, was a traditionalist who opposed the philosophical and scientific thought of the Enlightenment by defending Christianity, morality, and the established social order. He was a founding member of the conservative Accademia dei Granelleschi, whose purpose it was to preserve the Tuscan idiom from foreign influence. As a playwright Gozzi rejected Carlo Goldoni's theatrical innovations by returning to the improvisational scenarios of the commedia dell'arte. His ten important satirical and moralistic plays, collectively called *Fiabe* (Fables, 1761–65), were based on Oriental and popular grotesque stories. *Re Turandot,* perhaps the most famous fable, was transformed into operas by Carl Maria von Weber, Ferruccio Busoni, and Giacomo Puccini; *L'Amore delle tre melarance* was the basis for Sergei Prokofiev's opera *The Love of Three Oranges.* CHRISTOPHER KLEINHENZ

Bibliography: Rusack, Hedwig Hoffmann, *Gozzi in Germany* (1930).

Gozzoli, Benozzo [goht-tsoh'-lee, bay-noht'-tsoh]

Benozzo Gozzoli (Benozzo di Lese, di Sandro), 1420-97, was an Italian Renaissance fresco painter and a pupil of Fra ANGELICO and Lorenzo GHIBERTI. From 1450 to 1452 he painted frescoes in the churches of San Fortunato and San Francesco in Montefalco, in Umbria. In 1459, Piero de'Medici commissioned him to decorate the walls of the chapel of the Medici-Riccardi palace in Florence. Here, in his best-known work, Benozzo painted on three walls a *Procession of the Magi* in which the three Magi and their attendants ride toward a Nativity scene by Fra Filippo Lippi, which once hung above an altar on the fourth wall. This animated and tapestrylike composition contains portraits of Gozzoli's contemporaries, including Lorenzo and Cosimo de'Medici. The artist appears in the crowd, with his signature on his cap. This charming and decorative work, packed with splendidly costumed figures in a rich Tuscan landscape, recalls the Gothic paintings GENTILE DA FABRIANO executed 30 years before.

From 1463 to 1467, Gozzoli worked in the Church of Sant' Agostino in San Gimignano, and from 1468 to 1485 he painted Old Testament scenes in the Campo Santo in Pisa. He spent the remaining years of his life in Pisa, occupied in decorating church furniture. TANIA MARIE BAYARD

Bibliography: Bargellini, Piero, *The Medici Palace and the Frescoes of Benozzo Gozzoli*, trans. by Gladys Hutton, rev. ed. (1954); De Wald, Ernest T., *Italian Painting: 1200-1600* (1961; repr. 1978); Marks, Claude, *From the Sketchbooks of the Great Artists* (1972); Marle, Raimond van, *The Development of the Italian Schools of Painting* (1929).

Grabbe, Christian Dietrich [grahb'-e, kris'-tee-ahn deet'-rik]

The German dramatist Christian Dietrich Grabbe, b. Dec. 11, 1801, d. Sept. 12, 1836, presents in his works a vision of reality as chaos and of history as a demonic and irrational force. His plays are written on an epic scale, and one of the best known is the satirical *Comedy, Satire, Irony, and Deeper Meaning* (1827; Eng. trans., 1955). His heroes, such as Napoleon in *Napoleon oder die hundert Tage* (Napoleon or the Hundred Days, 1831), are undone by the force of historical necessity; a powerful will and a vision of greatness are lost in a sea of irrational forces. In *Hannibal* (1835) a heroic individual is destroyed by the masses on whom he must largely rely and by the overwhelming power of circumstance. CARL R. MUELLER

Bibliography: Hornsey, A. W., *Idea and Reality in the Drama of Christian Dietrich Grabbe* (1966).

graben: see HORST AND GRABEN.

Gracchus (family) [grak'-uhs]

The Roman tribunes Tiberius Sempronius Gracchus, b. *c.*164 BC, and Gaius Sempronius Gracchus, b. *c.*154 BC, are famous for their radical reform program. They were sons of another Tiberius, a plebeian noble who served as consul (177) and censor (169). Their mother, Cornelia, was a daughter of SCIPIO AFRICANUS MAJOR, and their sister Sempronia married SCIPIO AFRICANUS MINOR.

Tiberius Sempronius Gracchus served with the younger Scipio at Carthage (146) but was offended when Scipio secured the rejection of a treaty that he (Tiberius) had negotiated (137) to save a Roman army from surrender to the Celt-Iberians at Numantia. Supported by his father-in-law, Scipio's rival Appius Claudius Pulcher, Tiberius was elected tribune for 133; he sponsored legislation to redistribute public lands held by the rich to poorer citizens. Opposition from rivals and vested interests, however, forced him into blatant violation of political customs. A mob led by fellow senators killed Tiberius in 133 BC as he sought a second tribunate.

Ten years later, **Gaius Sempronius Gracchus**, who had accompanied Scipio at Numantia (134), became tribune and promoted further reforms: grain subsidies, public-works employment, and further distributions of land to the poor; citizenship for Rome's Italian allies; and increased power for the wealthy, nonsenatorial class of equestrians, through control of the courts trying provincial officials and control of provincial tax collecting. Opponents appealed to disparate interests among these groups to deny Gaius their support. When he failed to win election to a third tribunate, Gaius gathered armed followers to oppose the repeal of his legislation. A murder resulted, and the Senate for the first time passed the *senatus consultum ultimum* (extreme decree of the senate), declaring a state of emergency. Gaius died (122 BC) during the subsequent violence.

The Gracchi intended their reforms to deal with urgent problems, but they also designed them to strengthen themselves in their rivalry with other senators. ALLEN M. WARD

Bibliography: Bernstein, A. H., *Tiberius Sempronius Gracchus: Tradition and Apostasy* (1978); Boren, Henry Charles, *The Gracchi* (1968); Earl, D. C., *Tiberius Gracchus: A Study in Politics* (1963).

grace

Grace, a central concept in Christian THEOLOGY, refers to God's granting SALVATION not in reward for the moral worth of the human but as a free and undeserved gift of love. This concept stands opposed, therefore, to any notion that salvation can be earned by human effort apart from God's help.

The Old Testament contains important themes related to God's undeserved love for his people, Israel. The chief architect of the early Christian church's theology of grace, however, was Saint Paul; *charis*, the Greek word for "grace," is infrequent in the non-Pauline writings of the New Testament. For Paul, grace means the free gift of salvation by which God liberates humans from SIN and frees them from death "through the redemption which is in Christ Jesus" (Romans 3:24). Paul deliberately sets grace in contrast to all human efforts to achieve favor with God.

In the subsequent development of the theology of grace, two conflicting views have predominated. The first, characteristic of medieval Christianity and continued in much Roman Catholic theology, has treated grace as a divine power that enters a person and, in cooperation with the person's own will, transforms him or her into one who loves God and is loved by God. This grace is transmitted especially, perhaps exclusively, through the church's SACRAMENTS (the "means of grace"); and it allows some room for human merit because the one who receives grace must also cooperate with it in the process of transformation.

The second view, often a reaction against the first, is particularly associated with the Protestant REFORMATION and Protestant theology. In contrast to the ideas that the sacraments transmit grace and that one must cooperate with grace, Protestant theologians have insisted that grace is given where God wills and is not conditional on a person's receptivity. Thus the sacraments are signs of grace, but do not impart it, and salvation depends entirely on God, not at all on human will—a theme close to the idea of PREDESTINATION. This grace, controlled only by God, is not a power that transforms a person; it is a love that receives a person directly into God's favor.

These two views are not totally incompatible. Both seek to understand the forms of God's unmerited love for people and their undeserved gift of salvation. WILLIAM S. BABCOCK

Bibliography: Fransen, Peter, *Divine Grace and Man*, trans. by George Dupont (1962); Journet, Charles, *The Meaning of Grace*, trans. by A. V. Littledale (1960); Moffatt, James, *Grace in the New Testament* (1932); Watson, Philip, *The Concept of Grace* (1959); Whitley, William T., ed., *The Doctrine of Grace* (1932).

Grace, W. R.

The founder of the Grace shipping lines, William Russell Grace, b. Ireland, May 10, 1832, d. Mar. 21, 1904, ran away to sea at age 14. After working as a clerk in New York City, he eventually moved to Peru, where he entered the shipping business with a brother. Eventually, this enterprise became (1865) W. R. Grace & Company and dominated merchant shipping between the United States and Latin America after 1895. By helping to underwrite Peru's national debt, the company acquired huge mineral, land, and railroad concessions there. Grace also served two terms (1880–88) as mayor of New York City. Running on a reform, anti-Tammany ticket, he was the first Roman Catholic to be elected mayor.

Bibliography: Grace, Joseph P., *W. R. Grace and the Enterprises He Created* (1953).

Graces

In Greek mythology the Graces were beautiful sister goddesses, most often represented as three in number. Their names are synonymous with their attributes: Aglaia ("brilliance"), Euphrosyne ("joy"), and Thalia ("bloom"). Their charm and winning manner made them welcome as the companions of the MUSES and the attendants of APHRODITE, EROS, and DIONYSUS. They presided over banquets, social gatherings, and polite entertainments. Their gentleness and agreeable dispositions enhanced the joys of life.

grackle [grak'-ul]

The common grackle, Q. quiscula, *a blackbird native to eastern and central North America, is considered an agricultural pest; large flocks descend on a wide variety of crops.*

Grackle is the common name for several species of New World blackbirds in the family Icteridae. The largest number of grackles, seven species, belong to the genus *Quiscalus,* including the common grackle, *Q. quiscula;* boat-tailed grackle, *Q. major;* and great-tailed grackle, *Q. mexicanus.* Other grackles are the South American red-bellied grackle, *Hypopyrrhus pyrohypogaster;* mountain grackle, *Macroagelaius subalaris;* golden-tufted grackle, *M. imthurni;* and velvet-fronted grackle, *Lampropsar tanagrinus.* The Ceylon grackle, *Graculus ptilogonys,* is actually a starling of the family Sturnidae.

Grackles are typically black. Males often have an iridescent sheen and have very long tails. Females are generally smaller, with shorter tails and little or no iridescence. Grackles have an extremely varied diet, feeding on insects, fruit, grain, and even crayfish, lizards, and the eggs and young of other birds.

The common grackle, found in North America east of the Rocky Mountains, is about 30 cm (1 ft) in overall length. It has a long, wedge-shaped tail, which the male often "keels" while in flight by depressing the central feathers. The common grackle is black with a blue, purple, green, or bronze iridescent sheen and has bright yellow eyes. Females are smaller and duller in color.

Common grackles feed on open ground, favoring wet areas. Most nesting is in colonies of up to 25 pairs of birds (the closely related South American carib grackle, *Q. lugubris,* may nest in colonies of up to 100 pairs). Common grackles breed from southern Canada to the southern United States, and winter from the central United States to the Gulf coast.

GARY D. SCHNELL

Bibliography: Bent, Arthur C., *Life History of North American Blackbirds, Orioles, Tanagers and Allies* (1958; repr. 1965).

gradient: see VECTOR ANALYSIS.

graduate education

Graduate education is rigorous, specialized training in particular academic and professional fields and is generally considered to include all postbaccalaureate programs with the exception of the first professional degree programs in medicine, veterinary medicine, dentistry, law, and theology. Traditional graduate education programs culminate with the award of a doctor's or master's degree (see DEGREE, ACADEMIC), although certificate programs at the postmaster's and postdoctoral levels have increased. Admission to graduate degree programs in the United States is usually based on students undergraduate records, recommendations by professors, and scores on the GRADUATE RECORD EXAMINATION.

Development of Graduate Education. Advanced education in law, medicine, and theology began in European universities during the Middle Ages, but modern graduate education, emphasizing scientific research, began in Germany in the early 19th century, and German universities remained preeminent until the 1890s. A few colleges in the United States experimented with graduate education before the Civil War, and Yale University awarded the first doctor of philosophy (Ph.D.) degree in the United States in 1861. The continuous growth of graduate education in the United States dates from the founding of The John Hopkins University in Baltimore in 1876, however. By then a national elite had emerged, secular in outlook and eager to foster German scholarly ideals. At first this elite received hostility from religious leaders who feared the effect of advanced learning on the Christian faith. By 1880, however, the prestige of science, under the impact of Darwinism, had grown in the urban centers, and the scholars were accepted.

Graduate students at Johns Hopkins worked in an atmosphere of idealistic dedication and had a strong sense of social mission. Other leading colleges and universities established similar graduate programs. Some did this enthusiastically, and some, such as Princeton University, more reluctantly. The latter clung to their traditional British-oriented definitions of education, yet feared that if they did not move to add doctoral programs they would be bypassed. Most early graduate schools were part of privately endowed universities; examples are Harvard University and Clark University (1887) and the University of Chicago (1892), which were established with great emphasis on graduate study. Only in Michigan, Wisconsin, and California did state universities initially try to compete in this area. Among the U.S. universities offering high-quality graduate education by 1900, 14—Catholic University of America, Clark, Columbia, Cornell, Harvard, Johns Hopkins, Princeton, Stanford, and Yale universities, and the universities of California, Chicago, Michigan, Pennsylvania, and Wisconsin—founded the Association of American Universities to coordinate mutual concerns. Graduate education grew rapidly during the 20th century, and today there are more than 300 universities in the United States that award the Ph.D. degree.

Doctorate. In general, doctoral programs in the United States consist of three stages. After completing a specified number of advanced courses in their fields of study, students prepare for and must pass an oral or written qualifying examination. A period of supervised research then follows and culminates with the submission and defense of a research dissertation, a book-length, scholarly work. In European universities doctoral programs generally consist of supervised individual study and research and the completion of a dissertation.

While the Ph.D. is the dominant doctoral degree associated with graduate education, other doctoral degrees are also awarded. For the most part, they are, as their titles suggest, professionally oriented: doctor of education (Ed.D.), doctor of business administration (D.B.A.), and doctor of psychology (D. Psych.). The doctor of arts (D.A.) degree was introduced in the 1960s. It emphasized college-teacher preparation and required the writing of an expository thesis instead of the traditional research dissertation. Since Carnegie-Mellon University offered the first D.A. in 1967, a relatively small number of institutions has followed.

The great advances in knowledge, especially in the sciences, have made it desirable for individuals to continue highly specialized study upon receiving the doctorate. Postdoctoral positions were created to accommodate this need. Such appointments, which have been funded primarily by government and industry, provide the individual the experience of concentrated and sophisticated research.

Master's Degree. The academic and intellectual achievement represented by the doctor's degree has long been recognized. The achievement represented by the master's degree, however, has long been a subject of controversy. Nevertheless, the master's degree has survived, in various forms, for eight centuries, and it is today the most widely awarded degree on the graduate level.

The University of Paris awarded the first master of arts (M.A.) degree in the 12th century. As the most advanced degree then offered by the faculty of arts, it entitled holders to join that faculty and also to pursue doctoral studies in medicine, law, or theology. Whereas in Europe the master's degree was gradually discontinued or awarded as an adjunct to the baccalaureate, with little or no additional scholarship, in the United States where, for a time, it remained the ultimate degree, the master's was more highly regarded. The degree represented exacting academic achievement—comprising three years of postbachelor's study—when it was first awarded by Harvard University in the 1640s. By the early 19th century, however, the degree's significance lessened in the United States as well.

The revival of the master's degree is often credited to a program established by the University of Michigan in 1858. It required the holder of a bachelor's degree to complete two courses in each of two semesters, to pass examinations in three of the four courses, and to submit a thesis. Those requirements, which were adopted soon thereafter by the state universities of Georgia and North Carolina, characterized, with some variation, master's degree programs at most institutions by the beginning of the 20th century.

Recognition of the master's degree as distinct from the doctorate increased as colleges and universities admitted greater numbers of students, especially women, and expanded their offerings in the field of education. During a 20-year period beginning in 1939, when approximately 75 percent of liberal arts master's degrees were awarded to public school teachers, growth of master's degree education was notably tied to the expansion of elementary and secondary education. An increase in career-oriented graduate education also contributed to the growth of master's degree programs and to the proliferation of degree titles, such as master of social work (M.S.W.), master of library science (M.L.S.), and master of education (M.Ed.). Many schools of education also provide a special program beyond the master's degree for further education of teachers and administrators. These programs do not ordinarily carry a degree designation; instead, advanced study is recognized by certificate.

In 1975 the Council of Graduate Schools in the United States characterized the master's degree as follows:

> Broadly speaking, the master's degree indicates that the holder has mastered a program in a particular field sufficiently to pursue creative projects in that specialty. In some areas, it may be a prerequisite for further study toward a more advanced degree such as the doctorate. The degree should be awarded for completion of a coherent program designed to assure the mastery of specified knowledge and skills, rather than for the random accumulation of a certain number of course credits after attaining the baccalaureate.

Administration of Graduate Education. Historically, the administration of graduate programs has been assigned to the dean of graduate school. The dean is assisted by a graduate council, which is elected by the graduate faculty. The increasing necessity for interdepartmental and interdisciplinary programs in graduate education argues for a centralized overview of graduate education and research. Therefore many universities assign administrative responsibility for the research program to the graduate school.

The decision to initiate a new graduate program requires a major commitment of resources. This is particularly true of doctoral level programs. The institution must be able to support an excellent faculty of sufficient size to offer the breadth of graduate level education for the particular subject area of the program. Equally significant are facilities needed for the program, such as library and information services, laboratories, and research instrumentation. In some states, statewide coordinating groups have the authority to approve or disapprove graduate programs proposed by individual universities.

Current Trends. Graduate education, particularly at the doctoral level, traditionally prepared students for academic careers. According to data from a recent survey by the National Research Council, career pathways are undergoing change. Holders of Ph.D.s in engineering, mathematics, computer science, and the physical sciences have experienced the greatest shift from academe: 53% of the 1977–80 graduates were working for business or industry in 1981, as compared to 35% of the 1960–64 graduates. Only 68% of the 1977–80 humanities graduates worked at four-year colleges and universities in 1981, compared to almost 90% of the graduates for the period 1960–64.

These changes are due in part to fewer teaching vacancies as colleges and universities face declining enrollments. They are also due to a recognition by nonacademic institutions of the value of critical thinking and of the specific knowledge and skills acquired during graduate education. Most such institutions also offer higher remuneration than academe. The increasing complexity of national and global issues highlights the need for more knowledge and a better understanding of this knowledge by more people if conditions for life are to improve. Graduate education has a central role in providing, interpreting, and implementing this new knowledge.

MICHAEL J. PELCZAR, JR.

Bibliography: Berelson, B., *Graduate Education in the United States* (1960); Council of Graduate Schools in the United States, *The Doctor of Philosophy Degree* (1977) and *The Organization and Administration of Graduate Schools in the U.S.* (1981); Frankena, William K., ed., *The Philosophy and Future of Graduate Education* (1979); Storr, R. J., *The Beginnings of Graduate Education in America* (1953; repr. 1969).

See also: UNIVERSITY.

Graduate Record Examination

The Graduate Record Examination (GRE) is a series of aptitude and achievement tests taken by applicants for admission to programs of GRADUATE EDUCATION and widely used by graduate schools in the selection of graduate students. The tests are administered by EDUCATIONAL TESTING SERVICE (ETS) at many sites in the United States on six dates each year. The tests also are administered at less frequent intervals in major cities throughout the world.

All students who register for the examinations must take three tests, the morning tests of the GRE, measuring verbal aptitude, quantitative aptitude, and analytical aptitude. In addition, students may elect an afternoon test designed to assess achievement in their major field of undergraduate study. Test scores are reported by ETS to the student and to admissions offices of graduate schools designated by the student.

The GRE program was established in 1948. Since 1966 it has been supervised by the GRE Board, which is responsible for all aspects of the testing program and also supports research activities to improve the validity of the tests. LYLE V. JONES

See also: EDUCATIONAL MEASUREMENT.

Grady, Henry Woodfin

Henry Woodfin Grady, b. May 24, 1850, d. Dec. 23, 1889, was a leading American Southern journalist and a noted orator of the Reconstruction period. As editor (1879–89) of the *Atlanta Constitution*, he achieved national recognition in 1886 with his address, "The New South," which he delivered in New

York City. In it he advocated investment, manufacturing, crop diversification, and other progressive measures for his economically depressed region. A superb reporter, Grady also had great talent as a managing editor. CHARLES T. DUNN

Bibliography: Harris, Joel C., ed., *The Life of Henry W. Grady* (1890; repr. 1972); Nixon, Raymond B., *Henry W. Grady* (1943; repr. 1969).

Graebner, Fritz [greb'-nur]

Fritz Graebner, b. Aug. 4, 1887, d. July 13, 1934, was a German ethnologist who developed a now obsolete theory on cross-cultural similarities and differences. He held that certain cultural traits diffused outward from the world's most ancient cultural complexes (called *Kulturkreise*, "culture circles"). Central was his notion that similarities between cultural elements in geographically separated areas were necessarily the result of cultural diffusion. Among his writings are *Die Methode der Ethnologie* (The Method of Ethnology, 1911) and *Das Weltbild der Primitiven* (The Worldview of Primitive Peoples, 1924). JAMES W. HERRICK

Graf, Steffi

West German tennis star Steffi Graf, b. June 14, 1969, was the world's top-ranked woman player in 1987–89. Armed with a powerful forehand, Graf won 11 of 13 tournaments, 75 of 77 matches, and the French Open in 1987. In 1988 she became only the 3d woman ever (after Maureen Connolly, 1953, and Margaret Court, 1970) to win the tennis Grand Slam—the Australian, French, Wimbledon, and U.S. Open singles titles—earning the Olympic gold medal as well. In 1989 she repeated her Australian, Wimbledon, and U.S. victories. STEVE FLINK

Graf, Urs [grahf, oors]

Urs Graf, *c.*1485–*c.*1527, was a Swiss engraver, etcher, designer of woodcuts, and goldsmith. His life was turbulent; he was imprisoned and saw combat as a mercenary soldier. Graf's artistic career developed in Strasbourg and Basel. Albrecht DÜRER and Johannes Wechtlin were important sources of inspiration. In 1525 he drew a series of dancing peasants, a theme favored by Dürer and others, but much of his work portrays violent subjects. He incorporated a dagger in his monogram signature, a reminder of his life as a soldier.

Bibliography: Anzelewski, Fedja, *Dürer and His Time* (1967).

Graf Zeppelin [grahf tsep'-e-lin]

The *Graf Zeppelin* was a German rigid AIRSHIP that was a commercial success for many years. Its first flight was on Sept. 18, 1928. It was 237 m (778 ft) long, was rendered airborne by hydrogen gas, and had a top speed of 111 km/h (69 mph). From 1928 to 1933, the airship made five trips to the United States, including one around-the-world flight and 22 flights to Brazil. During 1934–37 it operated a scheduled passenger and mail service between Germany and Brazil. In 1937, after the HINDENBURG disaster, the *Graf Zeppelin* was grounded. It was scrapped in May 1940. RICHARD K. SMITH

graffiti [gruh-fee'-tee]

In contemporary usage, *graffiti* (singular *graffito*, from the Italian *graffio*, a "scratch") refers to handwriting or images on the walls or surfaces of a public area, such as buildings, parks, toilets, and trains; they are usually political or sexual in content: a lover's pledge, a proposition, or obscene words. The word was originally used by archaeologists to describe drawings and inscriptions scratched on walls and other surfaces in ancient Pompeii and Rome.

Graffiti are ubiquitous, appearing in many places and times, including the walls and pillars of medieval churches. Some graffiti preserved today, such as those in churches around Cambridge, England, were wrought with great care and intricacy of pattern. Graffiti are characteristically urban, and today especially embody a reaction against the featureless, depersonalized character of modern architecture. The term also refers to an ancient technique of decorating architectural plaster or pottery surfaces, in which patterns are produced by incising a top layer of plaster or glaze to reveal a contrasting undercoat. VALENTIN TATRANSKY

Bibliography: Barclay, B., *A Dictionary of Graffiti* (1984); Chalfaut, H., *Spraycan Art* (1987); Pritchard, V., *English Medieval Graffiti* (1967).

graft

Something of value given to, and accepted by, public officials for dishonest or illegal purposes is commonly called graft. The practice may also involve corrupt officials directing the fraudulent expenditure of public funds for private benefit. In order for graft to be present in a transaction, one of the parties must occupy a position of public trust. The word probably reflects the idea that extra or illegal profits are something grafted onto a legitimate transaction. "Graft" is usually considered synonymous with "political corruption."

In its least offensive form, graft merely involves favored treatment or unfairness. It usually extends, however, to criminal activity such as blackmail, theft, fraud, and swindling. Whatever its form, graft is usually secretive and is almost always regarded as morally repugnant. MARTIN TORODASH

Bibliography: Amick, George, *The American Way of Graft* (1976); Chambliss, W. J., *On the Take* (1978); Drew, Elizabeth, *Politics and Money* (1983); Heidenheimer, A. J., et al., eds., *Political Corruption: A Handbook*, 2d, rev. ed. (1988).

grafting

Grafting is a method of plant propagation in which a scion (a bud or a stem containing several buds) of one plant is inserted into the stock (root, stem, or branch) of another plant so that they unite and grow as one plant. This technique of propagation is ordinarily used for biennial or perennial woody plants, not for annuals and soft succulent plants.

Purposes. Grafting is done to increase the numbers of plants of a desired variety when it is difficult or impossible to do so by seed germination; to adapt desired varieties to soil or climatic conditions that normally would be unsatisfactory for good growth; to increase a plant's resistance to insects and diseases; to control the size of a plant; to facilitate pollination; to repair damaged plants; to change the form of the plant; and to transmit diseases for purposes of research.

Principles and Methods. Grafting is not difficult if certain principles are followed. First, the cambium, or inner bark, of both the stock and the scion must be in contact to allow the tissues to knit together. Second, the cut surfaces must be protected from excessive moisture loss. Last, the stock and the scion must be compatible, or closely related; for example, a pear can be grafted to a pear or to a quince.

Many methods are commonly used in grafting. The whip graft, also called tongue or bench graft, is used with stocks of 2 cm (0.8 in) or less in diameter. To make a whip graft, a slanted cut three times the diameter of the stock is made on the stock and the scion. Next, the two slanted-cut surfaces are cut again. The stock and scion are then fitted together so that the cambium layers of both come into contact. They are then tied together with a budding band. This form of grafting is frequently used in the propagation of new woody ornamental plants and pear and apple trees.

Other methods of grafting depend on the size of the scion. The cleft graft, applied to stocks 2.5–5 cm (1–2 in) in diameter, is often used on large apple trees to change one variety to another. Stub or side grafting is used on a branch that is too small for a cleft graft and too large for a whip graft. The bark-graft is used on large branches more than 5 cm (2 in) in diameter. The inlay graft is used on large branches that have thick bark, during seasons when the bark is not slipping.

A bridge graft may be used to repair a type of plant damage known as girdling, in which the conducting tissues of the tree are cut apart by rodents or deer. All buds in the grafting area are removed, and a scion is grafted from the upper to the lower part of the wound so that there is a continuous flow from the lower to the upper conducting tissues. Inarch grafting is another method for repairing girdled trees; it is also used for repairing damaged root systems. A sucker or seedling

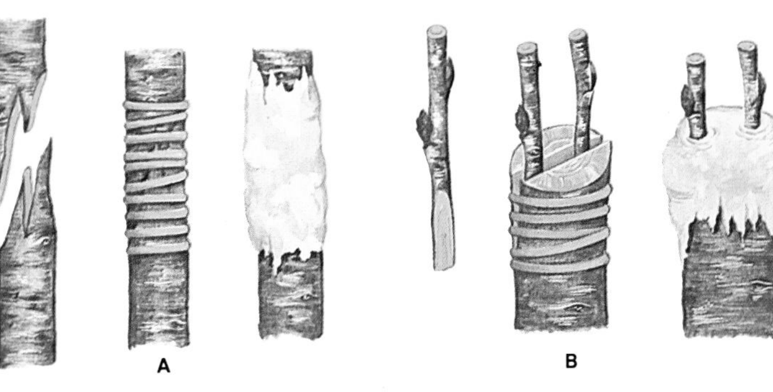

A whip graft (A) is formed by making a slanted, notched cut on both the scion and stock, and then fitting and tying them together. In a cleft graft (B), the scion, with a wedge-shaped lower end, is inserted into a split in the sawed-off end of the stock. Bridge grafting (C) reconnects conducting tissues between the stem and root of a girdled plant; scions reach from the lower to upper end of the wound. Inarching (D) involves the grafting of a rooted sucker or seedling onto the stem of another plant. T-budding (E) is done by inserting a bud into a T-shaped cut in the bark of the stock. In any graft, the cambium layer of stock and scion should be in close contact.

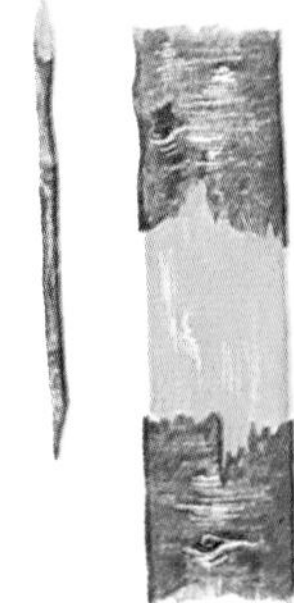
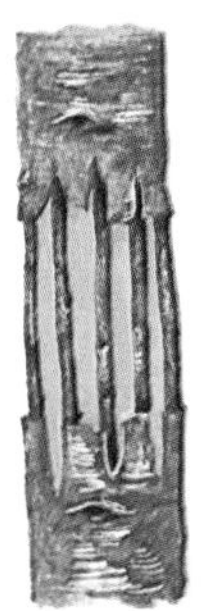
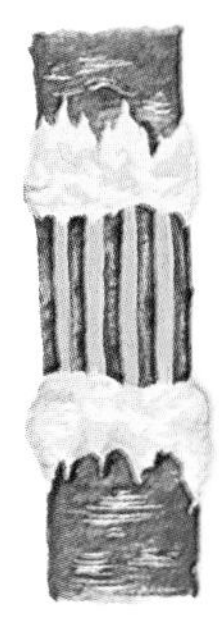

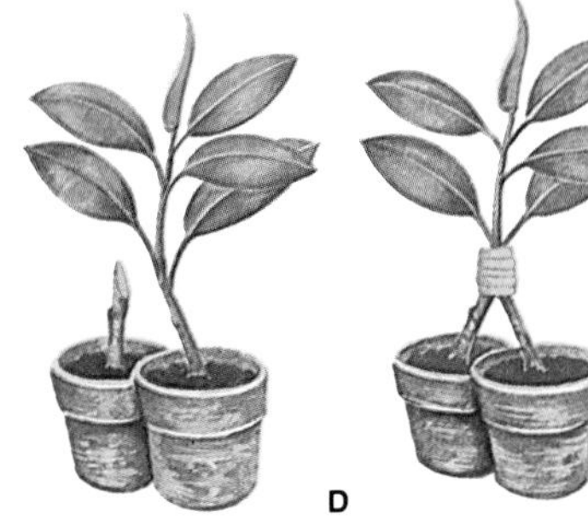

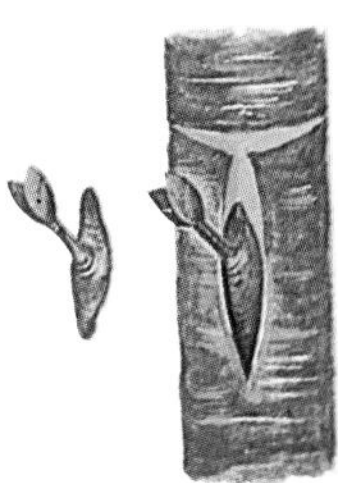

plant is grown next to the tree and is then grafted onto it. The seedling supplements or replaces the damaged system.

Budding is a specialized grafting method in which only one bud is used rather than a shoot with several buds. A detached bud of the desired variety is placed under the bark of the stock. Budding is most successful when the bark of the plant slips. The buds found at the base of the leaf petiole are used. In the most common budding method, T-budding, a T-cut is made on the stock, into which is inserted a single bud with a small piece of the bark surrounding the bud. The bud is held securely in place by rubber binding strips. Other methods of budding include plate budding and patch budding.

Natural grafting is also possible. Adjacent branches are tied so that they will grow naturally together and strengthen the top of the tree. RICHARD MERRITT

Bibliography: Garner, R. J., *Grafter's Handbook*, 3d ed. (1968); Kester, D. E., and Hartmann, H. T., *Plant Propagation*, 3d ed. (1975).

Graham, Billy [gray'-uhm]

The American evangelist Billy Graham has conducted revivalist crusades all over the world. Preaching to thousands at a time, with radio and television broadcasts reaching millions, he typically exhorts his listeners to make a life-changing commitment to Christ.

William Franklin (Billy) Graham, Jr., b. Charlotte, N.C., Nov. 7, 1918, is an American religious leader with a worldwide reputation for charismatic preaching and evangelistic crusades. After graduating from Wheaton College, Ill., in 1943, he entered the ministry as pastor of the First Baptist Church of Western Springs, Ill., and became a leader in the Youth for Christ movement.

In 1947 Graham organized a revival team in the style of Billy Sunday, and this group, which included George Beverly Shea as singer, began a series of revivals. His first big success came in Los Angeles in 1949, when several prominent Hollywood personalities were converted to Christianity.

The Billy Graham Evangelistic Association, founded in 1950, has promoted crusades, developed radio and television programs (including *The Hour of Decision*), and produced films. In 1969, Graham gave a prayer at the inauguration of President Richard Nixon, and he subsequently became a close advisor to the president. His many books include *Peace with God* (1953), *World Aflame* (1965), and *How To Be Born Again* (1977). JOHN F. PIPER, JR.

Bibliography: Frady, Marshall, *Billy Graham: A Parable of American Righteousness* (1979); Pollock, John, *Billy Graham: Evangelist to the World* (1979); Strober, Gerald, *Billy Graham: His Life and Faith* (1977).

Graham, George

The English instrument builder George Graham, b. *c.*1674, d. Nov. 16, 1751, gained international fame for the quality of his astronomical instruments. After a 7-year apprenticeship (1688–95), Graham was employed by the instrument maker Thomas Tompion, and with Tompion he constructed the first orrery, the forerunner of the modern PLANETARUIM. During the first half of the 1720s, Graham invented an improved pendulum and the deadbeat escapement for clocks, and a cylinder escapement for watches (see CLOCKS AND WATCHES). This was followed by his work on large astronomical quadrants, which Graham furnished with accurate graduations and micrometer screws, thus increasing the precision with which the positions of celestial bodies could be determined. He was buried in Westminster Abbey.

Graham, Katharine

Katherine Graham became (1963), on the death of her husband, publisher of the Washington Post, *one of the most respected newspapers in the United States. During her tenure the* Post *published (1971) the Pentagon Papers, a secret report on U.S. involvement in Vietnam, and spearheaded the investigation of the Watergate break-in (1972).*

Katharine Meyer Graham, b. New York City, June 16, 1917, is owner and chairwoman of the board of the influential WASHINGTON POST. The daughter of financier Eugene Meyer, who in 1933 purchased the newspaper, Graham learned all phases of newspaper management from him. Her husband, Philip L. Graham, was named publisher in 1946, and when he committed suicide in 1963 she became president, with control over the *Post, Newsweek* magazine, and several television stations. Under Graham's direction, the *Post* supported John F. Kennedy and Lyndon B. Johnson, employed more blacks than any other U.S. newspaper, and in 1971 won a major battle for freedom of the press when the Supreme Court supported the *Post*'s publication of the PENTAGON PAPERS, an exposé of high-echelon military activities. The *Post* gained world attention in 1972 by exposing the WATERGATE scandals, which marked the Nixon administration. Graham was succeeded as publisher of the *Washington Post* by her son, Donald Graham, in January 1979. RICHARD HIXSON

Bibliography: Emery, Edwin, and Emery, Michael, *The Press and America*, 5th ed. (1984); Leamer, Laurence, *Playing It for Keeps in Washington* (1977).

Graham, Martha

Martha Graham is one of the most innovative and influential American dancers and choreographers of the 20th century. Graham's brusque, emotion-laden style of movement, perpetuated in her dance company, became a major force in the evolution of modern dance.

More than any other individual, Martha Graham created the image and substance of the art form called MODERN DANCE. She developed a new vocabulary of movement and from it created a body of powerfully expressive dances.

Born in Pittsburgh, Pa., on May 11, 1894, Graham decided to become a dancer when she moved to California and as a teenager saw Ruth St. Denis perform. In 1916 she enrolled at the Denishawn school, and from 1919 to 1923 she toured with the Denishawn troupe. After dancing in vaudeville and teaching at the Eastman School of Music in Rochester, N.Y., Graham opened her own studio in New York City in 1927, working with the musician-composer Louis Horst.

Graham discarded the serpentine flourishes of Denishawn dancing and evolved a language of angular, percussive gestures originating in the contraction and release of the muscles of the lower torso. Body weight was emphasized; dancers moved on the floor and in space, using an unconcealed tension and effort that added to the impact of the dance.

In *Primitive Mysteries* (1931), Graham explored the individual's relation to the universe and society in a ritualized, austere, quasi-religious ceremony. Later she adopted specifically American themes, illustrating the bold pioneering spirit in *Frontier* (1935) and *Appalachian Spring* (1944), the New England heritage and art of Emily Dickinson in *Letter to the World* (1940), and the Southwestern culture in *El Penitente* (1940). Next, Graham explored universal psychological problems as they were expressed in mythology, using gestures depicting inner conflict and sets of symbolic sculptures. *Cave of the Heart* (1946) embodied Medea's overwhelming hate; in *Errand into the Maze* (1947), the Minotaur legend suggested the conquest of fear.

Graham was married to her partner, Erick HAWKINS, from 1948 to 1954.

As she grew older, Graham was reluctant to preserve her dances or pass on her roles, and in the early 1970s her company almost collapsed. She relented, however, and revivals of Graham classics, as well as new works, including *Acts of Light* (1981), *Andromache's Lament* (1982), and *Song* (1985), brought her fresh acclaim. EDWARD RICCO

Bibliography: Armitage, Merle, ed., *Martha Graham* (1937; repr. 1966); Graham, Martha, *The Notebooks of Martha Graham* (1973); Leatherman, Leroy, *Martha Graham* (1966); McDonagh, Don, *Martha Graham* (1973); Stodelle, Ernestine, *Deep Song* (1984).

Graham, Otto

Otto Everett Graham, b. Waukegan, Ill., Dec. 6, 1921, was an American professional football player who played quarterback for the Cleveland Browns for 10 years (1946–55). During this period the Browns won four All-America Football Conference championships and, after joining the National Football League, won six division titles and three league championships. Graham was known for his passing (he threw 174 touchdown passes in his career), but he also ran for 46 touchdowns. He retired from professional football in 1955 and in 1959 began coaching the U.S. Coast Guard Academy team. He coached briefly (1966–68) for the Washington Redskins. KEVIN LAMB

Bibliography: Heumann, William, *Famous Pro Football Stars* (1967).

Graham, Thomas

The Scottish inorganic and physical chemist Thomas Graham, b. Dec. 21, 1805, d. Sept. 16, 1869, was the founder of colloid chemistry and one of the chief founders of physical chemistry. He became professor of chemistry at Anderson's College in Glasgow (1830–37) and at University College, London (1837–54) and finally Master of the Mint (1854–69). From 1828 to 1833 he studied diffusion of gases and in 1833 proposed Graham's law, which states that the rate of diffusion of a gas is inversely proportional to the square root of its molecular weight.

In 1833, Graham distinguished the three phosphoric acids (ortho, pyro, and meta), and his discovery of their polybasicity led Justus von LIEBIG to his modern concept of polybasic acids. He studied the solubility of salts (1827), the adsorption of salts by charcoal (1830), and heats of reaction (1841–45). In his work on colloids (1849–61) he distinguished between crystalloids and colloids as different states of matter (see COLLOIDAL STATE) and devised a method for their dialysis (separation) by osmosis (both of these terms were coined by Graham).

GEORGE B. KAUFFMAN

Grahame, Kenneth [gray'-uhm]

Kenneth Grahame, b. Mar. 8, 1859, d. July 6, 1932, was a Scottish author best known for his juvenile classic THE WIND IN THE WILLOWS (1908). The book was written for his only son, Alastair, while Grahame served (1897–1908) as a secretary of the Bank of England. He wrote only three other books: *Pagan Papers* (1893), personal essays that reflect his private frustrations, and the short-story collections *The Golden Age* (1895) and *Dream Days* (1898). Although his works are noted for their graceful charm, the conflict between Grahame's aristocratic background and new social concerns lies just beneath the surface of his mythic tales. He also compiled the *Cambridge Book of Poetry for Children* (1916).

FRANCELIA BUTLER

Bibliography: Grahame, Kenneth, *The Penguin Kenneth Grahame* (1984); Green, Peter, *Kenneth Grahame* (1959) and *Beyond the Wild Wood* (1984); Kuznets, L. R., *Kenneth Grahame* (1987).

Grahn, Lucile [grahn]

Lucile Grahn, b. Copenhagen, Denmark, June 30, 1819, d. Munich, Germany, Apr. 4, 1907, one of the great ballerinas of the romantic ballet, made her debut at the age of seven. She studied with August BOURNONVILLE and created the title role in his version of *La Sylphide* (1836). She left Copenhagen in 1838 and became the first Danish ballerina to gain international fame. She danced in Paris, St. Petersburg, and London, where she appeared in the famous *Pas de Quatre* of 1845. Grahn retired from dancing in 1856 but worked as ballet mistress in Leipzig (1858–61) and Munich (1869–75), where she choreographed the bacchanale in Richard Wagner's *Tannhäuser* and assisted in the staging of *Rheingold* and *Die Meistersinger von Nürnberg*.

DAVID VAUGHAN

Bibliography: Migel, Parmenia, *The Ballerinas* (1972; repr. 1980).

Grail, Holy [grayl]

The Holy Grail, a symbolic talisman around which numerous medieval legends and poems revolve, probably originated in Celtic pagan tradition, but later became associated with the cup used at the Last Supper, in which Joseph of Arimathea gathered blood from Christ's wounds. The Grail was sought by the knights of King Arthur in several medieval romances, the earliest of which was the late-12th-century *Perceval* by CHRÉTIEN DE TROYES. The quest for the Grail, which can only be found by a hero free from sin, is treated at great length in Sir Thomas MALORY's *Morte Darthur* (*c.*1469) and in Wolfram von Eschenbach's epic, *Parzifal* (*c.*1210), which inspired Richard Wagner's opera *Parsifal* (1877–82).

Bibliography: Cavendish, Richard, *King Arthur and the Grail* (1985); Currer-Briggs, Noel, *The Shroud and the Grail* (1988); Weston, Jessie, *The Quest of the Holy Grail* (1913; repr. 1973).

See also: ARTHUR AND ARTHURIAN LEGEND.

grain

Grain is the seed or fruit of various cereal grasses of the family Gramineae. The principal grain crops are WHEAT, CORN (or maize), RICE, BARLEY, OATS, RYE, SORGHUM, and MILLET. Sometimes seeds other than grasses, such as BUCKWHEAT, WILD RICE, and SOYBEANS, are characterized as grains. Grains are grown under a wide range of environmental conditions from the equator to close to the Arctic Circle in the Northern Hemisphere and to the 40th parallel in the Southern Hemisphere. They can be grown with little labor, and in comparison to other crops, returns are high for the work required. Cereal grasses were among the first domesticated plants, and today grains are a mainstay of agricultural production.

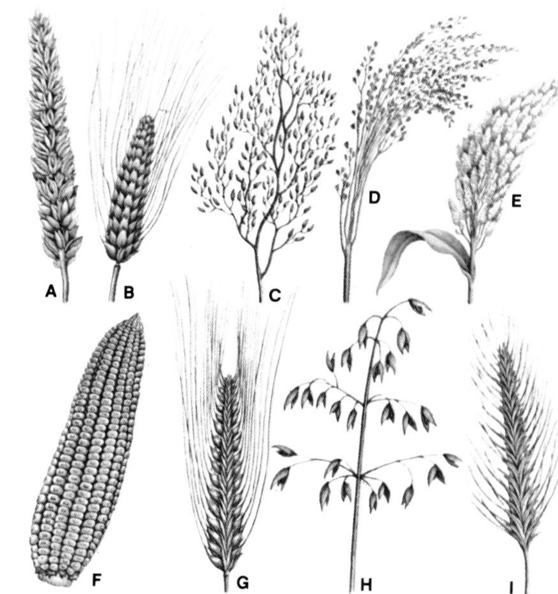

Grains, or cereal grasses, the most important of all food crops, are grown in almost every agricultural region. The chief grain crops are wheat, including Triticum vulgare (A) *and* Triticum durham (B); *rice,* Oryza sativa (C); *millet,* Panicum miliaceum (D); *sorghum,* Sorghum vulgare (E); *corn,* Zea mays (F); *barley,* Hordeum vulgare (G); *oats,* Avena sativa (H); *and rye,* Secale cereale (I).

Production. The principal grain-growing countries, in descending order of production, are the Soviet Union, India, China, the United States, Brazil, Canada, Australia, Turkey, and Indonesia.

The central part of the United States is the nation's major grain-producing region. Approximately one-third of the total agricultural exports of the United States are grains and grain products.

Nutritional Analysis. Cereal grains are the least expensive source of calories for human consumption. An important energy source, they supply most of the carbohydrates in the human diet throughout the world, and the proteins, lipids, vitamins, and minerals contained in cereals are also of considerable nutritional importance. The carbohydrate content of cereals ranges from 60% to 80%; lipid content ranges from 2% to 7%. The variability of the constituents is illustrated by the range of protein content within the grain: barley, 8% to 21%; corn, 8% to 17%; rye, 8% to 10%; wheat, 8% to 22%. The extent and method of processing drastically alter the relation between the vitamin, mineral, and lipid value.

Marketing. All grains can be handled, transported, and stored without deterioration when moisture content is below 14% and temperatures are below 38° C (100° F).

To facilitate orderly marketing, grain is graded by ranking certain quality characteristics, permitting both buyer and seller to know the grain's properties without actually seeing it. In the United States, Congress established fixed grain standards in 1916.

Grain Storage. Primitive societies stored grain as a way of maintaining a food supply. In modern agriculture grain is stored mostly because the grower wishes to control his product until he chooses to sell. On-farm storage of grain is an important aspect of grain marketing, and the United States has more than 15,000 off-farm grain storage facilities (see GRAIN ELEVATOR).

Grain Uses. Grains are used principally for food and feed, although they also have numerous industrial uses. Most grains are milled to separate the floury endosperm from the BRAN and germ, which can cause rancidity. The germ is nutritious, however, and is often added to food products after being dried and rolled. The oil extracted from the germ is refined for salad or cooking use. Most processed by-products of grain are used as feed.

FLOUR is used in various types of baked and cereal products, in pasta products, and in gravies. Pearled, rolled, flaked, ground, and cut grains are used in breakfast foods, soup, meal, hominy, and specialty items.

Food and feed grains are used industrially to manufacture starch, dextrins, malt, beer, liquors, oils, and glutens. Starch is used in paper and textile sizing, ore refining, pelletizing, and drilling fluids. The gluten protein of wheat is separated to produce a product that is used in the baking industry or for making condiments.

Bibliography: Leonard, W., and Martin, J., *Cereal Crops* (1962); Pomeranz, Y., *Introduction to Cereal Science* (1987); Stoskopf, N., *Cereal Grain Crops* (1985).

grain elevator

A grain elevator is a structure that stores large volumes of grain, which are moved into it by conveyor belts or pneumatic tubes. In North America the two most commonly stored grains are wheat and corn; elevators also store oats, barley, rice, sorghum, soybeans, and other commodities. Many large farms maintain their own elevators. They can then sell their grain for higher prices in the months between harvests and utilize stored crops for fattening livestock.

Large grain elevators are usually located at railroad sidings and at seaports, where they hold and rapidly transfer large grain tonnages into ships or freight cars. In addition, all elevators require adequate road access for trucks and trailers that deliver grain from the fields.

Farm trucks dump their cargoes into a pit next to the elevator. At the pit bottom, an electric-powered conveyor moves the grain to one of several cylindrical storage silos within the elevator.

Incoming grain is periodically sampled for quality, cleanliness, and moisture content. If the grain contains too much chaff, weed seeds, or other nongrain particles, it will be run through a cleaner. If the moisture content is too high, the grain is put through a drier while it is being transferred. Grain that is too moist and cannot be immediately dried or dehydrated tends to heat up, and must be moved frequently to preserve its quality and to avoid the production of inflammable gases. The accumulation of grain dust can cause a violent explosion if it should be ignited, and all elevators, therefore, have ventilator fans and equipment for fighting fire and preventing explosions.

The year 1986 set records for corn, wheat, and soybean production in the United States, and the glut created the worst storage shortage the country had ever seen. Grain elevators were filled to capacity. Fees for storage were high, to make up for a 5-year drop in agricultural exports that had cost storage companies (which also act as grain brokers) many millions of dollars. To keep up with the harvest, more elevators were built, grain was piled on empty barges, and farmers rushed to buy their own grain bins.

Grain growers found that the harvest bonanza kept prices low. Grain-elevator operators and barge owners, on the other hand, sold much of the harvest in foreign markets. The enormous new storage capacity also permitted extra stocks of grain to be kept and used during the poor harvest of 1988.

EDWARD W. FOSS

Grainger, Percy [grayn'-jur]

Percy Aldridge Grainger, b. Melbourne, Australia, July 8, 1882, d. Feb. 20, 1961, was a composer and pianist so thoroughly absorbed in folk music that it colored nearly every one of his compositions. He learned the piano from his mother and then studied (1895–1901) in Germany, but he began (1901) his concert career in England, afterward touring South Africa and Australia. He settled (1914) in the United States and taught at various academic institutions. Grainger tried to give his music the spontaneity of folksong and experimented with unorthodox scales and polyrhythmic combinations. His works include *Irish Tunes from County Derry* (1909), *Harvest Hymn* (1933), and *Suite on Danish Folksongs* (1937) for orchestra; *Marching Song of Democracy* (1917) and *Tribute to Foster* (1932) for chorus and orchestra; and *Handel in the Strand* (1913), *Spoon River* (1922), and *Free Music* (1935) for chamber groups. Most of the works listed above exist in arrangements by the composer for various other media.

Bibliography: Bird, John, *Percy Grainger* (1976); Slattery, Thomas C., *Percy Grainger: The Inveterate Innovator* (1974); Taylor, R. L., *The Running Pianist* (1950).

gramicidin: see ANTIBIOTICS.

grammar [gram'-ur]

Grammar is the study of the structure and meaning of human language; the term is also applied to books that set out rules governing a language's use. Grammar may be understood either in a traditional sense, designating an unbroken chain of theories about language extending back to ancient Greece, or in a more modern way. In current LINGUISTICS, grammar is defined as the body of tacit knowledge that constitutes a speaker's grasp of his language.

Grammar includes such specific subtopics as morphology (the principles of word formation; see PHONOLOGY AND MORPHOLOGY), SYNTAX (the principles of sentence structure), and the PARTS OF SPEECH. Descriptive grammar is observational and attempts to characterize the principles of word and sentence formation that speakers actually follow in using their language. On the other hand, prescriptive grammar, also called normative grammar, formulates rules about how people ought to speak. The prescriptive grammarian necessarily has preconceived notions of what is supposed to be right and wrong.

Traditional Grammar. Traditional grammar isolates and identifies language units of various sizes and develops rules for combining them into larger structures. A properly constituted structure—one formed according to the rules—is called grammatical; ungrammatical structures are those which violate the rules. For example, a morphological rule for English is that nouns but not verbs can end in the suffix *-ness.* Forms such as *quickness, fastness,* and *presentness* may or may not be nouns in English, but they cannot be verbs. A syntactic rule is that singular subjects take singular verbs. The sentence *he runs* is grammatical; *he run* is not.

The root of a word is its core—a minimal meaningful unit to which prefixes and suffixes can be progressively added to create larger forms. *Beat* can be expanded into *beatable,* which in turn can be enlarged to *unbeatable.* In the domain of sentence structure, words are traditionally divided into classes—the parts of speech—whose members perform similar grammatical functions. In accordance with rules specifying their order, form, and allowable combinations, words can be grouped into larger expressions, such as phrases, clauses, and sentences.

Linguistic Competence and Performance. Following the lead of Noam CHOMSKY, modern linguists tend to emphasize the status of language structure as a facet of human psychological organization. Linguistic competence is the subconscious ability to string words into grammatical sentences; linguistic performance can be measured by how grammatical the resulting spoken sentences are. To be understood, successful speakers must pair a meaning and a pronunciation. For example, to express the two different concepts, a speaker subconsciously learns to say *he runs* but *they run.*

Grammar Books. PANINI produced an elaborate grammar of Sanskrit about 400 BC. In the West, the SOPHISTS began their grammatical analysis of Greek at about the same time or a little earlier. Both Plato and Aristotle wrote on various aspects of language—particularly phonetics and etymology—but a far more comprehensive grammar was that of DIONYSIUS THRAX, from about 100 BC.

The Romans applied to their own language the grammatical categories developed for Greek. Priscian wrote an exhaustive Latin grammar in the early 6th century AD, but much more popular both in classical times and throughout the Middle Ages was the shorter grammar by Aelius DONATUS.

The Anglo-Saxon monk ÆLFRIC compiled a Latin grammar about 1000, but the first analyses of the English language date from almost 400 years later. Until the 20th century all English grammars were both prescriptive and heavily influenced by Latin. Probably the most important English grammarian was Bishop Robert Lowth (1710-87), who laid down the well-known rule that two negatives make a positive.

RONALD W. LANGACKER

Bibliography: Bolinger, Dwight, and Sears, Donald, *Aspects of Language*, 3d ed. (1981); Jackson, H., ed., *Discovering Grammar* (1985); Langacker, Ronald W., *Language and Its Structure*, 2d ed. (1973); Newmeyer, Frederick, *Grammatical Theory* (1983); Quirk, Randolph, and Greenbaum, Sidney, *A Concise Grammar of Contemporary English* (1973); Sapir, Edward, *Language* (1921).

Grammy Award [gram'-ee]

The National Academy of Recording Arts and Sciences established the Grammy Award in 1958 to give public honor to creative achievement in about 70 categories of recording. Awards are given for virtually every type of recorded music from jazz through opera.

Grampian [gram'-pee-uhn]

Grampian is an administrative region in northeastern Scotland bounded by the North Sea on the east and north. The region covers an area of 8,702 km^2 (3,360 mi^2) and has a population of 497,300 (1984 est.). Grampian's economy is based upon agriculture, fishing, distilling, and textile and paper manufacturing. ABERDEEN, the largest city, is the center of the North Sea oil industry. Grampian was created in 1975 from the former counties of ABERDEEN, BANFF, KINCARDINE, and part of MORAY.

Gramsci, Antonio [grahm'-shee]

A leading Marxist theoretician, Antonio Gramsci, b. Jan. 23, 1891, d. Apr. 27, 1937, played an important role in Italian revolutionary politics during the 1920s. He studied (1911-14) at the University of Turin, where he met Palmiro TOGLIATTI and other young socialists. After writing for the socialist papers *Avanti* and *L'Ordine Nuovo* ("The New Order," which he cofounded, 1919), Gramsci helped found the Italian Communist party in 1921 and became its leader in 1924. He worked for the Comintern in Moscow, Vienna, and Italy from 1922 to 1926. Elected (1924) to the Chamber of Deputies, Gramsci was arrested (1926) with other Communists in Rome after the Fascists outlawed their party. He remained in prison until shortly before his death. Since World War II, Gramsci's *Prison Notebooks* (1948-57; selections trans., 1971) and *Letters from Prison* (1947; trans., 1973), which deal with wide-ranging cultural and political issues, have been enormously influential among Italian intellectuals, both Marxist and non-Marxist.

Bibliography: Davidson, Alastair, *Antonio Gramsci* (1977); Femia, J. V., *Gramsci's Political Thought* (1981); Fiori, Giuseppe, *Antonio Gramsci: Life of a Revolutionary*, trans. by Tom Nairn (1971); Joll, James, *Antonio Gramsci* (1978).

Gran Chaco: see CHACO.

Granada (city in Nicaragua) [grah-nah'-dah]

Granada (1982 est. pop., 80,000), the capital of Granada department in southwestern Nicaragua, is situated beside Lake Nicaragua at the foot of Mombacho Volcano. It is an industrial center, and its chief products are furniture, soap, clothing, oil, rum, hides, coffee, and sugar. Granada, the oldest city in Nicaragua, was founded in 1523 by Francisco Fernández de Córdoba. In the 17th century, pirates from the Caribbean raided Granada frequently. In 1857 the U.S. filibusterer William Walker sacked the city. The city is Spanish in style, with many old mansions and churches remaining from its early days.

Granada (city in Spain)

Granada, a city in southern Spain, is the capital of the province of Granada. It is located on the Genil River, a tributary of the Guadalquivir, in a small but intensively cultivated plain. The city has a population of 262,182 (1981). It lies at an elevation of about 690 m (2,260 ft) and is overlooked from the south by the Sierra Nevada. Granada's industries include sugar refining, tanning, iron and copper working, and textile manufacturing. Granada enjoys a mild Mediterranean climate. The city's great architectural treasures make it one of Spain's most visited tourist centers.

The old city is spread around two steep hills. The Darro River, which flows here into the Genil, divides the old city into two quarters: the Antequeruela and the Albaicín. The Albaicín was the residence of the Moorish aristocracy. The Antequeruela was founded in the 15th century by refugees from Antequera. The modern city stretches over the flatter land to the north.

The city's most famous site is the beautiful ALHAMBRA palace (built 13th-14th centuries), the greatest Moorish monument in Spain. Other notable sights include several Moorish villas, the Renaissance cathedral (begun 1523), which contains the tombs of Ferdinand II of Aragon and Isabella I of Castile, and the unfinished palace of Charles V (begun 16th century). The University of Granada was chartered in 1531.

Granada first rose to prominence under the Moors. After the breakup of the Moorish caliphate in 1002, it became the seat of a kingdom (1031-90) ruled by the Banu Ziri, or Zirids, a local Muslim dynasty. After a period of Almoravid and Almohad domination, another local dynasty, the Nasrids, came to power in the 13th century. During the more than 250 years of Nasrid rule, Granada was a flourishing commercial and artistic center. The city fell to Christian forces in 1492, ending Moorish power in Spain. In the 17th century, after the Jews and the Moriscos (Muslim converts to Christianity) had been expelled, it entered a period of decline.

NORMAN J. G. POUNDS

Bibliography: Rosenthal, Earl E., *The Cathedral of Granada* (1961) and *The Palace of Charles V in Granada* (1985).

Granada (region in Spain)

Granada is a province in southern Spain forming part of the larger, historical region of Granada, which also includes the provinces of Almería and Málaga. In the 11th century, and again from the 13th to the 15th century, Granada was a Moorish kingdom. In 1492 it was conquered by forces of the Christian monarchs FERDINAND II of Aragon and ISABELLA I of Castile.

The province of Granada has an area of 12,531 km^2 (4,838 mi^2) and a population of 761,734 (1981). The capital city is Granada. The topography of the province is varied, with the Sierra Nevada in the north and fertile valleys in the central and southern portions.

Bibliography: Handler, Andrew, *The Zirids of Granada* (1974).

Granados, Enrique [grah-nah'-dohs, ayn-ree'-kay]

Enrique Granados, b. July 27, 1867, d. Mar. 24, 1916, was a Spanish composer and pianist. After piano studies at the Barcelona Conservatory, he studied composition in Madrid with Felipe Pedrell. He also studied the piano in Paris and soon gained wide recognition as a pianist. From 1889 he lived in Barcelona, where he established his own academy of music. His first opera, *María del Carmen*, was well received (1898) in Madrid, but the four that followed had little success. In 1892 he published the 12 *Spanish Dances* for piano, which have remained his most popular pieces, especially No. 5, *Andaluza*. On a larger scale is the suite for piano, *Goyescas* (2 vols., 1912-14), inspired by the paintings and tapestries of the Spanish artist Francisco Goya. Granados's opera, also titled *Goyescas*, was based on the music and the scenes represented in the piano suite. Although the outbreak of World War I delayed its premiere, it was produced (1916) at the Metropolitan Opera with the composer present. On the homeward voyage Granados and his wife perished when their ship was torpedoed by a German submarine.

GILBERT CHASE

Bibliography: Chase, Gilbert, *The Music of Spain*, 2d ed. (1959).

Grand Alliance, War of the

The War of the Grand Alliance, 1688–97, was the first war in which LOUIS XIV of France was confronted by a major European coalition. The latter, called initially the League of Augsburg, became known as the Grand Alliance in 1689; it included the Holy Roman Empire, the United Provinces, England, Spain, and Savoy.

The war began (September 1688) when Louis invaded the Palatinate, thus uniting the other powers against him. Louis provided support to the deposed English king JAMES II in Ireland, but the latter's forces were defeated by the new king WILLIAM III at the Battle of the BOYNE in 1690. At sea, too, although defeated by the French at Beachy Head (1690), the English were ultimately victorious in the Battle of La Hogue (1692). On the Continent the French were more successful. They won a series of victories, including Steenkerke (1692) and Neerwinden (1693), in the Low Countries. The French also defeated Duke VICTOR AMADEUS II of Savoy at Marsaglia (1693) and invaded Catalonia. Subsequent action was indecisive, and the war ended inconclusively in the Treaty of Ryswick (1697). Louis recognized William III as king of England and gave up most of his post-1679 conquests. The question of the succession to the Spanish throne remained a major issue in European affairs, however, and led directly to the War of the SPANISH SUCCESSION. K. M. SMOGORZEWSKI

Bibliography: Clark, G. N., *The Dutch Alliance and the War Against the French Trade, 1688–97* (1923; repr. 1971).

See also: AUGSBURG, LEAGUE OF.

Grand Army of the Republic

The Grand Army of the Republic (GAR), founded in Springfield, Ill., in April 1866, was the largest organization of Union veterans of the Civil War. Organized under the leadership of Dr. Benjamin F. Stephenson, a former army surgeon, the GAR sought to promote comradeship among veterans, to extend pension rights, to provide relief for war widows and orphans, and to maintain homes for old soldiers. In 1868, GAR commander in chief John A. LOGAN inaugurated the observance of MEMORIAL DAY in honor of fallen soldiers. Membership in the staunchly Republican organization peaked at more than 400,000 in 1890. Two years earlier it had undoubtedly helped defeat Democratic president Grover CLEVELAND, who had vetoed pension legislation. The GAR was dissolved in 1956.

Bibliography: Dearing, Mary R., *Veterans in Politics: The Story of G. A. R.* (1952; repr. 1974).

Grand Banks

The Grand Banks is a large (93,000 km²/36,000 mi²) area of submerged highlands located in the North Atlantic Ocean off the southeastern coast of Newfoundland and east of the Laurentian Channel. Noted for its thick fogs and hazardous icebergs, the area also has the reputation of being the world's best fishing grounds. The waters over the banks are relatively shallow, between 55 and 185 m (180 and 600 ft) deep; sunlight penetrates to the seabed, where small marine life thrives. In addition, the warm GULF STREAM, which meets the cold Labrador Current here, deposits sea plants, crabs, worms, and shrimp in the area, attracting cod, haddock, mackerel, herring, and flatfish. Fishing fleets have been drawn here for more than three centuries. In recent years, trawlers from the USSR and Japan have joined those from North America, northern Europe, and Britain. In 1929 a severe submarine earthquake shattered a large area of the fishing grounds, snapping transatlantic cables, sending TSUNAMIS washing over Newfoundland's Burin Peninsula, and creating turbidity that adversely affected fishing for a time.

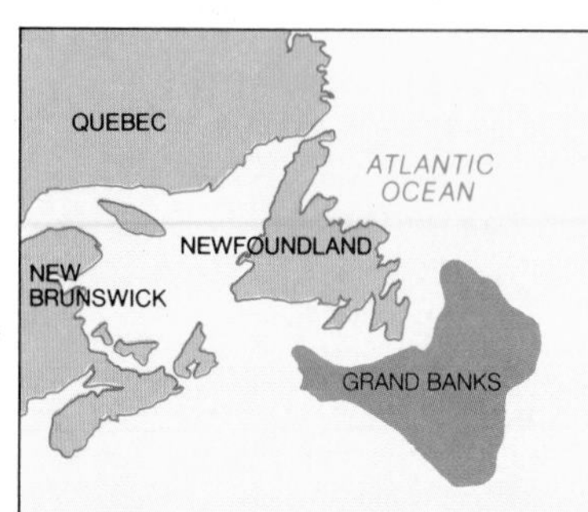

The map indicates the approximate boundaries of the Grand Banks, a portion of the North American continental shelf lying southeast of Newfoundland. Since the English explorer John Cabot first visited the area in 1498, it has become one of the most productive commercial fishing grounds.

See also: DENSITY CURRENT.

Grand Canal

The Grand Canal is an ancient Chinese waterway that extends for some 1,600 km (1,000 mi) from PEKING to HANGCHOW, roughly parallel to the coast of the Yellow Sea. Called the *Yunliang Ho* ("transport river") in Chinese, it is used to transport cargoes of coal, grain, lumber, and cotton.

The canal was dug in three stages. In the 6th century BC a prince of the later Chou dynasty began constructing a waterway 225 km (140 mi) long that would link the Yangtze and the Huai Ho. Approximately 1,200 years later, Emperor Yang Ti extended the canal southward 400 km (250 mi) to Hangchow. Kubla Khan further extended the canal to his capital city, Cambaluc (Peking), during the 13th century.

The growth of coastal shipping and the construction of railroads in the 19th century lessened the canal's importance. It was dredged and widened under the Communist regime, however, and is still used.

Grand Canyon

The Grand Canyon, located in northwestern Arizona, is a spectacular gorge carved by the COLORADO RIVER into rocks that represent over a billion years of Earth history. Its total length, from the Little Colorado River to Lake Mead, is 349 km (217 mi), of which 169 km (105 mi) is in Grand Canyon National Park.

The canyon is more than 1.6 km (1 mi) deep in places and from 6 to 29 km (4 to 18 mi) wide. Plateaus to the north and south rise 1,520 to 2,740 m (5,000 to 9,000 ft) above sea level,

The Grand Canyon, in northwestern Arizona, was accorded the protected status of a national park in 1919. The formations within the canyon are remnants of the plateau from which the gorge was carved by the Colorado River over millions of years.

partly as a result of regional uplift, which left the North Rim more than 305 m (1,000 ft) higher than the South Rim in places. On the bare walls, strata of limestone, sandstone, lava, and other rocks can be seen; they change color as the day passes.

García López de Cárdenas, a Spanish explorer, discovered the canyon in 1540, but systematic exploration did not begin until 1850. John Wesley Powell was the first to travel through the canyon by boat (1869). The national park, created in 1919, has an area of 4,931 km² (1,904 mi²).

Grand Central Terminal

New York City's Grand Central Terminal, a notable example of the Beaux-Arts style, was designed by Whitney Warren and constructed in 1907–13. Once the rival of New York's even more grandiose Pennsylvania Station (demolished in 1963), Grand Central still functions as a major railroad terminus and has been designated a landmark structure.

Bibliography: Middleton, William D., *Grand Central . . . the World's Greatest Railway Terminal* (1977).

Grand Coulee Dam [koo'-lee]

The most massive concrete structure in the world, Grand Coulee Dam on the Columbia River in Washington State contains over 7.6 million m³ (10 million yd³) of concrete. Opened in 1942, the 1.3-km-long (0.8 mi), 168-m-high (550-ft) gravity DAM serves the world's largest hydroelectric complex, recently enlarged to 9.7 million kilowatts. The dam's reservoir, Roosevelt Lake, stretches over 241 km (150 mi) toward the Canadian border. F. EUGENE MCJUNKIN

Bibliography: Smith, Norman, *The History of Dams* (1972); Sundberg, George, *Hail, Columbia* (1954).

Grand Forks

Grand Forks (1980 pop., 43,765) is the seat of Grand Forks County in eastern North Dakota. It is located at the junction of the Red River of the North and Red Lake River, 145 km (90 mi) south of the Canadian border. The city is the center of trade and processing for an agricultural region where wheat, potatoes, sugar beets, and livestock are produced. The University of North Dakota (1883), an Air Force base, a Minuteman missile complex, and a branch of the U.S. Bureau of Mines are located in or near the city. Grand Forks was settled in 1871 and incorporated in 1881.

Grand Guignol: see GUIGNOL, GRAND.

Grand Island

Located in southern Nebraska on the Platte River, Grand Island (1980 pop., 33,180) is the seat of Hall County. It is a rail, shipping, and manufacturing center. Grand Island was settled in 1857 by Germans and laid out in 1866, when the Union Pacific Railroad arrived.

grand jury

A grand JURY, a body of from 12 to 23 private citizens, hears accusations of crimes committed in a district or county. After hearing the evidence submitted by the prosecutor (it seldom hears the accused), the grand jury decides whether the evidence is sufficient to hold the accused for trial. If so, it authorizes an INDICTMENT that carefully spells out the charges against the accused so that a defense may be prepared. A grand jury may also initiate its own investigation and subpoena witnesses. Grand juries are often chosen by lot, and the process of selection must be fair. In POWELL V. ALABAMA the U.S. Supreme Court upset the convictions of several black youths on the grounds that blacks had been excluded from the grand jury that indicted them for rape.

The grand jury is part of the JURY institution developed in Anglo-American common law, although England abolished the grand jury in 1933. In the United States grand jury protection was guaranteed by the 5TH AMENDMENT of the Bill of Rights. In recent years the use of the grand jury has declined. The U.S. Supreme Court had ruled in *Hurtado* v. *California* (1884) that grand jury indictments were not required of the states, and prosecutors have increasingly presented accusations in the form of an information, a formal accusation that does not have to be made by a grand jury. Moreover, there have been charges that grand jury investigations have been improperly used as a means of persecution or to bypass constitutional protections.

Bibliography: Brant, Irving, *The Bill of Rights* (1965); Frankel, Marvin E., and Naftalis, Gary P., *The Grand Jury: An Institution on Trial* (1978); Trebach, Arnold, *The Rationing of Justice* (1964).

Grand Old Party: see REPUBLICAN PARTY.

Grand Ole Opry [ohl ahp'ree]

The Grand Ole Opry's rise from one among many square dance radio shows to an international musical and tourist institution parallels COUNTRY AND WESTERN MUSIC's climb to national eminence. In 1925 radio station WSM in Nashville, Tenn., began broadcasting hillbilly music weekly. At first, the mostly amateur musicians presented authentic regional music. The first star of the show—banjoist and singer "Uncle" Dave Macon, whose style reached back into the 19th century—achieved national acclaim during the 1930s.

The Grand Ole Opry's growth began when Roy Acuff joined the show in 1938 as its first singing star. During the 1940s the show was broadcast nationally over NBC radio and began to send out auxiliary touring companies.

By 1950 the Grand Ole Opry had become a supershow with a cast of about 120 performers. It was largely responsible for the growth of Nashville as the center of the country music recording industry and became the city's most famous tourist attraction. By this time the Opry had long since lost its regional, down-home quality, and in 1974 the last link with the past was cut when it moved to a new multimillion-dollar Opryland concert center on the outskirts of the city.

Bibliography: Krishef, Robert F., *Grand Ole Opry* (1978); Tassin, Myron, *Fifty Years at the Grand Ole' Opry* (1975).

Grand Rapids

A furniture-manufacturing center and the second largest city in Michigan, Grand Rapids is situated at the rapids (now largely dredged) of the Grand River in west central Michigan. Grand Rapids is the seat of Kent County and has a population of 181,843 (1980) within the city limits and 601,680 in the 2-county metropolitan area. In addition to furniture production, the city has several hundred diversified industries; it is the distribution, trade, and cultural focus for much of western Michigan. It is also the gateway to fishing and recreational areas. Several colleges are located there.

The city was established (1827) as a fur-trading post on the site of an Indian village. Abundant forests and waterpower fostered a thriving lumber industry, which led (by 1859) to furniture making; the many new Dutch immigrants excelled at this craft.

Grand Teton National Park [teet'-uhn]

Grand Teton National Park, containing the TETON RANGE of the Rocky Mountains, is situated in northwestern Wyoming, only 11 km (7 mi) south of YELLOWSTONE NATIONAL PARK. Established in 1929, it covers 1,256 km² (485 mi²). The mountains quickly rise more than 2,100 m (7,000 ft) from JACKSON HOLE, a flat plain at their base. The highest peak in the park, Grand Teton, reaches 4,196 m (13,766 ft). Glaciers, lakes, rivers, hot springs, and waterfalls add to the park's beauty. Elk, deer, moose, and bear inhabit the heavily forested park.

Bibliography: Murie, Margaret E., *Grand Teton* (1984).

grand unification theories

In theoretical physics, grand unification theories (GUTs) are attempts to describe three of the fundamental forces of nature—the strong, weak, and electromagnetic forces—as aspects of a single interaction (see FUNDAMENTAL INTERACTIONS). Grand unification theories also describe the two primary constituents of matter, QUARKS and LEPTONS, as manifestations of a single type of subatomic particle.

According to current theory, forces between subatomic particles are transmitted via the emission and absorption of vector BOSONS, particles with one unit of intrinsic angular momentum. Theorists use a mathematical structure known as a gauge field to describe these fundamental interactions. The weak, strong, and electromagnetic interactions differ mainly in their strengths, as measured by the rest energies of their bosons, and by the probability of boson emissions. In order of decreasing strength, the individual bosons are GLUONS (the strong force), PHOTONS (the electromagnetic force), and W and Z particles (the weak force).

In GUTs the differences between fundamental forces are seen to be the result of the fact that particles are observed at relatively low energies. If particles could be observed at very high energies, the three types of interaction would be found to have equal strength. In addition, quarks and leptons would behave similarly under those conditions. The energy at which this unification is expected is about 10^{14} GeV (giga electron volts), a trillion times higher than the energies of present-day experiments. While it may never be possible to examine such high-energy processes in the laboratory, it is thought that in the very early universe, a small fraction of a second after the Big Bang (see COSMOLOGY) the average energy of all particles was high enough for these particles to behave in the manner described by GUTs.

One startling prediction of GUTs is that new interactions may exist, involving vector bosons whose rest energy is 10^{14} GeV. These interactions would allow three quarks to convert into a lepton, inducing the decay of protons and neutrons into leptons. The result of such decays would be a proton lifetime of 10^{31} years, and evidence for this would defeat the long-held notion of the eternal stability of the proton. Experiments designed to detect these rare proton decays are being carried out, but no conclusive evidence has been obtained.

Although the validity of GUTs is not yet established, physicists are developing theories that will link the fourth force, gravitation (and its boson, the graviton), with the other three forces. These models are referred to as supersymmetry theories. GERALD FEINBERG

Bibliography: Feinberg, Gerald, *What is the World Made of?* (1977); Fritzsche, Harald, *Quarks* (1983); Pagels, Heinz, *The Cosmic Code* (1982); Weinberg, Steven, *Subatomic Particles* (1983).

See also: SYMMETRY (physics); UNIFIED FIELD THEORY.

grandfather clause

A grandfather clause exempts certain people from specific requirements in laws or regulations that normally have to be fulfilled in order to enter into an occupation, start a business, or assume a right. People who are declared exempt by a grandfather clause are privileged because of their status or their ancestors' status prior to enactment of the requirements. In 1895 several Southern states began to pass laws with grandfather clauses to allow whites to vote, in spite of the fact that they failed to meet literacy or poll-tax requirements, if they themselves, or their fathers or grandfathers, had been entitled to vote on Jan. 1, 1867. Such laws, designed to keep blacks from voting, were declared unconstitutional under the 15TH AMENDMENT in *Guinn & Beal* v. *United States* (1915).

Grandma Moses: see MOSES, GRANDMA.

Grandville [grand'-veel]

Grandville, the pseudonym of Jean Ignace Isidore Gérard, b. Sept. 15, 1803, d. Mar. 17, 1847, was a French caricaturist, illustrator, and graphic artist noted for his inventive political and social satire. Like many of the famous caricaturists of the period such as Honoré Daumier, Grandville worked for Charles PHILIPON, contributing drawings to the periodicals *La Caricature* and *Le Charivari.* His satirical series included *Métamorphoses du jour* (Present-day Metamorphoses; 1829), *Un Autre Monde* (Another World; 1844), and *Scènes de la vie privée et publique des animaux* (1842; *Public and Private Life of Animals*; 1977). He created the illustrations for Jonathan Swift's *Gulliver's Travels* (1838) and Daniel Defoe's *Robinson Crusoe* (1840). Grandville's fantastic anthropomorphic figures combining human and animal characteristics may have inspired Sir John Tenniel's illustrations for Lewis Carroll's *Alice in Wonderland.*

Bibliography: Appelbaum, Stanley, ed., *Bizarreries and Fantasies of Grandville* (1974); Olmert, M. J., "Grandville's Phantasmagoric View of Humanity," *Smithsonian*, September 1978.

Grange, National

The National Grange is the popular name of the Order of the Patrons of Husbandry, the oldest general farm organization in the United States. It was established in Washington, D.C., on Dec. 4, 1867, largely through the efforts of Oliver Hudson Kelley, a Minnesota farmer who was deeply affected by the poverty and isolation of the farmers he saw while inspecting farm areas in the South for the U.S. Department of Agriculture in 1866. He felt they had to unite and promote their interests collectively. The organization, which acquired the character of a FRATERNAL SOCIETY, provided lectures and entertainment for farm men and women. It also experimented in COOPERATIVE buying and selling of farm products and supplies and carried on educational programs, setting up Grange units for children as well as adults.

In the 1870s the Grange was prominent in the broader Granger movement, which campaigned against extortionate charges by monopolistic railroads and warehouses and helped bring about laws regulating these charges in some states in the upper Mississippi Valley. Although challenged, the constitutionality of such laws was upheld by the U.S. Supreme Court in MUNN V. ILLINOIS (1876).

In general, the policies adopted by the Grange have been fairly conservative. The organization has favored the commodity-by-commodity approach to farm supports but aims at freeing the farmer from governmental supports and controls. In 1985 the Grange had about 425,000 members in 5,500 local granges in 37 states.

Bibliography: Gardner, Charles M., *The Grange: Friend of the Farmer* (1949); Nordin, D. Sven, *Rich Harvest: A History of the Grange, 1867-1900* (1974).

Grange, Red

Harold Edward Grange, b. Forksville, Pa., June 13, 1903, was a legendary American football player. Red Grange became nationally known in his football seasons at the University of Illinois (1923–25) as he rushed for 3,637 yards and scored 31 touchdowns. In his most famous game, against the University of Michigan in 1924, Grange scored five touchdowns and set

Red Grange, one of the outstanding running backs in the history of collegiate football, led the University of Illinois to a national championship during his first season with the varsity squad and won All-American honors three times (1923–25). Grange became the focus of a bitter controversy when he left school before graduating to play professional football for the Chicago Bears.

up a sixth in a 39–14 upset. Grange joined the professional ranks after his last college game in 1925 and went on a 19-game tour in which he drew record-breaking professional crowds in many cities. He is credited with making professional football a major spectator sport. Grange played with the New York Yankees of the American Football League and the Chicago Bears of the National Football League until 1934. He was a brilliant broken-field runner and was thus nicknamed (by sportswriter Grantland Rice) "The Galloping Ghost."

Bibliography: Cope, Myron, *The Game That Was: The Early Days of Pro Football* (1970); Danzig, Allison, *Oh, How They Played the Game* (1971); Morton, Ira, *The Galloping Ghost* (1984).

Granger movement: see GRANGE, NATIONAL.

granite [gran'-it]

Granite is a light-colored plutonic rock found throughout the continental crust, most commonly in mountainous areas. It consists of coarse grains of QUARTZ (10–50%), potassium FELDSPAR, and sodium feldspar. These minerals make up more than 80% of the rock. Other common minerals include MICA (muscovite and biotite) and hornblende (see AMPHIBOLE). The chemical composition of granite is typically 70–77% SiO_2, 11–13% Al_2O_3, 3–5% K_2O, 3–5% Na_2O, 1% CaO, 2–3% total iron, and less than 1% MgO and TiO_2. Volcanic rock of equivalent chemical composition and mineralogy is called RHYOLITE.

Granites are the most abundant plutonic rocks of mountain belts and continental shield areas. They occur in great BATHOLITHS that may occupy thousands of square kilometers and are usually closely associated with quartz monzonite, granodiorite, diorite, and gabbro.

Debate has long centered on whether granite is IGNEOUS or METAMORPHIC in origin. Originally granite was thought to form mainly from magmatic differentiation of basaltic MAGMA, but geologists now believe there is simply too much of it for it to have formed this way, except locally. Most granite seems to have formed either by melting, partial melting, or metamorphism of deeply buried shale and sandstone. Granite dikes are clearly igneous, and granite emplaced in the upper few kilometers of the Earth's crust also often shows evidence of forceful intrusion into surrounding rocks, whereas some granites that formed deeper within the crust seem not to have been forcefully emplaced. Evidence of intrusion or great mobility is considered to indicate an igneous origin that stems from melting of sediments; but where no good evidence of either a magma chamber or of fluidity is observed, a metamorphic origin must be considered.

Granite is used as a building and ornamental stone. Many ore deposits (copper, lead, zinc, gold, and silver, for example) were produced by hydrothermal solutions created during late stages of cooling of granite bodies. These may be emplaced around the peripheries or related to fissures and fractures within bodies of granite. WILLIAM D. ROMEY

Bibliography: Marmo, V., *Granite Petrology and the Granite Problem* (1971); Marre, J., *The Structural Analysis of Granitic Rocks* (1986).

granodiorite [gran-oh-dy'-uh-rite]

Granodiorite is a plutonic rock composed mainly of coarse plagioclase, QUARTZ, and a little potassium FELDSPAR. Hornblende (see AMPHIBOLE) and biotite (see MICA) may constitute about 20 percent of the rock, with small amounts of other accessory minerals. Granodiorite is intermediate between QUARTZ MONZONITE and quartz DIORITE. Batholiths in the Sierra Nevada containing large amounts of granodiorite often show intrusive relationships. They probably formed from the melting or transformation of sedimentary rocks in deep zones of mountain belts. WILLIAM D. ROMEY

Bibliography: Hyndman, Donald W., *The Petrology of Igneous and Metamorphic Rocks*, 2d ed. (1985).

Grant, Cary

Cary Grant was the professional name of English-born Archibald Alexander Leach, b. Jan. 18, 1904, d. Nov. 29, 1986, who won world fame in dozens of Hollywood movies as the quintessentially debonair, self-confident sophisticate. Appearing in films from 1932 on, he played roles particularly suited to his talents in *The Awful Truth* (1937) and *My Favorite Wife* (1940) opposite Irene Dunne, in *The Philadelphia Story* (1940) with Katharine Hepburn, and in such Alfred Hitchcock thrillers as *Suspicion* (1941), *Notorious* (1946), *To Catch a Thief* (1955), and *North by Northwest* (1959). Grant retired in 1970.

Cary Grant shares a romantic moment with leading lady Ingrid Bergman in this scene from the spy drama Notorious *(1946). Throughout his film career the urbane, British-born actor gave performances characterized by sophisticated nonchalance.*

Bibliography: Deschner, Donald, *The Films of Cary Grant* (1973); Wansell, Geoffrey, *Haunted Idol* (1984).

Grant, Ulysses S.

Ulysses Simpson Grant, the best-known Federal general in the CIVIL WAR, served also as 18th president of the United States. He was born in the Ohio River village of Point Pleasant, Ohio, on Apr. 27, 1822, the son of a tanner. Although baptized Hiram Ulysses, Grant was listed by the congressman who secured his appointment to West Point as Ulysses Simpson, the latter being his mother's maiden name.

Having helped in farm work and developed skill in hauling wood, Grant made some mark as an equestrian at the military academy; otherwise his performance there was undistinguished. He graduated 21st in a class of 39 in 1843. In the Mexican War, Grant served effectively with Zachary Taylor's army at Monterey and then with Winfield Scott's army in the campaign for Mexico City; he won two brevets for meritorious conduct at Molino del Rey and Chapultepec.

After the war, Grant was assigned to garrison duty. His early postings in the Great Lakes region were happy because he was with his new wife, Julia Dent Grant (1826–1902), whom he married on Aug. 22, 1848. In 1852, however, he was sent to the Pacific Northwest, where he was unable to have his family with him. He apparently so overindulged in alcohol that he was impelled to resign from the army in 1854. For six years he struggled in Missouri as a farmer, real estate salesman, unsuccessful candidate for county engineer, and agent in a customhouse. In 1860 he was obliged to accept a clerkship in his brothers' leather-goods store in Galena, Ill.

Civil War. After the outbreak of the Civil War, Grant tried in vain to obtain a position on the staff of Gen. George B. MCCLELLAN. He initially received the colonelcy of an Illinois regiment, but his effective leadership of that soon brought him appointment (Aug. 7, 1861) as a brigadier general of volunteers. Grant's Civil War career revealed him as a man of serious, self-contained, determined bearing. Confident yet humble, he demonstrated consistent, unflinching courage, both physical and moral. In November 1861 he launched an ill-prepared attack on Belmont, Mo., where, after an initial advantage, he was forced to fall back with losses. A few months la-

ULYSSES SIMPSON GRANT
18th President of the United States (1869-77)

Nickname: "Hero of Appomattox"
Born: Apr. 27, 1822, Point Pleasant, Ohio
Education: U.S. Military Academy, West Point, N.Y. (graduated 1843)
Profession: Soldier
Religious Affiliation: Methodist
Marriage: Aug. 22, 1848, to Julia Boggs Dent (1826-1902)
Children: Frederick Dent Grant (1850-1912); Ulysses Simpson Grant (1852-1929); Ellen Wrenshall Grant (1855-1922); Jesse Root Grant (1858-1934)
Political Affiliation: Republican
Writings: *Personal Memoirs* (2 vols., 1885-86); *Papers* (4 vols., 1967-), ed. by John Y. Simon
Died: July 23, 1885, Mount McGregor, N.Y.
Buried: Grant's Tomb, New York City

Vice-President and Cabinet Members
Vice-President: Schuyler Colfax (1869-73); Henry Wilson (1873-75)
Secretary of State: Elihu B. Washburne (1869); Hamilton Fish (1869-77)
Secretary of the Treasury: George S. Boutwell (1869-73); William A. Richardson (1873-74); Benjamin H. Bristow (1874-76); Lot M. Morrill (1876-77)
Secretary of War: John A. Rawlins (1869); William T. Sherman (1869); William W. Belknap (1869-76); Alphonso Taft (1876); James D. Cameron (1876-77)
Attorney General: Ebenezer R. Hoar (1869-70); Amos T. Akerman (1870-71); George H. Williams (1871-75); Edwards Pierrepont (1875-76); Alphonso Taft (1876-77)
Postmaster General: John A. J. Creswell (1869-74); James W. Marshall (1874); Marshall Jewell (1874-76); James N. Tyner (1876-77)
Secretary of the Navy: Adolph E. Borie (1869); George M. Robeson (1869-77)
Secretary of the Interior: Jacob D. Cox, Jr. (1869-70); Columbus Delano (1870-75); Zachariah Chandler (1875-77)

er, however, with considerable help from the Federal navy, Grant captured FORT HENRY AND FORT DONELSON on the Tennessee and Cumberland rivers, respectively. This success of February 1862 brought him new prominence, and he was advanced to major general.

In early April, Grant moved incautiously southward along the Tennessee River to Pittsburg Landing, or SHILOH, Tenn. There his carelessly disposed army was surprised by a sudden and shattering attack by Albert Sidney JOHNSTON, who was mortally wounded at the height of the Confederate advance. Near defeat on the first day of battle, Grant was reinforced by Maj. Gen. Don Carlos BUELL and counterattacked the following day. The Unionists were able to turn the tide and slowly to push the enemy back toward Corinth. Grant's army was just one of three that made the snail-paced advance on Corinth, which the Southerners evacuated. Gen. Henry HALLECK had taken personal command and Grant was largely ignored. He was subsequently shelved for several months as unfounded rumors to the effect that he was again drinking caused several of his superiors to hesitate in giving him another important command.

On Oct. 25, 1862, Grant was restored to a vital position. Appointed commander of the Department of Tennessee, he was instructed to take Vicksburg, Miss., the great enemy bastion on the east bank of the Mississippi River. The VICKSBURG CAMPAIGN began badly for Grant. An enterprising cavalry raid by Confederate Maj. Gen. Earl Van Dorn captured Grant's base at Holly Springs and compelled his retreat in December. Grant's approaches to the north of Vicksburg were also ineffective and resulted in the abortive "Bayou Expeditions" in the spring of 1863. Then, however, in a masterpiece of planning and bold execution, Grant crossed the Mississippi south of Vicksburg, marched northeastward to insert his army between John C. PEMBERTON's at Vicksburg and Joseph E. JOHNSTON's at Jackson, and fought five victorious battles. This permitted his investiture of Vicksburg, which, after a stern 47-day siege, capitulated on July 4, 1863.

In September 1863, Grant went to the rescue of the beleaguered Union army under William ROSECRANS at Chattanooga. He reinforced this army, replacing Rosecrans with George H. THOMAS, and opened up new lines of supply and communication. Then, in battles at Lookout Mountain and Missionary Ridge in November 1863, he defeated Braxton BRAGG and opened the way toward Dalton, Ga., and eventually for William T. SHERMAN's advance on Atlanta and Savannah. (See CHATTANOOGA, BATTLES OF.)

Thus far during the war, Grant, although ambitious for advancement in the army, had remained largely disinterested in politics. He had, however, impressed Abraham LINCOLN with his self-reliance, bulldog tenacity, and confidence in final victory; so early in 1864 he was promoted to lieutenant general and named general in chief of all the Federal armies. Grant did well in this top command; he was able to see the big picture of the war as well as its parts and skillfully coordinate the movements of the many armies of the Union. Leaving Sherman in command in the West, Grant established his headquarters with George G. MEADE's Army of the Potomac in the East. In effect, he commanded that army in its driving campaigns of 1864 against Robert E. LEE's army in Virginia. Although the command structure was at times awkward, Grant and Meade were usually able to work together harmoniously and to complement each other's activities.

With troops outnumbering Lee's almost two to one, Grant launched the so-called WILDERNESS CAMPAIGN in early May 1864. He tried to bludgeon his way through the Virginia Wilderness, but he was checked and forced to sidestep toward Spotsylvania Court House. Here, in several days of desperate fighting, Grant's gains were negligible and he suffered numerous casualties. At Cold Harbor he was massively repulsed, again with high losses, as morale sagged in the Army of the Potomac. Finally outguessing Lee and stealing a march on him across the James River (June 12-18), Grant and his subordinate generals missed an opportunity to take Petersburg, the railroad key to Richmond, by surprise. After the 9-month PETERSBURG CAMPAIGN (June 18, 1864, to Apr. 2, 1865), conducted while Philip SHERIDAN cleared the Shenandoah Valley of Jubal EARLY's forces, Grant was finally able to force Lee back from Petersburg and Richmond. A 142-km (88-mi) pursuit to the west-southwest ended in final triumph when Lee was obliged to surrender to Grant at APPOMATTOX COURT HOUSE on Apr. 9, 1865. Grant's generous terms were accepted immediately by Lee.

Presidency. After the war, Grant was advanced to full general and served not only as general in chief but also, briefly, as interim secretary of war after President Andrew JOHNSON suspended Edwin M. STANTON in 1867. Grant's attempts to protect the army of occupation in the South deflected him from Johnson and toward the Radical Republicans with their more rigorous RECONSTRUCTION policies. This helped secure for him the Republican presidential nomination in 1868. In the election of that year he defeated the Democrat Horatio SEYMOUR and began an 8-year administration in the White House.

As president, Grant seemed at times torpid and irresolute, and many of his appointments left much to be desired. He had 25 men in his small cabinet in eight years. Despite campaign pledges for civil service reform, Grant was largely responsible for scuttling such a program. At first conciliatory toward the South, he pushed for the unconditional readmission of Virginia to the Union. He relentlessly opposed the KU KLUX KLAN, however, in which he was aided when Congress passed the so-called Force Acts of 1870–71.

Grant's hard-money stand delighted business and banking interests and helped him win reelection over Horace GREELEY in 1872. Although at first slow to react, he had been able in 1869 to block the attempts of Jay GOULD and James FISK to corner the gold market. However, his second term came under a cloud of graft, scandal, and corruption. The scandal that came closest to the White House itself was that of the WHISKEY RING, in which Grant's private secretary, Orville Babcock, was implicated. Grant's chief successes, due largely to his capable secretary of state, Hamilton Fish (see FISH family), were scored in the field of foreign affairs. They included favorable settlement of the ALABAMA CLAIMS dispute with Britain.

Later Years. After leaving office, Grant made a 2-year cruise. In 1880 he was unsuccessful in securing the Republican nomination for a third-term bid as president. Subsequently, he was exploited in business and failed. To get his family out of debt he undertook to write his memoirs. These were completed while he was dying of throat cancer and were published in two volumes as the *Personal Memoirs of U. S. Grant* (1885–86). Not only were they profitable, netting his family $450,000, but they also have become an American classic. Grant died at Mount McGregor, N.Y., on July 23, 1885, and his body was finally laid to rest in an imposing tomb on Riverside Drive in New York City. WARREN W. HASSLER, JR.

Bibliography: Badeau, Adam, *Military History of Ulysses S. Grant*, 3 vols. (1885); Barber, James G., *U. S. Grant: The Man and the Image* (1986); Catton, Bruce, *Grant Moves South* (1960) and *Grant Takes Command* (1969); Conger, Arthur L., *The Rise of U. S. Grant* (1931); Frassanito, William A., *Grant and Lee: The Virginia Campaigns, 1864–1865* (1983); Fuller, J. F. C., *The Generalship of Ulysses S. Grant* (1958); Goldhurst, Richard, *Many Are the Hearts: The Agony and Triumph of Ulysses S. Grant* (1975); Lewis, Lloyd, *Captain Sam Grant* (1950); McFeeley, William S., *Grant: A Biography* (1981); Pitkin, Thomas M., *The Captain Departs* (1973).

granulation, solar [gran'-yoo'-lay-shuhn]

The Sun is covered by a pattern of quasi-polygonal shapes called granules, which are columns of upward-moving gas with a bright interior 300° C (580° F) hotter than the darker surrounding background. Each has a lifetime of less than 10 minutes and is about 1,000 km (620 mi) across. The gas moves at about 0.5 km/sec (0.3 mi/sec). The entire pattern is in constant oscillatory motion, each granule moving up and down with a period of almost exactly 5 minutes. This pulsation may be the outer manifestation of pulses emerging from the depths of the solar interior. The granules seem to be part of more complex structures of rising and falling gas columns about 33,000 km (20,000 mi) across, called supergranules.

See also: SUNSPOTS.

Granville, John Carteret, 1st Earl: see CARTERET, JOHN, 1ST EARL OF GRANVILLE.

Granville-Barker, Harley [gran-vil-bar'-kur, har'-lee]

Harley Granville-Barker, b. London, Nov. 25, 1877, d. Aug. 31, 1946, was an English actor, dramatist, producer, and critic whose work invigorated English theater during the Edwardian period. As manager of London's Royal Court Theatre (1904–07), Granville-Barker developed a progressive repertoire that included many of the first English stage productions of George Bernard Shaw, Maurice Maeterlinck, Gerhart Hauptmann, and Henrik Ibsen. His productions of Shakespeare at the Savoy Theatre (1912–14) were noted for their simplicity of stage design and acting technique. Granville-Barker's own plays, including *The Voysey Inheritance* (1905), *Waste* (1907), and *The Madras House* (1910), though not greatly successful, supported the new realism in early 20th-century English drama. As a literary critic, he is best remembered for his six-volume work, *Prefaces to Shakespeare* (1927–47), which is still considered an important critical study of Shakespeare and Shakespearean theater. COLETTE BROOKS

Bibliography: Kennedy, Dennis, *Granville-Barker and the Dream of Theatre* (1985); Salenius, E. W., *Harley Granville-Barker* (1982).

grape

The grape is the fruit of vines of the genus *Vitis* of the family Vitaceae; the genera *Cissus* and *Rhoicissus* also belong to this family. Classified botanically as berries, domesticated grapes grow in clusters, range in color from pale green to black, and contain sugar in varying quantities. Grapes with about 20 percent sugar are used to make WINE. Other types are eaten fresh, dried as raisins, or canned. Unfermented grape juice is processed for drinking or for use in jellies. More than 90 percent of all cultivated grapes are varieties of *V. vinifera*, the Old World or European grape, which produces most of the world's wine. Originating in Anatolia, this species has been spread by humans into all temperate regions and recently into subtropical areas. At least 5,000 varieties of grapes have been derived from this species, although the most widely grown wine grapes are selected from perhaps 100 varieties.

Whereas European grapes derive exclusively from *V. vinifera*, native American grapes come from many wild species of *Vitis*. These grapes differ markedly from European types; they are characterized by their musky, or "foxy," odor and flavor,

Pictured here are two important varieties of the Old World wine grape, V. vinifera: *the white Pinot Chardonnay and the red Pinot Noir. Native American species, such as the Concord* (V. labrusca), *are generally less sweet and, unlike the wine grapes shown here, their skins slip readily from the pulp.*

and by the fact that, unlike *V. vinifera,* their skins slip from the fruit pulp.

Specimens of the European grape were brought by the Spanish into areas of present-day California and Mexico and by the English to settlements along the Atlantic seaboard. The latter plantings failed mainly because of climatic extremes; fungus diseases that thrive in the hot, humid summers; and the plant's susceptibility to root aphids *(Phylloxera)* that are less harmful to native American grapes. *Phylloxera* were accidentally introduced into Europe in the mid-19th century, almost completely destroying vineyards in France, Germany, and Italy. Most wine grapes in Europe and America are grown on vines grafted onto resistant rootstocks.

Derivations of American species or hybrids of American grapes and *V. vinifera* are cultivated throughout the United States. They fall into three broad categories: American cultivars, the most important of which are varieties with *V. labrusca* as one parent, including Catawba, Niagara, and Concord grapes, with Concord by far the most widely grown; the Muscadine cultivars, from the American *V. rotundifolia,* which includes scuppernong; and the group known as "French hybrids," crosses of *V. vinifera* and native American species grown in European vineyards for bulk wine production and in the eastern United States for winter hardiness.

California produces most of the table grapes grown in the United States, and it provides about 80 percent of the world's production of raisins. Other U.S. grape-producing states are New York, Washington, Michigan, Pennsylvania, Arizona, and Ohio.

In 1985 world grape production exceeded 62 billion metric tons (68.3 billion U.S. tons). Italy, France, Spain, the USSR, and Turkey were the largest contributors; the United States produced 7.5% of the total. ROBERT J. WEAVER

Bibliography: Weaver, Robert J., *Grape Growing* (1976); Winkler A. J., et al., *General Viticulture* (1962; rev. ed., 1974).

grape hyacinth [grayp hy'-uh-sinth]

Grape hyacinth, *Muscari,* is any of several spring-blooming bulbous plants that belong to the lily family, Liliaceae. *M. armeniacum* bears deep cobalt blue flowers. *M. azureum* blooms in very early spring with bright, azure blue flowers. The common grape hyacinth, *M. botryoides,* has blue flowers densely clustered at the end of the stem; it grows well in full sunlight or partial shade.

grapefruit

The grapefruit is an evergreen tree, *Citrus paradisi,* of the Rutaceae family, and its fruit is the largest of the commercially grown CITRUS FRUITS. A descendant of the pomelo—a citrus species that grows in Southeast Asia and was brought to the

The grapefruit tree, C. paradisi, *a member of the orange family, was so named because of the grapelike clusters in which its large fruit grows.*

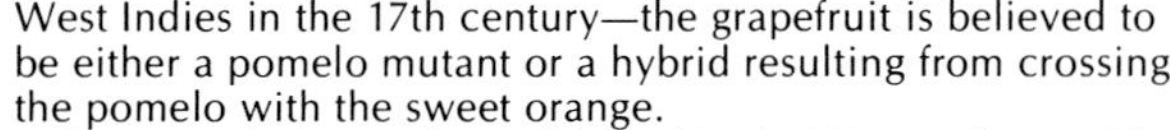

West Indies in the 17th century—the grapefruit is believed to be either a pomelo mutant or a hybrid resulting from crossing the pomelo with the sweet orange.

The grapefruit was first cultivated in the West Indies and introduced into the Florida area in the 1820s. Only in the 1900s, however, did the fruit become commercially significant, and among citrus fruits it now ranks fourth in the world in economic importance. World production reached more than 4 million metric tons (4.4 million U.S. tons) in 1985, with the United States producing 50 percent of the total, followed by Israel, Thailand, Costa Rica, China, and Argentina. About 2 million metric tons (2.2 million U.S. tons) were produced in the United States in 1985: 75 percent of the crop in Florida, and the remainder in Texas, California, and Arizona.

The globular fruit usually grows in clusters somewhat like bunches of grapes, although some grapefruit are borne singly. Mature grapefruits reach 8 to 15 cm (3 to 6 in) in diameter, with a pale yellow rind and pale yellow or yellow-pink pulp. Juice content ranges from 35 to 50 percent, with more acid and slightly less vitamin C than orange juice. More than half the U.S. production is processed into canned and frozen fruit or juice. Processing residues are used to produce peel oil, cattle feed, and various chemicals. WALTER REUTHER

Bibliography: Sinclair, Walton B., *The Grapefruit: Its Composition, Physiology, and Products* (1972); Wardowski, Wilfred F., et al., *Fresh Citrus Fruits* (1986).

Grapes of Wrath, The

The Grapes of Wrath (1939) by U.S. novelist John STEINBECK is one of the most powerful chronicles in American literature of the Depression of the 1930s. It deals with the Joads, a family that loses its farm through foreclosure and leaves the Oklahoma Dust Bowl for California in the hope of finding work. The eldest generation has the comfort of religion, the next one has a dogged perseverance, but the youngest has little to believe in. Embittered by the brutal exploitation of migrant workers, Tom, who had been jailed for murder and who later kills again, becomes a labor organizer. In this Pulitzer Prize-winning (1940) novel, Steinbeck alternates his narrative with serious discussion of the problems of migrant laborers.

CHARLOTTE D. SOLOMON

Bibliography: Donohue, Agnes M., ed., *A Casebook on "The Grapes of Wrath"* (1969); French, Warren, *John Steinbeck* (1961).

graph

A graph is a pictorial representation of numerical data. It is a diagram representing interrelationships between two, three, or more quantities by the use of a number of distinctive features such as points, lines, and bars. Types of graphs include HISTOGRAMS (bar graphs), circular (pie) graphs, and line graphs. A histogram consists of a series of bars or rectangles, the lengths of which are proportional to the data being presented. In a line graph the data are represented by points that are joined by straight-line segments. A "pie" graph presents data in the form of slices of a pie, with the size, or angle, of each slice proportional to the quantity it represents. A pictorial representation displays at a glance much of the quantitative behavior of the variables involved; at times graphs can be misleading, and care must be used in interpreting them. Branches of mathematics such as ANALYTIC GEOMETRY, STATISTICS, and TRIGONOMETRY deal with the study of various graphs.

The graph of an EQUATION in two variables is the set of points in a plane whose coordinates satisfy the equation. The graphic representation of an equation in three variables is a surface in space. For example, the graph of the equation $x^2 + y^2 = 1$ is a circle with the center at the origin; the graph of the equation $x^2 + y^2 + z^2 = 1$ is the surface of a sphere. The graph of an inequality is the set of all points whose coordinates satisfy the inequality; in two dimensions it is the region on one side of a plane. Inequality graphs are often used in economics and operations research.

The graph of an equation shows pictorially the relation of members of one group (independent variables) to members of

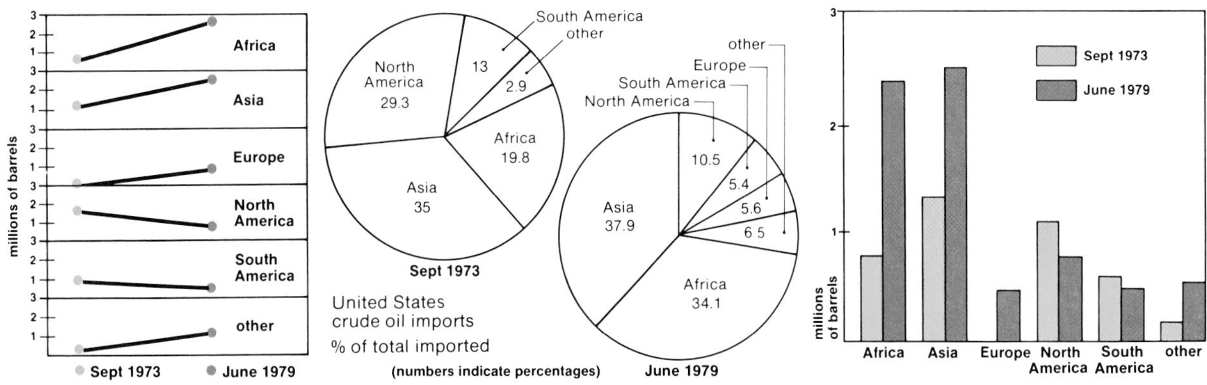

Bar, pie, and line graphs indicate amount of U.S. crude oil imports from various areas in September 1973 and June 1979.

another group (dependent variables). If a variable y is a FUNCTION of a variable x written as $y = f(x)$, then the graph of the function will represent the LOCUS of all points (x, y) that satisfy the relationship.

The graph of a function f from a set A to a set B is the set of all ordered pairs, x, $f(x)$, where x varies in the set A. Set A is the domain of the graph of f. The range of the graph is $f(A)$, and the graph of f is a subset of the Cartesian product of A and B (see SET THEORY). V. K. BALAKRISHNAN

Bibliography: Hackworth, Robert D., and Howland, Joseph, *Introductory College Mathematics* (1976); Ore, Oystein, *Theory of Graphs* (1983); Selby, Peter H., *Interpreting Graphs and Tables* (1976).

graphic arts

In a general sense, the term *graphic arts* includes all forms of artistic visual representation executed on a two-dimensional surface by such means as painting, drawing, or photography. More specifically, the term is a synonym for printmaking. In this application, the graphic arts include all works of art that begin with an original impression of any kind of imagery or design executed by the artist and intended to be reproduced by any one of a number of printing processes.

Among the many reproduction processes used by artists, those involving INTAGLIO techniques, where the design is cut into the surface of a metal plate or wood block, are among the most important. In ENGRAVING, the design is cut directly into the surface of a copper or zinc plate, using a tool called a burin, which leaves a minute shaving along both sides of the line it cuts. The shaving may be brushed away. Prints made from plates where the shavings have been deliberately created and left on the plate surface are called DRYPOINT engravings. They have a generally softer, more shaded line. In ETCHING, the plate is first covered with a "ground," usually a wax mixture, and the artist draws the design through the ground with etching needles of various sizes, exposing the metal underneath. The plate is then immersed in acid, and where the ground has been scratched away, the acid eats into the exposed metal, leaving the design etched below the plate surface.

The three processes—engraving, drypoint, and etching—are very often used together, and sometimes in conjunction with other intaglio processes. With AQUATINT, which is used to create greater tonal gradation or to add color, a layer of rosin is poured on the plate and then heated, so that the grains fuse to the surface. When immersed in acid, the metal between the grains is eaten away, forming tiny holes which print as a soft-toned background. The MEZZOTINT has even softer, more shaded qualities, produced by first pitting the entire plate surface with a "rocker," then scraping and burnishing where the design is to appear.

Woodblocks can also be carved with intaglio designs, although more commonly the blocks are carved in relief: that is, the design stands up from the surface of the block, all non-design areas having been cut away (see WOODCUTS AND WOOD ENGRAVING).

In lithography, an oily paint is used to draw on a smooth stone surface. An acid treatment leaves the design area capable of holding and printing ink. (See LITHOGRAPH.) The silk-screen printing process involves cutting the design out of fine silk stretched within a frame, and then squeezing paint through the open portions of the silk onto the surface to be printed (see SILK-SCREEN PRINTING).

Woodcut. The woodcut is the oldest form of printmaking. In the 2d century AD paper was developed in China, and wood blocks were used to create book illustrations. Japanese woodcuts achieved their greatest refinement in the masterful, multicolored 18th- and 19th-century *ukiyo-e* prints that depict landscapes and scenes of everyday life by such masters as HIROSHIGE, HOKUSAI, and UTAMARO (see also JAPANESE ART AND ARCHITECTURE).

The woodcut was developed as a pictorial art in Europe at the end of the 14th century, when the process was used to make simple religious pictures for mass distribution. They were executed by skilled craftsmen after original designs by painters and sculptors. With the mid-15th century invention of the printing press, woodcuts were used for BOOK ILLUSTRATIONS.

Among the first great European artists to use the woodcut were the German Renaissance masters Albrecht DÜRER and Hans HOLBEIN the Younger. Dürer's *Life of the Virgin* (1509–11) and Holbein's *Dance of Death* (1523–26) demonstrate refined technique and a combination of energy and solidity. The same period saw the development of woodcut *chiaroscuro,* which created contrasts of light and shade by using several blocks. Developed by Hans BURGKMAIR and Jobst de Negker, Albrecht ALTDORFER, Lucas CRANACH the Elder, and

Albrecht Dürer's minutely detailed engraving of a rhinoceros (1515) shows the naturalism characteristic of his work. Dürer, one of the most eminent German artists of the Renaissance, was especially known for his woodcuts and engravings. (British Museum, London.)

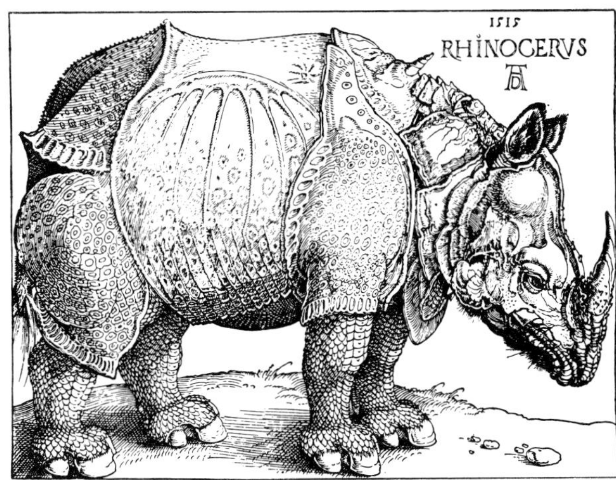

Hans BALDUNG-GRIEN also produced woodcuts. The first Italian chiaroscuro woodcut is credited to Ugo Da Carpi (*c.*1450–1525), who, like others of the time, worked from the designs of master painters such as Raphael.

Woodcut declined as a fine art after the mid-16th century, when it was replaced by line engraving and etching. During the late 19th century, however, it had its greatest revival, chiefly in the works of Frenchmen Paul GAUGUIN and Félix VALLOTTON and the Norwegian artist Edvard MUNCH. Unlike most previous woodcuts—which had been reproductions of the drawings of the masters by craftsmen—these were executed by the artists themselves. The symbolist Gauguin, mainly influenced by Japanese woodcuts and the primitive art of the South Seas, produced many of his greatest woodcuts in the South Pacific, for example, his *Offerings of Gratitude* (*c.*1891–93). Munch produced psychologically powerful, visionary colored woodcuts of rhythmic line, such as *The Kiss* (one version, 1902). He had great influence on the German expressionists, who, like Munch, closely followed the tradition of the German medieval woodcut. Members of Die BRÜCKE, such as Ernst KIRCHNER and Emil NOLDE, produced a large number of highly emotive woodcuts, which greatly expanded the potentials of the medium. The German graphic artist Käthe KOLLWITZ made black-and-white woodcuts depicting the lower classes in the German expressionist tradition.

(Left) Portrait of a Man *(1919), a woodcut by Erich Heckel, reflects the simple, linear composition characteristic of the medium. Multicolored woodcuts must be printed by as many blocks as there are colors in the print.*

(Below) *Martin Schongauer's* Temptation of St. Anthony *(c.1480–90) shows the kind of meticulous detail he was able to introduce into his engravings. One of the first artists to use a copperplate matrix, Schongauer contributed greatly to the development of intaglio printing. (Metropolitan Museum of Art, New York.)*

Related to the art of woodcut are Pablo PICASSO's linocuts (using linoleum blocks) of the 1950s, the wood engravings of American Leonard BASKIN, and the cellocuts (using plastic plates) developed by Boris Margo. New techniques and forms have kept woodcut a vital medium in contemporary art.

Engraving and Etching. The technique of engraving metal surfaces with pictorial designs dates back to classical antiquity and was practiced continually throughout the Middle Ages by such skilled craftsmen as goldsmiths and armorers. The engraved and enameled plaques of the Klosterneuburg (1181) by NICHOLAS OF VERDUN are a prime example of the highly developed sculptural style of metalwork that had evolved in the Meuse Valley since the Carolingian period.

The earliest datable engravings on paper are from about 1430 and show the influence of the Flemish master painters of the period. The German artist Martin SCHONGAUER was the first printmaker, who was also a painter, to gain international acclaim for his finely detailed, late Gothic engravings, including *Death of the Virgin* (*c.*1471; Metropolitan Museum of Art, New York City) and *Temptation of St. Anthony* (*c.*1480–90; Metropolitan Museum of Art). Also of the same period was the MASTER OF THE HOUSEBOOK, who in engravings such as *Holy Family* (*c.*1480–90) pioneered the technique known as drypoint to achieve prints of a sketchy spontaneity, which prefigure the work of Rembrandt. The outstanding engravers of late-15th-century Italy were Antonio Pollaiuolo (see POLLAIUOLO family) and Andrea MANTEGNA. Pollaiuolo's only surviving engraving, *Battle of Ten Naked Men* (*c.*1465–70; Metropolitan Museum of Art), exemplifies his achievement in the study of anatomy in movement. Mantegna's engraving *Battle of the Sea Gods* (*c.*1493) had great influence on the work of Albrecht Dürer. In such engravings as *Adam and Eve* (1504; Museum of Fine Arts, Boston), Dürer used classical subject matter to depict the ideal human proportions in the Renaissance manner. The etchings that he produced between about 1515 and 1518 are among the earliest important examples of the art, also practiced with great refinement by Altdorfer.

The greatest etcher of the 17th century, and perhaps the greatest in the entire history of art, was the Dutch master REMBRANDT van Rijn. His style of dramatic chiaroscuro—in rich, dark tones executed with a vigorous spontaneity—is exemplified in his almost 300 etchings of landscapes.

Another important 17th-century graphic artist was the innovative French printmaker Jacques CALLOT, who developed the hard-varnish ground technique. Callot is particularly noted for his skillful use of numerous elements within a small space, for example, his series the *Miseries of War* (1633).

During the 18th century outstanding etchings were produced by three Italian artists. A master of the decorative fresco, Giovanni Battista Tiepolo (see TIEPOLO family) was one of two Venetians of the period to produce etchings of great technical skill. The other is CANALETTO, a master draftsman who produced finely detailed, linear, and accurate scenes of Venetian architecture. The etcher and architect Giovanni Battista PIRANESI spent most of his life in Rome, where he engraved scenes of both the modern and ancient city with grandeur and accuracy and made imaginative reconstructions of Roman monuments. Also during the 18th century, the English painter William HOGARTH engraved a series of biting, satirical paintings—*The Harlot's Progress* (1732) and *The Rake's Progress* (1735).

(Below) *Rembrandt's etching* The Three Crosses *(c.1661) displays a fine control of line and light and a powerful evocation of atmosphere that make him one of the greatest masters of the graphic arts. (Rijksprentenkabinet, Amsterdam.)*

(Above) *"Can Nobody Liberate Us?" is one of Francisco Goya's series of 80 bitterly satirical etchings,* Los Caprichos *(1797–98), all but one executed on an aquatint ground. The aquatint technique uses a granular plate to create a solid background and produce a textured effect that simulates watercolor technique. (Rijksmuseum, Amsterdam.)*

During the late 18th and early 19th centuries, the great Spanish painter Francisco de GOYA produced several series of powerful black-and-white etchings of grotesque figures, which satirized the contemporary social situation, titled *Los caprichos* (1796–98), *The Disasters of War* (1810–14), *La tauromaquia* (The Bullfight; 1815–16), and *Los proverbios* (*c.*1813–18). Goya's neobaroque style of great individual visionary strength was derived from those of Diego VELÁZQUEZ and Rembrandt, using techniques learned from Tiepolo.

Among the outstanding mid-19th-century etchers was the French artist Charles MERYON, whose works combined architectural settings of structural clarity and grotesque figures. His most famous series is the 22 etchings of the old section of Paris, *Eaux-Fortes sur Paris* (1850–54).

More than 400 plates remain of the etchings of James McNeill WHISTLER, who was perhaps the most innovative of the graphic artists during the late 19th century. His delicate, summary impressions exemplify his technical mastery of the medium and his great contribution to modernist abstraction.

James ENSOR and Edvard Munch are among the many artists to use etching as part of their oeuvres during the early 20th century. The etchings of Paul KLEE are also of particular importance. A major part of his multimedia work, Klee's etchings are rich in technique and texture and combine abstraction with fantastic images of great wit and originality. The graphic designs of M. C. ESCHER are especially notable for their creation of unusual perspectives and optical illusions and for their exploration of the theme of metamorphosis.

Related to the history of etching is the inventive exploration of new intaglio techniques by Stanley William HAYTER's Atelier 17 in pre-World War II Paris, in New York City during the 1940s, and in Paris during the 1950s and '60s.

Lithography. The earliest lithographic process was developed (1796–98) by the German playwright Aloys SENEFELDER, whose main objective was the inexpensive duplication of his works. His partners, Philipp and Johann André, introduced the technique in England, where linear works on the lithographic stone were done by William BLAKE, Henry FUSELI, and Benjamin WEST. The ability of lithography to reproduce a more expressive line was used to its best advantage in the 19th century by the French, first by Théodore GÉRICAULT and Eugène DELACROIX and later by Honoré DAUMIER. Daumier produced about 4,000 lithographs; boldly personal caricatures of the lower and middle classes, they were influenced by Rembrandt and grew out of Daumier's early political cartoons. These caricatures were reproduced in Paris periodicals, *Le Charivari* and *La Caricature*. The celebrated posters of Henri de TOULOUSE-LAUTREC are among the finest examples of 19th-century French lithography. Lautrec's lithographs—like some of the finest works of Pierre BONNARD, Edgar DEGAS, Édouard MANET, and Edouard VUILLARD—are highly colored works, greatly influenced by Japanese prints. Also of note in the late 19th century are Odilon REDON's symbolist lithographs, such as his series dedicated to Edgar Allan Poe (1882).

Early-20th-century accomplishments in lithography include those by the German expressionists Karl SCHMIDT-ROTTLUFF,

In works such as Marcelle Lender *(1895) Henri de Toulouse-Lautrec exploited the possibilities of color lithography, elevating a commercial printing technique to an art form. In the lithographic process, a design executed in greasy crayon is transferred from a stone or other flat surface to the paper. (Musée Toulouse-Lautrec, Albi, France.)*

Andy Warhol's screen-printed Flowers *(1964) shows how much fine detail is possible in modern methods of silk screening. Originally a commercial process, silk screening, printing from a stencil and mesh screen, permits numerous duplications. (Private collection.)*

Emil Nolde, and Ernst Kirchner (all members of Die Brücke) and by Käthe Kollwitz. Related to these are the works by Edvard Munch and Austrian artist Oskar KOKOSCHKA.

In the United States CURRIER AND IVES and Joseph PENNELL are outstanding in the area of 19th-century lithography, followed by such 20th-century artists as Arthur B. DAVIES and George BELLOWS. The lithographic process has been widely used in recent years to record body prints, for example Kenneth J. Butler's *Cherrie V* (1968), a work influenced by Robert RAUSCHENBERG's earlier use of this technique. The lithograph has also been widely used by other New York painters of the 1960s, including Jasper JOHNS in works such as *Light Bulb* (1966) and James ROSENQUIST.

Silk-Screen Printing. The technique of silk-screen printing originated during the Middle Ages in the art of stencil printing of China and Japan, where it was practiced with great delicacy and intricacy. Until the 20th century, screen printing was a decorative and commercial medium, used to enhance fabrics, wallpaper, furnishings, and advertising.

In 1936 screen printing was seen as a means of artistic expression by a group of American artists working on the Works Progress Administration (WPA) under the leadership of Anthony Velonis. The art historian Carl Zigrosser coined the term *serigraph* to identify the new screen prints as a fine art.

Op artists of the 1960s, such as Richard ANUSZKIEWICZ and Victor de VASARELY, have used silk-screen printing in their style of precise form and color. The two most important artists of the 1960s to use silk-screen printing as a major medium in their art were Robert Rauschenberg and Andy WARHOL, both of whom used screen printing in combination with photographic processes to achieve significant works of contemporary art. BARBARA CAVALIERE

Bibliography: Blanchard, R. W., *Graphic Design* (1984); Brunner, F., *A Handbook of Graphic Reproduction Processes* (1986); Castleman, R., *Prints of the 20th Century* (1976); Carter, D. E., *Evolution of Design* (1985); Eichenberg, F., *The Art of the Print* (1976); Graham, Jacqui, *Studio Secrets for the Graphic Artist* (1986); Hind, A. M., *A History of Engraving and Etching from the 15th Century to 1914* (1923; repr. 1963), and *An Introduction to the History of Woodcut,* 2 vols. (1935; repr. 1963); Horn, M., *Contemporary Graphic Artists,* 2 vols. (1986); Meggs, P. B., *History of Graphic Design* (1983); Narazaki, M., *The Japanese Print* (1966); Roger-Marx, C., *Graphic Art of the 19th Century* (1962); Sotriffer, K., *Printmaking: History and Technique* (1968); Weber, W., *A History of Lithography* (1964); Zigrosser, C., *The Book of Fine Prints* (1956).

See also: BLOCK PRINTING; PRINTING.

graphite: see CARBON.

graptolite [grap'-tuh-lyt]

Graptolites are the remains of extinct, colonial invertebrate animals that inhabited a number of marine habitats and were especially abundant during the early Paleozoic Era. The most commonly found graptolites superficially resemble small hacksaw blades impressed in rock. Others appear as small, bushy structures pressed onto the rock matrix. Those resembling hacksaw blades are commonly about 15 to 44 mm (½ to 1½ in) long; the smallest of the bushlike structures are about 25 mm (1 in) across; larger ones are several centimeters across.

The floating graptolites have been useful in correlating stratigraphic units because they have wide geographic distribution. Since the floating graptolite colonies changed shape rapidly, they are also particularly valuable as indicators of geologic time. Graptolites are among the few fossils that may be preserved in metamorphic rocks and thus can be used to date terrains of otherwise undatable rock.

Graptolites lived from the middle of the Cambrian Period into the Carboniferous, some 200 million years. The longest-lived graptolites were those which had bushy growth habits resembling those of seaweed and lived attached to shallow-shelf sea bottoms.

Species that had a planktonic life habit are the most widely distributed; they have been found in rocks ranging from Early Ordovician to Early Devonian times (about 500 to 390 million years old). Most of them floated in waters over the outer parts of continental shelves, but some lived in shallower seas or in the surface waters of the deep oceans. Most of the latter are found in dark shales rich in organic matter deposited in oxygen-poor environments. The biological relationships of graptolites are uncertain. They most closely resemble shells of the modern rhabdopleurans, tiny colonial marine animals belonging to the phylum Hemichordata. WILLIAM B. N. BERRY

Bibliography: Bulman, O. M. B., *Graptolina,* Part V of *Treatise on Invertebrate Paleontology,* 2d ed. by Curt Teichert (1970); Dyer, J. and Schram, F., *A Manual of Invertebrate Paleontology* (1983); Tasch, P., *Paleobiology of the Invertebrates,* 2d ed. (1980).

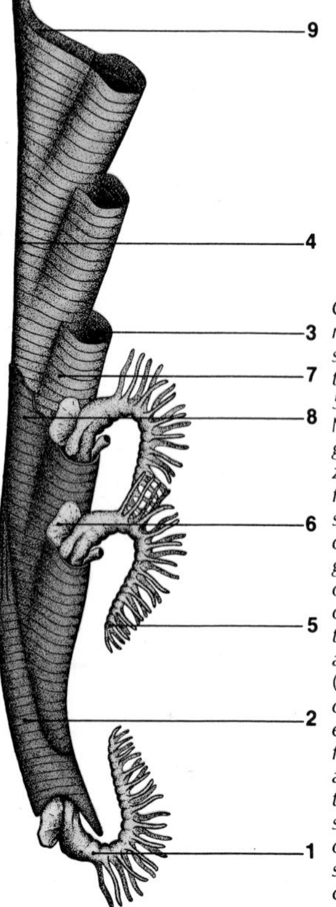

Graptolites were common, small, marine animals that lived in slender, threadlike colonies in all the oceans of the world 390 to 500 million years ago. In a typical Monograptus *colony of graptolites, the first animal, or zooid* (1), *formed a conical, fibrous, protein skeleton, or sicula* (2), *that opened downward. Subsequent zooids grew from the side of the original, budding off from each other to form a series of cups, or thecae* (3). *These cups grew along a threadlike tube, or nema* (4), *that extended from the end of the sicula and ran through the entire colony. Each zooid had a feeding organ, or lophophore* (5), *and a disk* (6), *which secreted the growth bands of an inner shell layer* (7). *The skeleton's outer layer* (8) *probably was secreted by an external skin. A canal* (9) *connected the thecae.*

grass

Grasses, family Gramineae, are the most variable, widespread, and useful plant groups and comprise over 600 genera and 7,500 species. The soft, velvety turf plants that form lawns bear little resemblance to the huge, woody bamboos towering 40 m (132 ft) or more in height. Submerged aquatic plants growing on the sea seem quite different from the small, tender shoots emerging from a snowbank in the alpine tundra above timberline. Yet all these may be grasses.

To the average urban dweller, grass may mean only the green carpet covering a lawn or courtyard. To a farmer in the Great Plains, on the other hand, grass cereal grains such as wheat may be the major cash crop. Grasses produce the bulk of forage for the world's livestock industry, and they provide building materials for houses in tropical areas.

Grasses grow on all continents. They are found in the sea, in freshwater marshes, in deserts, above the treeline on high mountains, and in arctic areas. In some regions grasses constitute the dominant vegetation type. As a group, grasses are among the most successful and actively evolving of all plants. Their great flexibility and adaptability permit them to live in most situations. Their adaptive radiation has evolved treelike forms, intermediate tufts that compete with understory in forests and savanna, and horizontally spreading perennials that form either dense sod or loose ground cover.

STRUCTURE

Stems. The grass plant is composed of stems, leaves, roots, and fruiting structures. Stems of grasses have two parts: nodes and internodes. The node is a joint in the stem at the place where leaves are attached. The internode, or area between where leaves are attached, may be either pithy, hollow, or solid. The erect stem of a grass is called a culm. Lateral shoots immediately above the ground may produce creeping prostrate stems called stolons. Stoloniferous grasses may reproduce asexually by stolons growing into new territory and establishing roots at the nodes.

Lateral buds immediately below the ground may produce subterranean stems called rhizomes. Rhizomes are a major source of asexual reproduction and allow a plant to persist even under heavy defoliation. Lateral shoots of cultivated grasses may be called tillers (usually in wheat, oats, and other cereals) or suckers (in maize and sorghum).

Most perennial grasses have herbaceous culms that die back each year and are replaced by new shoots. The resulting colony of individual grass shoots is often called a "plant" or a clone. The clone grows from the center outward, with the older plants in the center becoming weakened from competition. In extreme cases the "plant" may actually develop into a ring of healthy plants with a dead open center. Not all perennial grasses die back each year; some have developed a woody stem that stores nutrients, and the grass behaves much like a woody shrub. Bamboos are the most common woody grasses.

Leaves. The leaves of grasses are two-ranked, a characteristic that separates them from other families that they closely resemble, such as sedges (*Cyperaceae*) with three-ranked leaves. The grass blade itself consists of a sheath and a blade, or lamina. The sheath, the lower portion of the leaf, tightly enfolds the culm from its attachment at the node almost to the next node. The blade is the flattened, elongated portion of the leaf that extends away from the culm. A membranous or hairy structure on the leaf at the side toward the axis where the sheath and blade come together is called a ligule. Lateral projections at the base of the leaf or the apex of the sheath are auricles. Photosynthesis and respiration are carried out in both the sheath and the blade. The growing point of the new shoot, the apical meristem, is usually enclosed by several older leaves that give the new shoot some protection from the extremes of a harsh environment.

Roots. Most grass roots are fibrous. When the seed first sprouts it produces primary, or seminal, roots. These roots are usually of little importance after the first few weeks. Early in the development of the grass plant, adventitious roots (roots growing from stems or leaves) are produced at the lower nodes of the shoot. The root systems of most native grass plants are almost entirely adventitious. The size of the root system is usually related to the amount of shoot growth. Plants with large root-to-shoot ratios appear to be more drought-tolerant than those with smaller ratios.

Fruiting Structures. The flowering and fruiting structure of a grass is called the inflorescence. Its basic unit is the spikelet, which may contain one or more flowers, or florets, on a shortened stem axis, or rachilla, enclosed by two flora, or "empty," bracts called glumes.

There are three basic types of inflorescences: spikes, racemes, and panicles. A spike is an inflorescence in which all spikelets are attached directly to the main axis. Wheat and rye are good examples of this type. In a raceme, the florets are borne on short flower stalks, or pedicels, on the major axis; barley is an example. When the flower stalk branches, as in oats, it is called a panicle. Grasses have wind-pollinated flowers. The grass fruit varies greatly in size, from the very small grains of *Sporobolus* and *Muhlenbergia* to common grains of corn, wheat, and rice. Regardless of size, all have a high percentage of stored nutrients, making them attractive to insects, birds, and mammals.

Some species of grass produce large amounts of highly fertile seeds that can quickly colonize disturbed areas. Other species rely on rhizomes or stolons to move the plants into new environments. This wide variation in grasses has resulted in many uses.

USES

Human Consumption. Grass seeds have a large quantity of nutrients stored in them that allow new shoots and roots to develop quickly upon germination. These large, nutritious seeds are ideally suited as food for animals and human beings alike. Grass seed, or GRAIN, is grown on about three-fourths of the world's arable land. Three species of cereal grass—wheat, rice, and maize—form the basis of the staple human food for most of the world.

Wheat (*Triticum aestivum*) is a grass of temperate origin, ideally suited to the cooler climates of the world. Although it probably originated in Europe, where many wild varieties occur, it was widely cultivated as early as 3000 BC in both Europe and Asia. Many specialized varieties have been developed through controlled breeding for bread, cereal foods, and animal feed, so that today it is not only a major food but an important trade item in world commerce.

Rice (*Oryza sativa*) is a grass of tropical origin whose grain probably feeds more people than any other plant. Although rice is one of the oldest cultivated plants, production changed little for centuries. Then new varieties were developed by the International Rice Research Institute in the Philippines, and yields have been dramatically increased.

Maize (*Zea mays*) probably originated in Mexico from tropical grasses. It was not known in Europe before Columbus's voyages to the New World. Now maize, or corn (as it is known in the United States), is a major crop on all continents. Yields have been increased dramatically following the development of hybrids and controlled breeding programs. Today hundreds of varieties are available. Some are bred especially for grain production, some as a table vegetable, some for popcorn, and others for silage or forage production. Recent development of a corn that is rich in the amino acid lysine offers the promise of a complete human food available in a single crop, maize.

Other cool-season cereal grasses such as oats (*Avena sativa*), rye (*Secale cereale*), and barley (*Hordeum vulgare*) are important grain crops in temperate regions of the world. Tropical cereals such as sorghum (*Sorghum bicolor*) and pearl millet (*Pennisetum americanum*) form the basis of human diets in much of Africa and other tropical areas.

Sugarcane (*Saccharum officinarum*) produces much of the world's refined molasses and sugar. It is cultivated in tropical areas throughout the world. The high production levels possible, combined with the large amount of tropical land suitable for sugarcane production, make the regulation of sugar production a topic for discussion in international trade.

Animal Feed. Although grasses produce a large part of the

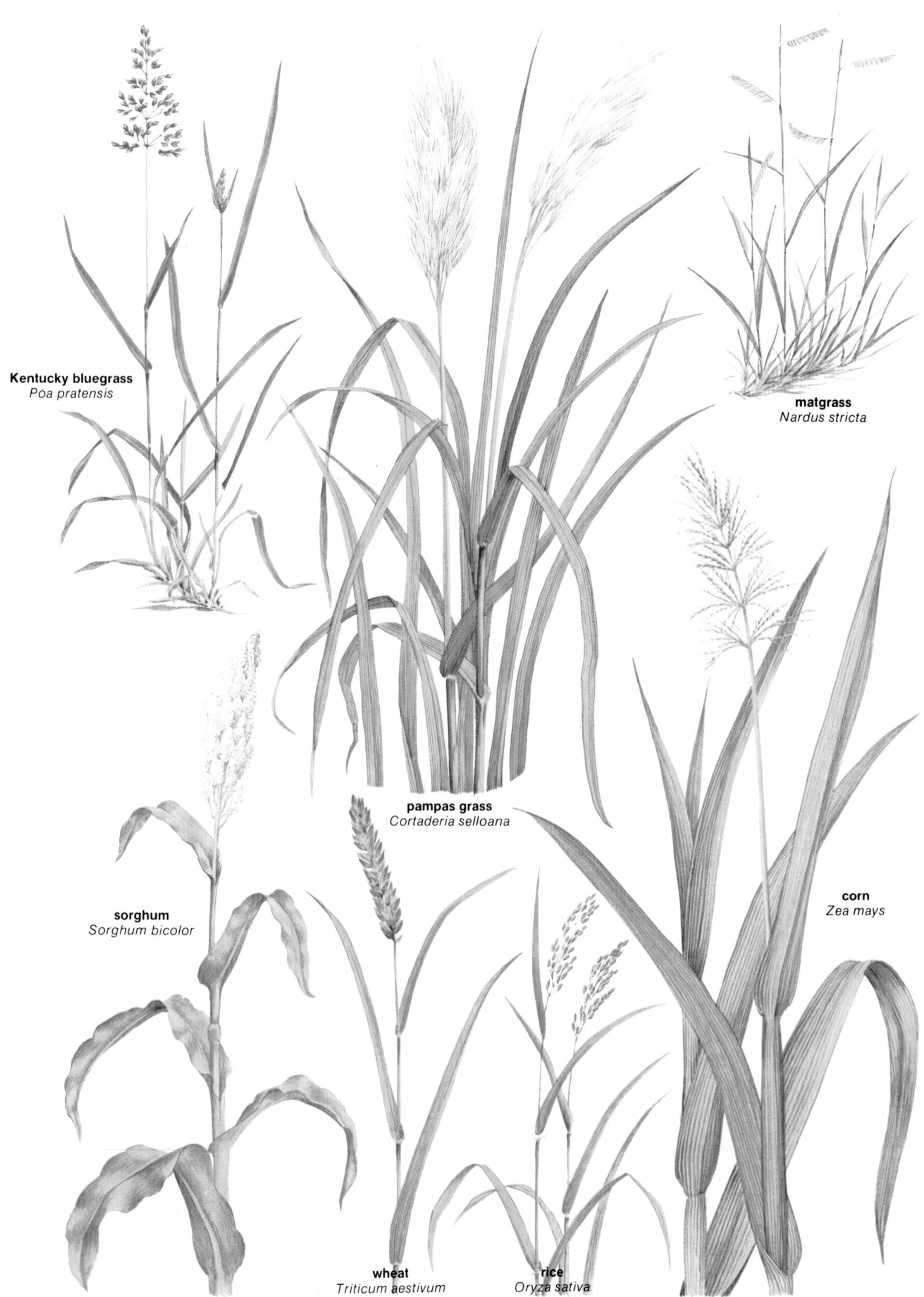
Kentucky bluegrass
Poa pratensis
matgrass
Nardus stricta
pampas grass
Cortaderia selloana
corn
Zea mays
sorghum
Sorghum bicolor
wheat
Triticum aestivum
rice
Oryza sativa

(Opposite page) *Some of the better-known grasses are economically important plants and are a rich source of food and forage. The grasses, constituting the family Graminae, include such major crops as wheat, rice, and corn. Grasses are also the basic diet of many farm animals and provide needed ground cover.*

world's diet, only relatively small amounts are consumed directly by humans. Most grasses are used as animal feed. While animals are fed some grain, the bulk of animal feed comes from specialized varieties of grass that are not very palatable to human beings. In addition, grass varieties such as sorghum and maize are raised as fodder crops. Several tons per hectare of palatable forage can be produced, stored, and used at a later date.

By far the largest amount of grass is consumed by grazing animals. Thoughout history grasses and grazing animals have coevolved. In North America the fossil remains of the earliest known member of the horse family are found to have been present in the Eocene Epoch (154–38 million years ago), causing some scientists to theorize that grasses probably existed before that time, and grasslands apparently became abundant by the Miocene Epoch (26–12 million years ago). When the first Europeans arrived, the North American grasslands were stocked with bison, elk, and other grazing animals. Australia and New Zealand are the only major grassland areas that do not have a recent history of grazing by wild ruminant animals, but Australia does have wild grazing marsupials such as kangaroos. Grassland and savanna areas still provide feed for wild game herds in Africa, North America, and elsewhere.

Native grasses provide a major source of feed for domestic livestock on all continents. The nomadic herd-keepers of Africa, station operators in outback Australia, dairy farmers in Norway, and ranchers in Nevada all depend on grass for their animal production. The species of grass growing in each area varies, but a sustained yield of products from these lands depends upon the application of the rules of ecology to perpetuate healthy populations of both plants and animals. The science of managing plants while observing ecological principles is called range management. Almost 30 percent of the Earth's land surface is grazed by animals: grazing is the most widespread of all land uses.

Some grasses are grown under cultivation and grazed by animals. These cultivated pastures are managed as farms. In cool temperate areas species of *Poa* (bluegrass), *Festuca, Phleum* (timothy), and *Dactylis* (orchard grass) are the most common forage plants. In tropical climates *Sorghum, Paspalum, Panicum,* and *Cynodon* are more important. Selective breeding has developed improved varieties and cultivars of most of the common species of forage grasses. In some species, such as Bermuda grass (*Cynodon dactylon*), hybrids have been developed that give much higher yields than the parent species.

Turf. Turf for aesthetic and recreation purposes is a major use of grass. Most lawns are of grass. The cool regions of the world regularly use plants of the genera *Poa* and *Agrostis* for turf. Kentucky bluegrass (*Poa pratensis*) is by far the most widely used lawn grass in the northern United States. Creeping bent grass (*Agrostis palustris*) is also used, but it is more popular for golf greens and specialty turfs than for home lawns. Bermuda grass is the popular lawn in much of the warm temperate to tropical areas. In hot areas, Saint Augustine grass (*Stenotaphrum secundatum*) is a popular grass, but because of its coarse leaves and high water use it has not challenged the finer-leafed varieties in areas where they can be grown. Other turf species include *Zoysia*, centipede grass (*Eremochloa ophiuroides*), and Bahia grass (*Paspalum notatum*) in warm areas and fescues (*Festuca*) and ryegrass (*Lolium*) in cool areas. Some native sod-forming grasses such as buffalo grass (*Buchloë dactyloides*) and curly mesquite grass (*Hilaria belangeri*) are used as minimum maintenance turfs in the drier portions of the U.S. Great Plains.

Other Uses. There are many nonfood or nonfeed uses of grasses. Grass skirts are used in the South Pacific Islands, and grass huts in many tropical regions. Other grasses, particularly bamboos, are used in construction and industry. Houses, bridges, and boat masts are sometimes constructed from the poles and posts of large bamboos. Furniture, window shades, mats and floor coverings, water pipes, and cooking utensils made from grass are found in homes throughout the world. In addition, recreational equipment such as fishing poles, musical instruments, toys, and pipes have been made of grass. The grass plant has evolved to fill many human uses, and its widespread abundance in many forms will continue to contribute to civilization.

GRASSES AS WEEDS

Grasses that invade new habitats and spread rapidly may become unwanted plants, or weeds. Crabgrass (*Digitaria sanguinalis, D. adscendens*) is a major weed in lawns and gardens throughout temperate areas. Quack grass (*Agropyron repens*), native to Europe, has become a major weed throughout temperate areas.

Many of the annual grasses become weeds on overgrazed rangeland. Cheatgrass (*Bromus tectorum*) is an aggressive annual from the European area that has invaded the dry ranges of the western United States wherever fire or heavy grazing has left the soil bare. Other introduced annual grasses may be locally important.

Grasses fill many ecological niches throughout the world. As humans create new niches, it is probable that grasses—either brought from other parts of the world or bred specifically for new conditions—will fill them. THADIS W. BOX

Bibliography: Bews, John W., *The World's Grasses: Their Differentiation, Distribution, Economics* (1977); Emmons, Robert D., *Turfgrass Science and Management* (1984); Gould, Frank W., and Shaw, Robert B., *Grass Systematics,* 2d ed. (1983); Hitchcock, A. S., *Manual of Grasses of the United States,* 2d ed. rev. by Agnes Chase (1950; repr. 1971); Langer, R. H., *How Grasses Grow,* 2d ed. (1979).

See also: GRASSLANDS; individual articles on grass species.

Grass, Günter [grahs, gun'-tur]

Günter Grass, here addressing a political rally, is considered one of the foremost literary figures of postwar Germany. His strong commitment to political ideals is manifested in satiric, Rabelaisian novels and plays. The Tin Drum *(1959) and* The Flounder *(1977) are among his most acclaimed works.*

Günter Wilhelm Grass, b. Danzig, Oct. 16, 1927, Germany's prominent contemporary writer, has been called the conscience of his country's postwar generation. Drafted into the Labor Service toward the end of World War II, he was wounded and taken prisoner in 1945. After the war he moved (1947) to Düsseldorf where he studied sculpture and painting, supporting himself as an apprentice stonecutter and jazz drummer. In 1953, Grass settled in Berlin, where he has since devoted himself to writing, the graphic arts, and, increasingly, to socialist politics. As a committed artist and antifascist, he said that "to be engaged is to act." Grass's strong moral convictions are never far beneath the biting irony and grotesque satire of his works.

Grass has written novels, poetry and plays. His first novel, *The Tin Drum* (1959; Eng. trans., 1962; film, 1980), for which he earned the 1958 prize of the GRUPPE 47, brought him immediate worldwide recognition. An epic work, the novel is characterized by a bawdy exuberance, its author delighting in the ribald parody of a variety of literary styles and traditions. Grass's complex and self-contradictory narrator, the dwarf drummer Oskar, is an amoral, picaresque hero who narrates the events of the war and postwar eras through a distorted and exaggerated perspective. *Cat and Mouse* (1961; Eng. trans., 1963) and *Dog Years* (1963; Eng. trans., 1965) have many characteristics in common with the earlier work and, like it, are set in Danzig. Together, the three novels are referred to as the Danzig Trilogy. Grass's poetry has been translated in *Selected Poems* (1966) and *In the Egg and Other Poems* (1977).

Grass's dramatic works reveal the influence of the theater of the absurd and the epic theater of Bertolt Brecht. The grotesque is dominant in *Mister, Mister* (1957; Eng. trans., 1967), *Only Ten Minutes to Buffalo* (1959; Eng. trans., 1967), and *The Wicked Cooks* (1957; Eng. trans., 1967). In *Flood* (1957; Eng. trans., 1967), Grass depicts the varied reactions and decisions of representatives of two generations as they watch the floodwaters rise around them—a symbolic enactment of the dilemma of postwar Germany.

In his most controversial play, *The Plebeians Rehearse the Uprising: A German Tragedy* (1965; Eng. trans., 1967), Grass points an ironically critical finger at Bertolt Brecht. The play concerns the role of the committed artist vis-à-vis society, a question that has continually preoccupied Grass and that led in the 1960s to his direct participation in the political process in support of leftist politician Willy Brandt.

Grass's political activities and his sense of commitment inform his later works as well. *From the Diary of a Snail* (1972; Eng. trans., 1978) is a fictionalized account of his involvement with Brandt's 1969 campaign. *The Flounder* (1977; Eng. trans., 1978) is simultaneously novel, fairy tale, diary, political commentary, and a history of women's emancipation. The satire *Headbirths; or, The Germans Are Dying Out* (1980; Eng. trans., 1983), the historical novel *The Meeting at Telgte* (1979; Eng. trans., 1981), and the apocalyptic fiction *The Rat* (1986; Eng. trans., 1987) all contribute to Grass's vision of a world that, because it is not better, is inevitably going to be worse.

MARILYN SIBLEY FREIS

Bibliography: Hayman, Ronald, *Günter Grass* (1985); Lawson, Richard H., *Günter Grass* (1984); O'Neill, Patrick, ed., *Critical Essays on Günter Grass* (1987); Reddick, J., *The "Danzig Trilogy" of Günter Grass* (1974).

grass finch

Grass finches are small, colorful, finchlike birds that constitute the tribe Erythurini, including the genus *Poephila*, of the family Estrildidae. Native to Australia and New Guinea, most grass finches inhabit grasslands or other relatively open areas and feed on insects and small seeds. They are hardy in captivity, and include such popular pets as the Gouldian finch, the zebra finch, the long-tailed grass finch, and the red-tailed grass finch.

ROBERT J. RAIKOW

grass tree

Grass tree is the common name for the Australian genus *Xanthorrhoea* in the lily family, Liliaceae. The genus contains about 12 species of woody plants whose stems, or trunks, increase in diameter, palmlike, by the addition of old leaf bases. Grass trees grow to a height of about 4.5 m (15 ft) and bear long, narrow leaves in a tuft at the top of the trunk. White flowers are produced in a dense spike above the leaves. The plants yield acaroid resins, which are used in varnish and as a paper sizing.

OLIN S. FEARING

Grasse, François Joseph Paul, Comte de
[grahs]

The comte de Grasse, b. Sept. 13, 1722, d. Jan. 14, 1788, was a French naval officer who commanded the French Atlantic fleet during the AMERICAN REVOLUTION. He won a series of battles against British Caribbean fleets in 1781 before going north to ensure the Franco-American victory against Charles CORNWALLIS in the YORKTOWN CAMPAIGN by turning back a British relief fleet in the Battle of Chesapeake Bay (Sept. 5–9, 1781). Resuming Caribbean duties, de Grasse was soundly defeated and captured by the British in 1782. After his release he was court-martialed in 1784; although acquitted, he did not recover his command.

A. LLOYD MOOTE

Bibliography: Lewis, Charles Lee, *Admiral de Grasse and American Independence* (1945; repr. 1980).

grasshopper

A grasshopper has large compound eyes, leathery forewings that protect its veined, membranous hind wings, and long, powerful hind legs used for jumping. Its coloration enables the grasshopper to blend into its habitat, mainly bushes and grass.

Grasshoppers are members of two different superfamilies in the order Orthoptera characterized by long, slender bodies, hind legs specialized for jumping, chewing mouthparts, and production of sound, or singing, typically only in the males. When four wings are present, the front pair, called tegmina (singular, tegmen), are usually somewhat thickened, long, and slender. The hind wings are wide and membranous.

One superfamily is the Acridoidea, or short-horned grasshoppers, which include the LOCUSTS. These are characterized by antennae shorter than the body and by ears (tympana) set in the abdominal wall. The male's song is generally produced by rubbing a row of stubby comblike teeth on the inside of the hind leg against a hardened edge on the front wing. One group, however, the band-winged grasshoppers (Oedipodinae), sings by snapping the hind wings while in flight. The second superfamily is the Tettigonioidea, the long-horned grasshoppers (KATYDIDS), which have antennae longer than the body, the ears in the front legs, and a bladelike extension (ovipositor) of the female's abdomen. In this group, the males sing by rubbing a scraper on the base of one front wing against a filelike ridge on the underside of the other front wing.

A female short-horned grasshopper lays her eggs in the soil, a few dozen at a time, and embeds them in froth as an egg pod. Waterlogging is fatal to the eggs, but the embryos have to take in some water or their development stops. The newly hatched larva is wormlike and inches its way to the soil surface where it quickly molts to become a hopper. It then passes through approximately five or six larval, or nymph, stages and becomes progressively more like the adult, which is readily distinguished only by the complete wings and genitalia. Growth continues for some time in the adult stage, especially in the exoskeleton and muscles, before sexual maturation begins. Mating occurs with the male riding the female and curling his abdomen tip beneath hers to insert the spermatophore, a specially secreted package containing the sperm. One such insemination suffices to fertilize all the eggs the female will lay in her lifetime, which may total more than a thousand but usually much less.

Development may be suspended in any stage of the life history, for weeks or months, in unfavorable seasons. The egg stage usually continues through cold winters, and in continental climates the eggs may remain dormant from the start of the hot, dry season until the following spring. Where winters are milder, hibernation occurs in the hopper or adult stage. In the dry tropics the adults remain sexually immature through the dry season, and sexual development proceeds only when, or just before, the rains come. Night migrations by winged adults to extend their geographical range is another way many grasshoppers escape unfavorable conditions and gain access to favorable ones. They have been sighted by radar taking off in enormous numbers as night falls and flying with the wind at altitudes up to one thousand meters. They may travel hundreds of kilometers in a few days.

The key to the life history, ecology, pest status, and geographical distribution of short-horned grasshoppers lies in their requirement of a variety of environments for the different stages of their life cycle. Their eggs are laid in ground that is largely without vegetation, and bare patches are also used during active stages (hopper and adult) for basking. Hoppers and adults also need vegetation for food and shelter, however. Thus, suitable grasshopper habitats consist of a vegetal mosaic that gives both uniform plantcover and bare ground.

Short-horned grasshoppers have adapted to a great range of habitats, but the great majority of species are largely *xerophilous,* inhabiting the arid and semiarid regions of the world. They are therefore favored, and some of them are liable to become pests, when forest or bush is cleared for human cultivation and when grasslands are overgrazed. Among the thousands of species only a few are pests, but these can cause severe damage to field crops and pastures throughout the temperate and tropical zones. The most notorious of these pests are the swarming locusts, but the damage done by the less conspicuous nonswarming grasshoppers is more insidious and, in the long run, much greater. J. S. KENNEDY

Bibliography: Richards, O. W., and Davies, R. G., *Imms' General Textbook of Entomology,* 10th ed., 2 vols. (1977); Uvarov, B. P., *Grasshoppers and Locusts. A Handbook of General Acridology,* 2 vols. (1966–77).

grasslands

Grasslands, a major world BIOME of Earth, are characterized by the dominance of grasses, the smooth cover they provide, and the monotony of flat to rolling terrain. Trees and shrubs occur as scattered individuals or are concentrated along streams or in low areas. Resident wildlife must be adapted to distinct wet and dry seasons, temperature extremes, drying winds, and prolonged droughts. With decreased rainfall deserts form; with increased annual rainfall forests and savannas form. Grasslands are usually found in the interior areas of continents. They occupy a high percentage of the total land surface area.

Environment. The fluctuating environment ensures that grasslands change in the abundance and distribution of wildlife. Plants become dormant in the dry seasons or develop extensive root systems that can tap water at greater depths. With drought, the grass cover, flowering, and seed production decline, and drought-tolerant plants spread; most animals migrate in search of food and water. With rainfall recovery is rapid, as the dormant plants resume growth and animals have more food available.

Periodic fires commonly spread across grasslands and play an important role in the maintenance and character of these ecosystems. Most growing parts of the grasses are below ground and survive the fires. Shrubs, trees, and herbs are eliminated temporarily, and browsing animals must look elsewhere for food. Release of nutrients by burning stimulates grass growth, and animals dependent upon grass for food and cover increase in number and diversity.

Life below the soil surface is essential to grassland survival. Of the total living plant matter in a grassland, one-half or more may be produced below ground as underground stems (rhizomes) and dense, fibrous root systems. This mass of plant material and the activity of the millions of microbes, thousands of invertebrate animals, and hundreds of burrowing rodents account for a dynamic portion of the grasslands. They ensure availability of water and nutrients to above-ground vegetation. The death and decomposition of these plants and animals lead to the accumulation of considerable organic soil matter and high soil fertility.

Temperate Grasslands. The temperate central North American grasslands are rich in warm-season grasses and broad-leafed herbs; during the summer months over 70 species may be flowering at any one time. In the more humid tallgrass prairie the dominant grasses are bluestems, Indiangrass, switchgrass, and needlegrasses, while the drier plains are characterized by the shorter grama grasses and buffalograss. Throughout these grasslands, members of the sunflower and legume plant families provide the largest number of colorful flowers.

Major herbivores found in temperate grasslands are pronghorn, rodents, and rabbits. Coyotes, bobcats, badgers, and snakes are also present and depend on the rodent population for food. Grassland birds include lark bunting, meadowlarks, plovers, and several species of predatory hawks and owls. Marshes, sloughs, and potholes (poorly drained depressions) provide essential habitats for numerous ducks, geese, coots,

Grassland vegetation reduces competition between species for water and nutrients by concentrating each species' roots and foliage at different, noncompetitive levels (called layering). In root layering, for example, some species have short, surface root systems that exploit only precipitation, and others have extremely long taproots that may absorb no precipitation (taking water only from underground sources). Grassland soils, in order of depth, are litter (yellow), *fine loam* (dark brown), *two layers of dense loam* (light brown *and* gray brown), *calcerous loam* (light gray brown to yellow brown), *and sandy clay* (light gray to yellow).

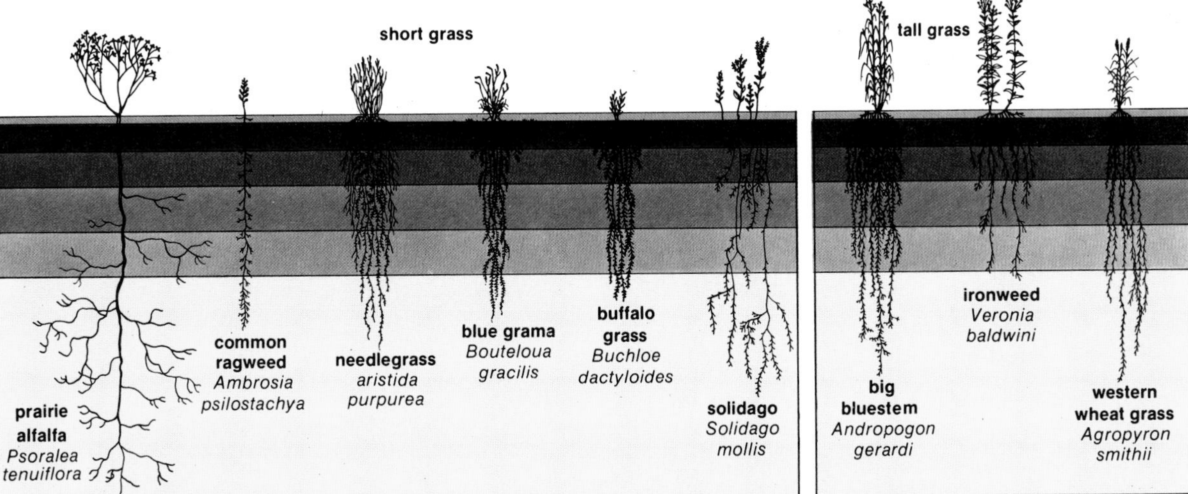

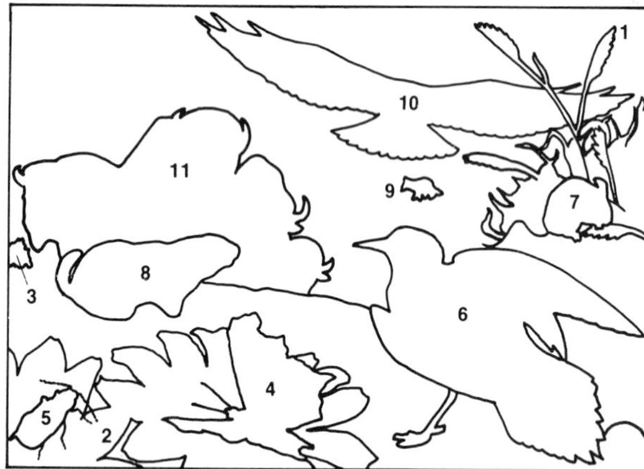

The varied species of plants and animals inhabiting the North American prairies all contribute to the ecological balance of this grassland ecosystem. Grasses, the climax vegetation of the prairies, have evolved to take full advantage of the moderately dry climate. The narrow leaves and short stems of such species as buffalo grass (1) minimize loss of moisture, and their small flowers are readily pollinated by the winds. Plants such as sunflowers (2) and the leguminous Lambert crazyweed (3) develop colorful blossoms that attract the insects that pollinate them, including the fritillary butterfly (4) and the cucumber beetle (5). These insects, in turn, provide the diet of such birds as the killdeer (6), which nests in small depressions of the prairie soil. The seeds and stems of prairie grasses and plants are consumed by insects and such rodents as the deer mouse (7) and the prairie dog (8). Predators such as the coyote (9) and scavengers such as the red-tailed hawk (10) scour the plains for these smaller prey. Large grazing animals such as the North American bison (11) were once abundant in these regions. The migratory habits of the bison prevented overgrazing and subsequent erosion of the land. Insects and burrowing rodents play a vital role in improving drainage and restoring fertility to the soil.

and other waterfowl. Herbivores such as the bison, wapiti (elk), prairie chickens, and prairie dogs, as well as predatory wolves and mountain lions, have almost become extinct, and their range is greatly constricted. The occupation of the prairies and plains by greater numbers of people and domestic livestock and plants has reduced the number and extent of native animals.

The temperate grasslands of Argentina (pampas), Russia, China, and Siberia (steppes) are also rich in plant species. Dominant sod-forming, cool-season grasses include several species of needlegrass and fescue in the Asian grasslands, whereas related grasses form tussocks (bunches) in Argentina, Uruguay, New Zealand, and Australia. Large herds of grazing ungulates (hoofed animals) are absent in South America and Australia, but a number of them are important to the maintenance of the Asian steppe, where gazelles and antelope are numerous and widely distributed. Wild horses and wild asses, though present, are few and face extinction. Burrowing rodents, such as marmots and ground squirrels, affect the steppe vegetation with their consumptive grazing and underground activity, although they provide food for predatory birds and mammals. Locusts and grasshoppers provide food for the flocks of cranes, starlings, and huge birds called bustards (see STEPPE LIFE). The unique kangaroos and wallabies of Australia are ecological equivalents of the ungulates of Asia.

Tropical Grasslands. Plants and animals of tropical grasslands are adapted to longer growing seasons. Tropical grasslands of Latin America are dominated by *Panicum* and *Paspalum* grasses. Worldwide they represent more than 1,000 species of grasses. In Africa the major warm-season grasses—red oat grass, dropseeds, and bluestems—extend from the tropical savannas into the southern African grassland (veld). On the East African Serengeti Plains more than 100 grass species support a diverse grassland wildlife. Tall red oat grass, elephant grass, and the bluestems dominate the moist western area. With increasing dryness, shortgrass vegetation prevails, predominantly Bermuda grass and dropseed grasses. Major broad-leaved herbs on the plains are members of the mint and Acanthus plant families. Cactus plants of temperate grasslands are absent, but fleshy euphorbias are abundant.

The greatest concentration of mixed plains wildlife in the world exists on the Serengeti Plains. Wildebeests, gazelles, impalas, zebras, and about 25 other species, along with predatory lions, hyenas, cheetahs, leopards, and other carnivores, constitute the more than 1 million large animals that share the plains with numerous species of birds, rodents, and insects. The ungulates move in large herds across the plains on the basis of grass palatability and dry seasons.

Tundra Grasslands. The treeless polar and alpine tundras are characterized by plants and animals that must survive short growing seasons, low temperatures, and drying winds. Many of these habitats have an abundance of broad-leaved herbs associated with grasses, such as hairgrass and fescue and grasslike rushes and sedges. Herbivores of polar tundra include rodents, caribou, and reindeer, which are prey to wolves, foxes, and eagles. In mountainous areas, species of sheep, goats, and rodents provide food for large predator cats and wolves.

Human Influence. Human utilization of the world's grasslands for cropland, grazing of livestock, and living space places considerable pressure on grassland life. Several species of plants and animals are threatened with extinction as habitats critical to their survival decline and illegal collecting continues. Examples are the white lady's-slipper orchid of North American prairies, wild horses in Asia, and the African cheetah.

Overgrazing reduces vegetative cover, and under prolonged drought desertlike conditions may spread. Overgrazing also permits invasion of unpalatable species and nonnative weeds. As grazers avoid them, these plants begin to dominate and exclude the original species, which contributes to a drop in grazing and wildlife potential.

Conversion of the perennial grass cover into row crops eliminates wildlife habitats and accelerates soil erosion. During droughts the annual crops fail, the land is exposed to wind erosion, and the productivity of once fertile grasslands is greatly reduced. WILLIAM H. MARTIN

Bibliography: Brown, Lauren, *Grasslands* (1985); Cloudsley-Thompson, John, and Duffey, Eric, *Deserts and Grasslands: The World's Open Spaces* (1976); Duffey, Eric, et al., *Grassland Ecology and Wildlife Management* (1974); Estes, James R., et al., *Grasses and Grasslands* (1982); Hayes, Harold, *The Last Place On Earth* (1977); Spedding, C. R. W., *Grassland Ecology* (1971); Sprague, Howard B., ed., *Grasslands of the United States: Their Economic and Ecologic Importance* (1974); Wali, M. K., ed., *Prairie: A Multiple View* (1975).

Grasso, Ella T. [gras'-oh]

Ella Tambussi Grasso, b. Windsor Locks, Conn., May 10, 1919, d. Feb. 5, 1981, became governor of Connecticut in 1975, the first woman to be elected a state governor in her own right. A Democrat, she held other state elective offices (1952–70) and served in the U.S. House of Representatives (1971–75). She was reelected governor in 1978 but resigned at the end of 1980 because of ill health.

Grateful Dead, The

The Grateful Dead, one of America's most enduring rock-music bands, helped create the "acid-rock" sound of the 1960s and later pioneered "country rock." Their free San Francisco concerts were among the first of the giant, multimedia rock happenings. The Dead's first album, *The Grateful Dead,* was released in 1967. Two 1970 albums, *Workingman's Dead* and *American Beauty,* along with the 1987 album *In the Dark,* are rated among their best works. Original members still with the group are Jerry Garcia, b. San Francisco, Aug. 1, 1942, and Bob Weir, b. San Francisco, Oct. 16, 1947, guitars and vocals; Phil Lesh, b. Berkeley, Calif., Mar. 15, 1940, bass; and Bill Kreutzmann, b. Palo Alto, Calif., June 7, 1946, drums.

JONATHAN KAMIN

Gratian [gray'-shuhn]

Gratian, a 12th-century Italian monk and legal scholar, is considered the father of CANON LAW. Very few details of his life are known other than that he taught at the Camaldolese monastery in Bologna and was a consultant to a papal judge in 1143. His greatest work is the *Concordia discordantium canonum,* commonly known as the *Decretum Gratiani,* a collection of canon law. This was not the first such compilation, but it was the most original in its attempt to analyze conflicting authorities and arrive at some specific conclusion in the case of each question at issue. His collection quickly became standard, was taught in the law schools by the end of the 12th century, and became the manual used in the papal curia under the pontificate of Pope Alexander III. DAVID HENRY MILLER

Bibliography: Carlyle, Alexander J., *A History of the Medieval Political Theory in the West,* 6 vols. (1909–36); Tierney, Brian, *Foundations of the Conciliar Theory: The Contribution of the Medieval Canonists from Gratian to the Great Schism* (1955).

Gratian, Roman Emperor in the West

Flavius Gratianus, AD 359–383, was Roman emperor of the West from 367 to 383. He was coemperor with his father, VALENTINIAN I, until the latter's death (375); then he divided his father's empire with his young half-brother, VALENTINIAN II. Gratian ruled over Gaul, Spain, and Britain and successfully defended Gaul against barbarian invaders. He was a devout Christian and relied upon Saint AMBROSE as one of his chief advisors. He declined the title of *pontifex maximus* and removed the statue of Victory from the Senate. His power declined, and he was assassinated by the supporters of Magnus Maximus.

Bibliography: Jones, A. H. M., *The Later Roman Empire, 284–602: A Social, Economic and Administrative Survey,* 3 vols. (1964).

Grattan, Henry [grat'-uhn]

Henry Grattan, b. July 3, 1746, d. June 4, 1820, was a brilliant Irish orator who led the fight for Irish legislative independence. Such independence was achieved in 1782 when the British Parliament repealed Poynings's Law, a medieval statute that placed the Irish legislature under the control of the English privy council, but it was lost again in 1800, when the Irish and British parliaments were united. A member of the Irish Parliament (1775–97, 1800) and the United Parliament (1805–20), Grattan also fought for CATHOLIC EMANCIPATION.

Bibliography: O'Brien, Gerard, *Anglo-Irish Politics in the Age of Grattan and Pitt* (1986).

Grau, Shirley Ann [grow]

The novelist and short-story writer Shirley Ann Grau, b. New Orleans, La., July 8, 1928, writes tough, realistic stories about the American South. *The Black Prince and Other Stories* (1955), her first collection, has been described as "Southern Gothic." *The Hard Blue Sky* (1958), a novel, was praised for its view of a Gulf Coast Cajun community. *The Keepers of the House* (1964), a powerful story of a Southern dynasty with a history of miscegenation, won a 1965 Pulitzer Prize and led critics to compare Grau with William Faulkner. Later works include the novels *The Condor Passes* (1971) and *Evidence of Love* (1977) and the short-story collections *The Wind Shifting West* (1973) and *Nine Women* (1985).

Grau San Martín, Ramón [grow sahn mar-teen', rah-mohn']

Ramón Grau San Martín, b. Sept. 13, 1887, d. July 28, 1969, was twice president of Cuba. A professor of medicine at the University of Havana and a political progressive, he participated in the overthrow of dictator Gerardo MACHADO in August 1933. A month later, after Fulgencio BATISTA's sergeants' revolt had driven out President Carlos Manuel de CÉSPEDES,

Grau San Martín became provisional president. The United States considered his government too radical and refused to recognize it, however, and Grau was forced to resign in January 1934.

Leading Cuba's non-Communist left, Grau lost the 1940 presidential election to Batista but won in 1944. Widespread corruption within his government hampered implementation of promised social reforms, but his nominee won the election of 1948. In 1954, Grau ran again for the presidency against Batista, but, charging fraud, he withdrew before the election.

Bibliography: Ruiz, Ramón Eduardo, *Cuba: The Making of a Revolution* (1968); Stokes, William S., *Latin American Politics* (1959).

Graun, Karl Heinrich [grown]

Karl Heinrich Graun, b. May 7, 1704, d. Aug. 8, 1759, was a German baroque composer and singer. After training in Dresden, he worked there (1714–21), in Braunschweig (1725–35), and in Rheinsberg (1735–40), where his employer was the crown prince of Prussia, later Frederick the Great, who appointed him court choirmaster in Berlin in 1740. Vocal music, with 30 operas and approximately 100 secular cantatas, dominates his work as a composer, and he is best known for two religious compositions, the oratorio *The Death of Jesus* (1755) and a *Te deum* (1756). Graun's brother Johann Gottlieb (1703–71), a prominent violinist and composer, was also connected with the Prussian court. A third brother, August Friedrich (1699–1765), was an organist and composer. F. E. Kirby

Bibliography: Grout, Donald J., *A Short History of Opera*, 2d ed. (1965); Weinandt, Elwyn A., *Choral Music of the Church* (1965).

Graupner, Christoph [growp'-nur, kris'-tohf]

Johann Christoph Graupner, b. Jan. 13, 1683, d. May 10, 1760, was a prominent German composer. After studies in Leipzig at the St. Thomas School, he worked at the Hamburg opera as harpsichordist and then in Darmstadt, where he became music director in 1712 and remained the rest of his life. In 1722 he refused an offer to become cantor at St. Thomas School, and the post went to Johann Sebastian Bach. Although known for his harpsichord suites, Graupner was also distinguished for his operas and cantatas. F. E. Kirby

Bibliography: Fortune, Nigel, and Lewis, Anthony, eds., *Opera and Church Music, 1630–1750,* vol. 5 in *The New Oxford History of Music* (1975); Kirby, F. E., *A Short History of Keyboard Music* (1966).

gravel [grav'-ul]

In geology, any loose, or unconsolidated, natural accumulation of rounded rock fragments with individual sizes greater than 2 mm (0.08 in) in diameter is called gravel. The size distribution of the fragments is not necessarily uniform; pebbles, cobbles, and boulders may predominate, and fragments of intermediate size may not occur. Sand, which is less coarse than gravel, often fills the spaces between pebbles.

The bedding, jointing, and cleaving characteristics of the parent rock may influence the fragment's original shape, whereas the distance a fragment has traveled may be reflected in its ultimate degree of roundness. For engineering purposes the term *gravel* is restricted to rounded fragments ranging from 4.76 mm (0.19 in; retained on U.S. standard sieve no. 4) to 76 mm (3 in) in diameter. Gravel is used in concrete work and road surfacing.

Gravelot, Hubert François [grahv-loh']

The French draftsman and engraver Hubert François Gravelot, b. Mar. 26, 1699, d. Apr. 20, 1773, became famous as a book illustrator. His father sent him as a youth to the island of Santo Domingo to cure his extravagance. On returning to Paris he studied painting with François Boucher and became his favorite pupil. From 1732 he worked in England for 13 years, illustrating English novels and an edition of Shakespeare and caricaturing public figures in association with William Hogarth. In Paris once again in 1745 he undertook decorative designs, but he was most acclaimed for illustrating books, among them editions of Boccaccio's *Decameron* and Tasso's *Jerusalem Liberated.* Gravelot's style had a pronounced influence on his pupil Thomas Gainsborough. Philip Gould

Bibliography: Salomons, Vera, *Gravelot* (1911).

Graves, Michael [grayvz]

The Portland Building (1982), with its cube shape and exuberantly colored facade, exemplifies the style of Michael Graves, one of the leading exponents of postmodern architecture. This controversial structure, containing the municipal offices of the city of Portland, Oreg., was Graves's first major public building.

Michael Graves, b. Indianapolis, Ind., July 9, 1934, is a leading theorist and practitioner of POSTMODERN ARCHITECTURE. He studied at the University of Cincinnati and Harvard University before becoming one of the New York Five group of architects. His work has always stressed the historical continuity of architecture and preserves close relationships with traditional modes of design and decoration. He has taught at Princeton University since 1962. His major buildings include the San Juan Capistrano, Calif., public library (1983) and the Humana Building (1985) in Louisville, Ky.

Bibliography: Graves, Michael, *Buildings and Projects, 1966–1981* (1983) and *Buildings and Projects, 1980–1985* (1985).

Graves, Morris

The American painter Morris Graves, b. Fox Valley, Oreg., Aug. 28, 1910, works in a highly individual vein expressive of the values of Oriental philosophy, particularly Zen Buddhism and Taoism. In cultivating his interest in these philosophies he made three trips to the Orient. The artist who influenced Graves most strongly was the American painter Mark Tobey. From Tobey he derived the mode of "white writing," a kind of calligraphy as fine in its touch as filigree, which he used with striking effect in *Bird Singing in the Moonlight* (1938–40) and *Blind Bird* (1940), both in the Museum of Modern Art, New York City. Graves never tires of painting birds, which have been recognized as symbols of this extremely private, introspective artist who leads a rather isolated life in the woods north of Seattle, Wash.

Bibliography: Kass, Ray, *Morris Graves: Vision of the Inner Eye* (1983).

Graves, Nancy

The American artist Nancy Stevenson Graves, b. Pittsfield, Mass., Dec. 23, 1940, first established her reputation with sculptures of Bactrian camels (1966–71) in a variety of materials; some sculptures resembled ancient camel bones (such as the 36-piece *Variability of Similar Forms,* 1970). Her paintings of the 1970s, first inspired by maps (of Mars, of the ocean floor), evolved to complete abstraction. In the 1980s Graves concentrated on bronze sculptures, based on direct casts of natural objects and specimens.

Bibliography: Cathcart, Linda L., *Nancy Graves* (1980).

Graves, Robert

The novelist, poet, and scholar Robert Ranke Graves, b. Wimbledon, Greater London, July 24, 1895, d. Dec. 7, 1985, went straight from Charterhouse School to the horrors of trench warfare. Seriously wounded in France during the first Battle of the Somme, he wrote poetry during his convalesence to identify his feelings about the war. After taking a degree (1926) at Oxford, Graves devoted his life to writing, study, and teaching. Prose works range from his autobiography, *Goodbye to All That* (1929), and a critical study, *The White Goddess* (1948), which sets forth his theory of poetry and poetic inspiration, to a series of historical novels, most notably the celebrated *I, Claudius* (1934), *Claudius the God* (1934), and *King Jesus* (1946). He taught English literature at Cairo University (1926–27) and was professor of poetry at Oxford (1961–66).

During the 1930s, Graves worked closely with the American poet Laura Riding, collaborating with her on the influential *Survey of Modernist Poetry* (1927). Graves's own best poetry, while following traditional forms, combines irony and vision in a highly individual manner. In his later years he became more and more the poet of personal relationships, especially of love between a man and a woman. Graves published more than 15 volumes of poetry, but *Collected Poems, 1959* represents what he wished to preserve. His highly popular *Greek Myths* (1955) contains translations and commentary; and with Omar Ali-Shah he translated the *Rubáiyát of Omar Khayyám* in 1967. Graves lived for most of his life on the Balearic island of Majorca. JEROME KLINKOWITZ

Bibliography: Keane, P. J., *A Wild Civility: Interactions in the Poetry and Thought of Robert Graves* (1980); Seymour-Smith, Michael, *Robert Graves* (1956; repr. 1983); Winzinger, Anita, *Graves as a Critic* (1982).

Gravettian [gruh-vet'-ee-uhn]

In archaeology, Gravettian is the name given to an advanced tool industry that succeeded the AURIGNACIAN in the Upper PALEOLITHIC PERIOD. In France, where it was first described and named after the site of La Gravette, it has come to be known as the Upper PERIGORDIAN and is recognized as bearing little typological relationship to central and eastern European assemblages subsequently termed Gravettian.

Characteristic Gravettian stone tools include burins (chisel tools), simple end scrapers, and numerous backed blades and bladelets. The burins are of several different types and occur in greater frequency than in earlier industries. Their function is usually considered to have been the manufacture of various bone and antler tools that occur in Gravettian assemblages. Some art objects have been found in Gravettian sites (notably at DOLNÍ VĚSTONICE in Czechoslovakia), the most well-known being female figurines thought to be fertility symbols. Assemblages described as Gravettian date from between 27,000 and 17,000 years ago. DAVID BROSE

Bibliography: Bordes, François, *The Old Stone Age*, trans. by J. E. Anderson (1968); Klein, Richard G., *Ice-Age Hunters of the Ukraine* (1973); Piggott, Stuart, and Daniel, Glyn, *France Before the Romans* (1975).

gravimeter [gruh-vim'-uht-ur]

Gravimeters measure differences in the magnitude of the Earth's gravity field. Measurement of gravity involves balancing the gravity force on a so-called proof mass contained in the meter against the force exerted by a spring. Such a force on a mass is called the acceleration of gravity. The net acceleration that the meter feels is the sum of the effects of all surrounding masses.

Gravimeter Measurements. The first step in using a gravimeter is to level the meter and change the spring tension so that the gravitational force on the proof mass is balanced. The meter is then moved to another location, leveled, and balanced again.

The change in spring tension required to bring the meter back into balance at the new location is measured—in effect, measuring the change in the acceleration of gravity between the two locations. Gravity values are usually referenced to some starting point.

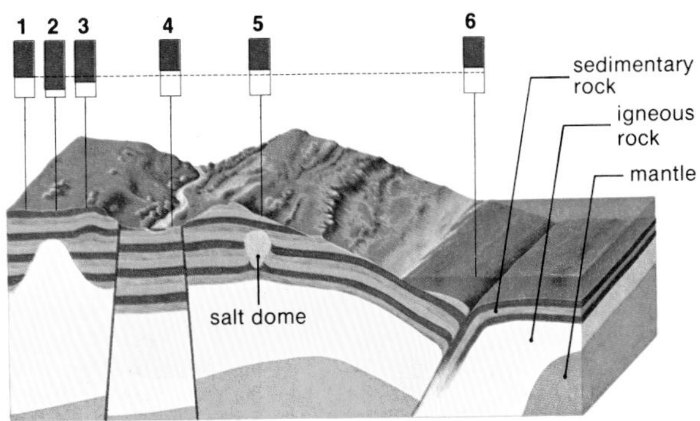

Gravimetric readings are often compared to a "normal" value (1). Higher readings indicate a stronger gravitational pull from regions of heavy igneous rock (2) or from an anticline (3), an arch of stratified rock. Lower readings occur above a rift valley (4), where lighter sedimentary rocks reach a greater depth; a salt dome (5), a mass of relatively light material; and an oceanic trough (6), where the Earth's crust extends into the mantle.

The unit of gravity measurement is the milligal (mgal), named after Galileo. One mgal is equivalent to an acceleration of 0.001 cm/sec^2, or 0.001 dyn/gm. Sometimes a "gravity unit," equal to 0.1 mgal, is used. The attraction of the Earth as a whole is about 980,000 mgal, and a typical gravity meter can be read to 0.01 mgal. Thus a gravimeter measures to about 1 part in 100 million.

Gravity readings are usually intended to locate regions of light or dense rocks; such readings may indicate structural features such as basins, uplift areas, and faults. Gravity anomalies of exploration interest are generally 0.5–10 mgal in magnitude.

Corrections to Gravimeter Measurements. Corrections need to be made to gravity measurements for a number of factors. These corrections must be accurate if the survey is to be reliable. Among the factors to be considered are meter drift and tidal effects, which are easily corrected.

In addition, the rotation of the Earth introduces a centrifugal force effect that makes gravity measurements smaller than they would be if the Earth were not spinning. Since the Earth is not a perfect sphere, latitude corrections must also be made.

Nearby landmasses, such as hills, that protrude above the level of the meter exert an upward attraction and make the meter read less than usual; nearby valleys below the meter level fail to attract and thus also make the meter read less. Corrections for masses above or voids below the meter are called terrain corrections. They are very difficult to account for and are responsible for most limitations of gravity survey accuracy.

Gravity readings also change with elevation, since the distance to the center of the Earth changes. A mass between the meter location and the reference elevation makes the meter read more than it would if such a mass were not present. The attraction of this mass depends on its density and thickness and is corrected for by what is called a Bouguer correction. Gravity data with the Bouguer and other corrections applied are called Bouguer anomaly values; they indicate gravity effects for reasons other than those for which the corrections have been applied. Most anomaly maps used in petroleum exploration are Bouguer anomaly maps. Readings from gravimeters that are in motion during a measurement, such as shipboard meters, require an additional adjustment, called an Eötvös correction. R. E. SHERIFF

Bibliography: Nettleton, Lewis Lomat, *Gravity and Magnetics in Oil Prospecting* (1976); Telford, W. M., et al., *Applied Geophysics* (1976).

gravimetric analysis: see QUANTITATIVE CHEMICAL ANALYSIS.

gravitation

Gravitation, or gravity, is a force that attracts all objects in the universe; it is the most familiar of the four FUNDAMENTAL INTERACTIONS of matter. Gravitation has several basic characteristics that distinguish it from the other fundamental interactions. First, it is universal, affecting all forms of matter and energy in essentially the same way, whereas all the other interactions directly affect only certain types of particles; the electromagnetic force, for example, affects only charged particles. Second, gravity is always attractive, since it interacts with mass-energy, which is always positive; in electromagnetism, on the other hand, charges can either attract or repel. Third, gravitation is a long-range interaction; electromagnetism is also long-range, but the strong and weak nuclear forces generally operate only within a distance the size of an atomic nucleus. Fourth, gravity is the weakest of the four fundamental forces. It has a negligible effect on elementary particles; the electromagnetic attractive force between a proton and an electron is nearly 10^{40} times greater than the gravitational force at the same separation. Because gravity is a long-range attractive force affecting all matter, however, it is the dominant force in the universe.

HISTORICAL THEORIES

Throughout history there have been many attempts to describe or explain gravitation. About 330 BC, Aristotle claimed that the four elements—earth, water, air, and fire—have their natural places, toward which they tend to travel. He argued that objects containing greater amounts of earth than others would fall toward the Earth faster and that their speed would increase as they neared their natural place.

GALILEO GALILEI deduced (1604) that gravity imparts a definite acceleration, rather than a velocity, and that this acceleration is the same for all objects traveling in a vacuum. The universality of gravitational acceleration is known as the weak equivalence principle.

Sir Isaac NEWTON made the most significant contribution to gravitational theory when he perceived (1666) that the orbit of the Moon depended on the same type of force that causes an apple to fall on Earth. This proposition required that the magnitude of the force decrease in inverse proportion to the square of the distance from the Earth's center. Newton combined the inverse-square law with his three LAWS OF MOTION to formulate a theory of universal gravitation, which stated that there is a gravitational attraction between every pair of objects, directly proportional to the square of the distance between them.

René Descartes (1596–1650) had earlier proposed a nonquantitative theory of gravitation based on the inward pressure of vortices on planets (see PHYSICS, HISTORY OF), but Newton did not offer a cause for the attraction. In fact, he avoided even calling it an attraction, speaking instead of "bodies gravitating towards one another." This description was sufficient to deduce KEPLER'S LAWS of planetary motion, the oceanic TIDES, and the PRECESSION OF THE EQUINOXES. In 1846 it was used to predict and discover a new planet, Neptune. Thus Newton's theory of gravitation stands as one of the greatest advancements of scientific knowledge.

Expressed mathematically, Newton's theory states that there is an attractive force F, given by $F = Gm_1m_2/r^2$, between two particles having masses m_1 and m_2 and separation distance r. G is the gravitational constant of proportionality, an unknown quantity that could not be determined by solar-system observations, which give only ratios of masses and thus the product of G and some mass. The value of G was first determined in 1798 by Henry Cavendish, who measured the force of gravitational attraction between two spheres of known mass. This experiment has come to be known as "weighing the Earth," because once G was determined, the Earth's mass, m_e, could be determined from the astronomically known value for Gm_e. The experiment has been repeated many times with increasing precision; the currently accepted value of G is 6.67259×10^{-8} $cm^3/g\ sec^2$.

MODERN THEORIES

In 1905, Albert EINSTEIN developed his theory of special RELATIVITY, which modified Newton's theory of gravitation. Seek-

According to Newton's law of universal gravitation (A), all bodies attract each other with a force that varies inversely as the square of the distance between them (1). Thus a planet (2) that is one astronomical unit (AU) away from the Sun, S, is attracted by a force that is four times as great as that experienced by a planet (3) two AUs away. A planet near the Sun moves faster than one farther away, as indicated by the length of the arrows; increasing length corresponds to increasing velocity. The orbit (B) of an artificial satellite at a given height above the Earth is dependent on the relationship between the Earth's gravitational field and the satellite's inertial or centrifugal reaction force resulting from its velocity, v, at that point. A circular orbit (1) results at a critical velocity, v_1. A slightly greater velocity, v_2, produces an elliptical orbit (2). At a specific higher velocity, v_3, called the escape velocity, the orbit is a parabola (3) with the Earth at one focus, and the satellite will escape the Earth's gravity. The orbit becomes hyperbolic (4) at any velocity, v_4, greater than the escape velocity. Newton's laws of gravity and mechanics also explain Kepler's laws of planetary motion (C); the equatorial bulging (D) of rotating planets, such as Jupiter; the parabolic paths (E) of ballistic missiles on Earth; and the hyperbolic paths (F) of nonrecurring comets.

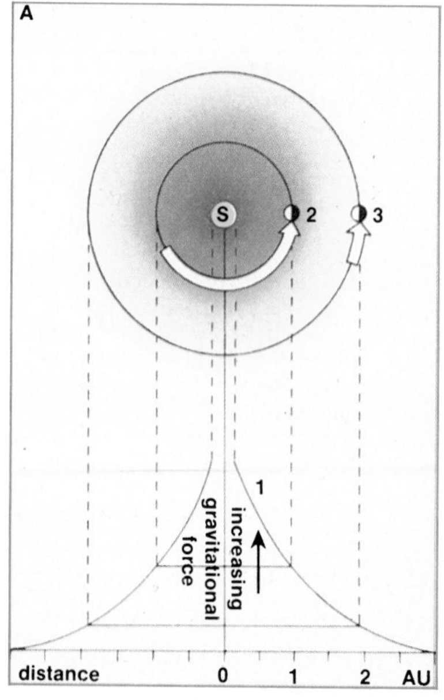

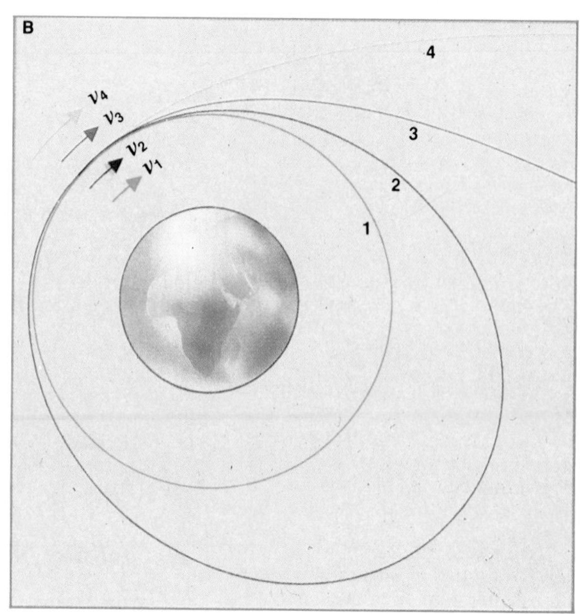

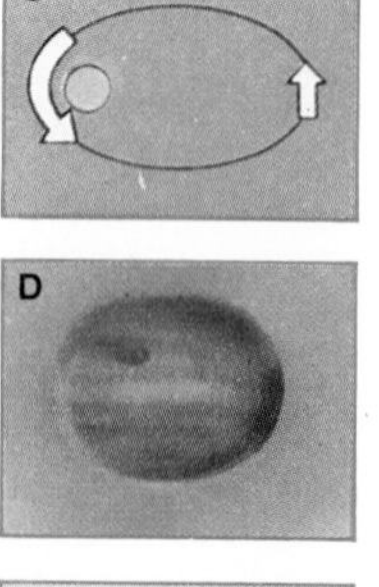

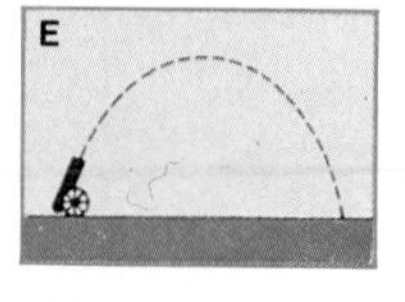

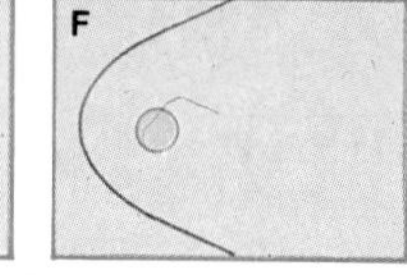

ing to describe gravitation in a way that was independent of the motion of observers and of the coordinates chosen to label events, Einstein's work led him to describe gravity purely by the structure of the SPACE-TIME CONTINUUM. According to this geometrical theory, gravity affects all forms of matter and energy, all of which move in space-time. Thus this theory obeys the weak equivalence principle and gives the same gravitational acceleration for all freely falling objects.

In addition to describing the effect of gravity on matter, Einstein described the effect of matter on gravity. This theory, completed in 1915, is called general relativity. Although Einstein's theory is much different from Newton's, it predicts nearly the same effects in systems in which gravitational fields are weak and velocities are slow compared to the velocity of light. Einstein's theory, however, accounts for some solar-system phenomena not considered by Newton.

One such phenomenon is the perihelion precession of Mercury. In the 19th century, it was observed that the rate of precession differed by 43" per century from what Newton's theory predicts; Einstein's theory predicts precisely such a difference in the precession rate. Another such phenomenon is the bending of light rays by the Sun's gravitational field, which Newton's theory does not predict at all. Einstein's prediction was confirmed by Arthur S. Eddington during a total eclipse in 1919, and later by others to 1% accuracy. Einstein also predicted the gravitational RED SHIFT, a change in the frequency of electromagnetic waves escaping from a strong gravitational field, which was confirmed by Robert Pound and Glen Rebka in 1960. In 1964, Irving Shapiro used general relativity to predict a time delay of signals passing near the Sun, an effect since confirmed by sending radar signals to and from planets and spacecraft.

In addition, Einstein's theory of general relativity predicts several qualitatively new effects in other systems and is especially useful in dealing with COSMOLOGY. Relativity asserts that the universe must be either expanding or contracting. Einstein was not sufficiently bold to believe this prediction and thus modified his equations to allow for a static universe. In 1929, though, Edwin Hubble discovered that the universe is expanding. Whether gravity will eventually cause it to collapse is a subject of current investigation and debate. General relativity also predicts GRAVITATIONAL WAVES from masses in nonuniform motion, but these waves are so weak that they have not yet been definitely detected. Finally, the theory predicts GRAVITATIONAL COLLAPSE of sufficiently massive objects into BLACK HOLES. Today there is mounting evidence that several astronomical systems may contain black holes.

Einstein's general relativity is not the only 20th-century theory of gravity, though it is perhaps the simplest and most elegant. All viable theories of gravity must, like Einstein's, be complete, self-consistent, and relativistic. They must also have the correct Newtonian limit, uphold the weak equivalence principle, and predict the same Einstein shift as measured by all ideal clocks at the same position. There is strong experimental evidence for accepting these criteria as fundamental, and L. I. Schiff has conjectured that they can be satisfied only by geometrical, or metric, theories.

The strongest rival theory has been the Brans-Dicke theory. Like general relativity, it is a geometrical theory that satisfies the fundamental criteria. Its field equations are different, however, and it claims that the geometry of space-time is affected not only by matter but also by an additional scalar field. Unlike Einstein's calculations, the Brans-Dicke theory cannot predict the perihelion shift of Mercury.

Some recent theories attempt to explain gravitation nongeometrically, proposing instead that particles (or waves) called gravitons are responsible. Such supergravity, or supersymmetry, theories place gravitational phenomena within the realm of quantum physics. They are part of an attempt to show that the four FUNDAMENTAL INTERACTIONS of nature are related, and that they were a single, united force at the birth of the universe (see UNIFIED FIELD THEORY). Some mathematical theories use up to 13 separate dimensions in the effort to unite the four interactions.

Multidimensional analysis has also raised the issue of the constancy of the gravitational constant G. This idea was proposed earlier by British physicist Paul Dirac in his so-called "large numbers" hypothesis. Dirac noted that the ratio of the strength of the electromagnetic force to that of the gravitational force (approximately 10^{40}) is roughly equivalent to the age of the universe in atomic terms. He wondered whether there might be a deep physical connection requiring this similarity and proposed that this would be the case if G slowly decreased as the age of the universe increased. If G were decreasing, however, gravitational time would change with respect to atomic time; thus far, experiments have not shown this to be happening.

DON N. PAGE

Bibliography: Berry, Michael, *Principles of Cosmology and Gravitation* (1976); Kaufmann, William, III, *Relativity and Cosmology*, 2d ed. (1977); Misner, Charles, et al., *Gravitation* (1973); Nicolson, Iain, *Gravity, Black Holes and the Universe* (1981); Weinberg, Steven, *Gravitation and Cosmology* (1972); Will, Clifford, *Theory and Experiment in Gravitational Physics* (1981).

gravitational collapse

Gravitational collapse is the catastrophic fate that befalls a massive object when its own gravity completely overwhelms all other forces. During most of a stars lifetime, its tendency to contract as a result of its gravity is balanced by the outward pressure produced by the heat of its nuclear reactions. Eventually, however, the nuclear fuel will be exhausted. If the star's mass is less than about 3 solar masses, it will eventually contract to a stable configuration as either a WHITE DWARF (about the size of the Earth but hundreds of thousands times denser) or a NEUTRON STAR (a similar mass compressed into a sphere only a few miles across). More massive stars, however, will continue to shrink even further when their thermal and rotational energy is exhausted. Unless the star sheds its excess mass, gravity will overcome all conceivable pressure forces and gravitational collapse will occur.

Once gravity exceeds the other forces, the star will fall in on itself in a few hours. When the size of the collapsing star falls below what is called the SCHWARZSCHILD RADIUS, the escape velocity becomes equal to the velocity of light. When not even light can escape from the surface, the star is said to be inside a black hole. Theorems by Roger PENROSE and Stephen HAWKING show that, according to general RELATIVITY and similar theories of GRAVITATION, a singularity, or edge to the space-time continuum must then occur. It is believed, but has not been proved, that everything inside the black hole will hit the singularity and be utterly destroyed within a few microseconds; however, some claim that matter and energy may reappear in another universe.

The collapse of a star or a dense cluster of stars can release large amounts of energy, perhaps 10% of the total rest-mass energy of the system if the collapse is nonspherical. Most of the energy will probably be emitted as GRAVITATIONAL WAVES. Matter falling into a black hole already formed can also release much electromagnetic energy. This is a possible source of X rays from Cygnus X-1 in our galaxy (see X-RAY ASTRONOMY) and of visible light and radio waves from quasars and from certain distant galaxies.

The universe as a whole may also undergo gravitational collapse. The universe is presently expanding as distant galaxies move apart, but if they do not have escape velocity relative to each other they will eventually fall back together and bring the universe to an end. Whether this will happen depends on the density of matter in the universe, which is not precisely known (see COSMOLOGY).

DON N. PAGE

Bibliography: Asimov, Isaac, *The Collapsing Universe: The Story of Black Holes* (1977); Davies, P. C. W., *Space and Time in the Modern Universe* (1977); Peratt, Anthony L., "Are Black Holes Necessary?" *Sky & Telescope*, July 1983; Wald, Robert, *Space, Time and Gravity: The Theory of the Big Bang and Black Holes* (1977).

gravitational lens

Albert Einstein's theory of general RELATIVITY predicts that starlight is deflected by the gravitational field of an intermediate massive body. A predicted deflection of 1.75 seconds of arc at the Sun's edge has been observed at numerous solar eclipses since 1919. Einstein's theory also predicted that a massive intervening body, such as the nucleus of a galaxy, would tend to deflect the light from a more distant object and act as a gravitational lens. An "Einstein ring" of light could be produced by a precise alignment of objects. Much more likely would be the observation of one or more distorted images of the more distant object lying to one side or another of the intervening mass.

A gravitational lens was first identified in 1979, when two nearly identical quasar images were observed lying only about 6 seconds of arc apart in the sky. The intervening galaxy producing these images was later also identified. A number of other lens effects have been observed since then. They include the 1987 sighting of giant luminous arcs in distant galaxy clusters, the arcs apparently being distortions of still more distant galaxies by the clusters. In 1988 an apparent Einstein ring produced by perfectly aligned objects was also observed.

JOHN B. IRWIN

Bibliography: Chaffee, F. H., "The Discovery of a Gravitational Lens," *Scientific American,* November 1980; Falco, Emilio, "Gravity Makes a Spectacle of Itself," *New Scientist,* Mar. 10, 1987; Turner, E. L., "Gravitational Lenses," *Scientific American,* July 1988; Waldrop, M. M., "Einstein's Impossible Ring: Found," *Science,* June 24, 1988.

gravitational waves

Gravitational waves are theoretical perturbations in a gravitational field. According to the theory of general RELATIVITY, when an object changes its configuration, its gravitational field changes; because nothing can travel faster than light, the gravitational field cannot change instantaneously over all space. Instead, the changes in the field spread out from the source in the form of gravitational waves. The strongest waves should come from massive objects changing configuration at high velocity, as during the GRAVITATIONAL COLLAPSE into BLACK HOLES of stars, star clusters, the central regions of galaxies, and matter that condensed before galaxy formation. Even these strongest waves, however, are predicted to be very weak by the time they reach the Earth and would produce distortion amplitudes of less than one part per 10^{15}.

Gravitational waves distort objects in a way that depends upon the forces between the object's constituent particles. The distortion is simplest when the particles are free. Then the change in separation between particles at any one time is proportional to the separation itself but does not necessarily occur in the same direction. The proportionality, which is equal to the local distortion amplitude of the wave, depends upon the direction of separation of particles. For example, free particles initially at rest in a spherical configuration are distorted into an ellipsoid. According to general relativity, the ellipsoid should have the same volume as the initial sphere and its longest and shortest axes should be perpendicular to the direction of wave motion. There is no motion along the wave direction. Other theories of gravitation predict that the distortion ellipsoid should have different axes.

American physicist Joseph Weber built the first gravitational-wave detectors in the 1960s. They consisted of massive aluminum cylinders, cooled to low temperatures, that were expected to oscillate in response to the waves. The gravitational-wave detectors built since then have been either of this type (sometimes using niobium instead of aluminum) or separated-mass instruments that extend over distances of several kilometers. Thus far no conclusive evidence for gravitational waves has been found.

To detect low-frequency waves from massive black-hole events, scientists have suggested using the Earth and interplanetary spacecraft as free particles. An observer would look for oscillations in the time radio signals take to travel between them.

DON N. PAGE

Bibliography: Davies, Paul, *The Search for Gravity Waves* (1980); Jeffries, A. D., et al., "Gravitational Wave Observatories," *Scientific American,* June 1987; Trimble, Virginia, "Gravity Waves: A Progress Report," *Sky & Telescope,* October 1987.

gravity: see GRAVITATION.

gravity, center of: see CENTER OF GRAVITY.

Gravity's Rainbow

In *Gravity's Rainbow* (1973), Thomas PYNCHON expands the monumental theme taken up in his earlier novels, *V.* (1963) and *The Crying of Lot 49* (1966): the dehumanizing effects of technology, supported by the modern obsession with stability and control. Set at the end of World War II, the ambitious *Gravity's Rainbow* seeks to show that bureaucracies have used the war to extend their power over science, religion, language, history, and all the forms of life and culture that are bound up in them. The novel itself resists this "movement toward death and stillness" by its variety of styles, complexity of structure, and fantastic comedy.

BRUCE HERZBERG

Bibliography: Hume, K., *Pynchon's Mythography: An Approach to Gravity's Rainbow* (1987); Mackey, D. A., *The Rainbow Quest of Thomas Pynchon* (1980); Moore, T., *The Style of Connectedness* (1987).

gravure: see INTAGLIO.

Gray, Asa

Asa Gray, b. Sauquoit, N.Y., Nov. 18, 1810, d. Jan. 30, 1888, an American botanist, wrote the comprehensive *Manual of the Botany of the Northern United States* (1848), commonly known as *Gray's Manual of Botany.* He edited the *American Journal of Science* for several years and in 1842 accepted the chair of natural history at Harvard University. He supported Charles Darwin's theory of evolution.

Bibliography: Dupree, A. Hunter, *Asa Gray* (1968); Gray, Asa, *Letters of Asa Gray,* 2 vols., ed. by Jane L. Gray (1893; repr. 1973).

Gray, Elisha

The American inventor Elisha Gray, b. Barnesville, Ohio, Aug. 2, 1835, d. Jan. 21, 1901, contested the invention of the telephone in a famous patent litigation suit against Alexander Graham Bell. Gray was interested in electricity and in 1867 received a patent for a self-adjusting telegraph relay. In 1888 he invented the telautograph, an electrical device for reproducing and transmitting handwriting and line drawing. On Feb. 14, 1876, Gray filed with the U.S. Patent Office a caveat announcing his intention to file a patent for a telephone. A few hours earlier, Bell had filed just such a patent. Extensive patent litigation followed and was brought to an end only when the U.S. Supreme Court ruled that Bell was the inventor. Trial testimony showed, however, that Bell's first transmission of the human voice could not have taken place with the device that he patented, whereas the device that Gray intended to patent was workable.

Bibliography: Brooks, John, *Telephone* (1976); Hounshell, David, "Two Paths to the Telephone," *Scientific American,* January 1981.

Gray, Francine du Plessix

An American essayist and novelist, Francine du Plessix Gray, b. in France, Sept. 25, 1930, has ranged widely in her writings. The essays collected in *Divine Disobedience: Profiles in Catholic Radicalism* (1970) are based on her Catholic background. *Hawaii: The Sugar-Coated Fortress* (1977) deals with militarism and racism, and *Adam and Eve and the City* (1987) is a collection of her writings for journals. Her works of fiction, *Lovers and Tyrants* (1976), *World without End* (1981), and *October Blood* (1985), are primarily novels of ideas.

Gray, Robert

The American navigator Robert Gray, b. Tiverton, R.I., May 10, 1755, d. 1806, was the first seaman to carry the U.S. flag around the world—on a 35-month voyage ending in 1790. In May 1792, Gray sailed his ship, the *Columbia,* into the mouth of what came to be called the Columbia River, his discovery forming the basis of the U.S. claim to the Oregon Territory.

Gray, Simon

Simon Gray, b. Oct. 21, 1936, is an English dramatist whose work is marked by sardonic wit and tragic overtones. His plays include *Wise Child* (1968), *Butley* (1971; film, 1974), *Spoiled* (1971), *Otherwise Engaged* (1975), *Quartermaine's Terms* (1983), and *The Common Pursuit* (1987). He studied at Cambridge and has taught at the University of London. He has also written several novels. ROBIN BUSS

Gray, Thomas

The lyricism, wit, and intensity of the British poet Thomas Gray place him in the vanguard of the 18th-century romantic movement. A refined, highly disciplined style of restrained emotion characterizes Gray's work, the best known of which is "Elegy Written in a Country Churchyard" (1751). He appears here in a portrait by J. G. Eckardt. (National Portrait Gallery, London.)

Of all English poets to achieve greatness, Thomas Gray, b. Dec. 26, 1716, d. July 30, 1771, was the least productive. Indifferent to fame and financial reward, he wrote few poems and published even fewer. Yet the small number that did appear in his lifetime were sufficient to earn him the undisputed title of foremost poet of his time. Gray's ELEGY WRITTEN IN A COUNTRY CHURCHYARD (1751), his Pindaric odes (1757), and "Ode on the Death of a Favorite Cat, Drowned in a Tub of Gold Fishes" (1748) are not only the finest of their kind, but have no parallel in English. For Gray, who refused the title of poet laureate, poetry was an accomplishment, not a vocation; it was an activity to which he was occasionally inspired at intervals between scholarly studies of architecture, history, and natural science. He led a reclusive life, and his studious and retiring nature can be glimpsed only through his copious letters to a few close friends.

Gray entered Eton College at the age of eight, where he met Horace Walpole and Richard West, both precocious scholars and poets. He attended (1734-38) Cambridge University, then toured Europe with Walpole. Cambridge was his home from 1742, and he became Regius Professor of Modern History in 1768. There he began to write poems, among which were "Ode on a Distant Prospect of Eton College" and "Sonnet on the Death of Mr. Richard West," both occasioned by the premature death of his friend in 1742. These poems revealed gifts that his later poetry was to refine but hardly excel: dignified ease of expression, noble diction, and a remarkable facility for the memorable statement of moral truth. These qualities have made the plangently melancholy "Elegy Written in a Country Churchyard" one of the most celebrated short poems in English. Gray's later Pindaric odes "The Bard" and "The Progress of Poesy" exploit a taste for picturesque imagery and historical allusion anticipating the romantic movement. Gray turned his prodigious learning to lighter purposes in the mock-heroic ode on the death of his friend Walpole's cat, and in his somber but witty denunciation of a venal politician, "On Lord Holland's Seat near Margate, Kent," he recalled the brilliance of Alexander Pope's satiric verses.

HOWARD BATCHELOR

Bibliography: Cecil, Lord David, *The Poetry of Thomas Gray* (1945; repr. 1974); Gray, Thomas, *Correspondence*, ed. by Paget Toynbee and Leonard Whibley, 3 vols. (1935; repr. 1971); Ketton-Cremer, R. W., *Thomas Gray: A Biography* (1955; repr. 1973); Sells, A. L., *Thomas Gray: His Life and Works* (1980).

Gray Panthers

The Gray Panthers is a U.S. organization that seeks to combat discrimination against people on the basis of age. Founded in 1971, the group, which includes both old and young members, conducts discussion meetings, does research, lobbies local, state, and federal governments, and maintains an information and referral service. The headquarters of the Gray Panthers is in Philadelphia.

grayling

The grayling is a cold-water fish, related to the salmons, that has a very large and colorful dorsal fin and that supposedly smells like the herb thyme. Because of the combination of its habits of schooling, feeding on surface insects, and leaping, it is a popular sport fish in northern Canada. ALAN R. EMERY

Gray's Anatomy

A standard study of descriptive anatomy, *Gray's Anatomy* has been used by medical students for more than 100 years. It was first published in London in 1858, and an American edition followed in 1859. The original work contained 363 figures drawn by Dr. Henry Vandyke Carter (1831–97). Since then it has gone through numerous editions and revisions, adding photographs, more drawings, and current bibliographic entries, as well as keeping in step with new medical methods.

JANE COLVILLE BETTS

Grayson, David: see BAKER, RAY STANNARD.

graywacke [gray'-wak]

Graywackes are SANDSTONES composed of a mixture of abundant mineral and rock fragments, together with a fine-grained clay matrix that constitutes from 15 to 50 percent of the rock. Graywackes vary widely in their mineral composition and may include fragments of biotite, chlorite, feldspar, hornblende, magnetite, pyroxene, quartz, and serpentine. Their color, as the name implies, is various shadings of gray. Graywacke beds, probably formed by DENSITY CURRENTS, are thin and graded, and they are generally found in geosynclinal areas of thick sediment accumulation. They date from nearly all geological ages, from the Precambrian Time to the Pleistocene Epoch.

Bibliography: Bouma, A. H., and Brouwer, A., eds., *Turbidites* (1964); Dzulynski, S., and Walton, E. K., *Sedimentary Features of Flysch and Greywackes* (1967).

Graz [grahts]

Graz is the capital of Styria province in southeastern Austria. Situated on the Mur River at the foot of the Styrian Alps, it is Austria's second largest city, with a population of 243,166 (1981). It is a rail, cultural, and industrial center with iron and steel works and breweries. Graz manufactures machinery, paper, leather, and optical instruments. Its name is derived from the fortress that was located on top of the Schlossberg (475 m/1,558 ft high), a defensive site since ancient times. During the Middle Ages Graz became the principal city of Styria, and the Leopoldine Habsburgs made it their seat (1379). Noted for its clock tower (1561) and belfry (1588), Graz was founded in 1586.

Graziani, Rodolfo [graht-see-ahn'-ee]

Rodolfo Graziani, b. Aug. 11, 1882, d. Jan. 11, 1955, was an Italian field marshal and supporter of Benito MUSSOLINI. He was commander of the Italian forces in Libya (1930–34), governor of Somaliland (1935–36), viceroy of Ethiopia (1936–37), and governor of Italian East Africa (1938). Commanding Italian forces in Libya in 1940, he advanced into Egypt but soon resigned (March 1941) when defeated by the British under Archibald WAVELL. After the Italian armistice of 1943, Graziani

became defense minister in Mussolini's northern Italian Republic. Sentenced to prison after World War II, he was granted amnesty in 1950 and later headed Italy's neo-Fascist movement.
CHARLES F. DELZELL

greasewood [grees'-wud]

Greasewood is a western North American shrub, *Sarcobatus vermiculatus,* in the goosefoot family, Chenopodiaceae. It grows to about 3 m (10 ft) high, with erect, much-branched stems that turn gray with age. The leaves are stalkless, about 40 mm (1.5 in) long, and fleshy at the tips. The tiny male flowers are borne in catkinlike spikes about 32 mm (1.25 in) long; the small female flowers are produced singly or in pairs at the bases of the leaves. The fruit is a tannish or reddish nutlike achene, up to 5 mm (0.2 in) long, with a coiled-up, or wormlike, embryo. Greasewood contains soluble oxalates, and in quantity it has been toxic to domestic animals, especially sheep.
OLIN S. FEARING

Great Artesian Basin

The Great Artesian Basin, or Great Australian Basin, the world's largest artesian-water area, is situated in east central Australia. This vast, arid lowland covers some 1,751,488 km^2 (676,250 mi^2), more than one-fifth the territory of Australia. The artesian water comes from deep, underground rivers that originate principally in the GREAT DIVIDING RANGE to the east. The water is pumped from depths of as far down as 1,500 m (4,900 ft) and used to irrigate pasture lands. The daily discharge, 1,300,000,000 l (350,000,000 gal), is mostly lost through evaporation and seepage.

Great Australian Bight

The Great Australian Bight is the shallow indentation of the Indian Ocean on the southern coast of Australia. The bight extends from Cape Pasley in Western Australia on the west to Cape Carnot in Southern Australia, on the east, a distance of 1,160 km (720 mi). Its coast is inhospitable, and the waters of the bight are subject to severe storms.

Great Awakening

Between 1720 and 1750 a widespread and intense revival of interest in religion occurred in the American colonies, a phenomenon that supporters called the Great Awakening. The most famous contributor to this contagious religious response was the English itinerant preacher George WHITEFIELD, who became the leader of Calvinistic METHODISM. Other important figures included Theodorus Frelinghuysen, a Dutch Reformed minister of New Brunswick, N.J., and Gilbert TENNENT, a Presbyterian minister in the same town. They were joined in their common preaching effort by Jonathan EDWARDS of Northampton, Mass., who provided the best intellectual defense of the new emphasis on personal religious experience. Together with many other clergymen who shared a heritage of Calvinistic doctrine, these men stressed the importance of vital religious experience as the cornerstone of effective religious life.

More conservative ministers did not welcome the turmoil occasioned by the Great Awakening. Many resented traveling preachers who invaded their parishes and held competitive religious services. Charles CHAUNCY of Boston argued that the new enthusiasm was a form of spiritual derangement where emotions destroyed man's rational control of his destiny. In spite of these opponents, thousands of individuals experienced a new sense of dependence on God's will. Many churches were revitalized, and new converts were added to the lists of faithful members.

Religious enthusiasm tended to wane after 1750, but it did not entirely disappear. During the Revolutionary period many Methodist preachers kept the tradition alive in their congregations. Beginning in 1795 and expanding tremendously through the 1840s, a new revival known as the Second Great Awakening appeared. Evangelists such as Charles G. FINNEY emphasized free will, divine forgiveness for all, and the need of each person to freely accept or reject salvation. The First Great Awakening drew on Calvinist theology, while the Second relied on ARMINIANISM, which allowed human decisions in the salvation process. But their common emphasis made revivals a central feature of American religion through the years
HENRY WARNER BOWDEN

Bibliography: Gaustad, Edwin S., *The Great Awakening in New England* (1968); Rutman, Darrett B., *Great Awakening: Event and Exegesis* (1970).

Great Barrier Reef

The Great Barrier Reef, a formation composed of living coral polyps and their skeletal remains, extends for 2,000 km (1,250 mi) along the northeastern coast of Australia. The reefs contain many islands, including Fairfax Island (foreground), *that are popular tourist resorts.*

The Great Barrier Reef lies in the Coral Sea 15-160 km (10-100 mi) off the eastern coast of QUEENSLAND, Australia. Often called the longest coral reef in the world, it is actually a series of coral islands, reefs, and shoals that extend north to southeast for over 2,000 km (1,250 mi). The coral formations are based on the outer, eastern edge of the CONTINENTAL SHELF, once part of the Queensland coast. They largely consist of the calcified remains of coral polyp built up in strange and beautiful formations over millions of years; there are more than 350 species of coral. Between the Main Reef and the mainland lies the Lagoon, a shallow body of water dotted with hundreds of islands, some of them coral cays, others summits of a drowned coastal mountain range. Vividly colored fish, shells, and giant clams, all clearly visible in the crystalline waters, are a great tourist attraction. The reef was discovered by Capt. James COOK on June 11, 1770, when his ship, the *Endeavour,* ran aground on the reef that now bears the ship's name.

Bibliography: McGregor, Craig, *The Great Barrier Reef* (1973).

Great Basin

The Great Basin, an arid region of the Western United States between the Sierra Nevada Range and the Rocky Mts., covers an area of about 489,500 km^2 (186,000 mi^2). Mountain ranges, with peaks over 3,050 m (10,000 ft), divide it into small deserts, including DEATH VALLEY, the lowest point. John Charles FRÉMONT explored the region in 1843-45 and gave it its name.

Valley floors are PLAYAS or salt flats, often as hard as pavement, but the slopes are covered with mixed deposits of salt and sand. Borax, potash, gold, silver, and tin have been mined at various times. Annual temperatures average 7° C (45° F) in the north and are much higher in the south. Shielded from rainfall by the Sierra Nevadas, the region receives only about 100 to 515 mm (4-20 in) annually. During the PLEISTOCENE EPOCH, the basin held two huge glacial lakes, Lahontan and Bonneville, of which GREAT SALT LAKE is the largest remnant. Rivers, such as the Humboldt, Carson, and Sevier, flow for short distances, ending in salty lakes. Sagebrush and coarse grasses grow on the slopes and juniper and pine in the mountains. Pronghorn, ground squirrels, rabbits, spadefoot toads, quail, and grasshoppers live in the basin. Paiute and Shoshone Indians were early human inhabitants. Today, except in the south, the border areas are populous, since irrigation makes farming possible.

Bibliography: Cline, Gloria G., *Exploring the Great Basin* (1972).

Great Bear Lake

Great Bear Lake is a large, deep freshwater body on the Arctic Circle in the NORTHWEST TERRITORIES of Canada. It covers an area of 31,791 km^2 (12,275 mi^2) and has a maximum depth of 413 m (1,356 ft). Approximately 320 km (200 mi) long and up to 177 km (110 mi) wide, it has an irregular shape with several long arms. One arm extends westward 113 km (70 mi) to Great Bear River, which drains into the MacKenzie River. Radium ores were mined on its eastern shores from 1930 to 1961. Great Bear Lake becomes an important transportation conduit during its four ice-free months. Discovered in about 1800, the lake was first explored (1825) by Sir John FRANKLIN.

Great Books Program

The Great Books Program is an educational system based on readings and discussions of the classics of Western literature. Developed by Robert M. HUTCHINS and Mortimer J. ADLER at The University of Chicago, the program substituted for the traditional lecture the Socratic method of teaching by questioning. Hutchins and Adler selected and edited (1945-52) *Great Books of the Western World*, a 54-volume set that included 443 works by 74 authors from HOMER to Sigmund FREUD. A similar program, which has the works of more than 100 authors on its list of Great Books, is the core of the curriculum at St. John's College in Annapolis, Md., and Santa Fe, N.M.

Great Britain

Great Britain, comprising ENGLAND, SCOTLAND, and WALES, is the principal island of the BRITISH ISLES and the largest island of Europe. The term *Great Britain,* or *Britain*, is popularly used to refer to the UNITED KINGDOM of Great Britain and Northern Ireland.

Great Britain, history of

The story of the British Isles is that of a creative mixture of peoples. In modern times their insularity gave these islands security and enabled them to influence the world more than any other islands in history. Until the Norman Conquest in 1066, however, insularity was no bar to settlement within the islands by peoples from the European continent, since movement by sea was then easier than by land.

ISLAND PEOPLES—TO 1066

Various peoples of different stocks entered Britain in the early stages of its history. It is convenient to call them, from their speech, CELTS and ANGLO-SAXONS. The earlier Celts are now represented by the Irish and Gaelic Scots, the later Celts by the Welsh and Cornish. In addition to the main Germanic element of Angles, Saxons, and Jutes, Scandinavian peoples also settled in Britain—Danes in eastern ENGLAND and Norse (Norwegians) in the northwest, the Hebrides, and around the Irish coast.

Within Britain significant differences have long persisted between the highland and lowland zones. These zones may be demarcated by drawing an imaginary line from the Tyne River in the northeast to Exeter in the southwest. All the land to the south is the lowland zone, and all to the north and west—including WALES, SCOTLAND, and IRELAND—is the highland zone. There is a marked contrast in climate and culture between the two. The lowland was more accessible and open to influences from Europe, while the highland was more isolated and thus more conservative and inward-looking.

Romans. The Roman occupation of Britain illustrates this division. Present in England from AD 43 to *c.*400, the Romans were effectively confined to the lowland zone. Many signs of those four centuries of occupation can be seen today—in the road system that converges on London, in the remarkable resort city of BATH, in HADRIAN'S WALL and other rich archaeological remains, and, most of all, in Christianity, which continued in Britain after the withdrawal of the Romans. In the 5th century, Saint Ninian missionized in Scotland, Saint PATRICK in Ireland. The Britons also produced a significant figure in Pelagius (*c.*355-425), whose heresy of PELAGIANISM upheld the essential goodness of human nature as against the orthodox emphasis on sin as man's condition.

Germanic Settlements. Even before the Roman withdrawal, immigration of the Germanic peoples from across the English Channel and North Sea had begun. Two main waves brought the Anglo-Saxons (English), from *c.*450 to 550, and the Scandinavian VIKINGS, from *c.*800 to 1000. The English gradually pushed the Britons ("Welsh" to them) westward until the former reached (*c.*600) the Mersey and the Bristol Channel. This fragmented the Celtic peoples, who were now concentrated in the areas of Wales, Scotland, and Ireland. Thenceforward the English were the dominant stock in what had become England. The process consisted not only of war and conquest but of colonization. There remained Celtic elements in a gradual fusion of peoples, particularly in WESSEX, which became the dominant kingdom in the later Anglo-Saxon period.

The Roman influence returned in 597, when Saint AUGUSTINE OF CANTERBURY began to convert the pagan English and to gradually organize the English church. Celtic influence also returned from the northwest, as missionaries from Iona, a center of Celtic Christianity, penetrated the Anglo-Saxon kingdoms of NORTHUMBRIA and MERCIA. Rivalry between the Ro-

During the 8th century, Mercia and Northumbria vied to extend their hegemony over the various Anglo-Saxon kingdoms. The country was finally unified under the kings of Wessex, but Anglo-Saxon power was shattered during the 11th century by the Norman Conquest.

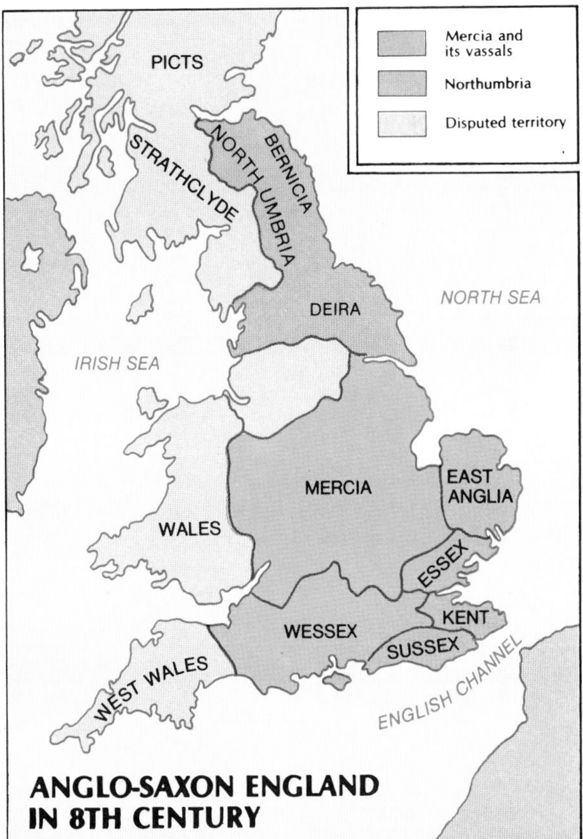

man and Celtic churches ensued, but the Synod of Whitby (664), at which King Oswy of Northumbria adopted Roman usages, set the pattern for the development of the English church. In this period northern England produced one of the greatest European scholars, Saint BEDE, who wrote a classic account of his people's conquest of Britain. And from the southwest came the influential Saint BONIFACE, who was a missionary to the Germans along the Rhine and organized the German church for Rome.

The brilliant early Anglo-Saxon period was ended by the destructive Viking invasions. Responsibility for organizing the English resistance fell to the kings of Wessex. The most notable of these rulers was ALFRED (r. 871-899), who held the line against the Danes and restricted their settlement to the DANELAW, mainly eastern counties where Danes settled alongside of the English. Anglo-Saxon England was much weakened by the continuing Danish raids, and for a time (1016-42) the country was part of the North Sea empire of King CANUTE and his sons.

Norman Conquest. The Vikings, or Norsemen, raided all around northwestern Europe and made their most important settlement across the English Channel in Normandy. The duchy of Normandy became the most highly organized and militarily efficient state in Europe.

The NORMANS decided the future of England. Norman influence was already gaining ground under the last English king, EDWARD THE CONFESSOR, to whom the Norman duke William regarded himself as heir. On Edward's death (1066) William invaded England to claim the throne from the half-Danish HAROLD II. Harold was defeated at the Battle of HASTINGS. The Norman conqueror assumed the English crown as WILLIAM I.

The Norman conquest brought England close to continental Europe in terms of cross-Channel relations with Normandy, France, and the Low Countries. However, the Norman genius for military and political organization meant that England was at last tightly pulled together under an enforced unity and rendered secure from outside invasion. It could now work out its own destiny.

THE MIDDLE AGES, 1066-1485

Norman Rule. For much of the medieval period, England—and, increasingly, Wales, Scotland, and Ireland—was dominated by a French-speaking military aristocracy. The Norman Conquest virtually destroyed the Anglo-Saxon governing class. Their lands were seized, and all resistance was crushed. William the Conqueror devastated northern England in particular. As they destroyed, so also the Normans built—more firmly and efficiently than had been done before. The TOWER OF LONDON, intended to protect the capital and also to overawe it, remains as visual evidence of this. In the north a splendid acropolis, a vast cathedral and castle together, was built at DURHAM to rule the border country and defend it against the Scots.

A detail from the Bayeux Tapestry depicts a scene from the Battle of Hastings (1066), the key engagement of the Norman Conquest. At Hastings, William the Conqueror routed the English defenders under King Harold, the last Anglo-Saxon ruler. (Musée de Bayeux, France.)

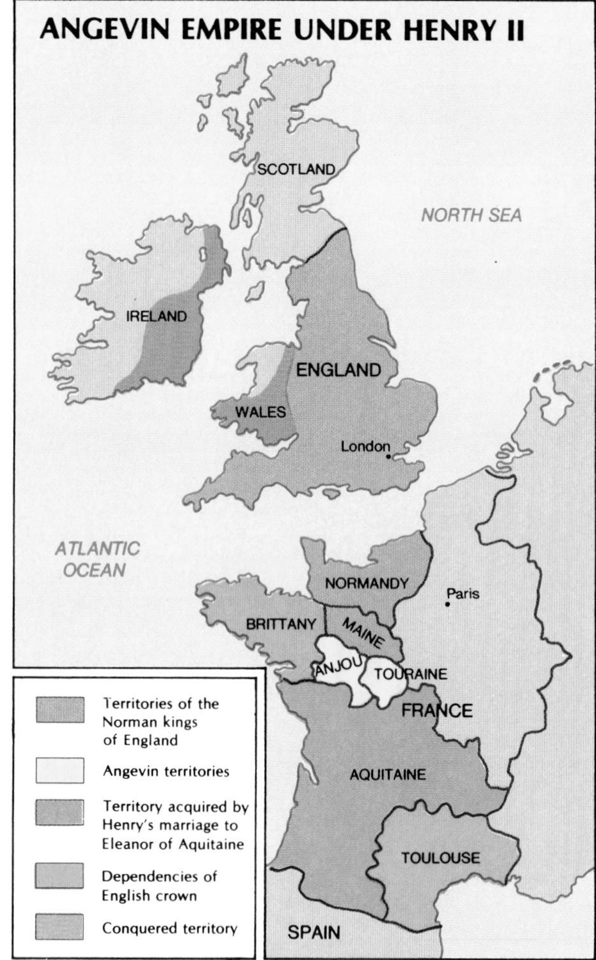

Shaded areas represent the English landholdings in France during the 12th century. With the succession (1154) of Henry II to the English throne, the area of France under English control was more extensive than that under the royal domain of the French sovereign Louis VII.

An even more remarkable monument is DOMESDAY BOOK, which testifies to the Norman genius for administration. Compiled (1085-86) by order of William the Conqueror, it was a complete survey of the land, its holdings, tenures, and services, wealth, population, animals, resources, and taxable capacity. A Russian historian has called the Domesday Book "the greatest record of medieval Europe." The history of British administration is no less remarkable than its constitutional history, which has had widespread influence abroad.

The English hated Domesday Book, Norman taxation, and the harsh Norman rule. They lived their own lives and spoke their own language—or, rather, various dialects of what is now regarded as Middle English. For some years English monks continued to record events in the ANGLO-SAXON CHRONICLE. The English also continued to produce alliterative poetry, which later surfaced in the masterpiece PIERS PLOWMAN.

The lasting achievement of the 12th century was the internal colonization of the land. The new monastic order of the CISTERCIANS contributed to this process; they built their monasteries in sequestered areas, cultivated the land around, and bred great flocks of sheep on hills and wolds. England became the chief supplier of fine wool to the cloth industries of the Low Countries and Italy. The wool trade, which was easily taxable by government (the lord chancellor's seat in the House of Lords is still called a woolsack), was the chief strength of the medieval economy.

Church and State. Along with efficient government, the Normans reformed the church; they brought in men like LANFRANC and Saint ANSELM to set new standards in religion and thought. All over the country splendid cathedrals and monasteries were built as well as the Norman castles that held the country together in a tight spider's web. From these centers a feudal society was organized; most of the land was held by and owed service to Norman lords, who in turn owed allegiance and service to the king (see FEUDALISM).

The reform of the church led to a clash between its claims and those of the state. Both WILLIAM II (r. 1087–1100) and HENRY I (r. 1100–35) fought Anselm in the INVESTITURE CONTROVERSY. Later the church-state conflict was renewed by HENRY II (r. 1154–89) and Thomas BECKET, archbishop of Canterbury. The murder (1170) of Becket by four of Henry's knights created a European furor and forced Henry to confirm the privileges of the church. Canterbury became the shrine of the canonized Becket, whose cult spread all over Europe. He was depicted in stained glass, painted fresco, and manuscript illumination as a prime English saint, although actually he was pure Norman.

Expansion of Influence. Henry II was the heir not only to England and Normandy but to the vast ANGEVIN territories in France. By marriage to ELEANOR OF AQUITAINE he also secured AQUITAINE, whose chief city, Bordeaux, was the center of the wine trade with England. As a result, England's foreign relations focused more than ever upon France.

Meanwhile the powerful Norman military caste pursued expansionist aims closer to home. Normans settled in and gradually feudalized Scotland. Eventually a Norman family, the STUARTS, was to succeed (1371) to the Scottish throne. Norman barons also conquered the Welsh border and much of South Wales. An expedition under Richard de Clare, 2d earl of Pembroke, known as Strongbow, began the Anglo-Norman conquest of Celtic Ireland in 1170. This brought into existence Norman-Celtic feudal families—Fitzgeralds, Butlers, Burkes—who ruled much of Ireland under nominal suzerainty from England.

Legal and Constitutional Developments. Within England an increasingly firm and diverse society flowered, made possible by the internal peace maintained by a strong monarchy. (When the monarch was not strong—as in the reign of STEPHEN and later of John and Henry III—there came periods of confusion and barons' wars.) Henry II gave significant impetus to the development of a system of royal justice that superseded feudal courts. From this there grew up the system of COMMON LAW, based on the decisions of the king's judges, who traveled around the country. In contrast to Roman civil law and the church's canon law, common law reflected the customs and instincts of the English people, who were beginning to recover influence. Norman lawyers, like Ranulf de Glanvill (d. 1190) and Henry de Bracton (d.1268), helped to codify it. Its very flexibility and adaptability (like the empirical spirit of British philosophy later) was to ensure its future importance among English-speaking peoples all over the world, especially in the United States.

A step of later constitutional significance was taken with the granting of MAGNA CARTA in 1215. The document itself registered feudal concessions extracted by the barons and the church from King JOHN (r. 1199–1216), whose position had been drastically weakened by the loss of Normandy. The fact that Magna Carta set forth certain 'liberties," however, opened the way to greater liberties later. Magna Carta became more important in time, especially with the development of PARLIAMENT.

This institution was also to have major significance in all English-speaking countries. Many medieval states had comparable institutions, but none with such a future. Parliament was in origin an extension of the royal council (*curia regis*), in which the king consulted magnates from all over the realm. In 1265, during the BARONS' WAR between HENRY III (r. 1216–72) and the nobility, the baronial leader Simon de MONTFORT summoned a Parliament that also included local gentry from each county (knights of the shire) and middle-class people of the leading towns (burgesses). Thus for the

King Edward I (r. 1272–1307) presides over an early Parliament in this medieval miniature. Edward was obliged to convene Parliaments of varying compositions on several occasions in order to secure the funds to conduct his military campaigns against Wales, Scotland, and France.

first time the whole country was represented—or, at least, all the active elements who ran it. Thereafter, these representatives were generally consulted in times of national emergency—as during foreign wars or rebellions—that necessitated the raising of money.

This gradually strengthened the lower elements in Parliament, the Commons (knights and burgesses), to whom it fell to raise the money. Financial power gave them some control over the executive and eventually won them a share in it. In the end, many centuries later, the House of Commons came to provide the executive—the system called parliamentary government. But the origin was, and the essence has always been, REPRESENTATION. Thus, from this medieval institution flowed the idea of representative government, which is a chief contribution of English-speaking peoples to political practice and thinking throughout the world.

Cultural Development. Universities are another legacy from the Middle Ages. Medieval England had two. Oxford was already a center of learning in the 12th century, when GEOFFREY OF MONMOUTH wrote his *History of the Kings of Britain,* which spread the Arthurian stories into the literatures and arts of Europe. In the 1160s students began to form a university at Oxford, and in the early 13th century a group emigrated from Oxford to start another university at Cambridge. Medieval Oxford was one of the great universities of Europe; its philosophers Roger BACON, John DUNS SCOTUS, and WILLIAM OF OCCAM, among others, were leading European thinkers. This succession ended with John WYCLIFFE, who challenged the foundations of the church and medieval religious thought. His followers exerted marked influence with John HUSS in central Europe; the LOLLARDS, with their translation of the Bible and their preaching, heralded the eventual Reformation.

The 13th century may be regarded as the meridian of medieval culture. It saw not only the rise of the universities but the establishment of new religious orders, the DOMINICANS and FRANCISCANS, who made contributions to philosophic thought. The architectural achievements of the age included WESTMINSTER ABBEY and SALISBURY CATHEDRAL.

The Battle of Poitiers (Sept. 19, 1356) marked a decisive English victory over the French during the Hundred Years' War over territorial rivalries. It was at Poitiers, in France, that Edward, the Black Prince, defeated and captured John II of France.

Renewal of Expansion. The reign (1272-1307) of EDWARD I is important in terms of major legal reforms that further asserted the judicial supremacy of the crown. It also saw the renewal of expansion with Edward's militant aggression against Wales and Scotland. He conquered the mountain fastness of North Wales, building a girdle of splendid castles, the most notable of which was CAERNARVON, seat of the principality that he created for the eldest son of ruling monarchs. Edward also annexed Scotland. This did not last, however. At the Battle of BANNOCKBURN (1314) the Scots under ROBERT I confirmed their independence.

Between 1347 and 1349 the Black Death (see BUBONIC PLAGUE) killed a quarter of the English population. This profoundly disturbed feudal society, leading the peasantry and artisans to demand more for their labor. Ultimately the discontent produced the PEASANTS' REVOLT of 1381.

EDWARD III (r. 1327-77) revived the claims of his ancestors to the French territories and thus began the HUNDRED YEARS' WAR with France. There was an interlude under pacific, art-loving RICHARD II, during whose reign (1377-99) English literature reached new heights with the work of Geoffrey CHAUCER. Richard was, however, an incompetent king, and he was deposed by his cousin HENRY IV (r. 1399-1413), who brought the house of LANCASTER to the throne. Henry's son HENRY V (r. 1413-22) renewed the claims on France. A soldier and ruler of great ability, he defeated the French in the Battle of AGINCOURT (1415) and won the right of succession to the French throne.

Lancaster Versus York. Henry V's extraordinary achievement proved a mirage, for he died young and was succeeded by his infant son, HENRY VI. In France the tide was turned against

KINGS AND QUEENS OF ENGLAND SINCE 871

Anglo-Saxon and Danish Rulers	
Alfred	871-99
Edward the Elder	899-924?
Athelstan	924?-39
Edmund	939-46
Edred	946-55
Edwy	955-59
Edgar	959-75
Edward the Martyr	975-78?
Æthelred the Unready	978?-1013, 1014-16
Sweyn Forkbeard (Danish)	1013-14
Edmund Ironside	1016
Canute (Danish)	1016-35
Harold Harefoot (Danish)	1035-40
Harthacanute (Danish)	1040-42
Edward the Confessor	1042-66
Harold II	1066
Normans	
William I	1066-87
William II	1087-1100
Henry I	1100-35
Stephen	1135-54
Angevins (Plantagenets)	
Henry II	1154-89
Richard I	1189-99
John	1199-1216
Henry III	1216-72
Edward I	1272-1307
Edward II	1307-27
Edward III	1327-77
Richard II	1377-99
House of Lancaster	
Henry IV	1399-1413
Henry V	1413-22
Henry VI	1422-61
House of York	
Edward IV	1461-83
Edward V	1483
Richard III	1483-85
Tudors	
Henry VII	1485-1509
Henry VIII	1509-47
Edward VI	1547-53
Mary I	1553-58
Elizabeth I	1558-1603
Stuarts	
James I	1603-25
Charles I	1625-49
Commonwealth and Protectorate	1649-60
Charles II	1660-85
James II	1685-88
William III and (until 1694) Mary II	1689-1702
Anne	1702-14
Hanoverians	
George I	1714-27
George II	1727-60
George III	1760-1820
George IV	1820-30
William IV	1830-37
Victoria	1837-1901
House of Saxe-Coburg (Windsor)	
Edward VII	1901-10
George V	1910-36
Edward VIII	1936
George VI	1936-52
Elizabeth II	1952-

(Above) *In 1520, Henry VIII* (left) *met with the French king Francis I on the Field of the Cloth of Gold. Henry subsequently allied with Emperor Charles V against France, although he concluded another alliance with France in 1527. The enmity of Charles impeded Henry's attempt to divorce his first wife, Catherine of Aragon, who was Charles's aunt.* (Right) *Elizabeth I enhanced England's power by diplomatic maneuvers designed to pit Spain and France against each other. The ermine on her sleeve in this painting by Nicholas Hilliard is a symbol of virginity. Elizabeth is known as the Virgin Queen.*

the English invaders with the appearance of Joan of Arc, and by 1450 the English were driven out of France (except for Calais, which they held until 1558). This eventuality, combined with the incapacity of Henry VI, produced a dynastic conflict between the royal houses of Lancaster and York resulting in the Wars of the Roses.

These wars (1455-85) distracted the country at intervals without disturbing its social life. The wool industry continued to flourish; in addition to wool production, there was a gradual turn to manufacture in the clothing areas of East Anglia and the West Country. The great churches and civic buildings of such provincial capitals as York, Norwich, and Bristol testify to the period's prosperity. The Perpendicular Gothic Style of these buildings was a specifically English contribution to architecture. The same period produced a monument of English prose in Sir Thomas Malory's Arthurian romances.

The conflict was brought to an end by the victory of the Lancastrian heir, Henry Tudor, over Richard III at Bosworth Field in 1485. The new king, Henry VII, united the two houses by marrying Elizabeth of York, daughter of Richard's predecessor, Edward IV.

THE NATION STATE, 1485-1688

The fact that Henry VII was a Welsh Tudor reconciled Wales to union with England, formalized by the Act of Union (1536). Wales was organized into counties and came under the English system of local government, by which the gentry served as justices of the peace, and received representation in Parliament.

Reformation. Farsighted Henry VII backed the early voyages of John Cabot from Bristol to North America. However, the promise of these early discoveries was not immediately followed up because of Henry VIII's absorption in the English Reformation. Although the Reformation stemmed from Henry's desire to divorce his first wife, Catherine of Aragon, it became a controlled revolution, supervised by the able minister Thomas Cromwell. Henry broke with Rome, subordinated the church to the state, ended monasticism, and annexed vast church properties to the crown. The last were gradually sold and came into the hands of the gentry and middle classes, immensely increasing their economic strength and leading them to claim greater political power through the House of Commons.

Some of these resources were also used to strengthen the nation-state. Henry VIII built a powerful navy and fortified the whole Channel coast. The struggle over the Reformation—Edward VI's reign advanced it, Mary I's retarded it—was resolved by the long and successful reign (1558-1603) of Elizabeth I. During these years the Church of England achieved its permanent character; its intellectual position was defined by the great work of Richard Hooker in *The Laws of Ecclesiastical Polity* (1593). (See England, Church of.)

Elizabethan Age. That issue settled, the Elizabethans were able to renew voyages across the Atlantic and, with Sir Francis Drake and Thomas Cavendish, around the world. Expansive energies drove them to challenge Spain's monopoly of the New World, leading to conflict in the Caribbean and elsewhere. Sir Humphrey Gilbert and Sir Walter Raleigh led the campaign to establish English settlements in North America, taking possession of Newfoundland in 1583 and sending out colonies to Roanoke Island (now in North Carolina) from 1585 on. Many voyages explored the American coasts, and several penetrated the Davis Strait in search of a Northwest Passage to China and the Far East.

Voyages searching for a Northeast Passage opened up direct sea routes to Russia. The English were given privileges in Russian trade that extended to the Caspian Sea and Persia. From 1580 strong expeditions into the Mediterranean produced direct trade with Turkey and the Middle East; companies were formed in London for this purpose. In 1600 the British East India Company was founded to make trading voyages around the Cape of Good Hope; from these beginnings British interests in the East rapidly expanded.

Spain was determined to keep other Europeans out of the New World. Moreover, its efforts to suppress the revolt

English ships approach Roanoke Island, which lies between the mainland of North Carolina and the treacherous Outer Banks. The first English settlement in the New World was founded on Roanoke in 1585, but the small colony had disappeared by 1591.

against Spanish rule in the Netherlands posed a direct threat to nearby England, especially since the Spanish king, Philip II, supported revolt against Elizabeth I. These factors precipitated a long war between England and Spain from 1585 to 1604. The defeat of the Spanish Armada of 1588 increased the self-confidence of the Elizabethans and gave a patriotic inspiration to the brilliant Elizabethan Age. This was expressed creatively in literature and the arts, in a general cultural renaissance, and in scientific development, particularly in cosmography and navigation. The work of William Shakespeare and others made the Elizabethan era one of the most creative periods in the history of drama.

In the conflict with Spain, Ireland lay strategically open to Spanish incursion, the more so since it remained overwhelmingly Roman Catholic. Under Queen Elizabeth, therefore, Ireland was increasingly subjugated, a process completed by the reduction of Ulster and the latter's partial plantation with Scottish settlers after the accession of James I.

Plantation in Ireland served as a blueprint for colonization in North America. After the war with Spain ended (1604), the London Company was founded, and Jamestown was established (1607) in Virginia. Efforts in New England were begun, but development there awaited the arrival of the Pilgrims in 1620 and the larger settlement of Puritans (see Puritanism) in the 1630s.

Union and Division. The accession (1603) of the Stuart, James VI of Scotland, to the English throne as James I brought the personal union of the Scottish and English crowns. Although institutional union of the two kingdoms did not occur until 1707, the whole of Great Britain was now united under a Scottish dynasty. It proved almost impossible, however, to hold the kingdoms together on one course. They differed in religion, even within each country, and this exacerbated political differences and produced conflicts, civil war, and rebellions at intervals throughout the 17th century.

England was largely Anglican. Scotland had been won over to the Calvinist Reformation by John Knox and emerged predominantly Presbyterian. Ireland remained Catholic, except for the now-Scottish Presbyterian northeast.

There were also religio-political divisions within each country. The most dynamic movement was that of the Puritans in England, who wanted a Presbyterian established church. They were a minority, but they continued to increase their strength in eastern England, among the growing urban middle class, and, above all, in London, whose commercial and financial resources held the key to the situation. Puritan sympathies in Parliament won a narrow majority in the House of Commons,

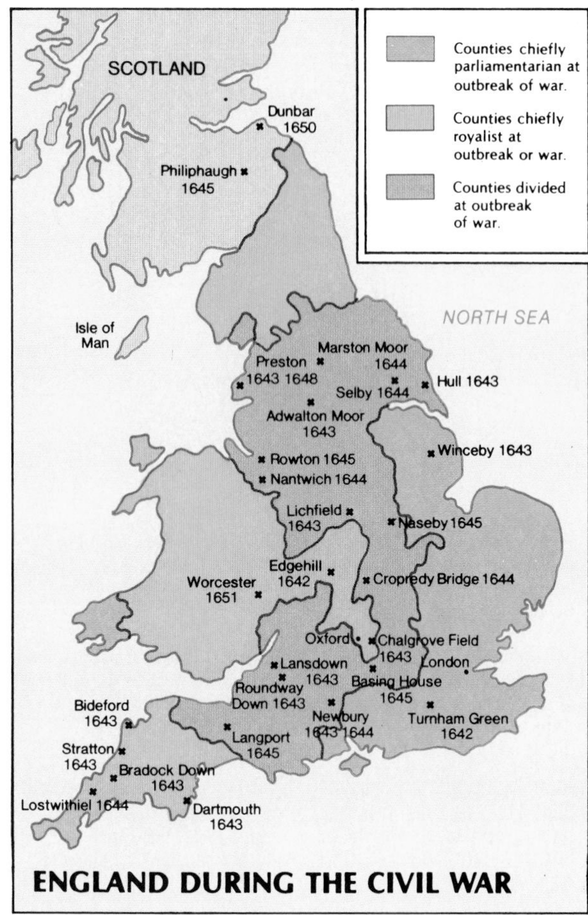

(Above) *The map indicates the major battles of the English Civil War (1642-51) and the political sympathies of the English counties at the beginning of the struggle between the king and Parliament. The victory of the parliamentarians led to the establishment of a republic.*

which was soon pitted against CHARLES I (r. 1625-49) and the Anglican church. Puritan intellectual leadership was provided largely by Cambridge University, which had risen to prominence in the Reformation. And, of course, the Puritan parliamentarians had allies in New England and, above all, in Scotland.

Conflict finally erupted in the ENGLISH CIVIL WAR. In the first war (1642-46), the Puritans brought in the Scottish Presbyterians to turn the tide and decide the issue of power. They already had far superior resources—economic, military, and naval—but they were divided among themselves—moderates against radicals, Presbyterians against Independents (Congregationalists), and Parliament against the army headed by Oliver CROMWELL. In 1648 civil war was renewed, with the defeated King Charles now in alliance with the Scots. Charles was again defeated, and Cromwell's army, having seized control from Parliament, brought about the judicial murder of the king. After this act no reconciliation was possible.

The army next proceeded to subdue (1649-50) the royalists in Ireland. The lands of royalists and Catholics were expropriated on a large scale and granted to Cromwellian soldiers and settlers, who provided a nucleus for the Protestant ascendancy that controlled Ireland until 1922. The Presbyterian Scots revolted and invaded England to restore the monarchy under CHARLES II. However, Cromwell defeated the Scots at both Dunbar (1650) and Worcester (1651); Scotland was occupied and an enforced union imposed. England, Scotland, and Ireland became a republic—called first the Commonwealth, later the Protectorate, with Cromwell as lord protector.

Republic and Restoration. The dynamic impulse of the English republic was seen in its aggressive expansion, as well as its military and naval efficiency. Puritans had earlier been in the fore of colonizing and imperialist enterprises; now the same spirit directed national policy. The first of the ANGLO-DUTCH WARS was fought (1652-54) for commercial and maritime supremacy; parity was achieved. In addition, Cromwell renewed war against Spain both in the Caribbean and the Mediterranean.

Cromwell's army dictatorship could not last, however. It rested on a small minority in the country, strained the nation's resources, and was bound to end with Cromwell himself, who could neither find a civilian basis for his rule nor reconcile England—let alone Scotland or Ireland—to it. The restoration of both the monarchy and Parliament was the only hope for a permanent solution. Royalists and parliamentarians came together to effect it with the RESTORATION of Charles II in 1660. This move marked the restoration of the governing classes and the Anglican church. The Puritan Revolution had proved abortive; henceforth Puritanism took the form of minority sects of NONCONFORMISTS.

Restored Stuart rule rested on a compromise between the crown and Parliament—the terrible civil war had at least achieved this balance. The crown continued to provide the executive, but it had to rule on the basis—and with the support—of Parliament. With this settled, the ruling elements in the nation, with the commercial and maritime interests constantly increasing in power, renewed their drive for trade and colonies overseas.

The second Anglo-Dutch War (1664-67) added New York to the growing chain of English North American colonies. English trading factories in India—particularly Calcutta, Madras, and Bombay—portended the extension of British rule from these bases.

JAMES II, who succeeded Charles II in 1685, attempted to overturn the political and religious balance by his Catholicizing policy—he was himself a Roman Catholic—and his attempt to gain greater power for the monarchy. This united the governing classes of both the WHIG and TORY parties—which had just developed—against him. They called in his son-in-law, the Dutch and Protestant William of Orange, to replace him as WILLIAM III. This was effected by the so-called GLORIOUS REVOLUTION of 1688.

Once again the decision in England was contested in Ireland, but imposed by force upon it— James's supporters were defeated at the Battle of the BOYNE in 1690. A compromise was effected in Scotland by recognition of Presbyterianism as the national Church of Scotland (see SCOTLAND, CHURCH OF). This rendered possible the subsequent Act of Union (1707),

King Charles I was tried by a parliamentary court and beheaded in 1649, becoming the only reigning British monarch to be executed. Charles had assured his fate by secretly inviting a Scottish army to invade England after his own royalist forces had been defeated.

(Above) *An equestrian statue of King George III is toppled by jubilant New Yorkers on receiving news of the adoption of the Declaration of Independence in 1776. The loss of the American colonies changed the focus of British imperialism, which in the 19th century was directed primarily toward Asia and Africa.*

(Right) *A British infantry unit defends its position against a French cavalry charge in a scene from the Battle of Waterloo (June 18, 1815), which marked the final defeat of Napoleon I. Britain waged almost continuous war from 1793.*

which made Scotland an equal partner with England in economic and colonial enterprise and gave it representation in Parliament. The way was now open to Scottish participation in government and trade—in London and throughout the growing empire.

The constitutional settlement of the Glorious Revolution, which in effect ensured the supremacy of Parliament, besides barring Catholics from the throne, gave England enough stability to take the lead—with Holland—in the European resistance to the ascendancy of France. This struggle was to be fought out in a series of wars lasting from 1689 to 1815.

EMPIRE AND INDUSTRIAL REVOLUTION, 1688-1837

A cardinal principle of British policy was to maintain the balance of power against any state that was so strong as to threaten the independence of others. In that principle Britain found its own security—as against Philip II's Spain and later against LOUIS XIV's France.

French Wars and American Revolution. Britain began its participation in the wars against Louis XIV with the War of the GRAND ALLIANCE (1689-97). This was followed by the larger-scaled War of the SPANISH SUCCESSION, which began (1702) after Louis had claimed the inheritance of the whole Spanish Empire for his grandson Philip V. For the British this conflict was known as Marlborough's war. John Churchill, 1st duke of MARLBOROUGH, won a succession of victories, the most striking of which was the Battle of BLENHEIM (1704) in Bavaria. By the Peace of Utrecht (1713; see UTRECHT, PEACE OF) some restraint was placed upon France, although the Bourbon dynasty retained the Spanish throne. This led to a series of alliances—Family Compacts—by which France and Spain fought several wars against Britain and its allies.

In 1714 the death of the last Stuart monarch, ANNE, brought to the throne the elector of Hanover, GEORGE I. Rebellions (1715, 1745) by the JACOBITES (supporters of James II's descendants) could not unseat the new German dynasty. The Hanoverian connection involved Britain even more closely in European affairs and wars.

Although the War of the AUSTRIAN SUCCESSION (1742-48) resulted in little change, the SEVEN YEARS' WAR (1756-63) was a different matter. Through the exercise of sea power and under the inspired leadership of William PITT the Elder, Britain won Canada (1760) and eliminated French power in India. This constituted the apogee of the first BRITISH EMPIRE, which now included much of North America.

With the threat from French Canada removed, however, the American colonies moved toward independence. The London government's determination to make the colonies bear part of the expense of the wars (called the FRENCH AND INDIAN WARS in America) raised colonial protests against taxation without representation. An impasse was reached, which resulted in the AMERICAN REVOLUTION and, ultimately, British recognition (1783) of the independence of the United States of America.

France had aided the colonies in the American Revolution, and ten years later Britain was again engaged in war with France. This time it was a mortal struggle with Revolutionary and later Napoleonic France (see FRENCH REVOLUTIONARY WARS; NAPOLEONIC WARS). Britain's command of the sea narrowly averted invasion by NAPOLEON I and finally helped to overthrow France's rule over Europe. The long duel with France was over.

During the crisis of the American war British rule in India was saved by a great proconsul, Warren HASTINGS. Upon the collapse of the MOGUL empire, Britain filled the vacuum, and gradually and reluctantly the British government took over responsibility for rule from the East India Company. At the conclusion of the Napoleonic Wars, Britain retained Cape Colony (South Africa), which it had captured from the Dutch, as a station on the route to India. The British Empire was set for a new stage of development.

Economic Development. Certain internal developments had

PRIME MINISTERS OF GREAT BRITAIN

Ministers	Party	Dates	Ministers	Party	Dates
Sir Robert Walpole	Whig	1721-42	Earl Russell	Liberal	1865-66
Earl of Wilmington	Whig	1742-43	Earl of Derby	Conservative	1866-68
Henry Pelham	Whig	1743-54	Benjamin Disraeli	Conservative	1868
Duke of Newcastle	Whig	1754-56	William E. Gladstone	Liberal	1868-74
Duke of Devonshire	Whig	1756-57	Benjamin Disraeli (Earl of Beaconsfield)	Conservative	1874-80
Duke of Newcastle	Whig	1757-62	William E. Gladstone	Liberal	1880-85
Earl of Bute	Tory	1762-63	Marquess of Salisbury	Conservative	1885-86
George Grenville	Whig	1763-65	William E. Gladstone	Liberal	1886
Marquess of Rockingham	Whig	1765-66	Marquess of Salisbury	Conservative	1886-92
William Pitt the Elder (Earl of Chatham)	Whig	1766-68	William E. Gladstone	Liberal	1892-94
Duke of Grafton	Whig	1768-70	Earl of Rosebery	Liberal	1894-95
Lord North	Tory	1770-82	Marquess of Salisbury	Conservative	1895-1902
Marquess of Rockingham	Whig	1782	Arthur J. Balfour	Conservative	1902-05
Earl of Shelburne	Whig	1782-83	Sir Henry Campbell-Bannerman	Liberal	1905-08
Duke of Portland	Coalition	1783	Herbert H. Asquith	Liberal	1908-15
William Pitt the Younger	Tory	1783-1801	Herbert H. Asquith	Coalition	1915-16
Henry Addington	Tory	1801-04	David Lloyd George	Coalition	1916-22
William Pitt the Younger	Tory	1804-06	Andrew Bonar Law	Conservative	1922-23
William Wyndham Grenville, Baron Grenville	Whig	1806-07	Stanley Baldwin	Conservative	1923-24
Duke of Portland	Tory	1807-09	Ramsay MacDonald	Labour	1924
Spencer Perceval	Tory	1809-12	Stanley Baldwin	Conservative	1924-29
Earl of Liverpool	Tory	1812-27	Ramsay MacDonald	Labour	1929-31
George Canning	Tory	1827	Ramsay MacDonald	Coalition	1931-35
Viscount Goderich	Tory	1827-28	Stanley Baldwin	Coalition	1935-37
Duke of Wellington	Tory	1828-30	Neville Chamberlain	Coalition	1937-40
Earl Grey	Whig	1830-34	Winston Churchill	Coalition	1940-45
Viscount Melbourne	Whig	1834	Winston Churchill	Conservative	1945
Sir Robert Peel	Tory	1834-35	Clement Attlee	Labour	1945-51
Viscount Melbourne	Whig	1835-41	Sir Winston Churchill	Conservative	1951-55
Sir Robert Peel	Tory	1841-46	Sir Anthony Eden	Conservative	1955-57
Lord John Russell (later Earl Russell)	Whig	1846-52	Harold Macmillan	Conservative	1957-63
Earl of Derby	Tory	1852	Sir Alec Douglas-Home	Conservative	1963-64
Earl of Aberdeen	Peelite Coalition	1852-55	Harold Wilson	Labour	1964-70
Viscount Palmerston	Liberal	1855-58	Edward Heath	Conservative	1970-74
Earl of Derby	Conservative	1858-59	Harold Wilson	Labour	1974-76
Viscount Palmerston	Liberal	1859-65	James Callaghan	Labour	1976-79
			Margaret Thatcher	Conservative	1979-

enabled Britain to defeat France, which was three times its size and had more than twice its population. Scotland was making rapid progress in commerce, agriculture, and manufacturing.

In the late 18th and early 19th century a brilliant cultural epoch centered upon Edinburgh, "the Athens of the North."

An 1814 print depicts a Yorkshire miner against the background of a pithead, with a pit railroad and steam-driven winding gear. Technological advances of the period made Great Britain the world's first industrialized nation, but also intensified social problems.

In Ireland, Dublin became a cultural center, as is reflected in its architectural distinction.

England developed tremendous power with its INDUSTRIAL REVOLUTION. In essence this meant the application of mechanical power to every form of manufacture and industry. Water power gave Yorkshire a lead in woolens; Lancashire became a world center for cottons, importing the raw material from America; and BELFAST, in northeast Ireland, was the center of the linen industry.

Communications were facilitated by a network of canals and a new road system. Vast deposits of coal and iron in various parts of Britain led to the growth of heavy industry, particularly steel. The application of steam power revolutionized mining and soon led to the invention of the steam locomotive and the development of railroads. Next, steel revolutionized shipbuilding.

Britain was not only becoming the workshop of the world but was also creating the foundation of its modern industrial civilization.

Concurrently agriculture was transformed and productivity increased by large-scale ENCLOSURE of land and improved rotation of crops; steam power was also applied to operations on the land. Country-house civilization and the planned beauty of the countryside reached a peak about 1800. The population doubled, while large numbers emigrated to America and to new colonies in Australia and New Zealand.

Social and Political Change. The social and political consequences of economic change were profound and were, in time, to transform society in both islands. The Irish emigrated both to industrial Britain and overseas. The growth of the middle classes challenged the rule of landed aristocracy and gentry. The middle class demanded reform and a widening of

William Ewart Gladstone, leader of the Liberal party and four times prime minister of Great Britain, consults with Queen Victoria over issues of state. Gladstone was often at odds with his sovereign, who preferred his Conservative rival, the flamboyant Benjamin Disraeli.

opportunities in every sphere—political, social, educational, and religious, as well as in public health, medicine, and nutrition.

John WESLEY, a religious leader and brilliant organizer, worked among the new industrial masses and created—unwillingly—the Methodist church, which took root both at home and in America (see METHODISM). The expanding lower classes swelled Methodist membership as well as that of other nonconformist sects. The Church of England was also revived by the Evangelical movement— inspired from Cambridge—among Low Churchmen, and by the OXFORD MOVEMENT among High Churchmen. Both had their influence and following overseas; the former inspired the abolition of the slave trade in 1807 and of slavery throughout British dominions by 1834.

The middle-class demand to share in government created agitation for reform from the late 18th century on. William PITT the Younger, who was prime minister from 1783 to 1801 and again in 1804-05, favored reform in most spheres but was frustrated by the long struggle against revolutionary France. Pitt brought to an end an experiment, begun in 1782, of nominal self-government in Ireland. The intended effect of his act (1801), to unite the Irish in a British parliament, was ruined by the refusal of King GEORGE III to allow enfranchisement of the Catholic population. CATHOLIC EMANCIPATION was not conceded until 1829—too late to avert increasing unrest among the Irish. In Britain the REFORM ACT of 1832 broadened parliamentary representation and opened the way for the middle class to share in power.

Reform was now underway in every area: administration, local and municipal government, the POOR LAWS, sanitation, and factory conditions. The Anglican monopoly of the old universities was ended, and new universities were started. Reform lagged behind in the army and navy and in lower education.

VICTORIAN AND MODERN ERAS

The Victorian Age—named for Queen VICTORIA, who reigned from 1837 to 1901—saw another peak reached, economically, politically, and culturally, with the diffusion of the English language and literature throughout the world. The growth of the United States helped make the fortune of Britain, for during this time, which has been called the Railway Age, British entrepreneurs built railroads at home and overseas as well.

Free Trade and Further Reform. The growth of the industrial working class necessitated cheaper food. In 1846 the repeal of the CORN LAWS initiated the era of FREE TRADE. British agricultural interests were further hit when wheat from the American Middle West, transported by rail and steamship, poured into Britain from the 1870s on.

The unfortunate CRIMEAN WAR (1854-56), brought on by Russian expansion in the Middle East, revealed the inefficiency of aristocratic government and speeded up army reform. Benjamin DISRAELI sought to broaden the appeal of the old Tory party and, building on the beginnings made by Sir Robert PEEL, created the modern CONSERVATIVE PARTY. On the other side the Whigs gradually developed into the LIBERAL PARTY, led for many years by William Ewart GLADSTONE.

Gladstone, the champion of reform, began the task of dismantling the old regime in England as well as in Ireland, where he disestablished the Anglican Church of Ireland and began to dispossess the landlords in hopes of creating a society of peasant proprietors. He favored self-government for Ireland, but his HOME RULE BILLS were defeated (1886 and 1894) by Unionist opposition. Gladstone championed liberalism and self-government everywhere (including South Africa). He was the antithesis of his contempory Otto von BISMARCK, whose unification of Germany by "blood and iron" portended ill for the future.

During this period the civil service was transformed by the introduction of an examination system. Numerous "public schools" (actually private institutions) were founded for the growing middle class. In 1870 a national system of primary education was belatedly created; not until 1902 was a complete nationwide system of secondary education brought into existence. (See BRITISH EDUCATION.)

The Empire. The INDIAN MUTINY of 1857 ended the rule of the East India Company in India, and administration there was taken over directly by the crown. In Canada, where the Scottish element was large and provided many political leaders, the provinces formed a confederation in 1867. Australia achieved a similar federal union in 1901. Hopes of collaboration between the Dutch Boers and the British in South Africa were disastrously set back by the SOUTH AFRICAN WAR of 1899-1902. The British won the war, but the establishment (1910) of the Union of South Africa gave the Boers (Afrikaners) effective control. Britain obtained substantial colonial holdings elsewhere in Africa as a result of the late-19th-century partition of that continent by the European powers.

World Wars. Britain had enjoyed a century of unprecedented security behind the shelter of naval supremacy, which was no threat to others and indeed gave security to both North and South America. The determination of the new German Empire to build a powerful navy gravely threatened Britain's existence, since it depended on overseas imports to feed its population. This, more than anything, caused Britain to end its isolationist policy toward Europe and align itself with France and Russia in the TRIPLE ENTENTE (1904, 1907).

In the ensuing WORLD WAR I (1914-18) Britain lost the large part of a generation of young men. The domestic effect of the war was to accelerate many social and political developments.

A Labour party campaign poster in the 1920s extols Ramsay MacDonald's abilities as a peacemaker. MacDonald, who served three terms as prime minister of Great Britain (1924, 1929-31, 1931-35), demonstrated considerable skill in the formulation and implementation of foreign policy but split the Labour party when he formed a coalition with the Conservatives in 1931.

Sir Winston Churchill, who provided strong leadership when Britain stood alone against Nazi Germany during World War II, flashes his famous "V for victory" sign. Churchill regulated the nation's wartime economy, coordinated military strategy with Britain's allies, and played a vital role in the agreements that shaped the postwar world.

Women, who worked in various industries during the war, won limited (1918) and then full (1928) suffrage. The issue of Irish home rule, which had brought Ireland to the brink of civil war in 1914, was placed on the political back stage for the duration of the war; however, increasing nationalist revolutionary activity and unionist resistance led to the partition (1920) of Ireland and the creation (1922) of the Irish Free State in the south. The war also split the old Liberal party, and after the defeat of its renegade leader David LLOYD GEORGE in 1922, it dwindled and never regained strength. Its place was taken by the LABOUR PARTY, which formed its first government in 1924 and its second in 1929-31.

Economic dislocation caused widespread hardship and industrial unrest in the early 1920s, and in 1926 there was a GENERAL STRIKE. Economic difficulties increased with the worldwide depression of the 1930s. Ramsay MACDONALD's second Labour government was converted into a coalition in 1931, and coalitions, soon dominated by the Conservatives, ruled the country until 1945. The abdication (1936) of King EDWARD VIII—so that he might marry an American divorcée—provided temporary distraction from economic woes and the mounting threat of Nazi Germany. The appeasement policy of Prime Minister Neville CHAMBERLAIN failed, and in September 1939, Britain again declared war on Germany. Wartime leadership was soon assumed by Winston CHURCHILL.

As a result of WORLD WAR II, European primacy in the world came to an end. The creation (1947) of the independent states of India and Pakistan set in train the achievement of independence by nearly all Britain's colonies in the following 2 decades. Most, however, retained some ties with Britain in the COMMONWEALTH OF NATIONS.

Welfare State. The end of the war in 1945 brought to power the first majority Labour government. Britain already had a system of old-age pensions and health and unemployment insurance, first enacted by the Liberal government just prior to World War I. The post-World War II Labour government greatly extended social services and created (1948) the National Health Service, a system of socialized medicine. It also nationalized the Bank of England, the coal and steel industries, the railroads, communications facilities, and a number of other vital enterprises. The denationalization and then renationalization of some of these industries by subsequent Conservative (1951-64, 1970-74, 1979-) and Labour (1964-70, 1974-79) governments were not conducive to economic stability. The social services of the WELFARE STATE, however, have been maintained.

Since the mid-1960s, Britain has been subject to mounting economic problems—partly the product of its loss of colonial markets, partly the result of its failure to keep pace in both plant and labor and managerial practices with more recently industrialized nations. Britain entered the European Economic Community in 1973, thus loosening Commonwealth ties. These ties were further affected by the imposition, beginning in the 1960s, of restrictions on immigration from Commonwealth countries. In part this reflected the racial tensions afflicting Britain's efforts to absorb a growing nonwhite minority during a time of economic austerity.

Britain entered the 1980s under its first woman prime minister, Conservative Margaret THATCHER, whose policies of economic retrenchment were under heavy attack by 1981. The government rallied support when it sent a British force to retake the crown colony of the FALKLAND ISLANDS, seized by Argentina in April 1982. In June 1983 the Conservatives won a decisive victory at the polls; despite a sluggish economy, and record unemployment, they retained their majority against a divided opposition in the 1987 elections, with Thatcher winning a third term. Tensions in NORTHERN IRELAND continued despite the 1985 signing of an Anglo-Irish accord granting Ireland a consultative role in determining the future of that long-troubled area.

A. L. ROWSE

Bibliography: Briggs, A., *A Social History of England* (1985); Childs, D., *Britain since 1945* (1980; repr. 1984); Churchill, Sir Winston, *History of the English-Speaking Peoples,* 4 vols. (1956-58); Clark, G. N., ed., *Oxford History of England,* 15 vols. (1937-65); Haigh, C., ed., *The Cambridge Historical Encyclopedia of Great Britain and Ireland* (1985); Havighurst, A. F., *Britain in Transition,* 4th ed. (1985); Morgan, K. O., ed., *The Oxford Illustrated History of England* (1984); Porter, B., *Britain, Europe and the World 1850-1982* (1984).

See also: IRELAND, HISTORY OF; UNITED KINGDOM.

great circle

A great circle is a circle on the surface of a sphere that divides the sphere into two equal hemispheres. The shortest distance between two points on a spherical surface is always along the arc of a great circle. On Earth, lines of longitude and the equator are great circles.

Great Dane

The Great Dane is one of the largest of all dogs. Its accepted minimum height at the shoulders is 71.1 cm (28 in) for females and 76.2 cm (30 in) for males. Despite the origin implied by its name, the Great Dane was first bred in Germany and was used initially to hunt wild boar.

The Great Dane is one of the most distinguished breeds of giant dogs. Egyptian monuments from about 3000 BC supposedly contain drawings of dogs like the Great Dane. The modern breed reached its present state in Germany in the late 19th century. There is no known reason for connecting the Great Dane with Denmark. The name was adopted by the English from the French, *grand Danois.* Males must be 76.2 cm (30 in) at the shoulder and females 71.1 cm (28 in), but it is preferable that males be at least 81.3 cm (32 in) and females at least 76.2 cm (30 in). The Dane is powerful and smooth-coated, with a massive rectangular head, cropped ears (except in Britain), and a long, curved tail carried low. Its broad range of colors include brindle, fawn, blue, black, and harlequin (in which a white dog has black patches of color).

JOHN MANDEVILLE

Bibliography: Draper, Nancy-Carroll, *The Great Dane: Dogdom's Apollo* (1981); Lanning, Jean, *The Great Dane,* 3d ed. (1974).

Great Dividing Range

The Great Dividing Range, a series of ranges and plateaus in Australia, extends 3,700 km (2,300 mi) from Cape York Peninsula through central Victoria to Tasmania. The ranges are between 160 km (100 mi) and 320 km (200 mi) wide and vary in elevation from 610 to 2,135 m (2,000 to 7,000 ft). The highest point, Mount Kosciusko, rises to 2,228 m (7,310 ft).

The belt of highlands acts as a watershed between the short, swift, eastern streams and the longer, west-flowing rivers that compose the Murray-Darling drainage system. The rocks, mostly sedimentary, are covered by substantial amounts of fertile volcanic soils, and vegetation varies from tropical rain forest to alpine meadows. Coal mining, forestry, agriculture, winter sports, and the production of hydroelectric power are important regional industries. Once a barrier to migration into the Australian interior, the highlands were first crossed (1813) by William Lawson, Gregory Blaxland, and William Charles Wentworth.

Great Eastern

A forerunner of the ocean liner, the British iron steamship *Great Eastern* was the largest ship in the world when it was launched in 1858 and was not surpassed in size for more than 40 years. It was 211 m (692 ft) long, displacing 18,915 tons—27,400 tons when fully loaded. Designed by the engineers Isambard Kingdom BRUNEL and John Scott Russell, the ship carried sails on six masts to supplement two sets of engines powering 18-m (59-ft) paddlewheels and a 7.2-m (24-ft) screw propeller. It had an enormous coal-carrying capacity to enable it to cruise to Australia without refueling. The first ship built without ribs, the *Great Eastern* relied for strength on two hulls, one inside the other; longitudinal and transverse bulkheads divided the interior into 12 compartments.

Beset with misfortunes from the first attempts at launching in 1857, the ship bankrupted its backers and may have contributed to Brunel's fatal stroke in 1859. Finally commissioned for the transatlantic trade, the *Great Eastern* made its maiden voyage in June 1860 from Southampton to New York in 11 days. The ship made several more Atlantic crossings but did not have enough power for adequate control in severe storms, and the service lost money. In 1865–66 it successfully laid the transatlantic cables; in 1870 it rounded the Cape of Good Hope to lay the Bombay-to-Aden cables to Europe. In 1867, Napoleon III chartered it to carry Americans to the Paris Exhibition. Among the passengers was young Jules Verne, who was inspired to write *Une Ville flottante (A Floating City),* published in 1871. Superseded by a custom-built cable ship in 1874, the *Great Eastern* was used for a time as a showboat but was finally broken up for scrap metal in 1888.

FRANCES GIES

Bibliography: Dugan, James, *The Great Iron Ship* (1954).

Great Expectations

Great Expectations (1860–61) is a late novel by Charles DICKENS that takes as its subject youth's delusive assumptions about success and innocence. The early involvement of the protagonist, Pip, with two worlds of exile—that of the escaped convict Magwitch and that of the reclusive Miss Havisham—is the central experience in his maturation, which is marked as much by false pride and guilt as by flattering prospects. In branding failures of love (in Pip's sister, in Miss Havisham, in Estella, and in the flawed hero himself) as worse transgressions than the infractions of the victimized Magwitch, Dickens here condemns what he considers ignoble and unrealistic aloofness from humbleness and degradation. Evocative descriptions of the Kent Marshes, of the Thames, and of London legal life symbolically enhance the theme. The author's rich humor, celebrating eccentricity and deflating humbug, offsets his melodramatic lapses in this suspenseful, psychologically ambitious work.

MARGARET GANZ

Bibliography: Collins, P., ed., *Dickens: The Critical Heritage* (1971); Miller, J. Hillis, *Charles Dickens: The World of His Novels* (1958).

Great Falls

Great Falls (1980 pop., 56,725) is the seat of Cascade County in west central Montana. Located on the Missouri River at an altitude of 1,015 m (3,330 ft), it is near the 28-m (93-ft) falls for which it is named. The city has a diversified economy. Copper, zinc, and aluminum are processed, flour is milled from nearby wheatfields, and there is a large crude-oil refinery. Malmstrom Air Force Base, site of an intercontinental ballistic missile installation, is located nearby.

Great Gatsby, The [gats'-bee]

The Great Gatsby (1925), F. Scott FITZGERALD's most famous novel, is considered by many his finest single work. In the protagonist, Jay Gatsby, Fitzgerald effectively embodies a romantic idealism that is sustained and destroyed by the intensity of his own dreams. The story is narrated by a Fitzgerald-like character, Nick Carraway, who engages the reader in the depiction of Gatsby's flawed grandeur and in the characterizations of Gatsby's love, Daisy, Daisy's husband, Tom Buchanan, Tom's mistress, Myrtle Wilson, and Myrtle's pallid husband. Expertly constructed and marvelously evocative of the inner emptiness of the Jazz Age's beautiful people, the novel has the air of myth. Few readers can escape perceiving in it the conflict between materialism and idealism that created and still defines the American character.

KENNETH EBLE

Bibliography: Hoffman, F., ed., *"The Great Gatsby"* (1962); Long, Robert C., *The Achieving of the Great Gatsby: F. Scott Fitzgerald, 1920–25* (1981); Piper, H., ed., *Fitzgerald's "The Great Gatsby"* (1970).

Great Lakes

SUPERIOR, MICHIGAN, HURON, ERIE, and ONTARIO, the Great Lakes, are located in east central North America at the border

The Great Eastern, *a forerunner of the modern ocean liner, was the largest vessel in the world when launched in 1858. Despite three means of propulsion—six masts of sails, two paddlewheels, and a screw propeller—the ship had barely sufficient power to weather storms at sea.*

between Canada and the United States. With an area of 246,490 km^2 (95,145 mi^2), they are collectively the world's largest body of fresh water. The lakes' drainage basin of some 765,000 km^2 (295,000 mi^2) extends 1,110 km (690 mi) north to south and 1,385 km (860 mi) west to east. The lakes drain generally from west to east into the Atlantic Ocean. The lakes were created by the scouring of Ice Age glaciers, the last of which melted and retreated approximately 18,000 years ago.

The first European to explore the Great Lakes was Samuel de CHAMPLAIN in 1615, and the lakes played a crucial role as a route for settlers traveling to the interior of the North American continent. The lakes are connected by straits or canals and are navigable for 1,930 km (1,200 mi) from Duluth, Minn., at their western tip to the eastern end of Lake Ontario. Ocean-going vessels from the Atlantic Ocean can reach the lakes through the ST. LAWRENCE SEAWAY. In recent years measures have been taken to combat pollution of the lakes (especially Lake Erie); large and hard-to-predict water-level fluctuations are also a concern to those around the lakes.

Bibliography: Rousmaniere, J., ed., *The Enduring Great Lakes* (1979).

Great Lakes Naval Training Center

The Great Lakes Naval Training Center is located on Lake Michigan just south of Waukegan, Ill. With an area of approximately 607 ha (1,500 acres), it is a major basic-training center for U.S. Navy recruits, commissioned in 1911.

Great Leap Forward

A radical program instituted in 1958 by MAO TSE-TUNG, the Great Leap Foward was intended to demonstrate that China could "catch up with Britain" in industrial production in 15 years and "bypass the Soviet Union" in creating a truly communal society. The masses were exhorted to heroic effort, "backyard furnaces" for the production of iron were started, and collective farms were merged into vast communes. The endeavor, however, was a fiasco. Even the official claims for agricultural production had to be revised downward the following year. In 1959, LIU SHAO-CH'I replaced Mao as the head of state, and although Mao retained leadership of the Communist party, his standing was severely shaken. He used the CULTURAL REVOLUTION (1966–69) to recover his full power.

Bibliography: Eckstein, A., *China's Economic Revolution* (1977); MacFarquhar, R., *The Origins of the Cultural Revolution* (1983).

Great Plains

A vast, semiarid grassland in west central North America, the Great Plains extend from southwest Texas 4,830 km (3,000 mi) north to the MACKENZIE RIVER delta in Canada; their east to west extent is from the border of the Laurentian Highlands and the Central Plains to the ROCKY MOUNTAINS, varying in width from 485 to 1,125 km (300 to 700 mi). Rising well above sea level, the Great Plains begin at an elevation of about 460 m (1,500 ft) in the east and rise gradually to over 1,800 m (about 6,000 ft) in the foothills of the Rockies. The terrain is generally level, although broken in places by buttes, badlands, and small, isolated mountain groups such as the BLACK HILLS of South Dakota. Precipitation, which averages less than 510 mm (20 in) a year, decreases from east to west and from south to north. Most rain occurs in the spring; summers are dry, often with severe wind erosion and occasional, violent thunderstorms. The climate is continental steppe, with strong winds and great temperature variations in winter and summer. The population is relatively sparse; DENVER (1984 est. pop., 504,588) is the largest city.

Rivers, including the MISSOURI and its tributaries, the ARKANSAS and the RIO GRANDE, rise in the Rocky Mountains and flow east or southeast. Full to flooding in the spring from rain and melted snow, many streams dry to a trickle in the summer. Hydroelectric projects provide power, flood control, and irrigation. The Great Plains were a vast inland sea in the remote past; marine sediments underlie much of the area. Now grass-covered, with scattered trees found only along the streams, it is excellent grazing country, supporting large herds of cattle and sheep on sprawling ranches, some larger than 40,500 ha (100,000 acres). Wheat is grown in the east where farms are large and highly mechanized. Mineral resources include oil, natural gas, coal, iron, helium, and gold.

First inhabited by nomadic Indians, the Great Plains attracted buffalo hunters and ranchers. Permanent settlement came in the last half of the 19th century, spurred by massive immigration and the building of railroads.

Bibliography: Webb, Walter P., *The Great Plains* (1981).

Great Purge

The Great Purge is the name given to Joseph STALIN's liquidation of much of Soviet Russia's political and military leadership between 1936 and 1938. The Russian name for this period of terror is the *Yezhovshchina.*

The purges actually began after the 1934 assassination of Sergei Kirov, the Leningrad party leader, whose murder was probably arranged by Stalin as a pretext for eliminating all opponents—suspected or real—of the dictator's rule. At first the process was secret: people were arrested and simply disappeared. However, beginning in 1936 a series of show trials were held. Under the questioning of public prosecutor Andrei VYSHINSKY, the victims "confessed" to such crimes as counterrevolutionary conspiracy and association with Stalin's exiled archenemy Leon TROTSKY. Among the most prominent victims of the Great Purge were the former Bolshevik leaders Grigory ZINOVIEV, Lev KAMENEV, and Nikolai BUKHARIN (all exonerated in 1988 by the Gorbachev regime). Altogether, an estimated 3 million people lost their lives in the Great Purge. The number who died in Stalin's forced labor camps will probably never be known (see GULAG).

The purges weakened the USSR on the eve of World War II and disillusioned many intellectuals and others in the West who had admired the Bolshevik revolutionary experiment.

Bibliography: Conquest, Robert, *The Great Terror* (1968); Getty, J., *Origins of the Great Purges* (1985).

Great Pyrenees [pir'-uh-neez]

The Great Pyrenees is a working dog developed in southwestern France. Proclaimed the royal dog of France by Louis XIV in 1675, it has been used as a shepherd and a watchdog and to haul guns, ammunition, and medical supplies during both world wars.

The Great Pyrenees is a breed of dog thought to be descended from the central Asian mastiff dogs whose remains have been found in Europe and that date from the Bronze Age (about 1800 to 1000 BC). The breed reached its present state of development in the isolated reaches of the Pyrenees Mountains, where it was used to guard shepherd's flocks, a job for which it was ideally suited because of its great size and its strength. The breed stands up to 81.3 cm (32 in) at the shoulder and weighs up to 56.7 kg (125 lb). The head is large and strong, with triangular ears; the thick coat is flat and straight; and the tail is heavily plumed. Great Pyrenees are always white or white with gray or tan markings on the head. The first Great Pyrenees were brought to the United States by General Lafayette in 1824, and the American Kennel Club officially recognized the breed in 1933. JOHN MANDEVILLE

Bibliography: Strang, P. D., and Griffin, J. M., *The Complete Great Pyrenees* (1977).

Great Red Spot

The Great Red Spot is a salmon-colored elliptical feature on JUPITER. It has been observed since the 17th century when it was discovered concurrently by Robert HOOKE and Giovanni CASSINI. Centered at about 22° south latitude, the spot is about 40,000 km (about 25,000 mi) from east to west and 13,000 km (about 8,000 mi) from north to south. Its surface area is about the same as Earth's. The spot's color and brightness vary extensively—it is sometimes nearly invisible—and even its longitudinal position and period of rotation vary somewhat. The Voyager spacecraft confirmed that the Great Red Spot is a hurricanelike disturbance in Jupiter's atmosphere, surrounded by smaller vortices and similar in structure to other spots observed on the planet that have finite lifetimes. But the Great Red Spot is a permanent feature, as has been demonstrated through both computer and physical models.

Great Rift Valley

The Great Rift Valley of eastern Africa and the Middle East is the largest fault system on Earth, extending 4,800 km (3,000 mi) from Syria to Mozambique. The valley, which averages 56 km (35 mi) in width, includes deep lakes and is lined in some areas by sheer cliffs.

The Great Rift Valley, a succession of RIFT VALLEYS that extend from near the mouth of the Zambezi River northward through East Africa to the Red Sea and farther north into the Jordan Valley, is an enormous depression that accounts for nearly one-fourth of the Earth's longitudinal dimension. More than 4,800 km (3,000 mi) long, it is a continental branch of the worldwide MID-OCEANIC RIDGE system, and its major portion is called the EAST AFRICAN RIFT SYSTEM.

The Great Rift Valley was formed in the PLEISTOCENE EPOCH when the African CONTINENTAL SHIELD was compressed, producing major thrust FAULTS, and sections of the crust dropped to form rifts or were forced upward to form HORSTS. Its lakes include RUDOLF (Turkana), Nakuru, Magadi (completely dry and the source of the world's largest soda deposits), NYASA (Malawi), and TANGANYIKA. Lake VICTORIA lies between the eastern and western branches of the valley in east-central Africa. The western rift valley lakes are nearly all fresh water. The great horst of RUWENZORI, situated between Lakes ALBERT and EDWARD in western Uganda, is the most imposing feature of the East African Rift Valley. Although in the midst of the rift valley system, the horst still rises to 5,109 m (16,763 ft) at its highest point, Mount Stanley's snow- and ice-capped Margherita peak. G. N. UZOIGWE

Bibliography: Baker, G. H., et al., *Geology of the Eastern Rift System of Africa* (1971); Dixey, F., *The East African System* (1956).

Great Salt Lake

The Great Salt Lake, a shallow, saline inland sea, lies in northwestern Utah between the Wasatch Mountains and the Great Salt Lake Desert to the west. Always subject to significant fluctuation, the lake's area grew from 4,248 km^2 (1,640 mi^2) in 1982 to 6,345 km^2 (2,450 mi^2) in 1986. Its surface is approximately 1,280 m (4,200 ft) above sea level, but this, too, fluctuates: in June 1986 it reached a record high of 1,283.7 m (4,211.65 ft) above sea level. By then the encroaching lake had destroyed farmland on the eastern side and threatened bird sanctuaries. Beginning in April 1987, with the completion of the $60-million West Desert project, lake water was pumped westward to create an evaporation pond on the Bonneville Salt Flats. Although it receives fresh water from the Bear, Jordan, and Weber rivers, the lake has no outlet and is highly saline. Table salt, which constitutes three-quarters of its mineral salts, has been harvested for years.

The Great Salt Lake is a remnant of the glacial lake Bonneville, which covered approximately 51,800 km^2 (20,000 mi^2) during the Pleistocene Epoch. The high salt concentration precludes most marine life except for colonial algae and brine shrimp. Many birds, however, including gulls, pelicans, blue herons, double-crested cormorants, and Caspian terns, nest on the lake's islets. Lucin Cutoff traverses the lake, connecting the towns of Lucin and Ogden by rail. The Great Salt Lake was discovered in 1824 by James Bridger.

Bibliography: Morgan, D. L., *The Great Salt Lake* (1986); Price, R. C., *Barrier of Salt: The Story of the Great Salt Lake*, 2d ed. (1976).

Great Sandy Desert

The Great Sandy Desert, a barren region of sandhills and salt marshes in northern Western Australia, extends from the Indian Ocean at Eighty Mile Beach inland for about 565 km (350 mi). It has an average elevation of 210 m (790 ft) and an area of about 520,000 km^2 (about 200,000 mi^2). A riverless land of scattered grasses and acaias, it is nearly coextensive with the Canning Basin. Peter E. Warburton explored it in 1873.

Great Schism: see SCHISM, GREAT.

Great Seal of the United States

The Great Seal of the United States is used mainly for diplomatic purposes. It is affixed to treaties, commissions of diplomatic personnel, and letters from the president to foreign leaders. The design was adopted by the Continental Congress on June 20, 1782, and by the U.S. Congress on Sept. 15, 1789.

The obverse of the seal was designed by William Barton, a Philadelphia lawyer and numismatist; the reverse was designed by Charles Thomson, secretary of the Continental Congress. The obverse has a shield with 13 alternate red and white stripes superimposed on the breast of an American bald eagle. In his right talon the eagle holds an olive branch, for peace, and in his left talon, a bundle of 13 arrows, symbolizing armed might. His beak holds a scroll inscribed with the motto *E pluribus unum* ("Out of many, one"). Over the head of the eagle appears a constellation of 13 stars against a blue sky, representing the 13 original states.

The reverse contains an unfinished 13-step pyramid, topped with an eye, supposedly of God, within a triangle. Over the triangle are the words *Annuit cœptis* ("He has favored our undertakings"). On the base of the pyramid are the Roman numerals MDCCLXXVI (1776), and below is a scroll with the motto *Novus ordo seclorum* ("A new order of the ages").

Engravings of both sides of the Great Seal can be seen on the back of dollar bills. MARTIN TORODASH

Bibliography: Hunt, Gaillard, *History of the Seal of the U.S.* (1909); Patterson, Richard S., and Richardson, Dougall, *The Eagle and the Shield: A History of the United States Seal* (1976).

Great Slave Lake

Great Slave Lake, located in the southwestern Northwest Territories of Canada, encompasses an area of 28,930 km^2 (11,170 mi^2). Named for the Slave Indians, the lake was discovered in 1771 by Samuel Hearne. It is about 480 km (300 mi) long, between 48 and 225 km (30 and 140 mi) wide, and has a maximum depth of 610 m (2,000 ft). The lake is drained by the MACKENZIE RIVER, and tributaries include the Yellowknife, Slave, and Hay rivers. During the four ice-free months of the year, Great Slave Lake is an important transportation conduit of the Mackenzie River waterway. Gold mining and a small fishing industry support the main settlements on its shore.

Great Smoky Mountains

The Great Smoky Mountains, in Tennessee and North Carolina, are part of the Appalachian Mountains. They are known for a bluish haze that gives them their name, virgin forest, and bald-topped peaks. The highest mountain, Clingmans Dome (2,025 m/ 6,644 ft), is in eastern Tennessee. Spruce, buckeye, hemlock, birch, rhododendron, and dogwood are the major vegetation. Black bear, white-tailed deer, turkey, ruffed grouse, bass, and trout are among the animal life that interest sportsmen and other visitors. Thomas L. Clingman and Arnold Guyot explored the region in the late 19th century, and Great Smoky Mountains National Park was established in 1930.

Great Trek

The Great Trek denotes a series of migrations undertaken by AFRIKANER farmers (Boers) in South Africa from the Cape Colony into the interior, beginning in 1835 and lasting into the 1840s. The participants in the trek (an Afrikaans term denoting a journey by ox wagon) moved inland in wagon trains and, after great hardships, settled as far afield as Natal, the Orange Free State, and the Transvaal.

The migrations were prompted by several circumstances. The Afrikaners traditionally made their living from extensive pastoral farming, from hunting, and from trade. As their herds grew and as they exhausted the soil, they needed more land. Cheap land, however, was available only in the interior. The trekkers also had political grievances. The British had permanently occupied the Cape in 1806, and in 1833 they decreed the abolition of slavery, a measure widely resented at the Cape. The Boers also objected to the relatively liberal terms prescribed by the British for the handling of Khoikhoi (Hottentot) laborers. In addition, widespread fear existed that the British were hostile to the interests of the Boer frontiersmen, that the British would not adequately protect pioneers against African stock raiders, and that British policy was determined by missionaries and humanitarians blind to the realities of South Africa. Some Afrikaner historians now regard the Great Trek as a milestone in the building of Afrikaner national consciousness.

About 14,000 people, mostly from the eastern region of the Cape, participated in the movement. Most slaveowners stayed at home, whereas a good many ex-slaves and free blacks took part in the trek. The movement may best be interpreted as a local solution for local frontier problems. L. H. GANN

Bibliography: Walker, E.A., *The Great Trek*, 4th ed. (1960).

Great Victoria Desert

The Great Victoria Desert is a region of sandy hills stretching from western South Australia into southeastern Western Australia. It has a length of about 725 km (450 mi) and an average elevation of about 230 m (755 ft). Ernest Giles, exploring in 1875, named it for Queen Victoria. Opal is found in volcanic and sedimentary rocks at the eastern end. In the north and east is a reserve for Aborigines, and part of the desert is used for tracking and recovering missiles fired at the Woomera testing range.

Great Wall of China

The Great Wall of China winds some 2,400 km (1,500 mi) along the edge of the Mongolian plateau from Kansu province in the west to the Yellow Sea in the east. Its width ranges from 4 to 12 m (12 to 40 ft) and its height from 6 to 15 m (20 to 50 ft).

Shih Huang-ti of the CH'IN dynasty (221-206 BC), first to unify the Chinese empire, built the original wall in the 3d century BC by linking the earlier walls of states along the northern frontier to demarcate Chinese territory and to thwart invasion. Gates through the wall, such as the main one at Nan-k'ou near Peking, became centers of trade and of contact with the northern nomads. The wall was extended to Yu-men ("Jade Gate") in Kansu province during the Han dynasty (202 BC-AD 220) and was reconstructed during the Northern Wei (386-534) and Sui (581-618) dynasties. Its present appearance is a result of repairs and additions by the Ming emperors (1368-1644). Ironically, the Manchu conquerors of the Ming were let through a gate in the wall by a traitor.

The Great Wall of China, a line of earth and brick fortifications, extends 2,400 km (1,500 mi) across northern China from the Gulf of Chihli to Kansu Province. The first continuous wall was built in the late 3d century BC by linking earlier sections. The Great Wall was only partially effective in preventing invasions from the north.

Bibliography: Fryer, Jonathan, *The Great Wall of China* (1978).

Greater Antilles: see ANTILLES, GREATER AND LESSER.

grebe [greeb]

The grebe is an aquatic bird, sometimes called a dabchick, 18 to 76 cm (7 to 30 in) long, with short wings, a very short tail, and a pointed bill. The plumage is satiny, commonly black,

The great crested grebe, Podiceps cristatus, *builds floating nests in spring and carries newborn chicks on its back. If danger causes the grebe to dive, it takes the chicks underwater.*

gray, or sometimes reddish above, with white underparts. Both sexes are colored alike. The legs are set far back on the body, making it difficult for grebes to maneuver on land, which they rarely visit. The most distinctive feature of the grebe is the toes, which are united by a web only near their base, the remaining portions bearing lobed flaps. The claws of many species are markedly flattened. Grebes feed on fish and other aquatic animals. These excellent swimmers use their feet only for propulsion underwater. Although the grebe is considered a weak flier, many species migrate long distances.

Courtship involves elaborate vocal and visual displays. The nest is a floating platform of vegetation, in which two to ten eggs are laid. The eggs are white but soon become stained from the decaying vegetation. Both sexes incubate and care for the young. Young birds are conspicuously striped.

The 18 species of living grebes are nearly worldwide in distribution. They and the 20 extinct species are classified in the family Podicipedidae, order Podicipediformes.

GARY D. SCHNELL

Bibliography: Huxley, Julian, *The Courtship Habits of the Great Crested Grebe* (1968); Palmer, R. S., ed., *Handbook of North American Birds,* vol. 1 (1962).

Grechko, Georgy Mikhailovich [grech'-koh, gyor'-gee meek-hy'-loh-vich]

The Soviet civilian cosmonaut Georgy Mikhailovich Grechko, b. May 25, 1931, made two record-breaking SALYUT flights in 1975 and 1977–78. Grechko was a computer engineer in the Soviet space program when he was selected to become a cosmonaut in 1966. Together with crew commander Aleksei GUBAREV, he was launched into space on *Soyuz 17* (see SOYUZ) on Jan. 10, 1975; they were the first crew to board the *Salyut 4* space station. Subsequently chosen to make the second attempt to break the world space-endurance record, he was launched into space with Yuri ROMANENKO on board *Soyuz 26* on Dec. 10, 1977, and successfully completed a 96-day space mission aboard *Salyut 6.*

JAMES OBERG

Greco, El: see EL GRECO.

Greco, José [grek'-oh]

José Greco, b. Dec. 23, 1918, is considered the finest male Spanish dancer of modern times. Born in Italy and raised in Brooklyn, N.Y., he danced in nightclubs until chosen by La Argentinita to be her partner. Performing in her ballets until her death in 1945, Greco then traveled to Spain and formed his own company, which made its debut in 1949. On its first appearance in the United States in 1951, the company achieved instant popularity with a revue of Spanish ballet and classical, folk, flamenco, and gypsy dances. Greco relied on clarity of line and pattern rather than a flamboyant personality to convey the intensity of all forms of Spanish dance.

JOHN HOWELL

Greece

Greece (modern Greek, Ellás) is a country in southeastern Europe that forms the southern extremity of the Balkan Peninsula (see BALKANS). It is bordered by the Ionian, Mediterranean, and Aegean seas on the west, south, and east, and on the north by Albania, Yugoslavia, Bulgaria, and Turkey. Greece encompasses many island groups, including the Ionian Islands to the west and the Sporades (Sporádhes) and CYCLADES (Kikládhes) to the east, as well as the larger islands of CRETE (Kríti), LESBOS (Lésvos), RHODES (Ródhos), SAMOS, SAMOTHRACE (Samothráki), Chios (Khíos), and Lemnos (Límnos), which lie within sight of the Turkish coast. The name *Greece* is derived from the Latin name *Graeci,* applied to a people who lived in ancient times in the northwest part of the country.

Greece is predominantly an agricultural country, although less than one-third of its area is cultivated. The country is self-sufficient in basic foodstuffs, and agricultural products make up most of Greece's exports. Tourism is well developed and is economically important.

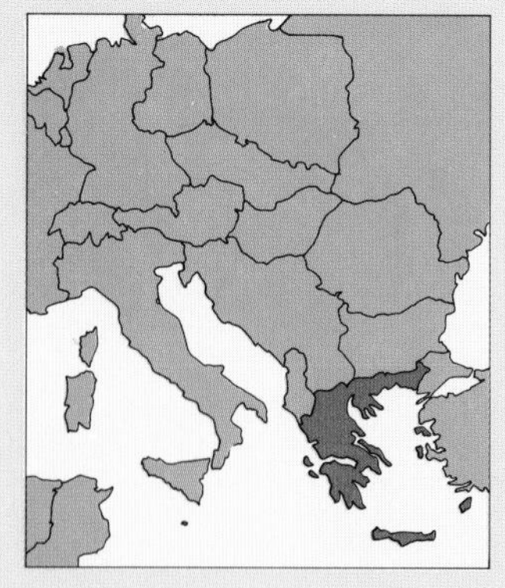

HELLENIC REPUBLIC

LAND. Area: 131,944 km^2 (50,944 mi^2). Capital and largest city: Athens (1981 pop., 885,136).
PEOPLE. Population (1987 est.): 10,000,000; density (1987 est.): 75.8 persons per km^2 (196.2 per mi^2). Distribution (1987 est.): 70% urban, 30% rural. Annual growth (1987): 0.2%. Official language: Greek. Major religion: Orthodoxy.
EDUCATION AND HEALTH. Literacy (1985): 92.3%. Universities (1987): 9. Hospital beds (1983): 57,081. Physicians (1983): 27,607. Life expectancy (1987): 74. Infant mortality (1987): 14 per 1,000 live births.
ECONOMY. GNP (1985): $35.5 billion; $3,550 per capita. Labor force (1981): services—39%; agriculture—31%; industry—30%. Foreign trade (1985): imports—$10.7 billion; exports—$4.8 billion; principal trade partners—West Germany, Italy, United States, Saudi Arabia. Currency: 1 drachma=100 leptae.
GOVERNMENT. Type: republic. Legislature: Parliament. Political subdivisions: 10 regions, 1 self-governing district.
COMMUNICATIONS. Railroads (1986): 2,557 km (1,589 mi) total. Roads (1985): 34,492 km (21,432 mi) total. Major ports: 2. Major airfields: 9.

Modern Greece came into being in 1830, following a war of independence against the Ottoman Empire. The country has since greatly expanded its territory at the expense of its northern neighbors, with whom its relations have been generally unfriendly.

LAND AND RESOURCES

Greece is a mountainous country, with flat land restricted to many small coastal plains. The mountains, which form part of the Alpine system, generally stretch from northwest to southeast. They are highest and most rugged in the northwest, where the Grámmos Mountains rise to 2,519 m (8,265 ft) and the Pindus (Píndhos) to over 2,285 m (7,500 ft), although the highest mountain in the country (Mount OLYMPUS; 2,917 m/

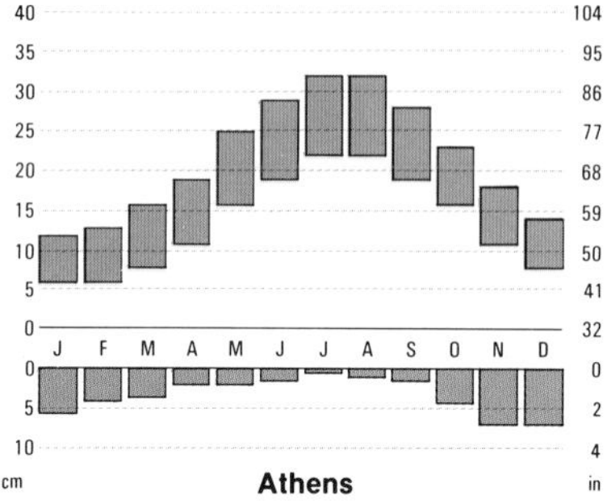

Bars indicate monthly ranges of temperature (red) *and precipitation* (blue) *of Athens, Greece. The mediterranean climate of Greece's capital is moderated by mountains and sea breezes.*

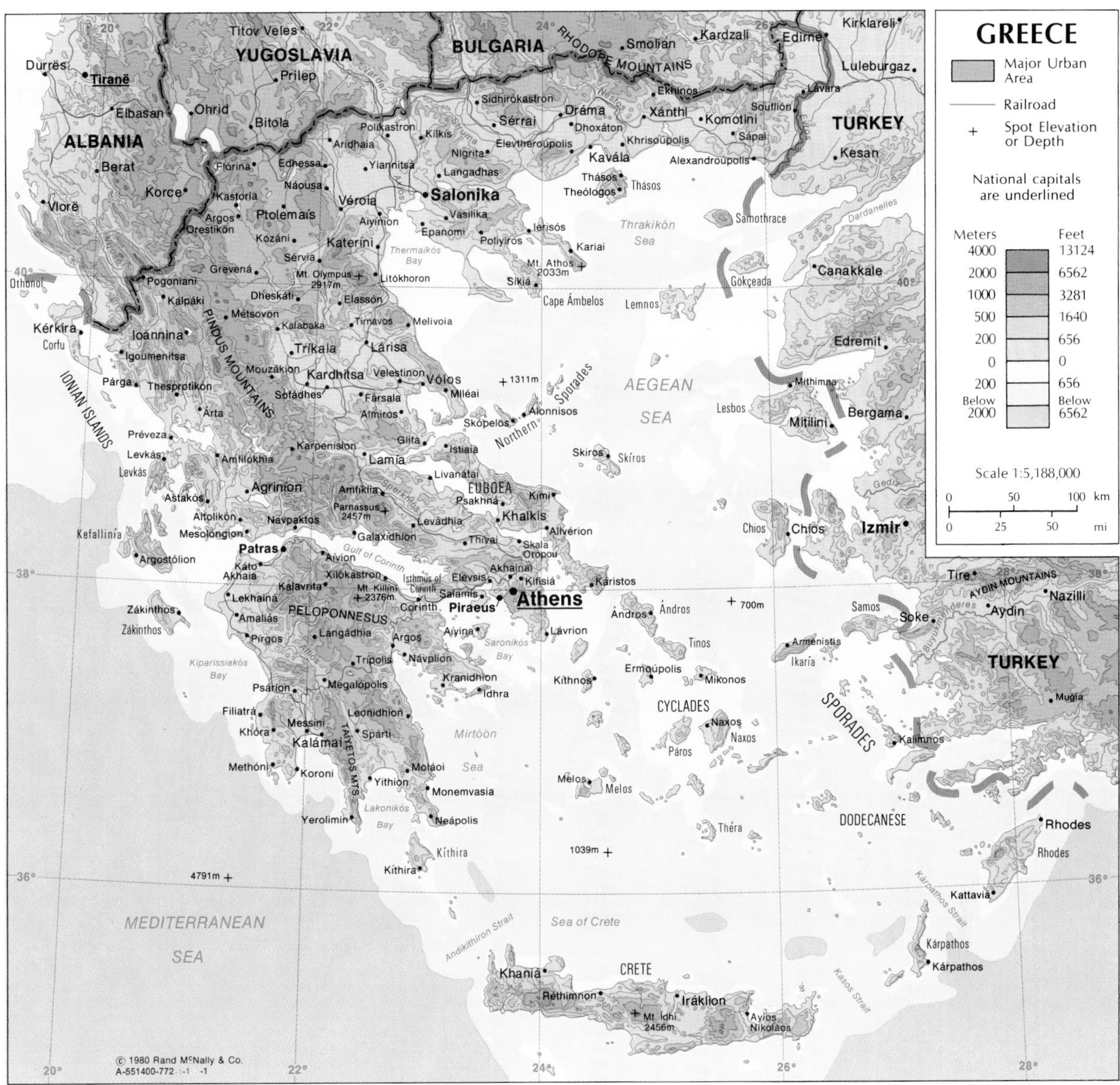

9,573 ft) is in east central Greece. The mountains are interrupted by the long, narrow Gulf of Corinth, which almost cuts off southern Greece—the PELOPONNESUS—from the rest of the peninsula. But the mountains continue south of the gulf and terminate in the three headlands of southern Greece.

The mountain ranges, extending in the same direction, are continued offshore, and their highest portions appear as the chains and groups of islands that dot the Aegean. The Cyclades continue the eastern ranges toward the Turkish mainland, and Crete and Rhodes are continuations of the more westerly ranges. Both mountains and islands are composed of sedimentary rocks, mainly limestone and sandstone, most of which were deposited during the Mesozoic Era (230 to 65 million years ago). Only near the northern boundary of Greece are igneous rocks significant in the landscape. The largest plains are those of MACEDONIA, THESSALY, and THRACE, all of which border the Aegean Sea.

The soils of Greece, as Plato noted more than 2,000 years ago, are thin and poor, and over much of the country the bare rock shows at the surface. The only good soils are on the small coastal lowlands. These are mainly alluvial soils, but their productivity is greatly reduced by the long summer drought.

Climate. The climate of Greece is typically Mediterranean. Summers are long, hot, and dry. The average temperature in July is 26.7° C (80° F), in Athens, the capital, but is much lower in the mountains. Winters are mild; the average January temperature is 9.2° C (48.5° F). Winter temperatures are also much lower in the interior; in mountain valleys averages are close to freezing, and prolonged frosts may occur. Snow is not uncommon away from the coasts. Precipitation varies greatly. In Athens it averages 394 mm (16 in) annually, but it is much higher away from the east coast and rises to more than 1,200 mm (47 in) in the higher mountains. In all parts of the country rainfall is seasonal, most of it coming in late fall and winter. Only in Macedonia and Thrace is there a significant summer rainfall; almost no rain falls in the rest of the country.

Drainage. Few rivers exist in peninsular Greece; all are small, and most dry up in the summer. Only those rivers which rise farther north in the Balkan Peninsula and flow through northern Greece to the sea, for example, the Vardar and Struma, have any significant summer discharge. The small size and seasonal character of most rivers is the primary reason for the limited use of irrigation. Of the several lakes within the mountains—many of them in northern Greece—most occupy basins that were formed by the dissolution of limestone.

Vegetation. Naturally occurring vegetation is adapted to the climate and consists largely of xerophytes, which are plants that are able to withstand the summer drought by the storage of water. Spring is the primary growing season, and flowering plants make a brilliant show during this time, before withering under the summer heat. The mountains are mostly clothed with a relatively dense scrub brush (called maquis). Evergreen forests may once have covered much of the land but have been largely destroyed in southern Greece. Extensive forest is found only in the mountains of northwestern Greece, where large stands of fir occur. About 19% of the total area is forested.

Resources. Greece is poorly endowed with minerals and fuel. Although some lignite (a soft coal) is produced, no economically significant coal deposits exist. Oil has been found in northwestern Greece and on the floor of the Aegean Sea. The Pinos oilfield, off the island of Thásos, has been producing petroleum since 1981. Reserves of hydroelectric power are slight because of the small size and seasonal flow of most rivers. Iron ore and bauxite are the most important mineral resources; bauxite is quarried to the north of the Gulf of Corinth, and most of it is exported. Small amounts of pyrites (used in making sulfuric acid), lead, zinc, magnesite, manganese, chrome, and silver are also mined. In most cases the ore is exported for smelting elsewhere.

PEOPLE

Ethnic Groups, Language, and Religion. The present population is derived mainly from the inhabitants of ancient Greece, but there has been a strong infusion of Slavic and Turkish blood. Greek is spoken by about 97% of the population. The modern language is derived from classical Greek of Attica and Ionia and exists today in two forms. The popular, or demotic, form has evolved naturally and has incorporated Slavic, Turkish, and Italian words. The Katharevousa, "pure," form of Greek has resulted from a conscious attempt to revive ancient Greek. The latter had been taught in the schools and used by the civil service and church until its official demise in 1976 in favor of the demotic form.

Crete, Greece's largest island, lies at the southern limit of the Aegean Sea, 100 km (60 mi) from the Peloponnese. The Lévka Óri (White Mountains) appear in the background of this view of the remote village of Khóra Sfakíon, on the southwestern coast of Crete.

The non-Greek population includes a small Albanian community close to the Albanian frontier in the northwest; some Macedonian and Bulgarian Slavs near the northern frontier; and a few Turks, who remained after the exchange of population of 1923. Small communities of Vlachs, a seminomadic people who speak a Romance language, live in the northern mountains.

After World War I, Greece and Bulgaria agreed to exchange their ethnic minorities; about 92,000 Bulgarians left Greece for Bulgaria, and 46,000 Greeks emigrated from Bulgaria to Greece. In 1922 a large-scale exodus of Greeks from Anatolia, followed by a more orderly exchange of populations, occurred. In all, about 1,500,000 refugees came to Greece, and about 800,000 Turks were transferred from Greece to Turkey. Although the settlement of the newcomers presented great difficulties, the country eventually benefited from the resulting increase in economic productivity.

More than 95% of the population belongs to the Greek Orthodox church, which is the established religion of the country. In 1987 the Socialist-controlled parliament enacted legislation confiscating most of the church's land and placing its other property (except for the self-governing monastic territory of Mount Athos) under lay control.

Demography and Education. Greece is one of the least urbanized countries in Europe and has only two large cities, ATHENS (with its contiguous port city of PIRAEUS) and SALONIKA (Thessaloníki). Most Greek cities are small—even the well-known city of CORINTH had only 22,658 people in 1981.

The population has grown rapidly during the past century. Many rural areas have become overpopulated, and there has been a large migration, especially to the United States. Temporary migration by men to work in northern Europe is also common.

Education is free and compulsory until the age of 15, with provision for further secondary education in high schools or in gymnasiums. Nevertheless, illiteracy remains higher than is usual in Europe.

Culture. The cultural history of Greece goes back to the artists, historians, philosophers, playwrights, and poets of ancient times. Classical Greek culture was probably the greatest formative influence in the development of European civilization. Greek cultural traditions continued through the Hellenistic, Roman, and Byzantine periods and reemerged in modern forms after the centuries of domination by the Ottoman Empire. See separate articles on BYZANTINE ART AND ARCHITECTURE; BYZANTINE MUSIC; GREEK ARCHITECTURE; GREEK ART; GREEK LITERATURE, ANCIENT; GREEK LITERATURE, MODERN; GREEK MUSIC.

ECONOMIC ACTIVITY

Little economic growth occurred during the long period of Turkish rule (1456–1830), and when Greece gained independence in 1830, it was a backward, peasant country with no industry above the level of rural crafts. Athens was little more than a large village. Economic growth was slow in the 19th century. Greece offered little scope for industrial development, having only scanty resources in metals and solid fuels. Economic development began following World War II and was assisted by massive foreign aid from the United States. In 1962, Greece became an associate member of the European Economic Community (EEC); it was admitted as a full member in 1981 but has had difficulty working within a system geared to the more economically advanced countries that predominate in the EEC.

Agriculture and Fishing. Agriculture continues to be the most important economic activity, although in recent years there has been a movement from the land to the cities. Agricultural activities are typically carried on by peasants, who cultivate holdings that are uneconomically small, using old-fashioned, if not primitive, methods. In remote areas, plows similar to those represented on classical Greek vases continue to be used. The average size of holdings is less than one ha (2.4 acres), although as some peasants forsake the land, others are able to acquire larger holdings. A land redistribution program instituted in the late 1950s has also enlarged some holdings. The primary agricultural products are wheat; fruit, such as grapes, olives, and citrus fruit; and industrial crops, such as

Greek Macedonia, in northeastern Greece, is the largest of the country's ten administrative regions. The seclusion of this mountainous area provides a natural refuge for the monastic life. This monastery is one of many found in the Macedonian countryside.

(Below) *This view of Athens, the capital and largest city of Greece, is taken from the hill of the Acropolis, which overlooks the city's densely populated metropolitan area. In the background is Lycabettus Hill, with the Church of Saint George (Agios Georgios).*

cotton and tobacco. Greece is generally self-sufficient in bread grains, and large amounts of tobacco and dried grapes (raisins and sultanas) are exported. Rice is grown in some damp deltaic regions, but Greek agriculture in general suffers from a shortage of water during the growing season.

Animal rearing is restricted by a shortage of grass and fodder. Sheep and goats, which can subsist on the coarse grass of the hills, are by far the most numerous farm stock; there are few cattle. Cheese is made from sheep's and goats' milk.

Fishing is important around the coast of Greece. Among the fish caught are tunny and octopus, considered a delicacy.

Manufacturing. Manufacturing is largely related to domestic agricultural production. It includes canning and drying fruit; wine making and distilling; and tobacco preparation. All these activities are carried out in small units of production. Most factory industries are found near the two large cities, Athens and Salonika. Cement, fertilizers, simple chemical products, and china and glass are made for the domestic market. A small aluminum industry exists, and an oil refinery has been built near Salonika.

Transportation and Trade. Greece has only a skeletal railroad network, which focuses on Athens. The main roads that link Athens with the principal provincial centers are well built, but only about half of the road system is surfaced, and much of it is in poor condition. A canal, used by small ships, cuts through the Isthmus of Corinth, linking the Ionian Sea with the Aegean. Greece has a large fleet of merchant ships and tankers that contribute to Greece's balance of payments but have little relationship to the country's foreign trade.

Greece has a small volume of foreign trade. Exports consist mainly of fruit, alcoholic drinks, and tobacco. Imports include fuel and manufactured goods. In the 1980s, the value of imports has been more than double that of exports, creating a large balance-of-payments deficit. Most foreign trade is with other members of the EEC.

GOVERNMENT

Until 1973, Greece was a constitutional monarchy. In 1967, King CONSTANTINE II withdrew after failing to unseat the military junta that had seized power a short time before. In 1973, Greece was declared a republic, and the action was ratified by a plebiscite. In the following year the junta was overthrown, and the previous constitution was restored under a new prime minister, Konstantinos KARAMANLIS. A new constitution was introduced later, in June 1975. Greece is now governed by a prime minister and a cabinet responsible to the 300-member unicameral legislature whose members are elected by universal adult suffrage to 4-year terms. The president, whose post was made largely ceremonial in March 1986, is chosen for a 5-year term by the legislature.

For purposes of local administration the country is divided into 10 regions, each subdivided into *nomoí* ("departments"). Local government rests essentially with the 51 *nomoí*, which have been granted increasing autonomy.

HISTORY

Ancient Greece. Although modern Greece has been an independent state only since 1830, the country has a long and distinguished history and virtually provided the foundations of Western civilization. Early civilizations emerged in the Greek world in the second millennium BC and were centered first in Crete and then in MYCENAE (see AEGEAN CIVILIZATION). Little is known of the following several centuries; the *Iliad* and the *Odyssey*, ascribed to HOMER, probably date from this period, however. By the 6th century BC, the Greek world around the Aegean Sea comprised several hundred small, autonomous CITY-STATES. Most were little more than village communities, but all tried, within the limits of their resources, to build temples and marketplaces and to create an urban civilization.

Such larger cities as Athens and Corinth succeeded in establishing a highly ordered civilization, and in the 5th century BC, Athens came to dominate the Greek world. This dominance was possible in part because the territory of Athens

In Nemea, an agricultural village in the northeastern Peloponnesus, residents enjoy the traditional folk dancing and lamb roasting of the Easter celebration. The Greek Orthodox church figures prominently in preserving a Greek identity and cultural unity.

Boeotia, a province in east central Greece, consists of two wide plains divided by a spur of Mount Helicon. The fertile central region of the province is primarily agricultural; in the southern coastal area along the Gulf of Corinth tourism is gaining in importance.

was larger and more populous than that of its rivals, and in part because of the prestige and power Athens had earned by successfully resisting Persian invasions. The city-states were weak, however, because they were small and because of their wrangling. In 338 BC they were all overcome by the large and powerful state of Macedonia.

The Hellenistic period, as the age of Macedonian domination is called, was followed by the Roman conquest of Greece in 146 BC. Greece, divided into the provinces of EPIRUS, ACHAEA, and Macedonia, remained part of the Roman Empire until the empire's collapse.

Greece's great period of artistic achievement was in the 5th century BC, but literary and architectural creativity continued, albeit on a less exalted plane, throughout the Hellenistic period. The Romans themselves showed a deep appreciation of the Greek achievement. (See GREECE, ANCIENT.)

From the Byzantine to the Ottoman Empire. When Diocletian divided the Roman Empire into two parts, Greece fell to the Eastern, or BYZANTINE, EMPIRE. From the 5th to the 7th century it was invaded by Goths, Huns, and Slavs, whose depradations destroyed urban life as the Greeks had known it and brought Greek civilization to an end.

In the late 11th century Greece again came under Western influence. Normans from Sicily invaded Greece. The Crusaders crossed it on their way to the Middle East, and in 1204 the Fourth Crusade was diverted to an attack on the Byzantine Empire. All of Greece, except the rugged interior, was occupied and divided into states ruled by Western princes or was controlled by the commercial republics of Venice and Genoa. This domination continued until the Ottoman Turkish invasion in the 15th century. The Turkish conquest (1456) was not, however, total. Some islands, notably Rhodes and Crete, held out until 1522 and 1669, respectively, and in the mountains of Epirus, Turkish rule was little more than nominal. Nevertheless, Greece remained part of the OTTOMAN EMPIRE for nearly 400 years.

The Modern Greek State. Modern Greek nationalism first manifested itself in the late 18th century in literary activity; but it soon acquired political overtones, and in 1821 the Greek revolt against Turkish rule began. With assistance from Russia and West European powers, Greece achieved independence in 1830 and was presented (1833) by these powers with a king from Bavaria, Otto (see OTTO, KING OF GREECE).

Greece at this time consisted only of the southern part of the peninsula and the Cyclades. In 1864 the Ionian Islands were ceded to Greece by Great Britain. Northern Greece was annexed in successive stages in 1881, 1913, and 1922. The DODECANESE and Rhodes were acquired from Italy in 1945.

Modern Greece has had a disruptive internal history. Its democratic constitution worked imperfectly. In 1862, King Otto was driven out and was replaced by King GEORGE I, a member of the Danish royal house. Under his rule (1863–1913) the frontiers were greatly expanded, particularly as a result of the BALKAN WARS of 1912–13, but there was little internal development.

During World War I, Salonika was used as a base for Allied campaigns in the Balkans from 1915, although Greece did not fully enter the war until 1917, under the leadership of Prime Minister Eleuthérios VENIZELOS. At the end of the war the Greeks overextended themselves: their attempt to incorporate part of Anatolia led to violent Turkish reaction and the expulsion of the Greeks from Turkey.

The internal political scene continued to be disturbed between the two world wars by repeated coups and a period of military rule. From 1925 to 1935, Greece was a republic. After the restoration of the monarchy (in the person of GEORGE II), a right-wing dictatorial regime was established (1936) by Ioánnis METAXAS. In October 1940, however, Greece was attacked by the Italians, and in April 1941 it was overrun by the Germans (see WORLD WAR II).

The war years were disastrous for Greece and were followed by a bitter civil war, in which the EAM-ELAS, the Communist-inspired liberation forces, attempted to seize power. The task of protecting constitutional liberties in Greece was assumed in 1947 by the United States. The civil war ended in 1949, and a period of reconstruction followed. Although Greece was a monarchy, republicanism remained strong, and in 1964 an antiroyalist, Georgios PAPANDRÉOU, became prime minister. King Constantine II forced his resignation in 1965, precipitating a period of instability that culminated (1967) in the establishment of another military dictatorship. Claiming that it was protecting Greece from communism, the new regime, led by Georgios Papadopoulos, imprisoned its opponents and imposed rigid controls on all aspects of Greek life. When the king attempted a countercoup in December 1967, he was forced to flee the country, and a republic was proclaimed in 1973. The following year the government's involvement in a pro-Greek coup d'etat in CYPRUS brought Greece to the brink of war with Turkey and led to the downfall of the military regime. Democracy was restored under a conservative civilian government headed by Karamanlis, who also brought (1981) Greece into the European Community. Karamanlis was replaced (1981) by Socialist Andreas PAPANDRÉOU, who remained in office until brought down by a series of scandals in 1989. His successor, the conservative New Democrat Tzinnis Tzannetakis, formed a coalition with the Communists. NORMAN J. G. POUNDS

Bibliography: Clogg, Richard, *Parties and Elections in Greece* (1988); Kourvetaris, George, *A Profile of Modern Greece* (1987); McNeill, William, *The Metamorphosis of Greece since World War II* (1978); Mavrogordatos, George, *The Stillborn Republic* (1983); Toynbee, Arnold, *The Greeks and Their Heritages* (1981); Woodhouse, C. M., *Modern Greece: A Short History* (1977).

Greece, ancient

The first Greek-speaking peoples are thought to have migrated into the Balkan peninsula shortly before 2200 BC, during the Aegean Bronze Age. Their arrival is attested by signs of violent destruction in the vicinity of Argos, most notably at Lerna. By 1500 their descendants in mainland Greece had established a civilization that reached as far as RHODES and was in contact with Near Eastern kingdoms. The Mycenaeans, as these people are known, were much influenced by the Minoan Cretans, whose importance was remembered in such myths as stories about King MINOS and THESEUS of Athens. By the middle of the 15th century, KNOSSOS, Crete's greatest city, had fallen into Mycenaean hands, as is known from the discovery in the palace of Knossos of clay tablets inscribed in LINEAR B, an early Greek script. Knossos was destroyed about 1400; other Cretan cities had been destroyed about a century before. (See also AEGEAN CIVILIZATION.)

MYCENAEAN CIVILIZATION

Mycenaean civilization is best known from the remains of MYCENAE, although many other sites exist in the Peloponnesus as well as in south central Greece, on the islands of the Aegean, and on the coast of Anatolia. The graves at Mycenae have yielded many precious objects of great beauty. Golden crowns, diadems, and cups, some in raised relief, were found with vessels of silver and alabaster and numerous bronze weapons. Some tombs, called beehive tombs because of their shape, show developed architectural skill. The most monumental tomb is the so-called Treasury of Atreus. Like Mycenae's Lion Gate and the palace remains, this tomb reflects the Mycenaeans' ability to organize their resources on a large scale. The great palaces of the mainland were built in the 14th century BC. They were enclosed in fortified citadels defended by strong walls. Major palaces have been excavated at

This detail of The Warrior Vase, *a clay krater dating from c.1200 BC, portrays Mycenaean soldiers in battle armor. The Mycenaeans were culturally dominant throughout the Aegean from about 1400 to 1200 BC, when the Dorians overran the area. (National Museum, Athens.)*

Ruins of the Agora, which served as the central meeting place for commerce and public assembly in ancient Athens, can be seen in this view of the city. The official public buildings of the city-state, including the assembly house and law courts, surrounded the Agora.

TIRYNS and PYLOS as well as at Mycenae. The Linear B tablets found at Knossos and Pylos attest the existence of an elaborate palace bureaucracy headed by a king. Matters of cult were overseen by a priest or priestess, and the work force was highly specialized and regimented. The workers lived beyond the walls of the palaces, the king and nobles within. Archaeological evidence indicates that the Mycenaeans enjoyed their greatest prosperity during the 14th and early 13th centuries BC. They pursued trade with east and west, establishing footholds in both areas of the Aegean.

As their fortifications suggest, the Mycenaeans were a warlike people. Battle scenes are prominent in their art, and they took their weapons with them to their graves. HOMER made one of their military expeditions famous when he sang about the TROJAN WAR. TROY, in northwest Anatolia, was in fact violently destroyed shortly after 1300, apparently after a siege, and there is no reason to doubt that this destruction was brought by the Mycenaeans. It is unknown, however, whether the town of Mycenae ever acquired the leadership of Greece, as Homer supposed, or whether each palace was autonomous. The homogeneity of the civilization is not conclusive evidence that there was a dominant imperial city.

ARCHAIC PERIOD

In the 13th century a dark age set in, although the precise cause of Mycenaean decline is unknown. There may have been some intercity warfare; wandering peoples certainly brought war by sea into both the Near East and Greece. The main Mycenaean cities were destroyed by the end of the century. The DORIANS, themselves a Greek people, took possession of much of the Peloponnesus, and though some Mycenaean sites lingered on for a considerable period, civilization was swept away and population decreased. The art of writing was lost, not to be regained until the Greeks adapted it from the Phoenician script about 400 years later. Many Mycenaeans fled from Greece to the coast of Anatolia, which later

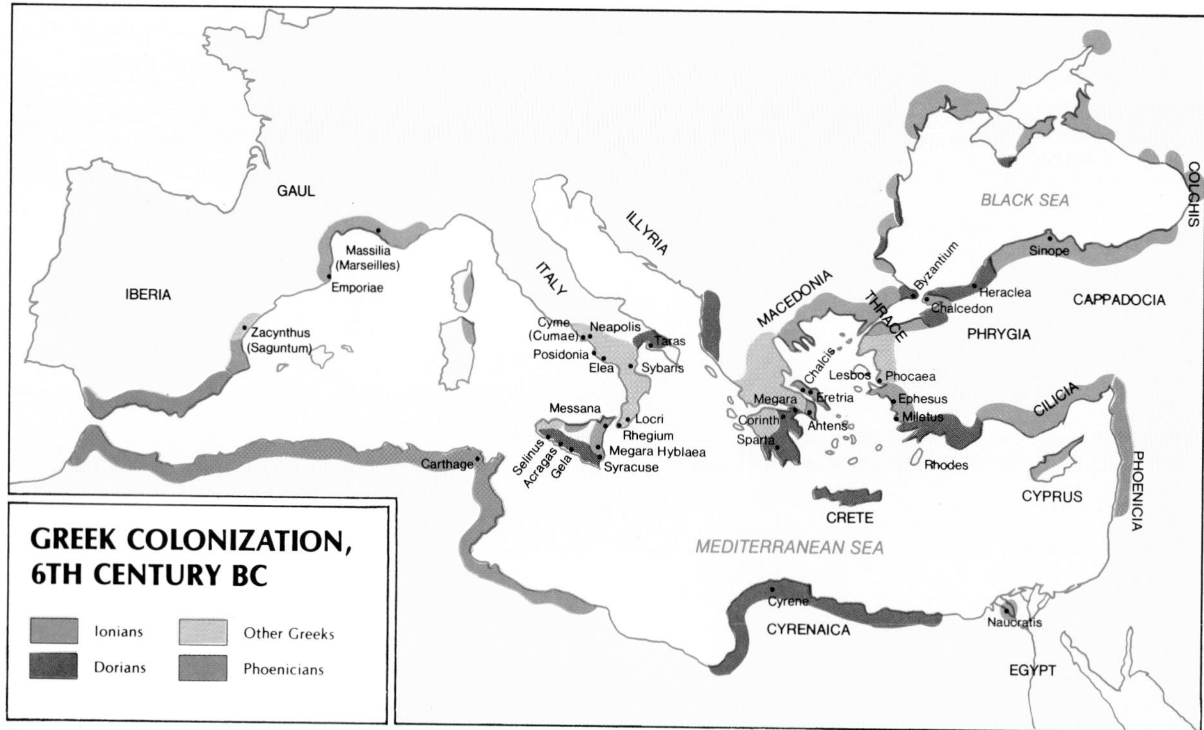

The extensive areas of Greek colonization in the 6th century BC *are illustrated in this map. The Greek colonizing movement, which began during the mid-8th century* BC*, was originally initiated to expand territorial holdings and led to wide-scale commercial enterprise.*

came to be called IONIA. Athens, which was immune from Dorian conquest, was the embarkation point. These refugees took with them a recollection of their traditions, which crystallized into the oral and epic poetry best known from Homer.

A new aristocratic social structure, less rigid than the Mycenaean, began to take root—in Ionia, as well as in Greece itself. The Dorians—some of whom passed from the Peloponnesus to Crete, other islands in the Aegean, southwest Anatolia, and Rhodes—lived in tribal communities led by a hereditary king who commanded in war and served as chief priest. The king heeded the advice of a council of elders, and the warrior class ratified major decisions about war and peace. Hunting and war were the main business of life. The non-Dorian Greeks of BOEOTIA and elsewhere led a similar existence.

Establishment of City-States. In Ionia, where kingship was also the early rule, the refugees remained on the seacoast and quickly organized themselves into cities, probably in order to defend themselves better from the adjacent Near Eastern population, though there must have been considerable cultural interchange between the two peoples. The walled cities, which served as the focus of the surrounding population, began to evolve into the CITY-STATE (the *polis*). The defensible city, with its citadel, central shrine, hearth and sacred fire, and marketplace (*agora*), became the center of government for town and country. One's city, not one's village or race, determined one's political identity. A similar process occurred in Greece itself, though in some areas, such as Arcadia in the center of the Peloponnesus, village life continued; in other areas exceptional or fortunate cities assimilated a relatively large surrounding area. Thus ATHENS and SPARTA absorbed Attica and Laconia, respectively.

The Greeks on both sides of the Aegean early frequented common shrines. APOLLO was worshipped at DELPHI, ZEUS at OLYMPIA, Apollo and ARTEMIS at DELOS. The Greeks celebrated festivals at these shrines with dance, song, and athletics. These meetings reinforced their common identity and prompted them to formulate some basic rules of interstate behavior concerning warfare, religious truces, and the sanctity of heralds or messengers. Delphi became the center of a league that initially comprised only the surrounding peoples but eventually came to include both Athens and Sparta. The oracle at Delphi was much consulted throughout ancient times. In the archaic period it was very influential, fixing the site of prospective colonies and helping to formulate major policies for cities as well as individuals.

Colonization. Increasing stability and prosperity caused a growth of population; a great wave of colonization ensued between 750 and 500 BC. Greek culture spread throughout the Mediterranean and even into the southern Ukraine. Markets were opened for Greek oil, wine, and other wares in return for precious metals, timber, grain, and other goods. One major center of colonization was Sicily and southern Italy. CORINTH founded SYRACUSE, the greatest Greek city in the west; Chalcis (modern Khalkis), in EUBOEA, settled many other cities in the area. The region of the Black Sea was settled from Ionia, MILETUS being the chief colonizer. The small island of THERA founded the great kingdom of CYRENE in northeast Libya. Further expansion in Africa was blocked by CARTHAGE; PHOENICIA proved impermeable; in Egypt the Greeks were able to establish a commercial emporium, Naucratis, on the Nile delta. Neither Sparta nor Athens were colonial powers.

Aristocracy and Tyranny. This was also a time of great social upheaval. The landholding aristocracy, which had already wrested power from the kings, found their own supremacy challenged by those beneath them. People of less-distinguished birth became increasingly dissatisfied with the prevailing aristocratic order and were acquiring power in their own right. The rise of literacy, the increased concentration of economic power in the hands of traders and artisans, and the introduction of the phalanx—a mass of men fighting in unison in heavy armor, which made discipline and manpower the key element of success in war—shifted the balance of power to the general citizenry.

By the 7th century BC, ambitious or sympathetic individuals from the circle of the aristocracy were capitalizing on the general discontent, especially in prosperous cities, and establishing tyrannies. Cypselus (d. 625) seized control of Corinth and built a colonial empire, founding cities on the west coast of Greece and modern Albania. Tyrants also arose in Megara, EPIDAURUS, and SICYON, just northwest of Corinth. In the Aegean, Polycrates (d. c.522), tyrant of SAMOS, made his island a major naval power.

Early Athenian and Spartan Development. Athens's tyranny developed after a long series of troubles. Cylon's early attempt to establish a tyranny, probably in 632, ended in failure. The social discontent reflected in his attempt, and perhaps also the sacreligious murder of his partisans, which brought a curse on the murders and led to a vendetta, apparently prompted DRACO to draw up and publish a code of laws in 621. Even that proved ineffective, however; the oppression of the poor, some of whom suffered debt-slavery, the exclusion of the middle class from political office, and other factors combined to precipitate a crisis. In 594, SOLON was given unique powers as *diallaktēs,* or mediator; he cancelled debts, abolished debt-slavery, and made wealth the criterion of public office. But his reforms were only temporarily successful; civil strife soon broke out again.

PEISISTRATUS seized the tyranny in 561 by defeating his aristocratic rivals. Though exiled twice, he ended his days as tyrant of Athens in 527, after a continuous rule of 19 years. He was succeeded by his sons Hippias and Hipparchus; the assassination of the latter in 514 ended the benign character of the tyranny. In 510, Hippias was expelled from Athens with Spartan assistance. Three years later CLEISTHENES established the Athenian democracy, which in many respects fulfilled the tendencies begun by Solon and enforced by Peisistratus.

Despite the modern connotation of the word, tyranny was generally a beneficial stage in the evolution of government. Though the tyrant seized power illegally and ruled extraconstitutionally, his power ultimately derived from popular support. The first tyrants centralized the city-state, repressed the aristocracy, fostered commerce and the arts, and brought civic pride to the citizenry. Their heirs, however, ruled despotically and brought about their own destruction. Most tyrants were removed from power by the end of the 6th century, except in Sicily and other areas on the periphery of Greece, where they became monarchs rather than true tyrants.

Tyranny failed to develop at SPARTA in archaic times, undoubtedly because of that city's unique social order. Discontent seems to have arisen by the middle of the 7th century, when Sparta was engaged in the Second Messenian War. While suppressing this rebellion in MESSENIA, which Sparta had conquered c.735-15, the Spartans effected changes in their constitution. They abolished the right of the people to contradict their leaders, the two kings and the 28-member council of elders. At some point thereafter the power of the five EPHORS, overseers, was increased at the expense of the power of the kings. The Spartans also instituted a sweeping social reform, which they attributed to LYCURGUS, facilitating the virtually total subordination of the citizenry to the military demands of the state. HELOTS, or serfs, supplied the Spartans with their material needs, and the use of money was forbidden. By the middle of the 6th century, after taking the southeast portion of the Peloponnesus from Argos, Sparta began to form a series of alliances with other city-states and localities, which it turned into a league under its leadership. Sparta's policy from c.550 was to oppose and overthrow the tyrannies. This policy was generally successful.

THE 5TH CENTURY

Persian Wars. A threat to Greek liberty arose in the last half of the 6th century when CYRUS THE GREAT, king of Persia, defeated CROESUS in 546 and conquered his kingdom of LYDIA, in Anatolia. The subjugation of Ionia, already begun by Croesus, entered its final phase. The Ionians, who became tributary to Cyrus and his successors, CAMBYSES II and DARIUS I, rebelled in 499. They were granted token aid, which was swiftly withdrawn, by Athens and Eretria, but nevertheless struggled for six years until the Persians sacked Miletus and gained command of the sea.

Darius, alleging Athenian participation in the revolt, dispatched an army across the Aegean to conquer Athens. After Athens won a splendid victory in the Battle of MARATHON in 490, a new expedition, on a grander scale, was readied by Darius' son, XERXES I. It too was defeated, in the Great PERSIAN WAR of 480-79. Though a small band of Spartans led by King LEONIDAS was destroyed at the narrow pass of THERMOPYLAE, a sea battle fought simultaneously off Artemesium, the northern tip of Euboea, resulted in the destruction of a considerable portion of Xerxes' fleet. The Greeks withdrew to the isthmus of Corinth while the Persians sacked Athens. Later in the same year, the Greeks annihilated Xerxes' fleet at SALAMIS; in 479, they destroyed his land army at PLATAEA in Boeotia. The battle of Mycale, on the southern coast of Anatolia, opened up Ionia to the Greeks. Athens continued the Ionian war, liberated the Greeks, and, in 478-77, organized the DELIAN LEAGUE. The Greeks always remembered the defeat of Xerxes as their finest achievement.

Athenian-Spartan Rivalry. The 5th century also saw a great conflict between Athens and Sparta, the strongest powers in Greece and the proponents of two different systems of government and society—progressively radical democracy and oligarchy, respectively. By the middle of the century Athens had used its mighty naval force to transform the Delian League into an empire. Athens's new prosperity and pride in its achievements, particularly under the leadership of PERICLES, led to an outpouring of creativity, especially in drama, and allowed the city to adorn itself with public buildings of unsurpassable beauty such as the PARTHENON, begun in 447.

In the 450s, while Athens was attempting to deprive Persia of Egypt, it entered into a sporadically fought and inconclusive war with the Peloponnesians for the possession of Megara and AEGINA. Sparta was largely inactive in this war, though

This fragment from a sarcophagus captures the action of the Battle of Marathon (490 BC), a decisive Athenian victory during the Persian Wars. Although the Athenian army was greatly outnumbered, under the strategic command of Miltiades and with the aid of Plataean troops they defeated the Persian army on the Plain of Marathon, 32 km (20 mi) from Athens.

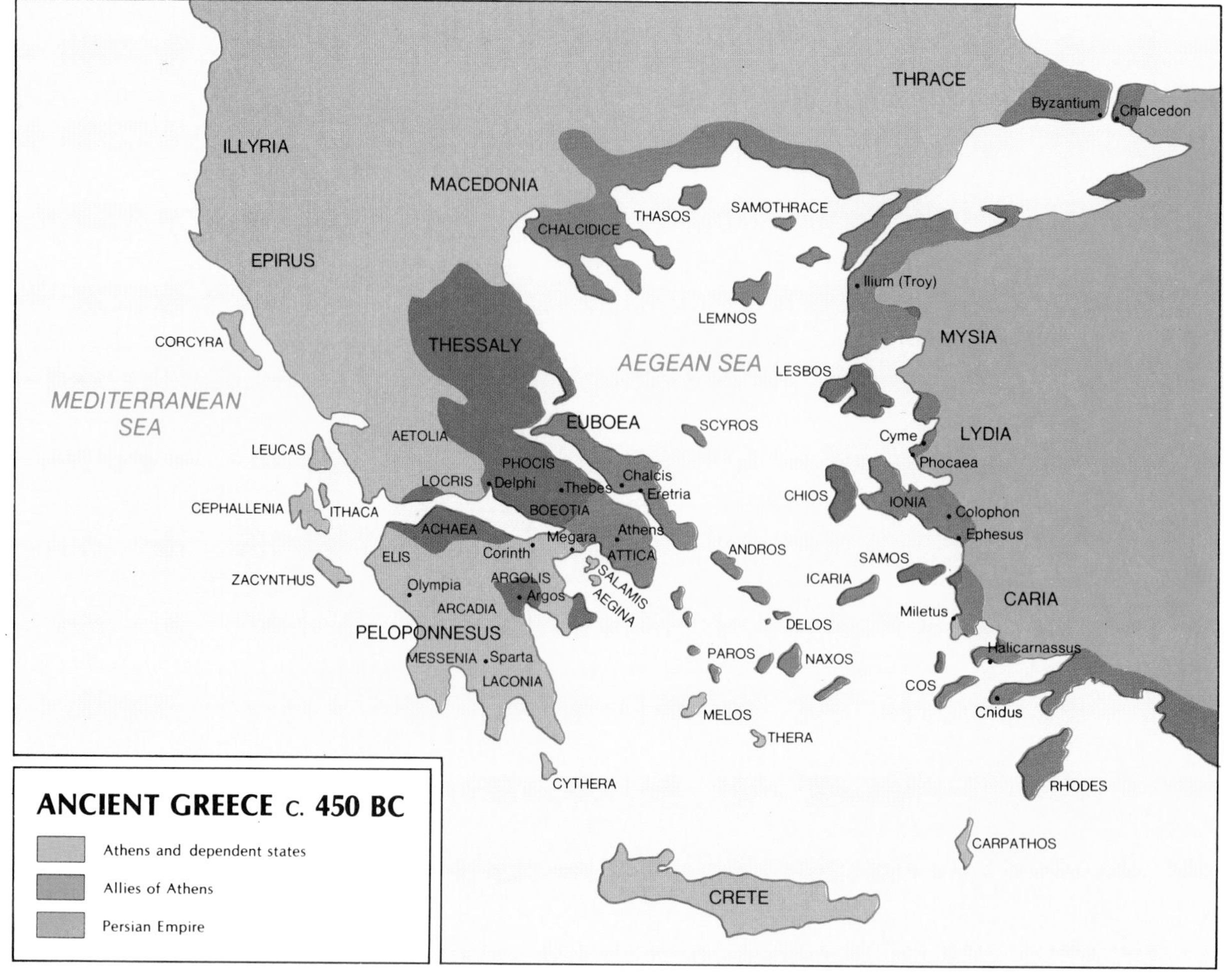

The allies and dependent states of Athens are represented in this map of Greece c.450 BC. The Athenian Empire had its roots in the Delian League, a confederation of Greek city-states formed under Athenian control in 478 for the purpose of opposing Persia. A period of peace followed with the end of the Persian Wars in 449 BC, but Athenian hegemony was broken by Sparta in the Peloponnesian War (431–404).

it fought and defeated the Athenians in the Battle of Tanagra (c.457). Sparta was probably distracted (or left weakened) by the great helot revolt that had erupted in 464 and lasted for ten (or possibly only four) years.

The war ended in the winter of 446–45 with the so-called Thirty Years' Peace. However, the peace was broken in 431, when the PELOPONNESIAN WAR began; it was to last until 404. This destructive conflict, which is chronicled by THUCYDIDES, brought revolution to many cities and resulted in increasingly brutal acts perpetrated by both sides. After the Spartans invaded Attica and sought to incite Athens's subjects to rebellion, Athens retaliated by raiding the Peloponnesian coast. The Athenians sought to retain control of the sea and attacked Corinthian settlements in northwestern Greece. After Athens's disastrous defeat in Sicily in 413, Sparta itself became a naval power and gradually drove Athens from the sea. Under siege, Athens capitulated in 404. It consented to the destruction of its fortifications and gave up its navy and empire. Meanwhile, Persia had succeeded in reasserting its presence in Ionia by financing the Spartan fleet.

THE 4TH CENTURY

Spartan and Theban Ascendancy. The Spartans, now leaders of the Greeks, soon aroused widespread enmity by their high-handed rule. In 395, Thebes and Corinth, which had been fierce enemies of Athens in the Peloponnesian War, formed a coalition with Argos to wage war against Sparta. To maintain its predominance, Sparta had to bargain with Persia. In 386 the Persians dictated the so-called King's Peace, which asserted Persia's ancestral claim to Ionia and acknowledged, in exchange, Spartan supremacy in Greece. Nevertheless, THEBES defeated Sparta at Leuctra in 371. The Theban army under EPAMINONDAS then drove into the Peloponnesus and liberated Messenia from Sparta in 369—a devastating blow to the Spartans. Meanwhile, the Athenians partially regained their naval leadership by forming the Second Athenian Confederacy in 377. The confederacy was too decentralized to permit Athens to regain its earlier dominance, however; within 20 years it virtually disintegrated.

Rise of Macedonia. A monarchy in the north soon arose to dictate the fortunes of the Greeks. The brilliant statesman and warrior PHILIP II became regent of MACEDONIA in 359 and its king in 356. Under his leadership this newly centralized kingdom gradually overwhelmed the disunited land. By easy stages Philip advanced into central Greece, winning control of Delphi as a result of the Third Sacred War (355–47) against PHOCIS. In 338 he destroyed a Theban and Athenian army on the field of CHAERONEA. He imposed a short-lived federal union on the Greeks and made himself their commander in chief in anticipation of a war against Persia. He was assassinated in 336, however, before the war could be fought.

The defeat of the Greek city-states at Chaeronea ended an era of Greek history. Neither Sparta, Athens, nor any other city-state had proved capable of uniting Greece under its leadership. Intense mutual jealousies, sharpened by the egoistic abuse each *polis* dealt the others whenever circumstances permitted, made unity a hopeless dream.

Under Pericles (left), *who was leader of the Athenian city-state from 445 to 430 BC, Athens became the center of intellectual life and the dominant imperial power of Greece. During the last years of Pericles' rule, however, the Peloponnesian War (431–404 BC) began between Athens and Sparta. The map below illustrates the division of Greece between the principal combatants and their allies.*

HELLENISTIC AND ROMAN PERIODS

ALEXANDER THE GREAT, Philip's son and successor, continued his father's plans. Aided by a battle-hardened Macedonian army that possessed the cavalry necessary for a campaign against the Persians, Alexander conquered the entire Persian Empire in ten years (334–25). He created an empire stretching from Macedonia to the Indus River, a magnificent achievement that had even more important, far-reaching effects. Alexander initiated the systematic Hellenization of the East. Greek and non-Greek culture fused together over the centuries, promoting new concepts of ethics and new religions, including Christianity.

Hellenistic Kingdoms. Alexander's huge empire broke apart at his death in 323 BC. His generals, known as the *Diadochi* (successors), claimed his legacy. By 275 three Macedonian dynasties had established themselves in the natural units of the empire. The successors of ANTIGONUS I (the Antigonids) ruled Macedonia; those of SELEUCUS I (the Seleucids), the Asian provinces; and those of PTOLEMY I (the Ptolemies), Egypt.

Meanwhile, in Greece itself, two leagues developed as important political entities. It is notable that neither was created by a former major city-state. The Achaean League comprised the cities of ACHAEA and most of the rest of the Peloponnesus except for Corinth, which remained a Macedonian possession, and Sparta, which remained independent. Founded in 280, the league was headed at first by two generals, later by one, who were elected annually. Voting was by cities, with representation proportionate to population. In AETOLIA, north of the Bay of Corinth, the cities had joined together in a federal state in the 4th century; in the 3d century they acquired control over Delphi. The structure of the Aetolian League was similar to that of the Achaean. Both leagues conferred equal citizenship upon members of participating cities. This experiment in federalism was new to the Greeks.

In the struggles among the Hellenistic monarchs of Macedonia, Asia, and Egypt between 275 and 200, the Seleucids were the chief losers. In addition to an inconclusive contest waged with the Ptolemies for the possession of Syria, the Seleucids were beset by rebellions in the eastern provinces of Asia, leaving them with only southern Anatolia, northern Syria, and Mesopotamia. In western Anatolia the rival Attalid dynasty established the kingdom of PERGAMUM.

In Greece the Antigonids enjoyed greater success. The defeat of Sparta by ANTIGONUS III at Sellasia in 222 not only overthrew CLEOMENES III but placed the Achaean League under Antigonus' control.

Roman Intervention. Rome became the decisive factor in Greek affairs after 200. It conquered PHILIP V of Macedonia in 200–196, charging that Philip had supported Rome's Carthaginian enemy, Hannibal, and was mistreating Pergamum and RHODES, powers friendly with Rome. The liberty of the Greeks was proclaimed by the Roman general Titus Quinctius FLAMI-

Alexander the Great of Macedonia, who conquered the Greek city-states and the Persian Empire and established an empire that stretched to the Indus River, is portrayed in this floor mosaic found in the House of the Faun at Pompeii. He is shown during his decisive battle against the Persian king Darius III at Issus in 333 BC.

NINUS at the Isthmian Games of 196, but it was not long before Rome intruded again in both Macedonia and Asia. Macedonia became a Roman province in 148, and the Achaean and Aetolian leagues were dissolved in 146. Meanwhile, the Seleucid ruler ANTIOCHUS III had been defeated by the Romans in 189, and the diminution of his authority led many of his subjects to rebel. By 100 BC, the Jews had established a state in Palestine and the Parthians had acquired Mesopotamia. Pergamum was bequeathed to the Romans by Attalus III in 133.

By the end of the 1st century BC, POMPEY THE GREAT, Julius CAESAR, and AUGUSTUS had settled the eastern provinces of the Roman Empire into their final form. The old Greek city-states, though subject to Rome, enjoyed local autonomy. The propertied classes controlled the local governments and Greek was retained as the official language. For a time there was much prosperity. Many cities were patronized by the Roman emperors, and Athens, especially, flourished as a university town.

However, Greece suffered terribly when Rome entered its period of great crisis in the 3d century AD. Weakness on the frontiers allowed GOTHS to invade the Balkans in the middle of the century and pirates ravaged the Aegean. Simultaneously, the SASSANIANS of Persia overran Syria, and their capture of the Roman emperor VALERIAN in 259 opened Anatolia to Persian invasion.

The Goths were defeated in 269, and the emperor DIOCLETIAN (r. 284-305) restored order in the Roman provinces. His administrative division of the empire into East and West was completed by CONSTANTINE I, who made BYZANTIUM (renamed Constantinople) his capital in 324. Even so, later in the 4th century, the Greeks were once more subjected to Gothic invasion. Afterward, the Greeks, increasingly divorced from the West, entered a new social order in which their attenuated prosperity depended on the strength or the weakness of the BYZANTINE EMPIRE.

CHARLES W. FORNARA

Bibliography: Andrews, Anthony, *Greek Society* (1967); Baker, Ernest, *Greek Political Theory*, rev. ed. (1960); Bury, J. B., *The History of Greece*, ed. by Russell Meiggs, 4th ed. (1975); Ehrenberg, Victor, *The Greek State* (1961); Forrest, W. G., *The Emergence of Greek Democracy, 800-400 B.C.* (1967); Grote, George, *The History of Greece*, 12 vols., rev. ed. (1906-38); Hopper, R. J., *The Early Greeks* (1976); Kitto, Humphrey D., *The Greeks* (1958); Lévêque, Pierre, *The Greek Adventure*, trans. by Miriam Kochan (1968); Rostovtseff, M. I., *History of the Ancient World*, 2 vols., 2d ed. (1930-33; repr. 1971); Seeley, Raphael, *A History of the Greek City States, 800-338 B.C.* (1976); Tarn, William, and Griffith, Guy, *Hellenistic Civilization*, 3d ed. (1966).

See also: PERSIA, ANCIENT; ROME, ANCIENT.

Greek architecture

The architecture of ancient Greece is represented by buildings in the sanctuaries and cities of mainland Greece, the Aegean islands, southern Italy and Sicily, and the Ionian coast of Turkey. Monumental Greek architecture began in the archaic period (7th-6th century BC), flourished through the classical and Hellenistic periods (5th-2d century BC), and saw the first of many revivals during the Roman Empire. The roots of Greek architecture lie in the tradition of local Bronze Age houses and palaces; the megaron of the Mycenaean princes, with its columned porch, forehall, and throne room, provided the basic plan of the Greek TEMPLE. Epic poems, such as the *Odyssey* of Homer, which were recited by traveling bards, kept alive the legends of the Bronze Age palaces, some of which became sites of archaic temples or shrines.

The history of Greek architecture is known from the writings of ancient authors and from carved stone inscriptions, from the accounts and drawings of 18th- and 19th-century European travelers, and from the direct study of building remains by scholars. The portable stone elements of Greek buildings (the CAPITALS, COLUMNS, and ENTABLATURE), the quantities of architectural SCULPTURE taken to Italy by the Roman army, and galleries of classical art still form the basis of most European museum collections.

GREEK BUILDING TYPES

Sacred Architecture. The Greeks conceived of their gods in human form, as anthropomorphic representations of the forces and elements of the natural world. These gods and goddesses were worshiped with sacrifices made at an outdoor ALTAR. At many sanctuaries, the altar was much older than the temple, and some sanctuaries had only an altar. The temple was designed simply as a shelter or home for the cult statue and as a storehouse for offerings. The statue stood or was seated against the back wall of the CELLA (NAOS) in view of the altar. In front of the cella was a columned porch (*pronaos*). The side walls of the cella were often extended to form a similar enclosure at the back of the temple (opisthodomus). The porches were usually secured with bronze grills hung between the columns and the projecting end walls (*antae*). The temple was often enclosed by a COLONNADE that provided shelter for visitors and supported the pitched roof.

The earliest monumental buildings in Greek architecture were the temples. Since these were solidly built and carefully maintained, they had to be replaced only if destroyed by fire, earthquake, or an attacking enemy. The architectural orders (see ARCHITECTURE), Doric on the mainland and Ionic in the eastern Aegean, were developed in the archaic temples, and their lasting example tended to make Greek architecture conservative toward changes in design or in building technology.

Greek sanctuaries were located within the cities, as on the ACROPOLIS of Athens, or at isolated sacred spots in the countryside. Some rural sanctuaries were famous healing centers, and others had oracles whose advice was sought by both Greeks and foreigners. Many sanctuaries held regular athletic contests, which were followed very seriously. These Panhellenic centers required large functional buildings to shelter visitors, to store equipment, and to serve as meeting places. The sanctuaries, as well as the developing cities, encouraged the growth of Greek civic architecture.

Secular Architecture. Greek cities were commercial, social, and governmental centers for large farming or seafaring communities, as well as homes for townspeople. As political and

The megaron (A) formed the principal element of Mycenean palaces and produced the plan of early Greek temples. It featured an outer (1) and inner (2) vestibule leading to a frescoed, rectangular room (3) housing the throne. One of the earliest Greek peristyle temples (B) at the Sanctuary of Hera on the island of Samos dates from the 9th-8th century BC. A second row of columns at the entrance (4) served as the model for later colonnaded porches. The Temple of Zeus (C) at Olympia, constructed c.470 BC, is considered an exemplar of the Doric temple. It rested upon a crepidoma (5) of several steps and was approached by a ramp (6). A standard 6 × 13 Doric colonnade (7) surrounded the temple. The cella (8) was prefaced and backed by two smaller porches, the pronaos (9) and the opisthodomos (10).

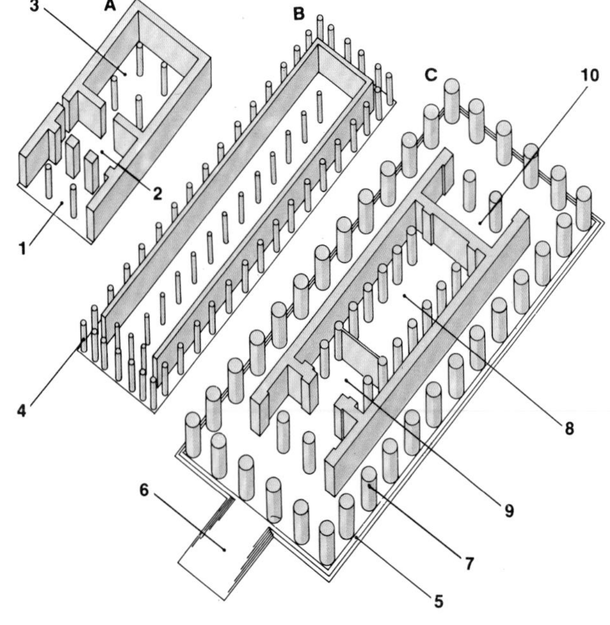

cultural institutions evolved, the forms of civic buildings became as regular as the temple form.

In Athens the AGORA began as a large public space on either side of the sacred way leading from the western city gate to the Acropolis. In the hillside south of the agora there were springs that were piped down into sheltered draw basins (fountain houses). Along the western side a nondescript group of rooms housed the Athenian council before the construction of a theaterlike assembly hall (bouleuterion) and the circular building (tholos) in which the council members ate their meals. The most characteristic and versatile civic building was the STOA—a long hall with an open colonnaded front and shops or a closed wall on the back.

Elsewhere in a Greek city were the public BATHS, GYMNASIUM, STADIUM, and theater. Greek festivals involved music and dancing performed outdoors, and the early theater consisted simply of a circular dance floor at the foot of a hillside where the audience sat. By the 4th century BC the hillside was scooped out to form a semicircular cavea furnished with stone benches and aisles. As the actors became more prominent in Greek drama, a low stage was built at the back of the dance floor, or orchestra (see THEATER ARCHITECTURE AND STAGING).

The Temple of Hera (c.460 BC) at Paestum, Italy, is a well-preserved example of a Doric temple. The temple, at one time incorrectly identified as a temple of Poseidon, is typically Doric in its plan, featuring a crepidoma, peristyle, cella, pronaos, and opisthodomos.

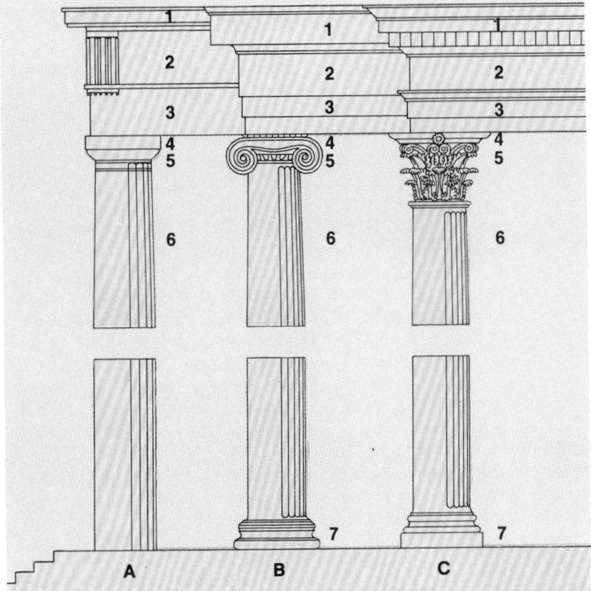

(Above) *Greek architectural orders, consisting originally of the Doric* (A) *and the Ionic* (B) *and joined by an Ionic variation, the Corinthian* (C), *during the 5th century BC, share certain compositional elements. The entablature, comprised of the cornice* (1), *frieze* (2), *and architrave* (3), *rests upon the abacus* (4). *Beneath the abacus the capital* (5) *surmounts the shaft* (6), *which is often fluted, or grooved. Only the Ionic and the Corinthian orders feature a base* (7). (Below) *The Doric capital* (A) *is formed by a square abacus and a rounded echinus* (8). *The Ionic capital* (B) *is distinguished by its spiral, or volute* (9). *The Corinthian capital* (C) *is an inverted bell featuring two rows of acanthus leaves* (10), *from which arise small spirals.*

ARCHAIC PERIOD

After the sudden collapse of the Mycenaean palace period about 1200 BC (see AEGEAN CIVILIZATION), there followed a so-called dark age lasting about 300 years, during which the surviving Greek people reestablished their communities but the fine arts languished. At many sanctuaries, remains of primitive temples have been found dating from near the end of this period. These buildings, with rubble foundations in a horseshoe-shaped plan, timber and mud-brick walls, and a thatched roof, resemble some Bronze Age houses. Remains of such buildings have been found beneath the archaic temples at Eretria and Thermon and separately in other sanctuaries. Clay house models dedicated in the sanctuaries complete the picture of the primitive temples: a single room sometimes furnished with a cult figure, a shallow columned porch, a rounded hip roof, and exterior walls painted with geometric patterns.

Doric Order. In the succeeding archaic temples, stone gradually replaced wood, and some of the structural details of the early buildings appear to have been copied in stone. At Thermon, in northwestern Greece, a succession of buildings from the Late Bronze Age through the 6th century BC show the evolution of the Doric temple from a hall shaped like a hairpin to a long rectangular building with a porch at either end and surrounded by columns. The latest temple had a tile roof, a painted terra-cotta sima (gutter), and painted panels (metopes) probably set between the ends of the rafters; these

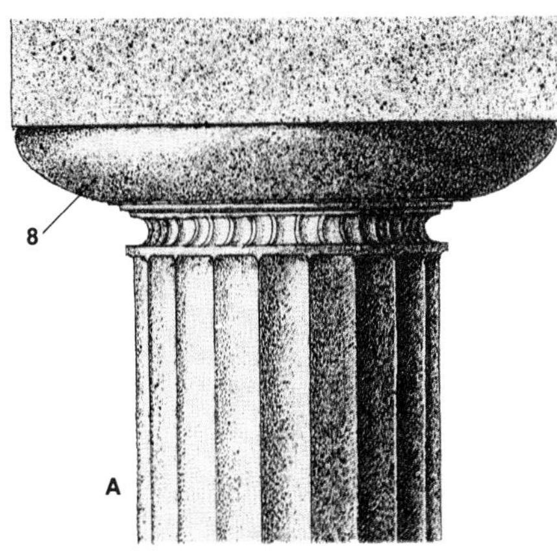

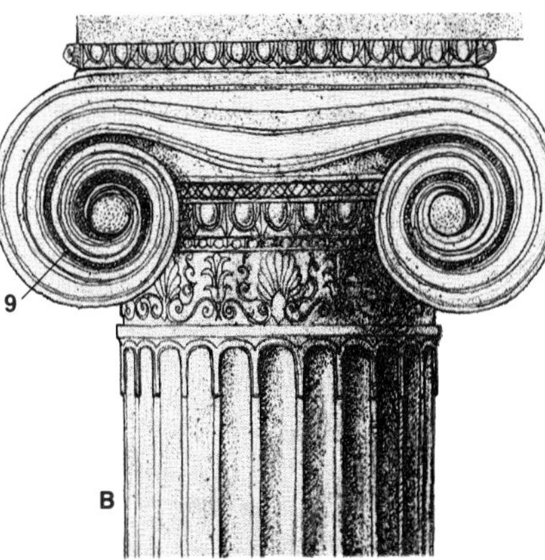

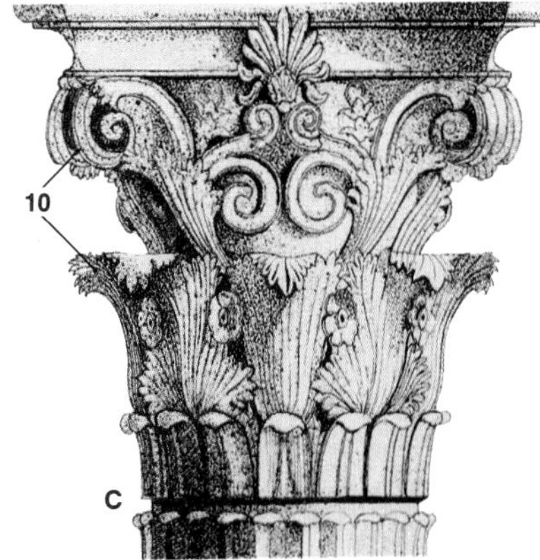

timbers must have rested on a horizontal beam (ARCHITRAVE) supported by the colonnade. The exposed rafter ends were sheathed with terra-cotta panels (triglyphs), and the line or FRIEZE of alternating triglyphs and metopes became a fixed part of the Doric order.

Ornaments and moldings were prominent decorative elements in Greek architecture. Mythological figures, such as the gorgon (1), often appeared as sculptural decoration. Ornamental blocks, such as the antefix (2) and the acroterion (3), were used to cover the ends of roof tiles and to decorate the apex of the roof. Sima recta moldings (4) often featured a honeysuckle motif. A fret (5), or key pattern, was a geometric ornament. Some of the moldings most commonly found on Greek architecture were the astragal (6); the ovolo (7); and both the sima reversa (8) and the sima recta (9), which alternated convex with concave, or concave with convex, curves. A patera (10), a small, flat ornament, sometimes featured a small central rosette.

The temple of Hera at OLYMPIA, built about 600 BC, had wooden columns that were gradually replaced by stone ones, probably as votive gifts. The variety of column and capital shapes illustrates the evolution of the Doric order. The earliest columns had a heavy, bulging profile, and their capitals were broad and low.

In the 5th and 4th centuries BC the column shaft became straighter and more slender, and the capitals smaller with a more angular profile. The columns rested on a platform (stylobate) built of limestone blocks, two steps above ground level. The lowest course of the cella wall was made of a double thickness of limestone blocks (*orthostates*). Above this level the walls were made of sun-dried mud brick, braced with PIERS on the interior. The projecting wall ends (antae) and the doorways were sheathed in wood. Above the level of the column capitals the temple was finished in wood and brick and roofed with terra-cotta tiles. Above the eastern pediment was a huge terra-cotta disk acroterion (roof ornament) painted with geometric patterns.

Although the plan of the Doric temple was formalized during the archaic period, between about 650 and 490 BC, with pronaos, cella, and opisthodomus surrounded by a colonnade having six columns at each end and thirteen along the flanks, there were many exceptions to the rule. The elements of the Doric order seen in elevation, however, varied only in the curved profiles and proportions of height to thickness.

During the archaic period, limestone became the standard building material for foundations, steps, walls, columns, and the Doric entablature (architrave, triglyph/metope frieze, and CORNICE). Simas and roof tiles were usually made of terra-cotta, formed in molds and fired in closed kilns like coarse pottery. Archaic temples often had limestone pedimental sculpture, which was carved in the round and brightly painted, depicting battle scenes or vignettes from the life of the god or goddess. Metope panels were sometimes carved to illustrate events in the lives of heroes or demigods, such as scenes from the labors of Hercules or the struggles of the Lapiths and Centaurs.

The Temple of Aphaia on Aegina, built about 500 BC, illustrates how the interior columns, which had to reach a greater height than the exterior colonnade, could be constructed in two tiers. The floral acroteria and pedimental sculptures were carved from marble, which had been introduced by sculptors during the late 6th century BC.

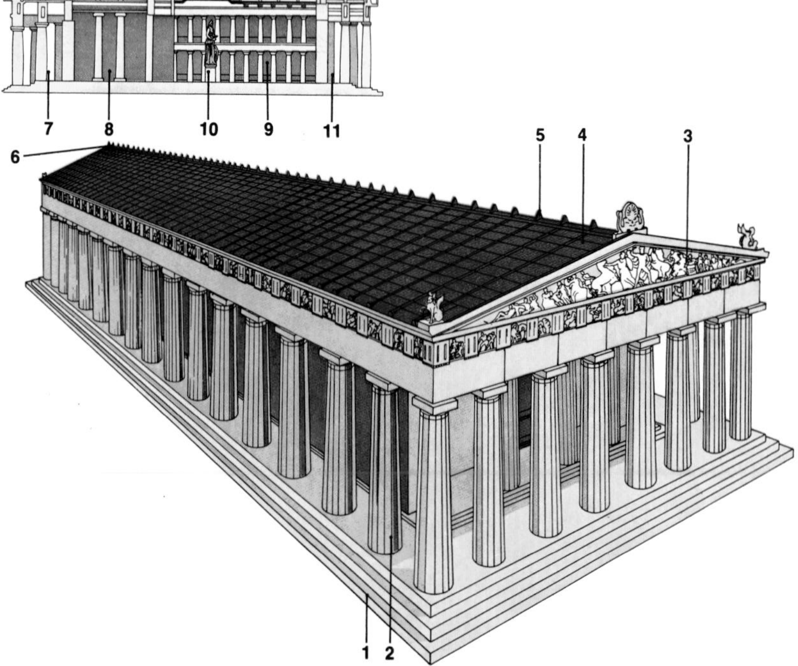

The Parthenon (447–432 BC) on the Acropolis in Athens, dedicated to Athena Parthenos, is the supreme example of classical architecture. Although Doric in plan, many Ionic elements, such as the sculptured friezes, are integrated into the structure. The crepidoma (1) rises to the temple floor on which the 8 x 17 Doric colonnade (2) stands. The pediments (3) were brightly colored, those on the east depicting the birth of Athena and those on the west her struggle with Poseidon for Attica. The roof (4) was made of marble slabs; palmette ridge tiles (5) were placed along its ridge. Acroteria (6) were placed at the apex, and antefixes at the corners of the roof. The opisthodomos (7) is situated behind the Parthenon (8), the chamber from which the building takes its name. Four Ionic pillars stand in the Parthenon. The majestic gold and ivory statue of Athena Parthenos (10) stood in the naos, or cella (9), which is reached through the pronaos (11). Both the pronaos and opisthodomos served as municipal treasuries.

Ionic Order. As the Doric order became the standard for mainland Greece, the Ionian colonies in the eastern Aegean were developing a very different system of columns and entablature based on Egyptian and Near Eastern architecture. The Ionic column is taller and more slender, stands on a profiled base, and has a volute (spiral) capital. The entablature of the archaic temples in Anatolia was relatively low, consisting of an architrave, egg-and-dart molding, and a cornice, but no sculptured frieze course. The 6th-century BC Ionic temples at Samos, Ephesus, and Didyma were unprecedented in size, as large as 55 by 112 m (180 by 367 ft). The long, narrow cellas were enclosed by double rows of columns and had deep, densely columned porches.

The western Greek colonies in Sicily and southern Italy (together called *Magna Graecia*) adopted the Doric order for most purposes. The entablature of temples was sometimes raised by adding decorative moldings, and the cornice revetments and simas were made of brightly painted terra-cotta. Buildings were made entirely of limestone coated with white stucco to look like marble; cornices, triglyphs, and moldings were often painted red or blue. Wealthy cities such as PAESTUM, SELINUS, SYRACUSE, Akragas, and Metapontum each had as many as six major temples, sometimes arranged in a regular sequence, in addition to the standard civic buildings.

CLASSICAL PERIOD

Athenian Dominance. The war between the Greek city-states and Persia (499–480 BC) interrupted almost all temple building for a generation while the Greeks concentrated on restoring their defensive walls, civic buildings, and the fleet. ATHENS emerged as the leader, controlling the war chest of the Delian League, a Panhellenic league; the city initiated an extravagant program to rebuild the sanctuary of Athena on the Acropolis. The PARTHENON (temple of Athena Parthenos), Propylaea (entrance gates), Temple of Athena Nike (goddess of victory), and the Erechtheum (a complex temple dedicated to Athena Polias and a series of minor deities) were built entirely of marble and elaborately decorated with carved moldings and sculpture. The architects were CALLICRATES and ICTINUS, and the chief sculptor was PHIDIAS.

A large school of builders and sculptors developed in Athens during the second half of the 5th century BC. Most of these craft workers were freed slaves (metics) from the eastern Mediterranean. Perhaps as a consequence there developed in Attica a unique blend of the Doric and Ionic orders seen in the fortified sanctuaries at ELEUSIS, Rhamnus, and Sounion, as well as in Athens. On the Acropolis the Propylaea had tall Ionic columns in the western corridor; the tiny Athena Nike temple and the Erechtheum were built in the Ionic order, with the addition of a sculptured frieze course and a more complex column base.

Corinthian Order. A succession of long civil wars during the late 5th and 4th centuries BC eclipsed monumental architecture in mainland Greece, although old temples were repaired and some innovative building was done in the Peloponnesian cities and sanctuaries of ARGOS, EPIDAURUS, NEMEA, and TEGEA. The Corinthian column, probably first used by Ictinus in the Temple of Apollo at Bassae, was used for interior colonnades and for the exterior of circular monuments called tholoi. The design was inspired by the sight of ACANTHUS leaves growing from a basket set on a grave column, according to legend.

The Ionian cities recovered more quickly during the 4th century BC under Persian sovereignty. The colossal 6th-century BC temples and altars were replaced on a grander scale. Several Ionian cities were rebuilt on a grid plan that has been credited to HIPPODAMUS OF MILETUS but was employed in most colonial new towns. In small temples, sculptors and architects were employing strict canons of proportion, as seen in the Ionic temple of Athena at Priene designed about 340 BC by Pythius, who also wrote a theoretical book that was known to the Roman architect VITRUVIUS.

HELLENISTIC PERIOD

The rise of Macedonia and the conquests of Alexander the Great heralded the Hellenistic period (usually dated 323–86 BC), when royal patrons favored the Panhellenic sanctuaries, founded new cities in Syria and Egypt, and embellished such cities as EPHESUS and PERGAMUM in Anatolia. Old building types became more complex: altars, gate buildings, council houses, stoas with two or three levels, and theaters with large attached stage buildings. Many new building types were introduced, including the nymphaeum (a sculptured facade with fountains), monumental tomb, columned hall, choragic monument (a circular tower celebrating the winners of a choral dance competition), clock tower, and lighthouse. Many of these structures were decorated with dramatic marble sculpture.

Hellenistic architects made imaginative variations on the standard temple forms, introducing APSES, high podia (stepped or square platforms), and subtle combinations of Doric and Ionic features. Several temples had exterior Corinthian columns, such as the colossal temple of Zeus Olympius in Athens, begun in 174 BC. In the Ionic order, Hermogenes of Priene evolved new canons of proportion concerning the temple plan and the height and spacing of columns. His writings were also passed down to Roman architects who emulated his designs. Long after the Roman army captured Athens, the principles of Greek architecture continued to govern building designs in mainland Greece and in Anatolia and strongly influenced ROMAN ARCHITECTURE throughout the empire.

W. WILLSON CUMMER

Bibliography: Berve, Helmut, and Gruben, Gottfried, *Greek Temples, Theatres and Shrines* (1963); Boardman, John, et al., *The Art and Architecture of Ancient Greece* (1967); Coulton, J. J., *Ancient Greek Architects at Work* (1977); Dinsmoor, William B., *The Architecture of Ancient Greece*, 3d ed. (1950; repr. 1975); Lawrence, Arnold W., *Greek Architecture*, rev. ed. (1975); Pollitt, J. J., *Art and Experience in Classical Greece* (1972); Robertson, D. S., *Greek and Roman Architecture*, 2d ed. (1969); Scranton, Robert L., *Greek Architecture* (1962); Scully, Vincent, *The Earth, the Temple and the Gods: Greek Sacred Architecture*, rev. ed. (1970); Wycherley, R. E., *How the Greeks Built Cities* (1976).

See also: ARCHAEOLOGY; ELGIN MARBLES; GREEK REVIVAL; MINOAN ART; ROMAN ART.

Greek art

Ancient Greek art developed and flourished between about 1000 and 31 BC in mainland Greece and in the Greek colonies of the eastern Mediterranean, southern Italy, Sicily, and the Aegean. The earlier date is associated with the transitional period following the decline of the prehistoric Minoan and Mycenean civilizations (see AEGEAN CIVILIZATION; MINOAN ART); the battle of Actium in 31 BC represents the time of transition into ROMAN ART. Greek art developed within the framework of the Greek city-state, the evolution of which falls into the chronological period defined above.

The Doric, Ionic, and Corinthian orders, which had profound influence on the history of architecture, developed in monumental Greek religious and civic architecture. Greek sculpture progressed from stylization to naturalism and from naturalism to realism, creating some of the greatest works in

Geometric sculpture consisted of human and animal figures made of terra-cotta and bronze. This small bronze piece, Mare Suckling Her Foal *(c. 750–700 BC), was found at Olympia, one of the richest centers of geometric sculpture. It shows great clarity of line and form. (National Museum, Athens.)*

(Right) *Decorated pottery was an important ancient Greek art form, with Athens, Corinth, and Chalchis as the chief centers of potterymaking. Four main groups of vessel were produced for various functions: holders, including the amphora* (1), *urns* (2), *and kraters* (3), *which were used for mixing wine and water; dippers, such as the hydria* (4); *pourers, represented by the oinoche* (5) *and the lekythos* (6); *and drinking vessels, including the kylis* (7) *and the kantharos* (8), two-handed drinking cups, *and the rhyton* (9), *or drinking horn.*

(Left) *The Dipylon Krater is a classic representative of Attic geometric pottery. Dated after 750* BC, *this large vase was a grave monument decorated with a chariot funeral procession painted on a circumferential band. (Metropolitan Museum of Art, New York.)*

the history of art. Greek painting developed in two channels: monumental painting and painting on pottery. Because little remains of the former type, scholars rely mainly on vase painting to trace the development of Greek drawing. The early study of Greek art, which was seen mainly through the works of Roman copyists, had enormous influence in 16th-century Italy and was of fundamental importance in the development of RENAISSANCE ART AND ARCHITECTURE.

GEOMETRIC PERIOD (10TH–8TH CENTURY BC)

The beginning of the Iron Age in Greece coincided with the dissolution of the prehistoric cultures of the area. The material remains of the new culture are rather sparse; there is little surviving monumental architecture, which was mainly in the form of primitive temples, no wall painting, and no large-scale sculpture. Existing sculpture is small, mainly bronze, terra-cotta, or ivory statuettes that served as dedications at religious sanctuaries or as grave offerings. Pottery, however, is plentiful and, particularly in Attica, of good quality. The geometric period is named for the pottery with its geometric decoration. Bands of decoration drawn in black on the light-colored clay included a rich repertoire of geometric designs, such as meanders, swastikas, chevrons, and elaborations of these patterns. Animal forms began to intrude gradually into the abstract decoration, and by the 8th century BC human figures appeared in stylized silhouette. These figures included dancers, processions of horsemen and chariots, battle scenes, and men and women lamenting the dead, as in the *Dipylon Krater* (8th century BC; Metropolitan Museum of Art, New York City), a large vase that was originally used as a grave monument.

ARCHAIC PERIOD (7TH–6TH CENTURY BC)

The beginning of the archaic period is sometimes called the Orientalizing phase because of the great influence of the Near East on the figurative arts. The full development of the *polis*, or city-state, occurred during the archaic period. The cities, through colonization and trade, became acquainted with Egyptian stone carving and the decorative arts of Assyria and Mesopotamia.

Painting. The Eastern motifs, probably transmitted through

One of the techniques developed by Athenian artists during the archaic period was black-figure pottery, which flourished c.580–530 BC. *Exekias, who blended archaic traditions with classic styles, was one of the greatest artists in this genre.* (Left) *This Attic amphora by Exekias, dating from c.530* BC, *portrays a domestic scene involving Tyndareos, Leda, and their sons, Castor and Pollux. Exekias's refined style infuses the figures with deep emotion, visible in the detail* (below) *of Leda. (Vatican Museum, Rome.)*

This detail from a red-figure amphora from Vulci, Etruria, dates from c.445–440 BC. It was executed by the Achilles painter, whose classical portrayal of the Greek hero Achilles has been compared to the style of the Parthenon frieze in its manifest strength and calm. Unlike the earlier black-figure style, the details on red-figure pottery were painted rather than incised, allowing for a heightened sense of perspective. (Vatican Museum, Rome.)

imports of metalwork or textiles, blossomed into a painting style that replaced the geometric style in pottery decoration. The abstraction of the geometric vases, in which the human and animal figures were subjugated to the overall design, disappeared. Human figures appeared in compositions that told a story, often a familiar one from Greek legend, and inscriptions painted on the vase identified the heroes and divinities represented. Corinth was the most important pottery center; Corinthian miniature vessels for perfumed oil, as well as larger vases, were exported in great quantities during the 7th and 6th centuries BC. By the middle of the 6th century, however, Athens assumed the lead in the pottery industry.

Athenian potters experimented with different techniques, such as silhouette, outline drawing, and the use of white in their vase paintings. They gradually concentrated on black figure, a technique borrowed from the Corinthian animal style. The black-figure style consisted of painting figures in silhouette on a light ground and then incising details in the black with a fine instrument. Black-figure vases were decorated with scenes from mythology as well as from daily life. The style, which was particularly suited to a decorative medium such as pottery, was used by numerous excellent artists, some of whom signed their vases, as did CLEITIAS, the painter of the *François Vase* (c.570 BC; Archaeological Museum, Florence). The best black-figure artist was EXEKIAS, who painted elegant and sometimes somber scenes on vases and terra-cotta plaques—an amphora that shows Achilles and Ajax playing at droughts (c.550–540 BC; Vatican Museum, Rome) is particularly noteworthy.

During the late archaic period, about 530 BC, the red-figure style was introduced. In this technique the background of the picture, rather than the picture itself, was covered with black glaze. The figures were preserved in the color of the clay; details were painted rather than incised on the light ground. This technique gave painters greater freedom to perfect their rendering of anatomy and perspective.

Sculpture. Monumental sculpture in limestone and marble appeared in Greece during the archaic period. The first statues were influenced by Egyptian sculpture, which in the 7th century BC already had a long tradition. Egyptian sculpture, however, showed little stylistic change over the centuries. Greek sculptors used the prototype of a standing figure with one foot advanced and the hands clenched to the sides and developed it so that within a hundred years the same general type was no longer stylized but had become a naturalistic rendering with subtle modeling. This type of figure is usually called a *kouros* (Greek: "boy") and is pictured in the nude, for example, the *Kritios Boy* (c.490–480 BC; Acropolis Museum, Athens). The female equivalent, or *kore*, is always dressed in rich drapery enhanced by incision and color. Color was also used for the hair and facial features of both male and female statues. The figures do not seem to represent a divinity, nor are they usually portraits, but instead are images of the ideal masculine or feminine form.

The great artists of the period also created other types of sculpture; the *Rampin Horseman* (c.560 BC; Acropolis Museum, Athens; the head is in the Louvre, Paris) was an early example of a man-animal composition. The architectural sculptures, which were carved in relief or in the round and designed to decorate stone temples, were even more com-

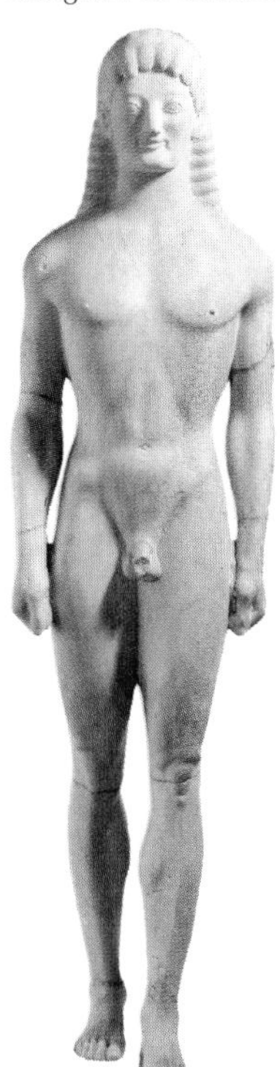

Archaic sculpture is represented by (left) *the young male* kouros *from Tenea (Staatliche Antikesammlungen, Munich) and* (above) *the painted marble* kore *from the Acropolis. (Acropolis Museum, Athens.)*

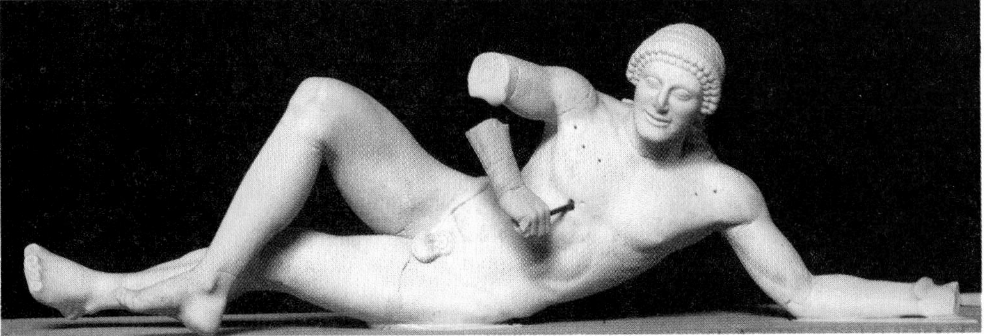

The most fully developed of the archaic temples is that of Aphaia at Aegina. Shown is a marble sculpture of a wounded warrior, in the tradition of bronze statuary. The figure occupied the right angle of the west pediment, and the facial expression is archaic in style. (Staatliche Antikesammlungen, Munich.)

The idealism typical of the classical period in Greek art is captured by this fragment from the Parthenon frieze. The horse and rider were part of a long cavalcade representing the Panathenaic procession, which surrounded the top of the outer wall of the cella. The frieze, in Ionic style, was carved in low relief, balancing the more powerful Doric architecture of the rest of the Parthenon.

plex. Early gable sculptures show a predilection for monsters; the limestone statue of a three-headed monster (*c.*560–550 BC; Acropolis Museum), striking in the preservation of its gay colors, belonged to such a gable. Gradually fighting scenes began to predominate, as in the late-6th- or early-5th-century gables from the Aphaia temple on the island of Aegina (Glyptothek, Munich). Battle scenes were used to decorate the frieze of the marble treasury dedicated to the sanctuary of Apollo by the island city-state of Siphnos (*c.*525 BC; Delphi Museum). In these reliefs, as well as in freestanding statues, there was a striking clarity of contour and a predilection for pattern that characterize archaic sculpture.

Monumental Greek architecture was a development of the archaic period that coincided with the beginning of monumental sculpture. During this period the Doric style of mainland Greece and the western colonies and the Ionic style of the Aegean islands and the Ionian colonies came into being. Both styles reached their culmination in Attica during the 5th century.

CLASSICAL PERIOD (5TH–4TH CENTURY BC)

The culmination of the tendencies of the preceding centuries in all fields of art occurred during the classical period. The standardization of the temple form permitted only minor innovations—chiefly in the ornamentation of buildings, including the creation of the Corinthian order—and Greek architects turned their efforts toward creating the subtleties of proportion that were to make Greek architecture one of the greatest in the world.

Sculpture. Two buildings and their decoration exemplify what was achieved by the Greeks in architecture and sculpture. The first is the temple of Zeus at Olympia (468–456 BC); the other is the PARTHENON on the Athenian ACROPOLIS (447–432 BC). The temple of Zeus is a Doric building, imposing in size and in the magnificence of its architectural sculpture. The compositions on the two gables and on the metopes over the inner porches are representative of the early-5th-century severe style, with rather simple, severe forms,

The early classical period (c.480–450 BC) of Greek art is exemplified by the bronze Charioteer of Delphi (right). *The statue's naturalistic style represents a shift from archaic formalism. (Museum, Delphi.) Classical sculpture culminated in the 4th-century works of Praxiteles. His* Hermes and the Infant Dionysus (left) *(Museum, Olympia) displays a deftly balanced composition further developed in his* Apollo Sauroktonos (center). *(Villa Albani, Rome.)*

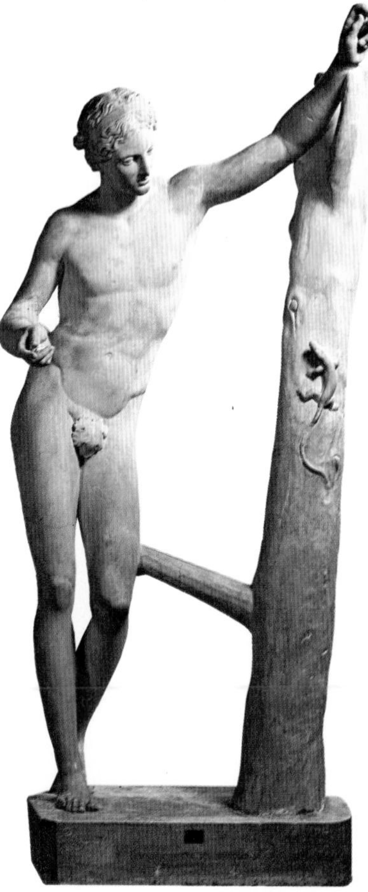

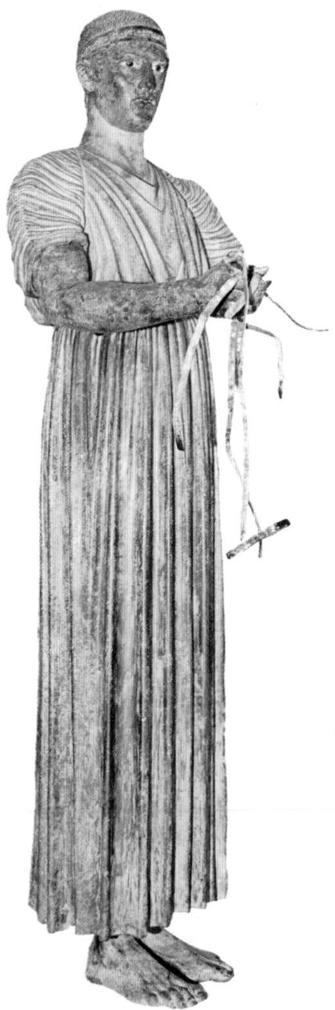

heavy drapery, an interest in emotion and characterization, and contrasts of texture and age. The Doric architecture of the Parthenon was tempered by Ionic intrusions, including the Ionic frieze. Most of the frieze is in the British Museum in London, together with some of the metopes and gable figures (see ELGIN MARBLES).

The Parthenon represented the high point in Greek sculpture. A calm idealism pervaded the exquisitely carved figures, which were based on Greek mythology. The Ionic frieze portrayed the procession during the great Panathenaic festival. Although executed by many artists, it was conceived by one designer, probably PHIDIAS, the eminent Athenian sculptor who was the overseer of the building program on the Acropolis and who created the gold-and-ivory cult statue of Athena for the Parthenon. Because of a lack of original works by the great sculptors of the 5th century BC—MYRON and POLYCLITUS—and of the 4th century BC—LYSIPPUS and SCOPAS—scholars rely mainly on Roman copies and on ancient descriptions. One possible exception is the *Hermes and the Infant Dionysus* (*c.*340 BC; Olympia Museum, Greece), which is believed by some to be an original. Classical sculpture was characterized by a more relaxed attitude of the human body with a balanced composition, idealized treatment of the head, and increasingly slender proportions.

Some great bronzes have survived, such as the *Charioteer of Delphi* (*c.*480-475 BC; Delphi Museum) and the *Zeus*, or *Poseidon, of Artemision* (*c.*460 BC; National Museum, Athens).

Painting. No trace exists of the work of the great painters of the classical period—APELLES, MICON, PARRHASIUS, POLYGNOTUS,

A significant development in classical Greek painting during the second half of the 5th century was the creation of white-ground lekythoi. This detail of a lekythos by the Achilles painter portrays a muse on Mount Helicon. Lekythoi, vases with cylindrical bodies and long necks, were used as grave offerings. The muse's spiritual calm is typical of the refined style of the Achilles painter. (Staatliche Antikesammlungen, Munich.)

The Hellenistic period of Greek art, 323 to 31 BC, is characterized by wide eclecticism, with the great artistic centers spreading from the mainland to the islands. The Aphrodite of Melos *(Venus de Milo)* (left) *dates from the 2d or 1st century BC and is typically Hellenistic in its idealization of form. (Louvre, Paris.)* (Below) *The* Laocoön, *created by three Rhodian sculptors during the mid-2d century BC, skillfully captures the intense emotionalism and movements of the agony and death of Laocoön and his sons. (Vatican Museums, Rome.)*

and ZEUXIS. A pale glimmer of their type of work can be discerned in the drawing of the vase painters who worked in the red-figure style and in the white-ground technique suitable for grave offerings. The vase painters perfected the rendering of anatomy and introduced and developed perspective and shading. The Berlin Painter, the Brygos Painter, the Niobid Painter, and the Penthesileia Painter are just a few who worked in Athens, especially during the earlier years of the period, when red-figure ware was at its best.

HELLENISTIC PERIOD (323-31 BC)

After the death (323 BC) of Alexander the Great, his extensive empire was dissolved into many different kingdoms. This fragmentation was symbolic of the diversity and multiplicity of artistic tendencies in the Hellenistic period. The great art centers were no longer in mainland Greece but in the islands, such as Rhodes, and the cities in the eastern Mediterranean—Alexandria, Antioch, and Pergamum.

Sculpture. The variety of artistic directions makes a general statement about the sculpture of the period rather difficult. There was a tendency toward classicism, but also another toward the baroque or even the rococo; a tendency toward idealization, but also a tendency toward realism. The Hellenistic period was, above all, a period of eclecticism. Art still served a religious function or to glorify athletes, but sculpture and painting were also used to decorate the homes of the rich. There was an interest in heroic portraits and in colossal groups, but also in humbler subjects. The human being was portrayed in every stage and walk of life; there was even an interest in caricature.

The awareness of space that characterized architecture also began to emerge in sculpture and painting. As a result landscapes and interiors appeared for the first time in both reliefs and painted panels. The great Altar of Zeus from Pergamum (*c.*180 BC; State Museum, East Berlin), created by Greek artists for King Eumenes II, was enclosed by a high podium decorated with a monumental frieze of the battle between the gods and giants. Many Hellenistic tendencies were realized in this work. The basis for its iconography was firmly rooted in classical tradition. The baroque style of the sculpture was characteristic of the time in its exaggeration of movement, physical pain, and emotion, all set against a background of swirling draperies.

Painting. Some of the painting of the time has been preserved, mainly in chamber tombs with painted facades and interiors. Other examples were echoed in Roman copies and in adaptations of the originals from Rome and Pompeii, or they survived in MOSAICS, which were already being produced in the classical period and reached their highest point in Pella and Delos during the Hellenistic period.

ANASTASIA DINSMOOR

Bibliography: Arias, P. E., *A History of Greek Vase Painting* (1962); Boardman, John, et al., *The Art and Architecture of Ancient Greece* (1967); Brilliant, Richard, *Arts of the Ancient Greeks* (1973); Charbonneaux, Jean, et al., *Archaic Greek Art: 620-480 BC* (1971); Lullies, Reinhard, and Hirmer, Max, *Greek Sculpture*, trans. by Michael Bullock, 2d ed. (1960); Pollitt, J. J., *Art and Experience in Classical Greece* (1972); Richter, Gisela M. A., *A Handbook of Greek Art*, 7th ed. (1974; repr. 1977) and *Sculpture and Sculptors of the Greeks*, 4th ed. (1970); Robertson, C. M., *A History of Greek Art*, 2 vols. (1975); Webster, Thomas B., *The Art of Greece: The Age of Hellenism* (1966).

See also: PAINTING; POTTERY AND PORCELAIN; SCULPTURE.

Greek fire

Greek fire, an incendiary substance that bursts into flame when wet, was first used on a large scale by the Byzantine Greeks in the late 7th century A.D. It was used at Constantinople to set fire to invading ships and was so effective that its formula was kept a state secret. Presumably, it was a mixture of flammable materials such as sulfur and pitch, with quicklime added to react with water and catch fire.

Greek fire was also known as wet, or sea, fire. Liquid fire, a mixture of incendiary materials that was first set afire and then thrown against enemy ships or troops or against besieged fortifications, was used by the Greeks as early as the 4th century BC.

Greek fire, an incendiary composition that ignited when exposed to water, was used in warfare as early as the 4th century BC. It was hurled in pots as grenades or forced through tubes and sprayed, as in this illustration of a 10th-century naval battle.

Greek language

The Greek language (both ancient and modern) is a member of the Indo-European family of languages; its closest relatives are Armenian, Indo-Iranian, and Italic. The historical evolution of Greek reveals a unity paralleled only in Chinese, and the major changes can be charted in an unbroken literary tradition.

Ancient Greek was spoken in Greece, on Crete and Cyprus, in parts of the eastern Mediterranean and western and northern Anatolia, on Sicily and in southern Italy, on the northern Black Sea coast, and sporadically along the African coast and the French Riviera. Modern Greek is the language of about 9,340,000 people in Greece and the Greek islands and about 480,000 on Cyprus; it is also spoken in isolated villages of Turkey, Sicily, and southern Italy, and in many areas throughout the world to which Greeks have immigrated, notably Australia and North America.

History. From about 1500 BC to the present day, Greek has gone through a slow, organic, and uninterrupted growth, with four major stages of evolution: prehistoric, classical, Byzantine, and modern. Prehistoric Greek was introduced into the Aegean by a series of immigrations throughout the second millennium. The language can be reconstructed in outline from a comparison of ancient dialects and from Mycenaean inscriptions, such as LINEAR B, now generally agreed to be an early form of Greek. Ancient Greek includes classical Greek, recorded in inscriptions and literary works from the 7th century BC to the death of Alexander the Great in 323 BC, and Hellenistic Greek. Classical Greek is known in four main dialect groups—Attic-Ionic, Arcado-Cyprian, Aeolic, and Doric—spoken in independent city-states and creatively adapted for particular genres in the great works of classical literature. Homeric Greek was a traditional literary language, comprising elements from several dialects, but was never the spoken language of any one people. The Hellenistic *koine,* or common tongue, was based on a late form of Attic, and became the official language of the unified Greek-speaking world, later extending to peoples whose native language was not Greek. Invaluable evidence of its spoken form exists in papyrus letters: its best known literary expression is in the New Testament.

Byzantine Greek is notable mainly for its heterogeneity. The *koine* remained the basis of the language of the early church and of the spoken tongue. Learned writers, however, adhered to an obsolete form of Attic, revived in the aftermath of the Roman conquest in opposition to the *koine*. Their archaizing Greek replaced Latin as the official language of the Byzantine Empire in the 6th century.

Modern Greek appears in verse from the 12th century and was creatively adapted in Cretan Renaissance literature. The question of a national language did not arise, however, until the 19th century with the emergence of the newly independent Greek state. *Katharévousa* ("purifying" Greek), an artificial compromise between the archaizing and the spoken forms, was imposed as the official language from 1834 until

1976. After 1976, *demotiké*, the language used in speech and creative literature, became the officially taught language. *Katharévousa* is now used in official documents. The division between them has its roots in the first centuries of the present era and presents a series of ever-changing oppositions that affect both speech and writing. The four major dialect groups—Peloponnesian, Northern Greek, Cretan, and Dodecanesian-Cypriot—all derive from the Hellenistic *koine*.

The transition from ancient to modern Greek was gradual and uneven, beginning in the 5th century BC and completed by the 10th century AD. Hellenistic Greek is closer to modern Greek than it is to prehistoric Greek. The differences between classical and modern Greek are scarcely greater than those between middle English and modern English.

Phonology and Morphology. Ancient Greek had an accentual system based on pitch with three tones: rising, falling, and rising/falling. Its phonology was characterized by a tendency to move vowels forward from the back to the front of the mouth (a>ē : Latin *mater*, Greek *mḗtēr*); loss of initial *s* before vowels (Latin *sex*, Greek *hex*=six); and weakening of final consonants. Its inflectional system was highly developed, with five cases (nominative, vocative, accusative, genitive, dative), three genders (masculine, feminine, neuter), three numbers (singular, plural, dual), five moods (indicative, imperative, infinitive, subjunctive, optative), and a verbal distinction in oblique moods between tense (time) and aspect (mode of action).

The principal changes that distinguish modern Greek are superseding of pitch-accent by stress; further iotacism of vowels (ai>e, oi>ü>i, ei>i, ē>i); transforming the voiced plosives *b* and *d* to the voiced fricatives *v* and *dh;* loss of modal particles; and less variable word order because of replacement of pitch-accent by stress. Morphological groups that were originally distinct have become unified, with a consequent reduction in the number of inflections. Its vocabulary remains basically Greek, with many Latin loanwords and later borrowings, mainly from Italian and Turkish.

MARGARET ALEXIOU

Bibliography: Allen, William Sidney, *Vox Graeca,* 2d ed. (1974); Bien, Peter, *Kazantzakis and the Linguistic Revolution in Greek Literature* (1972); Browning, R. A., *Medieval and Modern Greek* (1969); Buck, Carl, *The Greek Dialects,* rev. ed. (1955); Costas, Procope S., *An Outline of the History of the Greek Language* (1936); Thomson, George D., *The Greek Language* (1960).

Greek literature, ancient

The earliest European literature was produced by Greek-speaking Indo-European peoples who began to settle in the eastern Mediterranean in the second millennium BC. Virtually all Western literary forms, both prose and verse, were established and brought to a high degree of perfection by the ancient Greeks, and the first systematic Western historiography, philosophy, literary criticism, and scientific speculation were undertaken by Greek thinkers. Greek literature, along with

Homer, one of the greatest poets of all time, established the form of the epic with his monumental tales of the Trojan War and its aftermath, the Iliad *and the* Odyssey. *Although little is known of his life, he is believed to have lived during the 8th century BC and to have based his work on a vast body of oral tradition. Legend portrays him as blind.*

Roman literature, survived the catastrophes of late antiquity and the Middle Ages and made possible the rebirth of learning in the Renaissance by furnishing indispensable models for rebuilding the European tradition.

THE ARCHAIC PERIOD (8TH-6TH CENTURIES BC)

Greeks had used writing since *c.*1400 BC, but it was not until the late 8th century BC that their literature was first written down. Greek literature began in Ionia with the brilliant epics of HOMER, the ILIAD and the ODYSSEY. These mature products of a long tradition of oral poetry brought together a vast body of divine and heroic myths and sagas that served as a foundation for much subsequent Greek literature. The epic view of humankind had a lasting influence on Greek thought; indeed, it has been said that later Greek literature is but a series of footnotes to Homer. But the Archaic Period, a great age of Greek colonization and expansion, was also productive in other areas. Ionia was the cradle not only of the first philosophy and science (ANAXIMANDER, EMPEDOCLES, HERACLITUS, PARMENIDES, THALES, XENOPHANES) but also of historiography (Hecataeus). Lyric poetry became an independent art form with the choral songs of ALCMAN of Sparta, IBYCUS, SIMONIDES, and STESICHORUS in western Greece, and BACCHYLIDES in Ionia. Personal monodic lyrics were perfected by ALCAEUS and SAPPHO of Lesbos and later by the Ionian ANACREON. The Ionians ARCHILOCHUS and Hipponax wrote personal iambic and elegiac poetry, as did THEOGNIS of Megara. The epic poetry of the Boeotian HESIOD explored the poet's role as social and religious teacher. The city of Athens, which was to become the literary colossus of the Greek world, was relatively quiet during this period. But the great literary movements of the Greek world were beginning to converge there; in the early 6th century Solon wrote his great personal and political poems, and in the late 6th century the earliest forms of European drama, both tragedy and comedy, were developing on Attic soil. Of the great figures of the classical period, only the lyric poet PINDAR, from Thebes, was non-Athenian.

THE CLASSICAL PERIOD (5TH-4TH CENTURIES BC)

Catapulted from relative obscurity into a leading position among the Greek states by its part in the Persian Wars, Athens entered a golden age of empire and expansion during the 5th century BC. Until its defeat in the ruinous war with Sparta (431-04), Athens enjoyed a period of unprecedented artistic creativity. Every variety of literary composition was performed at the Athenian festivals, but the highlight was tragic DRAMA. In these plays poets used the archetypal figures of heroic myth to illuminate the life of man and his position in the universe. The three greatest tragedians were AESCHYLUS, EURIPIDES, and SOPHOCLES, and through their works the spiritual progress of the Athenians can be followed through this great century. A different light is shed on Athens by the topical comedies of ARISTOPHANES, but they too reflect the heroic spirit and larger-than-life forces of a society caught in a period of dizzying change.

Because the extreme democracy of Athens encouraged public speaking, the 5th century was a great age of orators and rhetoricians, such as GORGIAS, LYSIAS, ANDOCIDES, and ANTIPHON. Old beliefs were questioned by the philosophers PROTAGORAS and Prodicus, and the resulting climate of intense ethical and moral debate set the stage for SOCRATES, one of the most influential thinkers in Western history. Thus the scientific and philosophical speculation begun in Ionia, like so much earlier Greek art and thought, was to converge and be carried forward in Athens: the Ionian physician HIPPOCRATES, like the Ionian historian HERODOTUS, lived and wrote in the great city. Herodotus's history of the Persian Wars chronicles Athens's days of triumph. THUCYDIDES' account of the war with Sparta, on the other hand, records the decline from the golden age of Pericles. By the end of the century, Athens's political supremacy had come to an end, and its enormous creativity had been sapped of its vital forces.

Much great Athenian literature, however, was still to be written. Although in the 4th century many of the traditional poetic forms, such as choral lyric, ceased to be produced or, like tragedy, were no longer of sufficiently high quality to ensure their survival, the art of prose reached its greatest height.

Two friends of Socrates went on to become prominent writers of very different kinds: XENOPHON turned to history, popular philosophy, and other areas of interest to educated Athenian gentlemen. But PLATO turned his back on civic life and created a school (the Academy) and an immortal philosophical literature based on the personality and teachings of Socrates. Later, Plato's pupil ARISTOTLE founded his own school (the Lyceum) and further extended the compass of philosophy. Both Plato and Aristotle exerted an enormous influence on later European religion, science, philosophy, and literature, and their formulations continue to serve as a basis for modern philosophical speculation. The 4th century also witnessed the perfection of oratorical prose in the works of AESCHINES, DEMOSTHENES and ISOCRATES. Demosthenes' fiery speeches hardened Athenian opposition to Philip of Macedon, opposition that was finally crushed at the battle of Chaeronea in 338 BC. Although Philip was killed before he could conquer all of the eastern Mediterranean and East Asia, his son Alexander the Great lived to realize that dream.

THE HELLENISTIC PERIOD (3D AND 2D CENTURIES BC)

The death of Alexander in 323 ushered in a new literary age. Mainland Greece was overshadowed in importance by the vast Greek empires in Asia, Macedonia, and Egypt. This was an age not of the individual but of increasing cosmopolitanism, as many of the barriers that had long separated the Greek cities fell away. Feeling that people could no longer confidently control their lives or those of others, writers turned from the great panoramic style of earlier days and focused more and more on the personal. The goal of philosophy became the attainment of individual happiness: Epicureans, Cynics, and Stoics all offered programs for right living, and Attic New Comedy, which has survived in the plays of MENANDER, showed a social and ethical concern with the dilemmas of everyday people. Literature finally began to withdraw from the center of community life. Scholars and artists from all over Greece were attracted to the famous library at Alexandria, where poets such as APOLLONIUS OF RHODES and CALLIMACHUS created the first Greek literature written especially for the educated, rather than for the public at large. The bucolic poetry of THEOCRITUS, the mimes of Herodas, and the witty epigrams of the Greek Anthology were also directed toward a learned audience. The stage was now set for the absorption of the Greek world into the sphere of the Roman colossus to the west. Greek writers continued to flourish during the Roman period: POLYBIUS, the historian of Rome's rise to great power status; PLUTARCH, the biographer of matching pairs of Greek and Roman lives; LUCIAN, the author of satiric dialogues; LONGUS, the inventor of the prose pastoral romance; and PLOTINUS, the exemplar in philosophy of Neoplatonism. Through them, as well as through Roman adaptations of Greek models, ancient Greek literature was to have a new birth and a far wider impact than Homer ever dreamed of.

JEFFREY HENDERSON

Bibliography: Bowra, C. M., *Ancient Greek Literature* (1933) and *Greek Lyric Poetry from Alcman to Simonides,* 2d ed. (1961); Ferguson, John, *A Companion to Greek Tragedy* (1972); Gould, T. G., and Herington, C. J., eds., *Greek Tragedy* (1977); Hadas, Moses, *A History of Greek Literature* (1950); Highet, Gilbert, *The Classical Tradition* (1949); Jaeger, Werner, *Paideia: The Ideals of Greek Culture,* 3 vols., trans. by Gilbert Highet (1943-1945); Kitto, H. D. F., *Form and Meaning in Drama: A Study of Six Greek Plays and of Hamlet* (1960), *Greek Tragedy, A Literary Study,* 3d ed. (1961), and *Poiesis; Structure and Thought* (1966); Lesky, Albin, *A History of Greek Literature,* trans. by James Willis and Cornelis de Heer (1966); Murray, Gilbert, *The Rise of the Greek Epic,* 4th ed. (1960); Norwood, Gilbert, *Greek Comedy* (1963); Rose, Herbert J., *A Handbook of Greek Literature,* 4th ed. (1950); Webster, T. B. L., *Studies in Later Greek Comedy* (1970).

See also: GREEK LANGUAGE.

Greek literature, modern

Literature, especially poetry, has been written in Greek uninterruptedly from before the time of Homer to the present.

About AD 1000, popular poetry began to appear in vernacular Greek. This tradition culminated in an exceptional flowering in Crete during the 17th century, under Renaissance influence, which, together with the oral tradition, served as the source of modern Greek literature.

During and after the Greek War of Independence (1821-29), Greek writers set about laying the foundations of a national literature. This nationalistic effort underlay Greek literature from 1830 to 1920. During the next 60 years Greek literature assumed a more modern, cosmopolitan outlook.

During the 19th century Greek literary activity was concentrated in two main geographical areas, Athens and the Ionian Islands. Whereas most writers in the capital used the artificial language, Katharévousa, those in the Ionian Islands (under British rule until 1863) wrote in the spoken, or demotic, language. This is one reason why the poetry of Dionysios SOLOMOS far surpasses anything produced by his contemporaries in Athens. Like them, Solomos was inspired by the War of Independence, but his work contains an added spiritual dimension lacking in theirs. A group of poets and prose writers continued Solomos's tradition in the Ionian Islands. Athens produced only a few writers of worth, including Aristotle Valaoritis, himself from the Ionian Islands, who wrote patriotic epic-lyric poems in demotic, and Emmanuel Roidis, notorious for his anticlerical novel *Pope Joan* (1866; Eng. trans., 1972).

The traditions of Athens and the Ionian Islands merged fruitfully in Athens from the 1880s onward, when a generation of poets and prose writers abandoned Katharévousa and turned for inspiration to the traditions of Greek folk culture and the demotic language. The writers of this period, led by Kostis PALAMAS, created a synthesis of the ancient, Byzantine, and modern folk traditions that has formed much of the basis of subsequent Greek literature.

Verse has always been the predominant medium of Greek literature, and the leading Greek writers of the period 1900-30 were all poets, such as the idiosyncratic Constantine CAVAFY, who lived in Alexandria, outside the Greek literary world, and the mystic Angelos SIKELIANOS. Leading poets of the generation of 1930 included George SEFERIS, Odysseus ELYTIS, and Yannis RITSOS. Several noteworthy prose writers were also associated with this group, including Stratis Myrivilis (1892-1969), famous for his antiwar novel *Life in the Tomb* (1924; Eng. trans., 1977); Kosmas Politis (1888-1974), who wrote the influential novel of adolescence *Eroica* (1937); and Pandelis Prevelakis, b. 1909, best known for his Cretan novel *The Sun of Death* (1959; Eng. trans., 1965). All these writers opened themselves to contemporary foreign influences without losing their essentially Greek character.

Postwar Greek literature has been characterized by works inspired by the Greco-Italian War of 1940-41, the German occupation, the civil war, and, more recently, by writings expressing modern urban malaise. These works, which abandon the rural setting of earlier Greek literature, lack the traditional local color; however, the novels of Nikos KAZANTZAKIS, who was himself a member of an earlier generation, stand out as notable exceptions.

P. A. MACKRIDGE

Bibliography: Dimaras, C. T., *A History of Modern Greek Literature,* trans. by Mary Gianos (1972); Friar, Kimon, *Modern Greek Poetry* (1973); Keeley, Edmund, and Bien, Peter, eds., *Modern Greek Writers* (1972); Keeley, Edmund, and Sherrard, Philip, trans. and eds., *Six Poets of Modern Greece* (1961); Politis, Linos, *A History of Modern Greek Literature* (1973).

See also: GREEK LANGUAGE.

Greek music

The musical culture of ancient Greece is known more through literary references than through preserved musical documents. About 20 fragments of music are extant written in a relatively late Greek notational system, but references to music performed at various rites and social occasions abound in the works of ancient Greek authors. Consequently, most modern discussions of Greek music either speculate about the sound of the music itself, or deal with the role and nature of music in that society.

Dance, poetry, rite, and music seem inseparably associated in the early history of music in ancient Greece. Homer's *Iliad* and *Odyssey* report vintners' songs, dirges, and hymns of praise to Apollo (paeans). Music was described as an art exerting great power (*ethos*) over human beings, and certain musical styles came to be associated with particular peoples and deities. The KITHARA, a plucked string instrument, came to be linked with Apollo, the god of the Sun and reason, while the aulos, a loud double-reed instrument, came to be identified with Dionysus, the god of wine and ecstatic revelry. The most important of mythic musicians in ancient Greek culture was ORPHEUS, whose music had the power to cause inanimate objects to move and even influence the forces of Hades.

Among the earliest Greek musicians whose existence and accomplishments seem to be rooted in reality as well as legend are TERPANDER of Lesbos (7th century BC), the founder of lyric kithara performance, PINDAR of Thebes (6th–5th century BC), whose odes represent the rise of Greek choral music, and Timotheus of Miletus (5th–4th century BC), a virtuoso performer on the kithara whose inventions contributed to his infamy as well as his fame. The musical and lyrical tradition represented by these personalities reached its apex in the Athenian drama of the 5th and 4th centuries BC, a dramatic tradition in which solo and choral singing, instrumental music, and dance all played essential roles.

Although many names of musicians are recorded in ancient sources, none played a more important role in the development of Greek musical thought than the mathematician and philosopher PYTHAGORAS OF SAMOS (6th–5th century BC). According to legend, Pythagoras, by divine guidance, discovered the mathematical rationale of musical consonance from the weights of hammers used by smiths. He is thus given credit for discovering that the interval of an octave is rooted in the ratio 2:1, that of the fifth in 3:2, that of the fourth in 4:3, and that of the whole tone in 9:8. Followers of Pythagoras applied these ratios to lengths of a string on an instrument called a canon, or monochord, and thereby were able to determine mathematically the intonation of an entire musical system. The Pythagoreans saw these ratios as governing forces in the cosmos as well as in sounds, and Plato's *Timaeus* describes the soul of the world as structured according to these same musical ratios. For the Pythagoreans, as well as for Plato, music consequently became a branch of mathematics as well as an art; this tradition of musical thought flourished throughout antiquity in such theorists as Nicomachus of Gerasa (2d century AD) and PTOLEMY (2d century AD) and was transmitted into the Middle Ages by BOETHIUS (6th century AD). The mathematics and intonation of the Pythagorean tradition consequently became a crucial influence in the development of music in medieval Europe. Followers of the peripatetic tradition, especially Aristoxenus (4th century BC), found the Pythagorean ratios too archaic and restrictive and began a more empirical tradition of ancient musical thought.

Although little of ancient Greek music survives, Greek musical thought has profoundly affected the manner in which Western culture has expressed itself in this art.

CALVIN BOWER

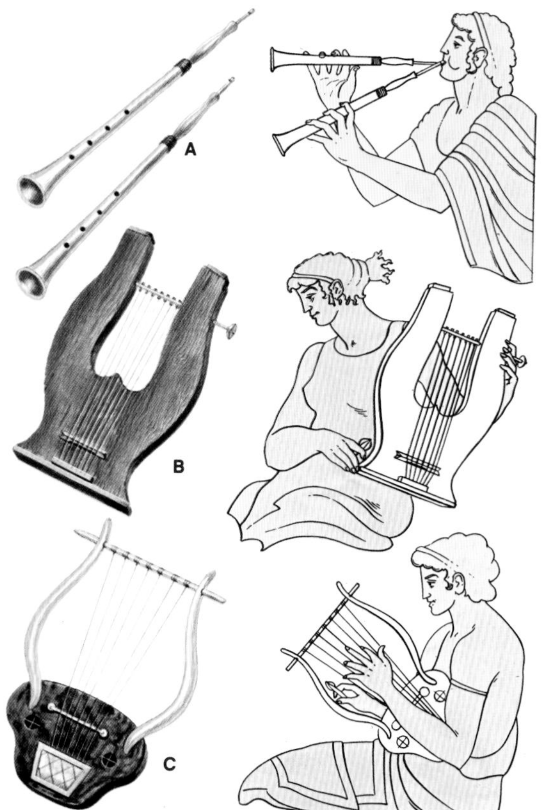

Evidence of the importance of musical instruments in ancient Greek culture is found in many paintings and vases. The aulos (A), *a double-reed wind instrument and an ancestor of the oboe, was adopted for music associated with Dionysus. Two auloi were played together, one probably providing the melody and the other perhaps a drone bass. The kithara* (B), *a large string instrument associated with Apollo, was traditionally regarded as the national instrument of classical Greece. The strings, numbering from three to eleven, were plucked by a plectrum. The lyra* (C), *another string instrument, was of a much lighter construction than the kithara. Both were used as accompaniment in the recitation of poetry.*

The buzuki is a popular folk instrument of Greece. When plucked with a plectrum, its six metal strings yield a clear singing tone.

Bibliography: Burkhalter, A. Louis, *Ancient and Oriental Music* (1968); Henderson, M. Isobel, "Ancient Greek Music," *Ancient and Oriental Music*, ed. by Egon Wellesz (1957); Hipkins, Alfred J., *Greek Music* (1930; repr. 1977); Lippman, Edward A., *Musical Thought in Ancient Greece* (1964; repr. 1975); Michaelides, Solon, *The Music of Ancient Greece: An Encyclopedia* (1978); Sachs, Curt, *The Rise of Music in the Ancient World* (1943); Williams, Charles F., *Music in Ancient Greek Drama* (1921; repr. 1977).

Greek mythology: see MYTHOLOGY.

Greek Orthodox church: see ORTHODOX CHURCH.

Greek Revival

Greek Revival architecture, a style of British origin directly based on the monuments of ancient Greece, was foreshadowed in the buildings of Robert ADAM, who combined the Greek and Roman orders in such mansions as Syon House, Middlesex (*c*.1760–69), and Harewood House, Yorkshire (*c*.1758–71). Adam used classical forms with great freedom, but James Stuart (1713–88) and Nicolas Revett (1720–1804), who had studied Greek architecture firsthand, faithfully reproduced classical forms in the Doric and Ionic temples that they constructed in English landscape gardens during the 1760s and '70s. Stuart and Revett's *Antiquities of Athens*, a series of publications that began to appear in 1762, provided a vocabulary for the many other architects who then took up the style. The popularity of the Greek architectural forms, associated with aesthetic purity, democratic freedom, and rational proportion, was part of a widespread enthusiasm for Hellenism (see HELLENISM, art).

William Strickland's design for the Second Bank of the United States (completed 1824) in Philadelphia, derived from the Parthenon in Athens, exemplifies the Greek Revival style. Strickland was one of the leading exponents of the 19th-century revival of classical architecture.

The major architects Henry HOLLAND, James WYATT, and Sir John SOANE adopted Greek style but used it with greater flexibility than did Stuart and Revett, frequently including forms derived from the work of Robert Adam and from Roman architecture. Wyatt's Radcliffe Observatory in Oxford (1773-94) and Soane's Bank of England in London (1788-1823) contain both replicas and free adaptations of Greek orders. The Greek Revival persisted in the REGENCY STYLE, exemplified in the work of John NASH, and found its most rigorous exponents in Sir Robert SMIRKE and William Wilkins (1778-1839). Wilkins's finest works are Downing College, Cambridge (begun 1806), and the National Gallery, London (1823-38). The facade of Smirke's British Museum (1823-47) is an imposing Ionic portico.

European interest in Greek architecture was also strong in Germany, where King Louis I of Bavaria was a champion of Hellenism. Among the notable contributors to the German Greek revival were Carl Gotthard LANGHANS, designer of the Brandenburg Gate in Berlin (1789-94); Karl Friedrich SCHINKEL, whose many neoclassical works include the elegant facade of the Berlin Altes Museum (begun 1823); and Leo von KLENZE, architect of the Munic Glyptothek (1816-30).

In the United States, classical styles were already well known through the work of Thomas JEFFERSON, but it was Benjamin Henry LATROBE who began the Greek Revival. Latrobe's work in Philadelphia and Baltimore, and on the CAPITOL OF THE UNITED STATES, had an abiding influence on American architecture. Greek styles were used extensively throughout the 19th century by Robert MILLS, William STRICKLAND, and Thomas WALTER, and became a feature of large public buildings, such as banks and churches, or of private houses.

HOWARD BATCHELOR

Bibliography: Crook, J. Mordaunt, *Greek Revival: Neo-Classical Attitudes in British Architecture, 1760-1870* (1972); Hamlin, Talbot F., *Greek Revival Architecture in America* (1944); Wiebenson, Dora, *Sources of Greek Revival Architecture* (1969).

See also: AMERICAN ART AND ARCHITECTURE; ENGLISH ART AND ARCHITECTURE; FRENCH ART AND ARCHITECTURE; GERMAN ART AND ARCHITECTURE.

Greeley, Horace [gree'-lee, hor'-uhs]

Horace Greeley was a renowned American newspaper editor who founded the influential New York *Tribune*. His voice in national affairs was of great significance in the critical years before and during the Civil War. Few issues of the time escaped his notice. On all of them he had strong opinions, which he vigorously expounded in his widely read editorials. "For 35 years Horace Greeley was probably the greatest political force this country has ever known except Thomas Jefferson," said the New York *World* on the 100th anniversary of Greeley's birth.

Born in poverty in New Hampshire on Feb. 3, 1811, Greeley became an apprentice printer at the age of 15 in East Poultney, Vt. He was an insatiable reader, and early in life he developed a consuming interest in politics and social issues. He went to New York as a penniless young printer in 1831. Ten years later, after several publishing ventures brought him considerable prominence but little financial gain, he founded the *Tribune*. With heavy emphasis on serious news and open to a wide variety of opinions, the *Tribune* represented a new step forward in journalism. It was successful from the start, especially the weekly edition, which circulated widely throughout rural America and in time made "Uncle Horace" a household name.

Greeley was forceful and outspoken on the many causes he espoused, sometimes with apparent inconsistency. He championed equality for women in employment and education but was adamantly opposed to woman suffrage and liberalized divorce laws. He advocated agrarianism but recognized the need for industrialization, and although he believed in free trade, he favored protective tariffs. Favorite targets for his condemnation included monopolies, liquor and tobacco, capital punishment, and the theater. He gave generous space in the *Tribune* to the socialistic doctrine of Charles Fourier. Above all, Greeley fought unceasingly against slavery.

In 1860, as a delegate to the convention of the new Republican party, which Greeley, long a loyal Whig, had helped form, he was instrumental in securing the nomination of Abraham Lincoln. Later, as the war progressed, he was somewhat erratic in his support of the president's policies. His influence on Lincoln has thus been the subject of much debate. For taking several unpopular stands, Greeley and the *Tribune* were the targets of much abuse, the most violent being two mob attacks on the *Tribune* building during the bloody New York draft riots of 1863. After the war ended, Greeley urged universal amnesty and impartial suffrage (male) as the basis for reconstruction. He also personally signed a bail bond for Confederate president Jefferson Davis.

Under Greeley's guidance, the *Tribune* developed a staff of distinguished writers unmatched in intellectual depth and versatility by any other newspaper of that time, if not since. Among them were Margaret Fuller, Charles A. Dana, Bayard Taylor, George Ripley, Henry J. Raymond, Carl Schurz, John Hay, Albert Brisbane, Whitelaw Reid, Henry James, and Charles T. Congdon. For a time Karl Marx wrote for the paper from London.

Obsessed with politics all his life, Greeley frequently sought, but rarely won, public office. He served a brief term in Congress (1848-49), filling a vacancy, and was twice an unsuccessful candidate for the Senate (1860 and 1866) and twice for the House (1866 and 1870). His political aspirations came

The American journalist Horace Greeley founded (1841) one of the most influential newspapers in the United States, the New York Tribune. *Using its editorial page to advocate his socially progressive views, Greeley became a national celebrity and in 1872 was persuaded to run for president against Ulysses S. Grant.*

to a devastating climax in 1872. Disillusioned with President Grant's administration and the Republican party, Greeley helped form the new Liberal Republican party and received its nomination for the presidency. Oddly enough, he was also endorsed by the Democratic party, his longtime political foes. He was overwhelmed at the polls, carrying only 6 states to Grant's 31. Exhausted by the campaign and from sleeplessly caring for his wife, who had died only a week before the election (Oct. 30, 1872), Greeley collapsed, became demented, and died Nov. 29, 1872. Chief among the dignitaries at his funeral, for which huge crowds thronged the streets of New York, was President Grant. CHARLES T. DUNCAN

Bibliography: Lunde, Erik S., *Horace Greeley* (1981); Parton, James, *The Life of Horace Greeley* (1855; repr. 1972); Seitz, Don Carlos, *Horace Greeley: Founder of the New York Tribune* (1926; repr. 1970); Van Deusen, Glyndon G., *Horace Greeley: Nineteenth-Century Crusader* (1953; repr. 1964).

Greely, Adolphus Washington [gree'-lee, uh-dawl'-fuhs]

Adolphus Washington Greely, b. Newburyport, Mass., Mar. 27, 1844, d. Oct. 20, 1935, was an officer of the U.S. Army signal service who won fame as an Arctic explorer. In 1882-83 he headed an expedition to set up a meteorological research station in the Arctic and in doing so discovered new regions, including parts of Ellesmere Island, Canada, and coastal Greenland. When a relief effort finally reached the party in 1884, only Greely and six other men were alive. Greely helped found the American Geographical Society in 1888, and he was in charge of relief work after the San Francisco earthquake and fire of 1906.

Green, Henry

The English novelist Henry Green (pseudonym of Henry Vincent Yorke), b. Oct. 29, 1905, d. Dec. 13, 1973, was educated at Eton College and Oxford University and published his first novel, *Blindness,* at the age of 21. His second novel, *Living* (1929), was based on the experience of working in his father's Birmingham factory, of which he later became managing director. Like almost all Green's subsequent work, *Living* portrays its subject—the daily lives of working people—through dialogue. Green avoids authorial description, allowing his narrative to proceed entirely through conversation. He was acutely aware of the intricate class structure of his own society, and subtle distinctions of speech, behavior, and morality lie at the heart of his humane and comic vision. *Party Going* (1939), a portrait of wealthy London socialites, and *Loving* (1945), set in the servant's quarters of an Irish castle during World War II, are among his finest works. Green wrote nine novels and an autobiography, *Pack my Bag* (1940).

Bibliography: Odom, Keith C., *Henry Green* (1978); Ryf, Robert S., *Henry Green* (1968).

Green, Hetty

The American financier and New York Stock Exchange member Hetty Green, b. Henrietta Howland Robinson in New Bedford, Mass., Nov. 21, 1835, d. July 3, 1916, was thought to be the richest woman of her day, and was regarded with awe by her contemporaries. She inherited a whaling and trade fortune of $10 million, and by shrewd investments in stocks and real estate she increased it to more than $100 million by the time of her death. Her fortune went to her son and daughter.

Green, Julian

The novelist and dramatist Julian Green, b. Paris, Sept. 6, 1900, of American parents, blends realistic descriptions with the nightmarish hallucinations of his heroes. His novels *Adrienne Mesurat* (1927), *Léviathan* (1929), and *Moïra* (1950) address the problem of sin and the conflict between the spirit and the senses. In 1971, Green became the first American elected to the Académie Française. JOSEPH A. REITER

Bibliography: Burne, Glenn, *Julian Green* (1972); Stokes, S. E., *Julian Green and the Thorn of Puritanism* (1955; repr. 1972).

Green, Paul

Paul Eliot Green, b. Lillington, N.C., March 17, 1894, d. May 4, 1981, is an American dramatist, most of whose plays are set in the South. In his two most successful plays, the Pulitzer Prize-winning *In Abraham's Bosom* (1926) and *The House of Connelly* (1931), Green wrote about the aftermath of the Civil War. The former is a tragedy on the theme of social inequality; the latter is an account of one farmer's attempt at a new beginning. Green is also the author of elaborate pageants on historical events. MALCOLM GOLDSTEIN

Bibliography: Adams, Agatha Boyd, *Paul Green of Chapel Hill* (1951); Green, Paul, *Five Plays of the South,* ed. by John Gassner (1963).

Green, Theodore Francis

Theodore Francis Green, b. Providence, R.I., Oct. 2, 1867, d. May 19, 1966, was a U.S. political leader. After a career in law, business, and banking, he was elected governor of Rhode Island in 1932 and reelected in 1934. A Democrat, he served in the U.S. Senate from 1937 to 1961. He retired at the age of 93, the oldest senator in the history of the institution.

Bibliography: Lenine, Erwin, *Theodore Francis Green,* 2 vols. (1963, 1971).

Green, Thomas Hill

Thomas Hill Green, b. Apr. 7, 1836, d. Mar. 26, 1882, was an English idealist philosopher. He studied at Oxford and was eventually appointed a professor there. The tradition of empiricism was deeply rooted in British philosophy, and Green produced a major critique of this tradition in the introduction to an 1875 edition of the works of David HUME, of which he was coeditor. He concluded his introduction with an expression of hope that young Englishmen would turn from Hume to G. W. F. Hegel. Green's positive philosophy strongly reflected Hegel's IDEALISM. Through Green's influence, idealism enjoyed a period of prominence in British philosophy. F. H. BRADLEY and Bernard BOSANQUET, leading members of this movement, were both indebted to Green.
THOMAS K. HEARN, JR.

Bibliography: Greengarten, I. M., *Thomas Hill Green and the Development of Liberal Democratic Thought* (1981); Richter, Melvin, *The Politics of Conscience: T. H. Green and His Age* (1964).

Green, William

William Green, b. Coshocton, Ohio, Mar. 3, 1873, d. Nov. 21, 1952, was president of the American Federation of Labor (AFL) from 1924 until his death. A coal miner and official of the United Mine Workers, he was chosen as a compromise to succeed Samuel GOMPERS as president of the AFL. In the struggle between craft and industrial unions in the 1930s, Green was unable to prevent a split that resulted in the expulsion of the industrial unions from the AFL and the formation of the Congress of Industrial Organizations (CIO).

See also: AMERICAN FEDERATION OF LABOR AND CONGRESS OF INDUSTRIAL ORGANIZATIONS.

Green Bank Observatory: see NATIONAL RADIO ASTRONOMY OBSERVATORY.

Green Bay

Green Bay is an inlet in eastern Wisconsin separated from Lake Michigan by the Door Peninsula. It is 190 km (118 mi) long and 16 to 32 km (10 to 20 mi) wide; the Fox and Menominee rivers flow into it. Jean Nicolet is known to have reached it in 1634.

Green Bay (city)

Green Bay, the seat of Brown County, is a port city in northeastern Wisconsin, located where the Fox River empties into Green Bay, an inlet of Lake Michigan. Its population is 87,899 (1980). Green Bay is Wisconsin's oldest settlement; in

1634 the area was named La Baye and claimed by the French, who established a mission here. It then became an active fur-trading center, and British traders renamed the site Green Bay. In 1825, as a result of the opening of the Erie Canal, the city developed as an agricultural and lumbering center. Today paper and cheese are the city's main products, and it is a heavy shipping port as well as a large wholesale and distribution center. Its professional football team, the Green Bay Packers, has been playing at Lambeau Field since 1919. The University of Wisconsin, Green Bay (1961), is located here.

green frog

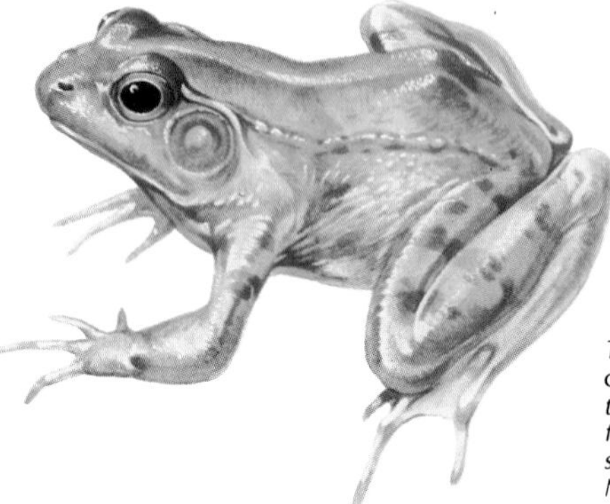

The green frog, R. clamitans, *is common to the shallow freshwater ponds and streams of eastern North America.*

The green frog, *Rana clamitans,* in the family Ranidae, is divided into two subspecies: the bronze frog, *R. c. clamitans,* and the green frog, *R. c. melanota.* The bronze frog, found from the coastal plain of North Carolina to east Texas, exclusive of most of peninsular Florida, is brown or bronze above and has a white belly marked with dark, wormlike lines. Males have yellowish throats at breeding time. The green frog, found from the Canadian maritime provinces south to the Carolinas and Oklahoma, is green or greenish brown and usually spotted above and white below, often with spots on the lower lip and legs. The upper lip is usually green. In both subspecies the tympanum, or eardrum, is as large as, or larger than, the eye, and the prominent ridges on the upper sides of the body do not extend to the groin. Adults attain lengths of 6.3 to 9.0 cm (2.5 to 3.5 in). The legs of this species constitute a small percentage of the commercial froglegs trade.

Green frogs are abundant and long-lived, surviving for up to 10 years. Insects account for about 75 percent of their diet. The frog's call is a single loud sound, often repeated three or four times, that is said to resemble the sound made by the lowest string on a banjo. Males defend breeding territories, and breeding takes place from April to August. Tadpoles may winter over, particularly in the northern localities.

JONATHAN CAMPBELL

Bibliography: Conant, Roger, *A Field Guide to Reptiles and Amphibians of Eastern and Central North America,* 2d ed. (1975); Dickerson, Mary C., *The Frog Book* (1969).

Green Mansions

Green Mansions (1904) is a romance by the Anglo-American novelist and naturalist William Henry HUDSON. Set in the South American jungles, the story is told in retrospect by a Mr. Abel, who relates his sad love affair with Rima the "bird girl," who seems to be as much an embodiment of nature and the forest as a human being. Abel awakens love in the spritelike creature only to lose her when she is killed by savages.

CHARLOTTE D. SOLOMON

Bibliography: Frederick, John T., *William Henry Hudson* (1972).

Green Mountain Boys

Commanded by Ethan ALLEN, the Green Mountain Boys, an irregular military force from Vermont, captured Fort TICONDEROGA from the British in 1775. They also helped win the Battle of Bennington (1777).

Green Mountains

The Green Mountains extend from north to south through central Vermont. They rise from the Champlain lowlands on the west and slope to the Connecticut River in the east. A folded and metamorphosed extension of the Appalachians, the Green Mountains owe their name to the forest of spruce, maple, birch, and beech that covers most of the area. Although 32 of the summits are over 915 m (3,000 ft), the highest, Mount Mansfield, is only 1,340 m (4,393 ft) above sea level. The area is famous for winter sports at Stowe, Killington, and surrounding locations, and for summer hiking along the Appalachian Trail.

ALLEN R. SMITH

green revolution

The *green revolution* is a popular term coined in the 1960s to describe the recent transfer and diffusion of agricultural technology from the technologically developed countries to less technologically advanced agricultural areas. The most dramatic example of this transfer is the development and rapid diffusion of high-yielding crop cultivars (cultivated varieties) of rice and wheat in tropical areas. These new cultivars have the ability to respond to fertilizer application, with dramatic increases in productivity. Many of them have an insensitivity to photoperiod (length of day) that makes them readily adaptable throughout large areas, and because they are short-stemmed, they withstand wind damage and can be more easily harvested by machine. Wheat seed from Mexico and rice seed from the Philippines have greatly increased grain production in India, Pakistan, Malaysia, and Turkey.

The wheat program originated from breeding studies begun in Mexico in the 1940s by the Rockefeller Foundation. This program is now carried out by the International Maize and Wheat Improvement Center, established in 1966 by the Rockefeller Foundation and the government of Mexico. Dr. Norman E. BORLAUG, the center's director, received the Nobel Peace Prize in 1970 for his contributions to the wheat-breeding program. The center also conducts significant research in corn (maize) improvement.

The International Rice Research Institute (IRRI) was founded in the Philippines by the Ford and Rockefeller foundations in cooperation with the government of the Philippines. The so-called miracle rice, IR-8, and the introduction of related rice-growing technology are widely heralded achievements of this institute. The IRRI also trains Asian scientists and technicians and directs technical assistance to other rice-growing nations of tropical Asia.

Within recent years, certain serious problems have become apparent to large-scale users of these new high-yield seeds.

Plant breeders have developed the new cereal grain triticale by crossing wheat, Triticum, *with rye,* Secale. *This intergeneric hybrid is fertile because of chemical treatment that doubles the number of chromosomes. Triticale has a high yield and a rich protein content.*

The precipitous rise in the cost of artificial fertilizers, which must be applied in large quantities, has reduced the import of these new cultivars. Also, the production of only one or two grain cultivars within a region increases the vulnerability of the crop to new pests and diseases.

The green revolution has been partially successful, however. In parts of Asia where soils are fertile and rain is plentiful, some countries are more or less self-sufficient in food. In contrast, areas of Africa with poor soils and recurrent drought are characterized by periodic famine. The social, political, and economic problems that beset such areas complicate the pursuit of the green revolution in Africa. JULES JANICK

Bibliography: Frankel, O. H., and Bennett, E., eds., *Genetic Resources in Plants: Their Exploration and Conservation* (1970); Frankel, O. H., and Hawkes, J. G., eds., *Crop Genetic Resources for Today and Tomorrow* (1975); Glaeser, B., ed., *The Green Revolution Revisited* (1987); Glissant, E., "Biotechnology, Agriculture, and Development," UNESCO *Courier* 40 (March 1987); Tangley, L., "Beyond the Green Revolution," *BioScience* 37 (March 1987).

See also: GENE BANK; PLANT BREEDING.

Green River

The 1,175-km-long (730-mi) Green River is the largest tributary of the COLORADO RIVER. Noted for its rugged canyon course, it rises in the Wind River range of the Rocky Mountains in west central Wyoming and flows south through Wyoming, Utah, and northwest Colorado before joining the Colorado River in southeastern Utah. Its principal tributaries are the Yampa, White, and San Rafael rivers. Several dams in its catchment area of 116,500 km^2 (45,000 mi^2) supply water for irrigation and hydroelectric power.

green turtle: see SEA TURTLE.

Greenaway, Kate

Catherine Greenaway, b. Mar. 17, 1846, d. Nov. 6, 1901, was an English artist of the Victorian period noted for her delicately colored and finely detailed illustrations for children's books. Her charming and sentimental drawings show children clothed in a quaint, vaguely 18th-century style in fanciful idyllic settings; she portrayed a fairy-tale world of fantasy that existed only in the imagination. Her style, which has had some imitators but few rivals, remained fairly constant throughout her career.

Greenaway remains one of the most popular and influential illustrators of children's books; some of her works are still in print. Among her most popular works are *Mother Goose or the Old Nursery Rhymes* (1881), *Language of Flowers* (1884), *Kate Greenaway's Album* (1885), and *April Baby's Book of Tunes* (1900). Her first success was *Under the Window: Pictures and Rhymes for Children* (1879), which sold 70,000 copies in England. RAYMOND LISTER

Bibliography: Kiger, Robert, et al., eds., *Kate Greenaway* (1980); Spielmann, M. H., and Layard, G. S., *Kate Greenaway* (1905; repr. 1968); Thomson, Susan R., ed., *Kate Greenaway* (1977).

greenback

The greenback was a green paper note issued by the United States government during the Civil War to finance the war effort. Greenbacks were the earliest paper money in U.S. history that were not redeemable in either coin or gold. Congress passed three Legal Tender Acts in 1862 and 1863 authorizing the printing of a total of $450 million in denominations ranging from $1 to $1,000. The issuing of greenbacks was intended to be a temporary measure, but their life was extended—against the opposition of conservatives—under the pressure of the hard times of the late 1860s and the political pressure of debtor farmers, who eventually organized the Greenback party. A compromise with conservatives in 1869 lowered the level of greenbacks in circulation to $356 million. Attempts to expand the supply in 1874 were unsuccessful, and in 1875 Congress set a date after which greenbacks would be convertible to gold. (Convertibility was revoked in 1968.) Greenbacks were made permanent in 1878 at a level of $346,681,016. Few greenbacks were redeemed in 1879, and in 1933 they became full legal tender.

Bibliography: Nugent, Walter T. K., *Money Question during Reconstruction* (1967); Unger, Irwin, *The Greenback Era, 1865–1879* (1964).

Greenback party

The Greenback party was an American political party that advocated currency reform from 1874 to 1888. Greenbacks were U.S. paper currency notes issued in 1862–65, during the Civil War. After the war, spokesmen for inflationary policies, primarily midwestern debtor farmers, opposed retiring the greenbacks and favored issuing more of them.

The greenbackers organized their party during the depression of the 1870s and nominated Peter COOPER as their first presidential candidate in 1876. Labor unrest in 1877 and continued depression brought the movement to its peak in the 1878 congressional elections, when it elected 14 congressmen. After the federal government began retiring some of the greenbacks in 1879, however, FREE SILVER became the inflationists' preferred scheme. Although the party broadened its platform in 1880 and 1884, its strength declined steadily. It held its last national convention in 1888, but did not nominate a presidential candidate. GERALD W. MCFARLAND

Bibliography: Barrett, Don Carlos, *The Greenbacks and Resumption of Specie Payments, 1862–1879* (1931); Unger, Irwin, *The Greenback Era: A Social and Political History of American Finance, 1865–1879* (1964).

greenbelt

A greenbelt is a space of open land within an urbanized area. It has been used most extensively in England. When the rapid growth of London threatened to engulf parts of the nearby countryside, British planners decided to introduce greenbelts—open spaces where the people of the city and town could enjoy nature. The first new town to incorporate the greenbelt principle was Letchworth, Hertfordshire, founded in 1903 by Sir Ebenezer HOWARD. Called a GARDEN CITY, it set the pattern for many more. By setting aside areas free of both commercial and residential development, urban planners have given city dwellers access to open spaces that would otherwise be found only beyond the suburban zone. Commuters from the suburbs travel through the greenbelt to reach the central city.

Greenbelts have been used in European cities, including the suburbs of Praunheim and Roemerstadt near Frankfurt, West Germany, and in Dutch housing developments in Amsterdam, Rotterdam, Hilversum, and The Hague. They have also been introduced in the United States in Radburn, N.J., now part of Fairlawn, and in the forest preserves surrounding Chicago. In the 1930s the federal government built the greenbelt communities of Greenbelt, Md., near Washington, D.C., Greenhills, Ohio, near Cincinnati, and Greendale, Wis., near Milwaukee.

Bibliography: Osborne, Frederick J., *Green-Belt Cities,* 2d ed. (1971).

See also: URBAN PLANNING.

Greenberg, Clement

The leading American art critic Clement Greenberg, b. Bronx, N.Y., Jan. 16, 1909, was an early supporter of ABSTRACT EXPRESSIONISM. A frequent contributor to the *Partisan Review* during the 1930s, he was one of the first to provide theoretical support to American abstract painting in the postwar era. The emphasis of his criticism is on the formal properties of artworks, to the almost total exclusion of expressive and iconographic content. Chief among his contributions is the concept of the "allover," or unified pictorial field. From roughly 1945 to 1970, "allover" imagery distinguished much American abstract painting from its European counterparts, which continued to show traditional pictorial composition. Greenberg is the author of several books, including *Joan Miró* (1945), *Art and Culture* (1961), *Hans Hofmann* (1961), and *Collected Essays and Criticism* (2 vols., 1986). CARTER RATCLIFF

Greenberg, Joseph H.

Joseph Harold Greenberg, b. May 28, 1915, a professor of anthropology and linguistics at Stanford University, is best known for his widely accepted classification of the languages of Africa. A search for universal relationships in languages has been a focus of his research. Greenberg's writings include *Universals of Language* (1963), *The Languages of Africa* (1963), and *Language, Culture and Communication* (1971).

JAMES W. HERRICK

greenbrier [green'-bry-ur]

Greenbrier is the common name for the genus *Smilax*, in the lily family, Liliaceae, a group of herbaceous or woody vines with fleshy, tuberous roots and often prickly or thorny stems with grasping, stringlike tendrils. Separate male and female flowers are borne in clusters on different plants. The fruit is a berry with one to six seeds. The genus contains about 200 species, mostly tropical, with some occurring in temperate North America and Asia. Extracts of the roots of some species yield sarsaparilla and sapogenin.

OLIN S. FEARING

Greene, Charles and Henry: see GREENE AND GREENE.

Greene, Graham

Graham Greene, an English writer, has achieved distinction as a master of the short story. His suspenseful novels and stories frequently treat the theme of evil through characters whose religious faith has eroded or completely disappeared. Greene has adapted several of his novels for film, including Confidential Agent *(1939; film, 1945) and* Our Man in Havana *(1958; film, 1960).*

Graham Greene, b. Berkhamsted, England, Oct. 2, 1904, one of the most distinguished and widely read English novelists of the 20th century, has, since the early 1930s, been producing works that reveal his abiding moral concerns, his pessimism, and his profound insight into the ironies and ambivalences of life. Equally known for his "entertainments" (whether spy stories or comedies) and more serious novels, Greene has fashioned a distinctive fiction through repeated use of a highly visual style, the conventions of the modern spy thriller, and settings and characters that together convey a palpable sense of evil, guilt, or futility. The seedy tropical city or drab London expanse, the failed middle-aged man, the inescapable force of unseen presences: all announce the unmistakable landscape of Graham Greene's private world.

Greene's first published novel, *The Man Within* (1929), was written in a lush romantic style. In *Stamboul Train* (1932; U.S. title, *Orient Express*) he first used the more colloquial, cinematic techniques that were to become his trademark in subsequent fast-paced suspense novels such as *The Confidential Agent* (1939) and *The Ministry of Fear* (1943). After a trip to the Liberian interior in 1934, described in *Journey without Maps* (1936), and an even more important trip to Mexico in 1934, which formed the basis for the travel book *The Lawless Roads* (1939; U.S. title, *Another Mexico*) and his moving fictional account of an alcoholic priest in revolutionary Mexico, *The Power and the Glory* (1940), Greene began to use the novel for more serious purposes. His conversion (1926) to Roman Catholicism was reflected in *Brighton Rock* (1938), in which the conflict between the corrupt individual will and the imperious grace of God first appeared as a major theme. *The Heart of the Matter* (1948) and *The End of the Affair* (1951), often considered his two best novels, brought him widespread, if not always friendly, recognition as a leading Catholic writer. This position was confirmed by his plays *The Living Room* (1953) and *The Potting Shed* (1957), but he later rejected it with the novel *A Burnt-Out Case* (1961).

In *The Quiet American* (1955), based on his experience as a journalist in French Indochina, Greene subordinated religious to political themes. Later, in a series of novels set in South America, he emphasized the claims of the private self against those of governmental or conventional morality. All the old elements—from the built-in terrors of the intelligence agent to the "grace" of a private (and objectively antisocial) morality—were combined in *The Human Factor* (1978). Greene's lighter novels include *Travels with My Aunt* (1969) and *Monsignor Quixote* (1982). He has also published three books of short stories and written several screenplays, most notably *The Fallen Idol* (1948) and *The Third Man* (1950). His film reviews are collected in *The Pleasure Dome* (1972). *A Sort of Life* (1971) and *Ways of Escape* (1980) together constitute his autobiography.

Bibliography: Atkins, John, *Graham Greene*, rev. ed. (1966); De Vitis, A. A., *Graham Greene* (1964); Hynes, Samuel L., *Graham Greene: A Collection of Critical Essays* (1973); Kulshrestha, J. R., *Graham Greene, the Novelist* (1977); Kunkel, Francis, *The Labyrinthine Ways of Graham Greene*, 2d ed. (1959; repr. 1973); Lodge, David, *Graham Greene* (1966); Stratford, Philip, ed., *The Portable Graham Greene* (1973).

Greene, Nathanael

The American general Nathanael Greene figured prominently both as an advisor to General George Washington and as a military strategic expert during the American Revolution (1775–83). As commander of the southern war theater, he was instrumental in weakening the British forces during the Carolina campaign (1780–81).

Nathanael Greene, b. Aug. 7, 1742, d. June 19, 1786, is thought to have been the best general in the Continental Army, next to George Washington. Son of a Rhode Island ironmaster, Greene entered the family business and served in the colonial legislature. When the AMERICAN REVOLUTION began he was made a brigadier general. In 1776 he participated in the defense of New York City, was promoted to major general, and, in December, played an important role in Washington's surprise attack on Trenton. During 1777–78 he worked closely with Washington at Morristown, Brandywine, Germantown, Valley Forge, and Monmouth. He was quartermaster general from 1778 until 1780.

Greene's generalship was largely responsible for the triumph of the American forces in the South. He assumed command of a shattered army in 1780 and rebuilt it. His strategy succeeded in dividing the British forces under Charles CORNWALLIS, making possible the victory at COWPENS in January

1781. Within eight months, Greene freed most of the Carolinas from British control. His engagements at Guilford Court House and Hobkirk's Hill drained the enemy's strength, and though the British defeated him at Eutaw Springs in September 1781, their heavy losses forced them to withdraw. In 1785, Greene retired to a plantation near Savannah given to him by Georgia. GEORGE ATHAN BILLIAS

Bibliography: Greene, George, *Life of Nathanael Greene*, 3 vols. (1867–71; repr. 1972); Showman, R. K., et al., eds., *The Papers of Nathanael Greene*, 3 vols. (1976–86); Thayer, T. G., *Nathanael Greene* (1960).

Greene, Robert

A prolific writer of prose romances, poetry, and plays, the English writer Robert Greene, b. *c.*1558, d. Sept. 3, 1592, was perhaps even better known for his pamphlets. Some of these give a vivid picture of Elizabethan low life; others deal with religious controversies of the day. His story *Pandosto* (1588) provided the plot for Shakespeare's *A Winter's Tale*. His plays, especially *Friar Bacon and Friar Bungay* (1594), suggest the influence of Christopher Marlowe. ROBIN BUSS

Bibliography: Dean, James S., *Robert Greene: A Reference Guide* (1984); Jordan, John C., *Robert Greene* (1965).

Greene and Greene

In the first decade of the 20th century the American architectural firm of Greene and Greene, consisting of the brothers Charles Sumner Greene, b. Oct. 12, 1868, d. June 11, 1957, and Henry Mather Greene, b. Jan. 23, 1870, d. Oct. 2, 1954, produced elegant versions of the California bungalow equaled only by the finest work of Bernard MAYBECK in the Berkeley area. The Greenes, both born in Brighton, Ohio, graduated from Massachusetts Institute of Technology in 1891. They began their architectural practice in Boston but soon joined their parents in Pasadena, Calif., where, between 1902 and 1915, they produced a series of large residences characterized by open, spacious floor plans and deep, overhanging roofs. Although Charles Greene retired to Carmel in 1922, Henry Greene continued building, in the popular Spanish Colonial style, until his own retirement in 1933.

The David B. Gamble House (1908), presented to the city of Pasadena in 1966 with its fittings, furniture, and gardens intact, is the Greenes' collaborative masterwork. In the Gamble House their profound understanding of Japanese architectural principles is combined with their active interest in the Arts and Crafts movement. Entirely handcrafted in rare woods, with ceramics, fabrics, glass, and even linens designed by the architects, the house is a rare example of a fully realized architectural and interior design project.

Bibliography: Current, Karen, *Greene & Greene* (1974); Makinson, Randell L., *Greene & Greene*, 2 vols. (1977–79).

greenhouse

A greenhouse is a structure designed to provide a protected, controlled environment for raising plants indoors. It is made of glass or a clear plastic that transmits the Sun's light and traps its heat. Large commercial greenhouses raise and sell flowering plants and vegetables out of season. Often such greenhouses use sophisticated techniques for controlling the levels of heat and light—both natural and artificial—and have complex systems for watering and feeding plants (see FLORICULTURE). Greenhouses built to supplement a home garden are increasingly popular. Situated against the south wall of a house, a greenhouse may share its heat with adjacent rooms on sunny days and borrow house heat at night. A solar greenhouse, built on an insulated foundation and equipped with a curtain to cut heat loss at night and with walls or a floor containing built-in heat storage units (such as tanks of water or heat-absorbing masonry), can heat itself solely from the Sun and can retain heat for up to a week of sunless days.

Bibliography: Mastalerz, J. W., *The Greenhouse Environment*, 2d ed. (1988); Nelson, P. V., *Greenhouse Operations and Management*, 3d ed. (1985); Smith, M., *Greenhouse Gardening* (1985); Tanner, O., *Garden Rooms: Greenhouses, Sunrooms, and Solariums* (1986).

The Sun's heat is trapped by the glass walls and roof of this lean-to greenhouse. The heat will remain inside, although on sunny summer days the air may become too hot without insulation. In winter some of the stored heat will pass through the house wall to the rooms inside.

greenhouse effect

In environmental science, the *greenhouse effect* is a popular term for the role that the variable atmospheric constituents carbon dioxide (CO_2), water vapor (H_2O), and trace gases play in keeping the Earth's surface warmer than it would be without their presence. The atmosphere, when clear, is nearly transparent to the primarily shortwave radiation from the Sun, most of which is absorbed at the Earth's surface. The Earth, being much cooler than the Sun, reemits radiation most strongly at shortwave (infrared) wavelengths. The atmosphere's CO_2, H_2O, and trace gases then absorb much of this radiation and reemit a large proportion of it back toward the Earth. The atmosphere thus acts as a kind of blanket (although one with holes in it). Without its presence, the Earth's average ground temperature of 15° C (60° F) would fall to −28° C (−20° F). The term *greenhouse effect* implies that a comparable effect keeps the interior of a greenhouse warm. Actually, the main role of the glass in a greenhouse, besides that of admitting solar radiation, is to prevent convection currents from mixing cooler air outside with the warm air inside.

Although H_2O is an important atmospheric constituent contributing to the greenhouse effect—it is a major reason why humid regions experience less cooling at night than do dry regions—variations in CO_2, in particular, have played an important role in climatic changes (see PALEOCLIMATOLOGY). For this reason many environmental scientists have expressed concern over the global increase in amounts of atmospheric CO_2 in recent decades, largely as a result of the burning of fossil fuels. If the many other determinants of the Earth's present global climate remain more or less constant, the CO_2 increase should raise the average temperature at the Earth's surface. Because warm air can contain more H_2O before reaching saturation than can cooler air, the amount of H_2O would probably also increase as the atmosphere warmed (see HYDROLOGIC CYCLE). Conceivably, such a process could go on indefinitely. Some natural checks might develop. For example, negative feedbacks such as increased cloud cover and increased sea absorption of CO_2 could lower temperatures. Even a limited rise in average surface temperature, however, might lead to a significant rise in sea level and result in other environmental disruptions.

A great deal remains unknown about the cycling of carbon through the environment, and particularly about the role of oceans in this CARBON CYCLE. Further uncertainty occurs in greenhouse-effect studies because the historical temperature records being used tend to represent warmer urban areas rather than the environment as a whole. In addition, the effects of trace gases such as methane are only beginning to be understood. Despite such problems, a number of scientists maintain

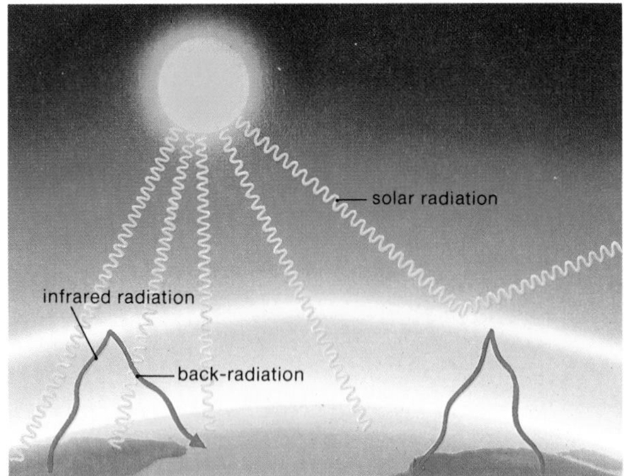

The greenhouse effect is related to the absorption of solar energy by a planet and its ultimate reradiation as longer-wavelength infrared energy. Atmospheric water vapor or carbon dioxide can trap infrared energy, thus increasing the planet's surface temperature.

that the rise in global temperatures in the 1980s is indeed a result of the greenhouse effect. A report issued in 1988 by three major international organizations called for further research into the effect and at the same time urged immediate governmental action to counteract the apparent global warming trend. By the end of the 1980s, no government had yet adopted any of the radical measures proposed by the report. In the United States, however, President George Bush did announce plans in 1989 for hosting an international workshop on the greenhouse effect and on possible ways to deal with it.

RICHARD A. ANTHES

Bibliography: Berner, R. A., and Lasag, A. C., "Modeling the Geochemical Carbon Cycle," *Scientific American*, March 1989; Bolin, Bert, et al., eds., *The Greenhouse Effect, Climatic Change and Ecosystems* (1986); Houghton, R. A., and Woodwell, G. M., "Global Climatic Change," *Scientific American*, April 1989; Sands, W. E., and Hoffman, J. S., *The Greenhouse Effect, Climate Change, and U.S. Forests* (1987).

Greenland

Greenland, or Kalaallit Nunaat, the world's largest island, lies northeast of the North American continent. More than two-thirds of its area is north of the Arctic Circle. About 2,650 km (1,650 mi) long and 1,200 km (750 mi) wide, its northernmost point is less than 800 km (500 mi) across the Arctic Ocean from the North Pole. Greenland is separated in the northwest corner from Canada's Ellesmere Island by the 26-km-wide (16-mi) Kennedy Channel. Greenland is an integral part of Denmark, although since 1979 it has enjoyed home rule.

LAND AND PEOPLE

Approximately 85% of Greenland lies beneath an enormous ice cap that averages about 1,500 m (4,900 ft) in depth. With an area of about 2,175,600 km² (840,004 mi²), it is the largest ice mass outside of Antarctica. Snow in the interior never melts but turns into ice from the weight of succeeding snowfalls. The pressure also pushes the ice cap slowly outward, creating glaciers that flow into fjords along the coast. The Jacobshavn Glacier, at 30 m (100 ft) per day, is one of the fastest-moving glaciers in the world.

Much of Greenland is ringed by mountains that contain the ice cap to the interior. The highest peak is Gunnbjørnsfjaeld (3,700 m/12,140 ft). The heavily indented coastline, 39,310 km (24,430 mi) long, is the only habitable portion. The largest settlement is GODTHÅB, or Nuuk, the capital.

Climate and Vegetation. Greenland's climate differs greatly between the coast and the interior. The temperature along the southern coast ranges from an average of −8° C (18° F) in January to 10° C (50° F) in July; comparable figures for the northern coast are −22° C (−8° F) and 5° C (41° F). Inland temperatures range from a February average of −47° C (−53° F) to a July average of −12° C (10° F). Precipitation ranges from about 760 mm (30 in) in the south to 125 mm (5 in) in the north. The arctic vegetation, located only in the south, consists mainly of grass and low-lying stands of birch, willow, and alder.

People. The vast majority of the inhabitants of Greenland are Greenlanders, a mixture of Eskimo and European immigrants—primarily from Denmark—who have gone there since the 18th century. Some isolated communities of pure Eskimo are still found, primarily in the north. The two major languages are Danish and Greenlandic, the latter based on the mid-19th-century creation of a single literary language out of many similar Eskimo dialects. Since 1979 the Greenlandic forms of place-names have been used increasingly. The Lutheran Church of Denmark is the official religion.

ECONOMIC ACTIVITY

Greenland's climate prohibits extensive agricultural development, although a few crops, such as cabbage and potatoes, are grown in southern sections for home consumption. Hayfields provide fodder for small herds of cattle and sheep. A small reindeer herd, introduced in 1953, has flourished.

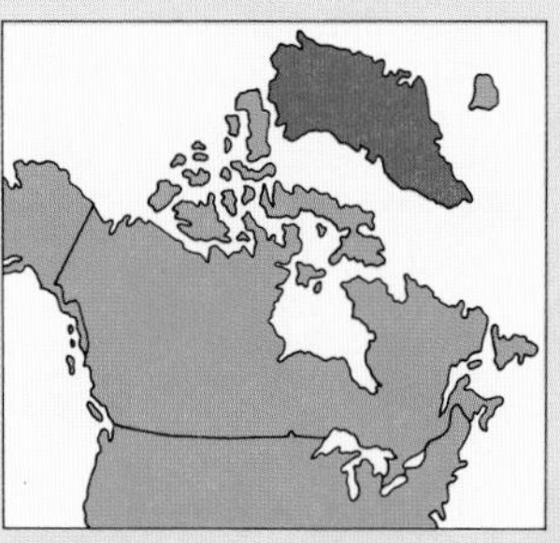

GREENLAND, or KALAALLIT NUNAAT

LAND. Area: 2,175,600 km² (840,004 mi²). Capital and largest city: Godthåb, or Nuuk (1988 est. pop., 11,615).

PEOPLE. Population (1988 est.): 54,790; density: 0.025 persons per km² (0.065 per mi²). Distribution (1988): 79.3% urban, 20.7% rural. Annual growth (1988): 1.13%. Official languages: Danish, Greenlandic. Major religion: Evangelical Lutheranism.

EDUCATION AND HEALTH. Literacy (1987): 99% of adult population. Universities (1988): 1. Hospital beds (1986): 570. Physicians (1986): 61. Life expectancy (1981–85): women—66.3; men—60.4. Infant mortality (1986): 23.4 per 1,000 live births.

ECONOMY. GNP (1986): $470 million; $8,790 per capita. Labor distribution (1976): agriculture, hunting, and fishing—15%; manufacturing—14%; construction—15%; government and services—33%. Foreign trade (1987): imports—$507 million; exports—$346 million; principal trade partners—Denmark, France, Sweden, Norway, West Germany. Currency: 1 Danish krone = 100 øre.

GOVERNMENT. Type: self-governing part of Denmark. Legislature: Landsting. Political subdivisions: 3 counties.

COMMUNICATIONS. Railroads (1989): none. Roads (1987): 80 km (50 mi) total. Major ports: 1. Major airfields: 2.

The village of Igaliko, located on Greenland's southern coast, is one of many small settlements dotting the island's perimeter. More than 90% of Greenland's population live along the south and west coasts, where the influence of the Gulf Stream permits fishing and some animal raising.

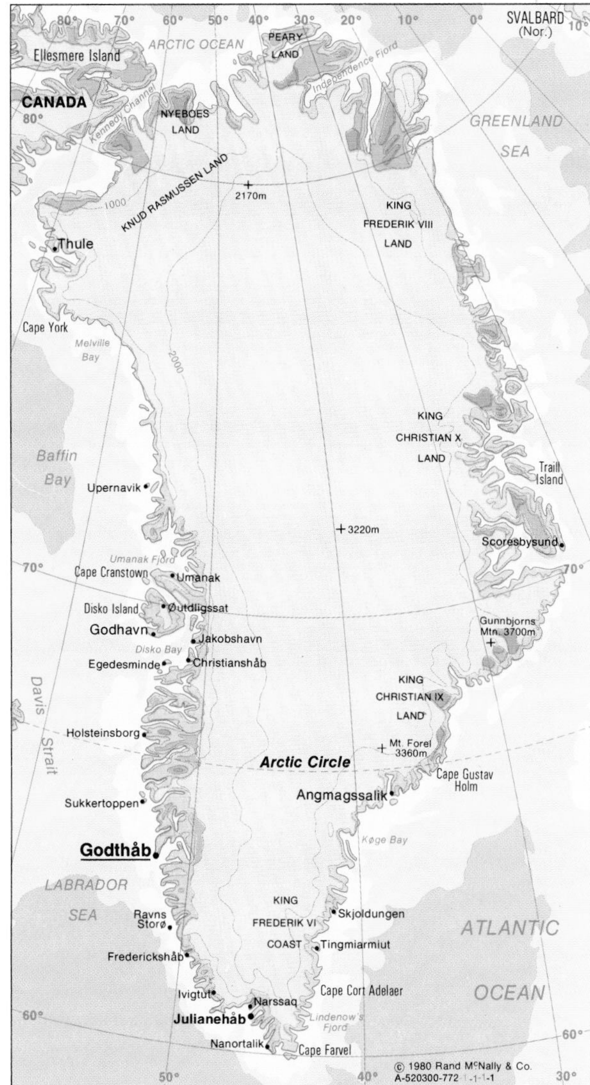

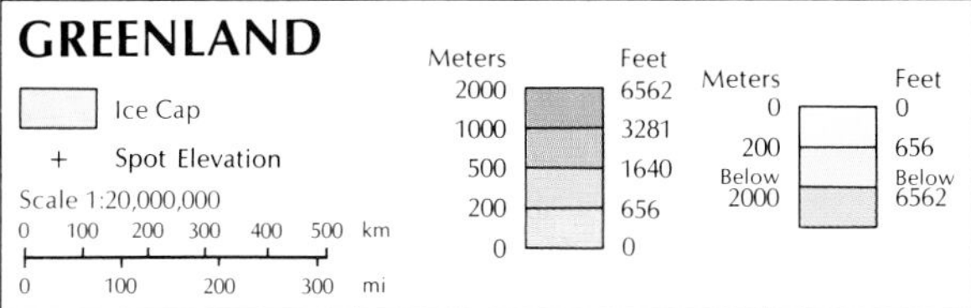

For many Greenlanders, fishing, for cod, shrimp, and salmon, and hunting, for white and blue fox, polar bear, and seals, provide a livelihood today, as they have for centuries. A sizable portion of the labor force, however, is employed in manufacturing, construction, or services. Cryolite is mined, and Greenland also possesses mineral deposits of uranium, molybdenum, and lead, although at present the cost of extraction is still too high to make mining worthwhile. Exploration for offshore oil is currently taking place.

Greenland must import many goods, including machinery and transportation equipment, fuel, and foodstuffs. Denmark supplies 98% of the island's imports. Processed and fresh fish and minerals are the only exports, half of which are shipped to Denmark. Greenland suffers from a large trade deficit.

Transportation and Communications. Greenland has no land transportation network of roads or railways. All travel is by sea along the coast, air, or by dogsled. The island possesses an excellent telephone and radiotelegraph system.

HISTORY AND GOVERNMENT

Between 4000 BC and AD 1000, Greenland's Eskimo migrated here from North America. Between 980 and 985, Norse settlers led by ERIC THE RED established a colony. The settlement ceased to exist around 1400 because of increasingly severe winters and trade problems. European explorers charted Greenland's coast during the 16th century, and the island was settled in 1721 by the Norwegian missionary Hans Egede under the aegis of the Danish crown. In 1729 the Danish crown assumed control of the colony and, from 1774, established a state monopoly on all trade with Greenland, which remained in effect until 1951.

During World War II, when Denmark was under German occupation, the U.S. government took over Greenland as a protectorate. In 1946 the United States offered to buy Greenland, but the Danish government refused. The United States was given permission to retain and develop its major radar and weather patrol base at Thule.

In 1975 a commission was appointed to work out terms for home rule. These were approved by Danish voters in 1978, and home rule was instituted in 1979. The popularly elected Landsting determines the internal affairs of Greenland. Greenland holds two seats in the Danish national assembly, and the Danish government handles some of Greenland's external affairs. In 1985 Greenland withdrew from full membership in the European community. PAUL C. HELMREICH

Bibliography: Banks, Michael, *Greenland* (1975); Erngaard, Erik, *Greenland Then and Now* (1972); Gad, Finn, *The History of Greenland*, 3 vols. (1971, 1973, 1983); Jones, Gwyn, *The Norse Atlantic Saga* (1964); Rink, Hinrich, *Danish Greenland: Its People and Its Products* (1877; repr. 1975).

greenling

The greenlings, family Hexagrammidae, order Scorpaeniformes, are elongated fishes endemic to the cold waters of the North Pacific. Most species live near rocky shores overgrown with algae, but some are found as deep as 400 m (1,310 ft). They have long dorsal and anal fins and small mouths with fine, pointed teeth; some species have five sensory lateral bones on each side of the body. Adults are usually 25–60 cm (10–24 in) long, but some reach a length of 150 cm (60 in). Males and females are differently colored. Species of the genus *Pleurogrammus,* which have a high vitamin A content, are of great commercial value, and up to 159,000 metric tons (175,000 U.S. tons) are taken each year in Japan.

CAMM SWIFT

Greenock [green'-uhk]

Greenock (1981 pop., 57,324) is a seaport and industrial city in Strathclyde region of southwestern Scotland, situated on the south shore of the Firth of Clyde. Local industries include textile, paper, and electronics manufacturing and shipbuilding.

Greenock was a small village until 1670, when it became a thriving port exporting herring. James Watt, inventor of the steam engine, was born here in 1736. The city suffered heavy bombing during World War II.

Greenough, Horatio [green'-oh]

Horatio Greenough, b. Boston, Sept. 6, 1805, d. Sept. 18, 1852, was America's first professional sculptor. After leaving Harvard University in 1824 he studied in Rome, where he was encouraged by the Danish neoclassical (see NEOCLASSICISM, art) sculptor Bertel THORVALDSEN, and in Florence, where Lorenzo Bartolini (1777–1850) taught him to work from nature. Greenough's marble portrait of *Evan Philip Thomas* (1837; Maryland Historical Society, Baltimore, Md.) combines the sitter's features with the bare chest and drapery reminiscent of a Roman bust in order to instill in Americans the civic virtue that upheld the ancient republic.

In 1842, Greenough's marble *George Washington* (1832–40; Smithsonian Institution, Washington, D.C.) was installed in

George Washington, *Horatio Greenough's marble statue, was intended for the Capitol rotunda but met with strong criticism. It was permanently installed in the Museum of History and Technology of the Smithsonian Institution, Washington, D.C.*

the Capitol rotunda. The partially nude figure emulated the gigantic statue of the *Olympian Zeus* (now destroyed) created by Phidias during Greece's Golden Age in the 5th century BC. Greenough intended his statue to inspire the spectator with Washington's steadfast patriotism. The work was poorly received by the American public, whose puritan sensibilities were offended by the sight of the father of their country undressed in public. Greenough is also recognized as a pioneer in the concept of functionalism—the fundamental relationship between form and function. JOAN C. SIEGFRIED

Bibliography: Crane, S., *White Silence: Greenough, Powers, and Crawford* (1972); Greenough, H., *Form and Function* (1947) and *The Travels: Observations and Experiences of a Yankee Stonecutter* (1852; repr. 1958); Matthiessen, F. O., *American Renaissance* (1941); Wright, N., *Horatio Greenough* (1963).

Greenpeace

Greenpeace is an international environmental organization founded in 1969 by a group of Canadian environmentalists. It advocates direct, nonviolent action to halt threats to the environment, and its confrontational tactics have earned the group widespread publicity for its causes, which include ending commercial whaling and the slaughter of baby seals, halting the dumping of toxic wastes, and creating a nuclear-free world. On July 10, 1985, the Greenpeace ship *Rainbow Warrior,* en route to protest nuclear testing in French Polynesia, was sunk by French agents in the harbor at Auckland, New Zealand, creating an international incident.

Bibliography: Dyson, J., with J. Fitchett, *Sink the Rainbow!* (1986).

Greensboro [greenz'-buhr-uh]

Located in the piedmont of north central North Carolina, Greensboro is the seat of Guilford County and the state's second largest city, with a population of 155,642 (1980) within the city and 827,385 in the 6-county metropolitan area. Greensboro is a diversified industrial city and an insurance and distribution center. Its many educational institutions include the University of North Carolina at Greensboro (1891), North Carolina Agricultural and Technical State University (1891), and Greensboro College (1838).

Greensboro was settled in 1749 and named for Gen. Nathanael GREENE; the battle of Guilford Courthouse was fought nearby on Mar. 15, 1781. Greensboro served as the temporary capital of the Confederacy in 1865. After 1890 the city grew rapidly, becoming a textile center.

Greenspan, Alan

The U.S. economist Alan Greenspan, b. New York City, Mar. 6, 1926, became chairman of the Federal Reserve Board in 1987. A free-market advocate educated at New York University, Greenspan headed President Gerald Ford's Council of Economic Advisers (1974–77) and consulted privately before President Ronald Reagan named him to succeed Paul VOLCKER as chairman.

Greenville

Greenville (1980 pop., 58,242) is a city in South Carolina on the Reedy River in the southern foothills of the Blue Ridge Mountains. It is the seat of Greenville County. Diversified commercial expansion has taken place since the late 1960s, although manufacturing of cotton textiles and related products has long been the leading industry. Lumber processing is also important. Greenville is the site of Furman University (1826) and Bob Jones University (1927). Paris Mountain State Park is nearby. Greenville was settled in the 1760s.

Greenwich (Connecticut) [gren'-ich]

Greenwich (1980 pop., 59,578) is a town in southwest Connecticut, on Long Island Sound adjacent to the New York border. Settled in 1640, it is an affluent suburb of New York City.

Greenwich (England)

Greenwich, located on the south bank of the River Thames, is a borough of Greater London and has a population of 216,000 (1984 est.). The borough, into which Woolwich was merged (1965), has docks and industrial plants. Greenwich was the site of the ROYAL GREENWICH OBSERVATORY from 1675 to 1958. The former observatory building, designed by Sir Christopher WREN, contains a brass strip marking the PRIME MERIDIAN (0° longitude). It is now part of the National Maritime Museum (founded 1937), which also includes the Queen's House (1616–35), designed by Inigo JONES. Wren's Royal Hospital became (1873) the Royal Naval College.

Greenwich mean time

Greenwich mean time (GMT) is the time on the Greenwich meridian, used as the zero for longitudinal measurement, according to the Mean Sun. The Mean Sun is an imaginary body that moves around the celestial equator with constant angular speed, making a complete circuit with respect to the vernal equinox in one tropical year. GMT was established as the world standard in 1884. In 1928 it was also given the name universal time; the International Time Bureau in Paris now coordinates astronomical measurements and atomic clock readings from around the world to arrive at coordinated universal TIME. J. M. A. DANBY

Greenwich Observatory: see ROYAL GREENWICH OBSERVATORY.

Greenwich Village

A residential area of lower Manhattan, bounded by 14th and Houston streets to the north and south, and by West Broadway and the Hudson River from east to west, Greenwich Village has long been a unique section of New York City. A separate settlement in colonial times, the area became a country retreat for the rich, then a tenement district, and finally a haven for artists and students. Recent high-rise construction has altered the area's ambience somewhat, but tourists still visit the shops and small restaurants that remain a Village attraction. Washington Square Park and New York University are located within the Village.

Bibliography: Delaney, Edmund T., *New York's Greenwich Village* (1968); McDarrogh, Fred W., *Greenwich Village* (1963).

Greer, Germaine [greer, jur-mayn']

Australian writer and feminist Germaine Greer, b. Jan. 29, 1939, was a successful teacher, journalist, and actress when her first book, *The Female Eunuch* (1970), made her a star of the feminist movement of the early 1970s. In that book, Greer argues that the feminine characteristics traditionally valued by males (delicacy, timidity, languor, and so on) are evidence of "the castration of our true female personality"—a castration accomplished by women themselves. *The Obstacle Race: The Fortunes of Women Painters and Their Work* (1979) is an examination of the almost always obscure histories of talented female artists. *Sex and Destiny* (1984) is revisionist feminism, in which Greer claims that Western society is profoundly hostile to children and attempts to manipulate and control sexuality by making it yet another consumer commodity.

Gregg, J. R.: see SHORTHAND.

Gregg, William

William Gregg, b. Monongalia County, Va. (now W. Va.), Feb. 2, 1800, d. Sept. 13, 1867, is often considered the father of cotton manufacturing in the southern United States. He started as a watchmaker in South Carolina but quit in his mid-thirties and began writing on the need to industrialize the south. His articles were published as *Essays on Domestic Industry* (1845). In 1846 he erected a cotton mill near Aiken, S.C., drawing workers from among the unpropertied whites in the area. His example was followed widely in the South. His factory ran successfully for 20 years, operating throughout the Civil War. He died after a flood had damaged the mill.

Bibliography: Mitchell, Broadus, *William Gregg, Factory Master* (1966).

Gregorian chant: see PLAINSONG.

Gregory, Cynthia

The American ballet dancer Cynthia Kathleen Gregory, b. Los Angeles, July 8, 1946, was trained by Eva Lorraine and Carmelita Maracci. Awarded a Ford Foundation Fellowship to study at the school connected with the San Francisco Ballet, she became a member of that company in 1961 in addition to dancing with the San Francisco Opera. In 1965 she joined American Ballet Theatre, where she has been a principal since 1967, except for periods in the mid-1970s of subsequently reconsidered retirement. Known particularly for her physical security and beauty of line, Gregory is naturally suited to such majestic classical roles as Odette-Odile in *Swan Lake*, the Queen of the Wilis in *Giselle*, and Nikiya in *La Bayadère*. She has also been effective in other classical and romantic ballets as well as Antony Tudor's dramatic *Undertow*, *Dark Elegies*, and *Jardin aux Lilas*. She is equally at home in a broad range of contemporary works, including those of Eliot Feld, who created roles for her in his *Harbinger* and *At Midnight*.

TOBI TOBIAS

Gregory, Dick

Dick Gregory, b. St. Louis, Mo., Oct. 12, 1932, was one of the first black comedians to use topical, nonstereotyped material. During the 1960s his satirical wit brought him wide success in night clubs, college concerts, and on television. Gregory was in the forefront of the antiwar movement and has long been an activist for civil rights causes. In 1968 the radical Peace and Freedom party nominated him as its candidate for the U.S. presidency. Gregory's writings include *From the Back of the Bus* (1962), *Write Me In* (1968), *Dick Gregory's Political Primer* (1971), and *The Murder of Dr. Martin Luther King, Jr.* (1977).

Bibliography: Gregory, Dick, with Robert Lipsyt, *Nigger: An Autobiography*, rev. ed. (1970), and *Up from Nigger* (1976).

Gregory, Horace

Poet, translator, critic, and editor Horace Victor Gregory, b. Milwaukee, Wis., Apr. 10, 1898, d. Mar. 11, 1982, was best known for the interior monologue "Dempsey, Dempsey" that appeared in his 1930 volume of poems, *Chelsea Rooming House*. A lyric gift and heroic attitude toward life permeate his poetry, which, as *Collected Poems* (1964), won him the Bollingen Prize in 1965. Gregory also translated the poetry of Catullus and *The Metamorphoses* of Ovid and wrote critical studies of D. H. Lawrence, Amy Lowell, and e. e. cummings. *The House on Jefferson Street* (1971) is a memoir of his youth.

Gregory, Isabella Augusta, Lady

Lady Gregory, b. Mar. 5, 1852, d. May 22, 1932, was an Irish playwright, folklorist, and a founder of the ABBEY THEATRE. In 1880 she married the elderly Sir William Gregory, a noted member of Parliament, and after his death, turned her abundant energies to the collection of Irish folktales and the movement called the IRISH LITERARY RENAISSANCE. In 1898 she met William Butler YEATS and the next year, with Yeats and others, helped develop the Irish Literary Theatre, which subsequently became the Abbey Theatre.

For more than 30 years Lady Gregory directed the fortunes of the Abbey—conducted rehearsals, wrote letters, read scripts, led the company on American tours, and, most importantly, wrote about 40 plays for it. Her highly regarded *Our Irish Theatre* (1913) is a history of the Irish dramatic movement. As a playwright her range was wide—short plays, long plays, comedies, tragedies, histories, children's plays, and translations, adaptations, and collaborations with Yeats and Douglas HYDE. She was an uneven writer and some of her work now seems dull and arcane, exploiting peasant folkways and Irish myths and history. Her best short comedies, however, *Spreading the News* (1904), *Hyacinth Halvey* (1906), *The Rising of the Moon* (1907), and *The Workhouse Ward* (1908), resemble the works of a miniature Molière; and her short tragedy *The Gaol Gate* (1906) is comparable to John Millington Synge's masterly *Riders to the Sea*. She translated Molière and encouraged the work of Synge and younger Irish writers.

ROBERT HOGAN

Bibliography: Coxhead, Elizabeth, *Lady Gregory: A Literary Portrait*, rev. ed. (1966); Mikhail, E. H., ed., *Lady Gregory, Interviews and Recollections* (1977); Saddlemyer, Ann, *In Defence of Lady Gregory* (1966).

Gregory, James

James Gregory, b. November 1638, d. October 1675, was a Scottish mathematician whose work on infinite series and analytic geometry led to the calculus. He also invented a reflecting telescope and solved some important problems in theoretical astronomy.

STEVEN LUBAR

Gregory of Nazianzus, Saint [nay-zee-an'-zuhs]

Gregory of Nazianzus, *c*.330–389, one of the FATHERS OF THE CHURCH, is known especially for his contributions to the theological definition of the TRINITY and the nature of Christ. He, BASIL THE GREAT, and Gregory of Nyssa are called the Cappadocian Fathers. Brought up in the Cappadocian town of Nazianzus (present-day Bekar, Turkey), where his father was bishop, Gregory as a young man was reluctant to take a position of responsibility in the church, retiring instead to a monastic community started by Basil in Pontus. He explained this action in his *Defense of the Flight to Pontus*, which became the basis for works on the priesthood by Saint John CHRYSOSTOM and Pope GREGORY I. Gregory was consecrated a bishop *c*.371 but did not become actively involved in ecclesiastical affairs until he assumed leadership (379) of the orthodox community in Constantinople, at a time when the city was divided by controversy between rival Christian groups. He played a leading role at the first Council of Constantinople (381; see CONSTANTINOPLE, COUNCILS OF), which continued the definition of Christian teaching begun at the Council of NICAEA, but opposition at the council to Gregory's claim to the bishopric of Constantinople made him decide to return to Nazianzus. In 384 he again retired to monastic life.

Gregory was not a systematic writer, and his works consist primarily of orations and letters. In the ORTHODOX CHURCH he is known as "the Theologian" because of his influential sermons dealing with the Trinity and Christology. His development of terminology helped to clarify the language of Nicaea and lay the foundation for the debates of the 5th-century ecumenical councils. Feast days: Jan. 25 and 30 (Eastern); Jan. 2 (Western). JOHN L. BOOJAMRA

Gregory of Nyssa, Saint [nis'-uh]

Gregory of Nyssa, *c.*330–*c.*395, was one of the FATHERS OF THE CHURCH; his theological and mystical writings had a strong influence on later Christian thought and spirituality, especially in the ORTHODOX CHURCH. Born in Caesarea, Cappadocia (present-day Kayseri, Turkey), Gregory belonged to an eminent Christian family, defenders of orthodoxy against ARIANISM. He, his brother BASIL THE GREAT, and Gregory of Nazianzus, are known as the Cappadocian Fathers. In 371 he was elected bishop of the Cappadocian town of Nyssa. Deposed from his bishopric by the Arians in 376, he was restored in 378 and took part in the first Council of Constantinople (381; see CONSTANTINOPLE, COUNCILS OF).

Gregory of Nyssa was a prolific writer. His *Great Catechesis* is one of the earliest systematic outlines of Christian theology. In his treatises *On the Holy Spirit* and *Ad Ablabium* (or *Not Three Gods*), he defended the orthodox doctrine of the TRINITY. His interpretations of the Bible include *The Creation of Man,* which was designed to complete his brother Basil's *Hexaemeron* ("Six Days"), and the *Life of Moses,* in which he treats the journey of the Israelites to the Promised Land as an allegory of the soul's progress toward God. Gregory is also known for his mystical commentaries on the Psalms, and he has been called the father of mysticism. His writings on asceticism include *On Virginity* and a biography of his sister, Saint Macrina. Feast day: Mar. 9. JOHN L. BOOJAMRA

Gregory Thaumaturgus, Saint [thaw-muh-tur'-guhs]

Gregory, *c.*213–*c.*270, was one of the Greek Fathers of the Church. After early studies in law and rhetoric, he went (*c.*233) to Caesarea in Palestine, where he fell under the influence of ORIGEN and converted to Christianity. On his return to his native city of Neocaesarea five years later, he was consecrated bishop. The many legends that were told about him earned him the name *Thaumaturgus* (Greek for "wonder-worker"). His writings include the *Panegyric to Origen,* which gives an attractive picture of Gregory's teacher, and the *Exposition of the Faith,* which was directed against the teachings of SABELLIANISM on the Trinity. His biography was written by Saint Gregory of Nyssa. Feast day: Nov. 17. ROSS MACKENZIE

Gregory of Tours, Saint

Saint Gregory of Tours, b. Nov. 30, 538, d. Nov. 17, 594, was a Frankish bishop and historian. As bishop of Tours he became a leading advisor to King Guntram in the king's struggle with his rebellious aristocracy. He is primarily remembered for his *Historia Francorum* (History of the Franks), a valuable source for the details of early French history. Feast day: Nov. 17.

Gregory I, Pope

Gregory I, known as Gregory the Great, was pope from 590 to 604. Born *c.*540 to a wealthy patrician family in Rome, he chose to follow a public career. At the age of 30 he was named prefect of Rome. Dissatisfied with worldly success, Gregory turned to a life of piety and contemplation. He became a monk (*c.*574) in one of the seven monasteries he had built with his own money, following the Rule of Saint Benedict. After several years in the cloister, he was summoned, first by Pope Benedict I, to serve as cardinal deacon (*c.*578) in Rome and later, by Pope Pelagius II, to serve as permanent ambassador (*c.*579) at the court of Emperor Tiberius in Constantinople. On his return (*c.*584) to the monastery, he was elected abbot. At a time when the church was in turmoil and the empire was in a state of disorder from natural disasters, wars, and invasions, Gregory was once again called out of the monastery and was elected pope in 590. He was the first monk to attain this high office. In his new position, he chose to be known as the "servant of the servants of God" (*servus servorum Dei*). He was an able administrator.

Pope Gregory I, known as Saint Gregory the Great, is credited with laying the foundations of the medieval papacy. The first monk to be elected (590) pope, Gregory asserted the temporal power of the papacy by consolidation of papal lands and independent diplomacy. Gregory also ministered to the poor, sought reform of both clergy and liturgy, and promoted missionary activity. (Library of Douai, France.)

As pope, Gregory strengthened his office by affirming his supremacy in the church and by asserting the right of the papacy to intervene in secular affairs. He appointed the governors of Italian cities, laying the foundation of medieval papal practices. As bishop, he sought practical solutions to the social misery of the day by using the revenues from the Roman ecclesiastical estates, which he organized and increased. Gregory's primary interests were pastoral. He sought to bring about reform of the clergy, of the liturgy, and of church practices. He was also interested in missionary work; one of the great successes of his pontificate was the conversion of England by Saint AUGUSTINE OF CANTERBURY. Gregory is credited with promoting plainsong, later called Gregorian chant.

Gregory wrote many theological, liturgical, and devotional works, including a biography of Saint Benedict. His thought was strongly influenced by Saint Augustine of Hippo. Gregory died Mar. 12, 604. He is one of the Doctors of the Church. Feast day: Mar. 12. AGNES CUNNINGHAM

Bibliography: Batiffol, P., *Saint Gregory the Great* (1928; Eng. trans., 1929); Dudden, F., *Gregory the Great,* 2 vols. (1905; repr. 1967).

Gregory II, Pope

Gregory II, b. *c.*669, d. Feb. 11, 731, was pope from 715 to 731. He sponsored Saint BONIFACE and other missionaries in their efforts to Christianize the Germans. Gregory resisted (727) the order of Byzantine Emperor LEO III (728) that all holy images be destroyed (see ICONOCLASM). Through his friendship with the Lombard king Liutprand, Gregory tried to restrain Lombard expansion in Italy. He built and renovated many churches in Rome and encouraged monasticism. Feast day: Feb. 13.

Gregory V (Patriarch of Constantinople)

Gregory V, b. George Aggelopoulos, *c.*1746, d. Apr. 22, 1821, was a Greek Orthodox bishop who held the position of ecumenical patriarch of Constantinople three times (1779–98,

1806–08, 1818–21) during a period when the patriarchate was largely subject to the vagaries of Turkish politics. During his tenures, Gregory acquired fame as a devoted and saintly prelate who was concerned with the spiritual progress of his people. In 1821 the Greeks rebelled against Turkish rule and eventually established an independent Greek state. Residing in Constantinople, which remained the sultan's capital, Gregory condemned the Greek revolution. However, on Easter Sunday 1821, he was hanged by the Turks on the main gate of the patriarchal basilica. He is venerated as a saint by the Orthodox church. JOHN MEYENDORFF

Gregory VII, Pope

Gregory VII, pope from 1073 to 1085, was a major reformer of the medieval church, noted for asserting the absolute rights of the PAPACY over the church and prohibiting secular interference in church affairs. A Tuscan named Ildebrando (Hildebrand), he became a Benedictine monk at an early age and was one of the reformers brought to Rome in 1049 by Pope LEO IX. He served in various official and advisory capacities to succeeding popes until his own election in 1073.

One of Gregory's first acts as pope was to implement a program of radical reform directed at the widespread corruption in the church. He issued decrees against SIMONY and clerical concubinage. In the following year he began his struggle to assert papal supremacy within Christian society at large. Gregory found the root problem of the time in the practice of lay investiture—the conferral of church offices by the Holy Roman emperor and other secular rulers. Gregory condemned the practice in 1075, initiating the prolonged dispute called the INVESTITURE CONTROVERSY.

The pope's chief opponent was Holy Roman Emperor HENRY IV, who attempted to depose Gregory in 1076. Gregory replied by excommunicating Henry. Losing his popular support, Henry was forced to seek absolution and the lifting of the ban of excommunication by appealing to Gregory as a suppliant at Canossa in January 1077. Nevertheless, Gregory lost control of the situation, since the German nobles used the excommunication of Henry as an excuse to elect a rival king. In the civil war that followed, Gregory tried to act as a mediator, but did not succeed. In the Lenten Synod of 1080, he once more excommunicated the victorious Henry and declared him deposed. In return, Henry elected an "antipope," Clement III, whom he installed in Rome, sending Gregory into exile among the Norman lords of south Italy. Gregory died in Salerno on May 25, 1085. He was canonized in 1606. Feast day: May 25. DAVID HARRY MILLER

Bibliography: Barraclough, Geoffrey, *The Medieval Papacy* (1968; repr. 1979); Emerton, Ephraim, trans., *The Correspondence of Pope Gregory VII* (1969); MacDonald, Allan J., *Hildebrand: A Life of Gregory the Seventh* (1932; repr. 1977); Tellenbach, G., *Church, State, and Christian Society at the Time of the Investiture Contest,* trans. by R. Bennett (1970); Ullmann, Walter, *The Growth of Papal Government in the Middle Ages,* 2d ed. (1962).

Gregory IX, Pope

Gregory IX, b. *c.*1170, d. Aug. 22, 1241, was pope from 1227 to 1241. He was named Ugolino dei conti di Segni. A native of Anagni, Italy, he was made a cardinal deacon by his uncle, Pope INNOCENT III, in 1198.

Gregory's pontificate was marked by stormy relations with Holy Roman Emperor FREDERICK II. A few months after becoming pope, Gregory excommunicated Frederick for reneging on his promise to go on crusade. Frederick was reinstated in the church, but was again excommunicated in 1239 after he invaded Lombardy. When Gregory died in Rome, Frederick was about to attack the city.

Gregory was a personal friend of Saint Francis of Assisi and, both as cardinal and pope, was protector of the Franciscans. He centralized the Inquisition in 1232 and placed the Dominicans in charge of it. During his pontificate, Gregory tried unsuccessfully to reunite the Eastern and Western churches, had the papal decretals collected and published, and commissioned expurgated editions of the works of Aristotle.

Gregory XI, Pope

Gregory XI, b. 1329, d. Mar. 27, 1378, was pope from 1370 to 1389. He was a Frenchman named Pierre Roger de Beaufort. Gregory's great achievement was returning the PAPACY to Italy in 1377, after its long exile at Avignon. Trained as a canon lawyer, he emerged as a resolute pope who endeavored to pacify the papal states and to make possible the return to Rome. The confusion and dissension that prevailed there after his death gave rise to the Great SCHISM of the West.
FRANCIS OAKLEY

Bibliography: Thibault, P. R., *Pope Gregory XI: The Failure of Tradition* (1986).

Gregory XIII, Pope

Gregory XIII, b. Jan. 1, 1502, d. April 10, 1585, was pope from 1572 to 1585. He was born in Bologna and originally was named Ugo Boncompagni. He was a respected canonist and advanced in the church's hierarchy even though he had fathered an illegitimate son before his ordination. As pope, he promoted missionary efforts and tried to implement the reforms of the Council of TRENT (1545–63), in which he took part. He founded several educational institutions for the clergy, including the Gregorian University in Rome. His diplomatic activities and his financial administration were generally inept. He is best remembered for his reform (1582) of the CALENDAR; the Gregorian calendar, named for him, is still in effect today. JOHN W. O'MALLEY

Grein, J. T. [gryn]

Jacob Thomas Grein, b. Oct. 11, 1862, d. June 22, 1935, was a Dutch-born theater critic who in 1891 established London's Independent Theatre, modeled after André Antoine's Théâtre Libre in Paris. His goal was to elevate the English stage by presenting the new realistic dramas. Grein's first production, Ibsen's *Ghosts* on May 13, 1891, drew a hostile critical reaction. The Independent Theatre, however, was later successful in launching the theatrical career of George Bernard Shaw. To avoid censorship, Grein organized his theater on a private subscription basis, performing on Sundays in vacant professional theaters. ALVIN GOLDFARB

Bibliography: Schoonderwoerd, N. H. G., *J. T. Grein* (1963).

Grenada [gruh-nay'-duh]

Grenada is an independent island nation in the WINDWARD ISLANDS of the Caribbean, located about 150 km (90 mi) north of the South American coast.

LAND, PEOPLE, AND ECONOMY

In addition to the main island of Grenada, the nation also includes the nearby smaller islands of Carriacou, Petit Martinique, and several islets of the GRENADINE ISLANDS. Grenada is a volcanic, mountainous island with little level land. Numerous streams, springs, and mountain lakes are found on Grenada, and alluvial river valleys provide fertile soil for farming. The island is heavily wooded with teak and mahogany. Grenada's climate is tropical, with an average annual temperature of 23° C (78° F) and with rainfall ranging from 1,525 mm (60 in) on the coast to 4,190 mm (165 in) in the mountains.

About 75% of the population are of black African descent; the remainder are chiefly mulatto or of East Indian descent. English is the official language, but many Grenadians speak a French patois. The majority of the population is Roman Catholic. Education is free and compulsory for children between the ages of 6 and 14.

Agriculture is the mainstay of the economy. The chief export crops are nutmegs and mace, cocoa, and bananas. Food crops are also produced for local consumption. Tourism is increasingly important to the economy, helped by a new airport (1984). Grenada must import many products and commodities to satisfy its needs; imports consistently far exceed exports. The nation is also heavily dependent on foreign aid.

HISTORY AND GOVERNMENT

Christopher Columbus was the first European to discover Gre-

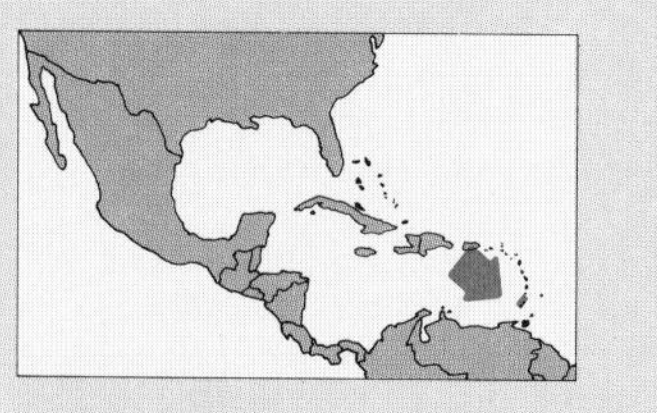

GRENADA

LAND. Area: 344 km^2 (133 mi^2). Capital and largest city: Saint George's (1980 est. pop., 7,500).

PEOPLE. Population (1986 est.): 86,000; density (1986 est.): 250 persons per km^2 (647 per mi^2). Distr. (1980): 5.4% urban, 94.6% rural. Annual growth (1983): 2.3%. Official language: English. Major religions: Roman Catholicism, Anglicanism.

EDUCATION AND HEALTH. Literacy (1985): 85%. Universities (1987): 1. Hospital beds (1982): 320. Physicians (1981): 38. Life expectancy (1980–85): women—72.5; men—68.5. Infant mortality (1985): 16.7 per 1,000 live births.

ECONOMY. GDP (1984 est.): $86.8 million; $940 per capita. Labor distribution (1985): services—31%; agriculture—24%; construction—8%; manufacturing—5%. Foreign trade (1983): imports—$55.6 million; exports—$18.9 million; principal trade partners—United Kingdom, United States, Trinidad and Tobago. Currency: 1 East Caribbean dollar = 100 cents.

GOVERNMENT. Type: independent state within the Commonwealth of Nations. Legislature: Parliament. Political subdivisions: 7 parishes.

COMMUNICATIONS. Railroads (1987): none. Roads (1984): 980 km (609 mi) total. Major ports: 1. Major airfields: 1.

GRENADA

+ Spot Elevation or Depth

National capital is underlined

Scale 1:787,000

© 1980 Rand McNally & Co.

nada, in 1498. The island was settled by the French in 1650; subsequently it was held alternately by English and French until 1783, when the island was ceded by treaty to Britain. Grenada remained a separate British colony until 1958 when it joined the Federation of the West Indies; in 1967, Grenada became one of the West Indies Associated States. Independence, within the Commonwealth, was achieved in 1974.

Sir Eric M. Gairy was prime minister of Grenada until 1979, when his eccentric regime was overthrown by the Marxist New Jewel Movement. The latter, led by Maurice Bishop, established a People's Revolutionary Government. On Oct. 14, 1983, Bishop was ousted by another New Jewel faction and then murdered. On October 25 a U.S. task force invaded the island, acting allegedly to forestall a Cuban and Soviet military buildup there. This controversial action was followed by the appointment of an interim government by the governor general, Sir Paul Scoon. By December all U.S. combat troops had been withdrawn. Following elections in December 1984, Herbert A. Blaize became prime minister. Thomas D. Boswell

Bibliography: O'Shaughnessy, Hugh, *Grenada* (1984).

grenade [gruh-nayd']

A grenade is a small bomb filled with explosives or chemicals. It can be thrown by hand or launched from a rifle or a special launcher. Used as early as the 15th century, the grenade was abandoned after 1750 because of increased musketry range. With the trench warfare of the early 20th century, however, they became effective weapons again.

The British Mills bomb (1915) is characteristic of the type of hand grenade used in both world wars. Pineapple-shaped, its iron body was deeply grooved for fragmentation; it had a time-delayed fuse. During the Korean War the U.S. Army adopted a grenade with a smooth outer surface lined with a serrated-steel spring for fragmentation. Special purpose grenades include illumination, tear gas, and other chemical-agent types. Rifle grenades usually have a streamlined body and fins at the rear. Russell J. Parkinson

Bibliography: Kershaw, Andrew A., and Close, Ian, eds., *Weapons and War Machines* (1976).

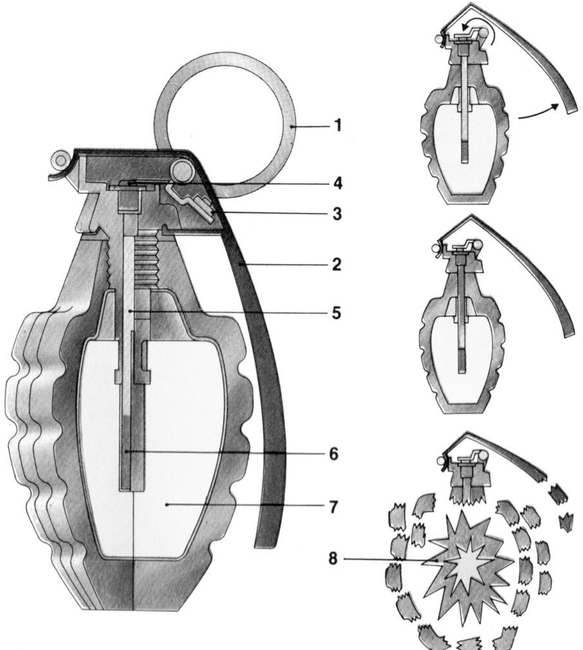

As the ring (1) of a hand grenade is removed and the weapon is hurled, a lever (2) is released. Its movement activates a striker (3), which detonates a percussion cap (4). The powder train (5) ignites, firing a detonator (6) set in the main charge (7). The resulting explosion (8) scatters fragments of the grenade's iron casing.

grenadier (military) [gren-uh-dir']

In the 17th century a grenadier was a soldier assigned to throw grenades against the enemy. By 1672, each French infantry regiment contained a grenadier company. During the 18th century the original function of the grenadier was lost, and since then the name has been applied to elite troops.

grenadier (zoology)

The grenadier, *Nezumis bairdi,* of the family Macruridae, order Gadiformes, is a deep-water fish found in depths of

145–2,200 m (480–7,200 ft) and ranges along the continental slope from the West Indies north to the Grand Banks; it is commonly found on soft mud bottoms. Little is known about the life history of this fish. Pelagic shrimp have been reported to be part of its diet. It is thought to spawn in summer and autumn. ALFRED PERLMUTTER

Grenadine Islands

The Grenadine Islands, a chain of about 600 islets in the Caribbean Sea, are part of the WINDWARD ISLANDS. They extend for more than 100 km (60 mi) from north to south; the northern portion is part of SAINT VINCENT AND THE GRENADINES, and the southern half is part of GRENADA. The largest island is Carriacou, on which Hillsborough, the principal village, is situated. Boat building and fishing are the principal economic activities, and tourism is becoming important.

Grenfell, Sir Wilfred [gren'-fel]

Wilfred Thomason Grenfell, b. Feb. 28, 1865, d. Oct. 9, 1940, was an English physician who spent his life as a medical missionary. Responding (1885) to a challenge by evangelist Dwight L. MOODY, he joined the Mission to Deep Sea Fishermen and ministered to the fishermen of the North Sea. Moving to Labrador (1892), he devoted himself for over 40 years to the welfare of its inhabitants. When he retired (1935), he had founded five hospitals, seven nursing stations, three orphanage boarding schools, cooperative stores, industrial centers, agricultural stations, and the King George V Seaman's Institute (1912). Grenfell was the author of many books, including his autobiography, *Forty Years for Labrador* (1932).

Bibliography: Kerr, James L., *Wilfred Grenfell* (1959; repr. 1977).

Grenoble [gruh-noh'-bul]

Grenoble is the capital of the French department of Isère, located in the Alps about 217 km (135 mi) north of Marseille on the Isère River. The city's population is 160,000, and the greater metropolitan area has a population of 392,000 (1982). The climate is characterized by warm, dry summers and relatively mild winters. Easy access to the winter sports regions of the Dauphiné Alps makes Grenoble a major tourist resort.

Grenoble is a cultural and industrial center and is noted for the manufacturing of gloves. Hydroelectric power from Alpine rivers provides much of the energy for the production of machinery, electrical transmission equipment, cement, paper and textiles, and for food processing. The University of Grenoble (1339) is a leading educational institution in southern France. In recent years the university has become noted for its contributions to scientific research, especially in physics.

Grenoble was the seat of a bishopric from the 4th century on and contains a number of buildings dating from the 11th to the 15th century. The city was a stronghold of Napoleon I after his return from Elba in 1815. The winter Olympic Games were held there in 1968. LAWRENCE M. SOMMERS

Grenville, George [gren'-vil]

George Grenville, b. Oct. 14, 1712, d. Nov. 13, 1770, chief minister of Great Britain from 1763 to 1765, set Britain's American colonies on the road to the American Revolution by imposing the Sugar Act of 1764 and the STAMP ACT of 1765. Entering parliament in 1741, he held various ministerial offices before succeeding the earl of Bute (1713–92) as chief minister. His prosecution of John WILKES, as well as his taxation of the colonies, provoked much criticism from reformers. In addition, he alienated King GEORGE III by his autocratic manner and was forced to resign.

Grenville, Sir Richard

Sir Richard Grenville, b. *c.*1542, d. Sept. 12, 1591, was an English naval hero in the service of Queen Elizabeth I. He was a cousin of Sir Walter Raleigh, and in 1585 he led the expedition that founded Raleigh's "Lost Colony" on Roanoke Island, N.C. In 1591, Grenville joined an English fleet intending to intercept Spanish treasure ships off the Azores. His ship, the *Revenge*, was separated from the rest and forced to engage a Spanish war fleet by itself. Grenville fought a 15-hour battle, but he was mortally wounded and his ship was captured.

Gresham's law [gresh'-uhm]

In economics, Gresham's law observes that "bad money drives out good"—in effect, that "good" money (coins made from gold or silver) will be hoarded or melted down for its metal when the value of that metal rises higher than the nominal value of the coins. Although named for Sir Thomas Gresham (1517–79), an English banker and merchant, the "law" had been stated as early as the 14th century and was restated by Copernicus in 1526.

Gressley, Amanz [gres'-lee, ah'-mahnts]

Amanz Gressley, b. July 17, 1814, d. Apr. 13, 1865, was a Swiss geologist whose work in the Jura Mountains led to development of key principles in modern STRATIGRAPHY. He is now recognized as one of the founders of the science of PALEOGEOGRAPHY on the basis of his reconstruction of the ancient environments in which facies, or different rock formations, developed. The naturalist Louis Agassiz hired Gressley as an assistant at the Musée de Neuchâtel. There Gressley concentrated on a study of sedimentary facies. When Agassiz went to the United States in 1846 he took with him much of the extensive collection of fossils his assistant had assembled, and Gressley turned to the more practical work of surveying Alpine railroad tunnels. ANNE MILLBROOKE

Grétry, André [gray-tree']

The Belgian composer André Ernest Modeste Grétry, b. Feb. 11, 1741, d. Sept. 24, 1813, was the chief composer of French opera of his generation. He studied (1759–66) in Rome, and in 1768 he began to produce operas in Paris, becoming one of the original members (1795) of the Institut de France. Most of his operas are examples of *opéra comique*, the further development of which he greatly influenced. His most successful opera was *Richard Coeur de Lion* (1784). He also wrote symphonies, sonatas, and church music.

Gretzky, Wayne

The Canadian professional ice hockey player Wayne "The Kid" Gretzky, b. Brantford, Ontario, Jan. 26, 1961, entered the National Hockey League (NHL) in 1979–80 and quickly became one of its best players ever. A center for the Edmonton Oilers (1979–88) and Los Angeles Kings (1988–), Gretzky won the league MVP award in nine of his first ten seasons and in his third set NHL season records for goals (92), assists (120), and points (212). Subsequently, he had 163 (1986) assists, combining with 52 goals for a new seasonal point record, 215. In all, he holds about 50 NHL records. The Oilers won the Stanley Cup in 1984, 1985, 1987, and 1988.

Greuze, Jean Baptiste [gruz]

Jean Baptiste Greuze, b. Aug. 21, 1725, d. Mar. 21, 1805, was a fashionable late-18th-century painter of anecdotal genre scenes and portraits (see GENRE PAINTING). After early training in Lyon, Greuze studied at the Royal Academy in Paris and the French Academy in Rome. He first exhibited at the Paris Salon in 1755 and won immediate acclaim for *The Father Reading the Bible to His Children* (1755; Louvre, Paris), a painting whose sentimental morality is typical of his style. Espousing the philosophy of Jean Jacques Rousseau, who believed that the purpose of art is to inculcate moral virtue, Greuze strained to convey platitudinous morality through his scenes of everyday life. Paintings such as *The Paralytic Cared for by His Children* (1763; The Hermitage, Leningrad) and *Young Girl Weeping over Her Dead Bird* (1765; National Gallery of Scotland, Edinburgh) were widely sought after at the time but find few admirers today. Greuze's many paintings of girls now seem repellently contrived and even prurient, obscuring his genuine talent, which is evident in forceful portraits such as *Etienne Jeaurat* (1769; Louvre, Paris).

Greuze's popularity dwindled abruptly during the French Revolution, when the neoclassical theories of Jacques Louis DAVID caused a reversal in French taste.

HOWARD BATCHELOR

Bibliography: Brookner, Anita, *Greuze: The Rise and Fall of an Eighteenth-Century Phenomenon* (1972); Schwarz, Michael, *The Age of Rococo*, trans. by Gerald Onn (1971).

Greville, Fulke, 1st Baron Brooke [grev'-il, fulk]

Fulke Greville, b. Oct. 3, 1554, was a noble and austere English poet and the author of a biography (1652) of his friend Sir Phillip Sidney, a work that contains a fine portrait of Queen Elizabeth I. His poems, included in *Certaine Learned and Elegant Works* (1633), have mainly religious, philosophical, and political themes. Greville also wrote a political tragedy, *Mustapha* (1609). He was killed by a servant on Sept. 30, 1628.

ROBIN BUSS

Bibliography: Rees, Joan, *Fulke Greville, Lord Brooke, 1554-1628* (1971).

Grew, Nehemiah [groo, nee-uh-my'-uh]

Nehemiah Grew, b. September 1641, d. Mar. 25, 1712, an English botanist and physician, observed and described the reproductive structures in plants and noted that pollen is produced by the stamen, or male organ. He wrote a book on the gastrointestinal systems of several animals and was the first to use the phrase "comparative anatomy."

Grey, Albert Henry George Grey, 4th Earl

Albert Henry George Grey, b. Nov. 28, 1851, d. Aug. 29, 1917, was a British administrator who served (1904-11) as governor-general of Canada. A Liberal, he sat (1880-86) in the British House of Commons before succeeding to his earldom (1894). He also served (1896-97) as administrator of Rhodesia. In Canada, Grey was extremely popular as governor-general, and a Canadian football trophy, the Grey Cup, bears his name.

Grey, Charles Grey, 2d Earl

The British statesman Lord Grey, b. Mar. 13, 1764, d. July 17, 1845, though briefly foreign secretary (1806), is chiefly remembered as the prime minister who secured passage of the first REFORM ACT (1832). He had advocated electoral reform from the 1790s and, inheriting the mantle of Charles James FOX, was regarded for a quarter of a century as the leader of the Whig reformers.

When the duke of WELLINGTON's rejection of parliamentary reform brought the fall of his ministry in 1830, Grey formed a government that incorporated Canningite Tories—though he had despised the lowborn George CANNING—as well as Whigs. Lacking a majority in the House of Commons for his Reform Bill, he secured one by a new general election (1831) and then induced WILLIAM IV to create enough new peers to pass the measure in the House of Lords. Ancillary reforms followed, but Grey, anxious to retire to his country estate, took advantage of a crisis over Irish affairs to resign in 1834.

DONALD SOUTHGATE

Bibliography: Trevelyan, G. M., *Lord Grey of the Reform Bill* (1920; repr. 1971).

Grey, Sir Edward

Sir Edward Grey, b. Apr. 25, 1862, d. Sept. 7, 1933, was foreign minister (1905-16) of Great Britain in the years preceding World War I. A Liberal, he continued the policies, begun by the Conservatives, of cooperation with France, authorizing secret military talks, and standing by France in the MOROCCAN CRISES of 1905 and 1912. In 1907 he concluded an entente with Russia (see TRIPLE ENTENTE). In August 1914, Grey persuaded the hesitant British cabinet that Britain should enter the war because of the German violation of Belgian neutrality. Created 1st Viscount Grey of Fallodon in 1916, he was later a strong supporter of the League of Nations.

Bibliography: Hinsley, F. H., ed., *British Foreign Policy Under Sir Edward Grey* (1977); Trevelyan, G. M., *Grey of Fallodon* (1937; repr. 1948).

Grey, Sir George

George Grey, b. Apr. 4, 1812, d. Sept. 19, 1898, was a British colonial administrator in Australia and New Zealand. After a military career in England, he led (1837-38 and 1839) two exploratory expeditions to northwestern Australia. He remained as resident magistrate and was appointed (1841) colonial governor of South Australia, where he rescued the colony from disaster by vigorous economies.

As governor of New Zealand (1845), Grey successfully suppressed the rebellious Maoris. He was knighted in 1848 and appointed governor of Cape Colony in 1854. An advocate of federation for the South African colonies, he was recalled for disobeying instructions and sent again to New Zealand in 1861 to end the new Maori uprising. After quarreling with the military and again defying instructions he was dismissed in 1868. Later, returning to New Zealand, he sat in Parliament for 20 years and was prime minister from 1877-79. Although autocratic in manner, Grey was politically liberal and a patron of education. His writings include *Polynesian Mythology and Ancient Traditional History of the New Zealand Race* (1855).

E. J. TAPP

Bibliography: Rutherford, James, *Sir George Grey, K.C.B. 1812-1898* (1961).

Grey, Lady Jane

Lady Jane Grey became the "nine days' queen" of England in 1553. She was only 15 when she was proclaimed queen—at the instigation of her father-in-law, the duke of Northumberland—on the death of Edward VI. Within a few days the supporters of Edward's sister Mary I gained control, and Jane was charged with high treason. She was beheaded.

Lady Jane Grey, b. October 1537, d. Feb. 12, 1554, was queen of England for nine days in 1553. She was a great-granddaughter of HENRY VII and a cousin of EDWARD VI. Shortly before his death, Edward was persuaded to name Jane his successor in preference to his half-sisters Mary and Elizabeth. John Dudley, duke of NORTHUMBERLAND, who dominated the government, arranged Jane's marriage to his son Lord Guildford Dudley and proclaimed her accession in July 1553, but few supported this scheme, and Mary Tudor soon secured the throne as MARY I. Jane and Guildford were charged with treason and beheaded. Widely praised for her beauty and learning, Jane was not herself a conspirator but rather an innocent victim of a political plot.

STANFORD E. LEHMBERG

Bibliography: Chapman, Hester W., *Lady Jane Grey* (1963); Malvern, Gladys, *The World of Lady Jane Grey* (1964).

Grey, Zane

The author of about 60 western adventure stories, Zane Grey, b. Zanesville, Ohio, Jan. 31, 1872, d. Oct. 23, 1939, remains popular for his formulaic novels pitting strong, independent heroes against dastardly opponents. Starting with *The Spirit of the Border* (1905), Grey produced a long line of best-sellers that easily lent themselves to film and, later, television adapta-

Zane Grey, an American writer of adventure stories, abandoned a career in dentistry when his action-filled novels about life in the Wild West became best-sellers. An avid outdoorsman, he also wrote nonfiction works on camping and game fishing.

tion. Strong in local color, if weak in characterization, his greatest successes include *The Last of the Plainsmen* (1908) and *Riders of the Purple Sage* (1912).

Bibliography: Farley, G. M., *Zane Grey* (1985).

greyhound

The greyhound is a breed of dog that was known in both ancient Egypt and Greece. Greyhound types were known in the British Isles by the 9th century AD.

This dog has been used to run down many kinds of small game, primarily hare. Since 1776, when the first known dog coursing club was founded at Swaffham, Norfolk, in England, the greyhound has been valued as a coursing dog. Greyhound racing became popular after 1876.

A large breed, measuring up to 76 cm (30 in) at the shoulder and weighing about 32 kg (70 lb), the greyhound is considered to be the epitome of elegance and grace among canines. A greyhound is smooth-coated, any color being acceptable, and has small, folded ears, and a long, down-carried tail. Its roached back assists the dog in galloping flat out. A greyhound is both very fast and extremely agile. It can be raised as a gentle and well-mannered house dog.

JOHN MANDEVILLE

Bibliography: Freund, J. L., *Greyhound Champions: 1952–1986* (1987).

The greyhound is one of the oldest breeds of dog. With its highly developed sense of sight and its sleek, smooth-coated body and long legs adapted for speed, it is popular for coursing, racing, and show.

greyhound racing: see DOG RACING.

gribble [grib'-ul]

Gribbles, genus *Limnoria,* are marine isopod crustaceans in the family Limnoriidae, suborder Flabellifera, that live on submerged wood. About 5 mm (0.2 in) long, they are known to have destroyed the wooden hulls of ships, bridge piles, and wharfs by burrowing at close intervals. Gribbles digest wood with the help of an intestinal enzyme that breaks down the polysaccharide cellulose, an important constituent of cell walls.

Griboyedov, Aleksandr Sergeyevich [greeb-uh-yed'-uhf, uhl-yik-sahn'-dur sir-gay'-uh-vich]

Aleksandr Sergeyevich Griboyedov, b. Jan. 15, 1795, d. Feb. 11, 1829, a Russian playwright and diplomat, is best remembered for his brilliant satirical comedy *The Misfortune of Being Clever* (1833; Eng. trans., 1914). Written in lively verse and pungent dialogue, the play attacks the conservatism of the contemporary Russian aristocracy. Several lines from the play have entered Russian speech as common expressions.

Griboyedov was a professional diplomat with extensive service in the Near East. In 1828 he became the Russian ambassador to Persia and the following year was murdered in Tehran by an enraged anti-Russian mob.

HAROLD B. SEGEL

grid

The grid of an ELECTRON TUBE is a metal ELECTRODE located between the tube's CATHODE, or filament, and its anode, or plate. This basic configuration constitutes a TRIODE. A voltage applied to the grid establishes an electrostatic field that controls the flow of electrons from the cathode to the plate, making the tube an AMPLIFIER. If a varying voltage is applied to the grid, the resulting current between the cathode and plate is an amplified version of the grid voltage. When a sufficiently negative voltage (called the grid-cutoff voltage) is applied to the grid, the cathode-plate current vanishes. This switching effect is the basis of operation of the thyratron.

The term *grid* also refers to a network of electrical conductors such as that which comprises a telephone or power distribution system. Local and regional grids may be interconnected with one another to form even more complex national grids.

FORREST M. MIMS, III

Grieg, Edvard [greeg, ed'-var]

Edvard Hagerup Grieg, b. Bergen, June 15, 1843, d. Sept. 4, 1907, was Norway's greatest composer. At the suggestion of the famous violinist Ole Bull he went to study in Leipzig (1858–62). An attack of pleurisy in 1860 undermined his health for the rest of his life. He worked (1863–66) with Niels Gade and Johann Peter Hartmann in Copenhagen, where he developed his interest in Norwegian folk music. Upon his return (1866) to Norway he conducted a successful concert in Christiana (Oslo) that led to his appointment there as conductor of the Harmonic Society.

The following year he founded the Norwegian Academy of Music and also married his cousin Nina Hagerup, an accomplished singer. An annual grant from the Norwegian government, commencing in 1874, enabled him to give most of his time to composition, and he returned to Bergen. There he became conductor (1880–82) of the Bergen Harmonic Society, the last such position he held. Throughout his life he traveled extensively, associating with the most celebrated musicians of his time, notably Franz Liszt, Richard Wagner, Gabriel Fauré, and Claude Debussy.

Grieg generally worked within the traditions of German romanticism—as represented by Felix Mendelssohn and Robert Schumann—which he absorbed in Leipzig. His chief works include the piano sonata in E minor (1865), the piano concerto in A minor (1868), the *Holberg Suite* (1884), and several

The Norwegian composer Edvard Grieg, much admired for his art songs, accompanies his wife, singer Nina Hagerup Grieg, a leading interpreter of them. Using Norwegian folk music, Grieg infused his compositions with a romantic nationalism and rich lyricism, which has made them very popular with critics and public alike.

works of chamber music. The piano concerto is modeled on Schumann's work in that form. Grieg, however, was essentially a miniaturist, as can be inferred from songs and solo piano pieces, particularly the 10 books of *Lyric Pieces.* His elegiac melodies, with their chromatic harmonic accompaniments, are characteristic of his style.

Of prime significance is Grieg's involvement with Norwegian folk music, which determined the character of much of his music. The largest and best-known work in this category is the incidental music for Ibsen's *Peer Gynt* (1874–75). Other works include the "Ballade in the Form of Variations on a Norwegian Folk Song" (1875) and arrangements of songs and dances, including the "Slåtter" (1902), in which the sound of the Hardanger fiddle (a Norwegian folk instrument) is ingeniously imitated on the piano. F. E. KIRBY

Bibliography: Abraham, G., ed., *Grieg: A Symposium* (1948; repr. 1972); Finck, H. T., *Grieg and His Music* (1929; repr. 1971); Horton, J., *Grieg* (1974); Monrad-Johansen, D., *Edvard Grieg,* trans. by M. Robinson (1938; repr. 1945); Schjedlerup-Ebbe, D., *Edvard Grieg, 1858–1867* (1964).

Grieg, Nordahl Brun [nor'-dahl broon]

Johan Nordahl Brun Grieg, b. Nov. 1, 1902, d. Dec. 2, 1943, was a Norwegian writer, seaman, war correspondent, and patriot. Influenced by Rudyard Kipling, Johannes V. Jensen, and the romantic mythos of "young death" represented in the works of Percy Bysshe Shelley and Rupert Brooke, Grieg conveyed a strong lyrical sense and social conscience in the book of poems *Rundt Kap det Gode Haab* (Around the Cape of Good Hope, 1922) and the vivid sea novel *The Ship Sails On* (1924; Eng. trans., 1927)—perhaps his best works. He embraced communism, but after living in the USSR (1933–34) rejected it. His novel *Men ung må verden ennu vaere* (But the World Must Be Young, 1938) refutes Stalinism. Influenced by Russian theater and film, he dramatized class conflict in such epic plays as *The Defeat* (1937; Eng. trans., 1945), which deals with the rise and fall of the Paris Commune. RAYMOND JARVI

Grierson, John

Scottish filmmaker John Grierson, b. Apr. 26, 1898, d. Feb. 19, 1972, was—more than any other person—responsible for the growth of the DOCUMENTARY film as a medium for social analysis and as an art form. In 1927, Grierson persuaded the Empire Marketing Board (EMB) that such films could illustrate in a most positive way the life and work of Britain's people. Grierson set up the EMB Film Unit as a group effort involving some of the most talented filmmakers of the day. Although Grierson himself made only one film (*The Drifters,* 1929, a study of fishermen in the North Sea), others in the unit made a series of fascinating films on such unlikely subjects as salmon fishing, harvesting bananas, and English markets.

In 1933 the EMB Film Unit was replaced by a group working through the General Post Office (GPO). Here, Grierson and his colleagues made two sound masterpieces, *Song of Ceylon* (1934) and *Night Mail* (1936), the latter with music by Benjamin Britten and a verse narrative by W. H. Auden. Grierson's reviews and essays were widely influential; many were collected in *Grierson on Documentary* (1947).

grievance procedure

A grievance procedure, an important aspect of INDUSTRIAL RELATIONS, provides a way of settling disputes between workers and their employers. Individual employees or committees of workers may seek redress of grievances by following specified methods within their department or company. If talks between labor and management cannot settle a dispute, an outside mediator or arbitrator may be consulted. Arbitration became the normal method of settling disputes in the United States after Congress passed (1935) the National Labor Relations Act, which obligated employers to bargain collectively with their employees. Grievance procedures have become a part of most collective bargaining agreements.

Bibliography: International Labour Office, *Grievance Arbitration* (1982).

Griffes, Charles Tomlinson [grif'-is]

Charles Tomlinson Griffes, b. Elmira, N.Y., Sept. 17, 1884, d. Apr. 8, 1920, was an American composer best known for his impressionist orchestral works and piano pieces. As a young man he studied piano and composition in Berlin. He returned to the United States in 1907 and taught music at the Hackley School for Boys in Tarrytown, N.Y., until his death. His best-known piano work is the *Four Roman Sketches* (1915–16), the first one being the familiar *White Peacock.* His most important orchestral work, *The Pleasure Dome of Kubla Khan* (1920), was based on the Samuel Taylor Coleridge poem. Griffes also wrote stage works, chamber music, and songs.

Bibliography: Anderson, D. K., *The Works of C. T. Griffes* (1983); Maisel, Edward M., *Charles T. Griffes* (1943; repr. 1984).

griffin [grif'-in]

In Greek mythology, the griffin was a creature with the body of a lion and the head and wings of an eagle. Griffins drew the chariot of the sun; they also guarded a golden treasure that the Arimaspians, a one-eyed Scythian people, tried to steal. Griffins probably originated in Indo-Iranian mythology.

Griffin, Marion Mahony

Marion Mahony, 1871–1961, was one of the first women to graduate from the School of Architecture at Massachusetts Institute of Technology and was the first woman licensed to practice architecture in Illinois. She worked as a collaborative designer with Frank Lloyd WRIGHT on many of his prairie-style homes (see PRAIRIE SCHOOL) in the early 20th century. The famous monograph on Wright's work, published (1910) by Wasmuth in Berlin, contained a great body of drawings, half of which are attributed to Mahony. In 1911, Mahony married a fellow architect in Wright's office, Walter Burley Griffin.
RONALD WIEDENHOEFT

Bibliography: Brooks, H. A., *Frank Lloyd Wright and the Prairie School* (1984); Torre, Susana, ed., *Women in American Architecture* (1977).

Griffin, Walter Burley

Walter Burley Griffin, b. Maywood, Ill., Nov. 24, 1876, d. Feb. 11, 1937, was a member of the PRAIRIE SCHOOL of architecture, which flourished in the Midwest in the early 20th century. After studying architecture ar the University of Illinois, he served as Frank Lloyd Wright's assistant from 1901 to 1906. He then established his own practice in Chicaco, and foremost among his commissions was the Rock Crest-Rock Glen development in Mason City, Iowa (begun 1912). In 1912, Griffin won the competition for the commission to plan the new Australian capital of CANBERRA. He worked in Australia from 1914 to 1936, when he went to India.

Bibliography: Birrell, James, *Walter Burley Griffin* (1964); Peisch, Mark, *The Chicago School of Architecture* (1964).

Griffith, Arthur

Arthur Griffith, b. Mar. 31, 1872, d. Aug. 12, 1922, founded (1905) the Irish nationalist party SINN FEIN and was president (1922) of the Irish Free State. One of the more moderate nationalist leaders, Griffith took no part in the EASTER RISING (1916), but he joined other Sinn Fein members in establishing the Irish legislature, Dáil Éireann, in 1918. He helped negotiate (1921) the treaty that created the Irish Free State and, although not satisfied with it, became president under its terms in January 1922. He died soon after the outbreak of the Irish civil war.

Griffith, D. W.

David Lewelyn Wark Griffith, b. La Grange, Ky., Jan. 23, 1875, d. July 23, 1948, is recognized as the greatest single film director and most consistently innovative artist of the early American film industry. His influence on the development of cinema was worldwide.

After gaining experience with a Louisville stock company, he was employed as an actor and writer by the Biograph Film Company of New York in 1907. The following year he was offered a director-producer contract and, for the next five years, oversaw the production of more than 400 one- and two-reel films. As his ideas grew bolder, however, he felt increasingly frustrated by the limitations imposed by his employers. Griffith left Biograph in 1913 to join Reliance-Majestic as head of production, and in 1914, he began his most famous film, based on the novel *The Clansman* by Thomas Dixon. This Civil War Reconstruction epic, known as *The Birth of a Nation* (1915), became a landmark in American filmmaking, both for its artistic merits and for its unprecedented use of such innovative techniques as flashbacks, fade-outs, and close-ups. The film was harshly condemned, however, for its racial bias and glorification of the Ku Klux Klan; several subsequent lynchings were blamed on the film. In response to this criticism, Griffith made what many consider his finest film, *Intolerance* (1916), in which the evils of intolerance were depicted in four parallel stories—a framework that required a scope of vision and production never before approached.

Although Griffith made numerous other films up to 1931, none ranked with his first two classics. Among the best of these later efforts were *Hearts of the World* (1918); *Broken Blossoms* (1919), released by his own newly formed corporation, United Artists; *Way Down East* (1920); *Orphans of the Storm* (1922); *America* (1924); *Isn't Life Wonderful?* (1924);

The American film director D. W. Griffith (left) appears here with Billy Bitzer, his cameraman, during the filming of The Birth of a Nation *(1915), one of Griffith's most acclaimed films. Griffith's pioneering techniques, which included montage, cross-cutting, and tracking shots, greatly influenced the development of cinema into an art form.*

Griffith's Intolerance *(1916) was an epic of spectacular proportions, as may be seen in this scene of Belshazzar's feast from one of the Babylonian sequences. Although a critical and financial failure at the time,* Intolerance *is now considered one of the finest silent films.*

and *Abraham Lincoln* (1930). Of the many actors trained by Griffith and associated with his name, Mary PICKFORD, Dorothy and Lillian GISH, and Lionel Barrymore (see BARRYMORE family) are the most famous. In 1935, Griffith was honored by the Academy of Motion Picture Arts and Sciences with a special award.

Bibliography: Barry, Iris, *D. W. Griffith, American Film Master* (1940); Brown, Karl, *Adventures with D. W. Griffith* (1976); Geduld, Harry M., ed., *Focus on D. W. Griffith* (1971); Gish, Lillian, *Lillian Gish: The Movies, Mr. Griffith and Me* (1969); Henderson, Robert M., *D. W. Griffith: His Life and Work* (1972) and *D. W. Griffith: The Years at Biograph* (1970); O'Dell, Paul, *Griffith and the Rise of Hollywood* (1970); Wagenknecht, Edward C., *The Films of D. W. Griffith* (1975).

Grignard, Victor [green-yar', veek-tor']

The French chemist François Auguste Victor Grignard, b. May 16, 1871, d. Dec. 13, 1935, developed a method for using magnesium as a catalyst in organic synthesis. He became assistant to P. A. Barbier, with whom he published his first paper on the reactions of organomagnesium compounds in anhydrous ether (1901). The active agent that he discovered, known as the Grignard reagent, has a hydrocarbon group and a halogen attached to magnesium. It is highly reactive and is one of the most versatile reagents used in organic synthesis. For this work, Grignard was awarded the Nobel Prize for chemistry in 1912. VIRGINIA F. MCCONNELL

Grignard reagents

The reaction discovered by Victor Grignard yields a class of organic magnesium compounds remarkable in their versatility in many organic syntheses. These Grignard reagents are prepared by reacting magnesium metal with an organic halogen compound, RX. The exact structure of the product is still uncertain and is usually represented as RMgX. The reaction is carried out in ether, which not only serves as a solvent but is believed to be a component of the final product. Grignard reagents are too reactive to store and must be used immediately. The most important use of Grignard reagents is in reactions with carbonyl compounds to form new carbon-carbon bonds. Addition of carbon dioxide, aldehydes, ketones, and

$$\underset{\text{ethyl bromide}}{CH_3CH_2Br} + Mg \rightarrow \underset{\text{ethyl magnesium bromide}}{CH_3CH_2MgBr}$$

$$\underset{\text{ethyl magnesium bromide}}{CH_3CH_2MgBr} + \underset{\text{ethylene oxide}}{CH_2 \overset{O}{-} CH_2} \rightarrow CH_3CH_2CH_2CH_2OMgBr$$

$$CH_3CH_2CH_2CH_2MgBr + H_2O \rightarrow \underset{n\text{-butyl alcohol}}{CH_3CH_2CH_2CH_2OH} + MgBrOH$$

ethylene oxide leads to a lengthening of the original carbon chain, and the alcohol thus formed can be converted to the corresponding hydrocarbon, halide, carboxylic acid, or other derivative. Reviewed by JOHN TURKEVICH

Bibliography: Roberts, John D., and Caserio, Marjorie C., *Basic Principles of Organic Chemistry,* 2d ed. (1977).

Grigorovich, Dmitry Vasilievich [grig-uh-roh'-vich, duh-meet'-ree vuh-seel'-yeh-vich]

Dmitry Vasilievich Grigorovich, b. Mar. 31 (N.S.), 1822, d. Jan. 3 (N.S.), 1900, was a Russian author and art historian known for his sympathetic depiction of peasant life in imperial Russia. His short novel *Derevnya* (The Village, 1846) and tales such as *Anton Goremyka* (1847) and *The Fishermen* (1853; Eng. trans., 1916), published in the *Annals of the Fatherland* and the *Contemporary,* won him literary fame. Within his collected work, several volumes contain articles on the history and theory of art. His *Literary Reminiscences* (1892–93) contains valuable biographical material on his friend Fyodor Dostoyevsky and other leading Russian literary figures of the mid-19th century. RALPH E. MATLAW

Grigorovich, Yury Nikolayevich [yoo'-ree neek-uh-ly'-uh-vich]

Yury Nikolayevich Grigorovich, b. Jan. 2, 1927, is a leading contemporary Soviet choreographer and teacher. He graduated from the Leningrad Choreographic School in 1946 and joined the Kirov Ballet, where he choreographed a new version of Sergei Prokofiev's *The Stone Flower* (1957). He was appointed artistic director and chief choreographer of the Bolshoi Ballet in 1964. His works include *Spartacus* (1968) and *Ivan the Terrible* (1975) as well as revised versions of the classics. As a guest choreographer at the Paris Opéra he has mounted *Ivan the Terrible* and, in 1977, a new version of Prokofiev's *Romeo and Juliet.* He is married to the ballerina Natalia Bessmertnova. DAVID VAUGHAN

Grillparzer, Franz [gril'-part-sur, frahnts]

Franz Grillparzer, b. Jan. 15, 1791, d. Jan. 21, 1872, is generally considered one of the greatest Austrian poetic dramatists. During much of his life Grillparzer worked (1814–56) as a civil servant, but his dramatic output of 12 tragedies and one comedy represents the foundation of Austrian high drama. Grillparzer's unhappy childhood and adult life infused his work with a sense of gloom and melancholy, and the censorship and harsh criticism that greeted his plays only added to his severe psychological instability.

His first play, *Die Ahnfrau* (The Ancestress, 1817), was a tragedy of fate written in verse. Like many of his dramas, it represented characters in conflict with warring emotions. *Sappho* (1818; Eng. trans., 1953) followed. His trilogy *The Golden Fleece* (1821; Eng. trans., 1942), written soon after Grillparzer's mother committed suicide in 1819, is a pessimistic and open-ended version of the Medea story. Two later tragedies, *King Ottocar, His Rise and Fall* (1825; Eng. trans., 1953) and *The Waves of Sea and Love* (1831; Eng. trans., 1947), are particularly noted for their probing psychological insight and near-perfect dramatic form. Among his final works, however, *The Jewess of Toledo* (1855; Eng. trans., 1953) and *Family Strife in Habsburg* (1855; Eng. trans., 1940) perhaps best represent in mythical and dramatic terms Grillparzer's own personal strife. CARL R. MUELLER

Bibliography: Wells, G. A., *The Plays of Grillparzer* (1969); Yates, Douglas, *Franz Grillparzer: A Critical Biography* (1946; repr. 1980).

See also: AUSTRIAN LITERATURE.

Grimaldi, Francesco Maria [gree-mahl'-dee]

The Italian physicist Francesco Maria Grimaldi, b. Apr. 2, 1618, d. Dec. 28, 1663, is best known for his discovery of the phenomenon of optical DIFFRACTION and for his wave theory of light. A Jesuit who was professor of philosophy at Bologna, Grimaldi described his optical experiments in *De lumine* (1665). First, he noticed that shadows are larger than they ought to be if light travels in straight lines. Secondly, he observed that the edges of shadows are bordered by colored bands. This led him to suggest that light moves in waves like a fine fluid, with different velocities representing different colors. Grimaldi also did work in astronomy with G. B. RICCIOLI. He measured the heights of lunar mountains, constructed one of the earliest lunar maps, and instituted the practice of naming lunar features after eminent scientists.

CATHERINE WILSON

Grimaldi, Joseph [grim-al'-dee]

Joseph Grimaldi, b. Dec. 18, 1778, d. May 31, 1837, was an English comic singer, dancer, mime, and sometime actor in melodramas. He was famous above all for his creation of Clown, the white-faced, grotesquely costumed character who figured prominently in the English harlequinade as performed by Grimaldi at London theaters between 1800 and 1823. In England Grimaldi's nickname "Joey" is to this day synonymous with "clown." After an illustrious career he was forced into early retirement by a crippling disease. A. H. SAXON

Bibliography: Dickens, Charles, *Memoirs of Joseph Grimaldi,* ed. by Richard Findlater (1968); Findlater, Richard, *Grimaldi, King of Clowns* (1955) and *Joe Grimaldi: His Life and Theatre* (1979).

Grimaldi man

In the late 19th and early 20th centuries, 14 prehistoric human skeletons, collectively referred to as Grimaldi man, were unearthed in caves outside of the village of Grimaldi, Italy, near the French border. Found in graves filled with stone and bone tools of the Upper Paleolithic AURIGNACIAN tradition, the skeletons, which belong to the species *Homo sapiens sapiens,* were sprinkled with red ocher and decorated with jewelry made of shell and animal bones. Excavators discovered traces of an animal pelt surrounding one individual. The Grimaldi burials date to the latter part of the Pleistocene Epoch, about 20,000 years ago.

At the time of their discovery, the Grimaldi specimens were thought to possess many physical characteristics similar to those of present-day populations of Africa. More recent analyses of the bones and other fossil discoveries indicate that the Grimaldi skeletons are representative of a physical type not markedly different from that of Mediterranean peoples inhabiting the region today. ALAN MANN AND NANCY MINUGH

Bibliography: Howells, William W., *Evolution of the Genus Homo* (1973).

Grimes Graves [grymz grayvz]

Grimes Graves is the site of the largest known Neolithic flint mine in Britain (see CHERTS AND FLINTS). Radiocarbon dating indicates that the site flourished in the late 3d millennium BC, with intermittent Bronze Age settlement thereafter until about 1700 BC. It is located some 8 km (5 mi) northwest of Thetford, in Norfolk, and covers an area of 35–40 ha (87–99 acres), within which approximately 500 mine shafts have been recognized. Some shafts are relatively shallow; others are sunk to depths of 13 m (43 ft), evidently depending upon the depth of the flint bed. From the base of the deeper shafts, side galleries have been discovered along which the miners apparently followed the productive beds rather than engage in the labor of excavating new shafts. Lateral post-sockets indicate that timber staging was built in order to remove flint and waste materials from the mines.

Artifacts at the site include picks, principally of deer antler, as well as axes of flint or other stone. Primitive chalk lamps and torches were probably used to illuminate the galleries, and in one a votive deposit had been placed before a small altar of flint.

DENNIS W. HARDING

Grimké, Sarah Moore and Angelina Emily [grim'-kee]

Angelina Emily (left) and Sarah Moore (right) Grimké were American abolitionists and pioneers in the women's rights movement. They rejected a life of Southern gentility to become outspoken reformers and campaigners for the enfranchisement of women and slaves.

Sarah Moore Grimké, and her sister, Angelina Emily, were American ABOLITIONISTS and pioneers of women's rights. Born in Charleston, S.C., on Nov. 26, 1792, and Feb. 20, 1805, respectively, they were temperamentally rebellious and soon became sensitive to the injustices of slavery. Sarah's conversion to Quakerism led her to leave (1821) the South for Philadelphia, where she was joined (1829) by Angelina. As lecturers for the American Anti-Slavery Society (1836-38), they told of the abuses in a system that they had experienced firsthand and drew audiences numbering in the thousands.

The sisters expanded their interests to include social justice for women after they were criticized for addressing audiences that included both sexes. Angelina's *Letters to Catherine Beecher in Reply to an Essay on Slavery and Abolitionism* and Sarah's *Letters on the Equality of the Sexes, and the Condition of Woman*, both published in 1838, constituted perhaps the first written advocacy for women's rights in the United States. After Angelina's marriage (1838) to the abolitionist Theodore WELD, the sisters withdrew from the lecture circuit and turned their attention to education. But until Sarah's death on Dec. 23, 1873, and Angelina's six years later on Oct. 26, 1879, they retained their interest in and concern for reform.

LORETTA ELLEN ZIMMERMAN

Bibliography: Barnes, Gilbert H., and Dumond, Dwight L., eds., *Letters of Theodore Dwight Weld, Angelina Grimké Weld, and Sarah Grimké, 1822-1844*, 2 vols. (1934); Birney, Catherine H., *The Grimké Sisters* (1885; repr. 1969); Lerner, Gerda, *The Grimke Sisters from South Carolina* (1967).

Grimm, Jacob and Wilhelm [grim, yah'-kohp, vil'-helm]

Although the Grimm brothers, Jacob, b. Jan. 4, 1785, d. Sept. 20, 1863, and Wilhelm, b. Feb. 24, 1786, d. Dec. 16, 1859, were largely responsible for establishing such philological studies as folklore, comparative and historical linguistics, lexicography, and the scholarly editing of older texts on a scientific basis, they are more widely remembered as the authors of GRIMM'S FAIRY TALES. These stories—collected mostly from oral sources—were first published in German as *Kinder- und Hausmärchen* (2 vols., 1812-15) and have since been translated into innumerable languages, sometimes faithfully, sometimes in adapted form. The most famous tales were contained in the original volumes, but the Grimms continually revised and expanded the collection so that it eventually contained a total of 210 tales. A third volume of scholarly commentary, published in 1822, did not become a permanent part of the work.

The brothers lived and worked together virtually throughout their lives. Jacob remained a bachelor, but Wilhelm married and had children. Jacob was the more prolific and scholarly brother, but Wilhelm had the greater poetic gift and was principally responsible for putting the *Fairy Tales* in their published form. Although Wilhelm's only major scholarly treatise was *Die deutsche Heldensage* (German Heroic Legends, 1829), he collaborated with Jacob on many scholarly projects, most notably the *Deutsches Wörterbuch* (German Dictionary). This work, the first installment of which appeared in 1852, established a norm for historical dictionaries in all languages, including the *Oxford English Dictionary*. The Grimms did not live to see the completion of this monumental undertaking, which was finished in 1960.

Among linguists Jacob is best remembered for GRIMM'S LAW, which provided a scientific explanation of the relation between consonants in the INDO-EUROPEAN LANGUAGES. Jacob's most important scholarly treatises were his *Deutsche Grammatik* (German Grammar, 4 vols., 1819-37), which systematically explained the relation of German to other Germanic and Indo-European languages; *Deutsche Rechtsaltertümer* (1828), a study of ancient Germanic law; *Deutsche Mythologie* (1835), which contrasted ancient Germanic beliefs and superstitions with those of Christianity and classical antiquity; and *Geschichte der deutschen Sprache* (History of the German Language, 2 vols., 1848).

In the post-Napoleonic years the Grimms served as librarians to the Elector of Hesse at Kassel, then left these positions to become faculty members at the University of Göttingen.

The German philologists and folklorists Jacob (right) and Wilhelm Grimm, best known for their compilation of folktales in Grimm's Fairy Tales *(1812-15), made major contributions to the study of the grammar, linguistics, and morphology of Germanic languages in their* Deutsches Wörterbuch *and Jacob's* Deutsche Grammatik *(1819-37). They appear here in a portrait by Elisabeth Jerichau-Bauman.*

Their tenure there (1830–37) was terminated after they joined five fellow professors in protesting the king of Hanover's abrogation of the constitution. The Grimms were subsequently appointed to the Prussian Academy of Sciences in Berlin, where they spent their remaining years. JAMES M. MCGLATHERY

Bibliography: Ellis, John, *One Fairy Story Too Many* (1983); Michaelis-Jena, Ruth, *The Brothers Grimm* (1970); Peppard, Murray, *Paths through the Forest: A Biography of the Brothers Grimm* (1971).

Grimm, Melchior, Baron von [mel'-kee-or]

A German diplomat and critic who lived in Paris, Friedrich Melchior von Grimm, b. Sept. 25, 1723, d. Dec. 19, 1807, was a friend of Rousseau and Diderot, and a key figure in the intellectual exchange between France and Germany before the French Revolution. The semimonthly newsletter of cultural and political affairs, which he wrote and edited for influential readers in Germany, Scandinavia, and Russia, is an invaluable source of information on every aspect of his age. His writings were collected in *Correspondance littéraire, philosophique et critique* (1877–82). JAMES M. MCGLATHERY

Grimmelshausen, Hans Jakob Christoffel von [grim'-ulz-how-zen, hahns yah'-kohp kris'-toh-fel fuhn]

Hans Jakob Christoffel von Grimmelshausen, b. *c.*1622, d. Aug. 17, 1676, was one of the most important 17th-century German writers of prose fiction. He spent his early years as a roving soldier and became a village mayor rather late in life. After the Thirty Years' War he anonymously published a cycle of novels, *Simplicianische Schriften.* Of these, *The Adventures of a Simpleton* (1669; Eng. trans., 1967) is the best known. Largely autobiographical, it is a picaresque parody of the then-fashionable adventure romance, depicting the motley career of an ignorant peasant who becomes a soldier of fortune in a gruesome war. Enormously popular in Grimmelshausen's day, it provided Bertolt Brecht with the central character for his play *Mother Courage.* HUGO BEKKER

Bibliography: Hayens, K. C., *Grimmelshausen* (1948); Negus, Kenneth, *H. J. C. Von Grimmelshausen* (1974).

Grimm's Fairy Tales [grimz]

Grimm's Fairy Tales (German, *Kinder- und Hausmärchen,* 1812–15) is a collection of German folk tales gathered by Jacob and Wilhelm GRIMM. Most of the tales (which include the adventures of such personages as Rapunzel, Hansel and Gretel, and Rumpelstiltskin) were derived from oral peasant narrations, and in the original publication many appeared in dialect. Although other German writers of the period had written their own *Kunstmärchen* (artistic fairy tales), Grimm's were the first to be drawn directly from folk sources and to have been transmuted into literature without degrading the originals. Translated into many languages (some had appeared in English by 1823), they have become an essential element of CHILDREN'S LITERATURE and have had a significant influence on folklore studies and on literature in general. The discovery of the unpublished manuscript of an additional Grimm's tale was announced in 1983.

Bibliography: Bettelheim, Bruno, *The Uses of Enchantment* (1976); Lüthi, Max, *Once Upon a Time: On the Nature of Fairy Tales,* trans. by L. Chadeayne and P. Gottwald (1970); Manheim, Ralph, trans., *Grimm's Tales for Young and Old* (1983); Segal, Lore, and Jarrell, Randall, trans., *The Juniper Tree and Other Tales from Grimm* (1973).

Grimm's law

To explain why the initial consonants of such words as Latin *piscis, dentis,* and *fundus* differ from those of their cognates fish, tooth, and bottom, Grimm's law states that in prehistoric times (1) the INDO-EUROPEAN voiceless stops *p, t,* and *k* became the GERMANIC fricatives *f, th,* and χ; (2) the voiced stops *b, d,* and *g* became the voiceless stops *p, t,* and *k*; and (3) the fricatives *bh, dh,* and *gh* became the voiced stops *b, d,* and *g.* Rasmus RASK came close to formulating these consonant shifts in 1814, but Jacob GRIMM made the decisive breakthrough in the second edition of his *Deutsche Grammatik* (1822). Working from the first part of Grimm's law, Karl Adolf VERNER was able to trace subsequent developments of the Germanic fricatives *f, th,* and χ. DAVID YERKES

Bibliography: Anderson, James M., *Structural Aspects of Language Change* (1973); Anttila, Raimo, *An Introduction to Historical and Comparative Linguistics* (1972); Lehmann, Winfred P., *Historical Linguistics,* 2d ed. (1973).

Grimsby [grimz'-bee]

Grimsby (1981 pop., 92,596) is a city and seaport in Humberside county in eastern England. It is located on the North Sea coast about 30 km (20 mi) southeast of Hull. Fishing, food processing, shipbuilding, and chemical manufacturing are the principal industries. Originally a Danish settlement, Grimsby grew rapidly during the 19th century after docks were constructed (1800) and the railroad arrived (1848).

Grindal, Edmund [grin'-dul]

Edmund Grindal, b. *c.*1519, d. July 6, 1583, was archbishop of Canterbury from 1576. A Puritan sympathizer, he sought a reformed episcopacy with close relationships between bishops and clergy. He had been chaplain to Edward VI and a canon of Westminster but was exiled by Mary I. During his exile, he sought to reconcile the party of John Knox with defenders of the 1552 Book of Common Prayer. Later, as archbishop of Canterbury, he refused to suppress Puritan prophesying and was suspended (1577) from his administrative duties by Elizabeth I. Although he was reinstated in 1582, no real reconciliation was ever achieved.

Bibliography: Collinson, Patrick, *The Elizabethan Puritan Movement* (1967).

grinding and polishing: see MACHINE TOOLS.

Grinnell, Josiah Bushnell [grih-nel', juh-zy'-uh bush'-nul]

Josiah Bushnell Grinnell, b. Dec. 22, 1821, d. Mar. 31, 1891, was an American Congregational minister and abolitionist. Because of his antislavery sermons, he lost his pastorate in Washington, D.C., and Horace GREELEY gave him his famous advice, "Go West, young man, go West!" Grinnell went West, founded (1854) Grinnell, Iowa, and by donating land and buildings, persuaded Iowa College to relocate there in 1859. He served in the U.S. Congress from 1863 to 1867.

Grinnell College

Established in 1846 by the United Church of Christ as Iowa College in Davenport, Grinnell College (enrollment: 1,200; library; 250,000 volumes) is now a private independent 4-year liberal arts school for men and women in Grinnell, Iowa.

Gris, Juan [grees]

The Spanish artist Juan Gris, b. Mar. 13, 1887, d. May 11, 1927, was, with Pablo Picasso and Georges Braque, one of the first and greatest exponents of the cubist idiom in painting (see CUBISM). Originally named José Victoriano Gonzalez, he adopted the pseudonym by which he is known after moving (1906) to Paris, where he lived as Picasso's friend and neighbor. Between 1907 and 1912 he watched closely the development of the cubist style and in 1912 exhibited his *Homage to Picasso* (collection of Mr. and Mrs. Leigh Block, Chicago), which established his reputation as a painter of the first rank. He worked closely with Picasso and Braque until the outbreak of World War I, adapting what had been their intuitively generated innovations to his own methodical temperament.

In the 1920s, Gris designed costumes and scenery for Serge DIAGHILEV's Ballets Russes. He also completed some of the

The Dice (1922) was painted by Juan Gris, a major exponent of the cubist style. This geometric still-life composition shows his virtuosity in the "synthetic" phase of the style. Using a tight structure to synthesize his simple, planar components, Gris produced a work that is both mathematically precise in design and rich in decoration. (Musée National d'Art Moderne, Paris.)

boldest and most mature statements of his cubist style, with landscape-still lifes that compress interiors and exteriors into synthetic cubist compositions, such as *Le Canigou* (1921; Albright-Knox Art Gallery, Buffalo, N.Y.), and figure paintings, especially the fine series of clowns that includes *Two Pierrots* (1922; collection of Mr. and Mrs. Harold Hecht, Beverly Hills, Calif.). IRMA B. JAFFE

Bibliography: Golding, John, *Cubism: A History and an Analysis* (1959); Kahnweiler, Henry David, *Juan Gris: His Life and Work*, trans. by Douglas Cooper (1969); Soby, James Thrall, *Juan Gris* (1958).

Gris-Nez, Cape [gree-nay']

Cape Gris-Nez (French: "gray nose") is a promontory about 24 km (15 mi) southwest of Calais in Pas-de-Calais department, France. Its lighthouse marks the point of France closest to England; here the Strait of Dover is only 34 km (21 mi) wide.

grisaille [grih-zy']

Grisaille is a monochromatic painting technique in which images are formed entirely in shades of gray, either to give the illusion of relief sculpture or as a preliminary stage in the execution of an oil painting. The technique was used by GIOTTO DI BONDONE in his cycle of fresco paintings (*c.*1304–05) in the Arena Chapel, Padua, and was also popular with 15th-century Flemish painters. In the 18th century grisaille was used extensively in the interior decoration of houses to emulate classical friezes, notably by the Venetian painter Giovanni Battista Tiepolo (see TIEPOLO family), and the technique has frequently been revived in glass painting and enamelwork, notably by the 16th-century artisans of Limoges. ADELHEID M. GEALT

griseofulvin: see ANTIBIOTICS.

Grisi, Carlotta [gree'-zee, kar-loht'-tah]

The Italian dancer Carlotta Grisi, b. June 28, 1819, d. May 20, 1899, was one of the great ballerinas of the romantic ballet and the creator of the role of *Giselle* (Paris, 1841). She made her debut at La Scala in 1829. Jules PERROT, her teacher and lover, choreographed her role in *Giselle* (the ballet was originally credited to Jean Coralli); the libretto was coauthored by Coralli and the poet and critic Théophile Gautier, who was infatuated with Grisi. She also danced in London, Vienna, and St. Petersburg, creating such ballets as *La Péri* (1843), *La Esmeralda* (1844), and *Paquita* (1846) before retiring in 1853. DAVID VAUGHAN

Bibliography: Lifar, Serge, *Carlotta Grisi*, trans. by Doris Langley Moore (1947); Migel, Parmenia, *The Ballerinas* (1972).

Grisi, Giulia [gree'-zee, jool'-yah]

The Italian soprano Giulia Grisi, b. July 28, 1811, d. Nov. 29, 1869, reigned as prima donna of the Paris and London operatic stages from 1835 to 1860. Born into a family of dancers and musicians, she made her debut (1828) in Milan as Emma in Rossini's *Zelmira*. She sang coloratura, lyric, and dramatic leads and created the roles of Norina in Donizetti's *Don Pasquale*, Adalgisa in Bellini's *Norma*, Juliet in Bellini's *I Capuletti ed i Montecchi*, and Elvira in Bellini's *I Puritani*. Grisi was memorable in other operas by those composers as well as operas by Mozart. ELLA A. MALIN

grison [griz'-uhn]

The grison, Galictis vittata, *eats fruit and small animals. During the 19th century it was used to control chinchillas in South America.*

The grison is either of two species, *Galictis vittata* or *G. cuja*, of slender-bodied, short-legged carnivores of the weasel family, Mustelidae. Grisons are found from southern Mexico to southern South America. The slightly larger *G. vittata* reaches 55 cm (22 in) in length plus a 16-cm (6-in) tail, and weighs up to 3.5 kg (7 lbs). A dramatic white or yellow stripe across the forehead and down the sides of the neck separates the black face, legs, and underparts from the gray or brown back. The grison lives in both forests and open areas and feeds on rodents, birds, and other small animals. EVERETT SENTMAN

Grissom, Virgil I. [gris'-uhm]

The astronaut Virgil Ivan ("Gus") Grissom, b. Apr. 3, 1926, d. Jan. 27, 1967, was the second American in space and one of three astronauts killed in the first fatal U.S. space-program accident. Grissom, veteran of air combat over Korea, was an Air Force test pilot when selected in 1959 to be one of the original seven ASTRONAUTS. His 15-minute suborbital flight into space aboard Liberty Bell 7 (1961) was the second flight in the MERCURY PROGRAM. During recovery the hatch accidentally blew off, causing the craft to sink. Grissom jumped overboard and nearly drowned.

On Gemini 3 (1965), with John YOUNG, Grissom commanded the first manned test of the two-man spacecraft (see GEMINI PROGRAM). He was selected in 1966 to command the first manned Apollo mission (see APOLLO PROGRAM). But during a launch simulation a fire broke out in the spacecraft cabin, asphyxiating Grissom, Edward H. WHITE, and Roger CHAFFEE before they could open the complex hatch. DAVID DOOLING

Bibliography: Grissom, Betty, and Still, Henry, *Starfall* (1974).

Griswold v. Connecticut

In the case of *Griswold* v. *Connecticut* (1965) the U.S. Supreme Court expanded the meaning of the DUE PROCESS clause of the 14TH AMENDMENT to encompass the right of privacy in the marital relationship. A Connecticut statute prohibited the use of birth control devices and made it a criminal offense for anyone to give information or instructions concerning contraceptive use or practice. Estelle Griswold and Dr. Buxton, two officers of a planned parenthood league, were convicted and fined $100 for dispensing birth control information to married persons.

Speaking through Justice William O. Douglas, the Court reversed the convictions and declared the statute unconstitutional. Douglas reasoned that the marital relationship was protected by a constitutional right of privacy emanating from the "penumbras" of several specific guarantees of the Bill of Rights. The right of association contained in the penumbra of the 1ST AMENDMENT, the prohibition of the quartering of troops in private homes of the 3D AMENDMENT, the prohibition against searches and seizures of the 4TH AMENDMENT, and the SELF-INCRIMINATION clause of the 5TH AMENDMENT all combine to create a zone of privacy for the individual. Douglas and Justice Arthur Goldberg also invoked the 9TH AMENDMENT ("The enumeration in the Constitution, of certain rights, shall not be construed to deny or disparage others retained by the people") to justify the judicial creation of a new right. In subsequent cases the right of privacy was extended to individuals and was the basis of the controversial ROE V. WADE (1973) decision on abortion. ROBERT J. STEAMER

grizzly bear: see BEAR.

Grock [grahk]

Grock was the stage name of Charles Adrien Wettach, b. Jan. 10, 1880, d. July 14, 1959, a celebrated Swiss clown who performed in both circuses and music halls. After working as an acrobat and tightrope walker, he discovered his true vocation and developed a distinctive type of CLOWN, derived from the clumsy but nonetheless often intelligent Auguste, who usually got the better of his white-faced colleague. Grock, who could play 24 instruments, often built his comic routines around musical performances. A. H. SAXON

Bibliography: Grock, *Grock: King of Clowns,* trans. by Basil Creighton (1957), and *Life's a Lark,* trans. by Madge Pemberton (1931).

Groener, Wilhelm [groh'-nur, vil'-helm]

Wilhelm Groener, b. Nov. 22, 1867, d. May 3, 1939, was the German general who at the end of World War I gave army support to the new Social Democratic government of Germany to prevent a Communist revolution. During the war he had been in charge of army railroad arrangements before succeeding (Oct. 25, 1918) Erich LUDENDORFF as quartermaster general. He insisted on the abdication of Emperor WILLIAM II and handled the difficult task of bringing home the defeated German troops. Groener subsequently served as minister of transport (1920–23), minister of defense (1928–32), and minister of the interior (1931–32). He helped rebuild the German army (*Reichswehr*) by circumventing the restrictions imposed by the Treaty of Versailles. K. M. SMOGORZEWSKI

Bibliography: Carsten, F. L., *The Reichswehr and Politics, 1918–1933* (1966); Garoon, Harold J., *The Reichswehr and the German Republic 1919–1926* (1957; repr. 1971).

Grofé, Ferde [groh-fay', fur'-dee]

Ferde Grofé, b. New York City, Mar. 27, 1892, d. Apr. 3, 1972, was an American composer, pianist, and arranger. For ten years he was a violist in the Los Angeles Symphony and also played the piano and conducted in theaters and cafes. In 1920 he became the pianist-arranger in the Paul Whiteman band, and in 1924 he orchestrated Gershwin's *Rhapsody in Blue.* Grofé is best known for his *Grand Canyon Suite* (1931) for orchestra. Many of his works incorporate nonmusical elements, such as the sound of jackhammers and sirens. CAROLYNN BAILEY

Grolier, Jean [grohl-ee-ay']

Jean Grolier, vicomte d'Aguisy, 1479–1565, was a French bibliophile and patron of writers and printers. Between 1499 and 1521 he was treasurer of the French army in Italy and of the French duchy of Milan, and he later became treasurer-general of France. He was a friend and patron of Aldus MANUTIUS, a Venetian master printer, editor, and publisher who specialized in Greek and Latin texts.

Grolier's library, which was dispersed in 1676, contained about 3,000 volumes, of which 561 are known to exist today. Their bindings are of fine leather decorated with geometric designs tooled in gold and bright colors. Grolier was well known for his generosity, and the volumes contain the inscription, "belonging to Jean Grolier and his friends"; some also contain his motto, "Lord, may my portion be in the land of the living." He also amassed a large and famous collection of medals and coins.

Bibliography: Austin, Gabriel, *The Library of Jean Grolier* (1971).

Gromyko, Andrei [groh-mee'-koh, uhn-dray']

Andrei Andreyevich Gromyko, b. July 18 (N.S.), 1909, d. July 2, 1989, was Soviet foreign minister from 1957 to 1985 and president of the USSR from 1985 to 1988. Gromyko began his professional career at the Institute of Economics of the Soviet Academy of Sciences. In 1931 he became a member of the Communist party. He entered the diplomatic corps in 1939 and, in 1943, replaced Maksim LITVINOV as ambassador to the United States. Gromyko led the Soviet delegation at the founding of the United Nations at Dunbarton Oaks in 1944, and took part in the Yalta and Potsdam conferences. He was made permanent representative of the USSR to the United Nations in 1946, first deputy foreign minister in 1949, and foreign minister in 1957, by which time he had become (1956) a full member of the Central Committee of the Communist party. A member of the ruling Politburo from 1973 and chief executor of the Soviet policy of DÉTENTE with the United States, he was a key ally of Mikhail GORBACHEV, who became party leader in 1985. Gromyko then held the office of president until his retirement in October 1988.

Groningen [groh'-ning-en]

Groningen, a city in the northeastern Netherlands, is the capital of Groningen province. The population of the city is 167,929 (1988 est.). A concentration of highways, railroads, and especially rivers and canals that connect Groningen to the North Sea and the Ems River makes the city a commercial and exporting center. Grains, cattle, and wood products constitute much of the trade. Industries process agricultural goods and also produce chemicals, bicycles, and clothing. Development of a nearby gas field has given added economic importance to Groningen.

First mentioned in the 11th century, Groningen joined the Hanseatic League about 1284 and enjoyed considerable independence for over two more centuries. It came under Habsburg rule in 1536 and fell to Maurice of Nassau in 1594. The city's noted university was founded in 1614 and became a state institution in 1815. JONATHAN E. HELMREICH

Grooms, Red

Charles Roger "Red" Grooms, b. Nashville, Tenn., June 2, 1937, was involved in the early HAPPENINGS, such as *Burning Building* (1959), in New York City during the late 1950s and early 1960s before developing an individual, cartoonlike, sculptural style. He is best known for his playful constructions, such as *Discount Store* (1970) and *Ruckus Manhattan* (1975), huge distorted models of people and buildings executed in papier-mâché, plywood, and paint. These witty constructions, which Grooms did with associates, satirize the worlds they depict. He continues to exhibit widely and frequently.

Bibliography: Stein, Judith, et al., eds., *Red Grooms: A Retrospective* (1986); Tully, Judd, *Red Grooms and Ruckus Manhattan* (1977).

Groote, Gerhard [groh'-teh, gayr'-art]

Gerhard Groote, b. October 1340, d. Aug. 20, 1384, was a Dutch Roman Catholic mystic and founder of the Brothers of the Common Life, or *Devotio Moderna.* After studying at Paris, he retired to a Carthusian monastery for two years. He was then ordained a deacon and began to preach, denouncing abuses in the church. His attacks were not well received and protests grew, but he died of the plague before any action was taken. In his sermons and writings, Groote stressed poverty and communal life. He soon had followers who attempted to live out his teachings at Windesheim, which became the center for the *Devotio Moderna.* His ideas are clearly reflected in *The Imitation of Christ,* often attributed to Groote but traditionally ascribed to THOMAS À KEMPIS.

THOMAS E. MORRISSEY

Bibliography: Van Zijl, T. P., *Gerard Groote: Ascetic and Reformer, 1340-1384* (1963).

Gropius, Walter [groh'-pee-us, vahl'-tur]

Walter Gropius, b. Berlin, May 18, 1883, d. July 1969, was one of the most important architects and educators of the 20th century. The son of a successful architect, Gropius received his professional training in Munich. After a year of travel through Spain and Italy, he joined the office of Peter BEHRENS, the most important European architect of the day, in Berlin.

In 1910, Gropius left Behrens to work in partnership with Adolf Meyer until 1924-25. This period was the most fruitful of Gropius's long career; he designed most of his significant buildings during this time. The Fagus factory in Alfeld-an-der-Leine (1911) immediately established his reputation as an important architect. Notable for its extensive glass exterior and narrow piers, the facade of the main wing is the forerunner of the modern metal and glass curtain wall. The omission of solid elements at the corners of the structure heightens the impression of the building as a glass-enclosed, transparent volume. In his next major work, the Administration Building for the Werkbund Exhibition in Cologne (1914), Gropius carried the idea further by glazing the entire facade including the corner stairwells. His entry in the Chicago Tribune competition of 1922 was an application of these principles to skyscraper design. In contrast to the winning Gothic design by Raymond Hood, Gropius's solution was free of all eclectic or historical detail. Using the rectangular Chicago window employed by architects like Louis SULLIVAN, Gropius offered a significant European solution to the design problem posed by America's most innovative structure, the skyscraper.

The Harvard University Graduate Center (1950) was designed by Walter Gropius and The Architects Collaborative (TAC). The complex's architectural style is based on Gropius's Bauhaus designs and contains the Harkness Commons and groupings of dormitories. The German-born Gropius became a professor of architecture at Harvard in 1937.

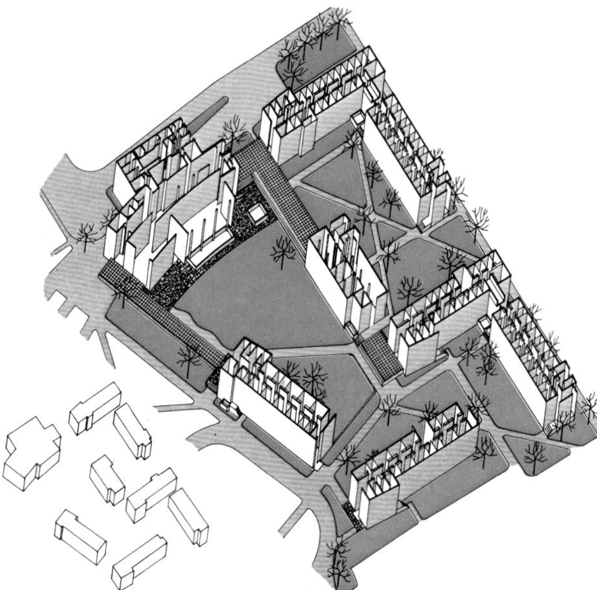

Gropius's educational philosophy encompassed the designing of all functional objects. His goal was to raise the level of product design by combining art and industry. Although these principles were inherited from English reformers like William MORRIS, Gropius was able to implement them when he reorganized the Arts and Crafts School in Weimar, which became the world-famous BAUHAUS. The unique educational program of the school sought a balance between practical training in the crafts and theoretical training in design. The integration of the arts was stressed, as is evidenced by the faculty who were attracted there—Josef ALBERS, Marc CHAGALL, Lyonel FEININGER, Wassily KANDINSKY, Paul KLEE, and László MOHOLY-NAGY. In 1925 the Bauhaus was forced to move to Dessau, where a landmark of modern architecture was constructed: the Bauhaus in Dessau (1925-26). Asymmetrical in its overall composition, the Bauhaus consists of several connected buildings, each containing an important part of the school (including administration, classrooms, and studio space). The workshop wing, a 4-story glazed box, is the most striking part of the complex.

With Adolf Hitler's rise to power in 1933, Gropius fled to England, where he practiced briefly with Edwin Maxwell FRY. In 1937, Gropius was appointed to teach at Harvard. He was widely respected as a teacher and designed a number of American buildings, including the Harvard University Graduate Center (1950). Gropius espoused collaborative effort in the design process and founded a firm that he worked with until his death in 1969.

LEON SATKOWSKI

Bibliography: Busignani, Alberto, *Gropius* (1973); Fitch, James M., *Walter Gropius* (1960); Franciscono, Marcel, *Walter Gropius and the Creation of the Bauhaus in Weimar* (1971); Giedion, S., *Walter Gropius, Work and Teamwork* (1954); Gropius, Walter, *The New Architecture and the Bauhaus,* trans. by P. Morton Shand (1935).

Gropper, William [grahp'-ur]

The "American Daumier" William Gropper, b. New York City, Dec. 3, 1897, d. Jan. 6, 1977, was a cartoonist, painter, and graphic artist whose work was often concerned with political corruption and social satire. He began (1919) as a cartoonist for the *New York Tribune.* In 1927 he made a trip to the USSR and in 1928 published *Fifty-six Drawings of the U.S.S.R.,* based on his travels. He also contributed cartoons to radical periodicals such as *New Masses.* In his satirical work, Gropper created an exaggerated type of human being, often using lawyers, judges, and politicians as targets, as, for example, in the painting *The Senate* (1935; Museum of Modern Art, New York City).

ABRAHAM A. DAVIDSON

Bibliography: Freundlich, August L., *William Gropper: Retrospective* (1968).

Gros, Antoine Jean, Baron [groh]

Antoine Jean, Baron Gros, b. Paris, Mar. 16, 1771, was a painter of Napoleonic battle scenes who studied under Jacques Louis DAVID. From 1793 to 1799 he traveled in Italy, where he painted *Bonaparte at Arcole* (1796; Versailles). After returning to Paris, Gros exhibited a nocturnal scene, *Sappho* (1801; Musée Baron-Gérard, Bayeux), and painted a series of monumental works that celebrated Napoleon's victories and virtues in a grandiose, baroque manner. Among these were *Napoleon in the Plague House at Jaffa* (1804; Louvre, Paris) and *The Battle of Aboukir* (1806; Versailles), which display a romantic intensity, vivid colors, and a taste for Levantine subjects that later influenced Eugène Delacroix and Théodore Géricault. *The Battle of Eylau* (1808; Louvre) depicts a merciful Napoleon standing in an icy wasteland.

After Napoleon's downfall, Gros's style became less energetic; he returned to themes of Greek mythology and strove to uphold the classical ideals of David. He continued to receive commissions from the new government, completing the decorations of the Pantheon, Paris (1824), and painting *Louis XVIII Leaving the Tuileries* (1817; Versailles). On June 26, 1835, following the poor reception of *Hercules and Diomedes* (1835; Musée des Augustins, Toulouse), Gros drowned himself in the River Seine. KENNETH BENDINER

Bibliography: Friedlaender, Walter F., *David to Delacroix*, trans. by Robert Goldwater (1952); Muehsam, Gerd, ed., *French Painters and Paintings from the 14th Century to Post-Impressionism* (1978).

Gros Ventres [groh van'-truh]

Gros Ventres (French for "big bellies") refers to two North American Indian tribes, the Siouan-speaking HIDATSA and the Algonquian-speaking Atsina. The term arose from the misinterpretation by early French traders of similar gestures used to denote the two tribes in Indian sign language. The Atsina broke from the ARAPAHO as early as 1700. Their language suggests that they originated in the Eastern Woodlands, but by the 18th century they roamed the plains between the Saskatchewan and Missouri rivers as mounted bison hunters. Together with their allies the BLACKFOOT, they dominated the fur trade in the early 1800s. The Atsina borrowed some ceremonial rites from the MANDAN or Hidatsa, notably those associated with the SUN DANCE and Medicine Lodge.

European traders reported (1780) 1,200 Atsina divided into southern and northern bands. Smallpox struck them the following year. Warfare with the ASSINIBOIN, CREE, and CROW soon further reduced their population. In 1827 two-thirds of the tribe moved to the Yellowstone River and with the Arapaho ranged southward. The PAWNEE joined their list of enemies, but epidemics accounted for most deaths. Eventually, they returned to the area of their homeland in northern Montana, where they numbered 534 in 1904. They now live with the Assiniboin on the Fort Belknap Reservation, with a combined population of more than 2,000 (1981 est.). In 1968 the Atsina and the Blackfoot were awarded more than $8.5 million in a land-settlements claim. ERNEST L. SCHUSKY

Bibliography: Flannery, Regina, *The Gros Ventre of Montana*, 2 vols. (1953); Kroeber, Alfred L., *The Ethnology of the Gros Ventre* (1908; repr. 1977).

grosbeak [groh'-beek]

Grosbeak is the common name applied to at least 25 different species of finches, family Fringillidae, order Passeriformes, characterized by a large, powerful, conical bill. Grosbeak means "thick bill." The grosbeaks are primarily seedeaters and range from 15 to 23 cm (6 to 9 in) in length. North America has the rose-breasted grosbeak, *Pheucticus ludovicianus*; the black-headed grosbeak, *P. melanocephalus*; the blue grosbeak, *Guiraca caerulea*; the evening grosbeak, *Hesperiphona vespertina*; and the pine grosbeak, *Pinicola enucleator*. The latter also inhabits Europe and Asia. Among the grosbeaks of Central and South America are the crimson-collared grosbeak, *Rhodothraupis celaeno*; the black-faced grosbeak, *Caryothraustes poliogaster*; and the yellow grosbeak, *Pheucticus chrysopeplus*, which has an extremely large triangular bill. In the Old World, several species of hawfinches, *Coccothraustes*, are also called grosbeaks.

The pine grosbeak, the largest of the North American grosbeaks, is approximately the size of the American robin. The males are rose pink with two white wing bars. The females are gray with yellow green heads and rumps and two white wing bars. The pine grosbeak is found mostly along coniferous forest edges, where it feeds on buds and seeds. These birds may gather in flocks of up to 100 individuals. Pine grosbeaks range from Alaska to the northern contiguous United States in summer and as far south as Pennsylvania and Kansas in winter. GARY D. SCHNELL

Bibliography: Bent, Arthur C., *Life Histories of North American Cardinals, Grosbeaks, Buntings, Towhees, Finches, Sparrows and Allies*, 3 vols. (1968).

Grosman, Tatyana [grohs'-muhn, taht-yah'-nuh]

Tatyana Grosman, b. Tatyana Aguschewitsch, in Sverdlovsk, Russia, June 17 (N.S.), 1904, has been instrumental in the development of contemporary American fine art printing. She left Russia in 1918 and eventually settled in Dresden, where she married the painter Maurice Grosman in 1931; together they emigrated to the United States in 1943. In 1957 she founded Universal Limited Art Editions in West Islip, N.Y., thus establishing lithography (see LITHOGRAPH) as a medium for contemporary American art. Grosman has collaborated with such artists as Larry Rivers, Jasper Johns, Robert Rauschenberg, Robert Motherwell, and Jim Dine. HARRY RAND

Bibliography: Tomkins, Calvin, *The Scene: Reports on Post-Modern Art*, rev. ed. (1976).

Gross, Chaim [grohs]

The sculptor Chaim Gross, b. Czechoslovakia, Mar. 17, 1904, studied art in Budapest, and immigrated to the United States in 1921, where he studied at the Educational Alliance Art School and the Beaux Arts Institute of Design in New York

Grosbeaks (females at top, males at bottom) *are finches that are identified by their deep, stout beaks. Rose-breasted grosbeaks,* P. ludovicianus (left), *named for the male's summer plumage, aid farmers by ridding fields of potato bugs and other pests. The evening grosbeak,* H. vespertina (center), *is a finch native to North American coniferous forests. Pine grosbeaks,* P. enucleator (right), *feed on seeds and fruit.*

City. His earliest work was in clay, but he soon began to sculpt in wood and stone and since the late 1950s has worked in plaster and cast bronze. His roughly executed human figures frequently reflect a preoccupation with traditional Jewish themes. BARBARA CAVALIERE

Bibliography: Gross, Chaim, and Robinson, Peter, *Sculpture In Progress* (1972).

gross national product

Considered a basic statistical measure of a nation's economic performance, the gross national product (GNP) is the total market value of all goods and services produced within a given period, usually a year. Its components include capital investment, such as that for new factories, machinery, or houses; personal consumption of goods and services; government expenditures for goods and services; and net exports (exports less imports). Only final products are included: the value of the flour to be made into bread, for example, is considered part of the value of the bread itself.

As computed yearly by the Department of Commerce, the U.S. GNP has included part of the value of goods and services produced abroad by United States-based companies. Another economic statistic, the Gross Domestic Product (GDP), counts only output produced within the country, and this measure is now being used more frequently as a means for evaluating the size of the economy.

Bibliography: Samuelson, Paul, and Nordhaus, W., *Economics*, 12th ed. (1985).

See also: INCOME, NATIONAL.

Grosseteste, Robert [grohs'-test]

Robert Grosseteste, b. *c.*1175, d. Oct. 9, 1253, was an English theologian, scientist, and mathematician. The first chancellor of the University of Oxford, he was appointed bishop of Lincoln in 1235. As bishop, he was a reformer and especially opposed the appointment of Italians to English ecclesiastical positions. His struggles to preserve the independence of the English church brought him into fierce conflict with both HENRY III of England and Pope INNOCENT IV.

Grosseteste's commentaries on and his translations of Aristotle influenced the development of scholasticism during the Middle Ages. He wrote many works in theology and philosophy, as well as treatises on physics, astronomy, and mathematics. Thus he is sometimes called the founder of the modern scientific method. His scholarly reputation was such that his name was forged to at least 65 spurious works.
DAVID HARRY MILLER

Bibliography: McEvoy, James, *The Philosophy of Robert Grosseteste* (1982); Southern, Richard, *Robert Grosseteste* (1986).

grossular: see GARNET.

Grosvenor, Gilbert Hovey [grohv'-nur]

Gilbert Hovey Grosvenor, b. Oct. 28, 1875, d. Feb. 4, 1966, served as editor in chief (1903–54) of NATIONAL GEOGRAPHIC MAGAZINE and as president (1920–54) of its parent organization, the NATIONAL GEOGRAPHIC SOCIETY, during their greatest period of development. During his tenure the magazine became noted for its popular coverage of geography, exploration, and travel and for its pioneering efforts in color photography. ERNEST C. HYNDS

Grosz, George [grohs]

The German-American painter, caricaturist, and graphic artist George Grosz, b. Berlin, July 26, 1893, d. July 6, 1959, is best known for his ascerbic satires of German society.

After studying at the Dresden Academy of Fine Arts, Grosz moved (1912) to Berlin to attend art school and to work as a magazine and book illustrator. He studied the work of Honoré Daumier, Francisco de Goya, and Henri de Toulouse-Lautrec. He served in the German army during World War I and spent time in a military mental institution; his experiences motivated the publication of his antiestablishment caricatures. In 1919, Grosz joined the Club DADA in Berlin and in 1920 organized the First International Dada Fair. His kaleidoscopic images of postwar Berlin give a strident portrait of a dislocated society, as in *Dedicated to Oskar Panizza* (1917–18; Staatsgalerie, Stuttgart).

The first of Grosz's many portfolios to be confiscated by the police was *God with Us* (1920), a satire on German society. In 1921 he was fined for slandering the German army and in 1924 for obscenity in *Ecce Homo* (1923). Grosz's graphic images of grimacing, lewdly gesticulating figures—murderers, sadists, alcoholics, prostitutes, and addicts—and caricatures of judges, generals, capitalist bosses, war profiteers, and patriots portrayed a spiritually bankrupt society.

Because of the rise of the Nazi party, Grosz left Germany in 1932 to live in the United States. He was invited (1933) to teach at the Art Students League of New York and became a U.S. citizen in 1938. Away from his German sources of inspiration, Grosz's work became less strident and more realistic, as in *Couple* (1934; Whitney Museum of American Art, New York City). The outbreak of World War II, however, caused him to resume his social commentary, in, for example, *Peace, II* (1946; Whitney Museum of American Art). His autobiography, *A Little Yes and a Big No: The Autobiography of George Grosz*, was published in 1946. IDA K. RIGBY

Bibliography: Flavell, M. Kay, *George Grosz* (1988); Hess, Hans, *George Grosz* (1974); Scheede, Uwe M., et al., *George Grosz: His Life and Work*, trans. by Susanne Flatauer (1980); Whitford, Frank, *Grosz* (1981).

George Grosz's caricature Beauty, I Cherish You *(1919) is a scathing attack on the moral disintegration of postwar German society. Grosz was a prominent member of the Dada movement, and his satirical drawings reflect his disillusionment and bitterness. (Private collection.)*

Grosz, Karoly

Karoly Grosz, b. 1930, became general secretary of the Hungarian Socialist Workers' (Communist) party in 1988. A native of the Miskolc region, Grosz was elected to the party's Central Committee in 1980, became a member of the Politburo in 1985, and was named prime minister in 1987. The following year he succeeded the aging János Kádár as party leader.

Grote, George [groht]

George Grote, b. Nov. 17, 1794, d. June 18, 1871, was an English historian whose *History of Greece* was for many years the definitive English work on ancient Greece. An associate of Jeremy Bentham and James Mill, he helped found (1826) University College, London. He also sat in Parliament as a Radical (1832–41) and fought for parliamentary reform. Grote's political liberalism colored his *History of Greece* (12 vols., 1846–56), which covers the period up to Alexander the Great. The work won instant acclaim for its careful scholarship and sympathetic depiction of Greek life.

Bibliography: Clarke, Martin Lowither, *George Grote: A Biography* (1962).

Grotefend, Georg Friedrich [groht'-eh-fent]

Georg Friedrich Grotefend, b. June 9, 1775, d. Dec. 15, 1853, a German philologist and epigrapher, made early contributions to the decipherment of the Old Persian CUNEIFORM script. Through his study of texts copied from Persepolis, he recognized that many Persian inscriptions were trilingual and that the characters were alphabetic rather than syllabic. His findings, first presented in 1802 to the Göttingen Academy, were not generally accepted until after 1837, when Sir Henry Creswicke Rawlinson, working independently, began his successful decipherment of the BEHISTUN inscription.

grotesque [groh-tesk']

The term *grotesque*, an English borrowing from the Italian *grottesca*, was first applied by Renaissance archaeologists to classical Roman fresco paintings discovered in excavations then called *grotte*, or caves. The extravagant combinations of animal, plant, and human forms found in such paintings were quickly imitated by Mannerist artists (see MANNERISM) and followers of RAPHAEL.

Since the 18th century the term has gained a wide and imprecise literary currency and refers to fanciful or distorted images of natural forms used for comic or alarming effect. Franz KAFKA'S *Metamorphoses*, which opens with a man's realization that he has become an insect, is a memorable instance of the grotesque used as a literary strategy. Similar devices may be found in the novels of Charles DICKENS and the plays of Eugène IONESCO.

Bibliography: Barasche, Frances, *The Grotesque: A Study in Meanings* (1971); Hollington, Michael, *Dickens and the Grotesque* (1984); Kayser, Wolfgang, *The Grotesque in Art and Literature*, trans. by Ulrich Weisstein (1963; repr. 1981); Thompson, Philip, *The Grotesque* (1972; repr. 1979).

Grotius, Hugo [groh'-shuhs]

Hugo Grotius (Huigh de Groot), b. Delft, Apr. 10, 1583, d. Aug. 28, 1645, was a Dutch jurist and humanist whose *On the Law of War and Peace* (1625; Eng. trans., 1925) was the first comprehensive text on international law. Grotius maintained that NATURAL LAW prescribes a *jus gentium* ("law of nations"), or rules of behavior for nations as well as individuals. Using biblical, classical, and scholarly (especially Alberico Gentili's *De jure belli*, 1598) sources, Grotius set forth an international law that recognized the necessity for war under certain conditions (his doctrine of the just war) but attempted to make its impact less devastating on individuals. His emphasis on a precise, secular natural law was influential in political philosophy.

The Dutch jurist Hugo Grotius is credited with synthesizing the tenets of international law. A philosopher and a poet, Grotius applied natural law to both political and individual conduct. (Trippenhuis, Amsterdam.)

Grotius was a precocious child; he wrote Latin and Greek poems at an early age, became a student at the University of Leiden at age 11, at age 15 was described by King Henry IV of France as "the marvel of Holland," received his doctorate in law at age 16 from the University of Orléans, and was appointed official historiographer of Holland at age 18. In 1604, Grotius wrote *De jure praedae* (*On the Law of Prizes*, 1950), a chapter of which, "Mare Liberum" ("Open Seas"), was an important defense of freedom of the high seas. He served (1607–13) as *advocaat fiscaal* (deputy attorney general) at the highest law court in the province of Holland and then became pensionary (chief magistrate) of Rotterdam.

In 1619, as a result of having aligned himself with Johan van OLDENBARNEVELDT in his unsuccessful political and religious struggle against MAURICE OF NASSAU, Grotius was sentenced to life imprisonment in the fortress of Loevestein. He escaped in 1621 by hiding in a chest of books and fled to France. He returned to Holland in 1631 but was again forced to flee, going first to Hamburg and later to Stockholm where Swedish chancellor Count Axel Oxenstierna appointed him the Swedish ambassador (1633) at the French court. Grotius relinquished the post in 1645 and was offered by Queen Christina of Sweden a position on the Swedish council of state, an honor that he declined. On the way back to Holland from Sweden, Grotius was shipwrecked and died two days later in Rostock, Germany. In addition to his legal writings, he wrote poetry and history, translated Greek and Latin poetry, and discoursed on ecclesiastical matters.

Bibliography: Dumbauld, Edward, *Life and Legal Writings of Hugo Grotius* (1969); Edwards, Charles S., *Hugo Grotius, the Miracle of Holland: A Study of Political and Legal Thought* (1981); Vreeland, Hamilton, Jr., *Hugo Grotius* (1917; repr. 1986).

Groton [graht'-uhn]

Groton (1980 pop., 10,086), in eastern Connecticut, is a town on Long Island Sound that is bounded by the Thames River on the west and the Mystic River on the east. Founded *c.*1650, it was long a fishing port. The modern town is the site of a large U.S. Navy submarine base and of the Electric Boat division of General Dynamics, builders of ships and submarines. Groton township (1980 pop., 41,062) includes Groton and the nearby villages of Noank, West Mystic, Groton Long Point, and Conning Towers.

Grotowski, Jerzy [graw-tawf'-skee, zher'-zhi]

A Polish theater director and theoretician who founded the POLISH LABORATORY THEATER, Jerzy Grotowski, b. Aug. 11, 1933, has profoundly influenced experimental theater since the late 1960s. His disciplined, ritualistic, communal productions, usually limited to between 34 and 40 spectators, have been admired and adapted by theater groups throughout Europe and America.

After attending (1951–59) Kraków's National Theater Academy, Grotowski in 1959 founded the Theater with 13 Rows in the industrial city of Opole; in 1965 this group re-formed in

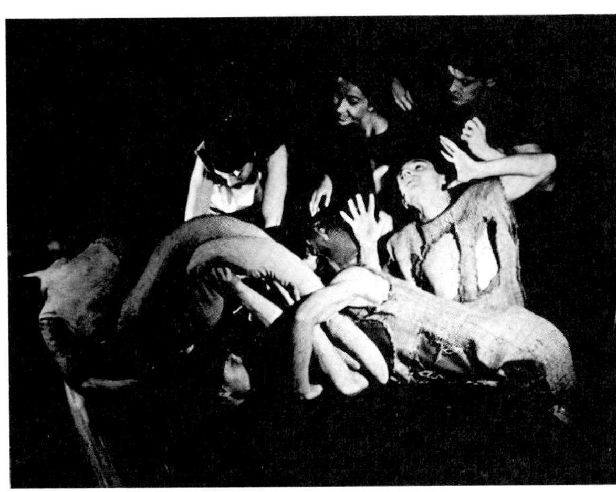

The director Jerzy Grotowski, an innovator in experimental theater, founded the Polish Laboratory Theater of Wrocław in 1959. The group is shown in a 1962 performance of Stanisław Wyspianski's Akropolis *(1904), in which audience involvement was an integral element.*

Wrocław as an acting workshop called the Polish Laboratory Theater. It was then that Grotowski set down the theoretical ideas later collected in *Towards a Poor Theater* (1968; Eng. trans., 1968), in which he championed productions that were reduced to their essential elements and a style of acting that would probe the audience's subconscious by exposing it to scenes of unbearable pain.

ground, electrical

In a circuit, a ground is an electrical conductor that has zero electrical potential with respect to all voltages applied to the circuit. This type of ground is sometimes called a chassis ground. A ground may also be a massive conductor of electricity, such as the frame of an automobile, the girders in a large building, or the Earth itself.

An electrical current will flow into a conductor at ground potential if given the opportunity by defective insulation or by a short-circuit—an inadvertent electrical path provided by an uninsulated conductor. For this reason electrical devices are grounded as a safety measure to provide a harmless path for stray currents. FORREST M. MIMS, III

ground bass [bays]

The ground bass (Italian, *basso ostinato*) belongs to the musical class of continuous variations. In this style the bass does not state a complete theme but repeats a pattern, usually four to eight measures in length, over which written or improvised variations are created. In the late Renaissance and early baroque periods the ground bass was an important device for unifying and extending compositions that were neither strophic nor contrapuntal. The passacaglia (see PASSACAGLIA AND CHACONNE), an important repeated-bass form of the baroque, has been revived in the 20th century.

The ground bass was used in England in the 16th and 17th centuries as the basis for variations for keyboard instruments and viols, especially the division VIOL. William Byrd, John Blow, Henry Purcell, and others employed it in church and theater as well as in chamber music. Ground-bass patterns have come into wide use with rock music; in rock the insistent repetition of a short passage serves as the foundation for an entire piece. ELWYN A. WIENANDT

ground-cherry: see CHINESE LANTERN PLANT.

ground temperature

Ground temperatures range from those at the surface to those inside solids (soils, rocks, building materials) down to depths where no daily or annual change exists (about 1 m/3 ft and 20 m/65 ft, respectively). These temperatures are but one part of the soil-plant-atmosphere continuum or boundary layer (see MICROCLIMATE).

The ground temperature fluctuates in accordance with the surface energy budget, the rate of change in internal energy of the soil volume near the surface. The energy budget for a thin surface layer is made up of the changing intensity of absorbed short-wave and long-wave radiation minus the reradiation at the surface, plus the sums of the net rates of conduction (see HEAT AND HEAT TRANSFER), CONVECTION, and latent heat flux (the amount of energy used to evaporate water). The internal energy, via its heat-capacity component, determines how much the temperature will change in a certain time interval. For example, a flat surface of bare soil becomes, in regard to deeper portions of the soil, a heat source during the day and a heat sink at night.

Below the surface, conduction is the only major mode of energy transfer. For each layer, the rate of heat inflow equals the rate of heat outflow plus the rate of internal-energy change of a particular soil volume. Temperatures in the upper layers fluctuate in the course of the time corresponding to the alternating intervals of heat storage and heat release. These fluctuations are not truly periodic, because of daily weather variation.

Fluctuations are most pronounced for clear conditions and for bare soils (or other fully exposed surfaces) and are least noticeable for vegetation-covered surfaces under cloudy weather. Daily (or annual) waves of energy, according to the surface-temperature variation, are transmitted downward into the soil, with an exponentially decreasing temperature range between highest and lowest soil temperatures at a particular level. This transmission is accompanied by an increasing time lag compared to the time of the surface event. Ground temperatures tend to be most extreme (hottest or coldest) at, and are closely related to, the time of maximum radiation input at the surface. Such excesses become quickly dampened with depth and are out of time phase with the original input of energy. WERNER H. TERJUNG

Bibliography: Leet, Don L., and Judson, Sheldon, *Physical Geology*, 5th ed. (1978).

ground wave

The ground wave is the component of radiation from an ANTENNA that travels parallel to the Earth's surface. Its electric field tends to be vertically polarized, the lower ends of the field lines terminating at an angle to the ground that depends on the Earth's surface resistance. Over seawater the angle is almost 90°; it becomes progressively smaller with increasing ground resistance. The ground wave has two components: a surface wave, which travels along the Earth's surface, and a space wave. The space wave itself may be considered as composed of two components, a direct wave and a ground-reflected wave. Because of ground losses, ground-wave propagation is not employed at high frequencies but is primarily used in standard radio broadcasting. FRANK G. SPREADBURY

groundhog

The groundhog, or woodchuck, Marmota monax, *is a North American rodent with a plump body, short legs, and a bushy tail. Active in the daytime for most of the year, it hibernates in a burrow during winter.*

The groundhog, or woodchuck, *Marmota monax*, is a North American MARMOT, a ground-dwelling member of the squirrel family, Sciuridae, order Rodentia. Groundhogs grow to 65 cm (26 in) long, plus a 15-cm (6-in) tail, and up to 6.5 kg (14 lb) in weight. The coat is coarse, grizzled brown above, and pale below. Groundhogs feed on plants and occasionally on snails and insects. They dig burrows with numerous exits and hibernate in winter. Mating occurs in the spring, and usually 4 to 5 young are born after a gestation period of 31-32 days.

Groundhog Day

According to popular legend, the groundhog, or woodchuck, emerges from hibernation on Groundhog Day, February 2. If the day is sunny and he sees his shadow, he will return to his burrow to sleep through 6 more weeks of winter weather. A cloudy day, on the other hand, signals an early spring. European folklore assigns this weather-predicting ability to the bear and the badger. A similar tradition—where snow and dark skies presage a quick end to winter—is observed in northern Europe on Candlemas Day, which also falls on February 2 and in some areas marks the beginning of spring planting.

groundsel [grownd'-suhl]

Groundsel is the common name for the genus *Senecio* in the sunflower family, Compositae. It is a genus of worldwide distribution and contains up to 3,000 species, making it one of the largest genera of flowering plants. Groundsels are annual or perennial herbs, sometimes vines or shrubs; in East Africa, a few are treelike in form. Some species demonstrate adaptations to dry conditions by having fleshy stems, leaves, or roots. The flowerheads are daisylike, commonly yellow in color, and occur singly or in clusters. The fruit, a small nutlike achene, bears a crown (pappus) of numerous soft white bristles. Some groundsels are poisonous and have been responsible for the death of humans and grazing animals in Africa and the West Indies. An alkaloid, retrorsine, a pyrrolizidine reported to cause liver cancer, has been isolated from several species.

OLIN S. FEARING

groundwater

Underground water found in the pore spaces of rocks and sediments in fully saturated zones is called groundwater. Although not used as extensively as surface water worldwide, groundwater is the most important source of water for rural domestic use. In many areas groundwater constitutes the largest reserve of potable water; it provides drinking water for about half the population of the United States. In arid regions, such as the Middle East, groundwater is the only source of water for irrigation and municipal and industrial use. Even in humid regions, cities such as Miami, Tokyo, London, and Houston extract large amounts of groundwater for various purposes. Groundwater is generally preferred to surface water because it is less contaminated by pathogenic organisms, is usually found only a short distance below the surface, has a nearly constant temperature, and is available in many areas even after several years of severe DROUGHT.

ORIGIN

Most shallow groundwater originates directly from the downward percolation of small amounts of rain and snowmelt into the subsurface. Very deep groundwater, on the other hand, may be held in pore spaces in an almost static condition for thousands or million of years. Some of this water contains large amounts of dissolved salts and may be ancient seawater trapped during the formation of enclosing rocks. In most geologic settings, however, the deep, saline water has migrated slowly, and it does not represent the water trapped when the rocks were formed. In volcanic areas, small amounts of water may come from bodies of molten igneous rock (magma) in the deeper subsurface. Even in areas of hot springs and geysers, however, the amount of water derived directly from molten rock sources is generally less than 1% of the total amount of hot water discharged at the surface.

MOVEMENT

The rate of movement of groundwater is controlled by the permeability of the rock or sediment in which it is contained (see PERMEABILITY, ROCK) and by the slope of the WATER TABLE, just as a river's flow rate depends on the slope of the riverbed. The movement of groundwater is much slower than that of surface water, however—usually only a few centimeters per day. This slow movement is an important characteristic, for it means that water is held in the ground, available for human use, for relatively long periods before making its way to the sea. If suitable AQUIFERS are present, groundwater may travel hundreds of kilometers from its source region.

DISCHARGE AND RECHARGE

Groundwater is discharged at the surface through SPRINGS, by slow, diffuse seepage into streams and lakes, by vegetation that sends roots into the water table, and by wells and drainage galleries. Vegetation can discharge very large amounts of water vapor into the atmosphere, and may be a serious drain on water supplies in arid climates.

Most precipitation either returns to the atmosphere by evapotranspiration or runs off the surface into nearby stream channels. In most areas less than 10 cm (4 in) per year percolates through the soil to eventually recharge the groundwater reservoir. In arid regions the amount of water that eventually becomes recharge averages less than 1 cm (3/8 in) per year. Unusually high recharge rates, more than 100 cm (40 in) per year, may take place locally in humid regions where surface materials are very permeable, as in streambeds and recent lava flows.

The natural balance between recharge and discharge, part of the HYDROLOGIC CYCLE, can be drastically upset by pumping too much water from wells, particularly near large cities and in such regions as the southwestern United States, where water is pumped for irrigation. Natural recharge may be so slow in arid regions that water that has taken several thousand years to accumulate may be exhausted by deep wells in one or two decades. The drop in groundwater levels in many areas exceeds 3 m (10 ft) per year because of overextraction. A potentially dangerous side effect of groundwater depletion is earth subsidence, which occurs when the ground sinks and deep fissures form as the result of too much water being pumped from below the surface.

QUALITY

All groundwater, including that fit for drinking, contains dissolved chemical substances. The exact composition of groundwater depends on the original composition of the precipitation before it enters the ground, the nature of the soil that first comes in contact with the precipitation, the minerals that make up the rocks in the saturated zone, the water temperature, and the presence of human contaminants. In general, more than 90% of the dissolved substances consists of Ca^{2+}, Mg^{2+}, Na^{+}, H_4SiO_4, N_2, HCO_3^{-}, SO_4^{2-}, and Cl^{-}. Total dissolved substances in groundwater range from about 20 to more than 300,000 milligrams per liter.

The temperature of groundwater almost everywhere is only 1 to 5 C (1.8 to 9 F) degrees higher than mean annual air temperature. Exceptions are found in HOT SPRINGS, which obtain added heat from either volcanic activity or exceptionally deep circulation in the subsurface.

CONTAMINATION

Almost all human activity alters water quality somewhat, but not necessarily as a result of pollution by human materials. For instance, in some areas reduction of water levels in the subsurface by pumping may allow saline water to flow toward the wells; this happens most often in coastal areas. Domestic waste (sewage and solid trash), however, is, worldwide, the most serious source of groundwater contamination. Although within the acceptable range of potable (suitable for drinking) water in terms of chemical composition, sewage commonly contains excessive amounts of solid organic material and large numbers of pathogenic (disease-causing) organisms. Filtration of solids and adsorption of dissolved heavy metals by soils and other natural materials may render sewage potable by the time it reaches groundwater supplies. Unfortunately, natural materials can filter and absorb only so

In geology, groundwater is water—mainly from rain and melted snow—that has penetrated the Earth's surface and completely filled zones of porous rocks and voids beneath it. In certain regions where beds of dense, nonporous limestone rock near the surface normally prevent penetration, rainwater can enter the ground along small cracks in the limestone. The chemical action of the water and carbon dioxide from the air gradually dissolves the limestone and enlarges the cracks to form wide surface grooves, or grikes (1), *and large underground caves* (2). *If the limestone* (3) *lies on impermeable rock* (4), *the water eventually emerges as springs* (5). *Below the water table* (6), *or the top of the saturated rock layer* (7), *the groundwater moves downward under the influence of gravity* (light blue arrows). *Additional rainwater* (dark blue arrows) *may flow downward along the water table to a lower level and seep into a perennial stream* (8). *Other groundwater may enter an inclined waterbearing rock zone, or aquifer* (9), *between two impermeable rock layers* (10). *If an artesian well* (11) *is drilled into the aquifer at a lower level, the pressure of overlying water will usually be sufficient to raise at least some water above the ground level* (12).

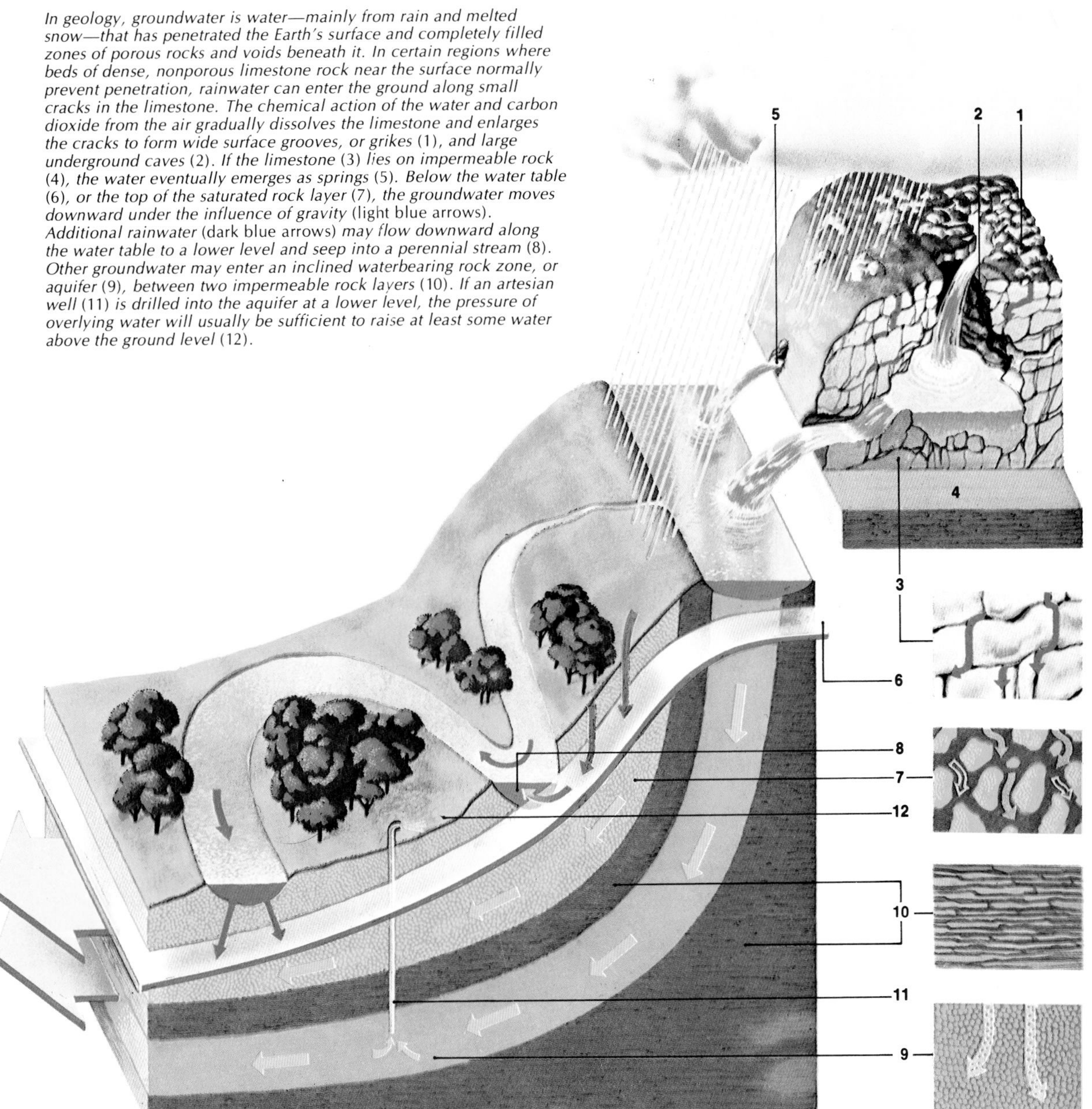

much. For this reason, sewage-disposal systems for more than a single-family residence must be more elaborate than the usual septic tank. Solid trash, if accumulated in large amounts in humid regions, is a major source of concentrated pollution. Water moving through the decaying trash can dissolve thousands of milligrams per liter of noxious material, including poisonous metals and flammable methane. Modern sanitary landfills are carefully engineered so that surface water cannot move through trash and enter the groundwater supply.

Other common sources of groundwater contamination are industrial wash water, fluids used in metal plating, pickling brines, and strong acids. Hazardous chemicals stored in waste-disposal areas can leak into groundwater supplies unless disposal sites are carefully chosen so as to isolate their contents from the water table (see POLLUTANTS, CHEMICAL). Agricultural practices can also pollute groundwater. The three most common agricultural sources are animal waste in barnyards and feed lots; chemicals, such as ammonia fertilizers; and excess return irrigation water, which is needed to keep salts from accumulating in the soil.

The U.S. government has adopted measures to reduce groundwater contamination and protect public health. In compliance with the Safe Drinking Water Act of 1974, which was amended in 1986, the Environmental Protection Agency has set standards limiting the presence of eight hazardous chemicals, including benzene, carbon tetrachloride, and vinyl chloride, in drinking water. The Clean Water Act enacted in 1987 provides funds for the control of such runoff pollutants as fertilizers, pesticides, and petroleum products.

DEVELOPMENT

Most groundwater used today comes from wells, the rest from springs and horizontal collection galleries. The first stage in developing a groundwater supply is to inventory the existing wells and springs and, with geologic and geophysical studies, to estimate the groundwater resources available in the region. Test drilling is then conducted to check on the data that have been gathered, and previously existing wells and new wells are pumped to determine the storage and water-transmitting properties of the subsurface materials. At this point it was formerly customary to drill wells for final groundwater production. It has become increasingly common to construct mathematical models to simulate future behavior of the groundwater reservoir. These models can then be used to manage the groundwater resources. Agricultural scientists are evaluating new irrigation techniques and constructing models in studies of groundwater quality. This research will help ensure the beneficial use of groundwater, a precious resource. STANLEY N. DAVIS

Bibliography: Kovacs, G., et al., *Subterranean Hydrology* (1981); LaFleur, R. G., ed., *Groundwater as a Geomorphic Agent* (1984); Pinneker, E. V., ed., *General Hydrogeology,* trans. by D. E. Howard (1983); Raghunath, H. M., *Ground Water Hydrology* (1982).

See also: ARTESIAN WELL; POLLUTION, ENVIRONMENTAL; POLLUTION CONTROL; WATER QUALITY; WATER RESOURCES; WATER SUPPLY.

group dynamics

Group dynamics is the social science that attempts to understand and improve the nature of human groups and the psychological and social forces associated with groups. The term was first used (1939) by Kurt LEWIN to refer to the psychological and social forces arising from the interaction of people in such groups as families, committees, and athletic teams and in work, educational, therapeutic, religious, racial, and ethnic groups.

One of the basic properties of any group is its level of cohesiveness, or the degree to which members are attracted to it. When cohesiveness is high, members are motivated to participate in the group's activities and to help the group attain its goals and objectives. Such a group gives its members a sense of security and identity and a feeling of personal worth, or in Lewin's words, "the ground on which the person stands."

With the passage of time, groups develop social norms (see NORM, SOCIAL) for the behavior, attitudes, and values of their members; and exert social pressures by rewarding CONFORMITY to the norms and rejecting DEVIANCE from the norms. The strength of these pressures is greater in more cohesive groups. The uniformity resulting from these pressures has both desirable and detrimental effects: it facilitates social interaction and the attainment of group goals, but may at the same time foster a group mentality that limits creativity.

Well-established groups have an internal structure that provides stability for interaction among members, who tend to enact particular roles, to perform specific functions, to communicate more often with certain other members, and to form subgroups and cliques. Most groups have status structure, or pecking order; in other words, some members have more prestige than others and exert more influence on the life of the group. The productivity of problem-solving groups is often impaired by this structure, since it tends to inhibit contributions by low-status members.

Acts of leadership are those which strengthen the group and contribute to effective group performance. Although they may be performed by any member, they are often restricted to one person who is designated as the official leader. A democratic leader encourages participation in decision making, fosters group cohesiveness, and facilitates social interaction. Even though an autocratically led group is often efficient, that kind of leadership tends to breed hostility or apathy among the members.

The size of a group also has important consequences for its functioning. Larger groups have more resources and can accomplish more than smaller ones. But as size increases, a smaller proportion of the group's members take part in group discussion and decision making, interaction becomes more impersonal, satisfaction declines, group cohesiveness is reduced, and the group tends to become divided into factions. The optimal number of members depends upon the group's objectives, but for most problem-solving groups and committees it is generally regarded as being approximately seven. DORWIN CARTWRIGHT

Bibliography: Brown, Hedy, *People, Groups and Society* (1985); Cartwright, Dorwin, and Zander, Alvin, eds., *Group Dynamics,* 3d ed. (1968); Forsyth, Donelson R., *An Introduction to Group Dynamics* (1982); Luft, Joseph, *Group Processes: An Introduction to Group Dynamics,* 3d ed. (1984); Ridgeway, Cecilia L., *Dynamics of Small Groups* (1983); Shaw, Marvin, *Group Dynamics,* 3d ed. (1980).

See also: SOCIAL PSYCHOLOGY.

Group of Seven

J. E. H. MacDonald's The Solemn Land *(1921) celebrates the grandeur of Canada's landscape. MacDonald was an original member of the Group of Seven, an association of artists committed to representing Canada's natural beauty. (National Gallery of Canada, Ottawa.)*

The Group of Seven was founded in 1920 by the Canadian painters Frank CARMICHAEL, Lawren HARRIS, A. Y. JACKSON, Franz JOHNSTON, Arthur LISMER, J. E. H. MACDONALD, and Frederick VARLEY. Reacting against the European dominance of Canadian painting traditions, the members of the Group of Seven sought to paint their native landscape in a distinctly Canadian manner. The rocks, trees, and lakes of Canada's north, rather than the urban centers, became for them symbols of national pride and greatness. Shortly before World War I, the artists began sketching the rugged terrain of northern Ontario's Algonquin Park and the Georgian Bay and Algoma regions. After the group was founded, several members traveled nationwide, painting in Quebec, the Maritime Provinces, the Rocky Mountains, and the Arctic. The works completed during these trips are characterized by vivid coloration and expressive brushwork, often accompanied by a simplification of form reminiscent of Art Nouveau.

The Group of Seven gained international fame in 1924, when its members exhibited at Wembley, England. Although it disbanded in 1931, the Group, together with Tom THOMSON, who died before its formation, has not only continued to influence subsequent generations of painters, but has also affected the way in which all Canadians today view their native land. DAVID WISTOW

Bibliography: Mellen, Peter, *The Group of Seven* (1970); National Gallery of Canada, Ottawa, *The Group of Seven* (1970); Reid, Dennis, *A Bibliography of the Group of Seven* (1971).

Group Theatre, The

The Group Theatre (1931–41), one of the foremost American theater companies in the period between the world wars, was founded in New York by Harold CLURMAN, Cheryl CRAWFORD, and Lee STRASBERG. It was dedicated to forming a permanent acting company to present professional productions of dramas of social and political relevance. During its 10-year history the group produced 25 original plays by American authors. Characteristic of the Group Theatre was its approach to acting, founded on the principles of the Russian acting teacher and director Konstantin STANISLAVSKY. The Group produced plays of liberal or socialist sympathies and took a collaborative approach to creation.

Members of the Group Theatre included the actors Morris Carnovsky, Luther and Stella ADLER, Robert Lewis, and Margaret Barker. Among the playwrights it produced were Clifford ODETS (*Awake and Sing*, 1935; *Waiting for Lefty*, 1935; and *Golden Boy*, 1937; film, 1939), whom the company discovered and nurtured; Paul GREEN (*The House of Connelly*, 1931); Sidney Kingsley (*Men in White*, 1933); and William SAROYAN (*My Heart's in the Highlands*, 1939).

When the Group Theatre broke up in 1941, its members dispersed into filmmaking, teaching, directing, and acting. Their influence, however, largely in the area of acting technique, is still felt. BONNIE MARRANCA

Bibliography: Clurman, Harold, *The Fervent Years: The Story of the Group Theatre and the Thirties* (1945; rev. ed. 1957).

group theory

Group theory studies algebraic objects called groups. Like many basic mathematical ideas, the definition of a group arose out of the comparison of numerous examples occurring in many different subjects. For instance, groups of geometrical transformations, of numbers, and of permutations all share the three basic axioms of group theory. Thus a single theorem in group theory will be applicable to all groups, regardless of the branch of mathematics or physics in which the group has arisen.

One of the basic concepts of group theory is the set. A set is a collection of objects called elements; the study of such elements is the subject of SET THEORY. A group is a mathematical system that consists of a set G together with a binary operation satisfying three axioms. A binary operation is a rule that assigns to each ordered pair (g, h) of elements in G another element of G. This new element, usually written as gh, should be thought of as the result of combining g and h in that order. If a set has a binary operation, the set is said to be closed (or have the closure property) with respect to the operation. The three axioms are: (1) $g(hk) = (gh)k$ for all g, h, and k in G (ASSOCIATIVE LAW); (2) there exists in G some element e, called the identity element, such that $eg = ge = g$ for all g in G; and (3) for any x in G there exists some element y in G such that $xy = yx = e$. Such an element y is unique; it is called the inverse of x and is denoted x^{-1}. A simple example is the set of integers, with addition as the binary operation; the element gh is defined to be the sum of g and h for any two integers g and h. The identity element is zero, since zero added to any number leaves that number unchanged, that is, $0 + a = a + 0 = a$. The inverse of any number is its negative; symbolically, $a + (-a) = (-a) + a = 0$.

A mathematical object in which axiom (3) does not hold is called a semigroup. The set of positive numbers under addition is an example of a semigroup, because the inverse of a positive number is a negative number, which is not a member of the original set. Semigroups have many applications in computer science.

Groups can be classified in many ways. If, for every pair of elements g and h in the group G, the COMMUTATIVE LAW $gh = hg$ holds, then G is called a commutative, or abelian, group. For example, the integers under addition are an abelian group.

If the group G contains a finite set of elements, G is called a finite group. For example, the hours marked off on the face of a clock form a finite abelian group with 12 elements, when addition is defined as the addition of time. For instance, $3 + 11 = 2$ in this arithmetic, in which the identity element is 12. Finite groups are especially important in the theory of polynomial equations (Galois theory) and in physics.

If the group G contains an infinite set of elements, G is called an infinite group. The most familiar example of an infinite group is the integers, which can be used in counting. Also important are topological groups, which consist of sets that are both groups and topological spaces.

If F is a function from a group G to another group satisfying $F(gh) = F(g)F(h)$ for every g and h in G, then F is called a homomorphism. Homomorphisms allow the comparison of different groups. If, for instance, a homomorphism is discovered between some obscure new group in physics and some well-known group from geometry, much knowledge about the old group may be applicable to studying the new one.

AVNER ASH

Bibliography: Adler, Irving, *Groups in the New Mathematics* (1967); Herstein, I. N., *Topics in Algebra*, 2d ed. (1975).

See also: Groups section under ALGEBRA.

group therapy

Group therapy is a popular form of PSYCHOTHERAPY in which a number of patients—usually 4 to 12—meet together with a therapist. The term *group therapy* is reserved, strictly speaking, for groups in which individuals with emotional disorders seek help from a mental health professional. More broadly, the term describes groups with other purposes. Encounter groups, consciousness-raising groups, and ALCOHOLICS ANONYMOUS are forms of group therapy that each have a different purpose and structure. People join these groups to improve their lives or become more aware of particular issues.

There are many theoretical approaches to group therapy, such as psychodynamic or analytic, Gestalt (see GESTALT PSYCHOLOGY), TRANSACTIONAL ANALYSIS, t-group, behavioral, and psychodrama. While the approaches vary in rationale, procedure, and content, they all tend to view the group format as having characteristics that make it different from individual therapy. In addition to being a more economical format, groups can serve five therapeutic functions. First, the group, a small sample of society at large, provides an interpersonal context in which each patient may reveal his or her problematic styles of relating to others. Second, the group can provide a sample of social response to each individual. Third, the group can be a source of ideas exchanged between people with similar problems. Fourth, the group can act as a stage on which individuals are able to practice new behavior. And fifth, the group provides a foundation of emotional support for its members, who may gain a sense of not being alone in their problems and of being accepted despite difficulties in overcoming their problems.

Therapists attempt to guide the group in helping themselves and one another. A therapist sets basic rules and interprets events within the group in ways that provide the participants with a language system for understanding their behavior. In some groups, therapists provide exercises by which the group may facilitate interactions. LYNN REHM

Bibliography: Appley, D. G., and Winder, Alvin, *T-Groups and Therapy Groups in a Changing Society* (1973); Berne, Eric, *Principles of Group Treatment* (1966); Egan, Gerard, ed., *Encounter Groups: Basic Readings* (1971); Gazda, George M., ed., *Basic Approaches to Group Psychotherapy and Group Counselling*, 2d ed. (1977); Yalom, Irving D., *The Theory and Practice of Group Psychotherapy*, 2d ed. (1975).

grouper [groop'-ur]

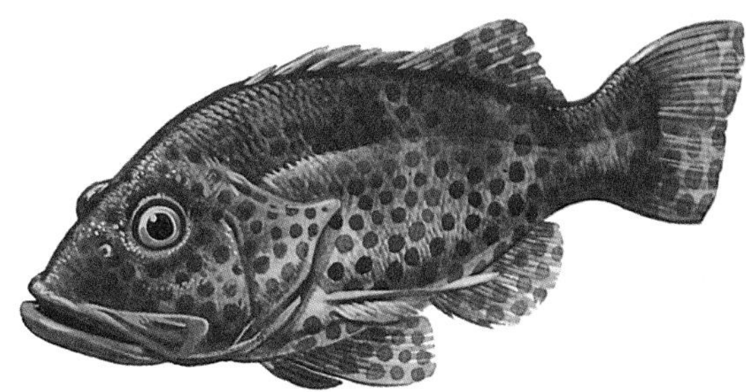

The spotted grouper, Epinephelus elongatus, *is a carnivorous, nonschooling sea bass that has a spiny first dorsal fin and a second dorsal fin with soft rays. Groupers are important food and game fish.*

Groupers, family Serranidae, are large, predatory marine fishes found in tropical and temperate seas worldwide. They are noted for their slightly compressed bodies, large mouths, and a wide variation in color patterns. They range from 2.5 cm to 366 cm (1 to 144 in) in length. The genus *Epinephelus* also contains jewfish.
EDWARD O. WILEY

grouse [grows]

The sage grouse, C. urophasianus, *feeds primarily on sagebrush. Characteristic of all members of the grouse family are feather-covered nostrils and legs. The elaborate courtship of the male* (left) *involves the use of a collective display site called a lek.*

Grouse, order Galliformes, are popular game birds of the family Tetraonidae and are related to the other gallinaceous birds including turkey and quail. Like their relatives, grouse are heavy-bodied, chickenlike ground dwellers and have a short, heavy bill and short, rounded wings. They are medium sized, 30.5–88.9 cm (12–35 in) long. The feet and nostrils are covered with feathers. They eat seeds, insects, bark, and buds.

The tetraonids include the PTARMIGANS—the willow ptarmigan, *Lagopus lagopus*, and the rock ptarmigan, *L. mutus*, in Arctic regions; and the white-tailed ptarmigan, *L. leucurus*, in the high Rockies. All species have insulating double feathers and feathered feet; even the toes are feathered in the ptarmigans. So-called snowshoes, shed in summer, are characteristic of some species. Tetraonids also have erectile feathers—ruffs or pinnae—on the sides of the neck, and some have inflatable cervical pouches for producing the booming sounds characteristic of some species. They lay large clutches of eggs. Intestinal ceca harbor bacteria that function in the microbial decomposition of cellulose, prominent in their diet.
GEORGE J. WALLACE

Bibliography: Johnsgard, Paul A., *The Grouse of the World* (1983).

Grove, Frederick Philip

Frederick Philip Grove, b. Felix Paul Greve in Rodomno, Prussia (now USSR), on Feb. 14, 1879, d. Aug. 19, 1948, was a Canadian novelist whose books are of great documentary value and give a vivid picture of the pioneers and the settlement of western Canada. He published eight novels, including *Settlers of the Marsh* (1925) and *The Yoke of Life* (1930), and an autobiography, *In Search of Myself* (1946), which won the Governor General's Award.

Grove, Sir George

George Grove, b. Aug. 13, 1820, d. May 28, 1900, was an eminent English writer on music. For 40 years (1856–96) he wrote program notes and analyses for the Crystal Palace concerts, in a suburb of London. In 1882, Grove became the first director of the newly founded Royal College of Music, serving for 12 years; he was knighted by Queen Victoria in 1883. His most important work was *Grove's Dictionary of Music and Musicians* (1879–89), which was published in five volumes and was followed by several increasingly larger editions (6th ed., 1980).
HOMER ULRICH

Bibliography: Graves, C. L., *The Life and Letters of Sir George Grove* (1904; repr. 1977).

Grove, Lefty

Some experts consider Hall of Fame member Robert Moses Grove, b. Lonaconing, Md., Mar. 6, 1900, d. May 23, 1975, the greatest baseball pitcher ever. In an American League career with the Philadelphia Athletics (1925–33) and Boston Braves (1934–41), Grove led his league in winning percentage 5 times and in earned run average (ERA) 9 times, both totals unapproached. His career record was 300 games won and 141 lost. In his Most Valuable Player season (1931), Grove was 31-4, with 27 complete games, 175 strikeouts, and an ERA of 2.06—all league-leading statistics.

growth

Growth in single-celled organisms may refer either to an increase in size of the CELL or to an increase in number of cells in one location (population growth). In an organism with many cells, growth is an increase in the size of the entire organism or of one of its organs or tissues. This growth may result from an increase in the size of individual cells, from an increase in the number of cells, from an increase in production of materials between cells—whether mineral (as in bones), fibrous (as in tendon or scar tissue), or gelatinous ground substance (as in cartilage)—or from any combination of these. Growth depends on intake of food, which is metabolically converted to suitable chemical building components. Animal cells are not surrounded by the rigid cellulose wall found in plants and thus retain the ability to grow and divide as well as to change position. In plants these properties are restricted to specific growing cells.

In general, in animals, growth is chiefly due to new cells, although the increased muscle mass from exercise is the result of increased cell size. Plants, however, typically produce very small cells that then massively enlarge. Animal and plant growth differ in another striking way: in most animals, the growth period ends with maturity (completed development), whereas plants maintain embryonic tissues, called meristems, throughout their lives, and growth may occur at any time.

CELL GROWTH

Growth involving the production of new cells may occur by fission, budding, or filamentous growth. In fission, the parent cell divides into two smaller but equivalent cells. In budding, which is typical of certain fungi such as yeast, a small new cell (the bud) is pinched off from the parent cell and then grows into a duplicate of its parent. Filamentous growth, seen in certain algae, occurs when hairlike filaments of two or more algal cells join end to end; enlargement of the tip of the filament forms new cells.

Most animal and plant cells undergo fission through a process called MITOSIS, in which each daughter cell receives one copy of each gene present in the parent, plus approximately one-half of the cellular structures (organelles) and materials of the parent. In gonadal tissues that form the egg and sperm, cells undergo a process termed MEIOSIS in which the genes are divided between the daughter cells. Growth of a cell occurs in two phases: immediately after mitosis, each new cell grows to adult size and remains at this size until shortly before it is to undergo mitosis. At this time, it duplicates its DNA, which contains most of the cell's genetic information (see GENETIC CODE), and increases to a little less than twice normal size.

The first period of growth is the most variable phase of the cell cycle. The cytoplasm of the cell must have a specific size relative to the size of the nucleus before cell division can occur, and the growth period must be long enough to achieve the proper relative proportions. Cell division can be prevented indefinitely by periodically cutting away portions of the cytoplasm or by starving the cell.

DIFFERENTIATION

Growth in animals and plants results in the development of the shape and structures characteristic of the organism, as well as an increase in size or mass. The development of shape and structures, called morphogenesis, is brought about by the coordinated action of growth and differentiation, the process by which cells develop into such specialized types as muscle, nerve, skin, leaf, or root cells. In a developing organism, different centers of growth are active at different times and proceed at different rates. This pattern of growth is called differential growth and results in the "sculpturing" of various kinds of body parts. For example, when the rate and amount of growth varies in different directions, new shapes can arise, such as elongations and altering contours; a solid mass can become hollow if the outer layers of the mass grow faster than the core; and a hollow structure can become solid if the inner layers of the rind grow faster than the outer.

Differential, or relative, growth in the embryo (see DEVELOPMENT) is responsible for forming the vertebrate eye from a hollow ball of ectoderm (outermost of the three primary tissue layers of an embryo) and for forming the heart from a spongy sheet of mesoderm (middle layer of embryonic tissue). In plants, changes in shape result almost entirely from differential growth; the petiole (stalk) of a leaf, for example, develops at a rate different from that of the blade (see PLANT).

Differential growth stops when a certain size, proportional to the whole organism, is reached. In MAMMALS, growth in overall length ends after ossification (conversion to bone) of the epiphyseal plate (an area near the ends of a bone where new bone is made). At the same time, other organs and tissues cease growing, indicating that the total supply of body cells (approximately 1,000 trillion in adult humans) is limited by a central regulatory system. The constancy of size of organs or whole organisms merely indicates that the death of cells is balanced by the production of new cells.

Some animal tissues are capable of growth throughout life, whereas others lose this capacity after formation in the embryo. In humans, red blood cells die and are replaced by blood-forming tissue in the bone marrow at the rate of 3 million cells per second. Cells in the skin and in the lining of the digestive tract continually die and are renewed by growth. If a portion of the liver is surgically removed, cells of the remaining part multiply until the original mass is restored, and then growth ceases. Most nerve cells are formed before or soon after birth and cease multiplying soon after birth.

Organs or tissues forced to function at higher than normal levels may grow to compensate for the increased demands placed on them. For example, when one kidney is lost, the other undergoes compensatory growth and enlarges; constant stress may cause enlargement (hypertrophy) of the adrenal gland, and the heart often enlarges by hypertrophy when it is forced to work harder.

The factors resulting in balanced growth and morphogenesis have not yet been identified, nor is it known how the different parts of an adult retain correct proportions and shapes. CANCER is a term for a class of diseases in which growth escapes normal controls limiting cell multiplication; the uncontrolled growth results in tumors (masses of cells).

ALLOMETRIC GROWTH

The growth of various parts of the animal body at different rates is called allometric growth. The role of allometric growth in evolution was first described by the Scottish biologist d'Arcy W. Thompson in *On Growth and Form* (1915). Thompson found that the varied body shapes of animals belonging to the same family could be represented by proportionate distortions of a single basic shape, much like the stretching of a figure drawn on a rubber sheet. The distortions, or transformations, could be expressed by simple mathematical formulas. Among the primates, for example, Thompson found that the differing skull shapes of humans, gorillas, chimpanzees, and baboons, if drawn on an imaginary rubber sheet, are simply different proportionate distortions of the same basic skull. This finding indicates, according to Thompson, that the modifications of jaws, braincase, and the regions between are regulated by a center in the body coordinating their relative growth.

REGENERATION

All plants and animals have some ability to survive injury by regenerating lost tissue to heal wounds. Some animals, however, have the extraordinary ability to restore lost body parts. (See REGENERATION.) Certain lizards can regenerate entire limbs and tails, a new hydra can grow from a fragment of its original tissue, and flatworms and starfish can do the same. Plants can repair or replace many lost parts, and sometimes new plants can grow from cuttings.

Little is known about how regeneration occurs. Experiments with the salamander and axolotl have shown that regeneration of an amputated limb occurs only if a critical mass of the leg nerve is present in the regenerating stump. Similar experiments with mammals are more difficult; reportedly, however, some regrowth of the amputated hind limb of the opossum is possible under experimental conditions. It is conjectured that such experiments could eventually provide knowledge enabling medical scientists to induce regeneration of lost limbs and other structures in humans.

ANIMAL GROWTH

At birth or hatching, the vertebrate is usually far from mature. The final stages of development involve the growth of tissues and organs formed in the embryo. Young mammals, for example, possess the elements of a reproductive system, but the system is not fully developed until the onset of puberty and the accompanying maturation of these existing structures (see REPRODUCTIVE SYSTEM, HUMAN).

Hormonal Control. Animal growth requires the coordinated action of various kinds of HORMONES. The hormones active in regulating growth in higher animals are produced by glands in the ENDOCRINE SYSTEM. Two animal groups are known to possess specialized glands that synthesize and release growth factors—the insects and the vertebrates.

A hormone called the GROWTH HORMONE, secreted by the PITUITARY GLAND in vertebrates, stimulates mitosis in experimental animals and tissue cultures (tissues grown on a nutrient medium in the laboratory). Presumably by accelerating mitosis, growth hormone effects an increase in body growth. An excess or deficiency of this hormone in humans and other higher animals results in gigantism or dwarfism. Many circus giants or dwarfs are of this "pituitary" type—their growth was accelerated or retarded abnormally during early life.

In young animals in which the epiphyseal plates have not yet ossified, growth hormone stimulates growth, and surgical removal of the pituitary gland inhibits growth. If growth hormone reaches excessive concentrations in an adult, characteristic overgrowth (in thickness, not length) of facial bones and bones of the hands and feet occurs, resulting in the coarse features of a disorder called acromegaly. (See ENDOCRINE SYSTEM, DISEASES OF THE.)

Another hormone essential for normal growth and maturation in animals is thyroxine, secreted by the thyroid gland. In children with a deficiency of thyroxine, bone growth is slowed, secretion of growth hormone is suppressed, and cretinism results. Tadpoles never become frogs if their thyroid glands are removed.

The hormone INSULIN, secreted by the PANCREAS, stimulates growth by accelerating the manufacture of protein. Failure to grow can be a symptom of insulin deficiency (DIABETES mellitus) in children.

SEX HORMONES, produced in mature ovaries and testes of vertebrates, maintain secondary male-female characteristics, including different patterns of growth, and differences in muscular development and the amount of fat under the skin.

Invertebrate Growth. The postembryonic development of invertebrates can be markedly different from that of vertebrates. The young of many insects hatch in a larval form bearing little resemblance to the adults of their species. (This occurs rarely in some vertebrates, such as the frog, which passes through a larval tadpole stage.) In the development of the adult butterfly, for example, the process of METAMORPHOSIS converts the larva (caterpillar) to its adult form. The caterpillar grows to many times its original size and then forms a pupa, from which the adult arises. The wings and other structures are developed internally through a series of larval molts (shedding of the hard outer cuticle; see MOLTING). Such development is called complete metamorphosis.

Other insects, such as grasshoppers and cockroaches, undergo incomplete metamorphosis: the young resemble the adult except for poorly developed wings and other organs, and development occurs through both relative growth of various parts and a series of molts.

Insect metamorphosis has been studied extensively and has been found to be regulated by two hormones: JUVENILE HORMONE, secreted by cells behind the brain and so named because it blocks the development of the adult form; and ecdysone, secreted by a gland in the thorax and initiating molting. Insect form is determined by the balance between the levels of the two hormones. Ecdysone appears to be the molting hormone for all other arthropods, as well. Juvenile hormone is more specific; the juvenile hormone active in one insect group may have no effect in other insects.

HUMAN GROWTH

At birth, a child weighs about 3.4 kg (7.5 lb), an increase of about 3 million times the weight at conception. Each child has an inherited pattern of skeletal development. In the embryo, most bones begin as connective tissue and gradually change to cartilage, which forms the model for the hard bones of the adult. Deposition of fibers and salts, chiefly a calcium salt similar to the mineral apatite, causes the cartilage to ossify. Ossification begins in spots called ossification centers; the rate of ossification is an index of growth because the maturation of the skeleton is an indicator of the development of the remainder of the body. The "bone age," determined by X rays, therefore indicates the state of the individual's maturation.

Growth patterns and the ultimate height attained by an individual are also influenced by hormones, nutrients required for growth, and even the individual's emotional environment. The most important environmental factor affecting growth is diet, which must include adequate protein, essential vitamins and minerals, and calories. Injury and disease stunt growth because they increase protein catabolism (breakdown of body protein in metabolism, as a response to stress).

The yearly growth in height, or "height velocity," measured in inches or centimeters per year, is determined by the net effect of hereditary, hormonal, and environmental factors. Height velocity is not evenly spaced over the 12 months of the year, and periods of rapid growth may follow periods of slow growth and vice versa. Following an illness, children can experience a period of "catch-up growth."

Puberty. The number of years during which growth occurs is largely dictated by the age at which puberty occurs, because the hormones initiating puberty also terminate the process of physical growth. These hormones are the sex hormones: androgens, secreted by the testes in males and by the adrenal gland in females; and estrogens, secreted by the ovaries in females and formed by the muscle, adipose (fatty) tissue, and liver in males. Androgens initially stimulate growth but ultimately terminate growth by causing the epiphyses to fuse. A growth spurt occurs at the time of puberty, due largely to stimulation of protein synthesis by androgens.

The body changes that develop in girls at puberty, in addition to enlargement of the breasts, uterus, and vagina, are due in part to estrogens and in part to the absence of testicular androgens. Women tend to have narrow shoulders, broad hips, and thighs that converge and arms that diverge ("wide carrying angle"). This body pattern, plus the female distribution of fat in the breasts and buttocks, is seen also in castrated males. The presence of testicular androgens in males is responsible for the typical male body pattern of broad shoulders, enlarged muscles, and lengthened and thickened vocal cords, which deepen the voice.

Before puberty, however, most children of the same age grow at the same rate. The child who seems too short or too tall may actually have a normal growth velocity for his or her age. Exceptionally short or tall children may simply represent one extreme or the other of the normal range of sizes. The range of normal heights at each age of childhood has been well established and is the basis for the growth curves known as the Wetzel grid. The grid is a chart indicating the normal range of heights at each age and is used by physicians for predicting the growth of children. The average height of a 2-year-old boy, for example, is about 87.5 cm (35 in), but most children will be between 80 and 97.5 cm (32 and 37 in) tall. From the third year of life until puberty, growth velocity for most children continues at a rate of approximately 6.25 cm (2.5 in) per year.

Growth in height stops only after pubertal changes are complete. By the time of the first menstrual period (usually at the age of 11 or 12), the growth velocity of girls is already slowing down. Puberty starts and finishes about 2 years later in boys. If puberty occurs at an unusually early age, growth will cease earlier than it does with other children the same age and may result in short stature. If puberty is delayed, growth will continue for a longer period of time than is the case with other children of the same age. The bone age, determined by an X ray, may be used to estimate the chronologic age at which puberty will occur and the number of years of growth potential remaining in a particular child.

Hormonal Effects. During the prenatal period, thyroxine stimulates the formation of bone from cartilage and affects the contours of the face and proportions of the body. A deficiency of thyroxine (hypothyroidism) results in a dwarfed adult with infantile features (cretinism). In adults, thyroxine is necessary to maintain a normal level of growth hormone secretion. African pygmies have been shown to have normal levels of growth hormone, but their tissues appear to be subnormally responsive to this hormone, probably due to a decrease in the number of receptor sites for the hormone on the surface of body cells.

Other causes of short stature include—in addition to pituitary insufficiency, hypothyroidism, and sexual precocity—the syndrome of inherited deficiency of growth hormone. Individuals with this syndrome are called sexual ateliotic dwarfs and remain short; however, they mature sexually and women with this disorder can become pregnant, deliver, and lactate (produce breast milk). Alterations in height are also seen in gonadal dysgenesis, a group of disorders in which there is an abnormal number of the sex chromosomes. Those having XO are dwarfed females, and those with XXY or XYY are very tall males. Normal females are XX, and normal males are XY. Various bone and metabolic diseases also cause stunted growth, and in many cases of stunted growth there is no known cause ("constitutional" delayed growth).

SIZE LIMITS OF ANIMALS

The possible range of size of animals is determined by such factors as the ability of the animal to support its own weight, the adequacy of blood circulation, metabolic rate, and whether the animal is homeothermic (maintains constant BODY TEMPERATURE) or poikilothermic (has a changeable body temperature, depending on the surroundings).

In the evolution of invertebrates, the development of an adequate circulatory system may have been the first requirement for growth beyond a certain size, except where the body is filamentous or greatly flattened. Circulation, together with branchial (relating to gills) respiration, permitted crustaceans and mollusks to grow to considerable size. Insects are severely limited in their ultimate size, as their respiratory system consists of tiny tubes that carry air from openings in the body wall to every cell.

Data compiled for many types of animals indicate that metabolic rate is a major factor limiting the size of animals. Within a given group of animals, the metabolic rate (per gram of body weight) invariably increases with diminishing body size; the higher metabolic rates require correspondingly higher food intake, faster digestion, and increased circulation. Hypothetically, an animal might be so small that it would have to eat so much so quickly and expend so much energy looking for food that it actually could not exist. For example, the smallest mammals, shrews, may weigh as little as 4 g (0.14 oz) and must consume nearly their own body weight in food each day; if deprived of food, a shrew's high metabolic rate consumes body reserves so fast that it starves to death in a day or less.

Land animals cannot increase to unlimited size, because their muscles and bones could not support the weight. As size increases, weight increases more rapidly than strength. The largest living land animal, the elephant, weighs about 3,600 kg (7,940 lb), whereas the largest of animals, the blue whale, weighing up to 130,000 kg (286,600 lb), is aquatic and fully supported by the surrounding water.

PLANT GROWTH

Plants grow by mitotic cell division from a single original egg cell that has been fertilized by pollination. In this growth, cells multiply and then enlarge and differentiate into specialized types as root, stem, and leaf cells. The formation of flowers, fruits, and seeds is usually considered an aspect of plant reproduction or plant propagation, not plant growth.

Plant growth occurs only in tissues called meristems, in which, under favorable conditions, new cells are more or less continually being formed as a result of repeated mitosis. The tip of every shoot or branch has a shoot-apical meristem, and each root tip has an analogous root-apical meristem. The shoot meristem ultimately forms leaves, and root meristems develop the more extensive root system needed for continued growth. Rapid mitosis in the shoot- and root-apical meristems of germinating seeds (see GERMINATION) produces the young seedling. These meristems maintain embryonic tissues capable of growth throughout the life of the plant, producing stem and root systems, leaves, and flowers. The growth activity of these meristems is called primary growth.

Stems thicken as a result of mitosis in another meristem called cambium, which is present in the stems of GYMNOSPERMS (seed plants in which the seed is not enclosed in an ovary) and most dicotyledons (plants whose seeds are enclosed in an ovary—ANGIOSPERM—and, in addition, contain two seed leaves, or COTYLEDONS). Cambium also generates the woody xylem, the tissue through which water and minerals flow upward from the roots to every leaf. Still another portion of cambium generates phloem, the tissue that transports products of photosynthesis from leaves to other parts of the plant. In trees, the so-called cork cambium produces most of the tissue called bark. The growth activity of the cambium producing other tissues is called secondary growth.

Embryonic Growth. The initial growth of the fertilized egg proceeds only until the resulting embryo is "packaged" in a seed case. Further growth into an adult occurs after germination.

The fertilized egg of a flowering plant, for example, first develops a short filament of cells, one end of which then burgeons to form a small spherical embryo. The remaining portion of the filament, called the suspensor, elongates and pushes the embryo into the surrounding nutrient tissues; because plant egg cells have no yolk, they are normally embedded in a mass of cells that contain nutrients for the developing embryo. Further cell divisions transform the embryo into a torpedo-shaped body. The surrounding tissues meanwhile develop into a seed coat and a storehouse of food. Finally, the embryo is packaged in the coat to await germination.

Growth Rings of Trees. It is well known that the age of a tree may be estimated by counting the "annual rings" showing on the face of a cut stump, allowing one ring for each year of age. The annual rings are more accurately called growth rings, because they are not necessarily formed at the rate of one per year. In temperate regions, a growth ring is formed by the difference in size between the xylem cells formed in the spring and those formed in the previous summer. In the spring, growth is rapid and the cells formed are large; as spring wears into summer, growth slows and smaller cells are formed. A dormant period occurs in the winter and is followed by a surge of new growth the following spring. In tropical forests, with no unfavorable growth season, trees do not normally show growth rings.

Light and Growth. Plants require light for photosynthesis, and so plant growth is attuned to the length of the day. The growth response of plants to changes in the duration of light is termed photoperiodism. Plants grown in temperate regions may be divided into three groups according to the effect of different exposures to daylight. So-called short-day plants develop flowers only if they are illuminated for less than 12 hours daily. Such plants include violets, asters, and some varieties of strawberries and wheat. Long-day plants develop flowers only if the daily photoperiod is longer than 12 hours. Long-day plants include clover, beets, lettuce, and other varieties of wheat. Some plants produce flowers regardless of the length of the daily photoperiod and are called indeterminate plants. Examples include tomatoes, cucumbers, cotton, dandelions, and sunflowers. Reviewed by LOUIS LEVINE

Bibliography: Black, Michael, and Edelman, Jack, *Plant Growth* (1976); Brookbank, John W., *Developmental Biology: Embryos, Plants and Regeneration* (1978); Fogg, G. E., *Growth of Plants* (1975); Graham, C. F., and Wareing, P. F., *The Developmental Biology of Plants and Animals* (1976); Gruelach, V., *Plant Structure and Function*, 2d ed. (1983); Sinclair, David, *Human Growth after Birth*, 2d ed. (1973); Smith, D. W., *Growth and its Disorders* (1977); Solomon, E. P., and Davis, P. W., *Human Anatomy and Physiology* (1983); Sussman, Maurice, *Animal Growth and Development* (1964); Tanner, J. M., *Fetus into Man* (1978).

growth hormone

Human growth hormone (HGH), also called somatotropin, is a single polypeptide chain containing 191 amino acids. It is produced by the anterior portion of the PITUITARY GLAND of the ENDOCRINE SYSTEM. A deficiency of the growth hormone in children produces dwarfism (maximum height of about 1.2 m/4 ft), whereas an overproduction of the hormone in children produces gigantism (maximum height of about 2.4 m/8 ft). An excess of the hormone in adults produces acromegaly (see ENDOCRINE SYSTEM, DISEASES OF THE).

In the past, children suffering from HGH deficiency could be treated with injections of the hormone, which was obtainable only from the pituitaries of cadavers. Unfortunately, it has been found that the virus causing Creutzfeldt-Jakob disease, a fatal infection of the brain, can be transmitted with such growth-hormone injections. Recently, however, it has become possible to transfer the human growth-hormone gene to the bacterium *Escherichia coli,* which then produces an effective form of the hormone that is free from the virus. This offers great promise for a continuing supply of the hormone for the 3,500 children in the United States and the many other thousands around the world who, each year, require periodic injections if they are to avoid dwarfism. LOUIS LEVINE

Bibliography: Bollin, A. P., *Recombinant DNA Products* (1984).

Groza, Lou [groh'-zuh]

The professional football player Louis Ray Groza, b. Martins Ferry, Ohio, Jan. 25, 1924, was an outstanding placekicker and offensive lineman during a career (1946–59, 1961–67) that spanned three decades. Groza initially joined the Cleveland Browns when the team was in the All-American Football Conference. After the Browns joined the National Football League in 1950, Groza accumulated 1,349 points (then a record) by kicking 641 points after touchdown and 234 field goals and scoring one touchdown. He led the league in field goals 5 times. An excellent offensive tackle, Groza was inducted into the Pro Football Hall of Fame in 1974.

grub

Grub is the name commonly applied to the immature larval stages of all BEETLES (order Coleoptera). Technically, a grub is a scarabaeiform larva, with a thick, soft, usually curved body, a well-developed head, thoracic legs, and no prolegs (leglike appendages on the abdomen). It is generally pale in color and is relatively inactive. Other types of beetle larvae are campodeiform (elongate and somewhat flattened, with well-developed antennae, thoracic legs, and cerci, or taillike projections), elateriform (elongate, cylindrical, hard-bodied, and short-legged), and vermiform (elongate and maggotlike, without legs). STEPHEN C. REINGOLD

See also: LARVA.

Grub Street

The term *Grub Street* was first used by 18th-century English satirists to refer to hack writers and hackwork. It is derived from Grub Street in London (now Milton Street), where writers once eked out a living by producing "small histories, dictionaries and temporary poems," as Samuel Johnson wrote in his dictionary. George Gissing's novel *New Grub Street* (1891) is a portrait of the hacks of Victorian London.

Gruen, Victor [grun]

During the 1960s, Victor Gruen, b. Vienna, July 18, 1903, d. Feb. 14, 1980, was at the forefront of architects concerned with the revitalization of U.S. cities through the union of architectural planning and commercial enterprise. Gruen received his training in Vienna under a leading German architect, Peter Behrens, and emigrated to the United States in 1933. His first U.S. building was the Lederer Store (1939; New York City). In 1950 he formed Victor Gruen Associates, a group of architects, designers, and engineers. The main features in his plans for the center cities of Fort Worth, Tex. (1957), Cincinnati, Ohio (1963), and Fresno, Calif. (1965), were landscaped streets or malls reserved for pedestrians. In some instances entire streets were vaulted over, creating an effect like that of the arcades of Naples and Milan. Gruen's major contribution to U.S. urban life was the development of the regional shopping center as a focus for suburban living. This aspect of his work is exemplified by the Northland Center (1954) near Detroit. Between 1963 and 1967, Gruen produced a design for the reconstruction and development of Tehran, Iran. Although Gruen's projects exhibit admirable planning, the buildings themselves are relatively conventional. LEON SATKOWSKI

Bibliography: Gruen, Victor, with Larry Smith, *Centers for the Urban Environment* (1973), *The Heart of Our Cities* (1964), and *Shoppingtown U.S.A.* (1960).

Gruenberg, Louis [groo'-en-burg]

Louis Gruenberg, b. Aug. 3 (N.S.), 1884, d. June 9, 1964, was an American composer of Russian birth. His parents brought him to New York as a child. As a youth he moved to Berlin, where he studied piano and composition with Ferruccio Busoni. Returning to the United States in 1919, he became active principally as a composer. He was one of the first to employ jazz elements in music for the symphony orchestra. For 3 years (1930–33) he taught composition at the Chicago Musical College, then moved to Santa Monica, Calif., where he became engaged in writing music for films. Gruenberg's first symphony (1919; rev. 1929) received the RCA-Victor prize in 1930. His opera *Emperor Jones*, based on Eugene O'Neill's play, was produced at the Metropolitan Opera in 1933. He also composed other stage works, songs, piano pieces, concertos, and chamber music. HOMER ULRICH

Gruenther, Alfred Maximilian [gruhn'-thur]

Alfred Maximilian Gruenther, b. Platte Center, Nebr., Mar. 3, 1899, d. May 30, 1983, was a U.S. general who achieved distinction as a strategist during World War II and as commander of the North Atlantic Treaty Organization (NATO) after the war. A graduate (1919) of West Point, Gruenther held several important staff posts during World War II. In 1950 he was appointed Dwight D. Eisenhower's chief of staff at Supreme Headquarters, Allied Powers, Europe (SHAPE). From 1953 until his retirement from the army in 1956, Gruenther served as NATO's supreme allied commander in Europe.

Grumiaux, Arthur [groom-ee-oh']

The eminent Belgian violinist Arthur Grumiaux, b. Mar. 21, 1921, d. Oct. 16, 1986, was best known as a leading exponent of the music of Mozart. At the age of 12 he entered the Brussels Conservatory, studying with Alfred Dubois. His debut in 1940 was almost immediately followed by the German invasion of Belgium; until the end of the war, he made no public appearances. From 1945, however, when he played his first concert in Britain, he became one of the world's most admired violinists. His fame was enhanced by his numerous recordings, most notably a series of Mozart and Beethoven sonatas in which he was accompanied by the great Romanian pianist Clara Haskil. Grumiaux's repertoire included contemporary works as well as music of the classical and romantic periods.

Grumman, Leroy [groo'-muhn]

Leroy Randle Grumman, b. Huntington, N.Y., Jan. 4, 1895, d. Oct. 4, 1982, founded the Grumman Aircraft Engineering Corporation. He learned to fly while serving in the U.S. Navy during World War I. After the war he spent nine years working for an aircraft company before going into business for himself in 1929. After some lean months he began getting contracts from the navy. During World War II, Grumman developed the folding wing for carrier-based aircraft. Grumman factories turned out as many as 605 planes a month for the navy during the war, the best-known models being the Avenger, the Wildcat, and the Hellcat.

Grumman TBF-1 Avenger

On Apr. 8, 1940, the U.S. Navy ordered two XTBF-1 prototypes from Grumman Aircraft Corporation. Prior to that, Grumman had concentrated on producing excellent fighters for the U.S. fleet but lacked experience in designing torpedo-carrying aircraft; it proceeded, however, to construct the three-seat TBF-1 Avenger, one of the most effective of all torpedo-bombers (see AIRCRAFT, MILITARY). Powered by a Wright R-2600 radial engine, the 16.5-m-span (54.2-ft) mid-wing monoplane had angular flying surfaces. Including those made by General Motors as TBMs, 9,836 Avengers were built. The Avenger remained operational for about 15 years. Variants produced included a target-tower (for towing aerial targets), special versions for night operation and for radar countermeasures, and a seven-seat carrier transport for delivering vital supplies or personnel. PETER M. H. LEWIS

Grundtvig, Nicolai Frederik Severin [grunt'-vig, nik-oh-ly' frith'-uh-rik sev-uh-reen']

Nicolai Frederik Severin Grundtvig, b. Sept. 8, 1783, d. Sept. 2, 1872, was a Danish bishop, poet, historian, educator, and hymn writer. His poetry and historical writings, including a Danish version of *Beowulf*, were specifically influenced by the Norse Eddas and early Anglo-Saxon literature and, in general, by the romantic movement. As a churchman he taught the historical revelation of Christianity and criticized the rationalist tendencies of the Danish church. As an educator he stressed knowledge of the national language and history and encouraged the founding of folk high schools. *Sang-Vaerk til den Danske Kirke* (Hymns for the Danish Church, 5 vols., 1837–81), an original collection of Christian hymns, established him as the greatest of Scandinavian hymn writers.

Bibliography: Knudsen, Johannes, ed., *Selected Writings* (1976).

Grünewald, Matthias [grun'-eh-vahlt, mah-tee'-ahs]

Matthias Grünewald, *c.*1475–1528, whose real name was Mathis Gothart, called Nithart or Neithardt, was a major figure in a generation of great northern German Renaissance painters that also included Albrecht Dürer, Lucas Cranach, and Albrecht Altdorfer. Grünewald remained relatively unknown until the 20th century; only about 13 of his paintings and some drawings survive. His present worldwide reputation, however, is based chiefly on his greatest masterpiece, the *Isenheim Altarpiece* (*c.*1513–15), which was long believed to have been painted by Dürer.

Grünewald grew up in Würzburg near Nuremberg, and

This Crucifixion, *from German Renaissance master Matthias Grünewald's polyptych,* Isenheim Altarpiece *(c.1510–15), is the view seen with the two outer movable wings of this three-layer work closed. The distorted, suffering body of Christ is in the center; at left, the swooning Virgin Mary is supported by St. John with the grieving Mary Magdalene at their feet; at right, St. John the Baptist, accompanied by the Lamb of God, points to Christ as the Savior. (Unterlinden Museum, Colmar, West Germany.)*

from 1501 until 1521 he was proprietor of a workshop in Seligenstadt. He traveled to Halle for commissions, and, although he was apparently a Protestant and a supporter of Martin Luther, he executed several commissions for two bishops of the Mainz diocese.

Grünewald's earliest datable work is the *Mocking of Christ* (1503; Alte Pinakothek, Munich), a colorful, vehemently expressive painting demonstrating his ability to create dazzling light effects. The painting depicts Christ blindfolded and being beaten by a band of grotesque men. The figures are thick-bodied, soft, and fleshy, done in a manner suggestive of the Italian High Renaissance. Elements of the work also show Grünewald's assimilation of Dürer, specifically his Apocalypse series. Different from High Renaissance idealism and humanism, however, are Grünewald's uses of figural distortion to portray violence and tragedy, thin fluttering drapery, highly contrasting areas of light and shadow (CHIAROSCURO), and unusually stark and iridescent color. It is these elements, already in evidence in this early work, that Grünewald was to develop into the masterful, individualistic style most fully realized in his *Isenheim Altarpiece*.

The *Isenheim Altarpiece* was executed for the hospital chapel of Saint Anthony's Monastery in Isenheim in Alsace and is now at the Unterlinden Museum in Colmar, a nearby town. It is a carved shrine with two sets of folding wings and three views. The first, with the wings closed, is a *Crucifixion* showing a harrowingly detailed, twisted, and bloody figure of Christ on the cross in the center flanked, on the left, by the mourning Madonna being comforted by John the Apostle, and Mary Magdelene kneeling with hands clasped in prayer, and, on the right, by a standing John the Baptist pointing to the dying Savior. At the feet of the Baptist is a lamb holding a cross, symbol of the "Lamb of God" slaughtered for man's sins. The drama of the scene, symbolizing the divine and human natures of Christ, is heightened by the stark contrast between the vibrantly lit foreground and the dark sky and bleak landscape of low mountains in the background. When the outer wings are opened, three scenes of celebration are revealed: the *Annunciation*, the *Angel Concert for Madonna and Child*, and the *Resurrection*. Grünewald's unsurpassed technique in painting colored light is epitomized in the figure of the rising Christ; his dramatic use of writhing forms in movement is also seen here in the figures of Christ, the arriving angel, and the Madonna. BARBARA CAVALIERE

Bibliography: Burkhard, Arthur, *Matthias Grünewald, Personality and Accomplishment* (1936; repr. 1976); Huysmans, J. K., and Ruhmer, Eberhard, *Grünewald: The Paintings* (1958); Pevsner, Nikolaus, and Meier, Michael, *Grünewald* (1958); Scheja, Georg, *The Isenheim Altarpiece*, trans. by R. E. Wolf (1969).

See also: GERMAN ART AND ARCHITECTURE; RENAISSANCE ART AND ARCHITECTURE.

grunion [gruhn'-yuhn]

Grunion is a common name for a small, elongated species of marine coastal fish, *Leuresthes tenuis*, of the silversides family, Atherinidae. They measure up to 20 cm (8 in) in length, have small mouths and no teeth, and live 3 to 4 years.

Grunion are famous for the nocturnal spawning runs they make onto sandy beaches in southern California and northern Baja California. These runs occur around midnight once every two weeks from March to August. Two to four days after a new or full moon thousands of grunion ride the waves up to the beach, and the females burrow tailfirst vertically into damp sand, laying 1,000 to 3,000 eggs apiece. One or more males encircle each female to fertilize the eggs, after which all the grunion ride the next wave back to the sea. The eggs continue to develop until the next high tide two weeks later washes them out of the sand and they hatch. In hunting for grunion, a popular sport, the spawning fish are caught by hand.

grunt

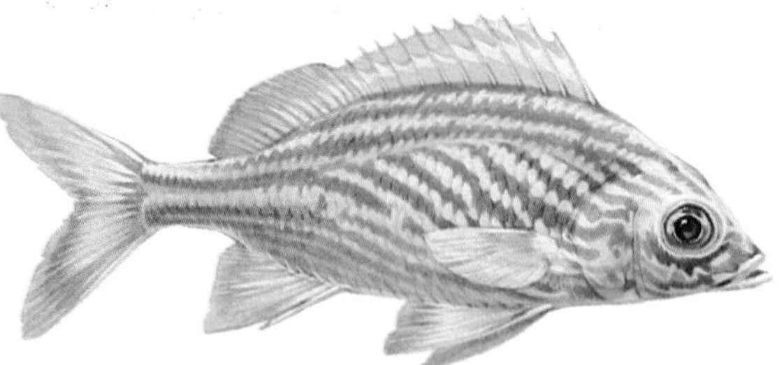

The French grunt, Haemulon flavolineatum, *is a tropical marine fish named for the noise it makes by grinding its teeth.*

Grunts, family Pomadasyidae, order Perciformes, are marine fishes that resemble snappers; they are called "grunts" because they make sounds by grinding their pharyngeal teeth together. The noises are amplified by their swim bladder. They range from Brazil to New England and are abundant in the West Indies and Florida. They are denizens of reefs and mangrove swamps and are esteemed as game and food fish. They may be seen in dense schools over the reefs during the day, dispersing at night over the flats to feed on small fish and crustaceans. Many species have fire-red-lined mouths. Individuals of certain species have been observed pressing their open mouths together in a manner resembling kissing. Many species are less than 0.3 m (1 ft) long, and very few are over 0.6 m (2 ft) in length. C. P. IDYLL

Gruppe 47

Motivated by the need to revitalize the German language and literature after their abuse by the Nazis, H. W. Richter, Alfred Andersch, and other writers founded Gruppe 47 in 1947 as an organization of German authors and critics whose goal was the promotion of works by young writers. Although the group was politically antiauthoritarian, it emphasized the writer's social commitment as a means of strengthening the ethical foundations of a new, democratic Germany. Gruppe 47 remained West Germany's most respected literary voice well into the 1960s. It awarded prizes for outstanding manuscripts and counted among its members more than 200 authors, including Heinrich Böll and Günter Grass.

MARILYN SIBLEY FRIES

Gryphius, Andreas [grif'-ee-us]

Andreas Gryphius, b. Oct. 2, 1616, d. July 16, 1664, the outstanding German poet of his generation, was educated in his hometown of Glogau, Silesia, in Görlitz, and in Danzig. A patron, Georg von Schönborn, enabled him to travel widely in Europe and study at the University of Leiden. After his return from travels in France and Italy, Gryphius declined offers of professorships in mathematics and astrology at the universities of Heidelberg and Uppsala, and became a legal advisor in Glogau in 1650.

Gryphius's intellectual pursuits were numerous: he wrote on legal and historical problems, and produced treatises on ghosts and mummies. His first literary endeavors consisted of Latin verse epics, but his German poetry is especially rich in odes and sonnets, many of them of a religious nature, and written in serialized form to trace a meditative process. In the collection *Kirchhoffsgedankcken* (Thoughts of the Cemetery, 1657), he examines the variety of the human condition and finds that true values can only be attained beyond the grave.

In his later years Gryphius was primarily a playwright. He wrote five tragedies in alexandrine verse, each with a chorus. His comedies, which are partly in verse, partly in prose, include the well-known *Peter Squentz* (1658)—based on an episode in Shakespeare's *Midsummer Night's Dream*—and *Horribilicribrifax* (1663). HUGO BEKKER

Bibliography: Bekker, Hugo, *Andreas Gryphius: Poet between Epochs* (1973); Schindler, Marvin S., *The Sonnets of Andreas Gryphius* (1971).

Guadalajara [gwah-dah-lah-hah'-rah]

Guadalajara is a city located in the Atemajac Valley in west central Mexico at an altitude of 1,552 m (5,092 ft). The capital and service center of Jalisco state, it has a population of 1,626,152 (1980). The surrounding area has rich volcanic soil and a mild climate, with an annual mean temperature of 12° C (53.8° F) and annual precipitation of 965 mm (38 in). As a result, agricultural productivity is high. Jalisco state is Mexico's leading producer of maize and beans, which are marketed in the city. Among the city's most important products are foodstuffs, iron and steel, textiles, and handicrafts, such as hand-blown glass, pottery, cloth, and leather goods.

A large colony of retirees from the United States lives in Guadalajara. They and the many tourists contribute substantially to the city's economy. Music is one of the main attractions of this part of Mexico. Guadalajara is regarded as the home of the mariachis—groups of strolling musicians who play instruments such as the guitar and trumpet. In the state capitol (1643) are murals by José Clemente OROZCO, a leading Mexican artist who lived and worked in the city for many years. Also of interest to visitors is the cathedral of Guadalajara, completed in 1618. Three universities, a cultural institute, and Agua Azul Park make Guadalajara a cultural center.

Guadalajara was founded in 1531 and established on its present site in 1542. Hidalgo y Costilla captured it in 1810, and for a short time it was the center of the Mexican independence movement. JAMES N. SNADEN

Guadalcanal [gwahd-ul-kuh-nal']

Guadalcanal, the largest island of the nation of Solomon Islands, lies in the southwest Pacific Ocean. The area is 5,302 km² (2,047 mi²), and the population is 41,030 (1985 est.). Honiara, the capital, is on the northern coast. The volcanic island has northern plains on which Melanesian peoples raise coconuts, oil palms, rice, and cattle. Forests cover the southern mountains, where some alluvial gold is found.

Sighted by Álvaro de Mendaña de Neira in 1568, Guadalcanal and most of the Solomon Islands chain became a British protectorate in 1893 and gained independence in 1978. During WORLD WAR II the Japanese occupied (1942) Guadalcanal; the island became the site of the first major Allied offen-

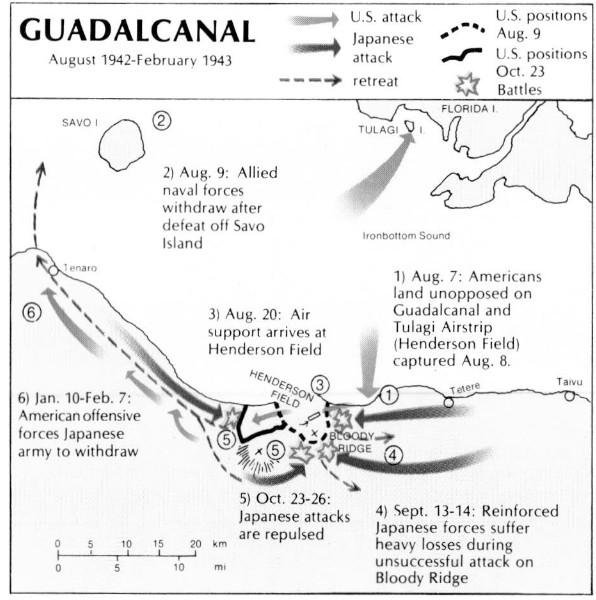

sive in the Pacific. After several months of fierce fighting (August 1942–February 1943) the Japanese were forced to evacuate, and the Allies made Guadalcanal a major base.

Bibliography: Hogbin, Herbert Ian, *A Guadalcanal Society* (1964); Miller, John, Jr., *Guadalcanal: The First Offensive* (1949).

Guadalquivir River [gwahd-ahl-kee-veer']

The Guadalquivir River rises in the Sierra de Cazorla in south central Spain and flows southwest past Córdoba and Seville, meeting the Atlantic Ocean at the Gulf of Cádiz. Tidal beyond Seville, it is canalized to allow navigation by oceangoing vessels. The principal tributaries along its 560-km (348-mi) course include the Guadalimar, Gaudiato, Guadiana Menor, and Genil rivers. There are over 80 hydroelectric stations on the river, and irrigation projects in its 57,394-km^2 (22,160-mi^2) basin support the olive groves, vineyards, fruit orchards, and grain fields of Spain's Andalusia region. The river's name is derived from the Arabic *Wadi al Kebir* ("great river").

Guadalupe Hidalgo, Treaty of [gwah-dah-loop'-ay ee-dahl'-goh]

The Treaty of Guadalupe Hidalgo, ending the MEXICAN WAR, was signed on Feb. 2, 1848, by Nicholas P. Trist (1800–74) for the United States and by a special commission representing the collapsed government of Mexico. Trist, who disregarded a recall to Washington, negotiated the treaty in violation of most of his instructions. The U.S. Senate approved the treaty reluctantly. Mexico ceded to the United States Upper California and New Mexico (including Arizona) and recognized U.S. claims over Texas, with the Rio Grande as its southern boundary. The United States in turn paid Mexico $15,000,000, assumed the claims of American citizens against Mexico, recognized prior land grants in the Southwest, and offered citizenship to any Mexicans residing in the area. Portions of the agreed boundary between the United States and Mexico proved unsurveyable and were adjusted by the GADSDEN PURCHASE.

SEYMOUR V. CONNOR

Bibliography: Connor, Seymour V., and Faulk, Odie B., *North America Divided: The Mexican War, 1846–1848* (1971).

Guadeloupe [gwah-dah-loop']

Guadeloupe, a French overseas department, consists of a group of eight islands in the Lesser Antilles chain in the eastern Caribbean Sea. The islands include Basse-Terre, Grande-Terre, and the smaller dependencies Marie-Galante, Îsles des Saintes, La Désirade, Saint-Barthélemy, and the northern half of SAINT MARTIN. Their combined area is 1,780 km^2 (687 mi^2), and their population is 332,000 (1985 est.).

Basse-Terre, of volcanic origin, has three summits exceeding 1,220 m (4,000 ft), the highest being La Soufrière (1,467 m/4,813 ft). Grande-Terre has low, limestone bluffs. The climate of all the islands is tropical with a rainy season in winter (July to October), and vegetation is dense. Sugarcane, bananas, pineapple, coffee, cacao, and vanilla are grown, processed, and exported. Tourism is a growing industry. The city of BASSE-TERRE is the capital (1982 pop., 13,656). Pointe-à-Pitre on Grande-Terre is the chief port.

The French, who eliminated the native Carib people when they colonized Guadeloupe in 1635, brought in African slaves and established sugarcane plantations. Despite several periods of British occupation in the late 1700s and early 1800s, the islands were confirmed as French possessions in 1815.

Guam [gwahm]

Guam, the largest, most populous, and southernmost of the MARIANA ISLANDS in the western Pacific Ocean, is an unincorporated territory of the United States and has a population of 123,700 (1985 est.). The area is 541 km^2 (209 mi^2), and the highest peak, Lamlam, reaches 407 m (1,334 ft). A volcanic island, Guam has a mountainous southern section and a high, limestone plateau in the north. Typhoons periodically threaten the area, which has an annual mean temperature of 26° C (78° F). The seat of government, Agana, is situated near Apra, the island's main harbor.

U.S. military installations occupy about one-third of Guam, which is important to Pacific defense, and U.S. military personnel constitute about 20% of the population. More than half of the indigenous CHAMORRO (some 40% of the total population) hold federal or local government jobs.

Probably sighted by Ferdinand Magellan in 1521, Guam was held by Spain from 1565 to 1898. It was placed under the U.S. Department of the Navy in 1917. Japan captured Guam in 1941 and surrendered it after fierce fighting in 1944. In 1950, under the Department of the Interior, it received autonomy, and Guamians enjoy U.S. citizenship. In 1982 the inhabitants voted to seek U.S. commonwealth status.

Guam, University of

The University of Guam (1952; enrollment: 2,692; library: 250,000 volumes) is a coeducational land-grant state school in Mangilao, Guam. It offers bachelor's and master's degree programs and operates the Micronesia Area Research Center and a marine laboratory.

guanaco [gwahn-ah'-koh]

The guanaco, L. guanacoe, *which is the only wild relative of the domestic llama and the alpaca, enjoys loitering in swiftly running streams.*

The guanaco, *Lama guanacoe*, is a member of the CAMEL family, Camelidae, order Artiodactyla. The guanaco's body is about 168 cm (5½ ft) long, with a slender neck and legs; the shoulder height is 102 cm (40 in), and the average weight 90 kg (198 lb). The long, woolly coat is dark brown above and white below. Guanacos roam the high grasslands of the Andes from Peru to Tierra del Fuego. They can run as fast as 56 km/h (35 mph) and are good swimmers.

EVERETT SENTMAN

Guanajuato (city) [gwah-nah-hwah'-toh]

Guanajuato (1984 est. pop., 83,586), capital of Guanajuato state in central Mexico, is located about 280 km (175 mi) northwest of Mexico City. Its economy is based upon silver mining and tourism. Guanajuato University (1945) is there.

Founded in 1554 by Spanish prospectors, it became one of the world's greatest silver-mining centers. The great wealth of the city led to the construction of many fine baroque churches and monuments that still stand.

Guanajuato (state)

Guanajuato is a state in central Mexico with a population of 3,358,000 (1984 est.) and an area of 30,590 km^2 (11,810 mi^2). The city of Guanajuato is the state capital. Lying at an average elevation of 1,830 m (6,000 ft), it is part of Mexico's central plateau. In the mountainous north, gold, silver, tin, lead, and copper are mined. Corn, barley, beans, and wheat are raised in the fertile plains of the south. Industries, concentrated in such urban centers as LEÓN and Celaya, produce petrochemicals, textiles, cement, processed foods, and leather. In 1810, Mexico's war for independence began in Guanajuato. It became a state in 1824.

Guangzhou: see CANTON.

guano [gwah'-noh]

The accumulated deposits of the dried droppings of seabirds and bats—deposits that have occasionally reached depths of over 30 m (100 ft)—guano has been used for centuries in parts of South America as a potent soil FERTILIZER. It is rich in nitrogen, phosphorus, and potassium. Nineteenth-century guano exporters dug and bagged the substance from the coastal islands off Peru, where large colonies of seabirds nest, and shipped it to Europe and America. But the depletion of guano reserves, and the development of artificial fertilizers in the early 20th century, brought the export to an end. Today sizable deposits still exist on the Galápagos Islands, in Arizona's Grand Canyon Bat Cave, and on a few Pacific islands.

Guantánamo [gwahn-tahn'-ah-moh]

Guantánamo (1983 est. pop., 171,065) is a city in the mountainous Oriente province in southeastern Cuba. It is located on the Guasco River about 16 km (10 mi) north of the U.S. naval base (established in 1903) at Guantánamo Bay on the coast. Guantánamo is linked to Santiago de Cuba 64 km (40 mi) to the southwest by rail and road. The economy is based on the processing of sugarcane and coffee grown on nearby plantations and on salt production. Guantánamo was founded in 1819 by French exiles from Haiti, an influence preserved in the city's architecture from this period.

Guantánamo Bay

Guantánamo Bay is a large deepwater harbor on the southeastern shore of Cuba, about 100 km (60 mi) from the eastern end of the island. One of the best-protected bays in the world, it covers 75 km^2 (30 mi^2). The bay was first used as a naval station by Britain. In 1903 it was granted to the United States by a treaty that cannot be annulled without the consent of both the United States and Cuba.

Guaraní [gwah-rah-nee']

The Guaraní are a Tupían-speaking people of southern Brazil, Paraguay, and the Rio de la Plata region of Argentina and Uruguay. When first encountered by the Spaniards in the 16th and 17th centuries, they were a large, dominant population in this region. Like the Amazonian TUPÍ, they had a reputation for being very warlike and practiced ritual cannibalism in the precolonial and early colonial periods. The Guaraní lived in villages made up of several households, each of which contained up to 60 families related through the paternal line. These communities were under the religious leadership of a SHAMAN and the political leadership of a chief. The main crops were manioc, maize, and beans; hunting, fishing, and gathering wild plants helped to supplement their diet. They possessed a rich folklore, expressed in song and dance, and an elaborate mythology.

By the 17th and 18th centuries, many Guaraní were encouraged to live in Jesuit missions. Like many other South American peoples, thousands succumbed to European diseases against which they had no immunity. An untold number were taken in Portuguese slave raids or died while resisting capture. Aside from small, surviving groups, the main concentration of Guaraní today consists of MESTIZO peasants in Paraguay. The tribal organization of the past has disappeared, but the Paraguayan peasants continue to speak the Guaraní language in many areas, and the influence of Guaraní musical traditions is apparent in contemporary folk music.

LOUIS C. FARON

Bibliography: Murphy, R. F., *Headhunter's Heritage* (1960); Steward, Julian H., and Faron, Louis C., *Native Peoples of South America* (1959).

guaranty [gair-uhn-tee']

In commercial law, a guaranty, or guarantee, is a promise by a person (the guarantor) to another to be responsible for payment of a debt or the performance of an undertaking by another person (the principal). The term *guaranty* is often used interchangeably with the common law term *suretyship*, and the laws in some jurisdictions have made them identical. Originally, however, a guaranty was a separate agreement that took effect upon the failure of the principal to carry out a contract, while a suretyship was part of the original contract, binding the guarantor directly as a codebtor. A guaranty company is a firm authorized to issue (upon payment of premiums) guaranties or suretyships. A guaranty is distinct from a warranty, which is an expressed or implied contract by a seller ensuring the title or quality of what is sold.

Guardi, Francesco [gwar'-dee]

Francesco Guardi's Ascension Day at Venice, *with its perfect balance between sea and sky, epitomizes 18th-century Venetian painting. Guardi's loose, painterly style captures the brilliantly flickering effects of water and sunlight. (Louvre, Paris.)*

The Venetian painter Francesco Guardi, b. 1712, d. Jan. 1, 1793, was a self-taught artist who created one of the most original painting styles of the 18th century. His enchanting views of Venice, for which he is best known, are painted with an extraordinary freedom. His unusual technique, almost like that of a sketch, used spots of brilliant color, rapid brush-strokes, and agitated, broken lines to evoke the Venetian scene.

Guardi began his career as a history painter in the studio of his older brother, Gianantonio, whose shop produced altarpieces for provincial churches and decorations for public and private buildings. About 1750, Francesco began to paint *vedutisti*, views of the city, at first attempting to imitate CANALETTO. Instead of following Canaletto's mode of precise delineation, however, Guardi developed a unique, interpretative approach that he applied both to evocative scenes of Venice, such as the magnificent *Piazza San Marco Decorated for the Feast of the Ascension* (*c*.1775; Gulbenkian Foundation, Lisbon), and elegiac imaginary views, such as the delicate *Lagoon Scene with Ruins* (*c*.1775–80; Metropolitan Museum, New York City). Although it is commonly noted that view painting declined with the advent of photography, no camera has ever captured the special character of Venice as convincingly as Guardi's tiny painting *Gondola on the Lagoon* (*c*.1780; Museo Poldi Pezzoli, Milan), one of the loveliest, most personal and poetic images of the century. LESLIE JONES

Bibliography: Binion, Alice, *Antonio and Francesco Guardi: Their Life and Milieu* (1976); Shaw, J. B., *The Drawings of Francesco Guardi* (1951).

guardian [gar'-dee-uhn]

A guardian, sometimes called a conservator, is charged with the duty of caring for the personal needs and property of another person (known as the ward). In common usage, the term most often refers to someone responsible for a minor's care. The natural guardians of a child are its parents, who usually name in their wills a relative or friend to serve as guardian if they should die. If no guardian is named, a PROBATE court appoints one, although above a certain age (usually 14) a child may have some say in the choice of a guardian. In some cases two guardians are named: a guardian of the person, who looks after the day-to-day needs of the ward, and a guardian of the property, who manages the estate or assets of the ward. If the ward becomes a plaintiff or defendant in a lawsuit, the court may appoint a special guardian *ad litem,* who represents the ward in the legal action.

A guardian may also be appointed to handle the affairs of someone who has been declared mentally incompetent or who, for some other reason, is incapable of managing his or her affairs.

Guare, John

The American playwright John Guare, b. New York City, Feb. 5, 1938, has written principally for New York's Off-Broadway, where his comic, satiric works have won acclaim since his first production, *Muzeeka,* in 1968. Other notable Guare plays include *The House of Blue Leaves* (1971), *Marco Polo Sings a Solo* (1973), and *Landscape of the Body* (1977), as well as his adaptation and lyrics for the musical version of *Two Gentlemen of Verona* (1971). Guare wrote the prizewinning screenplay for the film *Atlantic City* (1981), whose director, Louis Malle, also directed the Guare play *Lydie Breeze* in New York City in 1982.

Guarini, Giovanni Battista [gwah-ree'-nee]

Giovanni Battista Guarini, b. Dec. 10, 1538, d. Oct. 7, 1612, an Italian poet from an illustrious literary family, taught at the University of Ferrara and, like Torquato Tasso, was a member of the Paduan *Accademia degli Eterei.* From 1567 on he belonged to the court of Alfonso II d'Este, in Ferrara, whom he served as a diplomat. Guarini's main work is the pastoral tragicomedy *Il Pastor fido* (The Faithful Shepherd, 1590), written in the wake of, and in opposition to, Tasso's *Aminta.* The play influenced later European writers and was translated into English in 1647. A comedy in prose, *L'Idropica* (1613), never achieved the popularity of *Il Pastor fido.* OSCAR BÜDEL

Guarini, Guarino

Guarino Guarini, b. Modena, Jan. 17, 1624, d. Mar. 6, 1683, was an Italian scholar and architect. On entering (1639) the Theatine order of priests, he moved to Rome to study theology, philosophy, mathematics, and architecture. Between 1647 and 1666 he lived and worked at various times in Modena, Messina, Paris, and Lisbon, but unfortunately all of his works in those cities have since been destroyed. In Rome, Guarino seems to have known the work of Francesco BORROMINI; in Paris, he doubtless studied the new classicizing architecture of the Louvre.

His high reputation as a baroque architect is largely based on two churches he designed in Turin, Italy, where he settled in 1666 at the request of Duke Charles Emmanuel II of Savoy. For both works, the Capella della Santa Sindone (1667–90) and the Church of San Lorenzo (1668–87), Guarini used a centralized plan capped by a fantastic conical dome. The circular chapel seems almost to spin upward through a complicated grid of intersecting arches leading to the dome. This tendency toward fantastic and breathtaking effects also marks San Lorenzo; its vast dome rests on laced octagonal vaults cut by windows. As in Santa Sindone, the entire structure appears to rise in a mass of piers and columns along an elliptical path toward the apex. These remarkable buildings were much imitated—particularly by late-baroque Austrian and German architects—after the posthumous publication of Guarini's *Architettura civile* (1737).

Although in his writings Guarini sided with 18th-century rationalism, as a priest and an ecclesiastical architect he remained sympathetic to the ideas of infinity and irrationality. In all his structures he gave pride of place to the dome, which, for Guarino, may have signified all that was not measurable—a symbol of the infinity of heaven.

DAVID CAST

Bibliography: Wittkower, Rudolf, *Art and Architecture in Italy: 1600–1750*, rev. ed. (1973).

Guarneri (family) [gwar-nay'-ree]

A family of VIOLIN makers in Cremona, Italy, in the 17th and 18th centuries, the Guarneris, along with the AMATI and STRADIVARI families, brought the art of violin making to its peak. While the Amatis and Stradivaris confined themselves to Cremona, the Guarneris established branches in Mantua and Venice. Guarneri violins followed the patterns and traditions of the Amatis until the time of Giuseppe del Gesù, whereas the Stradivaris evolved their own lines. **Andrea Guarneri**, b. *c*.1626, d. Dec. 7, 1698, was a fellow apprentice of Antonio Stradivari in the Amati workshop. His sons **Pietro Giovanni Guarneri** (known as Peter of Mantua to avoid confusion with his nephew), b. Feb. 18, 1655, d. Mar. 26, 1720, and **Giuseppe Guarneri** (known as Josephi filius to avoid confusion with his son), b. Nov. 25, 1666, d. *c*.1740, continued their father's traditions with minor variations. In the third generation, **Pietro Guarneri** (Peter of Venice), b. Apr. 14, 1695, d. Apr. 7, 1762, incorporated aspects of Venetian instruments into his own, and his brother **Giuseppe Guarneri**, b. Aug. 21, 1698, d. Oct. 17, 1744, became the finest violin maker of the Amati line. Giuseppe is known as "del Gesù" because of the initials I. H. S. and a cross inscribed in his violins. He deviated widely from family tradition, developing instruments uniquely his own, second in quality only to those of Stradivari. Giuseppe del Gesù and Peter of Venice may have been cousins rather than brothers, and Peter of Venice may have been the son of Peter of Mantua. One of del Gesù's violins was played by Niccolò Paganini and is still on display in Genoa.

Bibliography: Hill, W. H., *Violin Makers of the Guarneri Family* (1931); Petherick, Horace, *Joseph Guarnerius: His Work and His Master* (1906; repr. 1977).

Guatemala [gwaht'-uh-mah'-luh]

Guatemala, the most populous country in Central America, is bordered on the north and west by Mexico, on the southeast by El Salvador and Honduras, on the south by the Pacific Ocean, and on the east by the Caribbean Sea and Belize. Once part of the great MAYA civilization and later a Spanish colony, Guatemala has been governed by military officers allied with a few wealthy landowners for most of its postindependence history. It is thought to have the most unequal structure of land ownership and income distribution in Latin America. In 1986, after years of violence by rural guerrillas, left-wing urban terrorists, and right-wing counterterrorists, the country installed its first civilian government in 16 years.

LAND AND PEOPLE

Most of the southern half of the country consists of mountains and plateaus. There is a narrow Pacific coastal plain and a small area of Caribbean lowlands. Guatemala also once claimed almost all of neighboring Belize, but in 1983 it reduced its claim to the southernmost part of that country, which would give Guatemala access to the Atlantic Ocean.

The great majority of the population and the major urban centers, including Guatemala City, are located in the highland area of the south, which is sometimes devastated by earthquakes. The principal range is an extension of the SIERRA MADRE; it includes the country's highest point, Mount Tajumulco (4,223 m/13,854 ft). The northern half of the country consists of Petén department, a sparsely populated lowland tropical area. Average temperatures range from 13° C to 28° C (55° F to 83° F), and annual rainfall averages 2,030 mm (80 in) on the plateaus and about half that in the east.

Some 50% of the population are Maya Indians. The remainder are *ladinos*, which include mestizos (people of mixed Indian and European descent) and westernized Maya. The Maya speak over 20 languages, and many do not speak Spanish.

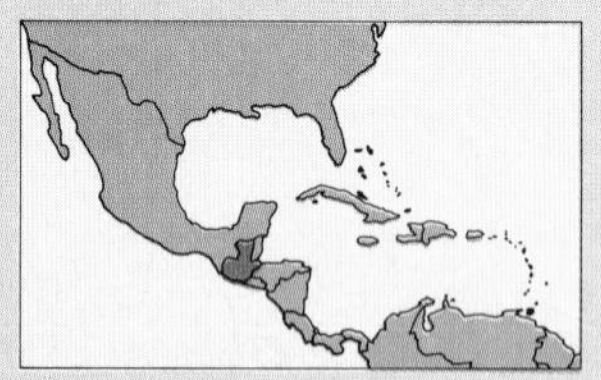

REPUBLIC OF GUATEMALA

LAND. Area: 108,889 km² (42,042 mi²). Capital and largest city: Guatemala City (1981 pop., 754,243).

PEOPLE. Population (1988 est.): 8,700,000. Density (1988 est.): 80 persons per km² (207 per mi²). Distribution (1988): 40% urban, 60% rural. Annual growth (1988): 3.2%. Official language: Spanish. Major religion: Roman Catholicism.

EDUCATION AND HEALTH. Literacy (1987): 50% of adult population. Universities (1987): 5. Hospital beds (1982): 9,881. Physicians (1982): 1,250. Life expectancy (1980–85): women—61.3; men—56.8. Infant mortality (1988): 65 per 1,000 live births.

ECONOMY. GNP (1986): $7.6 billion; $930 per capita. Labor distribution (1985): agriculture—57%; manufacturing—14%; services—13%; commerce—7%; construction—4%; transport—3%; utilities and mining—1%. Foreign trade: imports (1985)—$1.3 billion; exports (1985)—$1.2 billion; principal trade partners (1985)—United States, El Salvador, Netherland Antilles, Mexico, Venezuela, Honduras. Currency: 1 quetzal = 100 centavos.

GOVERNMENT. Type: republic. Legislature: National Congress. Political subdivisions: 22 departments.

COMMUNICATIONS. Railroads (1987): 870 km (541 mi) total. Roads (1987): 26,429 km (16,422 mi) total. Major ports: 2. Major airfields: 3.

Antigua, in southwestern Guatemala, became the Spanish colonial capital of Central America in 1542 after an eruption of Agua Volcano (background) *destroyed the nearby administrative center of Ciudad Vieja. The capital was moved to Guatemala City in 1776.*

ECONOMIC ACTIVITY

Until the late 19th century, when coffee was introduced, most people practiced subsistence agriculture. Coffee growing soon became the leading economic activity. The banana industry, introduced by the U.S.-based United Fruit Company, developed on both coasts during the early 20th century. United Fruit long dominated the economy, providing much of the nation's foreign exchange and controlling the only railroad and the principal port, Puerto Barrios. After World War II, however, a highway was built parallel to the railroad, which itself passed into Guatemalan hands, and the United Fruit banana lands were expropriated. Coffee has since resumed its place as the leading export, and the economy remains predominantly agricultural, although industry and mining are also important.

Since the 1960s, Guatemala has become one of the most industrialized nations in Central America, but manufacturing has been adversely affected by the 1982 collapse of the Central American Market and shortages of foreign exchange. Large deposits of petroleum and nickel in Petén have been exploited commercially since the 1970s. The country has a chronic balance-of-payments deficit, and domestic unrest and government-introduced economic austerity measures have led to a decline in the already low standard of living.

HISTORY AND GOVERNMENT

Impressive Maya ruins remain at TIKAL, UAXACTÚN, and the more recently discovered El Mirador, which dates back to about 300 BC. The area was conquered (1523–24) by the Spanish under Pedro de ALVARADO, who became the first captain general of Guatemala—a region that included most of Central America. Guatemala gained independence from Spain in 1821 and in 1824 became part of the CENTRAL AMERICAN FEDERATION. In 1838 the union broke up, and in 1839, Guatemala became an independent country. Until World War II it was ruled by CAUDILLOS, or military dictators. The most outstanding of these was Justo Rufino BARRIOS (president 1873–85), who enacted extensive anticlerical legislation and sponsored the beginning of the coffee industry.

The period of caudillo rule came to an end in 1944, and after a provisional regime, Juan José Arévalo was elected president in 1945. A 10-year period of basic reforms began, including a new constitution, the country's first labor code, and a democratic government. In 1951, Arévalo was succeeded as president by Col. Jacobo Arbenz Guzmán. His leftist regime began construction of a highway to the coast and carried out extensive agrarian reform, which brought Arbenz into direct conflict with the powerful United Fruit Company.

In 1954, Carlos Castillo Armas led a U.S.-supported revolt that overthrew Arbenz. For the next 30 years the country was governed principally by military men. Many of the Arévalo-Arbenz reforms were undone, including the agrarian reform

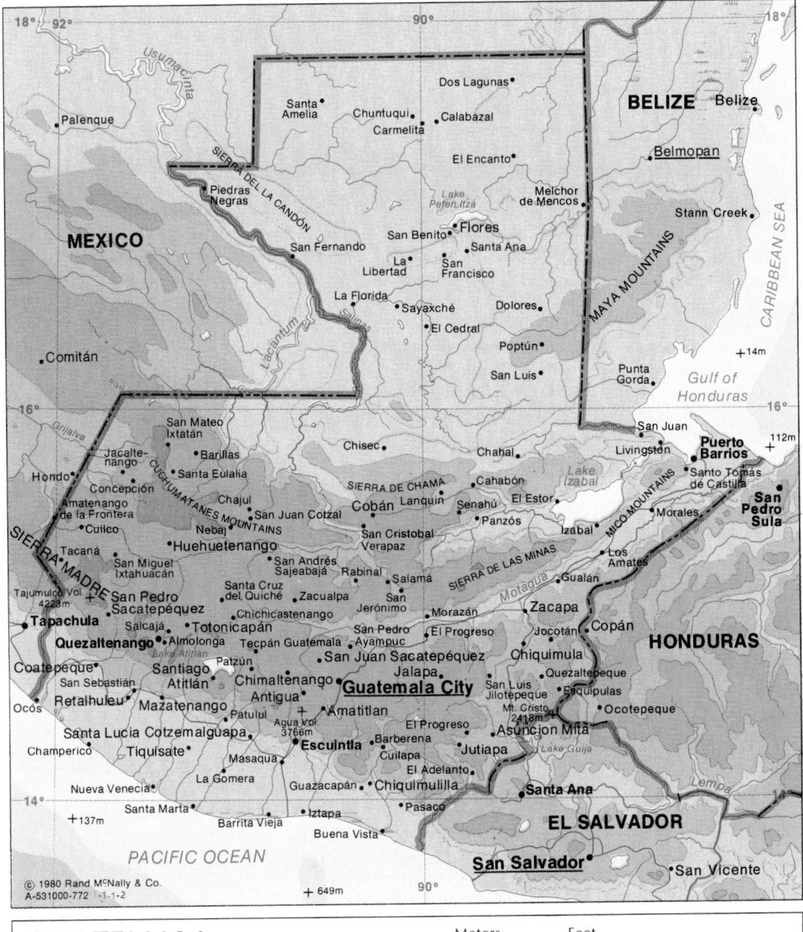

GUATEMALA

—— Railroad	National capitals are underlined	
+ Spot Elevation or Depth	City type size indicates relative importance	
Scale: 0 20 40 60 80 100 km / 0 20 40 60 mi	Scale 1:4,318,000	

Meters	Feet
Above 4000	Above 13124
2000	6562
1000	3281
500	1640
200	656
0	0

Meters	Feet
0	0
200	656
Below 2000	Below 6562

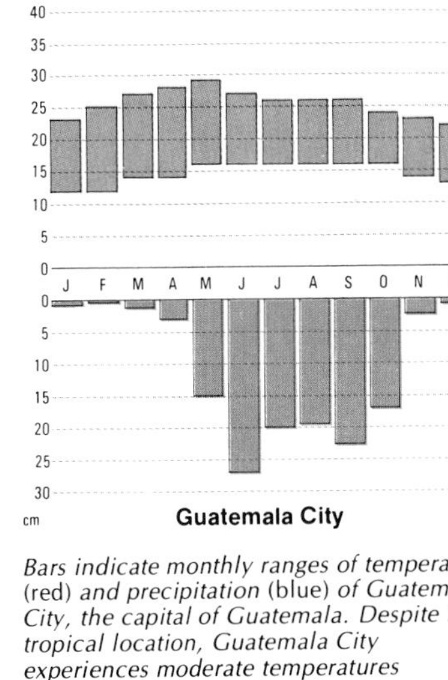

Bars indicate monthly ranges of temperature (red) and precipitation (blue) of Guatemala City, the capital of Guatemala. Despite its tropical location, Guatemala City experiences moderate temperatures year-round because of its elevation (1,480 m/4,855 ft).

Lake Atitlán is near the volcanoes of the southern range of Guatemala's Sierra Madre, at an elevation of 1,562 m (5,125 ft). The lake, located about 160 km (100 mi) west of Guatemala City, is a popular resort area.

and much of the labor legislation, and tens of thousands of Guatemalans, most of them civilians, lost their lives in political violence. In the early 1980s, in an attempt to undermine support for leftist guerrillas, more than one million Indian peasants were herded into army-run "model villages" and enlisted in civil-defense patrols.

President Efraín Ríos Montt, who had come to power in a military coup in 1982, was himself ousted by the army in August 1983 after he assumed increasingly dictatorial powers. His successor, Brig. Gen. Oscar Humberto Mejía Victores, supervised Guatemala's return to democratic rule. A constituent assembly elected in 1984 prepared a new constitution. It provided for a unicameral parliament and a president, both elected for 5-year terms by universal suffrage, and called for respect for human rights and an end to military involvement in politics. Legislative and presidential elections were held in 1985, and Marco Vinicio Cerezo Arévalo, a populist who had rebuilt Guatemala's Christian Democratic party, was sworn in as president on Jan. 15, 1986. Powerful conservative interests in the army and the private sector forced Cerezo to move slowly in implementing land reform, tax reform, and other changes. He concentrated on improving the economy and reducing political violence while agreeing not to prosecute army officers for past human rights abuses. Cerezo survived a coup attempt in May 1988. ROBERT J. ALEXANDER

Bibliography: American University, *Guatemala: A Country Study* (1983); Black, G., et al., *Garrison Guatemala* (1984); Brigham, W. T., *Guatemala: Land of the Quetzal*, ed. by W. Popenoe (1965); Calvert, P. A., *Guatemala* (1985); Fried, J., et al., eds., *Guatemala in Revolution* (1983); Hough, R., et al., *Land and Labor in Guatemala* (1982); Maslow, J. E., *Bird of Life, Bird of Death* (1986); Schlesinger, W., and Kinzer, S., *Bitter Fruit: The Untold Story of the American Coup in Guatemala* (1982); Simon, Jean-Marie, *Guatemala* (1988); Whetten, N. L., *Guatemala: The Land and the People* (1961; repr. 1974).

Guatemala City

Guatemala City is the capital of both the Republic of Guatemala and the department of the same name. Its population of 754,243 (1981) is the largest of any Central American city. Located on a fertile plateau 1,480 m (4,855 ft) high in south central Guatemala, it is the country's center for trade, industry, government, finance, and education. A modern urban center, Guatemala City is linked with other major Latin American cities by the PAN AMERICAN HIGHWAY. The city has five universities, including San Carlos University of Guatemala, founded in 1776. Four museums are located there.

Originally a Maya settlement, Guatemala City was founded in 1776 as the capital of Spanish Guatemala. Earthquakes in 1917 and 1918 destroyed the city, and another quake severely damaged it in February 1976.

guava [gwah'-vuh]

Guavas are the oval or pear-shaped berries of *Psidium*, a genus of small trees of the myrtle family that are native to tropical America and the West Indies. The most significant is *Psidium guajava*, indigenous to Brazil. Guavas have yellowish skin with many seeds in a gritty, sweet-acid pulp, either pink or white in color. Domestication occurred in Peru or Colombia about 1000 BC. The tree is now grown extensively in the American tropics and was widely introduced in the Old World by the Spanish and Portuguese. Naturally occurring trees are cropped in some places, but commercial plantations have been successful, for example, in Florida and California and in Brazil, Guyana, and India. Improvements by hybridization and artificial selection have proved possible. Eaten raw or in pies, or made into juice, pastes, or jellies, guavas have traditionally had only local significance in the areas of production. More recently, canning has enabled a small international trade to develop. P. M. SMITH

Guayaquil [gwy-ah-keel']

Guayaquil (Santiago de Guayaquil), Ecuador's largest city and chief port, is located on the Guayas River, about 65 km (40 mi) from the Gulf of Guayaquil. The population is 1,199,344 (1982). Guayaquil's industries include textile and cement manufacturing. Bananas and cacao are its primary exports. The University of Guayaquil (1867) and the Catholic University of Saint James of Guayaquil (1962) are located there.

Guayaquil was founded in 1535 on the feast day of Saint James (Santiago) by the Spanish conqueror Sebastian de Benalcazar. Pirate attacks, plagues, fires, and earthquakes have ravaged the city. Guayaquil was the site of a historic meeting between Simón BOLÍVAR and José de SAN MARTÍN in 1822.

guayule [wy-oo'-lee]

Guayule is the common name for the herb *Parthenium argentatum* in the sunflower family, Compositae. It is found in southwest Texas and northern Mexico, where it grows to 1 m (3 ft) high. Guayule was cultivated for rubber in northern Mexico between 1905 and 1910 and in the southwestern United States during World War II. Because imported natural rubber is costly and because guayule grows in areas not useful for other agriculture, the United States is conducting research on improved guayule strains and on increasing the productivity of the plant by chemical means. Guayule latex, unlike that of rubber trees, is contained in cells that must be crushed to extract it. OLIN S. FEARING

Bibliography: Hinman, C. Wiley, "New Crops for Arid Lands," *Science*, Sept. 28, 1984.

Gubarev, Aleksei

The Soviet cosmonaut Aleksei Aleksandrovich Gubarev, b. Mar. 29, 1931, was a Soviet navy jet pilot before becoming a cosmonaut in 1963. He made his first spaceflight, with Georgy GRECHKO, on *Soyuz 17*, which was launched on Jan. 10, 1975, and remained docked with the *Salyut 4* space station for nearly 30 days. On Mar. 2, 1978, he was launched on *Soyuz 28* with Vladimir REMEK and visited the already manned *Salyut 6* space station for one week. JAMES OBERG

Gucci, Aldo: see FASHION DESIGN.

Guderian, Heinz [goo-dayr'-ee-ahn, hynts]

Heinz Guderian, b. June 17, 1888, d. May 15, 1954, was a German army officer who devised the BLITZKRIEG strategy used by the Germans with great success in invading Poland, the Low Countries, and France in World War II. He served in World War I and remained in the German army after the war, developing his idea that highly mobile armored units should be used to breach enemy lines. By 1938 he was in command of all German armored forces, and the value of his strategy was proved in the opening campaigns of World War II. In the German invasion of Russia in 1941, Guderian's Panzer (tank) divisions were less successful, and he lost influence for a time. From July 1944 to March 1945, however, he was chief of the general staff. K. M. SMOGORZEWSKI

Bibliography: Carver, Michael, ed., *The War Lords: Military Commanders of the Twentieth Century* (1976); Keegan, John, *Guderian* (1973); Macksey, Kenneth John, *Guderian, Panzer General* (1975).

Gudrun [gud'-run]

In Norse mythology, Gudrun was princess of the Nibelungs (Niflungs) who married SIEGFRIED after her mother gave him a magic potion that made him forget his first love, BRUNHILD. After Brunhild had Siegfried murdered, Gudrun married Brunhild's brother Atli. But when Atli killed Gudrun's brothers, Gudrun slew her two sons by Atli, fed their hearts to him, and then killed him. In the German version of the myth, Gudrun appears as Kriemhild. Another Gudrun is the heroine of a 13th-century German epic, the *Gudrun Lied.*

Guelphs and Ghibellines [gwelfs, gib'-uh-linz]

The Guelphs and Ghibellines, the major political factions of late medieval Italy, arose from the followers of the two families contending for the Holy Roman Empire in the 12th century: the WELFS of Saxony and the HOHENSTAUFEN of Swabia. The name *Ghibelline* was derived from the name of the Hohenstaufen castle, Waiblingen.

In the early 13th century the Welfs, or Guelphs, became the allies of the PAPACY in its struggle against the Hohenstaufen emperor FREDERICK II for the control of Italy. In general, the Guelphs drew their Italian support from the merchant class of the central Italian communes and the Angevin rulers of Naples. The Ghibellines, composed of the imperial vicars of northern Italian cities, the communes of Siena and Pisa in Tuscany, and the feudal magnates of central Italy, attempted to regain control of the peninsula after Frederick's death in 1250. This cause failed when the Ghibellines were defeated by the Angevins of Naples and the Florentine Guelphs at Tagliacozzo in 1268. Thereafter, the names applied mainly to local factions or even families, although some cities in northern Italy, such as Milan under the Visconti and Verona under the Scala, were always Ghibelline, because their rulers were imperial vicars.

By about 1300 in Florence, membership in the Guelph party became a prerequisite for holding political office; thus Guelphism was elevated to the status of a political ideology. With the return of the papacy from Avignon to Italy and creation of regional states in the 15th century, the terms dropped from use. BENJAMIN G. KOHL

Bibliography: Hyde, J. K., *Society and Politics in Medieval Italy* (1973).

guenon [guh-nohn']

The moustached guenon, Cercopithecus cephus, *is a tree-dwelling African monkey. Distinctive features may include a blue nose, yellow whiskers, and a pale area resembling a moustache on its upper lip.*

The guenons, genus *Cercopithecus,* are about 12 species of colorful African monkeys belonging to the family Cercopithecidae, order Primates. These slim, graceful animals have bodies 30 to 69 cm (12 to 27 in) long, weigh approximately 7 kg (15 lb), and have nonprehensile tails 500–875 mm (20–34 in) longer than their bodies. Their faces are small, with large eyes, and some species look as though they were wearing dark glasses. The guenon's heavy, soft fur may be brown, red, gray, green, or yellow, with markings of white or other colors. For example, a ground-dwelling guenon called the green monkey, *C. aethiops sabaeus,* is a bright shade of green and has yellow whiskers, a yellow and black tail, and gray hands and feet. Other guenons have large, brightly colored noses that are in striking contrast with the hue of their body fur. Guenons are widely distributed in Africa. One new species, the sun-tailed guenon, *C. solatus,* was discovered as recently as 1988 in the forests of Gabon. It is named for the bright yellow orange color of its tail.

Most guenons are tree and rock-ledge dwellers. They mate at any time of the year, and after a gestation period of about seven months a single offspring is born. Guenons become sexually mature in about three years. The family unit is important to the guenons. During the day, families may mingle with other guenon families and also with other kinds of monkeys, but at night each family of guenons returns to its own area to sleep.

Guercino [gwayr-chee'-noh]

The Italian painter Giovanni Francesco Barbieri, 1591–1666, was called *il Guercino* (the squinter). He received his first training in his native Cento, near Ferrara. Travels to Venice and contact with the Carracci Academy in Bologna (see CARRACCI family) helped to shape his early style, which is characterized by freedom of execution and intensity of expression. At the age of 30, Guercino received a commission to paint the fresco of *Aurora* (1621–23) for the ceiling of the Casino Ludovisi at the Villa Ludovisi in Rome. This work is regarded as a marvel of illusionism with its bold foreshortening. After its completion, and owing to the death of his patron Pope Gregory XV, Guercino ended his stay in Rome.

Guercino returned to Cento where he remained until 1642, when the death of Guido RENI, the undisputed master of Bologna, may have prompted Guercino's move to that city. Guercino worked there until his own death, producing subdued paintings strongly influenced by Reni's restrained classicism. He also produced an immense oeuvre of bold, energetic pen-and-ink drawings and is now highly regarded for his graphic work as well as his painting. ADELHEID M. GEALT

Bibliography: Akserdjian, David, and Mahon, Denis, *Guercino Drawings from the Collections of Denis Mahon and the Ashmolean Museum* (1986); Haskell, Francis, *Patrons and Painters: Italian Art and Society in the Age of the Baroque* (1963; repr. 1971); Wittkower, Rudolf, *Art and Architecture in Italy, 1600–1750,* 3d ed. (1973).

Guericke, Otto von [gay'-rik-eh]

A natural philosopher who served as the mayor of Magdeburg, Germany, Otto von Guericke, b. Nov. 20, 1602, d. May 11, 1686, demonstrated experimentally the capacity of the atmosphere to do work and decisively refuted the long-held notion that it was impossible for a VACUUM to exist. Using hollow copper spheres and an air pump of his own construction, Guericke demonstrated that a partial vacuum could be created by pumping the air out of the sphere. He also proved that the air remaining in the sphere (at a pressure below that of the atmosphere) was distributed evenly throughout the vessel.

In 1657, Guericke carried out his famous demonstration that several teams of horses could not pull apart two joined hemispheres when the air within had been evacuated. Using a piston in a cylinder, he also showed that when a vacuum was created on one side of the piston, the atmosphere would move the piston and a considerable mass through a distance, thus performing work. This became the basic principle of the NEWCOMEN steam engine (1712). DAVID HOUNSHELL

Guérin, Pierre Narcisse, Baron [gay-ran', pyair nar-sees']

Baron Pierre Narcisse Guérin, b. Mar. 13, 1774, d. July 16, 1833, a French painter in the neoclassical tradition of the early 19th century, was celebrated for his elegant and polished style. After a period of study with Jean Baptiste Regnault, he won the Prix de Rome and spent the year 1799 in Italy. The painting he submitted to the Paris Salon in 1799, *Return of Marcus Sextus* (Louvre, Paris), was an immediate success, and he continued to exhibit at the Salon regularly thereafter. Guérin's studio in Paris was a meeting place for many artists of the romantic movement, such as Cogniet, Orsel, and Géricault. The Legion of Honor was conferred upon him in 1803. In 1815, Guérin became a professor at the École des Beaux-Arts. He accepted the directorship of the French Academy in Rome in 1822, a post he held until 1828. PHILIP GOULD

Bibliography: Friedlaender, Walter, *David to Delacroix* (1952); Rosenblum, Robert, *Transformations in Late Eighteenth Century Art* (1969).

Guernica: see PICASSO, PABLO.

Guernsey [gurn'-zee]

Guernsey is the second largest of the CHANNEL ISLANDS. It has an area of 62 km^2 (24 mi^2) and a population of 53,268 (1981). With all other Channel Islands except Jersey, it forms a bailiwick of the British crown. St. Peter Port is the chief town. The southern part of the island is a plateau, rising to 91 m (300 ft), and the northern part is low lying. Guernsey was first settled by the Romans, and in the 10th century, by the Normans. During World War II, the Germans occupied Guernsey. Tourism, flower and tomato growing, and the raising of Guernsey cattle are economically important.

Guerrero [gay-ray'-roh]

Guerrero is a state in southwestern Mexico along the Pacific coast. It has a population of 2,560,262 (1988 est.) and an area of 64,281 km^2 (24,819 mi^2). CHILPANCINGO is the state capital.

Most of the state is covered by the rugged Sierra Madre del Sur. The long, coastal margin and the Balsas River valley in the north, however, are so low that a tropical climate prevails; corn, cotton, tobacco, and coffee are grown there and in the fertile mountain valleys. Mining (gold, lead, iron, silver, and mercury) and forestry are carried on inland at higher elevations. Tourism is important at ACAPULCO and at Taxco, a mountain resort. Guerrero became a state in 1849.

guerrilla [guh-ri'-luh]

A guerrilla is a member of a small, mobile, irregular armed force that takes limited actions on a small scale, usually as part of a larger political and military strategy. Guerrillas often dress in civilian clothes, have some other occupation, such as farming, and use unconventional weapons. A populace sympathetic to the political goals of guerrillas favors their activities, as does irregular terrain that affords cover. Guerrilla warfare uses surprise attacks, ambushes, and the destruction of enemy supplies, rather than a massive direct confrontation as with regular armies. The strength of guerrillas lies in their unpredictability, mobility, and entrenchment in the terrain or populace. Guerrilla activities may constitute either partisan resistance to an enemy's army during wartime or a challenge to the government in power during peacetime.

Guerrilla fighting has a long history. Peasant bands sometimes took action against ruling powers during ancient and medieval times but rarely had much effect. During the American Revolution, American guerrillas such as Francis MARION harassed the more conventional British forces and inflicted considerable damage. These irregulars were incorporated into Washington's army as the war progressed; this merging of guerrilla and regular forces has become common.

During World War II, Ukrainian peasants formed bands and successfully battled large numbers of Nazi soldiers, contributing significantly to the German defeat on the eastern front.

TITO, a leader of Communist and other partisans in Yugoslavia during World War II, became Yugoslavia's leader after the war (1945); other guerrillas who succeeded and came to rule the countries whose governments they had challenged include MAO TSE-TUNG in China (1949) and Fidel CASTRO in Cuba (1959). VIET MINH guerrillas succeeded in bringing about a French withdrawal from Vietnam (1954); VIET CONG guerrillas together with North Vietnamese regulars brought about withdrawal (1975) of the United States. In Latin America, with the successful example provided by Castro and Ernesto (Che) GUEVARA in ousting the Batista government in Cuba, guerrilla activities continually recur, as in Nicaragua where Sandanista guerrillas came to power in 1979. The IRISH REPUBLICAN ARMY (IRA) continues to conduct guerrilla activity in Northern Ireland. The politically inspired bombings, kidnappings, and murders that occur in contemporary society are sometimes construed as acts of guerrilla warfare rather than terrorism.

guerrilla theater [guh-ril'-uh thee'-uh-tur]

Guerrilla theater, or street theater, evolving out of the politics of the New Left and the protest against U.S. involvement in Vietnam, first came to public attention in the late 1960s. The earliest radical theater companies were the San Francisco Mime Troupe, founded in 1959 by Ronnie Davis; the Bread and Puppet Theatre, in New York City, founded in 1961 by German artist Peter Schumann; and El Teatro Campesino (Farm Workers Theater) of Delano, Calif., founded by Luis Valdez. The goal of the movement was the creation of an alternate theater for a revolutionized society. Using mime, songs, puppets, speeches, masks, and a mixture of improvisational and rehearsed material, guerrilla theater companies sought to engage the emotional participation of audiences while teaching them a political or social lesson. In Europe the movement was represented by the *Grand Pantomime with Banners and Small and Medium Puppets*, an anti-fascist performance organized in 1969 by Italian playwright Dario FO.

Bibliography: Sainer, Arthur, *The Radical Theatre Notebook* (1975).

Guettard, Jean Étienne [get-ar']

A French botanist, mineralogist, and pioneer paleontologist, Jean Étienne Guettard, b. Sept. 27, 1715, d. Jan. 6, 1786, was the first to suspect the volcanic origin of the Auvergne region (1756) and thus figured prominently in the controversy over whether basalt was of volcanic or sedimentary origin. He produced (1751) the first maps of France showing surface geology, and helped prepare (1780) the *Atlas and Mineralogical Description of France.*

Guevara, Che [gay-vah'-rah, chay]

Ernesto "Che" Guevara, b. June 14, 1928, d. Oct. 9, 1967, was a Latin-American guerrilla leader who helped Fidel CASTRO achieve his revolution in Cuba. Argentinian by birth, he was trained as a doctor before becoming involved in agitation against the dictator Juan Perón. He went to Guatemala, where he joined the leftist regime of Jacobo Arbenz Guzmán in 1953. After Arbenz was overthrown (1954), Guevara met Fidel Castro in Mexico and joined his revolutionary cadre. From 1956 until the taking of Havana on Jan. 1, 1959, he fought as a member of the Castro army and helped shape its strategy.

Guevara held several important posts in the new Cuban government, including that of minister of industry (1961-65). He took more interest, however, in revolutionary warfare to spread communism in Latin America. In 1965 he dropped from public view; he had gone to Bolivia to train a guerrilla force. In 1967 his group was destroyed by Bolivian forces near Santa Cruz, and Guevara was captured and executed. His writings include *Guerrilla Warfare* (1961) and *Guerrilla Warfare: A Method* (1966).

Che Guevara (right), a Latin American revolutionary and theoretician, proved invaluable to Fidel Castro (left), first in the overthrow of Fulgencio Batista's Cuban government in 1959 and later in the administration of Castro's new socialist regime. Guevara was executed (1967) while attempting to foment revolution in Bolivia.

Bibliography: Debray, Regis, *Che's Guerrilla War* (1966); James, Daniel, *Che Guevara* (1969); Resnick, Marvin, *The Black Beret: The Life and Meaning of Che Guevara* (1970); Sauvage, Leo, *Che Guevara: The Failure of a Revolutionary* (1974).

Guggenheim (family) [goo'-gen-hime]

The Guggenheim family amassed its fortune in smelting and mining operations. **Meyer Guggenheim**, b. Feb. 1, 1828, d. Mar. 15, 1905, went to the United States from Switzerland at the age of 19 and settled in Philadelphia, where he became a successful importer of Swiss embroidery. In 1888, after he had invested in Colorado mining property, he formed the Philadelphia Smelting and Mining Company and, with the help of his seven sons, principally **Daniel** (b. July 9, 1856, d. Sept. 28, 1930), rapidly expanded the company's holdings and processing operations. In 1899, when the American Smelting and Refining Company was formed to consolidate leading companies in the field, Meyer refused to join; his company so successfully competed with the trust that by 1901 the Guggenheims were able to take it over. Daniel became head of the combine, which mined copper and nitrate in Chile, tin in Bolivia, gold in Alaska, and diamonds and rubies in Africa. Daniel retired in 1919; he founded the philanthropic Daniel and Florence Guggenheim Foundation and, in 1926, the Daniel Guggenheim Fund for the Promotion of Aeronautics. Another son, **Simon**, b. Dec. 30, 1867, d. Nov. 2, 1941, served a term as U.S. senator from Colorado (1907-13). He took over from Daniel in 1919 and served as president of American Smelting and Refining until his death. In memory of his son, who died in 1922, he founded (1925) the John Simon GUGGENHEIM MEMORIAL FOUNDATION, which gives financial aid to scholars and artists. Other members of the family noted for contributions to the arts are Solomon Robert—who established the GUGGENHEIM MUSEUM in New York City—and Peggy, a collector.

Bibliography: Davis, John H., *The Guggenheims: An American Epic* (1978); O'Connor, Harvey, *The Guggenheims: The Making of an American Dynasty* (1937; repr. 1976).

Guggenheim, Peggy

Peggy Guggenheim, b. New York City, Aug. 26, 1898, d. Venice, Dec. 23, 1979, was an art collector and patron of modern artists. The niece of Solomon Guggenheim, founder of the Guggenheim Museum in New York, she was educated in Paris, where she later became part of the international artistic milieu. In 1938 she opened a gallery in London called Guggenheim Jeune. Following her own taste for the most part, but occasionally aided by French artist Marcel DUCHAMP, she exhibited such renowned modern masters as Jean Arp, Constantin Brancusi, Alexander Calder, Wassily Kandinsky, and Henry Moore. In addition, she showed works by the German surrealist Max ERNST, whom she later married.

The outbreak of World War II forestalled Guggenheim's plan to convert her London gallery into a museum specializing in the modernist art movements to which she had given most of her support: cubism, geometric abstraction, and surrealism. In 1941 she moved to New York City, where she used her collection of major 20th-century paintings as the nucleus of a new gallery, Art of This Century. At this gallery she provided crucial support to such abstract expressionists as

Hans Hofmann, Mark Rothko, and Jackson Pollock. In 1946 she left New York for Venice, where she maintained her collection in the Palazzo Venier dei'Leoni. CARTER RATCLIFFE

Bibliography: Guggenheim, Peggy, *Out of This Century* (1979).

Guggenheim Memorial Foundation

The John Simon Guggenheim Memorial Foundation was established in 1925 by Mr. and Mrs. Simon Guggenheim (see GUGGENHEIM family) to provide fellowships for "advanced study in any field of knowledge, or in any of the fine arts . . . under the freest possible conditions." Grants are available to citizens and permanent residents of states and territories in the Western Hemisphere and the Philippines. In 1978 assets were $83,000,000, and 332 grants were made, totaling $4,997,500. The foundation is distinct from the Daniel and Florence and the Harry Frank Guggenheim foundations.

Guggenheim Museum

The Solomon R. Guggenheim Museum (1956-59) in New York City, designed by Frank Lloyd Wright, embodies Wright's ideal of continuous space in its dynamically expanding spiral gallery. Offices (foreground) were added in 1969, based on drawings by Wright.

The Solomon R. Guggenheim Museum, originally called the Museum of Non-objective Art, was established in New York City by Solomon R. Guggenheim for the purpose of promoting and encouraging modern art. The original holdings of the museum were assembled with the help of a young German artist, Hilla Rebay von Ehrenwiesen, who served as the museum's first director and curator. The new museum opened to the public on June 1, 1939. In 1959 it moved to its present building, designed by Frank Lloyd WRIGHT; the highly original circular structure is located on Fifth Avenue.

The nucleus of the collection, works by Kandinsky, Delaunay, Bauers, and other nonobjective painters, was enlarged in 1948 by the purchase of Karl Nierendorf's estate, which provided 18 additional Kandinskys, a famous Kokoshka, 110 Klees, 6 Chagalls, 24 Feiningers, and many other works. The collection was enriched by the Katherine Dreier bequest (1953) and by the works from Miss Rebay's estate (1971). Another important addition is the Justin K. Tannhauser collection, comprising 75 paintings and sculptures and including many important impressionist and postimpressionist works. Under the curatorship (1953-60) of James Johnson Sweeney, the collection's sculpture section was established with the acquisition of works by such major modern sculptors as Brancusi, Calder, Duchamp-Villon, Giacometti, and Moore. In recent years, the museum's holdings, which currently amount to about 3,500 works, have been expanded to include works by many important contemporary artists.

MAGDALENA DABROWKSI

Bibliography: Rudenstine, Angelica Z., *The Guggenheim Museum Collection: Paintings 1880-1945*, 2 vols. (1976); Wright, Frank Lloyd, *Solomon R. Guggenheim Museum* (1975).

Guicciardini, Francesco [gwit-char-dee'-nee]

Francesco Guicciardini, b. Mar. 6, 1483, d. May 22, 1540, was an Italian statesman, historian, and political thinker of the RENAISSANCE. Schooled in classics and law, Guicciardini wrote (1509) a history of his native city before embarking on a brilliant political career. In 1512 he served the Florentine Republic as ambassador to the court of Ferdinand II of Aragon. Pope Leo X appointed him governor of Modena in 1516 and of Reggio and Parma, in the Papal States, in 1517. In 1524 he was made president, or papal governor, of the Romagna. After the imperial defeat of the French at the Battle of Pavia (1525), he helped form the League of Cognac against Holy Roman Emperor Charles V.

Guicciardini supported the Medici at the restoration in 1530 but retired soon after to his country estate at Arcetri. There he wrote his lengthy eyewitness history of Italy from 1494 to 1534 and revised his *Ricordi*, maxims on politics and human nature. An even more cynical and realistic observer than his older contemporary Nicolò Machiavelli, Guicciardini has often been criticized for his lack of idealism and pessimistic view of humankind. BENJAMIN G. KOHL

Bibliography: Bondanella, Peter E., *Francesco Guicciardini* (1976); Ridolfi, Roberto, *The Life of Francesco Guicciardini*, trans. by Cecil Grayson (1967).

guidance, educational: see CAREER EDUCATION; SECONDARY EDUCATION.

guidance and control systems

Guidance and control systems are devices used to maneuver ships, aircraft, missiles, and spacecraft. Their development has been particularly stimulated in recent years by SPACE EXPLORATION. The concepts of navigation, guidance, and control, although often confused, have distinct meanings. NAVIGATION is the science of determining the position and path of a vehicle. This process involves the use of sensors, GYROSCOPES, and a knowledge of star and planetary emphemerides. Guidance is the logic by which the vehicle is steered and oriented along a planned path. It requires knowledge of a planned route and alternatives in case of changes.

Control is the application of guidance laws in conjunction with navigational information to make the vehicle behave in an acceptable manner. Implementation of control requires methods for the application of a force to bring about a change in orientation or course. SHIPS use rudders to steer. AIRCRAFT use elevators, ailerons, and rudders for changes in attitude and flight direction. SATELLITES and piloted spacecraft use thrusters, gyroscopes, and magnetic field interactions for their maneuvers.

METHODS OF SATELLITE GUIDANCE AND CONTROL

There are two general approaches to satellite guidance and control: passive and—for more complex missions—active.

Passive Control. A passive satellite has no propulsive capability once placed into orbit. It has no control elements and possibly no sensors. A more sophisticated, passively stabilized satellite might take advantage of a phenomenon known as gravity gradient when it is necessary to point the spacecraft along the local vertical direction (toward Earth). If a typical satellite is thought of as having a dumbbell shape with the two masses aligned with the local vertical direction, then any deviation from this orientation would cause a restoring torque to be produced. The reason is that the outer mass is experiencing less gravitational attraction and more centrifugal force than is the inner mass. Thus the outer mass "feels" a net force outward, and the inner mass, a net force inward. The method is effective only for circular or nearly circular orbits.

Another approach to passive stabilization is to spin the entire spacecraft about a single axis, much like a large gyroscope. The inherent stability thus produced would tend to keep the axis pointed along one direction in space. As periodic corrections are necessary to counter orientation drift due to solar pressure torque and other disturbances, this is not a purely passive approach. It is one that has been popular for communications satellites.

Active Control. Many elements and technologies are essential to active guidance and control systems. Precise guidance and control is required for most high-performance applications. During ascent from the launchpad, guidance systems are similar to those used on ballistic missiles. These are based on inertial navigation techniques, sometimes supplemented by stellar sensors. Once the spacecraft is in orbit, several maneuvers are usually required to achieve desired altitude and orientation. These are typically accomplished by means of commands, using telemetered radio data from onboard sensors.

GUIDANCE AND CONTROL DEVICES

Elements of guidance and control systems include sensors and actuators. The sensor is a device to gather information, and the actuator is a mechanism that acts on this information and moves the spacecraft. Most sensors take advantage of external reference sources or gyro instruments. The best gyros, however, are accurate only for limited time intervals and must be updated frequently by external reference souces, including the Sun, stars, and the Earth. Typical sensors used with these sources measure angular deviations by detecting electromagnetic radiations. Examples include Sun sensors, star trackers, and Earth horizon scanners.

Horizon scanners indicate the direction of the local vertical. This information is vital for orbiting satellites that must point an antenna or other instrument at the Earth. Horizon scanners can detect motion about two axes. Star trackers, which seek out specific stars and have very narrow viewing-windows, are generally very delicate, heavy, and expensive and are used only when no good alternatives exist. Fortunately, many automatic attitude-control systems in satellites can operate without these tracking devices. Sun sensors detect the Sun and can be simple, because the Sun is the largest source of electromagnetic energy detectable from a satellite.

Gyro or momentum devices can be used for control-implementation and sensing. Small gyros give displacement and rate information. Momentum and reaction wheels can generate control torques. A momentum wheel is a spinning rotor that tries to maintain a constant momentum but allows small variations in order to apply control torques about its spin axis. A reaction wheel is similar to a momentum wheel, except that it tries to maintain zero momentum. Both these devices are good when disturbances are small and persist over the mission life. When disturbances are large, propulsive devices, such as thrusters, may be more effective.

Some spacecraft, many missiles, and most intercontinental airliners employ a sophisticated inertial guidance device. It uses a combination of gyros, ACCELEROMETERS, and electronic circuits to keep a continuous record of vehicle position, velocity, and orientation. A pure inertial guidance system is entirely self-contained and requires no radio contact with the Earth. A combination of radio and inertial guidance is common in order to update the accuracy of an inertial guidance system periodically. M. H. KAPLAN

Bibliography: Battin, Richard Horace, *Astronautical Guidance* (1964); Kaplan, Marshall, H., *Modern Spacecraft: Dynamics and Control* (1976); Stearns; Edward V. B., *Navigation and Guidance in Space* (1963).

See also: ASTRONAUTICS.

guide dog

Guide dogs, or Seeing Eye Dogs (trademark of the organization, Seeing Eye, Inc.), are trained to act as guides for their blind masters. Although dogs had long been used to help the blind, the formal training of dogs for this purpose began only in 1916 in Germany, in an effort to help those blinded during World War I. Many organizations now train guide dogs, using breeds noted for their intelligence, responsiveness, and even temperament, particularly German shepherds and Labrador and golden retrievers. The dog begins a 3-to-5-month period of intensive training when it is about a year old. It learns to obey basic commands; is taught how to bring its future master safely through crowds, traffic, and other potentially hazardous obstacles; learns to disobey commands that will bring its master into danger; and becomes accustomed to its leather harness, which is designed to allow its owner to feel the dog's movements. Potential guide-dog owners are trained for about a month together with their dogs. A blind person's ability to use a guide dog is dependent on his or her physical fitness and degree of blindness—a person with a small amount of vision finds it difficult to work with a guide dog; thus the number of blind people using guide dogs in the United States is relatively low—perhaps some 5,000 in 1979.

Bibliography: Hartwell, Dickson, *Dogs Against Darkness*, 3d ed. (1968); Putnam, Peter B., *Love in the Lead: The Fifty-year Miracle of the Seeing Eye Dog* (1979).

guide fossil: see FOSSIL RECORD.

guided missile: see ROCKETS AND MISSILES.

Guido d'Arezzo [gwee'-doh dar-et'-tsoh]

Guido d'Arezzo, b. *c.*990, d. May 17, 1050, a renowned musical theorist, is credited with having perfected (*c.*1025) the STAFF system of MUSICAL NOTATION, which, with some modification, is still in use today. Possibly born in France, he became a Benedictine monk and went to Arezzo in Italy, where he lived for many years. His writings, notably the *Micrologus*, contain important information about the polyphony of his time, but it was his innovative teaching methods that brought him lasting fame. He formulated the concept of a scale pattern comprising six notes represented by the syllables *ut* (*do*), *re, mi, fa, sol, la*, and taught that the interval between each syllable is a whole tone except for the one between *mi* and *fa*, which is a half step. By associating syllables with the fixed pitches of the notes, singers were able to learn melodies much more quickly and accurately than previously. Guido's inventions revolutionized musical pedagogy and brought him to the attention of the papal court in Rome, where he successfully demonstrated his methods. FRANK D'ACCONE

Bibliography: Reese, Gustave, *Music in the Middle Ages* (1940).

Guiènne [gee-en']

Guiènne (also Guyenne) is a historic region in southwestern France on the Atlantic coast, north of the Spanish border. By the Treaty of Paris of 1259, Louis IX of France recognized the English king as his vassal for Guiènne and GASCONY, regions previously lumped together as AQUITAINE and under English control since 1154. Conflict over these regions was one of the principal causes of the HUNDRED YEARS' WAR (1337–1453). At the beginning of the war France retook Guiènne, but in 1360 the Treaty of Brétigny (see BRÉTIGNY, TREATY OF) restored it to England. By the end of the war France had conquered most of Guiènne once again.

In 1469 the French crown granted the region to the duc de Berry, but upon his death in 1472 it reverted to the crown. Guiènne was the scene of heavy fighting during the religious wars of the 16th century (see RELIGION, WARS OF). It was subsequently united with the region of Gascony. Following the French Revolution Guiènne was divided into the departments of Gironde and most of Dordogne, Lot, Lot-en-Garonne and Aveyron.

Guignol, Grand [geen-yohl', grahn]

Grand Guignol was a form of sensational entertainment that flourished in small Parisian theaters at the turn of the century and featured heavy doses of violence, madness, suicide, revenge, and trick apparitions. In its day it was the equivalent of such modern film styles as the horror movie or a psychological thriller like Alfred Hitchcock's *Psycho*. The form reached its zenith in 1897 when Oscar Méténier, a former police superintendent familiar with Parisian underworld vice, opened the Théâtre du Grand Guignol in Montmartre.

Guignol is the name of a French puppet known for his cruelty. He originated in Lyon and has been frequently compared with Punch of the commedia dell'arte. Guignol is also the generic name for the children's puppet theater in France.

The plays of the Grand Guignol were written according to a set form that depended on suspense, sensational revelations, emotional suffering, and finally violence of some sort. The stage tricks simulating gory acts were well-guarded secrets. Established authors wrote for the Grand Guignol, including Georges Courteline, Octave Mirbeau, Henri Lenormand, and André de Lorde; yet none of the plays were memorable. The Grand Guignol enjoyed brief success in London in 1908 and toured America in 1923, but graphic horror films contributed to its decline, then to its demise in 1962.

guilds [gildz]

Guilds were associations primarily of merchants and craftsmen, organized in medieval and early modern times. A guild normally comprised all the self-employed members of an occupation in one town or district; the members drew up the statutes of the guild, elected its officers, and contributed to its common purse. Once a guild was formed, only its members could practice that occupation. Parents contracted with guildsmen to take their sons as apprentices (see APPRENTICESHIP) and to teach them the mysteries of their professions. After 2 to 15 years, depending on the rules of the particular guild, apprentices completed their training and then became journeymen. (The term is derived from the French *journée*, meaning "day"; journeymen were paid by the day.) Because journeymen who were not the sons or sons-in-law of guildsmen often found it impossible to be admitted to full membership during the later Middle Ages, they sometimes organized journeymen's guilds, which operated like labor unions, but these were atypical.

The Twelve Great Companies of London, survivors of medieval craft guilds, represented by their coats of arms, are: (1) Mercers; (2) Grocers; (3) Drapers; (4) Fishmongers; (5) Goldsmiths; (6) Skinners; (7) Merchant Taylors; (8) Haberdashers; (9) Salters; (10) Ironmongers; (11) Vinters; and (12) Clothworkers.

1

2

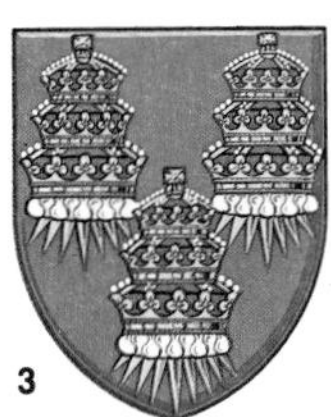
3

4

5

6

7

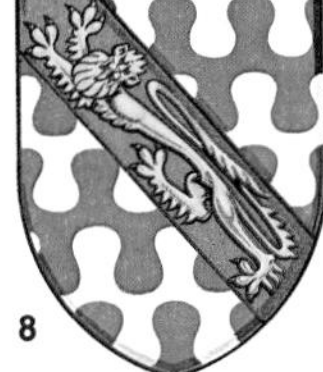
8

9

10

11

12

Guilds are so called from *gilds*, the name given to such groups in northern Europe. They can be traced to the social and religious associations found among the Germans in the 1st century AD. The church in the Carolingian empire tried to proscribe the gilds because the members took oaths to help one another and were accused of holding drunken orgies, not entirely free from pagan practices. The mutual help and the drinking, however, continued into later centuries. In southern Europe the guilds may have originated in *collegia* (economic and social groupings) of the Roman and later the Byzantine Empire.

The guilds took on new life in the towns of the 10th and 11th centuries as western Europe began its economic and social revival. Merchant guilds were most important at first, but in the 13th century and thereafter the craft guilds dominated. During the 14th and 15th centuries, guilds were increasingly made into agencies of the state, either of cities or of princes. At odds with the new capitalists of the early modern period, the guilds slowly declined. They were abolished over most of the continent by the Bonapartes, and the London livery companies are the best-known survivors.

At their height the guilds performed important functions. They engaged in political action to defend or police their towns and to secure liberties for themselves or their towns; they regulated trade and industry and provided professional education; they supported their members in sickness and in death gave them a good funeral; they enriched the religious and artistic life of their towns; and even their conviviality was not without its positive aspects. Their monopolistic character has often been condemned, but it ensured a considerable degree of economic stability, and because their monopoly did not extend beyond a single city-state, they usually could not interfere in any real way with the larger market economy.

FRED A. CAZEL, JR.

Bibliography: Clune, George, *The Medieval Gild System* (1943); Kramer, Stella, *The English Craft Gilds* (1927; repr. 1976); Sée, Henri, *Economic and Social Conditions in France during the Eighteenth Century* (1927; repr. 1968); Thrupp, Sylvia L., "The Gilds," in *The Cambridge Economic History of Europe*, Vol. 3 (1963); Unwin, George, *Gilds and Companies of London*, 4th ed. (1963).

See also: HANSEATIC LEAGUE.

Guillaume, Charles Édouard [gee-yohm', sharl ayd-war']

Charles Édouard Guillaume, b. Feb. 15, 1861, d. June 13, 1938, a Swiss-born physicist, won the 1920 Nobel Prize for physics. The award was for his discovery of metallic alloys with very little temperature expansion and unvarying elasticity, important properties for the construction of accurate timing devices.

MICHAEL MEO

Guillaume de Lorris [duh lor-ees']

Guillaume de Lorris was a 13th-century French poet who wrote the first 4,000 lines of Le ROMAN DE LA ROSE. His treatment of the allegory, in the tradition of COURTLY LOVE and notable for the beauty and lyricism of its descriptive passages, differs markedly from the erudite and satirical tone adopted by Jean de Meung in his later 22,000-line continuation of the romance.

Guillaumin, Armand [gee-yoh-man']

Jean Baptiste Armand Guillaumin, b. Feb. 16, 1841, d. June 26, 1927, a lesser known French impressionist (see IMPRESSIONISM), was principally a landscape painter and often worked with Paul CÉZANNE and Camille PISSARRO. Under Pissarro's tutelage Guillaumin evolved a style that incorporated textural effects and bright colors. In 1874 he participated in the first impressionist exhibition, and in 1884 he was the only member of that group to exhibit with the neoimpressionists (see NEOIMPRESSIONISM) at the newly formed Salon des Indépendents. During the 1880s, under the influence of Vincent van Gogh, Georges Seurat, and Paul Signac, Guillaumin developed a palette of brilliant intensity. PEARL GORDON

Bibliography: Rewald, John, *The History of Impressionism*, 4th rev. ed. (1980).

guillemot [gil'-uh-maht]

The "ringed" form of the guillemot known as the common murre, U. aalge, is found only in the North Atlantic region. When in breeding plumage it has a distinctive white eye-ring and postocular line. Like all auks, it is a diving bird that feeds on the sea bottom and propels itself through the water by means of its wings.

Guillemots are several species of diving birds of the auk family, Alcidae, order Charadriiformes. Like other alcids, they are cliff-nesting, oceanic birds of the Northern Hemisphere and feed on fishes, crustaceans, and plankton. They measure 33 to 46 cm (13 to 18 in) tall, with webbed feet and short wings used as flippers. They stand upright and have striking black and white plumage. The guillemot of Great Britain, *Uria aalge*, is known as the common murre in the United States. The black guillemot, *Cepphus grylle*, a circumpolar bird, has bright red legs and white wing patches. ROBERT RAIKOW

Guillén, Jorge [geel-yayn', hor'-hay]

Jorge Guillén, b. Jan. 18, 1893, d. Feb. 6, 1984, was a major Spanish poet and critic best known for his epic poem *Cántico*, first published in 1928 and revised several times before the definitive edition appeared in 1950 (Eng. trans., 1954, 1965). According to Guillén, this long yet economically crafted work is "a song in praise of the oneness of all being." A member of the so-called Generation of '27, which included García Lorca, Vicente Aleixandre, and Luis Cernuda, Guillén left Spain after the Civil War and taught and lived in England and the United States. ROBERTO GONZÁLEZ-ECHEVARRÍA

Guillén, Nicolás [nee-koh-lah']

Nicolás Guillén, b. July 10, 1902, d. July 16, 1989, was known as Cuba's national poet. His first published book of poems, *Motivos de son* (Motifs of Sound, 1930), revealed his concern over the difficult conditions endured by Cuba's black population and his ability to incorporate elements of Cuban popular culture into his poetry. Subsequent books of poetry showed a broadening sociopolitical vision. Guillén served as a deputy in the People's Assembly and in 1961 became president of the National Union of Writers and Artists of Cuba. His complete poetry, the two-volume *Obra poética 1920–1972*, appeared in 1974. In 1972, *Man-Making Words* was published in English. Other major works in translation include *Tengo* (1964; Eng. trans., 1974), *El gran zoo* (1967; *Patria o Muerte: The Great Zoo and Other Poems*, 1972), and *The Daily Daily* (1972; Eng. trans., 1989), a cultural and literary history of Cuba.
KEITH ELLIS

guillotine [gil'-uh-teen]

The guillotine, notorious from its use in the mass political executions of the French Revolution, was originally proposed as a humane and democratic device for capital punishment. Under the Old Regime, death by decapitation had been reserved for the aristocracy.

The guillotine is a device for cutting off peoples' heads. It was first used extensively during the French Revolution, although it had previously been used in Scotland, where it was called the maiden, and in other countries. The design is simple: a heavy, oblique blade falls between two uprights, slicing through the victim's neck. The French National Assembly adopted it in 1792 at the urging of Joseph Ignace Guillotin (1738–1814), a physician member who wanted all executions to be carried out in a uniform, painless way. It became the symbol of the Reign of Terror (1793–94), when thousands of people of all classes died under its blade. It remained the usual method of execution in France until the abolition of capital punishment there in 1981.

Guimard, Hector [gee-mar', ek-tor']

Hector Guimard, b. Mar. 10, 1867, d. May 20, 1942, was the foremost French architect working in the ART NOUVEAU style. The cast-iron and glass pavilions that he designed as entrances to the Paris Metro, the subway system, have become popularly identified with the style. Guimard was a fluent designer and theorist who believed that a work of architecture should synthesize many arts and achieve a unity of external appearance and interior design. This precept began to take shape during his study-tour of England (1894–95) and was confirmed by his early contact with the Belgian architect Victor HORTA, whose Tassel House, Brussels (1893), greatly influenced his development.

Guimard's particular version of Art Nouveau may be described as abstract naturalism—a style that draws its inspiration from organic forms such as leaves and flowers without closely reproducing them. The result, known as structural symbolism, is a building whose sinuous lines evoke natural growth. Guimard's use of these principles was supported by his skill in spatial and three-dimensional composition.

Starting with the Castel Béranger apartment building, Paris (1894–95), Guimard designed, constructed, and furnished a series of projects that constitute his finest work. These include the Coilliot house and store, Lille (1898–1900), the Castel Henriette in Sèvres (1899–1900), and such Parisian structures as the Humbert de Romans concert hall (1897–1901), the Metro entrances (1899–1900), the Nozal House (1902–05), the Jassedé apartments (1903–05), and finally, his own house (1909–10). Guimard's concern for the organic unity of his creations led him to study the materials and techniques of interior decoration. Some examples of his furniture, metalwork, ceramics, textiles, and other decorative arts are now preserved in the

Musée des Arts Decoratifs, Paris, and the Cooper-Hewitt Museum and Museum of Modern Art in New York City.

BETTY ELZEA

Bibliography: Dunster, David, ed., *Hector Guimard* (1978).

Guinea [gin'-ee]

Guinea is a state in West Africa along the Atlantic coast, bordered by Guinea-Bissau and Senegal to the north, Mali and Ivory Coast to the east, and Liberia and Sierra Leone to the south. It was a French colony until 1958, when it became independent under the leadership of Ahmed Sékou TOURÉ.

LAND AND PEOPLE

A narrow marsh adjacent to the Atlantic coast yields to a higher plain in the interior. Farther inland this open land is broken by the Fouta Djalon mountains where the headwaters of the Niger and Senegal rivers form. East of the mountains lie the savanna grasslands of Upper Guinea; to the south are the forest-covered Guinea Highlands. Mount Nimba, the highest point in Guinea, rises to 1,752 m (5,747 ft) in the south.

Guinea has a tropical climate with a rainy season from April to October. Annual precipitation ranges from 1,500 mm (59 in) in Upper Guinea to 4,320 mm (170 in) at CONAKRY, the capital, on the coast. The annual average temperature is 26° C (79° F) in most of the country.

The peoples of Guinea may be divided into 3 major ethnic groups and about 15 smaller ones. The coast and inland plain are home to the Susu, who constitute about 11% of the population, and other agricultural groups. Another 40% are FULANI cattle herders who live in the Fouta Djalon. The Malinke of Upper Guinea constitute roughly 26% of the population. The forest peoples include the Kissi, Guerze-Kpelle, Koma, Manon, and Loma. French is the official language, but it is understood by only a small portion of the population. Nearly two-thirds of the population are Muslim; traditional religions are practiced by most other inhabitants.

Guinea's annual growth rate, somewhat less than the average for Africa, is influenced by a very high infant mortality rate. A marked population migration from rural areas to the cities, especially Conakry, is taking place. Education is free, but only about 33% of children aged 7 to 12 attend.

ECONOMIC ACTIVITY

Guinea is one of the world's poorest nations. It is rich in mineral resources, however. About one-third of the world's bauxite (used to make aluminum) reserves are there, and Guinea is the world's second largest producer of bauxite (1981). The country also has substantial deposits of iron ore, uranium, diamonds, and gold. Minerals account for nearly 90% of all export revenue. Industry accounts for only a small portion of the national income, and the largest industry is bauxite processing. Although only a small proportion of the land is cultivable, more than 80% of the labor force are engaged in agriculture, growing chiefly subsistence crops. Commercial crops—coffee, pineapples, bananas, and palm kernels—contribute less than 5% of total exports. Touré placed almost every aspect of the economy under direct state control. After his death the government began to abolish many of the socialist economic structures he had established.

Guinea suffers from a chronic trade deficit. Transportation equipment, petroleum, textiles, and foodstuffs are the leading imports.

HISTORY AND GOVERNMENT

Neolithic stone carvings and artifacts throughout Guinea testify to a long period of human habitation. Parts of present-day Guinea were held by the kingdom of Ghana during the 11th century, the Mali empire during the 13th century, and the SONGHAI empire during the 16th century. In the early 1700s, northwestern Guinea became the core of an independent Fulani state; other similar states controlled the interior for the next two centuries.

During the 18th century, contact with French, Portuguese, and British traders along the coast began. A treaty signed by France and Britain in 1889 granted exclusive trading rights to

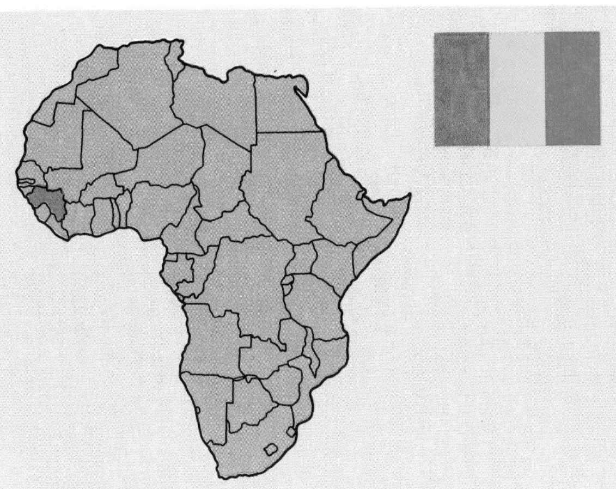

REPUBLIC OF GUINEA

LAND. Area: 245,857 km² (94,926 mi²). Capital and largest city: Conakry (1983 est. pop., 656,000).

PEOPLE. Population (1986 est.): 5,734,000; density (1986 est.): 23 persons per km² (60 per mi²). Distribution (1985): 22% urban, 78% rural. Annual growth (1980–85): 2.3%. Official language: French. Major religions: Islam, traditional religions.

EDUCATION AND HEALTH. Literacy (1983): 20% of adult population. Universities (1987): none. Hospital beds (1979): 6,858. Physicians (1981): 301. Life expectancy (1980–85): women—41.8; men—38.7. Infant mortality (1980–85): 159 per 1,000 live births.

ECONOMY. GDP (1984): $1,546 million; $300 per capita. Labor distribution (1983): agriculture—82%; industry and commerce—11%; services—5.4%; government—1.6%. Foreign trade (1984 est.): imports—$403 million; exports—$537 million; principal trade partners—France, West Germany, United States. Currency: 1 Sili = 100 cauris.

GOVERNMENT. Type: military rule. Legislature: National Assembly (suspended 1984). Political subdivisions: 8 provinces.

COMMUNICATIONS. Railroads (1984): 922 km (573 mi) total. Roads (1983): 28,400 km (17,600 mi) total. Major ports: 1. Major airfields: 1.

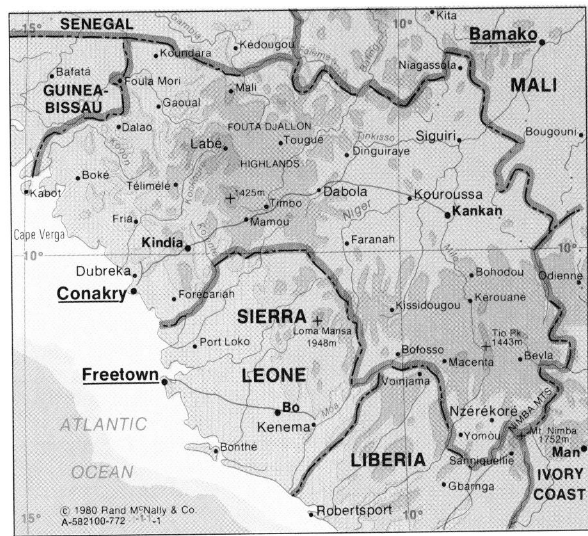

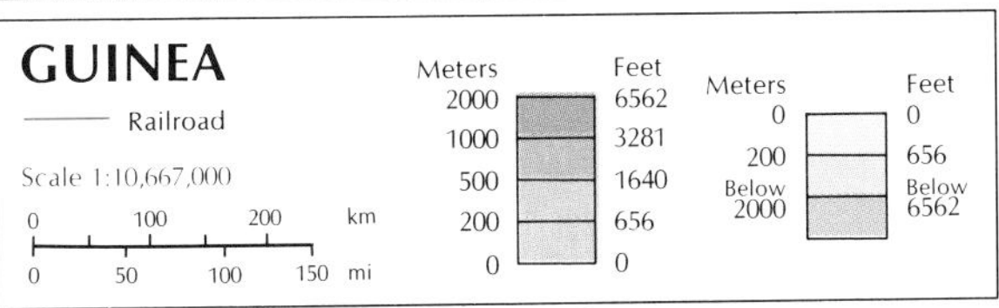

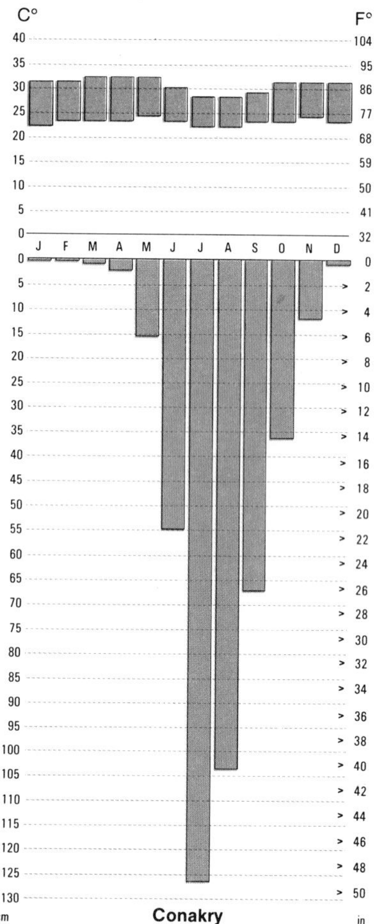

(Above) *Conakry, Guinea's capital and leading seaport, is a rapidly expanding urban center. Although the colonial French influence is still evident in the older part of the city, on Tombo Island, Conakry's industries and suburbs have spread to the nearby mainland.*

(Left) *Bars indicate monthly ranges of temperature* (red) *and precipitation* (blue) *of Conakry, Guinea. Located on the west coast of Africa, Conakry has a tropical wet-dry climate with monsoonal influences.*

France. In 1895, Guinea was incorporated into the colony of French West Africa. Following World War II the Parti Démocratique de Guinée (PDG), led by Sékou Touré, was formed. In 1958, Guineans voted in a referendum offering either independence or membership in the French Community, and Guinea became the only French colony in West Africa to choose independence.

Touré, president from independence until his death in 1984, held power longer than any other modern leader in black Africa. Known as a champion of African unity and socialism, Touré initially established close ties with the USSR and China but later espoused nonalignment and sought aid from Western nations. An estimated 1.5 million Guineans went into exile during his long rule.

After Touré's death a military junta seized power, suspending the constitution and dissolving the PDG and the National Assembly. The ruling Military Committee for National Recovery, headed by President Lansana Conté, appointed a cabinet that included civilians and represented all major ethnic groups. Guinea's new leaders pledged to restore human rights and encourage free enterprise. DENNIS D. CORDELL

Bibliography: Best, Alan C. G., and de Blij, Harm J., *African Survey* (1977); Hargreaves, John D., *West Africa: The Former French States* (1967); Nelson, Harold D., et al., *Area Handbook for Guinea*, 2d ed. (1975); Riviere, Claude, *Guinea: The Mobilization of a People*, trans. by Virginia Thompson and Richard Adloff (1977).

Guinea, Gulf of

The Gulf of Guinea is a large indentation of the Atlantic Ocean on the west central coast of Africa. The bights of Benin and Biafra (Bonny) are parts of the gulf. The Niger, Volta, and Sananga rivers terminate at the gulf. The low and swampy shoreline lacks natural harbors.

Guinea-Bissau [gin-ee-bis-ow']

The West African Republic of Guinea-Bissau is wedged between Senegal and Guinea on the Atlantic coast. It is commonly distinguished from Guinea by the addition of the name of its capital city, Bissau. It has a total area of 36,125 km^2 (13,948 mi^2), including a number of coastal islands, most of which are part of the Bijagós archipelago. Guinea-Bissau was a Portuguese colony until 1973, when independence was declared.

LAND AND PEOPLE

The country's deeply indented coastline does not rise significantly above sea level, and most of the country is subject to tidal flooding. Marshes and swamps suitable for growing rice make up much of the immediate hinterland, and there are heavy forests inland. The land rises only slightly in the southeast to 244 m (800 ft), the highest point in the country.

Guinea-Bissau has a tropical climate; the average temperature is about 27° C (80° F). Heavy rains fall from June to November, and the annual average precipitation is more than 1,015 mm (40 in).

Major ethnic groups are the Balante, the FULANI, the Malinke, the Mandyako, and the Pepel. The Cape Verdean mulatto community, numbering about 12,000, played a decisive role in the struggle for independence. The official language is Portuguese, and Crioulo, a creole dialect of Portuguese, is the common spoken language. The largest city and capital is BISSAU. Other major towns are Bafata, Bissorã, Bolama, Catió, Farim, Mansôa, and Madine do Boé.

ECONOMY, HISTORY, AND GOVERNMENT

About 80% of the population are engaged in subsistence agriculture, with rice, beans, corn, and sweet potatoes the major staple crops. Palm kernels and coconuts, produced along the coast, and peanuts, grown in the sandy-interior, are the chief cash crops; by 1983 the rapidly expanding fishing industry provided 24% of export earnings. Some timber is also exported, and cattle breeding is important in the interior. The government has encouraged the development of industry, particularly the processing of agricultural products.

Portuguese navigators established the first trading post in the region in 1446. During the 17th century, Cacheu became the center of an active slave trade. Until 1879, the area was administered from the CAPE VERDE ISLANDS, and Cape Verdeans

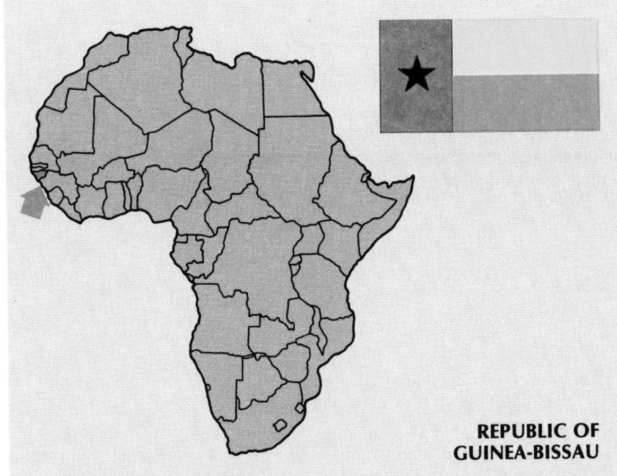

LAND. Area: 36,125 km² (13,948 mi²). Capital and largest city: Bissau (1979 pop., 109,486).

PEOPLE. Population (1986 est.): 875,000; density (1986 est.): 24 persons per km² (63 per mi²). Distribution (1985): 27% urban, 73% rural. Annual growth (1980–85): 1.9%. Official language: Portuguese. Major religions: traditional religions, Islam.

EDUCATION AND HEALTH. Literacy (1985): 9% of adult population. Universities (1987): none. Hospital beds (1981): 1,532. Physicians (1980): 108. Life expectancy (1980): women—42.6; men—39.4. Infant mortality (1985): 143 per 1,000 live births.

ECONOMY. GDP (1983): $154 million; $180 per capita. Labor distribution (1985): agriculture—90%; industry, services, and commerce—5%; government—5%. Foreign trade (1983): imports—$57.1 million; exports—$8.6 million; principal trade partners—Portugal, Italy, the Netherlands. Currency: 1 Guinea-Bissau peso = 100 centavos.

GOVERNMENT. Type: one-party state. Legislature: National People's Assembly. Political subdivisions: 8 regions, 1 municipality.

COMMUNICATIONS. Railroads (1987): none. Roads (1983): 2,500 km (1,553 mi) total. Major ports: 1. Major airfields: 1.

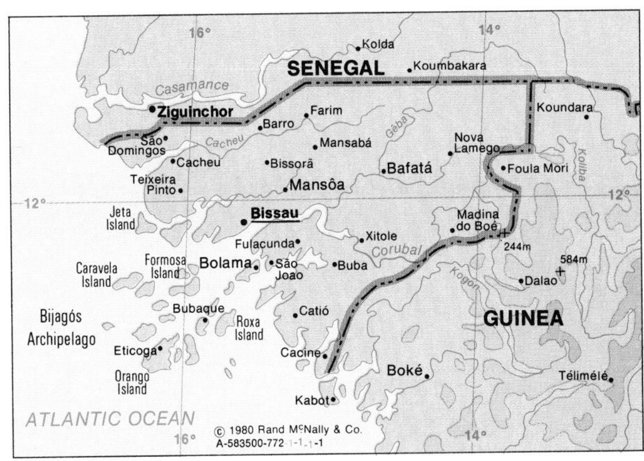

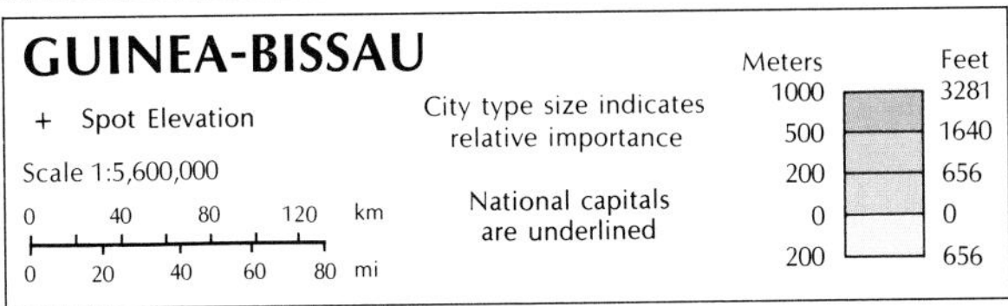

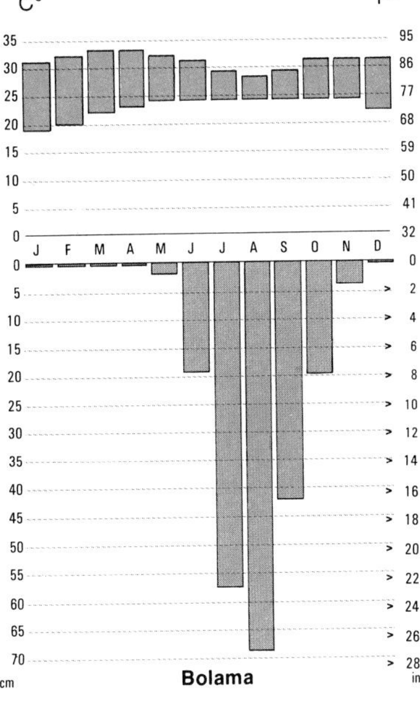

(Left) *Bars indicate monthly ranges of temperature* (red) *and precipitation* (blue) *of Bolama, Guinea-Bissau. Because of its location on an island off the west coast of Africa, Bolama has a tropical wet-dry climate with monsoonal influences.*

were widely used by the Portuguese to fill middle-ranking positions in the colonial bureaucracy. Guinea-Bissau's boundaries were not demarcated until 1905, and the Portuguese, who never settled in large numbers, did not effectively control the interior until 1915.

In 1956 a Cape Verdean, Amilcar Cabral, took the lead of a movement that called itself the African Party for the Independence of Guinea and Cape Verde (PAIGC, from its Portuguese name). Striking dockworkers clashed with the police in 1959, and by 1963 large-scale guerrilla warfare had broken out in the interior. Assisted by the government of neighboring Guinea, the PAIGC gradually extended its control over most of the countryside and organized an effective administration in the liberated areas. Cabral's assassination in 1973 did not end the movement, which unilaterally proclaimed the territory's independence on Sept. 24, 1973. Cabral's brother, Luis de Almeida Cabral, became president in 1974. The country's independent status was recognized by a number of countries. After the Portuguese revolution in April 1974, the new Portuguese regime negotiated with the PAIGC and recognized the independence of Guinea-Bissau as of Sept. 10, 1974.

In November 1980, Cabral was deposed in a coup led by João Bernardo Vieira. Diplomatic relations with Cape Verde were suspended until 1982. In 1984, under a new constitution that increased the powers of the president, the ruling Council of the Revolution was replaced by an indirectly elected National People's Assembly.

EDOUARD BUSTIN

Bibliography: Abshire, David M., and Samuels, Michael A., *Portuguese Africa: A Handbook* (1969); Chilcote, Ronald, *Portuguese Africa* (1967); Davidson, Basil, *No Fist Is Big Enough to Hide the Sky* (1981); Lopes, Carlos, *Guinea-Bissau* (1986); Rudebeck, Lars, *Guinea-Bissau: A Study of Political Mobilization* (1975).

guinea fowl

Guinea fowl are the 7 species of birds, closely related to pheasants, that constitute the family Numididae. They inhabit open forest and brush throughout most of Madagascar and sub-Saharan Africa.

Guinea fowl, which measure about 50 cm (20 in) in height, have bare necks and dark plumage, spotted or streaked with white. Their nests are ground scrapes lightly lined with grass. Guinea fowl lay 7 to 20 eggs; the precocial young leave the nest soon after hatching.

JOEL CRACRAFT

guinea pig

Guinea pigs are rodents of the genus *Cavia*, family Caviidae; the familiar pet guinea pigs are commonly *C. porcellus*. The compact body may be 25 to 36 cm (10 to 14 in) long; the weight ranges from 500 to 1,500 g (1 to 3 lb). The coat is brown or gray in wild guinea pigs, but the domesticated variety may exhibit a wide range of colors. The gestation period is about 68 days and life-span about 8 years. Guinea pigs are

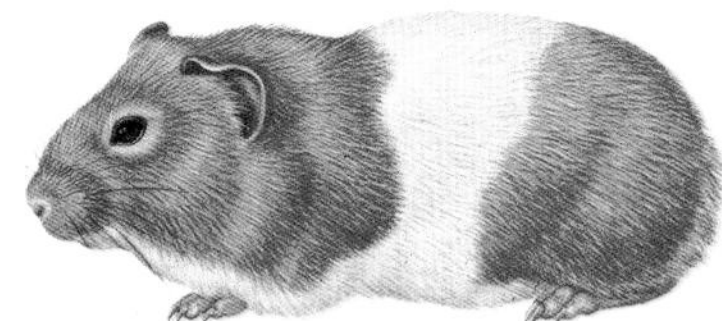
The domestic guinea pig, Cavia porcellus, often kept as a pet, is also used as a laboratory animal in toxicity and genetics studies.

native to South America and were domesticated for food centuries ago in Peru. In the wild, guinea pigs live in burrows and feed at night on plant material. Guinea pigs are used in laboratory studies and the production of serums.

EVERETT SENTMAN

Guinevere [gwin'-uh-vir]

Guinevere, wife of King Arthur, first appears in Geoffrey of Monmouth's *History of the Kings of Britain* (*c.*1135-39), where she is described as a noble Roman. Seized by Mordred, her husband's cousin, she is later reunited with Arthur and retires to a convent on his death. Later medieval poets such as Layamon and Sir Thomas Malory relate her adulterous affair with Sir Lancelot, with whom she bears a child, Sir Galahad. William Morris redeems her character in *The Defence of Guinevere* (1858), and one of Alfred Tennyson's *Idylls of the King* (1859) weaves a historical fantasy around this shadowy, romantic figure.

See also: ARTHUR AND ARTHURIAN LEGEND.

Guinicelli, Guido [gwee-nee-chel'-lee, gwee'-doh]

Guido Guinicelli, *c.*1230-*c.*1276, was an Italian jurist and poet whose style and thought influenced Dante Alighieri. Called the father of the *dolce stil nuovo* ("sweet new style"), he wrote sonnets and lyrics praising his lady's angelic qualities and proclaiming that only those born with a noble heart (defined by inner worth, not external circumstances) could experience love. He attempted to ennoble human love by transforming it into a "secular *caritas.*" This conception of the transcendental nature of earthly love eventually found full expression in Dante's *Divine Comedy*.

Bibliography: Goldin, Frederick, ed. and trans., *German and Italian Lyrics of the Middle Ages* (1973).

Guinness, Sir Alec [gin'-es]

Alec Guinness, b. Apr. 2, 1914, is an English stage and screen actor known particularly for his character roles and comic impersonations. He was a respected member of the Old Vic when roles in film adaptations of two Dickens novels—Herbert Pocket in *Great Expectations* (1946) and Fagin in *Oliver Twist* (1948)—brought him a larger public. He became better known through bravura performances in such British comedies as *Kind Hearts and Coronets* (1949), *The Lavender Hill Mob* (1951), *The Man in the White Suit* (1951), and *The Ladykillers* (1955).

Guinness received an Oscar for his performance in *The Bridge on the River Kwai* (1957) and was knighted in 1959. Guinness subsequently gave distinguished dramatic performances in *Tunes of Glory* (1960), *Lawrence of Arabia* (1962), and *Star Wars* (1977).

Bibliography: Tynan, Kenneth, *Alec Guinness: An Illustrated Study of His Work for Stage and Screen*, 3d ed. (1961).

Guinness Book of World Records, The

The Guinness Book of World Records, an annual publication since 1955, lists records for a wide variety of sports, stunts, and natural phenomena. Each record must be verified by an investigator before it can be included. The very existence of the Guinness Book generates a great number of attempts to establish records at feats that few people would otherwise attempt.

CHARLOTTE D. SOLOMON

Güiraldes, Ricardo [gweer-ahl'-days]

Ricardo Güiraldes, b. Feb. 13, 1886, d. Oct. 8, 1927, an Argentine poet and novelist, is chiefly remembered for the novel *Shadows on the Pampas* (1926; Eng. trans., 1935), a celebration of the vagabond existence of the *gaucho*, or cattle herder. Guiraldes's portrayal of this popular folk hero made him the leading figure in the *martinfierristas*, a group of writers who took their name from *Martin Fierro* (1872), a poem by José Hernández.

JAIME ALAZRAKI

Guise (family) [geez]

The French family of Guise rose to prominence in the 16th century. The founder was **Claude**, b. Oct. 20, 1496, d. Apr. 12, 1550, second son of René II, duc de Lorraine. He distinguished himself fighting in the Italian Wars and was created (1528) duc de Guise by King Francis I.

His title was inherited by his eldest son, **François**, b. Feb. 17, 1519, d. Feb. 24, 1563, who defended (1552) Metz against Holy Roman Emperor Charles V and captured Calais from the English in 1558. With his brother **Charles, Cardinal de Lorraine**, b. Feb. 17, 1524, d. Dec. 26, 1574, François became the head of the ultra-Catholic faction after the death of King Henry II. Their sister **Marie** (Mary of Guise), b. Nov. 22, 1515, d. June 11, 1560, had married (1538) JAMES V of Scotland, and the child of this match, MARY, QUEEN OF SCOTS, became the wife of Henry II's heir, FRANCIS II. This family connection enabled the Guise to rule France during Francis's short reign (1559-60).

In the third generation, **Henri, duc de Guise**, b. Dec. 31, 1550, d. Dec. 23, 1588, was also a Catholic leader in the Wars of Religion (see RELIGION, WARS OF) and opposed the more moderate king, HENRY III. When Henri was murdered by the king, his brother, **Charles de Mayenne**, b. Mar. 25, 1554, d. Oct. 3, 1611, assumed the leadership of the Catholic League, which Henri had created. The eldest son of Henri, **Charles, duc de Guise**, b. Aug. 20, 1571, d. Sept. 30, 1640, was considered by the league as a candidate to succeed Henry III, whose heir was the Protestant HENRY IV. Charles, however, proved loyal to Henry IV, who converted to Catholicism, and to his successor, Louis XIII. In the fifth generation, **Henri II, duc de Guise**, b. Apr. 4, 1614, d. June 2, 1664, the son of Charles, led unsuccessful invasions of Naples in 1647 and 1654. The main line of the family died out with François Joseph, 7th duc de Guise, in 1675.

J. H. M. SALMON

Bibliography: Sedgwick, H. D., *The House of Guise* (1938).

guitar [gi-tar']

The guitar, a fretted stringed instrument, is a member of the lute family. It originated in Persia and reached Spain during the 12th century, where its versatility as both a solo and accompanying instrument was established. The guitar shown here dates back to the 1790s.

The guitar is a chordophone (stringed musical instrument) with a neck. Classified as a "short lute" (see STRINGED INSTRUMENTS), the guitar is distinguished from other members of this family (the LUTE proper, the MANDOLIN, etc.) by its flat back, incurving sides, and flat peg disc with rear tuning pegs. The modern guitar has six strings; the upper three are made of gut or nylon, the lower three of silk overspun with metal—or all may be of metal. The strings are stretched over a fingerboard on the neck that has fixed metal frets; to the end of the neck is attached the peg disc, or "tuning head," which is fitted with mechanical tuning pins. The body is composed of a spruce soundboard and parallel hardwood back separated by curved hardwood ribs. A circular sound hole pierces the soundboard between the end of the fingerboard and the bridge to which the strings are fastened. Guitars are traditionally played with the bare fingers, but those strung in metal are usually played with a plectrum. The standard-sized modern guitar is approximately 90 cm (3 ft) in overall length and is actually the bass member of a complete choir of variously sized instruments that are still in use in Spain.

Although guitar-shaped lutes have been noted in iconography and in examples from excavations in Egypt between the 4th and 8th centuries AD, and even earlier in Western Asia, it was in the late Middle Ages that the guitar emerged in Europe. Cognate with the ancient Greek KITHARA through the Arabic *qītāra*, the word *guitar* was first used generically to refer to a number of plucked chordophones. In Renaissance Spain, where by the late 15th century the flat-backed, six-coursed *vihuela* had displaced the lute as the dominant plucked instrument, a smaller version of the *vihuela* with four courses (pairs of strings tuned in unison) came to be referred to specifically as the *guitar*. While the *vihuela*'s popularity was limited to Spain, the simpler guitar quickly gained acceptance all over Europe as an accompanying instrument and as a more easily played alternative to the lute. Late in the 16th century in Spain a fifth course was added, and the five-course guitar became widely popular in the rest of Europe during the 17th and 18th centuries. These early guitars had somewhat smaller bodies with less incurved waists than the modern instrument.

During the early 19th century in Spain the guitar underwent a transformation that included the adoption of six single strings, more pronounced "bouts" or bulges in the sides of the larger body, and mechanical (geared) tuning pegs. Antonio de Torres Jurado (1817-92) is credited with consolidating these advances into the coherent and elegant design that has been the basis for the sweetly voiced, modern classical guitar, as well as with establishing the modern form of the flamenco guitar with its smaller, lighter body and more brilliant sound.

Variants of the guitar with metal strings passed in and out of fashion during the instrument's long history in Europe, but it was in the United States in the early 20th century that the steel-strung guitar with its greater volume and "twangier" sound came to be preferred as the favorite popular instrument. The "arch-top" guitar developed by Orville Gibson introduced a violin-type arched soundboard to withstand the greater downbearing of the steel strings. This instrument was particularly popular in bands and orchestras of the 1920s and 1930s. The "flat-top" steel-strung guitar, as developed especially by the Martin Company, of Nazareth, Pa., around the turn of the century, is a slightly larger, more heavily built version of the classical guitar; it has become the favorite instrument of folk and popular singers, particularly since World War II.

Experimentation in the 1920s led to the development of the electric guitar. As developed in the 1930s and '40s, this instrument was a steel-strung acoustic guitar with an electromagnetic pick-up connected to an electronic amplification system. Pioneered by Les Paul in the 1940s, the solid-body electric guitar with its limitless volume and great sustaining power became increasingly popular in the 1950s and '60s with the advent of rock music. NICHOLAS RENOUF

Bibliography: Bellow, Alexander, *The Illustrated History of the Guitar* (1970); Evans, Tom and Mary Anne, *Guitars: from the Renaissance to Rock*, (1977); Grunfeld, Frederic, *The Art and Times of the Guitar* (1969); Turnbull, Harvey, *The Guitar from the Renaissance to the Present Day* (1974).

guitarfish [gih-tar'-fish]

Guitarfishes are a genera and 45 species of cartilaginous chondrichthyans in the family Rhinobatidae, which look like a cross between a shark and a ray. Because the gill slits are underneath the pectoral fins, guitarfishes are classified in the order Batoidei, as are the skates and rays. Their elongated, flattened bodies have extended pectoral fins, producing small, raylike wings. They have a wedge-shaped snout, and a tail that is difficult to distinguish from the body. They are generally considered harmless. Guitarfish have small and numerous teeth and primarily eat crustaceans. Like rays, guitarfishes are bottom feeders. They are found in tropical and subtropical seas worldwide. They are ovoviviparous. Adult guitarfishes normally reach a length of 1.5-1.8 m (5-6 ft). An Indo-Pacific species, *Rhynchobatus djiddensis*, reaches 3 m (10 ft) in length and 227 kg (500 lb) in weight. EDWARD O. WILEY

The Atlantic guitarfish, Rynchobatus lentiginosus, *common to warm areas of the Atlantic, has a grayish brown body with light spots.*

Guiteau, Charles Julius [gih-toh']

Charles Julius Guiteau, b. Sept. 8, 1841, d. June 30, 1882, assassinated U.S. President James A. GARFIELD on July 2, 1881. Guiteau's offers to help in Garfield's New York City campaign in 1880 were rebuffed, as were his attempts to find a job in the Garfield administration. He shot the president at the Washington, D.C., railroad station. Guiteau was hanged for the murder.

Bibliography: Rosenberg, Charles E., *Trial of the Assassin Guiteau: Psychiatry and the Law in the Gilded Age* (1968; repr. 1976).

Guitry, Sacha [gee-tree', sah-shah']

The French dramatist, producer, and actor Sacha Guitry, b. Feb. 21, 1885, d. July 24, 1957, first achieved success in 1905 with his play *Nono*. In all, he wrote about 130 plays, more than 90 of which were produced. The son of the noted actor Lucien Guitry, Sacha Guitry acted in most of his own plays and in many of the films that he wrote and directed. He was awarded the Legion of Honor in 1936.

Bibliography: Harding, James, *Sacha Guitry: The Last Boulevardier* (1968).

Guizot, François [gee-zoh']

François Pierre Guillaume Guizot, b. Oct. 4, 1787, d. Sept. 12, 1874, French statesman and historian, was first minister to King LOUIS PHILIPPE from 1840 to 1848. Born to a Protestant, bourgeois family, he began his career as a journalist in Paris in 1805 and in 1812 won appointment as professor of modern history in the University of Paris. From 1814 to 1820 he held administrative posts in the restored Bourbon government of Louis XVIII. Dismissed in 1820, he returned to teaching and writing and became increasingly active in opposition politics.

Guizot was elected to the Chamber of Deputies in January 1830, and when the Revolution of 1830 forced King Charles X to abdicate, he joined other opposition deputies in bringing Louis Philippe to the throne. In the 1830s he served in several ministries; his most notable achievement in this period was his drafting and winning parliamentary approval of the School Law of 1833, the foundation statute of the French public primary education system.

In 1840, Guizot became the effective head of the ministry that governed France for the duration of the monarchy. Believing that France had achieved the ultimate and ideal regime—government by men of substantial property—he resisted growing demands for electoral and parliamentary reform. Not surprisingly, his ministry was the first political casualty of the February REVOLUTION OF 1848.

As a historian Guizot won widespread acclaim. His books on the history of French and European civilization and on the English Civil War, published in the 1820s, brought to the writing of history in France an objectivity and a critical methodology that it had previously lacked. DAVID H. PINKNEY

Bibliography: Johnson, Douglas, *Guizot: Aspects of French History 1787–1874* (1963; repr. 1976).

Gujarat [guj-uh-raht']

Gujarat, a state in western India on the Arabian Sea coast, is bordered by Pakistan in the northwest. The population of Gujarat is 34,085,799 (1981), and the state covers an area of 195,984 km^2 (75,670 mi^2). Gandhinagar is the capital.

In the south the Tapti, Narmada, Mahi, and Sabarmati rivers create a fertile plain, where wheat, millet, cotton, and tobacco are grown. The hilly Kathiawar Peninsula, in the west, is largely arid. In the northwest the tidal marshes of the Rann of Kutch (see KUTCH, RANN OF) gradually give way to the Indian desert. The highly industrialized cities of AHMADABAD, BARODA, Surat, and Broach produce textiles, chemicals, and heavy machinery.

Relics of the INDUS CIVILIZATION of the 3d and 2d millennia BC have been found in Gujarat. The Maurya dynasty, considered by some the first truly "Indian" culture, controlled the area from the 3d century BC to the 2d century AD. The Gupta dynasty was dominant in the 4th and 5th centuries. Jainism flourished in the area under the Anhilvada kingdom from the 8th to the 13th centuries. Gujarat fell to the Delhi Sultanate in 1233 and became an independent sultanate in 1401. In 1572 it was annexed by the Moguls, but by the early 18th century control had passed to the Marathas. The region came under British rule in 1818. After independence (1947), Gujarat was a part of Bombay state until 1960, when a separate state was created along linguistic lines for Gujarati-speaking peoples. Mahatma Gandhi was born in Gujarat.

Gujarati: see INDO-IRANIAN LANGUAGES.

Gujranwala [guj-rahn'-vah-luh]

Gujranwala (1981 pop., 597,000) is a city in the Lahore division of Punjab province in northeast Pakistan. It was founded by the Gujars and became important during the reign (1792–1839) of the great Sikh ruler Ranjit Singh, who was born there. The economy is based on agriculture, especially rice, wheat, and fruit, as well as on the production of metal products and ceramics. The ashes of Ranjit Singh and his father, Mahan Singh, are kept in a mausoleum there.

Gulag [gu'-lahg]

Gulag is the Russian acronym for the Chief Administration of Corrective Labor Camps, a system of penal institutions in the USSR established (1918) after the Russian Revolution. Under Joseph STALIN, masses of people (an estimated 8 percent of the total work force) suspected of crimes against the state—which could mean anything from political dissidence to failure to cooperate with Stalin's schemes for collectivization—were sentenced to forced labor in the camps. Conditions were brutal and inhuman, and many people condemned to forced labor died of malnutrition and disease. Although much of the system has been dismantled, recent reports indicate that several thousand political prisoners remain confined in labor camps and in psychiatric institutions under harsh conditions.

The Gulag Archipelago, 1918–1956: An Experiment in Literary Investigation (1973–78), by Aleksandr SOLZHENITSYN, is a three-volume study of the Soviet penal system as it evolved between the 1920s and the 1950s. Based on the author's personal experiences the study is further documented by the letters, memoirs, and reports of 227 witnesses.

Bibliography: Conquest, Robert, *Kolyma* (1978); Fireside, Harvey, *Soviet Psychoprisons* (1979).

Gulbenkian, Calouste Sarkis [gul-beng'-kee-uhn]

The noted art collector and petroleum magnate Calouste Sarkis Gulbenkian, b. Mar. 23, 1869, d. July 20, 1955, was a Turkish citizen of Armenian descent who became a British citizen in 1902. An important presence in diplomatic, economic, and political circles, he was also acknowledged as a self-made expert in art and antiquities. He was especially active as a collector from 1910 until the outbreak of World War II, and his acquisitions included J. A. Houdon's *Diana* (1780) and Rembrandt's *Woman in Armor*, or *Pallas Athena* (1655), which had originally been in the Hermitage in Leningrad. A selection of Gulbenkian's collection of European paintings and Egyptian artifacts has been on loan to the National Gallery of Art in Washington, D.C., since the late 1940s. The rest of his collection is housed in Lisbon, at the Headquarters and Museum of the Gulbenkian Foundation, which has remained active since Gulbenkian's death as a supporter of artists and art institutions throughout Europe and America. CARTER RATCLIFF

Bibliography: Hewins, Ralph, *Mr. Five Per Cent: The Biography of Calouste Gulbenkian* (1957); Lodwin, John, and Young, Ralph, *Gulbenkian* (1958); Perdião, José de Azerdo, *Calouste Gulbenkian, Collector* (1969).

Guldberg, Cato Maximilian [gool'-bairg, kah'-toh mahk-sih-mil'-yahn]

The Norwegian physical chemist Cato Maximilian Guldberg, b. Aug. 11, 1836, d. Jan. 14, 1902, discovered, with his brother-in-law Peter WAAGE, the law of mass action, which states that the direction taken by a reaction is dependent not merely on the mass of the various components of the reaction, but upon the concentration, that is, upon the mass present in a given volume. The law, which was formulated in 1863, was generally ignored until it was translated into German in 1899. By this time, however, the Dutch chemist van't HOFF had already described it and gained initial credit. Guldberg also anticipated van't Hoff by introducing the ideal gas equation in 1867. JOHN T. BLACKMORE

gulf and bay

A gulf or bay is a body of water that is shaped by a concavity of a coastline and is a reentrant of a larger body of water. The larger water masses that fit this definition are usually called gulfs, while the smaller, affected to a greater extent by local conditions, are classified as bays. This convention, however, has many notable exceptions; for example, the Bay of Bengal (see BENGAL, BAY OF), an arm of the Indian Ocean, is much larger than the Gulf of Mexico (see MEXICO, GULF OF), which could itself almost be considered an inland sea.

An important distinction can be made between those bays and gulfs that are either deeper or shallower than the larger connecting water masses. The relative depth may be a controlling factor in the circulation, life forms, and water-mass properties, although the size, configuration, river runoff, isolation from an ocean, climate, and the depth of the connection, or strait, between the two bodies of water are also important factors. Thus the shallow PERSIAN GULF connects with the deeper Gulf of Oman (see OMAN, GULF OF); the Gulf of Guinea (see GUINEA, GULF OF) has a deep-water connection to the Atlantic Ocean; and the deep Gulf of Mexico has a narrow, shallow connection with the Atlantic Ocean at the Straits of Florida (see FLORIDA, STRAITS OF).

The circulation in gulfs and bays is typically of three types. The larger water bodies have current systems and water-temperature ranges similar to the adjoining oceans. The depth, structural configuration, and wide opening at the connection of these examples allow for normal oceanic circulation to dominate. As the size and depth of the body of water decrease and the isolation from the adjacent sea increases, the controlling factors become more local in character. The salinity and circulation of a small gulf may be drastically affected by local river runoff, which brings with it fresh water and a large sediment bedload, and by local climatic effects, which control the ratio of precipitation to evaporation. The third type of circulation common to some gulfs and bays is a strong TIDAL BORE caused by a funnellike shape and a bottom becoming more shallow toward the headland. Tides of 5 to 18 m (16 to 59 ft) are common in bays with this configuration.

Drowned river valleys or ESTUARIES—CHESAPEAKE BAY, the Gulf of St. Lawrence (see ST. LAWRENCE, GULF OF)—and drowned glacial valleys called FJORDS, found along the coasts of Norway and Sweden and in Canada, are sometimes classified as gulfs and bays. CRAIG AMERIGIAN

Bibliography: Hill, M. N., *The Sea*, vol. 2 (1963; repr. 1982); Huxley, Anthony, *Standard Encyclopedia of the World's Oceans and Islands* (1962; repr. 1969).

Gulf Stream

The Gulf Stream is a system of intense OCEAN CURRENTS that flow along the western boundary of the North Atlantic Ocean. A narrow, high-velocity flow, the Gulf Stream separates the colder, denser water of the continental slope from the warmer, less dense water of the SARGASSO SEA.

The Gulf Stream system is fed from the south by the broad westward-flowing North Equatorial Current. As this current enters the Caribbean, it is reinforced by the South Equatorial Current and becomes recognizably concentrated at approximately 20° N in the Yucatán Channel. This current usually follows a direct route through the Gulf of Mexico to the Florida Straits, where it becomes more intense. Near Miami the current is approximately 80 km (50 mi) wide at the surface, and the volume of water transported is approximately 3×10^7 m^3/sec (8×10^9 gal/sec). As the Florida Current, the Gulf Stream system then flows northward from the Florida Straits to Cape Hatteras in waters approximately 800 m (2,600 ft) deep. It is strong all the way to the bottom. Along the coast of Florida the Florida Current is joined by the Antilles Current.

From about 33° N until it reaches the vicinity of the Grand Banks (approximately 40° N, 50° W), the current is known properly as the Gulf Stream. Its width increases to approximately 150 km (90 mi) as it flows beneath the Grand Banks; the volume transport is more than double the amount transported through the Straits of Florida. Peak surface velocities exceed 250 cm/sec (5.5 mph), and appreciable current has been detected at depths greater than 2,000 m (6,600 ft). Evidence exists for a deep countercurrent off Cape Hatteras, flowing south to southwest at velocities between 9 and 18 cm/sec (0.2 and 0.4 mph). East of the Grand Banks the Gulf Stream becomes the diffuse North Atlantic Current.

Tracings (A) *of Gulf Stream sources* (broken lines) *and its flow patterns* (solid lines) *reveal meandering movement through the Gulf of Mexico eastward and northeastward toward Europe and Iceland. A water-temperature profile* (B) *discloses the warmer surface temperatures* (yellow area) *of the stream. The distribution of dissolved salts* (C), *in parts per thousand (ppt), and the variation in temperature* (D) *are graphed for various water depths, yielding an X-Y section of the stream extending from the eastern United States to Bermuda.*

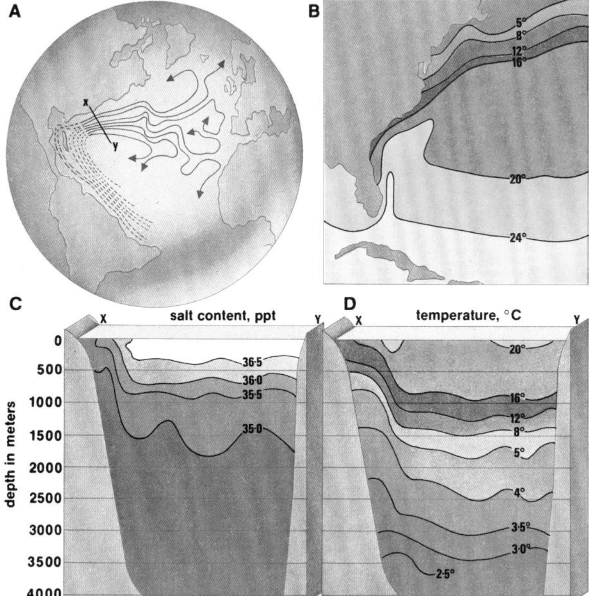

As the Gulf Stream leaves the vicinity of the continental shelf, it exhibits large meanders. These meanders pinch off and swirl around a core of warm or cold water extending down to the sea floor. According to recent analyses, dozens of large (up to 300 km/185 mi across) cold-water rings can be found south and east of the Gulf Stream and a few smaller warm-water eddies north of it. The rings rotate and move slowly toward the Gulf Stream. The cold-water rings survive three years, the warm-water rings typically less than one year. The rings slowly lose the energy "stored" in their temperature differences and are reabsorbed into the Gulf Stream.

The Gulf Stream system moderates the climate of land areas adjacent to it. Southwestern England and western Norway, for example, have winters much milder than would be expected from their latitudes.

Bibliography: Gaskell, Thomas Frohock, *The Gulf Stream* (1973); Stommel, Henry, *The Gulf Stream*, 2d ed. (1965; repr. 1977); Worthington, L. V., *On the North Atlantic Circulation* (1976).

Gulf war

The Persian Gulf war erupted on Sept. 22, 1980, when Iraq invaded Iran. The conflict had deep territorial, cultural, ethnic, and ideological roots and reflected a historic rivalry between Iraq and Iran for supremacy in the PERSIAN GULF area.

Iraq's stated war goal was to gain total control of the SHATT-AL-ARAB waterway dividing the two countries. However, Iraq's minority-based Sunnite government also feared the impact of Iran's 1979 Islamic revolution on its Shiite majority and hoped that Iran's military weakness and internal chaos would enable Iraq to reassert Arab claims to Iran's Khuzestan province and become the dominant power in the region. In June 1982, faced with strong Iranian resistance, Iraq withdrew its troops from most parts of Iran. Although Iran later launched several massive human wave attacks, the war essentially settled into a bloody stalemate with a death toll estimated at more than 1 million. In 1984, Iraq began attacks on Gulf shipping as part of its economic warfare against Iran. This strategy also helped draw other countries into the conflict, increasing pressure on Iran to accept a negotiated settlement. In response, Iran attacked ships carrying war material to Iraq and those belonging to countries that helped Iraq.

From the beginning there was fear that the war would expand and possibly spark a superpower confrontation. Iraq purchased arms mainly from France and the USSR and received Western credits and massive financial aid from other Gulf Arab states. Iran, supported by Syria and Libya, purchased most of its arms in the black market. The United States, officially neutral, gave nonmilitary aid and intelligence information to Iraq but also, in 1985 and 1986, supplied a few arms to Iran (see IRAN-CONTRA AFFAIR). In May 1987, after the U.S. frigate *Stark* was hit by an Iraqi missile, apparently by accident, the United States increased its naval presence in the Gulf and allowed 11 Kuwaiti tankers to fly the U.S. flag. Other nations later joined the patrols. In July 1987, Iraq accepted a UN resolution designed to end the war. Iran also accepted it in July 1988 after Iraqi air attacks on Iranian cities and several Iraqi ground victories, but Iraq continued its offensive. (On July 3 the U.S. cruiser *Vincennes* accidentally downed a commercial Iranian airliner, killing all 290 persons aboard.) A cease-fire took effect on Aug. 20, 1988, and talks aimed at achieving a permanent peace opened in Geneva on Aug. 25, 1988.

Gulfport

Gulfport, the seat of Harrison County, is a city in southeastern Mississippi with a population of 39,676 (1980). Located on Mississippi Sound of the Gulf of Mexico, Gulfport is a U.S.

port of entry. The city was founded in 1887 and developed because of its timber stands and natural deepwater harbor. Gulfport's modern economy includes seafood canning and aluminum and steel fabricating. Because of the city's fine beaches, tourism is also important.

Gulick, Luther Halsey [goo'-lik]

Luther Halsey Gulick, b. Honolulu, Dec. 4, 1865, d. Aug. 13, 1918, was a pioneer in American physical education. The son of American missionaries, Gulick was educated in the continental United States and served as secretary of physical training for the Young Men's Christian Association (YMCA) from 1887 to 1903. He helped James NAISMITH develop the game of basketball. From 1903 to 1908, he was director of physical education for the New York City public schools. He helped found the Camp Fire Girls in 1910. Gulick wrote several books and lectured extensively on physical education and hygiene.

Bibliography: Dorgan, Ethel J., *Luther Halsey Gulick, 1865–1918* (1934; repr. 1973).

gull

Gulls are approximately 43 species of birds belonging to the family Laridae, which includes the TERNS. They are uniform in size and coloration and range from about 28 to 81 cm (11 to 32 in) in length. Most have a gray or white mantle; some are black above (the black-backed and kelp gulls) and white below. Adults of several species have a black or brown hood. The bill is stout and hooked; the feet, except for the free hind toe, are fully webbed.

Gulls are mainly scavengers and prey on anything they can find, sometimes far inland. They forage along ocean and inland shores, where they pick up dead animal matter or catch fish in shallow waters. In some areas they are known to carry hard-shelled mollusks aloft and drop them on pavements or rocks to break the shell. Some species rob smaller birds of their catches, and gulls often gang up on wounded larger birds. Some species, such as the ring-billed, Bonaparte's, and Franklin's gulls, may follow a plow for upturned grubs or visit grainfields for insects, mice, and other prey.

Gulls usually nest in colonies on islands. Two or three eggs are laid in a shallow nest composed of stones, shells, seaweed, or stalks of vegetation. Incubation periods vary from 20 to 30 days, and the young, sparsely clothed with natal down, remain at or near the nest for several days before wandering off. Mortality is high in the nesting colonies, but survivors may live up to 30 years or more. The birds have been favorite subjects for behavior studies, and their movements and migrations are well known. GEORGE J. WALLACE

Bibliography: Graham, Frank, Jr., and Ayers, Christopher, *Gulls: A Social History* (1975); Grant, P. J., *Gulls: A Guide to Identification* (1981); Lockley, R. M., *Seabirds of the World* (1984).

Gulliver's Travels

Gulliver's Travels (1726), Jonathan SWIFT's best-known satire, was first published as *Travels into Several Remote Nations of the World, by Lemuel Gulliver.* Using the form of journal narrative recently popularized by Daniel Defoe's *Robinson Crusoe* (1709), Swift's naive but likable hero recounts his adventures on four fictitious voyages: to Lilliput, land of tiny people; to Brobdingnag, land of giants; to Laputa, land of scientists, sorcerers, and immortals; and finally to Houyhnhnmland, a country ruled by rational horses who dominate the Yahoos, a filthy and depraved race who bear a strong resemblance to human beings. Swift's topical allusions now require learned explanation, but the disturbing force of his mockery of such human failings as pride, selfishness, avarice, and dishonesty is undiminished. JEAN DWYER CORMICK

Bibliography: Brady, F., ed., *Twentieth-Century Interpretations of Gulliver's Travels* (1968); Lock, F., *The Politics of Gulliver's Travels* (1980).

gum

Gum, a sticky substance obtained from plants, is a complex compound derived from carbohydrates and is tasteless and odorless. Many gums are soluble in water; others absorb water to form a mucilaginous mass. Gum arabic, from an African tree of the genus *Acacia,* is the most commercially important water-soluble gum, followed by gum TRAGACANTH, ghatti gum, and karaya gum. Other sources of gums are seaweeds, such as ALGIN and agar, and plant seeds, including FLAX seed, TAMARIND, locust beans, quince seed, psyllium seed, and guar. Gums are used as emulsifiers, stabilizers, and thickeners in foods, cosmetics, medicines, water-based paints, and inks; as gelling agents and moisturizers in canned meats and fish, marshmallows, and jellied products; and as adhesives in postage stamps, envelopes, and cardboard. FRANCES GIES

Bibliography: Davidson, R., *Handbook of Water-Soluble Gums and Resins* (1980).

gum arabic

Gum arabic is a water-soluble plant gum obtained from the *Acacia senegal* and several other species of small acacia trees that grow in the dry areas of central and northern Africa. A

The great black-backed gull, Larus marinus (left), *is often seen with the smaller and more common herring gull,* Larus argentatus (center), *which often breaks the shells of clams and other mollusks by dropping them on rocks or paved areas. Franklin's gull,* Larus pipixcan (right), *found inland in freshwater habitats, feeds on insects and other small prey in plowed fields.*

colloidal polysaccharide substance that exudes from the tree, gum arabic is gelatinous when moist but becomes hard when dry. It is extracted by cutting into the bark, permitting the gum to ooze out in the form of "tears" that are collected after they dry. The color of the gum varies from white to red; the highest grades are a transparent white.

The thickening and film-forming properties of gum arabic are employed for a variety of commercial purposes: in the manufacture of adhesives, inks, and paper; as a sizing and filling in textile fabrics; and, in the pharmaceutical industry, as an emulsifier. The gum is also used as a gelling agent in cooking, especially in the production of candy and confections.

gumbo: see OKRA.

gumbo-limbo [guhm'-boh-lim'-boh]

The gumbo-limbo is a tropical tree, *Bursera simaruba*, of the bursera family, Burseraceae, found from southern Florida to Central America. It reaches 18 m (60 ft) high, with a smooth reddish bark that peels into thin shreds. It sheds its leaves in winter. Flowers are borne in slender clusters, and the fruit is a berrylike drupe.

Gumilev, Nikolai Stepanovich [goom-eel-yawf', neek-uh-ly' steep-ahn'-uh-vich]

The Russian poet Nikolai Gumilev, b. Apr. 15, 1886, was the husband of the poet Anna AKHMATOVA and a founder of the ACMEIST literary movement in 1912. He was executed on Aug. 24, 1921, for complicity in an anti-Soviet conspiracy. Gumilev's poetry, influenced by Théophile Gautier and Leconte de Lisle, is characterized by strength, concreteness, and clarity—qualities advocated by the acmeists. Much of his poetry glorifies soldiers and explorers of distant lands; his best works include *Ognenny Stolp* (The Pillar of Fire, 1921). His poetry remains banned in the Soviet Union. MAURICE FRIEDBERG

Bibliography: Raffel, Burton, *Russian Poetry under the Tsars* (1971).

gumweed

Gumweeds, also known as gumplants, rosinweeds, and tarweeds, are about 60 species of plants native to warm, semiarid regions of North and South America. They comprise the genus *Grindelia* in the sunflower family, Compositae. Some species grow to 1.4 m (4.5 ft) high; the gummy flower heads, which have as many as 45 florets extending from them, can be 5 cm (2 in) wide. Gumweeds are sometimes grown as ornamentals but have been considered of minor interest until recent research indicated their agricultural potential as a source for various RESINS. Such materials have numerous industrial uses, including the production of synthetic polymers, and natural sources are otherwise dwindling. Gumweed residues also show promise as animal feeds and as fuels.

Bibliography: Hinman, C. Wiley, "Potential New Crops," *Scientific American*, July 1986.

gun: see FIREARMS.

gun control

The introduction of legislation to curb the sale and possession of firearms, particularly handguns, in an effort to reduce violent crime has been a hotly debated issue in the United States in recent years. Opponents of gun control, including the 3 million-member NATIONAL RIFLE ASSOCIATION (NRA), argue that the RIGHT TO BEAR ARMS is guaranteed by the 2D AMENDMENT and that licensing restrictions penalize the law-abiding citizen while in no way preventing criminal use of handguns. Proponents of gun control argue that handguns have little value in self-defense, and range from those who favor an outright ban to those who wish to control sale and possession through strict licensing regulations, the deterrent to misuse being mandatory jail sentences for offenders.

The 1968 Federal Gun Control Act regulated interstate commerce in firearms and prohibited their sale to minors, felons, and addicts. Prodded by the NRA, Congress in 1986 eased some of these federal controls. Following a public uproar after a man killed five California schoolchildren with a semiautomatic assault rifle early in 1989, the Bush administration banned most foreign-made assault rifles. State and local laws regulating sale and possession of firearms vary greatly.

Bibliography: Kates, D. B., ed., *Firearms and Violence* (1984); Zimring, F. E., et al., eds., *The Citizen's Guide to Gun Control* (1987).

guncotton

Guncotton is a nitrocellulose EXPLOSIVE invented in 1845 by Christian Shönbein; it is used today in PROPELLANTS. Guncotton was first produced by nitrating cotton fibers in a solution of sulfuric and nitric acids; the resulting product contained approximately 13% nitrogen. Shönbein was seeking a propellant that could be used in firearms, but guncotton proved to be too potent for that purpose. In 1884 the Frenchman Paul Vieille synthesized the first successful smokeless powder from guncotton. Celluloses containing less than 13% nitrogen may also be used as explosives, but they are not termed *guncotton*. Although the term is still used, purified wood cellulose has virtually replaced cotton in its manufacture.

DAVID N. BUCKNER

Gunnarsson, Gunnar [gun'-ar-sohn, gun'-ar]

Principally known as an Icelandic novelist, Gunnar Gunnarsson, b. May 18, 1889, d. Nov. 21, 1975, wrote many of his works in Danish while living in Denmark from 1907 to 1939. His novels focus, however, on the Icelandic people and their culture and history. A recurrent theme is that human isolation may be overcome through faith and courage. Gunnarsson's works, which have been widely translated, include the four-volume *Borgslaegstens Historie* (The Borg Family Papers, 1912–14), the semiautobiographical five-volume *Kirken paa Bjerget* (Church on the Mountain, 1923–28), and *The Black Cliffs* (1929; Eng. trans., 1967).

gunnel [guhn'-ul]

Gunnels are small, eellike fishes found in shallow, rocky marine waters of the northern Pacific and Atlantic coasts. The rock gunnel of the North Atlantic, *Pholis gunnellus*, averages about 20 cm (8 in) long. The female rolls her eggs into a ball, which both parents guard. CAMM SWIFT

gunpowder

Gunpowder, or black powder, was the first true EXPLOSIVE. A mixture of 10% sulfur, 15% charcoal, and 75% saltpeter (potassium nitrate), it is generally thought to have originated in China, where explosive grenades and bombs were in use by AD 1000. The Arabs were acquainted with gunpowder by the 13th century, and Roger Bacon described its preparation in 1242. By the early 14th century, black powder and guns were being manufactured in Europe. Early FIREARMS were clumsy and of limited dependability, but they were rapidly improved. These weapons had great social impact, eventually sounding the death knell for the feudal system.

Because gunpowder is strictly a mechanical mixture of its separate components, its manufacture is a simple process. Gunpowder is, however, highly sensitive to sparks, whether mechanically or electrically produced, and extreme care must be exercised in its production. Gunpowder was originally mixed by hand and crushed into fine particles with wooden stamps. In time, water power mechanized the stamping stage, and metal stamps replaced the wooden ones. Accidental explosions often occurred. Today charcoal and saltpeter are mixed by the tumbling action of steel balls in a rotating hollow cylinder. The saltpeter is pulverized separately, and the ingredients are then mixed and ground. After further crushing between wooden rollers, the gunpowder is pressed into cakes that are rebroken in a corning mill to desired size. Finally, the grains are tumbled in wooden cylinders to wear off rough edges. During this process graphite is introduced, which coats the powder with a friction-reducing, moisture-resistant film.

By the beginning of the 20th century, black powder had been virtually replaced as the standard firearms propellant. Although it had served for centuries, it had many drawbacks. It produced a large cloud of white smoke when ignited, built up a bore-obstructing residue after relatively few shots, and absorbed moisture easily. Its replacement, nitrocellulose-based smokeless powders (see GUNCOTTON), eliminated most of these disadvantages. Gunpowder had already been largely replaced as a primary blasting explosive by DYNAMITE and TNT (see TNT). Black powder is still widely used, however, in artillery-shell primers, hand-grenade fuses, and FIREWORKS.

DAVID N. BUCKNER

Gunpowder Plot: see FAWKES, GUY.

Günther, Ignaz [gun'-tur, ig'-nahts]

Ignaz Günther, b. June 26, 1725, d. June 28, 1775, was the leading Bavarian sculptor of the 18th century working in the ROCOCO STYLE. Apprenticed (1743–50) to the sculptor Johann Baptist Straub (1704–84) in Munich, he later studied in Mannheim and at the Royal Academy in Vienna, where he was awarded first prize in 1753. Günther then returned to Munich, receiving commissions from churches and palaces throughout upper Bavaria. Working principally in carved-and-painted wood, he imbued his art with an exuberant emotional quality coupled with the statuesque sensuality associated with 16th-century Mannerism. His boldly expressive *Guardian Angel* group (*c.*1770; Burgersaal, Munich) displays the elongated proportions, sharply rendered folds of drapery, and lively pastel colors characteristic of Günther's style.

Günther, Johann Christian [gun'-tur]

Johann Christian Günther, b. Apr. 8, 1695, d. Mar. 15, 1723, was one of the most original German poets of his time. He wrote love poems, religious verse, satires, and drinking and student songs, including the German version of "Gaudeamus igitur." Goethe, one of the first to acknowledge his genius, recognized the importance of Günther's poetry to his own poetry.

LILIAN R. FURST

Gunther, John [guhn'-thur]

John Gunther, b. Chicago, Aug. 30, 1901, d. May 29, 1970, was a journalist and writer who interpreted the world to millions of Americans through his newspaper articles, radio broadcasts, and especially the books in his famous "Inside" series. *Inside Europe* (1936) was the first of these; later books concentrated on Asia (1939), Latin America (1941, 1967), the United States (1947, 1951, and 1956), Africa (1955), and Russia (1958). Gunther's *A Fragment of Autobiography* appeared in 1962.

ERNEST C. HYNDS

guppy [guhp'-ee]

The guppy, *Poecilia reticulata*, a MOLLY, is one of the most common freshwater aquarium fish. It lives in the ponds, swamps, and little streams of the southern Caribbean islands and in northern South America. It feeds on small aquatic insects. Careful breeding has enhanced the naturally beautiful colors and tail shapes of the male. The female guppy's eggs are fertilized internally, and offspring are born live; males grow to a length of 3 cm (1.2 in), females to 5 cm (2 in). Their birthrate is so high that they have been called "million fishes," and they have been widely introduced to control mosquito populations.

A. R. EMERY

The guppy, P. reticulata, *is a very hardy fish that is often seen in home aquariums. It was introduced commercially in 1908.*

Gupta (dynasty) [gup'-tuh]

The Guptas were a dynasty of northern Indian kings that flourished from the 4th to the 6th century. The house was founded by Chandragupta I (r. *c.*320–*c.*330), who took his name from the great Chandragupta Maurya, founder of the Maurya dynasty. The Gupta period is generally considered the golden age of ancient India. KALIDASA, author of *Sakuntala* and other outstanding dramas, was the greatest of the period's many eminent writers. Gupta sculpture was foremost in a general rejuvenation of the arts—including music, dance, painting, and architecture—not unlike that of the Italian Renaissance. Hindu philosophy was systematized into its present form in this period. Scientific accomplishments included the introduction of the zero and plastic surgery, as well as remarkable advances in metallurgy.

Politically, the Gupta empire reached its zenith under Chandragupta II (r. *c.*380–*c.*414), when it extended far into the Deccan and western India. It was greatly reduced by invading Hephthalites (White Huns) at the end of the 5th century but lingered in Bengal until *c.*544. A short-lived attempt was made by King Harsha of Thaneswar (r. 606–47) to revive the empire.

MARCUS FRANDA AND VONETTA J. FRANDA

Bibliography: Ganguly, D. K., *Imperial Guptas and Their Times* (1987).

Gurdjieff, George Ivanovich [goor'-jef]

George Ivanovich Gurdjieff, b. 1872?, d. Oct. 29, 1949, founded a movement based on doctrines of enlightenment through meditation and heightened self-awareness that attracted many prominent followers in Europe and the United States. Of Russian-Armenian origin, Gurdjieff established his Institute for the Harmonious Development of Man at Fontainebleau, France, where he settled in 1922. His disciples included architect Frank Lloyd Wright, painter Georgia O'Keefe, writer Katherine Mansfield, and journalist P. D. Ouspensky. Ouspensky's books helped to popularize Gurdjieff's teachings.

Gurkha [goor'-kuh]

Gurkha—from Gorkha, the name of the dynasty that has ruled Nepal since 1769—refers to those regiments of the British or Indian armies composed of mercenary soldiers recruited from various ethnic groups of Nepal, including the Magar, Gurung, Rai, and Limbu. The first Gurkha regiments were formed (1815) during the Anglo-Nepali War, when Nepali troops surrendering to the British Indian army at the Battle of Malaun were recruited to fight for their captors. They proved to be an unusually effective fighting force, and throughout the 19th century Gurkha regiments were used to support British colonial interests in Asia. During the two world wars, numerous Gurkha units served with distinction.

Since India gained independence in 1947, treaty arrangements have allowed both Great Britain and India to recruit Gurkha soldiers, although such recruitment has declined. In the mid-1980s, Nepali-speaking Indians began to agitate for the creation of a Gurkha state in West Bengal, adjacent to the Nepalese border; a 1988 accord granted this group greater control over their own affairs.

ROBERT A. PAUL

Bibliography: Bishop, E., *Better to Die* (1976); Northey, W. B., and Morris, C. J., *The Gurkhas* (1928; repr. 1975).

gurnard, flying [gur'-nurd]

The flying gurnards are marine tropical fishes belonging to the family Dactylopteridae, in the order Perciformes. Despite their common name, they are not known to fly. Their pectoral fins are greatly enlarged, and when folded they reach back to the base of the tail. If extended rigidly from the sides, they give the appearance of wings; however, these oversize fins merely serve to balance the fish as it glides along. The most common species of flying gurnard, *Dactylopterus volitans*, has

The flying gurnard, Dactylopterus volitans, *a bottom-dwelling fish found in tropical and subtropical waters, uses its stiff-spined pelvic fins to slowly "walk" along the ocean floor.*

been reported on both sides of the Atlantic and in the Mediterranean. In the western Atlantic it has been found from Massachusetts to Argentina but is more common in tropical waters. It reaches a length of 30 cm (1 ft) or greater. Crustaceans are its principal food.

Although the gurnard, like other species of fishes, swims by undulating movements of the body, it can also move either backward or forward by using the ventral fins. In this process the ventral fins move alternately, like legs, giving the animal the appearance of walking. A comparable method of locomotion is found in the sea robins, which belong to another family of fishes, Triglidae; however, in this family the detached lower rays of the pectoral fins serve as feet.

ALFRED PERLMUTTER

Gurney, Dan [gur'-nee]

The race car driver Daniel Sexton Gurney, b. Port Jefferson, N.Y., Apr. 13, 1931, became, in the 1960s, the first man to win championship races in Formula One, Indianapolis, stock, and sports cars. He was second in the standings for the 1961 Grand Prix World Driving Championship, won the Le Mans race in 1967, and finished second in the Indianapolis 500 in 1968 and 1969 in cars of his own design. In 1967 he became the first American since 1921 to win a Grand Prix race in an American car. He was also instrumental in introducing rear-engine race cars in the United States.

guru [goo'-roo]

In Hinduism, a guru is a religious teacher. Sometimes regarded as an incarnation of a Hindu god, the guru is generally looked upon as a mediator of divine truth. The title is also used for spiritual teachers in Buddhism, and was conferred upon the founders of the Sikh religion.

Gustav I, King of Sweden [gus'-tahv]

Gustav I, b. May 12, 1490, d. Sept. 29, 1560, of the VASA dynasty, was the king who made Sweden an independent Protestant country. He was descended from a great noble family that had become powerful in the days of Swedish autonomy under Danish kings. In 1521, with the support of the city of Lübeck, Gustav led a successful uprising to drive out the Danish king. He became lord protector of Sweden, and in 1523 he was elected king. At the diet of Västerås in 1527 he achieved control over the landed wealth of the bishops. This strengthened the crown, and it became the first step toward a Lutheran state church, which became firmly established during the following decade.

Gustav Vasa ruled for nearly 40 years, suppressed repeated internal risings, and established the first national standing army in Europe. The economic and political power of Sweden grew steadily during his reign. He was succeeded by his son, ERIC XIV.

J. R. CHRISTIANSON

Bibliography: Roberts, Michael, *The Early Vasas* (1968).

Gustav II Adolf, King of Sweden (Gustavus Adolphus) [ay'-dawlf]

Gustav II Adolf, b. Dec. 9, 1594, d. Nov. 6, 1632, was the king responsible for making Sweden a major European power. When his father, CHARLES IX, died in 1611, he left to Gustav a

Gustav II Adolf, king of Sweden (1611-32), made Sweden a major European power, dominating the Baltic. After concluding wars with the Danes and the Russians, he intervened decisively in the Thirty Years' War on the Protestant side. He was killed at the height of his success, however, in the Battle of Lützen.

kingdom at war with Denmark, Russia, and Poland, whose king SIGISMUND III had been deposed by Charles from the Swedish throne. Gustav ended the war with Denmark and temporarily suspended fighting with Poland, but continued the conflict with Russia. By 1617, Sweden controlled the whole Gulf of Finland, and Russia was cut off from the Baltic for the next century.

Working with Count OXENSTIERNA, Gustav transformed Sweden into one of the first bureaucratic states in modern Europe, strengthened the parliament and state council, and completely reorganized male secondary education. In 1620 he renewed the war against Poland, conquered Livonia, and in 1626 shifted the battlefield to Prussia. Sweden and Denmark united to aid the defense of Stralsund against the imperial army of WALLENSTEIN in 1628, and a truce with Poland (1629) allowed Gustav to devote his main energies to the THIRTY YEARS' WAR in Germany. His initial aim was to ward off the imperial Habsburg threat to the Baltic and to Lutheranism.

By early 1631, Gustav had won the support of Brandenburg, Saxony, and France, and in September 1631, at the famous Battle of Breitenfeld, he shattered the imperial army of TILLY and made himself master of Germany. Gustav's army had perfected its organization and tactics during the years of warfare in the Baltic regions. He marched relentlessly through Roman Catholic Germany and spent the winter in Mainz. All of Europe now stood in awe of the "Lion of the North," and Gustav began to plan a permanent Protestant league with himself as head. In 1632 he turned his army against that of Wallenstein. At Lützen on Nov. 6, 1632, they met and fought. The battle ended in another Swedish victory, but Gustav lay dead on the field. Oxenstierna took control of what was now a great Swedish empire, and the crown passed to Gustav's daughter, CHRISTINA.

J. R. CHRISTIANSON

Bibliography: Dupuy, Trevor N., *The Military Life of Gustavus Adolphus* (1969); Roberts, Michael, *Gustavus Adolphus: A History of Sweden 1611-1632*, 2 vols. (1953-58).

Gustav III, King of Sweden

Gustav III, b. Jan. 24, 1746, d. Mar. 29, 1792, was the king who established enlightened despotism in Sweden. He grew up in a kingdom torn by the squabbles of parliamentary factions. An intelligent and imaginative person, stimulated by a good education in French and Swedish literature, he became a poet, dramatist, and patron of the arts and music. When his father, Adolf Frederick, died in 1771, he hurried home from France to take the throne. The following year, he led a coup d'état that greatly increased his power. He carried through reforms in administration, currency, trade, and defense.

Meanwhile, strong opposition to his rule—encouraged by Russia—arose in aristocratic circles. In 1788, Gustav attacked Russia without warning. Soon after, Sweden was attacked by Denmark-Norway. Facing a war on two fronts, Gustav aroused a tremendous patriotic resistance in Sweden. The Dano-Norwegians were pushed back, and peace was negotiated with Russia in 1790. At this time Gustav began to consider forming a coalition to overthrow the French Revolution. Before this idea bore fruit, he was killed at a masquerade in Stockholm. Verdi's opera *A Masked Ball* (1859) is based on his assassination. His son, Gustav IV Adolf, succeeded him.

J. R. CHRISTIANSON

Bibliography: Sahlberg, Gardar, *Murder at the Masked Ball* (1969); Scott, Franklin D., *Sweden: The Nation's History* (1977).

Gustav IV Adolf, King of Sweden

Gustav IV Adolf, b. Nov. 1, 1778, d. Feb. 7, 1837, was king of Sweden from 1792 until 1809. Lacking the intellectual brilliance of his father, Gustav III, he tried nonetheless to carry on the enlightened and aggressive Gustavian traditions of his father's reign. In 1805 he joined Russia and Great Britain against NAPOLEON I, but in 1807, Russia changed sides and seized Finland from Sweden. Meanwhile, Great Britain attacked Denmark-Norway, and that realm, in retaliation, attacked Sweden. Overwhelmed by these difficulties, Gustav IV was deposed in 1809 and sent into exile. His uncle Charles XIII succeeded him, but the throne subsequently passed to the French Marshal Bernadotte as CHARLES XIV JOHN.

J. R. CHRISTIANSON

Bibliography: Scott, Franklin D., *Sweden: The Nation's History* (1977).

Gustav VI Adolf, King of Sweden

Gustav VI Adolf, b. Nov. 11, 1882, d. Sept. 5, 1973, succeeded to the Swedish throne on the death of his father, Gustav V, in 1950. An archaeologist and botanist, he was elected (1958) to the British Royal Academy. In 1971, Sweden adopted a new constitution, which removed the remaining powers of the monarchy. This became effective on the death of Gustav, who was succeeded by his grandson, Charles XVI Gustav.

Guston, Philip

Philip Guston, b. Montreal, June 13, 1913, d. June 7, 1980, a leading painter of the post-World War II era in New York City, is known for his works that make harsh comments on contemporary social conditions. He studied briefly at the Otis Art Institute, Los Angeles, in 1930. An art teacher in the federal Works Projects Administration from 1935 to 1940, Guston taught at a number of schools and colleges since then. An early example of his social commentary is the representational *If This Be Not I* (1945; Washington University, St. Louis). His earliest mature painting (1950s) is fully abstract. Brushstrokes of thick paint cluster in the middle of the canvas, producing lushly colored textures and evoking, as well, the effects of light in urban landscapes. During the 1970s, Guston's paint textures were organized like patterns of deliberately crude, cartoonlike drawings.

CARTER RATCLIFF

The loose handling of paint in Philip Guston's Cadran *(1956) typifies a principal characteristic of abstract expressionism. Guston modified the style, however, by curtailing slashing, linear strokes in favor of shorter patches of color. (Whitney Museum, New York.)*

Bibliography: Ashton, Dore, *Philip Guston* (1960) and *Yes, But. . .: A Critical Study of Philip Guston* (1976); O'Hara, Frank, *Art Chronicles, 1954–1966* (1975).

Gutenberg, Beno [goot'-en-bairk, bay'-noh]

Beno Gutenberg, b. June 4, 1889, d. Jan. 25, 1960, was a German-born American seismologist whose research on the Earth's internal structure led to the discovery (1913) of the boundary between the mantle and the core. Working with Charles Richter, he helped develop a method for determining earthquake intensity and focused attention on the predominance of earthquake activity in the Circum-Pacific Belt. He was associated with the California Institute of Technology's Seismological Institute at Pasadena from 1930 and served as its director from 1947 to 1958.

Gutenberg, Johann

Johann Gutenberg, b. c.1398, d. 1468, was a German goldsmith who is credited with the invention and development in Europe of PRINTING from movable type. His invention fulfilled the needs of the age for more and cheaper reading matter and foreshadowed the modern printing industry.

Gutenberg first experimented with printing about 1440 in Strasbourg, 160 km (100 mi) from his native Mainz. By 1450 he was back in Mainz, and his invention had been perfected to a point where it could be exploited commercially. To produce the large numbers of individual pieces of type that were needed for the composition of a BOOK, Gutenberg introduced the principle of replica-casting. Single letters were engraved in relief and then punched into slabs of brass to produce matrices from which replicas could be cast in molten metal. These were then combined to produce a flat printing surface, thus establishing the process of LETTERPRESS printing. The type was a rich decorative texture modeled on the Gothic handwriting of the period.

Gutenberg's second achievement lay in the development of an ink that would adhere to his metal type and that

The German artisan Johann Gutenberg is credited with the invention of movable type for use on a printing press. This development increased the availability of written material and furthered the dissemination of information and ideas. The only work ascribed to Gutenberg with any certainty is the magnificent 42-line Gutenberg Bible, *a Latin work whose type replicates the finest 15th-century calligraphy.*

needed to be completely different in chemical composition from existing woodblock printing inks. Gutenberg also transformed the winepress of the time into a screw-and-lever press capable of printing pages of type. While setting up his commercial press between 1450 and 1452, he borrowed a sum of money from Johann FUST to enable him to produce his type and presses but was unable to repay the debt promptly. Fust foreclosed on the mortgage in 1455 and obtained possession of the type and presses, setting himself up as a printer with his son-in-law, Peter Schöffer. Gutenberg apparently abandoned printing altogether after 1465, possibly because of blindness. He died on Feb. 3, 1468, in comparative poverty.

Only one major work can confidently be attributed to Gutenberg's own workshop. This is the Gutenberg Bible (also known as the 42-line Bible from the number of lines to each page), which was set and printed about 1455. M. C. FAIRLEY

Bibliography: McMurtrie, Douglas C., *The Book,* 3d ed. (1943); Scholderer, Victor, *Johann Gutenberg: The Inventor of Printing* (1963); Steinberg, S. H., *Five Hundred Years of Printing,* rev. ed. (1956).

Gutenberg Bible

The first book ever produced mechanically was a Bible printed in Europe about 1455 on a press invented by Johann Gutenberg. The actual printing is usually attributed to Gutenberg, but some scholars suggest that it may have been done by his partner, Johann FUST, and Fust's son-in-law, Peter Schöffer. Gutenberg (*c.*1398–1468), originally a goldsmith, developed his process of printing by using movable type made from punch-stamped matrices, a press similar to a wine press, and oil-based printing ink. The 42-line Bible, of which fewer than 50 copies are extant, comprised 1,284 pages, each with 2 columns of text containing 42 lines to a column. Each page held about 2,500 individual pieces of lead type, set by hand. The German Gothic type-style was modeled on manuscripts of the period. Six presses worked on the Bible simultaneously, printing 20 to 40 pages of type a day. The Psalter, generally regarded as Europe's second printed book, is sometimes attributed to Gutenberg because it includes his innovation of polychrome initial letters using multiple inking on a single metal block. The 36-line Bible (1458–59), of which 8 copies remain, and the Catholicon (1460), are sometimes also attributed to Gutenberg.

Bibliography: Scholderer, Victor, *Johann Gutenberg: The Inventor of Printing* (1963).

Guthrie, A. B., Jr. [guhth'-ree]

Alfred Bertram Guthrie, Jr., b. Bedford, Ind., Jan. 13, 1901, is an American writer best known for his panoramic Westerns, including *The Big Sky* (1947; film 1952), the 1950 Pulitzer Prize-winning *The Way West* (1949; film 1967), *These Thousand Hills* (1956; film 1959), and *Arfive* (1970). Guthrie also wrote the screenplays for the films *Shane* (1953) and *The Kentuckian* (1955) and an autobiography, *The Blue Hen's Chick* (1965).

Guthrie, Edwin Ray

Edwin Ray Guthrie, American psychologist, b. Lincoln, Nebr., Jan. 9, 1886, d. Apr. 23, 1959, deemphasized the importance of reinforcement in learning theory, holding that learning occurred when connections were established in the central nervous system between a given combination of stimuli and a response. Some interest has recently revived in Guthrie's empirical, parsimonious approach.

Guthrie, Janet

Janet Guthrie, b. Iowa City, Iowa, Mar. 7, 1938, was the first woman to drive in the Indianapolis 500 auto race. She was an aerospace engineer before she started competitive driving. Her major victories include the under-2-liter prototype class (1970) and the North Atlantic Road Racing Championship B sedan class (1973). During the 1977 and 1979 Indianapolis races mechanical trouble forced Guthrie to drop out before finishing; in 1978, however, she finished ninth.

Guthrie, Samuel

The American physician and chemist Samuel Guthrie, b. Brimfield, Mass., 1782, d. Oct. 19, 1848, discovered CHLOROFORM in 1831, independently of its simultaneous discovery by E. Soubeiran of France and Justus von LIEBIG of Germany. Guthrie also produced an early version of the percussion cap. After studying medicine with his father, Guthrie farmed, practiced medicine, and undertook chemical experiments, distilling alcohol and bleaching powder to produce a spiritous solution of chloric ether that was given the name *chloroform* in 1834 by the French chemist J. B. A. DUMAS.

Guthrie, Sir Tyrone

One of England's most prominent producers and directors, William Tyrone Guthrie, b. July 2, 1900, d. May 15, 1971, made his theatrical debut as an actor in 1924, but his most memorable achievements came after he turned to producing. During his tenure at the OLD VIC THEATRE as producer (1933–36), and later as administrator (1939–45), his successful productions included a modern-dress *Hamlet* (1939) with Alec Guinness and *Measure for Measure* (1933) with Charles Laughton. After leaving the Old Vic, Guthrie worked at several theaters and festivals, among them the Edinburgh Festival (1948 and 1949 seasons) and Sadler's Wells, where he produced grand opera. In 1953 he cofounded the Shakespeare Festival at Stratford, Ontario, serving as its first Artistic Director. In 1963, Guthrie founded the Guthrie Theater in Minneapolis, Minn., the most important regional theater in the United States. He was knighted in 1961. COLETTE BROOKS

Bibliography: Forsyth, James, *Tyrone Guthrie: A Biography* (1976); Guthrie, Tyrone, *A Life in the Theatre* (1959), *In Various Directions* (1965), and *Tyrone Guthrie on Acting* (1971).

Guthrie, Woody and Arlo

Woodrow Wilson "Woody" Guthrie, b. Okemah, Okla., July 14, 1912, d. Oct. 4, 1967, was a folksinger and songwriter who represents for later generations the quintessential folk poet. Guthrie was an itinerant laborer and wandering musician in his youth, and his works—more than 1,000 songs—reflect his life-long involvement with such issues as unemployment and social injustice. His relaxed, ironic, counterculture style provided a model for later singers, especially Bob Dylan, Phil Ochs, and Tom Paxton. Guthrie's songs fall into several broad categories: *Dust Bowl Ballads,* 12 records made in the 1930s for the Library of Congress Folk Song Archive; political and union songs; songs he wrote in support of various New Deal projects and for the American war effort; and a large group of children's songs. "This Land is Your Land" is perhaps his most famous work. His son, the composer and singer **Arlo Guthrie**, b. New York, July 10, 1947, continues in his father's profession, although his songs—including the 1967 hit "Alice's Restaurant"—are less overtly political. He played himself in the successful film *Alice's Restaurant* (1969).

Bibliography: Guthrie, Woody, *Bound for Glory* (1943; repr. 1976), *Born to Win* (1965; repr. 1974), and *The Seeds of Man* (1976); Yurchenko, Henrietta, and Guthrie, Marjorie, *A Mighty Hard Road* (1970).

Guthrie Theater: see REPERTORY THEATER.

gutta-percha [gut'-uh-pur'-chuh]

Gutta-percha is a rubbery solid prepared from the latex of various trees of Malaysia and the South Pacific. It is derived from the tree *Palaquium gutta* and related species of the family Sapotaceae, either as an exudate or by crushing and boiling the leaves. Gutta-percha is used in electrical insulation and dentistry. The South American tree *Mimusops balata* exudes a latex that is made into balata, which is similar to gutta-percha and is used in belting. At high temperatures, gutta-percha is soft and malleable; when cooled it becomes hard, nonbrittle, and water-resistant. FRANCES GIES

guttation [guh-tay'-shuhn]

Guttation is the exudation of water by the aerial parts of plants. When the humidity is so high that minimal amounts of water can be lost through evaporation, water is forced out of the leaves in liquid form through specialized structures (hydathodes). Guttation is common in such plants as grasses, strawberries, and roses. In many plants it is never apparent; in others it is rare.

JOSEPH BECKER

Guyana [gee-yah'-nuh]

Guyana is a republic on the northeast coast of South America, bordered on the west by Venezuela, on the south by Brazil, on the east by Suriname, and on the north by the Atlantic Ocean. First settled by the Dutch and then a British colony, Guyana became independent in 1966. Today this ethnically diverse, developing nation is a socialist state.

LAND AND RESOURCES

Guyana is divided into three physical regions. In the north, where nearly 90% of the people live and where GEORGETOWN, the capital and chief port, is located, is a low coastal belt, most of it below sea level but protected by dikes. Inland is a somewhat higher region, much of it covered by forests. In the south are the Guiana Highlands and related mountain areas, which extend along the border with Brazil. Mount Roriama, the highest point in the country, rises to 2,810 m (9,219 ft). The climate is humid tropical. Temperatures average 27° C (80° F), and annual rainfall averages 2,032 mm (80 in). The river systems flow generally south to north; the most important are the Essequibo, Berbice, and Courantyne. They are the principal lines of communication with the interior.

PEOPLE AND ECONOMY

There is a great diversity of racial and ethnic groups in Guyana. The two largest consist of people of African descent—called either Africans or creoles and making up about 40% of the population—and of the descendants of immigrants from India who constitute more than half the total population. The Africans are descended from slaves, imported to work sugar plantations. After emancipation in 1834, many of them deserted the plantations, and they were replaced by East Indians. The Africans are mostly concentrated in Georgetown and other urban centers, whereas the East Indians still constitute the great majority of the labor force in the sugar and rice industries. Two other groups are the Portuguese (generally mulattoes) and the Chinese, both descended from indentured servant populations and now generally businesspersons and artisans. In the interior live some indigenous Indians and Bush Negroes, descendants of escaped slaves.

The Guyanese economy depends overwhelmingly on exports. By value, bauxite is the most important export, followed by sugar. There are also other mineral exports, including gold and diamonds. The only important economic sector to remain in private hands is rice cultivation. In recent years industrial development has been modest.

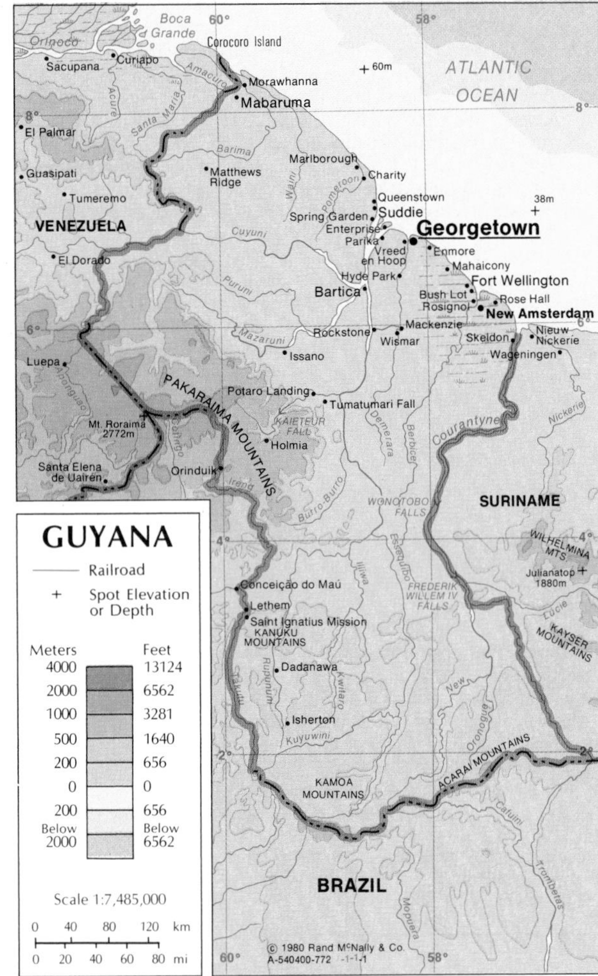

COOPERATIVE REPUBLIC OF GUYANA

LAND. Area: 214, 969 km^2 (83,000 mi^2). Capital and largest city: Georgetown (1985 est. pop., 200,000).

PEOPLE. Population (1986 est.): 771,000; density (1986 est.): 3.6 persons per km^2 (9.3 per mi^2). Distribution (1983): 28% urban, 72% rural. Annual growth (1983): 2.2%. Official language: English. Major religions: Christianity, Hinduism, Islam.

EDUCATION AND HEALTH. Literacy (1985): 85% of adult population. Universities (1987): 1. Hospital beds (1979): 4,002. Physicians (1980): 100. Life expectancy (1980–85): women—73.3; men—67.7. Infant mortality (1985): 41 per 1,000 live births.

ECONOMY. GNP (1984): $399 million; $510 per capita. Labor distribution (1983): industry and commerce—44%; agriculture—34%; services—22%. Foreign trade (1984): imports—$222 million; exports—$212 million; principal trade partners—Trinidad and Tobago, United Kingdom, United States. Currency: 1 Guyana dollar = 100 cents.

GOVERNMENT. Type: republic within the Commonwealth of Nations. Legislature: National Assembly. Political subdivisions: 10 districts.

COMMUNICATIONS. Railroads (1980): 130 km (80 mi) total. Roads (1983): 5,513 km (3,426 mi) total. Major ports: 1. Major airfields: 1.

(Above) *Georgetown, the capital and largest city of Guyana, was established in 1781 by British colonists on the banks of the Demerara River. Because the city is below sea level, a series of protective dikes has been constructed along the riverfront and the Atlantic coast.*

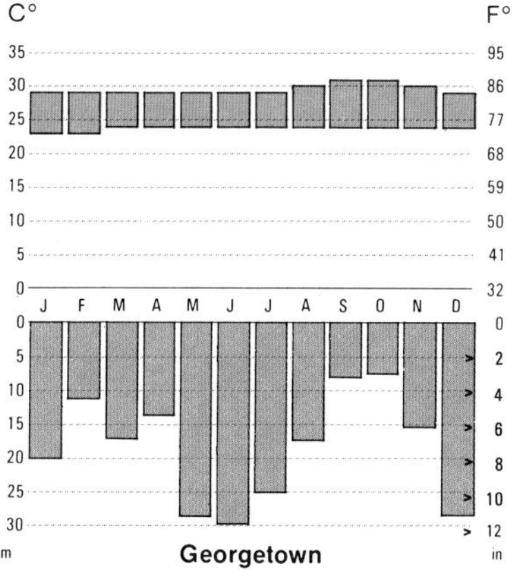

(Left) *Bars indicate monthly ranges of temperature* (red) *and precipitation* (blue) *of Georgetown, Guyana. Located on a narrow coastal strip of the northeastern coast of South America, Georgetown, the country's capital, has a tropical wet climate.*

HISTORY AND GOVERNMENT

The earliest inhabitants of the area were Arawak, Carib, and Warrau Indians. The first European settlers were the Dutch, in the early 17th century. In 1814 the Dutch ceded the colonies of Essequibo, Berbice, and Demerara to Britain; these became the crown colony of British Guiana in 1831.

In 1953 a popularly elected government headed by Cheddi JAGAN, of the People's Progressive party (PPP), took office. Soon ousted by the British on charges of attempting to set up a Communist regime, Jagan and the PPP returned to power in new elections after a 4-year interim government. The newly formed opposition People's National Congress (PNC), headed by former Jagan associate Forbes BURNHAM, won the 1964 elections, formed a coalition government with the United Force party, and led Guyana to independence in 1966.

Under a constitution adopted in 1980, Burnham became president, with power to appoint the prime minister and veto bills approved by the unicameral legislature. The Burnham government took control of the economy and adopted a nonaligned foreign policy. In the 1980s, efforts to settle a long-standing Venezuelan claim to more than half of Guyana met with little success, while the economy worsened, with a large foreign debt and trade deficit the major problems. Burnham died in August 1985; the interim president, Desmond Hoyte, was elected to a 5-year term in December 1985. ROBERT J. ALEXANDER

Bibliography: Baber, Colin, and Jeffrey, H. B., *The Co-operative Republic of Guyana* (1986); Burrowes, R., *The Wild Coast: An Account of Politics in Guyana* (1984); Manley, R. H., *Guyana Emergent* (1979; repr. 1982); Riviere, P., *Individual and Society in Guiana* (1984); Sukdeo, I. D., *The Emergence of a Multiracial Society* (1981).

guyot: see SEAMOUNT.

Guys, Constantin [gees, kahn-stahn-tan']

Constantin Guys, b. Dec. 3, 1805, d. Dec. 13, 1892, a self-taught French artist, left a memorable pictorial record of Parisian life during the Second Empire (1852–70) under Napoleon III. At the age of 18 he joined Lord Byron's expedition to Greece during the war of independence against the Turks. Not much more is known about his early life except that he spent some time in England and, during the Crimean War, became an artist-correspondent (1854–55) for the *Illustrated London News*. By 1860 he had settled in Paris, where he lived in relative anonymity, making hundreds of drawings of the Parisian scene. Charles Baudelaire published (1863) an essay based on Guys's life called "The Painter of Modern Life." Guys's drawings in pencil, ink, and watercolor washes, although rarely signed or dated, reveal a highly personal style that captured the movement and exhilaration of the brilliant life of the fashionable Parisian boulevards. PHILIP GOULD

Bibliography: Baudelaire, C. P., *The Painter of Victorian Life: A Study of Constantin Guys*, intro. and trans. by P. G. Konody (1930); Browse, Lillian, ed., *Constantin Guys* (1945).

Guzmán Blanco, Antonio [goos-mahn' blahn'-koh]

Gen. Antonio Guzmán Blanco, b. Feb. 28, 1829, d. July 20, 1899, was president of Venezuela from 1870 to 1888. Although his rule was despotic, he instituted numerous reforms that greatly improved the economic conditions of the country. He also made free education compulsory. Guzmán spent much of his time in Europe, ruling in his absence through puppets. In 1888, however, during one of his absences, a revolution broke out. He was forced to resign, and he spent the rest of his life in Paris.

Bibliography: Gilmore, Robert L., *Caudillism and Militarism in Venezuela, 1810–1910* (1964); Wise, George S., *Caudillo: A Portrait of Antonio Guzmán Blanco* (1951; repr. 1983).

Gwathmey, Charles [gwahth'-mee]

The architect Charles Gwathmey, b. Charlotte, N.C., June 19, 1938, has developed a highly respected residential architecture distinguished by a cubism based on the work of LE CORBUSIER—white intersecting planes and angled gables, cylinders and segments of cylinders, as in the Gwathmey residence, Amagansett, N.Y. (1967), or the Cogan residence, East Hampton, N.Y. (1972). He was among the "Five" of the New York school who became prominent leaders about 1970. First in partnership with Richard Henderson, then with Robert Siegel, Gwathmey has received commissions both for private houses and apartments and for offices, shops, restaurants, and large-scale housing, such as the dormitory at State University of New York, Purchase (1973). He also designed the proposed addition (1985) to the Guggenheim Museum, New York City. C. RAY SMITH

Bibliography: Jencks, Charles A., *The Language of Post-Modern Architecture* (1977).

Gwathmey, Robert

The American social realist painter and muralist Robert Gwathmey, b. Richmond, Va., Jan. 24, 1903, d. Sept. 21, 1988, was educated at the Maryland Institute and the Pennsylvania Academy of Fine Arts. Beginning in the 1930s, Gwathmey painted scenes from Southern life in which strong color and flattened, schematized forms express social concerns—especially those of rural black communities.

Gwent [gwent]

Gwent is a county in southeastern Wales bounded in the south by the Bristol Channel. Gwent's population is 441,800 (1986 est.), and the county covers an area of 1,376 km² (531 mi²). Cumbran is the county town. In the northwest the Black Mountains rise to more than 600 m (2,000 ft). The western hills comprise an important source of coal, supplying the heavily industrialized urban centers of Newport, Ebbw Vale, and Pontypool. The principal industries are iron, steel, aluminum, and textile manufacturing. The broad central plain, watered by the River Usk, supports dairy farming and agriculture. The low hills along the River Wye, in the east, are well-known for their natural scenery and castles, which attract many tourists.

Gwent was created in 1974 when the local government of Wales was reorganized. It is composed of the former counties of Monmouthshire and part of Brecknockshire.

Gwynedd [gwin'-eth]

Gwynedd, a county in northwest Wales, is bordered by the Irish Sea in the north and west. The population of Gwynedd is 232,700 (1984 est.), and the county covers an area of 3,870 km^2 (1,494 mi^2). CAERNARVON is the county town.

Lowlands on the Isle of Anglesey, the Lleyn Peninsula, and the Conway River valleys support agriculture and dairy farming. Summer resorts are located along the coast. Inland, the land rises abruptly to mountainous terrain. Tourism is also important here, where Snowdonia National Park includes the highest peak in Wales, Snowdon, which reaches 1,085 m (3,560 ft). Slate mining and wood production, the traditional economic mainstays, are being replaced by forestry and aluminum manufacturing.

Gwynedd was created in 1974 when the local government of Wales was reorganized. It includes the former counties of Anglesey, Caernarvon, and parts of Denbighshire and Merioneth.

Gwynne, Nell [gwin]

Nell Gwynne, b. Eleanor Gwyn, Feb. 2, 1650, d. Nov. 14, 1687, was a popular English comic actress and a celebrated mistress of King CHARLES II. Originally an orange-seller in the theater, she made her debut at London's Theatre Royal in John Dryden's *The Indian Emperor* (1665). Not a great actress, she was known for her charm and vivacity. She became Charles's mistress in 1668 and eventually bore him two sons. She made her last stage appearance in Dryden's *The Conquest of Granada* in 1670. According to John Evelyn, Charles's last words to his brother and successor James were, "Don't let poor Nelly starve."

ANDREW KELLY

Bibliography: Bevan, Bryan, *Nell Gwynn* (1969); Wilson, J. H., *Nell Gwynn: Royal Mistress* (1952).

Gymnasium [gim-nah'-zee-um]

Gymnasium is a German classical secondary school that prepares students to attend universities. In ancient Greece, gymnasia were places for athletics and discussions. There was a renewed interest in them during the Renaissance, and in Germany the first Gymnasium for academic purposes was founded in 1537. Gymnasia accept about 30% of secondary students in Germany and send 90% percent of their graduates to some form of higher education. Gymnasia now specialize in particular subjects, such as pedagogy, social sciences, and mathematics, but the curriculum in the first 5 to 6 years is the same for all, and for the first 4 or 5 years it is easy to transfer from one Gymnasium to another. Grades 11–13, the last three years of the 9-year secondary program, are specialized. Most students prefer the Gymnasia in modern languages, mathematics, and science.

Many students leave the Gymnasium with a certificate after grade 10. Others prepare for the Abitur, which serves as both a cumulative final examination and an entrance examination for higher education.

Other countries, including Czechoslovakia, Greece, Greek Cyprus, Denmark, Italy, Hungary, Sweden, Switzerland, and Yugoslavia, have similar secondary systems that are also called Gymnasia, but they differ in the range of grades included, the proportion of students accepted, and other features.

gymnasium [jim-nay'-zee-uhm]

Gymnasium, a word derived from ancient Greek, literally means a place where exercises are practiced by naked athletes. In ancient Greece and, later, in Rome gymnasiums were found in every important city. In addition to apparatus designed for physcial exercise, the ancient gymnasium usually included baths, porticoes, and dressing chambers. Imposing structures, they often were adorned with works of art and became meeting places for social events, lecture groups, and philosophers.

In the latter part of the 19th century, immigrants from Europe who were interested in physical fitness were foremost in making the gymnasium more important in the United States than it had been. The gymnasium became an important part of the American education scene. In the main exercise rooms were such pieces of equipment as weighted pulleys attached to walls, circus-type rings suspended from the ceiling, vaulting horses on which to practice springing, and horizontal and parallel bars designed to strengthen arms and legs. Many old gymnasiums even offered a banked, oval-shaped, indoor running track built around the perimeter of the main room's upper walls about 4.6 m (15 ft) above the floor.

Today's gymnasiums are larger, better equipped, and roomier than their earlier counterparts. Modern gymnasiums usually contain full-size basketball courts and spectators' bleachers, which can be folded or retracted against the walls when not in use. The modern gymnasium also can be outfitted for such sports as badminton, volleyball, and indoor soccer.

Many college, large high school, and athletic-club gymnasiums also have adjacent rooms that may be appointed for such activities as wrestling—by providing padded floor mats—body development, and fencing. Also included in the standard gymnasium complex are shower and locker rooms and a room where a trainer may tape an athlete's muscles or joints for prevention or protection of an injury, administer first aid, or give massages. Whirlpool baths for tired or sore muscles are now common.

Although outdoor sports are now more popular than ever, in the United States as well as elsewhere, the gymnasium remains the focal point for athletic endeavors. Gymnasiums are also used for an assortment of nonathletic functions. Many school gymnasiums serve as auditoriums, theaters, display areas, and workshops. Dances, meetings, conventions, rummage sales, and so on are often held in gymnasiums.

A recent alternative to the gymnasium, especially for adults, is the so-called health club, which has proliferated mainly in the 1980s. Usually not large enough to house a basketball court, a health club most often offers the following activities: racquetball (and sometimes squash), body building (both free weights and exercise machines), exercise classes, and swimming.

gymnastics

The sport of gymnastics, which derives its name from the ancient Greek word for disciplinary exercises, involves physical skills such as dexterity, gracefulness, and strength. It was introduced in early Greek civilization to facilitate bodily development through a series of exercises that included running, jumping, swimming, throwing, wrestling, and weight lifting. Modern international competition has fewer events. Men's events are the long horse, side horse, floor (or free) exercises, parallel bars, horizontal bar, and rings. Women's events are the vaulting horse, floor exercises, uneven parallel bars, and balance beam. In the United States, tumbling and trampoline exercises are also included in many competitions.

History. Many basic gymnastic events were practiced in some form before the introduction by the Greeks of *gymnazein*, literally, "to excercise naked." Physical fitness was a highly valued attribute in ancient Greece and both men and women participated in vigorous gymnastic exercises. The Romans, after conquering Greece, developed the activities into a more formal sport as they used the gymnasiums to physically prepare their legions for warfare. With the decline of Rome, however, interest in gymnastics dwindled.

Modern Gymnastics. In 1774, a Prussian, Johann Bernhard Basedow, included physical exercises with other forms of instruction at his school in Dessau, Saxony. With this action began the modernization of gymnastics, and also thrust the Germanic countries into the forefront in the sport. In the late 1700s, Friedrich Ludwig Jahn of Germany developed the side bar, the horizontal bar, the parallel bars, the balance beam, and jumping events. He, more than anyone else, is considered the "father of modern gymnastics." Gymnastics flourished in Germany in the 1800s, while in Sweden a more graceful form of the sport, stressing rhythmic movement, was developed by Guts Muth. The opening (1811) of Jahn's school in Berlin, to promote his version of the sport, was followed by the formation of many clubs in Europe and later in England. The sport was introduced to the United States by Dr. Dudley Allen Sargent, who taught gymnastics in several U.S. universities about the time of the Civil War, and who is credited with inventing more than 30 pieces of apparatus. Most of the growth of gymnastics in the United States centered on the activities of European immigrants, who introduced the sport in their new cities in the 1880s. Clubs were formed as Turnverein and Sokol groups, and gymnasts were often referred to as "turners." Modern gymnastics excluded some traditional events, such as weight lifting and wrestling, and emphasized form rather than personal rivalry. Gymnastics was on the schedule of the first modern OLYMPIC GAMES in 1896, and it has been on the Olympic agenda continually since 1924. Modern gymnastics gained considerable popularity because of the performance of Olga KORBUT of the Soviet Union in the 1972 Olympics. The widespread television coverage of her dramatic performance gave the sport publicity that it lacked in the past. Many countries other than the traditional mainstays—the USSR, Japan, East and West Germany, and other Eastern European nations—began to promote gymnastics, particularly for women; one of these countries was the United States.

Scoring. Gymnastic competitions are judged and scored on both an individual and a team basis. Judges award points to each participant in each event on a 0-to-10 scale, 10 being

Apparatuses used in gymnastic competition test a wide range of athletic skills. Men's routines on the parallel bars (1), horizontal bar (2), rings (5), vaulting horse, or long horse (6), and pommel-horse, or side horse (7), have traditionally emphasized upper body strength and required flexibility, precision, and form. Women's gymnastics, including routines on the uneven bars (3), balance beam (4), and vaulting horse (6), have increasingly stressed strength and precision over the traditional dancer's flexibility. Routines in these events and in the floor exercises, performed by both men and women, usually combine compulsory exercises with optional moves devised by the gymnast.

Sixteen-year-old American Mary Lou Retton executes a split on the balance beam during the 1984 Olympics in Los Angeles. Retton's strength and athleticism earned her the gold medal for the coveted all-around title; she also garnered a silver medal in the vault and two bronze medals, in the floor exercises and the uneven parallel bars. The U.S. women's team finished second overall—their best performance in the Olympics to date—for which Retton received another silver.

perfect. Judging is strictly subjective; however, guidelines are provided for the judges so that they can arrive at relatively unbiased scores.

Usually, there are four judges and the highest and lowest scores are dropped to provide a more objective evaluation. Gymnasts try to perform the most difficult routines in the most graceful way, thus impressing the judges with their mastery of the sport. MICHAEL STRAUSS

Bibliography: Fogel, Samuel J., *Gymnastics Handbook* (1971); Loken, Newton C., and Willoughby, Robert J., *The Complete Book of Gymnastics*, 3d ed. (1977); Price, Hartley D., et al., *Gymnastics and Tumbling*, 3d ed. (1959); Tatlow, Peter, et al., *The World of Gymnastics* (1978).

gymnosperm [jim'-nuh-spurm]

Gymnosperms are about 675 species of seed-bearing, woody PLANTS. They differ from the only other seed-bearing group of plants, the ANGIOSPERMS, in that their seeds are naked, or not enclosed in an ovary; and they usually bear POLLEN CONES, which carry the male sperm, and SEED CONES, which contain the female eggs. They are mostly softwoods and EVERGREENS that evolved about 250 million years earlier than angiosperms.

Four plant classes constitute gymnosperms, according to the Whittaker five-kingdom system of plant and animal classification: CYCADS (Cycadinae), the GINKGO (Ginkgoinae), gnetids (Gnetinae), and CONIFERS (Coniferinae). Some botanists, however, classify gnetids as conifers in other classification schemes. The earliest gymnosperms—seed ferns and fossil conifers—no longer exist. Cycads are evergreen, tropical shrubs and trees that have single, thick stems; large, leafy cones; and palmlike leaves. The nine surviving genera of cycads—the most primitive of gymnosperms—belong to the order Cycadales, three others being extinct. About 50 species of ginkgo existed 130 million years ago, of which only one, *Ginkgo biloba,* survives. This deciduous tree has fanlike leaves and rudimentary cones, the male cones resembling catkins and the female having two exposed ovules. Gnetids—of which no fossil record exists—comprise three highly diverse genera: joint firs, genus EPHEDRA, semiarid shrubs from which the drug ephedrine is derived; genus GNETUM, broad-leaved tropical trees and woody vines; and *Welwitschia mirabilis,* an African shrub having only two leathery leaves, which are never shed. Most conifers, which comprise about 50 genera, have branching stems and scalelike or needlelike leaves. They make up more than 30 percent of the world's forests and include such evergreens as pines, firs, and spruces as well as the deciduous larches, dawn redwood, and bald cypress. The pollen and seed cones are woody and in some species are carried on the same tree instead of on separate trees, as in the other classes.

The basic reproduction cycle of gymnosperms begins when male and female gametophytes develop from spores produced by the plants. Pollen is usually carried to the female cones by wind, and fertilization takes up to a year. The resulting embryos are scattered and develop into seedlings.

Bibliography: Sporne, K. R., *Morphology of Gymnosperms* (1967).

gymnotid [jim-noht'-id]

Gymnotids are a small group of teleost fishes related to minnows and characins. They are popularly known as KNIFE FISHES and gymnotid eels but are not closely related to true eels. They have long tails and a long anal fin that supplies much of their swimming power.

Knife fishes belong to three families: Gymnotidae, Apteronotidae, and Rhamphichthyidae. Several species of knife fishes are popular aquarium fishes. Gymnotids are found from Guatemala to northern Argentina. The most famous species of the group is the ELECTRIC EEL, *Electrophorus electricus,* a native of the Amazon Basin of South America, put in a family of its own, Electrophoridae. EDWARD O. WILEY

gymnure [jim'-nyur]

Gymnures are five species of Asiatic insectivores in the hedgehog family, Erinaceidae. They lack the spines found in the coats of hedgehogs. The Malayan gymnure, *Echinosorex gymnurus,* or moon rat, has a characteristic strong, unpleasant odor. It is usually black with whitish head and shoulders, and black spots near the eyes. It grows to a length of 44 cm (17.5 in), weighs up to 1.4 kg (3 lb), and has a scantily haired tail 21 cm (8 in) long. STEPHEN C. REINGOLD

gynecology [gy-nuh-kahl'-uh-jee]

Gynecology is the medical specialty dealing with the disorders of the female reproductive organs. It is often combined with the practice of OBSTETRICS, the branch of medicine dealing with the management of pregnancy and its problems. Among the most common disorders treated by gynecologists are those associated with menstruation, fertility, menopause, infection, and tumors, as well as endocrine disturbances. The most frequent complaints that bring patients to a gynecologist are DYSMENORRHEA (painful menstrual periods), amenorrhea (missed periods), metrorrhagia (vaginal bleeding at abnormal times), menorrhagia (excessive menstrual bleeding at normal times), leukorrhea (abnormal vaginal discharges), inability to conceive, and discomfort or pain in the pelvic or genital organs. In addition to treating such disorders, gynecologists provide counseling on BIRTH CONTROL and prescribe appropriate methods. In most practices the taking of a Papanicolaou smear (see PAP TEST) and the performing of BREAST examinations have become routine. PETER L. PETRAKIS

Bibliography: The Boston Women's Health Book Collective, *Our Bodies, Ourselves,* 2d ed. (1976); Lanson, Lucienne, *From Woman to Woman: A Gynecologist Answers Questions About You and Your Body,* rev. ed. (1981); Niels, Lauersen, and Whitney, Stephen, *It's Your Body: A Woman's Guide to Gynecology* (1977); Shephard, B. D., and Shephard, C. A., *The Complete Guide to Women's Health* (1982).

Gyokudo [gee-yoh'-kuh-doh]

Uragami Gyokudo, 1745–1820, was a Japanese painter of the Nanga school, which derived its artistic ideals from the literati tradition of China. A feudal retainer in central Japan, Gyokudo traveled to Edo and became a Confucian scholar versed in the gentlemanly arts of painting, poetry, and the koto (a type of zither). After 1794 he took up a life of wandering. His intensely personal mountain landscapes are marked by feathery, agitated brushstrokes, as in *Two Peaks Embracing Clouds* (Idemitsu Art Museum, Toyko). BARBARA BRENNAN FORD

Bibliography: Cahill, James, *Scholar Painters of Japan: The Nanga School* (1972).

Győr [dyur]

Győr (1985 est. pop., 128,252) is a city in northwestern Hungary 70 km (43 mi) west of Budapest. At Győr the Rábá and Répce rivers form the Moson tributary of the Danube, which flows 13 km (8 mi) to the north. A grain and livestock market center, the city also manufactures locomotives, farm equipment, furniture, food products, and liquor. Its cathedral (begun 12th century) and bishop's palace (built 13th century) are well-known historic landmarks. A Roman village, Arabona, existed on the site in early Christian times. Magyars established Győr at the beginning of the 10th century, and it was subsequently held by the Turks, French, Austrians, and Germans.

gypsies [jip'-seez]

Gypsies are a dark-complexioned Caucasoid people dispersed throughout the world and known for their distinctive customs and migratory way of life. Many gypsies speak Romany, an Indic language, and call themselves *Rom.* Others do not speak this language, but are still recognizable as gypsies because of their acknowledged origins and lifestyle. Those known as *manouches* in France and *sinti* in Germany speak a language similar to Romany but with a large admixture of German terms. Many gypsies in Great Britain and France speak a dialect of Spanish; in the Balkans some speak a language related to Turkish and others speak Romanian. Frequently, however, the only language spoken is that of the nation in which the gypsies reside. Groups such as the tinkers in Great Britain and the *jenisch* in Germany have nomadic lifestyles similar to that of the gypsies but have different ethnic origins.

Gypsies, known for their nomadic lifestyle, are depicted here at a caravan resting-place. Believed to have come originally from India, the gypsies migrated to Europe during the 15th century and now live all over the world, maintaining a distinctive folk culture and language.

It is believed that the gypsies originated in northwest India, where they were members of a low caste. In the 1st millennium of the Christian Era they migrated westward through the Middle East. The first written reference to gypsies in Europe dates from the 14th century. By the early 16th century they had been encountered in nearly every part of Europe. Most gypsies in North America arrived in the late 19th century or more recently.

To varying degrees, gypsies have become assimilated into the cultures of the nations they live in. Many are now industrial workers, particularly those in Soviet-dominated Eastern Europe, where the government requires that they convert to a sedentary way of life. Generally, however, they have carefully maintained their traditional identity and customs. Their bands are ruled by elders, and they have preferred trades that are consistent with nomadism. In many areas, especially agrarian Southern and Eastern Europe, they live as horse traders, peddlers, metal smiths, beggars, musicians, dancers, carnival workers, and fortune tellers. In industrialized Western Europe and North America they also often work as auto mechanics. In these areas the horse-drawn caravans by which they traditionally travel have been replaced by house trailers and recreational vehicles.

In many parts of the world gypsies historically have been stereotyped as undesirable aliens. Like the Jews, they were classified as an impure race in Nazi Germany. An estimated 500,000 Romanian, Hungarian, Polish, and Czech gypsies were killed in concentration camps during World War II. Today there are an estimated 5,000,000 gypsies in the world. Probably about 20,000 live in North America, mostly in the United States. ROBERT T. ANDERSON

Bibliography: Borrow, George, *The Romany Rye*, rev. ed. (1949; repr. 1959); Clébert, Jean-Paul, *The Gypsies*, trans. by Charles Duff (1963); Cohn, Werner, *The Gypsies* (1973); Sibley, David, *Outsiders in Urban Society* (1981); Sutherland, Anne, *Gypsies: The Hidden Americans* (1975; repr. 1986); Yoors, Jan, *The Gypsies* (1967; repr. 1983).

gypsum [jip'-suhm]

(Above) *Gypsum is a common water-containing compound of calcium sulfate. Often found as transparent-to-opaque deposits in the ceilings of caves, gypsum is usually white, but it may also be gray, yellow, or brown. Deposits of gypsum may be crystalline, massive granular, or fibrous.*

(Left) *Gypsum is found in different fibrous forms of silky luster, including a sheet variety called satin spar and these "rose" forms found in a cave in Mexico. Flower forms result from concentric groupings of mineral fibers that have spread and become rosette shaped.*

Gypsum, a hydrated calcium SULFATE MINERAL ($CaSO_4 \cdot 2H_2O$), is used as a raw material in plaster of Paris, as fertilizer, as an ornamental stone (alabaster and satin spar), and as optical material (selenite). Common gypsum is found as prismatic, curved, or twisting monoclinic crystals of vitreous luster and as earthy, foliated, or granular masses; alabaster as fine-grained masses; selenite as colorless, transparent crystals or foliated masses; and satin spar as pearly, fibrous masses. Gypsum is soft (hardness 2), clear, white, or tinted, and has a specific gravity of 2.3 and perfect cleavage in one direction. It occurs with halite and other evaporite minerals in extensive beds, often alternating with limestone and shale, deposited in seas or playa lakes.

gypsy moth [jip'-see mawth]

A male gypsy moth (top) *is brown in color and has feathery antennae. The larger female* (center) *which is a very weak flier, lays its eggs on tree trunks. The larvae, or caterpillars* (bottom), *which hatch the following spring, cause widespread damage to forest and shade trees. The drawings show actual sizes.*

The gypsy moth, *Porthetria dispar*, is a member of the family Lymantriidae, native to Europe and Asia. The female is white with black markings; the smaller male is dark. The gypsy moth was introduced to Massachusetts in 1866 and has spread to southern Canada, the midwestern United States, and Texas, with reported sightings in western states as well. The larvae feed on a wide range of deciduous and evergreen trees, defoliating and weakening or killing them; outbreaks have repeatedly caused serious damage. Attempted control measures include the use of pesticides, the introduction of parasitic wasps and other natural enemies, and, experimentally, the spreading of fungal and viral agents that are harmful to the moth.

ALEXANDER B. KLOTS

Bibliography: Gerardi, Michael H., and Grimm, James K., *The History, Biology, Damage and Control of the Gypsy Moth* (1978).

gyroscope [jy'-roh-skohp]

The gyroscope, often known as a gyro, was first introduced by J. B. L. FOUCAULT in 1852 and consists of a spinning device, usually in the form of a wheel, that exhibits strong ANGULAR MOMENTUM. This wheel, which may consist of the rotor of an electric motor, is mounted in a framework, or gimbal, that is in turn mounted in one or more frameworks whose axes are perpendicular to the spin axis of the rotor. The rotor is also free to rotate about these additional axes and is said to have one, two, or three degrees of freedom, depending on the number of axes it can rotate about in addition to the original spin axis. The gyroscope acts according to the law of conservation of angular momentum and will resist any attempt to change the direction of the axis about which the rotor spins. All true gyroscopes have in common a rotating mass.

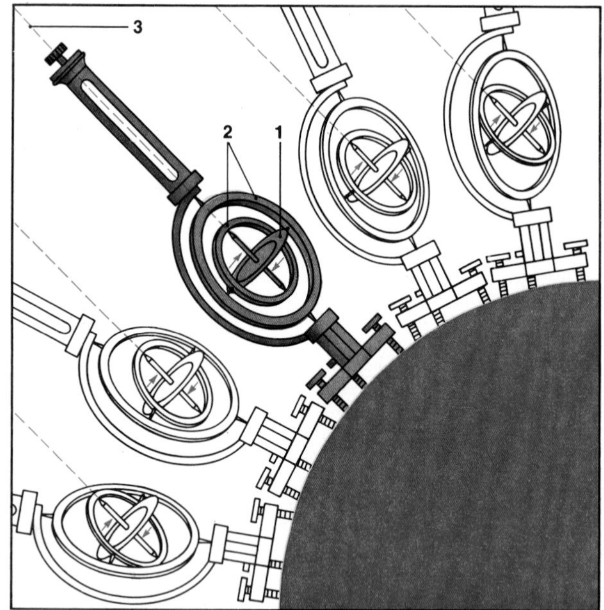

Used in automatic steering systems and ships' stabilizers, the gyroscope is an axle-mounted wheel with a massive rim (1) *and is supported with minimal friction in gimbal rings* (2) *so that it can be set in rotation with its axis* (3) *pointed in any direction. A distinctive property of a gyroscope is the stability of its rotational axis. As long as the wheel of a ground-based gyroscope is kept spinning at constant speed, its axis will continue pointing toward the position in the sky at which it was aimed when it started rotating. The gimbals, however, will change their angles relative to that point as the Earth turns.*

Gyros with two degrees of freedom, the earliest type used, have found applications in attitude instruments, fire control systems, and satellite stabilization. High-accuracy gyros can almost eliminate friction in the gimbals by floating the rotor in air, an electrostatic field, or a magnetic field.

Gyroscopic Instruments. A variety of aircraft and spacecraft orientation-measuring devices employ gyros as their principal reference element. Because a steadily spinning mass has an inherent tendency to point in only one direction in space, these devices are ideally suited to such applications. When properly mounted in different types of gimbals and restraints, they instantaneously measure angles and angular rates. A rate gyro gives a direct measure of the turning rate of every aircraft. A position, or displacement, gyro measures the angular deviation from a reference direction or orientation. The gyrocompass (see COMPASS, NAVIGATIONAL) and artificial horizon are two basic aircraft instruments that use a position gyro. Inertial platforms, used on most overseas flights, consist of a combination of gyro types to maintain a fixed direction without other navigation aids.

Gyros are also used as primary navigation and guidance devices in spacecraft, because magnetic compasses are useless and there is no local horizon to sight on. Astronauts piloting the SPACE SHUTTLE employ a set of gyro instruments.

Gyroscopic Actuators. A gyroscope may act as an actuator, a device that directly controls a vehicle, when the spinning wheel consists of very large rotating masses. In contrast to aircraft instruments, when a rotor takes on a size much larger than an attitude-measuring gyro, its stiffness can be used directly to maintain the orientation of a vehicle. Actuator gyros supply stiffness to many spacecraft and oceangoing ships. Most communications satellites use large rotors for controlling orientation.

M. H. KAPLAN

Bibliography: Crabtree, Harold, *Spinning Tops and Gyroscope Motion* (1977); Scarborough, James Blaine, *The Gyroscope: Theory and Applications* (1958); Wrigley, Walter, et al., *Gyroscopic Theory, Design and Instrumentation* (1969).

See also: GUIDANCE AND CONTROL SYSTEMS.